Social Problems

Most of the readers of this book are among the world's privileged people—those who have enough to eat, a comfortable place to sleep, and who have the special opportunity to study the human condition. I offer this book in the hope that it will stimulate thinking about those who are in need and the state of our world and spark action toward making our world a better place.

John J. Macionis

Social Problems

Sixth Edition

John J. Macionis
Kenyon College

PEARSON

Boston   Columbus   Indianapolis   New York   San Francisco
Amsterdam   Cape Town   Dubai   London   Madrid   Milan   Munich   Paris   Montréal   Toronto
Delhi   Mexico City   São Paulo   Sydney   Hong Kong   Seoul   Singapore   Taipei   Tokyo

Vice President of Product Development: Dickson Musslewhite
Senior Acquisitions Editor: Billy Grieco
Development Editor: Barbara Reilly
Data Research: Kimberlee Klesner
Program Manager Team Lead: Maureen Richardson
Program Manager: Emily Tamburri
Editorial Assistant: Amandria Guadalupe
Vice President of Marketing: Maggie Moylan
Director of Field Marketing: Jonathan Cottrell
Product Marketing Manager: Tricia Murphy
Field Marketing Manager: Brittany Pogue-Mohammed
Project Management Team Lead: Denise Forlow

Project Manager: Marianne Peters-Riordan
Senior Operations Specialist: Diane Peirano
Senior Art Director: Blair Brown
Cover Art Director: Maria Lange
Cover Design: Pentagram
Cartographer: International Mapping Associates
Digital Studio Product Manager: Claudine Bellanton
Senior Digital Studio Project Manager: Rich Barnes
Full-Service Project Manager: Melissa Sacco
Composition: Lumina Datamatics, Inc.
Printer/Binder: Manufactured in the United States by RR Donnelley
Cover Printer: Manufactured in the United States by RR Donnelley

Library of Congress Cataloging-in-Publication Data

Macionis, John J.
    Social Problems / John J. Macionis. — Sixth edition.
        pages cm
    Includes bibliographical references and index.
    ISBN 978-0-13-390959-3 — ISBN 0-13-390959-X
  1. Social problems.   2. Social problems—United States.   I. Title.
    HN16.M24 2016
    303.3'72—dc23
                                                    2014039844

10 9 8 7 6 5 4 3 2
V011

Student Edition
ISBN-10:   0-13-390959-X
ISBN-13: 978-0-13-390959-3

A la Carte Edition
ISBN-10:   0-13-391249-3
ISBN-13: 978-0-13391249-4

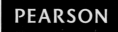

Brief Contents

Contents

Part III   Problems of Deviance, Conformity, and Well-Being

6   Crime, Violence, and Criminal Justice   159

7   Sexuality   199

11 Work and the Workplace   322

12 Family Life   354

13 Education   380

What's New in *Social Problems, Sixth Edition*

1. A "Tracking the Trends" figure at the beginning of each chapter identifies and graphically presents a key trend driving contemporary public debate, engaging students in chapter content from the outset. For example, Chapter 2, Poverty and Wealth, opens with a Tracking the Trends figure that reveals declining belief in the American Dream.

2. New learning objectives, which begin each major section of every chapter, alert students to the material they can expect to master in that section. All learning objectives are listed at the beginning of each chapter, and they organize the Making the Grade summary at the end of the chapter.

3. Several new, compelling chapter-opening vignettes draw students into the lives of people grappling with a situation or issue related to the topic of the chapter.

4. There is new and expanded discussions of issues that have commanded increased public attention in the last few years, such as gun violence, immigration, the decriminalization of marijuana, the Affordable Care Act, same-sex marriage, and the Common Core Initiative.

5. Writing prompts at the end of every chapter guide students in developing an essay in which they are asked to analyze the social trends discussed in the chapter and envision a better society.

6. All statistical material throughout the text has been updated to the latest available data. In addition, the sixth edition includes hundreds of new research references, many of them 2013 and 2014.

REVEL™

Educational technology designed for the way today's students read, think, and learn

When students are engaged deeply, they learn more effectively and perform better in their courses. This simple fact inspired the creation of REVEL: an immersive learning experience designed for the way today's students read, think, and learn. Built in collaboration with educators and students nationwide, REVEL is the newest, fully digital way to deliver respected Pearson content.

REVEL enlivens course content with media interactives and assessments—integrated directly within the author's narrative—that provide opportunities for students to read about and practice course material in tandem. This immersive educational technology boosts student engagement, which leads to better understanding of concepts and improved performance throughout the course.

Learn more about REVEL
http://www.pearsonhighered.com/revel/

Boxes

Maps

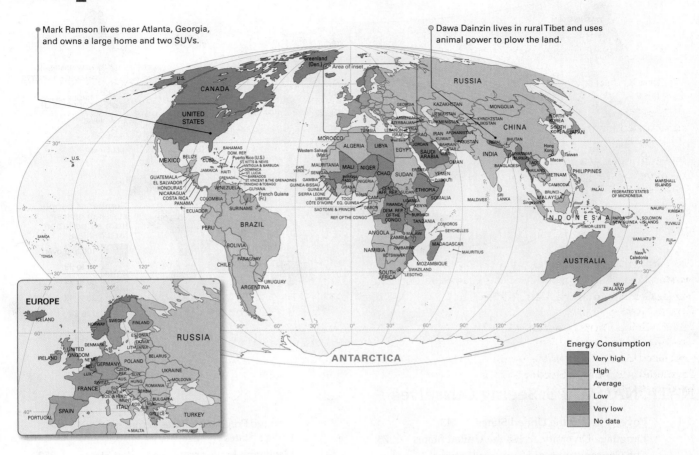

Mark Ramson lives near Atlanta, Georgia, and owns a large home and two SUVs.

Dawa Dainzin lives in rural Tibet and uses animal power to plow the land.

Energy Consumption
- Very high
- High
- Average
- Low
- Very low
- No data

GLOBAL MAPS: Window on the World

Number of people at risk of cancer from air pollution (in a million)

- 100 and over
- 75 to 99
- 50 to 74
- 25 to 49
- 1 to 24

U.S. average: 49.8

NATIONAL MAPS: Seeing Ourselves

Chapter 1
Sociology: Studying Social Problems

 ## Learning Objectives

1.1 Explain the benefits of learning about sociology and using the sociological imagination.

1.2 Define the concept "social problem" and explain how societies come to define some issues—and not others—as social problems.

1.3 Apply sociological theory to the study of social problems.

1.4 Discuss the methods sociologists use to study social problems.

1.5 Identify factors that shape how societies devise policy to respond to social problems.

1.6 Analyze how political attitudes shape how people define social problems and solutions.

Tracking the Trends

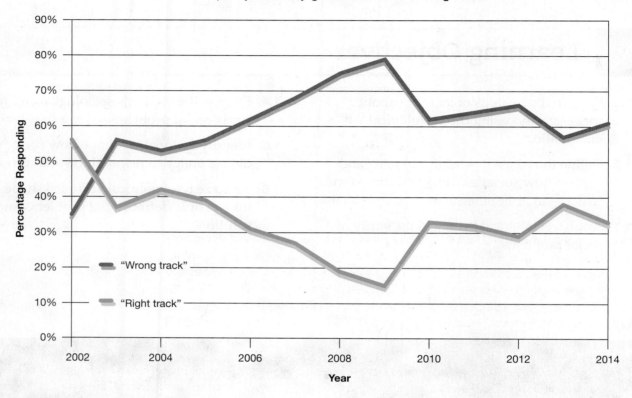

Survey Question: "Do you feel things in this country are generally going in the right direction or do you feel things have pretty seriously gotten off on the wrong track?"

SOURCE: New York Times/CBS News Poll (2014).

Researchers try to gauge the public's confidence in the country by asking general questions such as this one:

"Do you think the country is on the right track or the wrong track?"

In early 2014, 61 percent of U.S. adults said they thought that the country was "on the wrong track," almost twice the share who thought the country was "going in the right direction." Back in 2002, just 35 percent of U.S. adults said the country was on the wrong track. In recent years, dissatisfaction with government emerged as the most commonly cited social problem in the United States. Do you think the country can continue without the confidence of most people?

Constructing the Problem

What turns an issue into a social problem?

Social problems come into being as people define an issue as harmful and in need of change.

Aren't we always dealing with the same problems?

Most of today's problems differ from those that concerned the public several generations ago.

Isn't a social problem any condition that is harmful?

Many conditions harmful to thousands of people are never defined as social problems.

Chapter Overview

This chapter introduces the study of social problems by defining the sociological imagination, explaining sociology's theoretical approaches, and describing sociological methods of research. You will learn how people's political attitudes define the issues they are likely to view as social problems and what policies they are likely to favor as solutions. You will gain the ability to describe the political spectrum and to apply various positions on the political spectrum to social issues. ■

Marcos Jorman was already late as he rushed out the door of his apartment. He ran down the stairs, briefcase in hand, and crashed through the old wooden door of the apartment building. He looked north up Chestnut Street. What luck! The bus was right there, just half a block away! Catching his breath, Marcos climbed aboard as the bus pulled out into the heavy traffic. He saw Jan, a co-worker, a few seats back and he sat down next to her.

"I just got a text from Sandra," Jan explained looking a little desperate. "She says everyone is getting laid off. *We're all out.* The company is shutting down the whole division and moving operations out of the country." Her head dropped along with her spirit. "What am I going to do? How am I going to manage with my kids?"

Marcos checked his own phone. He, too, had messages—several from co-workers who had already arrived at work and confirmed the bad news. "Oh, man, it's true," he said softly. The two sat without speaking for the rest of the ride.

The day turned out to be one of the toughest in Marcos's entire life. He knew the start-up company was struggling with rising costs and heavy competition. Only two months earlier, new management had come in to "reorganize" and to cut costs. The decision to close operations was the result.

As he entered his workstation, he was handed a short letter spelling out the dismissal. He joined dozens of others at a short meeting with a human relations officer and then went back to pack up his things. He was home again by early afternoon.

Marcos sat in his apartment with a glass of tea looking out the window at nothing in particular. He felt weak, almost ill. He kept telling himself that times are tough. He knew the company was in trouble. But, somehow, he could not shake the idea that the job loss was his own fault, his own personal failure.

This story could be told millions of times, because millions of people—including those who worked in construction, sales, communications, management, and teaching—lost their jobs during the recession that hammered the U.S. economy starting at the end of 2007. ▪

Seeing Patterns: The Sociological Imagination

1.1 **Explain the benefits of learning about sociology and using the sociological imagination.**

Living in a society that teaches us to feel personally responsible for whatever happens to us—good or bad—we easily understand Marcos's reaction to being laid off. We imagine Marcos second-guessing himself: Should he have majored in something else? If only he had taken that other job in Atlanta! If only he had listened to his father and stayed in school. We all tend to personalize our lives and blame ourselves for our troubles.

However, when we apply the **sociological imagination**, *a point of view that highlights how society affects the experiences we have and the choices we make*, the picture changes. Using the sociological imagination, we see that the operation of U.S. society—in this case, a serious national recession—caused the loss of *millions* of jobs. This event, which changed the lives of people all over the country, can hardly be said to be simply a matter of bad personal choices.

Sociology is *the systematic study of human societies*. **Society** refers to *people who live within some territory and share many patterns of behavior*. As sociologists study society, they pay attention to **culture**, *a way of life including widespread values (about what is good and bad), beliefs (about what is true), and behavior (what people do every day)*.

Cultural patterns in the United States are diverse, but one widely shared value is the importance of individualism, the idea that for better or worse, people are responsible for their own lives. In the case of Marcos Jorman, it is easy to say, "Well, he lost his job because he decided to take a job with a start-up company in the first place. He really brought this on himself." In other words, our common sense often defines personal problems—even when the problems affect millions of people—as the result of *personal choice*. Without denying that individuals do make choices, sociologists point to ways in which society shapes all our lives. Thinking sociologically, we see that widespread unemployment may be a personal problem, but it is also a *social issue*.

Sociology's key insight is that *many of the personal troubles people face are really social issues with their roots in*

SOCIAL POLICY

C. Wright Mills: Turning Personal Troubles into Social Issues

All of us struggle with our own problems, which might include unemployment, falling into debt, falling out of love, drug or alcohol abuse, poor health, or suffering from violence. We experience these problems; we *feel* them, sometimes on a gut-wrenching level. Our problems are personal. But C. Wright Mills (1959) claimed that the roots of such "personal" problems lie in society itself, often involving the ways our economic and political systems work. After all, the normal operation of our society favors some categories of people over others: the rich over the poor, white people over people of color, middle-aged people over the very young and the very old. When people see their problems as personal, all they can do is try to deal with their troubles as one *individual*. Isolating one life in this way keeps people from seeing the bigger picture of how society operates. In the end, as Mills explained, people feel that "their lives are a series of traps. They sense that within their everyday worlds, they cannot overcome their troubles" (1959:3). Because we live in an individualistic culture, we are quick to conclude that the troubles we experience are simply our own fault.

A more accurate and more effective approach is to understand that it is society that shapes our lives. Using the sociological imagination transforms personal troubles into social issues by showing that these issues affect not only us but also countless people *like* us. This knowledge gives us power because, joining with others, we can improve our lives—and break free of our traps—as we set out to change society.

What Do You Think?

1. Provide three examples of personal problems that Mills would define as social issues.

2. To what extent do you think people in the United States believe that problems such as unemployment result from bad personal choices or even bad luck? Did this change during the recent recession? Explain.

3. Have you ever taken part in a movement seeking change? What was the movement trying to do? What were your reasons for joining?

the operation of the larger society. As the U.S. sociologist C. Wright Mills (1916–1963) explained, using the sociological imagination helps us "kick it up a level" and see how society shapes our personal lives. The Social Policy box takes a closer look at how sociology can help you do this for yourself.

By helping us to see the world in a new way, the sociological imagination gives us power to bring about change. But a sociological viewpoint can also be disturbing. A course in social problems asks us to face the fact that many people in our communities lose their jobs, become victims of crime, and go to bed hungry through no fault of their own. When the economy turns bad, as it did in 2008, millions of people suddenly find that they are out of work and many of them have not been able to find a good job since then. In this richest of nations, even during "good times," tens of millions of people (especially women and children) are poor. The study of social problems helps us see these truths more clearly. It also encourages us to play a part in shaping the future of our nation and the world.

Social Problems: The Basics

1.2 Define the concept "social problem" and explain how societies come to define some issues—and not others—as social problems.

A **social problem** is *a condition that undermines the well-being of some or all members of a society and is usually a matter of public controversy.* In this definition, the term "condition" refers to any situation that at least some people define as troublesome, such as not having a job, not having enough money, living in fear of crime, being overweight or living in poor health, or worrying about the effects of toxic wastes buried in the ground.

A condition that "undermines the well-being" hurts people, either by causing them immediate harm or, perhaps, by limiting their choices. For example, poverty not only deprives people of nutritious food and safe housing, but it also takes away their dignity, leaving them passive and powerless.

Because any issue affects various segments of our population differently, a particular social problem is rarely harmful to *everyone*. During the recent recession, some executives earned huge salaries and bonuses, just as some corporations (such as Walmart, which sells at very low prices) actually did pretty well. Even war that brings injury and death to young soldiers brings wealth to the companies that make and sell weapons and brings greater power to the military leaders who head our country's armed forces. As a result, the full consequences of any particular social problem are rarely simple or easy to understand.

Social problems spark public controversy. Sometimes a social problem (such as the earthquake and tsunami in

Japan in 2011 or the typhoon that devastated the Philippines in 2013) disturbs a significant number of people. In other cases (such as the outbreak of swine flu in Mexico and other regions of the world), a small number of significant people (researchers, public health officials, and government leaders) point out the problem and take action that affects the larger society (by, say, stockpiling vaccine and restricting travel to areas where infections have been reported).

Social Problems over Time

What are our country's most serious social problems? The answer depends on when you ask the question. As shown in Table 1–1, the public's view of problems changes over time. Back in 1935, a survey of U.S. adults identified the ten biggest problems facing the country, which we can compare to a similar survey completed near the end of 2013 (Gallup, 2013). In the mid-1930s, the Great Depression was the major concern because as much as 25 percent of U.S. adults were out of work. Not surprisingly, unemployment topped the list of problems that year. After years of gridlock in Washington, D.C., dissatisfaction with government topped the list in 2013, but several of the issues cited as serious social problems also reflected our country's weak economy.

Comparing the two lists in the table, we find four issues on both: the economy, unemployment, income inequality, and dissatisfaction with government. But the other issues are different, showing that the public's view of social problems changes over time. Of course, public opinion is always changing even over short periods. In the months after the onset of the recession at the end of 2007, the share of the people who said the economy was the country's most important problem jumped almost fivefold. Similarly, in reaction to the troubled rollout of the "Obamacare" Web site in the final months of 2013, an increasing share of the public identified health care as one of the nation's most serious social problems (Gallup, 2013).

Table 1–1 Serious Social Problems, 1935 and 2013

1935	2013
1. Unemployment and a poor economy	1. Dissatisfaction with government
2. Inefficient government	2. Health care
3. Danger of war	3. The economy
4. High taxes	4. Unemployment
5. Government overinvolvement	5. Federal budget deficit
6. Labor conflict	6. Moral/ethical decline
7. Poor farm conditions	7. Education
8. Inadequate pensions for the elderly	8. Welfare
9. High concentration of wealth	9. Lack of respect for others
10. Drinking alcohol	10. Gap between the rich and poor

SOURCE: Gallup (1935, 2013).

The Social-Constructionist Approach

The fact that people at different times define different issues as social problems points to the importance of the **social-constructionist approach**, *the assertion that social problems arise as people define conditions as undesirable and in need of change*. This approach states that social problems have a subjective foundation, reflecting people's judgments about their world. For example, the public has yet to include obesity on the list of serious social problems, even though health officials say that most adults in the United States are overweight. This is true despite the objective fact that illness brought on by obesity costs the lives of hundreds of thousands of people in our country each year, which is many times the number of our soldiers who were killed in Iraq or Afghanistan.

Figure 1–1 explains the subjective and objective foundations of social problems. Box A includes issues—such as homicide—that are objectively very harmful (almost 15,000 people are murdered each year in the United States) and cause widespread concern (polls show that a majority of U.S. adults worry about this kind of violent crime) (Smith et al., 2013). Box B includes issues—such as the use of automobiles—that, objectively speaking, cause even greater harm (more than 32,000 people in the United States die each year in auto accidents), and yet hardly anyone sees these issues as social problems. Of course, one reason people overlook the high death toll on our highways is that we think of automobiles as necessary to

our way of life. Box C represents issues—such as school shootings—that, objectively speaking, cause relatively limited harm (only a few dozen people have died from such incidents, which is actually fewer than the number of people who die each year from bee stings), but these issues are widely viewed as serious problems all the same (Federal Bureau of Investigation, 2013; National Highway Traffic Safety Administration, 2013). Finally, Box D includes the use of cell phones and other activities that are not thought to be harmful and also are not considered a problem.

Issues may move over time from one box to another. For years after the invention of cell phones, for example, few people worried much about their use even by those operating motor vehicles and there was little evidence that this practice posed a threat, placing the issue in Box D. Recently, however, studies are reporting that the use of cell phones by people driving automobiles plays some part in more than 1 million accidents a year, claiming several hundred lives. As the number of deaths linked to cell phone use continues to increase, this issue will move toward Box B. By 2013, as a result of increasing public concern, twelve states (California, Connecticut, Delaware, Hawaii, Illinois, Maryland, Nevada, New Jersey, New York, Oregon, Washington, and West Virginia) plus the District of Columbia have banned talking on handheld phones while driving; thirty-seven states have outlawed cell phone use by new drivers, and forty-one states have prohibited texting by anyone behind the wheel. Before long public opinion could define cell phone use in cars as a serious problem, moving the issue from Box B to Box A (Fitch et al., 2013; Governors Highway Safety Association, 2013).

Other issues that are not considered a problem now may be viewed quite differently at some point in the future. For example, in the wake of the 9/11 terrorist attacks, most people in the United States were only too glad that the National Security Administration and other government agencies were tracking people's movement, telephone calls, and Internet activity with the stated intention of identifying patterns pointing to the likelihood of terrorist activity. A decade ago, little was known of this tracking, and probably most people did not even realize the potential of computer technology to undermine personal privacy (Scherer, 2013). As a result, the government's use of computer technology fell in Box D. In recent years, revelations about the extent of government monitoring of people's movement and communication have convinced an increasing share of the public that this issue poses a real danger to personal freedom, suggesting that this issue is moving to Box B. Perhaps, at some point in the future, *most* people will consider this issue to be a serious social problem, placing the issue in Box A.

	Is it subjectively considered a very serious problem?	
	Yes	**No**
Yes	**A** Homicide	**B** Use of automobiles
No	**C** School shootings	**D** Use of cell phones

Does it objectively cause serious harm to thousands of people?

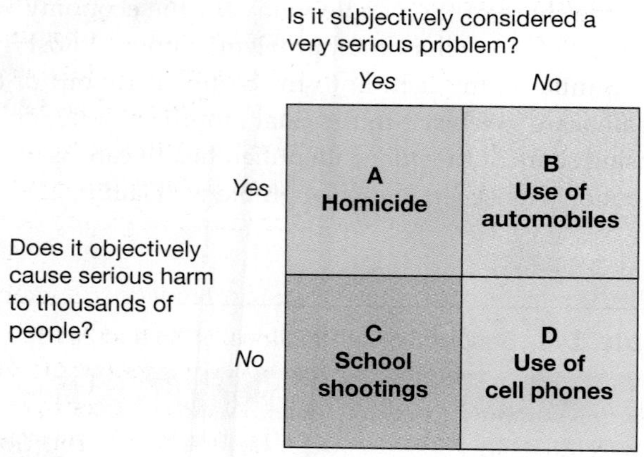

Figure 1–1 The Objective and Subjective Assessment of Social Issues

This figure shows that some issues (such as homicide) are both objectively harmful and widely seen as problems. But many issues that are objectively harmful (the use of automobiles results in more than 32,000 deaths each year) are not perceived as serious social problems. Likewise, some issues that are viewed as serious social problems (school shootings, for example) actually harm very few people. Many other issues (such as using cell phones) do not now appear to be harmful, although this may change at some point in the future.

Recognizing that the subjective and objective importance of social issues may be quite different opens the door for a deeper understanding of social change. Consider this curious pattern: A century ago, it was objectively true that the social standing of women was far below that of men. In 1900, nine out of ten adult men worked for income, and nine out of ten adult women stayed home doing housework and raising children. Women didn't even have the right to vote.

Although some people condemned what they saw as blatant inequality, most people did not define this situation as a problem. Why not? Most people believed that because women and men have some obvious biological differences, the two sexes must have different abilities. Thinking this way, it seemed natural for men to go out to earn a living while women—who were thought back then to be the "weaker sex"—stayed behind to manage the home. Objectively, gender inequality was huge; subjectively, however, it was rarely defined as a social problem.

Today, women and men are far closer to being socially equal than they were in 1900. Yet awareness of a "gender problem" in the United States has actually become greater. Why? Our cultural standards have changed, to the point that people now see the two sexes as mostly the same, and so we *expect* women and men to be socially equal. As a result, we perceive even small instances of gender inequality as a problem.

When we investigate social issues, it is important to consider both objective facts and subjective perceptions. Both factors play a part in the social construction of social problems.

Claims Making

Back in 1981, the Centers for Disease Control and Prevention began to receive reports of a strange disease that was killing people. The victims were mostly homosexual men. The disease came to be known as "acquired immune deficiency syndrome" (AIDS). For several years, even as the numbers of cases in the United States climbed into the thousands, AIDS received limited media coverage and there was little public outcry. By 1985, however, the public as a whole had become concerned about the danger of AIDS, and this disease was defined as a serious social problem.

What made this happen? For any condition to be defined as a social problem, people—usually a small number at first—make claims that the issue should be defined this way. In the case of AIDS, medical officials sounded the alarm and also the gay communities in large cities (notably San Francisco and New York) mobilized to spread information about the dangers posed by this deadly disease.

Claims making is *the process of convincing the public and important public officials that a particular issue or situation should be defined as a social problem.* Claims begin when people reject the *status quo* (Latin words meaning "the situation as it is"). The first step in claims making is to create controversy, beginning the process of change by convincing others that the existing situation is not acceptable. Claims making continues as people explain exactly *what* changes are needed and *why* they are needed.

Ordinary people can make claims more powerful by joining together. In 1980, women who had lost children in auto accidents caused by drunk drivers joined together to form Mothers Against Drunk Driving (MADD). This organization campaigned for tougher laws against drinking and driving in order to make the roads safer. In recent decades, students on college campuses have claimed that many women are victims of violence, trying to raise awareness by encouraging victims to speak out. This effort has been assisted by national organizations such as Take Back the Night.

The mass media are important to the process of claims making. Television, radio, newspapers, and the Internet can convey information to tens of millions of people and help mobilize individuals to join together in groups actively seeking change. The greater the media coverage of a topic and the more media stories argue for change, the more likely the issue in question is to develop into a social problem.

Success in claims making can occur quickly. After the economy went into a tailspin in 2008, government officials and the public quickly came to see the collapsing banking system and the rising unemployment rate as serious social problems. In other cases, the process may take years. As noted earlier, although experts estimate that driving while talking on handheld cell phones causes several hundred deaths every year, only twelve states have passed laws banning this practice (Governors Highway Safety Association, 2013).

As claims making gains public attention, it is likely to prompt counterclaims from opponents. In other words, most controversial issues involve claims making from at least two different positions. Take the abortion controversy, for example. One side of the debate claims that abortion is the wrongful killing of unborn babies. The other side claims that abortion is a woman's right, a reproductive choice that should be made only by the woman herself. Politics—how power plays out in a society—is usually a matter of claims and counterclaims about what should and should not be defined as social problems.

Success in claims making is often marked by the passing of a law. This act is a clear statement that some behavior is wrong, and it also enlists the power of government to oppose it. In recent decades, the passage of laws

Claims making is the process of defining certain issues as social problems. Economic inequality has existed in the United States throughout this country's entire history. Yet only in the last five years has this issue gained widespread public attention. In 2011, the Occupy Wall Street movement pointed to the "1 percent" who dominate U.S. society, and economic inequality was an issue debated in the 2012 presidential election. More recently, a number of left-leaning organizations have marched calling for government policies that would reduce the gap between the very rich and most working families.

against stalking and sexual harassment clearly defined these behaviors as problems and directed the criminal justice system to act against offenders (Welch, Dawson, & Nierobisz, 2002).

One important dimension of claims making is the deliberate use of language. Consider the case of the new health care law. Under this new law, insurance companies can no longer refuse insurance to someone who is already sick. Opponents of the law characterize this policy as "socializing" risk, meaning that the law forces other people to subsidize the cost of the sick individual's insurance. The word "socializing" (which sounds a lot like "socialism") suggests that this policy is outside this country's tradition of people taking personal responsibility for their own health and insurance. On the other hand, supporters of the health care law praise an end to what they call "discrimination against those with preexisting conditions." The use of the word "discrimination" implies that such refusal is unjust and a violation of people's basic rights.

The same careful use of language applies to debates about how to solve problems. In general, advocates choose language that makes their policy seem necessary and reasonable; by contrast, opponents describe the same policy in language that makes it seem unreasonable and perhaps even dangerous. In 2013, for example, Chicago mayor Rahm Emanuel tried to address his city's budget crisis by closing some public schools and moving their students to nearby schools. Supporters cheered what they saw as a necessary step toward a balanced budget. Opponents, alarmed at the thought of children having to walk through unfamiliar neighborhoods that might have gang activity, condemned the mayor's policy as "killing our children" (Rogers, 2013). In short, people on both sides of any issue use language to "spin" claims in one way or another.

Problems and Social Movements

The process of claims making almost always involves the deliberate efforts of many people working together. A **social movement** is *an organized effort at claims making that tries to shape the way people think about an issue in order to encourage or discourage social change*. Over the past several decades, social movements have played a key part in the construction of numerous social problems, including the AIDS epidemic, sexual harassment, family violence, and the debate over a national health insurance program.

Stages in Social Movements Typically, social movements progress through four distinct stages, shown in Figure 1–2, in the effort to define a condition as a social problem (Blumer, 1969; Mauss, 1975; Tilly, 1978):

1. **Emergence.** The emergence of a movement occurs when people (initially just a few) come together sharing their concern about the status quo and begin to make claims about the need for change. In 2011, for example, a group of activists in Canada proposed a gathering of people in New York City's Zuccotti Park and the result was the beginning of the Occupy Wall Street movement. The protestors drew attention to increasing economic inequality, corporate greed, and the great influence that corporations (especially those on Wall Street) have on the U.S. system of government.

2. **Coalescence.** The coalescence of a movement occurs as a new organization begins holding rallies and demonstrations, making public its beliefs, and engaging in political lobbying. After the initial "encampment" in the Wall Street area of New York, similar protests spread to dozens of other cities across the country and

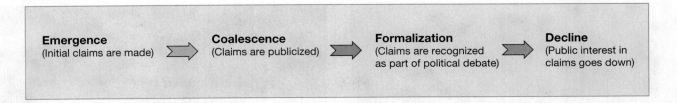

Figure 1–2   Four Stages in the Life Course of a Social Movement

Social movements typically pass through these four stages over time. How quickly this process unfolds varies from movement to movement.

in other nations. The mass media began to discuss the claims made by the Occupy movement.

3. **Formalization.** Social movements become formalized as they become established players on the political scene. Although social movements usually begin with only volunteers, at this stage the organization is likely to include a trained and salaried staff. The Occupy movement has attracted many volunteers and has developed a strong presence on Facebook and other social media. By 2014, however, Occupy was not as prominent as it had been years before, and it is not clear that it has developed the level of formalization that will be needed if it is to remain a part of the political scene in the future. But the message of the movement has certainly been adopted by the Democratic Party and the issue of economic inequality was widely discussed during the 2012 national elections.

4. **Decline.** Becoming established is no guarantee of continuing success. Social movements may decline because they run out of money, because their claims fail to catch on with the public, or because opposing organizations are more convincing. Sometimes, the powers-that-be simply have the clout to crush a social movement that threatens it. The future of the Occupy movement will depend partly on whether the trend toward income inequality continues and on the share of our population that is willing to become invested in change.

   At the same time, of course, a movement can decline simply because it is successful. If enough people demand greater economic equality, movements such as Occupy Wall Street may no longer be necessary. At the same time, organizations that succeed in reaching an initial goal often adopt new goals and continue to operate. The feminist movement began with the goal of getting women the right to vote and moved on to improving the standing of women in the workplace and in the home. More recently, MADD has shifted its attention from combating drunken driving to the goal of opposing another movement that seeks to lower the drinking age from twenty-one to eighteen.

Social Problems: Eight Assertions

To complete our discussion of the basics about social problems, the following eight assertions describe how sociologists approach social problems. These statements sum up much of what has already been presented in this chapter, and they form the foundation for everything that follows in this text.

1. **Social problems result from the ways in which society operates.** Society shapes the lives of each and every one of us. Because U.S. culture stresses individualism, we tend to think that people are responsible for their own lives. As C. Wright Mills (1959) pointed out, however, a sociological perspective shows us that social problems are caused less by personal failings than by the operation of society itself. For example, the increasing income inequality in the United States results not from the fact that some people are working harder than others but from corporate salary policies and government tax policies that are distributing income more and more unequally. In the same way, the tough economic climate means that millions of people are finding only low-paying jobs or no jobs at all. In other words, problems such as income inequality and unemployment have their roots in the way our economic and political systems operate. For this reason, correcting social problems requires change to society itself.

2. **Social problems are not caused by bad people.** This is the flip side of the first assertion. Especially when some individual harms a lot of innocent people—as when Bernard Madoff swindled investors out of $65 billion or when Adam Lanza shot and killed twenty-six people in a Connecticut elementary school—we think of the problem in terms of bad actions by evil people. The law holds us as individuals accountable for our actions.

   But, in general, pointing to "bad people" does not go very far toward explaining social problems. It is true that some people commit serious crimes that hurt others. But whether the crime rate is high or low depends not on individuals but on how society itself

Compared with women fifty years ago, women today are much more equal to men in terms of rights and opportunities. Yet today's women are more likely to see gender inequality as a problem. Can you explain this apparent contradiction?

is organized. As Chapter 6 ("Crime, Violence, and the Criminal Justice System") explains, how many police we hire, how many prisons we build, whether the economy is strong or not, and whether all categories of people have access to good jobs or not will go a long way toward explaining whether the crime rate is low or high.

3. **Problems are socially constructed as people define a condition as harmful and in need of change.** Whatever the objective facts of any situation, people must come to see the condition as a serious social problem. Claims making is the process of defining a condition as a social problem.

4. **People see problems differently.** Some issues, such as the high unemployment rate in recent years, are widely regarded as serious problems. But most issues are matters of controversy. For example, the Obama administration created the Affordable Care Act, which supporters see as a needed step toward the goal of proving everyone with health insurance. Opponents of this law, however, claim that inefficient government is unlikely to make care more "affordable" or to provide people with choice about their care. As this example suggests, one person's "solution" may be another's "problem."

5. **Definitions of problems change over time.** The public's views on what constitutes a serious problem change as time goes on. A century ago, the United States was a much poorer nation where no one was surprised to find many rural people living in shacks and many city people living on the streets. But as living standards rose, members of our society began to think of safe housing as a basic right, and so bad housing and homelessness emerged as social problems. Going in the other direction, some "problems" of the

past have largely gone away because people no longer think of them as problems. For example, sixty years ago, interracial marriage was illegal in many places and was widely defined as a social problem; such marriages, however, are now legal everywhere in the country and raise few eyebrows today.

6. **Problems involve subjective values as well as objective facts.** Today, 31 percent of people who have ever been married have also been divorced. But does this mean that there is a "divorce problem"? Facts are important, but so are subjective perceptions about any issue. People who value traditional families are likely to view a high divorce rate as a serious problem. But others who think family life can limit individual opportunities, especially those of women, may disagree.

7. **Many—but not all—social problems can be solved.** One good reason to study social problems is to improve society. Sociologists believe that many social problems can be effectively addressed, if not eliminated entirely. Back in 1960, for example, 35 percent of elderly men and women in the United States lived below the poverty line. Since then, rising Social Security benefits and better employer pensions have reduced the poverty rate among seniors to about 9 percent, which is about one-fourth of what it used to be.

But sociologists do not expect that every social problem will be solved. As already noted, situations that are problems for some people are advantageous to others, and sometimes those who benefit are powerful enough to slow the pace of change or to prevent change entirely.

The driving force behind the new Affordable Care Act is the fact that the United States remains the only industrial nation without a tax-funded system that helps pay for everyone's medical care. As the new system has come "online," 48 million people lack health insurance, and strong political opposition to universal health care (especially a system that is entirely government funded) remains on the part of organizations representing physicians and insurance companies and those who seek to limit the scope of government.

Even problems that everyone wants to solve sometimes defy solution. For instance, just about everyone hopes that we will find a cure for AIDS. But, despite advances that make "living with AIDS" a reality, the research breakthrough that finally cures this disease may lie years in the future.

8. **Various social problems are related.** Because social problems are rooted in the operation of society, many social problems are related to one another. This means that addressing one problem—say, reducing the number of children growing up in poverty—may in turn help solve other problems, such as the high rate of high school dropouts, drug abuse, and crime.

It is also true that solving one problem may create a new problem that we did not expect. For example, the invention of the automobile in the late 1800s helped people move about more easily, but as decades went by, automobiles were polluting the air and causing tens of thousands of traffic deaths every year (32,367 in 2011).

Together, these eight assertions form a sociological understanding of social problems. In the next section, we turn to another important idea: Addressing many social problems requires the use of a global perspective.

Social Problems: A Global Perspective

Many beginning students of sociology find it hard to imagine just how serious problems such as poverty and hunger are in the poorest regions of the world. To help you understand the seriousness of global problems, the Social Problems in Global Perspective box describes patterns of inequality in a world represented by a village of 1,000 people.

Adopting a global perspective also shows us that some social problems cross national boundaries. For example, Chapter 15 ("Population and Global Inequality") explains that the problem of Earth's increasing human population threatens the well-being of everyone on the planet. Chapter 16 ("Technology and the Environment") offers another example, showing how people living in rich countries are consuming the planet's resources very quickly and polluting the planet's air and water.

Finally, a global perspective shows that many dimensions of life—and many of life's challenges—may be quite different elsewhere. Global Map 1–1 on page 12 shows us

SOCIAL PROBLEMS IN GLOBAL PERSPECTIVE
The Global Village: Problems around the World

To see just how desperate the lives of many of the world's 7.1 billion people really are, imagine the entire planet reduced to the size of a "global village" of 1,000 people. The global village contains 603 Asians (including 190 citizens of the People's Republic of China), 154 Africans, 104 Europeans, 85 Latin Americans, 5 residents of Australia and the South Pacific, and 49 North Americans, 44 of them from the United States.

The village is a very rich place with a vast array of goods and services. Yet anything beyond the basics is too expensive for almost everyone. This is because of economic inequality: The richest 1 percent of all villagers—the ten richest people—earn 15 percent of all income and the richest 80 villagers (8 percent) earn half of all the income. By contrast, the worst-off 150 villagers (15 percent) earn just 1 percent of all income. These people are hungry every day and even lack safe drinking water. Because of their deprivation, the poorest villagers have little energy to work and fall victim to life-threatening diseases (Ortiz & Cummins, 2011; Milanovic, 2012).

Villagers boast of their fine schools, yet only 67 people (6.7 percent) have a college degree, and 175 of the village's adult population (17.5 percent) cannot read or write.

Many troubling issues such as health, illiteracy, and poverty are much worse elsewhere in the world than in a rich nation such as the United States. In fact, 41 percent of the world's people live on less than $2 a day—a standard of living far below what we in the United States consider "poor." This harsh reality of suffering—detailed in Chapter 15 ("Population and Global Inequality")—is one good reason to take a global perspective in our study of social problems (Milanovic, 2012; Population Reference Bureau, 2013; UNESCO, 2013; World Bank, 2013).

What Do You Think?

1. Do any of the facts presented in this box surprise you? Which ones? Why?
2. As a person living in a rich nation, do you think you have a responsibility to help solve problems in poor nations? Why or why not?
3. Can you see ways that you, personally, benefit from the economic inequality of our world? Can you point to ways that you are harmed by inequality? Explain.

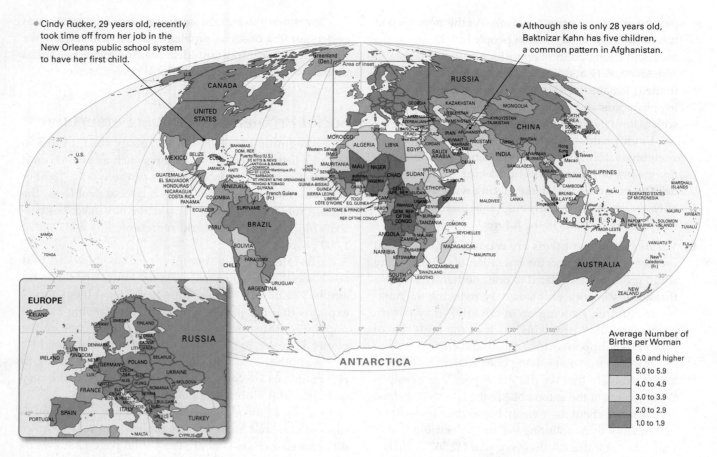

● Cindy Rucker, 29 years old, recently took time off from her job in the New Orleans public school system to have her first child.

● Although she is only 28 years old, Baktnizar Kahn has five children, a common pattern in Afghanistan.

Average Number of Births per Woman	
	6.0 and higher
	5.0 to 5.9
	4.0 to 4.9
	3.0 to 3.9
	2.0 to 2.9
	1.0 to 1.9

Window on the World

Global Map 1–1 Women's Childbearing in Global Perspective

How people live and the challenges they face differ dramatically around the world. If you are a woman living in a high-income nation, the chances are that you will have one or two children during your lifetime. But had you been born in one of the low-income nations of Africa, four, five, or even six children would be the rule. Can you point to several reasons for this global disparity?

SOURCE: Data from Hamilton, Martin, & Ventura (2013) and Population Reference Bureau (2013).

that in rich countries such as the United States, the typical woman has one or two children. But in a poorer country such as Guatemala, three children is the norm. In even poorer nations, the number goes even higher: In Ethiopia, four children is common; in Afghanistan, it's five; and in Nigeria, it's more than six.

Analyzing Social Problems: Sociological Theory

1.3 Apply sociological theory to the study of social problems.

Sociologists weave various facts into meaning using **theory**, *a statement of how and why specific facts are related.* Building a theory, in turn, depends on a **theoretical approach**, *a basic image of society that guides theory and research.*

Using a particular theoretical approach leads sociologists to ask certain questions. The following sections present the discipline's most widely used theoretical models: the structural-functional, social-conflict, feminist, and symbolic-interaction approaches.

The Structural-Functional Approach

The **structural-functional approach** is *a theoretical framework that sees society as a system of many interrelated parts.* Sociologists describe the main parts of this system as **social institutions**, *major spheres of social life, or societal subsystems, organized to meet a basic human need.* For example, the structural-functional approach might explore how the family is a system to ensure the care and raising of children, how schools provide young people with the skills they need for adult life, how the economy produces and distributes material goods, how the political system sets national goals and priorities, and how religion gives our lives purpose and meaning.

Early Functional Theory: Problems as Social Pathology

A century ago, the structural-functional approach looked on society as if it were a living organism. This view led to a *social pathology theory*, a model that treats social problems as a disruption in society's normal operation, in the same way that a disease upsets the operation of the human body. Crime, truancy, and premarital sex were all seen as pathologies (from a Greek word meaning "disease") that threatened the health of society.

What caused society to break down? Because early functionalists saw society as good and healthy, many were quick to assume that pathologies must be caused by bad or weak people. The English sociologist Herbert Spencer (1820–1903) made the claim that the problem of poverty was the result of some people lacking the ability and personal discipline to work. Spencer based his thinking on the ideas of the biologist Charles Darwin, who published a groundbreaking theory of evolution in 1859. Spencer's "social Darwinism" viewed the rich as society's most successful members and the poor as those who could not keep up. To Spencer, the harsh competition of the marketplace was good for society because it guaranteed the "survival of the fittest." For this reason, Spencer opposed social welfare programs as harmful to society because they transfer wealth from the people he considered the most able to the ones he regarded as the weakest.

There is no surprise in the fact that Spencer was very popular among the rich industrialist owners of his day. But sociologists gradually turned against Spencer because there is no scientific evidence that the rich and powerful are any more worthy than others or that a competitive economy benefits everyone. Social Darwinism has little support among sociologists today. But understanding this approach is important, if only because lots of people, including many politicians, still think this way.

The Chicago School: Problems as Disorganization

A second type of structural-functional theory—often called the "Chicago School" because it originated at the University of Chicago, home of the first sociology department in the United States—linked problems not to deficient people but to social "disorganization" (Park & Burgess, 1970, orig. 1921). *Social disorganization theory* holds that problems arise when society breaks down due to social change that occurs too rapidly.

A century ago, evidence of disorganization was easy to find as industrial cities grew rapidly with the arrival of millions of immigrants. Many saw traditional family patterns and long-held attitudes breaking down. Schools were filled to overflowing, there was not enough housing for everyone, and crime seemed to be rising out of control.

In response to such problems, many Chicago sociologists in the 1920s and 1930s became active reformers. They supported local settlement houses, set up programs to teach English to immigrants, and in a few cases even ran for public office (Faris, 1967).

More Recent Functionalism: Problems as Dysfunctions

By about 1950, the structural-functional approach had changed its emphasis from activism to scientific analysis. Sociologists then began to study the positive functions (or "eufunctions") of patterns like sports; they identified both functions that are intended and widely recognized (the "manifest functions") as well as others that are unintended and less well known (called "latent functions"). A manifest function of sports is improving physical fitness; a latent function of sports is strengthening the cultural values of individual effort and personal achievement. Sociologists noted that social patterns also have negative functions (called "dysfunctions"). For example, one dysfunction of sports on the campus is leaving college athletes with little time for their studies. From this point of view, social problems can be thought of as the dysfunctions of various social patterns.

These sociologists also pointed out that just as "good" things such as sports can have some bad consequences, "bad" things such as terrorism can sometimes do some good. For example, the terrorist attacks of September 11, 2001, cost thousands of lives but also had the effect of uniting the country behind the effort to combat terrorism. Similarly, one good thing to come out of the recent recession is reminding people that most of us can live with less.

EVALUATE

Although the structural-functional approach has been influential for more than a century, its importance has declined in recent decades. For one thing, many of today's sociologists have a renewed interest in activism and shy away from a "hands-off" approach that they think defends the status quo. For another, by viewing society as a smoothly functioning system, the structural-functional approach pays little attention to social divisions based on race, class, and gender. Since the 1960s, more attention has been paid to a second theoretical framework: the social-conflict approach.

CHECK YOUR LEARNING In a sentence, how does the structural-functional approach view society? How has this approach explained social problems in terms of social pathology, social disorganization, and social dysfunction?

The Social-Conflict Approach

The **social-conflict approach** is *a theoretical framework that sees society as divided by inequality and conflict.* In general, conflict theories claim that social problems arise from the fact that our society is divided into "haves" and "have-nots."

The structural-functional approach points to the contribution young people working in factories in Indonesia make to their families' income. The social-conflict approach provides a different insight: Many of the products popular in the United States are made by young people in sweatshops that pay pennies an hour to workers.

Marxist Theory: Problems and Class Conflict

Marxist theory, sometimes called "class conflict theory," is an explanation of social problems guided by Karl Marx's theory of class struggle. Marx (1818–1883), a German-born thinker and social activist, was amazed by how much the new industrial factories could produce. Yet Marx criticized society for concentrating most of this wealth in the hands of a few. How, he wondered, could a society so rich contain so many people who were so poor?

Marx devoted his life to analyzing *capitalism*, an economic system in which businesses are privately owned by people called "capitalists" who operate them for profit. To Marx, social problems are the inevitable result of the normal operation of a capitalist economy. The industrial technology of modern societies produces enough to meet everyone's needs; modern society therefore has the *productive* capacity to end human suffering. Yet, Marx observed, allowing this technology to operate under a capitalist economy means that this bounty will be *distributed* to only a few. Capitalism, explained Marx, is a system that does not serve the people but only seeks profit for the small share of people who own factories and other productive property. Therefore, he concluded, it is a system that does not operate to meet human needs. As a result, the normal operation of the capitalist system creates social problems such as poverty.

Marx was critical of modern society, but he was also optimistic about the future. He predicted that, as a system that failed to meet the needs of most people, capitalism would bring about its own destruction. In the short term, Marx concluded, the rich would become richer and richer, while the poor would have less and less. Industrial workers, whom he called "proletarians," performed hard labor in factories for low wages while facing the ever present threat of being replaced by machines. In the long term, Marx was certain that workers, holding little hope for the future, would join together, rise up, and end this oppressive system.

As Chapter 2 ("Poverty and Wealth") explains, however, such a revolution has not yet happened, at least not in industrial-capitalist nations. But followers of Marx still support a radical restructuring of society—especially the economy—as the best means to address most social problems.

Multiculturalism: Problems of Racial and Ethnic Inequality

Sociologists see conflict based not only on class but also on color and culture. Societies attach importance to skin color and cultural background, which leads to ranking people in a hierarchy based on race and ethnicity. *Multicultural theory* explains social problems in terms of racial and ethnic inequality.

The great social diversity of the United States and the rest of the Western Hemisphere is the result of centuries of immigration. Every person who lives anywhere in the Americas, from the northern reaches of Canada to the southern tip of Chile, either migrated here from someplace else or has an ancestor who did. Here in the United States, some categories of people (especially white Anglo-Saxon Protestants, or WASPs) have enjoyed higher social standing than others (especially people of color).

In 1865, the United States ended centuries of slavery, an important step in the process of giving people more equal standing before the law. Yet as Chapter 3 ("Racial and Ethnic Inequality") points out, racial and ethnic minorities remain disadvantaged today and at higher risk of poverty, poor health, street violence, and numerous other social problems. In addition, racial and ethnic prejudice is great enough on the part of some people that they see the very presence of minorities in their communities as a social problem.

EVALUATE

Offering a striking contrast to the structural-functional view of society as a well-integrated system, various social-conflict approaches now dominate the study of social problems. But taking a social-conflict approach also has limitations.

Critics fault this approach for overstating the extent of social divisions. They point out that, because of the general pattern of upward social mobility over the past century, few members of our society today show interest in Marxist class revolution. Although there is still much to be done, progress has been real: Over the last century, living standards have risen and African Americans and other minorities have far more opportunities than they did in the past.

A second criticism is that social-conflict analysis rejects scientific objectivity in favor of political activism, which calls into question the truth of some of its claims. Marxists and multiculturalists concede that their work is political, but as they see it, so is any theoretical approach, including structural-functionalism. They add that functionalism escapes the criticism of being biased only because it supports the status quo.

CHECK YOUR LEARNING   In a sentence, how does the social-conflict approach view society? Explain what Marxist theory and multicultural theory identify as the causes of social problems.

The Feminist Approach

The feminist approach, also called the "gender-conflict" approach, is another type of social-conflict approach in sociology. Because of its increasing importance to sociologists, this approach is appropriately treated on its own terms.

Feminism is *a political movement that seeks the social equality of women and men.* Feminists claim that women suffer more from poverty and many other social problems because society places men in positions of power over women. *Gender-conflict theory* explains social problems in terms of men's dominance over women.

Chapter 4 ("Gender Inequality") points out that although the social standing of women and men has become more equal during the past century, women working full time still earn just 77 percent as much as men do (U.S. Census Bureau, 2013). In recent decades, an increasing share of the poor is made up of women (especially single women) and their children. Just as important, working women remain concentrated in a number of low-paying jobs, and from childhood to old age, women are subject to everyday disadvantages—from subtle prejudice to outright violence—at the hands of men.

EVALUATE

Like Marxism and multiculturalism, feminism also seeks to change the status quo just as it challenges structural-functional view of society as a well-integrated system. In recent decades, feminism has become a widely supported point of view in sociology, and it is commonly used in the analysis of social problems. But, like Marxism and multiculturalism, this variant of the social-conflict approach also has limitations.

In the same way that critics fault Marxism for overstating "class warfare," critics claim that feminism overstates the degree of inequality that separates the sexes. Over the course of the last century, the opportunities for women—in politics, in the workplace, and in other arenas such as sports—have increased dramatically. Without denying that gender inequality is still a reality, critics claim that women (like other minorities) enjoy far greater opportunities than they did in the past.

The charge of political bias is also made against feminism by its critics. The fact that feminism explicitly seeks social change means that this approach is clearly a form of social activism. As in the case of Marxism and multiculturalism, defenders of feminism respond that they are committed to seeking greater social justice. They also point out that any analysis is political in that it either calls for social change or it does not.

A final criticism, which applies to both the structural-functional and all the social-conflict approaches, is that these macro-level approaches make use of broad generalities that seem removed from how individuals actually experience their world. This concern has led to the development of a third theoretical model: the symbolic-interaction approach.

CHECK YOUR LEARNING   In a sentence, how does feminist theory see the world? Explain how feminist theory understands social problems.

The Symbolic-Interaction Approach

The goal of describing society more in terms of how people experience the world underlies the **symbolic-interaction approach**, *a theoretical framework that sees society as the product of individuals interacting with one another.* We can apply this approach to social problems by asking two questions: How do people become involved in problematic behavior? And more generally, how do people come to define issues as social problems in the first place?

Learning Theory: Problems and the Social Environment

Why do young people in one neighborhood get into more trouble than those who live in another neighborhood? *Learning theory* claims that people learn troublesome attitudes and behaviors from others around them. The point here is that no one sets out to become a burglar, a Wall Street swindler, a drug abuser, or an industrial polluter; rather, people gradually engage in such behavior as they learn skills and attitudes from others.

A learning approach guided Nanette Davis (1980, 2000) in her study of thirty women working in prostitution. Interviewing these women, Davis discovered that no one simply decides to sell sex. A woman might turn to such a life for any number of reasons, perhaps as a way to cope with loneliness or as a means of economic survival. Whatever the reason, Davis found, the women she studied gradually "drifted" toward prostitution, usually taking years to learn the skills, norms, and attitudes that characterize the professional sex worker. In short, people learn such roles one step at a time, eventually reaching the point where the role becomes their livelihood as well as part of their social identity.

Reality is often less a matter of what people do than of how they define their own behavior. Studies show that many college students consume large amounts of alcohol on a regular basis. To these students, drinking heavily may just be "partying." College officials, however, may define such behavior as "binge drinking" or "alcohol abuse," which can result in serious penalties.

Labeling Theory: Problems and Social Definitions

The symbolic-interaction approach also explores how people socially construct reality. *Labeling theory* states that the reality of any particular situation depends on how people define it. For example, the spirited consumption of alcohol that young people view as normal partying may be labeled by college officials as dangerous binge drinking.

The distinction between a "social drinker" and a "problem drinker" often depends on which audience is watching (do parents view drinking the same way that friends do?), who the actor is (do we view women who drink the same as we view men who do?), where the action takes place (is drinking in a park the same as drinking at a bar?), and when the action occurs (is drinking on Sunday morning different from doing the same thing on Saturday night?). Obviously, many factors come into play as people socially define a given situation.

EVALUATE

The symbolic-interaction approach adds a micro-level or "real-world" view of social problems. But by highlighting how individuals differ in their perceptions, this approach overlooks the extent to which social structure, including class and race, shapes people's lives. In other words, pointing out that prostitution involves both learning and labeling is worthwhile, but we don't want to forget the broader issue that men dominate society and cast women into sexual roles in the first place.

CHECK YOUR LEARNING   How does the symbolic-interaction approach view society? How do learning theory and labeling theory help us to understand social problems?

This completes the introduction to sociology's major theoretical approaches, summarized in the Applying Theory table. But not only do sociologists use theory to analyze social problems, they also engage in research to gather relevant facts. We turn next to the ways in which sociologists conduct research.

Finding the Facts: Sociological Research

1.4   Discuss the methods sociologists use to study social problems.

Many sociologists devote their lives to investigating the nature and causes of social problems in the hope of making the world a better place. Barbara Ehrenreich (2001), for example, spent months working alongside low-wage workers in Florida, Maine, and Minnesota, documenting the many challenges faced by this country's "working poor." The willingness to work hard, she found, is sometimes not enough to escape poverty, as millions of people throughout the United States know all too well.

The sociologist Lois Benjamin (1991) investigated the problem of racial prejudice. Is prejudice directed only at poor people, or are successful people also victimized in this way? After interviewing 100 of the most successful African American men and women in the United States, Benjamin concluded that success provides no escape from racial prejudice. Even black people at the top of their fields encounter racial hostility in their daily lives.

William Julius Wilson (1996a) conducted interviews and examined available data in a major study of poor people living in Chicago. He found that people who have lived in poverty for many years contend with a host of social problems, including joblessness, unstable families, and, perhaps worst of all, a loss of hope. Wilson found that the major reason for this poverty is the disappearance of good jobs from Chicago's inner city.

APPLYING THEORY

Sociology's Major Theoretical Approaches

	Structural-Functional Approach	Social-Conflict and Feminist Approaches	Symbolic-Interaction Approach
What is the level of analysis?	Macro-level	Macro-level	Micro-level
What is the basic image of society?	Society is a system of interrelated parts, all of which contribute to its operation.	The social-conflict approach sees society as a system of social inequality in which some categories of people benefit at the expense of others. The feminist approach highlights inequality between men and women.	Through social interaction, we construct the variable and changing reality we experience.
How do we understand problems?	Society is basically good; problems are the result of deficient people, too rapid change, or dysfunctional consequences.	Problems result from inequality in terms of class (Marxism), gender (gender-conflict theory and feminism), and race (multiculturalism).	People learn attitudes and behavior for all patterns of behavior; this approach explores how people may or may not define situations as problems.

These brief accounts are just a few examples of the research being done by thousands of sociologists across the country. The following sections provide a brief description of the research methods used by Ehrenreich, Benjamin, Wilson, and many others to study social problems—and to make the world a better place.

Research Methods

Sociologists use four major research methods in their investigation of social problems: surveys, field research, experimental research, and secondary analysis.

Survey Research: Asking Questions   The most widely used research procedure is the **survey**, *a research method in which subjects respond to items on a questionnaire or in an interview*. A *questionnaire* is a series of items a researcher presents to subjects for their response. Researchers may deliver questionnaires in person, send them through the mail, or use e-mail.

Of course, the success of a project depends on your ability to locate the people you want to survey. If you are studying, say, homeless people, identifying and tracking down subjects may be difficult because many have no stable addresses. Alternatively, it would not be hard for researchers studying the medical system from the patient's point of view to find sick people in hospitals, but gaining access to them and getting them to complete a questionnaire may be challenging.

The *interview* is a more personal survey technique in which a researcher meets face to face with respondents to discuss some issue. This interactive format allows an investigator to probe people's opinions with follow-up questions. Interviews take a lot of time, of course, which usually limits the number of people one can survey in this way. A good way to think about surveys is this: Questionnaires offer the chance for greater *breadth* of opinion, and interviews can provide greater *depth* of understanding.

Whether you use a questionnaire or an interview format, the key to a successful survey is selecting a sample of people that represents the larger population of interest. For example, researchers try to reach conclusions about all the police officers in a city by studying only a small number of them. To make a sample representative of the larger population, researchers typically use various techniques to select subjects randomly.

Sometimes, researchers pursue a *case study*, in which they focus on a single case: a person (say, a divorced mother), an organization (a college or a gambling casino), or an event (a rock concert or a hurricane). The advantage of this approach is that focusing on a single case allows greater detail and depth of understanding. However, because this strategy involves a single case, researchers are not able to generalize their results.

Field Research: Joining In   Have you ever walked through an unfamiliar neighborhood and observed the people who lived there? If so, you have some experience with **field research** (also called participant observation), *a research method for observing people while joining them in their everyday activities*. Field research might mean investigating a particular community to understand the problems and hopes of the people who live there. Elijah Anderson (1999) did this when he studied families in some of Philadelphia's poor African American neighborhoods. Anderson discovered that although most people in these neighborhoods had "decent" values, some had come to accept what Anderson calls the "code of the streets." Such people were likely to have weak family ties, to use drugs, and especially if they were males, to engage in episodes of violence in an effort to defend themselves and to gain the respect of others.

Field studies involve a number of challenges. For example, the researcher benefits from observing people in their natural surroundings, but as Anderson's work suggests, fieldwork can be dangerous, especially to a researcher working alone. In addition, although this method makes sense for researchers with little money, it requires a lot of time, often a year or more. Finally, field researchers have to balance the demands of being a *participant*, who is personally involved in the setting, with those of an *observer*, who adopts a more detached role in order to assess a setting or situation more objectively.

Experimental Research: Looking for Causes   Why are this country's prisons so violent? Philip Zimbardo and his colleagues investigated this question using an **experiment**, *a research method for investigating cause-and-effect relationships under tightly controlled conditions*. Unlike field research, which takes place almost anywhere in the "real world," most experiments are carried out in a specially designed laboratory. There, researchers change one variable while keeping the others the same. Comparing results allows them to identify specific causes of patterns of behavior.

To investigate the causes of jailhouse violence, Zimbardo built an artificial prison in a basement at Stanford University. He recruited male students as volunteers and then assigned the most physically and mentally healthy subjects to the roles of inmates and guards. After the "prison" had been in operation for just a few days, Zimbardo was alarmed to see that on both sides of the bars, people performing their assigned roles were becoming hostile and violent. In fact, the aggression was so great that Zimbardo had to end the research for fear that someone would get seriously hurt.

Zimbardo's research highlights the responsibility researchers have for the safety and well-being of their subjects. His study also points to a fascinating conclusion: The prison system itself—not any personal problems on the part of inmates or guards—can trigger prison violence (Zimbardo, 1972; Haney, Banks, & Zimbardo, 1973).

Secondary Analysis: Using Available Data   Sometimes all that is needed to study social problems is a trip to the local library. Easier still is going online, where a vast amount of sociological information can be found. **Secondary analysis** is *a research method that makes use of data originally collected by others*. In simple terms, why go to the trouble and expense of collecting information for yourself if suitable data already exist?

Just because data are easy to find does not mean that the data are accurate. Much information that is readily available on the Internet, for example, is misleading, and some of it is just plain wrong. Always look carefully to learn as much as you can about the source: Is it a reputable organization? Does the organization have a political bias? Asking these types of questions and using more than one source will improve the quality of the data you find.

The federal government is a good source of data about almost all aspects of U.S. society. The Census Bureau continuously updates a statistical picture of the U.S. population—counting people, tracking immigration, assessing patterns of health, and reporting levels of employment, income, education, and much more. Other government agencies also collect specific information; for example, the Federal Bureau of Investigation publishes detailed statistics on crime in the United States.

Secondary analysis is often quick and easy, but this approach has its own problems. For one thing, a researcher who has not collected the data personally may be unaware of any bias or errors. Fortunately, however, the quality of most government data is high, and enough material is available to satisfy almost any researcher.

Truth, Science, and Politics

Once sociologists have data in hand, they must decide what to do with them. Sociologists turn to science in order to gather their data, but science cannot solve problems for us. Science can help us learn, say, *how many* U.S. families are poor and it may even yield some insights as to *why* they are poor. But science cannot tell us *what we should do* about poverty.

When we confront a social problem, we may use science to gather facts, which represent one kind of truth. But deciding how to respond to the problem always involves another kind of truth: our political values. How should sociologists tackle important and controversial issues such as poverty, family violence, and abortion? Should we simply try to discover the "facts"—reporting what is happening and perhaps why—and leave the political decisions about what the problems and solutions are to others? Or should we take a stand and actively try to change society for the better?

Sociologists have long debated how to square science and politics. No one wrestled more with this question than the German sociologist Max Weber (1864–1920), who urged his colleagues to focus on the facts in an effort to make research *value-free*. Weber knew that personal values lead people to choose one topic over another. But, Weber insisted, once a topic is selected and research is under way, social scientists should keep a professional objectivity in their work. This means that as much as possible, researchers should hold their personal politics in check to avoid distorting the results. In practice, for example, a researcher who personally supports the death penalty must be willing to accept any and all results—even those that show that capital punishment has little or no effect on the murder rate. For Weber, the sociologist's main goal should be discovering truth rather than engaging in politics and promoting change.

In recent decades, however, an increasing number of sociologists have taken an opposing view. Many believe that sociologists have a responsibility not just to learn about the world but also to help improve the lives of people who suffer from poverty and prejudice. This pursuit of social justice might seem like taking sides—and it is. In defense of this value commitment, many sociologists (especially those using the social-conflict approach) argue that "objective" research is impossible because whatever theory we use or whatever we may say (or not say) about the world, we end up taking some position (even if we do so by remaining silent). If this is true, then all knowledge is political, and trying to be neutral is itself a political position that ends up favoring the status quo. In the end, critics of Weber's view say, all sociologists must take one side or another on any issue they study. This activist orientation was the hallmark of Karl Marx, who summed up his view of this controversy in words placed on his tombstone: "The philosophers have only interpreted the world in various ways; the point, however, is to change it."

Truth and Statistics

Finally, a brief word about *statistics*, the numerical results that researchers often include when they report their findings. Statistics are easy ways to characterize a large number of subjects, as when a professor announces that members of a class had an average grade of 90 on a midterm examination.

Many of us have been brought up to think of statistics as "facts." How often have we been told that "numbers don't lie"? But numbers are not always so truthful, for two reasons.

First, like all research findings, numbers must be interpreted. A class exam average may be 90, but does that mean the students studied hard or that the exam was fairly easy? Similarly, one person can point out that the U.S. unemployment rate fell to almost 7 percent in late 2013 and interpret this as good news because the rate has come down in the last few years, or as bad news because it remains well above what it was in the decades before the recession began at the end of 2007.

Second, organizations, politicians, and even sociologists often present statistics that support some preferred conclusion.

How are we to know whether the statistics we read are presented in a misleading way? There is no easy answer, but here are three tips to make you a more critical reader:

1. **Check how researchers define their terms.** How people define terms affects the results. Even the most careful counts of the poor will vary widely, depending on how each researcher defines poverty.

2. **Remember that research is never perfect.** Even if we agree on how to define the poor, actually counting millions of poor women, men, and children is a very difficult task. This is especially true of those who are homeless and therefore difficult to contact. In most cases, researchers end up undercounting the poor and especially the homeless.

3. **Researchers may "spin" their statistics.** What does a "steep decrease" in the homicide rate really mean? "Low unemployment" means low in relation to what? There are countless ways to select and present statistics, and researchers often present their findings in a way that advances the argument they wish to make.

Use special care when reading tables and graphs. Figure 1–3 illustrates the problem with three graphs showing changes in the U.S. unemployment rate. All three figures are drawn using data from the U.S. government. Graph (a) might be titled "Unemployment Goes Up and Down!" because it presents data across a time frame that shows both a decreasing and an increasing rate of unemployment. Graph (b) uses the same time frame, but changes the scale to flatten the line supporting a title such as "Unemployment Holds Steady!" Graph (c) uses a limited time frame over just five years to display the decline in unemployment after 2009. Here we can announce "Unemployment Coming Down!"

Ideally, sociologists strive for accuracy, clarity, and fairness in their work and use statistical data with the

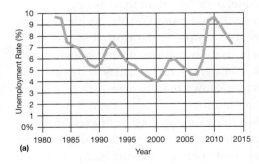
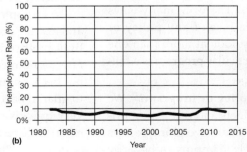
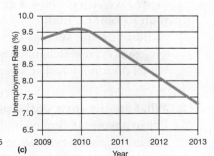

Figure 1–3 Do Statistics Lie?

Analysts, including sociologists, can "spin" their data to encourage readers to reach various conclusions. These three graphs are based on the same factual data. Yet the way we construct each graph suggests a different reality. The scale used in graph (a) gives the impression that the employment rate displays a lot of volatility, rising and falling over time. Graph (b) changes the scale to flatten the line, thus giving the impression that the unemployment rate has changed little. Graph (c) presents data only for the years 2009 through 2013, giving the impression that the unemployment rate is sharply falling.

SOURCE: Data from U.S. Department of Labor (2013).

intent to convey information rather than to mislead readers. But, keeping in mind that researchers have to make choices about how to present their numbers, you should always think critically about statistical information and how it is presented, whether it appears in textbooks or anywhere else. Never assume that statistics are the absolute truth.

Responding to Social Problems: Social Policy

1.5   Identify factors that shape how societies devise policy to respond to social problems.

How does a society respond to social problems? This question brings us to the topic of **social policy**, *formal strategies that affect how society operates*. Organizations, including governments and colleges, create social policy to get their work done and to address social problems. Sociologists play an important role in developing social policy. Over the years, sociologists have helped direct our nation's policy in dealing with racially segregated schools, poverty, pornography, health care, gun regulations, homelessness, racial discrimination, problems of family life, sexual harassment, and many other issues.

Policy Evaluation

How do we know whether a policy works? To evaluate any policy, we must answer the following, often difficult, questions:

1. **How do we measure "success"?**   There is more than one way to measure the success of any policy or program. Take, for example, a rehabilitation program for young people who abuse drugs. Does "success" mean that those completing the program stay "clean" for a year? Five years? Show a greater rate of completing high school? Or finding a job? There are many ways to measure the success or failure of any policy or program, so researchers must look at more than one before deciding whether a particular program is a failure or a success.

2. **What are the costs of the policy or program?**   We live in a world of limited budgets and competing priorities, so policy evaluation means weighing results against costs. It may be possible to improve schools by increasing funding, for example, but a local community may not support raising property taxes.

   The costs of any program involve not just money but ethical concerns as well. For example, installing surveillance cameras on public streets may reduce crime or at least drive criminal activity elsewhere. Yet many citizens object to having their movements—including which stores they visit and with whom they strike up a conversation—recorded in computer files by public officials. In short, street surveillance may be "successful" in reducing crime but may involve an unacceptable cost by taking away people's privacy.

3. **Who should get the help?**   In assessing a social policy, another key question is whom the policy should target for assistance. To combat poverty, should agencies work with adults who need jobs? Provide a good breakfast to poor children in school? Provide prenatal care to pregnant women? All of these things may be helpful, but limited budgets require agencies to make choices about whom to target.

   One guideline for making such decisions is Benjamin Franklin's old saying, "An ounce of prevention is worth a pound of cure." Generally, the earlier the intervention, the more successful a policy is and the lower the costs. For example, helping boys before they get into trouble costs less—and accomplishes more—than putting them in jail later on.

   Sherry Deane of the National Black Child Development Institute says that too many programs kick in too late: "We spend so much more money after the problem has occurred—after a baby is born at low birth weight, after a child begins to fail in school, after a child is in trouble with the law—instead of making an early investment in the child with prenatal care, preventive health care, early education" (Goldman, 1991:5).

Policy and Culture

Social policy is also shaped by cultural values. That is, societies respond to a social problem in a particular way not necessarily because that approach is cheapest or works best, but because a particular response seems, according to the society's culture, to be "the right thing to do."

As Chapter 2 ("Poverty and Wealth") explains, there are 46.5 million poor people in the United States, many living with inadequate nutrition, unsafe housing, and little or no medical care. Poverty persists in this country not because no one knows how to eliminate it; a policy to guarantee a minimum income would end the problem very quickly. But because our way of life stresses self-reliance, there is not much support for what would be widely criticized as "handout" policies. Guided by a culture that defines people as responsible for their social standing, we tend to see the poor as "undeserving" of assistance. As the next chapter describes in detail, such cultural values were at work in 1996 when Congress and the White House acted with widespread public support to change public assistance programs so that fewer people were dependent on government support.

Policy and Politics

The kinds of policies people favor depend on their political outlook. People with a politically conservative outlook usually turn to the past for guidelines about how to live in the present and how to shape the future. Conservative people try to limit the scope of societal change. Because the existing society is viewed as good, then problems arise mostly because of the actions and choices of bad individuals. This is why conservatives favor policies that treat problems as shortcomings of particular individuals rather than as shortcomings of society. If the problem is unemployment, for example, conservatives might suggest helping jobless people get more schooling or learn new skills in order to make them more attractive to employers. In taking an approach that places more responsibility on individuals to take care of themselves, conservatives are also saying that society is basically good the way it is so that they end up supporting the status quo.

By contrast, people with more liberal views see problems in the organization of society itself and favor greater social change. They are more likely to understand unemployment, for example, as caused by a society's economy. Therefore, to combat unemployment, liberals seek societal reforms, such as strengthening antidiscrimination laws, expanding the power of labor unions, or calling for government to create enough jobs to provide work for the people who need it.

People with radical-left views seek policies that go beyond the reforms suggested by liberals. From their point of view, social problems exist because the entire system is flawed in some basic way. For example, Marxists claim that replacing the market-based, capitalist economy with a government-controlled economy is the only real answer to problems such as high unemployment and increasing economic inequality. Because radical policies are, by definition, outside the political mainstream, they spark both committed support and widespread opposition.

We conclude this chapter—and each of the remaining chapters—with a discussion of how political attitudes lead people to define certain situations as problems in the first place and to define certain kinds of policies and programs as solutions to those problems.

⭐ POLITICS

Constructing Problems and Defining Solutions

1.6 **Analyze how political attitudes shape how people define social problems and solutions.**

The social-constructionist approach described earlier is useful for exploring how political views guide people as they define social problems and devise solutions. Let us begin with a look at the political spectrum.

The Political Spectrum

We become part of the political process as we form attitudes about various issues. Social scientists measure people's opinions using a model called the **political spectrum**, *a continuum representing a range of political attitudes, from "left" to "right."* As shown in Table 1–2, attitudes on the political spectrum range from the far left at one extreme through "middle of the road" views at the center to the far right at the other extreme.

The data in Table 1–2 show that 27 percent of people consider themselves liberal or left of center to some degree (adding the numbers at points 1, 2, and 3 together); 36.1 percent say they are moderates (falling in the middle at point 4); and 31.8 percent say that they are conservative or right of center to some degree (adding the numbers at points 5, 6, and 7 together). The remaining 5.1 percent of respondents did not know or were unable to answer the question. A majority of people place themselves near the middle of the political spectrum (points 3, 4, or 5), and just a small percentage describe themselves as holding what might be called a radical view, either at the far left (at point 1 on the continuum) or the far right (point 7 on the continuum) (Smith et al., 2013).

Over time, political attitudes may shift to the left (as they did during the 1960s) or to the right (as they did in the 1980s). In 2008, the election of Democratic candidate Barack Obama marked another shift to the left, and the Republican gains in the 2010 elections marked another shift

---

Table 1–2 The Political Spectrum: A National Survey, 2012

Survey Question: "We hear a lot of talk these days about liberals and conservatives. I'm going to show you a seven-point scale on which the political views people might hold are arranged from extremely liberal—point 1—to extremely conservative—point 7. Where would you place yourself on this scale?"

1	2	3	4	5	6	7
Extremely liberal	Liberal	Slightly liberal	Middle of the road	Slightly conservative	Conservative	Extremely conservative
4.1%	12.4%	10.5%	36.1%	13.6%	14.8%	3.4%

[*Don't know/no answer* 5.1%]

SOURCE: The data in this figure are from *General Social Surveys, 1972–2012.* (Chicago: National Opinion Research Center, 2013).

to the right. In 2012, President Obama was reelected in another shift leftward.

But at any time, there is always wide variation in people's political thinking. Some of this variation is regional: The people of Massachusetts and Minnesota almost always elect liberal candidates, just as those living in Mississippi and Texas usually elect conservatives. Similarly, some ethnic categories, such as African Americans and Jews, historically have favored liberal positions; others, such as Asian Americans, tend to be more conservative.

Conservatives, Liberals, and Radicals

What do labels such as "conservative," "liberal," and "radical" really mean? Here is a brief statement to get us going. The deeper meaning of these three concepts will become clear as you read through the chapters that follow, applying each point of view to various issues.

"Conservatives" look to the past for guidance on how to live. They believe that the past is a store of wisdom developed by countless generations who have already faced many of the same questions and issues that we face today. A "good" society, from the conservative point of view, is respectful of traditions and tries to conserve what earlier generations have learned. Conservatives have a special interest in the family and religion—the social institutions that transmit our moral traditions. Conservatives also typically seek to limit the size and scope of government. They tend to see "big government" as a problem because it threatens individual freedom and undermines people's responsibility for their own well-being. Typically, conservative people tend to support the Republican Party and the Libertarian Party more than the Democratic Party.

"Liberals" have a different view of the world. In simple terms, liberals (from a Latin word for "free") think people should be free from the past to decide, on their own, questions about how to live. A "good" society, from a liberal point of view, is one in which people are able to make choices for themselves. This requires that the society be both tolerant and respectful of individual rights. It also requires that categories of people be more or less equal in terms of basic rights and opportunities. Therefore, liberals have a special interest in the economy and politics because these are the social institutions that distribute wealth and power. Liberals typically seek to expand the size and scope of government. They see government power as a solution because it is an effective way to reduce inequality and to make other desirable changes in society. In general, liberal people support the Democratic Party more than the Republican Party.

Although liberals and conservatives differ in some important ways, both accept the existing political system, at least in most respects. In contrast, people with more extreme views seek more basic change in society. Such are the attitudes of "radicals" (from Latin meaning "of the root") because they hold that the system must be changed right down to its roots. Radicals point to some basic flaw in society that is responsible for any number of social problems. For people on the far right, the historical expansion of "big government" is the basic flaw, leading to claim that government is involved in far too many dimensions of our daily lives. In a few cases, people who hold such views withdraw away from the reach of government to remote places where they live as "survivalists." Radicals also include people on the far left. For Marxists, the basic flaw is the capitalist economic system that creates social classes; a socially just society could exist only after the abolition of capitalism. Similarly, for radical feminists, the basic flaw is the concept of gender that gives rise to patriarchy, the power of men over women. For them, a socially just society could exist only with the abolition of gender differences. Typically, people with radical views do not support either the more mainstream Democratic Party or Republican Party. Some may vote for the mainstream candidate closest to their political position; others may support "fringe" candidates; still others may choose not to vote at all.

Can we sum up these different views of the world in a single sentence? It might go something like this: Conservatives talk about the importance of traditions and keeping society the way it has been in many respects; liberals talk about the need to reform society to make it better; radicals talk about organizing society in some completely new way.

Social Issues

People hold political positions on two types of issues: social issues and economic issues. **Social issues** are *political debates involving moral judgments about how people should live*. Some of today's leading social issues include gender inequality, abortion, immigration, same-sex marriage, and the use of the death penalty.

Leaning Left People who lean to the left on social issues are called "social liberals." In general, social liberals think that people should be free to shape their lifestyles for themselves. In practice, then, social liberals are broadly tolerant of various "alternative" lifestyles. They also favor expanding opportunities for women, support the "pro-choice" side of the abortion controversy, look favorably on racial and ethnic diversity and welcome immigrants coming to the United States, and support legal marriage for gay and lesbian people. On the other hand, social liberals oppose the death penalty partly because, in the past, states have been more likely to execute African Americans than whites and the poor rather than the rich, even considering people convicted of the same crimes.

Lower-income people tend to be very concerned about economic issues, for the simple reason that they lack economic security. Members of the United Auto Workers recently engaged in this action against the auto companies to protest layoffs. Higher-income people, by contrast, take economic security for granted. They are likely to be most concerned about social issues, such as legalizing same-sex marriage.

Leaning Right People who lean to the right on social issues are called "social conservatives." Social conservatives are respectful of traditional values and want to conserve them. Conservatives criticize what they see as too much tolerance in today's society, which amounts to moral decline. Social conservatives favor the "pro-life" side of the abortion controversy. In addition, they are concerned about controlling this country's borders, both to uphold the law and also to protect our cultural traditions. Social conservatives also support the traditional family in which women and men have different roles and responsibilities. Social conservatives also endorse the death penalty as a necessary moral response to most brutal criminal acts.

Economic Issues

The second type of issues involves economics. **Economic issues** are *political debates about how a society should produce and distribute material resources*. These debates typically focus on the degree to which the economy should be under the control of government or a market system (Chapter 10, "Economy and Politics," explores these issues in depth).

Leaning Left In general, *economic liberals* (leaning to the left on economic issues) favor government regulation of the economy in order to reduce inequality. A free-market system, liberals claim, too often works to the advantage of a select few and harms everyone else. For this reason, economic liberals support strong government that is able to regulate the economy through policies such as raising the minimum wage, setting high taxes especially on the rich,

and using tax revenues to pay for health care and other social service programs that help average families and, especially, the poor.

Leaning Right By contrast, *economic conservatives* (who lean to the right on economic issues) call for a smaller role for government in the economy. From their point of view, the market—not government officials—can set wage levels more fairly and efficiently. In addition, conservatives claim that motivated individuals and the businesses they create (rather than government agencies) are the key to expanding the economy and generating wealth that benefits all of society. Government regulation of economic activity serves only to limit economic growth and to raise the cost of doing business and also limits personal choice and freedom. Economic conservatives support lower tax rates in the belief that people should be able to keep more of their own earnings and use this money as they choose to spend or to invest and expand the economy. In doing so, people take responsibility for their own well-being.

Who Thinks What?

What types of people are likely to fall on each side of the political spectrum? Social standing is a good predictor, but it turns out that most people are actually liberal on one kind of issue and conservative on another.

People of high social position, those with lots of schooling and above-average wealth, tend to be liberal on social issues. But they are split on economic issues. That is, most highly educated people are tolerant of lifestyle diversity (the liberal view), but many privileged people also seek to protect their wealth (the conservative position) whereas others support a progressive policy of reducing economic inequality (the liberal position).

People with less education and wealth show a different pattern. Typically they hold more traditional values so that they tend to see moral issues more as clear-cut choices that are right or wrong, which is the socially conservative view. At the same time, with less economic security, they are likely to support government-enacted economic programs that may benefit them, which makes them economically liberal (Kohut, 2012).

Keep in mind that most of us—whatever our social standing—tend to hold some combination of liberal and conservative attitudes. This inconsistency helps explain why so many people call themselves "moderates," "centrists," or "middle-of-the-roaders."

A Word about Gender   Finally, what about any differences between women and men? Political analysts have documented a modest "gender gap" in voting patterns that paints women as slightly more liberal than men. Surveys of voting behavior show that women are somewhat more likely to vote for Democratic candidates, and men are more likely to favor Republicans. In the 2008 presidential election, for example, 56 percent of women but only 49 percent of men voted for the Democratic candidate, Barack Obama. This pattern was repeated in 2012 with 55 percent of women compared to 45 of men voting for President Obama. In general, men express greater concern about having strong national security (generally viewed as a conservative or Republican issue), and women express greater concern about keeping an adequate social "safety net" to help those in need (a liberal or Democratic issue) (Pew Research Center, 2012).

Going On from Here

This chapter has presented important information that you will need in order to understand the rest of the book. Each chapter that follows focuses on important issues that are debated by politicians and the public across the country. To make better sense of these issues, each chapter will present research findings and will also apply sociology's major theoretical approaches—the structural-functional, social-conflict, feminist, and symbolic-interaction approaches—to the issues.

Always keep in mind this key fact: *Social problems are socially constructed.* Political attitudes guide what we define as a problem and what policies we are likely to support as solutions. Recognizing and respecting the diversity of political attitudes in the United States, this text does not assume that everyone will agree about what the problems are or what the best solutions might be. On the contrary, we expect and welcome disagreement. *The goal is to engage in conversation.* The word "conversation" is closely linked to the word "convert" meaning "to change." Engaging in good-faith conversation, therefore, implies not just stating one's opinion but also listening and asking questions and, most of all, having a willingness to change as a result of exchanging ideas with others.

The remaining chapters of this text present diverse analysis explaining how the libertarian, conservative, liberal, and left-radical political attitudes lead people to define social problems and to decide what we ought to do about them. Try to understand each of the various points of view. You will soon see for yourself that to come to a point where you can claim any one point of view as your own requires familiarity with *all* points of view. In addition, understanding various points of view helps to explain why we have such long-standing and intense debates over social issues. Finally, gaining a diverse understanding of politics also helps us understand that one person's solution often turns out to be another's problem.

What should you expect by the time you have finished this book? You will have learned a great deal about many of the social issues that command the attention of government officials and the public, both in the United States and around the world. You will gain familiarity with sociology's theoretical approaches so that you can apply them to new issues in the future. Finally, with a firm grasp of the various political positions and arguments, you will find it easy to analyze new issues as you confront them. With this ability, you become an active participant in the political process.

A social problems course is an invitation to get involved in political debates and political action. Each chapter of this text provides a feature called "Constructing Social Problems: A Defining Moment" that shows how easy—and how important—it is to become involved in the political life of our nation. At the end of each chapter, a photo essay provides a look at people and organizations making a difference in the country and in the world. You will find many examples of "ordinary" people like you or me who decided to take some action in a way that made a difference. Let us be inspired by them and live in a way that inspires others!

Essay: Envisioning a Better Society   Most people think about at least some social problems from a "common sense" point of view. What do you think are the benefits we gain from the sociological study of social problems? That is, what specific insights and information can we expect sociological study to provide to us? In what ways can sociology help improve U.S. society?

CONSTRUCTING SOCIAL PROBLEMS

A DEFINING MOMENT

A Call to Action: The Message of Martin Luther King Jr.

Martin Luther King Jr. (1929–1968) was born in Atlanta at a time when black people and white people were kept apart by a strict system of racial segregation. Taught in racially segregated classrooms, King graduated from high school at the age of fifteen. Then, like his father and grandfather, he earned a bachelor's degree from Morehouse College, a traditionally black institution.

Also like his father and grandfather, King set out to become a preacher. He enrolled at the Crozer Theological Seminary in Pennsylvania, where his mostly white classmates elected him president of the senior class. He received his theology degree in 1951. King continued his studies at Boston University, which awarded him a doctorate in 1955.

In 1954, King was appointed pastor at the Dexter Avenue Baptist Church in Montgomery, Alabama. Quickly, he became a community leader, heading up not only his church but also the local chapter of the National Association for the Advancement of Colored People (NAACP). The city of Montgomery—like the rest of the South—was still racially segregated, and people of color were restricted to their own businesses and neighborhoods and required to sit in separate sections at the rear of city buses. King condemned racial segregation as morally wrong and decided to take action to challenge the status quo. In December 1955, he led a nonviolent social movement that came to be known as the Montgomery bus boycott. Thousands of people pledged that they would no longer ride the buses until the city allowed all people equal access to seats on public transportation. The boycott continued for more than a year, ending only after the U.S. Supreme Court declared that the racial segregation of public transportation was unconstitutional.

King had won a great victory, but there was still powerful resistance to racial equality, which made his life difficult and dangerous. King faced hostility from not only members of the public but also from police. He was arrested dozens of times, his home was attacked, and some opponents of his cause made threats against King's life. But King held firm in his beliefs. In 1957, he was elected president of the Southern Christian Leadership Conference, emerging as the leader of the national civil rights movement. His activism continued for another decade, culminating in a civil rights march in Washington, D.C., that included more than 250,000 people who gathered to hear him deliver his famous "I Have a Dream" speech.

King was a great national and international change-maker, and he stands among a handful of people in the United States honored with a national holiday each year (celebrated on the third Monday in January, near King's birthday). But King was the first to say that his life should not be taken to mean that great people can accomplish great things; he believed that his life shows that the power to make a difference is within the reach of everyone. King believed that anyone can be great because anyone can serve others. He did not think that great people had to be rich or well educated. Rather, he reminded us that to serve others, all anyone needs is a heart full of grace and the desire to help.

King's message is an invitation to each and every one of us to learn more about our society and to recognize that, as human beings, our lives are bound up with the lives of everyone else around the corner and around the world. Following King's example, look for a way in which you can make a positive difference in the life of at least one other person. Get involved!

Dr. Martin Luther King Jr. is one of only four people in the history of our country whose birthday has become a national holiday (George Washington, Abraham Lincoln, and Christopher Columbus are the others). When we celebrate King's life, we are recognizing that our society has grappled with the issue of racial inequality for centuries and that this problem is still not solved.

CHAPTER 1   Sociology: Studying Social Problems

Whose problem is it?

This chapter has explained that different political attitudes lead people to disagree about what the problems are. And even when we do agree about the problems, we are likely to define different courses of action as solutions. Over the last several years, almost everyone has recognized that a major problem in the United States is the weak economy. Look at the accompanying photos to see two different approaches to fixing the problem.

The more we favor the left side of the political spectrum, the more we look to government to manage the economy. From a left point of view, a job is a right to be guaranteed by government, which should set a minimum wage of at least $15 an hour rather than allow pay to reflect market forces of supply and demand.

The more we favor the right side of the political spectrum, the more we expect people to set their own goals and to solve economic problems for themselves. To claim that a job is a personal responsibility, for example, suggests that people who want work have to ensure that they have the necessary personal skills and ambition as well as sufficient training for the type of job they are seeking.

Hint: A key difference between the two "sides" of the political spectrum is how economic life should be organized. Seen from the political "right," the economy should be based on a market system in which people freely act according to their individual interests. Therefore, primary responsibility for finding and holding a job lies with the individual. Conservatives tend to support the free market and they distrust "big government" as a threat to personal freedom and economic expansion. From the political "left," by contrast, the government should represent the interests of the public, regulating the economy through policies such as setting minimum wage levels and mandating working conditions. When left on its own, liberals claim, "big business" creates economic inequality and ends up favoring the rich. As for "personal responsibility," liberals believe that because many problems are rooted in society, individuals cannot solve such problems for themselves. In the 2012 electoral campaign, President Obama claimed that people's success or failure is not so much about who is smarter or works harder; rather, he claimed, everybody works hard and everyone deserves the assistance provided by a compassionate government. Mitt Romney, taking a more conservative position, claimed that a productive and free society rests on a market system that allows people to pursue their dreams and he called for limiting government taxation because it serves to discourage investment and economic growth.

Getting Involved: Applications and Exercises

1. Explain how the following slogans from bumper stickers are examples of claims making: (a) "We're the 99 percent!"; (b) "Guns Don't Kill People; People Kill People"; (c) "It's a Child, Not a Choice"; (d) "God is not spelled G.O.P."; and (e) "No War for Oil."

2. What kinds of questions might you ask about, say, poverty, using the structural-functional, symbolic-interaction, feminist, and Marxist social-conflict approaches?

3. Identify several national politicians—try to include your own members of Congress—who fall on the conservative and liberal sides of the political

spectrum. What are their views on social issues such as gay rights and on economic issues such as using tax money to stabilize the economy and raising taxes to reduce income inequality? Are there any radical politicians in Congress?

4. Explain how people's political attitudes affect the kinds of issues they are likely to define as social problems. For example, do conservatives or liberals see the "breakdown of the traditional family" as a social problem? Why? Are conservatives or liberals more concerned about economic inequality? Explain.

Making the Grade

A DEFINING MOMENT
A Call to Action: The Message of Martin Luther King Jr. **p. 25**

Seeing Patterns: The Sociological Imagination

1.1 Explain the benefits of learning about sociology and using the sociological imagination.

Sociology is the systematic study of human societies.

- Sociologist C. Wright Mills coined the expression "the sociological imagination" to encourage people to view their own personal problems as connected to the workings of society. **p. 4–5**

> **sociological imagination** (p. 4) a point of view that highlights how society affects the experiences we have and the choices we make
> **sociology** (p. 4) the systematic study of human societies
> **society** (p. 4) people who live within some territory and share many patterns of behavior
> **culture** (p. 4) a way of life including widespread values (about what is good and bad), beliefs (about what is true), and behavior (what people do every day)

Social Problems: The Basics

1.2 Define the concept "social problem" and explain how societies come to define some issues—and not others—as social problems.

A **social problem** is a condition that undermines the well-being of some or all members of a society and is usually controversial.

- A social-constructionist approach holds that a social problem is created as society defines some condition as undesirable and in need of change.

- The specific conditions defined as social problems change over time.

- At any particular time, the objective facts and the subjective perception of any social issue may or may not be the same.

- A global perspective is important because many social problems cross national boundaries. Also, many problems, such as poverty, are more serious elsewhere in the world than in the United States. **pp. 5–12**

Claims making is the process by which members of a social movement try to convince the public and public officials that a condition should be defined as a social problem. Claims made by one group of people typically prompt counterclaims by other groups. **pp. 7–8**

Social movements typically go through four stages:

- emergence
- coalescence
- formalization
- decline **pp. 8–9**

> **social problem** (p. 5) a condition that undermines the well-being of some or all members of a society and is usually a matter of public controversy
> **social-constructionist approach** (p. 6) the assertion that social problems arise as people define conditions as undesirable and in need of change
> **claims making** (p. 7) the process of convincing the public and important public officials that a particular issue or situation should be defined as a social problem
> **social movement** (p. 8) an organized effort at claims making that tries to shape the way people think about an issue in order to encourage or discourage social change

Analyzing Social Problems: Sociological Theory

1.3 Apply sociological theory to the study of social problems.

Sociologists use **theoretical approaches** to guide their research and theory building. The major theoretical approaches—structural-functional, social-conflict, feminist, and symbolic-interaction—all provide insights into various social problems. **pp. 12–16**

Macro-Level

The **structural-functional approach** sees society as a complex system of many different parts.

- Early *social pathology theory* viewed problems as disruptions in society's normal operation.

- Later, *social disorganization theory* linked social problems to rapid change.

- More recently, functionalism views social problems in terms of the dysfunctions of various social patterns. **pp. 12–13**

The **social-conflict approach** highlights social inequality, including inequality based on class and on race and ethnicity.

- *Class conflict theory*, based on the ideas of Karl Marx, links social problems to the operation of a capitalist economic system.
- *Multicultural theory* spotlights problems arising from inequality between people in various racial and ethnic categories. **pp. 13–15**

The **feminist approach** highlights social inequality based on gender.

Feminist theory links social problems to men's domination of women. **p. 15**

Micro-Level

The **symbolic-interaction** approach helps us understand how people experience social problems in their routine, everyday interactions.

- The *learning approach* links social problems to the learning of undesirable skills and attitudes from others.
- The *labeling approach* investigates how and why people come to define certain behaviors as problematic and others as normal. **pp. 15–16**

> **theory** (p. 12) a statement of how and why specific facts are related
> **theoretical approach** (p. 12) a basic image of society that guides theory and research
> **structural-functional approach** (p. 12) a theoretical framework that sees society as a system of many interrelated parts
> **social institution** (p. 12) a major sphere of social life, or a societal subsystem, organized to meet a basic human need
> **social-conflict approach** (p. 13) a theoretical framework that sees society as divided by inequality and conflict
> **feminism** (p. 15) a political movement that seeks the social equality of women and men
> **symbolic-interaction approach** (p. 15) a theoretical framework that sees society as the product of individuals interacting with one another

Finding the Facts: Sociological Research

1.4   Discuss the methods sociologists use to study social problems.

Sociologists use a variety of methods to investigate social problems.

Survey research can take different forms:

- A *questionnaire* is a series of items a researcher presents to subjects for their response.
- An *interview* is a more personal survey technique in which a researcher meets face-to-face with respondents to discuss some issue.
- A *case study* focuses on a single person, organization, or event. **p. 17**

Field research allows a researcher to observe people over a long period of time while joining them in their everyday activities. **pp. 17–18**

Experimental research is carried out in a specially designed laboratory. Researchers change one variable while keeping the others the same in order to identify specific causes of certain patterns of behavior. **p. 18**

Secondary analysis of existing data can be a quick and easy research method, but a researcher must be careful not to rely on data that may be incorrect or may contain a political bias. **p. 18**

> **survey** (p. 17) a research method in which subjects respond to items on a questionnaire or in an interview
> **field research (participant observation)** (p. 17) a research method for observing people while joining them in their everyday activities
> **experiment** (p. 18) a research method for investigating cause-and-effect relationships under tightly controlled conditions
> **secondary analysis** (p. 18) a research method that makes use of data originally collected by others

Responding to Social Problems: Social Policy

1.5   Identify factors that shape how societies devise policy to respond to social problems.

Social policy refers to strategies that societies use to address problems.

- A society evaluates a social policy based on its success, its cost, and whether the population it targets represents the best solution to a social problem.
- Societies favor social policy that reflects important cultural values.
- The kinds of policies individual people favor depend on their political attitudes. **pp. 20–21**

> **social policy** (p. 20) formal strategies that affect how society operates

★ POLITICS

Constructing Problems and Defining Solutions

1.6 **Analyze how political attitudes shape how people define social problems and solutions.**

The **political spectrum** is a model representing people's attitudes about social issues and economic issues. **pp. 21–22**

Conservatives claim that social problems arise from the shortcomings of particular individuals or the bad choices people make about how to live.

- Conservatives see the family and religion as important social institutions transmitting the moral traditions that guide people to live good lives. **p. 22**

Liberals claim that social problems arise from the operation of society, including patterns of social inequality that prevent categories of people from having equal opportunity.

- Liberals seek reform rather than radical change in social institutions. **p. 22**

On the **radical left**, Marxists claim that social problems result from the operation of the capitalist economic system.

- From this point of view, the solution to social problems requires radical change to our society's institutions, beginning with the economy.

The **radical right** claims that the most serious problem our society faces is the growth of big government, which threatens individual freedoms.

- Some people on the radical right withdraw from society altogether to live as "survivalists" in remote areas. **p. 22**

political spectrum (p. 21) a continuum representing a range of political attitudes from "left" to "right"

social issues (p. 22) political debates involving moral judgments about how people should live

economic issues (p. 23) political debates about how a society should produce and distribute material resources

Chapter 2
Poverty and Wealth

 Learning Objectives

2.1 Describe the distribution of income and wealth in the United States.

2.2 Assess the differences in the lives of the rich and the poor in the United States.

2.3 Analyze how poverty is linked to other social problems.

2.4 Explain the changing ways our society has used the social welfare system to respond to poverty.

2.5 Apply sociological theory to the issue of poverty.

2.6 Analyze economic inequality from various positions on the political spectrum.

Tracking the Trends

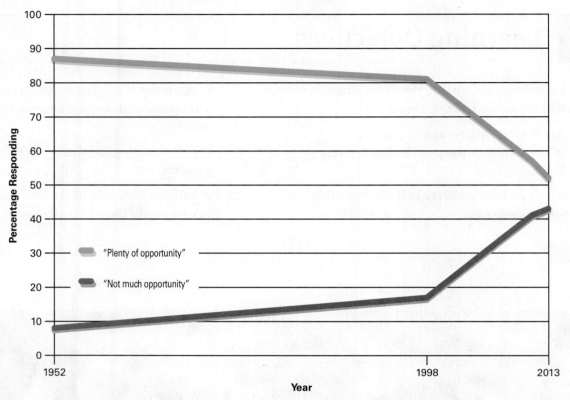

Survey Question: "How much opportunity does the average person have to get ahead?"

SOURCE: Gallup (2013).

One of the defining qualities of U.S. society has always been providing opportunity for people to get ahead. For decades, the Gallup (2013) organization has asked this survey question:

> "Some people say there's not much opportunity in America today—that the average person doesn't have much chance to really get ahead. Others say there's plenty of opportunity and anyone who works hard can go as far as they want. Which comes closer to the way you feel about this?"

In 1952, 87 percent of U.S. adults expressed the view that "there is plenty of opportunity" in the United States. As recently as 1998, 81 percent of people agreed with this view. Since then, however, this confidence has eroded with just 52 percent holding the same view in 2013. The flip side of this trend is that, back in 1952, just 8 percent of adults claimed that "there is *not* much opportunity." By 1998, that share had more than doubled, and by 2013, it had reached 43 percent. Do you think our society provides people who work hard the chance to get ahead?

Constructing the Problem

How much economic inequality is fair?

The richest 20 percent of U.S. families earn almost as much as the remaining 80 percent combined; the richest 5 percent of families control 63 percent of the country's wealth.

Do you think U.S. society is becoming more equal?

In recent decades, income inequality in the United States has increased.

Is there significant poverty in the United States?

In 2012, 46.5 million people were counted as poor.

Chapter Overview

How unequal is U.S. society in terms of income and wealth? This chapter documents the extent of economic inequality and describes the contrasting lives of this country's rich and poor. You will analyze a range of problems—including poor health, unsafe housing, and political alienation—linked to poverty. You will learn what our society has done—and has not done—to assist the poor over the course of our nation's history. Finally, you will carry out theoretical analysis of social inequality and learn how political attitudes guide people to construct certain "problems" and favor certain "solutions"? ■

Twelve-year-old Jennifer Muñoz Tello keeps an eye on her two-year-old sister as she looks down the street hoping to see a friend come out to join her. On this June afternoon in Palo Alto, California, the girls enjoy the sunshine in front of the stainless steel trailer where they live with their mother, Sandra, and their father, Roberto. Sandra works long days cleaning houses and Roberto works almost until sundown in construction.

The Muñoz Tello family is not like most of the people who live in their community. Palo Alto has a median income of about $165,000, making it one of the richest cities in the United States. Many of the local people drive around in BMWs, Audis, or one of the new Tesla electric cars. The average home sells for about $2 million. This affluence is rooted in the computer revolution, which transformed the whole Silicon Valley region into an economic growth machine.

This widespread affluence hides the reality of people like Jennifer and her family, who are earning barely enough to meet the high cost of living. Sandra could never hope to live in one of the houses she cleans or one of the new homes that Roberto helps to build. The Muñoz Tello family lives in a clean but decades old Airstream trailer in Buena Vista Mobile Home Park, paying $800 a month to rent a site.

Sandra and Roberto came to Palo Alto for the schools, which are among the best in the country. They know that if their daughters graduate from the local high school, the girls will have an excellent chance to get a college education, which, in turn, may provide a much richer life than their parents have known.

...mily's future in Palo Alto is now uncertain. ...ome park, like all the local land, has become ...e. The owners want to sell the land to a group ...rs who plan to close the mobile home park and ...uxury apartments. If the sale goes through, all of the roughly 400 people in Buena Vista will be forced to find other housing. As they know only too well, there is almost nothing else in town that any of them could afford.

Most want to stay and look to a number of community residents outside of the mobile home park to stand with them in opposition to the proposed sale. As many see it, closing this neighborhood—in which 80 percent of the people are Hispanic and almost all have relatively low incomes—would eliminate most of Palo Alto's low-income housing as well as the town's social diversity. For Jennifer and her sister, the thought of having to move has a more personal consequence—threatening their dreams for the future (Westervelt, 2013).

Economic differences can be found in every community across the United States and often the differences are striking. Just as importantly, economic inequality in the United States is increasing. This chapter examines poverty and wealth in this country, explaining how income and wealth are distributed. We begin with some basic facts about the unequal distribution of economic resources in the United States.

Economic Inequality in the United States

2.1 Describe the distribution of income and wealth in the United States.

It doesn't take a sociologist to point out that some people have much more money than others. The evidence of economic inequality is everywhere: Large, fancy houses with swimming pools and workout rooms in one neighborhood stand in striking contrast to small homes in need of repair across town. Some children dress in the latest styles, eat nutritious meals, have regular checkups at the doctor, and go on vacations to destinations around the world. But others wear hand-me-downs, eat poorly, go to the emergency room when they are injured or sick, and rarely travel anywhere.

These patterns are just some of the consequences of **social stratification**, *society's system of ranking categories of people in a hierarchy.* Stratification produces **social classes**, *categories of people who have similar access to resources and opportunities.* Being born into a particular social class affects people's *life chances,* including how much schooling they receive, the kind of work they will do (or their chances of not finding a job), and even how long they will live. Social stratification is a powerful system, and few people realize just how economically unequal people in the United States really are. We begin, then, with some important economic indicators.

Inequality of Income and Wealth

Any discussion of problems such as poverty must begin with a look at inequality in **income**, *salary or wages from a job plus earnings from investments and other sources.* According to the U.S. government, in 2012, the *median* family income—that is, the middle case of all families when ranked by income—was $62,241.

As the pie chart in Figure 2–1 on page 35 shows, the highest-earning 20 percent of U.S. families (with income of at least $119,000 a year and with a mean or average of $202,559) received 48.9 percent of all income. At the other end of the hierarchy, the lowest-paid 20 percent (with income below $28,000 a year and averaging $15,534) received just 3.8 percent of all income. Comparing these categories, we see that the high-income families earn thirteen times as much as the low-income families. From another angle, the highest-earning 20 percent of families earn nearly as much as the remaining 80 percent of families combined (U.S. Census Bureau, 2013).

The table at the left in Figure 2–1 gives a more detailed look at the U.S. income distribution. Families in the top 10 percent earn at least $169,000 annually, those in the top 5 percent earn at least $210,000, and families in the top 1 percent receive about $370,000 each year. At the very top, the highest-paid one-tenth of 1 percent of families earn at least $1.6 million each year. This means that a very small share of families earns as much money in a single year as a typical family earns in an entire lifetime.

Since about 1980, income inequality among U.S. families has been increasing. As shown in Figure 2–2 on page 35, between 1980 and 2012, the annual income of the highest-paid 20 percent of U.S. families (only about half of the families included in this category in 2012 were also in the category back in 1980) increased by 55 percent (from $130,656, on average, to $202,559). During this period, people in the middle of the income distribution typically saw gains of about 12 percent. The lowest-paid 20 percent of U.S. families, however, actually lost ground, making an average of $1,475 less in 2012 than they earned in 1980. This means that economic gains have been huge for the rich and small for most others. But the lowest-earning families today are actually living on less money than they were thirty years ago. Based on government data, income inequality is now greater than at any time in the past fifty years (U.S. Census Bureau, 2013). What do people think of this trend? The Social Problems in Focus box on page 36 provides some answers.

In the United States, economic inequality is even greater when it comes to **wealth**, *the value of all the economic*

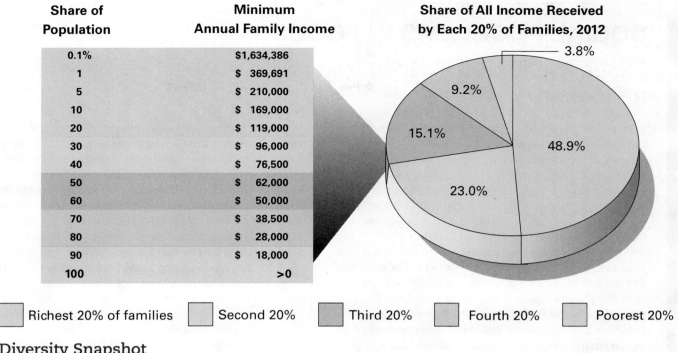

Share of Population	Minimum Annual Family Income
0.1%	$1,634,386
1	$ 369,691
5	$ 210,000
10	$ 169,000
20	$ 119,000
30	$ 96,000
40	$ 76,500
50	$ 62,000
60	$ 50,000
70	$ 38,500
80	$ 28,000
90	$ 18,000
100	>0

Share of All Income Received by Each 20% of Families, 2012

3.8%
9.2%
15.1%
48.9%
23.0%

☐ Richest 20% of families   ☐ Second 20%   ☐ Third 20%   ☐ Fourth 20%   ☐ Poorest 20%

Diversity Snapshot

Figure 2–1   Distribution of Income in the United States

Income is unequally distributed, with the highest-earning one-fifth of U.S. families receiving 48.9 percent of all income. This is thirteen times as much as the 3.8 percent of income earned by the bottom one-fifth of U.S. families.

SOURCES: Internal Revenue Service (2013) and U.S. Census Bureau (2013).

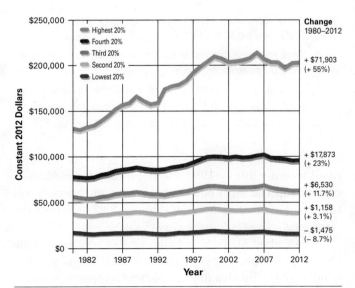

Figure 2–2   Mean Annual Income for U.S Families, 1980–2012 (in 2012 dollars, adjusted for inflation)

The highest-income families are now earning much more than they did in 1980, while average families have seen only small gains. The lowest-income families actually earned less in 2012 than in 1980.

SOURCE: U.S. Census Bureau (2013).

assets owned by a person or family, minus any debts. Wealth is made up of more than money earned; it also includes the value of homes, automobiles, stocks, bonds, real estate, and businesses. Figure 2–3 on page 37 shows that the wealthiest 20 percent of U.S. families own about 89 percent of all privately held wealth. Near the top, the very rich—those in the top 5 percent—own 63 percent of all wealth, and the super-rich, in the top 1 percent, control 35 percent of all private assets (Wolff, 2012).

The second 20 percent of U.S. families owns about 9 percent of all wealth. People in this category own some stocks and bonds, but most of their wealth is in the form of home equity and the value of automobiles and other consumer goods. Looking further down the economic hierarchy, however, about half of all U.S. families have barely any wealth at all. In other words, most ordinary families own a home and some other personal property, but the value of these assets is roughly balanced by what they owe. This fact means that most families live from paycheck to paycheck and lack cash reserves to carry them through an emergency. In a world in which illness or unemployment can strike unexpectedly, many families are only a paycheck or two away from poverty.

SOCIAL PROBLEMS IN FOCUS

Increasing Economic Inequality: When Does It Become a Problem?

In the poorest communities in the United States—such as rural Clay County, Kentucky; McDowell County, West Virginia; and Leflore County, Mississippi—the typical household manages to earn barely $20,000 a year. In a rich community such as Palo Alto, California, the average family earns eight time this much. And in the richest communities—such as urban Greenwich, Connecticut; Jupiter Island, Florida; and Winnetka, Illinois—the typical household earns more than ten times that much.

In 2012, the average compensation of the 100 highest-paid chief executive officers (CEOs) in the United States exceeded $29 million (more than the annual income of all 454 people who work in the White House, including the president). The very highest-paid people in the country—the twenty-five top-earning investment fund managers on Wall Street—averaged $566 million each in income, more than the state of Vermont pays all its public school teachers and more than 1,400 times what the nation's president earns (Taub, 2013; U.S. Census Bureau, 2013).

In any organization, we might well expect the people in charge to earn more than ordinary workers. But the leaders in some job situations earn much more than others. For example, public high school principals earn 1.8 times as much as public high school teachers. Similarly, hospital CEOs earn about 2.5 times as much as the average hospital physician. The presidents of small liberal arts colleges earn about 4 times as much as the faculty who teach there. The CEOs of investment banks earn 20 times as much as the typical investment banker. Among the largest 500 corporations, CEOs earn 92 times as much as typical middle managers. And the 25 top hedge-fund managers noted above earn more than 2,800 times as much as the average investment fund manager (and more than 20,000 times as much as the average U.S. worker).

Survey data indicate that an increasing share of U.S. adults have real concerns about economic inequality and the extent of opportunity for all. As we noted in the beginning of this chapter, a slight majority of people say there is opportunity for people who work hard, but this share has been declining steadily. About four in ten people now say that our society is "divided into two groups, the 'haves' and the 'have-nots.'" When asked about the gap between middle-class people and rich people, three-fourths of adults say that differences are greater than they were ten years ago.

Such data support the conclusion that economic inequality is now becoming widely defined as a serious social problem (see Table 1–1 on page 5). In addition, asked if "differences in income in America are too large," 63 percent agreed, 20 percent said they neither agreed nor disagreed, and 16 percent disagreed (1 percent had no opinion). Similarly, when asked if "there is too much power in the hands of a few rich people and large corporations," 77 percent of adults agreed that this was the case, and just 19 percent disagreed (again, the remainder had no opinion). These responses are even more striking when we keep in mind that the actual level of economic inequality is much greater than the average person thinks it is (Pew Research Center, 2012, 2013; Smith et al., 2013).

What Do You Think?

1. In your opinion, are economic differences in the United States too big or not?

2. What evidence can you point to that economic inequality is harmful to community life in this country?

3. What action, if any, should government take to address economic inequality?

The Trend toward Increasing Economic Inequality

In recent decades, the United States has experienced a rising level of economic inequality. In fact, economic inequality in this country has reached levels not seen in the country since 1929, just before the Great Depression. As shown in Figure 2–4 on page 38, the 1920s was a decade that saw steady gains in income for the highest-earning 1 percent of the population who, just before the stock market crash, were receiving almost 25 percent of all income.

As the Great Depression came to an end, the trend in the United States reversed itself and began to move toward greater income equality. By the 1970s, as the figure shows, the richest 1 percent received less than 10 percent of all income. But by 1980, the trend had reversed itself once again. The top 1 percent began earning a larger and larger share of all income, peaking in 2007 at almost the same level as just before the Great Depression.

The United States has always embraced a way of life that emphasizes competitive individualism, and so most people accept the idea that people should receive rewards in proportion to their talents, abilities, and efforts. But most people now say that our country's economic differences are too large (Smith et al., 2013). Even more disturbing, other surveys find that a large majority of people in the United States believe that there is now considerable conflict between rich and poor in this country and also that "this is a country in which the rich get richer and the poor get poorer" (Morin, 2012; Pew Research Center, 2012).

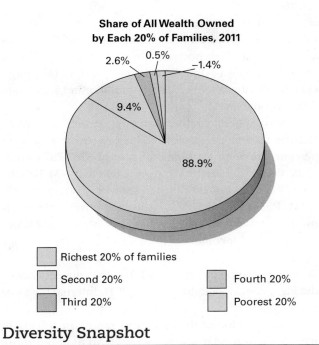

**Share of All Wealth Owned
by Each 20% of Families, 2011**

2.6% 0.5% −1.4%

9.4%

88.9%

☐ Richest 20% of families

☐ Second 20%   ☐ Fourth 20%

■ Third 20%   ☐ Poorest 20%

Diversity Snapshot

Figure 2–3   Distribution of Wealth in the
United States

Wealth is distributed much more unequally than income is. The
richest one-fifth of U.S. families control 88.9 percent of all privately
owned wealth; the poorest one-fifth of families are in debt.

SOURCE: Estimates based on Wolff (2012).

Income inequality is now widely viewed as a social problem. More people wonder whether the highest-paid individuals are really worth what they are receiving. People like Lady Gaga (who earns about $80 million a year) and Justin Bieber ($55 million), as well as athletes LeBron James ($58 million) and Serena Williams ($20 million), earn more money in a year than the rest of us are ever likely to see in a lifetime.

Is income always a good measure of talent, ability, and effort? In 2013, Alex Rodriguez of the New York Yankees topped the income scale of all major league ballplayers with $29 million in earnings. This amount was more than the season's pay for the entire Houston Astros team, whose players together surely offer more talent, ability, and effort than even the best single player on the Yankees. And the legendary Yankee Babe Ruth—arguably the greatest ballplayer of all time—earned only $80,000 (or $1.2 million in today's dollars) in his highest-paid seasons (1930 and 1931).

The Occupy Wall Street movement has called attention to the very high pay that goes to the leaders of large corporations. In 2012, according to *Forbes* magazine, John Hammergren, CEO of McKesson Pharmaceuticals, was the highest-earning CEO, receiving total compensation of $131 million in salary, bonus, stock options, and other perks. That year, the country's ten highest-paid CEOs averaged more than $60 million *each* in earnings. Noteworthy, in light of the Occupy movement's focus on Wall Street,

is the fact that no Wall Street CEOs made it into the top ten, although top hedge-fund managers made much more (DeCarlo, 2012).

Rising CEO pay is an important dimension of increasing economic inequality. In 1970, the compensation of top CEOs was about 40 times what the average company employee earned. By 2012, top CEOs earned 423 times the company average. This upward trend shows no signs of ending: In 2012, these top earners saw their pay increase by about another 11 percent, far more than the 3 percent increase received by the average U.S. worker (Helman, 2011; Roth, 2011; Corporate Library, 2013; U.S. Bureau of Economic Analysis, 2013).

Defenders of such high pay claim that companies pay what it takes to attract the most talented people to top leadership. A major league baseball pitcher may be just marginally better than a farm-team pitcher, but even a small difference helps win games and is important enough to warrant much higher pay. Similarly, in the corporate world, having the best leaders can help a company perform better (Fishman & Sullivan, 2013). Critics counter that company performance is not clearly linked to CEO rewards—half of the companies paying top salaries to CEOs actually lost money in their most recent year (Helman, 2011).

What about the rest of us? Do people who play by the rules and work hard at their jobs have the opportunity to get ahead? The idea that those willing to make the effort can enjoy economic security and expect to improve social standing over time is at the heart of the "American dream." In recent decades, while people at the top of the income hierarchy have been generously rewarded, average people who work hard have been struggling to hang on to what they have. With good-paying jobs harder to find, it is not surprising that the share of people who say that they believe their family can achieve the American dream has declined—from 76 percent in 2001 to 51 percent in 2013 (Gallup, 2013).

Taxation

Taxation is an important government policy that affects income inequality. The government levies a tax on what we earn and what we buy for three major reasons. First, taxes provide the government with the money it needs to operate. Taxes fund not only the salaries of government employees, including members of the military, but also pay for projects that benefit the public, such as building roads, bridges, and schools. Second, the government uses taxes to discourage certain types of behavior; for example, the high taxation placed on cigarettes discourages smoking by making tobacco more expensive. Third, and most important to this discussion, taxation can be a tool to redistribute income and to reduce economic inequality.

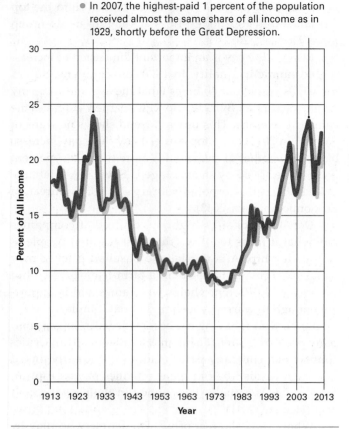

● In 2007, the highest-paid 1 percent of the population received almost the same share of all income as in 1929, shortly before the Great Depression.

Figure 2–4 Share of All U.S. Income Earned by the Richest 1 Percent, 1913–2012

In 1929, the richest 1 percent of the U.S. population earned almost one-fourth of all income. For several decades after that, the richest 1 percent's share of income declined. But by 1980, this share began to increase peaking in 2007 at almost the 1929 level. The share fell during the recent recession but then increased again to almost 23 percent in 2012.

SOURCE: Saez & Piketty (2013).

The government reduces economic inequality most effectively through **progressive taxation**, *a policy that raises tax rates as income increases.* The idea is a modern-day version of the story of Robin Hood, with government taking more from the rich in taxes and giving more to the poor in assistance and benefits. As shown in Table 2–1, the 1 percent of 2010 tax returns reporting the highest income ($369,691 or more) ended up paying 23 percent of this income in federal income taxes (federal inheritance taxes, state and local income taxes, and all sales taxes are not included in this figure). The top 10 percent of tax returns (reporting income of $116,623 or more) paid 18 percent of earnings in federal taxes (state, local, and sales taxes are not included). The bottom 50 percent of tax returns (reporting income of $34,337 or less) paid just 2 percent of earnings in federal taxes. Under this progressive system, families with lower incomes pay at a lower rate and receive more financial benefits from the government, and

those with high incomes pay at a higher rate and receive fewer benefits. When all deductions and benefits are considered, 58.4 million households (41 percent of all U.S. households) paid no federal income tax at all (although most of these households paid a payroll tax and some state or local income taxes).

Looking at dollars rather than rates, income tax returns reflecting income greater than $369,691 (the top-earning 1 percent) show an average payment of $262,757 in federal income tax. Households earning less than $34,337 (the bottom 50 percent of tax returns) show an average tax bill of $331. Rich families, who on average earn eighty times more than lower-income families, pay almost 800 times more in federal income tax. In other words, our county's progressive system taxes the rich ten times more heavily than lower-income people, which has the consequence of reducing income inequality (Luhby, 2011; Internal Revenue Service, 2012).

At the very top of the income pyramid, people earning $1.6 million or more per year (who average more than $5 million) typically paid about $1,256,000 in federal income taxes (Internal Revenue Service, 2012). The top one-tenth of 1 percent of households in terms of income actually paid 37.4 percent of all income taxes collected by the federal government, and the bottom half of all U.S. households paid only 2.4 percent of all such taxes. This contrast helps us see that tax cuts or tax increases typically have the biggest effect on high-income households.

Many high-income people make use of various legal strategies to lower their income taxes. For example, they may ask companies to defer their income until a later time, or they may make charitable contributions that, under the tax law, they can use to reduce their taxable income. Because high-income people must also pay a share of any inheritance that passes from one generation to the next, they make use of policies such as trusts and tax-free annual gifts to reduce these taxes. During the 2012 presidential election campaign, a lot was said about billionaires such as Warren Buffet who paid only about 17 percent of his 2010 income in taxes. This low tax rate reflects the fact that the very rich make most of their money not from salaries or wages (which are taxed at a top rate of 39.6 percent) but from investment or "unearned" income and capital gains, which are taxed at no more than 20 percent. So any one person's tax rate depends on not only the level of income but also the *source* of the income (Johnston, 2005; Moore & Anderson, 2005; Ohlmacher, 2011; Internal Revenue Service, 2012).

Not all taxes are progressive. The tax on gasoline, for example, is a set amount per gallon purchased. This makes the gasoline tax *regressive* because, although the tax per gallon is the same for everyone, whether they are filling up a new Rolls Royce or a beat-up Chevy pickup, the gasoline tax takes a bigger bite out of lower-income budgets. When all types of taxation are taken into account, however, our national tax policy is progressive, lessening income inequality to some extent, depending on the current tax rates. One reason for the trend toward increasing economic inequality is that our taxation policies are not as progressive as they were back in 1980.

The Rich and the Poor: A Social Profile

2.2 Assess the differences in the lives of the rich and the poor in the United States.

President Obama (2013) says that economic inequality is the "defining challenge of our time." The foundation for this claim is the fact that the differences between the rich and the poor are greater today than they have been for many decades. Of course, most families in this country are neither rich nor poor. But to sharpen your understanding of the extent of economic inequality in U.S. society, and to better understand the differences that economic standing makes, we now take a brief look at the two extremes: the rich and the poor.

The Rich

There is no standard definition of what it means to be "rich." To many of us, the rich are people who have a good bit more than we do. A more useful definition for this category of the population might be people with family income in the top 10 percent of the distribution. This means that a rich family has an income of at least $169,000, and rich families in this country, on average, earn about $277,000 per year. Many men and women with incomes in this range are successful in business; others are distinguished physicians, lawyers, and college deans and presidents (although rarely college professors). Over their working lives, a good portion of the rich will become millionaires. There are about 10 million households in the United States

(roughly 10 percent of the total) with at least $1 million in investment assets (excluding the value of a home; the number of millionaires is several times higher if you count home values) (Wolff, 2012).

Well-off people typically live in large and well-appointed homes, wear expensive clothes, and enjoy the high regard of people around them. Many in this category have the power to make a difference—they have access to political leaders and they are decision makers in their own right as members of governing boards of businesses and community organizations. High up in this elite category, we find a number of names familiar to people across the country and around the world. Oprah Winfrey, for example, is one of the highest-paid people on television and a highly successful businesswoman. Barack Obama is another. With taxable income of about $600,000 in 2012, the president earns far less than the $77 million received by Oprah Winfrey, but he lives in a bigger house and has more power to shape the world.

An estimate for 2013 placed the wealth of the ten richest individuals in the United States at more than $411 billion, which is as much as 15 million average people, or the entire populations of Hawaii, Oregon, Wyoming, New Mexico, Iowa, Kansas, Delaware, and Vermont combined. For some years, the richest of the rich has been Bill Gates, a founder of Microsoft Corporation and its single largest shareholder, whose wealth equals that of 2.7 million "ordinary" people, representing the entire population of Nevada (*Forbes*, 2013; U.S. Census Bureau, 2013).

Which categories of people are most likely to be rich? In general, because earnings rise through middle age and savings grow over time, older people have the most wealth. Men have more wealth than women do, a pattern detailed in Chapter 4 ("Gender Inequality") because, on average, a larger share of men work full time and, when they do, they earn 30 percent more than comparable women. Married couples out-earn single people because most of these couples benefit from double incomes and they save money by sharing their living expenses. Finally, white people in the United States fare better than people of

Table 2–1 Progressive Tax on Income, 2010

Share of Population	Adjusted Gross Income on Tax Return	Number of Tax Returns	Average Tax Rate	Share of Total Income Tax
Top 0.1%	$1,634,386 or more	135,033	23%	18%
Top 1%	369,691 or more	1,350,335	23	37
Top 5%	161,579 or more	6,751,675	21	59
Top 10%	116,623 or more	13,503,349	18	71
Top 25%	69,126 or more	33,758,373	15	87
Top 50%	34,338 or more	67,516,746	13	98
Bottom 50%	34,337 or less	67,516,746	2	2

SOURCE: Internal Revenue Service (2012).

color. The Census Bureau (2013) reports that 67 percent of white families earn more than $50,000 annually, compared with just 41 percent of African American and the same share of Hispanic families.

Should we define the rich as a social problem? On one hand, the rich are successful people, many of whom are living the American dream. Understandably, many people see such achievement as good. On the other hand, a society that distributes opportunity and wealth so unequally also leaves others behind: the poor.

The Poor

In this nation of great wealth, tens of millions of people living in cities and in rural areas scratch out a living on too little income. Every day across the United States, tens of millions of families struggle to get needed food, to pay the monthly rent, and to stay healthy. Some poor families experience the same daily struggle that is common in low-income countries in Latin America, Africa, and Asia. (A full discussion of global poverty and hunger is found in Chapter 15, "Population and Global Inequality.")

The Poverty Line   How many people in the United States are poor? Back in 1964, when the federal government launched a "war on poverty," officials devised what they called the **poverty line**, *an income level set by the U.S. government for the purpose of counting the poor*. The poverty line represents a dollar amount of annual income below which a person or family is defined as "poor" and may therefore become eligible for government assistance. In 2012, some 46.5 million people were counted among the poor, resulting in a *poverty rate* of 15 percent of the U.S. population. These people lived in a household with income below the official poverty line, not counting the value of benefits such as food stamps, Medicaid, and public housing.

The U.S Department of Agriculture set the poverty line to represent an annual income three times what a family has to spend in order to eat a basic, nutritious diet. Every year, government officials adjust this dollar amount to reflect the changing cost of living. In 2012, the poverty line for a nonfarm family of four was $23,492; poverty thresholds by family size are shown in Table 2–2.

The U.S. government uses what might be called an *absolute* poverty line—one directly linked to the cost of a basic diet. European governments, by contrast, use a *relative* poverty line, one set at 60 percent of the median income level. What does this difference mean? In the United States, poverty is seen as a condition in which people may not have enough to get by. How everyone else is doing does not figure in to the poverty rate. In Europe, where there is greater concern for the degree of economic inequality, poverty is seen as a relative condition that prevents people from being able to fully participate in social life. If the United States

Table 2–2 U.S. Government Poverty Threshold, by Family Type, 2012

Family Size	Annual Household Income
One person	$11,720
Two persons	14,937
Three persons	18,284
Four persons	23,492
Five persons	27,827
Six persons	31,471
Seven persons	35,473
Eight persons	39,688
Nine or more persons	47,297

SOURCE: U.S. Census Bureau (2013).

were to use the European standard, the poverty line for a family of four would be about $37,345 and our poverty rate would be more than twice as high at about 30 percent.

With the poverty line set so low, how easily can a family live on this level of income? Anyone who lives with this limited income knows that it is extremely difficult. Some analysts suggest that, to reach a minimum level of economic security, a U.S. family would need income at least 25 percent higher than the poverty line—something a step or two closer to the European standard. Some organizations go even further. A recent calculation by the Economic Policy Institute (2013) estimates that a two-parent family with two children living in a low-income region (such as Marshall County, Mississippi) would require an income of about $48,000—double the government's poverty line—in order "to secure an adequate but modest living standard." In a high-income region (such as New York City), this same family would need about $94,000 in annual income. Averaging across the United States, such a family would require about $63,000 in annual income, which is the national median figure.

Based on such data, critics (and many of the poor themselves) say the government should raise the poverty line to increase benefits to low-income people. As these critics see it, the government sets the poverty line at a very low level in order to make the poverty problem seem smaller. Yet this same policy harms the interests of the poor (Lichter & Crowley, 2002; Economic Policy Institute, 2013). The Personal Stories box lets you see for yourself to what extent a family can meet basic needs on income at the poverty line.

The Poverty Gap   The poverty line in the United States is set below a level that provides adequate income for families. Yet most poor families in the United States live on much less than poverty line income. The **poverty gap** is *the difference between the actual income of the typical poor household and the official poverty line*. The poverty gap has been growing in recent years.

PERSONAL STORIES

The Reality of Poverty: Living on the Edge

Zach Perkins, who lives in Richmond, Indiana, knows how hard it is to live at the poverty line. Zach had worked for seven years building school buses in a nearby factory before he was laid off eighteen months ago. He now looks after seven-year-old twins Michael and Sonya while Sandy Perkins, his wife, works in a fast-food restaurant. Sandy barely earns the minimum wage—she averages $7.50 an hour—for forty-eight hours each week, year round, for an annual income of $18,720. Zach earns another $500 per month doing part-time work, which boosts the family's total annual earnings to about $24,720, just above the official poverty line for a family of four, which in 2012 was $23,492.

To buy food, the Perkinses budget $6,000, almost one-third of their income, which amounts to $16 per day. For this amount to provide three meals for four people, the family can spend just $1.25 per meal. "You know," says Sandy with a look of pain, "that's not even enough to eat in the Burger King where I work." Although it is enough to buy low-cost foods (such as spaghetti, beans, and eggs), it is not enough to buy meals with wholesome meat and fresh vegetables.

If the Perkinses manage to stay within their annual food budget, they will have to meet all their other expenses for the year with $15,000, or about $1,250 per month. Their monthly rent on a simple but adequate mobile home is $700 (they were lucky to find a rental unit well below the national average rent level of about $850). But they also have to pay for utilities, including gas, electricity, and water, and these add another $200 monthly. Sandy also needs a car to get to work, and the gasoline, insurance, and repairs for their old Honda add another $200 to their monthly total. So far, total expenses come to $1,100, leaving the Perkins family with $150 (about $5 per day) to cover the cost of clothes for the entire family; everyone's medical and dental care; repairs on the washing machine, television, and other home appliances; school supplies and toys for the children; and other household items. Obviously, the family goes without most of these things.

At this income level, the family also has little money for entertainment, child care, or music lessons for the children. Zach and Sandy were glad to see the price of gas come down during the past year, but with the economy doing so badly, Zach has more trouble finding work, and Sandy is fearful that she could lose her job. Even if their income stays at the current level, they realize that sending a child to college or someday owning their home seems out of the question. "I have to be very careful with my clothes," jokes Zach. "By the time I can afford new ones, these will probably be back in style."

Zach knows how hard it is to make ends meet. But he adds firmly, "This family will never ask for a handout." Seated across the room, Sandy nods in agreement. Like everyone else, the poor are proud, even if they are barely able to pay their bills.

Can a family in the United States survive at the poverty level? Barely. Getting by month to month demands careful attention to every dollar spent. It also requires a bit of luck: The family must avoid unplanned expenses, which means everyone must manage to stay healthy. "Am I sure we can get by?" Zach wonders, looking down at the floor. "I guess not. But I do know one thing: We have to try."

What Do You Think?

1. Can a family survive on an income near the poverty line? Why or why not?

2. In what ways does growing up in a poor family limit the chances of children to succeed as adults?

3. Would you support policies or programs to assist a family like this? What should be done?

Considerable evidence suggests how hard it is to live on poverty line income. But in 2012, the average poor family with at least one child in the United States had an income of about $11,072, which is a poverty gap of $10,635 (U.S. Census Bureau, 2013). In human terms, the greater the poverty gap, the greater the hardship caused by poverty.

Who Are the Poor? A Closer Look

In 2012, the federal government counted 46.5 million men, women, and children—15 percent of the U.S. population—as poor. As shown in Figure 2–5 on page 42, the poverty rate was 22 percent in 1960, it fell to about 12 percent by the mid-1970s, and the rate has risen and fallen since then. Economic downturns, like the one that began in 2008, increase unemployment and raise the poverty rate.

As you might expect, the categories of people at greatest risk of being poor differ from those most likely to be rich. We can profile the poor in the United States according to age, race, gender, family patterns, and residence.

Age The age category at greatest risk of poverty is children, who make up 35 percent of the U.S. poor. In 2012, 16.1 million (22 percent) of young people under the age of eighteen were living in poor households. More seriously, almost half of these children live in families with incomes no more than *half* the poverty line ($12,000 or less for a family of four). A generation ago, the elderly were most likely to be poor. Today, however, poverty wears a youthful face, as the Diversity: Race, Class, & Gender box on page 42 explains.

Race Many people in the United States link being poor with being African American or Hispanic. But far more white people than black people are poor, and more non-Hispanic than Hispanic people live in poverty.

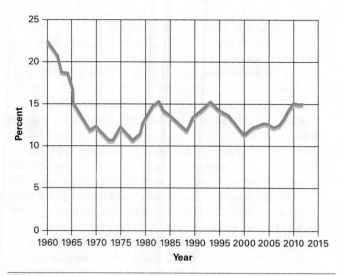

Figure 2–5 The Poverty Rate in the United States, 1960–2012

The poverty rate declined sharply in the 1960s, rising and falling since then but always staying above 10 percent of the U.S. population.

SOURCE: U.S. Census Bureau (2013).

It is true that the *percentage* of minority people who are poor is higher than that of whites. In 2012, 27.2 percent of African Americans (10.9 million people), 25.6 percent of Hispanics (13.6 million people), and 11.7 percent of Asian Americans (1.9 million people) were poor, compared to 9.7 percent of non-Hispanic whites (18.9 million people). Therefore, African Americans, Hispanics, and Asian Americans are at higher risk of being poor than whites. This is why more than half of all poor people in the United States fall into these disadvantaged categories (U.S. Census Bureau, 2013.)

Gender Women, too, are at greater risk of poverty: Fifty-seven percent of all U.S. adults who are poor are women, and 43 percent are men. The gender gap has become so large that sociologists speak of the **feminization of poverty** to refer to *the trend of women making up an increasing share of the poor*. In 1960, most poor families contained both men and women; today, by contrast, 50 percent of poor families are headed by a woman with no husband present, and just 11 percent are headed by a single man (U.S. Census Bureau, 2013).

Family Patterns Being married combines incomes and shares expenses to help build income and wealth. Therefore, marriage greatly reduces the risk of being poor. The poverty rate for married people is 6 percent, compared to

DIVERSITY: RACE, CLASS, & GENDER
The United States: A Land of Poor Children

The United States is the richest country in the world. Even so, more than one child in five under the age of eighteen—16.1 million boys and girls—is poor. Since the "war on poverty" began in 1964, the nation has managed to cut poverty among senior citizens by more than two-thirds (from 29 percent in 1966 to 9 percent in 2012). Yet the rate of child poverty is about the same today as it was then (23 percent in 1964 compared to 22 percent in 2012).

What is your mental picture of poor children? The common stereotype is of African American children living in an inner city with a teenage mother who is on welfare. But in truth, 62 percent of poor children are white, and 56 percent live not in inner cities but in other urban, suburban, and rural areas.

Why are there so many poor children? Liberals point to the loss of good-paying jobs in the United States. In inner cities, where factories have closed, and in declining rural communities, many people simply cannot find good jobs. Conservatives note the role of family breakdown in the rising tide of poverty. They point out that 62 percent of poor children live with a single parent, and 76 percent of these households have no adult working full time (U.S. Census Bureau, 2013).

Everyone agrees that children, wherever they live, are not to blame for their own poverty. Why, then, do we continue to tolerate their suffering? The moral case to care better for our children is compelling. And there are practical reasons, too. Isn't reducing the crushing experience of child poverty far easier and less costly than dealing with the problems that come later, such as unemployment, drug use, and crime?

What Do You Think?

1. Of the liberal and conservative explanations for the high rate of child poverty, which makes more sense to you? Why?

2. Few people think children themselves are responsible for being poor. Why, then, isn't there more popular support for increasing assistance to poor families with children?

3. As the unemployment rate increased rapidly during the recent recession, what do you think happened to the rate of child poverty? Why?

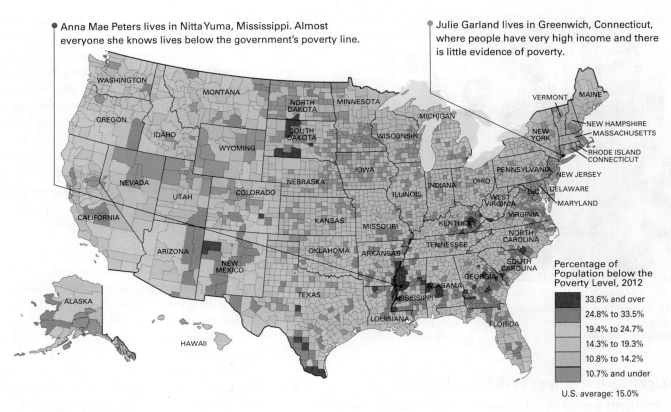

Anna Mae Peters lives in Nitta Yuma, Mississippi. Almost everyone she knows lives below the government's poverty line.

Julie Garland lives in Greenwich, Connecticut, where people have very high income and there is little evidence of poverty.

Percentage of Population below the Poverty Level, 2012

- 33.6% and over
- 24.8% to 33.5%
- 19.4% to 24.7%
- 14.3% to 19.3%
- 10.8% to 14.2%
- 10.7% and under

U.S. average: 15.0%

Seeing Ourselves

National Map 2–1   Poverty across the United States, 2012

This map shows that the poorest counties in the United States—where the poverty rate is more than twice the national average—are in Appalachia, spread across the Deep South, along the border with Mexico, near the Four Corners region of the Southwest, and in the Dakotas. Can you suggest some reasons for this pattern?

SOURCE: U.S. Census Bureau (2013).

21 percent for single men and 27 percent for single women (Zagorsky, 2006; U.S. Census Bureau, 2013).

Why are single women with children at higher risk of poverty? Because many single women (but rarely single men) stay at home to care for their children or because they cannot afford the child care they need to go to work. For all single mothers, the poverty rate in 2012 was 41 percent. Single minority women with children bear an added risk: About 47 percent of single, African American mothers and 49 percent of single, Hispanic American mothers had incomes below the poverty line. If the mother is also young and has not completed high school, poverty is almost a certainty (U.S. Census Bureau, 2013).

It is easy to see why divorce raises the odds of poverty for adults and, especially, children. One study found that within a year, one in eight children of divorcing parents had slipped below the poverty line. It is also true that most of these poor children live with their mothers in families that are likely to remain poor (Furstenberg & Cherlin, 1991).

Region   The official poverty rate varies from state to state, from a low of 8.1 percent in New Hampshire and 9.3 percent

in New Jersey to a high of 22.0 percent in Mississippi and 21.1 percent in Louisiana. By region, the South (16.5 percent) and the West (15.1 percent) have higher poverty rates, followed by the Northeast (13.6 percent) and the Midwest (13.3 percent) (U.S. Census Bureau, 2013).

Many people link poverty with the inner city. Most poor people—just like most affluent people—do live in urban areas. But as National Map 2–1 shows, rural areas have a greater share of the population living below the poverty level than do urban areas. Poverty is widespread across Appalachia (including West Virginia and Kentucky), along the Texas border with Mexico (where many new immigrants live), and in parts of the Great Plains and the Southwest (especially on American Indian lands). In 2012, some 17.7 percent of the rural population was poor, compared with 14.5 percent for people in urban areas or, looking more closely, 19.7 percent of people in central cities and 11.2 percent of people in suburbs (U.S. Census Bureau, 2013). Why do suburban areas show an advantage when it comes to income? By and large, poverty is lowest in areas that offer more jobs and more educational opportunity.

One way that we know that poverty is a social problem rather than simply an individual problem is by looking at poverty rates, which are very high in certain regions of the country. Economic opportunity is all but gone from a number of rural areas, especially in the Great Plains; as a result, entire communities suffer.

Working Families: Working Harder

Economic struggle is not limited to the poor. In recent decades, the American dream—the belief that with hard work, people can have a secure and improving way of life—has been shaken by some disturbing facts. Beginning about 1970, many U.S. families found themselves working harder than ever yet feeling that they were falling behind. The tough economy in recent years has only added to the struggle. No one should be surprised that, in a recent survey, the share of people who say they believe that their family can achieve the American dream declined from 71 percent in 2002 to 51 percent in 2013 (Gallup, 2013).

What's going on? For some families, of course, times have never been better. But for a large share of workers, income has nearly stalled. The earnings of a typical fifty-year-old man working full time jumped 72 percent between 1958 and 1973 (from $31,294 to $53,910 in constant 2012 dollars). Between 1973 and 2012, however, this same worker's income fell by 14 percent, to $46,466, so he had to work more hours to meet the rising costs of groceries, housing, college tuition, and medical care. Among younger workers, wage increases have been very small over the past twenty years. This is one major reason that, in 2013, 55 percent of women and men between the ages of eighteen and twenty-four were living with their parents (U.S. Census Bureau, 2013).

Underlying this pattern of stalled or declining earnings are changes in the economy detailed in Chapter 11 ("Work and the Workplace"). Through much of the twentieth century, the U.S. economy created jobs with *higher* pay; for example, low-paying farm jobs were replaced with higher-paying factory work. More recently, however, most new jobs have been in the service sector, including sales positions, computer data entry, and food service jobs that pay *less* than the factory jobs they are replacing. At the same time, as the economy has recovered from the recent recession, companies have not replaced all the people they had laid off, relying on computer technology and part-time workers to keep their labor costs down. A lower demand for labor puts downward pressure on wages.

The Working Poor

Barbara Ehrenreich, whom you met in Chapter 1, wanted to see for herself what it is like to be a low-wage worker, so she left her comfortable life as a writer to spend several months in Florida, Maine, and Minnesota, pretending to be in need of work, taking whatever jobs she could find, and trying to live on what she earned. Ehrenreich found that it was not easy. At the end of her journey, she explained (2001:220):

> I grew up hearing over and over . . . that hard work was the secret of success. "Work hard and you'll get ahead" or "It's hard work that got us where we are." No one ever said that you could work hard—harder than you ever thought possible—and still find yourself sinking ever deeper into debt and poverty.

In 2012, according to the government, 15 percent of the heads of poor families worked full time, at least fifty weeks during the year, yet remained below the poverty line. The reason is that low-wage work—Ehrenreich worked as a waitress, motel room cleaner, and sales clerk at a discount store—rarely pays much more than the (2013) federal minimum hourly wage of $7.25 per hour, which was set in 2009. In 2014, President Obama declared his intention to raise the minimum wage for federal workers to $10.10 an hour. At least twenty states already have set the minimum wage above $7.25, with Washington State paying the most at $9.19 per hour. But even at $10.10 an hour, full-time, year-round work yields just $21,000, about $2,000 below the poverty line for a nonfarm family of four (Rithholtz, 2013; U.S. Census Bureau, 2013; Hananel, 2014).

The Nonworking Poor

Many poor families do not have a steady income from work. Government data show that in 2012, 55 percent of the heads of poor families did not work at all; another 30 percent remained poor while doing part-time work (U.S. Census Bureau, 2013).

There are many reasons for not working. Some people have health problems; others lack the skills or self-confidence needed to hold a steady job. Some parents cannot afford to pay for child care because it costs more than they can earn at low-wage work. For many others, the problem is a lack of available employment. Most inner-city areas in the United States offer few jobs. Similarly, many rural areas and small towns are in economic decline, with stores and factories that have closed their doors. The recent recession has sent the unemployment rate in many communities to 15 and even 20 percent, which means a big increase in the number of non-working poor. Elkhart, Indiana, the town that makes most of the nation's recreational vehicles, is a case in point. As the bad economy has hurt the sales of RVs, the town's unemployment rate peaked above 20 percent in 2009 (W. J. Wilson, 1996a; O'Hare, 2002; Martin, 2009; U.S. Department of Labor, 2012).

The Underclass

Poverty is most severe among the **underclass**, *poor people who live in areas with high concentrations of poverty and limited opportunities for schooling or work.* The largest concentration of people in the underclass live in inner cities in a condition sociologists call *hypersegregation,* cut off from the larger society and having no access to either good schools or good-paying jobs. Under such conditions, children grow up poor, and most remain poor as adults (Massey & Denton, 1989; E. Anderson, 1999).

Hypersegregation is found in rural areas as well, which can be just as isolated from the larger world as the inner cities. Across the United States, the underclass includes perhaps one in seven poor people, or 1 to 2 percent of the total U.S. population.

For people who are part of the underclass, the reality of everyday life is *persistent poverty.* But most people in the United States who are poor are not part of the underclass. For the society as a whole, *temporary poverty* is more the rule. Over ten years, about one-fourth of the U.S. population falls below the poverty line, usually because of unemployment, illness, or divorce. When this happens, the typical pattern is for a household to remain poor for perhaps a year or two.

Whether poverty is a short-term or long-term experience, it is rarely a problem that exists all by itself. On the contrary, poverty brings with it a wide range of additional challenges, which we shall now examine.

Problems Linked to Poverty

2.3 Analyze how poverty is linked to other social problems.

When families lack the income needed for a safe and secure life, people suffer in many ways. The following sections take a closer look at six problems linked to poverty: poor health, substandard housing, homelessness, limited schooling, crime, and political alienation.

Poor Health

There is a strong link between income and health. In fact, there is a good deal of truth in the claim that "wealth means health." Poverty, disease, and illness often go together.

Good nutrition is the foundation of a healthy life. Yet many poor people cannot afford nutritious foods. In 2012, about 15 percent of U.S. households that have income below or near to the poverty line experienced "food insecurity" (U.S. Department of Agriculture, 2013). But the challenges of living poor go beyond having enough healthful food. In addition, poverty breeds stress, increasing the use of tobacco and alcohol and raising the risk of drug abuse and violence. Just as important, when illness or injury strikes, poor people have fewer resources to fight back. About 29 percent of poor people lack health insurance, which means that they cannot afford medical care. As a result, poor people may not seek medical care right away. A common pattern is for poor people to show up at an emergency room when faced with a serious condition that could have been cured easily had the person been treated much earlier (Center on Hunger and Poverty, 2000; Nord, Andrews, & Carlson, 2002; U.S. Census Bureau, 2013).

Poverty affects health throughout the life course. Among the poor, *infant mortality,* the risk of death during the first year of life, is double the rate among affluent people (Singh, 2010). Among the very poor in the United States, the death rate among newborns rises to levels we commonly find in low-income countries such as Nigeria and Vietnam.

Income continues to shape health into adulthood. When asked to rate their personal health, 82 percent of adults living in families with incomes over $100,000 replied "excellent" or "very good." But only 52 percent of people whose families had incomes of less than $35,000 could say the same (Adams, Kirzinger, & Martinez, 2012).

Finally, for people who are poor, life can be short. Low-income men and women are more likely to die young from infectious diseases, from violence, and even from natural disasters—almost all of the people who died in Hurricane Katrina were poor. By contrast, most rich people die of cancer and heart disease, diseases that typically take their toll in old age. For this reason, life expectancy for affluent people is almost five years greater than for low-income people, and this "health gap" has doubled in the years since 1980 (Congressional Budget Office, 2008).

Because poverty is linked to disease and early death, a nation with excessive economic inequality is likely to have less favorable patterns of health. One recent study found that, of twenty-one high-income nations, the United States was ranked last in terms of life expectancy at birth (Burtless, 2012).

Substandard Housing

In the United States, better housing is available to those who can pay for it. For this reason, poor people take what is left, sometimes living in crowded homes containing dangerous lead-based paint, faulty plumbing, inadequate heating, and even collapsing walls and crumbling ceilings.

Recent years have seen a steady decline in the number of low-rent apartments in the United States. As a result, many poor families are forced to spend most of what they earn for housing, leaving too little for food, clothing, and other needs. Not surprisingly, in large cities across the United States, tens of thousands of poor people are on waiting lists for programs that will help them secure better housing. In some affluent communities, including Palo Alto, the home of the Muñoz Tello family described in the chapter-opening story, there is little or no low-income housing (Ehrenreich, 2001; Westervelt, 2013).

After the onset of the housing crisis that began about 2007, a larger share of lower-income and middle-income people struggled to hold onto housing. After years of rising values, housing prices fell dramatically, in some cases losing half or more of previous value. With home values falling below the amount owed on a mortgage, many owners simply stopped making mortgage payments and walked away from their properties when banks foreclosed. Some states, including Florida, Arizona, and Nevada, experienced a full-blown crisis with more than five times the national foreclosure rate. The nation's recent housing crisis reduced the wealth of many families and added to the struggle to hold onto good housing (Christie, 2011).

Homeless shelters provide necessary housing to hundreds of thousands of people across the United States. But the larger question is why do so many people lack affordable housing in the first place?

Homelessness

In recent decades, the problem of **homelessness**, *the plight of poor people who lack shelter and live primarily on the streets*, has received a lot of attention. Researchers estimate that 610,000 people are homeless in the United States on any given night, and as many as 1.6 million people are homeless at some point during a year (U.S. Department of Housing and Urban Development, 2013).

There are many causes of homelessness, and how much emphasis is given to any particular cause depends on one's political outlook. Conservatives point to personal problems, noting that more than half of homeless people suffer from a mental disorder or abuse alcohol or some other drug. Liberals counter that homelessness has less to do with personal shortcomings than with poverty, and they point to increasing economic inequality, a rise in low-wage jobs, and a lack of affordable housing as major causes.

A large majority of homeless people report that they do not work; however, about 20 percent say that they do hold at least a part-time job. Average income for homeless individuals is low—just $350 per month; for families, the figure is about $475. Such income is simply not enough to pay for housing (U.S. Conference of Mayors, 2013: U.S. Department of Housing and Urban Development, 2013).

Limited Schooling

Poor children are less likely than rich children to complete high school. Therefore, the odds of going to college are low, and the chances of completing an advanced degree are smaller still. Too often, underperforming public schools transform low-income children into low-achieving students who grow up to be low-income adults. The public school systems in the fifty largest cities of the United States graduate just half of students on time (America's Promise Alliance, 2010). Under these conditions, it is easy to see how poor schooling can help pass poverty from one generation to the next.

Even for those who stay in school, rich and poor children typically have very unequal opportunities. Many schools use some form of *tracking*, by which the schools divide children into college-bound ("academic") and job-oriented ("vocational") coursework tracks. The stated goal of tracking is to teach according to each child's academic ability. But research suggests that school officials often see privileged children as more talented and label children as less able just because they are poor. The result is that the most privileged children get the best our public schools have to offer, while many poor children are taught in crowded classrooms with fewer computers, older books, and the weakest teachers (Kilgore, 1991; Kozol, 1991; Thornburgh, 2006).

Crime and Punishment

If you watch police "reality" shows on TV, you are bound to think that most criminals are poor people. Assault, robbery, burglary, auto theft—these so-called "street crimes" are the offenses that get most of the public's attention and are featured most in the mass media. As Chapter 6 ("Crime, Violence, and Criminal Justice") explains, when it comes to street crimes, the facts support the conclusion that poor people are involved more often than affluent people—not only as offenders but also as victims. But rich people, too, commit crimes. However, the public pays less attention to the crimes that are most likely to be committed by wealthy people, including tax evasion, stock fraud, false advertising, bribery, and environmental pollution. This is so despite the fact that such offenses almost certainly cause greater harm to society as a whole.

Our society's greater focus on street crime means that the poor are most likely to be arrested, go to trial, and face a prison sentence. Poor people who enter the criminal justice system must also rely on public defenders or court-appointed attorneys, typically lawyers who are underpaid and overworked. Wealthy people in trouble can afford to enlist the help of private lawyers who in turn employ other specialists to support their claims in court. Such an advantage does not always get people off the hook, but it does lower the chances of being charged with a crime or, if they are charged, of being convicted. Perhaps this is why not one of the executives of Wall Street's Lehman Brothers investment bank—the people widely thought to have engaged in the mortgage fraud that led to the collapse of the country's banking system—has faced prosecution (Holland, 2013).

Finally, for anyone who ends up serving time in jail, finding a good job later on will be more difficult. Just as poverty raises the risk of getting into trouble with the law, being convicted of a crime raises the odds that a low-income person will end up staying poor (Western, 2002).

Political Alienation

Given how hard the poor have to struggle to get by, you might expect that they would look for any chance to support causes and candidates that would bring about change.

The common view is that the poor are the most likely to commit crimes. But recent Wall Street scandals have gone a long way to changing that view. In 2014, stockbroker Michael Steinberg (*right*) was convicted of insider trading—using confidential information to make profitable stock trades—and was sentenced to three and a half years in prison.

Sometimes poor people do organize politically, but many do not even bother to vote. In the 2012 presidential election, almost 80 percent of people earning $100,000 or more voted; just 54 percent of people earning less than $40,000 did the same. This pattern suggests that many poor people feel alienated from a system that they think does not serve their interests (Samuelson, 2003; U.S. Census Bureau, 2013).

Responding to Poverty: The Welfare System

2.4 **Explain the changing ways our society has used the social welfare system to respond to poverty.**

To address the problem of poverty, all high-income countries rely on various kinds of **social welfare programs**, *organized efforts by government, private organizations, or individuals to assist needy people considered worthy of assistance.* Social welfare takes many forms, including government benefits for workers who lose their jobs, Red Cross benefits for flood victims, or simply people lending a hand to their neighbors after a tornado destroys many homes. The largest welfare programs, which are run by the federal government and state governments, typically have three characteristics:

1. **Social welfare programs benefit people or activities defined as worthy.** The public and its leaders debate and decide which categories of people or activities are most worthy of support. The categories of people who

Who gets government welfare? In 2009, the government's billion-dollar bailout of General Motors helped that corporation go through a short bankruptcy and reorganize in the hope of becoming a stronger company in the future. The government action meant that hundreds of thousands of autoworkers (who now own a share of the company) still have their jobs.

benefit from social welfare programs change along with the level of resources that government makes available according to swings in the political mood of the country.

2. **Social welfare programs benefit most of the U.S. population.** Welfare programs include not only assistance to poor families but also price supports for farmers, the oil depletion allowance to petroleum companies, the homeowner's tax deduction for home mortgage interest, pensions paid to the elderly, benefits for veterans, and low-interest loans for students. Government bailouts of GM and Chrysler as well as various financial corporations in recent years are all examples of massive social welfare assistance.

3. **Overall, social welfare programs reduce economic inequality, but only a little.** To fund social welfare programs, government takes from the rich (in taxes) and gives to the poor (in benefits), which has the effect of reducing economic inequality. But many programs, such as the recent corporate bailouts, benefit wealthier individuals and families. Even among

"ordinary" people, the tax deduction on home mortgage interest, worth about $70 billion annually, goes mostly to affluent people who own larger homes. The home mortgage deduction is worth several times more than what the government spends to provide food assistance to low-income people (Congressional Budget Office, 2013; U.S. Department of Health and Human Services, 2013).

The ongoing welfare debate points up a hard truth: People in this country like to think they are compassionate, but our cultural emphasis on personal responsibility makes many people uneasy with giving assistance to the poor. The Social Policy box evaluates six common assumptions about public assistance.

A Brief History of Welfare

Social welfare has a long and controversial history in the United States. The following discussion surveys welfare policies in three historical periods—the colonial era, the early industrial era, and the modern era after the Great Depression—and then highlights the 1996 welfare reforms (Trattner, 1980; Katz, 1990, 1996).

The Colonial Era   During the 1600s and 1700s, early immigrants who came to the United States settled in small communities where families struggled to survive in a strange and uncertain world. Because almost everyone was poor, family members and neighbors were quick to lend a helping hand to one another.

Even so, some colonists, including the early Puritans in New England, looked down on the very poor, seeing poverty as a sign of moral weakness. Throughout the colonies, free people looked down on slaves as personally inferior and therefore morally undeserving. During this period, there was hardly any government at all, and "welfare" was limited to acts of personal kindness between kin and neighbors.

The Early Industrial Era   As the Industrial Revolution began in the early 1800s, U.S. cities swelled with immigrants. The new industrial capitalist economy encouraged a spirit of individualism and self-reliance. As the idea that people were responsible for their own social position became more popular, attitudes toward the poor became more negative. As a result, the public criticized charity as a misguided policy that would only end up reducing people's need to work and encourage them to become lazy. Organizations such as the Salvation Army (founded in 1865) that did offer food and shelter to the poor included moral instruction reinforcing the belief that the poor were weak and of bad character and in need of reforming themselves.

But not everyone shared this harsh view of the poor. In the 1870s, the *scientific charity movement* (really an early form of sociology) began studying what categories of

SOCIAL POLICY

An Undeserved Handout? The Truth about "Welfare"

Are welfare assistance checks and food stamps just handouts for people too lazy to work? What are the facts? Let's evaluate six widespread assumptions about public assistance.

1. "Most welfare goes to the poor." Not true. If we look at *all* government income programs, we find hundreds that offer financial benefits—cash transfers or reduced taxes—to many categories of people at all income levels, including the wealthy. For example, almost all of the government "bailout" money given to banks in 2008 and 2009 ended up benefitting rich people. Overall, no more than half of all government benefits go to poor people.

    Furthermore, large corporations are able to pay such low wages only because workers whose earnings are below the poverty line can receive government assistance. Therefore, as some see it, companies such as Walmart and McDonald's benefit the most from welfare (Ritholtz, 2013).

2. "Most income assistance goes to able-bodied people who should be working." Not true. Most low-income people who benefit from government assistance are either too old or too young to work. Some programs do assist poor parents who do not work. But these funds are primarily for support of children, and this government assistance is provided only for a limited time.

3. "Once on welfare, always on welfare." Before the welfare reforms of 1996, there was some truth to this. Back then, half of families who ever enrolled in Aid for Families with Dependent Children received public assistance for four years or more. But because of limits in the current program (including a lifetime benefit limit of five years), this is no longer the case.

4. "Most welfare benefits go to African Americans and other minorities." True, but just barely. Non-Hispanic whites receive 49 percent of all food stamps; African Americans receive 31 percent, Hispanics receive 13 percent, and people of other races, including Asian Americans, receive 7 percent. So all the minority categories added together receive 51 percent of these benefits (U.S. Department of Agriculture, 2012). Minorities are more likely than whites to receive income assistance because, as we have already explained, these categories of the population are at higher risk for being poor.

5. "Welfare encourages single women to have children." Not true. The average number of children among women without husbands is the same whether or not families receive welfare support. The case has also been made that welfare assistance enabled some women to support children without marrying. This may be true, but the trend toward more single parenting is found among people of all income levels and is evident in all high-income nations.

6. "Welfare fraud is a serious national problem." Not really. Social service agency employees will tell you that a few people do take advantage of the system, but they will also confirm that the vast majority of benefits go to people who are truly needy.

What Do You Think?

1. Did any of the facts presented in this box surprise you? Which ones? Why?

2. In general, would you expand social welfare programs, keep them the same, or reduce them? Explain your answer.

3. Do you think that the recent economic recession affected how people think about poverty and welfare assistance? Explain your answer.

---

people were poor, why people were poor, and what could be done to help them. Researchers soon learned that most poor people were not lazy but were men and women for whom there were no jobs, children without parents, women without husbands, victims of factory accidents, and working people earning too little to support a family. In short, scientific charity claimed that most poverty was not the fault of the poor themselves but the result of how society operates.

This new thinking helped guide the *settlement house movement*. Settlement houses were buildings located in the worst slums of a city, where a staff of social scientists and reform-minded activists helped new immigrants get settled in their new surroundings. This social movement also tried to influence public opinion with the goal of making the public more compassionate toward the poor.

The Twentieth Century By 1900, millions of immigrants were streaming into the United States. The expansion of poor neighborhoods in large cities along the East Coast fueled hostility toward the poor. Within a few years, the outbreak of World War I (1914–18) made matters worse by raising suspicion about the "foreigners" in our midst. In this fearful climate, there was little public support for welfare programs of any kind.

Then, in 1929, the Great Depression rolled across the United States. As many as one-fourth of all working people lost their jobs, and the economic collapse suddenly sent millions of families into the swelling ranks of the poor. Banks closed, wiping out people's life savings, and families in debt lost their farms and were forced from their homes. Under such conditions, it became impossible to see poverty as caused by people who were lazy or "different." It was then that U.S. society began to define poverty as a *social* problem.

In 1996, Congress reformed the nation's welfare program, enacting the Personal Responsibility and Work Opportunity Reconciliation Act. As its name suggests, this policy requires people who seek public assistance to enroll either in school or in a job training program. Do you think that people who need income assistance should have to prepare for work in this way? Why or why not?

Franklin Roosevelt became president in 1933 and proposed a program he called the New Deal to help the millions made poor by the Depression. Throughout the 1930s, the federal government enacted many new programs to fight poverty, the most important of which was Social Security. Today, this program provides monthly income to 46 million people, most of whom are elderly.

Roosevelt's reforms eased the suffering, and World War II (1939–45) spurred the economy, ending the Depression and also directing public attention to other issues. Later, in the 1960s, researchers "rediscovered" poverty in both cities and the rural countryside (Harrington, 1962), prompting President Lyndon Johnson in 1964 to launch his War on Poverty. The Defining Moment feature takes a closer look at how two presidents prompted U.S. society to face up to the continuing reality of poverty.

A glance back at Figure 2–5 shows that the War on Poverty actually worked. The official poverty rate, which was about 22 percent in 1960, fell to about 11 percent by the early 1970s. But by the 1980s, the mood of the country again turned against social welfare programs. Beginning with the Reagan administration, the federal government scaled back assistance programs, claiming (like critics a century earlier) that welfare programs were discouraging personal initiative and creating "dependency."

The 1996 Welfare Reform

In the early 1990s, about 8 million poor households in the United States were receiving public assistance totaling some $40 billion annually, for an average of about $5,000 per family. The most important assistance program was Aid to Families with Dependent Children (AFDC), a program of the federal government that provided income to poor mothers with children.

Changes in the welfare system began to take shape in 1992, when President Bill Clinton pledged to "end welfare as we know it." In 1994, the Democratic president and a Republican Congress joined forces to produce the most sweeping welfare reform since the Roosevelt era. The purpose of the reform was suggested by its formal title: the 1996 Personal Responsibility and Work Opportunity Reconciliation Act. First, responsibility for helping the poor shifted from the federal government to the states. The old federal program, AFDC, was ended in favor of a state-level program called Temporary Assistance for Needy Families (TANF). The new rules were intended to increase the "personal responsibility" of the poor by requiring able-bodied people seeking benefits to find a job or enroll in job training. In addition, the program limits the period of time that families can receive benefits to two consecutive years, with a lifetime cap of five years.

Supporters of welfare reform (mainly conservatives) call the policy a success. They point to the fact that the nation's welfare rolls have fallen by half. In addition, half of those who have left welfare now have jobs, and most of the remainder are attending school or enrolled in training programs. But critics (mostly liberals) counter that most people who have left welfare for work now have low-wage jobs that leave them struggling to make ends meet. They claim that reform has reduced welfare assistance, but it has not done much to reduce *poverty* (Lichter & Crowley, 2002; Lichter & Jayakody, 2002).

Theories of Poverty

2.5 Apply sociological theory to the issue of poverty.

Why does poverty exist in the first place? Some answers can be found by applying sociology's major theoretical approaches to the issue of poverty.

Structural-Functional Analysis: Some Poverty Is Inevitable

Chapter 1 ("Sociology: Studying Social Problems") identified a number of structural-functional approaches to social problems. Each has something to say about why poverty exists.

CONSTRUCTING SOCIAL PROBLEMS

A DEFINING MOMENT

U.S. Society "Discovers" Poverty

During the first centuries of our country's history, so many people lived with so little. Most people today could barely imagine such widespread and extreme poverty. Back then, however, most poor people accepted their situation because when they looked around, everyone else was living pretty much the same way.

With the onset of the Industrial Revolution, living standards rose for the majority of the population. Yet, the gap between rich and poor became much bigger. Still, the poverty of those left behind—in urban neighborhoods and rural communities—provoked only passing public concern, probably because many of the poor were becoming defined as "different" (they were stereotyped as "immigrants" or "hillbillies") by those who were better off.

Another change took place with the Great Depression in 1929, when men and women in all social classes lost much of the security they had previously taken for granted. Suddenly, people started to talk about poverty as a serious social problem. This process was encouraged by Franklin D. Roosevelt, elected president in 1932, when he pointed out the problem of "one-third of a nation ill-clothed, ill-housed, and ill-fed." His economic programs

that came to be known as the New Deal—most importantly, the Works Progress Administration (WPA) employment projects and Social Security—addressed the problem of poverty by providing a social "safety net" for the U.S. population.

By the end of World War II, the Depression had given way to a period of economic prosperity. But despite the fact that the United States had become a very rich nation, a large underclass of poor people continued to live in both urban and rural areas. Lyndon B. Johnson, president from 1963 until 1968, mobilized the country once again to define poverty as a problem when he declared that the federal government would wage a "war on poverty." He pushed the government to "strike at the causes, not the consequences" of poverty, and Congress reacted by passing programs such as Title I federal funding for public schools in low-income districts, Head Start for preschool children, and the Job Corps training program for adults.

Together, Presidents Roosevelt and Johnson did more than any other U.S. leaders to define poverty as a social problem. Just as important, they directed the power of the government toward creating a solution.

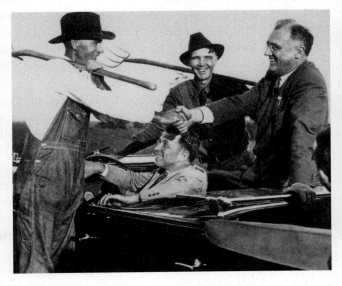 

Franklin Delano Roosevelt, who was president from 1933 until 1945, established Social Security and other programs that provide a social "safety net" to the U.S. population. A generation later, Lyndon Baines Johnson, who was president from 1963 until 1968, declared a national "War on Poverty" that succeeded in reducing the poverty rate.

Social Pathology Theories: Personal Deficiency Some early sociologists argued in favor of a "bad apple" theory that claimed that poverty was the result of personal flaws. For example, Herbert Spencer (1820–1903) developed an analysis, called *social Darwinism,* which viewed society as a competitive arena where the most able became rich and the

least able fell into poverty. Spencer described the operation of a competitive society as the "survival of the fittest" in which the "less fit" fell behind.

The social pathology approach is also found in the work of the anthropologist Oscar Lewis (1961, 1966). Lewis studied poor communities in San Juan (Puerto

Rico), Mexico City, and New York City, asking why some neighborhoods remained poor from generation to generation. His conclusion: They contain a **culture of poverty**, *cultural patterns that encourage poverty as a way of life.* Lewis claimed that people *adapt* to poverty, accepting their plight and giving up hope that life can improve. Thinking this way, Lewis continued, people may turn to alcohol or drugs, become violent, neglect their families, and end up living just for the moment. Doing so, they pass on the culture of poverty from one generation to the next.

A more recent social pathology theory is the "bell curve" thesis of Richard J. Herrnstein and Charles Murray (1994). Over the course of the twentieth century, they argue, the United States became more of a **meritocracy**, *a system of social inequality in which social standing corresponds to personal ability and effort.* In today's information age, intelligence matters more than ever in the world of work and corporations greatly reward personal ability. Therefore, the argument goes, the ranks of the rich are increasingly filled by people who are very smart, leaving behind the poor who are more and more likely to be people with limited intelligence. For this reason, Herrnstein and Murray conclude, government programs can do only so much to improve the plight of the poor: As Herbert Spencer said a century earlier, they are capable of little more.

More recently, Charles Murray (2013) has studied the diverging cultures of both high- and low-income communities. He studied high-income communities where he found that optimism about the future and a strong work ethic persist. By contrast, in white, working-class communities he found that pessimism about the future was widespread eroding industriousness (measured by a lower rate of employment), lowering rates of marriage, and weakening religious values. These trends combine to weaken the social fabric of these communities and to push poverty rates up. Overall, Murray concludes, the United States is more and more breaking apart into two societies—a small "new upper class" and an enlarging "new lower class."

Social Disorganization Theory: Too Much Change

In the 1920s and 1930s, sociologists at the University of Chicago linked poverty to **social disorganization**, *a breakdown in social order caused by rapid social change.* Industrial factories drew tens of millions of people—rural Midwesterners, men and women from towns in Appalachia, African Americans from the South's Cotton Belt, and immigrants from Europe—to the rapidly growing cities of the North and Midwest.

People arrived too fast for a city's neighborhoods, schools, and factories to absorb them. The result was overcrowded apartment buildings, overflowing classrooms, and too many people for the number of available jobs. The overall result was poverty and related social problems. Only with time could we expect local communities to respond to these imbalances to reduce the poverty problem.

In recent years, the high rate of immigration to the United States, especially from Latin America, has contributed to high poverty rates in the West (especially the Southwest), where new arrivals to this country struggle to find housing and work. In time, according to the social disorganization approach, we would expect most of these families to improve their situation.

Modern Functional Theory: Some Inequality Is Useful

Kingsley Davis and Wilbert Moore (1945) asked, "Why does inequality exist everywhere?" Their answer was that inequality—specifically, differences in the rewards given to people who perform various jobs—is useful for the operation of society. Davis and Moore explained that some jobs (say, work as a security guard) are not very important and can be performed by just about anyone. But other positions (for example, that of a surgeon) require rare talents and extensive training.

How can society draw talent toward more important work? How can society motivate people to develop their abilities and to gain the schooling they need to do important and demanding jobs? Only by giving them greater rewards, such as higher income, greater power, and more prestige. Linking rewards to the importance of various jobs is therefore useful. Therefore, social stratification—with some people having more resources than others—has some positive functions for a society.

Davis and Moore point out that any society could provide equal rewards to people regardless of what job they perform, but doing so would amount to saying that it makes no difference who does what job or how well the job is done. A society with no differences in rewards, they claim, would not be very productive because it would give people little incentive to strive for more important work or even to work hard at their present job. In sum, a system of unequal rewards is a strategy that actually helps society be productive.

Herbert Gans (1971) offers a critical response to Davis and Moore's theory, pointing out that inequality is useful but only to *affluent* people. The function of inequality, Gans claims, is to ensure that there is a supply of poor people willing to do almost any job, no matter how unpleasant. Other than poor people (who have few choices in their lives), he asks, who would want to perform farm labor, pick up garbage, or clean other people's homes? In addition, the poor also buy things no one else wants, including rundown housing, old cars, rebuilt appliances, and secondhand clothing. In short, Gans suggests, poverty exists because well-off people benefit from others being poor.

All structural-functional theories share a key argument: At least some poverty is a natural, expected part of life that has some useful consequences. Critics, especially people who are more liberal, take issue with these theories, especially the idea that poor individuals are somehow personally inferior. As they see it, poverty is not something that people bring on themselves, nor is it inevitable. Rather, poverty has economic causes, including unemployment, low wage levels that leave even full-time workers poor, and our nation's striking economic inequality.

Why, then, have such theories been popular? Perhaps because locating the causes of poverty in poor people themselves justifies the status quo and turns attention away from flaws in society itself. In addition, these theories tend to appeal to the rich and powerful, who (according to this analysis) are personally deserving of what they have.

CHECK YOUR LEARNING   Identify three types of functional theory and give a brief statement of what each has to say about poverty.

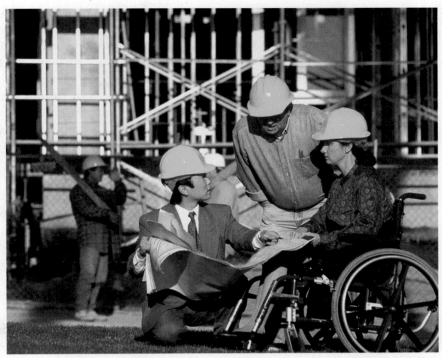

Engineers and architects are among the higher-paid workers in the U.S. labor force. From a structural-functional point of view, our society rewards work that requires rare skills and expensive education. As you read on, try to develop a critical response to this position based on social-conflict theory.

Symbolic-Interaction Analysis: Defining the Problem

Symbolic-interaction theory highlights the social construction of problems and solutions. This approach explores how members of a society build an understanding of the causes of poverty and how they view the poor.

For instance, the old structural-functional "personal deficiency" approach, which is still widespread in our society today, defines poverty as a reflection of the shortcomings of the poor themselves. From this point of view, poor people lack motivation or intelligence, or they are in some other way personally flawed, resulting in their low social standing. Given our society's individualistic culture, it's not surprising that many people today are quick to define the problem of poverty as resulting from traits of poor people themselves, people that they view as responsible for their own condition.

William Ryan (1976) describes how society can define people as responsible for their own poverty. He calls this process **blaming the victim**, *finding the cause of a social problem in the behavior of people who suffer from it*. He explains that the process of blaming the victim involves four simple steps:

1. **Pick an issue that you see as a social problem.** Almost any problem will do; here, our focus is poverty.

2. **Decide how people who suffer from the problem differ from everyone else.** It is easy to see that many poor people don't dress as well as others; many also don't speak English very well. Many have little schooling. Most poor people live in rundown housing. They sometimes get into trouble with the police. The list goes on and on.

3. **Define these differences as the cause of the problem.** Blaming the victim rests on claims such as, "*Of course* those people are poor! Just look at them! Listen to them speak! See where they live! Who is surprised that people like that are poor? They *deserve* to be where they are."

4. **Respond to the problem by trying to change the victims, not the larger society.** Think to yourself that people would not be poor if only they would dress better, speak better, live in better neighborhoods—in short, be more like those who are well off.

However, if we were to view the poor as people who are no different from anyone else, the picture would change. Poor people would now be seen as individuals who are struggling—often heroically—against disadvantages that they face through no fault of their own. When we view the poor this way, we come to see the society—not any personal failings of poor people themselves—as the main cause of poverty.

Ryan suggests that instead of shaking our heads at the rundown houses where poor people live, we should ask why U.S. society allows so many people to live in such inadequate housing. To offer another example, instead of pointing out how little schooling poor people have, we might ask why our society has an educational system that fails to provide adequate schooling to so many students.

EVALUATE

Symbolic-interaction theory is useful in showing that poverty is not simply an issue of money; it is also a matter of meanings, or how people come to understand the larger world. Whatever the issue we come to define as a problem, we can look for the causes of the situation in the people who suffer or, as William Ryan suggests, in the larger society. But saying that society is to blame goes only so far. We also need to know exactly how and why society makes some people poor. Such concerns bring us to the social-conflict approach.

CHECK YOUR LEARNING Explain the process of "blaming the victim," pointing to ways we tend to blame the poor for their own poverty.

Social-Conflict Analysis: Poverty Can Be Eliminated

Social-conflict theory takes the view that poverty is in no way inevitable or natural, and it is certainly a problem our society needs to fix. This approach also rejects the idea that poverty results from flaws in poor people themselves. On the contrary, it places the blame for poverty in the operation of society itself.

Marxist Theory: Poverty and Capitalism Karl Marx could see that the Industrial Revolution had greatly increased economic production. He pointed out that, applying industrial technology, society had the ability, for the first time in human history, to bring an end to poverty. But Marx explained that poverty was far from over. In fact, economic inequality was getting greater. Poverty continued, not because of any shortage of material goods, but because the industrial-capitalist economy placed almost all of this enormous wealth in the hands of very few people. In short, the owners of the means of production became ever more rich and powerful; the workers in the capitalist economy, with only their labor to sell, faced a life of low wages and powerlessness.

Marx pointed to what he called an *internal contradiction* in the capitalist economy: A system that produced so much ended up making the majority so poor. From this observation, Marx concluded that the only way to end poverty was to end the industrial-capitalist system. Therefore, he spent his life encouraging workers to join together to overthrow capitalism in favor of a more just system that would operate the economy in a way that would distribute wealth more equally (for details about how capitalism works, and how socialism differs from capitalism, see Chapter 10, "Economy and Politics").

In the century and a quarter since Marx's death, the United States and other high-income nations have seen living standards rise for all categories of people, a fact that helps explain why the workers' revolution that Marx predicted has not taken place, at least not yet. Even so, as noted earlier in this chapter, most income and wealth still go to a very small share of the people. Just as important, economic inequality has been increasing in recent decades and the poor in the United States have actually been losing ground. Following Marx's thinking, although U.S. society has managed to avoid a workers' revolution, the problem of poverty remains very real.

More Than Money: Cultural Capital More recent conflict theories have explained that social inequality involves not only income and wealth but also **cultural capital**, *skills, values, attitudes, and schooling that increase a person's chances of success.* Pierre Bourdieu and Jean-Claude Passeron (1977) argue that young people born into affluent families benefit from a rich cultural environment. The advantages that they gain, both at home and at school, all but ensure their success.

On the other hand, those born to low-income families have few such advantages and benefit from far less cultural capital. Children who grow up in poor families may receive less personal attention from parents (especially in activities such as reading). Such children may have less opportunity to develop their skills and imagination, they may see less of the world, and they may develop less confidence in their own abilities. As a result, low-income children are impoverished in more ways than one.

Multicultural Theory: Poverty, Race, and Ethnicity The social-conflict approach also includes multicultural theory, which links poverty to race and ethnicity. To see how race and ethnicity affect income, consider that, in 2012, the median income for non-Hispanic white families was $71,478. For African American families, however, median family income was $40,517, or 57 percent as much as white families. The figure for Hispanic families was $40,764, also 57 percent of the white income level.

As noted earlier, the risk of poverty for both African Americans (27.2 percent are poor) and Hispanics (25.6 percent) is almost three times higher than the risk of poverty among non-Hispanic white people (9.7 percent). Asian Americans and Pacific Islanders have above-average incomes ($77,864 in 2012) but a poverty rate of 11.7 percent,

What makes low-income children different from children born to affluent families? On the face of it, these children lack the material things others take for granted. In addition, however, many low-income children have less cultural capital—less attention from parents and other adults. Researchers have documented how children who lack social interaction with adults develop more slowly, acquire a smaller vocabulary, and gain fewer intellectual skills.

which is somewhat higher than the rate for non-Hispanic white people. Chapter 3 ("Racial and Ethnic Inequality") presents a full discussion of this issue.

EVALUATE

One of the earliest contributions of social-conflict theory is Karl Marx's claim that social inequality involves the struggle between owners and workers in a capitalist economy. More recently, social-conflict theorists have extended this analysis, pointing out how society unequally distributes not only money and power but also cultural capital. In addition, multicultural theory focuses on the inequality involving race, ethnicity, and gender.

Marx argued that poverty is a normal part of society, at least one with a capitalist economy. Yet critics of Marxist theory point out that Marx did not foresee ways that capitalist societies would improve living standards for working people and greatly reduce the extent of poverty. In fact, living standards for working people are far higher than they were during Marx's lifetime.

Critics (speaking from a conservative point of view) also ask, doesn't being rich or poor at least partly reflect the choices people make or the talents they have as individuals? If we deny people have any responsibility for their social standing, we all end up being little more than passive victims of society. Critics of the social-conflict approach also claim that there is considerable meritocracy—the ability to rise or fall based on individual talent and effort—in today's society so that social position reflects personal talent and effort.

Finally, multicultural theory points out how our society puts racial and ethnic minorities at high risk for poverty. But critics respond that, although social differences based on race and ethnicity remain, African Americans, Hispanic Americans, and people in other minority categories enjoy greater participation in our society than ever before. A century ago, after all, the segregation of African Americans from the larger society was a matter of law, and some categories of people had yet to earn the right to vote. Such blatant examples of inequality, say these critics, simply no longer exist.

CHECK YOUR LEARNING Why did Marx claim that poverty was rooted in the capitalist economic system? How is culture as well as money a dimension of poverty? What does multicultural theory tell us about poverty?

Feminist Analysis: Poverty and Patriarchy

Feminist theory is an important dimension of the social-conflict approach that focuses on social inequality involving gender. This theory begins with the fact of **patriarchy**, *a social pattern in which males dominate females*. In practice, patriarchy means that men typically enjoy more wealth, prestige, and power in our society than women do. In addition, women of all racial and ethnic categories are at higher risk of poverty than men.

The Feminization of Poverty We have already described the trend by which women make up an increasing share of the poor. A key reason for this trend is that the risk of being poor is especially high for single women. The rate of poverty among families with young children headed by a woman (with no man present) is 41 percent, nearly twice the rate of 23 percent among families headed by a man (with no woman present). For married-couple families, the rate is a much lower 9 percent.

Looking at this issue from another angle, while just 11 percent of all poor families are headed by a single man, 39 percent are headed by a married couple, and 50 percent are headed by a single woman (U.S. Census Bureau, 2013).

The link between gender and poverty is actually stronger than it was several generations ago. In 1960, just one in four poor families was headed by a woman;

in 2012, half were. What explains this trend, which sociologists call the *feminization of poverty*? One reason is that more of today's women are raising children by themselves, and single mothers have a tough time earning the money they need to support themselves and their children. But, as feminists see it, the underlying factor that links gender and poverty is that, even as more and more women have entered the labor force, U.S. society still provides more income, wealth, power, and prestige to men than to women. As Chapter 4 ("Gender Inequality") explains, our culture defines most high-paying jobs (such as doctors, airline pilots, and college presidents) as "men's work," while expecting that lower-paying positions (such as nurses, flight attendants, and clerical workers) will be filled by women.

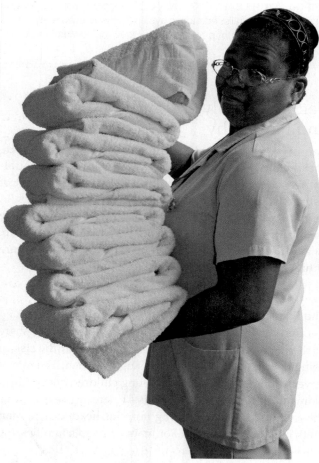

The basic insight of intersection theory is that various dimensions of social stratification—including race and gender—can add up to great disadvantages for some categories of people. Just as African Americans earn less than whites, women earn less than men. Thus, African American women face a "double disadvantage," earning just 62 cents for every dollar earned by non-Hispanic white men. How would you explain the fact that some categories of people are much more likely to end up in low-paying jobs like this one?

Intersection Theory: Multiple Disadvantages   If women are disadvantaged and African Americans and Hispanics are also disadvantaged, are African American or Hispanic women doubly disadvantaged? This question is the focus of **intersection theory**, *the investigation of the interplay of race, class, and gender often resulting in multiple dimensions of disadvantage.*

To see the intersection of various dimensions of inequality in action, let's start by noting the inequalities linked to race and ethnicity: The 2012 median income of non-Hispanic white men working full time was $56,247; African American men typically earned just $39,816, which is 71 percent as much; Hispanic men earned $32,516, or 58 percent as much.

Now add in gender. Compared with African American men, African American women (again, comparing just full-time workers) earned $35,090, or 88 percent as much. Hispanic women earned an average of $29,508, or 91 percent as much as Hispanic men. These disparities are linked to gender.

Now combine the two dimensions. Compared with non-Hispanic white men, African American women earned just 62 percent as much; Hispanic women earned only 53 percent as much. By comparing all these numbers, we see that race or ethnicity and gender not only operate alone but also combine so that certain categories of people are doubly disadvantaged (Saint Jean & Feagin, 1998; U.S. Census Bureau, 2013).

EVALUATE

Feminist theory is one type of social-conflict analysis that has gained enormous importance in recent decades. Just as Marxist theory highlights inequality based on class position, and multicultural theory shows inequality based on race and ethnicity, so feminist theory focuses on inequality based on gender. In addition, intersection theory combines these dimensions of inequality, explaining how some categories of people face multiple disadvantages based on a combination of class, race, ethnicity, and gender.

Critics of feminist theory point out that these approaches say little about how opportunities for women and minorities have improved in the past hundred years. A century ago, for example, few women in the United States worked for income and none even had the right to vote. Although it is true that gender inequality still exists, critics continue, some differences between the sexes reflect different choices people make, particularly about family obligations. Even so, the gap between the social standing of women and men has been steadily narrowing.

The Applying Theory table summarizes what each theoretical approach teaches us about poverty.

CHECK YOUR LEARNING   What does feminist theory tell us about social inequality? What additional insights do we gain from intersection theory?

APPLYING THEORY

Poverty

	Structural-Functional Theory	Symbolic-Interaction Theory	Social-Conflict Theory	Feminist Theory
What is the level of analysis?	Macro-level	Micro-level	Macro-level	Macro-level
What is the view of poverty?	Early social pathology theory and the later culture of poverty theory see personal flaws and the culture of poor communities as the causes of poverty. Social disorganization theory links poverty and other social problems to rapid social change. The Davis and Moore theory explains that a system of unequal rewards draws talent to important work and encourages effort, in the process creating social stratification. Gans points out that inequality is useful primarily to richer people.	Symbolic-interaction theory highlights the meanings people attach to the poor. Ryan describes a common view of the poor as "blaming the victim," which is finding the causes of poverty in the attitudes or behavior of the poor themselves. Viewing the poor as no different from anyone else encourages the view that society, rather than the poor themselves, is responsible for poverty.	Marx claimed that poverty results from the operation of the capitalist economic system. Poverty is a matter of not only a lack of material resources but a low level of cultural capital as well. Multicultural theory points to the high poverty rates of disadvantaged categories of people including African Americans and Latinos.	Feminist theory examines the link between social standing and gender. Feminists view the high rate of poverty among women as one consequence of patriarchy. Intersection theory links various dimensions of inequality, explaining how they result in a pattern of multiple disadvantages.

✪ POLITICS AND POVERTY

Constructing Problems and Defining Solutions

2.6 Analyze economic inequality from various positions on the political spectrum.

What are we to make of the fact that inequality in the United States is increasing? What about the fact that, in one of the richest nations on Earth, 46.5 million people are poor? Like every other issue we deal with in a social problems course, poverty and wealth are controversial. Some people consider income inequality as inevitable and link economic inequality to a free and productive society. Others are highly critical of income inequality and define poverty as a pressing national problem that can and must be reduced. Let us now examine how conservatives, liberals, and left-radicals construct the poverty problem and how they define solutions.

Conservatives: Personal Responsibility

Conservatives (more to the right on the political spectrum) point out that our way of life generates remarkable prosperity; therefore, almost all the poverty in the United States is *relative* poverty. That is, only a

small percentage of the people that the government defines as poor live anywhere close to *absolute* poverty, where day-to-day survival is at stake. According to one recent study, even the poorest 5 percent of U.S. families have more income than 60 percent of the world's people (Milanovic, 2011).

In the United States, "poverty" means having less than what government officials claim people living in our rich society *ought to have*. Conservatives point out that about one-third of families officially counted among the poor own their homes, almost two-thirds have at least one car, and almost all enjoy the use of a television set and a personal computer (U.S. Census Bureau, 2013). The big picture, as conservatives see it, is the dramatic increase in living standards over the past century; in this sense, our society has worked pretty well.

Conservatives hold the traditional value of self-reliance and therefore they support the idea that people should take responsibility for their personal well-being. They claim that U.S. society still offers opportunity and rewards both individual talent and personal effort. It is true that a few people in our society inherit great wealth; conservatives claim that families have a right to pass along their property to their children. But most successful people—and even most rich people—are men and women who have spent many years in school and who continue to work long and hard at their jobs (Stanley & Danko, 1996).

Speaking for conservatives, the retired general and former U.S. Secretary of State Colin Powell recalls that as a young boy, he began his working life pushing a broom. He explains that he always worked hard, doing his best and learning whatever he could from the job he had. As soon as he mastered one task, he asked for another one. He credits discipline and determination—learned from his parents—as the key to his success, helping him to rise to a top position in the U.S. military and become one of this country's political leaders. In short, Powell argues, the most effective way to prevent poverty may well be to teach children to value personal responsibility and hard work (Powell & Persico, 1995).

Conservatives see social character as one key to personal success. In addition, they support a market system that rewards individual effort as it provides not only a rich material life but also personal freedom. Is there a role for government in all this—especially in the fight against poverty? Because conservatives believe people should be responsible for their own social standing and support a market system, they want to limit the size of government. Still many "compassionate conservatives" support welfare programs that provide assistance to people who are poor through no fault of their own—those with disabilities, the elderly, and children. Most also think that the government should provide a helping hand to veterans who have sacrificed for their country and should make available short-term help to anyone thrown out of work. Conservatives supported the 1996 welfare reform in the belief that government assistance should be targeted and limited so that it never replaces personal responsibility. On the contrary, conservatives claim, expanding government welfare programs can make poverty worse by fostering dependency (Murray, 1984, 2013; Bennett, 1995; Connerly, 2000; Bork, 2008).

Liberals: Societal Responsibility

Conservatives point to personal responsibility and a market economy as the solutions to the problem of poverty. But liberals think that helping the poor is a job for everybody. From a liberal point of view, the causes of poverty lie in society rather than in the traits of poor individuals. Most people become poor not because they are lazy or because they make bad choices but because of the way society operates. As Chapter 11 ("Work and the Workplace") explains, most unemployment is caused by economic recession, corporate mergers, downsizing, or outsourcing of work overseas that reduces the number of available jobs. In addition, increasing economic inequality has swelled the ranks of the poor.

The ways in which society causes poverty are also evident in the specific categories of people who are at high risk of being poor. For example, because women are given fewer opportunities than men to work for income and because our society pays women less when they do work, women are at higher risk of being poor.

Because liberals define poverty as a societal problem, they look for societal solutions. They reject the conservative arguments that individuals must take responsibility for their own social position. According to the liberal viewpoint, the U.S. economy is highly productive, but it distributes income very unequally. In addition, many people are disadvantaged by racism and other forms of discrimination that limit their access to good education and high-paying work. Part of the liberal solution to poverty, then, is active enforcement of laws banning discrimination in education and the workplace.

In addition, liberals support government assistance programs that offer some measure of financial security to everyone—a "social safety net." Dismissing conservative worries about creating dependency, liberals view assistance programs as necessary; after all, they point out, millions of people—especially children—are poor through no fault of their own. Liberals also support higher taxes, especially on the rich, not only to pay for such programs but also to reduce economic inequality.

Liberals would direct tax revenue to social welfare programs that would lift millions of poor families above the poverty line. In 2010, public assistance benefits were small—the typical "welfare family" received only $391.93 per month—and provided people little help in improving their lives. On the other hand, more generous assistance might enable a poor working mother to commute to a better job in a nearby suburb, to purchase better medical care so that she loses fewer days each year to illness, or to finish a high school diploma by taking night courses.

Finally, liberals point out that millions of poor people never even apply for welfare benefits. Why not? In a culture that stresses personal responsibility, asking for help is regarded as an admission of personal failure and a source of shame (W. J. Wilson, 1996a; Mouw, 2000; H. Murray, 2000; U.S. Department of Health and Human Services, 2012).

The Radical Left: Change the System

Radicals on the left agree with liberals that poverty is a societal issue. Left-radicals also agree with liberals that we cannot expect poor people to improve their situation on their own. But they differ from those who share other political positions by claiming that the problem of poverty is built into a capitalist society (Liazos, 1982). In other words, vast differences between rich and poor

Conservatives claim that we should all take personal responsibility for our social standing; reducing poverty, then, depends on the choices and actions of the poor themselves. Liberals claim that poverty is mostly a matter of how society operates; according to this view, government should act to reduce poverty. Radicals on the left claim that ending poverty depends on replacing capitalism. Which view is closest to your own? Why?

result from the normal operation of a capitalist economic system. Left-radicals point to the increasing economic inequality in the United States—a trend that continues despite the welfare programs supported by liberals—and conclude that government assistance amounts to little more than a bandage applied to the body of a person with a terminal disease.

Karl Marx identified widespread poverty as one of the internal contradictions of capitalism. By the term "contradiction," Marx meant that industrial capitalism produces great wealth but places production under the control of an elite whose members gain most of the economic benefits. Working families, by contrast, get little for their efforts and, over time, have had to get by with less and less. For this reason, a very rich society such as the United States can contain millions of people who are desperately poor.

The radical left claims that the way to solve the problem of poverty is to replace capitalism with a more humane economic system that will greatly reduce economic inequality. The goal of such a system would not be to feed the greed of the few but to meet the needs of the many. In this way, radicals on the left reach the conclusion that nothing less than a basic reformulation of the U.S. economy will result in a solution to the problems of economic inequality and poverty.

The Left to Right table on page 60 sums up the views of all three political approaches. To understand each of the political positions, it is necessary to look closely at them all.

Going On from Here

This chapter describes the inequality of income and wealth that defines the rich and poor in the United States. It points out that certain categories of people—women,

children, and people of color—are at high risk of being poor and that all people who are economically disadvantaged contend with poor health, substandard housing, too little schooling, too few jobs, and a higher rate of crime and violence.

What can we expect in the future? Keep in mind that some trends are positive. Between 1960 and 2012, the official poverty rate fell by more than one-quarter, from 22.4 percent to 15.0 percent of the U.S. population. Among the elderly population, the poverty rate dropped by more than two-thirds, from 33.0 percent to 9.1 percent (U.S. Census Bureau, 2013). The recent recession, of course, pushed up the poverty rate for all categories of people.

Looking back at Figure 2–5 on page 42, we see that most of the decrease in poverty in the United States occurred between 1960 and the early 1970s. Since then, the overall trend has been slightly upward. Even more troubling, the age category at greatest risk of poverty is now children: Overall, 22 percent of U.S. children are poor, with much higher rates among African American (38 percent) and Hispanic American (34 percent) youngsters. Perhaps the most pressing question for the future is what to do about the "new poverty" in the United States involving households composed of women and children. The dramatic decline in the poverty rate among the elderly shows that this nation can reduce poverty when the public supports doing so. The question is whether we will do as much for our children as we have done for seniors.

Wealth and poverty in the United States have always been controversial, and the trend toward increasing economic inequality only makes the debate more important. Conservatives respond to increasing poverty by calling for a strong market economy and focusing on the need for personal responsibility and the importance of strong

LEFT TO RIGHT

The Politics of Income Inequality

	Radical-Left View	Liberal View	Conservative View
What is the problem?	The capitalist economic system concentrates most of the country's wealth in the hands of a small share of the population.	Millions of men, women, and children have too little income and need assistance.	Some "worthy" people are poor and should be helped, but social welfare programs can discourage people's desire to work and may foster dependency.
What is the solution?	The capitalist economic system must undergo fundamental changes toward greater governmental control of the economy.	Use higher taxes to expand government assistance programs and raise the income of the poor.	Provide short-term help to those who really need it; strengthen families and promote personal responsibility.

JOIN THE DEBATE

1. Assess the 1996 welfare reform from the radical-left, liberal, and conservative points of view. From each political position, has the reform been helpful or harmful? To whom? Why?

2. In recent years, many analysts have described a pattern of Congressional "gridlock." Conservatives (mostly Republicans) reject

the idea of raising taxes and liberals (mostly Democrats) reject the idea of cutting benefits provided by programs such as Medicare. Do you see these as issues on which people can compromise? Explain your view.

3. Which of the three political analyses of income inequality included here do you find the most convincing? Why?

---

families. They point out that not having a job or having children without being married raises the odds of being poor for both adults and their children. Liberals call for raising the minimum wage, expanding child care and job-training programs, and combating workplace discrimination that harms women and people of color. Liberals also support higher taxation, especially on the rich, as a strategy to fund greater benefits for the poor and to reduce economic inequality. Radical-left voices claim that as long as we have a capitalist economic system, our society will

always favor the few and leave more and more people behind. Whatever political position one favors, the fact that economic inequality is increasing can only increase the importance of ultimately resolving this debate.

Essay: Envisioning a Better Society Looking ahead fifty years, do you think economic inequality in the United States is likely to increase, stay about the same, or decrease? Which trend do you think improves U.S. society? What specific policies would you support in pursuit of this trend?

CHAPTER 2 Poverty and Wealth

Is social inequality a problem?

And whose problem is it? This chapter has explained that the way in which people understand social inequality depends on their political attitudes. What people say we ought to do about poverty and wealth also depends on politics. Look at the accompanying photos to see two different ways to respond to the contrast between poverty and wealth.

Is being rich a solution or a problem? If you were more liberal, what type of tax system would you support? What if you were more conservative?

How would you react to confronting this young woman on a New York City street? If your politics were more liberal, what would you say is the problem here? What would you think should be done about it? What if you were more conservative?

Hint: Liberals tend to see social structure (including class, gender, and race) as giving privileges to some people and putting others at a disadvantage. From this point of view, a young homeless woman needs assistance. A gift of money would be an act of kindness; but because the problem of inequality is based on the way society is organized, the real solution requires changes to society itself. Conservatives tend to see people as responsible for their own situations. Again, a gift of money might be kind, but as long as this young person is able-bodied and healthy, she should really take care of herself (and a handout only encourages more panhandling). As for the issue of taxation, conservatives typically see wealth as a product of personal talent and a lot of hard work; people are entitled to what they can earn. Liberals, on the other hand, see wealth and poverty as twin products of a free market that should be regulated by government, which should tax the rich (progressive taxation) to provide more for the poor (in government benefits).

Getting Involved: Applications and Exercises

1. We hear many people refer to the United States as a "middle-class society." Based on what you now know about social inequality in this country, to what extent is this description accurate? Offer specific evidence to support your position.

2. Find out more about the extent of poverty in your local area. U.S. Census Bureau reports are available from the local library, and you can find census data on the Internet at http://www.census.gov/did/www/saipe/data/interactive/ or by downloading the Census Bureau app called dwellr.

3. Have you ever had a low-wage job? If not, this is one good way to begin to understand what it means to be working but poor. Many low-wage jobs are available on or around campus. Whether you actually take such a job or not, work out a monthly household budget for a family of three, and see how far a minimum-wage job ($7.25 in 2014) takes you toward supporting a family.

4. Do you tend to favor the Democratic or the Republican Party? In the 2012 campaign, how did each of the major presidential candidates address the issue of economic inequality?

CHAPTER 2 Poverty and Wealth

A DEFINING MOMENT
U.S. Society Discovers Poverty **p. 51**

Economic Inequality in the United States

2.1 Describe the distribution of income and wealth in the United States.

Income is distributed unequally in the United States, with the richest 20% of families earning 48.9% of all income, thirteen times as much as the lowest-paid 20% of families. **p. 34**

Wealth is even more unequally distributed, with the richest 20% of families controlling 89% of all privately owned wealth, while the poorest 20% of families are actually in debt. **pp. 34–35**

The recent trend has been **increasing income inequality**. The top 20% of families have made strong gains while the bottom 20% have lost ground. **pp. 36–37**

social stratification (p. 34) society's system of ranking categories of people in a hierarchy
social classes (p. 34) categories of people who have similar access to resources and opportunities
income (p. 34) salary or wages from a job plus earnings from investments and other sources
wealth (p. 34) the value of all the economic assets owned by a person or family, minus any debts
progressive taxation (p. 38) a policy that raises tax rates as income increases

The Rich and the Poor: A Social Profile

2.2 Assess the differences in the lives of the rich and the poor in the United States.

- Rich families have incomes that average about $277,000 (with some ten times this much or more). Older people, white people, and men are overly represented among the rich.
- The government defines "poverty" as families living with income below a poverty line roughly equal to three times the cost of food. The 2012 **poverty line** was $23,492 for a nonfarm family of four.
- Income for the average poor family in the United States is about $11,000 less than the poverty line, a difference called the **poverty gap**.
- At the greatest risk of poverty are children, women who head households, and racial and ethnic minorities.
- The child poverty rate in the United States is high and now stands at 22%.

- Sociologists call the trend of women making up a rising share of the poor (now 57%) the **feminization of poverty**.
- The **underclass** represents a small share of the poor, cut off from the larger society, living in rural areas or inner cities where poverty is widespread. **pp. 39–45**

poverty line (p. 40) an income level set by the U.S. government for the purpose of counting the poor
poverty gap (p. 40) the difference between the actual income of the typical poor household and the official poverty line
feminization of poverty (p. 42) the trend of women making up an increasing share of the poor
underclass (p. 45) poor people who live in areas with high concentrations of poverty and limited opportunities for schooling or work

Problems Linked to Poverty

2.3 Analyze how poverty is linked to other social problems.

Poverty affects every aspect of life. The poor

- endure more illness
- receive less schooling
- experience more unemployment and crime
- are more likely to live in inadequate housing or to be homeless
- are less likely to vote **pp. 45–47**

homelessness (p. 46) the plight of poor people who lack shelter and live primarily on the streets

Responding to Poverty: The Welfare System

2.4 Explain the changing ways our society has used the social welfare system to respond to poverty.

Public attitudes toward the poor and support for **social welfare programs** have varied over the course of this nation's history.

- The settlement house movement in the late 1800s offered a helping hand to poor immigrants and tried to make the public more compassionate toward the poor.

- President Franklin Roosevelt's New Deal in the 1930s was the first of many government poverty programs, the most important of which was Social Security.

- In 1964, President Lyndon Johnson declared the War on Poverty to address the growing underclass of poor people in the United States.

- In 1996, welfare reform pushed people off welfare rolls and toward work and schooling. This reform decreased the number of people receiving benefits but did little to lower the poverty rate. **pp. 47–50**

social welfare programs (p. 47) organized efforts by government, private organizations, or individuals to assist needy people considered worthy of assistance

Theories of Poverty

2.5   Apply sociological theory to the issue of poverty.

Structural-Functional Analysis: Some Poverty Is Inevitable

Social pathology theories (including Spencer's *social Darwinism*, Lewis's *culture of poverty thesis*, and Herrnstein and Murray's *bell curve thesis*) view poverty mostly as the result of shortcomings on the part of the poor themselves. **pp. 51–52**

Social disorganization theory views poverty as the result of rapid social change, which makes society unable to meet the needs of all its members. **p. 52**

- More recent functionalism includes the *Davis and Moore thesis*, which argues that society uses unequal rewards to attract talent to the most important jobs.

- Herbert Gans states that the poor serve the needs of the nonpoor in various ways, including doing work that no one else wants to do.

Symbolic-Interaction Analysis: Defining the Problem

Symbolic-interaction theory highlights our socially constructed understandings of poverty. One common view is *blaming the victim*, which claims that poverty results from traits of the poor themselves. **pp. 53–54**

Social-Conflict Analysis: Poverty Can Be Eliminated

Karl Marx claimed that poverty follows from the operation of a capitalist economy. He believed the increasing misery of the working class would eventually lead people to overthrow the capitalist system. **p. 54**

More recent conflict theory explains that inequality involves not just money but also cultural capital—advantages in skills, attitudes, and schooling—that are not available to people born into poverty. **p. 54**

Multicultural theory highlights how African Americans and people in other disadvantaged racial and ethnic categories are at higher risk of poverty. **pp. 54–55**

Feminist Analysis: Poverty and Patriarchy

Feminist theory links the higher poverty rate among women to the fact that men dominate women in our society. **pp. 55–56**

Intersection theory highlights the fact that inequality based on the combined factors of race, class, and gender results in greater disadvantage for some categories of people. **p. 56**

culture of poverty (p. 52) cultural patterns that make poverty a way of life

meritocracy (p. 52) a system of social inequality in which social standing corresponds to personal ability and effort

social disorganization (p. 52) a breakdown in social order caused by rapid social change

blaming the victim (p. 53) finding the cause of a social problem in the behavior of people who suffer from it

cultural capital (p. 54) skills, values, attitudes, and schooling that increase a person's chances of success

patriarchy (p. 55) a social pattern in which males dominate females

intersection theory (p. 56) the investigation of the interplay of race, class, and gender, often resulting in multiple dimensions of disadvantage

✪ POLITICS AND POVERTY

Constructing Problems and Defining Solutions

2.6   Analyze economic inequality from various positions on the political spectrum.

Conservatives: Personal Responsibility

- **Conservatives** believe that social standing is a matter of personal responsibility; people can escape poverty by taking advantage of the opportunities U.S. society offers.

- Conservatives claim that government social welfare programs often make the poverty problem worse by fostering dependency. **pp. 57–58**

Liberals: Societal Responsibility

- **Liberals** believe that poverty is a societal problem, stemming mostly from a lack of good jobs.

- Liberals consider poverty a societal responsibility; they support government social programs that benefit the needy. **p. 58**

The Radical Left: Change the System

- **Radicals on the left** claim that poverty results from the normal operation of the capitalist economy, which benefits the capitalist elite.

- Radicals on the left argue that solving the poverty problem requires fundamental change to the economy so that production meets social needs rather than increases private profits. **pp. 58–59**

Chapter 3
Racial and Ethnic Inequality

Learning Objectives

3.1 Explain how race and ethnicity are socially constructed.

3.2 Describe four major societal patterns of interaction between majority and minority populations.

3.3 Analyze the social standing of major racial and ethnic categories of the U.S. population.

3.4 Discuss the causes and consequences of prejudice.

3.5 Distinguish discrimination from prejudice and show how the two concepts operate together.

3.6 Apply sociological theory to patterns of racial and ethnic inequality.

3.7 Analyze racial and ethnic inequality from various positions on the political spectrum.

Tracking the Trends

Relative Odds of Being a Financial Analyst, 2012

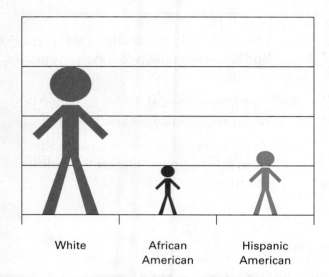

Relative Odds of Being a Custodian or Housekeeper, 2012

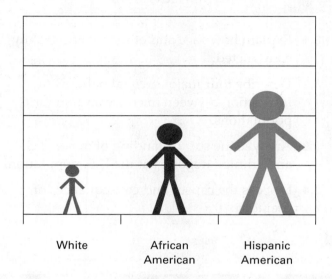

SOURCE: U.S. Department of Labor (2013).

Do race and ethnicity affect our life chances? We like to think that everyone in the United States has equal opportunity to succeed. But when it comes to the jobs people end up doing, the playing field is far from even. Take the sort of work that most of us would consider a "good" job, such as being a financial analyst. As the figure shows, the odds of a white person becoming a financial analyst are more than double the odds of a Hispanic American becoming a financial analyst. Compared to an African American, a white person has triple the odds of having this good job.

The pattern is reversed when it comes to jobs people view as less desirable. The typical African American has almost double the odds of a white person of ending up with a low-wage job as a janitor, maid, or house cleaner. A Hispanic American person has almost triple the odds of ending up doing this type of work as a white person. Do you think that race and ethnicity still matter in U.S. society?

Constructing the Problem

Is race simply a matter of skin color?

Race involves socially constructed categories that often give people advantages over others.

Is a "minority" just some category of people with small numbers?

Being a minority is mainly about power. Societies construct minorities by giving more power and privileges to some categories of people than to others.

Is prejudice simply about what people think?

Prejudice and discrimination do involve individual attitudes, but both are also built into the operation of society.

Chapter Overview

What is race and ethnicity? How are they related to social inequality, shaping people's access to jobs and income? This chapter explores the social standing of various racial and ethnic categories of the U.S. population. The chapter also explores the history of social diversity in the United States, interpreting this country's history using the concepts of genocide, segregation, assimilation, and pluralism. You will carry out theoretical analysis of racial and ethnic inequality and learn how people's political attitudes lead them to construct certain "problems" and favor certain "solutions." ■

"I'm sorry if this is not what you believe or what you want to hear," Samantha explained to her cousin as they worked their way through a pepperoni pizza, "but I don't think this country can have an 'open door' when it comes to immigration."

"What are you afraid of?" Justin spoke quietly in response.

"I'm not afraid of *anything*," Samantha responded, now on the defensive. "But I don't like people coming here illegally. Many immigrants get on welfare. They take places in our classrooms. They take jobs from Americans. We have enough to do taking care of our own people. We don't need to save the world."

Immigration is one of the most hotly debated issues in the United States today. With more than 1 million immigrants entering this country each year, most people have reason to hold some opinion. Surveys show that more than three-fourths of U.S. adults think that this country's immigration policies need major changes (Pew Research Center, 2013).

Most people know that the United States is a nation of immigrants. But most people do not have a good grasp of the relative size of the immigrant population. For example,

when surveys ask what share of the U.S. population was born in another country, averaging all the answers produces an overall response of "39 percent." The *actual* share is about 13 percent—so people greatly exaggerate the size of the immigrant population. A majority of U.S. adults also say that they think most people born elsewhere are living in this country illegally. This also is an exaggeration. The actual share of all U.S. immigrants who do not have legal documentation is about 30 percent (Harrell, 2011; Pew Research Center, 2011, 2013; Passel, Cohn, & Gonzalez-Barrera, 2013).

Most immigrants come to the United States to work. But the jobs they take are not likely to displace others in the labor force. In most cases, immigrants take jobs that people already living here do not want—because the work is hard and the pay is low. At the same time, some people who have better-paying jobs—such as work as an engineer—are also immigrants. Typically, this is because not nearly enough native-born people have the training to fill these necessary jobs.

The United States is and has always been a nation of immigrants. Everyone who lives in the United States has ancestors who came here from some other part of the world. But, as this opening story suggests, racial and ethnic differences are not only a source of strength for the United States, they are also a source of tension and conflict. Race and ethnicity are also important dimensions of social inequality.

Race and ethnicity are the foundation for many issues that people come to define as social problems. To understand why this is the case, first we must answer some basic questions: What are "race" and "ethnicity"? How do they affect our everyday lives? How do they figure into problems of social inequality? This chapter will also explore a range of related issues, including prejudice and discrimination, social processes such as assimilation and segregation,

and policies including affirmative action. We start with a look at the central concepts of race and ethnicity.

Race and Ethnicity

3.1   Explain how race and ethnicity are socially constructed.

In the United States and other countries, race and ethnicity are important aspects of social identity, just as they are major dimensions of social inequality. Yet many people are not quite sure what race and ethnicity are all about. Our first step is to clarify the meanings of the concepts.

Race

Race is *a socially constructed category of people who share biologically transmitted traits that members of a society define as important.* For hundreds of years, people in most societies have divided humanity into categories based on skin color, hair texture, facial features, and body shape.

Race has nothing to do with being human. All people everywhere belong to a single biological species, *Homo sapiens* (Latin words meaning "thinking person"), that first emerged in Africa some 250,000 years ago. As homo sapiens lost their body hair, our human ancestors developed darker skin from a natural pigment called "melanin." Over thousands of generations since then, physical differences developed among people living in different regions of the world. People who remained in Africa retained darker skin. Among those people who migrated away from Africa toward cooler regions of the world (such as northern Europe), skin color gradually became lighter. In some cases, people with lighter skin migrated back to hotter regions of the planet (such as India) and their descendants gradually developed darker skin (Johnson, 2014).

Migration continues today, of course. As people continue to move around the world, all the physical traits carried by human genes are spread ever more widely. This genetic diversity is especially pronounced among people living in the world's "crossroads" regions, such as the Middle East. On the other hand, historically isolated people have many physical traits in common. For example, almost all people who live on the island of Japan have black hair.

When Was Race Invented?   Centuries ago, as global trade brought the world's people into greater contact, awareness of human diversity increased. By the late 1500s, Europeans began using the term "race" to categorize people. By about 1800, European scientists settled on three broad classifications for humanity.

The fact that race is a socially constructed category means that any distinctive physical traits may be used to assign people to a racial category. In the early decades of the twentieth century, public opinion turned against European immigrants as their numbers grew. For a time, many southern Europeans—such as Italians—were "racialized" and defined as nonwhite.

They coined the terms *Caucasian* (meaning European and Western Asian) to designate people with light skin and fine hair; *Negroid* (derived from Latin meaning "black") to refer to people with dark skin and the coarse, curly hair typical of people living in sub-Saharan Africa; and *Mongoloid* (referring to the Mongolian region of Asia) to refer to people with yellow or brown skin and distinctive folds on the eyelids.

Are Races Real?   Sociologists are quick to point out that, at best, racial categories are misleading and, at worst, they are a harmful way to divide humanity. First, there are no biologically pure races. In fact, there is more genetic diversity *within* racial categories than *between* them. Second, because human beings have migrated and reproduced throughout the world, we find physical diversity everywhere. For example, Caucasian people can have very light skin (common in Scandinavia) or very dark skin (common in southern India). Similarly, Negroid people can be dark-skinned (common in Africa) or light-skinned (the Australian Aborigines).

Other physical traits often linked to race do not always line up the same way. For example, people with dark skin can have kinky hair (common in Africa) or straight hair (common in India). What this means is that from a scientific standpoint, physical variation is real, but racial categories simply do not describe human diversity very well (Boza, 2002; Harris & Sim, 2002).

Should Races Exist at All?   If racial categories are misleading or even harmful, why do they exist? Some sociologists argue that dividing humanity into racial categories is simply a strategy to allow some people to dominate others (Bonilla-Silva, 1999; Johnson, Rush, & Feagin, 2000; Zuberi, 2001). That is, Europeans attached cultural traits to skin color in order to set apart the "honest and rational" European from the "beastlike" African and the "devious" Asian. Race, in short, is a social device people that lets people define themselves as better than those they want to control. By defining people around the world as being of a different racial category, European colonists justified oppressing them. In North America, European colonists defined native peoples in less than human terms—as "red savages"—to justify killing them and taking their land. Even among Europeans, when people of English ancestry needed Irish and Italian immigrants to work for low pay, they defined them as racially different (Ignatiev, 1995; Camara, 2000; Brodkin, 2007).

Well into the twentieth century, laws in many southern states defined "colored" as anyone having as little as one-thirty-second African ancestry (that is, one African American great-great-great-grandparent). By 1970, such "one drop of blood" laws were overturned by the courts, allowing parents to declare the race of their child as they wish (usually stated on the birth certificate). Even today, however, most people still consider racial identity important.

Multiracial People   An important trend is the increasing number of people in this country who identify themselves as "multiracial." In a recent government survey, 9.1 million people in the United States described themselves as multiracial, identifying with more than one racial category (U.S. Census Bureau, 2013).

Marriage between people of different racial categories is becoming more common and now accounts for 8.2 percent of all marriages in the United States. One predictable result is that the official number of multiracial births has tripled over the past twenty years and represents about 6 percent of all births (U.S. Census Bureau, 2013). As time goes on, members of our society will have increasing difficulty seeing one another in terms of rigid racial categories.

Ethnicity

Race is a matter of what societies make of biological traits, but ethnicity is a matter of culture. **Ethnicity** is *a shared cultural heritage, which typically involves common ancestors, language, and religion.* Just as U.S. society is racially diverse, so the population contains hundreds of distinctive ethnic categories. Table 3–1 on page 70 shows the breadth of this nation's racial and ethnic diversity.

Although race and ethnicity are different, the two may go together. For example, Korean Americans, Native Americans, and people of Italian or Nigerian descent share not only certain physical traits but ethnic traits as well.

Immigration

This country's remarkable racial and ethnic diversity is a product of immigration. As noted earlier, everyone living in North America is descended from people who lived elsewhere. Immigration is one key reason our society is here at all. Even so, immigration is a source of difference causing conflict. This conflict is nothing new, as you will soon see.

The "Great Immigration"   What historians call the "Great Immigration" started with the end of the Civil War in 1865 and lasted until the outbreak of World War I in 1914. During this period, the Industrial Revolution created factory jobs that attracted some 25 million people who came to cities along the East Coast in search of economic opportunity. In 1900, fully 80 percent of the people living in New York City either had been born abroad or had parents who were (Glaab & Brown, 1967).

Nativists and the Quota System   Many people extended a welcome to the newcomers, but others—called "nativists"—opposed the high level of immigration (as some do today), fearing that it would endanger this country's mostly English culture. Nativist attitudes were especially common after 1900 when most immigrants came from southern and eastern Europe, where people had darker rather than lighter skin, spoke a language other than English, and were Catholic, Orthodox, or Jewish rather than Protestant.

Table 3–1 Racial and Ethnic Categories in the United States, 2012

Racial or Ethnic Classification*	Approximate U.S. Population	Percent of Total Population
Hispanic Descent	53,027,708	16.9%
Mexican	34,038,599	10.8
Puerto Rican	4,970,604	1.6
Cuban	1,957,557	0.6
Other Hispanic	12,060,948	3.8
African Descent	41,204,793	13.1%
Nigerian	277,631	0.1
Ethiopian	240,907	0.1
Somalian	124,431	<
Other African	40,561,824	12.9
Native American Descent	2,563,505	0.8%
American Indian	2,063,550	0.7
Alaska Native Tribes	119,627	<
Other Native American	380,328	0.1
Asian or Pacific Island Descent	16,145,821	5.1%
Chinese	3,660,659	1.2
Asian Indian	3,049,201	1.0
Filipino	2,658,354	0.8
Vietnamese	1,675,246	0.5
Korean	1,450,401	0.5
Japanese	780,210	0.2
Cambodian	256,956	0.1
Other Asian or Pacific Islander	2,614,794	0.8
West Indian descent	2,805,206	0.9%
Arab descent	1,860,341	0.6%
Non-Hispanic European descent	197,705,655	63.0%
German	46,882,727	14.9
Irish	37,266,657	11.9
English	25,262,644	8.0
Italian	17,361,780	5.5
Polish	9,500,696	3.0
French	8,475,576	2.7
Scottish	5,379,735	1.7
Norwegian	4,398,608	1.4
Dutch	4,351,210	1.4
Two or more races	9,073,614	2.9%

*People of Hispanic descent may be of any race. Many people also identify with more than one ethnic category. Figures therefore total more than 100 percent.
"<" indicates less than 1/10 of 1 percent.
SOURCE: U.S. Census Bureau (2013).

Pressured by nativists, during the 1920s Congress enacted laws, including the Immigration Act of 1924, which cut immigration and created a quota system that limited the number of people entering the United States from various countries around the world. These laws—coupled to the economic depression that began in 1929—reduced immigration to a trickle. The flow of immigrants to the United States stayed low until the mid-1960s.

The End of the Quota System   In 1965, Congress ended the quota system, leading to another wave of mass immigration. Again, the arrival of immigrants—by then mostly from Mexico and other nations in Latin America, as well as the Philippines, South Korea, and other Asian countries—became controversial. In 1986, Congress enacted the Immigrant Control and Reform Act in another effort to reduce the number of immigrants coming to this country. This act outlawed the hiring of undocumented immigrants and threatened businesses with fines for doing so. The idea was that if immigrants could not get jobs, they would not come here. But many workers produced fraudulent documents and were able to find work. In addition, the 1986 law granted amnesty to almost 3 million illegal immigrants already in the country, which allowed these people to join the mainstream of U.S. society and probably also encouraged more people to cross the border (Gamboa, 2003; Tumulty, 2006).

Nowhere is the immigration issue more important than in California, the state with the largest immigrant population, a total of more than 10 million people or 27 percent of the total population. In that state, 44 percent of the people speak a language other than English at home. In 1994, in reaction to the rising number of illegal immigrants, Californians enacted Proposition 187, designed to discourage illegal immigration by cutting off social service benefits, including schooling, health care, and food stamps, to anyone entering the country illegally. This law, however, was later declared to be unconstitutional by the courts and did reduce illegal immigration. The law also hurt those people already in California.

The Current Immigration Controversy   During the 1990s, Congress continued to debate the immigration issue as about 1 million people entered the United States each year. This flow represented a larger number of people entering the country than during the Great Immigration a century ago, although these recent immigrants joined a population five times larger. In 2012, the total U.S. population of about 314 million included about 41 million (13 percent) who were foreign-born. About the same number of people have at least one parent born abroad (U.S. Census Bureau, 2013).

In recent decades, immigration has become a major issue across the United States, with the focus of the debate on illegal immigration. From a total of about 500,000 people annually during the years after 2000, the number of unauthorized immigrants fell during the recent recession. As the flow of people declined, the total number of undocumented immigrants in the country decreased from a peak of 12.2 million in 2007 to about 11 million in 2009. The number of undocumented immigrants began to increase again in 2012 as the economy showed signs of improvement so that, by 2012, the total was about 11.7 million people (Pew Research Center, 2011; Passel, Cohn, & Gonzalez-Barrera, 2013).

Controlling the nation's southern border, which extends for almost 2,000 miles along the southern boundaries of California, Arizona, New Mexico, and Texas, is a monumental task. Much of the border has no fence or marking at all. In 2000, more than 1.5 million people were apprehended attempting to enter the country illegally. By 2012, as a result of both tighter border security and the recent recession, the number of people apprehended crossing the border had declined to about 300,000 annually. Estimating the number of people who manage to avoid apprehension is difficult, obviously, but it is likely that the number is at least 150,000 each year (Passel, Cohn, & Gonzalez-Barrera, 2013; Pew Research Center, 2013).

Congress has debated various proposals intended to improve control of the border as well as decide how to deal with illegal immigrants already living and working in the United States. The Social Problems in Focus box takes a closer look at the current immigration issue.

Minorities

Most immigrants to the United States have found more opportunity than they had in their homelands. But many have also discovered that their race and ethnicity keep them at the margins of U.S. society. Sociologists use the term **minority** to refer to *any category of people, identified by physical or cultural traits, that a society subjects to disadvantages.*

SOCIAL PROBLEMS IN FOCUS

Let Them Stay or Make Them Go? The Debate over Unauthorized Immigrants

For years, Congress has debated the issue of comprehensive immigration reform. As with many important issues facing the country, our legislatures in Washington, D.C., have accomplished very little.

Everyone agrees on one thing: The main reason people want to come to the United States is simple economics. Wages in the United States are about five times higher than in Mexico. Among all those who have entered the United States illegally, about 59 percent are from Mexico, 25 percent are from other Latin American nations or Canada, 12 percent are from an Asian country, and the remaining 4 percent are from African countries and elsewhere.

High levels of immigration—especially unauthorized immigration—are a troubling pattern to most people in the United States. In 2013, public opinion surveys found that about three-fourths of U.S. adults claimed that this country's immigration policy requires "major changes." About half of all adults say that immigration reform should be a "top priority" (Pew Research Center, 2013).

Although most people believe new policies are needed to deal with illegal immigration, the public is divided about exactly what the country should do. The most conservative people (including many people who identify with the Tea Party) claim that entering the country illegally is a crime so that illegal immigrants should face arrest and punishment or deportation. Almost 2 million unauthorized immigrants have been deported by the Obama administration, a fact that has won praise from conservatives but drawn criticism from liberals.

There are problems with such a "get tough" approach. For one thing, it is impractical to try to arrest some 11.7 million people who are in this country illegally. Even if they all could be identified, there are simply not enough jails to lock up this many people. In addition, any such effort would drive people into hiding and spread fear throughout immigrant communities. Finally, using arrests and deportation is likely to split up families.

Nonetheless, many conservatives claim that only tough measures will discourage even more people from coming to this country illegally. In addition, conservatives support efforts to make our borders more secure.

There is increasing support among moderate conservatives that illegal immigrants may be allowed to stay in the United States as guest workers if they pay a fine, pay back taxes on their earnings, and go to the end of the line among people seeking citizenship.

About 40 percent of U.S. adults hold conservative views on the immigration debate. Typically, they believe that immigrants are a burden to the country because they are likely to receive welfare assistance or, if they work, they will compete with the existing workforce for jobs. Immigrants may also overtax our schools, health care system, and housing supply. Some conservatives also worry that immigrants' ethnic differences will bring dramatic changes to U.S. culture. For this reason, conservatives want immigrants to learn to use the English language (Pew Research Center, 2013).

Liberals tend to see immigrants as a positive force in U.S. society. They point out that through their work, most immigrants (documented or not) contribute to our economy, often doing jobs that others in our country do not want to do. Much low-wage labor on farms, at hotels and restaurants, and in private homes is performed by immigrants. Liberals also remind us that more than 1 million of today's undocumented immigrants are children. In 2012, the Obama administration created a program called "Deferred Action for Childhood Arrivals," which allows children who came to the

United States illegally with their parents to apply for protection against deportation. To date, about 350,000 young people have made use of this program successfully (Pew Research Center, 2013).

What of children born to unauthorized immigrants after they come to this country? Under the Fourteenth Amendment to the Constitution, anyone born in the United States including the children of unauthorized immigrants are U.S. citizens, even if their parents are not. Over time, about 5 million children of people who entered the country illegally have claimed U.S. citizenship based on this law. Surveys find that most liberals and some moderate conservatives support citizenship for all children born on U.S. soil, although few conservatives would extend this right to the children of illegal immigrants (Passel & Cohn, 2011).

Strong liberals favor amnesty for unauthorized immigrants and want to give them a path to citizenship. They take this position as a way to free millions of men, women, and children from "living in the shadows," with no chance to apply for a scholarship to go to a community college or even to get a driver's license. Most seriously, liberals point out, illegal immigrants must live in constant fear that they or another family member may be arrested.

What is the radical-left position on the immigration debate? Radicals on the left oppose walling off this country from the rest of the world and support legalization and citizenship for all immigrants already here. Most important, they claim, the world must reduce the economic inequality that separates the United States from other countries. Until that happens, they claim, millions of people will keep coming to this country, many risking their lives in the process.

Keep in mind that the immigration debate has political consequences that could easily decide the outcome of presidential elections. Allowing all immigrants to become citizens would create more than 10 million new voters. In the 2012 presidential election, 71 percent of Hispanic or Latino voters supported Democrat Barack Obama while 27 percent voted for Republican Mitt Romney. This marked political leaning is one reason liberals are willing to extend citizenship to Latinos. At the same time, conservatives realize the importance of gaining favor within what is now this country's largest minority population (Pew Research Center, 2012).

What Do You Think?

1. Do you view immigrants as a benefit or a liability to our society? Why?

2. What would you do to address the almost 12 million unauthorized immigrants already living in this country? Why?

3. What do you think Congress will end up doing about this issue?

Visibility Minorities share a *distinctive identity*, which may be based on race (physical traits, which are difficult to change) or ethnicity (including dress or accent, which people can change). Men and women of Japanese ancestry provide an example of people changing their level of distinctive visibility. Many people of Japanese ancestry in the United States have little knowledge of their native language, most speak only English in their homes, and more than half of those who marry have non-Japanese spouses. Thus, Japanese Americans have become less of an ethnic category, and by marrying people of other backgrounds, they are becoming less distinctive as a racial category as well. A minority's ability to blend in with others depends on the minority members' desire to hold on to their traditions. It also depends on the willingness of other people to accept them. For instance, whites have a greater willingness to marry people of Japanese ancestry than to marry people of African descent (U.S. Census Bureau, 2013).

Power A second characteristic of minorities is *social disadvantage*. Because minorities typically have less schooling and hold lower-paying jobs, they experience higher rates of poverty. Of course, not all people in any minority category are disadvantaged. In other words, despite the statistical averages, some people of African, Asian, or Latino ancestry have very high social standing. But even the most successful individuals know that their membership in a minority category reduces their standing in some people's eyes (Benjamin, 1991).

Numbers About 37 percent of the U.S. population falls into a racial or ethnic minority category, and this share is increasing. Minorities have already become a majority in 65 of the country's 100 largest cities. A minority majority also exists in four states—Hawaii, California, New Mexico, and Texas—as well as the District of Columbia. Other states will be added to the list in years to come. In 2012, for the first time, a majority of the children born in the United States were minorities and, in 2013, a minority majority existed among children younger than five. Based on current trends, analysts predict that, by about 2043, racial and ethnic minorities will become a majority of the U.S. population (U.S. Census Bureau, 2013).

We take up the question of whether women—of any race or ethnicity—should also be counted as a minority in Chapter 4 ("Gender Inequality").

The United States has always been a nation of immigrants. But immigration has always been controversial. The Dream Act was first proposed in 2001 as a means to give young people who arrived in the United States illegally as minors a path to remain in the country legally. When the bill stalled in Congress, several states passed their own versions of the Dream Act to make college more affordable to undocumented students. Do you support or oppose this type of policy? Why?

Patterns of Majority–Minority Interaction

3.2 Describe four major societal patterns of interaction between majority and minority populations.

The way majority and minority populations interact can range from peaceful to deadly. In studying such patterns, sociologists use four models: genocide, segregation, assimilation, and pluralism.

Genocide

Genocide is *the systematic killing of one category of people by another*. Genocide amounts to mass murder. Even so, it has taken place time and again in human history, often condoned and sometimes even encouraged by governments and their people.

Beginning about 1500, the Spanish, Portuguese, English, French, and Dutch forcefully colonized North and South America, resulting in the deaths of thousands of native people. Although most native people died from diseases brought by Europeans to which they had no natural defenses, many were also killed outright (Matthiessen, 1984; Sale, 1990).

In the 1930s and 1940s, Adolf Hitler and his Nazi government murdered more than 6 million people that the Nazis defined as "undesirables," including homosexuals, people with disabilities, and most of Europe's Jews. The Soviet dictator Josef Stalin slaughtered his country's people on an even greater scale, killing some 30 million people, all of whom he defined as "enemies." Between 1975 and 1980, Cambodia's Communist regime butchered millions whom they saw as "Western" in their cultural patterns. More

recently, Hutus massacred Tutsis in the African nation of Rwanda, Serbs systematically killed Croats in Eastern Europe, and several hundred thousand people have been killed in the Darfur region of Africa's Sudan.

Segregation

Segregation is *the physical and social separation of categories of people*. Sometimes minority populations decide that they wish to segregate themselves; this is the case with religious orders such as the Amish. Usually, though, the majority population causes segregation by forcing minorities to the margins of society, where they have to "stay with their own."

Racial segregation in the United States began with slavery and later included legally separate hotels, restaurants, schools, buses, and trains for people according to race. A number of court cases have largely eliminated *de jure* (Latin words meaning "by law") segregation in the United States. However, *de facto* ("in fact") segregation remains common because most neighborhoods, schools, hospitals, and even cemeteries still contain mostly people of one race. For example, the city of Detroit is 82 percent African American, and Livonia, Michigan, right across the city's boundary, is 91 percent white (Emerson, Yancey, & Chai, 2001; Krysan, 2002; U.S. Census Bureau, 2013).

Intense segregation has been found in many inner-city areas. In 1989, Douglas Massey and Nancy Denton documented the *hypersegregation* of some African Americans who have little contact with people outside of their community. A study published a decade ago found that hypersegregation affected just a few percent of poor white people but it affected one in five African Americans living in about twenty-five of the largest U.S. cities (Massey & Denton, 1989;

CONSTRUCTING SOCIAL PROBLEMS

A DEFINING MOMENT

Rosa Parks: Saying No to Segregation

A huge change to U.S. society began so routinely that no one would have known history was being made. On December 1, 1955, Rosa Louise Parks, a young African American woman living in Montgomery, Alabama, had just finished a day of hard work as a seamstress. She was tired and eager to get home. She walked to the street and boarded a city bus. At that time, Montgomery city law required African Americans to ride in seats designated for "coloreds" near the back of the bus, and Parks did exactly that. Slowly the bus filled with people. As the bus pulled to the curb to pick up some additional white passengers, the driver turned and asked four black people to give up their seats so that the white people could sit down. Three did as he asked. But Parks refused to move.

Hearing Parks's response, the driver pulled to the curb, stepped out of the bus, and returned with a police officer, who arrested Parks for breaking the city's segregation law. She appeared in court, and a judge found her guilty as charged and fined her $14.

The story of Parks's stand (or sitting) for justice quickly spread throughout the African American community. In the age before cell phones and Twitter, activists printed and distributed thousands of handbills asking every African American to stay off the buses the following Monday in protest of the arrest and trial. "You can afford to stay out of school for one day. If you work, take a cab, or walk. But please, children and grown-ups, don't ride the bus at all on Monday. Please stay off the buses Monday."

A social movement was now under way. African Americans in Montgomery successfully boycotted city buses on that Monday and the next day and for 382 days after that. A year later, the city of Montgomery officially ended segregation on its buses. In 1964, the U.S. Supreme Court banned racial segregation in any and all public accommodations across the country.

Rosa Parks lived the rest of her life as a symbol of the quiet determination to achieve justice. When she died in 2005, she was hailed as the mother of the modern civil rights movement in the United States and her funeral was attended by national leaders including three presidents. She will be remembered as a leader of the civil rights movement and as proof of the power of people—even one at a time—to change the world.

This photo shows Rosa Parks being fingerprinted by police in Montgomery, Alabama. At the time of her arrest, the law defined Parks as the problem. But the bus boycott that followed her arrest soon changed that, defining racial segregation as the problem.

Wilkes & Iceland, 2004). More recent data from the 2010 census suggests that, although hypersegregation continues in the United States today, the recent trend involves declining racial segregation. According to the Census Bureau, in all of this country's largest urban areas, the level of racial segregation involving black people and white people declined between 2000 and 2010. Specifically, all-white neighborhoods that were common in urban areas in the 1960s now typically have at least some African American residents. Racial segregation is still widespread in urban places and even more so in rural places. But as a result of migration of African Americans (especially to suburbs and to Sun Belt cities), changes in mortgage lending policies that support racial integration, and a generally increasing social climate of racial acceptance, researchers claim that U.S. cities are now

less racially segregated than they have been in a century (Glaeser & Vigdor, 2012).

Because minorities, by definition, have little power, challenging segregation is not easy and may even be dangerous. Sometimes, however, the actions of a single person do make a difference. The Defining Moment box describes the actions of Rosa Parks, who sparked a social movement to end segregation on buses and other forms of public transportation throughout the South.

Assimilation

Assimilation is *the process by which minorities gradually adopt cultural patterns from the dominant majority population.* When minorities—especially new immigrants—assimilate, they

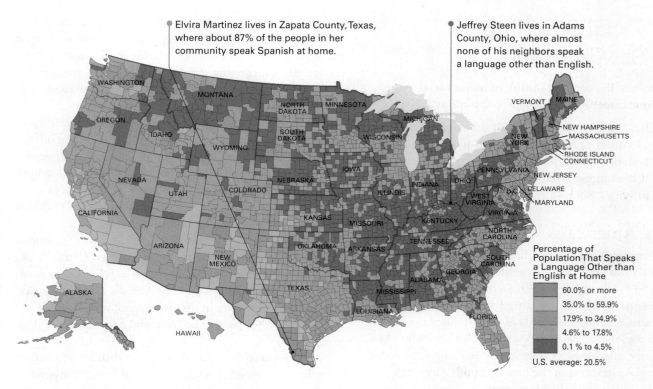

Elvira Martinez lives in Zapata County, Texas, where about 87% of the people in her community speak Spanish at home.

Jeffrey Steen lives in Adams County, Ohio, where almost none of his neighbors speak a language other than English.

Percentage of Population That Speaks a Language Other than English at Home

- 60.0% or more
- 35.0% to 59.9%
- 17.9% to 34.9%
- 4.6% to 17.8%
- 0.1% to 4.5%

U.S. average: 20.5%

Seeing Ourselves

National Map 3–1   Language Diversity across the United States

Of more than 294 million people age five or older in the United States, the Census Bureau reports that 62 million (21 percent) speak a language other than English at home. Of these, 62 percent speak Spanish and 16 percent use an Asian language (the Census Bureau lists thirty-nine languages and language categories, each of which is favored by more than 100,000 people). The map shows that non-English speakers are concentrated in certain regions of the country. Which ones? Can you explain this pattern?

SOURCE: U.S. Census Bureau (2013).

may change their styles of dress, use a new language, alter their cultural values, and even affiliate with a new religion.

Many people think of the United States as a "melting pot" where the different ways of immigrants blend to produce one national lifestyle. There is some truth to this image, but our history shows that minorities are the ones who do most of the changing as they adopt the cultural patterns of more powerful people who have been here longer. In some cases, minorities imitate people they regard as their "betters" in order to escape hostility and to move up socially. In many cases, however, the majority population forces change on minorities. For example, by 2014, legislatures in thirty-one states had enacted laws making English the official language. National Map 3–1 shows the share of people who speak a language other than English at home.

The amount of assimilation on the part of minorities also depends on where they live. Latinos living in Ohio or New Hampshire (where they represent a small part of the population) are more likely to speak English than their counterparts living in south Texas along the Mexican border (where, in many communities, Spanish-speaking people are a numerical majority). Of course, wherever they

live, some minority categories end up assimilating more than others. Looking back over the decades, we also see that German and Irish people have "melted" more than Italians, and Japanese people have assimilated more than people from China or Korea.

Pluralism

Pluralism is *a state in which people of all racial and ethnic categories have about the same overall social standing.* Pluralism represents a situation in which no minority category is subject to disadvantage. The United States is pluralistic to the extent that—officially, at least—all people have equal standing under the law. But in reality, tolerance for diversity (both among people in the majority and including one minority population's tolerance for another) is limited. As just noted, for example, thirty-one states have passed laws designating English as their official language. In addition, the United States is not truly pluralistic because the social standing of most minority populations is below that of the white, European-origin majority.

The Social Standing of U.S. Minorities

3.3 Analyze the social standing of major racial and ethnic categories of the U.S. population.

The United States is a nation built on racial and ethnic diversity. In order to better understand today's racial and ethnic inequality, it is important to know something of the history of the largest minority categories. The following sections provide brief historical profiles.

Native Americans

Native Americans (many of whom now prefer to be called "American Indians") are descendants of the first people to come to North America across the Bering Strait from Asia. Over thousands of years, they spread throughout the hemisphere, forming hundreds of distinct societies. These included the Aleuts and Eskimos (in Alaska), the Cherokee, Zuni, Sioux, and Iroquois (farther to the south), the Aztec (in Central America), and the Inca (in South America).

By 1500, the arrival of European explorers and colonizers began centuries of conflict. What some Europeans called "bringing civilization to the New World" was to Native Americans the destruction of their ancient and thriving civilizations. From a population in the millions before Europeans arrived, the number of "vanishing Americans" fell to barely 250,000 by 1900 (Dobyns, 1966; Tyler, 1973).

At first, the U.S. government viewed native peoples as independent nations and tried to gain land from them through treaties. But the government was quick to use superior military power against any who resisted. In the 1830s, soldiers forcibly removed the Cherokee and other Indian nations from their homelands in the southeastern United States, causing thousands of deaths along what came to be known as the Trail of Tears. By 1850, few native people remained along the East Coast.

In 1871, the United States declared American Indians wards of the federal government. At this point, the official goal was assimilation. This meant remaking native peoples as "Americans" by moving them to reservations where they were forced to adopt Christianity in place of their traditional religions and where schools taught children English in place of their ancestral language.

Since gaining full citizenship in 1924, many American Indians have assimilated, marrying people of other backgrounds. Yet many American Indians still live on reservations where poverty rates are very high. As Table 3–2 shows, American Indians remain disadvantaged, with below-average income, a high rate of poverty, and a low rate of college graduation.

In the past decade, American Indian organizations have received a large number of new membership applications, and many children are learning to speak native languages better than their parents (Nagel, 1996; Martin, 1997). Many American Indians operate a wide range of successful businesses, and some tribes have used the legal autonomy of reservations to build gambling casinos. But the enormous profits from these casinos have enriched only a few native people, with most profits going to non-Indian investors (Raymond, 2001; Bartlett & Steele, 2002). Overall, while some prosper, most American Indians remain severely disadvantaged and share a profound sense of historical injustice suffered at the hands of white people.

Despite media reports of the financial success that legal gambling on reservations has brought to some American Indians, the majority of Native people in the United States are greatly disadvantaged. Scenes such as this one from the Hopi reservation near Tuba City, Arizona, are more the rule than the exception.

African Americans

People of African ancestry arrived in the Americas along with the first European explorers. After 1619, however, when a Dutch trading ship delivered twenty Africans to Jamestown, Virginia, to work for whites, people came to see dark skin as a marker of subordination. In 1661, Virginia enacted the first slave law. By 1776, the year the United States declared its independence from Great Britain, slavery was legal in every state, and African Americans labored as slaves throughout the North as well as the South.

Table 3–2 The Social Standing of Native Americans, 2012

	Median Family Income	Percentage Living in Poverty	Percentage with Four or More Years of College (age 25 and over)
Entire U.S. Population	$62,241	15.0%	31.7%
Native Americans	41,361	29.1	13.5

SOURCE: U.S. Census Bureau (2013).

The demand for slaves was especially high in the South, where the plantation system required large numbers of people to work the cotton and tobacco fields. To meet this demand for labor, slave traders (including Arabs and Africans as well as Europeans and North Americans) legally transported human beings across the Atlantic Ocean, in chains and under horrific conditions. Before 1808, when the United States declared the slave trade illegal, 500,000 Africans were brought to the United States, and almost 10 million came to all of the Americas, North and South. Keep in mind that this total represents just half the number who left Africa—the other half died during the brutal journey (Tannenbaum, 1946; Franklin, 1967; Sowell, 1981).

Under the law and according to the norms of the time, owners administered what discipline they wished to slaves in order to force them to do just about anything. For their part, slaves had neither legal rights nor the opportunity to attend school. Slave owners routinely separated families as they traded men, women, and children for profit.

Not all people of African descent living in the United States were slaves. Roughly 1 million free persons of color lived in the North and the South. Most of these people farmed small parcels of land, worked at skilled jobs in cities, or operated shops or small businesses.

How could slavery exist in a society whose Declaration of Independence declared that "all men are created equal" and entitled to "life, liberty, and the pursuit of happiness"? The contradiction is obvious and had to be resolved. But rather than making all people free, our society decided that African Americans were not really people. In the 1857 *Dred Scott* case, the U.S. Supreme Court officially supported the widespread belief that slaves were not citizens entitled to the rights and protections of U.S. law (Lach, 2002).

In the northern states, where expanding industry meant that slavery had less economic value, the practice gradually came to an end. In the South, where the agrarian economy depended on human labor, it took the Civil War to abolish slavery. On January 1, 1863, as the guns of war roared, President Abraham Lincoln issued the Emancipation Proclamation, which declared that slavery was abolished in the breakaway southern Confederacy. When the fighting ended in 1865, Congress banned slavery everywhere in the country with the Thirteenth Amendment to the Constitution. In 1868, the Fourteenth Amendment reversed the *Dred Scott* decision, giving citizenship to all people, regardless of race, born in the United States.

But ending slavery did not mean ending racial discrimination. States soon enacted what came to be known as "Jim Crow laws," which barred black people from voting and sitting on juries and called for segregated trains, restaurants, hotels, and other public places (Woodward, 1974).

After World War I, when Congress closed the borders to further immigration, the need for labor in the booming factories sparked the "Great Migration," which drew tens of thousands of men and women of color from the rural South to the industrialized cities of the North. These were times of great achievements in African American life as, for example, the Harlem Renaissance (centered in Harlem, the large African American community in New York City) produced writers such as Langston Hughes and musicians such as Duke Ellington and Louis Armstrong. Even so, racial segregation in neighborhoods, schools, and jobs was a way of life in most of the United States.

But change was coming. In 1948, President Harry Truman declared an end to segregation in the U.S. military. Black legal scholars, including Thurgood Marshall (1908–1993), who later served for thirty years on the U.S. Supreme Court, led an attack on school segregation, leading to the 1954 case of *Brown v. Board of Education of Topeka* (Kansas). In this landmark decision, the Supreme Court rejected the practice of teaching black and white children in schools viewed as "separate but equal."

A year later, the heroic action of Rosa Parks sparked the bus boycott that desegregated public transportation in Montgomery, Alabama. In the next decade, the federal government passed the Civil Rights Act of 1964 (prohibiting segregation in employment and public accommodations), the Voting Rights Act of 1965 (banning voting requirements that prevented African Americans from having a political voice), and the Civil Rights Act of 1968 (which outlawed discrimination in housing). Together, these laws brought an end to most legal discrimination in public life.

But African Americans' struggle for full participation in U.S. society is far from over. People of African descent are still disadvantaged, a fact supported by the data shown in

Table 3–3 The Social Standing of African Americans, 2012

	Median Family Income	Percentage Living in Poverty	Percentage with Four or More Years of College (age 25 and over)
Entire U.S. Population	$62,241	15.0%	31.7%
African Americans	40,517	27.2	21.8

SOURCE: U.S. Census Bureau (2013).

Table 3–3. African American families still have below-average income, and the black poverty rate is almost three times as high as the white poverty rate. Although about 85 percent of African Americans now complete high school, their college graduation rate is well below the national average.

By 2012, 41 percent of African American families earned more than $50,000 a year. But most black families remain in the working class, and about one in four lives below the poverty line. On average, African American families earn just 57 percent as much as white families. One reason for the continued economic struggle of African Americans is that factory jobs, a key source of income for people living in central cities, have moved away from the United States to countries with lower labor costs. This loss of jobs helps to explain why black unemployment is double the rate among white people; among African American teenagers (aged 16 to 19), the unemployment rate in 2012 was 38.3 percent (W. J. Wilson, 1996a; R. A. Smith, 2002; U.S. Census Bureau, 2013; U.S. Department of Labor, 2013).

Asian Americans

Asian Americans include people with historical ties to any of several dozen Asian nations. The largest number have roots in China (3.7 million), India (3.0 million), the Philippines (2.7 million), Vietnam (1.6 million), South Korea (1.5 million), and Japan (780,000). In 2012, Asian Americans numbered more than 16 million, which was 5.1 percent of the total U.S. population. In 2012, according to the Census Bureau, Asian Americans comprised the fastest-increasing racial or ethnic category of the U.S. population, with most of the increase coming from immigration (U.S. Census Bureau, 2011, 2013).

The flow of immigrants from China and Japan to North America began back in 1849 when the Gold Rush in California created a demand for laborers. Chinese men answered the call, numbering 100,000 within a generation, and they were joined by a much smaller number of Japanese immigrants. As long as cheap labor was needed, whites welcomed them.

But as the economy slowed, whites began to view Asian immigrants as an economic threat and soon labeled them the "Yellow Peril." Legislatures and courts were pressured to bar Asians from certain jobs. In 1882, the federal government went even further and passed the Chinese Exclusion Act, which ended the flow of new immigrants from China. A similar law directed against Japan was enacted in 1908. These laws caused the Asian population in the United States to decline because almost all the people already here were men, and racial hostility prevented Asian men from marrying non-Asian women. Such norms were soon enacted into law, beginning in 1920, as California and other states passed laws banning interracial marriage outright.

Many Asians settled in urban neighborhoods where they could help one another. Chinatowns soon flourished in San Francisco, New York, and in other large cities, and many found work in Chinese-owned restaurants, laundries, and other small businesses. Self-employment has been popular not only among the Chinese but also among all minorities who find few employers willing to hire them for good wages.

World War II brought important changes to both the Japanese American and Chinese American populations. The war in the Pacific began when Japan attacked Hawaii's Pearl Harbor naval base. The military strike stunned the United States,

The mass media played a powerful role in the civil rights movement of the 1950s and 1960s. Televised scenes such as this one in Birmingham, Alabama, when police turned dogs and fire hoses on demonstrators, changed the mood of the nation in favor of the idea that all people should have equal opportunity and equal standing before the law.

and many people wondered which side Japanese Americans would take in the conflict. Japanese Americans always remained loyal to the United States. But fear of Japan's industrial and military might, coupled with racial hostility, pushed President Franklin Roosevelt to issue Executive Order 9066, forcibly relocating all people of Japanese ancestry to military camps in remote areas away from the coast. The order forced more than 100,000 Japanese Americans to sell their businesses, homes, and farms for a fraction of their true value. Taken to camps, they lived under the watchful eyes of armed soldiers until 1944, when the U.S. Supreme Court declared the relocation policy unconstitutional. In 1988, Congress declared that this action had been wrong and awarded a symbolic compensation of $20,000 to each surviving camp inmate (Ewers, 2008).

From 1942 until 1944, more than 100,000 men, women, and children of Japanese ancestry were forced to live in military detention camps. This policy took away not just Japanese Americans' liberty but also most of their property, as families were forced to sell homes and businesses for a small share of what they were really worth.

Because China joined the United States in the fight against Japan, in 1943 the federal government ended the 1882 ban on Chinese immigration and gave citizenship to Chinese Americans born abroad. After the war, in 1952, the same offer was extended to foreign-born Japanese Americans.

In the postwar period, many young people of Chinese and Japanese descent entered college, believing that more schooling was the key to success. By the 1980s, based on their cultural emphasis on study and hard work, Asian Americans were finding themselves described as the "model minority."

As Table 3–4 shows, all categories of Asian Americans now have above-average income and education. So there is some truth to the "model minority" notion. But poverty rates also are close to or even above the national average for some categories of Asian Americans. In addition, the "model minority" stereotype is misleading because many Asian families have multiple wage earners working long and hard in low-paying jobs.

Some Asian Americans live in distinctive communities. The Chinatowns and Little Tokyos found in some large cities may provide their people with social support, but they can also limit job opportunities by discouraging their residents from learning English (Kinkead, 1992; Gilbertson & Gurak, 1993).

Today, more than 41 percent of all immigrants to the United States each year are from an Asian nation. Many Asian Americans, especially those with high social standing, have assimilated into the larger cultural mix. For example, very few third- and fourth-generation Japanese Americans (the *Sansei* and *Yonsei*) live in racially segregated neighborhoods. In fact, most people of Japanese ancestry marry someone of another racial and ethnic background.

Keep in mind, too, that "Asian American" is a large category made up of many distinctive communities. Although most Japanese Americans have assimilated,

Table 3–4 The Social Standing of Asian Americans, 2012

	Median Family Income	Percentage Living in Poverty	Percentage with Four or More Years of College (age 25 and over)
Entire U.S. Population	$62,241	15.0%	31.7%
All Asian Americans	77,864	11.7	53.2
Chinese Americans	80,591	15.4	52.6
Japanese Americans	93,892	8.5	49.0
Korean Americans	66,488	14.9	53.6
Asian Indian Americans	103,642	8.1	72.2

SOURCE: U.S. Census Bureau (2013).

many Korean Americans follow the example of immigrants a century ago and settle in ethnic neighborhoods, sometimes for protection from racial and ethnic hostility.

In general, Asian Americans have fared better than most minorities. Even so, anti-Asian prejudice remains strong (Chua-Eoan, 2000; Parrillo, 2003; Parrillo & Donoghue, 2005, 2013). Many Asian Americans remain socially marginal, living in two worlds while fully belonging to neither one.

Hispanic Americans/Latinos

Hispanic Americans, also known as "Latinos" and "Latinas," are people with cultural roots in the nations of Central and South America, the Caribbean, and Spain. As a result, there are many Latino cultures. On the 2010 Census Bureau forms, people of any race could identify themselves as being Hispanic or Latino/a. In racial terms, about half of all Latinos described themselves as white; 6 percent said they are multiracial, 4 percent indicated that they are black. The

remainder claimed to identify primarily with Mexico, Puerto Rico, or some other nation (U.S. Census Bureau, 2011).

In 2012, the official Hispanic population of the United States stood at 53 million, making Hispanics the largest U.S. minority with 16.9 percent of the population (exceeding African Americans at 41.2 million, or 13.1 percent).

National Map 3–2 shows the geographical concentration of Latinos—as well as African Americans, Asian Americans, and Arab Americans—across the United States. Many Latinos reside in the Southwest because almost two-thirds (34 million) are of Mexican origin. Next in terms of numbers are Puerto Ricans (5 million) and Cuban Americans (2 million), and smaller numbers from dozens of other nations. Overall, Latinos are so numerous and their cultural contributions so great that Spanish has become the unofficial second language of the United States.

Many Mexican Americans had lived for centuries on lands that, following the Mexican War (1846–1848), were claimed by the United States and became what are now

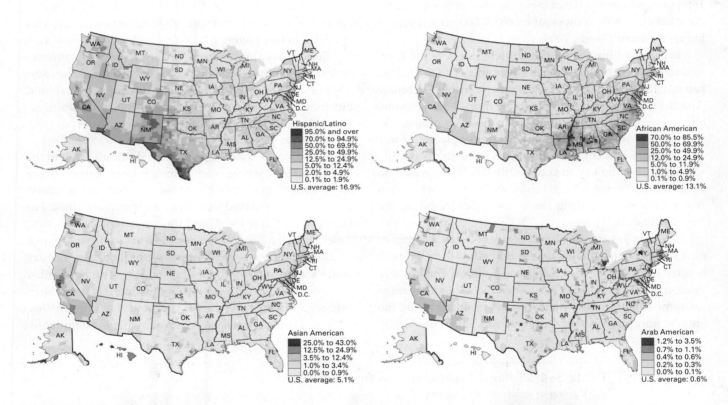

Seeing Ourselves

National Map 3–2 The Concentration of Hispanics/Latinos, African Americans, Asian Americans, and Arab Americans, by County

In 2012, Hispanic Americans represented 16.9 percent of the U.S. population, compared with 13.1 percent for African Americans, 5.1 percent for Asian Americans, and 0.6 percent for Arab Americans. These four maps show the geographic distribution of these categories of people in 2012. Comparing them, we see that the southern half of the United States is home to far more minorities than the northern half. But do the four minority categories concentrate in the same areas? What patterns do the maps reveal?

SOURCE: U.S. Census Bureau (2013).

Texas, New Mexico, Arizona, Nevada, Utah, California, and Colorado. Others are new arrivals, drawn to the United States by a desire for higher wages and greater economic opportunity.

Puerto Rico, an island controlled by Spain for about 300 years, became a U.S. territory in 1898 at the end of the Spanish-American War. Since 1917, all island residents have been U.S. citizens, although Puerto Rico is a commonwealth and not a state. The largest Puerto Rican community off the island is New York's Spanish Harlem. Since 1990, an outflow of people to the suburbs and also movement back to Puerto Rice reduced New York's Puerto Rican population from almost 900,000 to about 730,000 in 2012 (Marzán, Torres, & Luecke, 2008; U.S. Census Bureau, 2013).

Many Cubans fled to the United States after Fidel Castro gained control of their nation in 1959. These men and women, numbering several hundred thousand, included many affluent businesspeople and professionals. Most settled in Miami, Florida, where they established a vibrant Cuban American community.

Table 3–5 shows that the social standing of Hispanic Americans is below the U.S. average. However, various categories of Latinos have somewhat different rankings. The most advantaged are Cuban Americans, who have higher income and more schooling. Puerto Ricans occupy a middle position in terms of income, although recent immigrants have a low rate of high school completion. Mexican Americans have the lowest relative ranking, with median family income that is 65 percent of the national average. One reason for this disadvantage is that many Mexican Americans continue to speak only Spanish and not English, a pattern that can limit job opportunities.

Forty percent of Hispanic American families now earn at least $50,000 annually. But many challenges remain, including schools that do not do a very good job teaching students whose first language is Spanish. Chapter 13 ("Education") reports that 14 percent of Latinos between the ages of sixteen and twenty-four leave school without a high school diploma. In addition, their cultural differences—and, in some cases, dark skin—still spark hostility.

Overall, Hispanic Americans, now the largest ethnic category in the U.S. population, are a hugely important segment of our society. With more than 20 million Hispanic Americans eligible to vote in the 2012 elections, they represent 10 percent of all eligible voters and so they continue to draw the attention of leaders from all political parties (Pew Research Center, 2012, 2013).

Arab Americans

Arab Americans are another U.S. minority that is increasing in size. Like Asian Americans and Latinos, these are people who trace their ancestry to one of various nations around the world, in this case countries in northern Africa or the Middle East. It is important to remember, however, that some of the people who live in one of the twenty-two nations that are considered part of the "Arab world" are not Arabs. For example, Morocco in northwestern Africa is home to the Berber people, just as Iraq in the Middle East is home to the Kurds.

Arab cultures are diverse but share use of the Arabic alphabet and language, and Islam is the dominant religion. But once again, the term "Arab" refers to an ethnic category, and the word "Muslim" refers to a follower of Islam. A majority of the people living in Arab countries are Muslims, but some Arabs are Christians or followers of other religions. To make matters more complex, most of the world's Muslims actually live in Asia, rather than Africa or the Middle East, and they are not Arabs.

Immigration to the United States from many nations means that Arab Americans are culturally diverse. Some Arab Americans are Muslims and some are not; some speak Arabic and some do not; some maintain the traditions of their homeland and some do not. As is the case with Latinos and Asian Americans, some are recent immigrants and some have lived in the United States for decades or even for generations.

Officially, the government counts 1.86 million Arab Americans, but because many people may choose not to declare their ethnic background on a census form, the actual number might be twice this high. If so, Arab Americans represent roughly 1 percent of the population. The largest populations of Arab Americans have ancestral

Table 3–5 The Social Standing of Hispanic Americans, 2012

	Median Family Income	Percentage Living in Poverty	Percentage with Four or More Years of College (age 25 and over)
Entire U.S. Population	$62,241	15.0%	31.7%
All Hispanics	40,764	25.6	15.1
Mexican Americans	40,552	26.9	9.9
Puerto Ricans	41,505	27.3	16.8
Cuban Americans	47,449	19.6	24.3

SOURCE: U.S. Census Bureau (2013).

Some people in the United States link being Arab American or Muslim with support for anti-American terrorism. Why is this so? What can you suggest to eliminate this stereotype?

communities. Even so, many Arab Americans choose to downplay their ethnicity as a strategy to avoid prejudice and discrimination. The fact that many of the terrorist attacks against the United States and other nations have been carried out by Arabs encourages some people to link being Arab (or Muslim) with being a terrorist. This attitude is unfair because it blames an entire category of people for the actions of a few individuals. Since 2001, Arab Americans have been targets of a significant number of hate crimes, and many feel that they are subject to "ethnic profiling" that threatens their privacy and civil liberties (Ali & Juarez, 2003; Ali, Lipper, & Mack, 2004; Hagopian, 2004).

ties to Lebanon (27 percent of all Arab Americans), Egypt (13 percent), and Syria (9 percent). Most Arab Americans (65 percent) report ancestral ties to a single nation, but 35 percent report both Arab and non-Arab ancestry (U.S. Census Bureau, 2013). A look at National Map 3–2 shows the distribution of the Arab American population throughout the United States.

Arab Americans are diverse in terms of social class. Some are highly educated professionals who work as physicians, engineers, and professors; others are working-class people who perform various skilled jobs in factories or on construction sites; still others do service work in restaurants, hospitals, or other settings, or work in small family businesses. Overall, as shown in Table 3–6, median family income for Arab Americans is just slightly below the national average ($61,204 compared to a national median of $62,241 in 2012), but it is also true that Arab Americans have a higher than average poverty rate (23.4 percent versus 15 percent for the population as a whole). Arab Americans are highly educated; 47 percent over age twenty-five have a college degree, compared to about 32 percent of the population as a whole (U.S. Census Bureau, 2013).

A number of large U.S. cities—including New York, Chicago, Los Angeles, Houston, and Dearborn (Michigan)—have large and visible Arab American

Prejudice

3.4 Discuss the causes and consequences of prejudice.

The historical stories of various racial and ethnic minorities clearly illustrate the widespread problem of prejudice. Formally, **prejudice** is *any rigid and unfounded generalization about an entire category of people.* Prejudice is a prejudgment, an attitude one develops *before* interacting with the specific people in question. Because such attitudes are not based on direct experience, prejudices are not only wrong but also difficult to change.

Prejudice can be both positive and negative. Positive prejudices lead us to assume that certain people (usually others like ourselves) are better or smarter. Negative prejudices lead us to see those who differ from us as less worthy. Prejudices—both positive and negative—involve social class, gender, religion, age, sexual orientation, and political attitudes. But probably no dimensions of difference involve as many prejudices as race and ethnicity.

Stereotypes

A concept closely linked to prejudice is **stereotype**, *an exaggerated description applied to every person in some category.* The word *stereo* comes from the Greek word for "hard" or "solid,"

Table 3–6 The Social Standing of Arab Americans, 2012

	Median Family Income	Percentage Living in Poverty	Percentage with Four or More Years of College (age 25 and over)
Entire U.S. Population	$62,241	15.0%	31.7%
Arab Americans	61,204	23.4	46.7

SOURCE: U.S. Census Bureau (2013).

suggesting a rigid belief, one that is largely at odds with reality. For just about every racial or ethnic category, our culture contains stereotypes, which typically describe a category of people in negative terms. What stereotypes are conveyed in phrases such as "Dutch treat," "French kiss," "Russian roulette," and "getting gypped" (a reference to Gypsies)?

We all form opinions about the world, identifying people as "good" or "bad" in various ways. Generalizations about specific individuals that are based on actual experience may be quite valid. But racial or ethnic stereotypes are a problem to the extent that they assume that an entire category of people shares particular traits, as when a white person thinks all African Americans are unwilling to work hard or a person of color thinks every white person is hostile toward black people. Forming a judgment about another individual on the basis of actual personal experience is one thing, but when we place others in a category before we have a chance to judge them as individuals, stereotypes dehumanize people.

Racism

The most serious example of prejudice is **racism**, *the assertion that people of one race are less worthy than or even biologically inferior to others*. Over the course of human history, people the world over have assumed they were superior to those they viewed as lesser human beings.

Why is racism so widespread? Because the claim that people are *biologically* inferior, although entirely wrong, can be used to justify making them *socially* inferior. For example, Europeans used racism to support the often brutal colonization of much of Latin America, Asia, and Africa. When Europeans spoke of the "white man's burden," they were claiming to be superior beings who had the obligation to help "inferior" beings become more like them.

Even today, hundreds of hate groups in the United States continue to claim that minorities are inferior. In addition, subtle forms of racism are common in everyday life.

Measuring Prejudice: The Social Distance Scale

Prejudice shapes everyday life as it draws us toward some categories of people and away from others. Early in the twentieth century, Emory Bogardus (1925) developed the *social distance scale* to measure prejudice among students at U.S. colleges and universities. Bogardus asked students how closely they were willing to interact with people in thirty racial and ethnic categories. Figure 3–1 on page 84 shows the seven-point scale Bogardus used. At one extreme, people express very high social distance (high negative prejudice) when they say that some category of people should be barred from the country (point 7 in the figure). At the other extreme (little or no negative prejudice), people say they would accept members of some category into their family through marriage (Bogardus, 1925, 1967; Owen, Elsner, & McFaul, 1977).

Decades ago, Bogardus found that students, regardless of their own race and ethnicity, were most prejudiced against Latinos, African Americans, Asians, and Turks; they were willing to have these people as coworkers but not as neighbors, friends, or family members. At the other extreme, they were most accepting of the English, Scots, and Canadians, whom they were willing to have marry into their families.

Recently, Vincent Parrillo and Christopher Donoghue (2005, 2013) repeated the social distance study in 2001 and again in 2011 to see how more recent students felt about various minorities.[1] There were three major findings:

1. **The long-term trend is that students are more accepting of all minorities.** Figure 3–1 shows that the average (mean) response on the social distance scale was 2.14 in 1925 and 1946, dropping to 2.08 in 1956, 1.92 in 1966, 1.93 in 1977, and 1.44 in 2001. In 2011, however, the average response was 1.68, suggesting that tolerance may have declined somewhat by 2011. Even so, notice that in the 2011 study, students (74 percent of whom described themselves as white) expressed much more acceptance of minorities than students did in earlier studies. Regarding African Americans, for example, students in 2011 assigned African Americans a score of 1.42 (suggesting high acceptance, even higher than the acceptance given to the Irish or French). In 1925, Bogardus found the average score given to African Americans was about 4 (showing far lower acceptance, and giving African Americans the least amount of acceptance of any racial or ethnic category).

2. **Today's students see less difference between the various minorities.** In the earliest studies, although students were very accepting of some people (scores between 1 and 2), they were not very accepting of other minorities (scores between 4 and 5). In the 2011 study, no minority received a score greater than 2.23.

3. **The climate of concern over terrorism in the United States probably has increased prejudice against Arabs and Muslims.** The current generation of students has grown up in a nation concerned about terrorism. The fact that the 9/11 attacks in 2001 were carried out by nineteen attackers who were Arabs and Muslims probably explains why students expressed the greatest social distance toward these categories.

---

[1] In 2001, Parrillo and Donoghue dropped seven of Bogardus's original categories (Armenians, Czechs, Finns, Norwegians, Scots, Swedes, and Turks) because they are no longer visible minorities and added nine new categories (Africans, Arabs, Cubans, Dominicans, Haitians, Jamaicans, Muslims, Puerto Ricans, and Vietnamese). This change probably encouraged higher social distance scores, making the downward trend all the more significant.

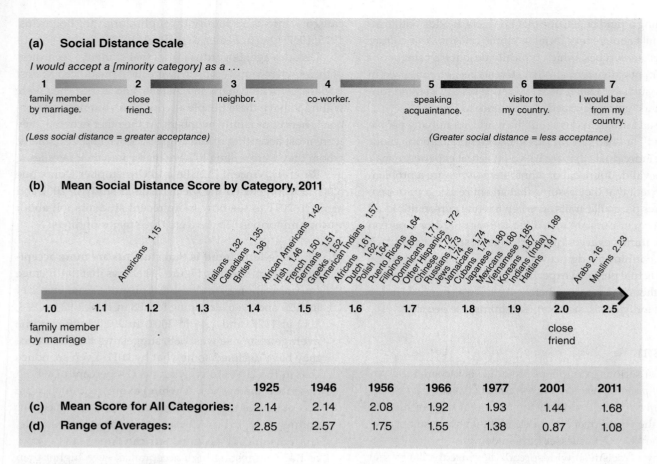

Diversity Snapshot

Figure 3–1   Bogardus Social Distance Scale

Using this seven-point scale, Emory Bogardus and others have shown that people feel much closer to some categories of people than they do to others. Between 1925, when the study was first carried out, and 2001, the average social distance response dropped from 2.14 to 1.44, showing increasing tolerance of diversity. When this research was repeated in 2011, the average response showed a modest increase to 1.68, suggesting a slight decline in tolerance.

SOURCE: Parrillo & Donoghue (2005, 2013).

(After World War II, Parrillo and Donoghue found, both Japanese and German people were scored lower on social acceptance; similarly, during the Cold War of the 1950s, Russians received low scores.) Even so, not one student in the study said that Arabs or Muslims should be barred from the United States. Also, even the most prejudiced score by today's students (Muslims, with a mean score of 2.23) shows much more tolerance than students back in 1977 expressed toward eighteen of the thirty minority categories.

Institutional Racism: The Case of Racial Profiling

The studies we have just looked at involve prejudice at the level of individual attitudes. But to the extent that those attitudes are widespread, prejudice can be described as *structural*, that is, built into the operation of society itself. This idea underlies the work of Stokely Carmichael and Charles Hamilton (1967), who described **institutional racism** as *racism at work in the operation of social institutions, including the economy, schools, hospitals, the military, and the criminal justice system.* Whenever race guides the operation of any social institution to the disadvantage of a minority, institutional racism is at work.

Racial profiling—in which police or others in power consider race or ethnicity to be, by itself, a sign of probable guilt—illustrates the operation of institutional racism. This is not a matter of one prejudiced police officer thinking that, say, African Americans are potential criminals. Prejudice is institutional when such attitudes are part of the culture and policy of a police department—so that police routinely assume that a black person who comes to their attention is likely to be engaged in wrongdoing. If the workplace culture or the unofficial policy of a police department is to consider black persons more dangerous than whites, they may be quicker to draw their weapons when confronting black people, perhaps with tragic results. In recent years, a number of African Americans who turned out to be neither armed nor guilty of any crime have been killed by police who may well have reacted at least partly to their skin color.

Challenging any case of institutionalized racism is difficult. Police departments are part of society's power structure and claim to serve the public interest. When institutional racism involves an organization with a lot of power, bringing about change can be difficult.

Causes of Prejudice

What causes people to become prejudiced in the first place? The research presented so far points to two key factors: the personality of individuals and the structure of society itself.

Personality Factors T. W. Adorno and his colleagues (1950) claimed that prejudice is strong in people with an *authoritarian personality*. Such people feel a lot of hostility, rigidly conform to conventional norms, and see the world in stark contrasts of "right" versus "wrong" and "us" versus "them." What creates such a personality? Adorno pointed to cold and demanding parents who fill their children with insecurity and anger. Such children, especially when they lack schooling, develop little tolerance of others and are quick to direct their anger at people who differ from themselves.

Societal Factors Prejudice also results from the structure of society itself. *Scapegoat theory*, for example, says that prejudice develops among people who are frustrated at their lack of control over their lives (Dollard et al., 1939). Working-class whites in southwestern Texas, for example, may feel anxious and angry at their lack of economic security, but where do they direct their anger? They might blame their political leaders, the people who run their communities, but speaking out against powerful people is often dangerous. A safer target would be the poor, illegal immigrants from Mexico who are willing to grab any job they can find, often at less than minimum wage. Scapegoat theory suggests that people direct their hostility at safe, less powerful targets such as illegal immigrants or other minorities. Because many of society's least powerful people are minorities, they often end up as scapegoats blamed for a host of troubles that are not their fault.

Cultural theory claims that prejudice is built into our culture. An illustration of this is the research using Emory Bogardus's social distance scale, described earlier in this chapter. Bogardus showed that most of us turn out to have the same kinds of prejudice, favoring certain categories of people and avoiding others. The fact that these attitudes are so widely shared suggests that prejudice is not a trait of deviant individuals as much as it is a normal part of our cultural system.

Many African Americans claim that skin color alone is enough to prompt a response from police. Often, this claim centers on black drivers being stopped for no apparent reason—the alleged crime of "driving while black." To what extent do you think this pattern exists in the United States? Explain.

Multiculturalism

Is there a way to address prejudice deeply rooted in our culture? One strategy for change is **multiculturalism**, *educational programs designed to recognize cultural diversity in the United States and to promote respect for all cultural traditions.*

Multiculturalism claims, first, that U.S. society has long down-played its cultural diversity. Schools have taught generations of children that the United States is a cultural "melting pot" that blends human diversity into a single culture we call "American." However, multiculturalism maintains that our diverse population has "melted" far less than most people think. More correctly, race and ethnicity have formed a hierarchy. At the top, Europeans (especially the English) represent the cultural ideal of the well-informed, well-groomed, and well-behaved man and woman. What we call assimilation, from this point of view, is really a process of *Anglicization* as immigrants try to become more like the privileged white Anglo-Saxon Protestants (WASPs).

In addition, U.S. institutions—including schools, law, and the economy, as well as dominant religions and family forms—are all modeled along Western European lines. Multiculturalists describe this bias as **Eurocentrism**, *the practice of using European (particularly English) cultural standards to judge everyone.* To multiculturalists, U.S. culture is itself an expression of prejudice against people in this country who differ from the dominant model. Multiculturalism asks that we rethink our national heritage and recognize the accomplishments not just of the cultural elite but of people of every race and ethnicity.

Although there is strong support for multiculturalism (especially among liberals) because it gives more visibility and power to minorities, others (especially conservatives) claim that this approach divides society by downplaying what we have in common. The Latin phrase that appears on all U.S. currency—*E pluribus unum*—literally means "out of many, one." Thus the controversy over multiculturalism is really about how much stress we should place on a single national identity and how much we should highlight differences.

Discrimination

3.5   Distinguish discrimination from prejudice and show how the two concepts operate together.

Discrimination involves *the unequal treatment of various categories of people.* Prejudice is a matter of *attitudes,* but discrimination is a matter of *actions.* Like prejudice, discrimination can be positive or negative. We discriminate in a positive way when we single out people who do especially good work or when we provide special favors to family members or friends. We discriminate in a negative way when we put down others or avoid entire categories of people based on their race or ethnicity.

Few people would object to an employer who hires a job applicant with more schooling over one with less. But what if an employer favors one category of people (say, Christians) over another (say, Jews)? Unless a person's religion is directly related to the job (for example, if a church is hiring a priest), ruling out an entire category of people is wrongful discrimination, which violates the law.

Institutional Discrimination

As in the case of prejudice, some discrimination involves the actions of individuals. For example, a restaurant

Wouldn't most people assume that the gloved hand holding the wine glass is white? Despite the outlawing of racial discrimination, there is still considerable social inequality between white and black people in U.S. society. The widespread pattern of people of color providing personal service to members of the dominant white majority goes all the way back to the beginnings of slavery.

owner might refuse to serve students with dark skin. Almost everyone condemns discrimination of this kind, and in a public setting such as a restaurant, it is against the law.

Institutional discrimination is *discrimination that is built into the operation of social institutions, including the economy, schools, and the legal system.* A well-known example of institutional discrimination is this nation's history of treating black and white children differently by placing them in separate schools. As noted earlier, not until 1954 did civil rights activists succeed in overturning the legal doctrine of "separate but equal" schools, which, in the landmark case of *Brown v. Board of Education of Topeka,* the U.S. Supreme Court concluded was unconstitutional. But that did not end racial segregation in our country; more than half a century after the *Brown* decision, most children attend school sitting in classrooms surrounded by students of the same race (Kozol, 2005).

Prejudice and Discrimination: A Vicious Circle

Prejudice and discrimination reinforce each other, maintaining social inequality over time. Let's begin with how prejudice can lead to discrimination: If prejudiced white police officers think that most African Americans are criminals, they may well engage in racial profiling, stopping a large number of black motorists and being quick to arrest black citizens on the street. Such discrimination, especially if it is widespread or institutionalized, will overly criminalize African Americans, reducing their chances of finding good jobs and raising their odds of living in neighborhoods marked by poverty, drug abuse, and crime. As people see minorities in such conditions, this discrimination unleashes a new round of prejudice. And so it goes, around and around, forming a vicious circle that harms minorities.

Affirmative Action: Reverse Discrimination or Cure for Prejudice?

One strategy aimed at breaking the vicious circle of prejudice and discrimination is **affirmative action**, *policies intended to improve the social standing of minorities subject to past prejudice and discrimination.* Affirmative action policies have changed over time, and they will continue to change in response to court rulings.

History of Affirmative Action   After World War II, the federal government assisted veterans by funding education under what was known as the GI Bill, and minorities who might not otherwise have gone to college were able to enter classrooms across the country. By 1960, almost 350,000 African Americans had used government help to earn a college degree. However, even with their schooling, many of these men and women were not getting the types of jobs for which they were qualified. The Kennedy administration concluded that education alone could not overcome deep-seated, institutionalized prejudice and discrimination against people of color. So they devised a policy of affirmative action requiring employers to "throw a wider net" to identify and hire qualified minority applicants. In the years that followed, employers hired thousands of African American women and men for good jobs, helping build the black middle class and reducing racial prejudice.

By the 1970s, affirmative action was extended to include college admissions, and many policies took the form of "quota systems" in which employers or colleges set aside a certain number of places for minorities. Categories of people assisted by this policy also increased to include women, Hispanics, veterans, and in some cases people with physical disabilities.

The expansion of affirmative action provoked opposition to this policy. In 1978, the Supreme Court heard the case of *University of California Regents v. Bakke,* brought by Allen Bakke, a white man who was denied admission to medical school at the University of California at Davis. The medical school had a policy of setting aside sixteen places (out of 100 in each entering class) for African Americans, Asian Americans, Native Americans, and Hispanic Americans.

The court declared such rigid quotas to be illegal, but the justices did endorse the use of race and ethnicity in the process of admitting students or hiring employees in order to increase minority representation in settings from which minorities had historically been excluded.

But opposition to affirmative action programs continued. In 1995, the University of California system declared it would no longer consider race and gender when making any decision involving admission, hiring, or awarding a business contract. The following year, California voters passed Proposition 209, which required state agencies to operate without paying attention to race, ethnicity, or gender. A similar proposition passed in the state of Washington. Also in 1996, a federal district court declared (in *Hopwood v. Texas*) that race and gender could no longer be considered by public colleges and universities in Texas, Louisiana, and Mississippi.

Seeking a socially diverse student body, many colleges and universities have tried to find a way around the new regulations. In Texas, for example, public universities admit all students in the top 10 percent of their high school class, a policy that ensures spaces for students from predominantly African American and Latino schools.

In 2003, the U.S. Supreme Court once again addressed the issue of affirmative action. The case involved admission policies at the University of Michigan, a state university. In the undergraduate admissions process, applicants of underrepresented minorities had received a numerical bonus that was added to a total score, which also reflected grades and College Board scores. The Supreme Court struck down this point system as too similar to the racial quota systems rejected by the Court in the past. However, the Court did say that colleges and universities could continue to take

Throughout much of the United States until the 1960s, public facilities, including bus and railroad stations, were segregated by law. But even today, more than fifty years later, many familiar social settings are largely segregated, with most of the people being of one racial category.

account of applicants' race, along with other factors, with the goal of creating a racially diverse student body. In this administrative process, rather than a rigid point system, race was treated as one of several variables used in giving each applicant individual consideration. In these decisions, the Court was affirming the national importance of allowing colleges and universities to create racially diverse campuses while at the same time stating that all applicants must be considered as individuals (Stout, 2003).

In 2013, the Supreme Court heard a case from Texas brought by Abigail Fisher, a white student who claimed that she was denied admission to the University of Texas while less qualified minority applicants were admitted. The Court did not rule on her complaint but instead sent the case back to a lower court with instructions that the court engage in "strict scrutiny" of the university admissions. This means that, rather than simply accepting the university's claim that race is considered only as part of a larger process, the court must gather facts to verify that racial preference is needed to ensure student diversity and that the program gives race no more importance than is necessary to achieve that goal.

The United States continues to wrestle with the issue of affirmative action. Most people agree that society needs to give real opportunity to people in every racial and ethnic category. But disagreement remains as to how to define affirmative action so that it becomes part of the solution rather than part of the problem (Fineman & Lipper, 2003; Kantrowitz & Wingert, 2003; NORC, 2007; Totenberg, 2013).

Theories of Racial and Ethnic Inequality

3.6   Apply sociological theory to patterns of racial and ethnic inequality.

Why do the various racial and ethnic categories of the U.S. population have unequal social standing? The following discussions draw answers from sociology's structural-functional, symbolic-interaction, and social-conflict approaches.

Structural-Functional Analysis: The Importance of Culture

Structural-functional theory places great importance on how culture guides people's behavior. To the extent that various racial and ethnic categories have different cultural orientations—for example, placing more or less emphasis on education—unequal social standing is the likely result.

The Culture of Poverty   Chapter 2 ("Poverty and Wealth") introduced the "culture of poverty" thesis of Oscar Lewis (1966). Lewis studied the low-income Puerto Rican population

of San Juan and New York and found a widespread way of thinking that he called "fatalism." This outlook leads people to accept their situation and to make the assumption that life is not likely to get better. Growing up poor and learning to accept that reality, young people develop low self-esteem, limited aspirations, and a sense of powerlessness. Over time, they grow into adults who are not likely to take advantage of any opportunities that society might offer them.

Joan Albon made a similar claim about American Indians, whose traditional cultures tend to be cooperative and nonentrepreneurial, "in direct opposition to the principles of the modern, competitive, capitalistic order" (1971:387). Some African American peer groups have also been described as having an "oppositional culture" that discourages members from excelling by defining school achievement as "acting white" (Fordham & Ogbu, 1992). In such an environment, adds Shelby Steele (1990), a successful man or woman of color risks being accused by others of not being a "real" African American.

EVALUATE

Few people doubt that culture matters in shaping people's lives. But critics of this theory claim that focusing on culture amounts to defining people as responsible for their own disadvantage—what Chapter 2 described as "blaming the victim." People who live in individualistic societies such as the United States find it easy to blame disadvantaged categories of the population for their own poverty. But do poor people really deserve to live as they do? If disadvantaged people lack some of the optimism and confidence found among people who are better off, critics suggest, this is more the *result* of being poor than it is the *cause* of their low social standing.

CHECK YOUR LEARNING   How does structural-functional theory explain the fact that some categories of the population have higher social standing than others?

The Applying Theory table summarizes the contributions of structural-functional theory, as well as social-interaction and social-conflict theory, which follow.

Symbolic-Interaction Analysis: The Personal Meaning of Race

Forty years after the end of slavery in the United States, the pioneering sociologist W. E. B. Du Bois published *The Souls of Black Folk,* an analysis of the social standing of African Americans. As Du Bois saw it, even though slavery was gone, most people of color were still living as second-class citizens.

Every time black people and white people met, said Du Bois, race hung in the air, defining each in the eyes of the other. From the African American perspective, race produces a "double-consciousness, [a] sense of always looking at oneself through the eyes of others, of

APPLYING THEORY

Racial and Ethnic Inequality

	Structural-Functional Theory	Symbolic-Interaction Theory	Social-Conflict Theory
What is the level of analysis?	Macro-level	Micro-level	Macro-level
What do we learn about racial and ethnic inequality?	Structural-functional theory highlights the importance of culture to social standing. Various categories of the population have differing cultural orientations that affect patterns of education and achievement. The "culture of poverty" thesis developed by Oscar Lewis is one example of a theory to explain why some low-income people have a fatalistic view of their situation.	Symbolic-interaction theory focuses on how people experience society in their everyday lives. Race and ethnicity affect the way we evaluate ourselves and others. W. E. B. Du Bois claimed that most people consider race a basic element of social identity, to the disadvantage of people of color.	Social-conflict theory links race and ethnicity to class—all are elements of social stratification. Marx and Engels claimed that race and ethnicity divided the working class. Multicultural theory claims that our culture has a European bias that pushes minority ways of life to the margins of society.
Are racial and ethnic differences helpful or harmful to society?	Ethnic differences are cultural and a source of identity and pride for most people. At the same time, traditional or fatalistic cultural orientations can be a barrier to achievement for some categories of people.	To the extent that race or ethnicity becomes a master status that devalues people, these social structures take away from our common humanity.	As elements of social stratification, race and ethnicity serve the interests of elites and are harmful to the operation of society.

measuring one's soul by the tape of a world that looks on in amused contempt and pity" (2001:227, orig. 1903). In effect, Du Bois said, U.S. society makes whites the standard by which others (including African Americans) should be measured. In daily encounters, race operates as a *master status*, a trait that defines and devalues any person of color.

Today, more than a century later, race continues to shape the everyday lives of everyone, regardless of their color. Manning Marable sums it up this way: "As long as I can remember, the fundamentally defining feature of my life, and the lives of my family, was the stark reality of race" (1995:1).

EVALUATE

Symbolic-interaction theory investigates how we use color (or in the case of ethnicity, cultural background) in the process of defining ourselves and evaluating other people. In short, race and ethnicity are key building blocks of the reality we construct in everyday life.

At the same time, race involves more than personal understandings. Race is also an important structure of society, a dimension of social stratification. This insight brings us to the social-conflict approach.

CHECK YOUR LEARNING   What did W. E. B. Du Bois mean when he said that African Americans have a "double-consciousness"?

Social-Conflict Analysis: The Structure of Inequality

Social-conflict theory claims that the unequal standing of minorities reflects the organization of society itself. Along with class, race and ethnicity operate as important dimensions of social inequality.

The Importance of Class   Karl Marx traced the roots of social inequality to a society's economy. As explained in Chapter 2 ("Poverty and Wealth"), Marx criticized capitalism for concentrating wealth and power in the hands of a small elite. He explained that the capitalist elite, realizing that the strength of the working class lies in its greater numbers, tries to divide the workers by playing up racial and ethnic differences. Marx and his colleague Friedrich Engels pointed to the racial and ethnic diversity of the United States as the main reason U.S. workers had not come together to form a socialist movement. "Immigration," Marx and Engels wrote,

> divides the workers into . . . the native born and the foreigners, and the latter . . . into (1) the Irish, (2) the Germans, (3) many small groups, each of which understands only itself: Czechs, Poles, Italians. . . . And then the Negroes. To form a single party out of these requires unusually powerful incentives (1959:458, orig. 1893).

Marx and Engels hoped that increasing misery would eventually provide the incentive for workers to unify themselves into a politically active class. To some degree, this has happened, and a number of unions and worker organizations have memberships that are black and white, Anglo and Latino. However, racial and ethnic differences still divide the U.S. workforce as they do workers around the world.

Multicultural Theory   Social-conflict theory also notes the importance of culture. A multicultural perspective claims that U.S. culture provides privileges to the dominant European, white majority while pushing racial and ethnic minorities to the margins of society.

Cultural hostility shaped the events of U.S. history. When Christopher Columbus landed in the Bahamas in 1492, he encountered Native Americans who were, on the whole, peaceful. Tragically, this gentleness made it easy for the more competitive and aggressive Europeans to take advantage of them. Yet, in another example of cultural bias, most of our historical accounts portray Europeans as heroic explorers and Native Americans as thieves and murderers (Matthiessen, 1984; Sale, 1990).

As W. E. B. Du Bois noted, bias involving race and ethnicity is still part of everyday life. Take the common case in which people assume that "classical music" refers only to European and not to Chinese, Indian, or Zulu compositions of a certain period. Cultural bias also leads people to apply the term "ethnic" to anyone not of English background or even to speak of "whites and blacks," placing the dominant category first (as we do for "husbands and wives").

EVALUATE

One criticism of social-conflict theory is that this approach downplays what people in the United States have in common. Whatever their color or cultural background, most people identify themselves as "Americans," and they have joined together over and over again to help each other in bad times and, in good times, to celebrate the principle of individual freedom that defines our way of life.

A second problem is that painting minorities as victims runs the risk of taking away people's responsibility for their own lives. It is true that minorities face serious barriers, but we need to remember that people also make choices about how to live and can act to raise their social standing and join together to improve their communities.

Third and finally, conflict theory all but ignores the significant strides this nation has made in dealing with its social diversity. Over time, U.S. society has moved closer to the ideals of political participation, public education, and equal standing before the law for everyone. As a result, the share of minorities who are well schooled, politically active, and affluent has steadily increased. In a 2013 survey, 81 percent of U.S. adults (including 71 percent of African Americans, 81 percent of Hispanic Americans, and 86 percent of whites) claimed that, over the last fifty years, his country has made "a lot" or "some" progress toward realizing Martin Luther King's dream of racial and ethnic equality (Pew Research Center, 2013). Although much remains to be done, there is also reason for pride and optimism. The election of Barack Obama, an African American man, as president of the United States is surely a sign that race is no longer the barrier it once was (West, 2008).

CHECK YOUR LEARNING How did Marx and Engels explain racial and ethnic conflict in capitalist societies such as the United States? What does multicultural theory add to our understanding of racial and ethnic inequality?

✪ POLITICS, RACE, AND ETHNICITY

Constructing Problems and Defining Solutions

3.7 Analyze racial and ethnic inequality from various positions on the political spectrum.

Should racial and ethnic inequality be defined as a problem? If so, what should be done about it? Conservative, liberal, and radical-left viewpoints, explored in the following section, produce different answers to these questions.

Conservatives: Culture and Effort Matter

Conservatives support the idea that all people should have equal standing before the law and that everyone should have the chance to improve their lives. Believing that our society, at least generally, does provide these benefits to all segments of the population, conservatives also believe that people are responsible for their own social standing.

If some racial and ethnic minorities are more successful than others, it is likely that cultural differences are at work. On average, people in various racial and ethnic categories place different emphasis on schooling, aspire to different kinds of jobs, and even attach different levels of importance to financial success. For instance, Italian Americans have long worked in the building trades, Irish Americans lean toward public service occupations, Jewish Americans have long dominated the garment industry and are well represented in most professions, and many Korean Americans operate retail businesses (Keister, 2003). Such differences make no one "better" than anyone else. But as conservatives see it, they do produce social inequality.

According to the conservative view, social standing should reflect people's level of ambition, the importance they place on schooling, and their commitment to hard work. In a society such as ours, people are free but they are also unequal. Conservatives claim that any society in which government tries to engineer rigid social equality would almost certainly offer little personal freedom.

The defense of individual freedom is the reason conservatives typically oppose affirmative action policies. They argue that instead of being an effective way to give everyone an equal chance—a path toward the goal of a color-blind society—affirmative action is really a system of "group preferences." In practice, as they see it, such policies amount to "reverse discrimination" that favors people based not on their individual qualifications and performance but on their race, ethnicity, or gender. If treating people according to color was wrong in the past, conservatives ask, how can it be right today?

Conservatives add that affirmative action harms minorities by calling into question their accomplishments: How would you feel, for example, if other people thought you had been admitted to college not because of your abilities and achievements but because of your skin color or ethnic background?

Finally, conservatives point out that affirmative action helps the minorities who need it least. Minorities on college campuses and in the corporate world are, by and large, already well off; affirmative action does less for the minority poor, who need help the most (Gilder, 1980; C. Murray, 1984; Sowell, 1987, 1990; Carter, 1991; Steele, 1990; B. L. Stone, 2000).

Liberals: Society and Government Matter

Liberals claim that societal factors such as prejudice and discrimination, rather than cultural differences, are the main causes of social inequality among various racial and ethnic categories. For this reason, liberals claim, it is simply not true (as conservatives claim) that everyone has the same chance to get ahead. Prejudice and discrimination are still very much a part of how our society operates and institutional bias can be found in education, the military, the corporate economy, and the nation's criminal justice system.

Liberals acknowledge that there may be cultural differences between various categories of the population. But liberals see such differences as more the *result* than the *cause* of social inequality. That is, people who are shut out of opportunity—whether they are inner-city or rural residents—may develop a sense of hopelessness about their situation. But minorities themselves are not the problem; the responsibility for this situation lies in the structure of power and privilege in the larger society.

If inequality is so deeply rooted in our society, we cannot expect minorities acting as individuals to improve their situation. Therefore, liberals look to government as the solution, supporting policies—including antidiscrimination laws—that reduce racial and ethnic inequality. This is why liberals favor greater spending to assist minorities.

This call for government action also helps to explain why liberals support affirmative action. As they see it, an affirmative action program is a necessary correction for historical prejudice and discrimination directed against minorities. African Americans today face the legacy of two centuries of slavery and an additional century and a half of racial segregation. In short, for most of its history, the United States has had a policy of *majority* preference, one

Everyday social interaction can be distorted by racial hostility. Sociologists have coined the term *microaggression* to refer to the pattern by which one person makes assumptions about the character, abilities, or behavior of another based on race. Do you think people at all points in the political spectrum are likely to consider "microaggression" to be a social problem? Why or why not?

reason the social standing of whites is higher than that of blacks and other minorities. For this reason, liberals think that minority preference is not only fair but also necessary as a step to help level the playing field.

Liberals see affirmative action as a policy that has had good consequences for this country. Where would minorities be today without the affirmative action that began in the 1960s? After all, major employers in government and corporate business began hiring large numbers of minorities and women only because of affirmative action, resulting in the growth of the African American middle class (Johnson, Rush, & Feagin, 2000; Kantrowitz & Wingert, 2003).

The Radical Left: Fundamental Changes Are Needed

Left radicals claim that much more than liberal reforms such as greater government spending is needed to end the problem of racial and ethnic inequality. Following Marx, radicals point out that as long as a capitalist society defines workers simply as a supply of labor, there is little reason to expect an end to exploitation and oppression, which is based on both class and race. Therefore, the radical left makes the argument that the only way to reduce racial and ethnic inequality is to attack the source of *all* inequality: capitalism itself (Liazos, 1982).

A more recent addition to radical thinking about racial inequality focuses not on economics but on culture. Some of today's activist scholars conclude that to end racial inequality, a society must eliminate the concept of race entirely. As they see it, as long as a society continues to recognize race, it will divide people, giving advantages to some at the expense of others.

Could we really leave behind the notion of race, which has been so basic to conventional ways of thinking? In time, perhaps. Doing so would certainly be a radical change because abolishing race will demand basic changes to the current white power structure. As one group of sociologists claims:

> A useful place to begin undoing racism is to address the social, economic, and political embeddedness of white racism within the foundation of the U.S. political system. . . . Thus, [we] call for a new constitutional convention, one that will represent fairly and equally, for the first time, all major groups of U.S. citizens. (Johnson, Rush, & Feagin, 2000:101)

At this convention, these critics propose, people representing all categories of the population might consider what all our social institutions would look like if this country set out to achieve the goal of meeting the needs of everyone, rather than supporting the privileges of the few.

The Left to Right table provides a summary of the three political perspectives applied to the issue of racial and ethnic inequality.

Going On from Here

For most people living in the lower-income nations of the world, everyday life is guided by their kin group, tribe, or traditions. In high-income countries, by contrast, people break free of the past and are more likely to say that their lives should be guided by personal choices, their talents and efforts, and their hope for the future. This is why most members of our society think that categorizing people on the basis of traits given at birth, such as skin color or cultural heritage, is wrong. That is also why, in our modern society, most people are likely to view traditional, race-based ranking of people as unfair prejudice and discrimination.

Social institutions in the United States have changed over time to reflect more modern and individualistic beliefs. Slavery was abolished (1865); soon after, African Americans gained citizenship (1868), as did Native Americans (1924), Chinese immigrants (1943), and Japanese immigrants (1952).

But as this chapter has explained, racial and ethnic inequality continues today. Minorities still suffer the consequences of prejudice and discrimination. These harmful biases exist not only in the attitudes and actions of individuals but also in the operation of society itself. For this reason, the inequality described in this chapter is carried from generation to generation, as too many young Latinos, African Americans, and native people grow up poor.

In 1903, W. E. B. Du Bois predicted that race would be the defining problem of the twentieth century. He was right. Could we say the same for the twenty-first century? How much importance will the traditional, so-called

---

LEFT TO RIGHT

The Politics of Racial and Ethnic Inequality

	Radical-Left View	Liberal View	Conservative View
What is the problem?	Striking inequality and racism are built into the very institutions of U.S. society.	Social and economic inequality places minorities at the margins of U.S. society.	Some people may hold prejudiced views of minorities, but all people make choices and must take responsibility for their own social standing.
What is the solution?	There must be fundamental change in economic, political, and other social institutions to eliminate racial hierarchy.	Government programs must attack prejudice and discrimination and provide assistance to minorities.	All people need to treat others as individuals. Some minorities must overcome cultural disadvantages through individual effort in order to realize higher achievement.

JOIN THE DEBATE

1. Consider the following statement: "Over the course of its history, the United States has moved closer to the ideal of being a color-blind society." Do you agree or disagree with this statement? Why? How would conservatives, liberals, and left radicals respond to this statement?

2. What does the election of Barack Obama, an African American, as this country's president suggest about the changing importance of race in our national life? Do you expect this event to encourage further change? Explain.

3. Which of the three political approaches regarding racial and ethnic inequality included here do you find most convincing? Why?

"color line" have a century from now? Just as important, what level of acceptance will our society extend to the millions of new immigrants from Mexico, Latin America, and Asia? Perhaps, as some analysts see it, the high level of immigration will increase the diversity of U.S. society to a point where race and ethnicity come to mean less and less. It seems likely that the steady increase of multiracial people—including a multiracial president—will have the same effect (Lee & Bean, 2010).

The conservative solution to problems of race amounts to focusing on individual achievement—that is, adopting a set of "color-blind" attitudes that treat people as individuals according to their skills, talents, and performance. Liberals also endorse the long-range "color-blind" goal, but they argue that to reach it, government action (including programs that take people's race and ethnicity into account) is needed to guarantee that all categories of people are full participants in society.

Radicals on the left weigh in with a greater challenge: Racism is too deeply entrenched in U.S. institutions to expect well-meaning individuals or even government reform to level the playing field. Therefore, as they see it, institutions must undergo fundamental change to ensure equality for all.

Throughout its history, U.S. society has debated issues related to racial and ethnic inequality. Let us hope that by the end of this century, we find answers that satisfy all categories of people.

Essay: Envisioning a Better Society How do you envision the racial and ethnic diversity of the United States fifty years from now? Do you think the trend toward a "minority majority" will reduce social problems related to race and ethnicity or make them worse? Why? What specific changes involving race and ethnicity do you feel would improve U.S. society?

CHAPTER 3   Racial and Ethnic Inequality

Is increased immigration to the United States a problem?

For many people, the answer to this question depends on whether the immigration is legal or illegal, and for everyone, it reflects political attitudes. What people say we ought to do about the current high level of immigration also depends on their political viewpoint. Look at the accompanying photos, which show two responses to this issue.

Do you see increased immigration as a threat to our way of life or as a source of national strength? If you are more liberal, you might well support legislation that would grant legal status to undocumented young people who were brought to the United States as children by their parents. From this point of view, why does immigration strengthen the country?

What about the idea that everyone should obey the law? If you are more conservative, you might think that the United States should do more to secure its southern border, which currently allows a steady flow of illegal immigrants to enter the country. From a conservative point of view, in what ways does not securing the borders threaten the country?

Hint: Liberals see the United States as the product of immigration. In addition, they view ethnic and racial diversity as good, and they seek to promote tolerance of different ways of life. Immigration is also a source of talent as newcomers to the country bring their skills, work hard, and pay taxes. Conservatives recognize that we're all immigrants, but they see increasing numbers of immigrants as bringing too much cultural change—a concern that leads many conservatives to support making English our nation's official language. In addition, conservatives point to the importance of the rule of law and believe that we cannot allow hundreds of thousands of people to break the law by entering this country illegally. They also say that only immigrants with legal status should be eligible to receive government benefits such as education and health care.

Getting Involved: Applications and Exercises

1. How do you describe yourself in terms of racial and ethnic identity? Write a short account of who you are in these terms. What importance do you assign to having a racial and ethnic identity? To what extent do you think this identity is important to others in your social world?

2. An easy and interesting research project is to watch ten or twenty hours of television over the next week or two while taking notes on the race of TV actors and the kinds of characters they play. Although your sample may not be representative of all shows, it will get you thinking about racial stereotypes in the mass media.

3. This chapter describes the steady increase in the rate of interracial marriage in the United States. What patterns do you see involving interracial socializing and dating on your campus or home community? Begin your analysis by keeping in mind the relative presence or absence of people representing various racial and ethnic categories in the campus community.

4. One of the reasons the changing racial and ethnic composition of the U.S. population matters is because minorities typically favor Democratic political candidates over Republicans. What do you think the long-term political consequences will be of the coming "minority majority"?

Making the Grade

A DEFINING MOMENT
Rosa Parks: Saying No to Segregation **p. 74**

Race and Ethnicity

3.1 Explain how race and ethnicity are socially constructed.

- **Race** is a socially constructed category based on physical traits that members of a society define as important.
- **Ethnicity** is a shared cultural heritage.
- Both race and ethnicity are important dimensions of inequality in the United States. **pp. 68–69**

The great racial and ethnic diversity of the United States is a product of **immigration** from other countries.

- The "Great Immigration" (1865–1914) brought 25 million people in search of economic opportunity.
- *Nativists*, fearing that high immigration would endanger this country's mostly English culture, pressured for a quota system, which Congress enacted in the 1920s.
- Congress ended the quota system in 1965, resulting in another large wave of immigration.
- Today, the issue of illegal immigration is a hotly debated topic. **pp. 69–71**

Minorities are categories of people that

- share a distinctive identity (which may be racial or ethnic)
- suffer disadvantages (such as poor schooling and low-paying jobs) **pp. 71–72**

> **race** (p. 68) a socially constructed category of people who share biologically transmitted traits that a society defines as important
> **ethnicity** (p. 69) a shared cultural heritage, which typically involves common ancestors, language, and religion
> **minority** (p. 71) any category of people, identified by physical or cultural traits, that a society subjects to disadvantages

Patterns of Majority–Minority Interaction

3.2 Describe four major societal patterns of interaction between majority and minority populations.

Genocide is the deliberate killing of a category of people. European colonization of the Americas resulted in the deaths of thousands of native people. **p. 73**

Segregation is the physical and social separation of some category of a population. *De jure* racial segregation existed in the U.S. until the 1960s. *De facto* segregation continues today. **pp. 73–74**

Assimilation is a process (a "melting pot") by which minorities adopt styles of dress, the language, cultural values, and even the religion of the dominant majority. **pp. 74–75**

Pluralism is a state in which racial and ethnic categories, though distinct, have equal social standing. In the U.S., all people have equal standing by law; however, social tolerance for diversity is limited. **p. 75**

> **genocide** (p. 73) the systematic killing of one category of people by another
> **segregation** (p. 73) the physical and social separation of categories of people
> **assimilation** (p. 74) the process by which minorities gradually adopt cultural patterns from the dominant majority population
> **pluralism** (p. 75) a state in which people of all racial and ethnic categories have about the same overall social standing

The Social Standing of U.S. Minorities

3.3 Analyze the social standing of major racial and ethnic categories of the U.S. population.

Native Americans suffered greatly at the hands of Europeans over the course of five hundred years. Even today, Native Americans have relatively low social standing. **p. 76**

African Americans came to the United States as cargo transported by slave traders. Despite substantial gains, African Americans are still, on average, disadvantaged. **pp. 76–78**

Asian Americans have lived in the United States for more than a century. Although their social standing is average or above average today, they still suffer from prejudice and discrimination. **pp. 78–80**

Hispanic Americans or Latinos are a diverse people sharing a cultural heritage. Some categories, such as Puerto Ricans, have low social standing; others, such as Cuban Americans, are better off. **pp. 80–81**

Arab Americans have ancestors in various nations. Like other categories of minorities, they are subject to both prejudice and discrimination. **pp. 81–82**

Prejudice

3.4 **Discuss the causes and consequences of prejudice.**

Prejudice consists of rigid prejudgments about some category of people.

- A **stereotype** is an exaggerated and unfair description.
- The study of prejudice using the *social distance scale* shows a trend toward greater tolerance on the part of U.S. college students.
- **Racism** is the assertion that people of one race are innately superior to people of another. Racism has been used throughout human history to justify the social inferiority of some category of people.
- Researchers have linked prejudice to individual traits (*authoritarian personality theory*) and to social structure (*scapegoat theory*) and patterns of belief (*cultural theory*). **pp. 82–86**

prejudice (p. 82) any rigid and unfounded generalization about an entire category of people

stereotype (p. 82) an exaggerated description applied to every person in some category

racism (p. 83) the assertion that people of one race are less worthy than or even biologically inferior to others

institutional racism (p. 84) racism at work in the operation of social institutions, including the economy, schools, hospitals, the military, and the criminal justice system

multiculturalism (p. 85) educational programs designed to recognize cultural diversity in the United States and to promote respect for all cultural traditions

Eurocentrism (p. 85) the practice of using European (particularly English) cultural standards to judge everyone

Discrimination

3.5 **Distinguish discrimination from prejudice and show how the two concepts operate together.**

Discrimination consists of actions that treat various categories of a population differently.

- *Example:* An employer refuses to consider job applications from people with Arabic-sounding names.

Institutional discrimination is bias built into the operation of the economy, legal system, or other social institution.

- *Example:* U.S. law prior to 1954 required black and white children to attend separate schools.

Affirmative action policies allow employers and universities to consider factors such as race in hiring and admissions decisions.

- Liberals favor affirmative action in order to increase minority representation in settings from which minorities have been excluded in the past, but conservatives criticize such policies as reverse discrimination. **pp. 86–88**

discrimination (p. 86) the unequal treatment of various categories of people

institutional discrimination (p. 86) discrimination that is built into the operation of social institutions, including the economy, schools, and the legal system

affirmative action (p. 86) policies intended to improve the social standing of minorities subject to past prejudice and discrimination

Theories of Racial and Ethnic Inequality

3.6 **Apply sociological theory to patterns of racial and ethnic inequality.**

Structural-Functional Analysis: The Importance of Culture

Structural-functional theory explains racial and ethnic inequality in terms of cultural values.

- The *"culture of poverty" theory* developed by Oscar Lewis claims that minorities develop a fatalistic cultural outlook that leads to a sense of hopelessness and low self-esteem. **p. 88**

Symbolic-Interaction Analysis: The Personal Meaning of Race

Symbolic-interaction theory highlights how race often operates as a *master status* in everyday interaction.

- W. E. B. Du Bois claimed that U.S. society makes whites the standard by which others should be measured and in so doing devalues any person of color. **pp. 88–89**

Social-Conflict Analysis: The Structure of Inequality

Social-conflict theory highlights how racial and ethnic inequality is built into the structure of society.

- *Marxist theory* argues that elites encourage racial and ethnic divisions as a strategy to weaken the working class.
- More recently, *multicultural theory* notes ways in which much U.S. culture is biased against minorities. **pp. 89–90**

⭐ POLITICS, RACE, AND ETHNICITY

Constructing Problems and Defining Solutions

3.7   Analyze racial and ethnic inequality from various positions on the political spectrum.

Conservatives: Culture and Effort Matter

- **Conservatives** point to cultural patterns, such as the importance given to education, as a cause of racial and ethnic inequality.

- Conservatives claim that individuals should be responsible for their social standing; they oppose government policies that treat categories of people differently. **pp. 90–91**

Liberals: Society and Government Matter

- **Liberals** point to social structure, including institutional prejudice and discrimination, as the cause of racial and ethnic inequality.

- Liberals endorse government reforms to promote equality, including enforcement of antidiscrimination laws and affirmative action. **p. 91**

The Radical Left: Fundamental Changes Are Needed

- **Radicals** on the left claim that capitalism is the root cause of racial and ethnic inequality.

- Radicals on the left call for basic change to all U.S. social institutions, including the capitalist economic system and the political system, so that they operate in the interests of all categories of people. **pp. 91–92**

Chapter 4
Gender Inequality

Learning Objectives

4.1 Define important concepts including gender and gender stratification.

4.2 Analyze the importance of gender in the operation of major social institutions.

4.3 Examine how gender stratification is found in many parts of everyday life.

4.4 Apply sociological theory to the issue of gender inequality.

4.5 Identify the foundations of feminism and distinguish three types of feminism.

4.6 Analyze gender inequality from various positions on the political spectrum.

Tracking the Trends

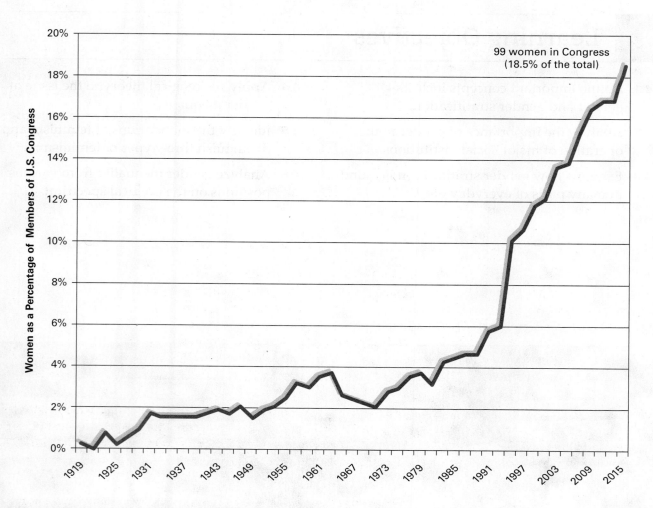

99 women in Congress
(18.5% of the total)

Women as a Percentage of Members of U.S. Congress

20%

18%

16%

14%

12%

10%

8%

6%

4%

2%

0%

1919 1925 1931 1937 1943 1949 1955 1961 1967 1973 1979 1985 1991 1997 2003 2009 2015

SOURCE: Center for American Women and Politics (2013).

Does gender affect our life chances? What about the odds of being elected to Congress? A century ago, no woman had ever served in Congress, either in the House or the Senate. It was in 1917 that the first woman was elected to Congress, which means women represented only a fraction of one percent of national leaders. In 2015, ninety nine women are serving in Congress but, as the figure shows, this number still represents less than 20 percent of the total. Do you think women have a fair share of political power in the United States?

Constructing the Problem

Are women and men equal in U.S. society?

Not in terms of income, with women on average earning 77 percent as much as men.

Can a woman be anything she wants to be?

Today's women have more choices, but many jobs are almost entirely done by people of one sex.

Is beauty just about looking good?

Women who are very concerned about beauty give men power over them.

Chapter Overview

What is gender? How is gender a dimension of social inequality that affects almost every aspect of everyday life? This chapter documents the different social standing of women and men. You will learn how income, housework, violence, and even ideas about beauty all reflect gender stratification. You will carry out theoretical analysis of gender inequality and learn how "problems" and "solutions" involving gender reflect people's political attitudes.

How might we assess a movie's portrayal of women and men? Alison Bechdel is a cartoonist with an interest in the way popular culture presents various categories of people. In 1985, she drew a cartoon outlining a simple test. A movie can be said to take women seriously if the film (1) has at least two female characters that have names, (2) the women talk to each other, and (3) they discuss something other than men.

Analysts who have applied the Bechdel test conclude that perhaps half of all popular movies during recent decades—from the *Star Wars* trilogy to *Avatar* to *The Social Network*, to *Harry Potter, Part II,* to all *The Lord of the Rings* films—fail this simple test. On the other hand, a number of recent films, including *The Heat, Blue Jasmine,* and *The Hunger Games* trilogy, have women in leading roles and clearly do pass the test. But, considering what the Bechdel test asks, is this really a very challenging standard for films to meet? Or, put the other way, must we conclude that many of the most popular films fail to present women as significant human beings (Cantrell, 2013; Gibson, 2014)?

In the world of films, there is a great deal of inequality between women and men. As this chapter explains, inequality can be found in almost every aspect of our social life. As the Tracking the Trends figure showed, a large majority of our national leaders—and all of our presidents—have been men. In the labor force, women earn much less than men. In addition, women deal with unwanted sexual attention in the workplace just as many women face outright violence at home. To understand many of the issues facing women and men today, we begin by looking at the important part that gender plays in the way society operates.

What Is Gender?

4.1 **Define important concepts including gender and gender stratification.**

In societies around the world, women and men lead lives that differ in important ways. Sociologists describe these differences using the concept of **gender**, *the personal traits and life chances that a society links to being female or male.* Gender is not the same as **sex**, *the biological distinction between females and males.* Sex is determined biologically

Patriarchy means that men have power to control the behavior of women. In some societies, this power can be almost absolute. This young Pakistani woman was mutilated by the men in her family, who declared that her behavior had dishonored them.

as an embryo is conceived. As Chapter 7 ("Sexuality") explains, specific biological differences are what give women and men the capacity to reproduce. Gender is a societal construction that shapes the entire lives of women and men, affecting the amount of schooling they receive, the kind of work they do, and how much money they earn. All societies define men and women as different types of people, in the process creating gender inequality. **Gender stratification** is *the unequal distribution of wealth, power, and privilege between men and women.* Throughout the world, gender is an important dimension of social inequality.

Patriarchy

Around the world, we find various degrees of **patriarchy** (literally, "rule by fathers"), *a social pattern in which males dominate females.* **Matriarchy**, *a social pattern in which females dominate males,* is extremely rare. Two centuries ago, among the North American Seneca (an American Indian nation), women provided most of the food and also required Seneca men to obtain their permission before engaging in a military campaign or making some other important decision. Today, the Musuo is a very small society in China's Yunnan province where women control most property, select their sexual partners, and make most decisions about everyday life (Arrighi, 2001; E. B. Freedman, 2002).

Global Map 4–1 surveys women's power relative to that of men around the world. A close look at the map shows that women living in poor countries are more disadvantaged relative to men than those living in high-income nations.

Explanations of Patriarchy Is patriarchy just a matter of men's greater body size? On average, according to government health data, males are 9 percent taller, 18 percent heavier, and 20 percent stronger than females (Fryar, Gu, & Ogden, 2012). Yet it is widely noted that women are catching up to men in almost every test of physical performance. Furthermore, to our cave-dwelling ancestors, physical strength may have made all the difference in survival, but muscles have little to do with success in today's high-technology societies.

Nor does patriarchy reflect differences in brain power. On the SAT, young men outperform young women on the math and reading tests, but women do better than men on the writing test. All in all, performance differences linked to sex are very small, and scientists find no overall differences in intelligence between men and women of similar social background (Tavris & Wade, 2001; Lewin, 2008; College Board, 2013).

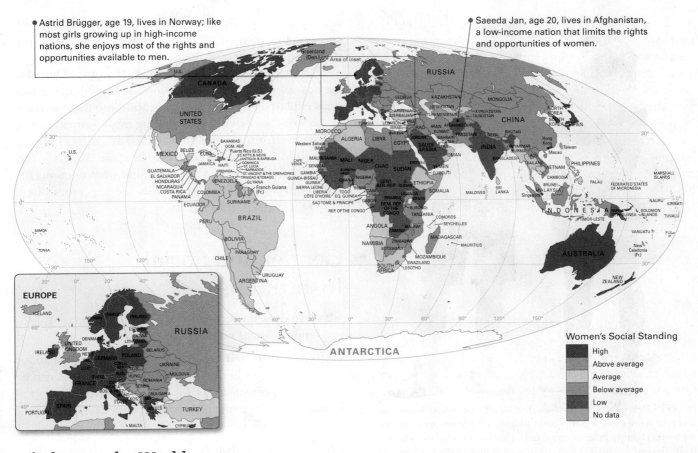

Astrid Brügger, age 19, lives in Norway; like most girls growing up in high-income nations, she enjoys most of the rights and opportunities available to men.

Saeeda Jan, age 20, lives in Afghanistan, a low-income nation that limits the rights and opportunities of women.

Women's Social Standing

- High
- Above average
- Average
- Below average
- Low
- No data

Window on the World

Global Map 4–1 Women's Power in Global Perspective

The social power of women in relation to that of men varies around the world. In general, women are closer to equality with men in high-income nations, and men have more control over women's lives in low-income nations. Where are women and men most equal? The answer is in the Netherlands, Sweden, and Denmark.

SOURCE: Data from United Nations Development Programme (2013).

Another theory links patriarchy to greater aggressiveness in males based on their higher levels of sex hormones (Goldberg, 1974; Maccoby & Jacklin, 1974; Popenoe, 1993b; Udry, 2000, 2001). Chapter 6 ("Crime, Violence, and Criminal Justice") reports that most murders are the work of young males, who generally have high levels of testosterone. But not everyone agrees with the testosterone theory. Barbara Ehrenreich (1999) counters that the male hormone testosterone and the female hormone estrogen are found to varying degrees in both sexes, and she point out that scientists have yet to explain the precise connection between these hormones and aggressive behavior.

Most sociologists reject the idea that any behavior is "hardwired" into human biology. On the contrary, we believe that patriarchy and all the behaviors linked to gender are mostly creations of society. In short, whatever biological forces are at work, societies can and do shape the social differences between the sexes.

Prejudice and Discrimination Like race and ethnicity, gender shapes the kinds of people we become. Familiar stereotypes cast women as dependent, sensitive, and emotional while portraying men as independent, rational, and competitive. Notice that gender stereotypes divide humanity by constructing femininity and masculinity in opposing terms.

Such stereotypes overlook the fact that most women and men exhibit a mixture of traits, being more "feminine" in some respects and more "masculine" in others. Also, does the capacity for showing emotions make anyone less rational? In truth, gender stereotypes do not describe real people very well.

In most sports played by both sexes, male athletes attract more fans and earn more money than female athletes. Fifty years ago, women who won championships earned only about one-third as much as men who did the same. Today, major tennis tournaments award equal prize money to women's and men's champions.

What is quite clear is that our culture assigns more worth to what we call "masculine" than what we call "feminine." For example, would anyone prefer being dependent to being independent? Being passive to being active? Being timid to being brave? Taken together, gender stereotypes amount to a form of prejudice against women.

In a society that devalues what is feminine, it is not surprising that discrimination against women is widespread. For centuries, U.S. society defined women as little more than the property of men. Women had to respect the authority of their fathers and, later, their husbands. To some degree, times have changed: A large majority of U.S. adults now say that they would support a qualified woman for president (Smith et al., 2013). Hillary Clinton, who came close to winning her party's nomination for president in 2008, will probably run again in 2016. So far, all of our country's forty-four presidents have been men. But this pattern is likely to change in the not-too-distant future.

The Problem of Sexism

Similar to racism, discussed in Chapter 3 ("Racial and Ethnic Inequality"), **sexism** is *the belief that one sex is innately superior to the other*. Sexism supports patriarchy by claiming that men are "better" than women and therefore should have power over them.

Sexism involves not just individual attitudes but also the operation of social institutions. As the following sections explain, male superiority is built into the operation of the workplace (with men running most companies and women performing most of the clerical support work), our political system (women may be more likely to vote, but most elected leaders are men), and even religious life (although women attend religious services more often, most religious leaders are men).

Gender and Social Institutions

4.2 **Analyze the importance of gender in the operation of major social institutions.**

Like class, race, and ethnicity, gender shapes just about every part of our lives. The importance of gender can be seen in the operation of all the social institutions, as the following survey explains. We begin with the family.

Gender and the Family

Do parents value boys more than girls? Traditionally, parents in the United States preferred boys to girls, although this bias has weakened in recent decades. But in poor countries around the world, a pro-male bias is still strong. In rural areas of India, for example, families benefit from the earnings of a son, but they have to pay a dowry to marry off a daughter. As a result, many pregnant women pay for ultrasound examinations to find out the sex of the fetus, and many who learn they are carrying a female request an abortion. Sometimes families may even kill an unwelcome newborn girl, the practice of *female infanticide*.

In the United States, gender shapes our experience of marriage. As Jessie Bernard (1982) explained in her classic study of traditional marriage, men's experience of marriage centers on providing economic support for the family and making key decisions. Women experience marriage differently, providing emotional support to husbands and raising children, sometimes to the point that they have little identity of their own. If Bernard was right that most marriages are unequal partnerships that favor men, why does it seem that women typically express greater eagerness than men to marry?

Gender and Education

By the time they begin school, children have learned a great deal about gender from books. Children's books

SOCIAL PROBLEMS IN GLOBAL PERSPECTIVE

Sweden Tries to Take Gender Out of the Classroom

Sweden has made remarkable strides in pursuit of gender equality. A gender gap in pay exists with women earning 86 percent of what men earn, but this is half the pay gap found in the United States. Almost half of Swedish legislators are women, making the country a world leader in sharing power between the sexes. Now, after passing a national law setting the goal of removing gender from schools, Sweden is moving into a postgender era by teaching children that they are *humans* rather than creatures fitting the mold of "girl" or "boy."

Annika Linder is a U.S. college student spending a year studying in Sweden. She is living and taking classes at a university in Stockholm. Her major is early childhood education, and she hopes that soon she will be teaching in an elementary school back in the United States.

On this particular day, Annika is beginning an assistantship at a local Swedish preschool. She has been in the classroom only for several hours, but already she cannot believe how different the schooling is in a country committed to gender equality. The Swedes speak of *gender neutrality,* which means that children may be one sex or the other, but sex should have nothing to do with the kinds of people they become. Right away, Annika notices a girl playing in a sandbox, slapping the sand with a plastic shovel. The girl is making a mess, but the teacher says nothing explaining to Annika that "We don't want to send the message that she cannot be physical or play with tools." In fact, Annika notices, the teacher always addresses the class as "children" and never as "boys and girls." There is no reason to

reinforce gender identity. Similarly, the Swedish words for "he" (*han*) and "she" (*hon*) are never used. In their place, children learn to use the pronoun *hen,* which is gender-neutral.

Looking around the classroom, the toys include plastic dinosaurs or Lego blocks, which have no evident gender. Even the dolls used to teach children the names of major emotions—facial expressions range from beaming smiles to dour frowns—lack clothing and have no physical traits that would suggest one sex or the other. All children do sports and take dancing classes, and they dress alike. But other changes are not so obvious. For example, school officials review all books in the library to ensure that the children find the same number of female and male characters (Abend, 2013).

The Swedish policy has critics. Some see the new policy as allowing officials to regulate almost all aspects of school life, crushing freedom and generating a mild sameness in people. But others see such efforts as necessary if the goal of ending gender inequality is to be taken seriously.

What Do You Think?

1. What appear to be the advantages of Sweden's gender policy for schooling? What are this policy's disadvantages?

2. Sweden's government includes a minister for gender equality. Do you think the U.S. president's Cabinet should include a similar post? Explain.

3. On balance, do you support this Swedish policy? Why or why not?

---

used to be full of gender stereotypes, showing girls and women mostly in the home while boys and men did almost everything else outside the home. Newer children's books present the two sexes in a more balanced way. More broadly, however, childhood education contains many messages about gender, from the presence of mostly women teachers in the lower grades to sex-linked activities both in the classroom and in recreation areas (Purcell & Stewart, 1990; F. Taylor, 2003; Abend, 2013). To get an idea of what could be done to eliminate gender bias in children's schools, we can look to Sweden. The Social Problems in Global Perspective box takes a closer look.

What about advanced education? As the figure at the beginning of this chapter shows, women have made remarkable gains in schooling, especially at the college level. In fact, women earn 62 percent of all associate's degrees and 57 percent of all bachelor's degrees. Even so, gender stereotyping still steers women to major in English,

education, health professions, dance, drama, or sociology while pushing men toward physics, economics, mathematics, computer science, and engineering (U.S. Department of Education, 2013).

Women have also made gains in postgraduate education. In the United States in 2014, women earned 60 percent of all master's degrees and 52 percent of all doctorates (including 63 percent of all Ph.D.'s in sociology). Women are now well represented in many graduate fields that used to be almost all male. Back in 1970, for example, hardly any women earned a master's of business administration (M.B.A.) degree; in 2011, more than 85,000 women did so, accounting for 46 percent of all M.B.A. degrees (U.S. Department of Education, 2013).

But gender still matters. Men slightly outnumber women in some professional fields, receiving 52 percent of medical (M.D.) degrees, 53 percent of law (LL.B. and J.D.) degrees, and 55 percent of dental (D.D.S. and D.M.D.) degrees (U.S. Department of Education, 2013).

Finally, gender stratification can be seen in the operation of higher education. In the case of law schools, for example, not only are most degrees earned by men but also men represent 70 percent of tenured professors and 80 percent of law school deans (American Bar Association, 2010).

Gender and College Sports Gender is at work on the playing fields as much as in the classroom. In decades past, extracurricular athletics was a male world, and females were expected to watch and cheer but not to play. In 1972, Congress passed Title IX, the Educational Amendment to the Civil Rights Act, banning sex discrimination in any educational program receiving federal funding. In recent years, colleges and universities have also tried to provide an equal number of sports for both women and men. Even so, men benefit from higher-paid coaches and enjoy larger crowds of spectators. In short, despite the federal policy outlawing gender bias, in few athletic programs is gender equality a reality.

Gender and the Mass Media

There are more than 300 million television sets in the United States (about equal to the country's total population) and people watch an average of more than four hours of television each day (TVB, 2012; Nielsen, 2013). Who can doubt the importance of the mass media in shaping how we think and act? What messages about gender do we find on TV?

When television became popular in the 1950s, almost all the starring roles belonged to men. Only in recent decades have television shows featured women as central characters. But we still find fewer women than men cast as talented athletes, successful executives, brilliant detectives, and skilled surgeons. More often than not, women have supporting roles as wives, assistants, and secretaries. Music videos also come in for criticism: Most performing groups are all men, and when women do appear on stage, they are often there for their sex appeal. In addition, many of today's song lyrics reinforce men's power over women.

Even among television stars, men typically earn more than women. Currently, the highest-paid actor is Ashton Kutcher, who earns $750,000 per episode in *Two and a Half Men*. The top-earning woman on television is Mariska Hargitay, earning $500,000 an episode for *Law & Order: SVU*.

What about mass media advertising? In the early years of television, advertisers targeted women during the day because so many women were at-home wives. In fact, because most of the commercials advertised laundry and household products, daytime TV dramas became known as "soap operas." On television and in newspaper and magazine advertising, even today, most ads still use female models to sell products such as clothing, cosmetics, cleaning products, and food to women and male models to pitch products such as automobiles, banking services, travel, and alcoholic beverages to men. Ads have always been more likely to show men in offices or in rugged outdoor scenes and women in the home.

Films also convey definitions of the two sexes in ways that favor men over women. As explained in the opening to this chapter, perhaps half of the most popular films today will fail the Bechdel test, which requires only that there be two named female characters who talk to each other about something other than a man. In response to this pattern the film industry in Sweden—a country in which gender inequality is widely defined as a serious problem—began in 2013 to rate films according to gender fairness (*Guardian*, 2013). In the United States, film ratings are primarily concerned with depicting sex and violence. Should gender inequality be assessed?

Finally, gender bias also exists in advertising. Sometimes the bias is obvious, as when only men are presented or the intended audience is just one sex or the other. But such bias can also be subtle. Look closely at ads and you will see that they often present men as taller than women, and women (but never men) often lie on sofas and beds or sit on the floor like children. In addition, men's facial expressions are likely to suggest competence and authority, whereas women laugh, pout, or strike childlike poses. Researchers have found that the men featured in advertising focus on the products they are promoting; women, as often as not, pay attention to men (Goffman, 1979; Cortese, 1999).

Gender and Politics

Patriarchy is about power. Because of patriarchy, women have played only a marginal role in the political history of our country. As Table 4–1 shows, the first woman to win election to the U.S. Congress joined the House of Representatives in 1917, after that body had existed for 128 years. In 1920, the country reached a political milestone with the passage of the Nineteenth Amendment to the U.S. Constitution, which permitted women to vote in national elections.

Since winning the right to vote, women have continued to move into the U.S. political mainstream. At the local level, thousands of women now serve as mayors of cities and towns and as members of other governing boards across the country. At the beginning of 2014, about 24 percent of state legislators were women (up from just 4 percent in 1970), and five of the fifty state governors were women (10 percent). National Map 4–1 on page 108 compares regions of the United States in terms of women's power in state government.

In national government, the picture is similar. At the beginning of 2014, a total of 79 of 435 members of the House of Representatives (18 percent) and 20 of 100 senators (20 percent) were women (Center for American Women and Politics, 2013).

Around the world, the pattern is much the same: Women hold just 21 percent of seats in the world's 188 parliaments. In only twenty-nine countries (about 15 percent of all countries), among them Sweden and Norway, do women make up more than one-third of the members of parliament (Inter-Parliamentary Union, 2013).

Gender and Religion

What does religion teach us about gender? When people in a national sample of U.S. adults were asked whether they tend to think of God as "Mother" or "Father," 7 percent replied they envision God more as "Mother." Two-thirds—nine times as many—favored "Father," with the remaining one-fourth imagining God equally in these terms (Smith et al., 2013).

The fact that most of us think of God as male is no surprise because societies give power and privilege to men. That's probably why all the Western religious traditions portray the divine in male terms. The Qur'an (Koran), the sacred text of Islam, clearly endorses patriarchy with these words: "Men are the protectors and maintainers of women. . . . Hence good women are devoutly obedient. . . . As for those whose rebelliousness you fear, admonish them, banish them from your bed, and scourge them" (quoted in W. Kaufman, 1976:163). Paul, perhaps the most influential leader of the early Christian church, also supported the social dominance of men over women:

> A man . . . is the image and glory of God; but woman is the glory of man. For man was not made from woman, but woman from man. Neither was man created for woman, but woman for man. (1 Corinthians 11:7–9)

> Wives, be subject to your husbands, as to the Lord. For the husband is the head of the wife as Christ is the head of the church. . . . As the church is subject to Christ, so let wives also be subject in everything to their husbands. (Ephesians 5:22–24)

Judaism also has a long history of supporting the social power of men. A daily prayer among Orthodox Jewish men includes the following words:

> Blessed art thou, O Lord our God, King of the Universe, that I was not born a gentile.

> Blessed art thou, O Lord our God, King of the Universe, that I was not born a slave.

> Blessed art thou, O Lord our God, King of the Universe, that I was not born a woman.

Table 4–1 Political "Firsts" for U.S. Women

1869	Law allows women to vote in Wyoming Territory.
1872	First woman to run for the presidency (Victoria Woodhull) represents the Equal Rights party.
1917	First woman elected to the House of Representatives (Jeannette Rankin of Montana).
1924	First women elected state governors (Nellie Taylor Ross of Wyoming and Miriam "Ma" Ferguson of Texas); both followed their husbands into office. First woman to have her name placed in nomination for the vice presidency at the convention of a major political party (Lena Jones Springs, a Democrat).
1931	First woman to serve in the Senate (Hattie Caraway of Arkansas); completed the term of her husband upon his death and won reelection in 1932.
1932	First woman appointed to the presidential Cabinet (Frances Perkins, secretary of labor in the Cabinet of President Franklin D. Roosevelt).
1964	First woman to have her name placed in nomination for the presidency at the convention of a major political party (Margaret Chase Smith, a Republican).
1972	First African American woman to have her name placed in nomination for the presidency at the convention of a major political party (Shirley Chisholm, a Democrat).
1981	First woman appointed to the U.S. Supreme Court (Sandra Day O'Connor).
1984	First woman to be successfully nominated for the vice presidency (Geraldine Ferraro, a Democrat).
1988	First woman chief executive to be elected to a consecutive third term (Madeleine Kunin, governor of Vermont).
1992	A record number of women in the Senate (six) and the House (forty-eight), as well as the first African American woman to win election to U.S. Senate (Carol Moseley-Braun of Illinois), the first state (California) to be served by two women senators (Barbara Boxer and Dianne Feinstein), and the first woman of Puerto Rican descent elected to the House (Nydia Velazquez of New York).
1996	First woman appointed secretary of state (Madeleine Albright).
2000	First former "First Lady" to win elected political office (Hillary Rodham Clinton, senator from New York).
2001	First woman to serve as national security adviser (Condoleezza Rice); first Asian American woman to serve in a presidential Cabinet (Elaine Chao, secretary of labor).
2005	First African American woman appointed secretary of state (Condoleezza Rice).
2007	First woman Speaker of the House (Nancy Pelosi).
2008	For the first time, women make up the majority of a state legislature (New Hampshire).
2013	Record number of women in the Senate (twenty) and the House (seventy-nine). Also, New Hampshire becomes the first state to have all-women leadership as the governor and all U.S. senators and members of Congress are women.
2014	First woman to head the Federal Reserve Board (Janet Yellen).

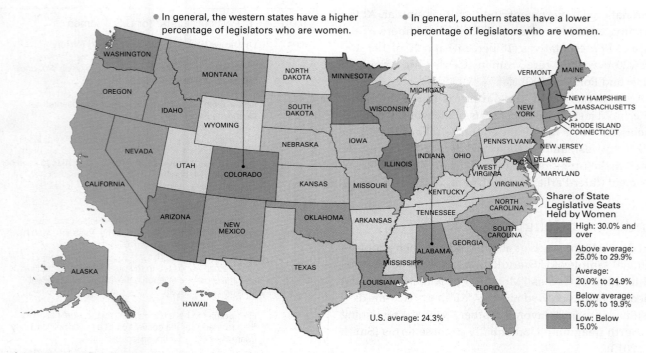

● In general, the western states have a higher percentage of legislators who are women.

● In general, southern states have a lower percentage of legislators who are women.

Share of State Legislative Seats Held by Women

High: 30.0% and over

Above average: 25.0% to 29.9%

Average: 20.0% to 24.9%

Below average: 15.0% to 19.9%

Low: Below 15.0%

U.S. average: 24.3%

Seeing Ourselves

National Map 4–1 Women's Political Power across the United States

Women represent slightly more than half of U.S. adults. Even so, women hold just 24.3 percent of seats in the state legislatures across the country. The map provides the state-by-state percentages. Looking at the map, what pattern can you detect? What factors can you think of that might account for this pattern?

SOURCE: Center for American Women and Politics, (2013).

In recent decades, more liberal denominations in the United States, including Episcopalians and Presbyterians, have moved toward greater gender equality. This liberal trend includes not only the revision of prayers, hymnals, and even the Bible to reduce sexist language but also the ordination of both women and men as priests and ministers. Not all religious organizations share in this spirit of change. Orthodox Judaism, Islam, and Roman Catholicism have retained traditional male leadership. But throughout the religious community, a lively debate surrounds the question of whether patriarchal traditions represent God's will or merely reflect patterns of the past.

Gender and the Military

Women have been part of the military since the Revolutionary War. During World War II, when the government officially opened the military to both sexes, women made up just 2 percent of the armed forces. By the Gulf War in 1991, that share had risen to almost 7 percent, and 5 of the 148 soldiers killed in that conflict were women. In the fall of 2012, women represented 15 percent of the U.S. military force in Iraq and Afghanistan. Between March 2003 and January 2014, the Iraq War claimed the lives of 110 women soldiers; another 49 died in Afghanistan. In these recent conflicts, women represent 3.6 percent of all U.S. military deaths (U.S. Department of Defense, 2014).

Today, almost all military assignments are open to women. In 2013, the Department of Defense decided that women would be permitted to engage in ground-combat operations, experience that is widely viewed as necessary to advance to top leadership in the military. But there is still resistance to expanding the role of women in the military. The traditional explanation for limiting women's opportunities is the claim that women are not as strong as men, although this argument makes much less sense in a high-technology military that depends less and less on muscle power. The real reason people oppose women in the military has to do with gender itself. Many people have difficulty with the idea of women—whom our culture defines as nurturers—being put in a position to kill and be killed.

In recent years, the nation has confronted a new problem involving women in the military—sexual assault. No one knows precisely the extent of this problem, but a survey carried out by the Pentagon concluded that about 26,000 women and men had been victims of sexual assault in 2012. Some activist organizations suggest that one in three military women may become a victim during her time of service. Officially, there were 5,061 reported cases of sexual assault in 2013. Perhaps even more disturbing is the fact that, according to official records, only 484 of these cases went to trial and 376 cases resulted in convictions. Critics of the military justice system claim that the armed forces are reluctant to pursue complaints and even more reluctant to punish offenders. Last year, one U.S. senator unsuccessfully proposed a law that would require complaints to be processed using civilian criminal courts rather than military courts. Defense Secretary Chuck Hagel sums up the matter, saying that "we have a long way to go before solving this problem" (Cooper, 2014).

The dangers women face as members of the military are not limited to armed conflict. Research suggests that as many as one in three women in the U.S. Armed Forces will experience sexual assault during her time of service.

Gender and Work

Many people still think of different kinds of jobs as either "men's work" or "women's work." A century ago in the United States, in fact, most people did not think women should work at all, at least not for pay. Back then, as the saying used to be, "a woman's place is in the home," and in 1900, just one woman in five worked for income. The most recent data, found in Figure 4–1 on page 110, show this share to be 57.7 percent, reflecting a slight decline since 2000. About 74 percent of women in today's labor force work full time. Since 1950, the share of adult men in the labor force has slowly but steadily declined (U.S. Department of Labor, 2013).

What accounts for this dramatic rise in the share of working women? Many factors are involved. At the beginning of the twentieth century, most people lived in rural areas where few people had electric power. Back then, women typically spent long hours cooking, cleaning, and raising large families. Today's typical home has a host of appliances, including washers, vacuums, and microwaves, and all this technology has dramatically reduced the time needed for housework so that women and men have more chance to work for income.

In addition, today's average woman has just two children, half the number that was typical a century ago. But that is not to say that having young children prevents today's women from working: 60 percent of married women with children under age six work, as do 70 percent of married women with children six to seventeen years old. From another angle, 52 percent of today's married couples include two partners working for income (U.S. Department of Labor, 2013).

Even though more women now work for pay, the range of jobs open to them is still limited, and our society still labels most jobs as either feminine or masculine (Bellas & Coventry, 2001; van der Lippe & van Dijk, 2002). Work that our society has defined as "masculine" involves physical danger (such as firefighting and police work), physical strength and endurance (construction work and truck driving), and leadership roles (clergy, judges, and business executives). Work defined as "feminine" includes support positions (secretarial work or medical assisting) or occupations requiring nurturing skills (child care and teaching young children). A number of jobs that are defined as feminine are performed almost entirely by women even today, as shown in Table 4–2 on page 110.

Gender discrimination was outlawed by the federal Equal Pay Act of 1963 and Title VII of the Civil Rights Act of 1964. This means that employers cannot discriminate between men and women in hiring or when setting pay. But gender inequality is deeply rooted in U.S. society; officials investigate thousands of discrimination complaints every year, and few doubt that the real number of cases of discrimination is far higher. The Social Problems in Focus box on page 111 takes a look at one well-known case.

Gender Stratification

4.3   Examine how gender stratification is found in many parts of everyday life.

As noted earlier, gender stratification is the unequal distribution of wealth, power, and privilege between men and women. Gender inequality is evident in the fact that, when compared to men, women have both less income and greater responsibility for housework. Women also contend

● In the middle of the last century, the world of paid work was mostly a world of men: More than 80% of men and only one-third of women were in the labor force.

● Working for income is now part of adult life for both men and women.

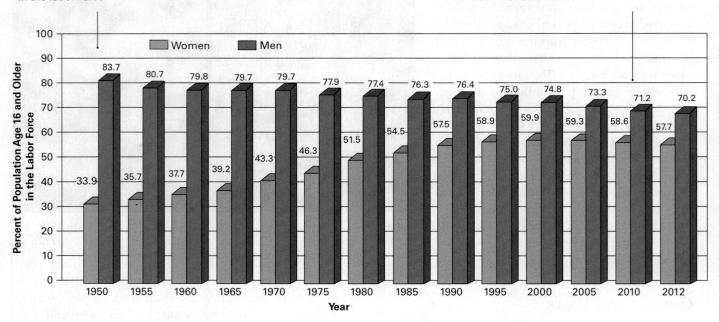

Diversity Snapshot

Figure 4–1 Women and Men in the U.S. Labor Force

Over the past half century, the share of men in the labor force has gone down (with men retiring earlier and living longer), while the share of women working for income went up rapidly, reaching a peak of about 60 percent in 2000 and declining slightly since then.

SOURCE: U.S. Department of Labor (2013).

with other disadvantages, including high risk of domestic violence and sexual harassment.

Income

Income is one important dimension of gender inequality. As you have learned, women and men perform different

Table 4–2 Gender Segregation in the Workplace: Jobs Defined as "Feminine"

Occupation	Percentage of Women in the Occupation
1. Dental hygienist	99.3%
2. Medical transcriptionist	98.2
3. Preschool or kindergarten teacher	98.1
4. Dental assistant	97.9
5. Secretary or administrative assistant	95.3
6. Speech-language pathologist	95.2
7. Licensed practical or vocational nurse	94.2
8. Child care worker	94.1
9. Occupational therapist	94.0
10. Medical assistant	93.8

SOURCE: U.S. Department of Labor (2013).

kinds of work, with women generally holding clerical and service jobs and men having most executive and professional positions. The predictable result is that women and men receive different levels of pay.

In 2012, the median pay for men working full time was $49,398; women working full time earned $37,791, or 77 percent as much. National Map 4–2 on page 112 shows that there are considerable differences among the states with regard to the female–male pay difference, but in every state men earn considerably more than women.

The gender gap in earnings means that women are more likely to be at the low end of the income scale. In 2012, 32 percent of full-time women workers earned less than $30,000, compared to 22 percent of men. The gender gap also provides advantages to men: More than twice as many men as women (16 percent versus 7 percent) earned more than $100,000 (U.S. Census Bureau, 2013).

Most women who share a household with a man depend on his earnings. For this reason, after separation, divorce, or the partner's death, a woman's income may fall dramatically. Especially if she has young children, the loss of a partner's income may cause financial hardship and raise her risk of falling into poverty.

SOCIAL PROBLEMS IN FOCUS

Sex Discrimination in the Workplace: The Hooters Controversy

Does a company have the right to hire anyone it wants to? That was the issue in 1991 when the Equal Employment Opportunity Commission (EEOC) decided to sue the Hooters restaurant chain for sex discrimination. Hooters stands apart from other restaurant chains because of its policy of hiring young, attractive women, who wait on tables while dressed in form-fitting, low-cut T-shirts and tight shorts. When men applied to work there, officials of the restaurant—dubbed a "breastaurant" by critics—pointed to this policy and turned them down.

But some of the men turned away thought the policy was unfair, and they joined with the EEOC to sue Hooters for sex discrimination. The suit pointed to Title VII of the 1964 Civil Rights Act, which bans hiring discrimination on the basis of race, color, sex, religion, or national origin. Following the letter of this law, a company cannot just hire only women any more than it could decide to hire only white people. But the law does recognize exceptions to this rule that involve what the law calls a "bona fide occupational qualification." This means that if a company can show that an applicant's sex is an important factor in doing the job that is being filled, hiring one category of people over another may be allowed.

It is easy to imagine situations where this exception makes obvious sense. A Jewish congregation looking for a new rabbi, for example, would hire a Jew and would not consider a Catholic or a Hindu. It would also hire a man if the denomination's religious doctrine permits only men to be ordained. But most cases are not this clear-cut. A department store in a largely white neighborhood cannot hire only white salespeople just because the management might think whites "fit in" better than people of color.

In a business like Hooters, is sex actually an occupational qualification? Deciding this case required the court to decide exactly what Hooters was really selling. If we define Hooters as simply a restaurant, its hiring policy would be a clear violation of the law. But Hooters claimed that customers come to their restaurants as much to see the women working as waitresses as they do to get a meal. For that reason, Hooters continued, hiring only women (and hiring only *certain* women) should be within the law.

When the case was settled in 1997, the court did not agree with the claims Hooters made—at least not entirely—and something of a compromise resulted. Because Hooters had provided employment to only one sex and excluded the other, the court found the restaurant chain guilty of sex discrimination and fined the corporation $3.75 million. But the court also found that the business of Hooters was not just food but "providing vicarious sexual recreation" to customers, which makes an applicant's sex relevant to the company's hiring. So the court ended up permitting Hooters to continue to hire attractive women as waitresses, but only if the company would create new categories of jobs—such as hosts and bartenders—that would provide employment opportunities to both men and women (Reiland, 1998; Bernstein, 2001).

What Do You Think?

1. When is a person's sex relevant to work? How would you assess whether or not a person's sex is relevant to a particular job?
2. Do you agree with the law stating that a college cannot legally refuse to hire a man to teach courses in women's studies or a woman to teach courses in men's studies? Why or why not?
3. Have you ever been the target of sex discrimination? Explain.

Three Reasons for the Gender Gap in Pay In the United States, why do men earn so much more than women? The first and biggest reason, noted earlier, is that men and women typically have different types of jobs. In general, what our society considers to be "men's work" commands higher pay (and more prestige) than "women's work."

A second reason is that everyone assigns importance to work in relation to other social roles and obligations. U.S. society assigns women most of the responsibility for raising children. Pregnancy, childbirth, and the task of raising small children effectively limit women's careers more than men's. Because women devote more of their time to the home—sometimes taking extended periods of time away from work to raise young children—men end up with more workplace seniority and career advancement. In addition, some women with young children or aging parents choose jobs, even at lower pay, that do not tie up their evenings and weekends or require them to travel far from home. Still other mothers (but rarely fathers) choose a job because it is nearby, offers a flexible schedule, or provides child care facilities. Family–work conflict is especially likely to come into play when women consider workplace leadership positions—many of which involve a workweek that may extend to sixty hours or more. When asked if they wanted to become a "boss or top manager," a larger share of young women (34 percent) than young men (22 percent) said "No, thanks" (Slaughter, 2012; Greenstone, 2013; Pew Research Center, 2013).

Women's greater family focus means that, especially during the time when they have young children, women are likely to fall behind men in their careers. Among young people just starting out in the labor force, women earn 90 percent as much as men, but the gap increases as women have children and typically step away from their jobs (Slaughter, 2012; Pew Research Center, 2013).

Nancy Willis works as a waitress in Laramie, Wyoming, earning less than $20,000 a year.

Karen Sachs works on the staff of a member of Congress, earning more than $70,000 a year.

Women's Earnings as a Percentage of Men's Earnings

	83.0% or more
	80.0% to 82.9%
	77.0% to 79.9%
	Less than 77.0%

U.S. average: 76.5%

Seeing Ourselves

National Map 4–2 The Earnings Gender Gap across the United States

Nationwide, women working full time earn about 77 percent as much as comparable men. In states with strong economies and younger populations (such as Florida and California), the gender gap is smaller; in states with weaker economies and older populations (such as West Virginia and Wyoming), the gender gap is greater. Why do you think age plays a part in this pattern?

SOURCE: U.S. Department of Labor (2013).

A similar pattern involves caring for aging parents, which, like child care, is defined as largely the responsibility of women rather than men. One study, for example, found that almost half of women in competitive jobs took time off from work to care for aging parents (Hewlett & Luce, 2005; Hewlett, 2009). Family–career conflict ends up creating an achievement gap: On the campus, for example, researchers find that young female professors with at least one child are less likely to have tenure than male professors in the same field (Shea, 2002; Ceci & Williams, 2011). This is why a recent survey found that, among people between the ages of eighteen and thirty-two, 59 percent of women but just 19 percent of men agreed with the statement that "being a working parent makes it harder to advance in a job or a career" (Pew Research Center, 2013). Taken together, these studies point to the long-term effects of family-based gender inequality: *Even if both sexes start out with exactly the same jobs,* over time women typically fall behind their male colleagues.

If women spend more time out of the labor force during important career-building years, what happens when they want to return to work? When the time comes to return to work, many women realize that simply getting back in the game is harder than they expected. The Personal Stories box takes a closer look.

The third reason for gender inequality is that women suffer from gender discrimination. This means that many employers pay women less than men simply because they can get away with it. Employment discrimination is illegal, and equal opportunity laws have reduced the blatant double standard that was common in the past. But more subtle discrimination continues, as in the case of a company in which male employees were invited to an out-of-town meeting while female employees were excluded because the company thought attending such an event might be too dangerous for a woman driving out of town at night alone (Benokraitis & Feagin, 1995:85).

The Glass Ceiling Today, when a company is looking to fill a top job, no one is likely to come right out and say, "Let's promote a man." But cultural bias against women affects many promotion decisions. Sociologists use the term **glass ceiling** to refer to *subtle discrimination that effectively blocks the movement of women into the highest positions in organizations.* According to one recent survey, just twenty-two of the Fortune 500 companies in the United States have a woman as their chief executive officer (Catalyst, 2014).

PERSONAL STORIES

After the Children: Getting Back in the Game

One major reason that women earn less than men involves society's expectation that they take on most family obligations. Consider the story of Catherine Strong, a well-educated and talented woman who had a career in banking and then took time off from work to have children (Chaker & Stout, 2004).

> Catherine Strong shifted nervously in her chair as the woman behind the large desk in front of her read through the papers in her hands. Strong remembered how she used to sit behind a big desk like that during her many years as an investment officer with several, high-profile banks in New York City. She thought about how she used to interview people seeking a promotion or eager to find a new job. That seemed a long time ago. Now it was her turn to be looking for work, and she had enlisted the help of a large search firm.
>
> The search-firm counselor completed the file, looked up, and with a serious expression, began to speak. She explained to Strong that she has a good education—a college degree from a well-known school and also an M.B.A. degree from a large university. Her résumé showing years of work for several large banks is also very impressive. But, the counselor continued, times are tight with the weak economy, and jobs are much harder to find than they once were. Even more important, she continued, is the fact that Strong has not taken home a paycheck for almost fifteen years. In the very competitive world of high finance, the odds were slim that Strong would find anything even close to the jobs she once had.

Catherine Strong is one of the millions of women who left the workforce to have children and to stay home raising them. At first, she expected to be away from work for perhaps a year. But she discovered that raising a newborn can be quite a challenge, and by the time her firstborn was two, she and her husband learned that they soon would be parents again.

Like most women, Strong does not regret the choices she made. But, also like most women, she does wish that her husband could have done more to share the parenting. She is quick to point out that once she stopped working, his paycheck was all the family had to live on, and he worked harder than ever. But she always thought that once the kids got into their teenage years, she could go back to the job she had loved. Now that dream seems to be far out of reach.

The recent recession has made job hunting hard for everyone. But women who have been out of the labor force (the polite expression is "having gaps in your résumé") have the toughest time of all. Their skills may be rusty or even completely out of date. Many women share the dismay experienced by Catherine Strong as they learn how much has changed in their field of work since the time they were last in the office. In addition, most women in this situation also learn that they have lost most of their networks and contacts.

Should companies do more to keep in touch with employees like Strong who leave to raise children? Are there other ways that companies (or society as a whole) should support women who have raised children and wish to return to work? Catherine Strong cringed when she heard her job counselor sum up her chances: "You're going to have to be realistic. You are not going to find the type of job you left fifteen years ago. You'll need to take a big step down." Does our society need to do more?

What Do You Think?

1. Should companies help women like Catherine Strong who are trying to return to work? How might they help?

2. What about fathers in all of this? Should they do more to share the work of parenting?

3. Have you or anyone you know ever been in Catherine Strong's position? If so, what happened?

Housework

Just as patriarchy gives men control of the workplace, it also assigns women most of the housework. In Japan, probably the most patriarchal of all high-income nations, women do almost all the shopping, cooking, cleaning, and child care. In the United States, where two incomes are the norm among married couples, women still do most of the housework (or pay other women to do it). A recent survey asked adults living with partners in a household who does the housework: 67 percent of women and just 10 percent of men answered "me" (Smith et al., 2013).

How much housework do men and women actually do? Figure 4–2 on page 114 shows that the answer depends on whether people are single or married and whether they work for pay or stay in the home. But looking at every one of these categories, women spend a lot more time doing housework than men—one reason that housework is sometimes called women's "second shift" (U.S. Department of Labor, 2013).

Violence against Women

Perhaps the most serious problem linked to patriarchy is men's physical violence against women. Assault, rape, and even murder are common enough that many sociologists view them as a dimension of men's domination of women.

The good news is that the rate of sexual assault fell by half between 1995 and 2005, a period during which crime rates in general fell. The sexual assault rate has remained about the same since 2005. The bad news is that the numbers are still high. The U.S. government estimates that some 2.2 million physical assaults against women take place each year, with an additional 425,000 aggravated (serious) assaults and 215,000 sexual assaults,

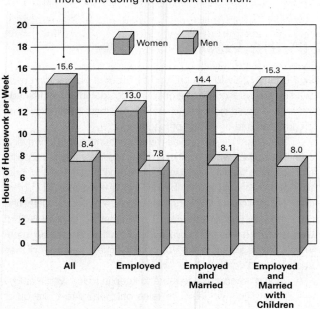

- On average, women spend considerably more time doing housework than men.

Diversity Snapshot

Figure 4–2 Gender and Housework

Regardless of employment or family status, women do more housework than men.

SOURCE: U.S. Department of Labor (2013).

including rape and attempted rape (Planty et al., 2013; U.S. Department of Justice, 2014). On campus, in any academic year, the government estimates that 3 percent of female college students were victims of rape or attempted rape. Another estimate is that, over a four- or five-year college career, about 20 percent of all women experience such a crime (National Institute of Justice, 2012).

Which categories of women are at greatest risk of sexual violence? Considering age, according to government data, women younger than thirty-five are at greatest risk. By income, poor women are at higher risk than affluent women. Finally, women in rural areas of the country are at higher risk than women living in cities and suburbs (U.S. Department of Justice, 2014).

Violence is a crime, but what makes it a gender issue? First, physical aggressiveness is part of our cultural definition of masculinity. Put simply, "real men" take control of a situation and do not allow themselves to be pushed around, one reason most violent crimes are committed by males (see Chapter 6, "Crime, Violence, and the Criminal Justice System"). Second, many people treat with contempt whatever a patriarchal society labels as "feminine" or less worthy (Goetting, 1999; Herman, 2001).

Gender violence ranges from annoying actions such as men whistling at a woman walking down a city street to unwanted physical contact such as "cornering" a

woman against a wall in a dorm hallway to outright violence such as an angry punch in a suburban home. In all cases, these assaults are not so much sexual—as is commonly thought—as they are displays of male power over women. For this reason, sexual violence is a dimension of gender stratification.

Looking over the statistics, the most dangerous setting for women turns out not to be the dark alley but the well-lit home, the very place where people are supposed to find peace and support (Smolowe, 1994; Frias & Angel, 2007).

In a number of countries, including the United States, families use violence to control the behavior of women. The Social Problems in Global Perspective box looks at the dramatic case of female genital mutilation.

Sexual Harassment

Sexual harassment refers to *unwanted comments, gestures, or physical contact of a sexual nature.* Only in the 1980s did U.S. society begin to define sexual harassment as a social problem. This issue was defined as a problem as more and more people rejected the traditional male practice of viewing women in sexual terms. Why? Because men who think of women in sexual terms ignore women's achievements and are unlikely to accept women as equals in the workplace, on the campus, or anywhere else.

Just as important, if society does not define sexual harassment as a problem, men in positions of power are free to coerce sex from women they supervise. Surveys show that about 4 percent of women claim that they have been harassed on the job in the last year and about 50 percent of women claim they have received unwanted sexual attention (Smith et al., 2013).

Sexual harassment can be blatant and direct: A professor pressures a student for sex, threatening a poor grade if she refuses. This is a clear case of *quid pro quo* sexual harassment (the Latin words mean "one thing in return for another"), which the law defines as a violation of civil rights. But sexual harassment can also involve subtle behavior—sexual teasing or off-color jokes—that someone may not even intend as harassment. Such behavior is still harmful if it has the effect of creating a *hostile environment* that prevents people from doing their work. In that case, the offender and the offended party may well interpret the behavior in question differently. For example, a man may view complimenting a co-worker on her appearance as simply a friendly gesture, but she may consider such comments intrusive and unprofessional.

Sexuality, Beauty, and Reproduction

A patriarchal culture teaches men to assess women not according to their abilities but on the basis of their sexual attractiveness. Of course, women live within this culture and they may also learn these lessons. Social norms encourage girls and women to wear figure-flattering clothing and shoes (whether or not they are comfortable or even safe) and to flirt with men and be attentive to them.

In recent years, sociologists have pointed out that beauty is not simply about looking good; it is about power and inequality. The Diversity: Race, Class, & Gender box on page 117 takes a closer look at what this means for women.

Our society has also debated who should control sexual reproduction. In the past, physicians and legislators, almost all of them men, restricted access to birth control technology. As late as the 1960s, state laws controlled even the sale of condoms and other birth control devices.

Today, however, many people are questioning older patterns: Should women have to consult a doctor to obtain birth control? Should women younger than a certain age have to obtain permission from parents? Should the government require all health insurance plans (including those of Catholic organizations, which officially oppose birth control) to provide birth control products and services to all women (Steinhauser, 2012)?

Abortion is perhaps an even more controversial practice, dividing the country along political lines. Conservatives see abortion as a moral issue and stress the need to protect unborn children. Liberals—especially feminists—see abortion as an issue of power and choice. Restricting access to abortion puts the decision about whether to continue a pregnancy in the hands of men—fathers, husbands, physicians, and legislators—rather than with the women whose bodies and lives will be affected by the decision. In the liberal view, access to birth control and safe abortion expands women's choices about their lives, including their ability to work, and helps reduce gender inequality.

Women: A Majority Minority?

Chapter 3 ("Racial and Ethnic Inequality") defined a minority as any distinctive category of people who are socially disadvantaged. Are women a minority? Numerically, women are a slight majority (about 51 percent) of the U.S. population. Even so, in a patriarchal society, women meet the test of being physically distinctive and socially disadvantaged.

Researchers have long noted that most women do not think of themselves as a minority (Hacker, 1951; Lengermann & Wallace, 1985). One explanation of this fact is that many women assess their relative privilege based on race, ethnicity, and class position. Another reason is that, although women do not have the same power as men, our society teaches women to think that they *should* defer to men, defining a husband's career or their children's happiness as more important than their own.

SOCIAL PROBLEMS IN GLOBAL PERSPECTIVE

Female Genital Mutilation: Using Violence to Control Women

In a poor home in the East African nation of Ethiopia, a little girl huddles in the corner of a small bed. Only eighteen months old, she is in pain and does not understand why.

Her suffering has been caused by a surgical clitoridectomy—sometimes incorrectly called "female circumcision"—which means the external clitoris is cut away. In its more extreme form, the clitoris is cut away entirely and the vagina is sewed almost completely shut, to be cut open again only on a woman's wedding night.

The procedure—sometimes performed by a doctor but usually carried out by a midwife or a tribal practitioner, typically without anesthesia—is common in Ethiopia, Nigeria, Togo, Somalia, Egypt, and three dozen other nations in Africa and the Middle East. More than 120 million girls worldwide have endured a clitoridectomy, now widely called "female genital mutilation" (UNICEF, 2013).

This so-called medical procedure is not about curing any illness or disorder; it is a means to control women. In highly patriarchal societies, men demand that the women they marry be virgins and that wives remain sexually faithful after that. Without the clitoris, a woman loses some or all of her ability to experience sexual pleasure. This procedure, some people believe, will make her unlikely to become sexually promiscuous or unfaithful and more likely to live by the rules of her society.

Throughout the United States, this procedure is illegal. Even so, thousands of young girls in immigrant families undergo a clitoridectomy each year. In fact, some immigrant mothers believe that this procedure is even *more* necessary once they are living in the United States, where women have far more sexual freedom.

What Do You Think?

1. How is the practice of female genital mutilation used to control the behavior of women?

2. What steps should be taken, in the United States and elsewhere, to eliminate this practice?

3. Does female genital mutilation amount to child abuse? Explain your view.

However women may feel about this matter, it is objectively the case that as a category of the population, women do have less income, wealth, and power than men. For this reason, it makes sense to define women as a minority.

Theories of Gender Inequality

4.4 **Apply sociological theory to the issue of gender inequality.**

A number of sociology's theoretical orientations—structural-functional, symbolic-interaction, social-conflict, and intersection theory—helps us understand gender inequality. As you have seen in earlier chapters, various theories highlight different facts and reach different conclusions.

Structural-Functional Analysis: Gender and Complementarity

According to functionalist theory, gender is society's recognition that women and men differ in some respects. This approach views gender in terms of *complementarity*. In other words, men and women are seen as different in limited but important ways, with each sex having somewhat different roles and responsibilities. As a result of this role differentiation, people of each sex need people of the other sex. More broadly, this mutual interdependence helps unite individuals into families and links families into larger communities. In short, gender helps tie together all of society.

Talcott Parsons: A Theory of Complementary Roles The best-known functional theory of gender was developed by Talcott Parsons (1942, 1951, 1954). To understand his ideas, it is helpful to begin with an historical look at human societies.

Among early hunters and gatherers, biological differences between the sexes had critical importance. Our distant ancestors had no way to control reproduction, so women experienced frequent pregnancies and spent much of their adult lives caring for children. As a result, women in these societies had little choice but to build their lives around the home, gathering vegetation as they raised the young. Men's greater size and strength placed them in charge of hunting and warfare, tasks that took them away from the home. Over many generations, this sex-based division of labor became *institutionalized,* meaning it became built into the culture and passed from generation to generation.

By the time of the Industrial Revolution, however, a gender-based division of labor was becoming less necessary. For one thing, societies had devised effective means

of birth control. As Chapter 7 ("Sexuality") explains, the rubber condom, invented about 1850, was a fairly reliable method of contraception. Industrial technology also reduced the importance of physical strength in the labor force, opening more jobs to women.

Parsons pointed to the historical trend by which gender differences become smaller over the course of human history and tied this pattern to another trend—that the biological facts of sex, including physical size and strength, matter less and less. Yet, Parsons suggested, modern societies still encourage some gender differences because they serve to integrate people and help them work together. Specifically, society defines the two sexes in *complementary* ways, which ensures that men and women need each other and benefit from joining together as families. In the family, women still bear the children, of course, and they take more responsibility for the household. By contrast, men do more to link the family to the larger world through their greater participation in the labor force.

To perpetuate this gender-based specialization, society guides parents to raise their boys and girls differently. Masculinity, explains Parsons, involves an *instrumental* orientation, emphasizing rationality, competition, and a focus on goals. Femininity involves an opposing *expressive* orientation: emotional responsiveness, cooperation, and concern for other people and relationships.

Young people soon learn that looking or acting too differently from society's standards of masculinity or femininity can bring sharp disapproval from others. As they grow older, boys and girls also learn that failure to display the right gender patterns may result in loss of sexual appeal. In short, society teaches men to favor women who display feminine qualities as it teaches women to favor men who are masculine. The end result is that men and women carry on the pattern of bringing different elements to a relationship and, in the process, integrating society.

EVALUATE

The structural-functional theory of gender was quite influential fifty years ago but is far less so today. Why? Because the functionalist argument that "gender differences help society to operate" strikes researchers today as supporting traditional gender roles. Many of today's sociologists interpret what Parsons called "complementary roles" as little more than male domination.

A second problem with this approach is that, by arguing that society benefits from conventional ideas about gender, structural-functional theory ignores the fact that men and women can and do relate to one another in a variety of ways that do not fit any norm. Is it reasonable—or desirable—to want everyone to fit into either the "instrumental" or "expressive" category? Today, for example, most people—including both men and women—have "instrumental" roles in the labor force and expressive roles within their relationships.

A third problem cited by critics is that functional thinking glosses over personal strains and social conflicts produced

DIVERSITY: RACE, CLASS, & GENDER
Beauty: What's It Really About?

Beauty is about good looks—what could be more obvious? But beauty is also about gender and power.

Naomi Wolf (1990) claims that our culture's ideas about beauty put men in a position of power over women. Women, she says, learn to measure their personal importance in terms of their physical appearance, a practice that discourages other avenues of personal development. Furthermore, the standards by which society encourages women to judge themselves are those created by the multimillion-dollar fashion, cosmetics, and diet industries. These standards (in the form of the *Playboy* "playmate" or the 100-pound New York fashion model) have little to do with the reality of most women's bodies or lives.

In addition, a focus on beauty teaches women to try to please men. The pursuit of beauty makes women highly sensitive to how men react to them and encourages them to view other women not as allies but as competitors.

Taken together, our cultural ideas about beauty amount to an effective strategy to maintain patriarchy. Much advertising directed at women on television and in magazines and newspapers is not simply about what women should buy and use. Rather, it is about what women *should be*. This cultural "beauty myth," Wolf charges, is a form of gender bias that is harmful to women.

What Do You Think?

1. The Duchess of Windsor once said, "A woman cannot be too rich or too thin." Does this advice apply in the same way to men? Why or why not?

2. Chapter 9 ("Physical and Mental Health") explains that almost all people suffering from eating disorders are women. Why do you think this is the case?

3. After reading this box, would you encourage or discourage your own daughter from thinking about beauty in conventional terms? Why?

---

by rigid gender patterns. They argue that in everyday life, we may experience gender as both helpful and harmful. How people actually experience gender in their lives brings us to symbolic-interaction theory.

CHECK YOUR LEARNING Explain how Parsons explains gender in terms of complementarity. How does this pattern help society to operate?

Symbolic-Interaction Analysis: Gender in Everyday Life

Symbolic-interaction theory provides a micro-level analysis of gender, which highlights how individuals experience gender in their everyday lives.

Gender and Personal Behavior How do people experience gender in everyday life? As we have seen, gender involves differences in power. The more power people have the more choices they have about how to behave. In general, then, our society gives men greater freedom in personal behavior. For example, would you react the same way to a man who uses foul language as you would to a woman who speaks the same way? Similarly, researchers have documented that, in everyday conversation, men have a tendency to interrupt others and especially women; women, by contrast, are more likely to listen politely, especially to men (Smith-Lovin & Brody, 1989; Henley, Hamilton, & Thorne, 1992; C. Johnson, 1994).

The same gender pattern is evident in facial expression. In addition to symbolizing pleasure, smiling expresses respect and a desire to make peace. Not surprisingly, then, researchers note that women tend to smile more than men (Henley, Hamilton, & Thorne, 1992).

Gender and the Use of Space Typically, people with more power also use more space in their everyday activities. In the classroom, for example, the professor can pace around the room while speaking, but students are expected to stay in their seats. Because men have greater social power, they typically use more space than women, whether the men are speaking in front of a group at work or relaxing on the sidelines at a sporting event. We learn to judge masculinity by how much space a man uses (the standard of "turf" by which "more is better"), and we learn to judge femininity by how little space a woman uses (the standard of "daintiness" by which "small is beautiful").

In addition, men's greater power gives them the option of moving closer to others, even to the point of breaking into what we consider people's "personal space." Women have to be more careful in this regard because "moving in on a man" is likely to be treated as a sexual come-on (Henley, Hamilton, & Thorne, 1992).

Gender and Language Finally, gender is at work in the language we use. When talking about proud possessions, many men use female pronouns, as when a young man shows off his new car, saying, "Isn't *she* a beauty?" Using a male pronoun in this case ("Isn't *he* a beauty?") seems awkward; this pattern reflects the fact that in a patriarchal culture, men control women, not the other way around.

People's names show the same pattern. Among opposite-sex newlyweds, the conventional practice is for the woman to take her husband's last name. The opposite pattern—a man taking his wife's last name—is extremely rare. Although few people today would claim that this pattern means that the man actually owns the woman, it does suggest that men expect to have control over their wives.

Finally, notice how the English language tends to give what is masculine more value than what is feminine. Traditional titles associated with men—such as *king* and *lord*—have positive meanings, but comparable titles associated with women—such as *queen, madam,* and *dame*—are often negative.

EVALUATE

The strength of symbolic-interaction theory lies in putting a human face on gender, showing how gender is at work in familiar dimensions of everyday life. This approach also shows that gender is an important building block of social reality.

At the same time, a limitation of this theory (and of all other microtheories) is that it overlooks the broad importance of gender as a structure of society. We now turn to social-conflict theory to examine broad issues of gender inequality and gender conflict.

CHECK YOUR LEARNING   Point to ways in which gender guides patterns of everyday interaction, including the ranges of choices available to people, use of space, and use of language.

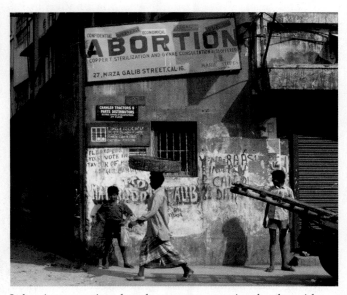

In low-income nations, boys have more economic value than girls because they can earn more money. Therefore, many poor families engage in sex-selective abortion to avoid giving birth to a daughter. In villages in India, clinics provide sonograms that usually reveal the sex of a fetus; they also provide abortions to women who choose to "try again" in the hopes of having a son.

Social-Conflict Analysis: Gender and Inequality

Social-conflict theory switches the focus from functionalism's horizontal imagery of gender differences as complementary to a more vertical view of gender as a dimension of social inequality. Rather than promoting social integration, conflict theory argues, gender generates conflict between male "haves" and female "have-nots."

Friedrich Engels: The Rise of Patriarchy   Friedrich Engels (1820–1895), Karl Marx's lifelong friend and collaborator, extended Marx's thinking about class conflict to include gender (Engels, 1902, orig. 1884). Engels argued that the same historical process that brings about a ruling class in which an elite dominates workers places men in a dominant position over women.

Early hunting and gathering societies assigned women and men different daily routines, but both sexes made vital contributions to daily life. That is, men may have done the hunting, but women collected the vegetation that provided most of the food. Therefore, just as these technologically simple societies lack distinct classes, they come close to gender equality.

Gaining the ability to raise animals and crops provided societies with a surplus—more than people needed just to survive. Typically, some families gained most of this surplus for themselves, and as this happened, social classes were born. Once some people had more than others, elites developed the idea of private property as a strategy to claim control over what they had. This same process of emerging hierarchy also led men to begin controlling the lives of women. Why? Because men who wish to pass on their wealth to their sons must both be confident in their claim to ownership of property and they also must be sure who their offspring are. Therefore, wealthy men devised the family as a way to control both property and to control the sexuality of women, who were to remain faithful and raise a man's children.

With the rise of capitalism, Engels continued, patriarchy became stronger than ever, taking the form of a male-dominated capitalist class. In short, men enjoy most wealth and power. In addition, to ensure an ever-expanding market for capitalist production, society teaches women that personal happiness lies in marriage and a domestic life as a consumer of products and services. Finally, because capitalism forced most men to work long hours in factories, men expected their wives to do all the housework. To Engels, the double problem of capitalism lies in exploiting men in factories for low pay and exploiting women in the home for no pay at all (K. Barry, 1983; Jagger, 1983; L. Vogel, 1983).

APPLYING THEORY

Gender Inequality

	Structural-Functional Theory	Symbolic-Interaction Theory	Social-Conflict Theory
What is the level of analysis?	Macro-level	Micro-level	Macro-level
What is gender?	As explained by Parsons, gender involves complementary patterns of thought and action on the part of women and men that help tie society together.	Gender is a system of meaning that shapes the everyday lives of women and men; how we interact with others, how we make use of space, and even our language all reflect gender.	Gender is a dimension of social stratification that benefits men at the expense of women. Engels explained that patriarchy arose to enable wealthy men to pass property on to their sons and to help all men work outside the home.
Is gender a problem?	Gender is not a problem; it is functional because it is helpful to the orderly operation of society.	From an individual point of view, gender may or may not be a problem; gender is a basic element of the social reality we experience every day.	Gender is a problem, especially for the half of the population that are women because they are disadvantaged by a system that gives wealth and power to men. As intersection theory explains, some categories of women experience especially great disadvantages.

EVALUATE

Social-conflict theory shows how gender developed into a major dimension of social stratification. Engels's work also highlights the close link between gender and class.

But Engels's theory has its critics. First, families may be patriarchal, but they perform the vital task of raising children. Second, the lives of men and women may be different, but not everyone defines these differences as unjust. In other words, say critics, social-conflict theory is likely to minimize the extent to which women and men live together cooperatively and, often enough, quite happily. Third, some challenge Engels's assertion that capitalism is at the heart of gender stratification. After all, patriarchy is also strong in socialist nations, including Cuba and the People's Republic of China.

CHECK YOUR LEARNING According to Friedrich Engels, how does patriarchy arise along with class differences as a system that allows wealthy men to pass property to their sons?

Intersection Theory: The Case of Minority Women

In recent decades, social-conflict theory has linked gender inequality to inequality based on race and ethnicity. **Intersection theory** is *analysis of how race, class, and gender interact, often creating multiple disadvantages for some categories of people.*

If women are disadvantaged and, as Chapter 3 ("Racial and Ethnic Inequality") explained, racial and ethnic minorities are also disadvantaged, what about minority women? Are they doubly disadvantaged? Intersection theory claims that the answer is yes.

To see how, consider data dealing with average income for various categories of the U.S. population. In 2012, the median income for non-Hispanic white women working full time was $41,184. But African American women earned $34,265, or 83 percent as much, and Hispanic women earned $28,981, or 70 percent as much. Among women, then, race and ethnicity are one source of disadvantage.

Then there is the second disadvantage based on gender. Within racial and ethnic categories, we see that in 2012, African American women earned 89 percent as much as African American men, just as Hispanic women earned 89 percent as much as Hispanic men.

Combining these two dimensions of inequality, African American women earned 64 percent as much as non-Hispanic white men and Hispanic women earned 54 percent as much as white men (U.S. Census Bureau, 2013). Therefore, the intersection of gender with race and ethnicity does result in even greater disadvantages for some categories of the U.S. population.

EVALUATE

Intersection theory is an important new social-conflict theory that warrants discussion on its own. By using income data, it is easy to see that dimensions of inequality combine so that specific categories of the U.S. population experience particular disadvantage.

At the same time, as Karl Marx might have said, *knowing* about a problem is all well and good. The point, however, is to change society to *reduce inequality*. This desire for change brings us to feminism, a study of gender with the purpose of bringing about change.

CHECK YOUR LEARNING What is intersection theory? How does it help us to understand the effect of various dimensions of social inequality? The Applying Theory table summarizes what each theoretical approach teaches us about gender.

Feminism

4.5 **Identify the foundations of feminism and distinguish three types of feminism.**

Since the 1960s, feminism has gained great importance in sociology. Formally defined, **feminism** is *a political movement that seeks the social equality of women and men.* Feminism therefore involves both theory and action.

The history of feminism in the United States goes back more than 150 years. The movement's first wave began in the 1840s as a spinoff of efforts to abolish slavery. Back then, Lucretia Mott (1793–1880) and Elizabeth Cady Stanton (1815–1902) saw parallels between whites oppressing people of color and men oppressing women. The Defining Moment box takes a closer look.

Feminist Foundations

There is more than one version of feminism. But almost all feminists agree on the following six general points:

1. **The importance of gender.** The lives of everyone, feminists claim, are shaped by gender. Men don't just

A woman enjoys the experience of sitting in a new convertible at an auto show in Jeddah, Saudi Arabia. She is able to buy the car, but will she be able to drive it on Saudi streets? In this patriarchal country, women face arrest and prosecution for driving.

choose to be competitive any more than women decide to be deferential; this kind of behavior has much to do with how our society defines masculine and feminine behavior.

2. **The importance of equality.** Feminists oppose the status quo in which U.S. society gives men both power and privilege. Therefore, feminism is an effort both to understand and to change the social world.

Feminists claim that everyone—women and men—would benefit from greater gender equality. Obviously, patriarchy limits the development and opportunities of women, who make up half the population. But men also suffer from a system that drives them to seek control of others, a pattern that results in high risk of death from suicide, violence, accidents, heart attacks, and other diseases related to stress. To a large degree, what psychologists call the *Type A personality* marked by impatience, driving ambition, and competitiveness—all of which increase the risk of heart disease—is the same behavior our culture defines as masculine (Ehrenreich, 1983).

3. **The importance of choice.** Feminists see gender as a societal creation that imposes a narrow set of opportunities on both women and men. Only by abandoning conventional ideas about the kinds of lives women and men "ought" to lead will all people be free to decide for themselves the direction of their own lives.

4. **The importance of sexual freedom.** Feminists claim that women have the right to control their sexuality and reproduction. Feminists support the wide availability of birth control information and technology and oppose legal restrictions on abortion. Many feminists also support the gay rights movement. As some feminists see it, lesbians, even more than gay men, are targets of prejudice and discrimination because they violate both the norm of heterosexuality and the expectation that men should control the sexuality of women (Hadley, 1996; Jackson & Scott, 1996; Herman, 2001; Armstrong, 2002).

5. **Activism against patriarchy.** Feminism actively opposes all forms of sexism and gender inequality. One important step in this process, as feminists see it, is for U.S. society to affirm the equal standing of women and men before the law. This is why, since its introduction in Congress in 1923, feminists have supported passage of the Equal Rights Amendment (ERA) to the U.S. Constitution. The ERA simply states, "Equality of rights under the law shall not be denied or abridged by the United States or any State on account of sex."

6. **Activism against gender violence.** As noted earlier in this chapter, many sociologists see violence against

women as a pressing social problem. Feminists claim that violence against women in the form of rape, sexual harassment, and domestic abuse can end only when society places women and men on the same level.

Types of Feminism

All feminists agree on the general goals just noted, but they favor various paths to achieving them. Generally speaking, there are three feminist solutions to the problem of patriarchy: liberal feminism, socialist feminism, and radical feminism (Jagger, 1983; A. Phillips, 1987; Lindsay, 1994 ; Armstrong, 2002; E. B. Freedman, 2002).

Liberal Feminism *Liberal feminism* seeks a society in which all people are treated as individuals so that both women and men can freely develop their talents and pursue their interests. Liberal feminism is a reform approach, meaning that it seeks change within existing social institutions. The goal of liberal feminism is for women to enjoy the same rights, opportunities, and rewards as men.

Passage of the Equal Rights Amendment is one objective. In addition, liberal feminists support laws to combat prejudice and discrimination against women. They also endorse policies such as providing birth control services as part of all health care, maternity leave for women workers, and child care facilities in the workplace so that women caring for young children can still hold a job.

Finally, liberal feminists do not expect that all women will have the same social standing. Individual talent and effort will always elevate some people above others. The liberal feminist position is that society should place no barriers in people's way simply because they are women or men. In short, all people should have opportunity based on their talent and effort and should be treated as individuals.

CONSTRUCTING SOCIAL PROBLEMS
A DEFINING MOMENT
Elizabeth Cady Stanton: Claiming Women's Right to Equality

It may be hard to imagine, but just a few generations ago, women in the United States were legally second-class citizens. Women could not vote and could not own property or enter into legal contracts. It was rare for women to earn an income, and the few women who did typically turned the money over to their husbands or fathers.

Many people who joined together to oppose the enslavement of African Americans by white people soon began to wonder if women were the slaves of men. Elizabeth Cady Stanton understood the second-class standing of women and decided to do something about it. In 1848, Stanton and her friend Lucretia Mott began the process of change by organizing a meeting in Seneca Falls, New York.

Some 300 women gathered at Wesleyan Chapel in the small town in upstate New York to hear more about "women's rights." Stanton led the meeting, asking why women did not have the same rights and opportunities as men, including the right to vote. Even many of those who thought women deserved something more were shocked by the suggestion that women's political voice should be equal to men's. Stanton's husband, Henry, muttering that, this time, his wife had gone too far, rode out of town in protest.

Stanton lived for another half century after her historic meeting without seeing her dream of women's equality come true. But she helped start a social movement that did make a difference. In 1920—eighteen years after Stanton's death—women did finally gain the right to vote. Of course, even after this victory,

many people realized that much work remained to be done. After all, the sexes remained unequal in so many other ways. As a result, a "second wave" of the feminist movement continues to this day, addressing issues such as equality in the workplace, domestic violence, and reproductive rights.

Here we see the beginnings of the feminist movement in the United States: Elizabeth Cady Stanton speaks to people who traveled great distances to attend the first women's rights convention in Seneca Falls, New York, in June 1848.

Socialist Feminism Further to the political left, other feminists doubt that reforming existing social institutions is enough to end patriarchy. Supporters of *socialist feminism* claim that Marxist class revolution is needed to secure equality not just for women but for all people. Recall from our earlier discussion that Friedrich Engels pointed to the roots of patriarchy in capitalist private property. That is, capitalism oppresses women by forcing them to do housework (which Engels called "domestic slavery") and to hold low-wage jobs. Without the ability to earn enough to support themselves, women are dependent on men for economic security.

From a socialist perspective, abolishing the capitalist class system means transforming economic production from private property to a collective enterprise. This process also means replacing the private household with collective living arrangements in which people come together to share tasks such as cooking and child care. If work were shared in this way, not only would there be no classes, but also men would no longer dominate women.

In short, socialist feminism sees class revolution as necessary for gender revolution. So, while liberal feminism accepts the basic institutions of U.S. society, socialist feminism does not. From this point of view, women's liberation can be achieved only through elimination of the broader economic conditions that have historically oppressed all humanity.

Radical Feminism A third strategy on the political left calls for the most basic change of all. *Radical feminism* argues that patriarchy is built into the concept of gender itself, and so nothing short of ending the distinction between female and male will bring about equality.

Why? Radical feminists begin with what may seem to be a surprising assertion: The roots of gender are the biological differences that allow women to bear children. In other words, the main reason that women have always been unequal to men is *motherhood*. From this point of view, the family is not so much an economic relationship (as Engels and socialist feminists claim) as it is a form of institutionalized heterosexuality that limits women's lives by demanding that they bear and raise children, which places women in the home.

But if the problem of patriarchy is rooted in human biology, what hope is there for change? Until recently, radical feminists explain, there was no hope at all, because societies had little control over reproduction. But that is no longer the case. With today's scientific technology, we have far more control over reproduction, so that people are able to reproduce outside of the conventional pattern of heterosexual parenting. For example, *in vitro* ("in glass") *fertilization*—surgically extracting a woman's ovum, fertilizing it manually in a glass dish, and then reinserting it into her body—has been a reality for decades, and the thousands of normal, healthy children produced in this way demonstrate that neither heterosexuality nor the traditional family is necessary to reproduce the human species (a more complete discussion of new reproductive technologies is found in Chapter 12, "Family Life").

The future imagined by radical feminism is more revolutionary than that imagined by socialists. Here we consider abolishing not only the traditional family but also all differences between women and men and perhaps even ending heterosexual relationships entirely.

Could this ever happen? If it did, social institutions would be very different from those we know today. The economy and political systems would have to evolve toward social equality. Families would take a new form, with collective responsibility for raising children. Some observers have suggested that, in order to limit the extent to which the lives of adults are defined by the task of parenting, children must gain greater rights and responsibilities for themselves (Jagger, 1983). Others, who see heterosexuality as part of the problem, claim that equality for women and men would require new thinking about sexuality itself. Andrea Dworkin (1987), for example, argued that an equal society would be one that gave up all sexual norms, including those that currently discourage masturbation, homosexuality, and sex outside marriage.

In the end, we can only imagine what a gender-free society would be like. But for many feminists, that is exactly the point. Whether or not one agrees with this view, radical feminism helps us see how deeply gender is woven into all aspects of our everyday lives.

Multicultural and Global Feminism In recent years, feminism has developed further to take account of the diversity of women around the world. Multicultural and global feminism asks that we recognize the common subordination of all women but also acknowledge the social differences among women within U.S. society and also the cultural differences among women throughout the world (Collins, 2000; hooks, 2000; Tong, 2009).

Multicultural feminism is informed by insights gained from intersection theory, described earlier in this chapter. Women share the common experience of oppression in relation to men, but women also have various racial and ethnic identities, just as they have differing class positions. It is important for feminism to recognize that social stratification involves various combinations of gender, race, ethnicity, and class that interact with one another.

Global feminism adds still another dimension of difference: Women live throughout the world in nations separated by a system of global stratification. Women living within the United States, for example, experience subordination to men but also enjoy the privileges provided by living in a high-income nation. The life chances and everyday experiences of women living in low-income nations of the world, by contrast, are shaped by both gender inequality and a disadvantaged position in the global economic system.

Feminism has always had an uneasy relationship to motherhood because, historically, bearing and raising children has been a barrier to social equality for women. Liberal feminists claim women should have children by choice. For socialist feminists, women may bear children by choice but societies should provide for collective child care. Radical feminists seek even greater change, exploring ways that technology can be used to replace conventional reproduction in the process of eliminating the concept of gender.

EVALUATE

Because feminism has become a powerful social movement throughout the United States, it is a major force in sociology. The contributions of feminism lie in showing how gender affects almost every aspect of our lives and also in bringing about change toward greater equality of women and men. The more recent development of multicultural feminism and global feminism also helps us appreciate not only the experiences common to all women but also the extensive diversity of women in the United States and around the world.

Like any successful social movement, feminism is controversial. Some critics claim that feminists focus too much attention on ways in which women remain unequal to men, ignoring the enormous progress women have made and the many opportunities they now enjoy (Sommers, 2003). Certainly, some men oppose feminism because this movement wants to take away their power and privileges. But there are also men—and women, too—who reject the idea that all differences between the sexes are unjust and oppressive. Some critics claim that differences between men and women, whether biological or cultural, provide useful ways to organize social life (this was the view, noted earlier, of Talcott Parsons). Others suggest that even though women can earn income, their choice to

remain at home makes a crucial contribution to the well-being of their children. Still others argue that feminism has wrongly sought to deny any differences between women and men; by contrast, we need to recognize the special strengths of women and build on them (Popenoe, 1993a; Ehrenreich, 1999; Slaughter, 2012).

CHECK YOUR LEARNING What assertions serve as the foundations of feminism? How does liberal feminism differ from socialist feminism and radical feminism? What contributions are made by multicultural feminism and global feminism?

In the end, of course, the view one takes of feminism—or of any issue related to gender—is a matter of values and politics. We now explore how politics shapes what people define as the social problems and solutions related to gender.

⭐ POLITICS AND GENDER

Constructing Problems and Defining Solutions

4.6 Analyze gender inequality from various positions on the political spectrum.

According to the Declaration of Independence, "All men are created equal." If we take this statement to mean that all *people* should be equal, we would have to define gender inequality as a problem. However, most historians claim that our founding fathers did not intend to include women in this statement. Remember that, at the time, all of our country's political leaders were men, and women had no political voice. But the issue of gender inequality has sparked controversy ever since, and people's views of this issue vary according to their political positions.

The Left to Right table on page 124 summarizes what we learn by applying the three political perspectives to the issue of gender inequality.

Conservatives: The Value of Families

Although many conservatives are cautious about change in gender roles, many accept and support the wider social role of today's women. Most conservatives realize that today's families depend on the income of both wives and husbands, and many applaud the fact that an increasing number of leaders in both the Democratic and Republican parties are women.

But many conservatives see the historical trend toward gender equality as causing a problem to the extent that it weakens the family. In this view, many conservatives agree with Talcott Parsons, whose structural-functional theory described gender as complementary roles that encourage men and women to depend on each other and to join together as they share a household. After the 1960s, as women entered college and the labor force in record numbers, the divorce rate went up, more people began living

LEFT TO RIGHT

The Politics of Gender Inequality

	Radical-Left View	Liberal View	Conservative View
What is the problem?	Serious gender inequality is built into not only the institutions of U.S. society but also the biological task of childbearing.	Although U.S. society has made strides toward greater equality for women and men, women still have lower social standing.	The trend toward gender equality has boosted incomes but has weakened families and reduced the importance of parenting in people's eyes.
What is the solution?	There must be fundamental change in economic, political, and family institutions in order to eliminate gender inequality. Some suggest that reproduction, too, must change to liberate women from childbearing.	Government programs (including passing the ERA) can combat prejudice and discrimination; affirmative action will open more doors to women; a comparable worth policy would reduce income differences between women and men.	Cultural values should encourage people to strengthen their commitment to marriage partners and children.

JOIN THE DEBATE

1. Can you identify areas on which the three political perspectives agree? What are they?

2. Do you think that a century from now, gender inequality will be greater, about the same, or less than it is now? Why?

3. Which of the three political analyses of gender inequality included here do you find most convincing? Explain.

---

alone, and a rising share of children were born to unwed parents (see Chapter 12, "Family Life").

A second important issue for conservatives involves child care. Now that most mothers have joined fathers in the workplace, who's minding the kids? Evidence suggests that today's children are getting less—some people say much too little—attention from adults. In an age of two-career couples, home life is often the interaction of weary men and women with little time and energy left for their children. No one doubts that most parents do the best they can to raise their daughters and sons, but conservatives see in the popular statement that people should share a little "quality time" with the kids an apology for fathers and mothers who do too little parenting. This retreat from parenting may be why, after 1960, important measures of well-being among children—including rates of poverty, arrest, and even suicide—trended up (Popenoe, 1993a; Blankenhorn, 1995; U.S. Census Bureau, 2013).

Although most conservatives support women in the workplace and also are willing to vote for women running for positions of national leadership, most conservatives would also like to see government policies that would strengthen traditional families. Sometimes what that means, according to conservatives, is government should not do for people what they and family members ought to do for themselves. Conservatives typically support policies, such as tax benefits that encourage people to marry,

that will raise the importance of families in our national life. In addition, conservatives encourage all women and men to make their parents, partners, and children the highest priority. In sum, conservatives claim that the choices people make about how to live should be guided by what is best for the entire family.

Liberals: The Pursuit of Equality

Liberals point out that at the time of the Declaration of Independence, the U.S. political system did not even define women (or African Americans and many other minorities) as full human beings. In a 2006 speech, Barack Obama (who was then a U.S. senator) reported meeting a 105-year-old African American woman who was born before women had the right to vote, which was also a time when people of color never expected to see one of their own in the U.S. Senate, never mind as president of the United States. Liberals speak out in favor of the slow but steady progress this country has made to expand the rights and opportunities available to women and to other minorities.

But liberals claim that, in this effort, there is still much work to do. As this chapter has shown, in the United States, most low-income jobs in this country are filled by women. In addition, almost ninety years after gaining the right to vote, only a small share of our national political leaders are women—19 percent of House and Senate members at the beginning of 2014. Looking at such numbers, liberals conclude that patriarchy is alive and well in the United States and gender inequality remains a serious social problem.

Liberals disagree with the conservative claim that the trend toward gender equality has weakened families. First, as liberals see it, conservatives have a nostalgic—and distorted—view of some "golden age" of family life built around visions drawn from the 1950s. Although television shows such as *Leave It to Beaver* celebrated the stay-at-home moms of that era, should we conclude that most women wanted to live that way? Furthermore, liberals view changes in families over recent decades not as families "in decline" but reflecting the reality that most families *need* two working adults to make ends meet (Stacey, 1990).

Liberals claim that theirs is the true "pro-family" position because they seek government support for the kinds of families that actually exist today. One pressing need is affordable child care. Liberals support the expansion of child care programs by both employers and government so that women can have the same career opportunities as men. Similarly, liberals supported the Affordable Care Act and other efforts to expand health care coverage to all people as a strategy to benefit families.

Second, liberals believe that, just as more women have entered the labor force, men must take greater responsibility for managing the home and caring for children. Liberals respond to conservative claims that working women neglect their children by suggesting that working men do more parenting—and also perform their fair share of housework.

Third, liberals place a high priority on policies that will raise the earning power of women. As they see it, raising the minimum wage and enforcing laws to eliminate workplace discrimination against women are both part of the solution. In addition, liberals support affirmative action (see Chapter 3, "Racial and Ethnic Inequality") as an effective strategy to increase the presence of women in workplace settings, such as executive positions, that have excluded them in the past.

In addition, the U.S. economy has long provided lower pay for some jobs simply because they are performed mostly by women. For example, laundry workers who wash clothes (typically women) are paid less than the laundry truck drivers (mostly men) who transport the laundry, showing that our culture attaches less value to "women's work" than to "men's work" even when both types of work require about the same level of schooling, skill, and effort.

To counter this form of institutionalized discrimination, some liberals support a policy of *comparable worth*, by which women and men would receive the same pay not just for doing the same work but also for doing different work that

has the same value. In other words, supporters of a comparable worth policy claim that it is possible to measure the worth of different jobs in objective terms, and they note that women currently earn about 25 percent less than men for work of equal value. Although courts have debated this policy, the United States—unlike Great Britain and Australia—has no comparable worth laws (England, 1992; Huffman, Velasco, & Bielby, 1996; England, Hermsen, & Cotter, 2000).

Liberals claim that all these efforts at increasing gender equality have the support of a majority of U.S. adults. Indeed, survey data show that most U.S. adults are committed, in principle, to equal rights for women and men (Smith et al., 2013).

The Radical Left: Change the System

Most people who support feminism identify with its liberal form, seeking greater gender equality within the bounds of our current social institutions. But others believe more basic change is needed to move U.S. society toward gender equality.

For some people, the target of basic change is the family. For example, Judith Stacey (1990: 269–70) states, "'The family' is *not* 'here to stay.' Nor should we wish it were. On the contrary, I believe that all democratic people, whatever their kinship preferences, should work to hasten its demise." The reason, Stacey explains, is that families perpetuate traditional forms of inequality based on class, race, and gender.

Conservatives argue that strong families and effective parenting depend on at least one parent spending much of the day in the home with young children. Liberals counter that most women want the chance to pursue careers just as men do. In your opinion, how should men and women share the responsibilities of work and parenting?

Most left-radicals, however, target the current economic and political systems. The socialist feminist solution to gender inequality, described earlier, seeks to transform the capitalist economy into a socialist system. This transformation would end the trend toward economic inequality and even eradicate class distinctions. At the same time, by encouraging people to perform domestic work collectively, men and women would become more equal and patriarchy would collapse.

Radical feminism offers the even more far-reaching vision of the elimination of gender itself. From this point of view, complete equality between women and men depends on liberating women from their historical task of childbearing and nurturing children. New reproductive technology makes such a vision theoretically possible.

Going On from Here

Imagine a woman living in the United States back in 1850—when the feminist movement was just beginning—stepping into a time machine and suddenly being transported forward in time to our society today. No doubt, she would be startled to learn that most women now work for pay, that women not only vote (at a slightly higher rate than men) but also hold elected office, and that women actually outnumber men on the nation's college campuses.

Our visitor from the past, knowing nothing about electricity, would expect most women to spend all day doing housework by hand. She would recall an average woman having about five children, a far cry from the one or two common now. She would be amazed to learn about birth control technology and would be pleased to learn that, in the United States today, very few women die in childbirth, which was a common occurrence in her day. In fact,

women are taller, healthier, and live decades longer than in the past, and women actually outlive men.

In light of such changes, perhaps our visitor from the past would be surprised to find that the social standing of women is still controversial. One reason that gender continues to be a matter of controversy is that our expectations have changed. Almost no one today accepts the centuries-old belief that women should remain in the home. Yet in many important ways, women are still unequal to men.

Where are we likely to be 150 years from now? Will the controversies surrounding gender inequality continue? Almost certainly, the answer is yes. The gender gap in pay has remained much the same for decades. It continues partly because many people continue to assume that men and women should do different types of work. In addition, many people think that family responsibilities fall more to women than to men. Given that such beliefs remain with us, it seems likely that, for the foreseeable future, women will not do exactly the same work as men, earn just as much as men, or share domestic chores equally with men. Keep in mind that the goal of gender equality has not yet been realized anywhere in the world.

At the same time, the worldwide trend is unmistakable and probably unstoppable. Women are moving closer to equality with men, and all indications are that the trend will continue.

Essay: Envisioning a Better Society Looking ahead fifty years, what changes involving gender inequality do you expect? Compared to men, what do you think will be women's place in the labor force? What about in higher education? With regard to doing housework? What specific changes involving gender do you feel would improve U.S. society?

CHAPTER 4 Gender Inequality

Is gender inequality in college athletics a problem?
If so, what is the solution?

Men have a dominant position in athletics at colleges and universities, just as they do in professional sports. Back in 1972, Title IX of the Civil Rights Act tried to eliminate gender inequality in college athletics by mandating equal opportunity for both sexes in sports programs. But almost forty years later, gender equality seems a distant goal—if it is a goal at all. Look at the accompanying photos, which show the reality of inequality and suggest ways to define a solution.

When the University of Alabama's football team takes to the field, the event can draw more than 100,000 spectators. If you are more conservative, you probably think people should freely attend the events they wish, and if men's sports generate more interest and revenue, so be it. But how do you square this view with the demands of Title IX?

Here, two Division I women's basketball teams face off in a mostly empty arena. If you are more liberal, this is clear evidence of the heart of the problem—men get the attention (and their sports get the money) and women are left to be cheerleaders or to play in front of small crowds. Title IX may be a good start, but more needs to be done. What additional steps would you suggest as a solution to this gender inequality?

Hint: Across the country, an undisputed fact is that the biggest crowds are drawn to male athletics, especially football and basketball. These are also the sports that earn the most revenues and pay the highest salaries to coaches. For example, the Alabama football program earned more than $80 million in 2012, and the head football coach earns more than $5 million a year. The more to the left you are, the more you would support government regulation that would make athletic opportunities the same for women and men. The more to the right you are, the greater your support for allowing the market, that is, people themselves, to decide what sports they wish to spend money to see; you would also point out that allowing universities to make tens of millions of dollars from men's basketball and football provides money to pay for other "nonrevenue" sports, both women's and men's.

Getting Involved: Applications and Exercises

1. Walk around your campus with an eye toward gender. Identify spaces (buildings, rooms, activities) that are dominated by men or women. Which are the men's and women's spaces? Which sex controls more space?

2. Visit a magazine rack in your local bookstore or supermarket. Examine popular magazines aimed at women. What images are on the covers? What topics—stories, features, and photographs—do magazines consider "women's issues"?

3. Identify an organization in your community or campus that deals with violence against women and visit its office. What are its goals and what strategies does it employ to achieve them?

4. Does popular music contain bias against women? Listen to at least two kinds of music (rap, hip-hop, rock, country, and so on), and see what messages about the life goals and relative power of females and males you can find.

CHAPTER 4 Gender Inequality

A DEFINING MOMENT

Elizabeth Cady Stanton: Claiming Women's Right to Equality **p. 121**

What Is Gender?

4.1 Define important concepts including gender and gender stratification.

Sex is the biological distinction between females and males.

- Sex is determined at the moment when an embryo is conceived. **p. 102**

Gender refers to the personal traits and life chances that a society links to each sex, creating the cultural concepts of "feminine" and "masculine."

- Gender is a dimension of social stratification. **p. 102**

Patriarchy is a social pattern in which males dominate females.

- Almost all societies display some degree of patriarchy.
- **Gender stereotypes** are one form of prejudice against women, which devalues what a society defines as feminine.
- **Sexism** is the assertion that one sex is less worthy than or even innately inferior to the other. **pp. 102–4**

> **gender** (p. 102) the personal traits and life chances that a society links to being female or male
>
> **sex** (p. 102) the biological distinction between females and males
>
> **gender stratification** (p. 102) the unequal distribution of wealth, power, and privilege between men and women
>
> **patriarchy** (p. 102) a social pattern in which males dominate females
>
> **matriarchy** (p. 102) a social pattern in which females dominate males
>
> **sexism** (p. 104) the belief that one sex is innately superior to the other

Gender and Social Institutions

4.2 Analyze the importance of gender in the operation of major social institutions.

Family

- In poor countries the world over, parents value sons more than daughters, encouraging selective abortions and, in some cases, female infanticide.

- In the United States, gender shapes people's experience of marriage, which is often an unequal partnership that favors the man. **p. 104**

Education

- Gender stereotyping steers women away from fields of study (such as engineering and physics) considered masculine.
- Despite policies against gender bias in college sports, men's sports typically receive more funding and public attention. **pp. 104–6**

Mass Media

- Historically, television and film have cast women mainly in supporting roles.
- Advertising reinforces gender stereotypes by pitching certain products (such as household cleansers) to women and others (such as cars and banking services) to men. **p. 106**

Politics

- Women hold only 21% of seats in the world's 188 parliaments.
- In the United States, until 1920 women were barred from voting in national elections.
- In 2012, a record number of women were elected to Congress. **p. 106–7**

Religion

- Traditional religions allow only men to be leaders.
- Many religious writings teach women to submit to the social dominance of men. **pp. 107–8**

Military

- Until recently, the claim that women are not as strong as men has allowed the military to bar women from certain assignments.
- Women represent 15% of the U.S. armed forces.
- Sexual assault directed at women is a serious problem in today's military. **p. 108–9**

Work

- Many people still think of certain jobs as "women's work" and others as "men's work."
- Although gender discrimination in the workplace is illegal, officials investigate thousands of discrimination complaints each year. **p. 109**

Gender Stratification

4.3   Examine how gender stratification is found in many parts of everyday life.

Income is an important dimension of gender inequality.

- In the United States, women working full time earn 77% as much as men.
- Child-rearing duties often cause women to fall behind their male colleagues in career advancement. **pp. 110–12**

Housework is still performed mainly by women, despite the fact that women have been entering the labor force in record numbers in recent years. **p. 113**

Violence against women is a serious problem in the United States and throughout the world. U.S. government agencies receive more than 2 million reports of nonsexual assaults and 215,000 reports of sexual assaults against women each year. **(pp. 113–14)**

Sexual harassment came to be defined as a social problem in the 1980s; about 50% of women surveyed claim to have received unwanted sexual attention in the workplace. **(p. 114)**

Our **ideas about sexuality and beauty** have consequences for giving men power over women. Reproduction is also an important issue because controlling reproduction gives women the freedom to work outside the home. **(pp. 114–15)**

> **glass ceiling** (p. 112) subtle discrimination that effectively blocks the movement of women into the highest positions in organizations
>
> **sexual harassment** (p. 114) unwanted comments, gestures, or physical contact of a sexual nature

Theories of Gender Inequality

4.4   Apply sociological theory to the issue of gender inequality.

Structural-Functional Analysis: Gender and Complementarity

Structural-functional theory views gender in terms of complementary roles linking men and women, building families, and integrating society as a whole.

- In traditional societies, women bear children and are primarily responsible for the household; men link the family to the larger world by their participation in the workforce.
- With greater control over reproduction, modern societies have less gender specialization. **pp. 116–17**

Symbolic-Interaction Analysis: Gender in Everyday Life

Symbolic-interaction theory highlights how gender influences people's actions in everyday situations.

- Gender involves social power: Our society gives men greater freedom in personal behavior and allows them to use more space than women do.
- Language also reflects the social dominance of males. **pp. 117–18**

Social-Conflict Analysis: Gender and Inequality

Social-conflict theory sees gender as a dimension of social inequality, with men having greater wealth, power, and privileges than women.

- Friedrich Engels linked gender stratification to men's desire to pass on property to their offspring.
- The rise of capitalism fostered patriarchy by forcing men to work long hours in factories; the burden of housework and child rearing fell to women. **pp. 118–19**

> **intersection theory** (p. 119) analysis of how race, class, and gender interact, often creating multiple disadvantages for some categories of people

Feminism

4.5   Identify the foundations of feminism and distinguish three types of feminism.

Feminism is an important social-conflict theory in sociology.

- *Liberal feminism* seeks reform within existing institutional arrangements.
- *Socialist feminism* links gender equality to broader class revolution, following Marxist principles.
- *Radical feminism* calls for the elimination of gender itself, partly through the use of new reproductive technologies to liberate women from childbearing. **pp. 120–23**

> **feminism** (p. 120) a political movement that seeks the social equality of women and men

⭐ POLITICS AND GENDER

Constructing Problems and Defining Solutions

4.6 Analyze gender inequality from various positions on the political spectrum.

Conservatives: The Value of Families

- **Conservatives** place great importance on the traditional family.
- Conservatives see the trend toward gender equality as a problem. They say that this trend weakens families and reduces the importance of parenting, and they claim that children may suffer when both parents work outside the home. **pp. 123–24**

Liberals: The Pursuit of Equality

- **Liberals** object to gender inequality that limits the earning power of women and discourages women from assuming leadership positions.

- Liberals look to government to raise the social standing of women by putting an end to gender discrimination and by increasing women's economic opportunities and providing affordable child care. **pp. 124–25**

The Radical Left: Change the System

- **Radicals on the left** claim that gender stratification is deeply rooted in present social institutions.
- Radicals on the left believe that reaching the goal of gender equality requires basic change in the economy, political system, and family life. Socialism would allow women and men to work collectively for the benefit of everyone. **pp. 125–26**

Chapter 5
Aging and Inequality

Learning Objectives

5.1 Explain the effects of industrialization on the process of growing old.

5.2 Discuss the graying of the United States and the social diversity of the older population.

5.3 Assess various problems faced by today's elderly population.

5.4 Apply sociological theory to issues of aging and age stratification.

5.5 Analyze aging and age stratification from various positions on the political spectrum.

Tracking the Trends

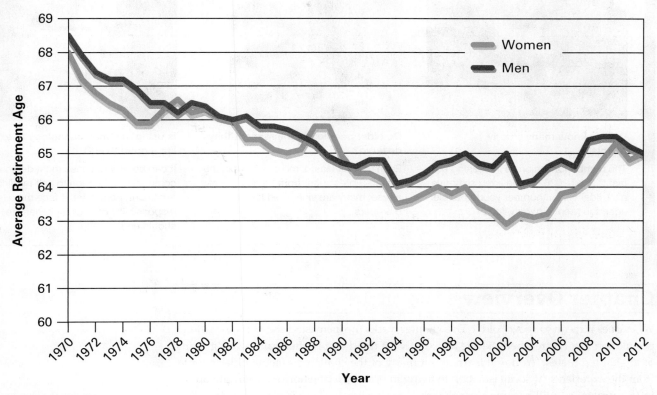

SOURCE: OECD (2013).

Is the decision to retire from paid work simply a personal choice? Back in 1970, the typical working woman retired at about the age of sixty-eight; the typical man was almost sixty-nine. In the decades that followed, economic prosperity helped to push the retirement age downward. In the first years of the new century, average retirement age had dropped to below sixty-five. But by about 2007, as the economy began to fall into recession, the retirement age began to move sharply upward. Today, as this chapter explains, many older workers are concerned that they do not have the financial security to retire (and many do not even have needed work). What programs or policies might increase the financial security of older workers?

Constructing the Problem

Do you know many elderly people?

The number of seniors is increasing so fast that by 2020 people aged sixty-five and older will outnumber young people aged fourteen to twenty-four.

Do older people get the respect they deserve?

Each year, at least 2 million elders in the United States suffer from some form of abuse; many are victimized by family members.

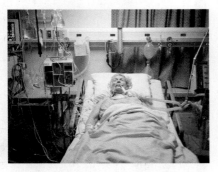

Is using medical technology to extend life a good thing?

It can be. But because most deaths come after a decision to halt medical treatment, people must face the difficult responsibility of deciding when life should end.

Chapter Overview

What does it mean to grow "old"? This chapter tracks the increasing share of our nation's population that has reached the age of sixty-five, a trend that is often called the "graying of the United States." You will learn about many of the challenges facing older people, from the experience of social isolation to living in poverty to the horror of outright abuse. In this process, it will become clear that the life process of aging is also a dimension of social stratification. You will carry out theoretical analysis of age-related inequality and learn how the process of defining certain issues as "problems" and particular programs and policies as "solutions" reflects people's political attitudes. ■

The Rolling Stones, a musical group that came on the scene in 1962, helped to define the tumultuous decade of the 1960s, an era of "sex, drugs, and rock-and-roll." This was also a decade in which popular culture celebrated youth and young people used to say "Don't trust anyone over thirty."

But times have changed. In 2014, Mick Jagger, the Stones' lead singer, turned seventy-one and became a great-grandfather. With Keith Richards and Charlie Watts (also in their seventies) and Ronnie Wood (the "youngster" of the group who is in his late sixties), the Rolling Stones continue to play rock-and-roll and serve to remind us that aging is what you make it to be (Coleman, 2013).

Here in the United States, more and more people are living into their seventies, eighties, nineties, and beyond. Many of them are active and some even go to Rolling Stones concerts. But not everyone finds that growing old is a happy time of life. As this chapter explains, the oldest members of our society face a number of challenges, including social isolation, prejudice and discrimination, a rising rate of poverty, and sometimes even outright violence. In addition, older people must face up to the sobering realization that their lives are nearing an end.

Growing Old

5.1 Explain the effects of industrialization on the process of growing old.

Old age is the final stage in the **life course**, the *socially constructed stages that people pass through as they live out their lives*. In our culture, commonly recognized stages of life include childhood, adolescence, adulthood, and old age. The last of these stages is the focus of this chapter and, more generally, of **gerontology**, *the study of aging and the elderly*.

We tend to think of the gradual physical, mental, and social changes that occur during the first half of the life course as "growing up." By about the age of forty, however, members of our society begin to define the process of aging in more negative terms, as if people start "growing down." After midlife, physical strength begins to decline, hair starts to turn gray and may also fall out, and the skin gradually becomes wrinkled. Among older men and women, injuries come more easily and they also take longer to heal. In addition, among older people, illnesses are more common, and the senses (sight, taste, hearing, and smell) become less sharp. There is truth to the idea that people "slow down" as they age. Compared with thirty-year-olds, people at age seventy-five have a bodily metabolism that has slowed by one-sixth; their heart and kidney functions are reduced by one-third; and their breathing capacity has fallen by half.

Older people can become seriously ill with something as common as the flu, an infection that a younger person would shake off in a day or two. Elderly people also suffer from more chronic (long-term) illnesses such as arthritis that, though not life-threatening, often cause pain and can make everyday activities difficult. Most seriously, the odds of a deadly disease, such as cancer, stroke, or heart disease, steadily increase with advancing age.

In terms of health, elderly people also differ among themselves. For those with higher income, health is typically better because they have more money to spend on safe housing, good nutrition, and high-quality health care. Well-being also reflects lifestyle and personal choices that are available to anyone: Factors such as regular exercise, not smoking cigarettes, and limiting use of alcohol all contribute to good health for people of any age (Holmes & Holmes, 1995; Medina, 1996).

Industrialization and Aging

The life course is "socially constructed" because growing old is not just a matter of biological changes. How a culture defines this stage of life makes a big difference in how people experience old age.

In traditional, agricultural communities, as in this rice-producing region of Japan, most wealth and power are held by older people, who typically continue working well into old age. Why does industrialization reduce the relative social standing of older people?

Preindustrial Societies: Elders as Social Elite In traditional, rural societies where many people engage in farming, ways of life change slowly. The knowledge gained by the oldest members of society remains valuable, so younger people look up to elders as wise and deserving of respect. In addition, the oldest people (typically, the oldest *men*) own most of the land, which gives them not only wisdom but also considerable wealth and power. For these reasons, preindustrial societies take the form of a **gerontocracy**, *a social system that gives a society's oldest members the most wealth, power, and prestige*.

In farming societies, seniors typically remain socially active both at work and as family leaders until they are unable to continue. At this point, elders can expect to live out their lives under the care of their children. In many societies, younger people continue to direct attention and respect toward elders even after the older generation has died in the religious pattern called ancestor worship.

Industrial Societies: Elderly as Social Problem The Industrial Revolution did much to raise everyone's living standards, but it also changed age stratification to reduce the social power and prestige of older people relative to those who are younger. This change happened because industrial technology speeds up the rate of cultural change, which encourages younger people to view the knowledge and skill of seniors as "old-fashioned" and unimportant to their lives. In preindustrial societies, people use the word "elder" as a term of respect for older people. Members of modern, industrial societies, by contrast, use the term "elderly," a word that has a more negative meaning. It is not far off the mark to say that in societies like our own, many younger people regard older people as something of a social problem.

SOCIAL PROBLEMS IN GLOBAL PERSPECTIVE

Will the Golden Years Lose Their Glow? Growing Old in Japan

Seventy-two-year-old Taizo Komurasaki grew up during the horrors of World War II. Later, he went to college and found a job with a trading company where he spent his whole career. At the age of sixty, he retired with a pension and looked forward to another twenty years or more of financial security.

But his golden years have already lost some of their glow. Even before the current economic crisis, his pension was only $1,625 per month ($19,500 per year)—not nearly enough to live comfortably in a country where the cost of living is among the highest in the world. To make matters worse, both corporations and government in Japan have been forced to reduce pensions during a long period of economic recession that began about 1990 and has recently become worse.

Another reason that the pressure to cut pensions has become intense is that the share of Japan's population that is over the age of sixty-five is increasing faster than in any country in the world. In 2014, 26 percent of Japanese people were over age sixty-five (compared with 14.5 percent in the United States); in 2025, the Japanese figure will be about 31 percent (19 percent in the United States).

The main reason for the rapid increase in the elderly population in Japan is the low birth rate. The birth rate has declined so much in Japan that the country's total population is projected to fall by more than 15 percent by 2050. Everyone understands an aging population means fewer workers to pay into a system that must provide pensions and other benefits to more people who have retired.

A long-standing Japanese tradition requires children (especially daughters) to provide care for aging parents. But tough economic times have left most couples wondering if they can afford to support aging mothers and fathers. Also, most of today's Japanese couples live in small apartments with little space for another person. Finally, as more Japanese women have joined the labor force, they have less time and energy to devote to elder care.

One sign of changing times is that the Japanese are now building facilities that were once unknown in that nation—nursing homes. As elders live longer, as pensions run low, and as families find they have less to offer to aging parents, the cultural taboo against placing parents in nursing homes is starting to break down.

What Do You Think?

1. In both Japan and the United States, the number of retired seniors drawing government funds is outpacing the number of younger workers paying into the system. What do you think should be done to head off a future financial crisis?

2. What responsibilities should families have to provide care for their elder members?

3. Do you see ways in which the recent economic recession has affected the lives of older people here in the United States? Explain.

SOURCES: Strom (2000) and U.S. Census Bureau (2014).

Industrialization also brings change to family relationships, separating the generations. In past centuries, for example, family members worked together on the farm, with the old teaching the young. In the nineteenth century, as factories sprang up, the lure of better pay caused younger workers to leave rural farming communities and migrate to the cities. In the new industrial economy, young people had less reason to look to their elders for work or for guidance about how to live. Just as important, as many younger men and women headed off for the growing cities and left their aging parents behind, the share of elderly people living in poverty began to rise.

Early in the twentieth century, the number of elderly people facing serious poverty steadily increased, and some older men and women ended up in poorhouses that were no better than prisons. Fortunately, as the century moved ahead, the economic standing of older people in the United States started getting better. Eventually, the poorhouses were closed, in part due to people who

formed a social movement demanding better treatment for older people.

Government also acted to assist older people. In 1935, the federal government passed the Social Security Act, which provides a monthly pension to everyone over a certain age (currently sixty-five). In addition to providing needed income, this program symbolizes our society's commitment to the idea that older people are worthy of support. By about 1970, the average income and wealth of older people began to climb and poverty rates began to fall to the point that, today, the poverty rate for the elderly is slightly below that for the population as a whole (Powell, Branco, & Williamson, 1996; U.S. Census Bureau, 2014).

But money, as they say, isn't everything. Today's older people have become better off economically, but many older men and women still feel devalued by today's "youth culture." The mass media typically focus on the lives, fashions, and attitudes of young people, making older people seem old-fashioned and of little value (Kosterlitz, 1997; Wise, 1997).

Not all industrial countries have been so hard on their oldest members. Japan stands out as a nation that still has some of its centuries-old respect for old people. But even in Japan, older people face challenges, as the Social Problems in Global Perspective box explains.

Life Expectancy

Life expectancy is *the average life span of a country's population*. Life expectancy has changed dramatically over the course of human history. In the earliest hunting and gathering societies, most people died in childhood; someone who lived to thirty had reached a "ripe old age." Today, life expectancy in the world's poorest nations, most of which are in found in Africa, can be as low as fifty-five years (U.S. Census Bureau, 2014).

In high-income countries, which have better nutrition, sanitation, and medical care, life expectancy is considerably greater. Today, males born in the United States can expect to live seventy-six years and females eighty-one years (Hoyert & Xu, 2012).

Just about everyone sees increasing life expectancy as good, of course, because we all have an interest in living longer. But this trend also means that societies must meet the needs of an increasing number of older people. This increase is especially pronounced in the United States, as we now explain.

The Graying of the United States

5.2 Discuss the graying of the United States and the social diversity of the older population.

When the United States won its independence in 1776, the country was very young in more ways than one. Half the new nation's people were under the age of sixteen, and it was then rare for someone to live to the age of sixty. Despite the familiar image of gray-haired "founding fathers," the great leaders of the colonial period were actually young by today's standards. When George Washington, who became our nation's first president, commanded the troops in the Revolutionary War, he was in his early forties, and when Thomas Jefferson wrote the Declaration of Independence, he was just thirty-three.

By 1900, about 3 million people in the United States were older than sixty-five, but they made up just 4 percent of the total population. As shown in Figure 5–1, the elderly share doubled by 1950 and it will double again by the year 2020, when the elderly population of this country will reach 56 million (U.S. Census Bureau, 2014). Against the trend of a rapidly increasing elderly population, the number of young people in the United States is staying about the same. The result is what sociologists call the "graying

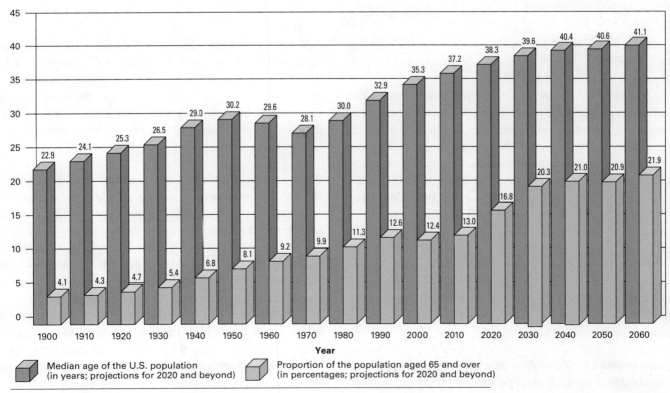

Figure 5–1 The Graying of U.S. Society

The Census Bureau projects that people aged sixty-five and older will reach about 20 percent of the U.S. population by 2030. At that point, almost half the U.S. population will be over the age of forty.

SOURCE: U.S. Census Bureau (2012, 2013).

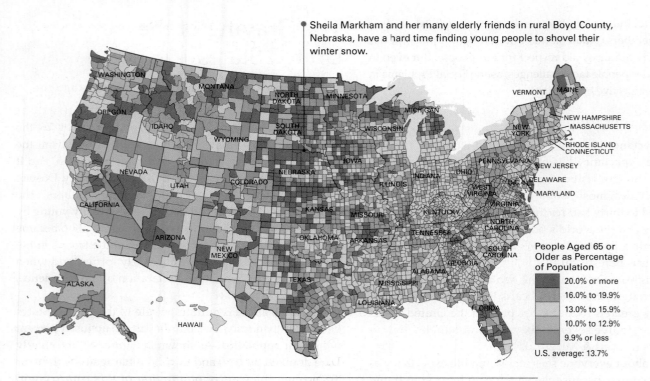

● Sheila Markham and her many elderly friends in rural Boyd County, Nebraska, have a hard time finding young people to shovel their winter snow.

People Aged 65 or Older as Percentage of Population

- 20.0% or more
- 16.0% to 19.9%
- 13.0% to 15.9%
- 10.0% to 12.9%
- 9.9% or less

U.S. average: 13.7%

National Map 5–1 The Elderly Population across the United States

Common sense suggests that elderly people live in the Sunbelt, enjoying the warmer climate of the South and Southwest. Although it is true that Florida has a disproportionate share of people over age sixty-five, it turns out that most counties with high percentages of older people are in the Midwest. What do you think accounts for this pattern? Hint: Which regions of the United States do younger people leave in search of jobs?

SOURCE: U.S. Census Bureau (2013).

of the United States." Figure 5–1 shows that the share of the U.S. population over age sixty-five is projected to reach 20 percent by about 2030.

As a result of this trend, all of us will have more contact with older people than ever before. Of course, the extent of contact with older people depends a great deal on where in the country we live. The elderly are a far larger share of the population in some regions, especially in the midsection, from North Dakota and Minnesota down to Texas, and a much lower share near the East Coast and West Coast. The patterns are shown in National Map 5–1.

Elders: A Diverse Population

Sociologists conduct research to understand the needs and problems of the elderly population of the United States. The evidence shows that elders in our society are socially quite diverse.

Three Levels of "Old" At a time of increasing life expectancy, one way in which older people differ from one another is age itself. Researchers divide the elderly into three categories. Most people sixty-five to seventy-four years of age—the "younger old"—live independently and enjoy good health. People aged seventy-five to eighty-four—the "older

old"—are more likely to need support services. Elders aged eighty-five and older—the "oldest old"—are those who need the most assistance. Of these three categories of elders, the oldest old are increasing in number the most rapidly. From just 0.1 percent of the U.S. population in 1900, by 2012 they made up 2 percent of our people, which represents a twenty-fold increase (U.S. Census Bureau, 2013).

Class, Race, Ethnicity, and Gender Social inequality shapes the lives of people of all ages. Older men and women who are well-off financially, especially when they are in good health, have lots of choices about where and how they want to live. Many of these fortunate people lead active lives including travel that provides both adventure and learning. Some well-off seniors retire to the South and Southwest to enjoy the mild weather and reasonable cost of living.

But these are the exceptions, not the rule. Just one in twenty older people ends up making a move to the Sunbelt. Why? Many (especially those with health problems) want to stay close to family members. For most, however, the reason comes down to money: They simply cannot afford it.

The elderly are also racially and ethnically diverse, and the older minority population faces the challenges that all minorities face—lower incomes, on average, as well as prejudice and discrimination.

Keep in mind that the older population of the United States is not as diverse as the younger population. One reason is that, on average, minorities do not live as long as white people. For example, life expectancy among African Americans is four years less than it is for whites. In addition, much of our country's racial and ethnic diversity results from immigration, and most immigrants are young people. Half of children under five years of age are now minorities (including African, Asian, Latino, and Native Americans), but the same is true of just 21 percent of those over age sixty-five (U.S. Census Bureau, 2013).

A final dimension of diversity among the elderly involves gender. Women tend to live longer than men. Therefore, although women are a slight majority of the total population (51 percent), they represent 56 percent of all people over the age of sixty-five. Among this country's 62,000 centenarians—people aged 100 years or older—82 percent are women (U.S. Census Bureau, 2013).

Problems of Aging

5.3   Assess various problems faced by today's elderly population.

We all experience change at every stage of life. But a common opinion among the elderly is that changes in old age present the greatest challenges they have ever faced. Although the physical health of seniors is, on the whole, far better than stereotypes of "frail old people" suggest, most older women and men spend a lot of time and money trying to improve their health. For many, pain from various ailments limits activity. Sooner or later, just about everyone has to learn the tough lesson that they now have to depend on others to carry out everyday routines. In addition, as family and friends die, older people face loneliness and the knowledge that the end of their own lives is drawing near. We now take a closer look at problems common to society's oldest members.

Social Isolation

At any age, being alone can provoke loneliness, anxiety, and depression. But of all the stages of life, old age presents the greatest risk of social isolation. Retirement from work closes off one important source of social activity. As people age, declining health limits their ability to get around, and a youth culture encourages negative stereotypes of the elderly as sickly, old-fashioned, or "out of touch," ideas that may discourage others from interacting with older people.

In addition, as time goes on, friends, neighbors, and family members die, shrinking an older

person's social world. Few human experiences are as difficult and isolating as the death of a close friend and, especially, a spouse. One study of older men and women who had lost a spouse found that three-fourths cited loneliness as a serious problem. This experience of social isolation is surely a key reason that, as researchers have long documented, the months following the death of a spouse place the surviving partner at high risk of death, sometimes by suicide (Benjamin & Wallis, 1963; Lund, 1989).

Gender figures into the problem of social isolation. This is because the experience of social isolation is more common to elderly women who typically outlive older men. Among people over sixty-five, 72 percent of men live with a wife, but only 42 percent of women live with a husband. From another angle, 19 percent of elderly men live alone, compared with 37 percent of older women (Federal Interagency Forum, 2012).

Another reason for this difference in social isolation is that widowers are more likely than widows to remarry. Men have better odds of finding another partner because U.S. culture supports the pairing of older men and younger women much more than the pairing of older women with younger men. In addition, given the difference in life expectancy, older women also outnumber older men.

Where do elders turn for support and companionship? Many elderly people look to community services provided by senior citizen centers as a source of social contact. But for most seniors, families are the main support system. Half of U.S. adults say that at some point in their lives they expect to care for an older family member. Almost half of all elders have at least one adult child who lives no more

A rising number of older women and men are in the paid labor force, a trend that increased during the recent economic downturn. How does ageism affect the types of jobs older people hold?

than twenty minutes away. According to researchers, the typical caregiver is a woman (most commonly a daughter or daughter-in-law of the elderly person) who is fifty years of age, married, and works for income. On top of her responsibilities to employer and husband, she typically provides almost twenty hours of care per week to an aging parent (AARP Public Policy Institute, 2009; Fox, Duggan, and Purcell, 2013).

Retirement

Industrialization made societies much more productive so that it was no longer necessary for almost everyone to work. As a result, the very young were excused from continuous labor. In fact, members of industrial societies came to view child labor (a practice still common in low-income nations around the world) as wrong, and they expect young people to spend much of their daily lives in school. At the other end of the life course, older people, too, began to step away from the labor force. And so it has become common for older people to retire from the labor force so that they can spend their remaining years doing what they wish.

When younger adults think about their future, most imagine that they will retire from paid work at about the age of sixty-five, an age that has become linked to retirement. Back in 1950, people in the United States typically retired about the age of sixty-eight; by 2005, however, the median age for retirement had fallen to sixty-three.

But beginning about 2006, this trend began to reverse itself especially after the onset of the economic recession by 2009. For many older workers, the weaker economy meant pay cuts or the loss of some (or even all) of a pension or retirement. As a result, more men and women remain in the labor force and they are also working longer hours. By 2012, the typical age of retirement for U.S. workers had moved back up to sixty-five for both men and women. In a world of economic uncertainty, people are now cautious about giving up paid work, perhaps not retiring at all or retiring in small steps, a pattern called *staged retirement* (Gendell, 2008; U.S. Census Bureau, 2013; Brown, 2013; OECD, 2013).

Even if you are decades away from retirement, it is a good idea to do some planning for this transition. The earlier one begins a program of regular savings, the greater the resources available to support life after retirement. But retirement involves more than a loss of income because work is also a source of personal satisfaction and social ties. Therefore, people must also consider how to replace work with other activities that provide similar personal benefits. Of course, there is no single formula for a satisfying retirement. Some people are eager to jump into entirely new activities, others are satisfied to spend much more time with children and grandchildren, and still others are content simply to sit back and relax. In nearly all cases, however, what people can and cannot do in retirement will depend on the state of their health and the extent of their financial resources (Neugarten, 1996; Gall, Evans, & Howard, 1997; Pitt, 2009).

Employers can play a part in a successful retirement, easing this transition by allowing people to retire in steps. For example, colleges and universities may allow professors nearing retirement to "step down" their teaching load. Schools may also provide support for retired professors to conduct research and to attend professional meetings.

PERSONAL STORIES
Is Aging a Disease?

A seventy-five-year-old man who loved to square dance suddenly had a sharp pain in his left knee. He went to his doctor to find out what the trouble was. The doctor noted his age, gave his knee a fairly superficial examination, and said, "I can't find anything obviously wrong with your knee. It must be due to your age." The man asked the doctor to explain. The doctor launched into a discussion of various theories of aging and how they might explain his knee problem, and concluded, "Now do you understand?" The old man replied, "No, I don't, because my right knee is just as old as my left knee, and it's not giving me a bit of trouble!"

The medical sociologist Erdman Palmore (1998:29) tells this story to make a point about subtle forms of ageism. Had this patient been twenty-five years old, Palmore explains, the doctor would never have treated him this way. The doctor probably would have ordered an X-ray or some other procedure immediately to find out what was causing the pain. But with elderly patients, doctors sometimes engage in a subtle form of ageism by acting as if aging itself were the problem. This response is not good medical practice; it is actually a form of age-based prejudice.

What Do You Think?

1. If it is true that people suffer more illnesses as they age, what's wrong with treating aging as a disease?

2. Can you point out other subtle forms of ageism? What about age-related stereotypes?

3. What do you think is a good solution to the problem of age-based prejudice?

Many colleges and universities also help older people by give retiring faculty members the title "emeritus professor" so that they keep their faculty standing, and many permit them to continue using an e-mail account, make use of the gym, and maybe even continue to park on campus. But most employers are not so helpful. In today's age of corporate downsizing, some companies simply push older (and often higher-paid) workers out the door. Such forced retirement usually offers the greatest challenges.

What is the government's retirement policy? Back in the 1930s, the U.S. government set the retirement age at sixty-five, which was about how long people lived at that time. But today, on average, people live about nineteen years beyond that. Recognizing the trend toward increasing life expectancy, in 1987 Congress enacted legislation phasing out mandatory retirement policies by 1994. Rigid retirement policies remain for only a small number of occupations, such as airline pilots, who must retire at age sixty-five (Bosworth & Burtless, 1998; Wyatt, 2000).

Among all high-income nations, we can expect to see the recent trend toward later retirement continue. For one thing, in Europe and Japan, lower birth rates will hold down the number of working-age people. Economic growth will depend on older people spending more years in the labor force. In addition, the rising costs of pensions and health care for an aging population threaten to overwhelm available resources. As a result, older people may have to work longer to ensure financial security. Currently in the United States, people can begin drawing on Social Security at the age of sixty-two, although full benefits kick in at age sixty-six (and, by 2026, age sixty-seven). Expect to see governments—both here and in other high-income nations—continue to push back the point of retirement (*The Economist*, 2011).

Ageism

Whether older people are working or retired, they may find that others look down on them simply because of their age. **Ageism** is *prejudice and discrimination directed toward older people* (Butler, 1975, 1994; E. Cohen, 2001). Like racism and sexism, ageism defines physical traits—in this case, graying hair, wrinkled skin, or any other signs of advancing age—as

evidence of being less worthy as a person. Certainly, ageism helps explain the fact that many older people turn to medications such as Botox and Viagra and even undergo cosmetic surgery in order to lessen the effects of aging on their looks and behavior.

Because our society is more likely to judge women than men by their physical appearance, ageism is often a bigger issue for women. But whenever anyone portrays elders of either sex as if they were old-fashioned, narrow-minded, or even senile, they devalue them as human beings.

Age-Based Prejudice Ageism involves prejudice—negative prejudgments about the elderly. Such prejudice can be blatant, as when employers pass over a job application from an older person because they prefer hiring someone younger. Prejudice can also be subtle, but just as harmful, as when a doctor assumes that an ailment is caused simply by a patient's age, a situation described in the Personal Stories box.

Prejudice directed toward the elderly may take the form of many stereotypes—all of them negative—depicting older people as "sick, senile, useless, sexually impotent, ugly, isolated, poor, or miserable" (Palmore, 1998:30–31). Such stereotypes are wrong because most elderly people are none of these things: Eighty-eight percent of people sixty-five and older live healthy and independent lives, and only about 4 percent of people over the age of sixty-five have health problems that confine them to nursing homes. Most seniors work as hard and as effectively as younger workers, and most employers rate older workers as more trustworthy and loyal. Most elderly men and women are also quite capable of having satisfying sexual relationships (American Health Care Association, 2013; National Center for Health Statistics, 2013).

Age-Based Discrimination Prejudice is an attitude that often leads to unfair treatment or discrimination. This is why, back in 1967, Congress passed the Age Discrimination in Employment Act, banning employers from discriminating against people because of their age. Because the average age of the U.S. workforce is going up—in 2012, 67 million workers (44 percent of the total) were age forty-five or older—the number of complaints of age-based

At least 2 million elders in the United States are victims of abuse every year. Countless others suffer from neglect and from treatment that robs them of their dignity. What are some of the causes of this problem? What do you think should be done about it?

discrimination is rising. In 2012 nearly 23,000 complaints of age discrimination were filed with the U.S. Equal Employment Opportunity Commission (2013), which represents a 38 percent increase over the number filed in 2006.

Keep in mind that even people in middle age experience age discrimination. In fact, the typical complaint of age discrimination now comes from people in their forties, not their sixties (U.S. Department of Labor, 2013; U.S. Equal Employment Opportunity Commission, 2013).

Whatever the age of victims, age discrimination is illegal. But this law is difficult to enforce because many people who are turned down for a job never know exactly why. In addition, companies can legally lay off higher-salaried workers in favor of those who are paid less, even though this policy usually hurts older people the most (Palmore, 1998; Labaton, 2000).

Ageism in the Mass Media Think about the older women and men you have seen on television and in films. Your first thought might well be, "There are not very many of them." When older people do appear on screen, it is often in stereotypical roles. In the Oscar-winning film *Driving Miss Daisy*, for example, Jessica Tandy played an old, lonely woman unable to cope with change.

But this pattern applies more to women than to men. Older men are seen on screen much more often—think of the many roles played by Harrison Ford, Sean Connery, and Clint Eastwood—and they usually appear (both on- and off-screen) opposite women half their age. Twenty-nine-year-old actress Mary McCormack recalled with excitement playing opposite Clint Eastwood, who was more than twice her age at the time. She explained that, although she was in only one scene with Eastwood, her part involved making out with him, and she found him—at age sixty-eight—to be extremely sexy. At the same time, she speculated that it would be highly unlikely that, when she reached that age, a twenty-nine-year-old actor would ever boast about making out with a sixty-eight-year-old Mary McCormack.

Race, too, figures into the way older people are presented by the mass media. Older people who do appear in the mass media are also likely to be white. More and more African Americans are on television and in the movies, but they are typically young people. Minorities become increasingly invisible once they pass the age of sixty-five.

Victimization of the Elderly

Only in the 1980s, with the increasing political power of older people, did our society begin to define *elder abuse* as a social problem. Elder abuse refers to a range of behavior that extends from passive neglect to active verbal and emotional mistreatment to life-threatening physical

---

SOCIAL POLICY

Nursing Home Abuse: What Should Be Done?

Few people disagree with the idea that society's oldest members deserve their fair share of kindness. Yet investigations show that, in 2012, 93.2 percent of nursing homes were cited for at least some violation of federal health and safety standards. About 22 percent of nursing homes had deficiencies that caused "actual harm or immediate jeopardy" to residents (Kaiser Family Foundation, 2014).

The details of abuse cases can be heartbreaking. One witness before a congressional committee was Leslie Olivia, who had been caring for her aging mother at home. When her mother's needs became greater than what Olivia could provide, she turned to a nursing home for help. Within months of her mother moving in, Olivia discovered that her mother suffered bruises, bedsores, and a broken pelvis. Sometimes attendants simply left a meal tray at the end of her bed, out of reach. Without adequate nutrition, her mother quickly lost weight. Olivia was so concerned that she moved her mother to another home. But problems continued, and her mother soon suffered from bedsores and severe dehydration. Olivia moved her mother yet again.

In the last of the homes, the staff called Olivia to report devastating news—her mother had choked to death on her food. In light of what had happened at the other nursing homes, Olivia was not sure that she should believe them. She soon learned that at the time of her death, her mother had been attached to a feeding tube. Clearly, the facts pointed to abuse.

Is this disturbing story an isolated case? Based on testimony by family members and also nursing home workers, the congressional committee concluded that elder abuse occurs much more frequently than we like to think and is commonly covered up (Thompson, 1998; U.S. House of Representatives, 2001; Pear, 2008).

Available evidence suggests that elder abuse is especially likely to occur in facilities that are understaffed and where employees are underpaid and have little training. As a result, tens of thousands of our society's oldest members are suffering needlessly, and many are in danger.

What Do You Think?

1. Why do you think the public is not more concerned about the problem of elder abuse?
2. What changes in the operation of nursing homes might prevent cases like that of Leslie Olivia's mother?
3. Have you had any experiences with elder abuse in care facilities? If so, explain.

violence. Experts estimate that at least 2 million people age sixty-five or older (about 5 percent of all elders) suffer some abuse each year, with about one-third of these cases involving serious, life-threatening abuse.

According to the federal government, half of all cases of elder abuse involve neglect of older people who cannot care for themselves. The remaining half involves a range of harmful actions, including active physical or psychological abuse (but rarely sexual abuse), wrongfully taking an older person's money, or unfairly taking some other property (Thompson, 1998; National Center on Elder Abuse, 2006).

Like other forms of family violence (discussed in Chapter 12, "Family Life"), elder abuse often goes undetected for the simple reason that victims are afraid to speak out. Many fear that if they were to file a complaint, their abusers might harm them even more or might try to have them institutionalized. For this reason, analysts estimate, only about 15 percent of all actual abuse cases are ever reported (Barnett, Miller-Perrin, & Perrin, 1997; National Center on Elder Abuse, 2006).

Causes of Elder Abuse   What would cause someone to neglect or abuse an older person? One important pattern is that many abusers are themselves victims of abuse. This vicious circle of abuse can be explained in simple terms: People who have experienced abuse in their own lives (often as children) are likely to re-create this pattern in response to the challenge of caring for an aging parent or other person (Greenberg, McKibben, & Raymond, 1990; Bendick, 1992; Barnett, Miller-Perrin, & Perrin, 1997).

People who abuse family members often face other challenges. They may be addicted to alcohol or other drugs; they may have emotional problems; or they may suffer from unhealthy personal relationships. Economic uncertainty adds stress to the lives of many people, a fact that only makes caring for others more difficult. But any person caught within the multiple demands of working, caring for young children, and looking after an aging parent may feel out of control and slip into abusive behavior (Hinrichsen, Hernandez, & Pollack, 1992; Barnett, Miller-Perrin, & Perrin, 1997).

Abuse also occurs in institutional settings such as nursing facilities. Sometimes this problem results from efforts to cut costs. For example, nursing home owners may try to operate their businesses with fewer workers or replace nurses with less trained aides. As a result of such policies, overburdened staff may end up neglecting patients (Manheimer, 1994). Like family members, in other words, staff employees who face patient demands they cannot meet may reach a point of desperation that triggers abuse. The Social Policy box describes a government investigation of nursing home abuse.

All of us, as we grow older, will require care from others. How does being poor affect your options for receiving care?

The Growing Need for Caregiving

As the share of the population over age sixty-five increases, so does the need for elder care. But most elders never live in a nursing home or other care facility. Rather, most elder care comes from other individuals. Understandably, then, sociologists are interested in **caregiving**, *informal and unpaid care provided to a dependent person by family members, other relatives, or friends* (Lund, 1993; Spillman, 2002).

Surveys show that more than one-third of U.S. adults are already providing some care to older people, and half of adults say they expect to do so at some point (Fox, Duggen, & Purcell, 2013). Today, middle-aged adults are a "sandwich generation" who may well spend as much time caring for their aging parents as they did raising their young children. Caregiving ranges from consulting the Internet or physicians about drugs, helping people get to medical appointments, and doing housework and cooking for an older person. Most of the hands-on care for an aging person is typically provided by one particular family member. Most caregivers are women, typically a wife, daughter, or daughter-in-law.

The demands of elder care can be great. Most caregivers have other family members to think about—and, of course, their own needs as well. In addition, three-fourths of all caregivers have jobs. Typically, then, a caregiver provides help for several hours a day on top of what is already a full day's work (Himes, 2001; AARP Public Policy Institute, 2009).

Poverty

In 2012, government data show 9.1 percent of people over age sixty-five—about 3.9 million women and men—were living below the government's poverty line. This figure represents a dramatic change from several generations ago: Back in 1965, the elderly poverty rate in the United States was almost 30 percent (U.S. Census Bureau, 2013).

What accounts for this long-term decline in elder poverty? The main reason is that seniors now receive better retirement benefits, such as Social Security payments with automatic cost-of-living adjustments. The reduction of poverty among the elderly is a success story that shows that, with effective policies, social problems can be improved. But of course, there is still much to be done.

Keep in mind that government poverty statistics do not include the relatively small share of elders who are institutionalized, most of whom are poor. Also worth noting is that the poverty line for an older person in 2012 was $11,011 for a person over sixty-five living alone, a number lower than for comparable people who are younger: $11,945 for a person below age sixty-five living alone. Therefore, the official poverty rate for elders almost certainly understates the actual extent of the problem (U.S. Census Bureau, 2013).

Age Stratification

Age stratification is *social inequality among various age categories within a society*. As explained earlier, in preindustrial societies elders have more wealth and power than younger people. In modern industrial societies, the opposite is true.

Figure 5–2 shows the average income and the poverty rates for the U.S. population according to age categories. In our society, as people get older, gaining education

and experience, their income typically goes up. This trend holds through middle age and income peaks about the age of fifty. Then the trend reverses itself, with income falling as people get older and enter old age. The poverty rate shows something of an inverse pattern. The highest rate of poverty (above 20 percent) is among children and young adults under the age of twenty-four. By contrast, the rate falls to 7.9 percent among people aged sixty-five to seventy-four. Then, with advancing age, the poverty rate rises, reaching 10.6 percent for people seventy-five and older. If we take all people over the age of sixty-five together, the poverty rate is just 9.1 percent, well below the figure of 15 percent for the country as a whole (U.S. Census Bureau, 2013).

Housing

Between 2015 and 2025, the U.S. elderly population will increase by more than 17 million, and the population over the age of eighty-five will grow by 1 million. According to social service providers, our nation will not have enough suitable housing for these numbers of elderly people (U.S. Census Bureau, 2012).

In the United States, nearly everyone, young or old, views keeping a home as one key to an independent and happy life. About 90 percent of today's older men and

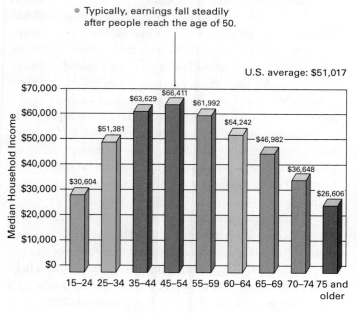

● Typically, earnings fall steadily after people reach the age of 50.

U.S. average: $51,017

(a) Age of Head of Household (in years)

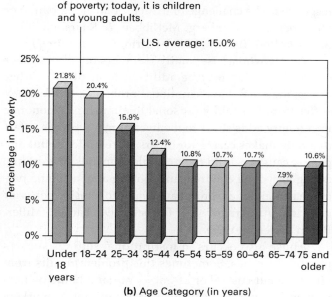

● A generation ago, it was the elderly who were at highest risk of poverty; today, it is children and young adults.

U.S. average: 15.0%

(b) Age Category (in years)

Diversity Snapshot

Figure 5–2 U.S. Household Income and Poverty Rate, by Age, 2012

In part (a), we see that median household income typically rises over the life course, peaking at around age fifty and falling as people enter old age. Part (b) shows that poverty rates go down as people get older, reaching a low point for people between the ages of sixty-five and seventy-four, and rising among people who have passed the age of seventy-five.

SOURCE: U.S. Census Bureau (2013).

80 percent of older women live independently with spouses or alone. About 80 percent of elders own their own homes, and most own them mortgage-free. Even so, older homeowners pay taxes and cover the costs of utilities, insurance, and home maintenance, all of which can leave elders "asset rich but income poor" (Federal Interagency Forum, 2013; U.S. Census Bureau, 2013).

Most elders prefer to "age in place," staying in the same homes they occupied while working and raising their children. Physical changes that occur in old age— including a loss of strength, a slowing of reaction time, and a weakening of eyesight—require safety modifications to a home. Stairways are a challenge commonly found in homes occupied by older people. But only a small share of this housing has safety and accessibility features such as grab bars in bathrooms (38 percent), entry-level bedrooms (36 percent), wide doorways that will accommodate walkers and wheelchairs (12 percent), and accessibility ramps (1 percent) (American Housing Survey, 2012).

As you might expect, the houses owned by seniors tend to be older than average. Many of these homes need maintenance and repairs, lack insulation, and require improvements to heating and air-conditioning systems. Homeowners most likely to face such problems are the categories of elders at higher risk of poverty: African Americans, women, and rural as well as inner-city people.

When housing is not up-to-date, the risk of accident or injury goes up. For example, a fall on dangerous stairs may cause a broken hip, landing an otherwise healthy person in a hospital or nursing facility. Trying to heat a drafty home with a space heater raises the risk of fire or death by asphyxiation. Government programs such as Medicare pay for some nonmedical equipment, such as safety seats for showers and tubs. But many elders are unaware of the federal programs that can help make their homes safer (U.S. Department of Housing and Urban Development, 2011; U.S. Census Bureau, 2013).

Access to shopping and services is another issue important to seniors. Suburban communities typically have limited public transportation, so that traveling around the area demands the use of an automobile. Yet many older people no longer drive. As a result, aging people may find that stores, businesses, churches, and recreational facilities are out of reach.

In a classic study of a declining neighborhood in southern California, Barbara Myerhoff (1979) found that elderly residents wanted, more than anything, to stay independent. But dressing, shopping, cooking, and cleaning an apartment are not easy for those challenged by arthritis or failing eyesight. Myerhoff found that the neighborhood had no large grocery store, forcing residents to take the bus to a shopping center. But the bus had high steps that were hard to climb and prevented older shoppers from taking a wheeled shopping cart. Such was the challenge of daily life.

Many elderly people prefer to "age in place." But homes that were comfortable for middle-aged people can become challenging to those who are entering old age. Alterations to make a home suitable for an older person can be very expensive, and alternatives such as moving to a retirement community can be more expensive still. Do you think U.S. society should expect individuals to meet these challenges for themselves?

Housing Programs for Older People   Across the United States, there are thousands of retirement communities that offer comfortable, accessible apartments with on-site health care services and help with cleaning, meals, and transportation. But the costs of living in such communities are high, typically between $2,000 and $6,000 per month for an apartment and meals. In addition, many such facilities require residents to pay up-front entrance fees of as much as $250,000. Clearly, such high cost puts this type of housing within reach of a very limited number of older people.

To make safe, accessible housing available to those with lower incomes, the federal government provides seniors with rental subsidies based on the individual's need. Elderly people occupy one-third of the 1.2 million public housing units. In 1990, Congress passed the National Affordable Housing Act, providing additional support to frail elders, a population that will increase quickly in the years to come as more seniors live past age eighty-five (U.S. Census Bureau, 2013; U.S. Department of Housing and Urban Development, 2013).

Passage of the National Affordable Housing Act also made available so-called reverse mortgages, financial arrangements that allow qualified elders to borrow against their home equity without making any monthly payments. Elders can use the cash as they wish—say, for home repairs, medical care, or housekeeping services. Eventually, after the person dies or moves elsewhere, the house is sold and the loan is paid back from the proceeds. This policy can turn the value of a home into cash needed for daily living. Even so, many seniors are not comfortable borrowing against their most important financial asset.

Finally, faced with the high cost of housing and declining income, many elders cut costs by sharing a home. About 11 percent of U.S. seniors live with a relative or an unrelated adult (U.S. Census Bureau, 2013).

Medical Care

As people grow old, they need much more medical care. Since 1965, the federal government has provided elders with assistance through Medicare, a program that pays for hospital care and other medical costs for people over age sixty-five. In 2003, Congress added a program to help pay for prescription drugs to Medicare coverage. However, Medicare has high deductibles and co-pay requirements and does not include dental or long-term care (Kaiser Family Foundation, 2010, 2012).

The cost of medical care has been rising steadily in the United States. In 2013, Medicare spending for elderly people reached almost $600 billion, a figure that will likely double by 2023. Seniors spend about 15 percent of their household budget on health care, triple the share among younger people. To help cover the cost of health care not covered by the government Medicare program, 56 percent of elders purchase private health insurance. Even with this additional coverage, many seniors face challenges in paying the bills. One key reason that this is the case is that as people get older, they face an increasing number of health-related problems (Cubanski et al., 2014; Kaiser Family Foundation, 2014).

The cost of medical care increases dramatically as people age and health declines. These costs are especially high for those who must move to a nursing facility. Although just 4 percent of U.S. elders live in a nursing facility at any given time, almost half will live in such a facility at some point. Here again, Medicare and private insurance typically pay only some of the costs, and the rest can easily overwhelm many people (Federal Interagency Forum, 2012).

Death and Dying

Sooner or later, we all face the reality of death. One of the most important challenges of growing old is coming to terms with the end of this life.

How people think about death and dying is shaped by culture. In low-income nations, many infants die at birth, and many as half of those born die before reaching their teenage years. Because medical professionals are few and far between, family members care for one another in times of illness. Therefore, people in low-income nations die in the company of family and friends. As a result, people in low-income societies come to accept death as a common part of everyday life.

Modern societies, however, gain greater control over health. But reliance on trained professionals removes death and dying from everyday life. Have you ever seen a person die? For most of us, the answer is no because family members and friends approaching death are whisked away to die behind closed doors in the company of medical specialists. Even in hospitals, morgues are well out of sight for patients and visitors (Ariès, 1974; F. R. Lee, 2002; Pew Research Center, 2013).

In our society, the work of preparing bodies for burial or cremation is not done by family members but by professional morticians, and most of our rituals dealing with death take place not in family homes but in the facilities of funeral businesses.

In sum, U.S. culture treats death as a topic to avoid. However, a new social movement, with elders leading the way, is trying to bring death and dying out in the open, raising some important questions that we now examine.

Euthanasia and the Right to Die Higher living standards and advanced medical technology mean people today live far longer than they did in the past. Modern life also transforms death from an event into a decision. In other words, more and more deaths in the United States result from a deliberate decision to cease life-extending treatment.

In recent decades, a right-to-die movement has developed, claiming that dying people—rather than doctors and hospital personnel—should decide when, where, and how people die (Morris, 1997; Ogden, 2001). It may not be possible to escape death, but the right-to-die movement claims that people with terminal diseases should be allowed to guide the process of dying and, if they wish, to ask others for help in bringing about their deaths. This policy is called **euthanasia** (from Greek words meaning "a good death"), *assisting in the death of a person suffering from an incurable disease.*

Euthanasia has two forms. *Passive euthanasia* involves doctors ending the treatment of a terminally ill person by, say, turning off respirators or other life-support machines. Passive euthanasia is generally accepted by lawmakers and is widely practiced by doctors. An increasing number of people expect to invoke passive euthanasia and have made their intentions known. More than 60 percent of U.S. adults say they have talked to another person about their wishes and 35 percent of all U.S. adults including 60 percent of those over the age of sixty-five have a *living will* that states which treatments they do and do not want if they are facing death and are unable to speak for themselves (Pew Research Center, 2013).

Active euthanasia, by contrast, involves a physician or other party actively bringing about a person's death. For example, a doctor might administer a lethal injection to a dying person to bring a painless end to life.

A middle ground between passive and active euthanasia is called *physician-assisted suicide*. In this case, a patient requests help in dying from a physician, who typically writes a prescription for lethal drugs. The doctor does nothing more and the patient decides if, when, and where to take the drugs.

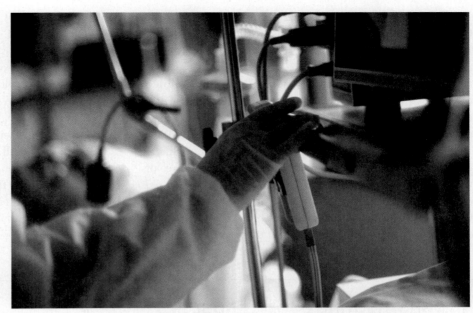

Public support for the claim that people have a right to die is increasing. Do you think people who are being kept alive by machines should be allowed to request that the machines be turned off? What about allowing a physician to prescribe lethal drugs that a terminally ill patient can choose to use?

Euthanasia in Europe Since 1981, the Netherlands has permitted active euthanasia under specific circumstances. Under Dutch law, patients can request euthanasia if they are dying with no hope of recovery, are suffering, and understand the medical options that are available. The participating doctor, in turn, must consult with another physician before acting to end a life (Tagliabue, 2008; Reuters, 2010). Dutch authorities report that about 2,000 people a year die with a physician's help. Because many cases are never reported, the actual number of cases may be twice as high.

Most people in the Netherlands support this policy of active euthanasia. Yet there is evidence that doctors do not always follow the rules. Critics point out that Dutch doctors assist in the deaths of people who, due to their illness, cannot clearly state that they want to die. In such cases, doctors help bring about death believing that this is in the patient's best interest, and usually nothing is reported to the government (Gillon, 1999; Barr, 2004). Still, this policy has the support of most Dutch people. In addition, in recent years, Belgium, Luxembourg, Switzerland, and Germany have enacted similar laws and active euthanasia is under discussion in other nations.

Another issue is whether euthanasia can be performed on people who are not terminally ill. In 2012, a Belgian physician euthanized two brothers, at their request. These men were both deaf and decided they wished to die after learning that they were also going blind. The physician defended the action as a proper response to patient suffering. Critics, however, fear that people may be pressured into choosing death by physicians or family members who are weary of providing care (Goldman, 2013).

Euthanasia in the United States The right-to-die debate continues in the United States, with people lining up to support or oppose active euthanasia. In 1997, the U.S. Supreme Court ruled (in *Vacco* v. *Quill* and *Washington* v. *Glucksberg*) that the Constitution does not recognize a right to die. This decision slowed the right-to-die movement that is seeking legalization of active euthanasia and supports the spread of physician-assisted suicide. Yet the state of Oregon passed a "death with dignity" law in 1997 permitting physicians to assist people in dying if the patients are judged to have less than six months to live. The number of cases of physician-assisted suicide in Oregon has remained low—about 673 in fifteen years. In 2008, the state of Washington also enacted a law permitting physician-assisted suicide and Vermont did so in 2013. Even more controversial is the idea of family members assisting in death. In 2013, a Pennsylvania woman was charged with helping her aged and ill father take a fatal dose of morphine. Her case has not yet come to trial (Leff, 2008; *New York Times*, 2013; Pew Research Center, 2013; State of Oregon, 2013).

The right-to-die movement remains controversial. Supporters claim that most people favor having a choice about when and how to die, and many people will welcome help from a doctor to bring about a "good death." National surveys show that two-thirds of people in the United States do support terminally ill people receiving help from doctors in bringing about a good death.

Critics of the right-to-die movement claim that the laws enacted in Oregon and Washington will create a "slippery slope" with the nation gradually sliding toward more and more assisted suicide. How could we be sure, for example, that a request to end a life is not prompted by depression on the part of the patient? Surveys confirm the public concern that doctors not assist in the death of people who are simply "tired of living" (Smith et al., 2013).

And what of pressuring people to die? Isn't it likely that family members, perhaps eager for an inheritance or wishing to avoid high medical bills, will encourage an old or sick parent to seek an end to life? How could we be sure that health insurance companies won't weigh in to encourage active euthanasia, knowing that they will earn bigger profits if patients opt to end their lives rather than continuing with months of expensive treatments? Finally, what about the poor? Many doctors and hospitals already view poor patients and people without health insurance as financial liabilities—would they not try to save money by "getting it over with"? In short, critics claim that it is difficult to set clear moral guidelines for euthanasia and even harder to prevent abuse (Kleinman, 1997).

So far, the small number of assisted suicide cases in Oregon, Washington, and Vermont does not confirm the fears of critics that this country is on a "slippery slope" toward widespread euthanasia. But as the elder population of the country rapidly increases, and medical costs continue to increase, the euthanasia debate is sure to continue.

CONSTRUCTING SOCIAL PROBLEMS

A DEFINING MOMENT

A Good Death: Cicely Saunders and the Birth of Hospice

Living in London during the height of the Industrial Revolution was not easy. Poverty was widespread, disease was common, and people moved about in a world teeming with strangers. With so many problems facing the living, why would anyone take time to think about people who were dying?

Cicely Saunders (1918–2005) was a nurse and physician who grew up in London early in the last century. She had struggled with her own illness and was motivated by a strong desire to help others. From her years of working with patients in hospitals, Saunders viewed illness not just as a medical or biological event but also as a social experience. Therefore, she fashioned her job into what we might call a medical social worker.

In 1948, Saunders began work with a patient, a refugee who had fled Poland for London during World War II. The two eventually became very close, but their personal relationship was doomed by the fact that the man was dying of cancer. During the time that they spent together, Saunders and he spoke about how dying people typically do not get what they need from hospitals, which, after all, were created with the goal of curing illness.

Dying people, Saunders concluded, have special needs that call for a new type of care center. This thought developed into the idea of hospice, a place where people will find the means to control pain and the compassionate care that can make their final stage of life as comfortable and peaceful as possible. In addition, Saunders learned from her patients, dying people need help in addressing their fears and in bringing closure to their lives. The vision of hospice can be summed up as *palliative care*, which involves helpfully addressing a dying person's symptoms and responding to their physical, emotional, social, and spiritual needs.

As her ideas came together, Saunders also completed her medical training. Based on her vision of hospice care, in 1967 Saunders founded St. Christopher's Hospice in London, the first facility devoted completely to the care of dying people. In the United States, the first hospice facility was started in 1974. Today, more than 1.5 million people in this country receive hospice care each year, which represents about 42 percent of people who die.

In 1979, Queen Elizabeth II recognized the efforts of Cicely Saunders by elevating her to knighthood. Saunders is celebrated as one who helped change the way the medical profession—and the public—thinks about dying.

Cicely Saunders was a nurse and physician who believed that our medical system did not serve dying people very well. By founding St. Christopher's Hospice in London, she helped the world understand the meaning of a "good death."

Hospice Another important development affecting patterns of death is the increasing use of **hospice**, *homelike care that provides physical and emotional comfort to dying people and their families*. The first hospice facility in the United States opened in 1974. The Defining Moment box describes the work of Cicely Saunders, who helped found the hospice movement.

Today, more than 5,500 hospice organizations care for more than 1.5 million people each year. Unlike a hospital, where medical personnel work to save lives and restore health, a hospice staff helps people die in comfort and with dignity. Some hospice organizations operate homes where dying people go to spend their final days; more often, hospice workers go to the homes (or residential facilities) of dying people to assist them and their families.

The growth of hospice reflects the fact that many people want to avoid the impersonal and highly regimented environment of a hospital. Typically, hospice personnel work with a doctor and family members to be sure that the dying person is comfortable, using drugs as necessary to control pain but making no efforts to extend life unnaturally. The work of hospice is to help the patient and family members accept death in an environment that is as comfortable as possible.

Theories of Aging and Inequality

5.4 Apply sociological theory to issues of aging and age stratification.

The following sections present structural-functional, symbolic-interaction, social-conflict, feminist, and intersection theories to help explain many of the issues raised in this chapter.

Structural-Functional Theory: The Need to Disengage

Structural-functional theory highlights ways in which social patterns help societies to operate smoothly. Faced with the reality that all people get old and eventually die, societies must develop ways to disengage older people from work just as they must train younger people for the future. In principle, the solution to the problem of eventual human decline is *disengaging* the elderly, which then allows for transferring workplace roles and other responsibilities to younger people. Disengagement is a strategy to ensure that the aging of the population does not disrupt the performance of important tasks.

Retirement is the main strategy for easing older people out of productive roles when they near the point when they will not be capable of performing them well. Retirement occurs in technologically advanced and rapidly changing societies, where many older workers lack recent knowledge and up-to-date skills. By contrast, younger workers will bring the benefits of the latest training. Formally stated, **disengagement theory** is *the idea that modern societies operate in an orderly way by removing people from positions of responsibility as they reach old age.*

Disengagement is functional for society as a whole. But it also provides older people, after years of hard work, with the chance to rest, relax, and explore opportunities for travel or spending more time with family (Cumming & Henry, 1961; Voltz, 2000).

EVALUATE

Disengagement theory provides a strategy for society to maintain its operation even as its individual members eventually grow old and die. The gradual disengagement of elderly people may be functional or necessary for society as a whole but, as critics of this idea point out, giving up a job or other responsibilities is not always good news for older men and women. Many enjoy their work, and most look to their jobs for needed income. Therefore, a criticism of this theory is that disengagement of the elderly may carry important personal costs, including loss of income, loss of social standing in the eyes of others, and rising risk of social isolation. The need for people to remain active and socially engaged in old age points us to symbolic-interaction theory.

CHECK YOUR LEARNING State the basic idea of disengagement theory. What is one criticism of it?

Symbolic-Interaction Theory: Staying Active

Symbolic-interaction theory focuses on the meaning people construct in their everyday lives. As aging people withdraw from some activities, especially those that are physically challenging, most try to find new things to do. For example, retiring from paid work can lead people to pick up a new hobby, travel, or perform volunteer work. Finding new activities is especially important because people in the United States who reach age sixty-five, on average, can look forward to another nineteen years of life (Robinson, Werner, & Godbey, 1997; Smart, 2001; Arias, 2014).

Researchers have found that personal satisfaction in old age depends on remaining socially active (Havinghurst, Neugarten, & Tobin, 1968; Neugarten, 1996). **Activity theory** is *the idea that people enhance personal satisfaction in old age by keeping up a high level of social activity.* Activity theory also reminds us that older people, like people of any age, are diverse with differing needs, abilities, and interests. For this reason, no single policy of disengagement is likely to fit everyone, nor should we expect seniors who choose to withdraw from work to agree on the kinds of activities they will enjoy most (Havinghurst, Neugarten, & Tobin, 1968; Palmore, 1979).

Activity theory helps us recognize the social diversity of older people. But keep in mind that at least some older people are not physically able to maintain a busy schedule. Even healthy older people may find that living in a care facility provides few options for interesting activity. Many elders with low incomes also face limited choices about how to live. In short, seniors who are disadvantaged in various ways may not be able to shape their lives as they may wish. This concern brings us to social-conflict theory.

CHECK YOUR LEARNING   State the basic idea of activity theory. What is one criticism of it?

Social-Conflict Theory: Age and Economic Inequality

Social-conflict theory focuses on age stratification, pointing to ways in which U.S. society limits the opportunities and resources available to elders. By and large, our society gives the most power and the greatest privileges to middle-aged people. As we have explained, modern societies tend to define elderly people in negative terms, giving rise to both prejudice and discrimination. The law bans age discrimination in the workplace, but even so, companies usually prefer hiring younger workers. Similarly, the law forbids employers from forcing most older workers to retire, but companies are often eager to replace older employees with younger, lower-paid employees as a strategy to control costs. In short, some analysts conclude that capitalist societies treat older people as second-class citizens in pursuit of profit. In addition, in a society that typically values human beings according to their economic productivity, anyone who withdraws from paid work risks being defined as unworthy (Atchley, 1982; Phillipson, 1982).

Age is one important dimension of social stratification. Yet by focusing on the relative disadvantages of some elders, social-conflict theory misses the larger picture that, on average, recent decades have brought major economic gains to seniors. In the United States, the poverty rate for seniors—even those over the age of seventy-five—is actually well below the rate for the society as a whole.

In addition, today's seniors have a lot of political clout because most of them vote. In the 2012 presidential election, 72 percent of people age sixty-five or older voted, compared to 41 percent of people between the ages of eighteen and twenty-four (U.S. Census Bureau, 2013). It is true that some elders live in poverty and that many encounter prejudice and discrimination. But critics of conflict theory point out that the system meets the needs of older people fairly well.

CHECK YOUR LEARNING   State the basic idea of social-conflict theory. What is one criticism of this approach?

Feminist Theory: Aging and Gender

Feminist theory is a social-conflict approach focused on gender. Sooner or later, the challenges of aging will affect everyone—at least those of us who are lucky enough to reach old age. From a feminist point of view, however, we see that women face greater disadvantages in old age than men. Yes, women do typically outlive men. But women struggle against gender stratification throughout their lives, including when they grow old.

In fact, among seniors, gender-based disadvantages may actually be greater. Recall from Chapter 4 ("Gender Inequality") that, among all adults who work full time, women earn 77 percent as much as men. Among people between the ages of twenty-five and forty-four, the gender gap is *smaller*, with women full-time workers earning 81 percent as much as men. By contrast, among older workers between the ages of forty-five to sixty four, the gender gap is *greater*, with women earning just 74 percent as much as men. Finally, among people aged sixty-five and older (who may or may not be working), the gender gap in income is *greater still*, with women receiving 70 percent as much income as men.

What explains women's greater disadvantage in old age? First, older women are more likely than older men to work in low-skill service jobs that provide lower pay and less in the way of pensions and other benefits. Second, gender stratification in our society defines family responsibilities

Disengagement theory suggests that society gradually removes responsibilities from people as they grow old. Activity theory counters that like people at any stage of life, elders find life worthwhile to the extent that they stay active. As a result, many older men and women seek out new jobs, hobbies, and social activities.

as women's work, which makes it harder for women to join (and remain in) the paid labor force. Finally, today's older women grew up at a time when gender stratification was even greater than it is today—a time that social norms actually kept many women off the campus and out of many jobs entirely. With less education and fewer occupational opportunities, today's older women now have lower income than men of the same age.

In the years ahead, with more women than men graduating from college, and to the extent that workplace discrimination diminishes, the income disparity between older women and older men will probably go down. But as long as gender stratification remains, a legacy of lifetime disadvantage will mean that, in old age, women will have a harder time than men (Neugarten, 1996; U.S. Census Bureau, 2013).

EVALUATE

Feminist theory is one type of social-conflict theory that is gaining importance in sociology. Gender stratification operates at all stages of the life course, so to understand the social standing of the older population of the United States, we must consider gender.

Critics of this approach remind us that, although older women are disadvantaged in relation to older men, the income gap between the sexes had grown smaller over the last century. By the time today's young women reach old age—especially with a larger share of women than men earning college degrees—we should expect the social standing of men and women to be more equal.

CHECK YOUR LEARNING Explain what we learn from applying feminist theory to old age. State one criticism of this approach.

Intersection Theory: Multiple Disadvantages

Just as elderly women are socially disadvantaged in relation to elderly men, some categories of women face greater challenges than others. Intersection theory examines the interplay of various dimensions of inequality to show that some elderly women are further disadvantaged by race and ethnicity.

Figure 5–3 contrasts the poverty rate for various categories of the elderly population in the United States. Among non-Hispanic whites over the age of sixty-five, women have a poverty rate (8.6 percent) that is almost double that for men (4.6 percent). However, African American women (21.2 percent) and Hispanic American women (21.8 percent) have poverty rates that are almost five times higher than those for white men (U.S. Census Bureau, 2013). In short, dimensions of social stratification

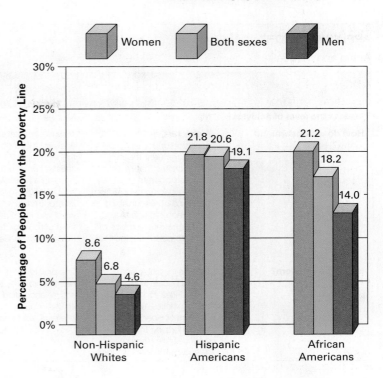

Diversity Snapshot

Figure 5–3 U.S. Poverty Rates by Race, Ethnicity, and Gender, Age 65 and Older, 2012

Among people over age sixty-five, Hispanic Americans and African Americans are more than twice as likely to be poor as non-Hispanic whites. In every category, older women are more likely to be poor than older men.

SOURCE: U.S. Census Bureau (2013).

involving gender, race, and ethnicity combine to shape the lives of older people.

EVALUATE

Intersection theory shows us that older women are a socially diverse category of the population, with some being much better off than others. The fact that there is no single "older woman" might well encourage us to investigate still other categories of the older population, including lesbians and people with disabilities. It is likely that all these categories of women have experiences that are distinctive in important ways.

Critics of this approach remind us that, although older women are disadvantaged in relation to older men, the income gap between the sexes has become smaller. By the time that today's younger people reach old age, we should expect the social standing of men and women to be more equal.

CHECK YOUR LEARNING What does intersection theory tell us about aging? State one criticism of this approach.

The Applying Theory table on page 152 sums up what each theoretical approach teaches us about aging and inequality.

APPLYING THEORY

Aging and Inequality

	Structural-Functional Theory	Symbolic-Interaction Theory	Social-Conflict Theory	Feminist Theory and Intersection Theory
What is the level of analysis?	Macro-level	Micro-level	Macro-level	Macro-level
How do we understand aging?	A structural-functional analysis supports disengagement theory, which claims that modern societies operate smoothly by disengaging people from positions of responsibility as they reach old age. Aging, then, amounts to a loss of ability to perform important roles.	A symbolic-interaction analysis supports activity theory, which links satisfaction in old age to keeping a high level of social activity. Aging is a time of transition during which people disengage from some activities and take on new ones.	Social-conflict theory focuses on age stratification. Society gives most power and privileges to people in midlife. In spite of age discrimination laws, most employers favor younger workers whom they can pay less.	Feminist theory points to the importance of gender stratification in old age. Intersection theory reminds us that dimensions of inequality combine to put some categories of people at greater disadvantage.
Is aging a problem?	Aging is inevitable and causes people to lose their abilities sooner or later. Societies avoid the problem of older people not performing their responsibilities through disengagement of the elderly.	The problems of aging can be minimized by remaining active, according to an individual's abilities, interests, and desires.	Many of the problems of aging are caused by our society's profit orientation, which devalues categories of people who are less economically productive.	Problems of aging are greater for women and other disadvantaged categories of the population who contend with more social problems throughout the life course.

 **POLITICS AND AGING**

Constructing Problems and Defining Solutions

5.5   Analyze aging and age stratification from various positions on the political spectrum.

As in other areas of social life, exactly how anyone views the social problems involving the elderly is guided by political attitudes. The Left to Right table summarizes how each political perspective—from radical left to conservative—defines age-related problems and solutions. We begin with conservative analysis.

Conservatives: More Family Responsibility

As conservatives see it, a healthy society is built, not on government looking after everyone (at the cost of personal freedom), but on personal responsibility. The social group that nurtures this sense of responsibility is the family. Conservatives also claim that our society's families have been getting weaker. In an age that celebrates individualism and independence, they say, the age-old system by which family members take care of their own is breaking down. This trend toward family decline is especially troubling because the elderly population is increasing and caregiving is now more necessary than ever. Weakening families is the conservative explanation for a number of social problems faced by older people, including social isolation, elder abuse, and poverty.

Women and men today are living longer and longer, which is good news. But this same trend also means that many families that are raising young children also find themselves having to care for aging parents. As conservatives see it, this is as it should be. But, conservatives argue, to face these challenges, we must reject a "me first" culture that makes many younger people less willing to take on family responsibilities. Here, conservatives part ways with feminists, claiming that feminism encourages women to view family life as less important than the workplace (Sommers, 2003).

Another important dimension of individual responsibility is planning for the future. Conservatives argue that people of all ages should plan ahead for their own old age through a program of saving and investment. With a long-term and disciplined savings plan, people will maximize the resources they have available for their old age.

All this is consistent with the conservative desire for limited government. Almost all conservatives support Social Security, although they point out that unless reforms are made, the current system will run out of money by about 2035. In recent years, conservatives who favor market solutions over government programs also argued for allowing people to invest some of their money in private accounts in order to earn a larger return. Such a reform of Social Security was tried by the Bush administration, but it became politically impossible with the onset of the recent recession. But some conservatives have supported expanded government assistance to older people. In 2003, for example, both Republicans and Democrats supported an extension of Medicare to help pay for prescription drugs.

In general, however, conservatives point to the soaring federal deficit and claim that we need to control

LEFT TO RIGHT

The Politics of Aging

	Radical-Left View	Liberal View	Conservative View
What is the problem?	Age stratification is one dimension of the striking social inequality caused by the capitalist U.S. economy.	Elders face a higher risk of poverty, as well as prejudice and discrimination based on their age, sometimes in combination with disadvantages based on class, race, and gender.	Although some seniors are poor, in general, older people do not face a host of social problems. In the United States, elders are more prosperous and live longer than they did in the past.
What is the solution?	Replacing the capitalist economy with a socialist system would end the practice of devaluing less productive people. Government must provide for the well-being of people of all ages.	Government programs (including Social Security and laws banning age discrimination) are crucial to meeting the needs of the rising elder population.	A culture of self-reliance will encourage most people to provide for their own old age; families should support elder members as necessary, and government programs should be a last resort.

JOIN THE DEBATE

1. To what extent, as radicals, liberals, and conservatives see it, are U.S. elders disadvantaged? What problems involving the elderly does each political position identify?

2. Compared to inequality based on gender, race, and class, how serious a problem do you think age-based inequality is? Provide specific facts to support your argument.

3. Of the three political analyses of aging and inequality included here, which do you find most convincing? Why?

government spending for various "entitlement" programs that provide income for various categories of people. In the 2012 presidential campaign, Republican candidates proposed raising the retirement age for receiving full Social Security benefits in the future; however, they were careful not to affect today's seniors, who are very likely to vote in presidential elections. Another strategy that finds favor with some conservatives, and that gains the support of liberals, is to limit or even cut off government benefits to well-off seniors who do not need them. As the number of seniors rises in the years to come, such policies would target Social Security on those who need it the most.

Liberals: More Government Assistance

Liberals differ from conservatives in their approach to problems involving older people because they reject the conservative idea that individuals and families should have to solve these problems for themselves. Liberals point out that many older people—especially those who have faced prejudice and discrimination their whole lives—simply have never had the opportunity to earn the money they need to carry them through old age.

Liberals also remind us that many of today's families depend on the earnings of both spouses just to meet their own needs, and too many men and women are out of work. Especially during tough economic times that have hurt average working families, most families have enough trouble taking care of themselves, never mind providing for older family members. Keep in mind, too, that many younger adults (especially women) come home from a day

of work exhausted. Stretched to the limit trying to meet their own needs and the needs of their children, can we really expect people to provide the care needed by family elders?

In addition, few older people want to depend on their children; indeed, the greatest fear of many older people is becoming a burden to their children. To help seniors remain independent, liberals conclude, the solution is not to limit social programs for the elderly but to expand them. Government programs that increase household income, ensure medical care coverage, and make affordable housing available—these are the "solutions" that would dramatically improve the quality of life for elders as well as their children. In an age of increasing economic inequality, liberals claim, government must raise more revenue by taxing those who earn the most and provide a broader safety net for everyone else.

The Radical Left: Capitalism and the Elderly

Radicals on the left have focused more on inequality based on class, race, and gender than on age stratification. But a left-radical analysis of aging was developed by Steven Spitzer (1980). Following Karl Marx, Spitzer argues that capitalist societies have an overriding focus on profits. For this reason, the culture of capitalism devalues any category of people that is economically less productive. To the extent that elderly people do not work—and to the extent that elders depend on pensions and other benefits—they are viewed as a costly burden to society. Understanding the culture of capitalism helps us to see why people typically define the elderly in negative terms and push them to the margins of society.

Conservatives believe that families should provide care as their members grow old. Liberals look to government to expand social programs that benefit seniors. Which political viewpoint do you think seniors themselves prefer? Why?

From the radical-left point of view, the solution to age-ism and other problems of inequality is to take the radical step of replacing the capitalist economy with one that values all people equally and meets the needs of everyone. In short, according to radicals on the left, a socialist economy would lessen all dimensions of inequality, including age stratification.

Going On from Here

This chapter has explained that older people suffer from a number of problems, including prejudice and discrimination, social isolation, poverty, and inadequate housing. Over the last two centuries, industrial societies raised living standards for everyone, but they also reduced the social standing of their oldest members relative to the young. Given the current trends, what can we expect in the future?

Looking ahead, perhaps the most important fact to keep in mind is the steadily increasing share of elders in the U.S. population. Elders are well organized and very active politically. As noted earlier, people over age sixty-five are much more likely to vote (72 percent cast a ballot in 2012) than those aged eighteen to twenty-four (41 percent). It is no surprise, then, that most politicians pay attention to the concerns of older people.

The political clout of seniors can also be seen in their improving economic standing. It is true that, as people move further into old age, income falls and the risk of poverty increases. Yet, in a dramatic change from fifty years

ago, the poverty rate for seniors as a whole (9.1 percent in 2012) is now below that for our society as a whole (15 percent) and well below that for young people (21.8 percent).

Still, there are grounds for concern. The greatest test for the elderly of tomorrow is likely to involve the Social Security system by which working people pay into the system and retired people collect benefits. Yet the rapid increase in the elderly population of the United States is placing demands on Social Security as never before. In 1950, there were six workers for every retired person. By 2050, projections indicate that there will be just two workers for every retiree, and most analysts believe that the current system will be bankrupt well before then. The strength of Social Security is especially important to African Americans and Latinos, who depend on the system for a larger share of their income in old age than non-Hispanic whites. The challenge is to ensure the financial security of all older people without placing an unfair burden on the young (Riche, 2000; Gendell, 2002; Andrews, 2005).

As government officials debate the future of Social Security, some critics—especially conservatives—point out that many older people are well-off. They would solve the Social Security problem by letting people set up private investment accounts and reducing benefits to well-off people who do not need government help. Liberals claim that more revenue must flow into Social Security to keep the current system operating so they would increase taxes, especially on the rich. Radicals on the left argue that only basic change to our economic and political systems will produce greater equality for everyone, regardless of age.

Most seniors are keenly interested in this debate over how much resources a society allocates to its oldest members and take an active part in political life. In the decades to come, of course, it is the younger majority—the elders of tomorrow—who will decide what changes are needed to improve their lives.

Essay: Envisioning a Better Society What changes to U.S. society do you expect to accompany the increasing share of our population that has reached the age of sixty-five? What policies or programs in support of seniors would you like to see in the future that would improve U.S. society?

CHAPTER 5 Aging and Inequality

Whose responsibility is it to support you in your old age?

This chapter has explained that people aged sixty-five and older, on average, face declining income. Although seniors overall are faring well in relation to younger people, most live on limited budgets even as they face higher costs for food and medical care. How our society should address the needs of the older population, as always, reflects people's political attitudes. Look at the accompanying photos, which show two general approaches to defining the solution.

Back in 1935, our society decided that government should provide part of the solution to economic security in old age. When President Franklin Delano Roosevelt signed the Social Security Bill as a cornerstone of his "New Deal," he established old-age pensions funded out of the earnings of younger workers. Today, however, as the ratio of older people (receiving benefits) to younger workers (paying into the system) keeps going up, the Social Security system needs more money—a problem that could be solved by raising Social Security taxes or by eliminating benefits to elderly people who are well-off. But the idea that the government should ensure everyone's basic economic security still has strong support from liberals.

Shouldn't you take responsibility for yourself? If you are more conservative, you are likely to see meeting your needs in old age (or, for that matter, at any age) as mostly your own responsibility. We expect people to give and receive support from family members. But, from this point of view, the solution to economic security in old age lies in personal financial planning and disciplined savings, and the earlier you get started the better.

Hint: Everyone who is lucky enough to live to old age will face the challenge of paying the costs of housing, food, and medical care. The question that our society wrestles with is how we should meet this challenge. In general, conservatives claim that individuals should take responsibility for themselves. From this point of view, people must ensure that they will have the resources they need—through working and a systematic plan to save for their retirement. Liberals claim that self-reliance is fine for well-off people, but what about those who have not been able to earn enough or who face lower income as pensions or benefits are cut? From their point of view, a government-centered approach is best. How conservative or liberal you are on this issue may come down to this: To what extent do you think higher-income people should help provide economic security for lower-income people?

Getting Involved: Applications and Exercises

1. Talk to someone who grew up in a culture outside the United States. Ask how members of that culture view the life course, and note how childhood and old age differ from what we understand.

2. Visit a senior citizen center in your community or near your campus. Ask about the social problems common to older people in your community. Why not volunteer to help out at the center once a week? This is an excellent way to get to know older people. Your efforts can be an enriching experience for all involved.

3. Ask your grandparents or other older people you know about their own experiences with aging. What do they say are the joys and sorrows of aging? What can they teach you about the experience of retirement?

4. Although there is more attention to death and dying today, this issue is still something of a social taboo. Are there any courses on your campus that deal with death and dying? Is there any organization such as a hospice in your community? If so, contact the organization to discover the range of services it provides.

CHAPTER 5   Aging and Inequality

A DEFINING MOMENT

A Good Death: Cicely Saunders and the Birth of Hospice **p. 148**

Growing Old

5.1   Explain the effects of industrialization on the process of growing old.

- The **life course** refers to the socially constructed stages that people pass through as they live out their lives. **Gerontology** is the study of old age, the final stage in the life course. **p. 135**

Aging is a biological fact of life, but the experience of growing old—and how people define "old"—is shaped by society.

- Preindustrial societies give most wealth and power to elders.
- Industrial societies confer lower social standing on the elderly. **pp. 135–37**

life course   (p. 135) the socially constructed stages that people pass through as they live out their lives
gerontology   (p. 135) the study of aging and the elderly
gerontocracy   (p. 135) a social system that gives a society's oldest members the most wealth, power, and prestige
life expectancy   (p. 137) the average life span of a country's population

The Graying of the United States

5.2   Discuss the graying of the United States and the social diversity of the older population.

The "**graying of the United States**" refers to the increasing share of the U.S. population over age sixty-five.

- People sixty-five to seventy-four—the "younger old"—are typically active and in good health.
- Older old" people—from seventy-five to eighty-four—experience more health-related problems and need more assistance.
- For the "oldest old"—people over eighty-five—staying healthy is the greatest problem. **pp. 137–39**

Problems of Aging

5.3   Assess various problems faced by today's elderly population.

Social isolation often occurs after retirement or the death of a spouse.

- Social isolation is more common among elderly women, who typically outlive their husbands. **pp. 139–40**

Retirement is an option in industrialized societies because a productive economy means that not everyone has to work.

- Corporate downsizing often results in forced retirement of older, higher-paid workers.
- Less economic security in recent years has resulted in many people finding themselves financially unable to retire. **pp. 140–41**

Ageism is prejudice and discrimination against older people.

- Ageism involves not just stereotypes but also discrimination in employment and housing.
- Ageism in the mass media casts older women and men in negative, stereotypical roles. **pp. 141–42**

Elder abuse, ranging from passive neglect to active verbal, emotional, and physical mistreatment, was recognized as a serious social problem only in the 1980s.

- At least 2 million elders suffer abuse each year, both from family members and from caretakers in institutional settings. **pp. 142–43**

The need for **caregiving** is growing as the share of the U.S population over age sixty-five steadily increases.

- Today's middle-aged people are a "sandwich generation" who will spend as much time caring for aging parents as they did raising children. **p. 143**

Poverty among elderly people is less common than it was fifty years ago because of improved retirement benefits and Social Security.

- In 2012, 9.1 percent of people over age sixty-five were living below the government's poverty line.
- A reflection of age stratification in our society, average income rises through middle age, peaks around age fifty, and falls as people enter old age. **pp. 143–44**

Safe, accessible, and affordable **housing** is a concern for many seniors.

- The United States lacks enough suitable housing to meet the needs of this nation's surging elder population. **pp. 144–46**

The rising cost of **medical care** is a growing concern for all categories of the U.S. population, but it is most pressing among older people.

- Government programs such as Medicare cover only some of the costs of medical care and nursing homes. **p. 146**

Facing the reality of **death and dying** is a challenge of growing old.

- Advances in medical technology that extend life now make death a decision; the right of very ill people to decide when to die is at the heart of the debate over euthanasia and physician-assisted suicide. **pp. 146–49**

ageism (p. 141) prejudice and discrimination directed toward older people

caregiving (p. 143) informal and unpaid care provided to a dependent person by family members, other relatives, or friends

age stratification (p. 144) social inequality among various age categories within a society

euthanasia (p. 146) assisting in the death of a person suffering from an incurable disease

hospice (p. 149) homelike care that provides physical and emotional comfort to dying people and their families

Theories of Aging and Inequality

5.4   Apply sociological theory to issues of aging and age stratification.

Structural-Functional Analysis: The Need to Disengage

Structural-functional theory highlights ways in which social patterns help societies operate smoothly.

- *Disengagement theo*ry argues that society must disengage elders from important roles, passing responsibilities from one generation to the next. **p. 149**

Symbolic-Interaction Analysis: Staying Active

Symbolic-interaction theory focuses on the meaning people find in their everyday lives.

- *Activity theory* states that elders who remain involved in many social activities have greater life satisfaction. **pp. 149–50**

Social-Conflict Analysis: Age and Economic Inequality

Social-conflict theory highlights age as a dimension of social stratification.

- Modern *societies define elderly people in negative* terms, causing both prejudice and discrimination. **p. 150**

Feminist Analysis: Aging and Gender

Feminist theory focuses on the importance of gender stratification in old age.

Intersection Theory: Multiple Disadvantages

Intersection theory explains that older women and other minorities are subject not only to ageism but also to sexism and racism.

disengagement theory (p. 149) the idea that modern societies operate in an orderly way by removing people from positions of responsibility as they reach old age

activity theory (p. 149) the idea that people enhance personal satisfaction in old age by keeping up a high level of social activity

⭐ POLITICS AND AGING

Constructing Problems and Defining Solutions

5.5   Analyze aging and age stratification from various positions on the political spectrum.

Conservatives: More Family Responsibility

- Conservatives support a society based on strong families in which people take responsibility for their own lives and future needs.
- Conservatives support a limited role for government in providing assistance to people in old age. **pp. 152–53**

Liberals: More Government Assistance

- **Liberals** point to many problems that challenge people in the United States as they reach old age.
- Liberals support an expansive role for government in providing assistance to people in old age. **p. 153**

The Radical Left: Capitalism and the Elderly

- **Radicals on the left** criticize capitalism's emphasis on efficiency and profit, claiming that this is why many look down on older people who are no longer economically productive.
- Radicals on the left believe the way to address poverty and other problems experienced by the elderly is to create a more equal society for the benefit of everyone. **pp. 153–54**

Chapter 6
Crime, Violence, and Criminal Justice

 ## Learning Objectives

6.1 Identify serious crimes, as well as trends and patterns in crime rates.

6.2 Define a number of specific types of crime.

6.3 Discuss the causes and consequences of violence in our society.

6.4 Analyze the operation of the U.S. criminal justice system.

6.5 Apply biological and psychological theories to the issue of crime.

6.6 Apply sociological theory to the issue of crime.

6.7 Analyze crime and violence from various positions on the political spectrum.

Tracking the Trends

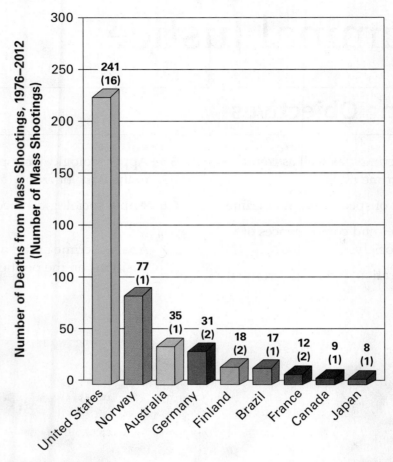

SOURCE: Statista (2014).

High-income nations provide a high quality of life in material terms. But when it comes to violence, some are far safer than others. Between the years 1976 and 2012, most high-income nations did not experience a single mass shooting. Others had one or two. The United States experienced sixteen shootings involving seven or more fatalities, resulting in 241 deaths, which is more than all the other nations combined. Compared to other rich nations, why is the United States a more violent society?

Constructing the Problem

Are you safe from crime?

Despite a downward trend in crime rates, more than 10 million serious crimes are recorded each year in the United States, and the actual number may be three times as high.

Is violence always wrong?

Our society defines some violence as a problem, but we also rely on violence as a way to solve problems.

Does our criminal justice system guarantee everyone accused of a crime a fair trial?

More than 97 percent of people charged with a crime never stand trial at all but are sentenced through a plea bargain.

Chapter Overview

What are the most serious types of crime? This chapter tracks trends in both violent and property crime. You will learn what categories of people are likely to be arrested as "street criminals" and you will recognize how people arrested for "street crime" differ from those involved in "organized crime" and "corporate crime." This chapter also explores the extent of violence in our society and explains why violence is sometimes defined as harmful and sometimes defined as useful. You will carry out theoretical analysis of crime and violence and understand the major justifications for punishment. Finally, you will learn how people's political attitudes lead them to define certain issues involving crime as "problems" and particular policies as "solutions."

On a warm Florida afternoon in early 2014, seventy-one-year-old Curtis Reeves settled into his seat in a movie theater for the matinee showing of *Lone Survivor*, a film that follows the exploits of Navy SEALS. Next to Reeves sat his wife. Another two dozen people were scattered about the small theater.

Two rows ahead sat forty-three-year-old Chad Oulson and his wife, Nicole Oulson. Concerned about their young daughter who was with a babysitter, Chad Oulson was sending a text message. Curtis Reeves became annoyed. He leaned forward and told Oulson to stop texting in the theater. Moments later, Reeves got up from his seat and went to the back of the theater, apparently to enlist the help of the manager. Finding the manager busy, Reeves returned to his seat. Oulson turned and ridiculed Reeves for trying to "report him."

The two men exchanged angry words. Then Oulson threw his popcorn bag at Reeves. Reeves stood up and drew a gun from his pants pocket. He fired a single shot that struck Chad Oulson in the chest and hit Nicole Oulson in the hand. Chad Oulson died later that day in a nearby hospital.

Reeves, a retired police captain, was soon standing in a county courtroom. Reeves claimed that his action was taken in self-defense, consistent with Florida law that allows citizens to "stand their ground" if threatened and to defend themselves. The judge did not agree and charged Reeves with murder in the second degree (Almasy & Fantz, 2014).

Barely a week goes by in the United States without a story of this kind appearing in the mass media. The details vary from case to case, but there is always pain and suffering, always wonder at how something so horrible could happen, and always wounds that may never heal. What is clear, however, is that we live in a society that experiences a considerable amount of crime and deadly violence. This chapter examines the problem of crime in the United States, asking what crime is, how much crime takes place, and who the offenders are. Special attention is given to violence, including the violent crime that causes so much fear among the public. Finally, we shall examine how our society responds to violations of the law through the criminal justice system, and we shall assess how well this system seems to respond to the crime problem. Let us begin by defining several important terms.

Understanding Crime

6.1 Identify serious crimes, as well as trends and patterns in crime rates.

Norms, Law, and Crime

All societies make rules defining what people should and should not do. **Norms** are *rules and expectations by which a society guides the behavior of its members*. Many everyday norms are informal and conformity is encouraged as people simply make a verbal comment or raise an eyebrow. A stricter type of norm is a **law**, a *norm formally created through a society's political system*. Most laws are enacted by a legislature (such as Congress), although laws also come into being through executive orders (by a local mayor, state governor, or national president) and also through international treaties.

A society's law includes both civil and criminal statutes. *Civil law* defines the legal rights and relationships involving individuals and businesses. Civil law comes into play when, say, an automobile accident prompts one person to sue another to receive payment for loss or damages. *Criminal law* defines everyone's responsibility to uphold public order. The driver of a car that runs off the road, if found to be intoxicated, is likely to face arrest for a criminal violation. So civil law involves claims of harm or loss leading to a financial settlement, and violations of criminal law involve charges of wrongdoing leading to arrest and punishment.

Crime is *the violation of a criminal law enacted by the federal, state, or local government*. Federal laws apply everywhere in the United States, and state and local laws apply within more defined areas or jurisdictions. Crime can be divided into two major categories. A **misdemeanor** is *a less serious crime punishable by less than one year in prison*. A **felony** is *a more serious crime punishable by at least one year in prison*.

Under our legal system, crime typically involves not only an action (or, sometimes, a failure to act) but also intention. In deciding whether a person has committed a crime, then, a court must establish not only what a person did but also the person's *intent*, that is, what the person meant to do. For example, a court can classify a killing in any number of ways, ranging from self-defense (in which someone acts with deadly force but with the intent only to escape serious injury or death) to murder in the first degree (in which someone plans and carries out the killing of another person). The killing described in the opening to this chapter led to a charge of second-degree murder because, although the judge did not see the shooting as self-defense, the killing was not planned in advance.

A recent survey found that 55 percent of U.S. adults consider dealing with crime to be a "top priority" for our society (Pew Research Center for the People & the Press, 2013). Each year, police record some 10 million serious crimes. At some point over a lifetime, just about everyone living in the United States is victimized by crime (Federal Bureau of Investigation, 2013). Because crime is so common and widely reported in the mass media, the fear of crime is widespread. In fact, fear of crime is itself a social problem because it limits the things people do and the places they go. For example, one-third of U.S. adults say they are afraid to walk alone at night in their own communities (Smith et al., 2013).

Crime Statistics

Police departments across the country make regular reports to the Federal Bureau of Investigation (FBI), which compiles an annual publication entitled *Crime in the United States: Uniform Crime Reports* (UCR). This report includes data on felonies or serious crimes of two types. The first is **crime against property**, which is *crime that involves theft of property belonging to others*. Crimes against property include burglary, larceny-theft, motor vehicle theft, and arson. The second type is **crime against persons**, *crime that involves violence or the threat of violence against others*. Crimes against persons include murder and manslaughter, aggravated assault, forcible rape, and robbery. Table 6–1 defines all of these serious crimes.

The UCR data are certainly useful, but there are two reasons to view these statistics with caution. First, the

UCR includes only crimes that are known to the police. But how many crimes are never reported? To answer this question, the FBI conducts the annual National Crime Victimization Survey. Researchers ask a random sample of the U.S. population whether they have been victims of serious crime within the past year. A comparison of survey responses with official crime reports suggests that about one-half of violent crimes and just one-third of property crimes are reported to the police. Realistically, then, a complete tally might show that as many as 20 million offenses actually occur each year (U.S. Department of Justice, 2013).

A second concern is that the UCR gathers statistics on "street crimes" but not "elite crimes," which include business fraud, insider stock trading, corruption, price fixing, and illegal dumping of toxic wastes. Elite crimes are the offenses more likely to be committed by rich people including corporate executives. When we put these shortcomings together, we see that the UCR not only underestimates the actual extent of street crime but, with a focus on street crime, it gives a biased picture of the typical criminal as well.

Violent Crime: Patterns and Trends

Violent crimes, that is, crimes against persons, account for just 12 percent of all serious offenses; crimes against property account for the remaining 88 percent. Put differently, the crime rate for property offenses is more than seven times higher than that for violent crimes against persons (U.S. Department of Justice, 2013). Figure 6–1 on page 164 shows the rates (the number of reported crimes per 100,000 people) for both crimes against persons and crimes against property.

From 1960 until the early 1990s, the rate of violent crime steadily increased. After that, the trend turned downward. (The rate of property offenses also went up after 1960 with a downturn in the early 1980s and further decline through 2012.) What accounts for the drop in crime rates? Analysts point to various factors, including a strong economy during the 1990s (although rates have continued to drop during the recent economic downturn). In addition, the downward trend in crime reflects a drop in the use of crack cocaine, the hiring of more police, and tougher sentences for criminal convictions (K. Johnson, 2000; Liptak, 2008; Antlfinger, 2009). We now take a closer look at trends for each offense covered by the UCR.

Murder In 2012, police recorded 14,827 murders, which means that on average, across the United States, a murder took place every thirty-six minutes. Looking back in time, however, the U.S. murder rate has been falling since 1993,

Table 6–1 Serious Crime in the *Uniform Crime Reports*

Crimes Against Property	
Burglary	The unlawful entry of a structure to commit a [serious crime] or theft
Larceny-theft	The unlawful taking, carrying, leading, or riding away of property from the possession … of another
Motor vehicle theft	The theft or attempted theft of a motor vehicle
Arson	Any willful or malicious burning or attempting to burn … the personal property of another
Crimes Against Persons	
Murder or nonnegligent manslaughter	The willful (nonnegligent) killing of one human being by another
Aggravated assault	An unlawful attack by one person upon another for the purpose of inflicting severe or aggravated bodily injury
Forcible rape	The carnal knowledge of a female forcibly and against her will*
Robbery	The taking or attempting to take anything of value from the care, custody, or control of a person or persons by force or threat of force or violence and/or by putting the victim in fear

*NOTE: In 2013, a new definition of forcible rape was adopted: "Penetration, no matter how slight, of the vagina or anus with any body part or object, or oral penetration by a sex organ of another person, without the consent of the victim." This definition expands the scope of acts defined as rape and also includes all people (not just females) as victims.

SOURCE: U.S. Department of Justice (2013).

and it now stands at about the same level as it did back in 1960 (U.S. Department of Justice, 2013).

The FBI also tracks the percentage of murders that are "cleared," meaning that the police arrested someone for the crime, whether or not that person was later found to be guilty. In 2012, police made arrests in 63 percent of all reported murders (U.S. Department of Justice, 2013).

Most murder victims (78 percent in 2012) are males. African Americans (about 13 percent of the population) are at especially high risk: The FBI reports that 51 percent of murder victims are black, 46 percent are white, and the remainder is of other racial categories. The statistics also show that murder is an intraracial crime, meaning that offenders and victims typically are of the same race. In 91 percent of cases involving an African American victim, the arrested suspect is of the same race; this pattern holds for 84 percent of murder cases involving a white victim (U.S. Department of Justice, 2013).

FBI data show that for murder cases in which the relationship of the victim to the offender could be determined, 78 percent of victims knew the offender. Furthermore, in 23 percent of the cases, victim and offender were actually related. A relationship between the victim and the offender is especially likely when the murder victim is a woman: 35 percent of female victims were murdered by husbands or boyfriends, but just 3 percent of male victims were killed by wives or girlfriends (U.S. Department of Justice, 2013).

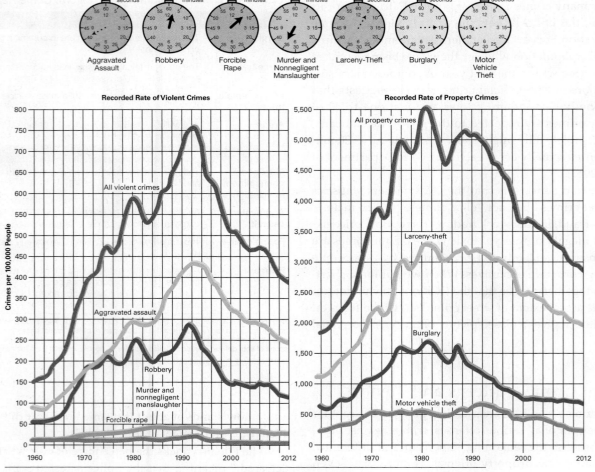

Figure 6–1   Crime Rates in the United States, 1960–2012

The graphs represent crime rates for various violent crimes and property crimes between 1960 and 2012. "Crime clocks," shown at the top of the figure, are another way of describing the frequency of crimes.

SOURCES: U.S. Department of Justice, Federal Bureau of Investigation (2013).

Many cases of homicide also include a history of the killer stalking the victim (Lowney & Best, 1995). **Stalking** is defined as *repeated efforts by someone to establish or reestablish a relationship against the will of the victim.* One study found that 3.3 million people say they have been stalked during the past year, and in some cases the stalking went on for five years or more. About 75 percent of these victims are women. Men (in most cases, celebrities) are usually stalked by strangers, but women are almost always stalked by people they know–typically, by former husbands or boyfriends. Most stalkers threaten their victims, some vandalize property, some harm or kill pets, and a few end up engaging in deadly violence (U.S. Department of Justice, 2012). The Personal Stories box takes a closer look at how stalking came to be defined as a serious social problem.

Forcible Rape   In 2012, the FBI recorded 84,376 rapes in the United States, which amounts to one every six minutes. Efforts by colleges and universities to educate students about "date rape"—sexual assault in which the offender and victim know one another—have encouraged more victims to come forward. Even so, across the country, only about 28 percent of women who are raped make a report to the police. Further, in just 21 percent of reported rape cases do police make an arrest despite the fact that most attackers are known to their victims. One reason for the low arrest rate is that the fear and shame experienced by some women discourage them from pursuing prosecution.

The FBI statistics do include attempted rape, but they do not include sex with a minor (typically a person under eighteen) when no force is used, which is a crime known as *statutory rape*. In addition, until 2013, the government's rape statistics did not reflect attacks on males, even though some researchers have found that male rape victims suffer greater physical injury than female victims. The government classified a sexual attack on a male either

PERSONAL STORIES

Stalking: The Construction of a Problem

Have you ever felt waves of fear, knowing that you are in real danger, and yet no one was there to help? That was the experience of a woman we will call Darlene Woodbury. Hers is a story of crime and violence, and it is also illustrates how our society defines a new social problem.

For two years, Darlene Woodbury lived with Richard. Early on, Darlene found Richard to be charming and kind. But gradually he changed, and soon Richard was trying to control her every movement, often erupting in explosive anger when Darlene did anything that displeased him.

Fearing for her safety, Woodbury moved out, stayed with relatives, and steered clear of Richard. But her absence only fueled Richard's anger, and he repeatedly tracked her down and threatened to harm her if she did not come back to him. Woodbury called the police and explained what was going on. But the police responded that they could not arrest Richard unless he actually became violent.

The threats continued. Again and again, Woodbury called the police. But the police kept insisting that Richard had broken no law and that they could do nothing as long as Richard was "only talking."

As you can probably guess, the story ends badly. One day, Richard called Darlene Woodbury to say he was leaving town and wanted to pick up some things from her. With a sense of relief, Darlene agreed to meet him in front of her aunt's house. When Richard arrived, she walked to the street and handed him a box.

Suddenly, he exploded with rage. Darlene turned and ran back toward the house. Richard started his van, drove up over the curb and across the lawn and ran down Woodbury, crushing her against the house. Her family looked on in horror as bricks from the front of the house tumbled down around her lifeless body.

This murder took place in 1980, when there were no laws requiring police to protect people like Darlene. But in the wake of this and similar incidents across the country, the social movement concerned with domestic violence began claiming that the law should protect victims of what we now call "stalking." This social movement created a new social problem and, in 1990, California lawmakers passed the nation's first antistalking law.

Within a few years, all fifty states enacted a similar law. Today, victims of stalkers can get police protection and a court order requiring that people like Richard stay away from them or face arrest and jail (Tjaden, 1997; Tjaden & Thoennes, 1998; U.S. Department of Justice, 2009).

What Do You Think?

1. This story illustrates the way society constructs social problems: What are the key steps in this process?

2. Why do you think no stalking law existed in the United States before 1990?

3. Can you think of other examples of social problems that were constructed in this way? Explain.

---

as an aggravated assault or as some other sexual offense (U.S. Department of Justice, 2013).

Aggravated Assault Aggravated assault is the most common crime against a person, accounting for 63 percent of all reported violent crime. Despite a downward trend in the assault rate after 1991, police recorded 760,739 aggravated assaults in 2012, which works out to one crime every forty-one seconds. Police make arrests in 51 percent of reported cases. Aggravated assault is a very male crime: A large majority of both victims and offenders are young men (U.S. Department of Justice, 2013).

Robbery Robbery involves both stealing and threatening another person, making this act both a property crime and a violent crime. In 2012, there were 354,520 robberies, with one occurring somewhere in the United States every ninety seconds. Since 1991, the general trend in the robbery rate has been downward.

Because victims usually do not know the people who rob them, of all violent offenses robbery is the least likely to result in an arrest: In 2012, police cleared just 29 percent of robberies. Again, almost all (87 percent) offenders were males, and most (62 percent) of these men were under age twenty-five. Race is also a factor in robbery: In 2012, African Americans accounted for 55 percent of arrests, whites represented 43 percent, and the remaining 2 percent were classified in some other racial category (U.S. Department of Justice, 2013).

What are your chances of becoming a victim of a violent crime? National Map 6–1 on page 166 shows the risks of violent crime for people living in counties across the United States.

Property Crime: Patterns and Trends

In 2012, law enforcement agencies across the United States recorded 9 million property crimes, which is

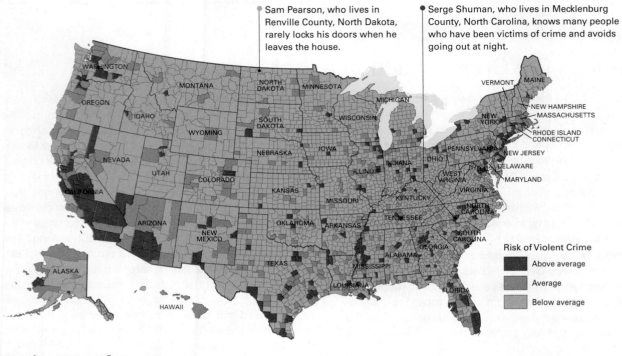

Sam Pearson, who lives in Renville County, North Dakota, rarely locks his doors when he leaves the house.

Serge Shuman, who lives in Mecklenburg County, North Carolina, knows many people who have been victims of crime and avoids going out at night.

Risk of Violent Crime
■ Above average
■ Average
■ Below average

Seeing Ourselves

National Map 6–1 The Risk of Violent Crime across the United States

The map shows the risk of falling victim to violent crime—in this case including murder, rape, and robbery but not aggravated assault—for all counties across the United States. In most places, the risk is below the national average, suggesting that violent crime is concentrated in certain areas of the country. Can you explain the pattern?

SOURCE: CAP Index, Inc. (2011).

more than seven times the number of violent crimes. Nationwide, a property crime occurs every four seconds, with annual losses of about $16 billion (U.S. Department of Justice, 2013).

Typically, the victim of a property crime never sees the offender. This is one reason that police make an arrest in only 18 percent of reported property crimes compared to 43 percent of reported violent crimes (U.S. Department of Justice, 2013). The following sections provide a brief look at each property crime.

Burglary Despite a decade-long decline in the burglary rate, there were still more than 2.1 million burglaries in 2012. This translates to one crime every fifteen seconds and an annual total property loss of more than $4.7 billion (the average loss per burglary is about $2,200).

In 2012, police cleared just 11 percent of known burglary cases. Of suspects arrested, 84 percent were male and 55 percent of these men were under the age of twenty-five (U.S. Department of Justice, 2013).

Larceny-Theft Larceny-theft includes familiar forms of stealing such as shoplifting, picking pockets, purse-snatching,

taking property from a motor vehicle, and stealing bicycles. Unlike burglary, such cases do not involve "breaking and entering," and offenders typically commit their crime in a public place and use no force or violence.

Larceny-theft is the most common of all the serious crimes tracked by the FBI and accounts for 60 percent of the total. In 2012, the FBI reported 6.2 million incidents of larceny-theft, which averages one such crime every five seconds. Even after a recent downward trend, the larceny-theft rate in 2012 was almost twice as high as it was in 1960. In 2012, the value of lost property from such crimes nationwide exceeded $6 billion (an average loss of $987 per incident).

In 2012, law enforcement agencies cleared 16 percent of larceny-theft cases. A slight majority of the suspects arrested were male (57 percent), with females making up the rest (43 percent) (U.S. Department of Justice, 2013).

Motor Vehicle Theft Here again, the recent trend for this crime has been downward. Yet, the number of motor vehicle thefts—including stealing cars, trucks, buses, motorcycles, and snowmobiles—still exceeded 720,000 in 2012. Nationally, one motor vehicle theft took place every forty-four seconds. The FBI estimated losses in 2012 at $4.3 billion (an average loss of $6,019).

In 2012, police cleared just 7.4 percent of motor vehicle thefts. Almost 50 percent of offenders who were arrested were under age twenty-five, and 81 percent were males (U.S. Department of Justice, 2013).

Arson Police and fire investigators determine whether a suspicious fire was caused by arson. The FBI does not have data on arson for the entire country, but some studies suggest that millions of cases of arson occur annually and that the rate has remained about the same in recent years. The FBI reports that about half of arsons involved structures (such as houses or businesses), with the remainder fairly evenly split between mobile property (such as cars) and other property (such as fences or crops). The average loss in arson cases came to $12,796, typically a much greater loss than in other types of property crime.

To what extent does the availability of firearms contribute to this country's high rate of violent crime? Especially since the election of President Obama, gun sales have been brisk, perhaps driven by a concern that tighter controls on firearms may be coming. Supporters of the constitutional right to bear arms consider gun ownership to be a basic freedom. Critics, however, claim that being able to reach for a gun often turns violence deadly.

In 2012, police cleared 19 percent of known cases of arson. Again, of suspects arrested, 82 percent were male, and 57 percent were under age twenty-five (U.S. Department of Justice, 2013).

"Street Crime": Who Are the Criminals?

Using FBI data, we can "profile" the typical street criminal in terms of age, gender, social class, race, and ethnicity. Keep in mind that this profile is based not on courtroom convictions but on arrest data provided by police.

Age For all offenses, those most likely to be arrested are the young. Arrest rates for both violent crime and property crime peak in the late teens and the rates have fallen dramatically by the time people reach middle age. People aged fifteen to twenty-four make up just 14 percent of the U.S. population, but in 2012, they accounted for 37 percent of arrests for violent crimes and 43 percent of arrests for property crimes (U.S. Department of Justice, 2013).

Gender Men make up about half of the general population, but in 2012, they accounted for 63 percent of arrests for property crimes. This means that police arrest men for property crimes almost twice as often as they arrest women. For violent crimes, gender is

even more important: Men represent 80 percent of all arrests, four times the women's share.

Women show up more often in the arrest data for certain crimes, including larceny-theft (43 percent of arrests are of women), fraud (41 percent), embezzlement (48 percent), and prostitution (68 percent). In addition, for all serious crimes, the gender gap is narrowing: From 2003 to 2012, the number of arrests of women *increased* by 3 percent, while arrests of men *fell* by 13 percent (U.S. Department of Justice, 2013).

Social Class Because there is no simple measure of someone's social class, the FBI does not track the class standing of people arrested for serious crime. But sociological research has long shown that people of lower social position are involved in most arrests for street crime (Thornberry & Farnsworth, 1982; Wolfgang, Thornberry, & Figlio, 1987; Reiman, 1998).

Crime and violence are serious problems in many low-income neighborhoods. But remember that most people who live in these neighborhoods obey the law. The sociologist Elijah Anderson (1994, 2002) conducted field research in inner-city Philadelphia and found that neighborhood contained mostly decent, hardworking families. Crime rates may be high in such communities, but most crime is committed by a small number of repeat offenders.

Keep in mind, too, that the link between class and criminality depends on the type of crime we are talking about. If we consider not just street crime but also the types of financial crimes that occur on Wall Street, the profile of the "common criminal" would include a much larger share of rich people.

Race and Ethnicity Both race and ethnicity are linked to crime rates. With regard to property crime, whites represent 68 percent of all arrests, and African Americans account for 29 percent. In the case of violent crime, whites represent 59 percent of arrests and African Americans 39 percent. In terms of actual numbers, then, most "street crime" arrests involve white suspects. But in proportion to their share of the population (about 13 percent), African Americans are more likely than whites to be arrested (U.S. Department of Justice, 2013).

African American men in the United States face a serious problem: Black males are six times more likely than white males to spend time in jail (U.S. Department of Justice, 2013). In fact, one study found that one-third of black men in their twenties were either in jail, on probation (sentenced to a period of court supervision), or on parole (under court supervision after release from prison) (Mauer, 1999).

Why does race play a large part in the crime picture? First and most important, African Americans have a high poverty rate. More than one-third of all black children grow up in poverty, compared with one-eighth of white children (U.S. Census Bureau, 2013). For some, a lack of hope for the future breeds hostility toward police and distrust of "the system." As a result, some young people adopt what Elijah Anderson calls the "code of the streets," which endorses crime and violence as a way to survive in what they see as a dangerous society.

The second reason for the high arrest rate among people of color is closely related to the first: More police patrols are found in poor neighborhoods, especially those with high African American populations. Prejudice based on race and class can prompt people to suspect blacks of criminal behavior simply on the basis of skin color (the practice of racial profiling discussed in Chapter 3, "Racial and Ethnic Inequality"). For example, although about the same share of black and white people report using illegal drugs, black people are four times as likely as white people to end up in jail after a drug conviction (U.S. Department of Justice, 2013; Cottom, 2014).

A third factor linking race and arrest involves family patterns. Seventy-two percent of black children are born to single mothers, compared with 29 percent of white children. Single parents have less time to supervise children. The fact that single mothers typically earn less money adds to family pressures. For these reasons, children who grow up in poor families without fathers are at higher risk for criminality (Piquero, MacDonald, & Parker, 2002; Martin et al., 2013).

Once again, when considering the link between crime and race, remember that street crimes are offenses for which police are likely to arrest low-income people. But white-collar crime, corporate crime, and organized crime—all discussed in the next section—typically involve a far larger share of white and wealthy offenders.

Finally, Asian Americans are underrepresented in street crime statistics. Making up 5.1 percent of the population, Asian Americans figured in just 1.2 percent of all arrests in 2012. This lower criminality is due to higher income levels and also a strong cultural emphasis on family, discipline, and honor, all of which tend to discourage criminal behavior.

Other Dimensions of the Crime Problem

6.2   Define a number of specific types of crime.

Although street crimes command the greatest attention from the U.S. public, there are additional types of crime. The following sections address problems of juvenile delinquency, hate crimes, white-collar crime, corporate crime, organized crime, and victimless crimes.

Juvenile Delinquency

Arrest data show that young people play a big part in the U.S. crime problem. **Juvenile delinquency** is *violation of the law by young people* (the definition of a "juvenile" varies from state to state, but it is generally someone under the age of eighteen). Any violation of criminal law by a young person can lead a court to declare the individual a delinquent. But some laws—such as curfews and truancy statutes that require school attendance—apply to young people but not to adults. Criminal cases involving juveniles are heard in a *juvenile court*, which focus on helping children straighten out rather than simply punishing them.

Similarly, when punishment is applied to juveniles, incarceration typically extends only to the legal age of adulthood (typically between eighteen and twenty-one). In addition, the offender is incarcerated at a juvenile detention center rather than in an adult prison. The assumption here is that, compared to older offenders, young people are better candidates for reform. Thus the goal of the juvenile justice system is to protect the community and also to serve the best interests of youthful offenders themselves.

A young person charged with a serious offense, such as robbery or murder, however, may face "adult charges." This means that the alleged offender is tried in an adult court and, if found guilty, is sentenced as an adult, held in a juvenile detention center until the legal age of adulthood, and then transferred to an adult prison to serve out the rest of the sentence.

In the past, U.S. courts have sentenced young people to death. But in 2005, the U.S. Supreme Court ruled that offenders who were under the age of eighteen when they committed their offenses cannot be sentenced to death, whatever their crime.

Larceny-theft—including shoplifting—is the most common of all serious crimes tracked by the FBI. In many cases, stealing is motivated by the "kicks" young people get if they are able to "beat the system." Because of the high-tech surveillance equipment used by stores today, the odds of getting caught are high. How do you think courts respond to offenders who claim that their actions were "only a game"?

Hate Crimes

Hate crimes as a societal problem did not exist until the mid-1980s, when civil rights groups successfully led campaigns for states to pass laws creating this new category of crime (Jenness & Grattet, 2001). By 2014, forty-five states and the federal government had passed statutes that mandate additional penalties for offenses if they also meet the criteria of a hate crime. According to the FBI, a **hate crime** is *a criminal offense against a person, property, or society motivated by the offender's bias against a race, religion, disability, sexual orientation, gender identity, or ethnicity or national origin*. Not all states have hate crime laws. In addition, only six states have hate crime laws that punish bias crimes involving *all* of the factors included in this definition. In 2009, the Matthew Shepard and James Byrd Jr. Hate Crimes Prevention Act (named for two victims of hate crimes) gave the federal government the power to investigate and prosecute hate crimes in localities that either had no such laws or were unable or unwilling to apply them.

Beginning in 1990, when Congress passed the Hate Crime Statistics Act, the U.S. attorney general has collected data from law enforcement agencies about bias-motivated crimes. In 2012, the government recorded about 5,800 hate crimes. Figure 6–2 on page 170 shows that just under half of hate crimes on record (48 percent) involve racial bias (U.S. Department of Justice, 2013).

Many—perhaps even most—hate crimes are not reported. For one thing, some police organizations do not record or submit hate crime data. For another, many victims—particularly gay men and lesbians—are reluctant to report their victimization. For these reasons, the problem of hate crimes is surely greater than official statistics indicate.

The odds of becoming a victim of a hate crime are especially high for people with multiple disadvantages, such as gay men of color. Even so, hate crimes can victimize anyone: The government reports that in 2012, 24 percent of the hate crimes based on race targeted white people (U.S Department of Justice, 2013).

Hate crime laws remain controversial. Critics argue that because acts such as assault are already against the law, special hate crime laws are unnecessary. In addition, because such laws end up punishing people's attitudes toward others, critics view such laws as a step in the direction of government "thought police," who try to control not just what we do but also how we think (A. Sullivan, 2002). Supporters of hate crime laws counter that the government must take extra steps to protect categories of people who are frequent targets of hostility and violence. They argue that because hate crimes harm not just a single victim but also inflame entire communities, they should bring more severe penalties.

White-Collar Crime

If you watch police "reality" shows on television, it is easy to think that every person arrested for a crime is poor. Beyond street crime, there is another type of crime that typically involves people who are much better off. **White-collar crime** refers to *illegal activities conducted by people of high social position during the course of their employment or regular business activities*. White-collar crime occurs in banks and corporations and often

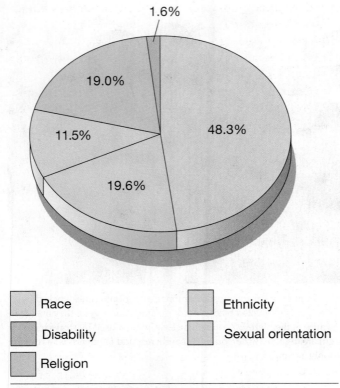

Figure 6–2 Bias-Motivated Offenses, 2012

Although the motivations for hate crimes vary, about half of all such crimes express racial bias.

SOURCES: U.S. Department of Justice, Federal Bureau of Investigation (2013).

involves offenders who are important members of a community. As compared with crime on the streets, then, white-collar crime is better described as "crime in the suites." The case of Bernard Madoff, convicted of numerous crimes after swindling investors out of more than $50 billion, provides a good example of white-collar crime.

Edwin Sutherland (1940), who pioneered the study of white-collar crime, noted that crimes ranging from fraud (obtaining money using false information) to insider trading (using restricted company information as the basis for a personal decision to buy or sell stock) to embezzlement (illegally taking money from one's employer) are far more common than people imagine.

Sutherland pointed out that the public often pays little attention to white-collar offenses. Historically, he explained, such cases have often been resolved in a civil court rather than a criminal court. This means that the person accused may have to pay damages but escapes being labeled a criminal and almost certainly will not go to prison. In today's world, we are all well aware of the Wall Street executives who do bad things—including breaking the law—but never face a judge or jury. Research confirms that white-collar offenders often

get off easy, so that even those who are convicted in a criminal court often serve no jail time. For example, just 54 percent of embezzlers convicted in the U.S. District Court system received any jail time at all; those remaining were placed on probation or fined (U.S. Department of Justice, 2014).

In recent years, some individuals have been sent to jail for engaging in fraud and other crimes. In 2012, for example, a federal judge sentenced Raj Rajaratnam, who was convicted of securities fraud and conspiracy, to eleven years in prison. Similarly, Lee B. Farkas, who was convicted of fraud in the housing and mortgage scandal, received a thirty-year sentence. To date, however, none of the CEOs of Wall Street banks involved in the financial crisis that threw the world into recession has faced criminal prosecution (Calabresi & Saporito, 2012; Eaglesham, 2012; Irwin, 2013).

Corporate Crime

Business crime involves not just the actions of individuals working within a company but also the policies and actions of companies themselves. **Corporate crime** is *an illegal act committed by a corporation or by persons acting on its behalf.* One example of corporate crime is *gross negligence*: knowingly producing a faulty or dangerous product. In one well-known case from the 1970s, Ford Motor Company continued to produce the Pinto, a subcompact automobile, despite the knowledge that a rear-end collision could rupture its gas tank causing an explosion and fire. Even after deadly accidents took place, Ford refused to order a recall that would have saved lives, deciding it would be cheaper to pay the legal claims resulting from future accidents. Eventually, lawsuits and a public outcry forced the recall and, soon after, also brought an end to the Pinto (Kitman, 2003).

Sometimes the line between white-collar crime (acts by individuals) and corporate crime (policies carried out by entire companies) is not clear. This is especially likely when the white-collar crimes are committed by top leaders in a company. The Enron corporation, which misstated its profits and losses to raise its stock price, eventually was forced to declare bankruptcy in 2001, and nineteen former executives subsequently pleaded guilty or were convicted of crimes. These convicted executives can be viewed as white-collar criminals, but the Enron collapse as a whole is also a case of corporate crime.

However we understand corporate crime, the losses it causes in the United States run into the hundreds of billions of dollars. The Enron case alone involved losses exceeding $50 billion. Of course, the losses involved in the collapse of the banking system in 2008 were far greater still, leading to government "bailouts" of well over $1 trillion.

For most of us, numbers this high are difficult to fully comprehend. But the simple fact is that the cost of white-collar and corporate crime is far greater than the costs of all the property crimes described earlier in this chapter. In terms of financial losses, white-collar and corporate offenses are the heart of this country's crime problem (Reiman, 1998; Lavella, 2002; CBS News, 2006).

Organized Crime

Organized crime is *a business that supplies illegal goods and services*. Such businesses profit from selling any number of goods and services that people want—including gambling, sex, and drugs—in violation of the law.

Organized crime in the United States expanded greatly during Prohibition (1919–33), when the federal government outlawed the manufacture and sale of alcoholic beverages throughout the United States. The ban on alcohol allowed the Mafia, also known as *La Cosa Nostra* (Italian for "our thing"), to gain wealth and power by illegally importing, producing, and distributing liquor to an eager public. With so much money to be made, criminal gangs—made up of people in just about every ethnic category—commonly protected their interest by using violence against members of opposing gangs as well as to frighten law enforcement officials.

Even after Prohibition was ended, members of organized crime continued to make huge profits, shifting their business from selling alcohol to selling illegal drugs. Mafia "families" became huge business enterprises, with profits rivaling those of legitimate corporations.

As the wealth and power of organized crime grew, Congress passed the Racketeer Influenced and Corrupt Organization Act (RICO) in 1970. This law gives police the authority to seize property such as cars, boats, or homes used in the commission of crimes involving gambling, prostitution, loan sharking, or illegal drugs.

In the decades since then, with the expansion of the global economy, organized crime has also become multinational in scale. The Social Problems in Global Perspective box takes a closer look.

Victimless Crime

Victimless crimes are *offenses that directly harm only the person who commits them*. Sometimes called *public order crimes*, victimless crime includes gambling, prostitution, public drunkenness, drug use, and vagrancy. These activities are against the law because they violate conventional norms and values, although people who engage in these things may not think of them as wrong. Still, victimless crimes can and do cause harm. For example, a large share

---

SOCIAL PROBLEMS IN GLOBAL PERSPECTIVE

Organized Crime: All Over the World

Corporations now operate as multinationals that do business all around the world. Organized crime, too, has "gone global," raking in huge profits that the early gangsters who ran local rackets in Brooklyn, New York, or the South Side of Chicago could never have imagined.

Today, organized crime's most profitable business is drug trafficking, which generates enough money to make the leaders of the biggest drug gangs richer than some entire countries. Just the sale of cocaine in the United States generates about $25 billion to drug cartels based in Colombia. However, drugs are not organized crime's only business. Gangs also pirate CDs and DVDs, sell weapons, smuggle illegal immigrants, kill people for profit, and even carry out acts of terrorism.

The Russian *mafiya* has a vast, worldwide business in weapons sales, car theft, illegal drug sales, money laundering, identity theft, and human slavery. Since the collapse of the Soviet Union in 1991, Russian crime organizations have expanded by forming partnerships with other criminal organizations around the world.

China's Six Great Triads are centuries-old organizations. Today, they have more than 100,000 members and stand as the world's largest criminal organizations. Based in Chinese communities around the world, the Triads deal in stolen cars, drugs, and weapons. They smuggle illegal immigrants, pirate electronics and software, and profit from gambling, loan sharking, and prostitution. Japan, too, has a vast criminal organization: The 60,000-member *Yakuza* engages in the same wide range of criminal activities.

All these organizations are active in the United States. In addition, drug-related violence in Mexico, which claims some 10,000 lives a year, has increased to the point that the U.S. Justice Department considers this violence to be the greatest crime threat to that country (Padgett, 2008, 2011; Grillo, 2013).

What Do You Think?

1. Do criminal organizations simply meet a demand from the public? Are they a real threat to the United States? Explain.

2. What actions, here and abroad, should the United States take to combat organized crime?

3. The drug-related death toll in Mexico threatens both that nation and the United States. Does our country have a legitimate interest in fighting the drug trade in Mexico? What could we do?

of prostitutes fall victim to violence at the hands of clients or pimps. In the same way, many "johns" who visit prostitutes pick up sexually transmitted diseases that they pass on to their wives or others.

Laws regulating the activities that are commonly considered to be victimless crimes vary from place to place. In most places, gambling is against the law, although thirty-nine states permit gambling in casinos, at racetracks, or on Indian reservations (American Gaming Association, 2013). Prostitution is illegal everywhere except for parts of rural Nevada. The purchase or possession of marijuana is now legal in Colorado and Washington and also in a few communities on the East and West Coasts. In addition, twenty-two states plus the District of Columbia have enacted medical marijuana laws that permit the purchase and use of marijuana under supervision of a physician (National Conference of State Legislatures, 2014). But where such activities are illegal, the enforcement of laws involving victimless crime is not consistent, usually taking the form of occasional crackdowns.

Many examples of violence exist within our society. The crash of a football tackle is certainly violent, and recent research is raising serious questions about the long-term effects of football on players' brain health. Yet few people consider football to be a social problem. Under what conditions is violence likely to be defined as a social problem?

Violence

6.3 Discuss the causes and consequences of violence in our society.

Violence is *behavior that causes injury to people or damage to property*. This chapter has already described many examples of criminal violence, including all the crimes against persons—homicide, rape, robbery, and aggravated assault.

But violence also plays a part in everyday life, often without anyone breaking the law. Many of our favorite sports (such as football) are quite violent, as are some forms of live entertainment (such as World Federation Wrestling) as well as many movies and video games.

Acting violently, then, may or may not be a crime, and people may or may not define violence as a social problem. Many of us consider some acts of violence to be quite normal and perhaps even desirable. Polls show, for example, that a majority of people in the United States have supported many wars as a necessary form of violence, and most people also support the death penalty (itself an act of deadly violence) as justified punishment for people

convicted of certain serious crimes. And there can be little doubt about the popularity of violent movies and violent sports.

Is Violence a Social Problem?

So when does violence become a social problem? A preliminary answer is that violence becomes a social problem to the extent that people define it that way. In other words, whether violence is or is not a problem has less to do with the violent act itself and more to do with how the action is defined by some audience.

But how do we decide which cases of violence are or are not a problem? In deciding how to define any act of violence, people commonly consider four basic factors:

1. **What do the actors intend by their actions?** A car crash is violent, but in most cases, people assume that the event was an accident and that the driver did not intend it to happen. We tend to be forgiving toward violence that we think is unintended. On the other hand, a driver who deliberately runs down a pedestrian almost certainly would face criminal prosecution.

2. **Does the violence conform to or violate social norms and values?** Many sports are violent without being seen as social problems. As the sociologist Harry Edwards (2000) explains, football is about as violent as hand-to-hand combat, causing personal harm including spinal cord injuries and brain damage. Even so, football fans crave the bone-crushing hits between rival teams. Why? Football, as Edwards explains, is a national ritual that upholds our cultural values of competitiveness, toughness, and masculinity.

3. **Does the violence support or threaten the social order?** Football may be violent, but it upholds our way of life. Football is also big business. Therefore, most people celebrate rather than condemn such violent sports. On the other hand, hazing incidents involving campus sororities and fraternities may disrupt the campus order and, if discovered by authorities, typically result in disciplinary action.

4. **Is the violence committed by or against the government?** In general, people accept government-sanctioned violence such as war, capital punishment, and the action of police SWAT teams because

they assume these actions benefit the public. In general, there is widespread support for **institutional violence**, *violence carried out by government representatives under the law*. In fact, most people believe that a certain amount of violence is actually necessary to keep society operating, whether it is used to oppose criminals or to defend our nation against foreign enemies. Of course, violence on the part of police or military personnel is not always lawful, as allegations of police brutality or U.S. soldiers intentionally killing innocent civilians remind us. But most people accept a considerable amount of violence carried out by "the system."

On the other hand, people are quick to condemn **anti-institutional violence**, *violence directed against the government in violation of the law*. The war on terrorism, which gained importance after the 9/11 terror attacks, has led us to define any violence directed against the U.S. government or its citizens as a serious problem. In the United States, most people were outraged by the anti-institutional violence of the 9/11 terrorists, yet most also supported the institutional violence of the U.S. military response in Afghanistan and Iraq. Of course, people will disagree about whether a violent campaign is just or unjust. The antiwar movement has worked to shift national opinion against the military presence in Iraq and Afghanistan.

Over time, members of a society carry on a debate about the right and wrong use of violence. In this process, a society comes to define new social problems. The Defining Moment box explains how this country came to define one type of violence—what we now call "child abuse"—as a serious problem.

CONSTRUCTING SOCIAL PROBLEMS

A DEFINING MOMENT

U.S. Society Discovers Child Abuse

In 1958, C. Henry Kempe was working as a physician in Denver's Colorado General Hospital. Every day, Kempe treated children for injuries such as lacerations and broken bones. Years of working in the emergency room and examining thousands of X-rays led Kempe to wonder if some children's injuries were really the "accidents" that the parents said they were. Kempe suspected that some of these wounds resulted from violence in the home.

At this time, the concept of "child abuse" did not exist. People assumed that parents had both the right and the duty to care for their children, including punishing children as they felt was necessary. What went on in the privacy of people's homes was a family matter, not a public issue.

Kempe decided to change that belief. To protect children from what he viewed as violence in the home, Kempe set up the hospital's first "child protection team," a group of people trained to investigate and evaluate children's injuries, deciding which might be the result of intentional violence. Three years later, he was able to document a surprisingly high level of deliberate violence against children, drawing the nation's attention to a new social problem he defined as "battered child syndrome."

Family violence obviously causes physical harm. Kempe explained that violence also results in psychological harm—including poor self-image and high risk of depression—that prevents injured children from forming trusting relationships.

Kempe's research prompted U.S. society to redefine violence against children from a private, family matter to a social problem. By 1966, every state had made child abuse a crime and required medical personnel to report suspected cases to authorities. As a result of these laws, about 3.1 million cases were reported in 2012, including about 686,000 confirmed to be serious and 1,640 fatalities. Kempe not only made a difference in the lives of children, but he also set the stage for our society, in the years ahead, to define two other types of family violence as social problems: violence against women and violence against the elderly (Kempe at al., 1962; U.S. Department of Health and Human Services, 2013).

Thanks to Dr. Kempe, doctors today routinely review medical data with an eye toward identifying cases of child abuse. This physician is using autopsy charts to describe the brain damage suffered by an abused six-year-old.

Serious Violence: Mass Murder and Serial Killings

Certain types of violence are almost always defined as serious social problems. Two examples of serious criminal violence are mass murder and serial killings.

Mass Murder A definition of **mass murder** is *the intentional, unlawful killing of four or more people at one time and place.* This type of violent crime is tragically frequent in the United States, with the mass media reporting a number of mass murders each year. The number of mass murders increased during the 1990s, with a number of deadly shootings occurring at a dozen public schools across the country. The worst case of mass murder was the killing of twenty children and six adults at the Sandy Hook Elementary School in Newtown, Connecticut, in 2012. Mass murder occurs not only in schools but also in the workplace when disgruntled workers vent their rage against a number of people they feel have wronged them.

Mass murder can also occur in the home. For example, in 2009, Graham Troyer's wife announced that she planned to divorce him. He responded by using a rifle to kill all five of his own children. He then searched for his wife and, unable to find her, turned the gun on himself. Mass murder can also take place in public, where it takes on the character of terrorism. In 2012, a disturbed young man wearing military clothing entered a movie theater in Aurora, Colorado, and fired guns into the crowd, killing twelve people and wounding fifty-eight. Mass murder takes place in other countries as well, although not as often as here in the United States. In 2011, a Norwegian man carried out two separate attacks on innocent people in the city of Oslo. First, he detonated a car bomb that killed eight people and then, dressed as a policeman, he systematically gunned down sixty-nine people in a rural area nearby. Although mass killing takes place in many nations, as the Tracking the Trends figure at the beginning of this chapter shows, such violence is much more common in the United States than in other high-income nations.

In most years, the death toll from mass murder in the United States is about fifty. This means that mass murder represents only about 0.2 percent of all the murders that take place in a year (in 2012, the total was 14,827 killings) (U.S. Department of Justice, 2013). But cases of mass murder are of great concern to the public because, for one thing, they receive extensive attention in the mass media. Just as important, most mass murders occur in schools, businesses, or homes, where people assume they are safe from violence.

What do mass murderers have in common? Almost all these offenders are men. School shootings typically involve young men—students or ex-students—who have experienced rejection by their peers. Mass murder in the workplace usually involves male employees or ex-employees, most of whom carry intense anger caused by perceived injustice and many of whom abuse alcohol or other drugs. Mass murder in the home typically involves men who have been rejected by spouses or other family members and who are emotionally distraught. Mass murderers are people with access to guns, and many were found to own many weapons (R. M. Holmes & S. T. Holmes, 1993; Hill, 2009).

Serial Murder Another type of killing that gets a great deal of public attention is **serial murder**, *the killing of several people by one offender over a period of time.* Typically, a serial killer commits one murder and then waits for a week or a month before killing again. Over time, however, the death toll—along with public fear—builds ever higher. In 2003, for example, Derrick Todd Lee was arrested and charged with the murder of five women in Louisiana. After a conviction on one of the killings, he was sentenced to death. The killings by the "Baton Rouge Serial Killer" made women in that urban region fearful for over a year (Deslatte, 2003).

A number of convicted serial killers have had even more victims. Back in the 1970s, Ted Bundy killed as many as thirty women. He was not the first serial killer to be identified, but it was his repeated crimes that prompted our society to define serial killing as a serious type of violence. Bundy was executed for his crimes in 1989. During the 1980s, Gary Ridgeway carried out a killing spree that involved at least forty-eight victims and may have involved twice that number. Ridgeway was sentenced to life in prison without parole. John Wayne Gacy, convicted of killing thirty-three young men, was executed in 1994. Jeffrey Dahmer was convicted of fifteen murders and in 1994 he died in a violent prison attack. In 2006, Robert Charles Browne, currently serving a life sentence in prison for one murder, confessed to forty-seven other killings putting Browne among the deadliest serial killers to date (Sarche, 2006).

Serial killers are probably the best known of all deadly offenders, and fictitious killers such as Hannibal "the Cannibal" Lecter have chilled millions of moviegoers. Although such cases grab the headlines, serial killers represent only a tiny fraction of all murderers.

What do we know about serial killers? Almost all are men. Most are mentally ill, suffering from psychotic disorders that distort their sense of reality and strip them of the ability to feel compassion for others. Some serial killers claim to hear voices or receive messages urging them to kill people in some specific category, such as women who are prostitutes or men who are gay. Others have an irresistible desire to control other people and gain great pleasure by putting others in fear. Still others cannot control their anger and strike out violently at anyone who might happen to get in their way. Finally, compared to those who commit single murders, most serial killers are somewhat older. These violent offenders are as likely to target men as women (P. Jenkins, 1994; R. M. Holmes & S. T. Holmes, 1998; Warf & Waddell, 2002).

The Mass Media and Violence

The mass media—radio, television, movies, and the Internet—have a huge influence on the way people—especially young people—view the world around them. Widespread violence in our society has no single cause, but many people wonder if the mass media play some part.

The basis of this concern is the enormous amount of violence in today's mass media. The typical young person in the United States watches about seven and one-half hours of media each day, and many television shows—even cartoons—contain plenty of violence. Over the course of a year, analysts estimate, a typical child observes roughly 12,000 violent acts (Groves, 1997; Rideout, Foehr, & Roberts, 2010).

Movies, on average, are even more violent than television shows. The high level of violence in the movies prompted the American Medical Association (American Medical Association, 1997) to declare that the mass media are hazardous to our health, reporting that three-fourths of U.S. adults say they have either turned off a television program or walked out of a movie because of high and disturbing levels of violence. Another survey found that two-thirds of parents are "very concerned" about the amount of violence that children see in the mass media. Making matters worse, this study found, characters that engage in violence typically are not punished, nor do they display any remorse (Rideout, 2007).

Does viewing violence make people commit violent acts? The answer may well be yes. A recent New Zealand study of 1,037 individuals over the course of twenty-six years found a significant link between the extent of childhood television watching and aggressive personality disorders as well as criminal convictions even when controlling for sex, intelligence, and social class (Robertson, McAnally, & Hancox, 2012). Other studies conclude that the more media violence children watch, the more they engage in rough play and the more likely they are to resort to violence when they become adults. In addition,

How much violence is presented on television? Researchers have concluded that most television shows contain at least some violence. Just as important, almost no shows contain antiviolence themes. At the very least, the high dose of violence that we receive from shows like *The Walking Dead* seems likely to reduce our reaction to violence, so we accept violence as an element of everyday life.

some offenders claim that, when committing their crimes, they were acting out behavior they saw in movies.

Watching violence in the mass media, then, may actually encourage people to be more violent. But perhaps an even more serious concern is that the media may end up *desensitizing* us all to violence. Living in a media-violence culture, in other words, we become so used to violence that the idea of people deliberately hurting each other no longer bothers us (Kromar & Valkenburg, 1999; Ritter, 2003; Federal Communication Commission, 2007; Pozios, Kambam, & Bender, 2013).

Poverty and Violence

Violence is also linked to poverty. Low-income people, who typically contend with poor nutrition, limited schooling, substandard housing, and lack of job opportunities, experience high levels of everyday stress. Most low-income people do not turn to crime or violence. But poverty does raise the *risk* of both. For this reason, some analysts claim poverty itself should be defined as a form of violence that harms tens of millions of people in the United States. Low-income people are highly represented among both offenders and victims of violent crime (Reiman, 1998; Parler & Pruitt, 2000; Hannon, 2005).

Youth Gangs and Violence

Especially in the poor neighborhoods of large U.S. cities, violence is linked to **youth gangs**, *groups of young people who identify with one another and with a particular territory*. Not all gangs are violent, of course. In fact, not all groups of young people are even called "gangs." We have a tendency to call middle-class groups "clubs" while calling groups of poor young people "gangs," regardless of how their members act.

A recent government study found 3,300 jurisdictions with "gang problems" and identified nearly 30,000 street gangs with 782,500 members (U.S. Department of Justice, 2013). Gangs range from nonviolent social groups to groups that sometimes clash over turf to all-out criminal organizations that engage in drug dealing, robbery, extortion, and even murder.

Who is likely to join a violent gang? The typical member comes from a poor, single-parent family in a neighborhood with high rates of crime and drug abuse and that offers few jobs. Many gang members have experienced violence in their own homes. Many young people look to gangs for opportunities, protection, and a positive self-image that they cannot find elsewhere (Zimring, 1998; Hixon, 1999).

Some low-income communities develop a "street culture" that teaches young people that the only way people will leave you alone is for you to be tough and quick to fight. In such a setting, young people—especially males—embrace violence as a strategy to avoid becoming a victim (E. Anderson, 1994, 2002).

The level of gang violence fell after about 1990, along with the overall crime rate. After 2002, however, gang-related violence in large cities was once again on the rise, with 1,824 gang-related killings in 2011. Police report that 87 percent of all gang-related homicides took place in larger cities and suburban counties. Some of the dead were innocent victims of stray bullets fired by people they never even saw (U.S. Office of Juvenile Justice and Delinquency Prevention, 2013).

Some cities have cracked down on gang violence. In Chicago—a city with a high level of gang violence—police have arrested many gang leaders. But this policy has not led to less violence. On the contrary, the loss of leaders caused a number of gangs to divide, fueling the level of violence (Altman, 2012).

Drugs and Violence

Violence is also fueled by the use of alcohol and other drugs. One government study found that 24 percent of the victims of violent crime thought their attackers were under the influence of alcohol or some other drug; another study found that 60 percent of people in prison for violent offenses said they were under the influence of a drug when they committed their crimes (U.S. Department of Justice, Bureau of Justice Statistics, 2011). The most recent study, based on urine tests of alleged offenders after arrest in five counties, reported that more than 60 percent of those arrested tested positive for illegal drugs (U.S. Office of National Drug Control Policy, 2013).

Drugs encourage violence by distorting judgment and reducing inhibitions. When a person already inclined to react to frustration and stress with violent behavior uses drugs, the odds of "losing it" go up (Gelles, 1997). In addition, some drugs are addictive and cause cravings so strong that people may turn violent in their search for the next high. In the process, drug abusers put those around them at risk, including children who may experience neglect or outright violence. In this way, drugs may create a cycle of violence that spills from one generation to the next.

Guns and Violence

Finally, many people blame our society's high level of violent crime on the easy availability of firearms. With at least 310 million guns in the United States, there are enough of these weapons to arm every man, woman, and child in the country. From another angle, about 34 percent of U.S. households have one or more guns. About 37 percent of these weapons are handguns, the type of gun most commonly used in cases of murder (Krouse, 2012; Smith et al., 2013). Figure 6–3 shows that, in 2012, half of all murders were committed using handguns. Thinking back to this chapter's opening story, if Curtis Reeves had not carried a handgun to the theater, the argument with Chad Oulson over texting would never have ended in deadly violence.

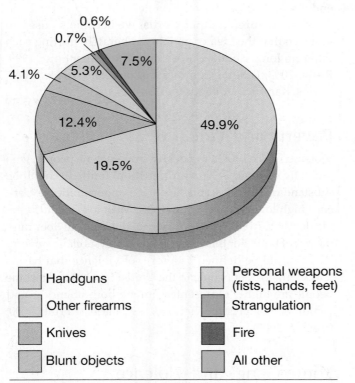

Figure 6–3 Murder: Type of Weapon Used

Firearms are used in two-thirds of all murders. Handguns are involved in almost as many killings as all other weapons combined.

SOURCES: U.S. Department of Justice, Federal Bureau of Investigation (2013).

These are the weapons used by Adam Lanza to kill twenty children and six adults at the Sandy Hook Elementary School in Newtown, Connecticut, in 2012. In a year and a half since that crime, seventy-four additional school shootings took place across the United States. Liberals point to the availability of guns as the main cause of these shootings; conservatives point to the difficulty in diagnosing and neutralizing people prone to violence due to mental illness.

Because many household guns find their way into the hands of criminals or even curious children, many people—especially liberals—define gun ownership itself as a serious social problem. They point out that many guns used in violent crime were readily purchased at a gun store.

Therefore, liberals continue, a solution to the problem of guns and violence is enacting laws that make guns harder to get. By restricting the availability of handguns, violence in the United States might not disappear, but it would become a whole lot less deadly. Supporters of gun control also favor laws requiring gun owners to apply trigger locks that make guns harder to use. In addition, they support a ban on military-style assault rifles and high-capacity ammunition clips. In a 2011 shooting spree, a man using a gun with a thirty-three cartridge ammunition clip had the firepower to gun down Representative Gabrielle Giffords and eighteen other people before anyone could attempt to disarm him.

Supporters of gun control point to Canada, where the government sharply restricts gun ownership (Canada has just 1.1 million handguns, compared with 114 million in the United States). There is no easy way to assess cause and effect here, but Canada's rate of firearms deaths is one-fourth that of the United States (Statistics Canada, 2013). In this country, not only are guns more readily available but also, as shown in National Map 6–2 on page 178, most states allow citizens to obtain a permit to carry a concealed handgun in public.

Reducing gun violence would provide enormous benefits to minority communities. Today, gun violence is the leading cause of death for African American and Latino males between the ages of fifteen and thirty-four (Williams, 2013).

Even so, not everyone thinks guns are part of the problem. Opponents of gun control—including many conservatives—point to the constitutional right to "keep and bear arms" as one of this country's basic freedoms. They claim that gun-control laws such as the 1993 Brady Bill, which requires a background check for anyone wishing to buy a gun, do little to keep weapons out of the hands of criminals, who typically obtain guns illegally. It is this thinking that underlies the popular bumper sticker that reads, "If guns are outlawed, only outlaws will have guns."

Some opponents of gun control go further and argue that gun ownership is actually part of the solution to the problem of violence. Why? When Ivan Lopez pulled out an unregistered handgun and opened fire on fellow soldiers on the Fort Hood military base in 2014, no one else was armed, allowing Lopez to kill three people and wound sixteen more before turning the gun on himself. Had other soldiers had weapons, it is likely that Lopez would have been stopped sooner, or perhaps never carried out his crime at all (Fishel & Pergram, 2014). The same logic applies to society as a whole, wherein widespread gun ownership may help to reduce crime because would-be criminals will think twice before they break into a home or rob a store where someone may be armed.

There is good news: Since 1993—the year that the rate peaked—the rate of gun violence has fallen by half. But that still leaves more than 10,000 killings a year involving guns. Keep in mind that about one-third of the murders in the United States do not involve guns at all. In fact, the number of people in the United States who are killed each year by someone wielding a knife is three times the number of Canadians killed by weapons of all kinds (Lott, 2000; Cohn et al., 2013; Statistics Canada, 2013; U.S. Department of Justice, 2013).

National Map 6–2 Who's Packin'? Concealed Weapon Laws across the United States

In only four states (Alaska, Arizona, Vermont, and Wyoming), any person can carry a concealed weapon without a permit. Nine other states (identified as "may issue" states) issue concealed weapon permits in cases of demonstrated special need. But in most states ("shall issue" states)—thirty-seven in all—permits are available to most people without special need. What regional pattern do you see? Can you explain this pattern?

SOURCES: Brady Campaign (2012) and Law Center to Prevent Gun Violence (2014).

The Criminal Justice System

6.4   Analyze the operation of the U.S. criminal justice system.

The **criminal justice system** is *society's use of due process, involving police, courts, and punishment, to enforce the law.* The following sections survey elements of the U.S. criminal justice system.

Due Process

The U.S. Constitution states that no person can be "deprived of life, liberty, or property without due process of law." In simple terms, *due process* means that the criminal justice system must operate within the bounds of law. The law recognizes that people charged with crimes have the right to confront their accusers and to defend themselves; they have a right to legal counsel and the right to a speedy, impartial, and public trial with a jury, if desired. Further, citizens can refuse to testify against themselves, and the criminal justice system cannot try a person twice for the same crime. In addition, the Constitution gives all people protection against excessive bail as well as cruel and unusual punishment

if they are found guilty of the charges against them (Inciardi, 2000).

Police

The first official response to crime involves police. The latest count tallied 670,439 police officers in the United States (U.S. Department of Justice, 2013). Still, even this many officers can provide only so much service to nearly 314 million people. Therefore, police must make decisions as to which situations are serious enough to require their attention.

Police Discretion   Police use discretion deciding whether or not to intervene in any situation. In a study of police discretion in five cities, Douglas Smith and Christy Visher (Smith, Visher, 1981; D. A. Smith, 1987) identified six factors that guided police in deciding whether or not to make an arrest:

1. **How serious is the crime?** The more serious a situation seems and the more it involves violence or the risk of violence, the greater the odds are that police will make an arrest.

Police must be allowed discretion if they are to handle effectively the many different situations they face every day. At the same time, it is important for police to treat people fairly. Here we see police deciding to make an arrest at an Occupy Wall Street rally in New York City in 2012. What factors do you think enter into this decision?

2. **What does the victim want?** If a victim demands that an arrest be made, police are more likely to do so.

3. **Is the suspect cooperative?** Police are more likely to arrest an uncooperative suspect.

4. **Does the suspect have a record?** Police are more likely to arrest someone they know has been arrested before.

5. **Are bystanders watching?** Police are more likely to make an arrest when people are watching. This gives police more control of the situation by moving it off the street.

6. **What is the suspect's race?** Smith and Visher argue that, all other factors being equal, police are more likely to arrest African American and Hispanic suspects than whites.

Changes in Police Policy Three recent changes in police work have contributed to the downturn in crime rates in U.S. cities. First, the practice of *community policing* makes police more visible to the public by moving some police officers from cars to bicycle or foot patrol. The idea is for officers to get to know local neighborhoods and for neighbors to get to know them; police and community cooperation is a proven strategy to reduce crime.

A second innovation in police work is a *zero-tolerance policy* under which police respond to any offense, no matter how minor. In recent years, for example, police in New York City have ticketed or arrested people for minor offenses including jaywalking and jumping turnstiles to enter the city's subway system. Supporters claim

that this policy deters crime because people who know any minor infraction may cause police to stop and search them are less likely to risk carrying an illegal weapon. Critics counter that a zero-tolerance policy encourages police to harass law-abiding citizens for minor infractions instead of concentrating on solving major crimes.

Courts

Arrest does not make someone a criminal. About half of suspects who are arrested are later released for various reasons, including a lack of evidence against them. The other half are formally charged and move through the criminal justice system toward trial in a court of law. In theory, the U.S. court system is an *adversarial process*, meaning that the prosecutor presents the state's case against the defendant and the defendant's attorney presents a defense against the charges. The judge or jury reaches a verdict based on the strength of the cases presented by the two sides.

Viewers of television shows such as *Law & Order* may imagine that this adversarial process is carried out carefully. In reality, it is rarely carried out at all. About 97 percent of all criminal cases are settled through **plea bargaining**, *a negotiation in which the state reduces a defendant's charge in exchange for a guilty plea.* Plea bargaining saves the time and expense of a trial, allowing courts to focus on the most serious cases. But a system that is efficient is not always just. This is especially true when dealing with low-income defendants. Under the law, the government must provide a public defender to any defendant who is unable to pay for a lawyer. Commonly, public defenders are young lawyers with limited experience; they are typically overworked and underpaid. As a result, a public defender may be eager to settle a case quickly. Without an aggressive defense, low-income defendants may feel that they have no choice but to "cop a plea." By relying so heavily on plea bargaining, our criminal justice system sometimes violates the ideal of due process by taking away a defendant's constitutional right to a trial in which the person is presumed innocent until proven guilty.

Punishment

In response to law breaking, the criminal justice system makes use of various forms of punishment, ranging from fines to jail time to death. In 2012, more than 2.3 million people were incarcerated in the United States, almost five times the number behind bars back in 1980 (U.S. Department of Justice, 2013). As shown in Figure 6–4, this

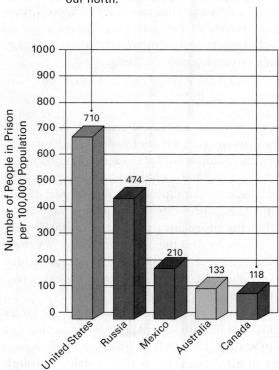

● The share of the U.S. population that is behind bars is six times higher than in Canada, the high-income country to our north.

Figure 6–4 Rates of Incarceration for Selected Countries

The 2012 rate of incarceration for the United States was 710 people for every 100,000 in the population. Among all the nations of the world, this country has the highest share of its people in prison.

SOURCES: U.S. Department of Justice (2013) and International Centre for Prison Studies (2014).

country now imprisons a larger share of its population than any other nation.

One reason for the increasing prison population is that many states have enacted tough sentencing laws. Twenty-eight states now have "three strikes and you're out" laws that require a life sentence for a third felony conviction. Another policy that raises the prison population is a mandatory prison sentence for specific serious crimes. The idea behind all these policies is to get people who commit serious crimes—especially repeat offenders—off the streets.

For decades, the debate over corrections has been dominated by voices favoring being "tough" on crime and accusing others of being "soft" on crime. A recent trend in the corrections field is moving past the old "tough" versus "soft" debate to being *smart* about crime. Conservatives make the point that recent increases in prison populations threaten to bankrupt states and cities. Liberals add that "three strike" laws and mandatory sentences laws are sending too many people who are not violent offenders to jail. Being "smart" about crime involves assessing the public threat that an offender represents and using prisons only for those who truly put the public at risk. In addition, prisons are not the only way to handle offenders. For some nonviolent offenders, community supervision may be an effective policy. For those with addiction and other personal issues, treatment strategies may make more sense than a lockup (National Conference of State Legislatures, 2011; Savage, 2011; Berman & Protass, 2013).

A larger question is why societies make use of prison and other forms of punishment. In principle, there are four justifications for punishing convicted offenders: retribution, deterrence, rehabilitation, and societal protection.

Retribution In human history, the oldest justification for punishment is to gain revenge against a criminal offender. **Retribution** is *moral vengeance by which society inflicts on the offender suffering comparable to that caused by the offense.* Retribution is based on the idea that the moral order of society is upset when someone commits a crime. But the moral balance can be restored by declaring the offender guilty and exacting a fitting punishment. The ancient saying "an eye for an eye, a tooth for a tooth" expresses this vision of justice and balance.

Deterrence A second reason to punish is **deterrence**, *using punishment to discourage further crime.* Deterrence is a more modern idea, emerging in the eighteenth century during the Enlightenment as people began to view themselves as rational decision makers. If society inflicts pain of punishment that outweighs the pleasure of the offense, people should realize that "crime does not pay" and behave themselves.

Punishment provides *specific deterrence* to the individual offender, who will think twice before offending again.

At the same time, punishment provides *general deterrence* by teaching everyone what happens to people who break the law. However, the success of deterrence rests on the assumption that people make rational decisions. For this reason, some offenders may not respond to punishment at all and, for most people, punishment may not deter so-called "crimes of passion." In addition, deterrence also works only to the extent that most offenders are caught, which, especially with respect to property crimes, is not the case in the United States today.

Rehabilitation A third justification for punishment is **rehabilitation**, *reforming an offender to prevent future offenses*. The idea of rehabilitation emerged during the nineteenth century along with the social sciences. If the reason people turn to crime in the first place is a bad environment, then we should expect a new and better environment to transform them into law-abiding citizens. It is easy to see why prisons built about this time were typically called *houses of correction* or *reformatories*.

Rehabilitation differs from retribution and deterrence in its positive intention: It tries to help people improve rather than to make them suffer. Rehabilitation also differs in another way: Retribution and deterrence demand that the punishment fit the crime, but rehabilitation means tailoring treatment to the personal needs of a specific offender.

Societal Protection The fourth reason to punish is **societal protection**, *protecting the public by using incarceration or execution to prevent an offender from committing further offenses*. In recent decades, the United States has built prisons at the rate of a new 1,000-bed facility every week. Placing more than 2 million people in jail, the argument goes, is bound to bring down the crime rate.

Does Punishment Work? We have now reviewed four justifications for punishment. But the question still remains whether or not punishment is an effective solution to the crime problem. Does punishment work? Or does punishment itself create problems? The answers are far from clear.

Retribution is based on the idea that responding to crime strengthens public morality. Some members of the public react to punishment with the comforting thought that justice is being done. Yet others argue that punishment— especially the death penalty—is not effective and only further brutalizes a society that already has too much violence.

Deterrence, too, is controversial. Although common sense suggests that punishment discourages crime, this

In recent years, the United States has imprisoned record numbers of people with the goal of controlling the crime problem. What arguments can you point to in support of this policy? On balance, do you think this policy works or not? Why?

country has a high rate of **criminal recidivism**, *later offenses by people previously convicted of crimes*. Studies suggest that roughly one-third of inmates who are released from prison are back in jail within three years either for committing a new crime or for violating the conditions of their release (Maruschak & Bonczar, 2013). A high rate of repeat offenders casts doubt on the idea that prison deters further crime.

What about rehabilitation? Again, prison may help some offenders "straighten out." But the high recidivism rate suggests that successful rehabilitation is the exception rather than the rule. Some critics claim that prison actually makes the crime problem worse. How? For one thing, putting offenders in jail with other offenders encourages them all to share their knowledge and skills with one another; prison is hardly a place that is going to reform anyone. In addition, the stigma of being an "ex-con" is likely to make getting a good job after release that much harder (Petersilia, 1997; DeFina & Arvanites, 2002).

Finally, punishment probably does result in societal protection. Few people doubt that in the short term, the rapidly increasing number of people in prisons has played a part in bringing down the crime rate. But whether this pattern holds for the long term—that is, as our large prison population is gradually released back into society—is less certain (K. Johnson, 2000).

Whatever the intentions of our system of punishment, there is increasing criticism of mass incarceration, by which an unprecedented 2.3 million people are behind bars. Conservatives typically point to the high costs of this practice. Liberals typically point to the harmful effects of incarceration, including subjecting people to the violence of prison life and breaking up families. In addition, the harmful effects of mass incarceration are targeted largely on people of color and minority communities. Perhaps, as some suggest, the money used to carry on the present policy of mass incarceration might better be used to invest in the low-income communities where street crime is most common (Justice Reinvestment, 2014).

Restorative Justice   A recent idea in the field of corrections is the concept of **restorative justice**, *a response to crime seeking to restore the well-being of the victim, offender, and larger communities lost due to crime*. The idea here is that, whatever conventional punishment may accomplish with regard to offenders, it does little to heal victims or the communities that are inflamed by crime. Therefore, courts that embrace restorative justice bring together offenders and victims to engage in dialogue about what happened, why it happened, and how the event affected each of them. Offenders are encouraged to understand their crime and to take responsibility for their actions. Victims have the opportunity to explain their loss, express their feelings, and assess their needs. No one expects victims to immediately forgive offenders. But the goal of restorative justice is a resolution that begins a long-term process of healing involving all parties ("Restoring Justice and Some Peace," 2013).

To conclude this discussion of punishment, one of the most important debates concerning punishment has centered on the death penalty. As Global Map 6–1 shows, the United States is one of the few high-income nations in the world that puts convicted offenders to death. The Social Policy box on page 184 takes a closer look at the controversy over the risk of innocent people being executed.

Restorative justice is a recent idea that seeks to move the judicial system from a focus on determining guilt and innocence to a focus on healing the victim, the offender, and the larger community. What advantages or disadvantages do you see in this response to crime?

Community–Based Corrections

Our society continues to rely on prisons to keep convicted criminals off the streets. But the weight of evidence suggests that prisons do little to rehabilitate most offenders. In addition, prisons are expensive: The cost of jailing one inmate exceeds $30,000 per year, not including the cost of building the prison in the first place (Vera Institute of Justice, 2012).

An alternative to the use of prison is **community-based corrections**, *correctional programs that take place in local communities rather than behind prison walls*. Community-based corrections have several advantages, including lower cost, reducing prison overcrowding, and supervising convicted offenders without applying the stigma that comes from imprisonment. However, the policy of allowing offenders to remain in the community is generally applied only to those who have been convicted of less serious, nonviolent crimes.

Probation   One form of community-based corrections is *probation*, a policy of letting a convicted offender stay in the community with regular supervision and under conditions imposed by a court. These conditions might include going to counseling sessions, enrolling in a drug treatment program, keeping a steady job, and avoiding contact with known criminals. Should the probationer fail to comply with these conditions, miss regular meetings with the probation officer, or commit another crime, the court may end probation and send the offender to prison.

Shock Probation   Another community-based corrections policy is *shock probation*. In this case, a judge imposes a substantial prison sentence but then orders that only part of the sentence will be served in prison and the rest will be served on probation. Shock probation mixes prison and probation with the goal of impressing on the offender the seriousness of the situation while avoiding a long prison term. In some cases, the lock-up portion of shock probation takes place in a special "boot camp" facility where offenders might spend several months in a military-style setting intended to teach discipline and respect for authority (Cole & Smith, 2002).

Parole   *Parole* is a policy of releasing inmates from prison to serve a remaining sentence under supervision in the local community. Most inmates become eligible for parole

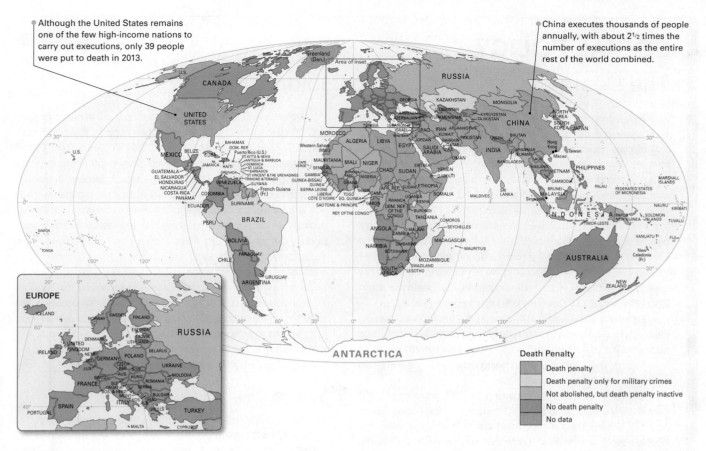

Although the United States remains one of the few high-income nations to carry out executions, only 39 people were put to death in 2013.

China executes thousands of people annually, with about 2¹/₂ times the number of executions as the entire rest of the world combined.

Death Penalty

Death penalty

Death penalty only for military crimes

Not abolished, but death penalty inactive

No death penalty

No data

Window on the World

Global Map 6–1 Capital Punishment in Global Perspective

The map identifies fifty-eight countries and territories in which the law allows the death penalty for ordinary crimes; in seven more, the death penalty is reserved for special crimes under military law or during times of war. There is no death penalty in ninety-eight countries and territories. In the remaining thirty-five countries, although the death penalty remains legal, no execution has taken place in more than ten years. Compare rich and poor nations: What general pattern do you see? In what way are the United States and Japan exceptions to this pattern?

SOURCE: Based on Amnesty International (2013).

after serving a specified portion of a prison term. At that time, a parole board evaluates the offender's chances of staying out of trouble, deciding to grant or to refuse parole. Should the offender not comply with conditions of parole or be arrested for another crime, the board can revoke parole and return the person to prison. In some cases of serious crimes, courts may sentence an offender to prison for a specified time without possibility of parole.

Do Probation and Parole Work? The evidence is mixed. Probation and parole cost much less than keeping someone in prison, and these policies do reduce prison overcrowding. It also makes sense to use prisons for offenders who commit serious crimes while monitoring those who commit less serious crimes in the community.

Probation and shock probation seem to be effective for some people. Parole is more controversial because

of the fact that so many people released on parole are soon arrested for another crime. For this reason, some states have abandoned the use of parole entirely. Yet this policy remains popular with prison officials because the chance to be released encourages good behavior among inmates.

Explaining Crime: Biological and Psychological Theories

6.5 Apply biological and psychological theories to the issue of crime.

Having examined both property crime and violent crime, we now turn to a basic question: Why does crime exist at all? Here, we review biological and psychological theories and, in the next major section, we turn to sociological explanations.

SOCIAL POLICY

The Death Penalty: Problem or Solution?

In 2000, Governor George Ryan of Illinois made a startling announcement. His state, he vowed, would stop all executions until officials could be sure that no innocent people would be put to death. Ryan had good reason for concern: Between 1987 and 2000, thirteen inmates in his state were released from death row after courts reviewed their cases and declared them to be innocent. Ryan, a longtime supporter of the death penalty, had come around to the view that Illinois "had a shameful record of convicting innocent people and placing them on death row." Before Governor Ryan left office in January 2003, he commuted the sentences of all 167 inmates on death row in Illinois to life in prison. In 2011, a new governor, Pat Quinn, signed a law outlawing the death penalty in Illinois (Babwin, 2003; Death Penalty Information Center, 2010).

Between 2006 and 2014, six states (Illinois, New Jersey, New York, Connecticut, Maryland, and New Mexico) have abolished the death penalty, bringing the total of states doing so to eighteen. The death penalty is being debated in the thirty-two states that retain death penalty laws.

Between 1977 and the beginning of 2014, more than 8,000 people were sentenced to death in courts across the United States, and 1,359 executions were carried out. At the same time, 144 people have had their death sentences overturned by the courts, including people found to have been innocent all along. The trend in sentencing offenders to the death penalty is downward, with 80 death sentences in 2013, down from 110 in 2010 and 224 in 2000. Similarly, just 39 executions were carried out in 2013, down from 46 in 2010 and 85 in 2000 (U.S. Department of Justice, 2013; Death Penalty Information Center, 2014). National Map 6–3 shows in which states more than 3,000 people across the country sit on death row.

When asked about using the death penalty in cases of murder, 65 percent of U.S. adults say they support it, and 35 percent say they do not (Smith et al., 2013). Supporters of the death penalty (typically conservatives) point out that this extreme form of punishment is used rarely—just 2 percent of people convicted of murder are executed—but that the death penalty is a necessary response to the most serious cases. Critics (typically liberals) counter that there is little evidence that the death penalty deters crime any more than a prison term. Even more important, there is mounting evidence that certain people—especially the poor, who rely on public defenders—are more likely to be sentenced to death, including some who are innocent. In addition, the extremely high cost of trials and appeals in death penalty cases is putting pressure on prosecutors not to seek capital punishment. In light of the mounting costs, questions about its effectiveness, and evidence that errors have been made, the question remains: Is the death penalty part of the solution or part of the problem?

What Do You Think?

1. Does the fact that juries can make mistakes mean there should be no death penalty, which, once inflicted, cannot be withdrawn? Why or why not?

2. Does the policy of providing public defenders for the accused who cannot afford an attorney ensure legal protection for all or does it mean "second-class justice" for the poor? Explain your answer.

3. Would you, as a member of a jury, be willing to vote for the death penalty? Why or why not?

Biological Causes

In the nineteenth century, an Italian doctor named Cesare Lombroso (1911, orig. 1876) came up with the idea that men in prison were physically different from law-abiding people. Lombroso pointed to several distinctive traits the men seemed to share: low foreheads, prominent jaws and cheekbones, protruding ears, excessively hairy bodies, and unusually long arms. Putting these traits together, Lombroso concluded that criminals appeared somewhat apelike. But Lombroso's work was flawed. He failed to see that the physical traits he found among prisoners were just as likely to be found in the general population.

Decades later, William Sheldon (Sheldon, Hartl, & McDermott, 1949) examined the body types of hundreds of young men, some criminal, some not. Sheldon found that men with athletic builds (he called such men *mesomorphs*) were more likely to be criminals than fat, round people (*endomorphs*) or thin, wiry people (*ectomorphs*). This pattern was later confirmed by Sheldon and Eleanor Glueck (1950). But the

Gluecks cautioned that a muscular build may not be the *cause* of criminal behavior. A more likely explanation, they thought, was that athletic boys become more independent. With more emotional distance from parents, perhaps muscular boys grow up less sensitive to others. The Gluecks also pointed out that people may expect muscular boys to act like bullies and treat them that way, creating a self-fulfilling prophecy that accounts for a higher rate of violence and criminal behavior.

By the 1960s, researchers began looking for a link between genetics and criminal behavior. An interesting finding is that men with an extra Y chromosome (XYY, a rare pattern compared with the normal XY pattern) may have a greater chance of criminal violence (L. Taylor, 1984; LaFree, 1998).

More recently, researchers in neurocriminology, a field that focuses on the biological causes of crime, have documented differences in the ventral prefrontal cortex of the brain—the area that controls emotional impulses—that distinguish criminal and noncriminal individuals. These researchers believe that mounting evidence links biology

Seeing Ourselves

National Map 6–3 Inmates on Death Row across the United States

In the United States, thirty-two states have laws permitting the death penalty. But some states apply these laws frequently, and others do not. For this reason, almost half (47 percent) of all prisoners on death row are in just three states. What regional pattern do you see for states that have condemned the most people? Can you explain this pattern?

SOURCE: U.S. Department of Justice (2013).

to criminal behavior. But they add that the way a child's brain develops is not simply a biological process but reflects the child's environment (Raine, 2013).

EVALUATE

Biological theories are gaining support in some circles. But they have yet to explain criminality. What is more likely is that genes, together with social influences, explain some types of criminality. Some research suggests that genetic factors (such as a defective gene that produces too much of an enzyme) together with environmental factors (such as abuse in early childhood) are linked to adult crime and violence (Lemonick, 2003; Pinker, 2003). But the major shortcoming of the biological approach is that most people convicted of crime turn out to be, biologically speaking, just like the rest of us.

CHECK YOUR LEARNING Describe ways in which researchers have tried to link biological traits to criminal behavior. Why is it fair to conclude that biological theories do not provide an adequate understanding of criminal behavior?

Psychological Causes

Like biological research, psychological study of crime focuses on the individual traits of offenders—in this case, abnormal personalities. Walter Reckless and Simon Dinitz explained male delinquency in terms of a boy's degree of moral conscience. These researchers began by asking

teachers to identify twelve-year-old male students who were likely to get in trouble with the law and those who were not. Researchers then interviewed all the boys and their mothers, trying to assess the boys' personalities and how they related to others. They found that the boys whom the teachers had identified as nondelinquent had a more positive self-concept and a stronger conscience. In practice, the "good boys" held to conventional norms and values and could handle frustration without becoming angry or violent. By contrast, the "bad boys" had weak belief in conventional norms and values and reacted angrily when frustrated.

As time went by, the "good boys" had many fewer contacts with police compared to the "bad boys." All of these boys lived in a high-delinquency area; therefore, Reckless and Dinitz attributed different outcomes to the "good boys" having a personality that allowed them to control or contain deviant impulses. Therefore, they called their analysis of delinquency *containment theory* (Reckless, Dinitz, & Murray, 1956, 1957; Dinitz, Scarpitti, & Reckless, 1962; Reckless & Dinitz, 1972; Reckless, 1973).

EVALUATE

Social workers and law enforcement officers give much attention to psychological theories. Few people doubt that personality traits play a part in encouraging or discouraging criminality. Some violent crimes are committed by people who are considered to be psychopaths because they apparently do not feel guilt or shame and they show little fear of punishment (Herpertz & Sass, 2000). But one problem with this approach, as with biological theories, is that many serious crimes are committed by people who are quite normal (Vito & Holmes, 1994). A second problem is that psychological theories focus on the individual, ignoring why a society defines some people as rule breakers in the first place. In short, to understand crime, we need to turn to sociological theories.

CHECK YOUR LEARNING   Explain "containment theory." Why does a psychological approach provide only a limited understanding of deviant behavior?

Explaining Crime: Sociological Theories

6.6   Apply sociological theory to the issue of crime.

Taking a sociological approach to deviance, we look for ways in which the organization of society itself gives rise to both particular laws and patterns of criminality. The

According to Emile Durkheim, one of the key functions of crime is uniting people with a shared sense of outrage. Here, students and parents link arms as they march to a high school in Chardon, Ohio, in March 2012, to honor the students who were killed in a mass shooting at the school. Has any similar event taken place in your community? Explain.

following discussions apply sociology's major theoretical approaches to the issue of crime.

Structural-Functional Analysis: Why Society Creates Crime

Structural-functionalist theory investigates how any social pattern contributes to the operation of society as a system. This approach guides several important theories of crime, beginning with the classic work of Emile Durkheim.

Emile Durkheim: The Functions of Crime   Emile Durkheim (1964a, orig. 1895; 1964b, orig. 1893), one of the first great sociologists, began by pointing out that crime exists everywhere. For this reason, he concluded, crime must somehow be useful to society. He went on to identify four functions of crime:

1. **Crime affirms a society's norms and values.** People cannot have a belief in what is good without having a corresponding understanding of what is bad. In short, any society can uphold a sense of morality only by recognizing crime.

2. **Recognizing crime helps everyone clarify the boundary between right and wrong.** When a college convicts a student of sexual harassment, that community is educating everyone on campus about where to draw the line between conventional behavior and behavior that will not be tolerated.

3. **Reacting to crime brings people together.** When an episode of crime victimizes a community, everyone is likely to come together in a shared sense of outrage.

4. **Crime encourages social change.** Deviance within any community suggests alternatives to the status quo. Behavior that people condemn as wrong at one point in time (whether it is rock-and-roll music or smoking marijuana) may turn out to become the norm later on.

Notice that Durkheim's theory asks not why some *individual* would engage in crime but why *society* defines some behavior as criminal. This insight helps us to understand the pattern noted earlier by which most people who are defined as criminals turn out to be quite normal. Durkheim concluded that crime is a creation of society, not individuals. In addition, he considered crime to be a normal and necessary element of society.

Robert Merton: Strain Theory   Robert Merton (1938, 1968) agreed that crime is a product of society itself. His theory also helps to explain how and why rule breaking takes various forms. Merton began by saying that our society sets up certain goals (such as gaining financial security) but does not always provide everyone with the means (including schooling and good jobs) to reach these goals. Therefore, Merton continues, patterns of rule breaking depend on, first, whether or not people accept society's goals and, second, whether or not society provides people with the opportunity to reach these goals. Merton identified five specific outcomes, which are shown in Figure 6–5.

Conformity is likely among people who accept society's goals and also have access to the conventional means to get there. For example, young people who strive for financial success and are willing and able to go to college and work hard to be successful are likely to be "conformists." But what if legitimate means to success are not available? Children growing up in poor, rural communities of Appalachia, for example, may see rich people on television but find few good jobs available locally. The strain between desiring cultural goals and having little or no conventional opportunity to achieve them will encourage people to engage in what Merton calls *innovation*, adopting some unconventional means to achieve a conventional goal. We can understand why some ambitious people living with little conventional opportunity in the Appalachian region of the country have turned to making moonshine or growing marijuana. People turning to theft and other property crimes can also be explained in this way.

Another option for people who have given up on the idea of achieving society's goals of success is *ritualism*, which Merton described as living almost obsessively by the rules. Living this way, even without expecting ever to be successful, at least offers some measure of respectability. A ritualist—for example, the local county clerk who never misses a day, takes exactly forty-five minutes for lunch, and never sends "texts" while at work—will never get rich but is proud to "do the right thing."

Still another response to a lack of opportunity is *retreatism*, turning away from both approved goals and legitimate means. In effect, retreatists "drop out" of society. Retreatists include some alcoholics, drug addicts, street people, and backwoods survivalists.

Finally, *rebellion* involves not just rejecting conventional goals and means but also advocating some entirely new system. Instead of dropping out of society the way retreatists do, rebels come up with a new vision of how to live, playing out their ideas as members of religious cults or revolutionary political groups.

Richard Cloward and Lloyd Ohlin: Opportunity Structure

Richard Cloward and Lloyd Ohlin (1966) extended Merton's theory, arguing that whether or not people turn to deviant behavior depends not only on access to legitimate opportunity (such as schooling or jobs) but also on access to *illegitimate* opportunity (such as the chance to learn how to carry out crime). In other words, people cut off from conventional opportunity might end up engaging in crime, but this is likely to the extent that they have the resources and opportunity to do so. In short, patterns of conformity

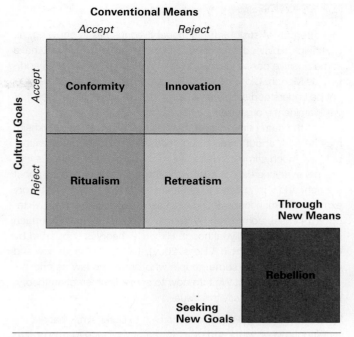

Figure 6–5   Merton's Strain Theory of Deviance

SOURCE: Created by the author, based on Merton (1968).

and criminality are likely to reflect what Cloward and Ohlin call people's *relative opportunity structure*.

Among people who have little legitimate opportunity to get to college but who do have illegitimate opportunity to make money through, say, prostitution or drug dealing, criminal activity is the likely outcome. On the other hand, people who are cut off from both legitimate and illegitimate opportunities may express their frustration through violence.

Travis Hirschi: Control Theory   Perhaps the best-known sociological theory of crime is Travis Hirschi's *control theory*. Hirschi (1969) argues that strong social and emotional attachments to others—that is, being well integrated into the community—discourage people from engaging in crime. Hirschi points out four kinds of social control that encourage conformity:

1. **Attachment to other people,** including parents, teachers, coaches, and friends

2. **Access to conventional opportunity,** so that people benefit from playing by the rules

3. **Involvement in conventional activities,** including holding a job, playing team sports, or participating in religious groups

4. **Belief in the rightness of cultural norms and values,** respecting authority figures, and seeing society as basically good

If these four types of social ties are strong, people are likely to resist the temptation of crime. To the extent that they are weak, the risk of drifting toward criminal behavior rises.

The strength of structural-functional theories lies in showing, as Durkheim explained, that crime and other forms of deviance have some positive consequences for the operation of society. In addition, as Merton, Cloward and Ohlin, and Hirschi explain, crime cannot be understood simply by looking at individuals but requires that we examine the organization of society itself.

At the same time, these theories have limitations. Durkheim may be right about crime being necessary to social organization, but how much crime is needed? Similarly, looking at Merton's theory, not everyone defines success in the same way or agrees about the right and wrong ways to get there. Cloward and Ohlin's theory explains common forms of crime but seems unable to explain white-collar offenses committed by people who already have so much going for them. Finally, although Hirschi's theory is supported by other research (Langbein & Bess, 2002), it says little about how and why society defines some people who break the law as criminal while ignoring others. We turn now to symbolic-interaction theory, which addresses exactly this issue.

CHECK YOUR LEARNING According to Durkheim, what are the four functions of crime and other forms of deviance for the operation of society?

Symbolic-Interaction Analysis: Socially Constructing Reality

Symbolic-interaction theory explores how people construct reality in everyday interaction. In part, this means that criminal or violent behavior is learned by individuals in the same way that people learn everything else: from

How might Travis Hirschi, who developed control theory, see something very important in this everyday scene on a community playground? Can you apply his theory to this situation?

their surroundings. In addition, what is defined as a crime and who is defined as a criminal result from a highly variable process of social definition.

Edwin Sutherland: Differential Association Theory
Edwin Sutherland (1940) pointed out that a great deal of learning takes place in social groups. Therefore, he continued, whether a person moves toward conformity or deviance depends on the relative degree of association with others who encourage or discourage conventional behavior. This is Sutherland's theory of *differential association*.

Researchers studying high school students have found a link between young people turning to drugs or becoming sexually active and the degree to which their peer groups encouraged such activity. In short, peer groups can be a powerful influence on young people, encouraging either conventional or delinquent behavior (Little & Rankin, 2001; Miller & Mathews, 2001).

Howard S. Becker: Labeling Theory How does deviant behavior come to exist? Howard S. Becker (1966:9) states that whether behavior is defined as deviant or not depends on how people define and respond to the behavior. In other words, the only real definition of "rule breaking" is behavior that people label that way.

Labeling theory is *the idea that crime and all other forms of rule breaking result not so much from what people do as from how others respond to those actions*. In other words, no action is right or wrong in any absolute sense. Consider the case of drinking alcohol: Is drinking likely to get a teenager into trouble? The answer depends on any number of factors, including whether anyone saw it; if so, how the observer defined it (taking into account *when* the drinking took place, *where* it took place, and *who* was doing the drinking); and whether the observer decided to do anything about it.

Labeling theory states that the "reality" of drinking, being sexually active, or taking something that belongs to someone else is a matter of how people label that behavior. Crime and other types of deviance are simply elements of socially constructed reality, which results from a highly variable process of detection, definition, and response. From Becker's point of view, the line separating crime from conformity is both thin and ever-changing.

Edwin Lemert: Primary versus Secondary Deviance Edwin Lemert (1951, 1972) explored how individuals can be changed by the labels that people apply to their behavior. To begin, many common norm violations—skipping school,

As soon as a person is accused of a crime and enters the criminal justice system, a process of labeling begins. People who hear that the person has been arrested may begin to reevaluate the person's character. What does being taken from one's home in handcuffs do for a person's reputation? Overall, criminal prosecution is a "degradation ceremony" that changes a person's social identity. Curiously, when a convicted criminal is released from prison, having paid a debt to society, there is no comparable ceremony to restore the person's good standing.

underage drinking, experimenting with drugs—bring little reaction from others. Lemert refers to these incidents, which may have only passing significance, as *primary* acts of deviance.

But what if others define these norm violations as a big deal? People might label a young man who tries an illegal drug as a "drug user" and keep their distance from him. Or a young woman who has a love affair might find herself being talked about as "easy" by others on campus. Such reactions often provoke confusion and anger and may have long-term consequences, such as the loss of friends. The person labeled in a negative way may then seek the company of people who are more accepting, perhaps those who have experienced rejection for similar behavior themselves. In this way, the reaction of others to primary deviance can provoke *secondary* deviance, in which the person begins to change, now basing choices on this deviant identity.

Erving Goffman: The Power of Stigma Growing up, we hear people say, "Sticks and stones can break your bones, but names can never hurt you." Erving Goffman (1963), for one, disagreed. Labeling someone as a "criminal" can be a form of **stigma**, *a powerful negative social label that radically changes a person's self-concept and social identity.* Once stigmatized, a person may find that friends and legitimate opportunities begin to disappear. In some cases, being stigmatized by others may launch a person on what sociologists call a *deviant career*, marked by an increasingly deviant identity and deeper involvement in rule-breaking behavior.

Criminal prosecution is a powerful ritual that stigmatizes a person. In a courtroom, the person stands before the community as the prosecutor presents the evidence, and if found guilty, a judge or jury may well declare the person unfit to remain in society. The stigma attached by this "degradation ceremony" may be very hard to lose (Garfinkel, 1956).

EVALUATE

Symbolic-interaction theories help us understand how people may come to define certain criminal behavior in positive terms and how some people end up defined as "criminal" by others. In each case, the reality of crime is socially constructed.

Even so, there is little disagreement that some behavior—such as intentionally killing a person—is a serious crime. Therefore, labeling theory is most usefully applied to milder offenses such as drug use or prostitution. Another problem is that by making crime seem highly relative, symbolic-interaction theory misses the fact that some categories of people are always at higher risk of being called criminal. This concern brings us to a third theoretical approach, social-conflict theory.

CHECK YOUR LEARNING In a sentence or two, state the essential idea of labeling theory. What is the difference between primary and secondary deviance?

Social-Conflict Analysis: Crime and Inequality

Social-conflict theory highlights how social inequality shapes who and what is defined as criminal. How laws are written, which neighborhoods police patrol, which categories of people end up being arrested—all these reflect who has power and who does not.

Karl Marx: Class and Crime Karl Marx understood social problems in terms of class conflict. In a capitalist society, he explained, the legal system protects the property of the capitalist class. Capitalists gain wealth legally simply by "doing business"; ordinary people who threaten capitalists' wealth risk arrest as "common criminals" or "political revolutionaries." Furthermore, with little wealth of their own, members of the working class may turn to crime simply in order to survive (Spitzer, 1980).

From a Marxist point of view, then, the solution to the crime problem is to eliminate capitalism in favor of a more egalitarian system that serves the interests of everyone (McClellan, 1985; Vito & Holmes, 1994).

The social-conflict approach claims that the criminal justice system serves the interests of powerful segments of the population. In the case of Marxist class-conflict theory, both the law and how it is applied are likely to favor the interests of the capitalist elite—in today's terminology, the "1 percent."

But this approach has limitations. For one thing, it has little to say about why well-off people engage in white-collar crime, corporate crime, and organized crime—and sometimes land in jail for doing so. In addition, if capitalism is the cause of crime, why do socialist societies have so many prisons?

CHECK YOUR LEARNING   What does the analysis of Karl Marx add to our understanding of crime?

Feminist Analysis: Crime and Gender

Feminist theory is another dimension of the social-conflict approach that has gained importance in recent years. As Chapter 4 ("Gender Inequality") explains, gender stratification is the pattern by which men have more wealth, prestige, and power than women. Feminists argue that gender stratification is also evident in patterns of crime.

Feminists claim that U.S. society subordinates women to men. Women have less access to good-paying jobs and hold fewer positions of power in our society. On one level, as second-class citizens, many women look to crime, including fraud, drug dealing, and prostitution, to increase their opportunity to make a living. Feminists point out that when law enforcement officials do take action against crimes such as prostitution, they are far more likely to arrest women (working

as prostitutes) than men (clients who also break the law) (Daly & Chesney-Lind, 1988; Simpson, 1989; Jenness, 1993). On a broader level, in a society shaped by patriarchy, everything defined as "feminine" is devalued as less important or less worthy than what is defined as "masculine." Finally, women are always at high risk of sexual violence. As one recent study concluded, about one in five college women becomes a victim of sexual violence (Krebs et al., 2007; Gray, 2014).

Some feminists—especially socialist feminists who support the ideas of Karl Marx—argue that capitalism exploits both men and women, who must turn to crime in their struggle to get by. Here again, the solution to the crime problem begins with eliminating capitalism.

Just as Marxist theory understands patterns of crime as serving the interests of elites in a society divided by class, so feminist theory understands patterns of crime in terms of the interests of men in a society divided by gender.

One limitation in feminist theory is that it does not easily explain why, if our society is dominated by men, men are many times more likely than women to end up in prison. Feminists suggest that women's lower crime rate reflects the fact that they are subject to greater social control than men; in addition, as our society is becoming more equal in terms of gender, the crime rates of women and men are also converging.

CHECK YOUR LEARNING   What does feminist theory add to our understanding of crime?

The Applying Theory table summarizes what each theoretical approach says about the crime problem.

APPLYING THEORY

Crime and Criminal Justice

	Structural-Functional Theory	Symbolic-Interaction Theory	Social-Conflict Theory	Feminist Theory
What is the level of analysis?	Macro-level	Micro-level	Macro-level	Macro-level
What is crime?	Durkheim said that as a society defines crime, it affirms norms and values, draws the line between right and wrong, brings people together, and encourages social change. Merton's strain theory linked types of rule breaking to a society's goals and the means available to attain them. Cloward and Ohlin's opportunity structure theory linked crime to legitimate and illegitimate opportunity. Hirschi's control theory states that strong social ties discourage crime.	Sutherland's differential association theory links crime and violence to patterns of learning. Labeling theory claims that rule breaking results from an audience defining some action in that way. Lemert explains how primary deviance can lead to secondary deviance and a deviant identity. Goffman pointed out that a deviant identity can be a powerful stigma.	Marx viewed the legal system as a way for capitalists to protect their wealth; criminals are those who threaten capitalism.	Feminism points to gender inequality as forcing poor women to engage in crime; male power is evident in the operation of the criminal justice system.
Who commits crime?	Durkheim claimed that all societies create crime. Merton, Cloward and Ohlin, and Hirschi all point to conditions that make crime more or less likely.	This approach claims that anyone or anything can be defined as deviant. All deviance results from a highly variable process of social definition on the part of some audience.	This approach claims that people with less social power—workers in relation to capitalists—are at greater risk of criminal involvement.	In cases such as prostitution, it is the less powerful women who are arrested more often than the more powerful men.

⭐ **POLITICS AND CRIME**

Constructing Problems and Defining Solutions

6.7 Analyze crime and violence from various positions on the political spectrum.

Crime has long been an issue of great public concern. But like so many social issues, how people see the crime problem, and what they consider to be effective solutions, depends on their political viewpoints. We now examine the crime problem from the conservative, liberal, and radical-left perspectives.

Young people growing up in low-income urban neighborhoods are at risk for getting into trouble with the law. Conservatives claim that the solution to crime lies in strong families, churches, and schools that teach moral values, including respect for the law. Liberals point to poverty caused by a lack of jobs that pressures people toward crime. Radicals on the left say that our capitalist society fails to support millions of people, forcing them to turn to crime to survive. Which view is closest to your own? Why?

Conservatives: Crime, Violence, and Morality

Conservatives believe that effective social controls are needed to keep people from engaging in violence or criminal behavior. The most effective type of control, as they see it, is *conscience*—a person's own internal sense of right and wrong. For this reason, conservatives emphasize the importance of families, churches, schools, and local communities teaching moral values to young people. Young women and men who learn from their families to respect the law, who gain strong religious values, and who are actively involved in community life are unlikely to get into trouble.

Conservatives see the rise in crime rates beginning in the 1960s as the result of a cultural shift toward growing permissiveness. Crime rates went up, they claim, because of a weakening of religious values, tradition, and neighborhood ties. In addition, at the same time, the share of families with two parents living in the home began a downward trend. It is no surprise to conservatives, for example, that a majority of young people arrested for violent crimes do not have a father living at home.

If some families fail to raise children with proper values, conservatives continue, society has little choice but to enact tougher laws, engage in more aggressive policing, and impose harsher penalties to keep crime and violence in check. But conservatives doubt that the criminal justice system, operating on its own, could ever solve the crime problem. The key to controlling crime always lies with parents who teach their children to make the right choices in a world filled with pressures to do the wrong thing.

Liberals: Crime, Violence, and Jobs

Liberals like to think that most people want to do the right thing, but many live in situations that put steady pressure on them to break the law. Thus, as liberals see it, crime and violence are caused by a harmful social environment, especially when lives are twisted by poverty. Millions of U.S. children are born into poor families, pass through substandard schools, and have few chances for a good job. It should be no surprise, then, that some young people lose hope, perhaps even adopting an "oppositional culture" that rejects authority figures or trying to gain some sense of importance through joining criminal gangs (E. Anderson, 1994, 2002). In short, liberals agree with conservatives that crime and violence are serious social problems, but they disagree about the cause.

Liberals also disagree with conservatives about the solution to the crime problem. They claim that our society must reinvest in whole districts of our cities and many rural regions that have lost jobs. It is jobs, liberals argue, that are the key to strong families and giving young people reason for hope so they will not turn to crime. Liberals claim that the same categories of people who suffer most from poverty and unemployment also suffer most from crime—both as offenders and as victims.

Finally, until our society can provide enough jobs for everyone, liberals see the criminal justice system as a revolving door: People with few legitimate opportunities turn to crime and many end up in prison; eventually, they leave prison only to return to crime because there is little in the way of good jobs. The overall result is the mass incarceration that we see today. The key to controlling crime lies in giving everybody the opportunity to succeed through honest work.

The Radical Left: Crime and Inequality

From a radical-left perspective, the real crime in this society is our nation's great economic inequality, a vast gap that has steadily increased in recent decades. The recent economic downturn, with millions of people losing their jobs and many even losing their homes, is only the latest chapter in the story of an economic system that fails to meet the needs of tens of millions of people. As left-radicals see it, economic insecurity is the real violence that is carried out against people every day. If some people resort to crime, it is because there may be no other way to get by.

From a left-radical perspective, the conservative claim linking crime to single parenting is a case of blaming the victims. They criticize liberals for seeking mere reform measures and for not recognizing that economic inequality and a lack of jobs are built into the capitalist system. Radicals on the left see the "get tough" policies of the criminal justice system—including proposals to add to the numbers of police and to build more prisons—as

simply one more way to oppress poor people and stabilize an inhuman system. The radical-left solution begins with restructuring the economic and political system toward an egalitarian social order that can make a real claim to justice.

The Left to Right table sums up the various political views of the crime problem and its solutions.

Going On from Here

Crime has been part of the human story since societies first enacted laws thousands of years ago. Although some crime helps society operate, as Emile Durkheim explained, few people deny that today's high crime rate is a serious social problem. Current debates over crime focus not only on street crimes (property crimes and violent crimes) but also on hate crimes and elite crime including white-collar crime and corporate crime. In addition, organized crime now operates on a global scale.

What is the likely future of crime? As you have seen, a decline in drug use, adding more police, and building more prisons have pushed the rates down in recent years. Politics guides the crime debate. Conservatives point to the need to strengthen families, but exactly how to do that has never been very clear. Liberals point to the need for government investment to produce more jobs, yet we see that the crime rate continued to fall even during the recent recession. Left-radicals call for a complete overhaul of the economic system, although even

---

LEFT TO RIGHT

The Politics of Crime, Violence, and Criminal Justice

	Radical-Left View	Liberal View	Conservative View
What is the problem?	The great economic inequality of a capitalist society promotes criminal activity by the underclass, individuals unable to succeed by legitimate means; the criminal justice system is used to maintain order and protect the interests of capitalist elites.	A lack of jobs is the major factor that forces people to break the law, often as a means to survive and to support their families.	The moral order of society is breaking down; because of the decline of the two-parent family, weakening religious values, and so much violence in the mass media, children are not being taught to behave responsibly.
What is the solution?	Crime and violence can never be controlled until class differences cease to exist. The real violence in our society is the oppression of capitalism. Therefore, the capitalist economy should be eliminated in favor of a more equitable system.	Government needs to use resources not to build more prisons but to expand economic opportunities in poor urban and rural areas where people are in desperate need of work.	The single most significant step toward reducing crime and violence is to strengthen families and increase the culture's emphasis on good parenting; tougher law enforcement is also necessary when crime has occurred.

JOIN THE DEBATE

1. About three-fourths of men in federal prisons grew up without a father present in the home. How would conservatives interpret this fact? How might liberals and radicals interpret it?

2. What trends in crime would people at various points on the political spectrum expect to see in the coming decades? Provide reasons for your predictions.

3. Which of the three political analyses of crime and violence presented here do you find most convincing? Why?

countries with far more economic equality than we have in the United States still have high crime rates and prisons filled to capacity.

In the foreseeable future, the burden of crime control is likely to remain squarely on the shoulders of the criminal justice system. Without doubt, the most popular idea in the United States when it comes to solving the problem of crime is to "get tough," which means adding more police, more prisons, and longer sentences for people convicted of serious crimes. So strong is this public opinion that no politician today would risk being viewed as "soft on crime." However, sociological research casts doubt on the idea that, operating on its own, the criminal justice system can solve the crime problem. We are likely to see various new initiatives that replace a "get tough on crime" approach with "get smart about crime" policies.

One example is the recent call by Attorney General Eric Holder to provide many nonviolent offenders (especially those abusing drugs) into treatment programs instead of prison. This "diversion" policy, he claims, would not only save money but also do a better job of reducing recidivism (Palazzolo & Jones, 2013).

Everyone hopes that the downward trend in the U.S. crime rate will continue. Looking ahead, population experts tell us that the share of the U.S. population in the "high-crime years" between the middle teens and middle twenties will fall in decades to come. Perhaps this trend will help control crime—at least until U.S. society develops a more effective solution.

Essay: Envisioning a Better Society What do you see as the future level of crime in the United States? What specific changes do you expect to see in the strategies and policies by which our society responds to crime? What changes would you like to see toward the goal of improving U.S. society?

CHAPTER 6 Crime, Violence, and Criminal Justice

What is the best way to keep crime in check?

As this chapter has explained, although the crime rate has declined in recent decades, crime and violence remain serious problems in much of the country. Look at the accompanying photos to see two different ways of defining solutions to these problems.

Liberals tend to see crime and violence as an economic issue, the result of too few jobs, leading young people to feel hopeless about their chances of succeeding in an unjust world. The solution to these problems lies in providing economic opportunity, so that young people have plenty of "legitimate opportunity" to lead productive and law-abiding lives as adults. Liberals look to government to set economic policy that benefits the population as a whole, to provide job counseling to young people, and to ensure that everyone receives a sound education.

Conservatives tend to see crime and violence as caused by greed or perhaps even aggressive human nature. The solution to these problems lies in society providing restraints. Parents should raise children to care about others and to respect the law, and all members of a community should look out for one another. Such thinking is embodied in the Guardian Angels, a nonprofit organization founded in New York City in 1979. Now active in a dozen cities and spreading around the world, the Guardian Angels are volunteers who patrol neighborhoods in their distinctive uniforms but without firearms. At the same time, the fatal shooting of Trayvon Martin in 2012 by an armed neighborhood watch volunteer cooled public support for such organizations.

Hint: Political attitudes guide how people view crime and violence and also lead them to prefer one solution over another. The conservative approach focuses on people themselves—the claim that individuals must make good choices—and supports solutions such as strong families and integrated communities. The liberal approach, and even more the approach of the radical left, focuses on the larger economic system as setting the stage for the opportunities we all have. From that point of view, a peaceful society must also be a just society, one in which there is equal opportunity for all. So which is it—a focus on individuals and the choices they make or a focus on structuring society in an equal way? Where do you fall on this important question?

Getting Involved: Applications and Exercises

1. Do some research about the developing problem of computer crime, including identity theft. How big a problem is identity theft now? What do analysts predict about the future? What new tactics will law enforcement need to control computer offenses?

2. The current debate over legalization of marijuana is not only about whether or not use of this drug is harmful. It is also about the fact that millions of people who use marijuana end up in jail. Do you think the use of soft drugs is a factor supporting the pattern of mass incarceration in the United States?

3. Watch several episodes of the television show *COPS*. How does this show portray the typical offender? Does this portrayal seem fair to you in light of what you have learned in this chapter? Why or why not?

4. The psychologist Philip Zimbardo conducted a famous prison study at Stanford University (see Chapter 1, "Studying Social Problems"). Look at reports of this research: One report is on the Web at http://www.prisonexp.org. What conclusions about prison does this research suggest?

Making the Grade

CHAPTER 6   Crime, Violence, and Criminal Justice

A DEFINING MOMENT
U.S. Society Discovers Child Abuse **p. 173**

Understanding Crime

6.1   Identify serious crimes, as well as trends and patterns in crime rates.

- Societies formally enact some **norms** in the form of **laws**.
- **Crime**, which is the violation of criminal law, includes more serious felonies and less serious misdemeanors. **p. 162**

> **norms** (p. 162) rules and expectations by which a society guides the behavior of its members
> **law** (p. 162) a norm formally created through a society's political system
> **crime** (p. 162) the violation of a criminal law enacted by federal, state, or local government
> **misdemeanor** (p. 162) a less serious crime punishable by less than one year in prison
> **felony** (p. 162) a more serious crime punishable by at least one year in prison

Arrests for violent crimes

- young people ages fifteen to twenty-four: 37 percent of all arrests
- males: 80 percent of all arrests
- whites: 59 percent of all arrests

Crimes against property include burglary, larceny-theft, motor vehicle theft, and arson.

Arrests for property crimes

- young people ages fifteen to twenty-four: 43 percent of all arrests
- males: 63 percent of all arrests
- whites: 68 percent of all arrests
  pp. 162–68

> **crime against property** (p. 162) crime that involves theft of property belonging to others
> **crime against persons** (p. 162) crime that involves violence or the threat of violence against others
> **stalking** (p. 164) repeated efforts by someone to establish or re-establish a relationship against the will of the victim

Other Dimensions of the Crime Problem

6.2   Define a number of specific types of crime.

Juvenile Delinquency

- The juvenile justice system seeks to reform rather than simply to punish offenders. **pp. 168–69**

Hate Crimes

- Forty-five states and the federal government have **hate crime** laws that provide more severe penalties for such crimes. **p. 169**

White-Collar Crime and Corporate Crime

- Typically, such wrongdoing is handled in civil courts, but a recent trend is toward the filing of criminal charges. **pp. 169–71**

Organized crime, which has a long history in the United States, also operates throughout most of the world. **p. 171**

Victimless crimes are offenses that directly harm only the offender. **pp. 171–72**

> **juvenile delinquency** (p. 168) violation of the law by young people
> **hate crime** (p. 169) a criminal offense against a person, property, or society motivated by the offender's bias against a race, religion, disability, sexual orientation, gender identity, or ethnicity or national origin
> **white-collar crime** (p. 169) illegal activities conducted by people of high social position during the course of their employment or regular business activities
> **corporate crime** (p. 170) an illegal act committed by a corporation or by persons acting on its behalf
> **organized crime** (p. 171) a business operation that supplies illegal goods and services
> **victimless crimes** (p. 171) offenses that directly harm only the person who commits them

Violence

6.3   Discuss the causes and consequences of violence in our society.

Violence is behavior that causes injury to people or damage to property. Whether people view violence as a problem depends on many factors, including

- the intentions of the actor
- whether the action conforms to cultural norms and values
- whether the action threatens the social order
- whether the actions are carried out by or against the government **pp. 172–73**

Most **murders** are committed by male offenders using guns. In many cases, offender and victim are of the same race.

- **Mass murder** usually occurs in homes, schools, or workplaces, where people expect to be safe.
- Most **serial killers** are considered mentally ill. **pp. 173–74**

violence (p. 172) behavior that causes injury to people or damage to property
institutional violence (p. 173) violence carried out by government representatives under the law
anti-institutional violence (p. 173) violence directed against the government in violation of the law
mass murder (p. 174) the intentional, unlawful killing of four or more people at one time and place
serial murder (p. 174) the killing of several people by one offender over a period of time
youth gangs (p. 175) groups of young people who identify with one another and with a particular territory

Social Dimensions of Violence

Research suggests that violence in the **mass media** raises the risk of deadly violence in some people, increases aggressiveness in many people, and desensitizes all of us to violence. **p. 175**

Poverty is linked to violence. Poor nutrition, inadequate schooling, substandard housing, and lack of jobs all raise the stress of daily living. **p. 175**

Government studies suggest there are almost 30,000 **youth gangs** in the United States. **pp. 175–76**

One study found that more than 60 percent of people arrested for a crime tested positive for the presence of an **illegal drug**. **p. 176**

There are some 310 million **guns** in the United States; 34 percent of U.S. households have at least one gun. **pp. 176–77**

The Criminal Justice System

6.4   Analyze the operation of the U.S. criminal justice system.

Police are the most visible part of the criminal justice system. Police officers use discretion, evaluating situations before deciding whether or not to intervene. **pp. 178–79**

Courts determine the innocence or guilt of people charged with crimes. Although the U.S. court system is an adversarial process, most cases are settled through plea bargaining. **pp. 179–80**

Punishment of offenders is carried out for four reasons: retribution, deterrence, rehabilitation, and societal protection. **pp. 180–82**

criminal justice system (p. 178) society's use of due process, police, courts, and punishment to enforce the law
plea bargaining (p. 179) a negotiation in which the state reduces a defendant's charge in exchange for a guilty plea
retribution (p. 180) moral vengeance by which society inflicts suffering on an offender comparable to that caused by the offense
deterrence (p. 180) using punishment to discourage further crime
rehabilitation (p. 181) reforming an offender to prevent future offenses
societal protection (p. 181) protecting the public by rendering an offender incapable of further offenses through incarceration or execution
criminal recidivism (p. 181) later offenses by people previously convicted of crimes
restorative justice (p. 182) a response to crime seeking to restore the well-being of the victim, offender, and larger communities lost due to crime
community-based corrections (p. 182) correctional programs that take place in local communities rather than behind prison walls

Explaining Crime: Biological and Psychological Theories

6.5   Apply biological and psychological theories to the issue of crime.

- Recent biological research in neurocriminology links differences in the ventral prefrontal cortex of the brain—the area that controls emotional impulses—to the likelihood that an individual will engage in criminal behavior.

- Psychological research links the risk of criminal behavior to an individual's capacity to control deviant impulses.

- A limitation of both biological and psychological research is that many serious crimes are committed by people who are clinically normal. **pp. 183–86**

Explaining Crime: Sociological Theories

6.6   Apply sociological theory to the issue of crime.

Structural-Functional Analysis: Why Society Creates Crime

- Durkheim argued that crime is a normal element of society's operation.

- Merton and Cloward and Ohlin described the role of opportunity in explaining patterns of rule breaking.

- Hirschi's **control theory** argues that social ties are important in helping a person resist temptation to break the law. **pp. 186–88**

Symbolic-Interaction Analysis: Socially Constructing Reality

- Sutherland's *differential association theory* states that people learn criminal or noncriminal attitudes from others in groups.
- *Labeling theory* argues that crime results less from what people do than from how others respond to the behavior.
- Lemert distinguishes between primary deviance, which may have only passing significance, and secondary deviance, in which individuals make choices that deepen their deviant identity.
- Goffman explained that being stigmatized as a rule breaker may deepen a person's deviant identity. **pp. 188–89**

Social-Conflict Analysis: Crime and Inequality

- Marxist theory highlights how capitalism provides most wealth and power to a small elite who use the criminal justice system against those who challenge the system. **pp. 189–90**

Feminist Analysis: Crime and Gender

- Feminist theory points to male domination of society as limiting women's opportunity and forcing women into lives of crime. **p. 190**

labeling theory (p. 188) the idea that crime and all other forms of rule breaking result not so much from what people do as from how others respond to those actions

stigma (p. 189) a powerful, negative, social label that radically changes a person's self-concept and social identity

✪ POLITICS AND CRIME

Constructing Problems and Defining Solutions

6.7 **Analyze crime and violence from various positions on the political spectrum.**

Conservatives: Crime, Violence, and Morality

Conservatives blame the rise in crime rates on the growing permissiveness in society that has resulted from a decline in traditional values. **p. 191**

Liberals: Crime, Violence, and Jobs

Liberals see crime as caused by a harmful environment that is the result of poverty and a lack of jobs. People resort to crime because there is no opportunity to succeed in life through honest work. **pp. 191–92**

The Radical Left: Crime and Inequality

Radicals on the left point to the injustice of economic inequality in capitalist societies as the reason for crime. **p. 192**

Chapter 7
Sexuality

Learning Objectives

7.1 Explain why sex is both a biological and cultural issue.

7.2 Discuss changes in sexual attitudes and practices over the history of the United States.

7.3 Describe four sexual orientations.

7.4 Discuss several current issues and controversies involving sexuality.

7.5 Apply sociological theory to issues involving sexuality.

7.6 Analyze issues involving sexuality from various positions on the political spectrum.

Tracking the Trends

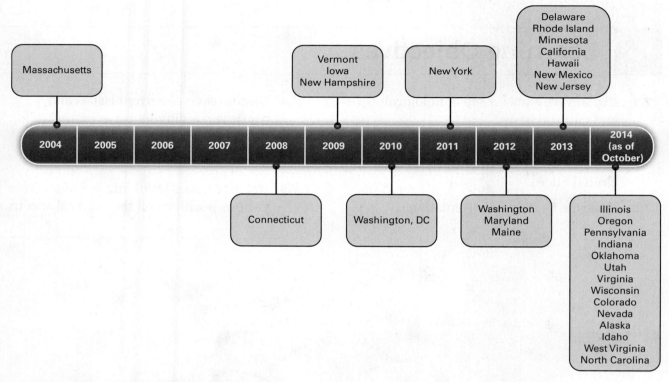

SOURCE: National Conference of State Legislatures (2014).

A decade ago, in 2004, only a handful of cities and towns allowed same-sex couples to marry, and these marriages were later declared to be illegal. Then, in 2004, Massachusetts became the first state to permit same-sex marriage. As of October, 2014, thirty states (and Washington, D.C.) enacted same-sex marriage laws. More states will follow suit in the months and years to come in what has been one of the most remarkable shifts in public opinion in this nation's history. Do you think same-sex marriage will become legal across the country in the near future?

Constructing the Problem

How can sex be the cause of social problems?

For most of our country's history, people didn't talk much about sex, and most people considered any sexual activity other than intercourse by married partners to be wrong.

Does the law decide how people can or cannot express their sexuality?

Yes. For example, during most of our country's history, homosexual activity was against the law; even today, same-sex couples are still denied the right to marry in many states.

Do you know all the dangers of sexual activity?

Sexual activity exposes people to the risk of infection by more than fifty diseases, including AIDS.

Chapter Overview

What is sex, and how is sex both a biological and a cultural issue? This chapter examines sexual attitudes and practices over the course of our nation's history, highlighting the sexual revolution and society's increasing support of gay rights. It also explores controversial sexuality-related issues such as pornography and prostitution and the issues of reproductive rights and abortion. You will learn about the major types of sexually transmitted diseases and behaviors that put people at risk. You will carry out theoretical analysis of sexuality, and also learn how "problems" and "solutions" involving sexuality reflect people's political attitudes.

In the small town of Jefferson City, Missouri, the biggest complaint among young people is that there is "nothing to do." But Peter Bearman, a sociologist who studied the students at Jefferson High, discovered there is certainly one thing that most of these young men and women do quite a bit: They have sex.

Interviews with 832 high school students revealed that, during the previous eighteen months, 573 (69 percent) had been involved in one or more "sexual and romantic relationships." The researchers, who were investigating the spread of sexually transmitted diseases (STDs), tracked the sexual partners of each of the students who reported being sexually active. The result: Students were linked by common sexual partners to a greater degree than anyone might have expected. In fact, half of the sexually active students (288 in all; in the diagram, red dots represent females and blue dots represent males) were "chained together" through other sexual partners (Bearman, Moody, & Stovel, 2004).

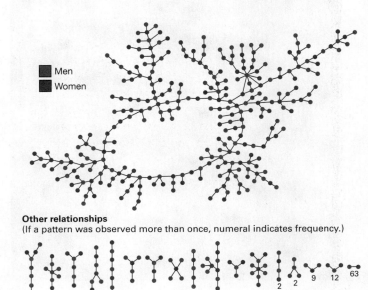

SOURCE: Bearman et al. (2004).

Sexual networks like this represent pathways through which STDs can be transmitted and suggest how STDs can spread from one individual to many additional people in a short period of time. This study also shows how sociological research can teach us about important social problems involving sexuality. This chapter explores many sexuality issues, including not only STDs but also gay marriage, prostitution, and pornography. We begin with some basic definitions.

What Is Sex?

7.1   Explain why sex is both a biological and cultural issue.

Sex is a concept that is rooted in both biology and culture. To better understand the meaning of sex, we need to examine sex from a biological and a cultural perspective.

Sex: A Biological Issue

Sex is *the biological distinction between females and males.* Biologically speaking, humanity is divided into two sexes, which have different reproductive organs—the *genitals*—that are also called *primary sex characteristics*. In addition, when people of each sex mature, they typically display other distinctive physical traits, which are called *secondary sex characteristics*. For example, females develop breasts and wider hips, and males develop more muscle and body hair.

Before the sexual revolution, U.S. society tolerated little in the way of public displays of sexuality, as suggested by this visiting day for World War II military personnel.

The term *sex* also refers to *activity that leads to sexual gratification and possibly reproduction.* From a biological point of view, reproduction is vital to the survival of a species. Among humans, a female provides an ovum, or egg, which is fertilized by a male's sperm through sexual intercourse to form a fertilized embryo. The embryo contains twenty-three matching chromosomes, which are the biological codes that determine a child's sex and other physical traits.

Sex: A Cultural Issue

Sociologists point out that sexual attitudes and practices, like all behavior, vary from one cultural setting to another. In addition, some of the most important cultural norms guide the selection of sexual partners. These norms involve *age* (some societies accept sexual activity on the part of children, although others define such behavior as a serious problem), *marital status* (some societies rigidly restrict sexual activity to married partners, but others are more permissive), and *sex of partner* (societies differ dramatically in their attitudes toward sexuality involving people of the same sex). In the United States, historical norms for sexual activity have favored adult, male–female married partners engaging in vaginal intercourse.

In reality, of course, much sexual behavior in our society does not conform to this model. People have sex within and without marriage, sexual relationships involve both other-sex and same-sex partners, and sexual activity includes anal as well as vaginal intercourse, oral-genital contact, and masturbation alone or with a partner. In addition, some people by choice or by circumstance engage in little or no sexual activity (Laumann et al., 1994).

Sexual Attitudes in the United States

7.2   Discuss changes in sexual attitudes and practices over the history of the United States.

Attitudes and behavior involving sex have changed over the course of this nation's history. During the colonial era, European settlers had no effective means of birth control. Therefore, most communities had strict norms allowing sex only by married couples for the purpose of reproduction. For example, the New England Puritans condemned sex outside marriage and considered any sex (including masturbation) not intended to result in conception to be sinful. Without strict rules to control people's behavior, they believed, the ever-present temptation of sex would lead to unwanted pregnancy, sex outside of marriage, and also prostitution.

Gradually, advances in technology led to more control over reproduction and societies then allowed more choice about sexual practices. Other factors also increased the level of sexual freedom. After 1920, the migration from farms and small towns across the United States to industrial cities meant that millions of young men and women lived and worked together beyond the control of parents. The result was an unprecedented level of sexual freedom, which is one of the reasons that this decade came to be known as the Roaring Twenties.

Researchers, too, played a part in this trend toward greater sexual freedom. After World War II, landmark research involving sexuality was carried out by Alfred Kinsey (1894–1956). To many people, it was remarkable that researchers were investigating *sex*, which had never even been widely discussed in public. The Defining Moment box on page 204 explains how Kinsey helped change a whole nation's way of thinking.

The Sexual Revolution

The first wave of sexual freedom during the Roaring Twenties and the groundbreaking Kinsey research of the 1940s and 1950s set the stage for even greater change. By the late 1960s, young people created a culture of freedom summed up in the cry "Sex, drugs, and rock-and-roll!" that came to be called the "sexual revolution."

Again, technology played a part, as 1960 saw the introduction of the birth control pill. Unlike condoms and diaphragms, both of which had to be applied at the time of intercourse, "the pill" could be taken at a woman's convenience, allowing her to more readily make a decision to engage in sex. This ease, combined with the pill's high effectiveness, effectively ended the historical connection between heterosexual intercourse and pregnancy.

Figure 7–1 confirms that, by the 1960s, the U.S. population became more free and easy about sex. Among those born between 1933 and 1942, people who reached the age of twenty *before* 1962, 56 percent of men and 16 percent of women reported having had two or more sexual partners before age twenty. But a single generation later, among people born between 1953 and 1962, 62 percent of men and 48 percent of women reported two or more sexual partners by age twenty (Laumann et al., 1994:198).

The Sexual Revolution and Feminism   Notice in Figure 7–1 how the gender gap in sexual activity became smaller among people who came of age during the sexual revolution. This trend suggests that greater sexual freedom also meant moving away from the traditional *double standard* by which men claimed some sexual freedom but women were expected to delay sex until they were married and, after that, forever to remain sexually faithful to their husbands.

During the 1960s, however, women organized in opposition to long-standing domination by men. In fact,

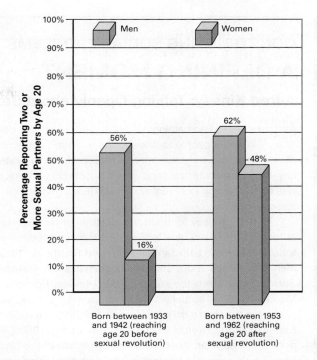

Diversity Snapshot

Figure 7–1   The Sexual Revolution: Moving Away from the Double Standard

Among people who came of age before the sexual revolution (shown on the left), a smaller share had two or more sexual partners by age twenty compared with people who came of age after the sexual revolution (shown on the right). The difference is especially marked among women.

SOURCE: Laumann et al. (1994).

many feminists placed attitudes about sexuality at the heart of male domination. Kate Millet (1970) summed up the argument, saying that sex is really about *power*: As long as men view women as mere sexual creatures and women accept this definition of themselves, men will dominate women. The word "sexism" emerged and became part of our society's vocabulary, thereby constructing a new social problem.

Feminists challenged male power in other ways as well, demanding equal pay for equal work, condemning pornography, and taking a stand against sexual violence, including rape and incest. In addition, women demanded access to contraception (which in the 1960s was still illegal in some states) and abortion (which was illegal everywhere in the United States until 1973). In short, out of the sexual revolution emerged the claim that only one person had the right to control a woman's body—the woman herself.

The Sexual Counterrevolution

Liberals typically supported feminism and the movement to increase sexual freedom. By the 1970s, however,

CONSTRUCTING SOCIAL PROBLEMS
A DEFINING MOMENT
Alfred Kinsey: Talking Openly about Sex

Alfred Kinsey did something no researcher before had dared to do: He asked people to talk about sex. From today's point of view, that may not seem very controversial. But in Kinsey's day—almost seventy years ago—most people did not think sex was a topic for polite conversation, much less a proper topic for scientific research.

In 1942, Kinsey founded the Institute for Sex Research at Indiana University, and in the years that followed, he and a dozen research assistants interviewed more than 11,000 men and women about their sexual practices. His first book, *Sexual Behavior in the Human Male* (Kinsey, Pomeroy, & Martin, 1948), is actually a fairly dry, scientific work, yet it sold more than half a million copies. A second volume, *Sexual Behavior in the Human Female* (Kinsey et al., 1953), was even more popular. Apparently, many people in the United States had a greater interest in sex than they were willing to admit.

Some of Kinsey's findings made news headlines, especially his discovery that people in the United States were far less conventional about sex than popularly believed. Kinsey's subjects confessed to breaking many cultural taboos of that time: Almost half of female subjects reported having sexual intercourse before they married, and one-third of married men said that they had been sexually unfaithful to their wives.

Looking back, there were flaws in the way Kinsey conducted his research. In his eagerness to find people willing to

talk about sexual experiences, Kinsey ended up using far too many college students. He also found willing participants among people in prison. At the same time, he almost totally ignored men and women who were older, rural, or poor. As a result, Kinsey's subjects were probably not representative of the U.S. population. But despite this shortcoming, this research marked a defining moment in our nation's history. Kinsey made a difference by bringing sex out of the closet.

Reports of Alfred Kinsey's survey of human sexual practices caused a sensation in the news media in the mid-1900s.

---

a conservative sexual counterrevolution was under way calling for a return to traditional "family values." As conservatives saw it, the 1960s had been a decade in which U.S. society had come apart, and what the country needed now was people taking more personal responsibility for their behavior and stronger families.

The conservative reaction to the sexual revolution did not turn back the clock; it only slowed the trend toward sexual freedom. In the decades since the 1960s, most adults still agree with the liberal idea that people should decide matters of sexual behavior for themselves. Today, 63 percent of young people (62.6 percent of men and 63.6 percent of women) report having sexual intercourse by their senior year in high school (CDC, 2013).

The Continuing Sexual Revolution: Older People

During the past decade, the men and women who began the sexual revolution of the 1960s—people who are now

in their sixties and seventies—are carrying that movement forward as they enter old age. An old stereotype presents older people as past their years of being sexually active. For many older men in their eighties and nineties, there is some truth to this claim. "Trying to have sex at ninety," quipped the comedian George Burns, "is like trying to shoot pool with a rope." But just as the birth control pill helped the 1960s generation spark a sexual revolution, another pill—this time in the form of Viagra, Levitra, and Cialis—offers the promise that the baby boomers will keep love alive as they grow old. These drugs that treat "erectile dysfunction," or ED for short, help otherwise healthy males achieve and maintain an erection, allowing more people to continue sexual activity in later life.

With or without drugs, researchers confirm, most older people remain sexually active well into old age. Among those between the ages of sixty-five and seventy-four, 85 percent of men and 62 of women report currently having a sexual partner. Among people between the ages of seventy-five and eighty-five, 78 percent of men and 41 percent of women said the same (Waite et al., 2009). The difference between the sexes reflects women's greater life expectancy—most older men live with a spouse and most older women do not.

The pharmaceutical industry has a financial interest in defining erectile dysfunction as a new problem. Their advertising may make increasing numbers of older men think they should be having more sex than they are, pushing up the sale of drugs to treat erectile dysfunction. Doctors now write almost 20 million such prescriptions each year, which send more than $1.5 billion to the drug companies.

The good news is that ED pills have extended sexual activity for millions of older people. Having more sex, say the researchers, means partners have a closer relationship and look and act in a more youthful way. At the same time, the "blue pill" is not a magic wand that allows a seventy-five-year-old male to perform sexually like he did in his twenties. In addition, like any other drug, these pills can cause side effects, which include headaches and even persistent and painful erections. Then, too, it is natural for the level of hormones that encourage sexual activity to decline as people move into old age. This fact raises the question as to whether the medical and pharmaceutical establishment should manipulate human biology in the interest of higher profits.

But given the popularity of these male drugs, many older men seem quite happy with their effects. Given the amount of money being made, there is little surprise in the fact that drug companies are working hard to create a new "pink pill"—for older women (Kotz, 2008).

Sexual Orientation

7.3   Describe four sexual orientations.

Sexual orientation refers to *a person's romantic and emotional attraction to another person*. Based on sexual orientation, people are drawn to partners of the same sex, the other sex, both sexes, or they feel no interest in any sexual partners.

The most common sexual orientation, approved by cultures the world over, is **heterosexuality** (*hetero* is Greek, meaning "other"), *sexual attraction to someone of the other sex*. In all societies, a small but significant share of people favor **homosexuality** (*homo* is Greek for "same"), which is *sexual attraction to someone of the same sex*.

Most people think of heterosexuality and homosexuality as opposites so that most people fall neatly into one category or the other. But as Kinsey discovered, many people have varying degrees of both sexual orientations. Also, keep in mind that sexual *attraction* is not the same as sexual *behavior*. Although most people have experienced some attraction to a person of the same sex, for example, only a small share of people have actually engaged in homosexual behavior. The fact that many people do not act on this attraction may reflect the operation of cultural norms that discourage same-sex relationships.

Kinsey's finding that sexual orientation is often not clear-cut calls attention to the existence of **bisexuality**, *sexual attraction to people of both sexes*. Some bisexual people experience equal attraction to females and males; others have a stronger attraction to people of one sex than the other. There are also many cases of bisexuals who experience attraction to both sexes but limit their sexual behavior to partners of one sex.

Finally, not everyone experiences sexual attraction at all. **Asexuality** is *the absence of sexual attraction to people of either sex*. Throughout the population, the extent of asexuality increases gradually as people get older.

We now take a closer look at issues related to homosexuality.

Homosexuality

Homosexuality is a natural sexual orientation found among a small share of a population. Because heterosexuality is the cultural norm, homosexual people—gay men and lesbians—are often pushed to the margins of society. Some people may even view homosexuality as a social problem because it conflicts with their moral standards. This attitude has long been a cause of prejudice and discrimination directed toward gay men and lesbians.

In the 1970s about three-fourths of U.S. adults claimed that same-sex relations were wrong. In recent decades, there has been a remarkable increase in the acceptance of homosexuality. In 2012, the share of adults saying homosexuality was wrong was no longer a majority, falling to 46 percent (Smith et al., 2013).

Today, reflecting the increasing acceptance of homosexuality, all states and the federal government have laws banning discrimination based on sexual orientation. In 2011, the U.S. military ended its historical ban on same-sex behavior. In addition, as shown in the Tracking the Trends figure at the beginning of this chapter, as of 2014, thirty states—Massachusetts, Vermont, New Hampshire, Connecticut, Iowa, New York, Washington, Maryland, Maine, Rhode Island, Delaware, Minnesota, California, New Jersey, Illinois, New Mexico, Hawaii, Oregon, Pennsylvania, Indiana, Oklahoma, Utah, Virginia, Wisconsin, Colorado, Nevada, Alaska, Idaho, West Virginia, North Carolina, and the District of Columbia—had changed their laws to permit same-sex marriage. About 60 percent of the U.S. population now lives in a state where same-sex marriage is legal. Even so, many states still ban same-sex marriage and, across the country, other forms of discrimination are within the law so that, for example, many religious organizations refuse to ordain gay men or lesbians as leaders.

Prejudice against gay men and lesbians also exists on college campuses. One study found that one-third of gay and lesbian students reported that they had experienced harassment in the past year (Rankin, 2003).

Hostility toward gay men and lesbians can fuel violence. The FBI (2013) records some 1,300 hate crimes against gays each year, and the true number is certainly far higher. Many of these violent acts—including assault and even murder—are directed at people simply because of their sexual orientation. According to the National Coalition of Anti-Violence Programs (2013), more than 2,000 lesbians and gay men in the United States said that they were the victims of anti-gay violence in 2012. This violence included twenty-five homicides that were defined as hate crimes. Almost all young lesbians and gay men report that they have experienced at least verbal abuse at some point in their lives.

People of color are especially likely to experience hateful action due to sexual orientation. Of all people who self-identify as LGBTQ (lesbian, gay, bisexual, transgender, and questioning), people of color were almost twice as likely as whites to report physical violence directed against them (National Coalition of Anti-Violence Programs, 2013).

The Extent of Homosexuality What share of the U.S. population has a homosexual orientation? This question is difficult to answer because, as we have already explained, sexual orientation is not a matter of neat categories. The extent of homosexuality, therefore, depends on exactly how you define the term.

Alfred Kinsey (1948) claimed that most women and men experience at least some same-sex attraction. Although most do not act on it, many do: Kinsey estimated that one-third of men and one-eighth of women engaged in one or more homosexual acts at some point in their lives, typically in adolescence. In addition, Kinsey estimated that 4 percent of men and 2 percent of women were exclusively homosexual in their orientation, meaning they had *only* same-sex desires, engaged in *only* same-sex sexual activity, and thought of themselves as gay men or lesbians.

More recent research by Edward Laumann and his colleagues (1994) provides a more precise estimate of homosexuality. Laumann concluded that 2.8 percent of men and 1.4 percent of women (about 6 million people) defined themselves as homosexual or bisexual. Figure 7–2 shows that about 5 percent of men and 14 percent of women between the ages of fifteen and forty-four reported engaging in at least some homosexual activity. At the same time, just 1.8 percent of men and 1.2 percent of women defined themselves as homosexual (CDC, 2014).

What Determines Sexual Orientation?

The causes of sexual orientation include many factors, such as genetics, brain structure, hormones, life experiences, and culture. Researchers point to both culture and biology as shaping sexual orientation.

Cultural Factors In earlier periods of history, most societies paid little attention to sexual orientation. The French social philosopher Michel Foucault (1990) notes that societies did not identify homosexuals as a specific category of the population until the late nineteenth century. This is not to say that people in earlier times did not have same-sex experiences; societies simply took little note of it. But once societies socially constructed the categories of "heterosexual" and "homosexual," people who had homosexual experiences began to be set apart as "different" and also became targets of prejudice and discrimination. This historical pattern provides evidence that how we express and experience sexuality is shaped by culture.

Sexual behavior also varies from culture to culture. Among the Chukchee Eskimo of Siberia, a man may

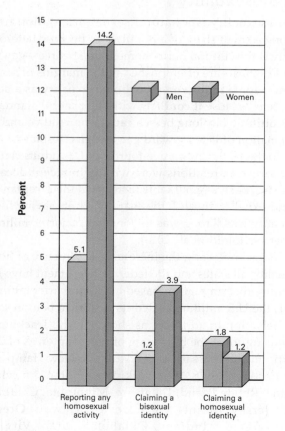

Diversity Snapshot

Figure 7–2 Measuring Homosexual Orientation

How one defines homosexual orientation affects the number of people considered to be homosexual.

SOURCE: Centers for Disease Control and Prevention (2014).

DIVERSITY: RACE, CLASS, & GENDER

Female, Male, or Something Else? The *Muxes* of Mexico

Alejandro Taledo, age sixteen, stands on a street corner in Juchitán, a small town in the state of Oaxaca, which is found in the middle of southern Mexico. Called Alex by her friends, she has finished a day of selling flowers with her mother and they now wait for the bus that will take them home for dinner.

As you already may have noticed, Alejandro is commonly a boy's name. In fact, this young Mexican was born a boy. But several years ago, Alex decided that she felt she was a girl, and she decided to live true to her own feelings.

In this community, she is not alone. Juchitán and the surrounding region are known not only for beautiful pottery and delicious food but also for the large number of gays, lesbians, and transgendered people who live there. This fact may surprise people who think of Mexico as a traditional country, especially when it comes to gender and sexuality. In Mexico, as the stereotype goes, men control the lives of women, especially when it comes to sex. But, as in the case of most stereotypes, this one misses some important facts. Nationally, Mexico has become more tolerant in matters of sexual orientation, and same-sex domestic partnerships are now legal in Mexico City, the nation's capital. Nowhere is tolerance for various sexual orientations as strong and widespread as it is in the region around Juchitán.

In this area of Mexico, transgendered people are called *muxes* (pronounced MOO-shay), which is based on the Spanish word *mujer* meaning "woman." This means that the local culture does not divide people into only the neat categories of "man" and "woman" but recognizes a third gender category as well. Some *muxes* wear women's clothing and act almost entirely in a feminine way. Others adopt a feminine look and behavior only on special occasions. One of the most popular events is a grand celebration that takes place every year in November and is attended by more than 2,000 *muxes* and their families. A highlight of the event is a competition won by the "transvestite of the year."

Anthropologists tell us that the acceptance of transgendered people in central Mexico has its roots in the culture that existed there centuries before the arrival of the Spanish. At that time, a person with ambiguous gender was viewed as especially wise and talented. The region's history includes accounts of Aztec priests and Mayan gods who cross-dressed and were considered to be both male and female. In the sixteenth century, the arrival of Spanish colonists and the Catholic Church reduced local gender tolerance. But the unusually high acceptance of mixed-sex identities continues to this day in Juchitán, a region where many people speak only their ancient Zapotec language rather than Spanish.

And so it is in Juchitán that *muxes* are respected, accepted, and, on special occasions, even celebrated. *Muxes* are successful in business and take leadership roles in the church and in politics. Most important, they are accepted by friends and family alike. Alejandro lives with her parents and five siblings and helps her mother both at home and working on the street selling flowers. Her father, Victor Martinez Jimenez, is a local construction worker who speaks only Zapotec. He still refers to Alex as "him" but says, "It was God who sent him, and why would I reject him? He helps his mother very much. Why would I get mad?" Alex's mother, Rosa Taledo Vicente, adds, "Every family considers it a blessing to have one gay son. While daughters marry and leave home, a *muxe* cares for his parents in their old age" (Gave, 2005; Lacey, 2008; Rosenberg, 2008).

What Do You Think?

1. To what extent do you think that U.S. society is tolerant of people wishing to combine male and female dress and qualities? Explain.

2. *Muxes* are people who are born males. How do you think the local people in this story would feel about women who want to dress and act like men? Do you think such people would enjoy the same degree of tolerance and support? Why or why not?

3. How do you personally feel about a third category of sexual identity? Explain your views.

take on the role known as a *berdache*, dressing and acting like a woman, doing women's work, even marrying another man. Among the Sambia of New Guinea, most boys engage in a sexual ritual in which they perform oral sex on older men with the idea that ingesting semen will enhance the young men's masculinity. In central Mexico, a region where religious traditions recognize gods who are both female and male, the local culture recognizes not only females and males but also *muxes* (pronounced "MOO-shays") as a third sexual category. *Muxes* are men who dress and act as women, some only on ritual occasions, some all the time. The Diversity: Race, Class, & Gender box takes a closer look. Such diversity of sexual expression around the world shows that sexual orientation has much to do with society itself (Herdt, 1993; Blackwood & Wieringa, 1999; Gave, 2005; Lacey, 2008; Rosenberg, 2008).

Finally, a few sociological studies claim that sexual orientation may reflect patterns of socialization. One study of opposite-sex twins found a higher likelihood of homosexual orientation among people raised in a gender-neutral environment than among those raised according to conventional ideas of masculine and feminine behavior (Bearman & Brückner, 2002).

Biological Factors Culture may play a part in the way societies think about sexuality, but on the individual level, most evidence points to the conclusion that sexual orientation is rooted in human biology. Like being left- or right-handed, sexual orientation appears to be largely fixed at birth.

The neurobiologist Simon LeVay (1993) claims that the key to sexual orientation is found in the brain. LeVay studied the brains of homosexual men and heterosexual men and noted a difference in the hypothalamus, an organ of the brain that regulates the body's hormone levels. Biologists have established that hormone levels—especially testosterone levels in men—affect sexual orientation. They claim that small differences in the brain can play a large part in establishing a person's sexual orientation (Grady, 1992).

Genes, as well as hormones, may affect sexual orientation. In a study of forty-four pairs of brothers, all homosexual, researchers found that thirty-three of the pairs had a unique feature on the X chromosome (one of the genetic traits affecting human sexuality). Some researchers think this might be evidence of a "gay gene," noting that the gay brothers had an unexpectedly high number of gay male relatives on their mother's side, the source of the X chromosome (Hamer & Copeland, 1994). To date, however, no research has conclusively identified such a gene. The most recent studies, called "epigenetic" research, suggest that sexual orientation is not caused directly by genes but by "epi-factors" that affect how genes are activated and how fetuses respond to hormones in the womb. The focus here is still on biology with the added claim that the fetal environment may affect how the biological process unfolds (Blue, 2012; Rice, Friberg, & Gavrilets, 2012).

EVALUATE

Scientists continue to debate the social and biological causes of sexual orientation. So far, the evidence supports the conclusion that biology plays a major part in how people experience sexual attraction. But there is still much to learn. Although biology may be the key to sexual orientation, keep in mind that many people do not fit into a simple category as being "gay" or "straight."

Why does it matter whether sexual orientation is caused by society or human biology? The reason is that, if sexual orientation is biological, it is as much beyond our control as the color of our skin. Therefore, gay men and lesbians are no more responsible for their sexual orientation than African American people are for their skin color, and both categories of people are entitled to the same legal protection from discrimination (Herek, 1991; Schmalz, 1993).

CHECK YOUR LEARNING What have researchers learned about the origin of sexual orientation? Why does it matter whether we consider sexual orientation to be mostly biological or simply a personal choice about how to live?

Homosexuality and Public Policy

Back in 1960, homosexuality was widely viewed as wrong almost everywhere in the United States. Many people also considered this sexual orientation to be a sickness; even the American Psychiatric Association included homosexuality in its list of mental disorders until 1973. Discrimination against gay men and lesbians was common and companies, schools, government agencies, and the military routinely refused to hire people thought to be homosexual. Just as important, employees found to be gay or lesbian were fired for no reason other than their sexual orientation. In this hostile environment, it is easy to see why most lesbians and gay men stayed "in the closet," keeping their homosexuality secret from all but a few close friends.

Since then, attitudes toward homosexuality have become more accepting. As shown in Figure 7–3, twenty years ago the percentage of U.S. adults who claimed that homosexuality is wrong was well over 70 percent; by 2012, this share had dropped to 46 percent (Smith et al., 2013). Such surveys also show that a majority of people now believe that homosexual people should have the same job opportunities and basic civil rights as everyone else.

The growing acceptance of homosexuality appears to have been on the minds of the justices of the U.S. Supreme Court when in 2003 they handed down a landmark ruling (*Lawrence et al.* v. *Texas*) that struck down the Texas law banning sodomy ("unnatural sex, especially anal intercourse") between same-sex couples. This ruling ended similar laws that had been on the books in other states.

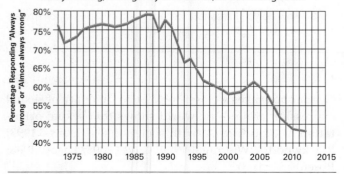

Survey Question: "What about sexual relations between two adults of the same sex—do you think it is always wrong, almost always wrong, wrong only sometimes, or not wrong at all?"

Figure 7–3 U.S. Attitudes toward Homosexual Relations, 1973–2012

In the United States, public acceptance of homosexual relations has increased dramatically since the early 1990s. In 2010, for the first time, a minority of U.S. adults characterized homosexual relations as wrong.

SOURCE: Smith et al. (2013).

Same-Sex Marriage

In 2004, the supreme court of Massachusetts ruled that gay men and lesbians had the right to marry. Gay rights advocates were elated by the Massachusetts decision and, since then, twenty-nine more states (Connecticut, Vermont, Iowa, New Hampshire, New York, Washington, Maryland, Maine, Rhode Island, Delaware, Minnesota, California, Oregon, New Jersey, Pennsylvania, Illinois, Hawaii, New Mexico, Indiana, Oklahoma, Utah, Virginia, Wisconsin, Colorado, Nevada, Alaska, Idaho, West Virginia, North Carolina, plus the District of Columbia) have enacted laws permitting same-sex marriage. Several other states recognize either "domestic partnerships" or "civil unions" that provide most or all of the benefits of marriage. In addition, many cities permit couples to register "domestic partnerships" that provide many of the rights of marriage, including family health care and inheritance rights (National Conference of State Legislatures, 2014).

The legal tide has turned in favor of same-sex marriage. Even so, many states have enacted laws saying that the state will not recognize gay marriages, even if they are performed in a state where they are legal. Efforts to overturn these laws are underway in all of these states. In 1996, Congress passed the Defense of Marriage Act, which allows any state to ignore a same-sex marriage performed elsewhere. In 2011, the Obama administration announced it would no longer support this law or defend it in court. In 2013, the Supreme Court struck down an important part of this law that denied federal benefits to same-sex couples who have legally married.

Organizations across the country—including major corporations, the federal government, and most colleges and universities—have also changed their policies to support same-sex relationships in places that do not allow same-sex marriage. Now these organizations extend to domestic partners the same employee benefits they give to married spouses.

Elsewhere in the world, seventeen countries (the Netherlands, Belgium, Canada, South Africa, Spain, Norway, Sweden, Portugal, Iceland, Argentina, Denmark, France, Brazil, Uruguay, New Zealand, Great Britain, and Luxembourg) recognize same-sex marriage. Another sixteen nations recognize same-sex partnerships or civil unions that extend to gays and lesbians many of the legal rights that married people have (Pew Research Center, 2014; Freedom to Marry, 2014).

In the United States, attitudes about same-sex marriage reflect people's position on the political spectrum. In general, liberals support extending the right to marry to same-sex couples everywhere. Many conservatives oppose this trend, claiming that the traditional idea of marriage in the United States has always been a union between a man and a woman (Thomas, 2003; Pew Research Center, 2010). But some people who hold conservative "family values" *do* favor gay marriage—as well as the right of gay couples to adopt children. These conservatives claim that, if families are good for people and good for society, we should encourage families for everyone, whether straight or gay (A. Sullivan, 2002).

The Gay Rights Movement

The increasing acceptance of gay men and lesbians reflects decades of struggle by people who have supported the gay rights movement. The first gay rights group formed in Chicago in 1924, but the movement did not gain widespread public attention until the 1950s (Chauncey, 1994). Like all social movements, the gay rights movement tried to construct a problem and define the solution in a particular way. This movement claimed that the problem is not homosexuality but the prejudice and discrimination directed against gay people. The solution, then, is public acceptance of homosexuality on equal terms with heterosexuality.

Back in the 1960s, despite the considerable risks of being identified as homosexual, more and more lesbians and gay men stepped forward demanding acceptance. A turning point occurred on June 27, 1969, when police raided the Stonewall Inn, a bar in New York's Greenwich Village. At that time, New York City police made a practice of raiding gay bars, arresting patrons, and recording their names, which often ended up in newspaper stories. This policy effectively discouraged most people from visiting gay clubs. In this case, however, the patrons of the Stonewall Inn openly resisted police harassment. Joined in the street by other people, these men and women battled the police for the better part of two days. This event, which came to be known as the Stonewall Riot, marked a new militancy in the gay rights movement.

Within a few years of the Stonewall Riot, the gay rights movement began using the term **homophobia** to describe *an aversion to or hostility toward people thought to be gay, lesbian, or bisexual*. This concept reinforced the idea that the problem was not homosexuality but people who were intolerant of that sexual orientation. The success of the gay rights movement is evident in the increasingly widespread condemnation of homophobia as a social problem today.

Transgender

The increasing acceptance of gay, lesbian, and bisexual people extends to a larger category of people who challenge conventional gender patterns. **Transgender** is a broad concept that refers to *appearing or behaving in*

The transgender movement is gaining importance in the United States and other high-income nations. On the most basic level, this movement seeks freedom for individuals to express their sexuality, not according to conventional norms about femininity and masculinity, but in ways that feel authentic to them.

ways that challenge conventional cultural norms concerning how females and males should look and act. People in the transgender community do not conform to conventional ideas about sexual identity or behavior. Rather, transgender people disregard any rigid and conventional ideas about femininity or masculinity in favor of combining feminine and masculine traits or perhaps embodying something entirely different.

Transgender is not the same as sexual orientation. Transgender people may think of themselves as gay or lesbian, heterosexual, bisexual, asexual, as some combination of these categories, or in entirely different terms.

Everyone, of course, breaks from conventional gender patterns in some way or another. However, according to research, about three in every 1,000 adults in the United States (perhaps 700,000 people) have a transgender identity. The common shorthand LGBTQ refers to people who claim to be lesbian, gay, bisexual, transgender, or questioning their own sexuality. Of course, because someone may identify with more than one of these categories, no exact number can be placed on the size of the total LGBTQ population. But estimates suggest that roughly 4 percent of the U.S. adult population—or about 9 million people—are within the LGBTQ community (Gates, 2011).

Sexual Issues and Controversies

7.4 Discuss several current issues and controversies involving sexuality.

Sexuality lies at the heart of a number of controversies in the United States today. Here we take a look at six key issues: pornography, sexual harassment, prostitution, teen pregnancy, abortion, and sexually transmitted diseases.

Pornography

Pornography refers to *words or images intended to cause sexual arousal*. This definition sounds clear enough, but people disagree about precisely what is and what is not pornographic. For one thing, sexual material comes in many forms. *Erotica* includes the artistic portrayal of nudity, although not necessarily sexual activity. Then there is *soft-core pornography*, which shows or describes nudity and suggests sexual activity. Finally, *hard-core pornography* contains explicit descriptions or images of sexual acts.

Laws regulate certain types of pornography, including the depiction of sexual violence and sexual acts with children. More broadly, pornography becomes illegal when it crosses the line into *obscenity*, meaning the content is offensive to public decency. Recognizing that what is acceptable in one place may be objectionable in another, the U.S. Supreme Court allows communities to ban sexual material as obscene if it violates "community standards of decency" and lacks any "redeeming social value." Even so, within a local community, people are likely to disagree about what the standards of decency should be.

Sexually explicit material is readily available in the United States. Most people are familiar with sexually explicit magazines, books, movies, and videos. In the Internet age, hundreds of thousands of websites portray every imaginable type of sexual behavior. The pornography industry as a whole is now a $13 billion-a-year industry, which is more than the total economic output of some countries.

Is Pornography a Social Problem? There is widespread opposition to sexual material involving children under age eighteen. Almost everywhere, police enforce federal and state laws against creating, selling, or possessing child pornography. There is also widespread concern about the effects of pornography on adults. Both conservatives and liberals take issue with pornography although, as we now explain, they do so for different reasons.

Conservatives: The Moral Issue   Conservatives view sex as a moral issue, emphasizing the importance of personal responsibility and public decency. Therefore, they define pornography as a social problem because it threatens conventional morality. Pornography encourages lustful behavior, they say, which can become an addiction, as it has for several million people in the United States. In addition, pornography weakens a society's moral fabric and may threaten the stability of marriage and family.

Only a minority of adults in the United States say that they find pornography to be morally acceptable, although the share varies according to age. Among young adults (eighteen to thirty-four years old), 42 percent make this claim; among middle-aged adults (thirty-five to fifty-four years old), 29 percent say so; among senior adults (fifty-five and older) just 19 percent find pornography morally acceptable (Gallup, 2011). Most people appear to share a conservative concern about pornography on moral grounds.

Liberals: Issues of Freedom and Power Liberals are divided over whether to define pornography as a social problem. Some liberals believe that what material people choose to read or view is their own business. Therefore, without claiming that pornography is necessarily good, liberals defend freedom of expression and support people's right to privacy. Liberals who share this position have been outspoken in defending government funding of the arts, including artists whose work may attract criticism as violating community standards of decency.

Although some liberals defend pornography on the grounds of protecting free speech, a growing number of feminist liberals object to pornography as demeaning to women. They see pornography as a power issue, noting that sexually explicit material typically depicts women as the playthings of men (Dworkin, 1991; MacKinnon, 2001).

In sum, many liberals defend the right of free expression and the idea that people should be free to choose whatever entertainment they want. But opposition to pornography has increased across the political spectrum. In this case, conservatives (who object to sexually explicit material on moral grounds) have joined with feminists (who object on political grounds) in their opposition to pornography.

Pornography and Violence Another widespread concern is that pornography promotes violence. Back in 1985, President Ronald Reagan created the Attorney General's Commission on Pornography (commonly called the Meese Commission, after Attorney General Edwin Meese) to investigate how people react to sexually explicit materials. The commission (1986) concluded that exposure to pornography causes sexual arousal, increases people's sexual activity, and encourages men to be aggressive and more accepting of violent acts such as rape. In addition, concluded the researchers, pornography involving children encourages some men to desire sexual activity with them (a crime called *pedophilia*).

Critics have challenged some of these conclusions, but the report found widespread acceptance among conservatives, who typically view sexually explicit material as encouraging immoral behavior. In addition, the report gained the support of some liberals including feminists who make the claim that rape is little more than "pornography put into practice."

Other researchers, however, claim that the evidence does not support a link between pornography and rape. Over the last twenty years, the availability of pornography has increased dramatically with the spread on the Internet. Yet, they point out, the level of rape has not increased; in fact, it has fallen substantially (Chapman, 2007).

Sexual Harassment

Sexual violence, which is examined in detail in Chapter 6 ("Crime, Violence, and Criminal Justice"), ranges from verbal abuse to forced sex and harms both women and men. In recent years, U.S. society has also recognized a new type of sexual violence: **sexual harassment**, *unwanted comments, gestures, or physical contact of a sexual nature*. In the television show *Mad Men*, men working in an advertising agency routinely make advances toward the women working as secretaries, suggesting how common what we now call sexual harassment was fifty years ago. In fact, sexual harassment was so much a part of our way of life that few men or women recognized this behavior as a social problem.

During the 1960s, the situation gradually changed along with the rise of the women's movement. In 1964, Congress passed the Civil Rights Act with the goal of protecting African Americans from employment discrimination. The women's movement successfully lobbied to extend the bill to defend people disadvantaged not just by their race but also by their sex. Thus Title VII of the Civil Rights Act prohibits discrimination in the terms, conditions, and privileges of employment on the basis of race and also sex. In 1972, Congress declared that schools, colleges, and universities follow this law by passing Title IX of the Higher Education Amendment, which banned sex discrimination in institutions receiving federal funds.

Congress then created the Equal Employment Opportunity Commission (EEOC) to investigate complaints of racial or sexual discrimination. In 1976, in the case of *Williams* v. *Saxbe*, a federal court recognized sexual harassment as one type of illegal sex discrimination. This decision brought sexual harassment to public attention, and it was soon defined as a serious problem.

The EEOC recognizes two types of sexual harassment. The first is *quid pro quo* (Latin, meaning "one thing for another") *harassment*, in which a person directs sexual advances or requests for sexual favors to an employee or other subordinate as a condition of employment or advancement. In this case, a boss might demand or imply that an employee is unlikely to receive a promotion unless she agrees to engage in a sexual relationship. The second type of harassment is more subtle behavior—including telling sexual jokes, displaying nude photos, engaging in unnecessary touching, or offering compliments on someone's good looks—that the offender may not intend to be harassing. But the law is concerned with not just an offender's intent but also with the *effect* of the behavior. Under the law, any behavior can be considered to be harassment, regardless of the actor's intent, if the behavior has the effect of *creating a hostile environment*. The point of the law is to protect people who are trying to do their jobs from having unwanted sexual attention imposed on them (U.S. Equal Employment Opportunity Commission, 2006).

Who Harasses Whom? A Court Case The fact that men hold most positions of power in U.S. society helps explain why 82 percent of known harassers are men who harass women (U.S. Equal Employment Opportunity Commission, 2014). But not all harassment follows this pattern. In *Oncale* v. *Sundowner Offshore Services* (1998), the U.S. Supreme Court stated that a person can be sexually harassed by someone of either sex. In the *Oncale* case, after male co-workers threatened a married man with rape, he reported the incident to his supervisor. When the company did not respond to the report, the man quit his job and filed a lawsuit against the company. This case shows us that in some circumstances, men sexually harass other men who do not display what harassers think of as typical "masculine" behavior. In this situation, sexual harassment was a form of control used by men to force others to conform to gender stereotypes (D. Lee, 2000).

Must Harassment Harm Victims? Other Court Cases
Does sexual harassment exist only when a victim suffers clear and obvious harm? In 1998, the U.S. Supreme Court addressed this question. In one case, *Ellerth* v. *Burlington Industries*, a woman complained that her supervisor made sexual advances in which he threatened that he could make her job easy or difficult, depending on whether she "loosened up." Although she resisted his advances, she did not report the behavior, and there was no evidence that her career had been harmed. Soon after, however, she quit her job and then filed suit, claiming she was a victim of sexual harassment.

In a second case, *Faragher* v. *City of Boca Raton*, three women who worked as lifeguards in that Florida city claimed their supervisors for years had created a hostile workplace environment, engaging in sexual comments and physical touching. Their employer, the city of Boca Raton, had a sexual harassment policy in place, but no one had informed the women of the policy. Subsequently, the women filed a lawsuit against the city, charging that they had been harassed on the job.

In considering the two cases, the Supreme Court ruled that employees can be victims of harassment even if they were not obviously harmed by, say, losing out on a promotion. The Court also stated that employers are responsible when a supervisor harasses another employee, even if the company was not aware of the behavior, unless the company can demonstrate that it had a well-publicized sexual harassment policy in place and that the employee knew about the policy but chose not to use it.

Prostitution

The cultural ideal of sex involves companionship and intimacy between two people. Therefore, although **prostitution**, *the selling of sexual services*, may be "the world's oldest profession," it has always been controversial. Offering to sell or to buy sexual services is against the law everywhere in the United States except in parts of rural Nevada.

Legal or not, prostitution is common. There is no accurate count of the number of people who work as prostitutes in the United States, but in national surveys about 9 percent of adult men (and just a very small share of women) say that they have paid someone for sex or have been paid for sex at least once (Smith et al., 2013). In global perspective, prostitution is most common in low-income nations, where women's economic opportunities are most limited.

Prostitution is another issue that brings together conservatives and liberals. From a conservative point of view, prostitution violates traditional moral standards. Many liberals, and especially feminists, object to prostitution as the exploitation of women. Which political approach is illustrated in this protest against the sex tourism industry in Kiev, Ukraine?

SOCIAL PROBLEMS IN GLOBAL PERSPECTIVE

Prostitutes and Johns in Sweden: Who Is Breaking the Law?

Just about everywhere in the United States, it is against the law to sell sex. This means that when they work, prostitutes break the law. It is also against the law to buy sex. This means that when they solicit sex, "johns" also break the law. In reality, in about 68 percent of all arrests involving sex for money, police nab women working as prostitutes. In most cases, police leave "johns" alone. Such a policy, in effect, defines the prostitution problem as *women selling sex*.

Sweden has a different approach to prostitution. For several decades, prostitution was legal in Sweden. Then, in 1999, that country passed a law that allows people to *sell* sex but makes it a crime to *buy* sex. As one of Sweden's police officials recently put it, "We don't have a problem with prostitutes. We have a problem with men who buy sex."

The government's policy is guided by feminist theory, which claims that prostitution is a form of male violence against women. In addition, the Swedish government explains, equality between the sexes can only be achieved when men do not exploit women in sexual ways. As for women, the law ended criminal prosecution for selling sex and created a wide range of social services available to women who wish to stop working in prostitution.

Critics of the new policy claim that this law encourages men cruising for sex to get women into a car quickly, a practice that gives women little opportunity to assess any possible danger.

In addition, the law has relocated most prostitution from visible city streets to the outskirts of town where women may be more vulnerable to violence. But almost everyone agrees that, under the new law, the number of women working as prostitutes has fallen by as much as half. In Stockholm, the capital, estimates suggest that prostitution is down 80 percent. Just as important, before the law was enacted, thousands of women were brought into the country each year to work as prostitutes. Since the law took effect, cases of sex trafficking are just a few hundred annually.

Most Swedes support the new law. Compared to the United States, where women working as prostitutes experience a "revolving door" of arrest followed by a return to working the streets, Sweden appears to have largely ended the problem by replacing the "male" policy of arresting women for selling sex with a "female" viewpoint of helping women get out of prostitution and arresting men who buy sex (Ritter, 2008; Women's Justice Center, 2009).

What Do You Think?

1. How does the Swedish policy on prostitution differ from that in the United States in terms of constructing the problem and defining the solution?

2. Do you think the United States is likely to adopt the Swedish policy? Why or why not?

3. Would you support such a change? Why or why not?

One high-income country stands out as having a successful record of reducing prostitution. The surprising solution is simpler than you might expect, as the Social Problems in Global Perspective box explains.

Prostitutes: A Profile Most prostitutes—many prefer to call themselves "sex workers"—are women. But they are a diverse category, with better or worse working conditions, depending on their degree of physical attractiveness, age, and social class position.

The most advantaged prostitutes are *call girls*, who arrange appointments with clients by text messaging or telephone. Typically, these women are young, attractive, and well educated, and they are also highly paid. Most call girls work independently rather than for a manager. Many advertise their services online or in the classified ads of big-city papers, typically calling themselves "escorts," which is a polite way of saying they offer an evening of charming company, gracious conversation, and for an additional fee, sex.

Less well-off are prostitutes who work in brothels or "massage parlors" or for large "escort services." These women are employees who must follow the direction of their superiors. In addition, most of these women turn over at least half their earnings to their employer.

The worst-off prostitutes—and the most numerous—are *streetwalkers*. These prostitutes work the streets, offering sex to drive-by "johns." Streetwalkers are mostly lower-class women, and they earn the least money. Although some of these women work on their own, they typically give most of their earnings to managers, or *pimps*, who control their lives. With little ability to choose their customers, streetwalkers are at high risk of violence and other abuse, as well as for acquiring and spreading sexually transmitted diseases. Researchers estimate that the majority of streetwalkers have histories as victims of rape, incest, or other forms of sexual abuse, often going back to childhood (Estes, 2001; Williamson & Cluse-Tolar, 2002).

Prostitutes typically offer the sexual service requested by the client. Research suggests that the most common sexual act performed by prostitutes is oral sex, followed by sexual intercourse (Monto, 2001).

What about men who work as prostitutes? About 10 percent of prostitutes are men, and almost all sell sex to other men. They, too, are a diverse category, ranging from well-paid "escorts" to young runaways trying to survive from day to day on the streets (Boyer, 1989; Strong & DeVault, 1994).

Arrests for Prostitution   Although prostitution is against the law almost everywhere in the United States, law enforcement is selective. About two-thirds of roughly 50,000 people arrested for prostitution in 2012 were women; the remaining one-third were men, including both male prostitutes and "johns" or male clients (U.S. Department of Justice, Federal Bureau of Investigation, 2013).

According to COYOTE (Call Off Your Old Tired Ethics, 2012), a sex workers' rights organization founded in 1973, fully 90 percent of women arrested for prostitution are streetwalkers from low-social-class backgrounds; very few are high-status call girls. Race also figures into the picture: COYOTE reports that although most prostitutes are white, most of those arrested are African Americans.

Should police and the courts get tougher in cases involving prostitution? Surveys suggest that most people think that prostitution is wrong even assuming that there were no health risks involved (Smith et al., 2013). Of course, health risks *are* involved and they include the danger of spreading sexually transmitted diseases, including AIDS. In addition, it is likely that there would be even less tolerance for prostitution if the public were aware of the extent of violence and the drug abuse that often accompany this way of life.

SOCIAL PROBLEMS IN GLOBAL PERSPECTIVE
Children and Sex Tourism

"On this trip, I had sex with a fourteen-year-old girl in Mexico and a fifteen-year-old in Colombia. I am helping them financially. If they don't have sex with me, they may not have enough food."

These words were spoken by a retired U.S. schoolteacher who had just returned from a "vacation" in Latin America, where he was part of the global sex tourism business.

We live in a world made ever smaller by faster and less expensive transportation. In the past fifty years, the number of people traveling all over the world has increased tenfold. But a troubling side of this trend is an increasing number of men from high-income countries who travel to low-income nations with the goal of having sex with children.

Sex tourism is big business. Although there are no exact figures, it is likely that about 10 percent of the gross domestic product of several Southeast Asian countries—including Malaysia, the Philippines, and Thailand—comes from sex tourism. Sex tourism is also increasing in Africa, Eastern Europe, and Latin America. Around the world, perhaps 1 million children are selling sex.

What accounts for the high level of sex tourism? One underlying cause is poverty. Sex tourism is most widespread in countries where the average person is very poor. With little economic opportunity, families are willing to allow their children to go to work, in many cases turning children over to "agents" who promise to find them jobs.

Gender stratification is also at work here. Most low-income countries are patriarchal, and boys get more schooling than girls do. This means that parents who need money may send their daughters off to work with many ending up in the sex trade.

A final factor that has increased sex tourism in recent years is the spread of the Internet. Not only do millions of men travel to have sex with children, but many of them share their experiences, posting detailed accounts on thousands of websites that attract even more people into this industry.

The plight of children working as prostitutes is tragic and can be shocking. Estimates suggest that most children have between 100 clients and 1,500 clients annually (the higher number would be almost five clients a day, working all year). Beyond being forced to have sex, these children face violence from clients and employers, fear of arrest by the police, and run a high risk of getting sexually transmitted diseases. Within months of going to work as prostitutes, most young children become depressed, lose their self-esteem, and view their situation as hopeless. Drug use and even suicide are common (U.S. Department of Justice, 2012).

In response to increasing sex tourism, many national governments are calling for an end to child prostitution and a full-scale assault on the entire sex tourism industry. In the United States, Immigration and Customs Enforcement (ICE) has launched "Operation Predator" and has successfully prosecuted about one hundred people for violating a 2003 law that bans traveling to engage in sex offenses involving children (ICE, 2012). But given the severe poverty that is widespread in many countries, not to mention the added problem of police corruption, great change is unlikely any time soon.

What Do You Think?

1. Many men who take part in sex tourism make excuses for their behavior, as we read at the beginning of this box. Can you think of ways to discourage men from high-income countries from traveling to have sex with children?

2. Some travelers feel that the social norms we recognize at home do not apply in foreign lands, so sex with children is somehow OK. Do you think people everywhere should declare sex tourism a "universal wrong"? Why or why not?

3. Children also sell sex in the United States. Have you heard of this practice, which has been documented at truck stops as well as business conventions? How do you explain this happening in high-income countries like our own?

Child Prostitution Few people defend prostitution when it involves children. Around the world, hundreds of thousands of children (most of them boys) live on the streets, and many sell sex to survive. Some of these children work to provide income for their families; others were orphaned by AIDS or war. Almost all are desperately poor (UNICEF, 2006).

The Southeast Asian nation of Thailand has become a center for the global "sex tourism" industry, where the number of prostitutes may be as high as 125,000. In countless brothels and sex shows on the streets of Bangkok, Thailand's capital city, half the women who are selling sex are not yet out of their teens (UNAIDS, 2013).

Why are child prostitutes so popular? Customers favor young women in the belief that they pose less risk of spreading AIDS. But the fact is that girls and women working as prostitutes are at high risk for AIDS and other sexually transmitted diseases. The share of sex workers with HIV has been declining, but the threat is real. In addition, many of these girls and women also suffer from other medical conditions caused by years of neglect and abuse (Renton, 2005; UNAIDS, 2011). The Social Problems in Global Perspective box takes a closer look at sex tourism involving children.

Teenage Pregnancy

In the United States there are about 15 million teenage girls, and about 768,000 of these young women become pregnant each year. Most did not plan the pregnancy, and neither did the young men they were involved with. More seriously, most of these young people are unprepared to face the responsibilities of parenthood. As Figure 7–4 shows, the rate of teenage births is much higher in the United States than in other high-income nations.

The good news is that compared to fifty years ago, the share of teens who became pregnant is much lower. Back then, cultural norms led people to marry at a younger age, and most teens who became pregnant were young wives who, with their husbands, were starting families. In the 1950s, there was widespread disapproval of having an "illegitimate" child, so many unmarried couples who learned they were expecting a baby married quickly (the so-called "shotgun wedding," often at the insistence of the woman's father). In other cases, the woman quietly moved away and, after the birth, put the child up for adoption. A few women obtained abortions, but this practice was against the law almost everywhere.

Today, most young women who become pregnant are not married. Few teenage girls who become pregnant rush to get married and few put their babies up for adoption.

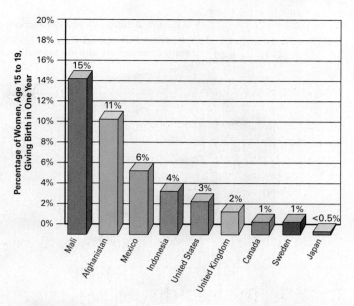

Global Snapshot

Figure 7–4   Births to Teenage Women

The share of women between the ages of fifteen and nineteen who have given birth in the past year is much higher in low-income nations than it is in high-income countries. Among the high-income nations, however, the United States stands out as having a higher share of young women who gave birth.

SOURCE: Population Reference Bureau (2011).

Research shows us this picture: Of all pregnant teens, 17 percent have miscarriages, 25 percent have abortions, and the majority (58 percent) keep their babies (Ventura et al., 2012).

In recent decades, the pregnancy rate among girls in their teens has fallen substantially, despite the fact that at least half of teenage girls and boys are sexually active. The main reason for the decline is almost certainly the increased use of contraceptives among sexually active teens.

The risk of unwanted pregnancy is greatest among girls who may be biologically mature but do not understand how their reproductive systems work. Such girls are likely to be from poor families. Compared with those from richer families, these girls are also more likely to keep their babies. Why? Researchers point out that most low-income girls and boys think that attending college and finding a good career is simply out of their reach. As a result, having a baby—being a parent—may seem to be the only way these young people can claim social standing as adults. Single motherhood is particularly common among poor African Americans, who are doubly disadvantaged by poverty and racism. For all racial and ethnic categories, becoming an unmarried teenage mother makes it harder to finish school and find a good job, dramatically increasing the odds of remaining

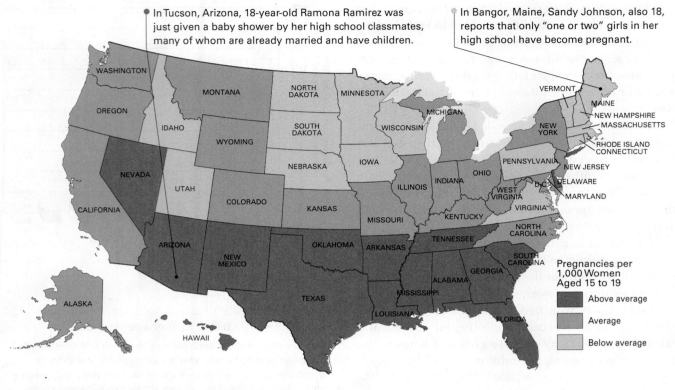

In Tucson, Arizona, 18-year-old Ramona Ramirez was just given a baby shower by her high school classmates, many of whom are already married and have children.

In Bangor, Maine, Sandy Johnson, also 18, reports that only "one or two" girls in her high school have become pregnant.

Pregnancies per
1,000 Women
Aged 15 to 19

Above average

Average

Below average

Seeing Ourselves

National Map 7–1 Teenage Pregnancy Rates across the United States

The map shows pregnancy rates for women ages fifteen to nineteen across the United States. What can you say about the regions of the country where rates are high? Where they are low? Can you explain these patterns?

SOURCE: Alan Guttmacher Institute (2013).

poor (Alan Guttmacher Institute, 2012; Ventura et al., 2012). National Map 7–1 shows the rate of teenage pregnancy across the United States.

The Costs of Teenage Pregnancy At its best, parenthood is a source of great joy. But for men and women who are young and poor, parenthood can bring a level of responsibility and economic pressure that they simply cannot handle. Many look to government for help, and the cost of income assistance, medical care, and other support for pregnant teenagers in the United States is about $11 billion each year (National Campaign, 2011).

The greatest burden of poverty, however, is borne by those who understand none of this—the babies. On average, infants born to poor teens have lower birthweight and higher risk of physical and developmental problems. Many such infants face a life of challenges that often accompany poverty, including poor nutrition, violence in the local neighborhood, little schooling, and inadequate health care. To make matters worse, most of these children face these hardships with little or no help from their fathers. Not surprisingly, these children grow up at high risk for becoming single parents themselves.

Sex Education: A Solution? What can society do to reduce unwanted teen pregnancy? One strategy looks to schools. Sex education programs teach young people how their bodies grow and change, present the biology of reproduction, and explain how to avoid pregnancy by using birth control or abstaining from sex.

Today, in most public schools, "sex ed" is an established part of the curriculum. Yet this program remains controversial. Critics (typically conservatives) point to what they see as a troubling pattern: Over the past two decades, as more schools have adopted sex education programs, the level of sexual activity among teenagers has gone up. Researchers tell us that, by their senior year, 63 percent of today's high school students have had sexual intercourse. Such data do show that the cause of this change is sex education, but they do raise doubts about whether this program is (as conservatives tend to say) part of the problem or (as liberals claim) part of the solution.

Supporters of sex education (typically, liberals) say that the biggest cause of teenage pregnancy is ignorance. It makes sense, they say, to teach young people—many of whom are sexually active—about birth control methods and the risks of contracting sexually transmitted diseases.

From this point of view, sex education is the main reason for the recent decline in unwanted teenage pregnancy.

Perhaps no sex education issue provokes more heated discussion than the policy of distributing condoms in school. Conservatives claim that this policy only encourages young people to rush headlong into sexual activity. Liberals respond that most young people will be sexually active one way or another; the point is to give them what they need to avoid pregnancy and sexually transmitted diseases (Alan Guttmacher Institute, 2012; CDC, 2013).

Finally, the mass media have a powerful effect on the attitudes and behavior of young people. In recent years, television shows including *16 and Pregnant* and *Teen Mom* have shown the reality of young motherhood. The viewing public may have picked up the message. Researchers note that, in the year and a half after this programming began, the teen pregnancy rate in the United States fell by 6 percent (National Bureau of Economic Research, 2014).

Abortion

Of all the issues surrounding sexuality in the United States, surely the most controversial is **abortion**, *the intentional termination of a pregnancy*. Each year in the United States, there are about 1.2 million abortions performed, which represents about one-fourth of all pregnancies. The typical woman receiving an abortion is in her twenties and about half of these women have had one or more abortions before. Data show that 85 percent are unmarried, and about half have income below or close to the poverty line. Finally, 36 percent of the women are white and 61 percent are African American or Hispanic American (Alan Guttmacher Institute, 2013).

Abortion: A Look Back   Abortion goes far back in history; this practice was common among the ancient Egyptians, Romans, and Greeks (Luker, 1984; Tannahill, 1992). In the United States, from the colonial era until the mid-nineteenth century, early-term abortion by midwives and other traditional practitioners was legal everywhere. The picture began to change in 1847, when the newly formed American Medical Association (AMA) pressed to outlaw the procedure. The AMA claimed that doctors were the best qualified to perform abortions, and the AMA was clearly trying to put midwives and other traditional healers who performed abortions out of business. This effort was successful. By the early twentieth century, every state in the country had enacted a law banning abortion (Luker, 1984).

These new laws did not end the practice of abortion, however. Women with money could find a doctor willing to perform a safe abortion. But for poor women, it was another story. They either endured an unwanted pregnancy or submitted to an inexpensive "back alley" procedure performed by an unlicensed practitioner with sometimes deadly results.

By the 1960s, all across the United States, a social movement was under way to repeal laws banning abortion. In 1973, the movement succeeded when the U.S. Supreme Court issued decisions in the cases of *Roe* v. *Wade* and *Doe* v. *Bolton*, which struck down all state abortion laws. Ever since, "pro-choice" people (typically liberals) have fought to keep abortion available to women. "Antiabortion" people (typically conservatives) are working just as hard to limit abortion and even to reverse the Supreme Court decision and once again make abortion illegal.

The Abortion Controversy Today   Since 1973, various laws and court decisions have limited women's access to abortion. In 1977, for example, Congress passed the Hyde Amendment prohibiting the use of Medicaid funds for abortions, except when necessary to save the life of the mother. In 1980, the U.S. Supreme Court ruled in *Harris* v. *McRae* that state and federal governments need not provide poor women with taxpayer-funded abortions. In 1989, the Supreme Court upheld a state law that banned public employees or public facilities from performing abortions, except to save the mother's life. In *Webster* v. *Reproductive Health Services* (1989), the Court also upheld state laws that require doctors, before performing an abortion, to conduct medical tests to see whether the fetus could survive outside the mother's body.

In 1992, the Court's decision in *Planned Parenthood of Southeastern Pennsylvania* v. *Casey* reaffirmed that states had wide latitude in setting abortion policy. Later in the 1990s, Congress twice proposed laws banning so-called partial-birth abortions performed in the third trimester of pregnancy, but President Clinton vetoed both bills. Finally, by 2014, thirteen states ban abortion after twenty-two weeks of pregnancy. In addition, thirty-nine states (most are in the South and Midwest) have enacted laws requiring some parental involvement in a minor's decision to have an abortion, including twenty-one states that require one or both parents to consent to the procedure (Pew Research Center, 2013).

Although there is no indication that the U.S. Supreme Court plans to overturn the *Roe* v. *Wade* decision, many supporters of abortion rights fear that this could happen. If so, control of abortion policy would go back to individual states. Currently, seven states have enacted laws that would keep abortion available if *Roe* were overturned. But twenty states have laws that would restrict or ban legal access to abortion (Alan Guttmacher Institute, 2014).

All the same, the public remains divided on this issue. Table 7–1 on page 218 shows the proportion of U.S. adults who support abortion under various circumstances. Although a large majority (81.8 percent) support

Table 7–1 U.S. Attitudes toward Abortion

Survey Question: "It should be possible for a woman to obtain a *legal* abortion ..."

	Percentage Answering Yes
". . . if the woman's own health is seriously endangered by the pregnancy."	81.8%
". . . if she becomes pregnant as a result of rape."	71.2
". . . if there is a strong chance of a serious defect in the baby."	69.1
". . . if she is married and does not want any more children."	42.7
". . . if the family has a very low income and cannot afford any more children."	40.2
". . . for any reason."	41.2
". . . if she is not married and does not want to marry the man."	39.1

SOURCE: Smith et al. (2013).

legal abortion if a woman's health is threatened by her pregnancy, less than half (41.2 percent) support legal abortion for any reason at all (Smith et al., 2013). Surprisingly, perhaps, support for abortion is almost the same among women (55 percent) as it is among men (53 percent). Support for abortion is greater among Democrats (69 percent) than among Republicans (35 percent). In addition, attitudes toward abortion vary by race and ethnicity. For example, people of Arab and Italian descent are more conservative on this issue, with only 29 percent supporting abortion for any reason. At the liberal end of the political spectrum, 89 percent of Jewish Americans support abortion in most or all cases (Zogby International, 2001; Pew Research Center, 2013).

Why is the abortion controversy so intense? From anyone's point of view, a lot is at stake. Antiabortion activists claim that abortion is nothing less than the killing of unborn children. On matters of life and death, many people will not compromise their beliefs. Yet pro-choice activists, too, have reason to stand firm. As they see it, legal access to abortion is the key to women's control over childbearing and therefore women's control over their lives. Only by avoiding unwanted pregnancy can women have the opportunity to earn income and establish their independence from men. In short, without legal abortion, women are unlikely ever to achieve social equality with men (Simon, 2003).

Sexually Transmitted Diseases

Sexually transmitted diseases (STDs) are *diseases spread by sexual contact*. In all, there are more than fifty STDs. Rates of infection of most STDs—including gonorrhea, syphilis, and genital herpes—began to rise during the sexual revolution of the 1960s. By the 1980s, the increasing danger of STDs played a part in encouraging the sexual counterrevolution, described earlier in this chapter.

The Centers for Disease Control and Prevention (2013) reports about 20 million new sexually transmitted infections each year. About half of the people infected are younger than twenty-five. Overall, the CDC estimates the number of sexually transmitted infections (both new and existing) in the United States at 110 million and about $16 billion annually is spent treating them. The following sections briefly describe several common sexually transmitted diseases.

Gonorrhea and Syphilis Gonorrhea and syphilis, among the oldest diseases to afflict humans, result from microscopic organisms typically transmitted during sexual activity. Untreated, gonorrhea can cause sterility; syphilis can result in blindness, mental disorders, and even death.

In 2012, the official record shows 334,826 cases of gonorrhea and 15,667 cases of syphilis in the United States, although the actual totals are probably much higher. Official data show that most cases involve non-Hispanic African Americans (63 percent), with lower numbers reported among non-Hispanic whites (23 percent), Latinos (12 percent), and Asian Americans and Native Americans (1 percent each) (CDC, 2013).

Doctors treat gonorrhea and syphilis effectively with antibiotics, such as penicillin. For this reason, neither disease is considered a major U.S. health problem today.

Genital Herpes Genital herpes (herpes simplex virus, type 2) is a virus that infects at least 25 million people, or about one in six (16 percent) of people in the United States between the ages of fourteen and forty-nine. Among people in their forties, about one in four is infected with the genital herpes virus. In this age category, the rate of infection is more than twice as high among African Americans (56 percent) than among non-Hispanic whites (21 percent) and Hispanic Americans (20 percent) (CDC, 2010).

Although herpes poses less danger to human health than gonorrhea and syphilis, it is a disease that has no cure. Some people with genital herpes have no symptoms at all, and many are unaware that they are infected with the virus. Others, however, experience periodic, painful blisters on the genitals accompanied by fever and headache.

One serious concern is that women with active genital herpes can transmit the disease to infants during vaginal delivery, and it can be deadly to a newborn. Therefore, doctors usually advise infected women to give birth by cesarean section.

AIDS The most serious of all sexually transmitted diseases is *acquired immune deficiency syndrome*, or *AIDS*. Soon

Sexually transmitted diseases are as old as humanity and they have long been defined as a social problem. More than fifty diseases are spread through sexual contact. Some diseases show no symptoms at all and some have obvious symptoms. Some may cause only periodic discomfort and some are deadly. Some can be easily cured using antibiotics and some have no cure at all. These young girls are being inoculated against human papilloma virus (HPV), which can produce warts on the genitals or other parts of the body and, in some cases, can cause cancer.

after identifying this disease in 1981, doctors concluded that it is incurable and, if untreated, it is usually fatal. AIDS is caused by the *human immunodeficiency virus*, or *HIV*, which destroys the body's immune system. AIDS itself does not kill; it makes a person unable to fight off a wide range of other diseases that eventually cause death.

Extent of the AIDS Problem in the United States Government officials recorded 15,529 deaths due to AIDS in the United States in 2010. Officials also noted 32,050 new cases in 2011. The number of cases reported each year has been decreasing. But the official count of people who have contracted AIDS stands at 1,155,792. Of these, 636,048 have died (CDC, 2013).

Non-Hispanic white people (63 percent of the population) account for 33 percent of patients with AIDS, and non-Hispanic African Americans (13 percent of the population) account for 43 percent of people with AIDS. Latinos also show high infection rates: They represent 17 percent of the total U.S. population and 20 percent of people with AIDS. In short, both African Americans and Hispanic Americans are at relatively high risk of HIV infection. This is especially true for women: About 79 percent of women and children with the disease are African Americans or Latinas. Asian Americans and Native Americans (together about 6 percent of the population) account for only about 2 percent of people with AIDS (CDC, 2013).

Extent of the AIDS Problem in the World In many regions of the world, AIDS is a medical catastrophe. Just how great is the global toll? Around the world, HIV infects some 35 million people, 3.2 million of whom are

under the age of fifteen, and these numbers continue to increase. Global Map 7–1 on page 220 shows that the countries with the highest rates of HIV infections are in sub-Saharan Africa, which accounts for 71 percent of the world's cases. According to the United Nations, in much of this region, 1.2 percent of young men (fifteen to twenty-four years of age) are infected with HIV as are 2.5 percent of young women. In these African nations, because heterosexual relations are the main way HIV is transmitted, girls are at higher risk than boys because HIV is more easily transmitted from males to females than the other way around (UNAIDS, 2013).

How HIV Is Transmitted People who become infected with HIV display no symptoms for a year or even longer. Therefore, most people with the virus remain unaware of their condition and may unknowingly spread the disease. Within five years, one-third of infected people develop full-blown AIDS; half do so within ten years, and almost all become sick within twenty years.

Although HIV is infectious, it is not contagious. This means that HIV is transmitted from person to person in only a few, specific ways: through blood, semen, or breast milk. It is not transmitted through casual contact such as shaking hands, hugging, sharing towels or dishes, swimming together, or even coughing or sneezing. The risk of transmitting the virus through saliva (as in kissing) is extremely low. One effective strategy to greatly reduce the risk of transmitting HIV through sexual activity is for males to use a latex condom. But the only sure way to stay safe from HIV is sexual abstinence or an exclusive relationship with an uninfected person.

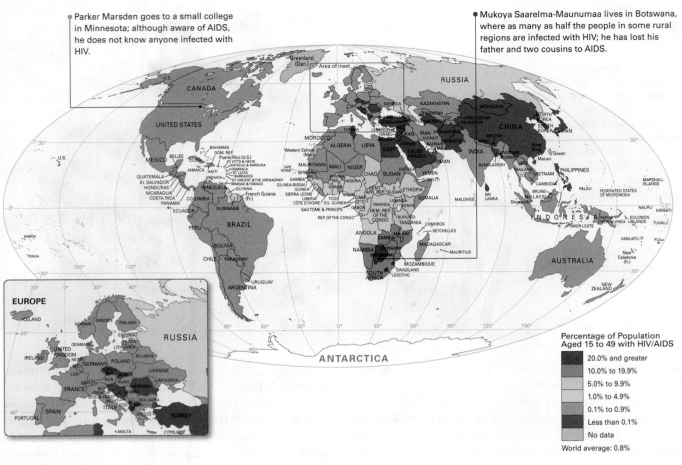

Parker Marsden goes to a small college in Minnesota; although aware of AIDS, he does not know anyone infected with HIV.

Mukoya Saarelma-Maunumaa lives in Botswana, where as many as half the people in some rural regions are infected with HIV; he has lost his father and two cousins to AIDS.

Percentage of Population Aged 15 to 49 with HIV/AIDS

- 20.0% and greater
- 10.0% to 19.9%
- 5.0% to 9.9%
- 1.0% to 4.9%
- 0.1% to 0.9%
- Less than 0.1%
- No data

World average: 0.8%

Window on the World

Global Map 7–1 HIV Infections in Global Perspective

The nations of sub-Saharan Africa contain 70 percent of the world's cases of HIV and 70 percent of all new infections. Currently, however, nations in Eastern Europe and Central Asia show the fastest increase in HIV infections and account for about 20 percent of all cases. Infection rates are fairly low in North and South America, which together account for 9 percent of global cases of HIV.

SOURCE: UNAIDS (2013).

Specific behaviors put people at high risk for HIV infection (CDC, 2010):

1. **Anal sex.** Anal intercourse is dangerous because it can cause rectal bleeding, which permits easy passage of HIV from one person to another. Because many homosexual and bisexual men engage in anal sex, these categories of people account for 48 percent of all cases diagnosed in 2010.

2. **Sharing needles.** Injecting a drug using a needle that is shared with other people is a high-risk behavior because users come into contact with each other's blood. Intravenous drug users account for about 25 percent of people with AIDS. For this reason, sex with an intravenous drug user is also a high-risk behavior. Because the rate of intravenous drug use is high among poor people in the United States, AIDS has become a disease of the economically disadvantaged.

3. **Using any drug.** The use of any drug, including alcohol, can put people at risk of acquiring any STD because it harms a person's judgment. Even people who understand the risks may act less responsibly if they are under the influence of alcohol, marijuana, or some other drug.

As Figure 7–5 shows, 25 percent of people with AIDS in the United States became infected through heterosexual contact. The risk goes up along with the number of sexual partners, especially if they fall into high-risk categories. Around the world, heterosexual activity accounts for two-thirds of all infections.

Combating AIDS In the early 1980s, the gay community was the first to call attention to the problem of AIDS. The government was slow to respond, perhaps because it was gay men who were most affected by the epidemic. Activists pressed for greater government funding for AIDS research and more social services for people with AIDS.

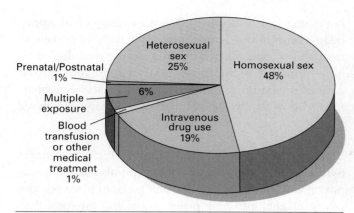

Figure 7–5   Types of Transmission for Reported U.S. AIDS Cases, 2011

Almost half the people with AIDS in the United States were infected through homosexual activity. However, there are many other ways to become infected.

SOURCE: Centers for Disease Control and Prevention (2013).

By the mid-1980s, when transfusions spread HIV into the heterosexual population, officials gave the problem greater attention and began screening the nation's blood supply for HIV.

As the death toll mounted, the gay and lesbian communities came together to begin outreach programs to encourage safer sex, and to explain what HIV is and how it is spread. These efforts succeeded as gay men began to reduce the number of sexual partners and avoid high-risk behaviors.

In recent years, new drug therapies have extended the lives of people with HIV. Antiretroviral therapy improves the health of people with HIV and can also prevent those people from further transmitting the virus. As the cost of such therapy has come down, this treatment is projected to reach 15 million people around the world by 2015 (World Health Organization, 2013).

Theories of Sexuality

7.5   **Apply sociological theory to issues involving sexuality.**

Sociological theory can help us understand various social problems more completely. The following sections look at sexuality using sociology's major theoretical approaches.

Structural-Functional Analysis: Controlling Sexuality

The most basic function of sexuality is human reproduction, which is the necessary process that allows our species to exist. But controlling sexuality is also important to social organization, which is why society demands that members select partners and reproduce according to specific norms. To see why controlling sexuality is important, imagine for a moment that people reproduced with just anybody. If this were to happen, the family as we know it would not exist, and kinship ties would become impossible to track. In such a chaotic state, no one would have clear obligations to anyone else, so that society as we know it would largely collapse.

Incest and Legitimacy   One important norm guiding reproduction is the *incest taboo*, the norm found in every society that forbids sex and reproduction between certain close family members. The incest taboo is found all over the world, although exactly which kin are included varies from one society to another. Why is this norm important? Again, if close blood kin were to reproduce, social relationships would soon become hopelessly confusing. If a father and a daughter reproduced and had a son, for example, what would the boy's relationship be to each of them?

In the same way, the traditional norms that defined as *legitimate* children born to married couples is a societal strategy to ensure that children are cared for within established families and that have legal ties, including rights of inheritance, to their biological parents. In short, structural-functional theory helps explain why societies define sexual relationships in various ways and why some types of relations, such as incest, are widely regarded as social problems in societies around the world.

The Functions of Prostitution   If certain sexual relationships are defined as social problems, it is also true that some sexual problems may not be entirely bad for everybody. Take the case of prostitution. As explained earlier in this chapter, most people view prostitution as a problem because it spreads disease and exploits women (Smith et al., 2013). But as Kingsley Davis (1971) pointed out many years ago, prostitution also performs a few useful, if less noticed, functions.

According to Davis, prostitution is one way to meet the sexual needs of those members of a society who do not have ready access to sex, including soldiers, travelers, as well as people who are for whatever reason unable to attract a partner. In addition, some people may favor prostitution simply because they want sex without the commitment of a relationship. As the saying goes: "Men don't pay for sex; they pay so they can leave."

EVALUATE

Structural-functional theory explains the importance of sexuality in the organization of society and especially why societies have always paid attention to who reproduces with whom. At the same time, now that modern technology has largely separated sex from reproduction, does society need to regulate sex as much as it once did?

Structural-functional theory sometimes ignores gender. When Kingsley Davis wrote of the benefits of prostitution for society, he was really talking about benefits to some *men*. Another limitation of this approach is that it ignores the diversity of sexual norms in the United States as well as how much patterns of sexual behavior change over time. To appreciate the varied and changeable character of sexuality, we now turn to symbolic-interaction theory.

CHECK YOUR LEARNING Applying structural-functional theory, why do societies control sexual behavior, especially when it involves reproduction? What is one limitation of this approach?

Symbolic-Interaction Analysis: Defining Sexuality

Symbolic-interaction theory highlights the fact that members of a society socially construct sexuality just as they create all other aspects of reality. As human creations, the meanings people attach to sexuality can vary quite a bit. One good way to see the different views people have about sex is to look back in history.

The Meaning of Virginity   A good example of the changing meanings attached to sex is the idea of *virginity*, that is, the state of never having had sexual intercourse. Through most of this nation's history, strong cultural norms demanded that people—or more precisely, *women*—remain virgins until marriage. Before modern methods of birth control were available, the norm of virginity was the only way men could be sure they were not marrying a woman who was carrying another man's child.

The development of effective birth control gradually separated sexuality from reproduction, so virginity did

Are chastity belts a thing of the past? In a clear case of society controlling sexuality, these women who work in massage parlors in one Indonesian city are required to wear padlocked trousers to prevent prostitution. Whose interests do you think are served by such a practice?

not matter nearly as much. One study shows that among people born in the decade after 1963, fully 84 percent of men and 80 percent of women reported that they were not virgins at first marriage. A century ago, most people defined premarital sexual intercourse as a social problem; today, however, this sexual pattern is widely considered the norm (Laumann et al., 1994).

Learning Sexual Roles: The Case of Topless Dancers
Symbolic-interaction theory not only points out that sexual norms vary from time to time and place to place but also offers insights into how people learn and interpret their own sexual behavior. For example, how do women become topless dancers? What do the women who do this work think of their jobs and themselves?

In a study of forty topless dancers in a southwestern city, researchers found that women came to this kind of work gradually, step by step, just as people enter any other career (Thompson & Harrod, 1999). Most of the women explained that their first experience with topless dancing was a brief episode, typically in response to a dare from someone else, and in most cases after having had a few drinks. The women reported receiving encouragement for their efforts, and more important, began to realize that they could earn more money dancing than through other "straight" work.

At that point, they made the decision to earn some or all of their income engaged in work that many people consider deviant. But most of the women insisted they were doing nothing wrong. Their clubs helped them think well of themselves by having strict "look but don't touch" policies, by which women defined themselves as entertainers, not prostitutes. In addition, all the women used stage names so that customers did not know their "real world" identities. Likewise, most women told only a few people outside the club what their job actually was; to the rest, including parents, they were simply "in the nightclub business."

Finally, almost all the women working as topless dancers learned to see their work as useful, pointing out that they provided entertainment that harmed no one and for which they were well paid. The women gradually built a world of meanings that both protected them and made them comfortable with their work (Thompson & Harrod, 1999).

EVALUATE

Symbolic-interaction theory highlights how people construct reality in their everyday lives, a process that applies to sexuality as it does to other forms of behavior. But although many aspects of sexuality vary over time and from place to place, some patterns are remarkably consistent, such as men's tendency to devalue women as sex objects. To understand this pattern, we turn to two important social-conflict theories.

CHECK YOUR LEARNING What insights do we gain by apply-ing symbolic-interaction theory to the issue of sexuality? What is one limitation of this approach?

Social-Conflict Analysis: Feminist Theory and Queer Theory

Social-conflict theory, as summarized in the Applying Theory table on page 224, highlights social inequality. Following this approach, feminist theory explains that sexuality involves inequality between women and men. Similarly, queer theory highlights inequality between homosexuals and heterosexuals.

Feminist Theory: Women as Sexual Objects Feminist the-ory points out that sexuality plays a part in men's domina-tion of women. Pornography, prostitution, and even topless dancing degrade women, casting them in the role of sexual objects that exist primarily for men's pleasure. Men who value women for their looks and submissiveness, in short, are unlikely to accept women as social equals. For this reason, the movement for gender equality has helped define sexual-ity in the workplace as a social problem, prompting govern-ments and companies to enact antiharassment policies.

Male domination often involves not just inequality but also violence. U.S. culture weaves sex and violence together, a fact evident in expressions such as "hitting on" or "banging" someone, which refer to both sexuality and physical violence. For this reason, social-conflict theory—especially feminism—has been sharply critical of conven-tional sexual norms. A few feminists reject sexual relations with men entirely, claiming that women who sleep with men are like slaves having sexual relationships with their masters (Dworkin, 1987).

Queer Theory A more recent devel-opment in sociology is **queer theory**, *a body of theory and research that chal-lenges the heterosexual bias in U.S. soci-ety.* Just as feminist theory seeks equal standing for women and men, queer theory seeks equal acceptance of homosexuality and heterosexuality.

Feminism defines the problem as *sexism*, with one sex superior to the other. *Queer* theory claims that our society is distorted by **heterosexism**, *bias that treats heterosexuality as the norm while stigmatizing anyone who violates this norm as "queer."* The heterosexism of U.S. society condemns not only gay men and lesbians but also bisexual people, asexual people, and transgender individuals who vio-late gender norms in any ways that they think, act, or relate to others. Heterosexist norms are common in everyday life, as when the mass media celebrate the "sex appeal" of popular movie stars, almost all of whom are portrayed as heterosexual. In 1998, the comedian and actress Ellen DeGeneres sparked controversy when she "came out" as a lesbian on her television show. Yet in recent years, popular shows like *Modern Family* feature openly gay characters, suggesting that attitudes are changing.

Although discrimination against women and African Americans is illegal, bias against people who differ in their sexuality is both common and, in many cases, within the law. But change is underway. Since the beginning of 2014, the Boy Scouts no longer exclude openly gay members. Similarly, in 2014 a California law took effect requiring schools to recognize and respect students' gender identity and allow them to fully participate in all school activities according to their gender identity.

EVALUATE

Feminist theory and queer theory highlight how closely sexuality is tied to various dimensions of social inequality. But critics of these social-conflict theories point out that not everyone thinks of sex-uality as a power issue. Rather, most people find that sexuality strengthens a relationship to another person. In addition, various social-conflict theories give little attention to the many steps U.S. society has taken to attack bias against women, gay men, and les-bians, including antidiscrimination policies and hate crime laws.

CHECK YOUR LEARNING What insights about sexuality do we gain from feminist theory? What about from queer theory? What is one limitation of each of these social-conflict theories?

From a social-conflict point of view, sexuality is not so much a "natural" part of our humanity as it is a socially constructed pattern of behavior. Sexuality plays an important part in social inequality: By defining women in sexual terms, men devalue them as objects. Would you consider the behavior shown here to be "natural" or socially directed? Why?

APPLYING THEORY

Sexuality

	Structural-Functional Theory	Symbolic-Interaction Theory	Social-Conflict Theory Including Feminist Theory and Queer Theory
What is the level of analysis?	Macro-level	Micro-level	Macro-level
What is important about sexuality?	Structural-functional theory begins pointing to the importance of sexuality for human reproduction. But society must control sexuality—that is, must control who reproduces with whom—to maintain social order.	Symbolic-interaction theory explains that, like all social patterns, sexuality involves meanings that people attach to their behavior. Patterns of sexuality and the way people understand them vary from place to place and over time. Sexual roles, including engaging in controversial behavior such as topless dancing, are learned over time.	All social-conflict theories focus on how sexuality is linked to social inequality. Both feminist theory and queer theory are efforts to make society more equal with regard to gender and sexual orientation.
Is sexuality a problem?	All societies make use of the incest taboo to regulate reproduction, preventing reproduction by closely related partners. To ensure that parents care for children and to ensure the right of offspring to inheritance, many societies also employ the idea of "legitimate" birth.	Meanings attached to sexual behavior change over time. Not being a virgin was defined as a problem in the past, especially for unmarried women, but virginity does not mean nearly as much today. To avoid the problem of negative labels, people who engage in controversial behavior involving sexuality, such as topless dancing, develop attitudes and behavior that protect their interests and self-esteem.	Feminist theory considers sexuality a problem to the extent that it allows men to dominate women. The problem of patriarchy contributes to other problems, such as prostitution and pornography, both of which involve men devaluing women. Queer theory opposes the heterosexism in our culture and seeks acceptance of homosexuality alongside heterosexuality.

✪ POLITICS AND SEXUALITY

Constructing Problems and Defining Solutions

7.6   Analyze issues involving sexuality from various positions on the political spectrum.

As always, the way in which people construct problems and what strategies they define as solutions depend on their political values. This holds for sexuality as well. This section explores the issues raised in this chapter from the conservative, liberal, and radical-left points of view.

Conservatives: The Value of Traditional Morality

The basic principle that defines the conservative view of sexuality is that people should be guided not by selfish desires but by established moral principles of right and wrong. To the extent that society encourages the traditional behavior we associate with "gentlemen" and "ladies," conservatives argue, most of the problems noted in this chapter can be avoided (Sommers, 2003).

Many conservatives support the conventional norms that place sexuality within the traditional bonds of marriage. For this reason, conservatives view premarital sex and extramarital sex as social problems, behavior that may lead to other problems such as teenage pregnancy and sexually transmitted diseases. Conservatives also condemn prostitution and pornography not only because they violate traditional standards of decency but also because they threaten marriages.

Conservatives oppose abortion on demand because this policy gives one person the power to end the life of another who is innocent and helpless: the unborn child. Rather than ending 1.2 million unwanted pregnancies each year through abortion, conservatives advocate greater personal responsibility so that fewer unwanted pregnancies occur in the first place.

Of course, conservatives do not all agree on every issue. Homosexuality is a case in point. Some conservatives condemn homosexuality as an immoral lifestyle and oppose same-sex marriage as a violation of tradition and, in the case of religious conservatives, biblical Scripture. Other, more moderate conservatives believe that sexual orientation cannot be a moral issue because it is not a matter of choice; they support same-sex marriage as a means of bringing the benefits of family life to all people, gay and straight.

Overall, the conservative answer to social problems involving sexuality is to have strong social institutions—including churches, schools, and especially families. These institutions teach personal responsibility so that young people can resist peer pressure and other temptations and do what is right. Today, conservatives support a number of policies that promise to strengthen families, such as child-support laws, laws requiring parental notification whenever young women seek abortions, and policies giving parents time away from work to care for family members. Most of all, conservatives claim, U.S. society would greatly benefit from a national effort to ensure that as many children as possible are raised in a home with both a father and a mother.

Liberals: Sex and Individual Choice

Liberals emphasize not the traditional morality that is so important to conservatives but individual freedom. As liberals see it, all people should be free to choose how they express their sexuality. This makes the liberal attitude toward sexuality one of tolerance. In the case of sexual orientation, for example, liberals avoid making judgments that a particular behavior is always right or always wrong; they favor allowing individuals to decide how to behave. For example, liberals are tolerant of premarital sex as long as the people involved have the maturity and the knowledge to make responsible choices.

The limits of liberal tolerance appear when someone threatens another with harm. Liberals define sexual violence, AIDS, and teenage pregnancy as social problems for this reason. Similarly, although liberals defend freedom of expression, many are concerned that pornography and prostitution are harmful to women.

Liberals look to government to address various social problems. Public schools should take the lead in teaching young people what they need to know to make responsible choices about sex. Liberals expect the criminal justice system to protect women from domestic violence and rape. In their view, government agencies should monitor the workplace to be sure that employees are free from sexual harassment. Finally, only the vast resources available to the government are likely to bring an eventual end to the AIDS epidemic.

Believing that individuals should be responsible for their own behavior, liberals support making abortion available to all and leaving the decision about abortion to the woman herself. Most liberals support government funding for abortions so that all pregnant women, regardless of their ability to pay, have choices.

The Radical Left: Go to the Root of the Problem

Radicals on the left view the issues in this chapter—including sexual orientation, pornography, sexual violence, and prostitution—as dimensions of social inequality. In their view, each problem comes about because some category of people has power over another.

Radical feminists explain that U.S. society is strongly patriarchal. Because male power runs deep into the structure

Is prostitution a problem? Conservatives tend to oppose the sale of sex on moral grounds. Many liberals support the idea that adults should be free to behave as they wish as long as they do not harm others. But other liberals—and most radicals—condemn the selling of sex because it perpetuates traditional gender stereotypes that harm women.

of U.S. society, radical feminists doubt that efforts at reform will ever create a society in which women and men stand as equals. As a result, radical feminists seek the elimination of gender itself. As noted in Chapter 4 ("Gender Inequality"), many radical feminists believe that to do this, society must rethink the biological process of reproduction. Perhaps, they suggest, new reproductive technologies will liberate women from their historical role in childbearing, which will open up the possibility of equal participation in social life.

In the short term, many radical feminists encourage women to work together to achieve political aims and to avoid dependency on men. Some even call for ending sexual ties to men, offering a strong voice on behalf of lesbians. It is lesbians, after all, who defy two basic structures of U.S. society: Their homosexuality challenges the heterosexual norm, and choosing to live without men is a direct challenge to male power.

Queer theory argues that U.S. society privileges heterosexuality while dismissing anyone who violates

LEFT TO RIGHT

The Politics of Sexuality

	Radical-Left View	Liberal View	Conservative View
What is the problem?	Men dominate women, just as heterosexuals dominate people with other sexual orientations.	Prostitution and pornography harm women, teen pregnancy is linked to poverty, and sexual harassment prevents people from doing their jobs.	Premarital sex, extramarital sex, and homosexuality violate traditional principles of right and wrong; abortion, too, is morally wrong.
What is the solution?	Because sexism and heterosexism are deeply rooted in the existing system, radical feminism advocates change in the direction of a gender-free society. Similarly, queer theory argues that equality for people of all sexual orientations will require a basic change in our culture.	Government must combat prostitution and pornography, keep sexuality out of the workplace, ensure that abortion is available to all women, and pursue a cure for AIDS.	Families—preferably with two active, involved parents—must teach children traditional virtues, such as personal responsibility in matters of sexuality. To the extent that they do, problems such as teen pregnancy and sexually transmitted diseases will decline.

JOIN THE DEBATE

1. In your opinion, which issues discussed in this chapter are the most serious social problems? Why?

2. Overall, do you think the sexual climate in the United States is getting better? Is it getting worse? Why?

3. Which of the three political analyses of sexuality included here do you find most convincing? Why?

that norm as "queer." So deep is this heterosexual bias, queer theory claims, that nothing less than challenging the roots of our way of life can produce an egalitarian society in which all people are equal participants in social life.

The Left to Right table summarizes issues related to sexuality as viewed from each of the three political perspectives.

Going On from Here

You might be tempted to conclude that, if anything is certain to be around a century from now, it is sex. Societies may change in many ways, but sex seems to remain a steady element of human experience.

But is it? This chapter has traced some remarkable changes in sexual practices and attitudes in the United States. From the rigid "sex as reproduction" view held by the earliest European settlers on our shores to the open, "anything goes" views of the sexual revolution, ideas about sex have been anything but static.

Change is also evident in the definition of sexual problems. At the beginning of the twentieth century, homosexuality was considered to be a social problem: No one talked about it openly, many people saw it as a sin or a sickness, and homosexual behavior was against the law almost everywhere. As the gay rights movement gained strength, an increasing tolerance of sexual diversity entered U.S. culture. Today, it is now possible to live an openly gay life, and millions of people do.

Several decades ago, few people considered sexual harassment to be a problem, accepting the idea that men should think of women primarily in sexual terms. As women have gained economic, political, and educational clout in the United States, such thinking has been replaced by the idea that women as well as men should be evaluated on the basis of their abilities rather than their looks. In the past decade, the widespread enactment of sexual harassment policies has sought to remove sexuality from workplace relationships.

Going on from here, what changes should we expect in the future? Although continued controversy is certain, the trend toward greater tolerance of homosexuality seems sure to continue. In the span of just a few years (and as of 2014), more than half the states and the District of Columbia have changed their laws to allow gay men and lesbians to form legal marriages; other states are likely to follow suit. Likewise, efforts to bring an end to the AIDS epidemic have expanded and shown promise. With time, this disease, which has caused more than 600,000 deaths in the United States, will be tamed. But what about the poor nations of the world, where the death toll since 1981 now exceeds 25 million? And back at home, what about the divisive issue of abortion? All that is certain is that this controversy will continue.

Sex may always be part of social life, but in this case, the more things stay the same, the more they change.

Essay: Envisioning a Better Society In what specific ways do you see our society's attitudes about sexuality changing? Is this change making society better or not? Why? Looking ahead fifty years, what further changes do you hope to see? What specific policies or cultural shifts would help bring about this change?

CHAPTER 7   Sexuality

Is it OK for young people to be sexually active?

Just about everyone has an opinion about this issue, if only because sexual activity can lead to a number of problems, including pregnancy and sexually transmitted diseases. Look at the accompanying photos to see two different approaches to defining a solution to these problems.

Liberals agree that unwanted pregnancy and sexually transmitted diseases are serious problems. They claim that the problem is not sex itself, however, but rather a lack of understanding about how to have "safe sex." For that reason, liberals favor solutions such as sex education and wide availability of condoms and other forms of birth control. Here, AIDS Healthcare Foundation staff and volunteers distribute condoms in Oakland, California, during a 2012 "Condom Nation" tour. What are the advantages and disadvantages of this approach?

Conservatives claim that our society has become too permissive with regard to sexual activity. Many favor the traditional idea that young people should delay sexual activity until marriage. If everyone followed this standard, they say, problems such as unwanted pregnancy and STDs would be very rare. The abstinence movement is one conservative solution that is asking young women to wear "chastity rings" that symbolize their pledge to abstain from sexual activity until marriage. What do you see as the "pros" and "cons" of this solution?

Hint: Both of these approaches will obviously "work" to some degree. At the same time, which one you would favor depends on your political attitudes. Conservatives take the position that traditional moral values, combined with personal responsibility, go a long way to solving problems. But what happens if young people are sexually active? The liberal approach assumes that young people will be sexually active. Liberals say that availability of condoms or other birth control, as well as sex education, will help young people make safer choices. But this approach offers little guidance to help a young person know whether and when getting into a sexual relationship with someone is a good idea. Where do you stand on this issue?

Getting Involved: Applications and Exercises

1. Almost every campus has student organizations involved in sexual issues discussed in this chapter, including gay rights, sexual violence, and abortion. Find out which organizations operate on your campus. What are their goals? What changes do they seek? How would you characterize them politically?

2. Ask an official in your college's student services office about the extent of sexual violence on campus. See what you can learn about the percentage of crimes reported and the policies and procedures to assist and protect victims.

3. Do some research in the library and on the Internet to learn more about past and present laws in your state and local community regarding a sexuality-related issue of interest to you, such as prostitution, sodomy, sexual violence, stalking, or sexual harassment.

4. In recent years, "hooking up" has emerged as a pattern of sexual behavior on college campuses. Organize a class discussion that explores what people think "hooking up" means, why this pattern has emerged, and what problems it involves.

Making the Grade

CHAPTER 7 Sexuality

A DEFINING MOMENT
Alfred Kinsey: Talking Openly about Sex **p. 204**

What Is Sex?

7.1 **Explain why sex is both a biological and cultural issue.**

Sex is a **biological** issue.

- Females and males have different organs used for reproduction and also different physical traits. **p. 202**

Sex is a **cultural** issue.

- Sexual attitudes and practices vary from one place to another and over time. **p. 202**

sex (p. 202) the biological distinction between females and males; also, activity that leads to physical gratification and possibly reproduction

Sexual Attitudes in the United States

7.2 **Discuss changes in sexual attitudes and practices over the history of the United States.**

Sexual attitudes have changed over the course of U.S. history:

- Early colonists viewed sex rigidly as intended solely for reproduction.

- In recent decades, sex has become more a matter of intimacy and personal pleasure.

- The **sexual revolution** that began in the 1960s encouraged people to be freer and more open about sexuality.

- By the 1980s, a **sexual counterrevolution** arose, reflecting the country's more conservative politics as well as fears about sexually transmitted diseases.

- The sexual revolution is continuing today among older people, sometimes making use of drugs that treat erectile dysfunction. **pp. 203–5**

Sexual Orientation

7.3 **Describe four sexual orientations.**

- Although the norm in all societies is heterosexuality, other sexual orientations—including homosexuality, bisexuality, and asexuality—are found as well.

- Although sexual orientation is partly a cultural issue, most evidence suggests that it is rooted in biology.

- The gay rights movement has been influential since the 1950s. A recent success was the legalization of same-sex marriage in several states. **pp. 205–10**

sexual orientation (p. 205) a person's romantic and emotional attraction to another person
heterosexuality (p. 205) sexual attraction to someone of the other sex
homosexuality (p. 205) sexual attraction to someone of the same sex
bisexuality (p. 205) sexual attraction to people of both sexes
asexuality (p. 205) the absence of sexual attraction to people of either sex
homophobia (p. 209) an aversion to or hostility toward people thought to be gay, lesbian, or bisexual
transgender (p. 209) appearing or behaving in ways that challenge conventional cultural norms concerning how females and males should look and act

Social Problems Related to Sexuality

7.4 **Discuss several current issues and controversies involving sexuality.**

Pornography

- Pornography consists of words or images that cause sexual arousal.

- Conservatives oppose pornography on moral grounds; many liberals object to it as demeaning to women.

- Some research links viewing pornography among males to higher aggression and greater acceptance of violence. **pp. 210–11**

Sexual Harassment

- In recent years, sexual harassment has been defined as a social problem.

- Today, laws protect people from sexual harassment, especially in the workplace.

- Most but not all cases of harassment involve men victimizing women. **pp. 211–12**

Prostitution

- Prostitution has long been widespread in the United States.
- Law enforcement usually targets female prostitutes rather than male clients and low-income streetwalkers rather than more affluent call girls.
- The extent of prostitution is even greater in Asia and many other poor regions of the world where sex tourism is widespread. **pp. 212–15**

Teenage Pregnancy

- About 768,000 U.S. teens become pregnant each year.
- Most teens who become pregnant are not married, and about half decide to keep their babies.
- Babies born to teens, especially young women who are poor, are at high risk for poverty as adults. **pp. 215–17**

Abortion

- Abortion is among the most divisive issues in the United States.
- The debate over abortion rights involves not just unintended pregnancy but also the social standing of women. **pp. 217–18**

Sexually Transmitted Diseases

- Unprotected sexual activity transmits some fifty diseases, including deadly AIDS.
- In global perspective, AIDS is a medical catastrophe, especially in Africa. **pp. 218–21**

> **pornography** (p. 210) words or images intended to cause sexual arousal
> **sexual harassment** (p. 211) unwanted comments, gestures, or physical contact of a sexual nature
> **prostitution** (p. 212) the selling of sexual services
> **abortion** (p. 217) the intentional termination of a pregnancy
> **sexually transmitted diseases (STDs)** (p. 218) diseases spread by sexual contact

Theories of Sexuality

7.5 **Apply sociological theory to issues involving sexuality.**

Structural-Functional Analysis: Controlling Sexuality

Structural-functional theory emphasizes society's need to control sexuality.

- The incest taboo and social norms regarding "legitimate" offspring help clarify social relationships and obligations between members of families.
- Some sexual patterns that are widely regarded as deviant, such as prostitution, may also have positive functions, at least for men. **pp. 221–22**

Symbolic-Interaction Analysis: Defining Sexuality

Symbolic-interaction theory highlights the fact that members of a society socially construct sexuality just as they create all reality.

- Sexual norms, such as those involving virginity, often change over time and also vary from place to place.
- People learn sexual behavior; the meaning they attach to sexuality affects how they think of themselves. **pp. 222–23**

Social-Conflict Analysis: Feminist Theory and Queer Theory

Social-conflict theory focuses on social inequality.

- **Feminist theory** points out that many aspects of sexuality reflect men's social domination of women.
- **Queer theory** claims that the heterosexist bias in U.S. culture stigmatizes gay men and lesbians, bisexual people, asexual people, and transgender individuals. **p. 223**

> **queer theory** (p. 223) a body of theory and research that challenges the heterosexual bias in U.S. society
> **heterosexism** (p. 223) bias that treats heterosexuality as the norm while stigmatizing anyone who violates this norm as "queer"

⊛ POLITICS AND SEXUALITY

Constructing Problems and Defining Solutions

7.6 **Analyze issues involving sexuality from various positions on the political spectrum.**

Conservatives: The Value of Traditional Morality

- **Conservatives** believe sexuality should be guided by traditional moral principles of right and wrong. They oppose abortion and premarital and extramarital sex, and many condemn homosexuality.
- Conservatives emphasize the importance of two-parent families in raising children with strong values and self-control. **pp. 224–25**

Liberals: Sex and Individual Choice

- **Liberals** emphasize the importance of individual freedoms. All people should be free to choose how they express their sexuality as long as their choices do not harm others.
- Liberals look to government to address social problems such as domestic violence and rape, sexual harassment, and the AIDS epidemic. **p. 225**

The Radical Left: Go to the Root of the Problem

- **Radicals on the left** point out that the root of many social problems related to sexuality is inequality.
- Radical feminism and queer theory argue the need for basic changes in U.S. society in pursuit of equality for all, female and male, gay and straight. **pp. 225–26**

Chapter 8
Alcohol and Other Drugs

Learning Objectives

8.1 Explain what a drug is and how culture, race, and ethnicity affect how a society views drug use.

8.2 Distinguish drug use from drug abuse as well as addiction from dependency.

8.3 Define various types of drugs.

8.4 Analyze the connections between drugs and various social problems.

8.5 Summarize the effectiveness of various drug-control strategies.

8.6 Apply sociological theory to issues involving drugs.

8.7 Analyze drug-related issues from various positions on the political spectrum.

Tracking the Trends

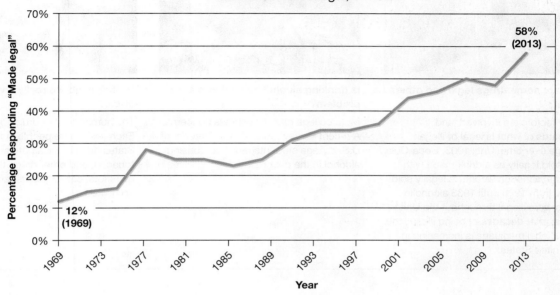

Survey Question: "Do you think the use of marijuana should be made legal, or not?"

58%
(2013)

12%
(1969)

Percentage Responding "Made legal"

Year

SOURCE: Gallup (2013).

By 1970, marijuana use had become widespread, especially among young people. But, as the figure shows, when asked "Do you think the use of marijuana should be made legal, or not?" only about 12 percent of U.S. adults thought pot should be legal. Over the next decade, this share roughly doubled but then declined through the 1980s. After that, support for legalizing marijuana began a slow but steady increase so that, by 2013, a majority of adults supported legal marijuana for the first time. Twenty-two states have legalized medical use of marijuana and, as of 2014, two states have legalized recreational marijuana. By the end of the next decade, do you think marijuana will become legal across the United States?

Constructing the Problem

Why are some drugs legal and others illegal?

Many factors are involved, and standards of what is legal or illegal change over time. Until 1903, Coca-Cola was sold legally as a drink made with cocaine; although alcohol is legally sold today, from 1920 until 1933 alcoholic drinks were illegal throughout the United States; after decades of being illegal, the sale of legal marijuana is increasing in the United States.

Is drinking alcohol by students a problem?

Most college officials express concerns. A recent survey found that 40 percent of U.S. college students reported abusing alcohol in the past month.

Isn't drug abuse really a victimless crime?

The human cost of drug abuse is high. Each year, more people in the United States die as a result of using alcohol, tobacco, and other drugs than from gunshots, car accidents, and AIDS combined.

Chapter Overview

What is a drug? This chapter identifies major categories of drugs and explains why some drugs are legal and others are not. You will learn how drug abuse is related to issues such as homelessness, crime, and global poverty. You will assess various strategies our government has used to counter illegal drug use. You will carry out theoretical analysis of drug use and learn how "problems" and "solutions" involving drugs reflect people's political attitudes. ■

It was a Sunday afternoon, four days before Thanksgiving. The president was 30,000 feet above South Dakota, on his way from Washington, D.C., to Seattle, where he would attend a series of fund-raising dinners. Seated in a high-back leather chair in his office near the front of the enormous airplane, he chatted with a journalist about the increasing public support for legalizing marijuana.

"As has been well documented," he began, "I smoked pot as a kid, and I view it as a bad habit and a vice, not very different from the cigarettes I smoked as a young person through a big chunk of my adult life. I don't think it is more dangerous than alcohol." Barack Obama paused and leaned back in his chair and continued, "I've told my daughters I think it is a bad idea, a waste of time, not very healthy." Then, sounding more sociological, he added, "Middle-class kids don't get locked up for smoking pot, and poor kids do" (quoted in Remnick, 2014).

A remarkable transformation is taking place in the United States. As the Tracking the Trends figure shows, support for legal marijuana is increasing, with a slight majority of U.S. adults now in favor. At the beginning of

2014, Colorado and Washington became the first two states to legalize this drug for recreational use. In the next few years, additional states are likely to do the same.

Marijuana is only one of many drugs that are part of popular culture in the United States. As the president's cautious remarks suggest, many people are not quite sure if legal marijuana is an entirely good idea. Many people feel the same way about legal alcohol, which is the most widely used (and abused) drug of all. As this chapter explains, the U.S. population is hooked on many types of drugs, from alcohol to pot to pills that promise you will lose weight, endure less pain, or have better sex.

Alcohol and other drugs, used wisely and in appropriate doses, can benefit both physical and mental health. Yet drugs also harm people of all ages, causing accidents, anxious trips to the emergency room, and even death. This chapter explains what drugs are, how they work, and the consequences of their use. We begin with a basic definition.

What Is a Drug?

8.1 Explain what a drug is and how culture, race, and ethnicity affect how people in our society view drug use.

Broadly defined, a **drug** is *any chemical substance other than food or water that affects the mind or body* (A. Goldstein, 1994). Throughout human history, people have used various natural substances to cause changes in the human body. In addition, with advancing technology, thousands of synthetic substances have been added to the list of available drugs. Today, most people use a number of drugs, from the caffeine in their morning coffee that helps them wake up to the aspirin that eases a headache at the end of the day.

Most of the time, drugs have effects that people think of as good. But 60 percent of adults in the United States worry about drug use and consider this issue to be a serious social problem. What people have in mind when they point to the "bad" side of drugs are illegal and "dangerous" drugs—substances such as crack cocaine and heroin (Gallup, 2013). In the case of still other drugs, such as marijuana, attitudes are evenly divided with slightly more than half of adults viewing marijuana use as a serious problem and the other half saying that marijuana should be legalized. About three-fourths of adults support making marijuana available to people for medical use (Pew Research Center, 2013).

Such divided opinions raise a basic question: When and why are drugs defined as good or as harmful? To find the answer, we first need to explore the link between drugs and culture.

Drugs and Culture

How people view any particular drug is a matter of culture, which is to say that it varies from one society to the next. Europeans, for example, have enjoyed drinking alcohol for thousands of years. But Native Americans, whose first experience with wine or hard liquor came just five centuries ago with the arrival of European colonists in North America, had no customs to guide the consumption of alcohol. As a result, many Native Americans drank too much, sometimes falling into a drunken stupor. For this reason, tribal leaders soon defined alcohol as a serious problem (Mancall, 1995; Unrau, 1996).

On the other hand, for centuries many Native people have used peyote in their religious rituals. Europeans learned about peyote from American Indians, and some Europeans began to use this drug. But having no experience with it, many became terrified by the hallucinations peyote produces and soon declared peyote to be a dangerous drug.

Cultural differences in defining drugs continue today. Coca, the plant used to make cocaine, has been grown for thousands of years in the South American nations of Bolivia, Peru, and Colombia, countries where it is legal today. In those nations, local farmers (and many tourists) chew the plant or make tea from it in order to give themselves a "lift." But laws in the

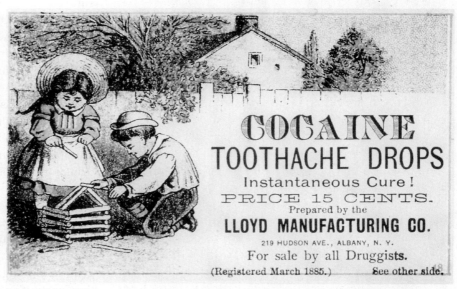

Whether a society defines a substance as a useful medication or a dangerous drug varies over time. It would surprise many people to learn that a century ago, cocaine was an ingredient in a number of readily available products, such as this remedy for toothaches.

United States ban the growing of coca and the sale or possession of cocaine, and most people here view this drug as a cause of violence and crime (Léons & Sanabria, 1997).

Just as the way people define a drug changes from one society to another, these definitions also change over time. A century ago, almost no one in the United States talked about a "cocaine problem," even though there was plenty of cocaine around. Famous people such as Sigmund Freud used cocaine openly, and anyone could stop by a corner drugstore to enjoy a glass of a popular "brain tonic" called Coca-Cola, which contained cocaine as one of its ingredients (Inciardi, 1996; Léons & Sanabria, 1997).

Drugs, Race, and Ethnicity

How people define drugs also has a lot to do with which categories of the population are using the drug. Here, we see the importance of race and ethnicity in the process of defining a "drug problem."

Drugs are part of our way of life, a fact that is evident in the collection of pills, capsules, and liquid medications found in most U.S. homes.

Late in the nineteenth century in the South, many white people feared that easily available cocaine would fall into the hands of African Americans, who might then commit crimes or become violent toward whites. Such racially linked fears were one reason that, in 1903, the Atlanta-based Coca-Cola Company stopped putting cocaine in its beverage. In the years that followed, state after state outlawed the use of cocaine (Goode, 1993; Bertram et al., 1996).

Race and ethnicity also shaped the public's opinion of other drugs. In other parts of the country, as ever-increasing numbers of immigrants came to the United States, they brought with them their culture, their dreams, and also their favored drugs. Since the 1850s, for example, many Chinese immigrants in California smoked opium (a practice they learned back in China from British colonists). Anti-Chinese feelings prompted public officials in eleven western states to ban opium. At the same time, in the East, where there were few Chinese people, there was no such ban. There, getting your hands on opium was as easy as going to the corner store or picking up a Sears, Roebuck mail-order catalogue and having the drug delivered to your door.

As the number of immigrants climbed, so did concern about drugs as a social problem. In 1914, Congress passed the Harrison Act, a national law restricting the sale of cocaine and heroin. By 1919, not even doctors could write prescriptions for these drugs. Then, in 1920, the nation's attention turned to a much more widely used drug: alcohol.

Changing Views of Alcohol

Alcohol has a long history in the United States, and ethnicity plays a central part in this story. Among the first Europeans to settle this land, alcohol (at least, when consumed in moderation) was defined as a good drug. But later in the nineteenth century, as the tide of immigration increased, opinions about alcohol began to turn negative.

Why did immigration change the public's view of alcohol? The answer is that common stereotypes linked alcohol with immigrants—the Germans drank beer, the Irish drank whiskey, and the Italians drank wine. In addition, immigration itself was highly controversial. In short, people who objected to the changes a million new arrivals a year were bringing to the country defined immigrants drinking alcohol as a serious social problem (Pleck, 1987; Unrau, 1996).

As opposition to immigration steadily increased (see Chapter 3, "Racial and Ethnic Inequality"), so did support for the *temperance movement*, a social movement seeking to ban alcohol. In 1920, the temperance movement reached this goal when Congress passed the Eighteenth Amendment to the Constitution, which outlawed the manufacture and sale of alcohol throughout the United States. This ban on alcohol was known as *Prohibition*.

Of course, many people, including those whose families had been in this country for centuries, enjoyed drinking alcohol. Therefore, Prohibition reduced alcohol consumption but it never was able to end it. But by ending the *legal* supply of alcoholic beverages, Prohibition created a demand for *illegal* booze that was made at home (the origin of the phrase "bathtub gin") or smuggled in from Canada. Throughout the urban North, notorious gangsters such as Al Capone made fortunes distributing illegal liquor to secret "speakeasy" nightclubs.

In the rural South, of course, homemade liquor had long been a local tradition. Especially after Prohibition began, poor people made corn-mash "moonshine" in local stills hidden in the mountains.

As Prohibition tried to solve the problem of alcohol, it created another—giving a huge boost to organized crime, which now gained more wealth and power than ever before. As the years went by, the public gradually came to see that Prohibition was more of a problem than it was a solution. In 1933, Congress passed the Twenty-First Amendment, repealing Prohibition and bringing an end to the failed "Great Experiment."

The Extent of Drug Use

8.2 Distinguish drug use from drug abuse as well as addiction from dependency.

What is the extent of drug use today? If we define drugs in a broad way to include aspirin and caffeine, almost everyone in the United States is a "user." Parents give analgesics to teething infants and Ritalin to overactive schoolchildren; college students take appetite suppressants to control their weight; adults reach for antidepressants and tranquilizers; and older people use pills to restore sexual functioning. Most people in the United States rely on drugs to help them to wake up, to stay alert, to relax, to ease aches and pains, and to go to sleep.

It is not far off the mark to say that we live in a "drug culture." At the same time, most people don't define this type of drug use as a problem. The positive view we have of most drugs reflects not only how widespread this use is but also the fact that most of us think such drugs make life better.

For most people in the United States, a "drug problem" means the use of *illegal* drugs. In 2012, according to government surveys, more than 24 million people—or about 9.2 percent of the population aged twelve and older—had used some illegal drug at least once in the past thirty days. Figure 8–1 provides the thirty-five-year trend in illegal drug use, as well as the use of alcohol and cigarettes, both of which are legal but regulated. The use of all these drugs declined after 1980. Since 2000, the use of alcohol and marijuana has been more widespread, the use of hallucinogens, cocaine, and heroin has been flat, and the share of people smoking cigarettes is leveling off after a long period of decline.

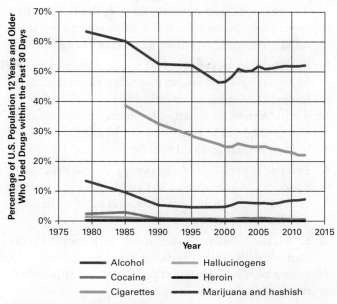

Legend:
— Alcohol — Hallucinogens
— Cocaine — Heroin
— Cigarettes — Marijuana and hashish

Diversity Snapshot

Figure 8–1   Use of Selected Drugs by the U.S. Population, 1979–2012

The most commonly used of the drugs listed here is alcohol, followed by cigarettes. The trend in overall drug use has been downward, with a slight upward turn in the last few years.

SOURCE: U.S. Department of Health and Human Services (2013).

Alcohol is by far the most widely used of these drugs, and it is the only drug that a majority of people report using in the last thirty days. Cigarettes are used at least occasionally by about 22 percent of adults. Among the illegal drugs, marijuana and hashish are used by a smaller share of the population (around 7 percent) and this share will certainly increase as more states legalize pot. Cocaine, hallucinogens (such as LSD), and heroin are used by less than 1 percent of people (U.S. Department of Health and Human Services, 2013).

Age is related to the likelihood that a person uses an illegal drug. The share of the population reporting illegal drug use peaks among people in their late teens, the time in life when people are experimenting with the limits of personal freedom. The use of illegal drugs declines as people get older and take on greater responsibilities involving jobs and families.

Why Do People Use Drugs?

People use drugs—including legal and illegal substances—for any number of reasons. The following are the most common reasons for drug use.

1. **Therapeutic uses.** Some drugs have therapeutic uses, meaning that they offer medical benefits such as controlling seizures, lessening depression, and reducing pain.

2. **Recreational uses.** Alcoholic beverages including beer or wine with a meal can make people feel more relaxed and can even make foods taste better.

3. **Spiritual or psychological uses.** Drugs can alter human consciousness, so that some people use them for psychological or spiritual reasons. Members of Native American societies, for example, use peyote to change their perception of the world around them and to deepen their spiritual experience.

4. **Escape.** Especially in large dosages, some drugs offer a form of escape from everyday life. People enduring serious trouble may turn to alcohol or other drugs to dull the pain of living.

5. **Social conformity.** Finally, drugs help people to conform—that is, to fit in socially. Peer pressure may lead young people to smoke cigarettes or older people to drink cocktails.

Of course, several of these factors may operate at once. Dining at a restaurant with business associates, people may enjoy a glass of wine to relax (recreational) and also because others expect it (social conformity). Whether they realize it or not, they may also be improving their health (therapeutic), because doctors report that consuming small amounts of red wine each day can reduce the risk of heart disease.

Use and Abuse

What is the line that separates the *use* of a drug from the *abuse* of a drug? Here is one way to think about this difference. Many people use the term "drug abuse" to refer to the use of any illegal substance or to the use of a legal substance (such as a prescription drug) in a way that violates accepted medical practice (Abadinsky, 1989). In this case, the distinction between using and abusing a drug is based on law and other social norms.

A second way to distinguish use and abuse is to focus on the *effect* of a drug. People who *use* a drug may function well in everyday life, but people who *abuse* a drug suffer physical, mental, or social harm. This definition means that any drug—legal or illegal—can be used or abused. After all, many people smoke a little marijuana without harmful consequences, but even a few legal glasses of wine can have devastating consequences for a person who gets behind the wheel of a car (Weil & Rosen, 1983; J. M. White, 1991; Goode, 1993).

Of course, assessing whether or not a drug causes harm is not always easy. For example, a person who regularly uses marijuana may get through the day just fine and may be convinced that this practice poses no personal danger. Friends, however, may shake their heads, noting that this drug use—or from their point of view, this drug *abuse*—is responsible for the person missing classes or failing to meet other daily obligations and perhaps risking trouble with the law.

Addiction and Dependency

Another term that is widely used but not always clearly understood is **addiction**, *a physical or psychological craving for a drug.* Doctors first began using this word back in the nineteenth century, describing people as "addicted" if they suffered physical distress—sometimes called *withdrawal symptoms*—when they stopped using the drug. Withdrawal symptoms caused by the use of opium and cocaine include chills, fever, diarrhea, twitching, nausea, vomiting, cramps, and aches and pains. The only quick way to eliminate these symptoms is to take more of the drug.

The precise point at which someone becomes addicted depends on a number of factors, including the dosage and the duration of the drug use. The onset of addiction is also likely to reflect a person's general physical and mental health, so that different people may react differently to the same amount of a drug.

Addictive drugs also affect the brain. Initially, drug use raises levels of a substance called dopamine, which gives the user the experience of euphoria. Eventually, however, the drug may cause unpleasant withdrawal symptoms (Begley, 2001).

Health professionals also use the term **dependency**, *a state in which a person's body has adjusted to regular use of a drug.* People who are drug dependent experience a need to continue using the drug in order to feel comfortable, so that they are sometimes characterized as having a drug "habit." Today, the terms "addiction" and "dependency" are applied not only to some illegal drugs but also to just about any substance—including food—over which a person seems to have little or no control (Goode, 1993; Milkman & Sunderwirth, 1995).

Types of Drugs

8.3   Define various types of drugs.

Various categories of drugs are defined based on the effects substances have on the body and brain. Here we briefly examine six types of drugs: stimulants, depressants, hallucinogens, cannabis, steroids, and prescription drugs.

Stimulants

Stimulants are *drugs that increase alertness, altering a person's mood by increasing energy.* Because U.S. culture values activity and achievement, stimulants are widely used in the United States.

Caffeine   Probably the single most popular drug in the United States is caffeine, which is available in coffee, tea, soft drinks, chocolate, and "stay alert" pills. Just about everybody—from long-distance truck drivers to college students facing an exam to workers trying to "wake up" before heading off to the office—depends on caffeine for alertness.

Nicotine Although legal in this country and almost everywhere else in the world, nicotine is both toxic and highly addictive. The most common way people ingest nicotine is through smoking cigarettes, a practice that became popular among U.S. men during World War I, when the armed forces issued free cigarettes to soldiers. Millions of people began smoking and, twenty years later, the health hazards of cigarette smoking were becoming clear in rising rates of illness and death. But the government did little to discourage cigarette smoking until the 1960s. At that time, 45 percent of U.S. adults smoked, and the rate of smoking among women had almost reached the same level as among men.

Since that time, people have become aware that smoking carries serious health risks. As a result, the share of adults who smoke cigarettes has steadily declined. By 2012, just 19.6 percent of U.S. adults (22 percent of men and 17 percent of women) were lighting up regularly (CDC, 2014). Generally, states in the Midwest and South have higher rates of cigarette smoking; western states (except for Nevada) have low rates.

Worldwide, about 30 percent of adults smoke cigarettes. According to the World Health Organization (2013), about 1 billion people smoke cigarettes and 80 percent of them live in middle- and low-income nations. While the trend in smoking in the United States is downward, the trend worldwide is upward, raising concerns about human health. Figure 8–2 shows that in some countries, a majority of men smoke, many with little awareness of the harm this smoking causes to the heart, lungs, and other organs of the body.

In the United States, cigarette smoking is far and away the single greatest preventable cause of death. Each year, according to the U.S. Surgeon General, nearly 500,000 people die prematurely due to tobacco use. This number exceeds not only the death toll from alcohol and all illegal drugs combined, but it exceeds the combined death toll from suicide, homicide, AIDS, and automobile accidents as well. Even secondhand smoke is blamed for some 50,000 deaths each year (U.S. Department of Health and Human Services, 2013).

In 1998, the U.S. tobacco companies reached a settlement with a number of states that had filed lawsuits seeking compensation for harm caused to people by smoking. The deal gave cigarette manufacturers protection from mounting lawsuits in exchange for paying billions of dollars toward the cost of providing medical care to smokers. The settlement also banned cigarette advertising targeting young people. Even so, thousands of young people start smoking every day. Given widespread concern about the rising cost of health care, efforts to reduce the rate of cigarette smoking take on an added urgency.

There is one clear solution to problems related to smoking: quitting. Although some researchers warn that

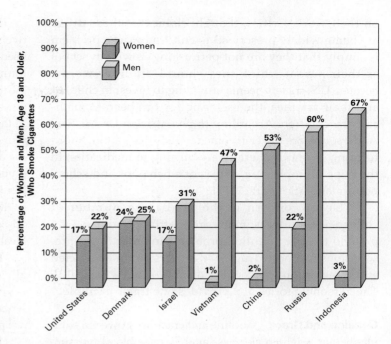

Global Snapshot

Figure 8–2 Cigarette Smoking in Selected Countries

In many of the world's low-income nations, cigarette smoking is more widespread among men than in the United States. At the same time, in these strongly patriarchal countries, gender norms limit the extent of smoking among women.

SOURCES: Centers for Disease Control and Prevention (2012) and World Health Organization (2013).

smoking during adolescence can permanently damage the lungs, a decade after quitting, most ex-smokers enjoy the same good health as people who never lit up in the first place (Recer, 1999).

Ritalin and Adderall Ritalin (the brand name for methylphenidate hydrochloride) and Adderall (the brand name for a combination of dextroamphetamine and amphetamine) are regulated drugs that are prescribed by doctors to treat children with attention deficit hyperactivity disorder (ADHD) or attention deficit disorder (ADD). These are disorders in which children are overactive, have trouble concentrating, or cannot focus attention on a teacher or another adult.

In recent years, the use of Ritalin and Adderall has increased sharply in the United States: Physicians write more than 50 million prescriptions a year for these drugs and sales revenues have almost doubled in the last five years to about $7.5 billion a year. About 8 percent of college students have a prescription for one of these drugs to treat a disorder, and probably just as many get these "study drugs" from others (Harris, 2012; Johnston et al., 2013).

This widespread use of Ritalin and Adderall has sparked controversy. Defenders of these drugs, which include drug companies and many parents, claim that the drugs help children to stay calm in school and to focus on their work. Critics, though, claim that these drugs are being widely prescribed to children whose problem is simply that they are not performing as well in school as their parents think they should. In other words, because U.S. society seems unwilling to invest in children and their families, the easier policy has been to medicate the children. According to pediatrician Dr. Michael Anderson, more lower-income families that cannot afford tutoring or family therapy are turning to medication in the hope of improving a student's behavior and school performance (Schwarz, 2012).

Also of concern is the increasing number of college-age students, many from affluent homes, who pretend to have attention problems in order to get prescriptions for these drugs. Some users become addicted and show serious personality disorders (Schwarz, 2013). The Personal Stories box provides one tragic example.

Cocaine and Crack   Cocaine and crack are powerful stimulants that heighten alertness as they raise blood pressure and pulse rate. These drugs keep people awake, reduce appetite, and cause some people to become agitated and perhaps even violent.

In 2012, about 1.8 percent of people over the age of twelve (including 2.6 percent of high school seniors) had used cocaine in some form during the past year. In powder form, cocaine can be snorted, which means inhaled through the nose. Cocaine is very addictive, and it can be harmful and even deadly because it can trigger a heart attack or stroke. In the United States, its use leads to about 3,000 deaths each year. Cocaine's popularity peaked in the 1980s, when it was the drug of choice among many young urban professionals ("yuppies"). The drug's popularity declined in the 1990s, but the typical cocaine user is still well-to-do, a fact that challenges the stereotype of drug abusers as people who are "down and out" (Johnston et al., 2013; U.S. Department of Health and Human Services, 2013; CDC, 2014).

Crack is a hardened form of cocaine that people usually smoke in a pipe. Although many people think crack is stronger than cocaine and more likely to provoke violence, research indicates that the effects of the two drugs are pretty much the same (Wren, 1996; Gómez, 1997).

During the 1980s, crack became popular in large cities in the United States, pushing crime rates sharply higher. As in the case of powdered cocaine, crack's popularity declined in the 1990s. However, experts estimate that about

PERSONAL STORIES
Dying for Attention: One Student's Story

Richard Fee was a good athlete, a well-liked student who won a full academic scholarship, and president of his college class. He worked hard and wanted to complete medical school and have a career as a physician. But Richard was also something else: He was an addict. He was addicted to the amphetamine-based medications Vyvanse and Adderall.

Adderall is an effective treatment for attention deficit hyperactivity disorder (ADHD). For young people with this disorder, the drug focuses attention on a task and allows the patient to get things done. Richard did not actually have ADHD, but he did have lots of things to get done. So, he began by getting pills from friends on campus, probably unaware that doing so is a federal crime. Eventually, to ensure his steady supply, he told physicians he needed help concentrating and the doctors wrote him a prescription. They did so without doing a detailed diagnosis. And they did so again and again.

Richard focused, and he got his work done. But Richard became addicted to the medication. His personality started coming apart. His mother, Kathy Fee, explained to Richard that he did not have ADHD and she insisted that he stop taking the medications. His father, Rick Fee, even pleaded with one doctor to stop writing the prescriptions, warning that the drug was likely to kill his son.

In 2011, while taking Adderall, Richard became delusional and violent. He ended up spending a week in a psychiatric hospital. But when Richard went to see his doctor, he received a prescription for another three months of Adderall. About two weeks after the pills ran out, Richard went into his bedroom closet and hanged himself.

No one doubts the value of drugs like Adderall for young people who have ADHD. But powerful drugs have powerful effects, and they can be addictive. Concern is increasing that too many young people feel they need drugs to help them focus and that the medical establishment is too quick to provide them. The rate of ADHD prescriptions has increased rapidly in recent years and our society now medicates some 35 percent of young people under the age of nineteen and about 17 percent of those between twenty and forty (Schwarz, 2013).

What Do You Think?

1. Do you realize that giving or receiving prescription drugs from other students is a federal crime? Do you think most students realize this?

2. Are you surprised to learn that about one-third of young people in the United States are medicated with drugs of the type described here? Explain.

3. What changes would you suggest making to reduce the risk of drug-related harm to young people?

921,000 people use crack for some period of time each year. African Americans have been about twice as likely as whites to use crack (U.S. Department of Health and Human Services, 2013).

Amphetamines Amphetamines were first developed for the medical treatment of personality disorders and also obesity. These drugs increase alertness, cause an excited sense of well-being, and reduce the desire to sleep and to eat. Because amphetamines are easy to make, many underground chemists operate highly profitable businesses selling drugs known on the street as "crank," "speed," "crystal," "go," "meth," or "ice." Surveys suggest that police officials regard methamphetamine use as the most serious drug problem partly because the drug is produced in vast quantities by "superlabs" in Mexico and in the United States. Another reason for concern is that use of amphetamines encourages some people to engage in serious crime (Hananel, 2006; Cave, 2012).

After cocaine, amphetamines are the most popular of the illegal stimulants. Official statistics suggest that more than 1 million people used amphetamines at least once in 2012, a decline of about one-third from the number back in 2002. Overall, more than 12 million people (about 5 percent of adults) claim to have tried amphetamines at some time in their lives.

Many people begin taking amphetamines under a doctor's supervision and some end up with problems of dependency or addiction. When people stop taking this type of drug, they typically experience withdrawal symptoms such as apathy, depression, irritability, and disorientation (U.S. Department of Health and Human Services, 2013). More seriously, as usage increases, amphetamines carry more and more risk of agitation, fever, hallucinations, and convulsions that stop the heart or breathing, leading to death.

Depressants

Depressants are *drugs that slow the operation of the central nervous system*. In short, depressants (sometimes called "downers") have an effect opposite to stimulants ("uppers").

Analgesics One class of depressants is analgesics, which are drugs that dull pain. The most widely used analgesics include familiar over-the-counter pain relievers such as aspirin, ibuprofen (Motrin and Advil), and acetaminophen (Tylenol). Although these drugs can be abused, they present little problem when used according to directions (Goode, 1993).

Heroin and other opiates are an increasing problem in largely rural states, including Vermont. In 2014, Vermont's governor declared that heroin was a serious threat to the people of his state and called for treatment and education programs as well as criminal prosecution. The photos shown here identify people arrested in a large drug sweep. Why do you think heroin use has been increasing?

More problematic are naturally occurring narcotics, or *opiates*, such as opium and opium derivatives, including morphine, codeine, and heroin. All of these drugs are highly addictive, and they are dangerous because of their capacity to disrupt the social world of abusers.

Heroin is made from morphine, which comes from the seed pods of poppy plants. A synthetic form of the drug is meperidine (marketed as Demerol). Although most people have heard of heroin, only a small share (0.1 percent) of the U.S. population are current users (see Figure 8–1). Even so, government data show a recent increase in heroin use and heroin deaths both in urban and rural areas. Recently, Vermont governor Peter Shumlin described what he termed a "full-blown heroin crisis" across much of New England. In many working-class cities and towns across this region, most of the population has been affected in some direct or indirect way by the recent rise in heroin use (SAMHSA, 2013; Gray, 2014; Seelye, 2014).

When injected, sniffed, or smoked, heroin quickly causes euphoria and drowsiness. Heroin is highly addictive and the law bans its use for any purpose. People who are addicted to heroin experience strong cravings and severe withdrawal symptoms. Another problem is that users can never be sure how pure their heroin is, so that overdoses are common and can be fatal (Leinwand, 2001; U.S. Department of Health and Human Services, 2011).

According to the Centers for Disease Control and Prevention (2012), the fastest-growing drug problem involves abuse of opioid analgesics. In the last decade, the number of deaths from unintentional drug overdoses involving opioid analgesics has reached 12,000 annually, exceeding the number of deaths involving heroin and cocaine combined. The danger of overdose is especially high among people who receive multiple prescriptions from multiple physicians and then take very high doses.

Sedatives, Hypnotics, and Alcohol Other depressants that can have a powerful effect on the central nervous system are sedatives and hypnotics. These drugs help people relax and, at higher dosages, they cause drowsiness and sleep. Examples of sedatives and hypnotics include barbiturates, such as secobarbital (Seconal) and pentobarbital, and tranquilizers, including alprazolam (Xanax), diazepam (Valium), and triazolam (Halcion). Overuse of these drugs, available by prescription, is dangerous, and when combined with alcohol or other drugs, they can be fatal.

Alcohol is the most widely used depressant in the United States. As noted in Figure 8–1 on page 237, about half the adult population aged twelve and over (including 26 percent of tenth-graders, 39 percent of twelfth-graders, and 68 percent of college students) consumes alcohol regularly. For many adults who drink responsibly and in moderation, alcohol poses no problem.

But this is not always the case. About half of all U.S. adults have been affected directly or indirectly (through the struggle of a close friend or family member) by **alcoholism**, *addiction to alcohol*. Estimates place the number of U.S. adults who become dependent on alcohol or who abuse this drug at about 18 million or 7 percent of the adult population. From another angle, 17 percent of men and 8 percent of women have such a problem at some point in their lives (CDC, 2013; U.S. Department of Health and Human Services, 2013).

Approximately 2.5 million people each year seek help for a problem related to alcohol. Many try to become sober, but many more continue to suffer from the problems related to alcoholism. Even more people face the daily challenges of living or working with an alcoholic person.

With the exception of nicotine, alcohol is the most addictive drug available legally without a prescription. Analysts put the total cost of alcoholism in the United States (reflecting everything from accidents to lost days at work) at about $225 billion per year (CDC, 2011).

Alcohol abuse is a serious problem at U.S. colleges and universities. A government study found that about 40 percent of college students said they had engaged in binge drinking, which is defined as having at least five drinks in a row for men or four drinks for women, at least once in the past month. In addition, almost one-third of these heavy-drinking students fell into the "extreme binge drinker" category, with five or more such drinking episodes in the past month. At the other end of the spectrum, about one-third of students reported drinking no alcohol in the past month (U.S. Department of Health and Human Services, 2013).

Researchers estimate that consuming alcohol—especially "drink till you drop" binge drinking—leads to 1,800 student deaths and 600,000 injuries each year. In addition, 400,000 students claim that after drinking alcohol, they had unprotected sex, putting them at risk for unwanted pregnancy and sexually transmitted diseases. Finally, by affecting people's judgment, alcohol also plays a part in about 100,000 cases of date rape each year (Hingson et al., 2005; Hingson, 2010).

The use of alcohol is related to other crimes as well: In 2012, police made about 400,000 arrests for public drunkenness and disorderly conduct involving alcohol and 340,000 arrests for violations of state or local liquor laws. More serious, police made 987,000 arrests for driving a motor vehicle while under the influence of alcohol. Police records also show that alcohol was involved in 31 percent of the 33,561 motor vehicle deaths on U.S. roads in 2012. In addition, about 33 percent of convicted jail inmates report that they were under the influence of alcohol when they committed their crimes (Rand et al., 2010; U.S. Department of Justice, Federal Bureau of Investigation, 2013; National Highway Traffic Safety Administration, 2014).

Finally, although an occasional alcoholic beverage may provide some health benefits, heavy drinking is harmful even to those who stay out of trouble. For one thing, drinking provides many calories but no nutrition, causing weight gain, and, as consumption increases, alcohol harms the heart and the liver. Pregnant women who consume alcohol also put their unborn child's health at risk (U.S. Department of Health and Human Services, 2008).

Antipsychotics Antipsychotics, such as haloperidol (Haldol), are powerful drugs that doctors prescribe to people with serious personality disorders (psychosis) such as schizophrenia. These substances are effective in reducing psychotic symptoms such as paranoia, visual hallucinations, and hearing voices. Supervised use of antipsychotic drugs allows hundreds of thousands of people who might otherwise need hospitalization to live independently. At the same time, if overused, these drugs can be dangerous (Goode, 1993).

Hallucinogens

Hallucinogens are stimulants, generally taken in pill or capsule form, that cause hallucinations. In the United States, the most commonly used hallucinogens include LSD, peyote, mescaline, psilocybin, phencyclidine (PCP, "angel dust"), and methylenedioxymethamphetamine (MDMA, "ecstasy"). Estimates suggest that by the end of high school, about 7 percent of young people have tried ecstasy (Johnston et al., 2013). Although about 15 percent of the U.S. population has tried a hallucinogenic drug at some point, only 1.7 percent of the U.S. population reports using one in the past year (U.S. Department of Health and Human Services, 2013).

Hallucinogens are nonaddictive but powerful. They can sharply elevate pulse rates, boost blood pressure, and alter perceptions of time and space. Hallucinogens produce vivid hallucinations, which can be pleasurable and even "consciousness-expanding." But these drugs can also trigger panic attacks, and many people find the experience terrifying. The fact is that, when people ingest hallucinogenic drugs, they can never be sure whether they will have a "good trip" or a "bad trip." Perhaps most seriously, hallucinogens can have long-term effects. People who use these drugs may experience "flashbacks"—unexpected hallucinations—months or even years after using the drug. For all these reasons, hallucinogens are dangerous. Overdoses can overpower the body's systems causing psychosis and even death.

In the United States, the use of hallucinogens peaked in the 1960s. Since then, the government reports a low but steady rate of use of these drugs mostly by teens. Race is linked to use of these drugs, with white people being twice as likely as African Americans and Hispanic Americans to use hallucinogens and American Indians being the most likely of all (U.S. Department of Health and Human Services, 2013).

Cannabis

Marijuana and hashish are two types of cannabis that have been used for several thousand years. Today, these two substances make up about 79 percent of this country's illegal drug use.

During the 1960s, both drugs gained widespread popularity in the United States. Although the rates fell in the decades that followed, marijuana use among young people has increased in the last few years. Estimates suggest that, in 2012, about 6.5 percent of high school students and about 5 percent of college students smoked marijuana almost every day. Figure 8–1 (page 237) shows 7.3 percent of U.S. adults using marijuana or hashish, but 43 percent (some 111 million people) say they have done so at some time in the past. In recent years, the use of synthetic marijuana—sometimes called "K2," "spice," or "bath salts"—gained popularity among young people, although use has declined as people learn of the serious health risks (Leger, 2011; Johnston et al., 2013; U.S. Department of Health and Human Services, 2013; Wadley & Barnes, 2013).

People smoke marijuana and hashish or consume the drugs in food items such as "magic" brownies or cookies. Both drugs produce a sense of euphoria, help people relax, and stimulate appetite. At higher dosages, however, these drugs can produce fatigue, disorientation, paranoia, and even serious personality disorders (U.S. Department of Health and Human Services, 2008).

As described at the beginning of this chapter, the movement to legalize marijuana has made huge gains. As of 2014, Colorado and Washington allow recreational use of small amounts of marijuana and more states are likely to do the same. At present, twenty-two states plus the District of Columbia permit the use of marijuana for medical purposes under the supervision of a doctor. For example, people undergoing chemotherapy for cancer or AIDS use marijuana to ease the nausea that is often a side effect of the treatment. Fifteen states have decriminalized marijuana, reducing penalties for possession, replacing jail terms with fines and, in some cases, involving no permanent criminal record. But twenty-three states continue to apply criminal penalties for possession of even small amounts of marijuana.

Twenty years ago, a majority of U.S. adults opposed legalizing marijuana. But by 2012, this pattern had changed with a majority now supporting legalization for recreational purposes. An even larger majority (77 percent) supports legalizing marijuana for medical purposes (Pew Research Center, 2013). It seems likely that the trend toward decriminalization will continue.

Steroids

The full name for this class of drugs is a mouthful: *androgenic* (promoting masculine characteristics) *anabolic* (building) *steroids*. Some professional and amateur athletes use steroids, although athletic programs ban their use. Typically, to avoid detection, athletes use steroids in cycles: a few weeks or months on, followed by a few weeks off before a drug test.

In twenty-two states plus the District of Columbia, people can legally use marijuana for medical purposes. This drug is now available in a wide range of products. Do you think this practice will spread throughout the country in years to come? Why or why not?

Surveys suggest that about 2 percent of high school seniors have used steroids at some time in their lives. Although 88 percent of these students disapprove of steroid use, more than one-quarter of students say that steroids are easy to obtain (Johnston et al., 2013).

Allegations of steroid use among professional athletes such as Lance Armstrong and Alex Rodriguez are well known. In 2007, the U.S. Senate issued a report concluding that steroid use was widespread in professional baseball and that the problem was widely ignored. The report called for more frequent drug testing as well as enforcement of a no-tolerance policy (Nightengale, 2007; Badenhausen, 2013).

The use of steroids can improve strength and athletic performance. But these drugs also pose significant dangers, ranging from acne and fluid retention to high blood pressure and liver tumors. In addition, some men who take steroids experience baldness, infertility, and breast development. Women using steroids may stop menstruating, grow facial hair, and experience an enlargement of the clitoris and a deepening of the voice. Among young people, use of steroids may cause the body to stop growing too soon. Finally, people who inject steroids and share needles are at high risk of contracting a range of diseases, including hepatitis and HIV (U.S. Department of Health and Human Services, 2005).

Prescription Drugs

Physicians prescribe a wide range of government-regulated drugs to patients, and almost everyone at some time has taken a drug as treatment for an illness, injury, or a psychological condition. But prescription drugs represent part of the drug problem in the United States because more than 16 million people use them in a nonmedical way, including taking a higher dosage than was prescribed, mixing drugs, or continuing to use a drug when the medical need no longer exists.

Many people feel that these drugs are safe because they are prescribed by doctors and sold by pharmacies. But prescription drugs are powerful and, when not used as directed, they can cause serious harm or death. In fact, the number of deaths in the United States caused by overdoses of prescription drugs is greater than deaths from overdoses of cocaine and heroin combined (U.S. Department of Health and Human Services, 2011; Johnston et al., 2013; CDC, 2014).

Today, the abuse of prescription drugs is the fastest-growing dimension of the drug problem. The number of people who are dependent on painkillers increased in recent years, to 1.6 million by 2012. The typical person who abuses prescription drugs is likely to be in the mid-twenties or older.

Of all prescription drugs, the most commonly abused are painkillers (analgesics) such as codeine, diazepam (Valium), and among college students, oxycodone (Percodan or OxyContin) and hydrocodone (Vicodin). Not only are these drugs widely prescribed, but people who build up tolerances to painkillers gradually take higher and higher dosages as well. Prescriptions limit the number of pills available, but many patients increase their supply by obtaining prescriptions from many physicians at the same time. In other cases, people who become addicted to prescription painkillers such as OxyContin move on to an illegal drug such as heroin, which has similar chemical properties (U.S. Department of Health and Human Services, 2011).

This completes our brief survey of types of drugs. We now turn to links between drugs and various other social problems.

Drugs and Other Social Problems

8.4 Analyze the connections between drugs and various social problems.

Government estimates put the direct cost of all illegal drug use—including the expense of medical treatment as well as time lost from work—at $193 billion annually (U.S. Office of National Drug Control Policy, 2014). If we added in the losses related to the use of legal substances including tobacco and alcohol, that number would be many times greater. In addition, drug use harms our society in a host of other ways, involving crime, poverty, and homelessness. We look first at the links between drugs and problems of family life.

Problems of Family Life

Drugs play a part in many cases of child neglect and family violence, both as a cause and as a consequence. Although it is difficult to specify cause and effect, drug abuse is closely linked to problems in family life. Why? Drugs reduce inhibitions and also affect judgment, raising the risk of abusive behavior (Gelles & Straus, 1988; Gelles, 1997). In extreme cases, the craving for drugs can be so strong that parents neglect or harm their own children.

Codependency The problem of drug abuse rarely affects only a single person. Typically, a drug problem involves an individual and also parents, brothers and sisters, partners, and children. Some people addicted to alcohol or other drugs spend their whole paychecks on the substances they crave; others cannot keep a job at all.

Drug abuse often provokes a pattern called **codependency**, *behavior on the part of others that helps a substance abuser continue the abuse.* In simple terms, codependency develops as members of a family change their behavior to make up for the shortcomings of the drug abuser. Codependent family members may try to earn extra money, hide evidence of accidents, "cover" for an abuser who misses work, or even provide drugs to the abuser in an effort to keep the peace in the home.

Jacqueline Wiseman (1991) studied the wives of male alcoholics and found that these women commonly experienced problems ranging from income uncertainty to outright violence. Children who live in a household with a substance abuser may lose their ability to trust others because the abuser has let them down so many times. These children often grow up too soon, taking over the tasks that are no longer performed by the older drug abuser and, in the process, sacrificing their own wants and needs. Not surprisingly, many young people in codependent situations drop out of school, get into trouble with the law, and some may even end up abusing drugs themselves. In this way, drugs begin a cycle of problems that stretches from one generation to the next.

The use of drugs—especially alcohol—by people who are homeless is widespread. Do you think such drug use is more often the cause or the result of being desperately poor?

Homelessness

Many people accept the idea that the use of drugs—especially alcohol—is commonplace among homeless people who live on the street. Research confirms that there is some truth to this belief: About half of homeless men and women have had a substance abuse problem (U.S. Department of Health and Human Services, 2011).

Recall from Chapter 2 ("Poverty and Wealth") that homelessness in the United States typically results from underemployment and a lack of affordable housing. Although U.S. culture encourages us to think that people are responsible for their social position, many individuals and families become homeless through no fault of their own. Certainly some people become homeless because they abuse drugs, but the opposite is often true: People who do not have work, who lose the support of neighbors, family, and friends, and who are forced to live alone on the streets may turn to alcohol or other drugs for comfort or escape.

There is also a historical link between drugs and homelessness. By the 1960s, physicians began giving antipsychotic drugs to people with mental illnesses to control their symptoms. These drugs allowed people challenged in this way to live on their own. Therefore, mental institutions began releasing such patients, with the condition that they make periodic visits to community mental health centers.

But less than half of the planned mental health centers were ever built. In addition, many patients who were released stopped taking their medications. In the end, many former patients were unable to land a job or to secure affordable housing. As a result, a number of these mental patients became homeless, and some ended up abusing alcohol and other drugs (Weiss, Griffin, & Mirin, 1992; Baum & Burnes, 1993).

Health Problems

Medical professionals prescribe drugs to treat illnesses, sometimes saving lives. At the same time, as many people die from the use of drugs (including tobacco and alcohol) as they die from gun violence, automobile accidents, and AIDS combined. Some drugs such as heroin harm people right away, damaging the brain or other vital organs. Other drugs harm people over the long haul: Years of alcohol abuse, for example, can lead to malnutrition and liver damage. Remember, too, that the distortion of judgment caused by drug use raises the risk of injury or death from accidents and from unsafe sex.

Prenatal Exposure to Drugs Some people suffer from drug problems that began before birth. Both physical and mental health problems can result from prenatal exposure to drugs, that is, the use of drugs by a pregnant woman. About 6 percent of pregnant women smoke marijuana or use some other illegal drug, 9 percent drink alcohol during pregnancy, and about 16 percent of pregnant women smoke cigarettes. As a result, almost 500,000 babies are born each year exposed to one or more harmful drugs (U.S. Department of Health and Human Services, 2013).

Many of the women who use drugs in this way do not know they are pregnant. This is especially true of women whose drug use is so heavy that it causes irregular menstrual cycles. Even when they do learn of their pregnancies, some women are unable to stop taking drugs. Even if they are able to stop, because an embryo's nervous system and major organs begin to develop within months of conception, some damage may already have been done (Gomby & Shiono, 1991; Gómez, 1997).

The global trade in illegal drugs has much to do with widespread poverty in lower-income nations. These children play soccer on a playground that is also used to dry coca leaves, which are later refined into cocaine. Cocaine production represents a bigger part of the national economy in Peru than wheat production is here in the United States.

Drug exposure during pregnancy greatly increases the risk of premature delivery, low-birthweight babies, and children born with birth defects. Longer-term problems for such children include retarded growth, poor physical coordination, learning disabilities, and emotional problems. Each year, the cost of hospital care for children with prenatal exposure to drugs and alcohol exceeds $4 billion (CDC, 2014).

Sharing Needles and HIV Transmission   Many people who abuse drugs use syringes and hypodermic needles to inject drugs directly into a vein. Entering the body in this way, drugs have an effect that is both immediate and intense. Intravenous (IV) drug users typically "shoot up" in groups, which invites the dangerous practice of sharing needles.

What makes sharing needles dangerous? Traces of blood retained in a needle can transmit the human immunodeficiency virus (HIV), which causes AIDS. In 1994, officials at the Centers for Disease Control and Prevention proposed—as a strategy to limit transmission of disease—a program of needle exchange: Local health centers would exchange used hypodermic needles for new ones. But this program never caught on because opponents claimed that this policy seemed to condone and encourage drug use. As an alternative, many local health departments adopted the policy of providing instructions on how to clean a used needle with a bleach solution to kill HIV and other dangerous agents.

Crime

The manufacture, distribution, or possession of an illegal drug is a crime. So is giving or receiving a prescription drug. More generally, both illegal substances such as cocaine and legal drugs such as alcohol are linked to other criminal behavior. Government officials report that about 60 percent of people in prison for violent offenses said they were under the influence of a drug when they committed their crimes. Similarly, a recent study found that 60 percent of people who were arrested tested positive for an illegal drug (Mumola & Karberg, 2007; U.S. Office of National Drug Control Policy, 2013).

Clearly, there is big money to be made in drugs and the rewards may outweigh the risk of arrest and jail, especially for someone with few other opportunities. At the same time, illegal drug dealers have disputes that they cannot settle in the courts, so they may turn to violence, harming themselves or innocent people. In recent years, the level of violence related to drug dealing has increased sharply in Mexico, where more than 47,000 people died in drug-related violence between 2006 and 2011. Each year, Mexico spends about $7 billion fighting illegal drug activity, but drug cartels take in perhaps $25 billion, wealth that allows them to recruit and equip large militias, bribe police and public officials, assassinate anyone who opposes their interests, and dig long tunnels under the U.S. border. Not surprisingly, drug-related violence has spilled into the United States (Padgett & Grillo, 2008; Cave, 2012; Dillon & Lovett, 2013).

In light of all of this evidence, some people reasonably conclude that drugs cause crime. But others counter that the enforcement of our nation's drug laws actually makes the crime problem worse. By limiting the supply of drugs, current laws drive up drug prices. High prices in turn lead users to commit crimes such as prostitution or burglary to get money for drugs. Government research shows that almost one in five federal prison inmates reports committing a violent crime to obtain money to buy drugs (U.S. Department of Justice, 2012). Just as important, enforcing drug laws turns millions of people into criminals. Currently, one-sixth of inmates in state and local prisons and half of those in federal prisons are there for drug offenses (U.S. Department of Justice, 2013). Because jail time stigmatizes people as "convicts" and makes getting a good job later on less likely, sending nonviolent people to jail for drug offenses may make them more likely to commit crimes later. The benefits of not sending drug users to jail will be especially great for low-income people, as President Obama noted in the chapter-opening story. African Americans and Hispanic Americans currently make up more than 60 percent of people in prison for drug offenses (U.S. Bureau of Justice Statistics, 2013).

Global Poverty

Drugs defined as illegal in the United States represent a significant share of the global economy. Millions of people in poor nations of the world with few other economic opportunities grow the plants and manufacture drugs that end up in rich nations such as the United States. For example, opiates from Afghanistan and other low-income countries in Asia are sold in the United States, Canada, the nations of Western Europe, and Australia. Hashish from the Middle East and western Africa moves readily to Western Europe, just as marijuana grown in Mexico, Cuba, and Central America is shipped to the United States. Finally, cocaine produced in mountainous regions of South America travels to both North America and Western Europe (Degenhardt & Hall, 2012).

Each year, people in the United States spend more than $100 billion on illegal drugs, including marijuana, hashish, cocaine, and heroin. This sum exceeds the total economic output of dozens of the world's countries. This enormous demand on the part of people living in high-income nations means that drugs can be a low-income country's biggest export and the major source of economic opportunity for its people. In Bolivia, for example, the "street price" of cocaine production represents more than half of that nation's gross domestic product (GDP). Cocaine has enormous economic importance in Peru, as does marijuana in Mexico and hashish in Afghanistan (U.S. Office of National Drug Control Policy, 2013).

Terrorism

Here in the United States, the Office of National Drug Control Policy links drug use and terrorism. Buying illegal drugs at home, officials argue, puts money in the hands of terrorists abroad. Terrorists may use this money to finance attacks on this country.

In the years after the September 11, 2001, terrorist attacks, the level of public concern about terrorism has remained high. But is the link between illegal drugs and terrorism real? Evidence suggests that almost one-half of organizations dealing in illegal drugs have direct ties to terrorist activity. Opium grown in Afghanistan, for example, is a major source of revenue for the Taliban.

Terrorism and illegal drug sales are certainly linked. Yet critics point out that most of the illegal drug trade is not carried out by terrorists and that most terrorist funding does not come from drug sales. Therefore, say critics, the federal government overstates the link between terrorism and drugs in an effort to discourage illegal drug use among young people (Lasseter, 2009; United Nations, 2012; U.S. Office of National Drug Control Policy, 2013).

Social Policy: Responding to the Drug Problem

8.5 Summarize the effectiveness of various drug-control strategies.

Despite changes in public behavior and attitudes, there has always been general agreement that U.S. society has to *do* something about illegal drug use. But there is far less agreement about exactly what our society should do in response to drug use.

Strategies to Control Drugs

Controlling the amount of illegal drugs in the United States is no easy task. For one thing, the United States has lots of political freedoms, which limit the power of government to intervene in people's lives. For another, there is a high demand for illegal drugs, which draws a huge supply. In the following sections, we take a closer look at four drug-control strategies: interdiction, prosecution, education, and treatment.

Interdiction *Interdiction* means preventing the movement of drugs across a country's borders. Interdiction efforts are carried out by the Drug Enforcement Administration, the Customs Service, the Border Patrol, and the U.S. military.

Consider the scope of this challenge: The United States has 12,000 miles of coastline and 7,500 miles of land borders. Each year, some 200,000 boats and ships, 600,000 aircraft, 200 million cars, and 500 million people cross this nation's borders.

Government agents work long and hard but they manage to seize only a tiny portion of the illegal drugs that enter the United States. No one doubts that the flow of drugs would be greater without efforts to control the border. But a fair assessment is that, although necessary, interdiction has limited success as a drug-control strategy.

Prosecution "Putting drug dealers where they belong—in jail!" is a popular idea in the United States. But catching drug dealers is easier said than done. More important, giving police more power to stop and search people can threaten our basic freedoms.

In addition, the policy of prosecuting drug dealers often unfairly punishes the poor and minorities. For example, government data show that African American and white people are about equally likely to say they use an illegal drug. But African Americans are about four times as likely as whites to be convicted of a drug offense (U.S. Department of Justice, 2011; U.S. Department of Health and Human Services, 2012).

The war on crack provides another example of racial bias in prosecution of drug cases. Why? The federal minimum mandatory sentencing guidelines, shown in

Table 8–1 Federal Minimum Mandatory Sentencing Guidelines

Type of Drug	Five-Year Sentence without Parole	Ten-Year Sentence without Parole
LSD	1 gram	10 grams
Marijuana	100 plants or	1,000 plants or
	100 kilograms	1,000 kilograms
Crack cocaine	28 grams	280 grams
Powder cocaine	500 grams	5 kilograms
Heroin	100 grams	1 kilogram
Methamphetamine, pure	5 grams	50 grams
PCP, pure ("angel dust")	10 grams	100 grams

SOURCE: United States Code, Title 21, Sec. 841 (2010).

Table 8–1, dictate prison sentences according to type of drug and quantity. Under the law, you will be sent to jail for five years for possessing 500 grams of cocaine, but only 28 grams of crack gets you the same jail time. White and middle-class people are more likely to use cocaine; black people and the poor are more likely to use crack. For this reason, critics claim, the sentencing law punishes one category of people more than another. In 2010, Congress passed the Fair Sentencing Act, which reduced what had been an even greater disparity in the sentences involving crack and cocaine (before, having just 5 grams of crack could result in a five-year prison sentence). Critics of the current system—even with the recent reform—continue to seek equal penalties for people convicted of dealing crack and powdered cocaine (Meyer, 2009; Cratty, 2011).

Treatment Rather than punishing offenders, another drug-control strategy tries to help drug users, especially people struggling with addiction. Beginning in the early 1970s, the United States expanded drug treatment programs, which offered methadone, a synthetic form of heroin, to treat heroin addicts. In practice, methadone programs replace one form of addiction with another. But the government can regulate the content of methadone; heroin bought on the street is of unknown strength and may be mixed with other chemicals. Also, by supplying methadone, the government reduces demand for heroin. Finally, programs offering methadone (and, more recently, a drug called buprenorphine) reduce a drug user's involvement in crime (Bowersox, 1995; Cloud, 1998; Hunt & Sun, 1998).

Treatment involves not just drug replacement but also counseling and group support (Cowley, 2001). No organization has done more to show the power of people to help those addicted to drugs than Alcoholics Anonymous. The Defining Moment box provides a look at Bill Wilson and the organization he founded.

The success of programs such as Alcoholics Anonymous confirms the importance of treatment in the efforts to control drug abuse. But treatment also has its limitations. For one thing, there are not enough treatment programs to serve everyone who needs assistance. Just as important, programs may help people stop using drugs, but they do little to change the environment that pushed them toward drugs in the first place. The risk of relapse (going back to drugs) helps explain the policy of Alcoholics Anonymous to teach its members that they are and will remain alcoholics who must actively control their addiction for the rest of their lives. A final problem is that although many people claim to support the policy of treatment for people who abuse drugs, U.S. public opinion has always favored prosecution over treatment for those who break the law.

Education A fourth strategy for controlling drug use is education. Unlike prosecution and treatment, which are both examples of a *reactive* policy that targets people after they use an illegal drug, education is a *proactive* policy aimed at discouraging people from using illegal drugs in the first place. Proactive policies are most effective when they target young people by, for example, operating in schools.

The most widespread drug education program is Drug Abuse Resistance Education (DARE), which began in 1983. This program, operating in about 75 percent of elementary schools in the United States and in forty-eight countries, has police officers instruct children on the dangers of drugs.

Police, school administrators, and parents all agree on the need to teach young people about illegal drugs. However, research raises doubts about the effectiveness of educational programs such as DARE. In 2001, DARE officials conceded as much as they launched a new, more interactive program aimed at drawing older students, those in middle school and high school, into discussions about drug use (Zernike, 2001; Rosenbaum, 2012).

The War on Drugs

All the strategies just described—interdiction, prosecution, treatment, and education—have played some part in U.S. drug policy. But the main focus has always been on prosecution: criminal penalties that target users and dealers.

This emphasis emerged back in 1968, when President Richard Nixon characterized illegal drugs as our nation's "public enemy number one." He backed up those words by creating the Drug Enforcement Administration (DEA), the federal antidrug organization that tries to keep other countries from producing illegal drugs and also works to keep drugs from entering the United States. The DEA has broad police powers to search private homes and seize illegal drugs.

The next two presidents (Gerald Ford and Jimmy Carter) viewed illegal drugs as less of a problem and there was some increase in treatment efforts. After his election in 1980, Ronald Reagan declared drugs to be a major moral challenge, and he funded vigorous prosecution efforts and also favored an educational strategy by urging parents to teach their children to avoid illegal substances, rallying the public with the slogan "Just say no to drugs." During Reagan's two terms in the White House, the federal budget for fighting illegal drugs increased tenfold (U.S. Department of Justice, 1993). In addition, the federal government adopted a policy of mandatory prison sentences for convicted drug offenders (see Table 8–1). As shown in Figure 8–3 on page 250, the result was a sharp increase

in the number of people convicted of federal drug crimes and sent to prison.

In addition, federal officials devised a new weapon to fight the war on drugs. Many drug dealers were using their enormous wealth to fight drug charges and avoid convictions and prison sentences. In 1984, Congress enacted a new law empowering police to seize drug dealers' property *before* they were convicted of any crime (Eldredge, 1998). Supporters of this law claim that seizing property is one effective way to put drug dealers out of business. But critics respond that such a law allows government agents to punish people before they are

CONSTRUCTING SOCIAL PROBLEMS

A DEFINING MOMENT

Bill Wilson: Alcoholics Can Learn to Be Sober

Bill Wilson was a successful stockbroker working in New York City. In many ways, he was living the good life. But he also had a serious drinking problem. He reached a point where alcohol had made his life unmanageable, and he needed a way out. In 1935, he envisioned a solution based on drawing support from others with similar experiences and adopting a new set of personal values. Wilson founded Alcoholics Anonymous (AA), and his idea spread quickly throughout the United States and abroad.

Today, AA is a global organization with 1.3 million members in 59,000 local groups in the United States and more than 2 million members in 115,000 groups worldwide. AA has helped millions of people stop drinking. It has also changed the way the rest of us look at alcoholism. A century ago, most people viewed alcoholics as morally weak people who gave in to the temptation of drink and, therefore, deserved little sympathy. AA redefined the problem of alcoholism as an *illness*—a sickness of the body and also of the mind and soul—that, like any other illness, can be treated and cured.

How does AA work? People who suffer from alcoholism are welcome to show up at an AA group's regular meeting. Having the support of others who face the same challenge can give someone a feeling of greater power on the road toward sobriety.

AA believes that alcoholics can learn to lead sober lives but cautions that they will always remain alcoholics. For that reason, AA members never call themselves "ex-alcoholics"; rather, they say they are "recovering from" their addiction.

The AA philosophy has been adapted by a number of similar organizations, including Al-Anon Family Groups (for friends and family members of addicts), Alateen (for teenagers whose parents are alcoholics), Adult Children of Alcoholics (for adults who grew up in an alcoholic home), Narcotics Anonymous (for people addicted to drugs other than alcohol), Gamblers Anonymous, and numerous programs aimed at helping people with eating disorders.

At thousands of AA meetings like this one, people throughout the United States learn to confront their alcoholism and to live a sober life.

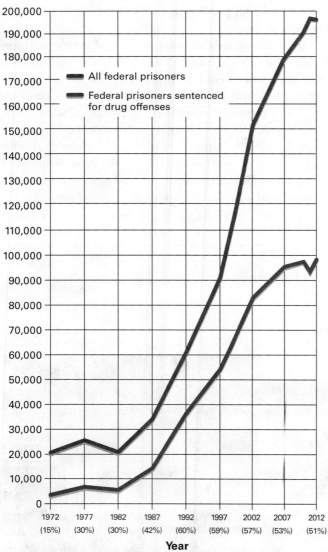

Figure 8–3   Total Federal Prison Population and Share of Drug Offenders, 1972–2012

The number of federal prisoners rose rapidly in the United States after 1982. (The total number of prisoners in federal, state, and local facilities is now about 2.3 million.) The increasing number of convictions for drug offenses has helped push up the total.

SOURCE: U.S. Bureau of Justice Statistics (2008, 2013).

convicted of a crime and—worse still—threatens people who have nothing to do with drugs. The Social Policy box takes a closer look.

In 1989, President George H. W. Bush created the Office of National Drug Control Policy, headed by William Bennett, who became known as the "drug czar." Getting tough on drugs remained the order of the day. Public opinion surveys at that time showed that two-thirds of U.S. adults considered illegal drugs the most serious social problem facing the country (Bertram at al., 1996).

When Bill Clinton entered the White House in 1993, he pointed out that once released from jail, most drug users go back to old habits. Therefore, he urged a step back from mandatory sentencing policies and pushed to make treatment the main strategy to deal with illegal drugs.

Conservatives charged that Clinton was "soft on drugs," a charge reinforced in the public's mind by the president's admission that he had smoked (but not inhaled) marijuana. When a top official in the Clinton administration suggested that perhaps government should consider legalizing some drugs, public reaction was quick and negative. Stung by this response, Clinton adopted a tougher line on drugs for the remainder of his presidency. More than 1 million people a year were arrested for drug offenses—almost twice as many as under the Reagan administration (U.S. Department of Justice, 2000).

George W. Bush focused more on terrorism than illegal drugs. But the Bush administration continued efforts to reduce the supply of drugs, especially the growing of coca (used to make cocaine) in Bolivia. At home, the country continued to rely on prosecution as the main drug-control strategy. During the Bush presidency, the United States spent $40 billion per year to seize illegal drugs at U.S. borders, to eliminate marijuana farms in California and elsewhere, and to prosecute and jail offenders (Alter, 2001; Roosevelt, 2001; Padgett, 2002).

More conservative administrations have focused their drug-control efforts on prosecution. The more liberal Obama administration has taken a treatment-focused approach. Turning away from a "war on drugs" strategy based on prosecution and mandatory sentences, the Obama administration has favored a treatment strategy for nonviolent drug offenders. In addition, the Obama administration has encouraged community-based programs in an effort to reduce the swelling prison population (Richman & Peele, 2013).

In addition, the Obama administration has sought to eliminate racial disparities in sentences imposed for drug convictions. In 2014, Congress is considering scaling back mandatory minimum sentences for drug offenses for nonviolent offenders. Congress is also at work to reduce the sentences imposed for possession of crack cocaine. As noted earlier, harsher sentences for use of crack cocaine (largely used by African Americans) compared to powder cocaine (largely used by whites) has resulted in a racial bias in punishment.

From another angle, the Obama administration has defined drug abuse more as an illness than as a crime and has relied on a combination of treatment, health care, and education programs to reduce the demand for illegal drugs (Meyer, 2009; Tierney, 2009; U.S. Office of National Drug Control Policy, 2013).

SOCIAL POLICY
The Drug Wars: Safer Streets or Police State?

Federal agents seized the home of seventy-five-year-old Mary Miller. She has never used illegal drugs; in fact, she would not know a joint if somebody handed one to her. But Mary Miller has a grandson who came to stay with her for a while, and during that time, he began selling soft drugs from the home. When federal agents became aware that the young man was selling drugs, they arrested him and, applying a law passed by Congress in 1984, officials seized the house where the drug dealing had taken place.

Only by taking their money, cars, boats, and other property, say supporters of this law, can police put drug dealers out of business. But critics counter that the law permits police to take property from people who have not have been convicted in a court of law and should be presumed innocent until proven guilty.

Critics also point out that, in practice, this law encourages police to investigate rich people for possible drug offenses and to effect a seizure of property even when evidence of someone's guilt may be weak. A case in point involved Donald Scott, a wealthy sixty-one-year-old man living on a $5 million, 200-acre ranch in Malibu, California. In 1991, someone told the Los Angeles County Sheriff's Department that Scott was growing marijuana plants on his land. The tip was false; later investigation confirmed that there were no illegal drugs anywhere at the ranch. But, after receiving the initial report, the sheriff's office sent a team to the property. Early in the morning, thirty heavily armed officers surrounded the Scott ranch. They knocked and then forced open the door, rushing through the house. They confronted Scott, who, holding his wife, was armed with a gun. In the scuffle that followed, agents fired twice, killing Scott. Police never found any illegal drugs at the ranch. Later, an investigation of the tragic incident suggested that the main reason for the police action was the chance to gain proceeds from the seizure and subsequent sale of the $5 million ranch (Blumenson, 1998:6).

What Do You Think?

1. How does the 1984 seizure law help the public? In what ways might it threaten basic freedoms?
2. Does this law seem likely to help people living in poor neighborhoods plagued by drug dealers? Why or why not?
3. Have a class discussion of this statement: "A society that provides extensive personal freedoms can never be drug-free."

A New Initiative: Decriminalization

During the last fifty years, this country's major drug-control strategies have been interdiction and prosecution. More conservative administrations supported a "war on drugs" and more liberal administrations have shifted the focus a bit toward treatment and education. But the reality remains that the U.S. prison population has soared with about half of all incarcerated people behind bars for a drug offense. Critics of the "war on drugs" point to the increasing number of people in jail for drug convictions as evidence that this strategy has actually made the drug and crime problem worse. What they see as the mass incarceration (especially of low-income and minority youth) for nonviolent drug offenses disrupts lives, stigmatizes people, and leaves them less likely to find good jobs. All of this adds up to a higher risk of engaging in future crime.

Such concerns have advanced the strategy of **decriminalization**, which refers to *reducing or removing severe criminal penalties that punish drug offenses, especially personal use of drugs*. In the United States, the focus of decriminalization has been marijuana, which is still listed as a "Schedule I" substance (the most heavily regulated) under the Controlled Substances Act. The idea of decriminalizing marijuana is not new. In 1973, Oregon was the first state to decriminalize the possession of small amounts of marijuana. Within five years, six other states passed similar laws and fifteen states did so by 2014. In addition, numerous local communities have decriminalized marijuana possession.

In practice, "decriminalizing" marijuana can mean reducing current penalties so that a first-time conviction for possession is a minor offense, punishable by a fine rather than jail time, creates no criminal record. In Ohio, for example, conviction for the possession of less than 100 grams of marijuana is punishable by a fine not to exceed $150 and results in no criminal record.

Another dimension of the decriminalization movement is permitting the medical use of marijuana. As of 2014, twenty-two states plus the District of Columbia have amended their laws to allow medical use of this drug.

Complete decriminalization means allowing people to buy and possess small amounts of marijuana as Colorado and Washington have done. Possessing greater amounts of the drug and selling the drug remain against the law without a state permit.

Decriminalization at some level has taken place in more than half the states. In twenty-three states, however, even possession of small amounts of marijuana is still a

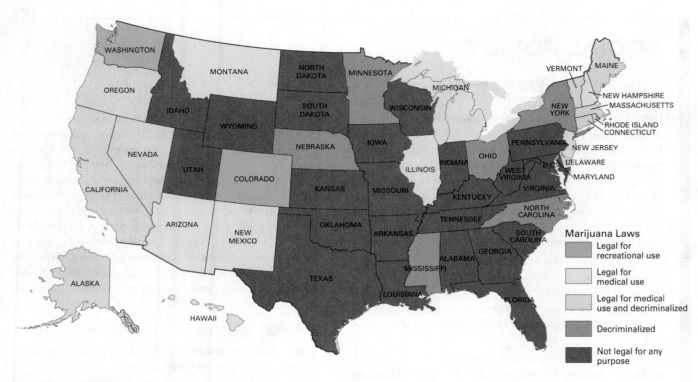

Seeing Ourselves

National Map 8–1 Marijuana Laws across the United States

Marijuana laws in the United States are in transition with change taking place each year and widely differing laws from one state to another. Twenty-three states apply criminal penalties for possession of marijuana. Twenty-two states plus the District of Columbia permit the use of marijuana for medical purposes. Fifteen states have taken steps to reduce criminal penalties for possession of small amounts of marijuana. In two states, possession of small amounts of marijuana for recreational purposes is legal. In general, the more liberal regions of the country have done the most to reduce criminal penalties for possession of marijuana.

SOURCE: National Conference of State Legislatures (2014).

serious crime subject to prosecution. National Map 8-1 shows the current (2014) marijuana laws in the states.

In a nation of contrasting marijuana laws, the debate over legalization will continue. Supporters (generally liberals) argue that the drug is not addictive and poses little danger to users. Therefore, society should treat marijuana in much the same way as alcohol and tobacco, which means that the government can regulate quality and ban sales to children. Legalization, supporters argue, would have three benefits. First, government regulation of quality should reduce the risk of injury or death from "bad" drugs. Second, the cost of a legal drug should go down, reducing the need for users to commit crimes to get drug money and also reducing violence among drug dealers. Third, our society would no longer bear the cost of locking up as many as 1 million people convicted of violating drug laws. Fourth, taxing the sale of marijuana can provide states and localities with badly needed revenue. Colorado, for example, levies a 10 percent tax on wholesale marijuana sales and an additional 15 percent tax on retail sales. During just the first month of Colorado's

"legal pot," that state received $1.25 million in new tax revenue (Sanders, 2014).

On the other side of the argument, opponents of legalization (generally conservatives) respond that marijuana is not harmless. They see widespread use of marijuana as raising many of the same health risks as tobacco and alcohol. In addition, legalizing marijuana will probably make use of this drug far more widespread, resulting in a population more "dazed and confused" with less responsibility and motivation. Legalizing marijuana, they suggest, may well increase rates of dropping out of school, poverty, and family problems. It is almost certain that increasing the availability of marijuana will increase the likelihood of people driving under the influence of this drug. As yet, no state has devised a plan to combat "driving while stoned" (Berkowitz, 2014; Brooks, 2014).

Reasonable people line up on both sides of this issue. But it is clear that decriminalization of marijuana now has considerable public support. As noted earlier, surveys show that 52 percent of U.S. adults support legalizing personal marijuana and 77 percent favor making the

Would legalization make the drug problem worse or better? When the Swiss permitted drug use in the city of Zurich (*left*), problems increased and officials reversed course. In the Netherlands (*right*), by contrast, legalization of soft drugs had a different result, and the policy continues to this day.

drug legal for medical purposes (Pew Research Center for the People & the Press, 2013). Note, too, that marijuana is not the only drug being considered for decriminalization. Congress is currently working to reduce criminal penalties for possession of crack cocaine, with the goal of bringing them into line with penalties for possession of powder cocaine. Beyond this change, however, there is little support in Congress or among the public for the idea of decriminalizing "hard" drugs.

The United States is not the only country wrestling with the issue of legalization. What lessons can we learn from other nations? Two interesting cases have played out in Europe.

Zurich: Decriminalization That Failed

In the 1970s, people began gathering in Zurich, Switzerland's capital city, to use illegal drugs. The word spread and, by the mid-1980s, drug activity became the central focus of one of the city's public spaces, which came to be called "Needle Park."

Then the AIDS epidemic began. Zurich's leaders feared that drug users sharing needles might spark a health nightmare. They reasoned that a police crackdown would be counterproductive because it would serve only to scatter drug users all over the city. Then they settled on the idea of decriminalization. Why not let people use drugs legally, as long as they stay in the park? That way, health officials thought they would be able to monitor their behavior.

And so Zurich became an experiment in the decriminalization of heroin. City police stopped making drug arrests, and city health stations provided heroin and methadone along with clean needles and condoms to addicts in the hope of limiting the spread of AIDS.

But the program had an unexpected result, drawing to the park drug users and dealers not only from all over Switzerland but from other European countries. It was far more than anyone had bargained for. By 1990, Zurich officials were handing out as many as 8,000 clean needles each and every day. As the number of people in the park continued to increase, it was clear that the experiment had failed. The park was completely overrun with drug users, vandalism was out of control, and everyone else in the city was afraid to go anywhere near the area.

In February 1992, government officials gave up and closed the park. The city of Zurich continues to offer small dosages of heroin to people dealing with addiction, but the city requires that they inject the drug at clinics rather than in public places. In 2008, voters in Switzerland passed a referendum continuing the free heroin program. At the same time, they voted to keep heroin—and also marijuana—illegal (Huber, 1994; Nadelmann, 1995; Bruppacher, 2008).

The Netherlands: Decriminalization That Mostly Works

The second case is the Netherlands, another European nation, where decriminalization appears to have worked far better than in Zurich. In 1976, Dutch officials enacted a drug policy that permits coffee shops ("cannabis cafés") to sell up to 5 grams of "soft" drugs such as marijuana or hashish (but not "hard" drugs such as heroin). Customers can legally buy and use (but not resell) these drugs as long as they remain orderly. Since 2004, clean-air regulations require customers who buy marijuana or hashish to smoke it outside (Ministry of Health, Welfare and Sport, 1998; van den Hurk, 1999; Henderson, 2003).

For several decades, Dutch decriminalization seems to have worked. The crime rate in the Netherlands remains well below that of the United States. In addition, although many people come to the Netherlands to smoke marijuana, the level of marijuana use among Dutch teenagers is roughly the same as in the United States. Perhaps most important, Dutch prisons are not filling with people convicted of drug offenses, as is the case in the United States (Common Sense for Drug Policy, 1999; MacCoun, 2001; Bruppacher, 2008).

Yet, opponents of decriminalization point out that Amsterdam also has a famous "red light" district in which prostitution is legal and, coupled to popular cannabis cafés, the drug and sex industry has been growing as well as becoming dominated by criminal organizations largely from Eastern Europe. In an effort to scale back drug sales, the city recently closed twenty-six of the seventy-six cannabis shops. Also, some Dutch cities now restrict drug sales to Dutch citizens who can present a "weed pass." Other European nations seem to think the Dutch policy is working. Belgium has made the possession of marijuana for personal use legal, and citizens can also grow their own plants. Copenhagen, the capital of Denmark, is moving ahead with a plan to allow cannabis cafés. In about half of European nations, criminal penalties for personal use of marijuana have either been eliminated or enforcement of the laws has been greatly reduced (Hoge, 2002; Tandy, 2009; Stanner, 2011).

The Dutch case is instructive because it shows that legalizing "soft" drugs did not create a host of serious social problems, at least in the Netherlands. By watching what unfolds in Colorado and Washington, we will soon see whether such a policy will work as well in the United States.

Theories of Drug-Related Social Problems

8.6 **Apply sociological theory to issues involving drugs.**

Each of sociology's major theoretical approaches offers insights into social problems involving drugs. As in earlier chapters, each theory highlights different facts and points toward a different conclusion.

Structural-Functional Analysis: Regulating Drug Use

Structural-functional theory highlights the functions of drugs for the operation of society. Some drugs, such as alcohol, ease social interaction, as when new neighbors enjoy a drink together. Other drugs—including caffeine, diazepam (Valium), or methylphenidate hydrochloride (Ritalin)—help people stay productive and cope with the day-to-day demands of modern life. Legal and illegal drugs also are a major source of economic activity, providing jobs and income for hundreds of thousands of people.

Because most drugs, when used to excess, are personally harmful or socially disruptive, societies establish social controls to regulate their use. In general, the more disruptive a drug's effects, the stronger are the efforts to control its use. Traditionally, the family, schools, and religion played a major part in regulating individual behavior. Perhaps a weakening in these social institutions—leaving people with less guidance and meaning in their lives—explains some of the rise in drug use over the past century. In any case, as families and religion have lost some of their power over individuals, the task of regulating drug use has fallen more and more to health care professionals and to the criminal justice system.

EVALUATE

Structural-functional theory suggests that drugs can be both helpful and harmful to the orderly operation of society. Yet this approach is unclear about precisely how one assesses the consequences of a particular drug for social life. In addition, functional theory takes such a broad and structural view that we learn little about the ways in which individuals understand drugs, which is the focus of symbolic-interaction theory.

CHECK YOUR LEARNING What insights do we gain about drugs and drug use from applying structural-functional theory? What is one limitation of this approach?

Symbolic-Interaction Analysis: The Meaning of Drug Use

Symbolic-interaction theory calls attention to the various meanings people attach to their surroundings. From this point of view, a drug that the members of one society define as a part of sacred, religious rituals, the members of another society may ban as a dangerous substance. Even within any one society, a drug (say, cocaine in the United States) may be legal at one point in time and outlawed later on. Conversely, a drug largely ignored may become popular (as with tobacco in the United States) or a drug once outlawed may become legal (as with cannabis in Colorado).

A second issue is how individuals come to use a drug. People do not simply become drug users; they gain skills and attitudes gradually through a learning process. In the case of marijuana smoking, for example, a novice smoker usually "turns on" in the presence of more experienced people, who explain how to smoke the drug, the proper behavior expected when doing so, and how to enjoy the experience of being "high" (Becker, 1966).

APPLYING THEORY

Alcohol and Other Drugs

	Structural-Functional Theory	Symbolic-Interaction Theory	Social-Conflict Theory
What is the level of analysis?	Macro-level	Micro-level	Macro-level
What is the approach to drugs?	Structural-functional theory directs attention to the societal consequences of using various drugs. Some drugs, including caffeine and alcohol, encourage social interaction and are viewed positively. Other drugs, including heroin and crack cocaine, are disruptive and are viewed negatively.	Symbolic-interaction theory explains that various societies attach various meanings to drugs and their use. The use of drugs, like other forms of behavior, is learned by people in various social settings. This learning involves both skills in using the drug as well as attitudes toward a drug and its use.	Social-conflict theory links society's view of various drugs to issues of social power and social inequality. Drugs that are highly profitable to powerful corporations are sold more freely, while those that are not are subject to greater legal controls.
Are drugs a problem?	All drugs can threaten social order if they are abused, so society must regulate drug use. Law enforcement is an important strategy to control drug use. Yet families, religious organizations, and schools should help regulate individual behavior to minimize problems related to drug use.	Whether drug use is defined as a problem depends on any number of situational factors. Therefore, what one society bans as a dangerous substance, members of another society may use as a part of sacred ritual. Finally, any society's view of a particular drug is subject to change over time.	Drugs favored by minorities with less social power are more likely to be defined as a problem and outlawed. Similarly, people with low social standing often receive more severe penalties for drug use than people with high social standing.

EVALUATE

Symbolic-interaction theory highlights the variable meanings people attach to all behavior, including drug use. From this point of view, we understand how people in one time and place take a view of a drug that differs from that of people in another time and place. Yet because of its situational focus, this approach runs the risk of missing broader patterns, especially those linked to social inequality. Such patterns are at the heart of social-conflict theory.

CHECK YOUR LEARNING What insights do we gain about drugs and drug use from applying symbolic-interaction theory? What is one limitation of this approach?

Social-Conflict Analysis: Power and Drug Use

Social-conflict theory understands issues in terms of social inequality. Throughout our own history, officials have outlawed the drugs favored by powerless people, especially minorities and immigrants. In the mid-nineteenth century, whites on the West Coast outlawed the opium used mainly by Chinese immigrants; about 1900, southern whites who feared black people succeeded in outlawing cocaine. By 1920, the tide of European immigration led to Prohibition, which banned alcohol until 1933.

On the other hand, powerful corporate interests sell highly profitable drugs—including tobacco and alcohol—with full protection of the law, even though these two drugs are linked to more deaths annually than all the illegal drugs combined.

Social-conflict theory also points out that the social standing of users has much to do with how severely illegal drug use is punished. Earlier we saw how racial inequality has played a part in explaining the harsher sentences handed down for use of crack (a less expensive cocaine derivative favored by African Americans and the poor) compared with those for the use of powder cocaine (a middle-class drug favored by white people). Similarly, young people who sell drugs to their friends are more likely to be arrested if they are poor and do business on the streets than if they are affluent and do business in their dorm on a college campus (Mohamed & Fritsvold, 2011; Cottom, 2014).

EVALUATE

Social-conflict theory links drug problems to social inequality, suggesting that the poor bear the greatest burden when it comes to the enforcement of drug laws. Yet it fails to account for the fact that many harmful drugs—such as nicotine and alcohol—are widely used by rich and poor alike. Similarly, the harm caused by alcohol—say, in contributing to automobile accidents—is not limited to any one class of people.

CHECK YOUR LEARNING What insights do we gain about drugs and drug use from applying social-conflict theory? What is one limitation of this approach?

The Applying Theory table summarizes what we learn from each theoretical approach.

✪ POLITICS AND DRUGS

Constructing Problems and Defining Solutions

8.7 Analyze drug-related issues from various positions on the political spectrum.

Theory helps us understand social problems, but the position anyone takes on drug-related policies is a matter of values and politics. The final section of this chapter explains how politics shapes views of drug-related problems and leads people to favor particular solutions.

Conservatives: Just Say No

In their analysis of all social problems, conservatives emphasize the importance of moral values in guiding individual behavior. Historically, the family, a religious community, and the local school were the main sources of moral instruction. From a conservative point of view, young people who are raised by committed, involved parents and who are guided by religious beliefs and caring teachers are usually able to resist any temptation presented by drugs.

As noted in earlier chapters, conservatives argue that the weakening of families, religious beliefs, and local communities since the 1960s has eroded our society's teaching of moral virtue. They see the rise of drug use in recent decades as one indication that, morally speaking, society has lost its way. The mass media and popular music, which fill more and more of the lives of young people, are as likely to glamorize drug use as to criticize it. In the past, most U.S. adults described marijuana use as a moral problem. Today, in a culture where "anything goes," a minority of people feel that way (Pew Research Center, 2013). The drug scene, as conservatives see it, amounts to a self-centered and pleasure-seeking way of life on the part of people who have too little understanding or appreciation of higher virtues, such as duty, self-control, and respect for authority figures. Most conservatives oppose the recent trend to decriminalize marijuana.

Conservatives define drug use as a serious social problem that both causes and results from weak families. Drug use also encourages divorce, crime, poverty, and dropping out of school. As a response to illegal drug sale, possession, and use, conservatives favor tough laws, aggressive enforcement, and

Conservatives claim that current drug laws are an effective tool to reduce the problem of illegal drugs. Liberals (and libertarians) argue that the main effect of our drug laws is putting people in jail. Do you favor enforcement or repeal of current drug laws? Why?

severe penalties. In the end, however, conservatives warn that there is only so much that police and other government agencies can do to control drugs. The major responsibility will always lie with parents, who must raise their children to make good moral choices in a world full of temptation.

Liberals: Reform Society

When it comes to questions about how people should live, liberals generally take a tolerant view. Liberals are uneasy with the moralistic tone of conservative arguments, which seem to apply traditional standards of right and wrong to everyone.

In addition, while conservatives typically point to the state of family and religion in explaining social problems, liberals turn to the economy. Liberals claim that drug use is the product of too much economic inequality and too much hopelessness on the part of ordinary people. Therefore, the liberal solution to the drug problem is reducing economic inequality and poverty, which would lead fewer people to turn to drugs in the first place.

Liberals take a tolerant view of "soft" drugs. Liberal support has been crucial in moving states toward decriminalization. Why, some liberals ask, should marijuana be against the law when it causes less harm than a legal drug such as tobacco?

Most liberals do support tough law enforcement when it comes to "hard" drugs—especially for big-time dealers. But liberals claim that our current policies criminalize hundreds of thousands of people who pose little harm to anyone and may not even be a danger to themselves. They call for less emphasis on police, courts, and prisons and more emphasis on programs of drug education for children and treatment programs for people struggling with drug addiction.

Radicals: Understanding Drugs from the Margins of Society

Both ends of the political spectrum figure into the national debate on drugs. First we look at the libertarian position on the far right; then we examine the socialist position on the far left.

The Radical Right: Libertarians In political terms, **libertarians** are *people who favor the greatest possible individual freedom.* Although some people who call themselves "libertarians" fall close to the political mainstream on many issues, most libertarians see government as the biggest threat to their core value of individual liberty. What they seek, therefore, is the smallest government possible in order to have the greatest degree of personal freedom.

Given this emphasis on personal freedom, libertarians oppose government efforts to regulate drugs (and almost anything else). As they see it, drug laws amount to a system by which government seeks to limit individual choice about how to live. Many libertarians believe that the government's war on drugs has greatly reduced our civil liberties, not only by limiting our choice about what to put in our own bodies but also by permitting widespread surveillance, searches, and seizure of property not to mention putting a million people in jail. In short, most libertarians see not a "drug problem" but a "government problem" that threatens everyone. Therefore, libertarians are at the forefront of the movement to legalize all drugs (Trebach & Inciardi, 1993).

The Radical Left: Socialists Radicals on the far left of the political spectrum also oppose current drug laws but for different reasons. From the point of view of socialists, drug laws (like all laws) reflect the interests of the rich and powerful members of society and target everyone else. Drug laws criminalize the poor—especially people of color—who now fill U.S. prisons in disproportionate numbers. In an effort to stabilize our society in crisis, the government has pushed the prisoner population to a level greater than at any time in our history. For this reason, the far left supports repeal of current drug laws.

But abolishing current drug laws is only a small part of the solution. From the radical left's point of view, society itself needs to be completely restructured. If a new society were created on the principles of economic and political equality for all people, left-radicals claim, there would be far less demand for drugs in the first place. The Left to Right table outlines the various political perspectives on drugs.

Going On from Here

Thousands of years ago, our ancestors discovered the powers of certain plants to alter human behavior and perceptions. Ever since, drugs have been part of human culture. Just as societies depend on the positive effects of some drugs, societies define other substances as problems that must be controlled.

There is little doubt that drugs, both illegal and legal, will remain controversial in the decades ahead. Drugs

---

LEFT TO RIGHT

The Politics of the Drug Problem

	Radical-Left View	Liberal View	Conservative View	Radical-Right (Libertarian) View
What is the problem?	Drug laws (like all laws) reflect the interests of the powerful and criminalize poor people and minorities.	Drug use is a symptom of the suffering of many people from various problems, such as poverty and powerlessness.	Drug use is a symptom of poor moral instruction to young people. Schools, churches, and especially families should raise children with the moral values that will give them the strength to resist the temptation to use drugs.	The government threatens civil liberties by using police power to make arrests, seize property, and monitor the lives of people suspected of using drugs.
What is the solution?	A fundamental reorganization of society to spread wealth, power, and opportunity to all would go a long way toward reducing the conditions that lead people to sell and use drugs in the first place.	As economic opportunity and social equality increase, drug use should go down. Government should fund treatment programs for people with addictions.	Enforcement of drug laws is important, but active parenting is the first line of defense against the threat of drugs. Schools, houses of worship, and community organizations must play a part in educating children about the dangers of drugs.	Most drug laws—especially those regulating "soft" drugs—should be abolished as a step toward providing people with greater personal freedom.

JOIN THE DEBATE

1. If you were put in charge of a national drug commission, what new policies would you enact to address this problem? Why?

2. Where on the political spectrum would you expect to find support for the various drug control strategies discussed in this chapter: interdiction, prosecution, education, treatment, and decriminalization?

3. Which of the four political analyses of the drug problem included here do you find most convincing? Why?

such as heroin and cocaine will continue to claim victims; the death toll from alcohol abuse—which is at a much higher level—will almost certainly remain a major problem.

The debate over the causes of drug abuse will also go on, with various political camps making different claims. With its focus on moral values, conservatives will point to family breakdown; with its focus on economic inequality, liberals will point to the increasing gap between rich and poor. Radical voices calling for liberty and freedom from government control (the far right) and the need for basic change to the economic system (the far left) will continue to be heard as well.

The movement toward decriminalization of marijuana is gaining speed. Part of the reason is support from the liberal Obama administration, which is concerned with the high rate of incarceration, especially for minority youth. But libertarian support (especially from young people) is also at work. Finally, state officials are well aware of the costs of keeping so many people incarcerated for drug offenses as well as the tax revenues that they may be able to generate through a system of government-regulated marijuana sales.

There are signs that the long history of widespread support for aggressive use of the criminal justice system—including police, courts, and prisons—to combat drugs may be weakening. While efforts at interdiction are likely to continue, we are likely to see greater focus on education and treatment rather than prosecution.

One additional fact: There is a large body of research showing that illegal drug use declines with age. In the next few decades, the average age of the U.S. population will continue to increase, raising the prospect of continuing the recent downward trend in most illegal drug use. But in light of the uncertain economy and the difficulty many families are having finding financial security, it is doubtful that aging alone will solve the drug problem in U.S. society.

Essay: Envisioning a Better Society Have you been surprised at the increasing public acceptance of legal marijuana? Do you think that this trend is making our society better or causing problems? Why? Looking ahead, do you support the legalization of marijuana nationally? Why or why not?

CHAPTER 8   Alcohol and Other Drugs

Are you concerned about drugs?

From almost anyone's point of view, at least some drugs are harmful to people and are, therefore, the basis of a social problem. But what's the best way to create a solution to the many troubling issues surrounding the use of drugs? Look at the two accompanying photos to see two different approaches to defining solutions.

From the liberal point of view, soft drugs themselves are not nearly as dangerous as the nation's response to them—specifically, the policy of locking up a million people for drug offenses. A large share of these people are minorities and those with low income. Many liberals therefore support relaxing marijuana laws and, in particular, legalizing the use of medical marijuana, a policy that has been adopted in twenty-two states and the District of Columbia. What do you see as advantages and disadvantages of this approach?

From a conservative point of view, there is entirely too much illegal drug use in our society, and these drugs weaken individual judgment and undermine families and communities. Of course, law enforcement is the policy of last resort for conservatives, who would prefer to guide behavior through moral education. These students have just completed the DARE antidrug education program in their local school. What do you see as the strengths and shortcomings of this approach?

Hint: As we have seen in earlier chapters, conservatives favor a solution based on personal responsibility ("Just say no!"), while liberals favor a solution based on making structural changes to our legal system. Decriminalizing marijuana would obviously reduce the number of drug offenses, but its effect on the rate of marijuana use remains unclear. Education programs such as DARE are also controversial, partly because the effect of such programs on children has not been established. What about libertarians on the far right? From their point of view, maximum freedom is the goal and keeping government at arm's length is the way to do that. Which of these two approaches do you think libertarians (perhaps surprisingly) would support? Why?

Getting Involved: Applications and Exercises

1. Take a walk around your campus with an eye toward drug use. What can you say about the places where people smoke cigarettes? Drink coffee? Drink alcohol? How are the places where each of these drugs is used different from one another? What does that tell you about the drugs?

2. Go online and do a Google image search for "old cigarette ads." What claims were made about the beneficial effects of smoking? How are medical professionals used in the ads to sell cigarettes? What, if any, statements are made by cigarette companies regarding the dangers of smoking tobacco?

3. Most communities have Alcoholics Anonymous and Al-Anon Family Group meetings. Look up the number for AA in your local phone directory, and ask about the time and location of a meeting open to the public. Attend a meeting and, afterward, talk to people about how AA helps them recover from alcoholism or helps them cope with a family member's addiction.

4. Go to your local library or do Internet research to see what you can learn about the extent of illegal drug use in your state. In what region of the state (for example, rural versus urban) is the arrest rate for drug offenses higher? Can you discover why?

Making the Grade

CHAPTER 8 Alcohol and Other Drugs

A DEFINING MOMENT
Bill Wilson: Alcoholics Can Learn to Be Sober **p. 249**

What Is a Drug?

8.1 **Explain what a drug is and how culture, race, and ethnicity affect how a society views drug use.**

Drugs are substances other than food and water that affect the body or the mind.

- Drugs have been a part of society throughout human history. **p. 235**

Drugs and **culture**

- Which drugs people use and which substances they define as helpful and harmful vary from society to society and over time. **pp. 235–36**

- One factor shaping attitudes about drugs in the United States is controversy over immigration; in the past, government has outlawed drugs favored by various categories of immigrants. **pp. 236–37**

> **drug** (p. 235) any chemical substance other than food or water that affects the mind or body

The Extent of Drug Use

8.2 **Distinguish drug use from drug abuse as well as addiction from dependency.**

- About 9.2% of the U.S. population aged twelve and older currently uses at least one illegal drug. The trend in drug use in recent decades has been downward, with an upswing in the last few years.

- People use drugs for various reasons, including recreation, therapy, escape, spiritual or psychological stimulation, and social conformity. **pp. 237–38**

> **addiction** (p. 238) a physical or psychological craving for a drug
> **dependency** (p. 238) a state in which a person's body has adjusted to regular use of a drug

Types of Drugs

8.3 **Define various types of drugs.**

Drugs fall into various categories according to their effect on the body and brain.

- **Stimulants** produce alertness and speed up activity (*examples:* caffeine, nicotine, cocaine, amphetamines).

- **Depressants** slow activity and dull pain (*examples:* aspirin, Valium, alcohol).

- **Hallucinogens** can distort sensory perceptions (*examples:* LSD, peyote, ecstasy).

- **Cannabis** helps people relax and increases appetite (*examples:* marijuana, hashish).

- **Steroids** build muscle and strength.

- Abuse of prescription drugs involving more than 16 million people is part of the drug problem in the United States. **pp. 238–44**

> **stimulants** (p. 238) drugs that increase alertness, changing a person's mood by increasing energy
> **depressants** (p. 241) drugs that slow the operation of the central nervous system
> **alcoholism** (p. 242) addiction to alcohol

Drugs and Other Social Problems

8.4 **Analyze the connections between drugs and various social problems.**

Problems of Family Life

- Drug use—and especially addiction—can lead to codependency among family members and friends.

- Parental addiction harms children, who are more likely to use drugs themselves, to drop out of school, and to get in trouble with the law.

- Drugs play a part in many cases of child neglect and family violence. **pp. 244–45**

Homelessness

- Drug and alcohol use is common among the homeless.

- Although some people become homeless because they abuse drugs, others turn to drugs and alcohol as a means of escape from the stresses of living on the streets. **p. 245**

Health Problems

- Drug abuse can damage the brain, liver, and other vital organs and lead to malnutrition.

261

- Among pregnant women, drug abuse increases the risk of premature delivery and birth defects.

- Drug users can transmit HIV by sharing needles.

- Research has shown that needle exchange programs reduce the transmission of HIV and other diseases, but critics claim that such programs encourage illegal drug use. **pp. 245–46**

Crime

- Most violent offenders report being under the influence of alcohol or other drugs when they committed their crimes.

- Drug laws contribute to crime by driving prices up so that addicted users of crack, cocaine, and heroin turn to crime to support their habit.

- Drug dealers often use violence to protect their profits against competition from other dealers. **p. 246**

Global Poverty

- People in poor nations grow and manufacture illegal drugs as a needed source of income.

- The $100 billion that people in the United States spend each year on illegal drugs exceeds the total economic output of dozens of the world's countries. **p. 247**

Terrorism

- Terrorist organizations may engage in drug trafficking to raise money for terrorist activities. **p. 247**

codependency (p. 244) behavior on the part of others that helps a substance abuser continue the abuse

Social Policy: Responding to the Drug Problem

8.5   Summarize the effectiveness of various drug-control strategies.

Four **strategies** for controlling illegal drugs in the United States are

- interdiction—stopping the movement of drugs across the border

- prosecution—enforcing laws that ban drug sale, possession, or use

- treatment—programs to help people overcome drug-related problems

- education—programs that try to convince people to stop using drugs or not to begin at all **pp. 247–48**

The **war on drugs** has resulted in an increase in the number of people jailed for drug offenses in the United States. People convicted of drug offenses now represent about half of all people in prison. **pp. 248–50**

Decriminalization as a strategy to eliminate drug-related social problems has met with varied success in countries around the world.

- Decriminalization has advanced in the United States, with two states recently legalizing the recreational use of marijuana. **pp. 251–54**

decriminalization (p. 251) reducing or removing severe criminal penalties that punish drug offenses, especially personal use of drugs

Theories of Drug-Related Social Problems

8.6   Apply sociological theory to issues involving drugs.

Structural-Functional Analysis: Regulating Drug Use

Structural-functional theory focuses on the functions of drugs for the normal operation of society.

- Societies rely on some drugs to ease social interaction and help people cope with the demands of modern living.

- Drugs are a source of economic activity, providing jobs and income for many people.

- Societies control drugs that have dangerous consequences. **p. 254**

Symbolic-Interaction Analysis: The Meaning of Drug Use

Symbolic-interaction theory highlights the various meanings people attach to drug use.

- A drug that one society defines as beneficial may be banned as dangerous in another society or at another time in history.

- People learn to use drugs in the same way that they learn other forms of behavior. **pp. 254–55**

Social-Conflict Analysis: Power and Drug Use

Social-conflict theory focuses on how the issue of social power shapes our drug policies.

- The United States has historically banned drugs favored by immigrants and other minorities.

- The degree to which illegal drug use is punished reflects the social standing of the drug users. **p. 255**

⊛ POLITICS AND DRUGS

Constructing Problems and Defining Solutions

8.7 **Analyze drug-related issues from various positions on the political spectrum.**

Conservatives: Just Say No

- **Conservatives** view illegal drug use as a serious social problem linked to the decline of traditional families and religion.
- Conservatives favor tough drug laws and urge parents to provide moral instruction to children. **p. 256**

Liberals: Reform Society

- **Liberals** claim that drug abuse is the product of too little economic opportunity, which creates hopelessness. They are generally tolerant of "soft" drug use.

- Liberals support expanded education and drug treatment programs. **p. 256**

The Radical Right: Libertarians

- **Libertarians**, radicals on the far right, believe that the government's war on drugs has reduced people's civil liberties.
- Libertarians oppose all drug laws in an effort to expand individual freedoms. **pp. 256–57**

The Radical Left: Socialists

- **Socialists**, radicals on the far left, argue that current drug laws tend to criminalize the poor.
- Socialists call for basic change in the U.S. economy leading to a more egalitarian society, which they believe would be characterized by far less demand for drugs. **p. 257**

libertarians (p. 256) people who favor the greatest individual freedom possible

Chapter 9
Physical and Mental Health

 Learning Objectives

9.1 Contrast patterns of human health in high- and low-income countries.

9.2 Describe how nations around the world pay the costs of health care.

9.3 Evaluate the performance of the health care system in the United States.

9.4 Summarize types of mental disorders as well as treatment strategies.

9.5 Apply sociological theory to issues involving physical and mental health.

9.6 Analyze physical and mental health issues from various positions on the political spectrum.

Tracking the Trends

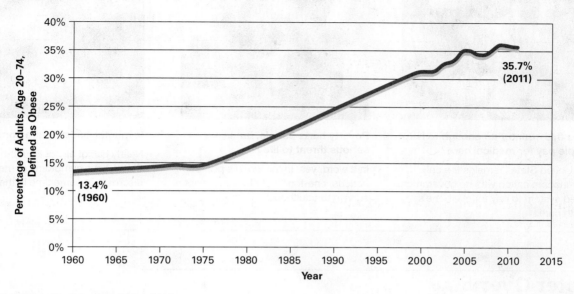

SOURCE: Fryar, Carroll, & Ogden (2012).

Can too much food be a problem? When people consume more calories than they burn in everyday activity, the result is weight gain. People who gain too much weight are at risk for a host of medical problems related to obesity. As the figure shows, among U.S. adults, the rate of obesity has increased dramatically over the last fifty years. From about 13 percent of adults in 1960, the obesity rate soared above 30 percent by 2000 and has continued to increase (more slowly) since then. What do you think are some of the reasons for this trend?

Constructing the Problem

Does this country do enough to help people pay for medical care?

The United States remains the only high-income nation with no government-based system to pay for everyone's health care.

Poverty hurts people, but is it a serious threat to life?

In a word, yes. In the world's poorest nations, one-fourth of children do not survive to adulthood.

Is mental illness a rare condition?

Nearly half of all adults in the United States have symptoms of mental disorders at some time in their lives.

Chapter Overview

Comparing high- and low-income nations, what differences in patterns of human health do we find? What about comparing rich and poor people here in the United States? This chapter explores these health patterns and also explains how people pay for health care. You will understand how inequality shapes health and also learn more about both physical and mental illness and various categories of disease and disorder. You will carry out theoretical analysis of health issues and also learn how the "problems" people identify as well as the "solutions" they favor reflect their political attitudes. ■

What category of people in the United States are we most likely to avoid, to stereotype, and to fear? In the past, the answer might have been gays and lesbians, physically handicapped people, or perhaps members of various racial and ethnic minorities.

Today, there is increasing acceptance of many categories of people once pushed to the margins. But there is still very little acceptance of one category of people—men and women with mental illness. Undoubtedly, the mass media play a part; everyone remembers "crazy" and genuinely scary characters in films from *Psycho* to *Friday the 13th* to *Silence of the Lambs*. Such movies frighten us precisely because they play on fears that lie deep within U.S. culture.

Mental illness may seem strange, but it is far from uncommon. More than 100 million people—almost one-half of the adult population in the United States—suffer from a mental illness at some point in their lives. Almost 20 percent of adults claimed that they had some type of mental illness in 2012 and 4 percent (9.6 million people) suffered from a mental disorder that was severe (U.S. Department

of Health and Human Services, 2013). Surprising, in light of these high numbers, is the fact that most people know very little about mental illness and its causes.

This chapter explores problems related to both mental and physical health. We begin by looking at problems of physical health in the United States. We also take a look at health in the poorest nations of the world, where illness

caused by poverty kills one-fourth of the people before they become adults. Then we survey health care systems, giving special attention to how people in various countries pay for care. Looking here at home, we consider why many people claim that the U.S. health care system is in crisis. Finally, we turn to mental health, explaining what mental illnesses are, what causes them, and why understanding of this widespread problem is limited. Although health is partly a matter of biology and medicine, society guides how we define people as "healthy" or "sick" and allows some categories of people to enjoy excellent health while stacking the odds against others from the day they are born.

Health and Illness: A Global Perspective

9.1 Contrast patterns of human health in high- and low-income countries.

Many of us think that being healthy simply means not being sick. However, the World Health Organization (1946:3) defines **health** as *a state of complete physical, mental, and social well-being*. In other words, just as there are degrees of illness, so there are degrees of health. Looking around the world, we see that one major predictor of people's level of health is their income. To put it in simple terms, the global pattern is "wealth brings health."

High-Income Nations

On average, people living in rich nations—in North America, Western Europe, or Japan—are far healthier than those living in poor countries. One good measure of a society's health is the **infant mortality rate**, *the number of babies, of every 1,000 born, who die before their first birthday*. In the world's rich nations, infant mortality rates are low, usually about five deaths for every 1,000 babies born. That means that a baby has at least a 99.5 percent chance of surviving the first year, and so infant deaths are quite rare. When they do occur, people view them as both unexpected and tragic. Global Map 9–1 on page 268 shows that the infant mortality rates for rich countries are quite low by world standards.

Another way to gauge global patterns of health is by calculating how long, on average, people live. **Life expectancy at birth** is *the number of years, on average, people in a society can expect to live*. In the United States, boys born in 2011 can expect to live seventy-six years, and girls born that year can expect to live eighty-one years. By contrast, in the world's poorest nations, life expectancy is about fifty-six years (Hoyert & Xu, 2012; Population Reference Bureau, 2013).

A society's average level of income also has a lot to do with the *types* of health problems its people face. People who live in rich societies typically don't worry too much about health until they are past middle age. In most cases, they live long enough to die in old age—typically, after age seventy-five—of some **chronic disease**, *an illness that has a long-term development*. Chronic diseases include heart disease, cancer, and stroke.

In most respects, being affluent is a lot better for human health than being poor. But a higher standard of living does carry some health dangers of its own. For example, people in the United States eat a high-fat diet; in addition, many of us do not engage in very much physical activity. Taken together, these factors help explain the fact—highlighted at the beginning of this chapter—almost two-thirds of adults in the United States are overweight including one-third of the adult population that is clinically obese. Being too heavy sets the stage for a number of other health problems, which helps to explain why rates of heart disease (the leading cause of death in this country) and diabetes have increased by more than 50 percent in the last ten years (Hoyert & Xu, 2012; CDC, 2014).

Low-Income Nations

Worldwide, according to the World Health Organization (2008), 1 billion people—one person in six—suffer from serious illness because they are poor. From another angle, while poverty is the cause of less than 10 percent of illness in rich nations, it causes about 70 percent of illness in poor countries (Institute for Health Metrics and Evaluation, 2013). Poor nutrition is one important factor that leaves low-income people—especially children—vulnerable to disease. Another is the lack of safe drinking water, which exposes poor people to disease-causing microorganisms.

The consequences of such conditions for human health are easy to see. Global Map 9–1 also shows that infant mortality rates in poor countries are far higher than they are in rich countries such as the United States. For example, the poor African nation of Sierra Leone has an infant mortality rate of 128, which means that more than one child in ten dies before the child's first birthday (Population Reference Bureau, 2013).

Life expectancy in poor countries is low by U.S. standards. In Sierra Leone, as in other extremely poor nations, disease brought on by poor nutrition and unsafe drinking water claims the lives of as many as one-fourth of all children before they reach age ten. Such high death rates among children hold down Sierra Leone's overall life expectancy to fifty-seven years (Population Reference Bureau, 2013; United Nations, 2013). In middle-income countries, such as Peru or India, people can

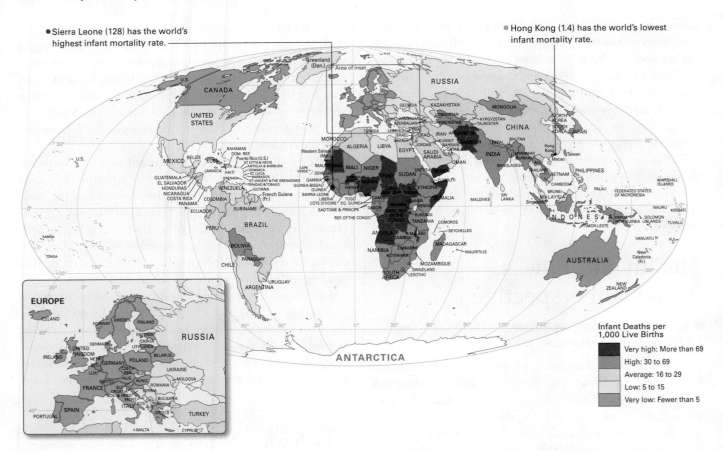

Sierra Leone (128) has the world's highest infant mortality rate.

Hong Kong (1.4) has the world's lowest infant mortality rate.

Infant Deaths per 1,000 Live Births
- Very high: More than 69
- High: 30 to 69
- Average: 16 to 29
- Low: 5 to 15
- Very low: Fewer than 5

Window on the World

Global Map 9–1 Infant Mortality in Global Perspective

A good measure of health for any nation is the rate of infant mortality: death in the first year of life. In rich nations, infant deaths are generally less than 10 per 1,000 live births. In poor nations, by contrast, infant mortality is high, with rates exceeding 100 in four African countries.

SOURCE: Population Reference Bureau (2013).

expect to live to their mid-sixties or early seventies. In rich nations, however, people live more than a decade longer.

Living standards shape not only when but how people die. How people die also reflects their standard of living. In rich nations, people typically die in old age of chronic conditions such as heart disease, cancer, or Alzheimer's disease. By contrast, in poor nations, people typically die at any time in the life course from an **acute disease**, *an illness that strikes suddenly.* Acute illnesses include various infectious and parasitic diseases such as Ebola, malaria, cholera, typhoid, measles, and diarrhea. Acute diseases were leading killers in the United States more than a century ago but rarely cause death today.

Rich and Poor Compared: The AIDS Epidemic

Investigating patterns of health is the work of **social epidemiology**, *the study of how health and disease are distributed*

throughout a society's population. Epidemiologists study the origin and spread of diseases, noting how the social environment shapes people's health.

The work of epidemiologists is especially important when a society experiences an **epidemic**, *the rapid spreading of a disease through a population.* Epidemics, from the plagues of medieval Europe to recent outbreaks of bird flu and swine flu, threaten the health of millions of people. Sometimes an epidemic is called a *pandemic* because, in an age of globalization, a disease can rapidly spread from one part of the world to another.

The most deadly pandemic is acquired immune deficiency syndrome (AIDS), which is discussed in Chapter 7 ("Sexuality"). First identified in 1981, AIDS is an incurable, deadly disease transmitted through bodily fluids, including blood, semen, vaginal secretions, and breast milk. We can illustrate the link between wealth and health by tracking the progression of AIDS, first in global perspective and then within the population of the United States.

AIDS: The Global View Global Map 7–1 on page 220, mapping the global distribution of roughly 35 million cases of HIV infection, shows that they are concentrated in low-income nations. Africa, the world's poorest continent, has 15 percent of the world's people but is home to 71 percent of the world's HIV-positive people.

Over the past decade, Presidents Clinton, Bush, and Obama have all declared AIDS to be a threat to the political and economic future of many African nations. About one-third of the world's people living with HIV reside in ten nations in southern Africa, and about one-third of new infections occur there. The AIDS epidemic has already wiped out 20 million people in Africa, dramatically dropping life expectancy in much of central and southern Africa to about fifty years. This epidemic has shattered these societies, overwhelming medical facilities, destroying families, and leaving huge numbers of orphaned children. The good news is that the number of new infections has been falling, with about 2.3 million reported in 2012 (down from 3.5 million a decade before). This decline reflects successful efforts to reduce transmission of HIV. In addition, the number of people living with HIV has increased to more than 30 million, as treatments are now available to more people with the disease who are living longer (Population Reference Bureau, 2013; UNAIDS, 2013).

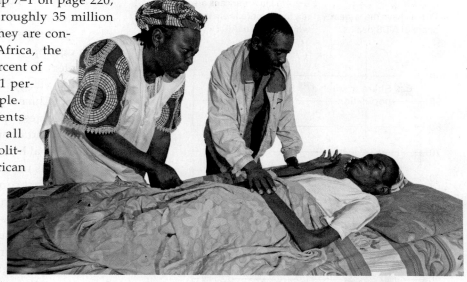

More than two-thirds of all people in the world who are infected with HIV live on the African continent. The epicenter of the global AIDs epidemic is sub-Saharan Africa, where life expectancy has fallen to as little as fifty-six years. In this region, medical facilities cannot cope with the crisis and families are left to do what they can. The only bright spot in this grim story is that the share of people receiving advanced medical treatment has been steadily increasing.

Why are many of the world's poorest nations so hard hit by AIDS? As already noted, poor people often have weakened health, so they are less resistant to infection. In addition, poor countries have few resources for education and prevention programs (say, to provide condoms and teach people the importance of using them). But cultural patterns—especially those involving gender—also have an impact. The Social Problems in Global Perspective box on page 271 takes a closer look at the problem of AIDS in Central Africa.

AIDS in the United States The AIDS epidemic is far less serious in the United States than it is in nations of southern Africa. The United States accounts for just 3 percent of the world's cases. Still, the government recorded 15,529 deaths due to AIDS in 2010. The total number of people who have contracted AIDS has reached 1,155,792 and, of these, 636,048 have died (CDC, 2013).

But a death toll exceeding half a million makes AIDS a deadly serious social problem. AIDS education programs, which have expanded since 1987, have reduced the incidence of high-risk sex, which includes behavior such as having multiple sex partners and having sex without using a condom. At the same time, health officials express concern that a new generation of young people may not take this deadly threat seriously. The Obama administration has asked Congress to spend about $30 billion annually to fight AIDS, including $23 billion at home and $7 billion around the world (Kaiser Family Foundation, 2014). Although researchers have yet to produce a cure for this deadly disease, they have developed drug treatments that delay the onset of full-blown AIDS among many people infected with HIV.

In the United States, as around the world, AIDS is primarily a disease of poor people. As Figure 9–1 on page 270 shows, African Americans and Hispanics, who together represent 30 percent of the U.S. population, account for 56 percent of all AIDS deaths. From another angle, non-Hispanic African Americans are ten times more likely than non-Hispanic whites to become infected; Latinos are three times as likely. Because of the higher poverty rates among African Americans and Hispanics, fewer people in these categories who become infected receive treatment, which can cost up to $100,000 a year. Predictably, the death toll among minorities is consequently also higher. A recent program, AIDS Drug Assistance Programs (ADAPs), provides HIV prescription drugs and other treatments to low-income people without sufficient insurance coverage (CDC, 2013; Kaiser Family Foundation, 2014).

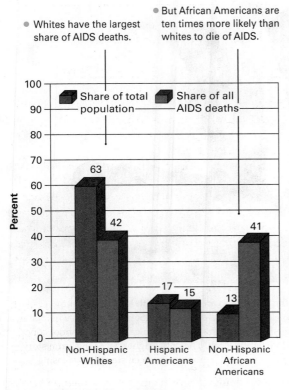

- Whites have the largest share of AIDS deaths.
- But African Americans are ten times more likely than whites to die of AIDS.

Diversity Snapshot

Figure 9–1 Deaths from AIDS in the United States

Death from AIDS among minorities is higher than population share would lead us to expect. Taken together, Hispanics and African Americans account for 30 percent of the U.S. population but 56 percent of all AIDS deaths.

SOURCE: Centers for Disease Control and Prevention (2013).

Health Policy: Paying for Care

9.2 Describe how nations around the world pay the costs of health care.

The expenses of health care can easily exceed what most people can afford. What policies should societies use to help cover the costs? Should a person's ability to pay determine the quality of health care available? The answers to these questions reflect a nation's political and economic systems.

Socialist Systems

In societies with *socialist economies*, the government controls most economic activity. This means that government agencies provide medical services and operate hospitals and clinics; doctors and other medical professionals are state employees who receive salaries for their services. Examples of socialist systems are found in China and the Russian Federation.

The People's Republic of China China is a middle-income country in the process of industrializing and is home to more than 1.4 billion people. In China, the government administers health care, operating hospitals and clinics in large population centers. In addition, China's famed "barefoot doctors" visit rural villages, providing basic health care to tens of millions of Chinese peasants.

The Chinese approach blends modern scientific medicine with traditional healing arts, including acupuncture and medicinal herbs. In most regions, China's traditional sexual norms remain strong, which has been a huge benefit to this vast country (especially inland regions away from large cities on the coast). Although China has so far escaped the AIDS epidemic that has ravaged other Asian nations to the south, China's medical establishment is facing the mounting costs of dealing with illnesses related to smoking: 53 percent of Chinese men (but only 2 percent of Chinese women) smoke, which takes its toll in high rates of cancer and heart disease (World Health Organization, 2013).

The Russian Federation Before the collapse of the Soviet Union in 1991, that nation had a government-controlled system of health care. Since then, the new Russian Federation—the largest of the former Soviet republics—has rebalanced its formerly government-controlled, socialist economy with a larger market-based system. Yet health care is still mostly under government control, so as is the case in China, people go to government-run clinics for treatment.

One consequence of state control is that physicians are paid much less for their work than their counterparts in the United States; many doctors in the Russian Federation earn only slightly more than skilled factory workers. Also worth noting is the fact that about 72 percent of the Russian Federation's doctors are women, compared with 34 percent in the United States.

Economic decline during the 1990s meant a sharp drop in the health of the Russian population. There has been a rebound in the past few years, but life expectancy remains about where it was back in 1990. The economic decline further strained a bureaucratic system that has long provided standardized and impersonal care. Perhaps, as market reforms proceed, living standards will rise and improve the quality of medical services. For the moment, however, health and health care in the Russian Federation are serious problems (Zuckerman, 2006; Population Reference Bureau, 2013; U.S. Census Bureau, 2014).

Capitalist Systems

Societies with mostly *capitalist economies* distribute health care—like other goods and services—through a market system. In practice, this means that individuals purchase

SOCIAL PROBLEMS IN GLOBAL PERSPECTIVE
The Social Roots of AIDS: Poverty, Culture, and Gender

Brigitte Syamaleuwe is a forty-year-old woman living in the African nation of Zambia. Several years ago, her life changed when she learned that she was HIV-positive. Like anyone else, her first question was, how could this have happened? Brigitte had never had sex with anyone but her husband, so she quickly came to the conclusion that it was he who had infected her.

Angrily, she confronted him. He was visibly shaken, but he reacted by accusing *her* of infidelity. Only after several weeks was he willing to admit that he had been unfaithful. He had become infected with HIV, and then, before he knew about his own infection, he infected his wife. The couple decided to devote the remainder of their lives to educating others about the dangers of HIV.

The United Nations states that reducing gender stratification is one key to reducing the spread of HIV and AIDS. As explained in Chapter 4 ("Gender Inequality"), low-income countries are typically strongly patriarchal. Women in these nations have little say in what their husbands or boyfriends do. Many men have traditionally seen little wrong with having extramarital sex, often with prostitutes, even though they now know that this behavior places them, their wives, and perhaps other women at high risk for infection with HIV.

Another factor that contributes to the AIDS epidemic in Africa and elsewhere is that many men—sometimes even men who know they are infected with HIV—do not use condoms when they have sex. Some women may not insist that men use condoms, either because they don't know that their partners are being unfaithful or because the men threaten violence if they don't get their way.

To make matters worse, traditional laws make it easy for men to divorce their wives for being unfaithful, but women have a hard time doing the same thing. Even when divorce is available, women think twice about it because a court often ends up giving men control over family property. For women, in short, divorce often means falling into poverty.

In poor countries, HIV infection usually results in death within several years. In the United States, well-off people with HIV now rely on expensive drugs to prolong their lives for a decade or more. These drugs are becoming less expensive and treatment is more widely available in poor countries. In sub-Saharan Africa, about 68 percent of people with HIV now receive some treatment. But in some nations, including Madagascar, Sierra Leone, and Mauritius, large majorities of people still go without the drugs that might extend their lives.

The larger answer to the problem of AIDS lies in research to discover a cure for this deadly disease. In addition, the death toll will come down faster to the extent that societies reduce patriarchy. Greater political and economic power would give women the ability to say no to sex, to insist on condom use, and even to demand that their men be faithful (UNAIDS, 2013).

What Do You Think?

1. How does the spread of AIDS in Africa, which has already claimed 20 million victims, confirm that health is a social as well as a medical problem?

2. Do you think education programs can change the ways men and women in high-risk countries think about sex? Explain.

3. What might rich nations such as the United States do to respond to the AIDS epidemic?

---

health care according to their particular needs and personal resources. But the high cost of health care can easily exceed the reach of even fairly well-off people, so capitalist nations such as Sweden, Great Britain, Canada, and Japan have additional strategies to help people cover the expense.

Sweden Although the Swedish economy is mostly market-based, for more than a century Sweden has taken a socialist approach by making health care a basic right for all citizens. The country raises money to fund its government-run health care system by taxation, making Swedish taxes among the highest in the world. Most physicians are government employees who receive salaries rather than collecting fees directly from patients or insurance companies. Government officials also manage most of the country's hospitals.

Because this system resembles that found in socialist countries, it is often called **socialized medicine**, *a medical care system in which the government owns and operates most medical facilities and employs most physicians*. How well does this system perform? The United Nations calculates a life expectancy index for world nations, which is a good measure of the overall health of a population. As Figure 9–2 on page 272 shows, the level of health in Sweden is high, and all Swedes receive much the same quality of care.

Great Britain Since 1948, Great Britain, too, has had a system of socialized medicine. However, the British did not do away with private care; rather, they created a dual system with government and a market-based system operating side by side. The government's National Health Service, funded by tax money, provides care to all British citizens and pays for a physician's services, hospital stays, and prescription drugs. At the same time, people who are able may pay for the services of private doctors and hospitals. Many British doctors work both sides of the system, splitting their time between the National Health Service and private practice.

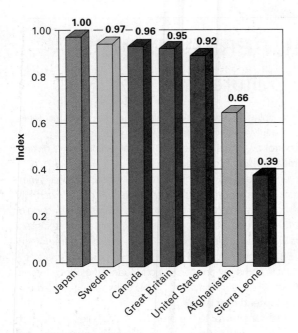

Global Snapshot

Figure 9–2   Life Expectancy Index for Selected Countries

Life expectancy in the United States is greater than what is typical of lower-income nations but less than that found in many other high-income nations.

SOURCE: United Nations Development Programme (2013).

The British system does a fairly good job of providing basic care to everyone. However, because only some people can afford the best private care, the British system is marked by a measure of inequality.

Canada   In Canada, the government has a major part in health care, but it does not control health care directly, as in Sweden or Britain. In Canada, the government operates rather like a large insurance company. In this "single-payer" system, the government sets fees and pays physicians and hospitals, with the funding coming from taxes. Like Great Britain, however, Canada permits doctors to work outside the government-funded system, setting their own fees for patients who can purchase care privately.

Figure 9–2 shows that public health in Canada is very good. The Canadian system also provides care at a lower cost than the U.S. system. Supporters applaud Canada's success in holding the line on doctors' fees and hospital costs. Critics, however, note that the lower costs reflect the fact that Canada uses less high-technology medicine. In addition, a shortage of practitioners means that people sometimes have to wait for care, especially in cases of major surgery.

In short, Canada may not match the United States in providing the most cutting-edge procedures to some of its people, but it outperforms the United States in providing

basic care to most of them (United Nations Development Programme, 2013; Macionis & Gerber, 2014).

Japan   Physicians and hospitals in Japan operate privately in a market system. At the same time, a combination of government programs and private health insurance pays most medical costs. Figure 9–2 shows that the Japanese people, with the highest life expectancy in the world, enjoy excellent health.

A look at Figure 9–3 shows that Japan and the other countries we have surveyed tax the population to distribute the cost of most health care over the entire population, with people who earn more paying more in taxes. But one high-income nation stands out from the rest: the United States, which does provide government support but treats medical care mostly as a product to be purchased on the open market.

Health Care in the United States: A System in Crisis?

9.3   Evaluate the performance of the health care system in the United States.

Probably future historians will look back on the Obama administration and point to the 2010 health care reform as its boldest domestic policy initiative. Why did that administration decide to focus on health care in this way? One reason is that this country ranks below most other high-income nations when it comes to the health of the overall population. A second reason is that the United States spends more money per person for health care than any other country in the world. A third reason is that health is unequally distributed, reflecting economic inequality.

Where do you think the United States ranks in life expectancy for its people? Global comparisons show that the nation ranks only thirty-eighth (United Nations Development Programme, 2013). This places the United States below not only Canada and almost every country in Western Europe but also behind a number of less-well-off nations, from Cuba and Costa Rica in Latin America to Singapore in Asia. In addition, despite our country's unmatched wealth, the United States barely breaks into the top fifty (with a ranking of 50th) in terms of infant mortality.

The U.S. health care system offers the best treatment in the world for people who can pay for it. But it does far less for the poor. What accounts for this mixed picture? The United States is the only high-income nation to rely primarily on a **direct-fee system**, *a medical care system in which patients or their insurers pay directly for the services of physicians and hospitals*. This means that people can obtain only the health care they can afford, with some having access to far better care than others.

According to some critics (typically, on the political left), the U.S. health care system is in a state of crisis. Two of the most pressing issues are soaring costs and limited access to health care.

The Cost Problem

The cost of medical care in this country has soared in recent decades, from about $12 billion in 1950 to more than $2.8 trillion in 2012. The U.S. population has doubled in size since 1950, but spending on health care has increased more than 230 times. Why has medical care become so expensive? There are six main reasons:

1. **The spread of private insurance.** Before World War II, most people in the United States paid for medical care out of their own pockets, so they went to doctors and hospitals only when they had to. During World War II, companies began to offer health insurance to employees, partly as a way to attract new workers because wages were frozen by the government. After the war, in the 1950s and 1960s, the system of private insurance grew rapidly. More insurance meant that people received more medical care, but it also gave most people little reason to question the cost of prescription drugs, office visits, and hospital stays. Under these conditions, doctors and hospitals faced little resistance to pushing prices upward (P. Starr, 1982).

2. **More doctors who specialize.** With the expansion of medical knowledge and advances in scientific technology, more doctors specialize in limited areas of medicine, such as internal medicine, cancer treatment, or cosmetic surgery. Specialists command higher fees, typically twice what a general practitioner earns. In a world of specialists, many patients see several physicians to treat a single problem and pay them all. Not surprisingly, the average income of physicians in the United States is high, ranging from about $175,000 for pediatricians to $400,000 for orthopedic surgeons. These figures have roughly doubled since 1990 (Medscape, 2013).

3. **More high technology.** Our medical system is technology driven. Medical personnel use high-tech medical treatments, such as computed axial tomography (CAT) scans to create images of internal organs and angioplasty to open clogged arteries. The medical establishment credits advanced technologies for most of the rise in health care spending since 1950.

   By contrast, both doctors and patients often overlook the value of everyday practices that promote good health, including changes in diet and exercise. This type of prevention costs little and is extremely effective in improving and maintaining well-being (Blank, 1997; Andrews, 2009).

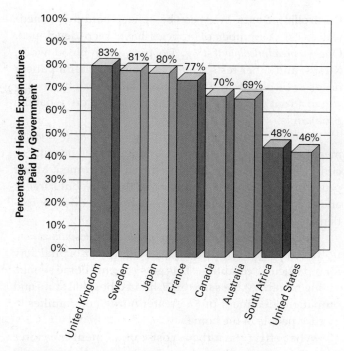

Global Snapshot

Figure 9–3 Extent of Socialized Medicine in Selected Countries

Compared with other high-income nations, government funding in the United States accounts for a far smaller share of health costs.

SOURCE: World Bank (2014).

4. **A lack of preventive care.** Many people, especially those with limited income, see doctors only when they face a medical crisis. People who go without preventive care, such as getting medication to control high blood pressure, often end up with a serious problem such as a stroke, which then requires a long and expensive hospital stay.

5. **An aging population.** As Chapter 5 ("Aging and Inequality") explains, the average age in the United States is increasing. As the baby boomers—more than 75 million people born between 1945 and 1964—enter old age, they spend more on health. This large age cohort is pushing medical spending ever higher.

6. **More lawsuits.** Many of us seem to believe that when accident or illness strikes, doctors and hospitals can always provide a cure. When treatment fails, patients or their families are likely to feel victimized and file a lawsuit, a trend that has driven up the cost of malpractice insurance, which doctors and hospitals pass along to patients. The fear of lawsuits raises costs in another way, too: Doctors who worry about being sued may order unnecessary tests and procedures just to protect themselves, a strategy called *defensive medicine* (Birenbaum, 1995).

Controlling Costs What can be done to hold down medical costs? A number of policies have been developed. One is *preadmission testing*. Doctors order blood work, X-rays, and other tests *before* deciding whether a patient needs to be admitted to a hospital. There may be no reason to admit people to a hospital just to find out what the problem is.

A second policy is performing *outpatient treatment*, meaning that the patient enters and leaves the hospital or clinic on the same day the procedure is performed. Minor procedures are routinely handled in this way, but surgery and cancer treatments can also be performed on an outpatient basis.

A third practice is *regulating the length of hospitalization*. In this case, insurance companies limit the hospital stay for a particular condition. This gets patients home sooner, saving money. At the same time, limited hospital stays and outpatient treatment put a greater burden on families to care for people in the home.

What effect have these cost-containment measures had? Going by numbers alone, they have probably slowed the increase in costs. But they have not brought about any reduction in this country's spending on medical care, which continues to rise every year.

Who Pays?

Every year, more than 35 million people in the United States enter the hospital and an average stay is five days. The overall bill for this care exceeds $880 billion. On a per-person basis, this hospital care is about $25,000, plus several thousand more in doctors' fees (CDC, 2013; Centers for Medicare and Medicaid Services, 2013). Clearly, such medical costs are a financial burden few families can easily afford. Who ends up paying the bills?

In the United States, people are responsible for most of their own medical expenses. To cover the costs, most rely on various types of health insurance.

Private Insurance Programs Private insurance companies, such as Blue Cross Blue Shield, sell policies to individuals and groups, usually through an employer. In 2012, some 199 million people (64 percent of the population) were covered by a private health insurance policy. Of that number, 86 percent received health insurance through an employer (their own or that of a family member); the remaining 14 percent bought policies on their own (U.S. Census Bureau, 2013).

Most employers require that people pay a share of the insurance premium. In addition, when people file claims, insurance companies rarely cover the entire bill. In recent years, the typical deductible has been increasing so that private insurance reduces but does not eliminate the financial burden caused by a serious accident or illness.

Health Maintenance Organizations Health maintenance organizations (HMOs) are *private insurance organizations that provide medical care to subscribers for a fixed fee*. In an effort to control costs, HMOs focus on disease prevention; they pay for weight-loss classes, immunizations, and treatments to help people quit smoking. But HMOs also limit patients' choices. As a type of *managed care*, HMOs require patients to choose medical care providers from a list of participating professionals, which often forces people to use doctors they do not know. In addition, nonemergency care must be preapproved by a *primary care physician*, who diagnoses the patient, provides some treatment, and makes referrals to specialists.

In short, HMOs try to keep costs down through managed care—that is, by controlling the treatment process. In some cases, HMOs will not pay for a treatment at all. For this reason, HMOs have become controversial.

Some 74 million individuals (24 percent of the U.S. population) are enrolled in HMOs (Kaiser Family Foundation, 2014). Most have mixed feelings about their health plan, worrying that they will be denied needed treatment, and many fear that their doctors will select a course of treatment based on what the HMO will cover rather than what they really need. Many physicians confirm that HMO rules sometimes deny patients needed treatment. Such concerns have led some states to enact a patients' "bill of rights" that requires a health care provider to pay for a minimum level of care and to disclose all its policies regarding payment to consumers.

Thus the success of HMOs comes at a price. But many employers favor HMOs because they typically cost less than traditional private insurance programs.

Government Insurance Programs In the United States, the federal government pays much of the health costs for some categories of the population. In 1965, Congress enacted tax-funded programs that pay part of the medical costs for the elderly or people with a disability (Medicare) and the poor (Medicaid). Overall, government insurance pays half of this country's medical bills.

Medicare is part of the Social Security system and serves people aged sixty-five or older as well as people of all ages who are totally and permanently disabled. In 2012, almost 49 million people (15.7 percent of the population) were enrolled in Medicare; more than 80 percent of these people were seniors over age sixty-five.

Medicaid serves poor people with special needs, including people who are blind, permanently disabled, pregnant, or aged or who live in families with dependent children. In 2012, some 51 million people (16 percent of the population) were enrolled in Medicaid. In addition, the nation's 14 million veterans (4 percent of the population) can obtain free care in government-operated hospitals (U.S. Census Bureau, 2013).

In all, 32.6 percent of U.S. citizens receive medical benefits from the government. Yet these programs provide only limited benefits (half of all medical expenses), which is why many people who are covered (especially by Medicare) purchase additional medical insurance from private companies.

The Coverage Problem

Even with medical insurance, many people are unable to pay all the costs of treating a serious accident or illness. But that's only part of the problem. More serious still is the fact that 48 million people—about 15 percent of the U.S. population—have no medical coverage at all.

One reason for the large population without insurance is that companies have been cutting back on benefits provided to workers. Several decades ago, most jobs in the United States offered vacation pay, sick leave, a retirement program, and health insurance. Today, fewer jobs offer all these benefits, and many jobs offer none at all. This trend leaves many workers to fend for themselves.

The larger question is whether the United States should remain the only high-income country in the world without a universal health care program. In 1994, the Clinton administration proposed a sweeping program of health care reform by which the government would ensure that everyone had medical insurance. The Clinton "managed competition" plan required employers to provide coverage to employees; employers could bargain with various providers to get the best plan. People not covered in this way (including those out of work) would be given insurance directly by the government.

Congress rejected the Clinton reforms, concluding that they would push medical spending even higher than it was already. In addition, critics objected to taking health from the control of patients and doctors and placing it under the control of a new government bureaucracy.

Fourteen years later, however, President Barack Obama was elected with the goal of extending health care coverage to everyone, and his efforts led to the 2010 Health Care Law.

The 2010 Health Care Law

In 2010, Congress enacted a law that significantly changed the way this country pays for health care. The act has a huge cost—estimated at almost $1 trillion by 2020—and change will take effect in stages.

Here is a summary of the major features of the new law, which was upheld by the U.S. Supreme Court in 2012:

1. All families now pay an insurance tax. Lower-income families, however, will receive subsidies to help pay the cost of the insurance; high-income families will pay higher taxes on their income to help fund the program.

2. Insurance companies are no longer permitted to drop existing customers because they get sick or legally refuse coverage to children because of preexisting conditions.

3. Insurance companies cannot limit the amount of money they will pay to any individual for medical expenses over a lifetime.

4. Parents can use their health care plans to include children up to the age of twenty-six.

5. Beginning in 2014, insurance companies will no longer be able to refuse coverage to anyone of any age due to preexisting health conditions.

6. Beginning in 2014, all families will be required to purchase insurance coverage. Government will regulate both the benefits available and the costs.

7. Beginning in 2014, people who do not buy insurance will be subject to penalties, which will increase over time.

Government estimates were that the new law would provide some insurance for about 32 million of the 48 million people in the United States who lack this protection. The rollout of the government health care plan late in 2013 was far from effective, with a poorly designed website that crashed under heavy user loads. In addition, millions of people had their coverage canceled by insurance companies that could not provide what the new law required at a reasonable price, and many more saw their premiums increase. Such experiences prompted half of adults to view the new law unfavorably, while one-third were favorable. By mid-2014, the number of people—especially young people—signing up for the new program was well below government projections. Nonetheless, the government remains firm in the belief that, with time, the Affordable Care Act, while falling short of the goal of universal health care coverage, will prove to be a major step forward (Drake, 2014).

Health: Class, Ethnicity, and Race

The health of affluent people in the United States is among the best in the world. But many poor people in this country are no better off than people who live in the world's low-income nations. For example, life expectancy among the Oglala Sioux Indians of South Dakota—among the poorest people in the United States—is just sixty-six years for women and fifty-six years for men. By contrast, life expectancy in the low-income Asian nation of Bangladesh is seventy-one years

How great a role should the federal government have in providing health care to people? The 2010 Affordable Care Act, commonly called Obamacare, expanded government's role by mandating what must be included in health care coverage. Some religious organizations, such as this one holding a rally in Washington, DC, have objected to being required to provide employees with contraception and abortion as part of their insurance. Do you think such organizations should be free to decide for themselves what coverage to provide or not provide? Why?

for women and sixty-nine years for men (Population Reference Bureau, 2013).

Chapter 2 ("Poverty and Wealth") pointed out that 46.5 million people in the United States—15 percent of the population—live below the poverty line. Most poor people cannot afford a healthful diet. Poor nutrition, in turn, leaves people (especially children) less able to fight off infectious diseases. But poverty harms health in other ways as well. Poor people are likely to live in a crowded and often unsafe environment marked by stress and violence. They may not have adequate heating and cooling, they may be exposed to poisoning from old, lead-based paint, and they suffer from a higher rate of accidents. National Map 9–1 presents life expectancy—a good indicator of overall health—for people across the United States.

Research confirms the strong connection between class position and health. When researchers asked people living in high-income families (those earning at least $100,000 annually) about their health, 78 percent reported it as "excellent" or "very good." By contrast, only 47 percent of low-income people (family income under $35,000) said the same (CDC, 2014).

This difference helps explain the fact that African Americans, who are almost three times as likely to be poor as white people, die an average of four years earlier than whites. Figure 9–4 on page 278 provides life expectancy data for black and white children born in 2011. Black males fare the worst of all these categories because not only is poverty a cause of poor health, but also being male puts these men at greater risk of violence. This fact helps explain

why the leading cause of death among African American men between the ages of fifteen and thirty-four is homicide (Heron, 2013). To get a better sense of how serious a health problem violence is in the African American community, note that in 2012 alone, 2,412 African Americans were killed by others of their own race—four times the number of black soldiers killed in the wars in Iraq and Afghanistan (U.S. Department of Justice, Federal Bureau of Investigation, 2013; U.S. Department of Defense, 2014).

The harmful effects of poverty begin early in life, often before birth. Because African Americans suffer from both higher poverty and higher unemployment, these families have less access to health insurance. One result is that African American women are twice as likely as white women to go without **prenatal care**, *health care for women during pregnancy*, and twice as likely to have low-birthweight infants, who are at high risk of dying soon after birth (Martin et al., 2013).

Racial bias plays a part in patterns of health even for African Americans who are not poor. For example, research shows that people of color often receive less thorough medical treatment than whites. One study, which focused on men who complained to doctors about chest pain, found that doctors were 40 percent less likely to order advanced tests for African Americans than for white patients among men who presented exactly the same symptoms. Such racial bias contributes to higher death rates (J. E. White, 1999a).

Health: The Importance of Gender

The numbers say that women have a health advantage over men: Figure 9–4 on page 278 shows that on average, women outlive men by at least five years. Notice that African American women—despite a much higher level of poverty—have a higher life expectancy than white men. Such facts highlight the importance of gender to human health.

One important factor is the way U.S. culture defines masculinity. Our society encourages men to be more individualistic and aggressive, placing them at higher risk of accidents, violence, and suicide. These facts help explain men's lower life expectancy.

But gender works against women too. Because women have lower social standing than men, women have often been ignored by medical researchers. For years, most research on heart disease, smoking, and the effects

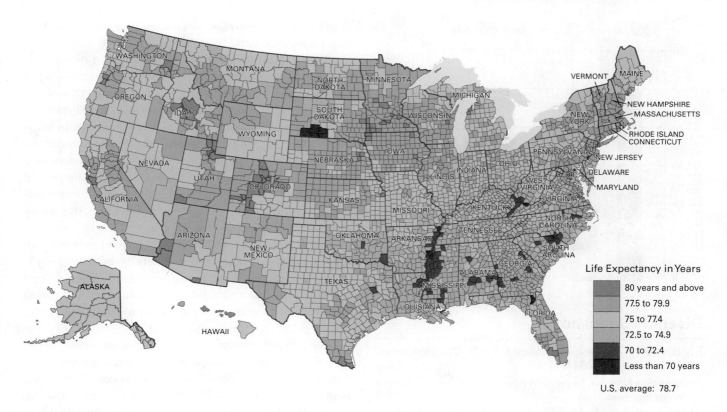

Life Expectancy in Years

- 80 years and above
- 77.5 to 79.9
- 75 to 77.4
- 72.5 to 74.9
- 70 to 72.4
- Less than 70 years

U.S. average: 78.7

Seeing Ourselves

National Map 9–1 Life Expectancy across the United States

How long people can expect to live is a good measure of the overall health of a population. Life expectancy, which varies from county to county throughout the United States, reflects factors such as nutritional diet and smoking habits. Looking at the map, what pattern do you see? Can you explain it?

SOURCE: U.S. Department of Health and Human Services (2009).

of medications was conducted only on male subjects. The result is that doctors know far less about the needs of women and how women respond to many treatments. This is why in 1990, the National Institutes of Health (NIH) created the Office of Research on Women's Health, a government agency that directs attention to women's health issues (Hafner-Eaton, 1994).

Gender stereotypes, even among modern scientists, distort medical treatment. Some critics claim that doctors turn normal life events, such as menopause, into medical "problems" that require long-term medication. In addition, they argue, women's health problems are sometimes not treated as aggressively as men's problems. For example, heart disease is the leading killer of U.S. women (Heron, 2013). According to the American Heart Association, however, doctors provide less care for women than for men with the same symptoms of heart disease.

Physicians also offer women less counseling about proper nutrition, exercise, and weight loss. Why? Perhaps because many doctors associate heart disease with men, they overlook potential problems in women. Perhaps part

of the reason for these patterns is that just 34 percent of physicians are women. But as the share continues to rise, doctors and hospitals should respond better to women's concerns (U.S. Department of Labor, 2013).

An Illustration: Eating Disorders A good illustration of the power of gender in shaping health involves eating disorders. In the United States, as many as 10 million people suffer from eating disorders, and about 90 percent of them are female (National Institute of Mental Health, 2014).

Experts estimate that about 2 percent of teenage girls suffer from *anorexia*, a form of compulsive dieting that leads people to eat too little to maintain a healthy body weight. Another 2 percent suffer from *bulimia*, a disease that involves binge–purge cycles of eating large amounts of food at one sitting and then purging by taking laxatives or inducing vomiting in order to avoid gaining weight (National Institute of Mental Health, 2014).

How is gender linked to eating disorders? The social roots of this disease lie in a culture that defines women's value in terms of physical attractiveness. In addition, girls

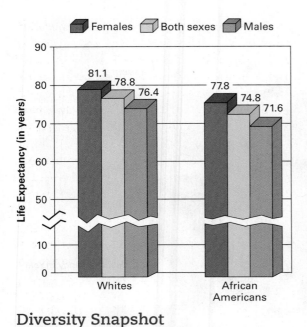

Diversity Snapshot

Figure 9–4   Life Expectancy for U.S. Children Born in 2011

On average, whites live longer than African Americans and women live longer than men.

SOURCE: Hoyert & Xu (2013).

grow up learning to judge their looks and assess their self-worth against an unrealistic, media-based image of thinness and beauty. Cultural beliefs run deep so that eating disorders can be difficult to cure and often end up causing serious health problems, including kidney damage, brittle bones, life-threatening infections, heart disease, and in extreme cases, death (Duffy, 1999; Lerner, 1999).

People with Disabilities

We have noted that people with lower social standing—women, minorities, and the poor—in the United States have greater health problems. Another category of the population that struggles with the health care system is people with any **disability**, *a physical or mental condition that limits everyday activities.*

To medical professionals, a disability is some impairment to the functioning of the mind or body. For sociologists, the question is how people construct the reality of a disability, that is, the meaning people attach to having a disability and how others react to them. Therefore, sociologists investigate how both the physical barriers of curbs and stairways, as well as the social barriers of prejudice and discrimination, affect the everyday lives of people with disabilities.

Sociologists note that physical disability often operates as a *master status*, meaning that other people may attach such importance to the disability that they overlook everything else that a person does and is. Thinking this way, people sometimes assume that those with physical disabilities must therefore have other limitations—such as low intelligence—and treat them accordingly.

Because there is no precise definition of disability, there is no exact count of people who are challenged in this way. One government tally estimates that about 4 percent of children, 10 percent of people aged eighteen to sixty-four, and 36 percent of the elderly suffer from some disability (U.S. Census Bureau, 2013). These numbers are increasing, in part because medical advances now save infants with birth defects who, several decades ago, might have died. The same is true for adults who suffer serious accidents and soldiers who are wounded in battle. Many more women and men who have lost a limb or sustained other serious injury now survive but have to contend with a permanent disability. More generally, because people in the United States are living longer, more people end up with a chronic and disabling condition, ranging from arthritis (inflammation of the joints) to Alzheimer's disease (loss of brain function).

Several generations ago, most people considered those with disabilities to be incapable of living normal lives. As a result, most people with disabilities were confined to their homes or even their beds. Today's more accepting attitudes are reflected in widespread use of barrier-free architecture—including wheelchair ramps, elevators, and bathrooms—that give everyone greater access to facilities, including schools and the workplace. In addition, new technology, ranging from motorized wheelchairs to computer-based communication systems, permits people with disabilities greater movement and ease of expression.

Like other dimensions of health, disability is linked to income. People with a severe disability have a poverty rate (22 percent) that is nearly twice the rate for people with no disability (13 percent) (U.S. Census Bureau, 2013).

Very thin fashion models are commonplace in the mass media. In the belief that these images increase the rate of eating disorders among young women, several European countries have recently banned such displays. Would you support similar restrictions here in the United States? Why or why not?

Disability Legislation In 1990, the disability rights movement, a political organization seeking to expand the rights and opportunities of people with disabilities, prompted Congress to pass the Americans with Disabilities Act (ADA). This law prohibits discrimination against people with disabilities in employment and public accommodations, including hotels, theaters, restaurants, and stores.

Proponents call the ADA the most important civil rights legislation since the 1964 Civil Rights Act, which banned discrimination based on race and sex. When President George H. W. Bush signed the bill into law, he expressed the hope that this act would make most public places accessible to people with disabilities. But two decades later, there is still work to do, as many people with disabilities have trouble riding a bus, attending school, watching a sports event, or even eating in a restaurant.

In 1997, the federal government expanded the definition of "disability" beyond physical problems to include a host of conditions from mental illness to learning disabilities to fear of open places. As a result, schools, colleges, and employers are engaged in debates about how to diagnose these disabilities and other conditions and what proper accommodations may be. In 2000, the U.S. Supreme Court narrowed the definition of a disability to exclude impairments that can be corrected or do not substantially limit everyday activities (Fujiura, 2001).

The Nursing Shortage

An additional problem facing the U.S. medical care system is a shortage of nurses. In 2013, there were 2.8 million registered nurses (people with an RN degree) in the United States. Currently, about 100,000 nursing positions remain unfilled, and projections indicate a need for more than 1 million new nurses by 2022 (U.S. Department of Health and Human Services, 2013; U.S. Department of Labor, 2013).

Why is there an increasing demand for nursing? Several factors are at work. First, technological advances in medicine mean that more illnesses can be treated, requiring more medical professionals to do the work. Second, there has been a rapid expansion in hospital outpatient services, such as same-day surgery, rehabilitation, and chemotherapy. Third, an increasing focus on preventative care, rather than simply treating disease or accidents, means that more people than ever are receiving care. Fourth, the passage of the Affordable Care Act should increase access to medical services for millions of additional people in the United States. Fifth, and most important of all, the population of the United States is aging and this means that people are consuming more and more medical services. For all these reasons, more people are coming to medical facilities, and more registered nurses (RNs) and advanced practice registered nurses (APRNs) are needed to provide care.

Since 2004, more than half a million people have begun careers in nursing and enrollments in nursing programs have increased each year. But the supply still falls short of demand. One reason is that nursing schools do not have as many teachers and classrooms as they need, which is one reason nursing programs turned away almost 80,000 qualified applicants in 2012. A broader reason for the nursing shortage is that women today have a wide range of job opportunities, and fewer are drawn to this traditionally female occupation. This fact is evident in the rising average age of working nurses, which is now forty-seven. In addition, many of today's nurses are unhappy with their working conditions, which typically involve heavy patient loads, required overtime, and a stressful working environment, sometimes coupled with a lack of recognition and respect from supervisors, physicians, and hospital managers.

Given the high demand for nurses, salaries are increasing. Currently, general-duty nurses earn about $65,000 a year, and many nurses with specialized skills (such as nurse-anesthetists and midwives) earn $100,000 a year or more. Many hospitals and private practice physicians offer hiring bonuses to nurses. In addition, nursing programs are trying to recruit a more diverse population, including more minorities (currently, about 25 percent of all nurses) as well

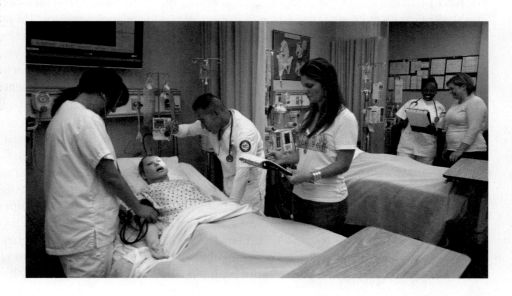

To address the shortage of nurses in the United States, hundreds of community colleges and four-year colleges now provide training in this important work. An increasing number of men as well as women are entering this field, which is expected to grow significantly during the next several decades.

as more men (just 9 percent of RNs) (U.S. Department of Health and Human Service, 2013; U.S. Department of Labor, 2013; American Association of Colleges of Nursing, 2014).

Mental Health and Illness

9.4 Summarize types of mental disorders as well as treatment strategies.

A **mental disorder** is *a condition involving thinking, mood, or behavior that causes distress and reduces a person's ability to function in everyday life* (U.S. Department of Health and Human Services, 1999:vii). The American Psychiatric Association recognizes more than 300 different mental disorders, including anxiety disorders, mood disorders, eating disorders, sleep disorders, personality disorders, disorders involving substance abuse, and mental retardation.

About 44 million adults (roughly one in five) suffer from a diagnosable mental illness in any given year, and nearly half of U.S. adults (100 million people) do so at some point in their lives. Most of these disorders are of minor importance and do not threaten a person's long-term well-being.

What about mental illnesses that are considered serious? Nearly 10 million U.S. adults (4 percent of the adult population) had a serious mental illness in 2012. Keep in mind that our society's lack of understanding concerning mental illness probably discourages many people who are suffering from a mental disorder from seeking treatment, so these estimates may well understate the extent of the problem (U.S. Department of Health and Human Services, 2013).

The experience of mental illness varies but may include extreme anxiety and fear, wild elation, mood swings, panic attacks, debilitating depression, or even hallucinations. Such symptoms are clearly troubling in themselves, but they also lead to other problems, including problems at work, strain in relationships, and even child neglect and outright violence.

For society as a whole, losses due to serious mental illness exceed $300 billion annually, mostly in terms of lost workplace productivity. The government estimates that the cost to our society of all mental illness exceeds that caused by all forms of cancer (U.S. Department of Health and Human Services, 2012).

As noted at the start of this chapter, mental illness sparks much confusion and fear. Why? Perhaps it is because some mental disorders prompt people to do the unexpected, which can frighten or disorient us. It is also true that we—doctors included—know much less about mental illness than about physical ailments. As a result, although we rarely stigmatize someone for having a broken leg or other physical ailment, people often do just that to those with mental disorders. We might label a person who experiences severe mood swings as "strange" or claim that someone who experiences hallucinations from time to time is "crazy." This type of stigma serves to socially isolate the person, which usually makes the problem worse.

Types of Mental Disorders

Effective treatment of any illness depends on accurate diagnosis. The most widely used classification of mental disorders, prepared by the American Psychiatric Association (2013), is the fifth edition of the *Diagnostic and Statistical Manual of Mental Disorders* (DSM-5). The DSM includes a wide range of disorders, as shown in Table 9–1.

As noted in the table, some mental disorders, such as those resulting from drug use, have an immediate cause. But most have many causes, both biological and social. In other words, all people are born with a relatively higher or lower risk of certain mental disorders, but social experiences beginning in childhood also play an important part in shaping everyone's mental health.

Mental Illness: A Myth?

Because mental disorders and their many causes are not well understood, the strongest critics claim that they are more a myth than real. The psychiatrist Thomas Szasz charges that people apply the label of "insanity" to behavior they find disturbing when in reality these patterns are only "different."

Consider a man who stands on a city street corner, shouting that God has told him that the end of the world is near. This action may be unusual, and if the man is jumping up and down, people standing nearby might even become a bit alarmed. But who is to say that the man is wrong? And whether he is right or not, is he mentally ill or just expressing deep religious convictions in an unusual way?

Szasz argues that we are quick to condemn as "crazy" behavior that fails to conform to what we would prefer. In this way, use of the label "mental illness" amounts to a form of social control. Therefore, Szasz concludes, we should abandon the whole idea of mental illness (1961, 1970, 1994, 1995). As he sees it, an illness is real only if it affects the body in a way we can see. In the absence of some physical abnormality, then, mental "illness" is simply a myth.

Szasz's claim is controversial, and most of his colleagues in the field of psychiatry reject the notion that mental illness is fiction. Still, many mental health professionals hail his work for pointing to the danger of using medicine to promote conformity. From time to time, just about everyone behaves in ways that disturb other people. But does this give others the right to force us to change? In addition, responding to "difference" with medical labels that stigmatize a person can do a great deal of harm—in the extreme, by defining those who are different as dangerous or less than fully human.

Table 9–1 Categories of Mental Disorders Listed in the *Diagnostic and Statistical Manual of Mental Disorders*

Disorders usually first diagnosed in infancy, childhood, or adolescence	Mental retardation, attention deficit hyperactivity disorder, dyslexia, stuttering, autism, Tourette syndrome, and bed-wetting
Cognitive disorders	Delirium and dementia: major changes in memory or the ability to think clearly, caused by brain damage or substance abuse
Mental disorders due to a medical condition that are not included in other categories	Symptoms such as delirium, dementia, amnesia, and sexual dysfunction that are a direct result of another medical condition
Substance-related disorders	Disorders such as intoxication, addiction, and withdrawal resulting from the use of alcohol or other drugs, such as heroin, cocaine, and amphetamines
Schizophrenia and other psychotic disorders	Disorders characterized by extreme paranoia, delusions, and hallucinations
Mood disorders	Major depression and bipolar disorder (manic depression)
Anxiety disorders	Obsessive-compulsive disorder and disorders characterized by extreme anxiety, panic, or phobia
Somatoform disorders	Disorders that manifest themselves as symptoms of physical disease, such as pain of an unidentifiable origin or hypochondria
Dissociative disorders	Disorders that involve a splitting or dissociation of normal consciousness, such as amnesia or multiple personality
Eating or sleeping disorders	Anorexia, bulimia, and insomnia
Sexual and gender identity disorders	An absence of sexual desire, the inability to function sexually, masochism, sadism, and gender identity disorders such as gender dysphoria (discontent)
Impulse control disorders	Disorders that manifest themselves in symptoms such as kleptomania (theft), pyromania (setting fires), and pathological gambling
Personality disorders	Chronic, inflexible, and maladaptive personality traits that are resistant to treatment, such as excessive dependency, paranoia, and narcissism (the need for constant admiration and a lack of empathy)

SOURCE: American Psychiatric Association (2000, 2013).

Mental Illness: Class, Race, and Gender

The pattern found throughout this chapter—that disadvantaged categories of people are more likely to suffer from illness—applies to mental as well as physical health. We now offer a closer look at patterns of mental health linked to class, race, and gender.

Mental Health and Class An early study documenting the link between class position and mental health dates to before World War II. Robert E. Faris and H. Warren Dunham (1939) identified 35,000 people living in Chicago who had received psychiatric care from private and public mental institutions and found that most of the people with serious disorders lived in the worst slums. This link between poverty and mental illness has been confirmed again and again by research since then, both in the United States and in other countries (Hollingshead & Redlich, 1958; Srole

et al., 1962; Rushing, 1969; Levy & Rowitz, 1973; Srole, 1975; Eaton, 1980; Ross, Mirowsky, & Cockerham, 1983; Wiersma et al., 1983; U.S. Department of Health and Human Services, SAMHSA, 2013).

We have all heard people call someone "crazy" for acting in a way that people find disturbing. Is such a label really an effort to discredit and control those who simply are different?

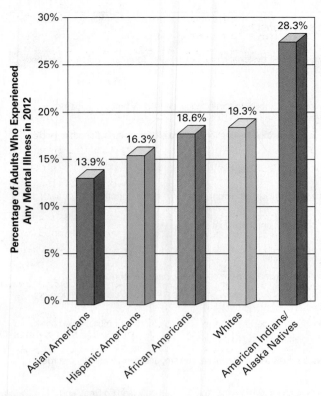

Diversity Snapshot

Figure 9–5 Patterns of Mental Health for Selected Racial and Ethnic Categories

For adults over the age of eighteen, the rates of reported mental illness in 2012 were slightly lower for African Americans and Hispanic Americans than for whites. Reports of any mental illness were made by a smaller share of Asian Americans and a larger share of American Indians and Alaskan Natives.

SOURCE: Based on U.S. Department of Health and Human Services (2013).

Poverty and mental illness are linked. But does poverty cause mental illness or is it the other way around? The truth cuts both ways. It is easy to see that mental illness reduces people's ability to earn a living. Faris and Dunham, however, documented the power of poverty to cause mental illness. Poverty breeds stress and social isolation, they explained, which in turn increases the risk of mental disorders. Research confirms that the isolation and stigma associated with being poor in the United States may be enough to harm the mental health of many people (Cockerham, 2007).

Mental Health, Race, and Ethnicity Sociologists have documented the lack of jobs that weakens many inner-city communities in the United States. People who struggle economically, often socially isolated by both low income and racial prejudice—in a society that claims to be color-blind—contend with high levels of stress and anxiety. This is the reality of life for many African Americans in the United States (W. J. Wilson, 1987; E. Anderson, 1994; Feagin & Hernán, 1995; Collins, 2009).

That said, it is important to notice that race and ethnicity *by themselves* do not seem to play a major part in patterns of mental health. Figure 9–5 shows the rates of any mental illness among adults of various racial and ethnic categories. As you can see, African Americans, Hispanic Americans, and non-Hispanic whites had about the same rate of mental illness in 2012. The exceptions to this pattern are American Indians and Alaskan Natives, with a higher level of mental illness, and Asian Americans, with a somewhat lower rate. Of course, the fact that major categories of our population showing similar rates of mental illness may reflect minorities being less likely to seek assistance for such conditions. But, for most of the U.S. population, it seems fair to conclude that, especially if we consider people of roughly the same social class position, race and ethnicity do not, in and of themselves, have a significant effect on levels of mental health (U.S. Department of Health and Human Services, 2013).

Treatment Strategies

During the Middle Ages, Europeans commonly viewed individuals who displayed symptoms of mental illness as possessed by demons or suffering punishment by God. Therefore, while a few mentally ill people were tolerated as "village idiots," many more were burned as witches (Cockerham, 2005).

By about 1600, a new strategy arose for dealing with mentally ill people: locking them away in prisons along with criminals and the poor. This era, sometimes called the Great Confinement, found people with mental disorders chained to walls or strapped into beds in dark, damp, rat-infested rooms, often without clothing or blankets, for years at a time (Foucault, 1965; Cockerham, 2005).

The Spread of the Asylum Reform came in the 1800s in large part because of the efforts of one woman, Dorothea Dix of the United States. Dix championed an alternative to what she saw as the punishment of people with mental illness. Rather than being shut away in prisons, she countered, people with mental illnesses should receive caring treatment. Such care should be provided in the *asylum*, a place of refuge for people in need. In practice, the asylum was an early version of today's mental hospital. Dix was successful in spreading the idea of asylums in the United States. Unfortunately, despite her success, the number of people who needed this kind of help far exceeded the capacity of the small number of available facilities. As a result, only a small share of people with mental illness received the humane care that Dix advocated. Most continued to be locked away in overcrowded prisons, out of sight and out of mind. The Defining Moment box takes a closer look at how Dix changed the way society viewed people with mental illness.

Psychotherapy The twentieth century saw the development of several new treatment strategies. One important advance was **psychotherapy,** *an approach to mental health in which patients talk with trained professionals to gain insight into the cause of their problems.* The famous psychologist Sigmund Freud (1856–1939) played an important part in the development of psychotherapy. Other practitioners helped develop psychotherapy in various directions since then and continue to do so today.

Medical Approaches Medical approaches to mental disorders also gained prominence during this time. One example is electroshock therapy, which was found to provide patients with temporary relief from severe depression. But the most important medical treatment was the development of *psychoactive drugs,* powerful substances that control symptoms of mental illness. In the 1950s, as these drugs came on the market, it was no longer necessary to confine people in institutions in order to control them.

Deinstitutionalization The development of psychoactive drugs prompted Congress, in 1963, to pass the Community Mental Health Centers Construction Act. This law mandated moving people out of big institutions and into communities where they could find outpatient treatment at local health centers. The law set off a stampede of **deinstitutionalization,** *the release of people from mental hospitals into local communities.* In just a few years, hundreds of thousands of men and women were released from mental hospitals based on claims that they could get by on their own as long as they took their drugs. But not everyone did take their drugs. In addition, not enough community health centers were built. Finally, little assistance was given to people with the greatest challenges—for example, those with bipolar disorder

CONSTRUCTING SOCIAL PROBLEMS

A DEFINING MOMENT

Dorothea Dix: Mentally Ill People Deserve Our Help

Dorothea Dix (1802–1887) was an extraordinary woman who made a difference. She began her career teaching at a girls' school and she rose to become head of the school. At that point in her life, Dix's attention turned to prisons.

She was shocked to learn that the prison population included not only criminals but also those with mental illness—people who were sick and had broken no law. Dix was deeply concerned about the uncaring treatment given to these innocent people. She pledged to change the way society viewed people with mental illness and devoted the remainder of her life to writing, speaking, and lobbying government officials on their behalf.

In 1840, when Dix began her crusade, the United States had only thirteen facilities that offered care to people with mental illness. Her efforts led twenty states to pass laws creating asylums where troubled people could find shelter and peace. By 1885, near the end of Dix's life, she could boast of 125 asylums in the United States.

Dix is remembered today as the person who opened people's hearts to those with mental illness. Rather than locking these people away, she showed society that people with illnesses need help and compassion, whether their illness affects the body or the mind.

For centuries, people with mental illness were locked up in prisons with dangerous criminals. Dorothea Dix pioneered the building of asylums, where such people could find protection and treatment. Unfortunately, many asylums were no more than warehouses that did little to improve the condition of those locked within.

and schizophrenia. The overall result was that, within a few years, many former patients ended up back in mental hospitals, in prison, or living on the streets (Roche, 2000; Fuller, 2013). The Personal Stories box describes an all-too-typical case.

Today, the government reports that 42 percent of people suffering from any mental illness and 63 percent of people with some serious mental disorder are receiving regular treatment (U.S. Department of Health and Human Services, 2013). Why is the percentage so low? Most communities still lack adequate mental health centers, and millions of people lack health insurance. In addition, many people who are struggling don't want to admit that they have a mental health problem.

In 1997, the federal government responded to this situation by expanding the Americans with Disabilities Act to include mental disorders. The law requires employers to make reasonable efforts to accommodate workers who suffer from depression, anxiety, or other mental disorders. Although assisting people in this way is not always easy, our society is now more successful in supporting people with mild mental illness.

Mental Illness on Campus

It is no surprise to college faculty that the number of students who suffer from mental health problems has been increasing. According to the American College Health Association (2013), 84 percent of U.S. college students admit to feeling overwhelmed from time to time, and 30 percent report that, at some time, they have been so depressed that they could not do their work. Across the country,

PERSONAL STORIES

Deinstitutionalization: When Good Intentions Have Bad Results

Martha Lester leans forward over the shopping cart that holds everything she owns. Evening has come to the cold Chicago street, and the fifty-nine-year-old woman pulls her coat tight against the wind, lowers her head, and pushes ahead into the gathering darkness. She is looking for a ventilation grate, where she can try to stay warm for the night without having to see anyone.

Martha Lester grew up in a working-class family in Illinois. Her parents worked hard and were often impatient with their daughter, who could be disruptive in school. Unable to discipline her, the parents turned to a doctor for help. Martha recalls telling the doctor that as long as she could remember, she had "heard voices." The doctor decided that Martha was mentally ill and diagnosed her problem as paranoid schizophrenia, with symptoms including paranoia, anxiety, and hallucinations.

Her parents and the doctor agreed that Martha should go to a large state mental hospital, where she spent the next five years. Every day, the staff gave her chlorpromazine, a powerful psychoactive drug, to calm her. Martha recalls that the chlorpromazine stopped her fears and ended the hallucinations. But she paid a price. As she puts it, "I felt like a zombie."

Then came the deinstitutionalization movement. Martha first learned about the new policy when a member of the hospital staff told all the patients that they would be released. Martha did not understand why, but she was glad when a social worker promised to help her find an apartment and apply for food stamps and government disability payments. The social worker promised to visit her every week.

Martha left the asylum with a supply of her new drugs. For a few years, things worked out pretty well. But then her social worker started missing visits, and Martha began to skip her medication. It didn't take long for the "voices" to come back,

which filled Martha with panic. Driven by fear, she left the apartment and ended up living on the street.

Martha spent her nights in an abandoned building or in a car. Within a week, she was arrested for stealing from a store. The court sent her back into the mental health care system, where she was assigned to a new social worker. She was given a new apartment and provided with a new supply of medication. But after several months, once again, she stopped taking the drugs. Then came a fight with her neighbors, which resulted in Martha being evicted from the apartment. And so the whole cycle has repeated itself, over and over.

Martha Lester's story shows us that policies formed with good intentions sometimes have unexpected bad consequences. Supporters of deinstitutionalization were hopeful that the new psychoactive drugs would bring an end to the need to confine people in mental hospitals, sometimes with the use of physical restraints. These drugs promised to allow people with mental illness to live normal lives in the community. But budget cuts and bureaucratic indifference left too many people to fend for themselves, and many of them could not handle life on their own. Some people have been helped, but others have become part of the problem of homelessness (Gagné, 1998).

What Do You Think?

1. Many people who are living on the streets or in prison suffer from mental illness. Do you think society owes these people something more? Explain.

2. What about people who may be mentally ill but do not want help from others? Do they have the right to live as they wish, even if it is on the street?

3. Can you think of other cases of social policy enacted with good intentions that ended up having bad consequences?

colleges are documenting a sharp rise in student demand for counseling.

Most serious is the problem of suicide. Researchers estimate that, in 2013, about 7 percent of students have thought seriously about suicide, and about 2 percent of students have attempted it, although the vast majority do not succeed (American College Health Association, 2013).

What accounts for the increase in mental health problems on campus? Everyone agrees that colleges themselves are not the main cause of the trend. More likely, we are seeing the effects of high rates of children living in poverty, rising pressures on today's young people, and low levels of parental involvement in children's lives. In addition, psychoactive drugs make it possible for more young people with mental health problems to attend college. Once on campus, however, they may not take their medications properly or they may find the demands of college work to be too great. Facing an increasing challenge, colleges are devoting more resources to providing health care for their students (Fujiura, 2001; Kelly, 2001; Shea, 2002).

Theories of Health and Illness

9.5 Apply sociological theory to issues involving physical and mental health.

Each of sociology's major theoretical approaches helps us to understand problems of physical and mental health. As you have seen in earlier chapters, each theoretical approach focuses on different aspects of the problem and provides important insights.

Structural-Functional Analysis: Health and Social Roles

Structural-functional theory views society as a complex system in which each individual takes on various social roles and completes important tasks. As individuals carry out their responsibilities, a society operates smoothly.

Illness interferes with people's ability to perform their roles as workers and as members of families. Consequently, when people are sidelined by illness, society allows them to assume the **sick role**, *a pattern of behavior expected of people defined as ill.* In practice, the sick role means that people are excused from carrying out routine, day-to-day duties and responsibilities. Unless there is some reason to think that people are to blame for an illness, explained Talcott Parsons (1951), society allows ill individuals to assume the sick role, which relieves them of most everyday obligations. At the same time, we expect the patient to try to get well by cooperating with medical personnel.

The sick role theory helps explain why some members of U.S. society feel little sympathy for people with mental disorders who are living on the streets. Some people think that living on the streets is evidence that individuals do not want help. Certainly sick people deserve help, but if it appears that they do not want treatment—and the public tends to conclude that living on the streets is evidence of that—then people deserve no special assistance. Of course, people may be on the streets because they have no money to pay for treatment; similarly, refusing to cooperate with medical personnel might be one symptom of a mental illness.

The structural-functional approach also explains that society's social institutions are linked, with change in one institution affecting other institutions. For example, families have changed so that more people are living alone and more single people are parents. These trends mean that people have less access to others who can provide daily support and caregiving, which can undermine health.

EVALUATE

Some illness is to be expected, and the sick role developed as a societal strategy to support people while they recover from illness. This strategy also encourages people who are ill to seek medical treatment.

However, taking on the sick role depends on a person's being able to afford to take time off from work and to seek medical care. Another limitation of the structural-functional approach is implying that doctors hold the key to good health. The trend toward emphasizing prevention rather than treatment after illness strikes highlights the fact that we can all make choices to improve our own health. For example, we promote health by eating a balanced diet, exercising regularly, and avoiding dangerous behavior such as smoking cigarettes or abusing alcohol and other drugs.

Finally, health is not a simple matter of being "sick" or staying "well." On the contrary, the reality of health is highly variable, a fact that brings us to the symbolic-interaction approach.

CHECK YOUR LEARNING What is the "sick role?" How is using the sick role a strategy for society to deal with illness? What is a limitation of structural-functional analysis of health and illness?

Symbolic-Interaction Analysis: The Meaning of Health

Symbolic-interaction theory highlights how people construct reality in their everyday lives. In low-income nations of the world, for example, poor people may consider inadequate nutrition and hunger to be a normal part of life. Although people living in high-income nations are generally healthier, they have become much more accepting of obesity. In the United States, 63 percent of adults are overweight (CDC, 2014). Obviously, what is considered "normal"—with regard to both physical and mental health—depends not only on medical fact but also on cultural standards that vary from place to place and from one point in history to another.

The variable reality of health and illness is also evident in the changing definitions used by medical professionals. For example, in the first half of the twentieth century, doctors defined homosexuality as a moral wrong, and the public followed their lead. In 1952, however, the first edition of the *Diagnostic and Statistical Manual of Mental Disorders* (DSM) defined homosexuality not in moral terms but as a "personality disorder," which redefined homosexuality as a form of mental illness. In 1974, the definition changed again when the DSM dropped homosexuality from its list of disorders. It is now considered simply one sexual orientation.

Finally, how people define any health situation may in fact affect how they feel physically. Doctors have long noted the existence of *psychosomatic* disorders, in which a person's state of mind affects the health of the body. When people believe they are sick or when they are convinced that they will get well, their belief often comes true.

EVALUATE

Because symbolic-interaction theory highlights the variable meanings people attach to health and illness, it tends to ignore structural factors such as social class position that play a major part in shaping the reality that people experience. Similarly, people tend to assign blame for poor health to people themselves, rather than asking why the U.S. medical care system does not provide more for poor people, or asking why tens of millions of people in the United States are poor in the first place. Such issues bring us to the social-conflict approach.

CHECK YOUR LEARNING   What insights do you gain from the symbolic-interaction analysis of health and illness? What is one limitation of this approach?

Social-Conflict Analysis: Health and Inequality

Social-conflict theory links health to inequality. A basic pattern, found everywhere in the world, is that having more wealth allows people to have better health. Social-conflict analysis points to ways in which social inequality shapes health and health care in the United States.

Perhaps the most basic issue is access to care. Because good health is necessary to be a productive member of society, everyone needs access to health care. Yet as this chapter has explained, the United States stands alone among rich nations as having no system to guarantee care to everyone. Researchers estimate that about one-third of U.S. adults struggle to pay the costs of medical care, and about 15 percent of the population lacks health insurance (Politz et al., 2014). In short, by linking care to the ability to pay, this country undermines the health of millions of people.

A second issue is that, in a capitalist economy, the medical system is based on profit. This fact goes a long way toward explaining why the United States overlooks the

health of the poor, who, by definition, have little money to pay for it. From this point of view, the profit motive ends up not only denying care to the poor but also corrupting medical practice for everyone. Doctors are always keenly aware of their financial interests when they make a diagnosis, decide on a treatment, or refer a patient to a hospital. Similarly, hospitals and insurance companies guide medical care with an eye on the bottom line, and pharmaceutical companies strive to convince doctors and the public as a whole that health depends not on how we live but on the pills we take (Pear & Eckholm, 1991; Cowley, 1995).

EVALUATE

Social-conflict theory reveals that the health of some people is better than that of others because of social inequality. Thus we can understand not only why people living in rich countries have relatively good health but also why the health of the poor in the United States is little better than that of people in many of the world's low-income nations.

With its focus on the failings of the U.S. health care system, the social-conflict approach overlooks the fact that the overall health of the U.S. population has improved dramatically over the course of the past century. Another criticism of this approach is that health care systems in countries with mostly socialist economies—presumably nations with less social inequality—do not perform all that well, typically because they provide little incentive for people to develop new treatments and technology.

CHECK YOUR LEARNING   What insights do you gain from the social-conflict analysis of health and illness? What is one limitation of this approach?

Feminist Analysis: Health and Gender

Feminist theory is an important dimension of social-conflict analysis that links patterns of health to gender inequality. As we have already explained, health is linked to wealth. Because women are disproportionately represented among the poor, women's risk of illness increases. In addition, as explained earlier in this chapter, women represent only 34 percent of physicians and medical research tends to focus on men more than women. As a result, medical professionals do not provide an equal level of care to women. Finally, eating disorders—a condition in which 90 percent of patients are females—illustrate the power of cultural standards of body shape and beauty to affect women's health.

What about mental health? Research shows that, over the course of their lifetimes, women and men have about the same rates of mental illness. However, some sociologists claim that members of our society are quicker to define women as mentally ill and they point to the fact that women are somewhat more likely than men to receive treatment for a mental illness. When women act in ways that appear to be "different," because they are a less powerful category of the population, women are at higher risk of having this

APPLYING THEORY
Physical and Mental Health

	Structural-Functional Theory	Symbolic-Interaction Theory	Social-Conflict Theory	Feminist Theory
What is the level of analysis?	Macro-level	Micro-level	Macro-level	Macro-level
What does the approach say about health and illness?	Structural-functional theory states that health is necessary for people to perform their daily roles. Illness threatens to disrupt the operation of a society by making the individual unable to carry out daily responsibilities.	Symbolic-interaction theory explains that the meaning of both health and illness varies from one setting to another, depending on what people define as normal.	Social-conflict theory links patterns of health and illness to social inequality. In general, people with more wealth have better health. Economic inequality is the major cause of poor health for millions of people.	Because women do not have equal social standing with men, they suffer from a number of health-related disadvantages. In addition, cultural standards of beauty and body shape contribute to eating disorders among young women.
How do we deal with illness as a social problem?	By allowing people to assume the sick role, society relieves people who are ill from daily responsibilities and encourages them to seek medical attention.	Because the reality of health and illness depends on situationally constructed meanings, illness (as well as health) is a social as well as a medical issue, which may or may not be defined as a social problem.	Under a capitalist economic system, the goal of the health care system is private profit rather than public well-being. To address the problem of illness, government would need to guarantee health care for all.	For our medical system to deal fairly with women, the social standing of women, in the medical profession and in society as a whole, must be equal to that of men.

difference labeled as deviant. Put another way, because men have more power, they have more freedom to behave as they wish without people calling their mental health into question. In addition, being relatively powerless means that women are more likely to worry about pleasing men. Perhaps this explains the fact that women have higher rates of anxiety and depression than men (Schur, 1984; Chesler, 1989; U.S. Department of Health and Human Services, 2013).

Feminist theorists also point out that traditionally masculine patterns of behavior carry risks of their own. U.S. culture defines "real men" as independent, tough, unemotional, and always in control. This cultural pattern subjects many males to stress and social isolation, both of which contribute to poor mental health. When men try to keep their troubles inside (as "real men" are taught to do), these problems are likely to become worse. Perhaps this is one reason that men have higher rates of aggression and substance abuse (Gupta, 1993; Kessler et al., 1994; U.S. Department of Health and Human Services, 2013).

EVALUATE

Feminist theory explains how gender shapes patterns of physical and mental health. Gender stratification plays a part in the health issues typically faced by women and men.

Feminists point out that women, as a subordinate category of our society's population, pay a price in terms of patterns of health. This is true, but we should remember that women's standing in our society has improved dramatically in recent decades. In addition, in one important dimension of health—life expectancy—women do considerably better than men.

CHECK YOUR LEARNING What insights about health do we gain from feminist theory? What is one limitation of this approach?

The Applying Theory table summarizes the contribution of each theoretical approach to our understanding of health and health care.

⭐ POLITICS AND HEALTH

Constructing Problems and Defining Solutions

9.6 Analyze physical and mental health issues from various positions on the political spectrum.

How well does the U.S. health care system perform? The answer depends on the politics of the person making the assessment. We turn now to how politics shapes what people across the political spectrum see as problems of health care and the solutions they propose.

Conservatives: Free Markets Provide the Best Care

Whatever the issue, be it housing or health care, conservatives favor the policy of allowing organizations, companies, and individuals to make choices and to compete freely in a market system. Choice means people can select their own doctors and choose their health care insurance. Competition encourages doctors, hospitals, and other health care providers to keep quality high and prices low giving more value to consumers. The opportunity for profit also means companies have the incentive to develop many new drugs, therapies, and technologies (Bartlett, 2000). Conservatives claim that the U.S.

free-market system offers the most advanced medical care in the world. Why else, they ask, do so many world leaders facing their own illnesses come to the United States for treatment?

Another conservative value that applies to health is the importance of individual responsibility. As conservatives see it, personal health reflects the choices we make about how to live. Making good choices helps to prevent disease before it happens. For example, choosing to avoid cigarettes reduces the risk of heart disease and cancer, just as choosing to eat healthy food in moderation goes a long way toward controlling one's weight and improving overall patterns of health. In the same way, choosing to have multiple sexual partners raises the risk of sexually transmitted diseases.

Given conservatives' support for free-market health care and their belief in taking personal responsibility for health, conservatives want only a limited role for government in this area. For the poorest people—especially the elderly or disabled—and for veterans who have served their country, the government should—and does—provide health care programs at little or no direct cost to patients.

People who are poor not only endure more illness but also "get old before their time." What do conservatives, liberals, and radicals support as solutions to the poor health of millions of people in the United States?

But, conservatives claim, to put government in charge for *everyone* is likely to do the same for health care as it has for public schools: reduce the quality of care and give people little choice about who provides the service. For this reason, conservatives point to loss of choice and rising costs as reasons for their opposition to the Affordable Care Act as well as the reasons for the low enrollment and lack of public support since this act took effect (Gingrich, 2009; Drake, 2014; Kesler, 2014).

Liberals: Government Must Ensure Universal Care

Liberals believe that a fair and just society should provide everyone with access to health care in a more or less equal way. As they see it, a market system serves the rich very well but does much less for average people and little for the poor. Liberals have long sought reform to the U.S. health care system because, even in 2014, 48 million people still lack adequate health insurance.

Most liberals accept the idea of doctors and hospitals operating for profit but they look to government to regulate the health care system and to ensure that everyone receives care. Liberals support the Affordable Care Act, with the idea that it will spread the cost of health insurance throughout the population so that lower-income people can also afford health insurance. Some liberals would like to see the government adopt an even larger role in the form of a single-payer system as in Canada or a national health care system similar to Great Britain's National Health Service.

Such a measure would certainly be expensive, at least in the short term, and it would limit people's choice. But liberals point to the long-term benefit of far better care for much of the population that is not well served now. If all pregnant women received prenatal care and all children had immunizations, regular checkups, and sound nutrition, this country's infant mortality rate would surely drop dramatically. Just as important, healthier people are more productive, leading to economic growth that, liberals claim, would offset much of the cost of this kind of program.

The Radical Left: Capitalism Is Unhealthy

As we might expect, the strongest criticism of the U.S. health care system comes from the radical left. From this point of view, the problem is the inequality in health care—both the gap between rich and poor in the United States and between the rich and poor nations of the world.

The cause of both of these patterns is capitalism. When health is considered to be a commodity to be purchased like automobiles rather defined as a basic need

LEFT TO RIGHT

The Politics of Health

	Radical-Left View	Liberal View	Conservative View
What is the problem?	The health of the rich is good, but the poor suffer. Not only is access to health care a problem, but also the medical establishment itself is distorted by the profit motive.	The average health of the U.S. population is good, but disadvantaged people are less healthy; 48 million people lack health insurance.	The health of the U.S. population has steadily improved and is very good by global standards. Individuals need to take greater responsibility for their own health.
What is the solution?	High-quality health care should be the right of everyone. Only radical change toward an economic and political system that meets the needs of all will end the health inequalities in the U.S. population.	Government must extend access by putting in place a universal health care program so that prenatal care, nutrition, and appropriate medical treatment are available to all, regardless of their ability to pay.	Encouraging responsible behavior is key to illness prevention. Programs to extend health care coverage can help but should be provided by employers or paid for by individuals in a free-market system.

JOIN THE DEBATE

1. Do you think the Affordable Care Act is a problem or a solution? Explain how the left and right answer this question. What is your view?

2. Why do liberals favor putting health insurance under government control? Why do conservatives favor using a market system? Why do

radicals on the left think that even a universal government health care program does not go far enough?

3. Which of the three political analyses of health care included here do you find most convincing? Why?

to be provided to all, wealthy people end up living long and healthy lives, but those with little income cannot even be certain of survival. In effect, left-radicals claim, the profit motive transforms physicians, hospitals, and the entire health care system into a multibillion-dollar industry that caters to the needs of the richest people.

From this perspective, the solution to the problem of unequal health care in the United States and in the world is to abandon capitalism— the source of the problem—in favor of an economic and political system that operates in the interests of the majority. Both the costs and the benefits of the health care system should be spread throughout the population or *socialized*. The promise of such a socialist system lies in providing a range of benefits, from safe drinking water to basic medical attention, to everyone on an equal basis.

The Left to Right table outlines the three political perspectives on health issues.

Going On from Here

The central theme of this chapter is that health is not simply a matter for medical professionals; it is also of concern to sociologists because patterns of health reflect how society operates. Over the last two centuries, economic growth has raised living standards, which has also improved human health. In addition, advances in science and medical technology have dramatically increased life expectancy.

But enormous health problems still exist, especially in countries where the problem of poverty is greatest. Around the world, about 1.2 billion people struggle to live on $1.25 a day in income, with little or no access to basic medical care. In these nations— especially in rural areas

of Latin America, Africa, and Asia— illness and poverty form a vicious circle. Poverty breeds disease, which in turn reduces people's ability to work, and so they and their children remain poor.

The greatest health crisis is in Central Africa, where many of the world's poorest countries are found. Nations including Burundi, Rwanda, Uganda, Kenya, and Sudan face the problems of unsafe drinking water and chronic hunger, made worse in recent years by warfare.

Perhaps most serious of all is the AIDS epidemic, which has spread through many African societies to infect as much as 20 percent of young people. The challenge lies in the fact that the greatest medical care needs are found in precisely the countries with the least capable health care systems.

Compared with the desperate struggle in poor countries, the outlook for the United States, home to the world's most advanced medical technology, is far brighter. Even so, the problem this country faces now is unequal access to the health care system, most dramatically evident in the fact that 48 million people have no health insurance. As noted in this chapter, the United States falls behind dozens of other nations— including those with much lower average incomes— on important health indicators. Where we stand in terms of health care a century from now will probably depend less on what happens in a high-tech laboratory than on the future extent of social inequality.

Essay: Envisioning a Better Society What is your prediction about the state of health care in the United States fifty years from now? Do you think that government will have a larger role in providing care or not? What do you think are the specific changes needed to improve the health of the U.S. population?

CHAPTER 9   Physical and Mental Health

We all want a society in which people have good health, but what is the best way to reach that goal?

The path people favor as the solution to our need for health care reflects their political attitudes and also their social standing. Look at the accompanying photos to see two approaches to providing health care to our population.

It may be that the United States offers the best care available anywhere in the world, but liberals point out that tens of millions of people make use of overcrowded and expensive emergency rooms like the one shown here, and others go without health care altogether because they lack health insurance. From this point of view, the core of the problem is the distribution of care. Striking inequality means that some people get little or no health care, which, in turn, is the reason that this country lags behind other high-income nations in measures of health. In the recent debate over our nation's health care, what solution do liberals support?

You already know that conservatives place great importance on individual responsibility for personal well- being. This means making good choices, including exercising regularly, eating nutritious food in moderation, and consulting regularly with medical professionals. From this point of view, this nation has the best medical care in the world, thanks largely to our free-market economy. The market economy makes good health care available to almost everyone, with government stepping in to give assistance to some categories of the population. In the recent debate over national health care, what solution do conservatives support?

Hint: The solution, as liberals see it, is to involve government to ensure that everyone has access to quality care. Whether government would operate clinics or simply pay for services, the goal is universal health care coverage. Conservatives are critical of extending government control into health care, believing that people should retain the right to select physicians and decide on treatment. Radicals on the left argue that basic changes to the economy are needed to eliminate the economic inequality that divides our population. Have you heard any radical-left voices in the recent health care debate?

Getting Involved: Applications and Exercises

1. Use the Internet and also contact your local public health clinic to learn about the extent of HIV infection and AIDS in your local community. In terms of policy, how much emphasis is given to prevention versus maintaining people after they become infected? What categories of people are most at risk in your community?

2. Go to a video search engine such as YouTube and search for videos concerned with women and body image. What seems to be the ideal body shape for a woman? What effect do you think such images have on women? How might these images play a part in the problem of eating disorders?

3. Most communities have a shelter or soup kitchen for poor and homeless people. Visit such a facility in your area, and ask the director about the role, if any, of mental disabilities among the people they serve. What programs does the facility offer to help clients cope with their problems? Consider helping out as a volunteer.

4. Do research on the deinstitutionalization of people with mental illnesses that took place in the United States in the 1960s. See what you can learn about the causes of this movement and its consequences.

Making the Grade

CHAPTER 9 Physical and Mental Health

A DEFINING MOMENT
Dorothea Dix: Mentally Ill People Deserve Our Help **p. 283**

Health and Illness: A Global Perspective

9.1 Contrast patterns of human health in high- and low-income countries.

Health is a state of complete mental, physical, and social well-being.

- The well-being of any population reflects the operation of society, including its level of technology and degree of social inequality. **p. 267**

High-Income Nations

- Low infant mortality
- High life expectancy
- Most people die after age 75 of chronic conditions such as heart disease or cancer. **p. 267**

Low-Income Nations

- High infant mortality
- Low life expectancy
- Most people die of acute diseases such as malaria, cholera, or measles, and as many as one-fourth of all children do not survive to adulthood. **pp. 267–68**

Rich and Poor Compared: The AIDS Epidemic

- World wide, some 35 million people are infected with HIV.
- The hardest-hit region is sub-Saharan Africa, with 71% of the world's AIDS cases.
- The United States accounts for about 3% of global AIDS. **pp. 268–70**

> **health** (p. 267) a state of complete physical, mental, and social well-being
>
> **infant mortality rate** (p. 267) the number of babies, of every 1,000 born, who die before their first birthday
>
> **life expectancy at birth** (p. 267) the number of years, on average, people in a society can expect to live
>
> **chronic disease** (p. 267) an illness that has a long-term development
>
> **acute disease** (p. 268) an illness that strikes suddenly
>
> **social epidemiology** (p. 268) the study of how health and disease are distributed throughout a society's population
>
> **epidemic** (p. 268) the rapid spread of a disease through a population
>
> **socialized medicine** (p. 271) a medical care system in which the government owns and operates most medical facilities and employs most physicians

Health Policy: Paying for Care

9.2 Describe how nations around the world pay the costs of health care.

Socialist societies, in which governments own hospitals and employ doctors, treat health care as a basic right. **p. 270**

Capitalist societies, in which doctors and hospitals operate privately, treat health care as a product to be purchased on the open market.

Of all high-income nations, only the United States lacks a universal coverage program to help pay the costs of everyone's medical care. **pp. 270–72**

Health Care in the United States: A System in Crisis?

9.3 Evaluate the performance of the health care system in the United States.

The Cost Problem

- The United States has a direct-fee system in which most doctors and hospitals operate on a for-profit basis.
- Health care spending in the United States has increased steadily and topped $2.8 trillion in 2012.
- Factors pushing up health care spending include the system of private insurance, the trend toward doctors specializing, increasing use of high-technology treatment, the aging U.S. population, a lack of preventive care, and a rising number of malpractice lawsuits.
- Despite the fact that this country spends more on health care than any other, the United States lags behind other rich nations in key indicators of health, including life expectancy and infant mortality. **pp. 273–75**

The Coverage Problem

- About 64% of the U.S. population have private health insurance.
- 23% have coverage from an HMO.
- 33% have some coverage from the government (categories overlap).
- 48 million people—15% of the population—lack any health care coverage.

- Projections suggest that 2010 health care reforms will extend health insurance to 32 million people. **p. 275**

Health: Class, Ethnicity, and Race

- Poverty means a lack of adequate nutrition, medical care, and safe housing; 46.5 million people in the United States live below the poverty line and most cannot afford a healthy diet.

- Poverty is also associated with violence, especially among men.

- Certain categories of poor people, including American Indians and African Americans, are at even greater risk of both physical and mental health problems. **pp. 275–76**

Health: The Importance of Gender

- On average, women outlive men by about five years. Even so, women's health concerns have often been treated less effectively and overlooked by researchers.

- Eating disorders, which are widespread among girls and women, illustrate the power of gender to harm health. **pp. 276–78**

People with Disabilities

- Physical disability often operates as a *master status*, dominating other aspects of a person's identity.

- Despite the 1990 Americans with Disabilities Act, many public places remain inaccessible to people with disabilities. **pp. 278–79**

The Nursing Shortage

- Many nurses are leaving the field, citing a stressful work environment and lack of respect from other hospital personnel. **pp. 279–80**

> **direct-fee system** (p. 272) a medical care system in which patients or their insurers pay directly for the services of physicians and hospitals
> **health maintenance organizations (HMOs)** (p. 274) private insurance organizations that provide medical care to subscribers for a fixed fee
> **prenatal care** (p. 276) health care for women during pregnancy
> **disability** (p. 278) a physical or mental condition that limits everyday activities

Mental Health and Illness

9.4 Summarize types of mental disorders as well as treatment strategies.

- Nearly half of all Americans have symptoms of a **mental disorder** at some time in their lives, and one-third of the population suffers from a serious mental disor-

der at some point. Less than half of those with serious mental illness ever receive treatment.

- Poverty, which is linked to stress and social isolation, puts people at greater risk of mental illness. **pp. 280–85**

> **mental disorder** (p. 280) a condition involving thinking, mood, or behavior that causes distress and reduces a person's ability to function in everyday life
> **psychotherapy** (p. 283) an approach to mental health in which patients talk with trained professionals to gain insight into the cause of their problems
> **deinstitutionalization** (p. 283) the release of people from mental hospitals into local communities

Theories of Health and Illness

9.5 Apply sociological theory to issues involving physical and mental health.

Structural-Functional Analysis: Health and Social Roles

Structural-functional theory highlights the functions of health and health care for the operation of society.

- Illness is a problem because it keeps people from fulfilling their social roles.

- People who become ill take on the **sick role**, which relieves them of most everyday social obligations as long as they make efforts to get well. **p. 285**

Symbolic-Interaction Analysis: The Meaning of Health

Symbolic-interaction theory focuses on the meanings people attach to health and illness.

- The meanings attached to various conditions change over time. Homosexuality has been viewed as a moral wrong, a mental illness, and finally, simply as a sexual orientation.

- The existence of *psychosomatic disorders* demonstrates that the way in which people define any health situation may affect how they actually feel. **pp. 285–86**

Social-Conflict Analysis: Health and Inequality

Social-conflict theory points out how social inequality shapes patterns of health.

- Both in the United States and throughout the world, poor people suffer the most from health problems.

- In a capitalist economy, medical practice is guided by the profit motive; many people in the United States lack health care because they cannot afford to pay for it. **p. 286**

Feminist Analysis: Health and Gender

Feminist theory points out how gender inequality shapes patterns of health.

- Women are underrepresented among physicians and medical research typically has focused on men. The medical care received by women suffers as a result.

- Eating disorders show the power of cultural standards of beauty to harm women's health.

- In cases of violating conventional norms, women are more likely than men to be viewed as being mentally ill. **pp. 286–87**

---

sick role (p. 286) a pattern of behavior expected of people defined as ill

---

✪ POLITICS AND HEALTH

Constructing Problems and Defining Solutions

9.6 **Analyze physical and mental health issues from various positions on the political spectrum.**

Conservatives: Free Markets Provide the Best Care

- Conservatives claim that competition in a free marketplace will result in high-quality, low-cost health care.

- **Conservatives** emphasize individual responsibility for health; they believe that good health results from wise decisions about how to live. **pp. 287–88**

Liberals: Government Must Ensure Universal Care

- **Liberals** focus on inequalities in the health care received by rich and poor people.

- Liberals favor making government responsible for more of the health care system to ensure access for everyone. **p. 288**

The Radical Left: Capitalism Is Unhealthy

- **Radicals on the left** blame the profit motive for inequalities in health care in the United States.

- Radicals on the left call for a rejection of capitalism in favor of a socialist system that would provide equal health care for all. **pp. 288–89**

Chapter 10
Economy and Politics

Learning Objectives

10.1 Distinguish between two economic models: capitalism and socialism.

10.2 Explain the links between the economy and politics.

10.3 Describe the operation of the U.S. political economy.

10.4 Apply sociological theory to the country's political and economic system.

10.5 Analyze the U.S. economic and political systems from various positions on the political spectrum.

Tracking the Trends

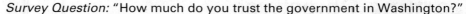

Survey Question: "How much do you trust the government in Washington?"

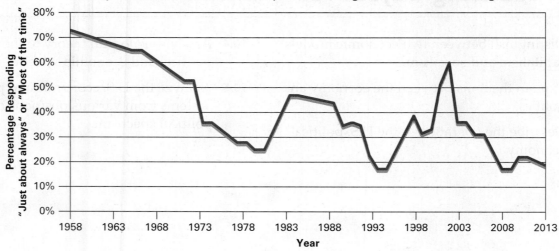

SOURCE: Pew Research Center for the People & the Press (2013).

Do you trust the government? If you have some doubts on that score, you are not alone. In a recent survey, only 19 percent of U.S. adults said they trusted the federal government to do what is right most of the time. In the last decade, trust in government has declined sharply. Over the last half-century, the decline is even more dramatic. How do you feel about the federal government's performance? What are some of the consequences of low public confidence in the government?

Constructing the Problem

Most government money goes to the poor in the form of "welfare," doesn't it?

The incentives provided to large corporations by federal, state, and local governments to encourage new types of production and to locate new production facilities in a local area far exceed the amount of money government provides to the nation's poor families.

Is our nation's system of financing political campaigns fair?

If "money talks," then we might be concerned that U.S. corporations give more money to political campaigns than any other type of organization, including labor unions, civil rights groups, and women's organizations.

Is the United States a true democracy?

In the 2012 national elections, only 58 percent of eligible voters went to the polls.

Chapter Overview

What are the advantages and disadvantages of a capitalist economy? What about a socialist system? This chapter describes these two types of economies and explains how the economy is linked to politics and the way power is used to make decisions and set policy. You will assess our society's economy and how our political system works. You will learn about our system of campaign financing and consider various explanations of why so many people do not bother to vote. You will carry out theoretical analysis of our country's political economy and learn how identifying "problems" and defining certain policies as "solutions" involving the economy and politics reflect people's political attitudes.

Nayef Habib rolled his eyes. "What is wrong with the people in Washington?" he said, turning from the television news to his wife, Fatima, who sat on the sofa next to him. "It's called 'gridlock'," Fatima replied, shaking her head. "Nobody wants to work together."

In simple terms, government is supposed to get things done. There has been a lot of talk about the need for bipartisanship—cooperation between leaders of the two major political parties. But many people are frustrated that our political leaders seem unable to agree on anything. In fact, in 2013, Congress passed just fifty-five laws. Back in 1948, President Harry Truman famously expressed frustration at what he called the "Do Nothing Congress." That year, Congress passed 511 laws—almost ten times more than Congress managed to do in 2013. Not only has there been little agreement in Congress, but the government actually had to shut down for several weeks

after legislators could not even agree on paying the bills. So there is something to the talk that our national leadership has become dangerously dysfunctional.

Nayef and Fatima Habib are disenchanted with politics and do not support either of the two major political parties. They are becoming more typical of the general U.S. population. In 2013, the share of people who identified strongly with either the Democratic Party or the Republican Party was down to about half the adult population. By contrast, people who claimed to be "independents" was at an all-time high (Viser, 2013; Jones, 2014).

Across the nation, schools teach young people that the United States is a democracy in which the government makes decisions in the interest of the entire population. But as this chapter explains, a lot of people in the United States are not so sure that our political system serves the people very well at all. People on the political left, including those who support the Occupy Wall Street movement, claim that the government speaks for the interests of the rich and powerful, especially the people who run the Wall Street investment banks and the multinational corporations. As they see it, the average citizen has little voice in politics. People on the political right, including those who support the Tea Party movement, claim that the government has become far too large and far too expensive and threatens to bankrupt the country. Even more important, expanding government now threatens people's basic freedoms.

The Occupy and Tea Party movements represent two very different political positions, and their supporters are not likely to agree on very much. But they do agree on one thing: Supporters of both movements claim that our elected officials in Washington, D.C., do not do a very good job of meeting the needs of ordinary women and men.

This chapter explores the operation of **politics**, *the social institution that guides a society's decision making about how to live.* As you will see, the political system has much to do with a country's **economy**, *the social institution that organizes the production, distribution, and consumption of goods and services.* By studying the operation of these two closely related social institutions—beginning with the economy and then turning to politics—we will learn more about many familiar problems that affect the lives of people across the United States.

Economic Systems: Defining Justice, Defining Problems

10.1 Distinguish between two economic models: capitalism and socialism.

One way to think about the economy is in terms of justice. The operation of the economic system determines who gets what and is built on claims about what is fair. The operation of the economy also has a lot to do with what issues end up being defined as social problems.

We begin with a brief look at the two broad economic models: capitalism and socialism. Keep in mind that these are economic models, not real economies. No nation is completely capitalist or totally socialist. Think of these models as opposite ends of a continuum with every country falling somewhere in between.

The Capitalist Model

Capitalism is *an economic system in which natural resources and the means of producing goods and services are privately owned.* In a capitalist system, individual men and women own a society's productive property, including investment banks, health care corporations, auto factories, large farms, and even fields and forests. Capitalism creates a special culture or way of thinking about the world. The culture of capitalism teaches people to think that everyone should behave according to their own self-interest. According to the Scottish economist Adam Smith (1723–1790), the pursuit of self-interest has widespread benefits because as people are guided by their self-interest, an economy ends up producing the greatest good for the greatest number of people (1937: 508, orig. 1776).

How does all this work? In theory, capitalism operates as a system of market competition in which people buy and sell goods and services from each other at the best prices they can get in a complex negotiation that economists call the "forces of supply and demand." In a free-market environment—sometimes described as *laissez-faire* (French words meaning "leave it alone")—producers compete with each other to sell goods and services, and consumers compete among themselves to purchase these resources. Everyone wants to get as much as possible for the money they spend. From the producers' or sellers' side of this process, businesses that offer high value in terms of quality and price are likely to do well because they will have many buyers; companies that offer products of little value will be met with little demand and likely soon fail. The overall result, explains Smith, is that the market system is economically efficient, making high-quality goods and services available to consumers at low prices.

Smith claimed that a market system is most productive when it operates with little or no interference of **government**, *a formal organization that directs the political life of a society.* Smith knew that countries need governments to perform some tasks, such as maintaining the borders and ensuring national defense. But he warned of government interfering with market forces by telling people, rather than letting them decide for themselves, what to produce or what to buy. Government regulation of the economy not only limits people's freedom but it reduces economic productivity as well, shortchanging consumers and holding down living standards.

Nations that have largely capitalist economies, including the United States, have been highly productive and have generated a high overall standard of living. At the same time, capitalism does create problems, at least for some people, when companies lay off workers in hard times or when producers develop machines that do a job more cheaply than human labor. In other words, what is economically efficient for producers is not always good for workers or for members of a local community.

In addition, as noted in Chapter 2 ("Poverty and Wealth"), a capitalist economy generates a high level of economic inequality. This is so because a market system may attach considerably different value to relatively small differences in personal talent and effort. In the United States, over the course of recent decades, economic resources have become more unequally distributed. In addition, as we shall see later in this chapter, capitalism has a tendency to concentrate not only wealth but also power, which can weaken democracy.

The Socialist Model

In contrast to capitalism, **socialism** is *an economic system in which natural resources and the means of producing goods and services are collectively owned.* In a socialist economy, government limits the right of individuals to own productive property. Instead, the government owns and operates factories, offices, and farms, claiming to do so in the interest of the people as a whole. Socialism also develops its own culture: In contrast to capitalism's individualistic orientation, socialism encourages a collective orientation, teaching people to be motivated not by self-interest but by a desire to serve the common good.

The idea of a socialist economic system arose largely as a criticism of capitalism and as a plan to solve capitalism's problems. This plan was the lifework of Karl Marx (1954, orig. 1848; 1964, orig. 1844), who claimed that capitalism's private ownership of productive property is what creates unequal social classes. By putting the *means of production* (such as factories and other productive property) in private hands, the capitalist economy serves the interests of these owners. That is, the operation of the economy serves the owners of productive property and not the interests of the large majority of people. As a way to change this situation, Marx envisioned an economic system that would replace private goals with social goals. This is the system we call socialism, and it operates with the goal of meeting the needs of everyone. The government, acting as an agent for all people, owns productive property and controls economic production. A socialist society expects everyone to work not out of self-interest but as a matter of social responsibility.

In practice, socialist nations such as China, Cuba, Laos, North Korea, and Vietnam have far less economic inequality than a capitalist society such as the United States. At the same time, socialist systems create problems of their own, including a relatively low standard of living. In addition, socialist societies have been criticized as highly regimented, with government limiting individual freedoms, including not only the chance to start a new business but also the freedom to speak out and the ability to move freely from place to place.

Mixed Systems

Remember that no nation in the world has an economy that is completely capitalist or completely socialist. A majority of the world's 194 nations—including the United States and Canada—have economies that are considerably closer to the capitalist model than to the socialist model. North Korea is probably the nation in which government most tightly operates the economy; about twenty countries—including Cuba, Algeria, Yemen, and China—can be described as mostly socialist. About forty

One way to "read" a nation's economic system is to examine housing in major cities. In the formerly socialist city of Bratislava, Slovakia, government policies mandated similar, basic housing for almost everyone. In the Philippines' capital city, Manila, a capitalist system provides luxurious housing for some while others live in shanty settlements or on the street.

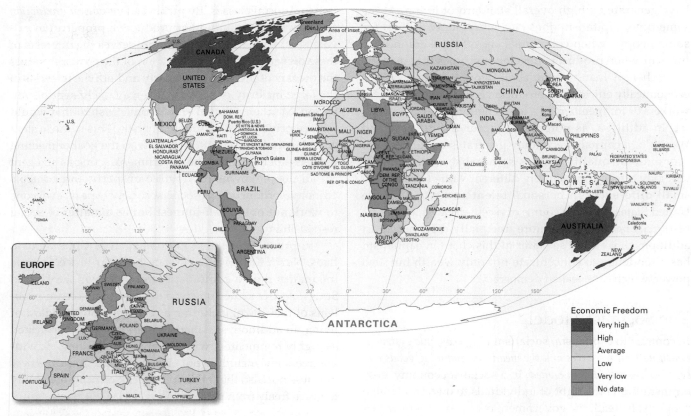

Window on the World

Global Map 10–1 Economic Freedom in Global Perspective

Economic freedom refers to workers, products, and capital moving freely with only the government constraint needed to maintain order and limit corruption. Nations with greater economic freedom are more capitalist.

SOURCE: Based on data from *The Wall Street Journal*/Heritage Foundation (2014).

of the world's countries—including Venezuela, Finland, and Russia—have a fairly balanced mix of capitalism and socialism (Freedom House, 2009; Heritage Foundation, 2012). Global Map 10–1 characterizes the world's nations in terms of the degree of economic freedom, which is one indicator of how capitalist an economy is.

Analysts have identified several distinctive mixed economic systems. In Asian countries, including Japan, South Korea, and Singapore, as well as in Middle Eastern nations such as Saudi Arabia and Kuwait, a mixed system known as *state capitalism* involves government working closely with large, privately owned companies. Although most property is privately owned, the government owns a few large companies, such as automobile producers, telephone services, and airlines. In some cases, typically in Asia, this public–private partnership is intended to make big companies more efficient and more competitive in global markets. In others, such as Saudi Arabia, the close ties between government and the private sector reflect something very different: There, a large royal family owns most of the country's productive wealth.

Another mixed system, common in Western Europe, including Italy, France, and Sweden, is *welfare capitalism*. Here, too, most production is carried out by privately owned

companies. But in welfare capitalist societies, government provides extensive welfare programs, funded by high taxes. In these nations, the government provides child care, housing, and medical care for the entire population. The goal here is to maintain high productivity by supporting the workforce while at the same time keeping economic inequality in check.

The U.S. economy is a mix of private and government activity, but as Figure 10–1 shows, the United States is among the most capitalist of all nations. The U.S. government carries out only about 18 percent of the country's production, with 82 percent of production in the privately owned sector of the economy. In tough economic times, however, the government can play a far larger role in the economy. In 2008, for example, in response to the onset of the recession, the federal government greatly expanded the role of government in the economy by bailing out financial companies deemed "too big to fail." The government also provided large loans of taxpayer money to several auto companies on the condition that these corporations restructure themselves following government guidelines.

Is government's involvement in the U.S. economy a problem or a solution? Your answer, of course, depends on politics. The more to the political left you are, the more you

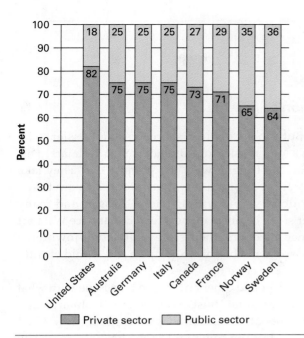

Figure 10–1 Percentage of Gross Domestic Product (GDP) in the Private Sector and the Public Sector

Compared with other high-income countries, the United States has a larger share of its economic productivity in the private sector, making this country more capitalist.

SOURCE: World Bank (2013).

are likely to see the free market as creating problems such as economic inequality, joblessness, and poverty. From that point of view, government intervention into the economy is a solution, by enforcing regulations that limit abuse driven by greed, as well as using tax policy to reduce economic inequality. By contrast, the more to the right you are, the more you are likely to see capitalism's market system as a solution because of how productive it is and how much personal freedom it provides to individuals. From this point of view, the government is viewed as a problem because excessive regulation of the marketplace stifles economic growth and limits individual freedom. In political campaigns, left-leaning candidates typically portray the market as a source of problems and the government as a solution; right-leaning candidates do just the opposite. Figure 10–2 illustrates this pattern.

It is probably fair to say that most people don't spend much time thinking about what kind of economic system they prefer. But in recent decades, the rapid expansion of the Walmart corporation has had the effect of making more people do just that. The Defining Moment box on page 302 explains how.

The Economy and Politics

10.2 Explain the links between the economy and politics.

How the economy operates says a lot about the way power is distributed throughout a society. For this reason,

analysts describe a society's **political economy,** *the closely linked economic and political life of a nation or world region.*

Supporters of capitalism claim that the limited role of government in a capitalist society provides people with lots of economic opportunity and affluence and also supports extensive political freedoms (Rueschemeyer, Stephens, & Stephens, 1992; Lipset, 1994). Peter Berger (1986), a sociologist who has examined the political consequences of capitalism, points out that limited government of a capitalist society typically provides people with not just the right to vote but also the freedom to work, travel, and speak according to their individual desires.

Supporters of socialism make other claims. Following the ideas of Karl Marx, they argue that capitalism actually reduces personal security, at least for most people (Domhoff, 1970; Bergsten, Horst, & Moran, 1978; Parenti, 1995). This is because capitalism concentrates wealth and power to such a degree that a small share of the population (Marx's "capitalist elite") has most of the wealth. In a capitalist society, the argument continues, people may have a legal right to vote, but real power lies with wealth. Therefore, the economic elite dominates the political life of the entire society. For ordinary people to have a voice in shaping their own lives, at least rough economic equality is necessary, which is not the case in capitalist societies.

Democracy

An important expression of political freedom is **democracy,** *a political system in which power is exercised by the people as a whole.* The conventional wisdom in the United States is that this country and other capitalist countries are

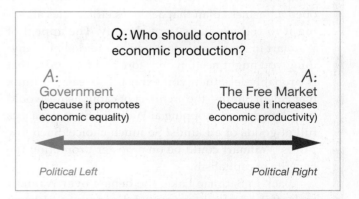

Figure 10–2 Who Should Control Production, the Market or the Government?

In the 1980s, conservative president Ronald Reagan claimed that freedom and prosperity were the result of a market economy in which people would turn loose their talent and creativity to produce abundance. In 2009, with a serious recession at hand, liberal president Barack Obama claimed that the steady hand of government could guide the nation away from years of greed, corruption, and rising economic inequality. How much control of the economy you would give to the market or to government reflects your position on the political spectrum.

CONSTRUCTING SOCIAL PROBLEMS

A DEFINING MOMENT

Store Wars: Is Walmart the Problem or the Solution?

About five years ago, the voters of Saranac Lake, a small community in the Adirondack Mountains of upstate New York, turned out at the polls like never before. It was not a presidential election; in fact, the election was not about political leaders at all. The issue was whether the local town council should let Walmart build a new store in the small town (Rosenbloom & Barbaro, 2009).

The local Ames store had closed a decade before, leaving the people of Saranac Lake with no place to buy sheets and bedding, underwear, or a pair of new jeans. With winter temperatures that can drop to –25°F, the locals are hardy people known for taking care of themselves. But few were willing to drive 50 miles to get to the nearest department store. So the town leaders began looking around for a large company willing to build a local store.

Walmart expressed interest in building a supercenter. But the offer divided the town when people realized that such a store was 120,000 square feet—a size that threatened to overwhelm the small community and crush local businesses.

Walmart certainly has a record of success. In 2014, the world's largest retailer had more than 4,200 stores and 1.3 million employees in the United States. Another 6,100 stores operate around the world. What makes Walmart so successful? The company developed a business plan that achieves efficiencies allowing it to sell products very cheaply. The appeal of Walmart to shoppers is that you can find almost anything you might need in one store and for a price that is probably less than you expect. It is easy to think that Adam Smith—the architect of capitalism—would have loved to go shopping at Walmart. So many aisles full of goods of all kinds! So much choice! Such low prices! Walmart could be on a poster promoting the benefits of capitalism.

Back in Saranac Lake, the debate over Walmart took off. Leslie Pruitt promoted the idea of a Walmart in town. "Today, we cannot find stuff we need," she explained. "We need children's clothes, we need bed sheets; you have to drive an hour to buy them." Sam Piro also claimed that Walmart would be good for the local economy. "A big-box store will bring people from all over the region to our town. As they drive through, they will also see the downtown and notice all the local shops and restaurants."

But other people disagreed. Jake Kessler, who runs a local music store, did not want a Walmart in his town. "No friggin' way," he stammered. "They take away from a community. They don't add anything; they don't give anything back." Kessler and many other small business owners feared that once Walmart opened its doors, their stores in the old downtown area would not be able to compete and would eventually have to close up.

Kessler and other critics also take issue with what they see as unfair business practices. Walmart starts new hires at minimum wage, which in now $7.25 an hour, but the company claims its average hourly wage for full-time workers in the state of New York is $13.09. But critics respond that, even at the level claimed by the company, working full time does not generate enough income to support a family. In fact, more than half of Walmart employees in the United States working full time earn less than $25,000 a year. Although some people who start in hourly jobs eventually earn higher salaries as managers, the critics claim that most of the Walmart workforce is paid too little for people ever to reach the middle class (Walmart, 2011; Berfield, 2013).

In the middle of the town's debate, something unexpected happened. Walmart said no. The corporation's management announced that they had decided not to build a store in Saranac Lake. Some people were disappointed; some were relieved. But there was still the problem of where to buy underwear and bedding.

Mickey Smith sat on a street corner in Saranac Lake and smiled. He was more philosophical than most local residents. "The Walmart episode was a defining moment for us, as it is for every town. The idea of bringing in Walmart forced us to decide who we are, what we want our town to be, what's really important to us." As Smith sees it, Walmart is pure capitalism—the stores are big, the selection of products is big, and the discounts are big. But he also thinks that the big corporations usually win at the expense of the "little guy." Smith does not want to live in a town where most of the local people end up shopping at and working for Walmart.

Many others agreed. So the people of Saranac Lake stopped debating whether or not to invite a big-box store to build in the area and decided that they would create their own Community Store. Residents of Saranac Lake turned an old restaurant on Main Street into the town's locally owned and operated Community Store. To bankroll the new business, they raised $500,000 by selling shares in the store for $100 each—a price low enough to entice 600 people in the town to be part owners (with an average investment of about $850 each). No one person is allowed to own more than $10,000 of the company stock. The store has three full-time employees, who earn salaries that are above average for the region with health benefits and paid sick days (Cortese, 2011).

On a cool October day in 2011, as the people of Saranac Lake braced for an early snowstorm, thousands of them turned out to take a look at their new Community Store. The word around town is that underwear, bedding, and jeans are already big sellers.

After a long debate about whether or not to allow a "big-box" store in their community, the people of Saranac Lake decided to "go local" and start their own community store.

democratic because they allow people to vote. By contrast, socialist countries are not democratic because people have no voice in selecting their leaders.

This view, of course, provides political support for the capitalist economy. But there is some truth to it: In mostly socialist nations, such as China, Cuba, Laos, North Korea, and Vietnam, people have no ability to vote leaders out of office. In recent years, however, several Latin American nations (including Nicaragua, Bolivia, Venezuela, and Ecuador) have elected leaders who support socialism. Keep in mind, too, that many countries in Africa, the Middle East, and Asia have mostly capitalist economies yet offer their people little voice in politics.

Authoritarianism and Monarchy

The opposite of democracy is **authoritarianism**, *a political system that denies popular participation in government.* Authoritarian countries can have various types of economies and power structures. Iran is an example of an authoritarian nation that is run by a religious elite. Malaysia and Singapore in Southeast Asia are authoritarian nations that have elections but have long been controlled by a single political party.

Another example of authoritarian nations includes Saudi Arabia in the Middle East, where power takes the form of **monarchy**, *a political system in which a single family rules from generation to generation.* In this oil-rich country of 30 million people (about the same population as Texas), most of the wealth is in the hands of an extended royal family of several thousand people, who dominate economic and political life.

There is little question that Saudi Arabia falls far short of the democratic ideal, which is a society in which all people have a political voice. But what about the United States? Is this country as democratic as many people like to think? We turn now to some of the economic and political problems in the "land of the free."

Problems of the U.S. Political Economy

10.3 Describe the operation of the U.S. political economy.

The following sections investigate the political economy of the United States. First, we look at the great power of large corporations. Then we assess how well this nation lives up to its democratic ideals.

The Power of Corporations

In the United States, most goods and services are produced by **corporations**, *businesses with a legal existence, including rights and liabilities, separate from that of their members.* In the United States, almost 6 million businesses (of a total exceeding 32 million) are incorporated. Of these, the largest 100 corporations are economic giants, each with at least $31 billion in annual revenue. Together, these 100 businesses are responsible for most corporate production in the United States, and this share has been increasing in recent decades (Internal Revenue Service, 2014).

As we would expect in a mostly capitalist society, the economic activity of corporations is far greater than that of government. Local, state, and federal governments in the United States do manage public resources, building highways, repairing bridges, running libraries and universities, and overseeing parks and beaches. In addition, the federal government operates the U.S. military. But most economic production takes place in the private sector, which is dominated by huge corporations.

Government also works with business, providing aid in the form of subsidies, price controls, loan guarantees, and outright cash grants, especially if officials see a national interest in their success. For example, the Obama administration has supported alternative energy production. In addition, government provides support to an industry in economic trouble, especially if it is viewed as "too important to fail," as in the case of big banks and automakers after the start of the recent recession (Drawbaugh, 2009).

Government is a partner to companies in other ways. For one thing, federal, state, and local governments are some of U.S. corporations' biggest customers. Especially in recent decades, as states and local communities have tried

How much power should corporations have over the operation of the U.S. economy? How much control should the federal government have over the operation of private corporations? These questions are now being asked by people in social movements such as Occupy Wall Street, and they were central to the debate during the 2012 presidential campaign. In general, the political left favors giving greater control of the economy to government and the political right favors allowing the "free" market to operate with little government oversight. Which side of this debate do you favor? Why?

to attract new business, corporations have also come to expect favors from government. As the Social Problems in Focus box on page 306 explains, government handouts to corporations are common, with far more taxpayer money in the United States going to wealthy corporations than to poor families.

The U.S. government also set interest rates, regulates the workplace, monitors foreign trade, and protects consumers. But, reflecting the capitalist model, actual government ownership of corporations has always been the exception rather than the rule. Given the fact that private corporations generate most of the economic output of the United States, we might well wonder: Are corporations more powerful than even the government? To the extent that this is the case, who really runs the country?

Monopoly and Oligopoly

At least until the emergence of the Occupy Wall Street movement, few people in our mostly capitalist society defined the size and power of business as a social problem. But, for more than a century, the law has banned *any one company* from controlling a market, because such control would void competition and defeat the market system.

Monopoly is *the domination of an entire market by a single company*. One result of the Industrial Revolution was the rise of monopolies during the final decades of the nineteenth century. A small number of individuals—sometimes called "robber barons" because they engaged in ruthless business tactics and lived like royalty—built enormous corporations that ended up controlling entire industries. For example, Andrew Carnegie (1835–1919) took control of the nation's steel industry, John D. Rockefeller (1839–1937) dominated oil production, and J. P. Morgan (1837–1913) took a leading role in banking. Not surprisingly, such men made enormous fortunes, earning tens of millions of dollars each year at a time when the average worker had an annual income of just $600 and there was no income tax.

In 1890, the federal government challenged the power of the giant monopolies when Congress passed the Sherman Antitrust Act. One result was that Rockefeller's Standard Oil Company was broken up into many smaller companies that would compete with one another. Almost a century later, the government broke up AT&T's monopoly in long-distance telephone service, creating the "Baby Bells" and setting the stage for Verizon, Sprint, and dozens of other long-distance companies to compete and bring down the price of long-distance calling. In 2002, federal and state governments settled action against the Microsoft Corporation based on alleged violations of antimonopoly laws.

Such actions have trimmed the power of giant corporations, but only to a point. The law forbids corporations from operating as outright monopolies because a single producer dominating a market that has no competition can set prices and exploit consumers. But the law does not prevent **oligopoly**, *the domination of a market by a few companies.* Today, for example, the manufacture of breakfast cereal is dominated by Kellogg and General Mills, which together control about 60 percent of all sales. Similarly, General Electric, Phillips, and Osram Sylvania dominate the market for electric lights; Goodyear, Bridgestone, and Michelin have a dominant position in the tire industry; and Microsoft, Apple, and Facebook all have a commanding position in their particular industries.

Conglomerates and Other Linkages

Many of today's corporations, by themselves, are powerful. But as businesses grow, they buy other businesses, becoming even larger and stronger. A **conglomerate** is *a giant corporation composed of many smaller corporations.* Examples of conglomerates include PepsiCo, the maker of Pepsi soft drinks, which also owns Taco Bell, KFC, and Pizza Hut restaurants as well as Quaker Oats, Frito-Lay, and other snack and fast-food companies. General Motors, which owns the German company Opel, the British company Vauxhall, and the Australian company Holden, has regional companies throughout Asia and has partnerships with Isuzu and Toyota in Japan and Daewoo in South Korea. Pearson, a large British corporation that is the publisher of this textbook, operates around the world, operating not only publishing companies but newspapers as well, including London's *Financial Times*.

Another way corporations work together is by sharing members of their boards of directors. **Interlocking directorates** are *social networks made up of people who serve as directors of several corporations at the same time.* A member of the Goldman Sachs board of directors, for example, might also serve on the board of directors of another financial corporation, such as Lehman Brothers. The world's biggest corporations are linked to hundreds of other corporations through common board members.

Conglomerates and interlocking directorates are perfectly legal and don't necessarily do anything wrong. But they may encourage oligopoly and illegal activities such as price fixing, in which various companies share information on pricing so they do not have to compete in the marketplace. Price fixing harms the public because consumers end up paying more than they would in a competitive economy.

The Power of Money

The enormous wealth of corporations brings us to the question of how money influences the political process. Corporations are not the only organizations with a voice in the political system. On the contrary, people across the United States join together to form many different types of

Toward the end of the nineteenth century, the ever-increasing influence of corporations reached the point at which the largest businesses had more power and money than the federal government. The government responded in 1890 by passing the Sherman Antitrust Act, which forbids single companies from controlling an entire market. In this cartoon from the early twentieth century, President Theodore Roosevelt plays Jack (from the fable "Jack and the Beanstalk"), out to slay the Wall Street giants who dominate the U.S. economy. Can you think of recent cases in which the government has charged that a particular corporation has gained control of an entire market?

organizations that seek to advance various political goals. A notable feature of the U.S. political system is the high number of **special-interest groups**, *political alliances of people interested in some economic or social issue.* We are all familiar with special-interest groups, including AARP (formerly the American Association of Retired Persons), the National Rifle Association (NRA), and the American Civil Liberties Union (ACLU).

For any organization, money buys political power through **lobbying**, *the efforts of special-interest groups and their representatives to influence government officials.* AARP, the NRA, and the ACLU all employ lobbyists in Washington, D.C., and elsewhere who pressure members of Congress to pass legislation that advances their interests. Corporations, too, employ lobbyists—Walmart, for example, has eight

SOCIAL PROBLEMS IN FOCUS

Corporate Welfare: Government Handouts for Big Business

Who benefits most from "welfare" in the United States? If you are like most people, you would probably say that most of the benefits go to needy people. In reality, however, government programs provide more benefits to corporations than to poor people.

Why do companies get such special treatment? With all their wealth, corporations have great power. In addition, with unemployment running high, state and local government officials are eager to attract new jobs. In this economic climate, many companies are willing to relocate to take advantage of offers from state and local governments—in the form of low-interest loans, tax relief, free utilities, and other benefits.

Supporters call government aid to corporations "public–private partnerships." Such aid, they explain, creates jobs that may be needed by communities hard hit by business closings. Critics view handouts for big business as unnecessary corporate welfare. Furthermore, the amount of assistance provided is often far greater than any promise of new jobs justifies. In 1991, for example, Indiana offered a $451 million incentive package to United Airlines to build an aircraft maintenance facility in that state. United built the facility and created 6,300 new jobs. Some simple math shows that the cost of these new jobs came to a whopping $72,000 per person hired. In 1993, much the same happened when Alabama offered $253 million to lure Mercedes-Benz to build an automobile assembly plant in Tuscaloosa. The corporation now has 3,000 workers at the plant, an average cost of $85,000 per job, but this includes many temporary workers.

Much the same pattern is found across the country. In 1997, Pennsylvania gave a $307 million incentive package to a Norwegian company to reopen part of Philadelphia's naval shipyard. Soon after, 950 people were hired, at a cost of $323,000 per new job. In 2002, Georgia spent $67,000 per job to close a deal on a new auto plant. In 2006, Indiana won the bidding for a new Honda plant near Indianapolis, spending $71,000 for each new job, and Nashville, Tennessee, closed a deal to bring a new Nissan plant to that city with an estimated 750 new jobs each costing $266,000 in incentives. In 2014, a number of southwestern states were bidding against each other in the hope of attracting a new Tesla plant (Bartlett & Steele, 1998; Sachs, 2009; Azok, 2014; Wilson, 2014).

Large Fortune 500 corporations have received more than $60 billion in government assistance. The government bailout of the auto industry and financial industry in 2008 and 2009 ran up an even bigger bill, topping $1 trillion, which is about fifty times the amount that the government spends on welfare programs that benefit poor families.

What Do You Think?

1. Did you support the recent government bailouts of the auto industry and several Wall Street firms? Why or why not?

2. Do you think state and local governments should offer financial assistance to lure new industry that will add jobs to your community?

3. What conditions, if any, would you attach to such financial assistance? For example, should government set a higher minimum wage, require full benefits, or limit the use of temporary workers? Explain.

---

lobbyists working from its office in Washington, D.C. In all, more than 12,000 lobbyists work to influence the operation of the federal government (Federal Election Commission, 2011; Center for Responsive Politics, 2014).

Lobbying is perfectly legal. But many lobbyists offer more than information to our elected leaders. When elected leaders accept money, other valuable items, or personal "favors" from lobbyists, both parties may well end up accused of committing a crime. The most controversial aspect of lobbying is making campaign contributions, as we now explain.

Campaign Financing

Concern about the power of money in politics involves not only the work of lobbyists but also the financing of political campaigns. A reality of political life in the United States is that running for office is very expensive. In the 2012 presidential elections, Barack Obama and Mitt Romney each spent more than $1 billion on their campaigns. In the 2012 congressional races, candidates for seats in the House and the Senate spent more than $1.8 billion. When all the state and local races are added in, the spending total for the 2012 elections was more than $7 billion (Federal Election Commission, 2014).

Where does all the money come from? Corporations provide more campaign contributions than all other organizations, including labor unions, civil rights groups, and women's organizations. Political parties also raise money for candidates. In addition, candidates are free to spend as much of their own money as they wish. Very rich people have a huge advantage over "ordinary" people, although great wealth is no guarantee of success. For example, in 1996 and 2000, Steve Forbes spent $66 million of his own money in unsuccessful runs for the presidency. In 2008, Mitt Romney spent some $40 million in his unsuccessful effort to win his party's nomination. The fact that these efforts were unsuccessful shows that money alone is no guarantee of winning an election. But, from another angle, being in office is always a huge advantage in fundraising. As president, Barack Obama raised far more money for his 2012 reelection effort than he was able to attract several years ago as a candidate (Perry, 2012).

Candidates at all levels of government receive money not only from individuals and organizations but also from **political action committees (PACs)**, *organizations formed by special-interest groups to raise and spend money in support of political goals*. There are currently about 5,700 PACs in the United States, representing a wide range of special-interest groups, including the pharmaceutical and tobacco industries, defense industries, labor unions, agribusinesses, religious organizations, senior citizens, and gun owners (Federal Election Commission, 2014).

As recently as 2000, campaign finance laws limited any PAC's contribution to a candidate to $5,000 in a primary election and an additional $5,000 in the general election. But PACs could solicit donations for candidates and pass along the donor's money directly to the candidate. Such *bundling* of checks, along with high-priced fundraising dinners and other strategies that get around legal limits on campaign contributions, generated an almost unlimited amount of campaign contributions called *soft money*.

In addition, there was no limit on how much a PAC could spend to assist candidates as long as the PAC did not operate under the control of candidates or their campaign committees (Conway & Green, 1998). For this reason, many PACs focused their spending on particular issues that helped the candidates they favored. For example, raising money in support of abortion rights typically helps more liberal (usually Democratic) candidates, and raising money to oppose abortion typically helps the electoral campaigns of more conservative (usually Republican) candidates.

Individuals, corporations, unions, and PACs were also able to donate larger sums of money to political parties. Although an individual could donate no more than $1,000 to any candidate in a specific political race, individuals were allowed to donate up to $20,000 per year to national parties and up to $5,000 to state parties (Herrnson, 1998). Federal law limited the amount an individual could contribute to all candidates for public office to $25,000 per year. Even so, by combining various methods of support, individuals could easily exceed any limit.

The 2002 Reforms In 2002, Congress passed the Bipartisan Campaign Reform Act, popularly known as the McCain-Feingold bill. This act ended the flow of soft money to candidates or political parties. Individuals are limited to gifts of $2,000 each to political candidates in any primary or general election. In addition, individuals can give no more than $95,000 in total gifts (a ceiling of $37,500 to all candidates and $57,500 to all political parties). PACs can give no more than $5,000 to any one candidate and $15,000 to any one political party, with

A number of major donors have access to this country's political leaders. To what extent is it true that wealthy people and powerful organizations shape the nation's political agenda?

no overall limit. PACs responded to this law by changing their strategy from collecting money and passing it along to candidates and parties to encouraging individuals to give money (under the limits noted earlier) directly to candidates and parties.

The Rise of Super PACs The effect of the 2002 reforms was greatly reduced in 2010, when the U.S. Supreme Court (*Citizens United* v. *Federal Election Commission*) ruled that the government cannot impose limits on financial contributions made by labor unions, corporations, other organizations, or individuals. This decision, seen by supporters as defending the constitutional right for people to engage in free speech and political activity, allowed the formation of Super PACs, or organizations that raise money on behalf of candidates. At the same time, Super PACs cannot work directly with candidates. The law continues to limit the amount organizations and individuals can contribute directly to candidates. But the operation of "independent expenditure" Super PACs means, in effect, there are no limits to the role money can play in today's elections.

In 2014, the Supreme Court took another step toward eliminating limits on campaign contributions. This time, the Court abolished limits on the amount of money that any individual can contribute to candidates in national elections. A majority of justices claimed that any such limits violate First Amendment rights that guarantee freedom of speech. The dissenting justices countered that eliminating limits threatened political democracy (Liptak, 2014).

Why have many people defined campaign financing as a serious problem? The simple answer is that both individuals as well as organizations representing the real estate industry, trial lawyers, or labor unions contribute tens of millions of dollars with the expectation that their money will advance certain political goals. In practice, few political officials write a law or even cast a vote without thinking about the effects of their decisions on fundraising for their next campaign. For this reason, say critics, our system of campaign financing puts the U.S. political system up for sale (Center for Responsive Politics, 2011; Federal Election Commission, 2012; Liptak, 2012; Confessore, 2014).

Voter Apathy

If money plays such a big part in U.S. politics, allowing special interests to dominate our political life, perhaps we should not be surprised that many people do not bother to vote. In the last five presidential elections, the share of eligible voters that actually went to the polls ranged from 52 percent (1996) to 63 percent (2008) for an average of about 57 percent. In 2012, 57.5 percent of those eligible voted (Center for the Study of the American Electorate, 2012). National Map 10–1 shows where in the United States people are most likely and least likely to vote.

Our country can be proud of a history of expanding voting rights. In 1870, the Fifteenth Amendment to the Constitution extended the vote to African American men; in 1920, the Nineteenth Amendment gave the vote to women; in 1971, the Twenty-Sixth Amendment lowered the voting age from twenty-one to eighteen.

In a society that has extended the right to vote to more and more people, why do so many of us not go to the polls? Conservatives suggest that the failure to vote is a sign of *indifference* on the part of people who are pretty much

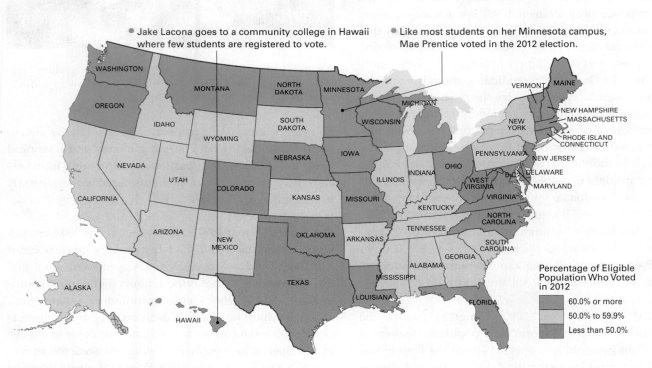

• Jake Lacona goes to a community college in Hawaii where few students are registered to vote.

• Like most students on her Minnesota campus, Mae Prentice voted in the 2012 election.

Percentage of Eligible Population Who Voted in 2012

- 60.0% or more
- 50.0% to 59.9%
- Less than 50.0%

Seeing Ourselves

National Map 10–1 Voter Turnout across the United States

Overall, 58 percent of voting-age people went to the polls in the 2012 presidential election. By state, people in Minnesota were most likely to vote (75.7 percent) and people in Hawaii were least likely to do so (44.2 percent). What pattern do you see for the country as a whole? Can you explain the pattern?

SOURCE: McDonald (2014).

satisfied with the way things are. Liberals and radicals on the left take a different view, arguing that low voter turnout is a sign of widespread *alienation* from politics. As they see it, many people are dissatisfied with the way things are, but they doubt that voting will make any difference. Especially in recent decades, corporate fraud, negative campaign advertising, and ongoing political "gridlock" so that little gets done in Washington have caused a decline in public confidence in "the system." As noted at the beginning of this chapter, a recent survey found that just 19 percent of U.S. adults trusted the federal government to do "what is right" most of the time (Pew Research Center, 2013). As shown in Figure 10–3, the share of the population expressing confidence in Congress has dropped to just 10 percent and most other institutions fare only somewhat better. Just the U.S. military has the confidence of a majority of U.S. adults (Gallup, 2013).

Perhaps the United States should follow the lead of Australia, Belgium, Italy, and other nations that have enacted laws that require people to vote. Another approach is to offer more political choices. Looking globally, higher voter turnouts are found where there are more political parties that represent a wider range of positions than found in the United States. Here, as some people see it, the two major parties have much in common. Considering that people such as Barack Obama and Rand Paul have attracted millions of new voters to the polls suggests that fresh faces and diverse policies may excite more voters.

Who Votes? Class, Age, Race, Ethnicity, and Gender

Low voter turnout not only weakens this country's democratic ideal but also reflects the fact that certain categories of people are especially likely to be left out of the political process.

Income and Age   Income is one important factor. In simple terms, most people with high incomes vote, but most people with low incomes do not. Figure 10–4 on page 310 shows that 78 percent of people earning more than $100,000 per year reported voting in the 2012 presidential election. By contrast, 47 percent of people earning less than $10,000 said that they had cast a vote (U.S. Census Bureau, 2013).

Why the difference? High-income people also have more schooling; college graduates are twice as likely to vote as high school dropouts. People with more schooling, income, and wealth have a greater stake in the system.

In addition, affluent people tend to be older because income rises over the life course. The older people are, the more likely they are to vote. People over the age of sixty-five are more likely to vote in presidential elections (72 percent voted in 2012) than college-age adults (41 percent), many of whom have not even registered (U.S. Census Bureau, 2013).

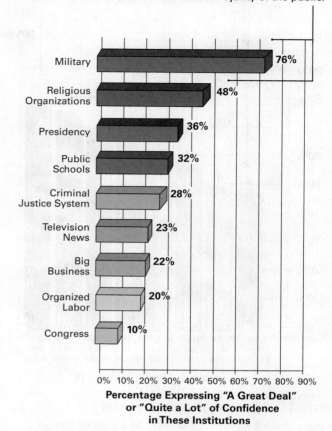

● Only one of these institutions receives a vote of confidence from a majority of the public.

- Military — 76%
- Religious Organizations — 48%
- Presidency — 36%
- Public Schools — 32%
- Criminal Justice System — 28%
- Television News — 23%
- Big Business — 22%
- Organized Labor — 20%
- Congress — 10%

Percentage Expressing "A Great Deal" or "Quite a Lot" of Confidence in These Institutions

Figure 10–3   Public Confidence in Selected Institutions, 2013

Public confidence in important organizations has declined in recent decades. Why do you think public confidence in most of our institutions is so low?

SOURCE: Gallup (2013).

Race   Historically, race has had much to do with whether or not people vote. Until 1865, no person of color could vote in the United States. African American men gained the right to vote in 1870, as did women of any race in 1920. In 2012, African Americans were more likely to vote (66 percent of eligible people voted) than white people (64 percent). African Americans provide strong support for Democratic candidates; in 2012, 93 percent voted for Barack Obama (Pew Research Center, 2012; U.S. Census Bureau, 2013).

Ethnicity   Compared to the population as a whole, people of Hispanic descent are less likely to vote (in 2012, just 48 percent of eligible voters did so). In part, this is because Hispanic Americans have a high rate of poverty. In addition, a sense of cultural marginality and a lack of fluency in English may discourage some Latinas and Latinos from voting. The political importance of Hispanic voters is increasing along with their population size. The recent trend has been for Hispanics to favor Democratic candidates (Cisneros, 2009; U.S. Census Bureau, 2013).

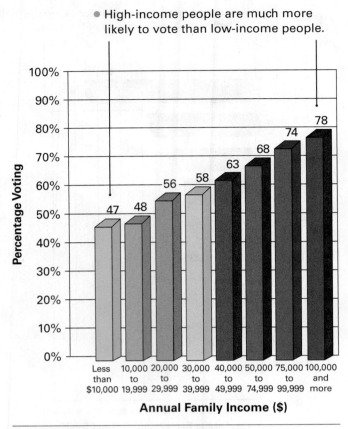

● High-income people are much more likely to vote than low-income people.

Figure 10–4 Voting by Income Level

The figure shows the percentage of adults who reported voting in the 2012 presidential election. A clear pattern is present. As income goes up, so does the likelihood of voting.

SOURCE: U.S. Census Bureau (2013).

Gender Gender matters in voting: In 2012, women were slightly more likely to vote (64 percent did so) than men (60 percent voted). In addition, women are more likely to support Democratic candidates. In 2012, women favored Obama over Romney by 55 percent to 44 percent. Men typically favor Republicans; in 2012, 52 percent supported Romney and 45 percent voted for Obama (Pew Research Center, 2012).

The Gender Gap: Seeing Problems Differently

In political terms, the **gender gap** is *the tendency for women and men to hold different opinions about certain issues and to support different candidates*. Women and men tend to have slightly different opinions of the problems our country faces and what should be done about them. In general, women are more likely than men to support so-called compassion issues that seek to protect vulnerable members of society (including children, older people, and people with disabilities). In addition, women are more likely to support gun control and to oppose the death penalty. Men, by contrast, are more likely to want a strong military, to support

the right to own a gun, and to favor a tough response to crime, including use of the death penalty.

Such differences make women more likely to support Democrats and men to vote for Republicans. In recent presidential elections, a larger share of women have supported the Democratic candidate and, except in 2008, a larger share of men have voted Republican.

Voting Laws for Persons Convicted of Serious Crimes

Today, there is only one category of adult citizens in the United States without the right to vote—convicted felons. These are men and women who have been convicted of committing serious crimes. Forty-eight of the fifty states (all except Vermont and Maine) have laws that bar people in prison from voting. Thirty-five states do not allow people to vote if they have been placed on probation after being convicted of a felony. Eleven states ban voting by people who have completed their prison sentences, subject to various appeals to restore their right to vote. These laws take away the right to vote for almost 6 million people in the United States (Sentencing Project, 2013).

Should people in prison—and even those who have served their time—lose their right to vote? Supporters of such policies claim that people who do not "play by the rules" do not deserve a political voice. But critics see this practice as politically motivated, because convicted felons include a high proportion of low-income people and racial and ethnic minorities, who show a strong preference for Democratic over Republican candidates. For this reason, giving political voice to people convicted of serious crimes would help elect Democratic candidates.

Social Movements: How Much Change?

Donating money and voting are not the only ways for people to be politically active. Other examples of political activism range from signing petitions to engaging in violent protest. Over the course of the twentieth century, social movements involving women, African Americans, gay men and lesbians, poor people, and workers led to important changes in social policy.

Early in the twentieth century, workers reacted to industrialization by demanding limited working hours and the right to form unions and to bargain collectively with employers. In the Great Depression of the 1930s and again in the 1960s, people successfully pressed for government programs to address problems such as poverty and homelessness.

In the 1950s and 1960s, African Americans joined together in the civil rights movement, demanding—and winning—an end to the legal segregation of schools and public facilities and protection from racial discrimination in employment, schooling, housing, and public

Elderly people in the United States have enormous political clout, based not just on their relative wealth but also on their high voter turnout. People over the age of sixty-five are much more likely to vote than young people in their late teens and twenties. How might the power of young people change if they, too, turned out to vote in large numbers?

accommodations. In the 1960s and 1970s, the women's movement gained similar protections from discrimination, guaranteeing women equal opportunities in schooling, athletics, employment, and expanding the availability of credit and the range of opportunities in the military. Since then, in some states and cities, the gay and lesbian movement has achieved protection from discrimination in the workplace and in access to housing; in more than half the states, same-sex partners have gained the right to marry. Finally, throughout the past century, senior citizens have worked to improve retirement and health care benefits.

No one can doubt that social movements have been a powerful political force in the United States, resulting in changes in the law and, over time, in public attitudes. But it is also true that none of the movements mentioned has altered the U.S. political economy in any fundamental way. In fact, in recent decades, the extent of economic inequality in the United States has increased. Nor has there been any notable reduction in the power of corporations in this country; on the contrary, corporations have increased in size along with the pay of corporate executives. Of course, it is precisely these trends that set the recent Occupy movement into motion. But this movement has yet to change our political and economic system in any significant way.

Theories of Economic and Political Problems

10.4 Apply sociological theory to the country's political and economic system.

Sociology's various macro-level theoretical approaches offer contrasting insights into economic and political

problems. Each approach highlights different facts and points to different conclusions.

Structural-Functional Analysis: Rule by the Many

Structural-functional theory views the economic system as a complex institution that operates to produce and distribute goods and services to the entire population. This approach has some similarity to the laissez-faire model that underlies capitalism because both share the idea that the economy serves the needs of individuals who make decisions about what to produce and what to consume. As Adam Smith argued, from individual decisions guided by self-interest the economy operates to produce the greatest good for the greatest number of people.

The structural-functional approach takes much the same view of politics. The theory most often linked to this approach is the pluralist model of Robert Dahl.

Robert Dahl: Pluralist Model The **pluralist model** is *an analysis of the political system that sees power widely distributed among various groups and organizations in a society*. This model, based largely on the work of Robert Dahl (1961, 1982), suggests that individuals and organizations compete in the political "marketplace" trying to win support from the people.

Dahl concedes that some organizations have more clout than others, but he claims that no organization is powerful enough to get its way all the time. This means that organizations achieve many of their goals, but most of the time, they operate as *veto groups*, working to keep their opponents from achieving all of *their* goals. In the pluralist model, various political organizations—including political parties, special-interest groups, and government agencies—compete for public support and also negotiate with one another, striking deals, forming alliances, and setting policy.

The pluralist model views society as an arena in which many organizations appeal to various segments of the population. In the same way that competition between businesses improves the economy, competition between parties and special-interest groups serves the public interest. Therefore, with so many organizations in operation, our political system is a chorus of many voices and ends up sounding rather democratic (Rothman & Black, 1998).

EVALUATE

In a test of the pluralist model, Nelson Polsby (1959) investigated political decision making in a number of large cities in the United States. Polsby confirmed that power is widely distributed among many organizations. He found that any specific group or organization in a city typically has some control over only a narrow range of issues (for example, the school board has influence in matters related to school policy but little else). Over the course of our history, the expansion of voting rights and the increase in the number of organizations, including special-interest groups, ensure that no one category of people has all the power and that just about everyone has some political voice.

But critics of the pluralist model claim that this view of U.S. society as highly democratic does not reflect political reality. Some very large and powerful corporations—including the Wall Street firms that manage the nation's money—have a huge influence throughout the political system. In addition, some categories of people—the rich in relation to the poor—clearly have much more political clout. Critics also point out that many people in this country—especially the poor—see little reason to vote and many never even bother to register. Such criticism that focuses on social inequality brings us to the social-conflict approach.

CHECK YOUR LEARNING What do we learn about politics and government by applying the pluralist model? What is one limitation of this approach?

Social-Conflict Analysis: Rule by the Few

Social-conflict theory sees an elite in control of the economic and political systems. From this perspective, the political economy of the United States operates not to serve the will of the people but in a manner that benefits just *some* of the people. Just as the economy concentrates wealth, so the political system concentrates power. This conclusion clearly challenges the pluralist claim that the United States is democratic. We briefly examine two social-conflict theories: the power-elite model of C. Wright Mills and the Marxist political economy model.

C. Wright Mills: The Power-Elite Model In 1961, as he prepared to leave office after eight years as president, Dwight D. Eisenhower gave a farewell address in which he warned the country of the growing power of what he called the **military-industrial complex**, *the close association of the federal government, the military, and the defense industries.*

In giving this warning, Eisenhower might well have been thinking of what the sociologist C. Wright Mills (1956) called the **power-elite model**, *an analysis of the political system that sees power as concentrated among members of a small elite.* Who is this elite group? According to Mills, the power elite is a small network of individuals and their families that includes top military officials, the heads of major corporations, and top political leaders. In fact, many of the top military, corporate, and political officials are actually the *same people* because elites often move from one sector to another. For example, Eisenhower himself moved from a top spot in the military to a top spot in the world of politics. Likewise, many corporate leaders move into politics and return to corporate boardrooms after leaving office. Dick Cheney left a cabinet position to become a corporate CEO and later moved back into government as vice president only to return to the business world once again. Many power-elite families are socially linked because they live in the same expensive communities, belong to the same exclusive clubs, and send their children to the same private schools.

Traveling in the same social circles, Mills added, children of the power elite stand a good chance of marrying one another and passing along their privileges to another generation. Were he alive today, Mills would

Throughout this country's history, people have banded together in an effort to gain power and change the system. In the 1950s and 1960s, African Americans mounted demonstrations, such as this march from Selma to Montgomery, Alabama, in an effort to gain a greater political voice. In your view, how much real change do such movements create?

probably point out that all the Republican candidates in the 2012 primary were millionaires (ranging from Rick Santorum who is worth $2 million to $3 million to Mitt Romney with some $200 million) as was Barack Obama, the Democratic president standing for reelection, whose wealth probably exceeds $5 million (Riley, 2012).

Based on such observations, the power-elite model rejects the pluralist claim that power is widely spread throughout society, with organizations preventing one another from gaining too much power. On the contrary, this model leads to the conclusion that both wealth and power in U.S. society are highly concentrated so that the power elite pretty much run the country as they wish.

Karl Marx: Capitalist Political Economy The **Marxist political-economy model** is *an analysis that sees the concentration of wealth and power in society as resulting from capitalism.* A Marxist approach accepts the power-elite model that U.S. society is far from democratic because it is dominated by an economic and political elite. But rather than focusing on the great power of certain individuals, the Marxist model takes a more radical approach and focuses on the institutional system that concentrates this wealth and power in the first place.

In Marx's view, the economy is the institution that guides the way the entire society operates. The concentration of wealth and power in the hands of a few results not from the unusual ability and exceptional efforts of certain individuals but from the routine operation of the capitalist economy. From this point of view, as long as the United States has a capitalist economy, the majority of people will be shut out of politics, just as they are exploited in the workplace.

Our national leaders represent differing political parties. According to the pluralist approach, our major parties represent different visions for the country and therefore give voters a real choice. The power-elite model sees all our leaders in Washington, D.C., as one ruling elite that represents mainly its own interests. The political-economy model claims that the political process is guided by the capitalist economy and the major parties differ to only an insignificant degree. Which position do you find most convincing? Why?

working-class family, and Barack Obama is the son of a single mother). Another criticism of this approach, particularly the Marxist analysis, comes from the observation that socialism seems to concentrate power even more than capitalism. After all, elites dominate the politics of nations with socialist economies such as China, Cuba, and North Korea, and leaders in these nations tolerate little opposition and many of the same people remain in power for decades.

CHECK YOUR LEARNING What do we learn about politics and government by applying the power-elite model and the Marxist political-economy model? What is one limitation of each of these approaches?

The Applying Theory table on page 314 summarizes what each theoretical approach teaches us about the economy and politics.

✪ POLITICS AND THE ECONOMY

Constructing Problems and Defining Solutions

10.5 Analyze the U.S. economic and political systems from various positions on the political spectrum.

Theory provides helpful insights about the economy and politics, but what the problems are and how to go about solving them are matters of political opinion. Here we explore conservative, liberal, and radical-left political positions on economic and political problems and solutions from each of these points of view.

EVALUATE

Social-conflict theory challenges the notion that U.S. society is democratic and highlights the extent of economic and political inequality. The power-elite model points to a small number of socially connected families that direct the operation of the political and economic system; the Marxist political-economy model points to the capitalist economy as concentrating wealth and power.

A limitation of this approach is that it gives little attention to the progress U.S. society has made toward extending both economic and political opportunity over the course of its history. This greater opportunity is evident in the rapidly increasing share of the population that has the right to vote and the increasing number of minorities and women who hold political office. Furthermore, although a few U.S. presidents were born into the upper class (George W. Bush is one example), many more rose from humble origins (for example, Bill Clinton was born into a

APPLYING THEORY

Economy and Politics

	Structural-Functional Theory	Social-Conflict Theory
What is the level of analysis?	Macro-level	Macro-level
How is power spread throughout U.S. society?	Structural-functional theory sees power as spread throughout society. Dahl's pluralist theory states that many diverse organizations operate as veto groups and compete for support so that just about everyone has some political voice.	One important social-conflict theory is the power-elite model developed by C. Wright Mills. This theory states that our society is run by a power elite made up of leaders in government, the economy, and the military. This alliance, or military-industrial complex, controls the political life of the nation. A more radical social-conflict theory is the political-economy model based on the ideas of Karl Marx. This approach claims that wealth and power are highly concentrated as a result of the operation of the capitalist economic system.
Is U.S. society democratic?	The pluralist model says yes because most organizations deal with only limited numbers of issues and no one organization gets its way all the time. Power is dispersed widely enough that our society can fairly claim to be democratic.	The power-elite model says no because power is concentrated within a small circle of families that make up the power elite. By controlling the government, the economy, and the military, these families effectively run the entire society. The Marxist political-economy model says no because power will always be highly concentrated as long as the United States has a capitalist economy. This means that radical change, not mere reform, is needed to make our society truly democratic.

Conservatives: The System Is Working

Believing that free competition is good for society, conservatives support the free market and want to limit government involvement in the economy. Likewise, they hold that competition between political candidates, who seek voter support, as well as competition between special-interest groups, is a pretty good definition of democracy.

Conservatives point out that our political system permits every adult citizen (except felons, in most states) to participate in the political process by voting—and the system leaves it up to each individual to register and cast a vote. People are free to engage in as much (or as little) political action as they wish. That is, people are free to join special-interest groups, contribute to campaigns, work for political parties, participate in social movements, and even join in political protests.

The foundation of these freedoms lies in the U.S. Constitution, which was ratified in 1788, and the first ten amendments to the Constitution (often called the Bill of Rights), which was ratified in 1791. In addition, in the years since then, the United States has steadily extended the right to vote to almost every adult. Never have there been as many special-interest groups on the political scene as there are today. In short, as conservatives see it, this nation is built on a foundation of freedoms and rights that continues to provide us with many opportunities to engage in political and economic life in pursuit of our own interests as we see them.

As a result, conservatives claim that the current economic and political systems work pretty well. As the old saying goes, the economic and political systems in the United States may not be perfect, but they are better than anything else out there. Conservatives do worry about the increasing scope of government with increasing regulation making it harder to start a new business and, overall, reducing the rate of economic growth (Ferguson, 2013). In addition, the increasing size of government threatens personal freedoms. In general, conservatives see the increase in the size of government as the major problem facing the U.S. political economy.

Liberals: The Need for Reform

Liberals also see benefits in the operation of a market economy, but they wish to ensure that the market is regulated by the government. As they see it, a laissez-faire economy concentrates wealth in the hands of the few. Those with the greatest wealth, in turn, are able to gain control of the political process so that government policy ends up mostly benefiting the rich and powerful interest groups such as large corporations.

To reduce the economic inequality produced by a market economy, and to provide for the needs of the poor and those not well served by the market, liberals support a **welfare state**, *a range of government policies and programs that transfer wealth from the rich to the poor and provide benefits to needy members of society.* A central part of welfare state policy is progressive taxation, a policy that raises the tax rate as income goes up (take a glance back at Table 2–1 on page 39). In practice, those with higher incomes provide money in the form of taxes to pay for programs that benefit people with lower incomes. The result of this policy is income transfer from rich to poor by which the government reduces the economic inequality created by the market and assists the needy.

Tax policy is a key part of any administration's political agenda. Liberal leaders typically try to make taxation more progressive to move the tax burden more toward high-income people. For example, the more liberal Obama administration raised tax rates on higher-income people just as the more conservative Bush administration had previously reduced rates.

Liberals also want to limit the political power of the corporate elites and other high-income people. To this end, liberals support a government strong enough to regulate both the economy and political system with the goal of ensuring that elites do not set the national agenda. Liberals support policies that benefit the "middle class" or "working people," such as raising the minimum wage, expanding child support programs, expanding access to higher education, and ensuring that health care is available to all. Liberals support a strong and activist government in the belief that it is government—not the marketplace—that works for the interests of ordinary people. Put another way, only government can effectively oppose the enormous power of special-interest groups such as large corporations.

It is true that liberals generally support "more government" than conservatives do. But a closer look shows that both liberals and conservatives favor using government power as a solution to what they define as social problems, as the Social Policy box on page 316 explains.

The Radical Left: A Call for Basic Change

Generally speaking, the further to the left you move on the political spectrum, the more you wish to place the economy under government control. Radicals on the left (following Karl Marx) sought to abolish the capitalist market system; they saw capitalism as a problem because it concentrates wealth in the hands of the few. Liberals close to the political center may support government regulation of the market, but radicals see such efforts as little more than helping the capitalist economy to operate and thereby protecting the wealth of the rich. Left-radicals claim that because government regulation cannot make much difference

under capitalism, government control of the economy must *replace* the capitalist market system.

From a radical-left perspective, the problem is not that a "power elite" has managed to seize control of the government, as liberals are inclined to say. Radicals believe that as long as a capitalist political economy exists in the United States, no small change—such as voters electing more liberal candidates or Congress passing campaign finance reform—will make much difference. For radicals, the only solution to capitalism's concentration of wealth and power is an end to capitalism itself, which means placing the entire economy under government control. For a society to be truly democratic, all people must be equally represented by the government; for that to happen, there must be economic equality.

Radicals on the left will certainly find the policies of the liberal Democrats preferable to those of conservative Republicans. But, from a radical point of view, the two parties are alike in their support of capitalism. For radicals on the left, meaningful change means working toward the goal of placing the economy entirely under government control. Only by ending private ownership of productive property will people share equally in everything our society produces (Eby, 2009).

The Left to Right table on page 317 views problems and issues of the political economy from various points of view.

Going On from Here

Over a century ago, during the Industrial Revolution, the emergence of huge corporations raised national concerns about the power of "big business" and "big money." Congress enacted various laws to combat corporate monopoly and to limit the power of big corporations. These laws ended huge near-monopolies such as Standard Oil, but permitted widespread oligopoly. For much of the twentieth century, therefore, corporations

Conservatives claim that by providing everyone with a vote and by linking rewards to personal ability and effort, our economic and political systems serve the entire population fairly. Liberals support government reforms to better serve the most needy people and reduce inequality. Radicals on the left call for a government-run economy that would meet everyone's basic needs equally. Which view comes closest to your own? Why?

SOCIAL POLICY

Who Favors "Big Government"? Everybody!

The conventional wisdom is that liberals (who typically vote Democratic) support a larger government than conservatives (who vote Republican). There is considerable truth to this statement. But it is also correct to point out that people on *both* sides of the political spectrum support the use of government power to pursue their particular political goals. After all, government has grown under *both* Democratic and Republican presidents.

The table illustrates the politics of big government. Liberals typically define social problems in terms of social inequality. For example, liberals are likely to think that the rich have too much and the poor have too little. Therefore, liberals support progressive taxation by the government with the funds used to pay for social welfare benefits for people in need. In addition, liberals support government enforcement of antidiscrimination laws that protect women and other minorities. To help everyone, liberals would like the government to mandate a universal health care program, putting health care under the control of government.

But conservatives, too, support big government—except that they want government to do different things. Conservatives typically define social problems in moral terms. For example,

conservatives see the world as threatening to the United States, and so they favor bigger government in the form of a larger military with more and better equipment. In the same way, many conservatives oppose abortion and gay marriage and would like the government to restrict access to abortion and some types of birth control and to enact a constitutional ban on same-sex marriage.

In the end, liberals and conservatives both try to use government power to advance their political objectives. This is because government power is a very effective way to address many social problems. This fact helps explain why government spending is high whether our leaders are mostly Republicans or Democrats.

What Do You Think?

1. Make a list of three problems liberals want government to solve. Do the same for conservatives.

2. After the 9/11 attacks, why did government spending increase under Republican president Bush? Why has it increased even faster under Democratic president Obama?

3. How would radicals on the left respond to both the liberal and conservative positions?

---

retained great power to shape the agenda in federal and state governments.

In the 1970s, Congress once again believed it was time to reduce corporate influence in U.S. politics. An important reform—the 1971 Federal Election Campaign Act—led to the creation of the political action committees (PACs) discussed earlier in this chapter. This law tried to level the playing field by placing limits on the political contributions of both rich individuals and large corporations.

The results of this bill fell short of its promise. For one thing, the costs of campaigning—now conducted primarily through paid advertising on television—have soared. Today's political candidates need more money than ever to be elected. Not surprisingly, in the past several decades, the number and influence of PACs have increased; PACs now provide more than four times as much money to members of Congress as they did in the 1970s. Although PACs represent a wide range of political interests, including labor unions, corporate PACs outnumber and give more money to candidates than any other type. With the

Supreme Court decision of 2010 that allows unlimited contributions to Super PACs, election-year spending hit new highs in 2012.

There can be little doubt that the operation of the U.S. economic and political systems will be debated for years to come. People on the right (in the spirit of the Tea Party movement) see a government that has grown too big, that intrudes into people's lives in too many ways, and spends so much money that it will eventually bankrupt the country. People on the left (in the spirit of the Occupy Wall Street movement) see a free market in which greed is the order of the day and in which the "1 percent" is running away with the country, while the "99 percent" are struggling to hold on to the little they have.

Surveys tell us that, in 2014, almost 90 percent of U.S. adults expressed little confidence in Congress (Gallup, 2014). In addition, almost 40 percent of all U.S. citizens are not engaged in the political process enough to bother casting a vote. Whether the people who do not vote believe that the candidates and policy options presented offer no real choice (as radicals on the left tend to say) or

LEFT TO RIGHT

The Politics of the Political Economy

	Radical-Left View	Liberal View	Conservative View
What is the problem?	The capitalist economy concentrates wealth in the hands of the few; the government serves the interests of the capitalist elite. Overall, U.S. society is neither economically just nor politically democratic.	The economy is productive, but some people fare much better than others; those with greater wealth have the most influence in the political system.	Politics and economics are not a problem. The economy provides a high standard of living and responds to consumer demand; the political system is based on elections in which individuals vote and various organizations negotiate to set public policy.
What is the solution?	Efforts to reform the capitalist political economy will have little effect. What is needed is fundamental change in the economic and political systems so that they reflect the interests and meet the needs of the majority.	Government social welfare programs should transfer wealth from rich to poor to lessen inequality. Political reforms are needed to reduce the role of corporate and individual wealth in the political process.	Market economics should be maintained because this provides the greatest good for the greatest number of people. The United States stands out among nations as a model of extensive rights and freedoms.

JOIN THE DEBATE

1. What, in your opinion, are the strengths and weaknesses of the U.S. economy? Provide specific facts to support your assessment.

2. To what degree do you think the United States can be described as a political democracy? What specific evidence can you present to support your assessment?

3. Which of the three political analyses of political economy included here do you find most convincing? Why?

---

whether they are basically satisfied with their lives (as conservatives to the right would have it) is hard to say.

In the end, perhaps we need to return to a basic question: What do we mean by "democracy"? Then we must face an even more difficult challenge: How can we as a nation get there?

Essay: Envisioning a Better Society Looking ahead fifty years, do you think government will control a larger or smaller share of the U.S. economy compared to today? What level of government control of the economy do you think would be in the best interest of the country? Why?

CHAPTER 10 Economy and Politics

What is the purpose of the economy?

The economy operates to provide goods and services to the people living in a society. That's easy enough, but the big question is what form should the economy take? All the great economic thinkers—including both Adam Smith on the right and Karl Marx on the left—understood that answering this question involves selecting a balance between a market economy and a government-operated economy. Look at the accompanying photos to see two distinct solutions to the question of how an economy should work.

From the point of view of the political left, the most important factor in the operation of the economy is how equally goods and services are distributed. The capitalist market economy, as Karl Marx explained, distributes everything unequally, thereby creating social classes. A market economy, as he saw it, was a problem rather than a solution. Only through government control of productive property, which allows an equal distribution of goods and services, can the needs of all people be met. Even capitalist countries such as the United States put government in control of national defense and building roadways and other public infrastructure.

From the point of view of the political right, the most important factor in the operation of the economy is its productivity. The market economy, as Adam Smith explained, is highly productive, generating the greatest good for the greatest number of people—as long as it is allowed to operate with minimal government interference. Market systems also provide extensive liberty, as individuals decide what to produce and people also should decide what to consume.

> **Hint:** Both Karl Marx and Adam Smith had it right, or at least partly right. The market economy is very productive, but it also generates considerable economic inequality. The question is where do you strike the balance between productivity and equality? Then there is the issue of freedom. Market systems provide extensive personal freedoms, but these freedoms mean less to the poor than to the rich. From another angle, government-run economies ensure freedom from want, but they attract criticism for limiting individual freedom. In your opinion, where should the balance be struck?

Getting Involved: Applications and Exercises

1. Go to http://www.cnn.com/election to find analysis of recent election results. Looking at the information presented there, try to discover how gender, race, income, and other variables shape patterns of voting. Can you develop a profile of the typical Democratic voter? What about the typical Republican voter?

2. Go to a search engine such as YouTube and search for short videos explaining the operation of oligopoly (try something like, "oligopoly market"). Identify traits of an oligopolistic market system. Why might oligopoly be encouraged by government, as when one business supplies electric power to a city or picks up everyone's trash?

3. Can you identify your representatives in the Senate and the House of Representatives? What party do they represent? How have they voted on recent political issues?

4. Go online and visit the home pages of several national and international political organizations such as the National Organization for Women (www.NOW.org), Amnesty International (www.Amnesty.org), the National Rifle Association (www.NRA.org), or Occupy Wall Street (www.occupywallst.org). Identify the organization's goals. What part might you play in the operation of any of these organizations?

CHAPTER 10 Economy and Politics

Economic Systems: Defining Justice, Defining Problems

10.1 Distinguish between two economic models: capitalism and socialism.

- The **economy** is the social institution that organizes the production, distribution, and consumption of goods and services.
- **Politics** is the social institution that guides a society's decision making about how to live.
- **Government** is the formal organization that directs the political life of a society. **p. 298**

Two major economic models are **capitalism** and **socialism**.

- Capitalism is based on the private ownership of productive property and a market system regulated by supply and demand.
- Socialism is based on collective ownership of productive property with government control of the economy. **pp. 298–99**

politics (p. 298) the social institution that guides a society's decision making about how to live

economy (p. 298) the social institution that organizes the production, distribution, and consumption of goods and services

capitalism (p. 298) an economic system in which natural resources and the means of producing goods and services are privately owned

government (p. 298) a formal organization that directs the political life of a society

socialism (p. 299) an economic system in which natural resources and the means of producing goods and services are collectively owned

The Economy and Politics

10.2 Explain the links between the economy and politics.

Democracy is a political system in which power is exercised by the people as a whole.

Authoritarian political systems give people little voice in government.

Are capitalist societies always democratic?

- Many conservatives and liberals point out that capitalism provides lots of personal freedom.

- Some liberals and people on the left counter that capitalism generates lots of economic inequality, which threatens democracy. **pp. 301–3**

political economy (p. 301) the closely linked economic and political life of a nation or world region

democracy (p. 301) a political system in which power is exercised by the people as a whole

authoritarianism (p. 303) a political system that denies popular participation in government

monarchy (p. 303) a political system in which a single family rules from generation to generation

Problems of the U.S. Political Economy

10.3 Describe the operation of the U.S. political economy.

Corporations stand at the center of the U.S. political economy.

- Government helps support corporations not only by buying corporate products but also with various incentives that critics call "corporate welfare." **pp. 303–4**

A century ago, some large corporations operated as **monopolies**, completely dominating a segment of the market.

- Today, government outlaws monopoly, but many large corporations operate as **oligopolies**, in which a few giant corporations dominate a market. **pp. 304–5**

Although **conglomerates** and **interlocking directorates** are within the law, they can encourage illegal activities such as price fixing, and they certainly increase corporate wealth and power. **p. 305**

Special-interest groups raise money for political candidates and lobby government officials to advance particular interests.

- Raising campaign funds is a major concern of public officials, who seek money from individual donors, political parties, and political action committees (PACs).
- The importance of fundraising makes us ask whose interests government officials should serve. **pp. 305–8**

Voter apathy is high in the United States, with only 58% of eligible people voting in the 2012 presidential election.

- Conservatives suggest that low voter turnout means that most people are content with their lives. Liberals and radicals counter that it means that people are dissatisfied but believe they have little power to bring about change.

- In general, voter apathy is greatest among the young, those with little education, and the poor. **pp. 308–10**

Social movements offer us all the opportunity to be politically active.

- Various movements have changed U.S. society in important ways but have not brought fundamental change to our political economy. **pp. 310–11**

> **corporations** (p. 303) businesses with a legal existence, including rights and liabilities, separate from that of their members
> **monopoly** (p. 304) the domination of an entire market by a single company
> **oligopoly** (p. 305) the domination of a market by a few companies
> **conglomerate** (p. 305) a giant corporation composed of many smaller corporations
> **interlocking directorates** (p. 305) social networks made up of people who serve as directors of several corporations at the same time
> **special-interest groups** (p. 305) political alliances of people interested in some economic or social issue
> **lobbying** (p. 305) the efforts of special-interest groups and their representatives to influence government officials
> **political action committees** (PACs) (p. 307) organizations formed by special-interest groups to raise and spend money in support of political goals
> **gender gap** (p. 310) the tendency for women and men to hold different opinions about certain issues and to support different candidates

Theories of Economic and Political Problems

10.4 Apply sociological theory to the country's political and economic system.

Structural-Functional Analysis: Rule by the Many
Guided by structural-functional theory, the **pluralist model** states that power is widely dispersed throughout U.S. society.

- Organizations compete for voter support and often operate as veto groups so that no single organization can dominate the political system.

- Just as economic competition results in the greatest good for the greatest number, competition between organizations and between candidates for popular support results in sound policy. **pp. 311–12**

Social-Conflict Analysis: Rule by the Few
Guided by social-conflict theory, the **power-elite model** states that the U.S. political system is dominated by a power elite made up of the top leaders in this country's corporations, military, and government.

- A more radical social-conflict approach is the **Marxist political-economy model**, which shifts the focus from elites to the capitalist system, which concentrates wealth and power in the hands of a few. **pp. 312–13**

> **pluralist model** (p. 311) an analysis of the political system that sees power widely distributed among various groups and organizations in a society
> **military-industrial complex** (p. 312) the close association of the federal government, the military, and the defense industries
> **power-elite model** (p. 312) an analysis of the political system that sees power as concentrated among members of a small elite
> **Marxist political-economy model** (p. 313) an analysis that sees the concentration of wealth and power in society as resulting from capitalism

⭐ POLITICS AND THE ECONOMY

Constructing Problems and Defining Solutions

10.5 Analyze the U.S. economic and political systems from various positions on the political spectrum.

Conservatives: The System Is Working

- **Conservatives** claim that the U.S. economic and political systems work well. Competition in the marketplace and in the political arena serves the public interest.

- Conservatives look to government to advance what they see as moral goals, such as national defense and restricting abortion and discouraging same-sex marriage. **p. 314**

Liberals: The Need for Reform

- **Liberals** point out that the U.S. economic and political systems produce significant social inequality.

- Liberals favor more government regulation of the economy and political system; they support social welfare programs funded by progressive taxation that redistribute income by providing various benefits to the poor. **p. 314–15**

The Radical Left: A Call for Basic Change

- **Radicals on the left** believe that the root cause of political and economic problems in the United States is capitalism's concentration of wealth and power.

- Radicals on the left maintain that reform will not solve these problems; they call for elimination of the capitalist system. **p. 315**

> **welfare state** (p. 314) a range of government policies and programs that transfer wealth from the rich to the poor and provide benefits to needy members of society

Chapter 11
Work and the Workplace

Learning Objectives

11.1 Explain how the Industrial Revolution, the Information Revolution, and globalization have changed the character of work.

11.2 Discuss widespread problems of the U.S. workplace.

11.3 Describe the effects of computer technology on the workplace.

11.4 Apply sociological theory to issues involving work and the workplace.

11.5 Analyze workplace issues from various positions on the political spectrum.

Tracking the Trends

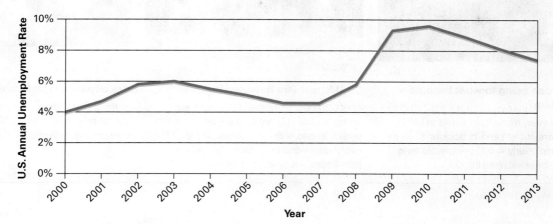

SOURCE: U.S. Department of Labor (2014).

Is there work for people who want jobs? To answer this question, we need to know about the state of the economy. As shown in the figure, the unemployment rate was less than 4 percent of the adult population at the beginning of this century. But soon after the onset of the recent recession, the unemployment rate jumped upwards to almost 10 percent. This means that more than 15 million people who wanted work were unable to find jobs, and this number does not count "discouraged workers" who had given up looking for work. Do you think that everyone who wants to work should have employment? How can our society create more economic opportunity?

Constructing the Problem

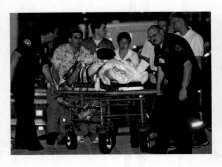

How can going to work become a problem?

Every year, more than 1 million U.S. workers suffer serious accidents on the job and nearly 4,400 people die as a result of workplace injuries.

Do U.S. workers have secure jobs?

About 20 percent of the U.S. labor force consists of temporary workers and part-timers. In bad economic times, just about everybody—and especially "temps" and part-timers—is at risk of a layoff.

Are all jobs available to everyone?

In the United States, 98 percent of dental hygienists—but just 31 percent of dentists—are women.

Chapter Overview

How does our economy shape people's jobs? This chapter looks at how major changes to the economy, including the Information Revolution and increasing globalization, affect each and every one of us. You will learn which types of jobs are likely to be available for tomorrow's workforce as well as which types of jobs are disappearing. In addition, you will learn which types of work are the most dangerous, why many workers feel on-the-job "alienation," and what's happening to labor unions. Finally, you will understand which categories of the population are at highest risk of unemployment and which categories of people have the most economic opportunity. You will carry out theoretical analysis of work and workplace issues and learn how the work-related "problems" people identify and the "solutions" they favor reflect their political attitudes.

The blast rumbled like 1,000 freight trains, collapsing a large section of the Sago coal mine near Tallmansville, West Virginia. One man, who was working near the point

of the explosion, died instantly. A dozen more men were trapped 2 miles inside, down the main shaft of the mine, more than half a mile below the surface.

As they had been trained to do, the men huddled together into what they hoped would be a safe spot in the mine and pulled a large sheet of cloth across the shaft to block the flow of toxic gases from the explosion. On the surface, workers and emergency personnel launched a rescue operation. But the rescuers ran into high concentrations of deadly carbon monoxide gas, forcing them back out of the mine until they could vent the gas.

The progress of the rescue effort was agonizingly slow. Inside the Sago Baptist Church, families had gathered, fearing the worst but hoping that the men would make it out alive. For two long days, rescuers cleared gas, moved debris, secured the shaft, and finally, located the men.

Hopes that the twelve men were still alive were dashed when the rescue workers reached the group of miners, finding only one man still breathing. Randal McCloy, the youngest of the twelve, lay motionless and clinging to life; he would spend months in recovery. Later, McCloy reported that the men in the mine passed the long hours quietly sitting together, using as little of the available oxygen as possible. Right to the point that they could no longer breathe and lost consciousness, they all believed that help would come.

The 2006 Sago mine disaster points to the serious problems that can surround the workplace. In recent years, this particular mine was cited for hundreds of safety violations. But this mining accident is far from an isolated case: In 2012, more than 3,700 miners suffered a work-related illness or injury, and 36 miners lost their lives (Levin, Frank, & Overberg, 2006; Vanden Brook & Nichols, 2006; U.S. Department of Labor, 2013).

Illness, injury, and death are all a reality in the U.S. workplace—especially in high-risk occupations such as mining. As this chapter explains, despite a long-term decline in workplace casualties, the dangers remain very real. In addition, a host of other work-related problems commands our attention. In recent decades, millions of men and women in the United States lost their factory jobs as computers and robots replaced workers on assembly lines and old industrial plants shut down entirely. And when the economy falls into recession, as it did in 2008, corporations engage in widespread layoffs, and not only factory workers but also managers and other highly skilled people with office jobs discover that they, too, are at risk of unemployment (Gumbel, 2009; McGeehan, 2009; Bui, 2013).

This chapter surveys all these social problems surrounding work and the workplace. But we might first ask a basic question: Why is work important? The obvious reason is that, for most people anyway, jobs provide the income needed to live. But work is more than a matter of money. A job gives many people a sense of pride and accomplishment. In addition, for almost everyone, what one does for a living is an important source of social identity and personal identity. Most people think of themselves in terms of their work, as firefighters, teachers, nurses, or carpenters, and they build the social world around the work they do every day.

Because work matters in so many ways, problems in the workplace take on special importance. To see the forces that shape the workplace and its problems, we begin by looking at broad, historical trends in the economy, which are beyond the control of ordinary people but which affect us all.

Structural Changes in the U.S. Economy

11.1 Explain how the Industrial Revolution, the Information Revolution, and globalization have changed the character of work.

The nature of work and the workplace in the United States reflect large-scale changes to the economy. Over our nation's history, two major structural changes have reshaped the economy. The first change, which began about 200 years ago, was the Industrial Revolution. The second change, which began in the 1950s and continues today, is the Information Revolution, which sparked both deindustrialization and the globalization of the economy. As you will see, both the Industrial Revolution and the Information Revolution transformed not just the economy but our entire way of life.

The Industrial Revolution

Throughout the nineteenth century, most people in the United States lived in rural areas and small towns where they worked in the *primary sector* of the economy, producing raw materials by farming, fishing, ranching, mining, or clearing forests. But as an increasing number of factories sprang up in the growing cities from New England to the Midwest, the nature of work changed. The Industrial Revolution pushed workers into the *secondary sector* of the economy, in which workers transformed raw materials into finished products: For example, factory workers turned wood into furniture and steel into railroad tracks and, later, into automobiles.

Figure 11–1 on page 326 shows that by 1900, the share of people working in industrial factories equaled the share working on the farm. Factories drew millions of people from rural areas to live in or near large cities. Many people, especially those who stayed behind, saw this migration as a serious problem because it drained the population of small, rural communities, many of which became "ghost towns." From this point of view, the Industrial Revolution threatened a traditional, rural way of life that had existed in the United States since the colonial period.

The Industrial Revolution brought further change to the workplace as new factories and rapidly growing cities attracted tens of millions of people from Europe and other parts of the world. These men and women came to the United States in search of work and a better life. Not all newcomers were welcomed, however. As explained in Chapter 3 ("Racial and Ethnic Inequality"), public opinion in this country was critical of what was described as a flood of foreign immigrants who threatened this country's established culture.

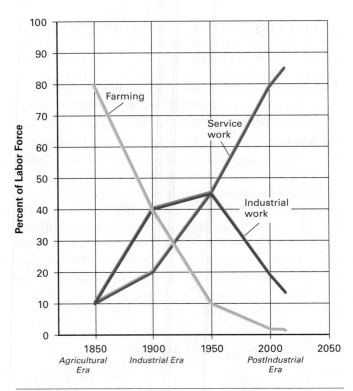

Figure 11–1 The Changing Nature of Work in the United States, 1850–2012

In 1850, 80 percent of U.S. workers were in the primary sector of the economy (farming); today, only a few percent of people in the labor force do such work. Industrial work in the secondary sector of the economy peaked about 1950 and has been in decline since then. Today, more than 80 percent of U.S. workers have service jobs in the tertiary sector of the economy.

SOURCE: Based on U.S. Department of Labor (2013).

Most who came to the new industrial cities to pursue their dreams did find work but their new lives were far from easy. Many had no choice but to take poor housing, sometimes with little heat and no sanitation. Factories offered jobs, but the pay was low, the hours were long, and the work was backbreaking and often dangerous. Many jobs involved repetitive routines in settings filled with smoke and deafening noise. Supervisors closely monitored their workers and tolerated no complaints. By and large, companies treated workers—especially immigrants who spoke little English—as little more than muscle power. But immigrant families needed wages to live, and with little or no ability to organize in pursuit of better working conditions, workers had little choice but to take whatever jobs they could find.

During the 1930s, the Great Depression swept across the country and this major economic collapse put one-quarter of the labor force out of work. Hardship and even hunger became commonplace. Not until World War II, a decade later, did the U.S. economy rebound and living standards start to improve.

In the 1950s and 1960s, the economy boomed. Many—perhaps most—working people in the United States enjoyed rising wages and a better standard of living. As Chapter 14 ("Urban Life") explains, even industrial workers with little schooling earned enough to afford a modest house in a new subdivision outside the city limits, and the population pushed outward from the central cities into the growing suburbs.

Overall, the Industrial Revolution moved work from farm to factory. People who once worked in families now took their place on vast and impersonal assembly lines. Living standards gradually went up, but so did the risk of layoffs.

The Information Revolution

Figure 11–1 shows that, by 1950, the economy was changing again. By that time, the share of the labor force in industrial jobs was matched by the share of workers in the *tertiary* (third) *sector* of the economy. Today, 81 percent of people in the labor force work not in factories but in offices, where they perform *service work* in sales, consulting, law, advertising, and other fields. Only about

In Pittsburgh, Pennsylvania, the tallest building in the city is a sign of the changing economic times by which service work has replaced industrial production. Originally the U.S. Steel building, this structure is now the University of Pittsburgh Medical Center, suggesting the transformation from an industrial to a postindustrial, service economy. Can you think of evidence of similar change in your city or town?

17 percent of the labor force is left in industrial jobs and less than 2 percent of workers remain in farming (U.S. Department of Labor, 2014).

Underlying this expansion of service work is the Information Revolution: the invention of the computer and the spread of computer technology into almost every aspect of life. The Information Revolution pulled workers from older, blue-collar industrial jobs toward newer, white-collar service work. Some of these service workers are established professionals—including doctors, lawyers, and college professors—who have long enjoyed good-paying careers. In addition, the ranks of new professionals—in advertising, consulting, and computer programming—have increased. But the Information Revolution has not been good news for all workers. Many of the office jobs—especially those typically held by women—offer low pay and little chance for advancement.

Deindustrialization

As the Information Revolution signaled the birth of new information technology, it marked the onset of **deindustrialization**, *the decline of industrial production that occurred in the United States after about 1950.* In simple terms, as the economy created new service jobs, it lost old industrial jobs. Many former assembly-line workers and machine operators were put out of work as their plants closed, where many ended up taking jobs as clerical workers, delivery personnel, maintenance workers, and fast-food employees. Almost all of these new jobs pay much less than industrial jobs do, and often the new jobs include fewer benefits. For this reason, many workers with industrial skills but without college degrees have found the last several decades to be tough economic times. For example, tens of thousands of skilled workers lost their jobs in the auto industry in the recent economic recession. Although some have been rehired as the auto industry has recovered, others have little hope of finding work that will offer them the same pay and benefits that they once enjoyed (Read, 2012).

Globalization

The Information Revolution and the deindustrialization of the United States are linked with another trend—economic globalization. With regard to the economy, **globalization** is *the expansion of economic activity around the world with little regard for national borders.* Today, the largest corporations produce and sell products in many countries, and more and more products made in one place cross national borders before they are purchased and consumed.

A century ago, more industrial production took place in the United States than in any other nation. Today,

however, lower wage levels in other countries have encouraged the "outsourcing" of industrial jobs. Consider, for example, that the average industrial worker in Mexico earns $6.48 an hour, far less than wages of more than $35 an hour in the United States. Just how much lower are wages in other countries? As Figure 11–2 shows, industrial workers in Mexico, Taiwan, and South Korea make only a fraction of what industrial workers in the United States earn. Such comparisons help explain why, in recent years, our economy has lost both factory jobs and also millions of white-collar jobs to Mexico, India, and other lower-wage countries (U.S. Department of Labor, 2012).

Saving money by paying lower wages is a powerful incentive for business to move factories and office operations abroad. Making use of new information technology,

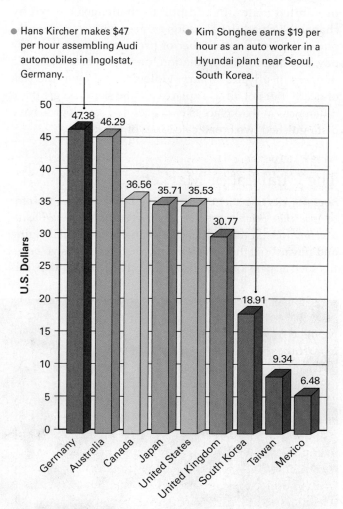

● Hans Kircher makes $47 per hour assembling Audi automobiles in Ingolstat, Germany.

● Kim Songhee earns $19 per hour as an auto worker in a Hyundai plant near Seoul, South Korea.

U.S. Dollars

Germany 47.38
Australia 46.29
Canada 36.56
Japan 35.71
United States 35.53
United Kingdom 30.77
South Korea 18.91
Taiwan 9.34
Mexico 6.48

Global Snapshot

Figure 11–2   Average Hourly Wages for Workers in Manufacturing, 2011

Workers in countries such as Taiwan and Mexico are paid far less than their counterparts in the United States. This disparity is a key reason that the United States has been losing industrial jobs to these nations.

SOURCE: U.S. Department of Labor (2013).

corporations can stay in instant communication with their facilities anywhere in the world.

In sum, global expansion of the economy has been good for most corporations, expanding their markets and raising profits for stockholders. At the same time, the loss of industrial and service jobs here in the United States has been bad for many U.S. working families.

Other Problems of the U.S. Workplace

11.2 Discuss widespread problems of the U.S. workplace.

Going to work is a daily fact of life for many people in the United States. In addition to challenges created by changes such as globalization of the economy, the workplace involves any number of problems, including low pay, alienation, discrimination, unemployment, and the dangers of physical injury, violence, and even the risk of death. But not all workplaces are the same. So great are differences in workplace experiences that sociologists have distinguished two broad categories of work.

The Dual Labor Market

Sociologists use the term **primary labor market** to refer to *jobs that provide workers with good pay and extensive benefits.* Jobs in the primary labor market are challenging and rewarding; they pay well and include extensive benefits such as pensions and health insurance. In addition, this type of work is secure and provides people with a good chance to move ahead. These are the jobs people perform with satisfaction and usually think of as *careers.*

At the top of the primary labor market are the *professions,* white-collar occupations, such as physician, lawyer, and college professor, requiring extensive schooling and offering good pay and lots of prestige. Also included in the primary labor market are positions as business managers and executives, airline pilots, accountants, newspaper editors, electrical engineers, and the good factory jobs that remain in the United States.

Other work in the U.S. economy is in the **secondary labor market,** *jobs that provide workers with low pay and few benefits.* Examples of this type of work include many service jobs, such as restaurant work, retail sales, telemarketing, and building maintenance. This low-paying type of work provides limited benefits, carries a high risk of layoffs, and offers little opportunity for advancement. Workers in the secondary labor market are economically insecure, knowing that they have limited income today and not being sure about having a job tomorrow. Typically, people who work in the secondary labor market are women and men with less schooling and fewer skills—in short, those members of our society with fewer options. The Social Policy box takes a closer look at the problems faced by workers in the secondary labor market.

Danger to Workers

A century ago, at the height of the industrial era, people who labored in steel mills and deep within coal mines were exposed workers to life-threatening danger every day. As amazing as it sounds, about 100 people died *every day* while working in coal mines, factories, burning office buildings, and on commercial fishing boats. Back then, employers and the government paid little attention to worker safety. Mining disasters, like the one described in the opening to this chapter, were almost daily events. In just the year 1907, for example, 3,242 U.S. workers lost their lives in coal mines. Accidents were commonplace not only in mines and in factories but also on farms across rural America, where the use of tractors, combines, and other powered machinery means that a careless moment can result in the loss of a limb or even a life (Mine Safety and Health Administration, 2009; von Drehle, 2011).

In the decades since then, workplace accidents have become less common,

In the United States and around the world, work in the primary sector of the economy has long carried the highest risk of injury and death. Today's mines are highly mechanized, so fewer people now work underground. But powerful equipment carries risks of its own, so that mining remains one of the most hazardous ways to make a living.

SOCIAL POLICY

Low-Wage Jobs: On (Not) Getting By in America

What is it like to work on the floor at Walmart, to clean motel rooms all day long, or to wait tables at a small diner? Low-pay jobs may seem easy—but are they? Even more importantly, can you live on $8 or $9 an hour?

Barbara Ehrenreich, a gifted writer who holds a Ph.D., has made her living for years working behind a desk writing about social issues, including poverty and problems of the workplace. Sharing lunch in New York City with a magazine editor, she was kicking around the idea of writing about low-wage jobs. Without thinking, she said that someone ought to do some old-fashioned research by going out there and actually doing some low-wage work. Her editor suddenly sat up and smiled, offering the simple reply: *"You!"*

So it was that Ehrenreich stepped out of her comfortable life to join the millions of people in the United States who work at low-income jobs. Her plan was simple but challenging: She would not fall back on her writing skills; she would take the best job she could find and do it as well as she could. She would try to live on what she earned, finding the cheapest housing available, as long as it was safe.

Ehrenreich began her adventure in Key West, Florida, by replying to twenty want ads in the local paper. She eventually landed a job waitressing on the 2 P.M. to 10 P.M. shift at a small restaurant connected to a motel. Her pay was $2.43 per hour plus tips. Her first day on the job, she learned an important lesson: *Working as a waitress is much harder than most people think.* Ehrenreich (2001) explains that she was peppered with requests from customers who sometimes seemed like bees swarming around her: more iced tea here, ketchup over there, a take-out box for table 14, a high-chair for the table by the door. She also had to master a touch screen ordering system that did not always work well. And then there was the work she never expected, including sweeping and scrubbing floors, slicing bread, refilling ketchup bottles, and restocking napkins and sugar packs. And she did all this while being constantly watched by the assistant manager for any signs of drug use, stealing, or simply slowing down to catch her breath.

When the tips were collected (and shared with the kitchen staff), Ehrenreich earned $6 to $10 per hour, which totaled about $1,200 for a month of hard work. The cheapest housing she could find was a half-size trailer home fifteen minutes from town for a monthly rent of $675, leaving her with $525 or less than $20 a day for food, clothing, transportation, telephone, health needs, and everything else.

In the months that followed, Ehrenreich performed low-wage work in Florida, Maine, and Minnesota. She swept hotel rooms, cleaned private homes, worked as an aide in a nursing home, and signed on as a sales associate at Walmart. She found that all these jobs, like the waitressing, require many skills and demand long hours of hard work. By the time her adventure came to an end, Ehrenreich had learned another important lesson: *Low-wage jobs do not pay enough to live on.* To have any kind of life, you need to work two of these jobs at the same time. And that—if you can do it—is no life at all.

What Do You Think?

1. Do you agree with Barbara Ehrenreich that low-wage work is much harder than most people think? Why or why not?

2. Should people who work full time have to live below the poverty line? If not, what should our society do about this fact?

3. How much of a chance do people who work in low-paying jobs have to get ahead? What about their chances to get a college degree? Explain.

---

mostly because of the change from industrial work to service jobs. But today's better safety record also reflects efforts by the government. In 1970, the federal government established the Occupational Safety and Health Administration (OSHA) to regulate workplace health and safety. In addition, the government created the National Institute for Occupational Safety and Health (NIOSH), an organization that conducts research on workplace hazards, ranging from toxic chemicals to ailments that result from repetitive motion or heavy lifting.

In 1976, Congress added another layer of worker protection, passing the Toxic Substances Control Act, which set guidelines for handling dangerous materials in the workplace. With corporations using an ever-increasing number of chemicals in the production of food, clothing, automobiles, and other goods, federal agencies face the challenge of not only regulating the use of substances known to be dangerous but also testing new substances to protect workers from those that may be harmful.

Despite the improvement, on-the-job accidents and injuries are still a serious social problem in the United States. In 2012, about 1.2 million workers suffered disabling accidents that required they take time off from work. More seriously, each year, about 4,400 workers lose their lives in workplace accidents. As Figure 11–3 on page 330 shows, the greatest risk of death is found in mining and agriculture (U.S. Department of Labor, 2013).

Mining As suggested in the opening of this chapter, mining has long been ranked as one of the most dangerous types of work a person can do. Mine workers labor

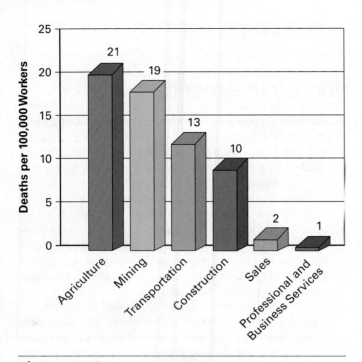

Figure 11–3 Risk of Death, by Type of Job, 2012

Of all categories of work, agriculture and mining have the highest rates of on-the-job fatalities.

SOURCE: U.S. Department of Labor (2013).

with heavy machinery deep underground, facing the ever-present dangers of cave-ins, explosions, fire, and poisonous fumes.

Events like the 2006 Sago coal mine disaster make headlines in the mass media. But even more deadly is something we rarely read about—the coal dust that miners breathe every day. Over many years, the coal dust that builds up in the lungs causes a number of respiratory diseases, which eventually take their toll on retired miners. As one man described working in the mines, "You die quick or you die slow but—either way—you're just as dead" (Gup, 1991:55).

Farming Farming poses risks to workers. Farm equipment is now far safer than it once was, but working with heavy machinery remains dangerous to life and limb. In addition, today's farmers work with more toxic chemicals. Note, too, that U.S. laws that ban child labor do not apply to farming. Therefore, farms and orchards place children at especially high risk of injury or death or harm from long-term exposure to toxic substances.

Toxic Substances and Radiation Human hazards are not limited to mines and farms. Toxic substances used in countless workplaces pose a hazard to workers. Nearly every factory or production facility in operation today contains at least some chemicals known to be hazardous to human health.

Radiation is another occupational hazard that places workers at risk of leukemia and other forms of cancer. The risk of being exposed to radiation exists at 100 nuclear power plants across the United States and also at dozens of factories that produce nuclear materials. The precise hazards are difficult to document because the effects of human exposure to radiation take many years to show up.

But sometimes workers take action. In 1999, fourteen former employees of Kentucky's Paducah Gaseous Diffusion Plant filed a $10 billion lawsuit, alleging that this plant exposed them to hazardous radiation and that the firm concealed this fact from workers and from the general public. A government investigation documented that the workers had reason for concern: They found potential radiation leaks at the plant and in some of 37,000 uranium-containing cylinders stored outdoors (Carroll, 1999a, 1999b).

Workplace Violence Some workplace hazards involve intentional violence. In 2012, across the United States, workplace murder claimed the lives of 463 people, with some killings carried out by robbers and others by fellow workers. Another 225 died from self-inflicted violence (U.S. Department of Labor, 2013).

Although men hold most of the hazardous jobs in mining and farming and suffer about 90 percent of workplace deaths in those occupations, women hold most clerical and other service jobs dealing with the public. For this reason, when a violent person enters a business, the first people at risk are typically women. This is why, of all causes of job-related deaths for women workers, homicide ranks first.

Workplace Alienation

Especially in the secondary labor market, workers have little control over what they do and how they do it. Therefore, for many workers, the main on-the-job experience is powerlessness. Different views of this problem were provided by Karl Marx and Max Weber.

Alienation: Marx's View Well over a century ago, Karl Marx (1818–1883) characterized this problem as **alienation**, *powerlessness in the workplace resulting in the experience of isolation and misery.* For Marx, the problem was not work itself. He believed work to be a natural and satisfying activity by which people meet their needs and develop their creative potential. Marx claimed that the problem of alienation stems from the ways work is shaped by the capitalist economic system.

How does capitalism produce worker alienation? Consider the job of making a coat. Traditionally, coats were made by highly skilled people who were responsible for the entire production of the garment and who could sell the final product, keeping whatever they could earn. Under the capitalist system, however, coat making falls under the control of mill owners, who break the work down into various low-skill tasks—some workers spin wool into yarn, others weave the yarn into cloth, others cut the cloth into patterns, and still others stitch the pieces together into the final coat. Under this system, work becomes a series of simple, repetitive tasks that allows no creativity and requires little skill. When the work is done, the coat is owned and then sold by the mill owner, who keeps whatever profit it brings. Under this system, workers have no say in what to make and how to produce it. Nor can they take any pride in the finished product.

With few skills, workers are easily replaced and have little job security. They end up competing with one another just to keep their jobs. In the end, Marx concluded, capitalism alienates workers in four ways: Capitalism alienates them from their jobs, it alienates them from the products they make, it alienates them from each other, and it alienates them from their human potential. No wonder, Marx observed, that workers in a capitalist economy find so little satisfaction in their jobs and look for pleasure only in their leisure time.

Alienation: Weber's View Max Weber (1864–1920) agreed with Marx that the modern workplace causes worker alienation, but he pointed to other causes of this problem. To Weber, **alienation** is *depersonalization not just in the workplace but throughout society as well brought on by a rational focus on efficiency*. For Weber, then, the cause of alienation is not capitalism, as it was for Marx, but something broader. The problem lies in the rationality—the impersonal focus on efficiency—that is a trait of all modern social life.

To Weber, the Industrial Revolution was one result of the **rationalization of society**, *the historical change from tradition to rationality and efficiency as the typical way people think about the world*. In the Middle Ages, tradition guided people's lives, so the "right" way to do something was simply to do it in the way it had been done in the past. Such an emphasis on tradition may not have resulted in efficient production, but it did bind people together into strong families and tightly knit communities, which gave workers a sense of belonging and purpose.

The modern world's emphasis on rationality is different, guiding individuals and organizations to make decisions not with an eye to the past or to the consequences for families or communities but on the basis of cool-headed calculations of what gets the job done most efficiently. In this way, the goal of efficiency directs the operation of the workplace with little concern for the human costs of any policy or practice. A bank teller, for example, is simply told to process transactions without taking time to get to know the people being served. Further, any worker's job will be at risk if the corporate office determines it can be done faster or cheaper by an automated teller machine (ATM). The result of such rationality may be higher productivity; however, Weber claimed that a single-minded focus on rationality strips us of our basic humanity.

McDonaldization and "McJobs"

Although Marx and Weber found different causes of alienation, they agreed that many people today find their work unsatisfying. Marx defined the problem as capitalism, with factory owners exploiting working people. Weber defined the problem as rationality, which makes production highly efficient but strips away a concern for our humanity. Both points of view help us understand the spread of the low-paying yet productive workplace system typical of McDonald's fast-food restaurants.

According to George Ritzer (1993, 1998), the concept of **McDonaldization** refers to *defining work in terms of the principles of efficiency, predictability, uniformity, and automation*:

1. **Efficiency:** McDonald's tries to serve food quickly and easily.
2. **Predictability:** McDonald's prepares all food the same way each time using set formulas.
3. **Uniformity:** McDonald's serves meals that look and taste exactly the same in all of its restaurants.
4. **Automation:** By automating all tasks, McDonald's is able to precisely control the production process, minimizing human decision making.

Ritzer points out that that the four principles of McDonaldization are found not only in fast-food companies; they guide people's work throughout the low-skill service sector of the U.S. economy. The result is that people now perform "McJobs" by doing a series of simple tasks (often involving pushing buttons on a computer or other machine) that the worker repeats over and over. Not surprisingly, most workers find little satisfaction in such work, and worker turnover rates are high.

McDonald's is a highly successful, multinational corporation serving meals to hundreds of millions of people all over the world. In addition, McDonald's (and similar companies) offer entry-level work experience to countless people—Ritzer estimates that one of every fifteen U.S. workers had a first job at a company like McDonald's, and one of every eight U.S. adults has worked at a fast-food restaurant at some point. But McJobs do not stimulate human creativity and imagination, and they often do not even encourage employees to think. It would not be too far off the mark to suggest that such jobs turn workers into robots for eight hours a day.

The Temping of the Workplace

After World War II, the U.S. economy was booming. Across Europe and in much of Japan, war had destroyed most factories and leveled many cities leaving survivors homeless and destitute. The United States was one of the few countries that could supply the goods

Most people find it easy to agree that many Information Age jobs generate worker alienation, meaning that workers find little to like in their work. Can you explain, from Marx's point of view, how this setting might alienate workers? What about from Weber's point of view?

demanded in war-torn nations as well as here at home. In the strong postwar economy, most jobs paid pretty well, and employers and employees alike assumed that people who worked hard could count on keeping their jobs for life.

Today, the rules have changed. The deindustrialization of the United States—the closing of factories and the loss of white-collar jobs to the "emerging economies" in Asia and elsewhere—means that more and more work in the U.S. economy is temporary. The economic downturns we have experienced in the past decade—especially the recession beginning in 2008—have made jobs less secure than ever. Many people, commonly called "temps," now hold jobs that are formally defined as temporary. These jobs typically pay low wages, give workers little say about their job, and provide no guarantees that their job will be there next year or even next month.

Every day, temp agencies such as Manpower and Kelly Services send 2.8 million people to work in temporary jobs. If we add in all part-timers and people contracted by companies from any outside agency, 21 percent of the U.S. labor force works without some of the benefits other workers count on, including retirement plans, sick leave, health insurance, and job security (U.S. Department of Labor, 2014).

Where can temps be found? Almost everywhere. Adjunct faculty at colleges and universities work year to year or even semester to semester to fill almost one-third of all teaching positions, and many of these men and women teach part time at several different colleges or universities at the same time (U.S. Department of Labor, 2011). Although all categories of the population are included in the ranks of temporary workers, women and other minorities are most likely to have such work, and they are over-represented in the least desirable jobs.

Not everyone finds temporary work to be a problem. Some people are glad to move from job to job. They may be looking for short-term employment—say, over the summer while they are out of school or perhaps an extra weekend job to help with unexpected expenses. Others may be seeking experience, trying out a line of work, and still others do not want the commitment of a permanent position. But overall, temporary work is a better deal for employers than it is for workers. By relying on temps, employers save the costs of training, health and retirement benefits, sick leave, and vacation time.

Unemployment

If many people are not getting all they need from a job, others have no work at all. In July 2008, just as the U.S. economy was falling into recession, the unemployment rate was 5.8 percent of the civilian labor force. That means that about 9 million people over the age of sixteen were without work. By the end of that year, however, another 5 million people had lost their jobs, and by late 2009, the unemployment rate had soared to almost 10 percent with 15.4 million people out of work. By late 2014, the unemployment rate had declined to 5.9 percent of the civilian labor force—still above the prerecession level—with about 10 million people officially out of work (Bui, 2013; U.S. Department of Labor, 2014).

But the official unemployment rate does not accurately describe the extent of the problem. To be counted among the ranks of the unemployed, a person must register with an unemployment office and actively seek work. Yet many people who are looking for jobs never register. Others become *discouraged workers* who start out looking for work but, finding no success, eventually give up so that they are dropped from the official unemployment statistics. For these reasons, the true unemployment rate is quite a bit higher than the government figure.

Reasons for Unemployment   Some unemployment occurs in every society for a number of reasons. Some people have been laid off, others are new to the labor force and looking for work, and still others are between jobs. This is why analysts often describe an unemployment rate between 4 and 5 percent to be normal, "full" employment.

Other analysts—especially on the far left—claim that a capitalist economy actually creates unemployment as a strategy to lower labor costs and increase profits. How? An economy that keeps some people out of work creates a reserve pool of unemployed labor. Having people eager to work means that employers can fill their positions paying as little as possible; after all, if one person won't work for a low wage, there is almost certainly someone else who will. Another benefit of having plenty of people without work is that there will always be someone willing to do even the least desirable job.

When the economy has a downturn, as it did beginning in 2008, the unemployment rate goes up. Most of the people out of work turn to unemployment benefits or welfare to get by. Frances Fox Piven and Richard Cloward (1971) argue that when the economy is weak, the government has little choice but to expand welfare assistance if only to keep people from rising up against the system. On the other hand, when times get better and demand for workers is high, as was the case in the mid-1990s, the government is likely to cut welfare programs to force more people into the labor force. The welfare reform of 1996 seems to provide support for Piven and Cloward's theory. Back then, government reacted to a strong economy by making cuts in welfare programs, as detailed in Chapter 2 ("Poverty and Wealth").

Unemployment can be a very challenging experience. As noted at the beginning of this chapter, work is important not only as a source of income but also as a basic element of social identity and a source of self-esteem. To be out of work robs people of all these things. In addition, in the individualistic and competitive culture of the United States, being out of work often carries the stigma of personal failure, which might be considered a "hidden injury" of unemployment.

Who Is at Risk for Unemployment? In the U.S. population, some categories of people are at higher risk of unemployment than others. Figure 11–4 shows that in 2013 the unemployment rates were slightly higher for men than for women (except for Hispanic Americans). Now look at race and ethnicity: The unemployment rates for African Americans (13.1 percent) and Hispanic Americans (9.1 percent) were notably above the rate for whites (6.5 percent).

Education also plays an important part for people in all racial and ethnic categories. According to government statistics, high school dropouts had an unemployment rate three times higher than that of college graduates (U.S. Department of Labor, 2014).

The "Jobless Recovery"

The U.S. economy operates in cycles, with periods of prosperity followed by periods of recession—what many

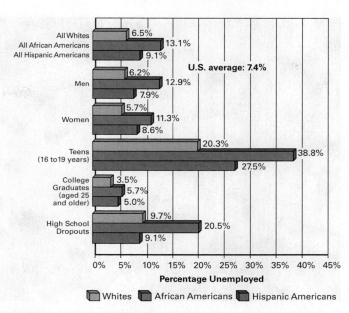

Diversity Snapshot

Figure 11–4 Unemployment Rates for Various Categories of the U.S. Population, 2013

Many factors affect the unemployment rate; among the largest categories of the U.S. population, unemployment affects African Americans most, followed by Hispanic Americans.

SOURCE: U.S. Department of Labor (2014).

people call "boom and bust." In the past, periods of high job loss during economic recession have typically been followed by good times that brought a rapid increase in jobs, with sharply falling unemployment.

This time around, the recovery in jobs has not been as quick. Corporate profits have returned to their prerecession levels, but U.S. corporations are now operating with about 7 million fewer workers than they had before the recession. This means that the nation's unemployment remains stubbornly high. As one recent analysis concluded, the official jobless rate is falling but one big reason for the decline is that millions of people are no longer counted among the unemployed because they appear to have dropped out of the labor force (Foroohar, 2014; Kurtz, 2014).

One reason for this pattern—sometimes described as the "jobless recovery"—is that, even before the economy went into recession, companies were finding ways to operate with a smaller workforce. Computer technology allows the typical employee to do more work. In addition, many companies now demand that their employees do more. Finally, companies are making more use of temporary workers, most of whom do not receive benefits.

Another reason that the United States has experienced continuing high unemployment is that more companies have opened factories and office hubs

In most workplace settings across the United States, minorities are disproportionately found in the jobs that provide the lowest pay and prestige. Based on your own observations in hospitals, hotels, or office buildings, do you think this pattern holds?

the recent recession provided enough pay and benefits to support what we might call a middle-class standard of living. But just half of the new jobs created during the last few years can support a family in the middle class. Millions of newly created jobs provide low wages and fewer benefits. This is especially true among the jobs typically taken by younger adults.

One way we can see this pattern is in the relatively weak levels of consumer spending. Simply put, fewer people have any extra money to spend, which is holding down retail sales and limiting economic growth. The recession may be officially over, in other words, but to millions of people across the United States, it does not feel that way (Casselman, 2013; Foroohar, 2014).

abroad—often in China, India, or Brazil, where wages and benefits will cost far less. In China, for example, labor costs are just 10 percent as much as they are in the United States. For this reason, many global corporations that are making record profits are adding almost no jobs here in the United States.

A third issue is that the U.S. economy is simply not growing fast enough—and has not been for many years—to absorb all the people looking for jobs. This is why, according to government reports, for every available job there are almost five people looking for work.

Fourth, and finally, in global terms, many U.S. workers are simply too expensive and yet not highly skilled enough to fare well in today's global economy. Perhaps, as some analysts suggest, large investments will have to be made in education and job training in order to get the unemployment rate here in the United States back to prerecession levels (Faroohar, 2011; Wessel, 2011; Zackaria, 2011).

The "Low-Wage Recovery"

During the last few years, many economic indicators have returned to prerecession levels. The stock market has recovered to hit all-time highs. Economic growth, although sluggish, has risen. Even the unemployment rate has come down although, as noted previously, the reason may have as much to do with people giving up on work as finding new jobs.

But for those who have found work, another crucial pattern is that many jobs pay less than in the past. One recent analysis concluded that two-thirds of the jobs lost in

Race, Ethnicity, and Gender

As Chapter 3 ("Racial and Ethnic Inequality") and Chapter 4 ("Gender Inequality") explained, prejudice, discrimination, and sometimes even U.S. law barred racial and ethnic minorities—as well as all women—from many good jobs throughout most of this country's history. Only in the 1950s and 1960s did social movements open the door to these categories of people for broader participation in the paid labor force.

Today, many earlier barriers have fallen. But women and other minorities are still not equally represented in many of the better jobs. Often enough, as the old saying goes, women and other minorities are "the last ones hired and the first ones fired." Why? Having the least seniority places these workers at higher risk for layoffs than white men, who, on average, have been in the labor force longer. In addition, as noted earlier, women and minorities are more likely to work as temps or part-timers and in low-skill "McJobs."

Women do have one advantage, however: Women are less likely than men to work in dangerous occupations such as mining or lumbering. This difference is the reason that fewer women than men die on the job. African Americans, too, have one advantage over white workers: They are more likely to be represented by a union (U.S. Department of Labor, 2014). The reason is simply that minorities are more likely to work in jobs where unionization is common.

Institutional Discrimination Why are women and other minorities concentrated in the secondary labor market? Some analysts see this pattern resulting from *institutional discrimination,* discussed in Chapter 3 ("Racial and Ethnic

Inequality") and 4 ("Gender Inequality"). Institutional discrimination refers to bias that is built into the operation of the economy, education, or other social institutions.

Institutional discrimination does not always involve people intentionally treating others unfairly, although this can be the case. Institutional discrimination often results from unfair treatment in the past. For example, through most of the twentieth century, the campus was considered a place for men, and women were underrepresented at colleges and universities as students and also as professors and as administrators. Today, most colleges and universities desire presidents with distinguished records of scholarly publications and lots of experience in academic leadership. But given that women were missing from the campus for so long, the number of very highly qualified female applicants is low. This fact helps explain why 74 percent of college and university presidents are men. Similarly, people of color account for only 13 percent of college and university presidents (*Chronicle of Higher Education*, 2012).

The Glass Ceiling In the past, women and other minorities were banned outright from many work settings. Today, such blatant discrimination is against the law and has become rare. But more subtle forms of discrimination are still widely practiced.

For example, most employers have ideas about what type of person is most suitable for various jobs. When hiring a secretary, a company almost always selects a woman. When hiring an executive, by contrast, a company almost always hires a white person, usually a man.

Of course, no corporation or other organization is likely to admit to blatant prejudice and discrimination. But as noted in Chapter 4 ("Gender Inequality"), many workplaces have a *glass ceiling*, a barrier—often involving institutional discrimination—that prevents women and other minorities from moving upward in the workplace.

Workplace Segregation

Consider the following jobs, which people in the United States rank near the bottom of the occupational ladder: shoe shiner, janitor, bellhop, and home health aide. Now try to imagine the race and ethnicity of most people who perform these jobs. What do you think is the case? Most people will quickly respond that such workers are typically minorities.

Or consider positions near the very top rung of the job ladder: physician, lawyer, judge, architect, and university professor. What are the race and ethnicity of most people who hold these jobs? Are most of these people women or men? In this case, most people will conclude that these workers are typically white and probably men.

It is easy to link race, ethnicity, and gender to various occupations because the U.S. workplace is actually highly segregated. Minorities are concentrated in the least desirable jobs, and white men predominate in the most desirable jobs. Figure 11–5 on page 336 shows the racial and ethnic composition of various occupations in the United States. These data show that African Americans and Hispanic Americans are overrepresented in lower-paying jobs (such as child care) and underrepresented in higher-paying jobs (such as physicians and dentists). Such differences in work are a major reason for disparities in income between the different racial and ethnic categories of the U.S. population. Among full-time workers in 2012, median income for whites ($53,629 for men and $41,184 for women) was well above that for African Americans ($38,670 and $34,265) and Hispanic Americans ($32,445 and $28,981) (U.S. Census Bureau, 2013).

In the U.S. workplace, women make out somewhat better than racial and ethnic minorities, with greater representation in many more desirable jobs. This is because minorities are overrepresented among the poor and among families just one generation removed from being poor, but women are found at all social class levels.

Women are still trailing men when it comes to leadership positions. Among business executives, clergy, judges, all the way up to national presidents, men dominate. At the same time, women are overrepresented in low-status positions in the business world, working as secretaries and other office employees, and in caring for the young, as child care workers and teachers.

Other notable examples of this male–female difference can be found in the health care field: 69 percent of dentists are men, but 98 percent of dental hygienists are women; 66 percent of physicians and surgeons are men, and 91 percent of nurses are women. Of course, such differences in work lead to sharp gender differences in income. Among full-time workers in 2012, median income for men was $49,398, compared with $37,791 (77 percent as much) for women (U.S. Census Bureau, 2013).

Finally, women are less likely than men to be in the paid labor force in any position at all. Women make up about 51 percent of the U.S. adult population but only 42 percent of the full-time labor force (47 percent of workers if we count not just full-time workers but part-timers as well) (U.S. Department of Labor, 2014).

Labor Unions

Faced with many problems in the workplace, can workers improve their situation? One of the most effective strategies for working people has been to join together to form **labor unions**, *worker organizations that seek to improve wages and working conditions through various strategies, including negotiations and strikes.*

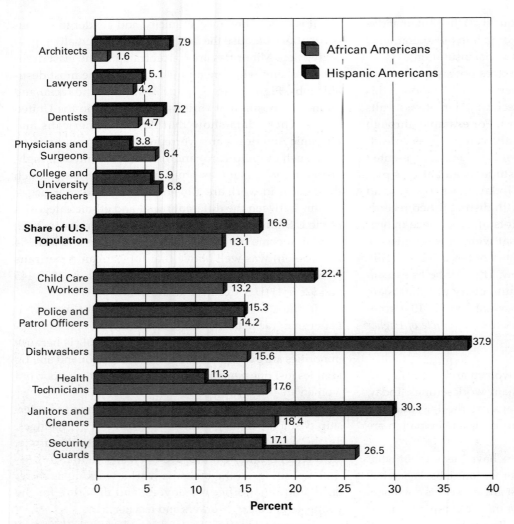

Diversity Snapshot

Figure 11–5   Percentage of Various U.S. Occupations Held by African
Americans and by Hispanic Americans, 2013

Minorities, including Hispanic Americans and African Americans, are underrepresented in jobs
that provide high income and prestige and overrepresented in jobs that offer lower income and prestige.

SOURCE: U.S. Department of Labor (2014).

A Brief History of Unions   The history of labor unions in
the United States extends back more than a century, with
the first large-scale organizations beginning during the
1880s at the height of the Industrial Revolution. At that
time, working conditions were tough—people labored for
long hours, faced many dangers, earned low wages, and
had almost no job security. Factory owners had little reason
to offer more because a steady stream of immigrants entering the United States provided plenty of people who were
eager to work.

Under the laws of that time, company officials could
fire workers for trying to form a union, and if employees
went out on strike, owners were often successful in getting a court to order workers back to the job. In short, a
century ago, employers held all the high cards.

Despite the challenges, a number of people devoted
their lives to promoting unions as a way to improve
the lives of working people. The Defining Moment box
explains how Eugene Debs advanced the cause of unions
in the United States.

With the coming of the Great Depression in the 1930s,
workers' organizations made important gains. The collapse of the economy put one-fourth of the U.S. labor force
out of work at one point, and government took notice of
the plight of working people. Congress passed several new
laws (the Railway Labor Act, the Norris-LaGuardia Act,
and the National Labor Relations Act) that guaranteed the
right of workers to organize and form labor unions.

Millions of working people responded to the union
call. Throughout the 1930s, union membership increased

CONSTRUCTING SOCIAL PROBLEMS

A DEFINING MOMENT

Eugene Debs: Standing Up for the Union

At the height of the Industrial Revolution, working conditions in the United States were a far cry from what most people experience today. People worked ten, twelve, or more hours per day, usually six days a week, earning 15 to 20 cents an hour. Workers labored near blast furnaces in steel mills or high atop towering steel buildings, where one misstep could turn deadly. But with many people eager to take any available job, employers gave little thought to worker safety.

Eugene Victor Debs (1855–1926) grew up in Indiana. He left school at age fourteen to work as a painter for the railroad. The longer Debs worked, the more he saw that workers were barely able to survive. But what could be done? The company had the power, and there were no laws protecting workers from exploitation. Standing alone, Debs realized, a worker had no chance. But standing together, workers could meet the bosses head on.

This realization led Debs to take a job with an early labor union called the Brotherhood of Locomotive Firemen. Soon after, Debs had become editor of the union's national magazine, and he helped found other railroad unions. A skillful writer and a powerful speaker, Debs poured his passion into his activism, and his success soon earned him a national reputation.

But opposition to unions was strong, and being an agent of change pushed Debs into a life of controversy. He led bitter strikes against the railroad companies, endured arrests by the police, and spent years in jail. In the final decades of his life, Debs spoke openly about the need for radical change in the United States and was a five-time presidential candidate representing the Socialist party. He ran his last campaign for the presidency from inside the federal prison in Atlanta, Georgia.

Debs's efforts to bring about socialism in the United States did not succeed. But he did bring about real change. As a result of his efforts, people accepted the idea that workers deserve a living wage, are entitled to safe working conditions, and have a legal right to organize and form unions. Today, Debs's home in Terre Haute, Indiana, is a National Historic Landmark—a museum documenting the struggle of early industrial workers.

Eugene Debs was a dynamic speaker who stirred the workers of his time to organize in pursuit of better lives.

---

sharply, and workers found strength in numbers. By 1950, unions claimed one-third of the entire U.S. nonfarm labor force. In terms of absolute numbers, union membership peaked in the 1970s at about 25 million people.

But union strength was not to last. One reason was falling support for unions at the highest level of government. In 1981, air traffic controllers, who are federal employees, went on strike. President Ronald Reagan responded by ordering them back to work. When they refused, Reagan fired them all, and replacements were hired. This incident was a major defeat for labor unions and dramatized the weakening of the labor movement.

Unions Today Perhaps the biggest challenge facing unions has been structural change in the U.S. economy. The number of factory jobs—work that is heavily unionized—declined after 1950. Since then, most new jobs have been in the service sector of the economy, and this work is not likely to be unionized. Therefore, in 2013, just 11 percent of nonfarm workers (14.5 million men and women) were members of labor unions—quite a drop from 33 percent in 1950 (U.S. Department of Labor, 2014). Another measure of the declining strength of the labor movement is the decreasing number of strikes in the United States in recent decades, as shown in Figure 11–6 on page 338.

But these downward trends may be turning around. In the past few years, unions have gained ground among government workers. In 2013, 35 percent of workers in the public sector of the economy were unionized. In addition, because many of today's service jobs provide low pay and few benefits (just as most industrial jobs did a century or so ago), more workers in the service sector are looking to unions to increase their bargaining

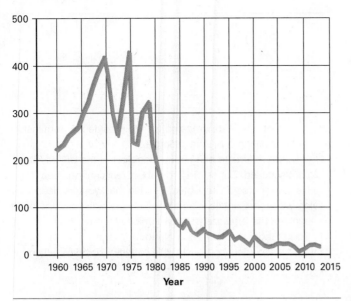

Figure 11–6 Number of Labor Strikes in the United States, 1960–2013

One indication of the declining power of unions in the U.S. workplace is the small number of labor strikes in recent decades.

SOURCE: U.S. Department of Labor (2014).

power, improve working conditions, and increase pay and benefits (Greenhouse, 2000; U.S. Department of Labor, 2014).

Historically, even when all workers indicated that they wished to form a union, companies were under no legal obligation to recognize the union. Efforts to increase unionization, therefore, have focused on a strategy called "majority sign-up." Under this policy, if a majority of workers in a plant or other bargaining unit sign a card saying that they want a union, a union will be formed, and all workers will be required to join and pay dues to the union. Supporters of this policy claim that unions provide benefits to workers. Therefore, they claim, requiring union membership of all workers is the only way to avoid giving "free rides" to people who benefit from union efforts yet do not pay dues. Many union leaders support a policy of asking workers to join a union through a system (sometimes called "card check") in which union representatives publicly ask each worker to sign a card supporting unionization.

On the other side of this controversy are people who support so-called "right to work" laws. "Right to work" activists see the secret ballot as a fundamental right and necessary to ensure that all workers have a true voice. They reject any system of signing up workers in public in the belief that union activists can intimidate many workers into signing up for a union they did not want.

In many states, "right to work" laws limit the power of unions to require membership and dues from workers as a condition of hiring or allowing workers to vote using a secret ballot. Supporters of "right to work" laws say that these laws give workers a fair chance to vote for or against a union and,

in addition, that "right to work" states attract more industry and have lower unemployment rates and higher average income levels. National Map 11–1 shows which states currently have "right to work" laws (Dalmia, 2008; Allen, 2009; Dolan, 2011; National Conference of State Legislatures, 2014).

The Recent Controversy over Public Employees On March 8, 2011, newly elected Ohio governor John Kasich gave his first "state of the state" speech claiming, "We're going to reform government." As he spoke, more than one thousand firefighters—state employees—crowded the lobby outside the doors of the legislative chamber and chanted in unison, "Kill the bill! Kill the bill! Kill the bill!"

So began the recent controversy over public-employee unions. Ohio's state government was $8 billion in debt, and the Republican governor claimed that one major cause of that enormous deficit is past agreements made between state officials and public-employee unions, including firefighters, police, and teachers.

As Kasich saw it, the problem is a system that has given public workers' unions too much power and now threatens to bankrupt the state. Under the current system, unions effectively require every public employee to be a union member and to pay dues through payroll deductions. Unions then spent millions of dollars to elect Democratic leaders who, in the past, have signed off on labor contracts that exceed what workers in the private sector earn and what the state can afford.

Kasich and the Republican-controlled state government sought reforms that would continue collective bargaining by public-employee unions for salary but not for job benefits. In addition, the governor sought to link employee pay to a performance-based merit system rather than seniority. Finally, public-employee unions would no longer be allowed to strike. Not surprisingly, labor leaders saw the "reforms" as nothing less than a war on unions.

A similar controversy unfolded in Wisconsin, where Governor Scott Walker was elected in 2010 on a platform of reducing that state's budget deficit by cutting the power of public-employee unions. In 2011, he signed a bill passed by that state's legislature (Act 10) limiting collective bargaining by public employees to wages (not benefits), limiting wage increases to the inflation rate, and decreasing the share the government contributes toward their health care and retirement pensions. The new law also gave government workers the right to join or not to join a union.

Across the country, thirty-four states mandate that public-employee unions engage in collectively bargaining for their workplace conditions; five states explicitly ban this practice. Most federal workers have no right to bargain collectively or to strike. Many states—as well as the federal government—are facing large budget deficits. So the debate over the power of public-employee unions has importance for the nation as a whole.

Seeing Ourselves

National Map 11–1 "Right to Work" Laws across the United States

In general, states that have enacted "right to work" laws are found in the South and in the central and western regions of the country. The date in the green states indicates the year in which a "right to work" law was passed. A few other states, such as New Hampshire, have some law that bans denying a job to someone who will not join a union or firing someone who refuses to pay union dues. In presidential elections, which political party do you think wins the popular vote in "right to work" states?

SOURCE: National Conference of State Legislatures (2014).

The public-employee unions mobilized in Ohio, and they successfully put the issue on the ballot in 2011, when it was soundly defeated by the voters. In Wisconsin, however, Governor Walker defeated his Democratic opponent in a 2012 union-led recall effort (Gray, 2011; Murphy, 2011; Ripley, 2011; Sulzberger, 2011).

New Information Technology: The Brave New Workplace

11.3 Describe the effects of computer technology on the workplace.

Just as the Industrial Revolution brought sweeping changes to the workplace in the 1800s, the Information Revolution is transforming the workplace today. As Global Map 11–1 on page 340 shows, access to the Internet has spread around the world, although it is far better in the United States and other high-income nations than in low-income regions (ITU, 2013).

Compared to the workplace a century ago, today's jobs require new types of skills. In the industrial age, people had to develop mechanical skills in order to make *things*; today, people in the postindustrial economy must develop literacy skills to create and manipulate *symbols*, including words, ideas, music, and computer code.

The Information Revolution is changing not only the character of work but also how and where we do it. As the following sections explain, many people experience these changes as positive. Others, however, face new challenges every bit as serious as those faced by industrial workers a century ago.

The Home as Workplace

In the centuries before the Industrial Revolution, most people worked in or near their homes. The development of industrial machinery changed this pattern, so that workers left home in the morning and traveled to factories. In this way, the Industrial Revolution *centralized* the workplace. Today, however, the trend is moving in the opposite direction. Using computers, iPads, and cellular telephones, workers can operate "offices" just about anywhere. One option becoming more common is for people armed with computer technology to work from home.

Only a small share of the U.S. labor force works exclusively in the home, but perhaps one in five workers spends at least some work time at home during the week. One recent survey found that many people who do some work at home are extending their working hours *beyond* the usual time in the office.

Who is likely to do work at home? As you might expect, it is people with "better" jobs in the primary labor market.

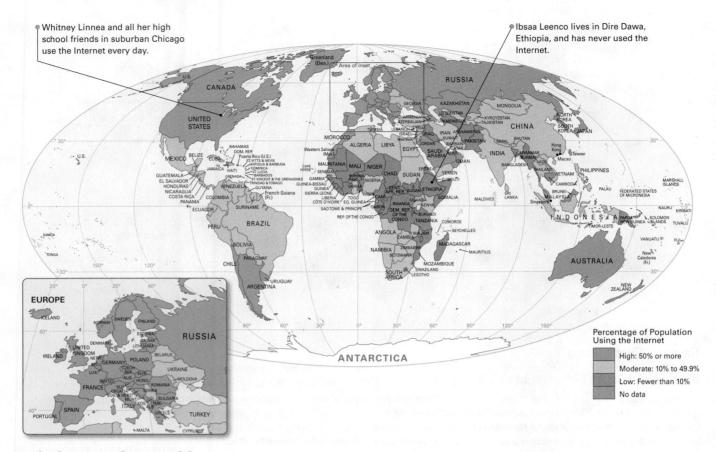

Whitney Linnea and all her high school friends in suburban Chicago use the Internet every day.

Ibsaa Leenco lives in Dire Dawa, Ethiopia, and has never used the Internet.

Percentage of Population Using the Internet

High: 50% or more
Moderate: 10% to 49.9%
Low: Fewer than 10%
No data

Window on the World

Global Map 11–1 Internet Users in Global Perspective

This map shows the state of the Information Revolution for countries around the world. In most high-income nations, at least one-half of the population uses the Internet. By contrast, only a small share of people in low-income nations does so. What effect does this lack of Internet access have for the future in terms of global inequality?

SOURCE: International Telecommunication Union (2013).

These are typically people earning higher salaries and those with more education. For example, while about 40 percent of workers with college degrees report doing some work at home, just 5 percent of people with less than a high school degree say the same (U.S. Department of Labor, 2013).

Working from home has obvious benefits, such as the time and expense workers save by not commuting to and from the office. It also has special appeal to people who want to hold a job but need to care for small children or aging parents. For many people, the home as workplace offers flexibility to balance career goals and family obligations.

Working at home may solve some problems, but it can create others. This practice blurs the line between home and work, so that the pressures of the job—which used to stay in the office—now invade our home space. In addition, workers who stay at home risk becoming isolated, left out of key decisions, and overlooked for promotion. In addition, because working from home is more popular with women (who have greater family responsibilities), this pattern has the potential to perpetuate gender inequality in the workplace.

Workplace Isolation

Even people who do their work in the office find that the Information Revolution is changing how they work. By connecting people in information networks, computer technology has greatly reduced the need for face-to-face interaction. Many workers communicate using e-mail, which reduces the need for face-to-face meetings and even for telephone calls. The result, for many workers, is a growing sense of workplace isolation.

In today's office setting, this pattern is easy to see. Many of today's office employees perform most of their work in small cubicles facing computer screens, having little contact with anyone else. Similarly, today's bank officials receive loan applications online, use computer programs to review the information, and make decisions as to whether to approve or reject customers they may never meet.

Workplace Supervision

We are all well aware that computer technology allows organizations to collect more information about us than ever before. This is especially true in the workplace. Using computer technology, employers can monitor worker output and keep an eye on workers' behavior.

For example, telemarketing companies routinely use computers to monitor the performance of their employees who sell products and services over the phone. In other words, computer technology allows supervisors to track how many calls their workers make each day, how long each call lasts, and the outcome of every call. In many cases, high-tech equipment records the actual conversation "for quality assurance purposes," which means that the company can listen in on what employees and customers say. Never before have organizations had more ability to control the working lives of employees.

Working at home can allow people with young children to manage both their careers and their family responsibilities. At the same time, what problems do you see in holding a job that requires you to work from home?

The "Deskilling" of Workers

Lower-level employees have long been aware that companies can use new technology to make them obsolete. Decades ago, robots replaced humans in many jobs on auto assembly lines. More recently, we have seen bank tellers replaced by ATMs and supermarket checkout clerks replaced by "self-checkout" scanners. The latest trend is using new information technology to replace the work of managers and executives. This is because many decisions once made by experienced managers are now made automatically by computers that are programmed to take account of every important consideration. Which car models should the assembly line build? Simply input data on profitability, projected interest rates, and the likely price of gasoline over the next ten years, and let the computer decide. When should a movie theater chain replenish its supplies of popcorn, soda, and candy? Computers monitor sales and automatically process orders for additional products. Given the proper input, computers are able to make more and more decisions without direct human assistance, which has the effect of *deskilling* managers and threatening their jobs. The final result is a decline in job security even for workers in the primary labor market.

Are computers capable of doing a better job of making business decisions than people? The answer to this question is unclear. Looking back at the collapse of so many financial companies and mortgage lenders during the last few years, perhaps there will be a trend away from allowing computers to manage risk, putting responsibility for business decisions back in the hands of people (Kivant, 2008). In any case, the increasing reliance on computers in business reminds us that

new technology is never socially neutral. It changes the relationships between people in the workplace, shapes the way we work, and often alters the balance of power between employers and employees.

Theories of Work and Work-Related Problems

11.4 Apply sociological theory to issues involving work and the workplace.

Each of sociology's major theoretical approaches helps us understand work-related problems. Each approach highlights different facts and points to different conclusions.

Structural-Functional Analysis: Finding a New Equilibrium

Structural-functional theory explains how technological change reshapes the economy. The Industrial Revolution was the driving force behind the economy of the twentieth century. In much the same way, the Information Revolution has set the stage for the economy of the twenty-first century. Now, as in the past, technology is a key factor shaping work and the workplace.

Another insight provided by structural-functional theory is that various social institutions are interrelated, so that change in one leads to adjustments in all the others. This chapter and Chapter 10 ("Economy and Politics") have explained how changes in the economy can cause hardship by causing people to lose their jobs. But structural-functional theory suggests that the disruption of past economic patterns eventually brings a new social

Computer technology makes workers more efficient, but it also has the effect of replacing many workers entirely. Using self-service scanners available in many discount stores and supermarkets, the customer simply scans a barcode on the product, and the computer does the rest. How close are we to seeing technology eliminate the need for checkout workers entirely?

order. This means that although the deindustrialization ended up eliminating millions of factory jobs, other institutions—especially education—responded by developing new courses of study to prepare workers for the new jobs being created in the postindustrial economy.

The changes now under way, like those in the past, will cause disruption in established ways of life. But we can expect social institutions to respond to these changes, addressing what we experience as short-term problems, to help us redirect our lives. In the long term, changes to the economy brought on by new technology are likely to make our society more productive, which will be good for almost everyone.

This approach reminds us that economic setbacks, although painful in the short term, may help bring about greater long-term stability. Many analysts, for example, see the rapid economic expansion that began after 1980 as having pushed up housing prices too much and too quickly. At the same time, the typical family began to spend more of its income and to save less. The recession that began in 2008 may well bring such patterns back to a more sustainable level (K. Andersen, 2009).

EVALUATE

The structural-functional approach takes a very positive view of society and its ability to rebound from the disruptions caused by structural changes in the workplace. For that reason, its greatest weakness may well be that it ends up being too optimistic. This approach downplays the human suffering caused by these disruptions, describing them as temporary, and makes the case that technological change and even economic recession are likely to strengthen society in the long run. Some of these predictions will likely turn out to be true, but this approach presents only one side of the story.

In addition, by treating society as a broad system, this macro-level approach provides little understanding about the ways in which individual people face everyday workplace problems. To better understand this issue, we turn to symbolic-interaction theory.

CHECK YOUR LEARNING   What insights about work do we gain from structural-functional theory? What is one limitation of this approach?

Symbolic-Interaction Analysis: The Meaning of Work

Symbolic-interaction theory focuses on the meanings people attach to the surrounding world as they construct everyday reality. Here, we consider the meaning people attach to the jobs they hold and the work they perform.

Typically, people with jobs in the primary labor market look forward to going to work every day and are motivated to advance; they think of their work as a *career*. Not only do such people attach positive meaning to their work, but they also believe that their work reflects well on them. Even after retiring from active work, teachers, doctors, and architects still hold on to the positive identity their work offered them. This fact helps explain why, for example, those who retire from teaching at colleges and universities are happy to enjoy a new status as professor *emeritus* (the male form) or *emerita* (the female form), which are Latin words meaning "fully earned."

At the same time, people doing unskilled, repetitive jobs—whether in factories or office buildings—usually find far less positive meaning in their work. These people are likely to go to work each day mostly because they have no choice. Hour to hour, they listen to the radio and may even watch the clock, looking forward to quitting time when they can do something else. Such work rarely provides a chance for advancement and positive identity. People with secondary labor market jobs talk little about their work to others, and the value of their job lies mainly in the paycheck it provides.

EVALUATE

Symbolic-interaction theory highlights the different meanings people attach to their work, helping us understand why some people look forward to going to work while others only look forward to "punching out."

Although the meaning people attach to work varies from person to person, the reality of work has much to do with people's social standing. To understand more about how and why work is linked to inequality, we turn to social-conflict theory.

CHECK YOUR LEARNING What insights about work do we gain from symbolic-interaction theory? What is one limitation of this approach?

Social-Conflict Analysis: Work and Inequality

The defining feature of social-conflict theory is its emphasis on social inequality. In the case of work, this approach highlights how the economy operates to provide very different opportunities and benefits for advantaged and disadvantaged categories of people.

Following the ideas of Karl Marx, the operation of a capitalist economy serves to concentrate wealth and power among members of a small elite. From this point of view, the most advantaged share of the labor force does not actually work but rather *owns* everything. The capitalist elite enjoys most of the benefits of economic production for the simple reason that it has total control over it. By contrast, most workers receive low wages and have little power in the production process. For most people, therefore, work is far from satisfying and produces only alienation.

As noted earlier, Max Weber took a different tack, arguing that capitalism was only one dimension of the larger pattern of increasing rationality, which defines modern society. A rational, matter-of-fact worldview stresses efficiency at the expense of meeting human needs and transforms the workplace into a highly regulated setting in which people have come to resemble machines. Weber would not have been surprised at the increasing number of McJobs found in today's world.

Both Weber and Marx agreed that, for most people, work is alienating rather than satisfying. For Marx, the root of the problem is the capitalist system and its effects on the working majority. For Weber, it is the historical trend toward greater rationality, which affects everybody. Differences aside, notice that both these theories reject the structural-functional claim that workplace problems result from temporary disruptions in the economy.

Perhaps both Weber and Marx might have expected to see the recent trend by which the share of jobs in the primary labor market has gone down and the share in the secondary market has gone up. The goal of rational efficiency (as Weber would put it) or of maximizing profit (as Marx might have said) encourages employers to exert

A society's economy changes as new technology creates new products and new types of work. One result of these shifts is that we can no longer assume that we will do only one type of job throughout our lives. A common experience for today's workers is retraining for a new career.

more and more control over workers and, when possible, to replace them with machines. No one should be surprised that an ever-greater number of workers are forced to settle for McJobs and that more of us worry whether, at some point in the future, we will have any work at all.

EVALUATE

Social-conflict theory helps us see how the operation of the economy affects people at various levels of our society differently. That is, the burden of workplace problems falls mostly on ordinary working families while the few enjoy most of the benefits.

At the same time, one limitation of this approach is that it downplays the real gains in living standards realized by average people over the course of the twentieth century. Today, average workers earn about five times as much as they did back in 1900 after controlling for inflation. In terms of standard of living, the typical U.S. family owns a house with air-conditioning, cable television, and at least one automobile parked in a garage—all of which was beyond the imagination of working families a century ago. Inequality is real, but in an absolute sense, just about everyone lives much better today than people did in the past.

CHECK YOUR LEARNING What insights about work do we gain from social-conflict theory? What is one limitation of this approach?

Feminist Analysis: Work and Gender

Feminist theory is one type of social-conflict analysis that focuses on gender inequality. From a feminist point of view, societies organize social life around the concept of gender. Gender has enormous importance in the world of work.

APPLYING THEORY

Work and the Workplace

	Structural-Functional Theory	Symbolic-Interaction Theory	Social-Conflict Theory	Feminist Theory
What is the level of analysis?	Macro-level	Micro-level	Macro-level	Macro-level
What does the theory say about the workplace?	Structural-functional theory links the operation of the workplace to other aspects of society, including technology. The Industrial Revolution shaped the workplace of the twentieth century, just as the Information Revolution is shaping the workplace of the twenty-first century.	Symbolic-interaction theory focuses on the meanings people attach to the world around them. People with jobs in the primary labor market define their work in positive terms and think that the work reflects well on them. People in the secondary labor market find little positive meaning in their work, seeing the job mostly as a source of income.	Social-conflict theory links the workplace to social inequality. Marx explained that the capitalist elite does no work at all yet gains the profit from the work done by others. As long as the workplace operates according to the rules of a capitalist economy, work is the exploitation of the many by the few.	Feminist theory explains that gender is a basic organizing principle of all of society, including the world of work. Just about every job is widely viewed as either "feminine" or "masculine" with men's work typically valued more than women's work.
How do we understand workplace problems?	Rapid change can disrupt the social order, causing problems. For example, new technology has caused the loss of many traditional types of jobs. But other social institutions such as education respond, preparing workers for new types of jobs.	The main problem is that workers with jobs in the secondary labor market are not able to find much positive meaning in their work. As a result, they must look for satisfaction outside of the workplace.	According to Marx, capitalism creates wealth for the few and alienation for the working majority. Weber agreed that alienation is a workplace problem, although he pointed to rationality in the modern world as the cause.	Gender segregates many workplaces according to sex. Jobs viewed as "masculine" provide the greatest wealth and power. In contrast, because women typically hold "feminine" jobs, they are disadvantaged in terms of income, power, and prestige.

The easiest way to see the power of gender in the workplace is to consider how our culture links certain types of work to one sex or the other. Jobs that involve assisting more important people—such as dental assistant or receptionist—are overwhelmingly performed by women. Similarly, jobs that involve working with children—including preschool teacher or child care worker—are almost entirely performed by women. By contrast, work that is associated with physical danger—such as police work—is mostly performed by men. Similarly, work that involves physical strength or endurance—such as construction work or long-distance truck driving—is mostly performed by men (U.S. Department of Labor, 2014).

More broadly, gender norms assign responsibility for the home to women, which is a major reason that a larger share of men than women are in the labor force. Finally, when it comes to positions that involve the greatest wealth and power—from corporate CEOs to the president of the United States—men vastly outnumber women.

EVALUATE

Feminist theory helps us appreciate the extent to which work is "gendered." In most cases, people see a specific job as either "feminine" or "masculine," and our society assigns greater importance as well as greater rewards to work defined as "masculine." Of

course, wealth and power themselves are typically viewed as masculine traits.

At the same time, it is important to recognize that gender no longer has anywhere near the importance it once had in shaping the world of work. A century ago, women were kept out of most jobs entirely; today, the occupational standing of women is steadily becoming more like that of men.

CHECK YOUR LEARNING   What insights about work do we gain from feminist theory? What is one limitation of this approach?

The Applying Theory table summarizes what each theoretical approach teaches us about the problems of the workplace.

✪ POLITICS AND THE WORKPLACE

Constructing Problems and Defining Solutions

11.5   Analyze workplace issues from various positions on the political spectrum.

Theory provides helpful insights about work, but exactly what people see as workplace problems and what they decide should be done about them is a matter of their political attitudes. Here we analyze issues involving work and the workplace using the conservative, liberal, and radical-left political perspectives.

Conservatives: Look to the Market

As noted in Chapter 10 ("Economy and Politics"), conservatives favor limited government regulation of the economy, believing that free competition makes society more productive, raises living standards, and increases the number of available jobs. The conservative claim is that free-market economics—with minimal regulation from government—generates the greatest good for the greatest number of people.

Like everyone else, conservatives recognize that economic downturns occur and recessions can push up the unemployment rate and that recessions can last for several years. They also know that technological change such as the Information Revolution causes problems for some people as old jobs disappear or move to other countries. But from this point of view, such dislocations turn out to be temporary problems because market forces will gradually provide solutions and offer new opportunities.

For example, a steep recession began in 2008. But households responded by spending less and saving more, which is good for families and strengthened the economy as a whole. Similarly, the housing market has gradually stabilized after the drop in prices to more realistic levels.

Conservatives also claim that the housing crisis and the recession were caused not by free-market greed but by government intervention in the market. For example, mortgage giants Fannie Mae and Freddie Mac were operated under government-mandated policies that required them and other banks to make more and more housing loans to people who could not afford to repay.

Similarly, conservatives claim that increasing government regulation has made starting new businesses harder than ever, and it is new small businesses that create the most jobs. Therefore, expanding government is the main reason that the recent recovery has yet to produce enough jobs for everyone who wishes to work. In the long run, conservatives believe, the operation of the market, rather than government, is the path to the greatest economic opportunity for everyone (Horwitz, 2008; Andersen, 2009; White, 2009; Kesler, 2014).

Another important conservative principle is individual responsibility. From this point of view, every able-bodied person should work, even at a low-paying job if that is all that is available. In general, conservatives claim that the market offers lots of opportunity and that it is up to individuals to prepare themselves to take advantage of jobs that are available. For workers with limited skills, this may mean starting out at an entry-level job—perhaps even at McDonald's—with the expectation that over time, gaining skills and developing good work habits will lead to advancement. Government may be able to help people in the short term by providing training or encouraging the construction of new businesses in a particular area, but people should never expect government to do for them what they are not willing to do for themselves. On the contrary, the more government expands in terms of business regulation and providing benefits to the population, the smaller the share of people who will work. This is why the states with the most extensive government regulation and the largest welfare benefits—including California, Illinois, and New York—are the states with the highest levels of long-term unemployment. Nationally, conservatives continue, as the size and scope of government expands, the share of the population working or looking for work declines. In 2013, just 62 percent of working-age people were working or looking for a job and just 47 percent held a full-time job (Bui, 2013; U.S. Department of Labor, 2014).

Such thinking helps explain why conservatives have opposed the expansion of government under the Obama administration as holding down job creation. Conservatives have also opposed the Affordable Care Act (widely called "Obamacare") as an unprecedented expansion of government into a large sector of the economy. Similarly, most conservatives oppose raising the legal minimum wage, in part because it is a form of government regulation but also because artificially increasing wages raises the cost of labor, which ends up decreasing the demand for labor and pushing up the unemployment rate. In short, conservatives see the operation of a free market as a solution to many of our needs; to them, extensive government regulation of the economy is the main problem.

Liberals: Look to Government

Liberals agree that a market-based economy is highly productive but they believe that, operating on its own, a market economy creates a number of workplace problems. Therefore, liberals see a need for government regulation to protect the interests of everyone, especially low-income people, immigrants, and others who are vulnerable.

Market systems generate unequal rewards, which results in economic inequality. In the interest of greater social justice, government must reduce economic inequality through progressive taxation (on the rich) paying for social welfare benefits (for the poor). Further, liberals claim, without government regulation a market system

Conservatives believe that the capitalist market system offers people a wide range of job opportunities. Liberals, by contrast, maintain that because the market system favors some people more than others, government action is needed to ensure that everyone has access to work. Radicals claim that the market system serves only the rich and the powerful; as they see it, we must devise a more egalitarian economic and political system before the interests of all will be served.

would leave most people at the mercy of the rich, resulting in problems such as low wages, loss of pensions and other benefits, and a host of workplace dangers. Liberals remind us that such problems were found throughout the United States before the 1930s, when government took a greater hand in regulating the economy and improving the lives of working people.

More recently, liberals see the recession that began in 2008 as mostly caused by runaway greed on the part of a few in the corporate world, and especially on Wall Street. Liberals look to greater government regulation as the way to protect the public (Pierson, 2008).

There is an old saying that the market provides "rough justice," meaning that a free market gives greater rewards to those who work harder and especially to people with rare talents that create value. But liberals look to the government to smooth the rough edges of market

justice to ensure that all workers are treated fairly. For this reason, liberals support increasing the federal minimum wage and President Obama proposes raising the minimum wage from $7.25 per hour to $10.10 (Morath, 2014). Liberals also seek government action to protect people from workplace hazards (so that workers are not harmed by, say, toxic chemicals) and to protect workers' right to join unions (so that they can collectively bargain for higher wages and better working conditions). Liberals also support government efforts to reduce prejudice and discrimination based on race and ethnicity because when workers are divided in this way, they lose power against management. To sum up, liberals see an important role for both the marketplace and the government in the operation of an economy that truly serves the interest of all.

In national political debate, Republicans make the conservative claim that people—rather than government—make the U.S. economy strong. Republicans typically describe government as the "problem," and point to the creative energy of the nation's people as well as the market economy as the "solution." From this point of view, government should get out of the way and let people make the economy grow. Democrats make the liberal counterargument that that most people—especially those in need—look to government to ensure their economic well-being. From this point of view, government must regulate the economy as well as provide programs such as educational benefits and health care that everyone needs. In this basic sense, government is not a problem but is part of the solution.

The Radical Left: Basic Change Is Needed

The further to the left people move on the political spectrum, the greater the role they give to government in the operation of the economy. On the far left, people take a radical position that seeks to eliminate the private market system completely, placing the entire economic system under the control of government.

From the radical-left point of view, the free market causes many serious problems. How? For one thing, by placing the economy in private hands so that individuals own factories and other businesses as their personal property, the economy operates to benefit the few rather than the many. Companies driven only by the goal of private profit will pay the lowest possible wages and show the least concern for worker well-being and workplace safety. Therefore, low wages, workplace hazards, and unemployment are predictable results of the operation of a privately owned, capitalist economy.

With this negative view of the market as the source of social problems, radicals on the left clearly reject the

LEFT TO RIGHT

The Politics of Work and the Workplace

	Radical-Left View	Liberal View	Conservative View
What is the problem?	The capitalist market system is the cause of most economic problems, including low wages, workplace hazards, and unemployment. By placing profits ahead of people, capitalism fails to meet the economic needs of the majority.	The market system is productive but it does not ensure the welfare of all. Low wages, unemployment, and discrimination based on gender, race, and ethnicity are all problems in the U.S. workplace.	The market system is highly productive and supports a high average living standard. Government regulation, however, reduces the productivity of the market. Therefore, government should regulate the economy as little as possible.
What is the solution?	Workers should own and control the means of economic production. Government, acting in the interest of the population as a whole, should be responsible for economic policy.	While allowing market forces to operate, government agencies must regulate the economy to ensure that workers receive a living wage and that the workplace is safe and free from discrimination.	The greatest number of people will benefit most if market forces are allowed to operate freely. The economy does a good job of regulating itself and moving workers from older industries to newer kinds of work.

JOIN THE DEBATE

1. How would people at each of the political positions understand the economic recession that began in 2008? What would they suggest as a solution to this problem?

2. Overall, do you think that the state of work in the United States improved over the course of the twentieth century? Why or why not? What new problems do workers face in the twenty-first century?

3. Which of the three political analyses of work and the workplace included here do you find most convincing? Why?

conservative claim that the free market provides "the greatest good for the greatest number." And they also do not think that liberals' demand for government regulation of the market goes far enough to be an effective solution. The radical left looks to what it sees as the real root of the problem, calling for the replacement of the capitalist economy with a political and economic system that makes people rather than profits its highest priority.

How will such a change occur? Karl Marx claimed that working people, pushed to action by their misery, would join together in opposition to the capitalists who oppress them and eventually overthrow the capitalist system itself. As Marx put it, capitalism fails to meet the needs of the majority of people and in this way sows the seeds of its own destruction. Only when workers collectively own and direct the workplace will they derive the rewards they should from a day's labor.

The Left to Right table outlines the three political perspectives on work and the workplace.

Going On from Here

In the early twentieth century, the black smoke that streamed from factory chimneys in the large cities of the Northeast and Midwest signaled that the U.S. economy was booming and the United States was on its way to becoming the world's most economically powerful nation.

The owners of this new industrial empire lived in mansions that rivaled the great castles of European monarchs. But all was not well with the majority of working people. Wages were low, and each year thousands of workers were injured and killed in factories and mines, and workers had little chance to organize and demand better working conditions.

In the 1930s, the Great Depression forced factories to close, and farmers who were unable to pay their mortgages lost their land. Back then, it must have seemed as if the problems of unemployment and poverty could not get any worse. Driven by such serious suffering, political support for radically changing the capitalist system was on the rise.

But that all changed in 1939 with the start of World War II, when the nation's attention turned to international problems. The war also provided a huge boost to the struggling economy so that when the war ended in 1945, this country entered a period of great economic prosperity.

There have been ups and downs in the economy ever since. But the overall record of the U.S. economy has been impressive. Despite the recent economic downturn, the historical trend is that the economic productivity of this nation has never been greater; nor have so many of us ever lived so well.

Without denying that many have prospered, many others have been left behind. As noted in Chapter 2 ("Poverty and Wealth"), the incomes of those already doing well have increased substantially in recent decades while tens of millions of working families have made little or no gains and the poorest segment of our population has actually lost ground. Furthermore, millions of jobs—both blue-collar jobs in factories and white-collar jobs in offices—have been lost. Most of the new service jobs being created provide low pay, few benefits, and no union representation. Most families now depend on the incomes of at least two people. With unemployment remaining high, economic insecurity—and for some families, even the loss of homes—remains a concern throughout the United States.

In the foreseeable future, it seems highly likely that the nation will continue to rely on a market economy because this system has generated so much wealth. The challenge will be whether the U.S. political and economic systems can be made to operate so that everyone, rather than just some of the population, can find economic security. In recent years, we have seen the Obama administration seek greater government involvement in the economy, not only in terms of "bailouts" and regulation but also by expanding health care and other government benefits. Liberals claim this expansion of government into the economy has improved people's lives; conservatives claims that it has held back economic recovery. Public debate over these two views will drive the outcome of the upcoming elections.

Essay: Envisioning a Better Society What specific changes in the jobs people have do you expect to see fifty years from now? What types of work will be more common? What types of work will be lost? What specific policies and program are needed to improve the economy moving forward?

CHAPTER 11 Work and the Workplace

Are unions necessary for workers to have good jobs?

As this chapter has explained, unions have been facing tough times, with union membership down as the economy has shifted from factory jobs (which were highly unionized) to service work (which is typically not unionized). Can unions make a comeback? Would that be good for this country's workers? Look at the accompanying photos to see two approaches to answering such questions.

Some jobs are highly unionized. Most government workers, and almost all public school teachers, are members of labor unions. From the union point of view—which is shared by most teachers— workers who are collectively organized can improve their pay and working conditions in ways that individuals acting alone almost never can. If you had a choice at your place of work, would you want to join a union?

As Walmart sees it, this giant corporation is doing pretty well by its workers. Walmart has created 1.3 million jobs and pays workers almost $300 billion in earnings each year. Wages for sales associates, according to the company, average more than $10 an hour. Walmart claims that its workers have a lot to be happy about and have little to gain from joining a union. As part of their effort to keep employees smiling, managers at each of more than 4,200 U.S. stores lead their workers through the Walmart cheer each morning. Do you expect to see stores like these with a unionized workforce?

> **Hint:** In today's service economy, many corporations—Walmart among them—are strongly opposed to unions organizing their workers. What about workers themselves? There have been efforts to organize Walmart employees, but so far, there is no groundswell of interest by workers in joining a union. Perhaps (as the company claims) this is because workers are getting pretty much what they want; perhaps (as unions claim) it is because workers fear losing their jobs if they try to organize. What most people can agree on is that the key to union success in today's service economy lies in being able to organize workers in "big-box" stores such as Walmart.

Getting Involved: Applications and Exercises

1. Do a little research about the faculty and staff at your college or university. What share of faculty have benefits such as health insurance, retirement pension, vacation time, and sick leave? Do adjunct faculty receive the same benefits as full-time professors? Compare the pay and benefits offered to teaching personnel to what is offered to skilled maintenance personnel and also to low-skill service workers, such as those in the campus food service.

2. Learn more about the two major political parties by visiting their websites. Visit the site of the Republican National Committee at www.GOP.com. The site for the Democratic National Committee is www.Democrats .org. In what ways do the two major parties appear to differ in the definition of the "problems" and the favored "solutions?"

3. Turn on your sociological imagination as you walk around campus and observe the people who work there. What can you say about the race and gender of faculty, administrators, secretarial staff, grounds workers, janitors, and cleaners on your campus? What patterns can you see?

4. Louisiana recently enacted legislation forbidding people receiving state welfare ATM cards from using them in businesses such as tattoo parlors, lingerie shops, nail salons, jewelry stores, bail bond shops, cruise ships, psychics, and video arcades. The benefits are intended to provide needy individuals and families with food, clothing, and housing. In Louisiana, average assistance payments total $192 per month for welfare assistance and $419 per month for family member assistance. What do you think is the reasoning behind this legislation? Do you think restriction of this type should be placed on how people spend assistance money? Why or why not?

CHAPTER 11 Work and the Workplace

A DEFINING MOMENT
Eugene Debs: Standing Up for the Union **p. 337**

Structural Changes in the U.S. Economy

11.1 Explain how the Industrial Revolution, the Information Revolution, and globalization have changed the character of work.

By 1800, the **Industrial Revolution** began changing the nature of work, moving people from *primary sector* jobs producing raw materials to *secondary sector* jobs turning raw materials into finished products. **pp. 325–26**

After 1950, the **Information Revolution** again changed the nature of work, this time through a process of deindustrialization as it moved people into service jobs in the *tertiary sector* of the economy. **pp. 326–27**

Deindustrialization resulted in the closing of many industrial factories. Many people whose factory jobs disappeared ended up with service jobs offering lower pay and fewer benefits. **p. 327**

Today's **global economy** is linked to deindustrialization in the United States:

- Many U.S. corporations moved manufacturing plants abroad, where they could pay lower wages. In recent years, white-collar jobs, too, have moved to lower-income countries. **pp. 327–28**

> **deindustrialization** (p. 327) the decline of industrial production that occurred in the United States after about 1950
>
> **globalization** (p. 327) the expansion of economic activity around the world with little regard for national borders

Other Problems of the U.S. Workplace

11.2 Discuss widespread problems of the U.S. workplace.

The Dual Labor Market
The **primary labor market** offers jobs with good pay and many benefits; jobs in the **secondary labor market** do not.

- Most of the new jobs created by today's service economy are in the secondary labor market. **p. 328**

Dangers to health and well-being exist in the workplace, especially in mining, agriculture, and construction work.

- Although the number of U.S. workplace fatalities fell over the past century, each year almost 4,400 workers die on the job. **pp. 328–30**

Alienation is a common workplace experience. Marx linked alienation to the powerlessness of workers in a capitalist economy. Weber linked alienation to modern rationality, which makes the workplace impersonal by emphasizing efficiency above all else. **pp. 330–31**

McDonaldization defines work in terms of efficiency, predictability, uniformity, and control of workers through automation. The simplified, repetitive occupations that result can be described as "McJobs," which resemble the low-skill factory jobs common a century ago. **p. 331**

The Temping of the Workplace
Counting temporary workers, contract employees, and part-timers, 21% of the U.S. labor force lack job security and have few benefits, such as employer-sponsored health insurance. This pattern benefits employers by reducing what they pay for wages and benefits. **pp. 331–32**

Some **unemployment** is normal as people enter the labor force or change jobs. Yet unemployment is also produced by the economy itself.

- The official U.S. unemployment rate in late 2014 was 5.9% of the labor force or about 10 million people. **pp. 331–32**

Race, Ethnicity, and Gender
Although a wider range of jobs is open to women and other minorities, minorities remain concentrated in lower-paying work.

- *Institutional prejudice and discrimination* generate workplace segregation and limit the advancement of minorities; informal and often invisible barriers of this kind are called the "glass ceiling." **pp. 334–35**

Labor Unions

- Labor unions gained strength along with the industrial economy in the twentieth century and, by 1950, claimed one-third of all U.S. nonfarm workers.

- Union membership has fallen due to deindustrialization and the expansion of service work. Today, just 11% of U.S. workers are union members. **pp. 335–39**

primary labor market (p. 328) jobs that provide good pay and extensive benefits to workers

secondary labor market (p. 328) jobs that provide low pay and few benefits to workers

alienation (Marx) (p. 330) powerlessness in the workplace resulting in the experience of isolation and misery

alienation (Weber) (p. 331) depersonalization not just in the workplace but throughout society as well brought on by a rational focus on efficiency

rationalization of society (Weber) (p. 331) the historical change from tradition to rationality and efficiency as the typical way people think about the world

McDonaldization (p. 331) defining work in terms of the principles of efficiency, predictability, uniformity, and automation

labor unions (p. 335) worker organizations that seek to improve wages and working conditions through various strategies, including negotiations and strikes

New Information Technology: The Brave New Workplace

11.3   Describe the effects of computer technology on the workplace.

Computers and other new information technology are redefining work in the United States:

- Working from home is becoming more common, especially among more educated workers.

- Computer technology can isolate workers and give employers greater ability to control worker activity.

- Computer technology also contributes to the "deskilling" of many jobs, including the work of managers. **pp. 339–41**

Theories of Work and Work-Related Problems

11.4   Apply sociological theory to issues involving work and the workplace.

Structural-Functional Analysis: Finding a New Equilibrium

Structural-functional theory looks at the importance of work for the operation of the economy.

- Changes (especially those brought on by new technology) can disrupt established patterns of work, causing problems such as unemployment.

- But other institutions, such as education, gradually retrain workers for new kinds of jobs, helping restore society's balance. **pp. 341–42**

Symbolic-Interaction Analysis: The Meaning of Work

Symbolic-interaction theory highlights the meaning people attach to work.

- In general, people in the primary labor market attach positive meaning to their work; their jobs are an important part of their social identity.

- People in the secondary labor market find less positive meaning in their work and value a job only for the income it provides. **pp. 342–43**

Social-Conflict Analysis: Work and Inequality

Social-conflict theory focuses on how wealth and power shape the workplace.

- A Marxist analysis argues that because factories and other productive property are privately owned, most people are powerless and find work alienating.

- Max Weber adds that modern rationality makes efficiency an all-important goal so that the workplace becomes impersonal, with workers coming to resemble machines. **p. 343**

Feminist Analysis: Work and Gender

Feminist theory focuses on how gender shapes social patterns involving work and the workplace.

- A feminist analysis points out that society links various types of work to people of each sex.

- In general, women predominate in jobs that involve less power and prestige and provide less pay. **pp. 343–44**

✪ POLITICS AND THE WORKPLACE

Constructing Problems and Defining Solutions

11.5   Analyze workplace issues from various positions on the political spectrum.

Conservatives: Look to the Market

- **Conservatives** hold that a free-market economy, with minimal government regulation, produces the greatest good for the greatest number of people.

- Conservatives believe that although new technology and downturns in the economy cause temporary disruptions, the market solves these problems over time, in the end creating a highly productive economy. **p. 345**

Liberals: Look to Government

- **Liberals** point out that a free-market economy, although productive, does not meet the needs of everyone. Rather, market systems cause problems, including dangerous working conditions, unemployment, and low wages.

- Liberals support government regulation of the economy and the workplace to enhance the well-being of all. **pp. 345–46**

The Radical Left: Basic Change Is Needed

- **Radicals on the left** see the free-market system as a source of problems. From this point of view, capitalism is concerned only with profits rather than the welfare of people.

- Radicals on the left believe that mere reform will not solve this problem; the capitalist system must be replaced with an economic system that operates in the interests of all workers. **pp. 346–47**

Chapter 12
Family Life

Learning Objectives

12.1 Explain sociological concepts used to describe family life.

12.2 Examine key changes and challenges to family life in the United States.

12.3 Apply sociological theory to issues of family life.

12.4 Analyze family life issues from various positions on the political spectrum.

Tracking the Trends

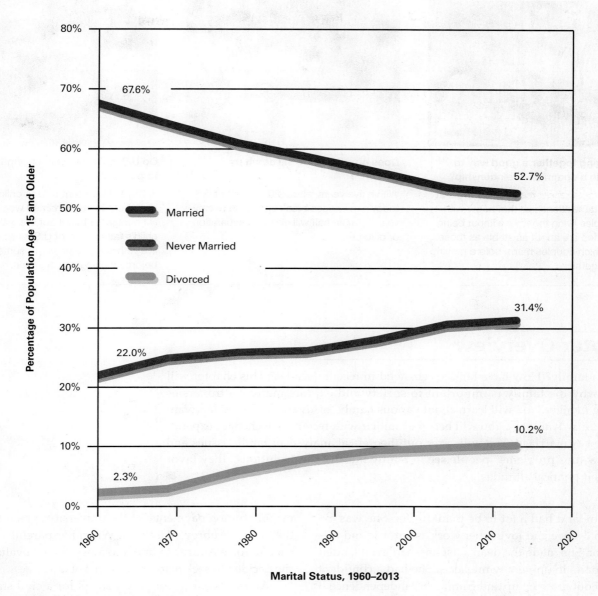

Marital Status, 1960–2013

SOURCE: U.S. Census Bureau (2014).

Is marriage becoming less popular? If you look at the numbers, you might think so. Back in 1960, more than two-thirds of U.S. adults were married. But, as shown in the figure, that share has been declining in recent decades. In 2013, about half of all adults were married—the lowest share on record. Over the same period of time, the share of adults who have never married has increased by nearly 50 percent and the share of people who are divorced has more than quadrupled. Do you think that these trends are good for the country or not? Why?

Constructing the Problem

Is living together a good way to begin a committed relationship?

The most recent research shows that marital relationships that begin with couples living together without being married are about as stable as those in which couples marry before moving in together.

Does marriage last "till death us do part"?

Within five years, about 20 percent of today's marriages break up; within twenty years, almost half will end with separation or divorce.

Do U.S. children have strong ties to parents?

In 2013, 41 percent of U.S. children were born to an unmarried woman (who might or might not live with the child's father); half of U.S. children live with just one parent at some time before reaching age eighteen.

Chapter Overview

What is a family? How have families changed in recent decades? This chapter will explain why the family is important to society and explore many controversies involving families. You will learn about various family forms and assess their advantages and disadvantages. You will become familiar with recent legal changes expanding same-sex marriage. You will carry out theoretical analysis of family issues and learn how the "problems" people see in family life and the "solutions" they favor reflect their political attitudes. ∎

Aubrey Ireland had a lot to be thankful for. She was excelling in college and loving her work as a music and theater major. She made the dean's list and had even landed leading parts in university musicals. She had a confident feeling about growing up and gaining her independence.

But there was a problem. Aubrey felt that her parents were not letting go. For one thing, David and Julie Ireland were coming to campus unexpectedly to see how their daughter was doing—driving 600 miles from their home in Kansas. Even more significantly, they installed software on her computer and cell phone to track her conversations and e-mails. They even requested that she sleep with her computer webcam turned on to monitor her actions.

Then, according to Aubrey, her parents began accusing her of bad behavior including illegal drug use, and confrontations with them became more heated, to the point of erupting in violence. That was too much, and Aubrey Ireland ended all contact with her parents. But they continued to show up, to the point that the university hired security guards to keep them away from her. Her parents stopped

making tuition payments, so the university agreed to pay the bill for Aubrey's last year. When her parents threatened to force Aubrey to undergo a psychiatric evaluation, she decided to seek help from a court of law.

Aubrey went to court and asked for a civil stalking protection order and the judge agreed that Aubrey was an adult who is entitled to live as she pleased without undue

interference from anyone—including her parents. The judge ordered the Irelands to remain at least 500 feet away from their daughter and to make no contact with her for a year. Aubrey Ireland went on to graduate in 2013—without her parents there to wish her well (Kuruvilla, 2012; Kana, 2013).

For centuries, people have looked to families as a "haven in a heartless world," a place to find love and support. For many people, families provide not only comfort but also great joy. But families also figure into many of the problems we face as individuals and as a society. This chapter explores the trends, issues, and challenges of family life in the United States. We begin by defining some basic terms.

What Is a Family?

12.1 Explain sociological concepts used to describe family life.

The **family** is *a social institution that unites individuals into cooperative groups that care for one another, including any children.* The related concept, **kinship**, refers to *a social bond, based on common ancestry, marriage, or adoption, that joins individuals into families.*

Families and kinship ties have existed since at least the beginning of recorded history, but the forms families take have varied over time as they do from place to place today. In modern, high-income societies such as the United States, most people think in terms of the **nuclear family**, *one or two parents and their children.* In lower-income nations around the world, however, people typically attach more importance to the **extended family**, *parents and children and also grandparents, aunts, uncles, and cousins who often live close to one another and operate as a family unit.*

Whatever the specific form, families are built around **marriage**, *a lawful relationship usually involving economic cooperation, sexual activity, and childbearing.* In the United States and throughout the world, people link marriage to having children, which explains why the word *matrimony* comes from the Latin word meaning "motherhood." This traditional link between marriage and having children is the reason a child born to an unwed mother was sometimes defined as "illegitimate." As we shall explain, single parenting has become more common in the United States and in other countries and, although a majority of U.S. adults express concern about the consequences of this pattern for society, it is now less likely to be defined as a problem (Pew Research Center, 2011).

Debate over Definitions

With families changing so much, we should not be surprised to find that people disagree about what a "family" ought to be. Fifty years ago, most people in the United States held the traditional view that a family was based on a married couple with children. Today, a large majority of people

still think that marriage and children are the foundations of family—but the two elements do not have to exist together. That is, most people say that a single parent with a child is a family, just as they say that a married couple without children is also a family. Most people also say that a child being raised by a same-sex couple—whether the couple is married or not—qualifies as a family (Pew Research Center, 2010). In short, people today have a broader and more inclusive idea of what "family" means to the point that many now favor recognizing a wide range of **families of affinity**, *people with or without legal or blood ties or children who feel they belong together and define themselves as a family.*

Does it matter how we define families? The answer is yes because the answer to this question makes a statement about which types of relationships are morally right or wrong. In addition, there are practical concerns, including whether all people who live together have the right to marry and whether they enjoy other rights that extend to family members, such as the right to adopt children, inherit property, or even visit a partner in the hospital. The remainder of this chapter explores many of these issues.

A Sociological Approach to Family Problems

When most people speak about "family problems" or "problems at home," they usually have in mind conflicts between individuals or perhaps a situation involving a family member who is struggling with alcohol or some other drug.

The sociological perspective looks at not just the behavior of individuals in families but takes a broader view of how family life is shaped by a society's standard of living and technology. Today, many U.S. adults find themselves torn by the demands of both work and family—spheres of life that computer technology tends to bring together. Sociology also explores how patterns of family life are linked to income, education, gender, and race. Today, for example, people with higher incomes and college degrees are more likely to marry than low-income people without college degrees (Pew Research Center, 2010). Similarly, a society in which most women as well as men work for income raises the odds that people will struggle to balance work and family responsibilities.

Family Life: Changes and Controversies

12.2 Examine key changes and challenges to family life in the United States.

How are U.S. families changing? The trends include a rising number of people living together without being married,

What does the modern family look like? If we look to the mass media, this is a difficult question to answer. In the television show *Modern Family*, Jay Pritchett's family includes his much younger wife, his stepson Manny, his daughter Claire (who is married with three children), and his son Mitchell (who, with his gay partner, has an adopted Vietnamese daughter). How would you define *family*?

people marrying later, an increase in the share of children born to single mothers, more mothers joining fathers in the labor force so that more young children spend the day in care programs, a divorce rate much higher than it was fifty years ago, an increase in the number of blended families following remarriage, gains by gay men and lesbians in their pursuit of legal marriage, and new medical technology that offers amazing new possibilities for reproduction. All these changes have sparked controversy. In the following sections, we examine all the trends in turn.

Living Together: Do We Need to Marry?

Fifty years ago, most people took it for granted that couples married before moving in together. But a recent trend favors **cohabitation**, *the sharing of a household by an unmarried couple*. The number of cohabiting couples in the United States has increased from about 500,000 in 1970 to more than 6.9 million (6.3 million heterosexual couples and 650,000 gay or lesbian couples). In all, cohabiting people represent 6 percent of all households (U.S. Census Bureau, 2013).

In some countries, especially Scandinavian nations such as Sweden, cohabitation is very common, even for couples with children. This practice is rare in more traditional (and Roman Catholic) nations such as Italy. In the United States, 49 percent of people between twenty-five and forty-four years of age (52 percent of women and 46 percent of men) cohabit at some point in their lives. Thirty-nine percent of these couples include at least one child under eighteen (U.S. Census Bureau, 2013; CDC, 2014).

Critics of cohabiting, typically political conservatives, claim that "living together" provides a less stable setting in which to raise children than marriage does. For one thing, most pregnancies that occur with cohabiting couples are unplanned. For another, the life span of the typical cohabiting relationship in the United States is barely two years. Putting these facts together, we can understand why research shows that just 5 percent of children born to cohabiting parents go on to live with both parents until age eighteen, compared with 70 percent of children born to married parents (M. Phillips, 2001; Manlove, 2012; Copen et al., 2013).

As critics see it, without the bond of marriage, men can more easily walk out on women and children. But, they add, cohabitation carries risks for men, too: When informal unions break up, men run the risk of losing legal rights to raise their children. Research shows that after three years, about 40 percent of cohabiting couples marry, 32 percent continue to cohabit, and 28 percent split up. In addition, initial research suggested that living together could weaken a later marriage because partners became used to relationships with less commitment. More recent research, however, suggests that this "cohabitation effect" is no longer very strong (Popenoe & Whitehead, 1999; Copen et al., 2013).

Supporters of cohabitation, typically liberals, argue that choices about sexual relationships are private matters that should be left to individuals. In addition, they ask, why would we think that one relational form—monogamous marriage—would meet the needs of everyone in a large and diverse population? They accept cohabitation in the interest of greater personal choice and freedom and also claim that cohabitation typically encourages a more equal relationship between a woman and a man. What about the well-being of children? Supporters of cohabitation argue that all parents who separate—whether married or not—must take responsibility for the support and care of their children (Brines & Joyner, 1999; Scommegna, 2002).

Postponing Marriage

The trend toward cohabitation is linked to another pattern: On average, people in the United States are delaying marriage. In 1950, the median age at first marriage in the United States was 20.3 years for women and 22.8 years for men. By 2013, these figures had jumped about six years to 26.6 years for women and 29.0 years for men (U.S. Census Bureau, 2013).

Why are people marrying later? One reason is the increasing share of young people who enroll in college and graduate school. Another is the increasing share of women who move into the labor force. A third factor is improvement in birth control technology and the availability of legal abortion. Unlike the 1950s, today's couples facing an unexpected pregnancy are not likely to feel forced to marry. A fourth factor is the recent climate of economic insecurity that makes it hard for many young people to live on their own. In 2013, 55 percent of young people between eighteen and twenty-four were still living with their parents.

This trend toward later marriage is not generally viewed as a problem, and it may well be a "solution" to other challenges. But postponing first marriage does have some important consequences. For one thing, men and, especially, women who marry later in life have somewhat lower odds of being able to have children. Those who choose to have children will be "older" parents, who may lack some of the energy of parents who are ten to twenty years younger. On the plus side, older parents typically have more maturity and life experience and older people also earn more money.

The trend toward delayed marriage has been accompanied by a drop in overall childbearing: A U.S. woman's average number of children dropped from 3.0 in 1976 to 1.9 in 2012. Other patterns linked to delayed marriage include a rising share of women who have not had a child by the time they reach their mid-forties (up from 9 percent in 1970 to about 20 percent in 2013) and a rising share of the population that remains single (almost tripling from 11 percent in 1950 to 27 percent in 2013) (U.S. Census Bureau, 2013).

Another consequence of delayed marriage is that by the time that people consider getting married, they have become more independent of their parents. With less parental input into the choice of partner, people are freer to form relationships that might have been discouraged in the past, such as same-sex or interracial unions.

Parenting: Is One Parent Enough?

In 2013, almost one in three families with children under eighteen years of age had just one parent in the household, a share that has more than doubled since 1970. About 28 percent of U.S. children live with a single parent; about half will do so at some point before reaching age eighteen (Solomon-Fears, 2014). Figure 12–1 shows the various arrangements that working women make to provide their children with care.

There is no doubt that most children raised by a single parent turn out just fine; similarly, having two parents in the home is no guarantee of a child's well-being. Still, a large majority of U.S. adults believe that children are best served by having two parents in the home (Pew, 2011). Research evidence is mounting in support of this belief. Some studies indicate that a

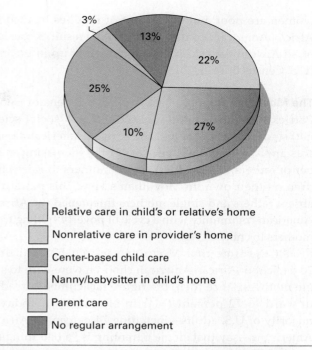

Figure 12–1 Child Care Arrangements for Working Mothers

Half of the young children of working mothers receive care from a parent, grandparent, or other relative.

SOURCE: U.S. Census Bureau (2013).

Legend:
- Relative care in child's or relative's home
- Nonrelative care in provider's home
- Center-based child care
- Nanny/babysitter in child's home
- Parent care
- No regular arrangement

father and a mother each make a distinctive contribution to a child's social development, so either parent alone cannot do as complete a job as two working together. In addition, it stands to reason that all else being equal, two parents can provide greater attention to children than one.

But the biggest problem confronting one-parent families—especially in the 77 percent of all cases where the single parent is a woman—is poverty. Of all children living in one-parent families, 41 percent are poor and, on average, they end up with less education and lower incomes when they become adults. Such disadvantages often develop into a vicious circle as boys and girls raised by single parents become single parents themselves (Popenoe, 1993a; Kantrowitz & Wingert, 2001; Pew Research Center, 2007; U.S. Census Bureau, 2013).

Families, Race, and Poverty

There are many reasons that children live with a single parent. Most white children live with a single parent as result of divorce or separation; among African American children, most have a mother who never married. Although the risk of being poor goes up in both situations, the problem of poverty is especially high for African American children. In the United States, about 33 percent of families with children headed by non-Hispanic white women are poor, but 47 percent of families headed by African American women are poor. As a result, 38 percent of all African American youngsters grow up in poverty (U.S. Census Bureau, 2013).

The Moynihan Report Back in 1965, U.S. senator Daniel Patrick Moynihan (who was trained as a social scientist) sounded an alarm that the African American family was approaching crisis because of the increasing number of fathers who had left single mothers to raise children on their own. In Moynihan's view, this pattern of absent fathers and single mothers threatened the African American community with a cycle of poverty spilling from mothers to children.

At the time that Moynihan issued his warning, 20 percent of African American children were born to single mothers; since then, the figure has climbed steadily upward to 72 percent (Martin et al., 2013). Today, a majority of U.S. adults—including 74 percent of African Americans—say that single parenting is "a bad thing for society" (Pew Research Center, 2010).

But, then as now, not everyone agrees with Moynihan. Critics claim that his concern reflected a traditional view of the two-parent family, rejecting anything different as "dysfunctional." There is no problem with a female-headed household, critics continue, at least nothing that adequate income cannot solve. In other words, liberal critics argue that single-parent families and poverty in the African American community are not so much *family* problems as they are *economic* and *racial prejudice* problems. Eleanor Holmes Norton (1985) argues that the "breakdown" of the African American family is the result of long-term racism, which results in discrimination in jobs, education, and housing. The sociologist William Julius Wilson (1987, 1996a) adds that African Americans who live within a disadvantaged urban "underclass" find that there are

simply not enough jobs to allow men and women to support a family. To claim that African Americans choose their family patterns (much less choose to be poor) amounts to blaming the victim (Hewlett & West, 1998).

African American Families: A Closer Look For years, the popular image of the average "welfare mother" was an unmarried African American woman. But this stereotype is not accurate. The simple fact is that most people in the United States who receive public assistance are white. The Diversity: Race, Class, & Gender box presents five more common but false stereotypes about African American families.

African American families—like families of people in any racial category—take many forms, and no single description is an accurate portrayal. In the United States, families—black and white, rich and poor—are much more diverse than most people realize.

Strengths of African American Families There is little doubt that African American families face more challenges—including low income, racial prejudice, and discrimination—than white families do. But research also shows that African American families, especially those struggling with poverty, have remarkable strengths. These families confront their challenges with a number of strategies, building strong kinship bonds, drawing strength from traditional religious beliefs, and using the resources of grandparents (especially grandmothers) to form three-generation households. In addition, many poor households form networks of mutual assistance that help everyone get by in hard times (Stack, 1975; Clemetson, 2000; Lofquist, 2012).

Conflict between Work and Family Life

For much of U.S. history, most people lived on farms where they combined work and family life. After the Industrial Revolution, people (mostly men) went off to work in factories, which created a "gender divide" that separated the home (dominated by women) from the workplace (dominated by men).

Starting in the 1950s, as increasing numbers of women entered the labor force, they began to feel new tensions between work and family life. Today, a majority (52 percent) of U.S. families have both parents working for income. Typically, today's women not only work for pay but also come home to perform close to another full-time job doing unpaid housework (Lewin, 2000; England, 2001; U.S. Census Bureau, 2013). This "double shift" means that many women are tired and overworked as they try to juggle their many responsibilities.

One of the strengths of African American families is the tendency to form multigenerational households. Why do you think this pattern is more common among African Americans than among whites?

DIVERSITY: RACE, CLASS, & GENDER

Reality Check: Five False Stereotypes about African American Families

In the United States, many people hold incorrect and stereotypical views of African American families. Here we do a reality check on five widespread stereotypes about African American families (U.S. Census Bureau, 2011, 2013).

Stereotype 1. African Americans do not form strong families.

Historical studies show that even under slavery, most African Americans lived in families with a father and a mother. This pattern of strong families continued well into the twentieth century. After about 1960, a combination of racial segregation (which trapped many African Americans in inner cities) and industrial decline (which meant that many inner-city communities lost a lot of jobs) resulted in a declining rate of marriage among African Americans and a rising rate of children born to single mothers. But in 2013, even against these odds, 46 percent of African American families still had both husband and wife in the home.

Stereotype 2. African American men do not make good husbands and fathers.

This stereotype is based on the fact that a larger share of families have no husband present among African Americans (44 percent) than among Latinos (26 percent), whites (14 percent), or Asians (13 percent). This stereotype assumes that the lack of a husband in the home reflects people's choices; yet many African American communities do not provide the jobs men need to support a family (W. J. Wilson, 1996b).

Stereotype 3. The African American family is a matriarchy: Women dominate family life.

History shows that African American men have played vital leadership roles both in their families and in their larger communities. It is also important to recognize that men or men and women together head a majority (56 percent) of African American families.

Stereotype 4. African American women have many children, often in order to increase welfare benefits.

Regardless of race, poor women receiving income assistance have more than twice as many children as women who do not receive public assistance. But this pattern holds for both black and white women. Overall, the birth rate for black women is just 10 percent higher than for non-Hispanic white women.

Stereotype 5. Today, African Americans have the same opportunities as everyone else.

Many white people believe, or want to believe, that racial prejudice and discrimination are things of the past. However, the evidence suggests that African American men and women—whether poor, middle class, or rich—continue to face barriers based on race.

What Do You Think?

1. Why do you think stereotypes about African American families are widespread? Can you add additional stereotypes to the list presented here?

2. How does sociology play a part in responding to stereotypes such as these?

3. What policies might the federal or state government follow to give more support to African American families? Explain.

As Chapter 11 ("Work and the Workplace") explains, the Information Revolution has changed the nature of work, and one-fifth of people in the labor force now spend some time each week working at home. Working at home saves travel time and expense, which can help to reduce work–family tensions. At the same time, as more people work at home or maintain home offices, workplace activities and concerns spill more and more into family life (Macionis, 2001; U.S. Department of Labor, 2013).

Child Care

A century ago, most families considered child care the job of the mother, who worked in the home. Today, with 58 percent of U.S. women in the labor force working for income, most mothers are working mothers—54 percent of married women with infants, 60 percent of married women with preschoolers, and 70 percent of married women with school-age children work for pay outside the home. The figures are a little higher for single women with children and higher still for widowed, divorced, or separated women with children (U.S. Department of Labor, 2013).

The increasing share of women and men working led members of our society to define child care as an important issue. Who provides care for children of mothers and fathers in the labor force? Figure 12–1 on page 359 shows that about

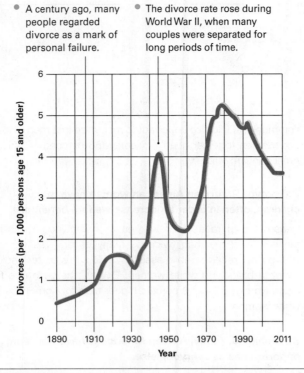

● A century ago, many people regarded divorce as a mark of personal failure.

● The divorce rate rose during World War II, when many couples were separated for long periods of time.

Figure 12–2 The U.S. Divorce Rate, 1890–2011

After 1890, the U.S. divorce rate climbed rapidly, especially during World War II (1939–1945). After falling in the 1950s, the rate rose again through the late 1970s and has since been on the decline.

SOURCE: Centers for Disease Control and Prevention (2013).

half (49 percent) of all children receive care from family—from a parent (22 percent) or from a grandparent or other relative (27 percent). An additional 25 percent of children go to a day care program or attend preschool, 10 percent receive care in a nonrelative's home, 3 percent receive care in their own home, and 13 percent have no regular arrangement (U.S. Census Bureau, 2013).

The range of options available to a particular family has a lot to do with income. Parents with higher incomes can afford to send their children to care programs that emphasize learning and early childhood development. By contrast, those with lower incomes turn to relatives or friends, piece together a patchwork of babysitters, or send their children to less costly care centers where the staff does not have much training and gives less attention to each child.

Older children, of course, spend most of the day at school. But after school, about 4.5 million youngsters (11 percent of five- to fourteen-year-olds) are "latchkey kids" who fend for themselves until a parent returns from work (U.S. Census Bureau, 2013). Some children adapt well to being alone after school, learning to become independent and self-reliant. But especially in neighborhoods prone to violence, unsupervised children are at high risk for becoming involved in drug use, crime, or sexual exploitation.

What role, if any, should the government play in ensuring that child care needs are met? In most high-income nations other than the United States, the government uses tax money to operate child care centers. In our country, government provides only indirect assistance to working parents by letting them deduct child care costs on income tax returns. In addition, states provide some financial assistance to poor families who need child care. Because of our country's cultural emphasis on self-sufficiency, the United States has yet to offer free or subsidized child care programs on a large scale.

Those who favor expanding government child care programs point out that many low-income families would welcome the assistance and more children could be well served. In addition, most existing child care centers operate only during business hours from Monday to Friday, which does not meet the needs of parents who work night shifts or "swing" shifts that change from week to week.

A small but increasing number of today's employers offer on-site child care programs. In most cases, employees pay for this care, but some employers provide this service as a workplace benefit. Most programs are of good quality and offer two added advantages: Parents can use work breaks to visit their children, and companies that provide workplace child care have the edge in attracting and retaining the best employees.

A final child care issue involves children whose parents cannot or will not care for them. Our society tries to assist these children through the foster care system. But the cost of doing so (roughly $11,000 a year per child) is high, and although in a majority of cases children are better off in foster care than they were before, the rate of neglect and abuse among foster children is far higher than among children living with biological parents.

Divorce

When they marry, many people recite a vow that they will stay together "till death us do part." But the reality today is that divorce is more likely than death to end a marriage. In the United States, about 20 percent of marriages end by separation, dissolution, or divorce within five years. Within twenty years, half of marriages break up. These rates are slightly higher for African Americans than for whites. At any given time, about 10 percent of adult men and 12 percent of adult women described their marital status as "divorced" (U.S. Census Bureau, 2013).

As Figure 12–2 shows, during and after World War II, the divorce rate pushed upward because the war forced millions of couples to live apart. Between 1960 and 1980, as more women entered the labor force, the divorce rate increased dramatically. During the last three decades, the divorce rate has eased downward.

The bigger picture is that today's divorce rate is almost four times higher than it was a century ago. Back

Seeing Ourselves

National Map 12–1 Divorce across the United States

The map shows the divorce rate (the number of divorces per 1,000 population), by state, for 2010. Divorce is far more common near the West Coast (and especially in Nevada, a state with very liberal divorce laws), somewhat less common in the East, and much less common in the middle of the country. Research suggests that divorce is more likely among people who are younger, who have weaker religious ties, and who move away from their parents' hometown. Can you apply these facts to make sense of this map?

SOURCE: Centers for Disease Control and Prevention (2012).

then, family members (especially the half of U.S. families who lived and worked on farms) relied on one another to get by, and this economic dependency kept married people together. In addition, because women had yet to enter the labor force in large numbers, unless a woman could turn to relatives for support, divorce often meant a life of poverty. Finally, the more traditional culture of that time defined divorce as sinful and a sign of personal failure, so moral pressure also helped keep couples together, whether they were happily married or not.

Today, of course, the share of women working for income is way up, and the average number of children per woman is way down. These trends made divorce a more realistic option, and gradually, public attitudes have become more accepting of divorce (Etzioni, 1993; Schoen at al., 2002; U.S. Census Bureau, 2013). National Map 12–1 shows the percentage of the population that is divorced for all the states.

No-Fault Divorce Increasing economic independence was not the only factor that gave women more opportunity to move on from an unhappy marriage. Changes in the law also helped make divorces easier to get. In 1969,

California became the first state to enact a new policy called "no-fault divorce." By 1985, every state in the country had done the same.

What is no-fault divorce? Perhaps the best way to answer this question is to explain that before this policy was in force, a couple could divorce only if one or both partners claimed in court that the other was at fault for *ruining* the marriage—typically, by one partner abandoning the other, committing adultery, or causing physical or emotional injury. Society viewed marriage in moral terms; therefore, for divorce to occur, someone had to have done something *very wrong*. Much was at stake in this "blame-game" because the courts took fault into account when dividing the couple's property and assigning custody of children. The "bad" person usually lost out.

No-fault divorce laws did away with this whole process. As marriage came to be defined less as a moral good and more as just an "agreement" between partners, no one had to accept blame for a failed marriage. On the contrary, couples could simply declare that their marriage is over due to "irreconcilable differences." The court then divides property fairly and places children where they seem best off. In addition, the court assigns *child support* according

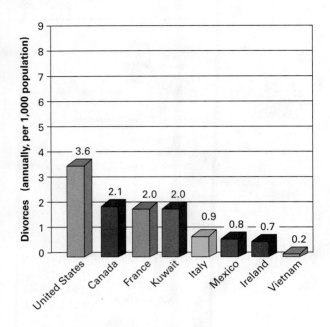

Global Snapshot

Figure 12–3 Divorce in Selected Countries

The odds of a marriage ending in divorce are higher in the United States than in other countries.

SOURCES: Centers for Disease Control and Prevention (2013), European Union (2013), United Nations (2013), and OECD (2014).

to the need of the custodial parent, the noncustodial parent's ability to pay, and the ability of both parents to work. Rarely does no-fault divorce involve *alimony*, payments traditionally made by one ex-spouse to the other.

By greatly reducing the payment of alimony, no-fault divorce ended the long-standing idea that men ought to take care of women. But this new policy does not mean that women are always better off. Researchers found that after divorce, the living standard of men typically went up, but the living standard of women and their children went down (Weitzman, 1985, 1996; Faludi, 1991; Holden & Smock, 1991). Why is this so? Allen Parkman (1992) claims that a weakness in no-fault divorce is that this policy ignores *cultural capital*, which includes skills and schooling that increase a person's earning power. In a traditional marriage, a wife may put little or no time into paid work, often devoting herself to helping her husband develop his career. Her focus on her husband makes sense only as long as she assumes that she will stay married and that her husband's success will benefit her as well. After divorce, the husband still has his job, but in most cases, the stay-at-home wife has few workplace skills to fall back on and also faces the expense of caring for the children.

Many people support no-fault divorce as a solution to the problem of unhappy marriages. In addition, supporters claim that this policy treats men and women as equals, reflecting the reality that most people of both sexes now work for income. But some people see no-fault divorce as a problem, claiming that it is harmful to women. Pointing to the fact that men still earn more money than women, critics say that we should bring back the system of alimony so that the person with the greater earning power (usually the man) helps support the ex-partner (typically, the woman) who stayed at home.

Finally, if divorce is always a possibility, should couples prepare for it? Many couples try to spell out the terms of any future divorce by writing a premarital agreement. The Social Problems in Focus box takes a closer look.

Too Much Divorce? Just about everyone today thinks that divorce is better than staying in an unhappy relationship. But is the U.S. divorce rate too high? In global perspective, this country has the highest divorce rate in the world. Figure 12–3 shows that the U.S. divorce rate is considerably higher than in Canada and more than four times higher than "low-divorce" nations such as Italy and Ireland (European Union, 2013; OECD, 2014).

In the United States, liberals generally do not view divorce as a problem. They tend to favor easy divorce as a means by which women can free themselves from unhappy or abusive relationships. Conservatives are more critical of a high divorce rate, claiming that families have become weaker due to a "me first" attitude that places individual needs and desires over obligations to others (Whitehead, 1997; Popenoe, 1999).

Then there is the effect of divorce on children. Again, the costs and benefits of ending a marriage vary from case to case, but the evidence suggests that many divorces end up being the most difficult for the children involved (Amato & Sobolewski, 2001).

So, is our present divorce rate a problem or not? The public is divided on the issue, but about half are concerned. When asked in a national survey whether divorce is too easy to get these days, 22 percent of U.S. adults say they are satisfied with the system as it is, 33 percent think divorce is still too hard to get, and 38 percent say that divorce is too easy to get, with the remaining 7 percent expressing no opinion (Smith et al., 2013).

Between 1997 and 2001, three fairly conservative states—Arkansas, Arizona, and Louisiana—responded to high divorce rates by enacting *covenant marriage* laws. These laws allow couples, when they marry, to choose a conventional marriage or a covenant marriage, which is harder to dissolve. Couples who choose a covenant marriage agree, first, to seek marital counseling if problems develop during the marriage. They agree to seek divorce only for limited reasons, including adultery, conviction for a serious felony, abandonment for at least one year or living separately for at least two years, habitual drug or alcohol abuse, or physical or sexual abuse of the spouse or a child. Covenant marriage rejects the "no-fault" idea that people ought to be able

SOCIAL PROBLEMS IN FOCUS

Should You Prepare a Premarital Agreement?

Any couple considering marriage today needs to face up to the fact that there is a significant chance that at some point in the future, the relationship will end in divorce. Therefore, lawyers suggest that couples prepare a premarital (prenuptial) agreement.

What should be included in such an agreement? The answer depends on the individuals involved and on how much property each person has going into the marriage.

1. **Property.** Start by making a list of each of your assets and liabilities. Will you retain separate ownership of existing property—including homes, furniture, jewelry, cash, cars, and investments—or combine everything as joint property? Will you keep your own savings and checking accounts or create new joint accounts? Will you be responsible for each other's existing debts, such as loans for college tuition or car payments? What about property that you accumulate during the marriage? In the event of divorce or death of one partner, what will happen to all property? If either of you entered the marriage with children, what property rights do those children have?

2. **Income.** Do you know your partner's income as well as your own? How will these incomes be applied to household expenses, savings and investments, and future purchases such as a new home? Who will be responsible for paying bills? For supporting children?

3. **Children.** Do you have children? Do you plan to have children together? How will you divide responsibility for child care? What are each partner's attitudes about disciplining children? Is it important to give children a religious upbringing? Will children from a previous relationship have the same

inheritance rights as any children you have with your new partner?

4. **Housework.** How much housework needs to be done? To answer this question, consider the likely size of your family and the size of your home. How will you divide responsibility for housework?

5. **In case of divorce.** Should your marriage end in divorce, how will you divide property? What marital property will be sold? What about assets (a house or investments) that may go up in value during the marriage? What about custody and care of any children? What share of either person's income would be reasonable as child support? Will you both share responsibility for paying for college? Do you or your partner expect to receive alimony? If so, how much and for how long?

Raising questions such as these may seem too business-like when people are deeply in love. This fact leads some people to wonder whether a couple is not inviting conflict by preparing a premarital agreement. Perhaps. But discussion and even written statements of expectations for the marriage will probably reduce the chances for conflict later on and may even increase the chances of a happy marriage.

What Do You Think?

1. Have you ever considered preparing a prenuptial agreement? If so, did you create one?

2. Do you think such an agreement is a good or bad idea? Why?

3. Would you support a law that requires any couples to prepare such an agreement prior to marriage? Why or why not?

---

to divorce simply because one of them no longer wants to stay married (Nock, Wright, & Sanchez, 1999; National Conference of State Legislatures, 2014).

In 2000 and 2001, covenant marriage bills were proposed in a dozen additional states, but no other state enacted such a law. In most cases, lawmakers simply passed a resolution encouraging couples to engage in premarital counseling. Further, in the three states that did enact covenant marriage laws, only a small share of people have chosen this type of marriage. Therefore, it seems safe to conclude that covenant marriage is not widely viewed as a solution to the high divorce rate.

Child Support

After parents divorce, many children do not receive adequate financial support. Failure to make an estimated

$14 billion in child support payments by the noncustodial parent (that is, the parent who does not have primary custody of a child) is one cause of high poverty rates among U.S. children.

After a separation or divorce, courts typically order noncustodial parents to help support their children. Such court orders are issued for 49 percent of the children of divorcing parents. Yet of the children who should receive this money, 57 percent receive only partial payments or no payments at all (U.S. Census Bureau, 2013).

When parents divorce, courts usually award custody of children to mothers. For this reason, most parents who fail to support their children are men, a fact that explains the national attention given to the problem of "deadbeat dads." However, noncustodial mothers (who fail to pay 32 percent of court-ordered support) are actually more likely than fathers (who fail to pay 25 percent of support) to fail to make child support payments, probably because single women have lower incomes (U.S. Census Bureau, 2013).

What should society do about parents who do not support their children? As this issue became defined as a social problem, states passed laws requiring an employer to withhold money from the earnings of a parent who fails to pay child support. Even so, some parents manage to duck their responsibilities by moving or switching jobs. In 1998, as a result, Congress passed the Deadbeat Parents Punishment Act, making it a serious crime to refuse to provide support payments to a child residing in another state or to move to another state in order to avoid making such payments. In addition, many states have begun publishing "Wanted" posters of delinquent parents on billboards or in newspapers in the hope that such publicity will shame them into paying up.

Remarriage: Problems of Blended Families

Because divorce is common in the United States, our society also has a lot of remarriage. In fact, three out of four people who divorce remarry, and most do so within four years. Nationwide, more than one-third of all marriages are remarriages for at least one partner (U.S. Census Bureau, 2013).

When partners with children from a previous relationship marry, they create **blended families**, *families in which children have some combination of biological parents and stepparents*. In the United States, about 10 percent of children with married parents are in a blended family; for African American children, the share is about 16 percent.

People in blended families face some special challenges. Children who become part of a blended family must learn new household rules and routines and build relationships with new siblings. Stepparents, too, must make adjustments, establishing relationships with a new spouse and unfamiliar children. Most couples also have to maintain a relationship with a child's other biological parent and perhaps that person's new partner.

Most blended families manage to cope with these challenges. But research shows that members of blended families carry some special risks. For children, stepparent families have a high rate of physical and sexual abuse. For spouses, the likelihood of divorce, especially among people who remarry at a younger age, is higher than for couples in first marriages (Fleming, Mullen, & Bammer, 1997; McLanahan, 2002).

Gay and Lesbian Families

Not all couples even have the choice of marrying. In 2004, Massachusetts became the first state to recognize same-sex marriage. The Defining Moment box takes a closer look at the Massachusetts decision.

As of the fall of 2014, twenty-nine more states (Connecticut, Vermont, New Hampshire, Iowa, New York, Washington, Maryland, Maine, Rhode Island, Delaware, Minnesota, California, New Jersey, Illinois, Hawaii, New Mexico, Oregon, Pennsylvania, Indiana, Oklahoma, Utah, Virginia, Wisconsin, Colorado, Nevada, West Virginia, Alaska, Idaho, and North Carolina) and the District of Columbia have also changed their laws to recognize same-sex marriage. At the same time, many states have enacted laws that ban same-sex marriage and also prevent recognizing same-sex marriages performed elsewhere.

Across the United States, about 640,000 same-sex couples have formed committed partnerships, including about 190,000 couples who are legally married and 450,000 who are not. About one-in-four same-sex couples are parents raising children under age eighteen. Typically, these children are offspring from a previous heterosexual relationship, although many gay couples adopt children of their own (U.S. Census Bureau, 2013; National Conference of State Legislatures, 2014).

Many people, both gay and straight, view the legal right to marry someone of the same sex as an important measure of society's acceptance of a same-sex orientation. Same-sex marriage also extends legal rights to spouses that range from hospital visitation rights to health insurance to child custody.

The first nation to give same-sex partners all the legal benefits of marriage was Denmark in 1989. Since then, thirty-four nations have followed suit. But only sixteen countries have extended marriage, in name as well as in practice, to same-sex couples: the Netherlands (2001), Belgium (2003), Canada (2005), Spain (2005), South Africa (2006), Norway (2009), Sweden (2009), Portugal (2010), Iceland (2010), Argentina (2010), Brazil (2011), Denmark (2012), France (2013), New Zealand (2013), Uruguay (2013), and United Kingdom except Northern Ireland (2014). Global Map 12–1 on page 368 shows the extent of legal same-sex partnerships around the world. The map reflects a "global divide" on same-sex marriage by which laws and public attitudes supporting same-sex marriage are most likely to be found in higher-income nations in North America, South America, and Western Europe. On the other side of the "global divide" are lower-income nation in Africa, Eastern Europe, and much of Asia (Pew Research Global Attitudes Project, 2013).

The same-sex marriage debate brings us again to the question of how to define a family. In general, social conservatives argue that same-sex marriage undermines the definition of the family that has guided societies for thousands of years. Conservatives argue, too, that such families do not offer the best setting in which to raise children (Knight, 1998). Most social liberals counter that all people who form committed relationships—whether straight or gay—want these ties to be recognized socially

CONSTRUCTING SOCIAL PROBLEMS

A DEFINING MOMENT

Same-Sex Marriage: The Massachusetts Decision

Hillary and Julie Goodridge had a wish. It had been three years since their daughter, Annie, asked her two mommies why they were not married. In response, the two women decided to take their case to the courts with the goal of obtaining the right to marry. The court supported their claim. The women's wish came true on May 17, 2004, as they became legally wedded spouses.

The Massachusetts case seeking legal marriage for same-sex partners was brought by the Goodridges and six other couples. The couples' lawsuit came down to a simple question: Why should having a same-sex orientation be grounds for denying people the right others have to marry? In the case of *Goodridge et al.* v. *Department of Public Health*, the Massachusetts Supreme Court ruled in a four-to-three decision that it was wrong to discriminate in this way against lesbians and gay men. The court's decision stated:

> Barred access to the protections, benefits, and obligations of civil marriage, a person who enters into an intimate, exclusive union with another of the same sex is arbitrarily deprived of membership in one of our community's most rewarding and cherished institutions. That exclusion is incompatible with the constitutional principles of respect for individual autonomy and equality under law.

The decision put to rest the contest over whether Massachusetts would allow same-sex marriage. But it did not end the debate. Polls at that time showed that a majority of people in Massachusetts did not support same-sex marriage. In light of this fact, there was much criticism of "activist judges" who, as critics saw it, were imposing their liberal politics on everyone else. President George Bush spoke out against the decision, describing marriage as "a sacred institution between a man and a woman" and pledging that the federal government would "protect the sanctity of marriage."

The impact of any state's decision to enact a gay marriage law is enhanced by the fact that the "full faith and credit" clause of the U.S. Constitution mandates that any contract (including marriage) performed in one state must be recognized by all states. For this reason, in 1996, congressional opponents of gay marriage passed the Defense of Marriage Act, which says that marriage must involve one man and one woman and that no state or other jurisdiction has to recognize a same-sex marriage law enacted by any other state or jurisdiction. By 2014, thirty-three states had passed some law restricting marriage to one man and one woman or preventing the recognition of same-sex marriages performed elsewhere. However, in 2011, the Obama administration announced that it opposed and would no longer support the Defense of Marriage Act; in 2013, the U.S. Supreme Court overturned a key part of that law denying federal benefits to same-sex couples.

The debate goes on, but gay rights activists have made remarkable progress in extending same-sex marriage, which is now legal in more than half the states and the District of Columbia. The rapid pace of change is evident in the fact that same-sex marriage laws took effect in at least fourteen states in 2014. Some analysts are already declaring that the battle to recognize same-sex marriage has been won (Von Drehle, 2013). That judgment may be premature. But the 2004 decision introducing legal same-sex marriage to the United States was a defining moment in the way our society views marriage and family life.

Hillary and Julie Goodridge were married in Boston in 2004, becoming the first same-sex couple to legally marry in the United States.

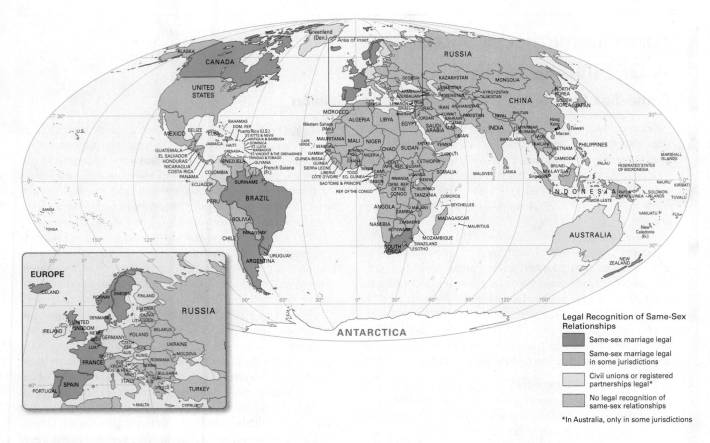

Legal Recognition of Same-Sex Relationships

■	Same-sex marriage legal
■	Same-sex marriage legal in some jurisdictions
□	Civil unions or registered partnerships legal*
■	No legal recognition of same-sex relationships

*In Australia, only in some jurisdictions

Window on the World

Global Map 12–1 Legal Same-Sex Marriage and Registered Partnerships in Global Perspective

Since Denmark recognized same-sex partnerships in 1989, thirty-four nations have enacted similar laws. Yet in only sixteen nations of the world—almost all of them high-income countries—is same-sex marriage legal.

SOURCES: Bruni (2011), European Union (2014), and Pew Research Center Project on Religion and Public Life (2014).

and legally, which leads liberals to support same-sex marriage. However, the political lines are not clearly drawn in this debate: Some social conservatives who believe in the importance of "family values" also support same-sex marriage, claiming that all people, whatever their sexual orientation, benefit from being married.

Same-Sex Parenting Roughly 160,000 same-sex couples in the United States are currently raising young children. From another angle, more than one-third of people who identify themselves as lesbian, gay, bisexual, or transgender (LGBT) have had a child at some point, and some 6 million U.S. children have an LGBT parent (Gates, 2013). Therefore, the diversity of U.S. families includes not only one-parent and two-parent families but also families in which children have two moms or two dads.

Public opinion is divided on whether gay parenting is in the best interest of children. About one-third of U.S. adults disapprove of gays and lesbians raising children; in recent years, this share has been declining. Some of these people fear that children living with homosexual parents are at higher risk of sexual abuse; however, research provides no evidence that this is the case. Quite the opposite: Research shows that gay and lesbian parents provide the same supportive and effective parenting as heterosexual couples. Nor is there any evidence that children raised by same-sex parents are any more likely to be gay themselves. In short, gay and lesbian families face problems, but the problems come more from the stigma society attaches to homosexuality than from the family form itself (Gates, 2013; Pew Research Center, 2013).

Brave New Families: High-Tech Reproduction

In 1978, Louise Brown became the world's first "test-tube baby." She was conceived not in the usual way but in a laboratory in England, where doctors placed a human ovum from her mother in a glass dish and fertilized it with a sperm cell from her father and then implanted the embryo in her mother's womb. The importance of test-tube babies is not just that they are conceived in a different way but that scientists can use medical screening to "design" their genetic makeup, which opens the door to parents having "designer children" with specific hair color or other traits. Advancing reproductive technology has created new choices for families and sparked new controversies as well.

By the end of 2014, more than half the states plus the District of Columbia had changed their laws to give legal support to same-sex marriage. As a result, this type of family life is now less likely to be viewed as a problem and is more likely to be defined as a happy solution for the partners involved.

In Vitro Fertilization So-called test-tube babies result from the process of **in vitro fertilization**, which involves *uniting egg and sperm in a laboratory* (*in vitro* is Latin for "in glass"). Once a fertilized embryo is produced, doctors may implant it in a woman's body, or they can freeze it for use at a later time.

Some 3 million couples in the United States are unable to conceive children in the normal way; in vitro fertilization provides such couples with the opportunity to become parents. However, the procedure is very expensive, so only 176,000 couples a year actually go through the process, resulting in about 65,000 births annually (CDC, 2014). Those who are finally able to have the child they want view this procedure as nothing short of miraculous. But critics point out that the cost places this procedure out of reach for most people. In addition, because new reproductive technology permits parents to select the physical and perhaps even mental traits of their children, we must face the troubling possibility of the creation of a "super-race" of genetically designed children.

Surrogate Motherhood One of the controversies arising from new reproductive technology is the issue of **surrogate motherhood**, *an arrangement by which one woman carries and bears a child for another woman.*

Surrogate motherhood came to national attention in 1986 with the case known as "Baby M." In that case, William Stern, whose wife was unable to bear children, agreed to pay Mary Beth Whitehead to bear a child conceived with his sperm via artificial insemination. Although Whitehead would be the baby's biological mother, she agreed to give up all claims to the child.

The pregnancy went according to plan, and Whitehead gave birth to a healthy child. But by that time, Whitehead had changed her mind and wanted to keep her baby. The Sterns reacted by filing a court case seeking custody of the baby and pointing to the signed agreement. In 1988, the New Jersey Supreme Court declared surrogacy contracts of this kind illegal in that state; furthermore, the court declared, the natural mother (in this case, Whitehead) should have custody of a child born from any such arrangement. A few states, however, permit such contracts, so there is no consistent policy across the United States, and in recent years, the issue has attracted relatively little attention. In a number of other countries—including India—laws permit paid surrogacy.

Cases of surrogate parenthood also raise questions about responsibility for child support. In California, John and Luanne Buzzanca, a married couple unable to have children, enlisted a woman to serve as a surrogate mother. In this case, both the egg and sperm came from unknown donors. In 1995, the surrogate mother gave birth to a baby who had no biological ties to either her or the Buzzancas. A month before the child's birth, however, John Buzzanca filed for divorce from his wife. Luanne Buzzanca took custody of the child and sought child support from her ex-husband. But John refused, claiming he was not the child's father.

In the court suit that followed, a California judge ruled that although they were not the child's biological parents, both John and Luanne Buzzanca were the child's "intended parents." Therefore, the court ruled, both parties who engage a surrogate mother are responsible for any child born in this way. In the end, Luanne Buzzanca received custody of the baby, and her ex-husband was ordered to pay monthly child support.

Cases such as these show that although new reproductive technology has obvious benefits for some couples, our society has yet to work out clear rules to guide its use. This disconnect illustrates a pattern sociologists call *cultural lag*, when scientific discoveries advance more quickly than our ideas about the acceptable ways to use them. The result is procedures that are scientifically possible but may or may not be considered morally right.

Theories of Families and Family Problems

12.3 Apply sociological theory to issues of family life.

We can increase our understanding of issues surrounding the family by applying sociology's major theoretical approaches: structural-functional theory, symbolic-interaction theory, social-conflict theory, and feminist theory. The following discussions are summarized in the Applying Theory table.

Structural-Functional Analysis: Family as Foundation

Structural-functional theory views the family as the foundation of all societies. Decades ago, George Murdock (1949) pointed out that families exist everywhere in the world because they perform four major tasks essential for the operation of society.

First, as explained in Chapter 7 ("Sexuality"), families are the means by which societies regulates reproduction, encouraging the birth of children to parents who have made a public commitment to one another. Second, families create a stable and caring environment for children. Third, families link spouses and other kin into units of economic cooperation. Fourth and finally, family members provide each other with emotional support in a world that can be uncaring and even dangerous.

Because families perform all these vital functions, structural-functional theory defines families as the foundation of a healthy society. If so, then any threat to family life is likely to be defined as a social problem. A structural-functional approach views many of the trends discussed in this chapter—including living together, single parenting, and high divorce rates—as potentially threatening to the stability of U.S. society.

One of the consequences of using fertility drugs and in vitro fertilization is a higher rate of multiple births. How would your life change if, all of a sudden, you were the mother or father of triplets?

EVALUATE

There is little doubt that families do matter: Research shows us, for example, that children who grow up in single-parent households complete less schooling and are at higher risk of poverty than those from two-parent households. In addition, it is hard to imagine how other social institutions could step in to perform the various functions that families perform now.

At the same time, critics claims that structural-functional theory overlooks the extent of conflict and violence in families, discussed in Chapter 6 ("Crime, Violence, and Criminal Justice"). In addition, critics point out, today's families also contribute to social inequality, typically supporting the dominance of men over women and perpetuating class inequality as parents pass along wealth and privileges to children.

Finally, the structural-functional approach takes a macro-level view of the family as a system, saying little about the individual experience of family life. This concern brings us to symbolic-interaction theory.

CHECK YOUR LEARNING What do we learn by applying structural-functional theory to families? What is one limitation of this approach?

APPLYING THEORY

Family Life

	Structural-Functional Theory	Symbolic-Interaction Theory	Social-Conflict Theory	Feminist Theory
What is the level of analysis?	Macro-level	Micro-level	Macro-level	Macro-level
What is the importance of the family to society?	Structural-functional theory views the family as the foundation of society because it has several important functions, including regulating sexuality and providing a committed parental relationship as the setting for raising children. Families also provide their members with economic and emotional support.	Symbolic-interaction theory focuses on the patterns of interaction by which people construct family life. Families have much to do with the type of self-image that every child develops. Gender can "script" behavior in married life, with the effect of reducing a couple's spontaneity and intimacy.	Social-conflict theory focuses on links between family and social inequality. Friedrich Engels explained that the family is a system that transmits wealth (or poverty) from one generation to another thereby reproducing the class structure in each generation.	Feminist theory links family to gender stratification. Feminism explains how the historical development of families gave men control over women and especially over women's sexuality.
What are the problems involving family?	Because of the importance of families to the operation of society, anything that threatens the strength or stability of families—the rise in divorce or the increase in single parenting—is likely to be defined as a social problem.	This approach highlights how individuals experience family life. People experience the family subjectively, subjectively defining their situation—whatever the objective facts—as a problem or not. Therefore, we cannot make broad generalizations about family problems.	From this point of view, the main problem is social inequality, and families contribute to this problem. The family is a system that helps to perpetuate a society's class structure from one generation to the next.	Feminist theory claims the main problem with families is that this social institution is a foundation of gender stratification. Families benefits men as they limit the wealth and power of women, including the power of women to control their own sexuality.

Symbolic-Interaction Analysis: Family and Learning

As a micro-level approach, symbolic-interaction theory views the family less as a societal institution and more as the ongoing interaction of individuals. From this perspective, we can appreciate how children develop their self-image within their families. Children raised with love and steady parental guidance develop a positive self-image and are likely to move through their lives with confidence. By contrast, children who experience a steady stream of criticism from parents may end up developing a paralyzing level of self-doubt.

A symbolic-interaction approach also highlights how people understand themselves and their partners. Ideally, marriage helps a couple build a relationship that is *intimate* (a word with Latin roots meaning "free from fear"), in which each partner finds comfort and support in the presence of the other and freely shares even personal fears. But the same marital ties that offer the promise of intimacy can work in the opposite direction to script the behavior of males (who then act "just like men") and females (who are constrained to act in "feminine" ways), with the result that the two sexes may live "unconsciously" without establishing personal identities and expressing personal feelings to one another

(Macionis, 1978). The importance of gender scripts in our everyday lives helps explain why women and men often have very different perceptions of the same marriage (Bernard, 1982).

Finally, symbolic-interaction theory reminds us that the experience of family life differs over time and also from person to person. Whatever the state of a family, objectively speaking, the subjective reality is likely to vary from one family member to another, reflecting factors including sex and age.

EVALUATE

Symbolic-interaction theory shows the varied ways in which individuals understand family life. A husband, wife, and child typically perceive the same family quite differently. Similarly, the experience of family life is likely to change over time just as it varies from place to place.

A limitation of this approach is that although family life is variable, a number of patterns are common. Social class, for example, greatly affects family life. Social-conflict theory offers a look at how the family is linked to dimensions of social inequality.

CHECK YOUR LEARNING   What do we learn by applying symbolic-interaction theory to families? What is one limitation of this approach?

Social-Conflict Analysis: Family and Social Class

As a macro-level approach, social-conflict theory shares with structural-functional theory the idea that the family plays an important part in the operation of society. But rather than highlighting ways in which family life benefits everyone, social-conflict theory points to how the family is linked to patterns of social inequality, especially how the family operates to benefit some categories of people and to disadvantage others.

An early social-conflict theory of family life comes from Friedrich Engels (1902, orig. 1884). As Engels saw it, the family actually came into being among wealthy people so that they would be able to pass their property from one generation to the next. Engels claimed that the family, in concert with the legal system, operates to protect inheritance. As the rich pass their money across generations—and other families transmit poverty—a society's class system is reproduced in each new generation.

A structural-functional analysis points to ways in which families unite individuals and provide a stable environment for raising children. A symbolic-interaction analysis might point to ways in which parents and children understand family life in different ways. A social-conflict analysis, as well as a feminist analysis, would point to ways in which family life gives unequal power and other resources to men and women. What insights into the family life shown here do you gain from each of these approaches?

Social-conflict theory suggests that the path toward an egalitarian society is to eliminate the family, at least in its current form. However, this approach overlooks the fact that a substantial majority of people in the United States claim a great deal of satisfaction from family life (Smith et al., 2013). It may be possible for a society to eliminate the family as a strategy to increase social equality, but it is far from clear how important tasks such as raising children in caring environments would be accomplished.

CHECK YOUR LEARNING   What do we learn about family life by applying social-conflict theory? What is one limitation of this approach?

Feminist Analysis: Family and Gender

Feminist theory highlights one important dimension of a social-conflict analysis, in this case focusing on gender. Feminist theory focuses on how the family is linked to gender stratification, which is the societal domination of women by men.

Friedrich Engels, who linked the family to class inequality, explained how the family supports gender inequality as well. First, by placing men in the position of being heads of households, the development of the family was an important way in which men gained power over women. Second, within a society of families, household wealth largely became *men's* wealth. Because men control wealth, as they think about passing on what they have, they need to be able to identify their offspring with certainty. Gaining this knowledge is the foundation of inheritance, which, in practical terms, is the transfer of wealth from fathers to sons.

But for men to be certain that their children are their own, Engels explained, men must control women, especially their sexuality. This fact goes a long way toward explaining the traditional concern that women be virgins before they marry and that women remain faithful wives afterward.

Finally, men have long expected women to care for their home and children while they work for income or do other things outside of the home. Putting all of this together, Engels concluded that the family turns women into the sexual and economic property of men.

Feminist theory explains that the family not only perpetuates class inequality from one generation to the next; it also perpetuates gender inequality. We see, in short, that class inequality and gender stratification developed together within the family.

One limitation of this theory is that, over the last century, women and men have become more and more equal in their family roles, with both husband and wife typically providing income to the family. In addition, women and men find family life to be a most pleasant setting for intimate living and not necessarily the arena of conflict described by Engels.

CHECK YOUR LEARNING What does feminist theory add to our understanding of families? What is one limitation of this approach?

⭐ POLITICS AND FAMILY LIFE

Constructing Problems and Defining Solutions

12.4 Analyze family life issues from various positions on the political spectrum.

Theory deepens our understanding of families, but exactly what people define as family problems and what they think we ought to do about them are matters of politics. We conclude this chapter by applying the conservative, liberal, and radical-left perspectives to issues surrounding families and family life.

Conservatives think that U.S. society should support the traditional family because families headed by both a father and a mother are good for individuals and good for society as a whole. Liberals support the expanding range of family forms, recognizing that no single family form is likely to be right for everyone. Radicals condemn traditional families for perpetuating social inequality and favor collective living arrangements that promote social equality.

Conservatives: Traditional "Family Values"

Conservatives see values as the core of any society because beliefs bind people together and define a way of life. To them, the family is the most important social institution because it does the most to instill basic values. For this reason, conservatives support what they call "family values" by emphasizing the importance of raising children well, which in turn depends on people getting married, remaining committed to their spouses and children, and avoiding divorce.

Conservatives point to evidence that marriage is good for adults as well as children. Compared with unmarried people, married spouses claim to be happier, are much better off financially, and even report having more sex (Waite & Gallagher, 2000; R. W. Simon, 2002; Fustos, 2010).

From a conservative point of view, anything that threatens the traditional family is likely to be defined as a social problem. One example is the rise in cohabitation, which conservatives claim spells trouble for U.S. society. Many conservatives do not approve of living together because such a relationship lacks the level of commitment typical of legal marriage. According to conservatives, the popularity of cohabitation signals the rise of "me first" values by which people favor individualism over commitment. More evidence of this trend is the fact that, for the first time, a majority of U.S. adults are unmarried. Conservatives claim that the greatest losers in this culture shift are often children, who have a greater chance of ending up in a single-parent family, raising their risk of poverty right away and pushing up their future risk of divorce (Popenoe & Whitehead, 1999; Glenn & Sylvester, 2005; U.S. Census Bureau, 2014.

Conservatives also see the high rate of divorce since the 1960s as a serious problem. Many conservatives oppose the spread of no-fault divorce throughout the country, claiming that this policy makes divorces too easy to obtain. More broadly, conservatives urge a change in our way of thinking from an individualistic culture favoring cohabitation and easy divorce to a culture favoring commitment and marriage. Favoring commitment over independence, they claim, gives men and women better mental health, strengthens families financially through greater earning power, and allows more children to grow up in a stable environment.

Supporting "family values" also means parents spending more time with children. Conservatives criticize the popular idea of parents spending a little "quality time" with children as an excuse for not making children a high enough priority. Conservatives recognize that many households depend on the earnings of both mothers and fathers, but they suggest that couples with young children consider limiting their combined workweek to, say, sixty hours so that they may be sure to meet the needs of their children (Broude, 1996; Whitehead, 1997; Popenoe, 1988, 1993a, 1999).

Liberals: Many Types of Families

Because liberals celebrate individual freedom, their take on today's families and family problems is very different from that of conservatives. Liberals claim that conservatives define only one type of relationship as a "true family" that would be best for everyone. But as liberals see it, this is imposing morality unfairly; different people favor different kinds of families—and some may even favor no family at all. Liberals point out that a wide range of families has existed throughout U.S. history, and this family diversity continues today (Kain, 1990; Koontz, 1992).

In support of family diversity, liberals say that people should have the right to choose from a wide range of family forms, including cohabitation, single-parent families, blended families, same-sex marriage, and singlehood. To liberals, and especially to feminists, these family patterns are not a problem as they are to conservatives. On the contrary, they are a solution. From a liberal point of view, locking people into "traditional families" is likely to make many people unhappy. Just as important, feminists claim that traditional families limit women's opportunities to earn a living and trap some women in abusive relationships. Therefore, liberals define the most serious family problems as poverty and domestic violence.

From a liberal perspective, then, the greater diversity in family forms is actually a solution to the historical problem of women remaining in the home under the control of men (Stacey, 1990, 1993; England, 2001). But what do liberals say about the fact that single-mother families have a higher risk of poverty? The liberal solution to this problem is to increase child care programs so that more women can work. In addition, government should act to eliminate gender discrimination so that working women are paid as much as working men. More broadly, a liberal "profamily" agenda would include raising the minimum wage and perhaps even setting a guaranteed minimum income as policies that would strengthen U.S. families.

The Radical Left: Replace the Family

The radical-left view begins with the close link between the family and social inequality. From a radical-left perspective, the family—at least in its current form—perpetuates social inequality in at least three ways.

First, recall the analysis of Friedrich Engels, who claimed that the family creates and maintains class stratification. Through the family, individuals pass private property from one generation to another. This process reproduces the class structure over time.

Second, Engels also explained that the family helps perpetuate gender stratification. According to this feminist analysis, for men to know who their heirs are, they must control the sexuality of women. In addition, so that men can leave home for the workplace, women must remain in the home to perform unpaid work as homemakers and mothers.

Third, although there has been significant change in recent years, legal marriage is still restricted to partners of the opposite sex in some states. To some extent, then, the current family system still pushes same-sex couples to the margins of society. This means that the family also perpetuates stratification based on sexual orientation.

Taken together, these arguments lead radicals on the left to support an end to the family as we know it in the interest of greater social equality. But what is their solution to the "problem" of the family? To eliminate class inequality, society would have to treat all children in the same manner by making child care a collective enterprise. In the same way, to eliminate gender inequality, society would have to redefine marriage as a partnership with equally shared responsibility for housework as well as earning income. Finally, as noted in Chapter 4 ("Gender Inequality"), radical feminists envision a future in which new reproductive technology allows women to break the bonds of biology that now require them to carry children.

The Left to Right table views family problems and solutions from the three political perspectives.

Going On from Here

The last century was a time of remarkable change for families in the United States. In 1900, the typical woman had five children, no job, and no right to vote. By and large, women were dependent on men. Today, women have, on average, just two children, and most childbearing is a matter of choice. Most women now work for income, and they do so at an ever-wider range of jobs. Women also have increasing political power. In short, within and beyond the family, women now live far more independently of men.

In the decades ahead, families will continue to change. We expect the share of women working for income to continue to rise and the birth rate to edge downward. These trends will continue to make the lives of women and men more alike, which is a key reason that conventional ideas about marriage and family life are giving way to a greater diversity in relationships.

Even if the divorce rate continues its recent downward trend, it seems likely that, for many people, marriage will not be a lifetime commitment. Rather, many family patterns—conventional marriage, living together, living alone, blended families, and raising children outside marriage—will all remain a part of U.S. society.

LEFT TO RIGHT

The Politics of Family Life

	Radical-Left View	Liberal View	Conservative View
What is the problem?	Family life is bound up with inequality: Families support inequality based on class, gender, and sexual orientation. All these types of inequality are unjust.	There is not enough tolerance for the broad range of family life in today's society; efforts to impose any model of an "ideal family" limit people's choices; poverty among women and children is a serious problem.	Conventional families are breaking down: Divorce, single parenting, and living together without marriage are symptoms of a "me first" culture that weakens society and places children at risk.
What is the solution?	Increasing social equality is possible only by radically restructuring the family as it exists today; society should enact collective arrangements for performing housework and child care.	Encourage tolerance for all types of families, including same-sex marriage. Increase women's economic opportunities. Enforce all antidiscrimination laws, and expand affordable child care programs.	Encourage the spread of a "culture of marriage": Encourage people to view commitment in a positive way. Abolish no-fault divorce laws, and discourage couples from living together in low-commitment relationships.

JOIN THE DEBATE

1. In the case of families, one person's problem is often another person's solution. Illustrate this idea using several issues examined in this chapter.

2. How do people who favor each of the three political perspectives define a "family"? Highlight areas of agreement and disagreement.

3. Which of the three political analyses of U.S. families included here do you find most convincing? Why?

One issue likely to remain controversial is the large share of U.S. children living in poverty. Both conservatives and liberals define this child poverty as a problem, although they support different solutions. As conservatives see it, the solution to child poverty is a return to a more traditional two-parent family. As liberals see it, the solution to child poverty lies in government policies that increase wages for low-income workers and expand women's economic opportunities.

A second important issue is the pace of change in giving gays and lesbians access to legal marriage. The fact that same-sex marriage is now legal in more than half the states plus the District of Columbia is a major victory for those supporting equal marriage rights for all citizens regardless of sexual orientation. At the same time, some states have taken measures to prevent recognition of same-sex marriage. Polls show that a slight majority (54 percent) of U.S. adults now support legal same-sex marriage, and there is every reason to expect that this share will increase because a substantial majority of young adults (68 percent) now support legal same-sex marriage (Pew Research Center, 2014).

Third and finally, the possibilities raised by new reproductive technology are sure to expand. The challenge here is to try to envision all the consequences of using genetic engineering. In short, with scientific advancement must come ethical reflection.

For all these reasons, there will be no lack of debate over the problems of family life and their solutions. A century from now, people will still be lining up on different sides as they try to answer the question "What is a family?"

Essay: Envisioning a Better Society In what specific ways do you expect families fifty years from now to differ from families today? What changes in family life would you support? Explain why the changes you identify would make society better.

CHAPTER 12 Family Life

Do the mass media present families from a conservative or a liberal point of view?

Or maybe the better question is: Do the media realistically portray the diversity of families in the United States today? Look at the two accompanying photos to gain some insights about family life as seen through the mass media.

The sitcom *The Middle* follows the everyday life adventures of the Heck family, including Frances "Frankie" Heck, Mike Heck, and their three children. The Hecks live in the midwestern town of Orson, Indiana. This family is "average" in any number of ways—they're middle class, they live in the Midwest, and the parents are halfway through their lives and the children halfway to adulthood. All the Hecks have their share of challenges, but the show focuses on many of the positive consequences of family life. From this point of view, the traditional family is the solution to many of life's problems, a point of view widely held by conservatives. Do you think this show is realistic? Do you support the way it presents family life?

In *Raising Hope*, James "Jimmy" Chance, who is just twenty-three years old and not yet very wise in the ways of the world, is raising his daughter Hope, who was conceived during a one-night stand with Lucy Carlyle, a woman who turned out to be a serial killer. Many of today's television shows are based on characters who either do not have families or have families that are very unconventional. A more liberal take on the family, conveyed in shows like this one, is that marriage and the family may not exactly be a problem, but neither are they necessary for a fulfilling life.

Hint: The Hecks are certainly closer to the norm as far as family life in the United States is concerned. But the Chance family may be a bit more typical of the highly diverse and often unconventional families that are portrayed in the mass media. From these two shows we learn something of the strengths and challenges that many people find in family life and we also are reminded of how diverse families can be.

Getting Involved: Applications and Exercises

1. Check the website of your local community's Department of Health and Human Services or another local social services agency to find out about the range of services the organization offers to assist families. Look for opportunities for you to become involved in helping local families.

2. Just about everyone has friends who live in blended families. Ask several people about the rewards and challenges of living with stepparents and stepsiblings.

3. Family life plays a part in almost every political campaign. Pay attention to the speeches and statements from candidates for national office, and note their views on family issues. What do Democrats see as family problems? What about Republicans? How are their solutions different?

4. Race and ethnicity affect people's view of family life. Review the material included in this chapter with the goal of showing ways in which race and ethnicity shape family form and family life.

Making the Grade

CHAPTER 12 Family Life

A DEFINING MOMENT
Same-Sex Marriage: The Massachusetts Decision **p. 367**

What Is a Family?

12.1 **Explain sociological concepts used to describe family life.**

- The **family** is a social institution that unites individuals into cooperative groups that care for members, regulate sexual relations, and oversee the raising of children.

- **Kinship** is a social bond, typically based on blood, marriage, or adoption, that joins individuals into families.

- In high-income countries including the United States, people's lives revolve around **nuclear families**.

- In the world's low-income nations, most people live in **extended families**.

- In recent decades, more people have broadened the definition of families to include **families of affinity**, made up of individuals who simply think of themselves as a family. **p. 357**

> **family** (p. 357) a social institution that unites individuals into cooperative groups that care for one another, including any children
> **kinship** (p. 357) a social bond, based on common ancestry, marriage, or adoption, that joins individuals into families
> **nuclear family** (p. 357) one or two parents and their children
> **extended family** (p. 357) parents and children, and also grandparents, aunts, uncles, and cousins, who often live close to one another and operate as a family unit
> **marriage** (p. 357) a lawful relationship usually involving economic cooperation, sexual activity, and childbearing
> **families of affinity** (p. 357) people with or without legal or blood ties or children who feel they belong together and define themselves as a family

Family Life: Changes and Controversies

12.2 **Examine key changes and challenges to family life in the United States.**

Living Together

Some 6.9 million U.S. couples cohabit (6% of all households).

- Many young people see cohabiting as a sensible way to try out a relationship.

- Current research shows that marital relationships that begin with couples living together without being married are about as stable as those in which couples marry before moving in together. **p. 358**

Postponing Marriage

A trend since 1950 has been for first marriages to occur later in life; currently, the age at first marriage is about 27 years for women and 29 years for men. **pp. 358–59**

Single Parenting

- Almost one-third of children live with one parent; about half will do so at some point before they reach age 18.

- Children raised in single-parent homes are at high risk of being poor and of being single parents themselves. **p. 359**

Race and Poverty

- Among white families, single-parent families typically result from divorce; among African American families, 72% of children are born to unmarried mothers.

- Research suggests that a lack of available jobs is the major reason for the high proportion of single-parent households in poor African American communities.

- African American families have a number of distinctive strengths: building strong kinship bonds, drawing on religious faith, and having grandparents who help in child rearing. **pp. 359–60**

Conflicts with Work

Because most women and men work for income, the demands of work and family life often conflict, especially for women, who bear more responsibility for housework and child care. **pp. 360–61**

Child Care

Securing affordable child care is a serious problem for millions of families, especially those with low income. **pp. 361–62**

Divorce

- About one in five of today's marriages will break up within five years; almost half will do so within twenty years. Today's divorce rate is almost four times greater than a century ago.

- Women's increasing financial independence from men, as well as no-fault divorce laws, has made divorce easier. **pp. 362–65**

Child Support

Courts order a parent to provide financial support to 49% of young children after parental divorce. Yet in 57% of all such cases, these children receive only partial payments or no payments at all. **pp. 365–66**

Remarriage

- Because three out of four people who divorce remarry, one-third of all of today's marriages are remarriages for at least one partner.
- Remarriage creates **blended families**, which present some special challenges, such as forming new relationships with stepparents and stepsiblings. **p. 366**

Gay and Lesbian Families

Some states and most other nations of the world prohibit same-sex couples from legally marrying. Still, in this country there are as many as 640,000 committed partnerships among gay men and lesbians, and these couples are steadily winning greater legal rights and social acceptance. **pp. 366–68**

In vitro fertilization and other **new reproductive technologies** help many infertile couples have children. But new reproductive technology also raises ethical questions about creating "designer" children. **pp. 369–70**

> **cohabitation** (p. 358) the sharing of a household by an unmarried couple
> **blended families** (p. 366) families in which children have some combination of biological parents and stepparents
> **in vitro fertilization** (p. 369) uniting eggs and sperm in a laboratory
> **surrogate motherhood** (p. 369) an arrangement by which one woman carries and bears a child for another woman

Theories of Families and Family Problems

12.3 Apply sociological theory to issues of family life.

Structural-Functional Analysis: Family as Foundation

Structural-functional theory points out the role that the family plays in the smooth operation of society.

- Families make a vital contribution to society's functioning by regulating sexual activity, overseeing the socialization of the young, fostering economic cooperation, and generating emotional support among kin.
- From this perspective, threats to family stability are defined as social problems. **p. 370**

Symbolic-Interaction Analysis: Family and Learning

Symbolic-interaction theory views family life as the interaction of individuals.

- The self-image of children and the degree of intimacy shared by couples are not fixed but variable outcomes of ongoing interactions.

- The experience of family life differs over time and from person to person. **p. 371**

Social-Conflict Analysis: Family and Social Class

Social-conflict theory highlights the link between families and social inequality.

- Friedrich Engels viewed the rise of families as a strategy by which families pass property from one generation to another.
- Families operate to reproduce the class structure. **p. 372**

Feminist Analysis: Family and Gender

Feminist theory highlights the link between families and gender inequality.

- By making men the heads of households, the family gives men power over women.
- The rise of families led men to control women and especially women's sexuality. **pp. 372–73**

⭐ POLITICS AND FAMILY LIFE

Constructing Problems and Defining Solutions

12.4 Analyze family life issues from various positions on the political spectrum.

Conservatives: Traditional "Family Values"

- **Conservatives** define the traditional family as the foundation of a healthy society and therefore define cohabitation, a high divorce rate, and single parenting as social problems.
- Conservatives support a return to traditional "family values" that rate commitment as more important than individualism. They urge parents to spend more time with their children. **p. 373**

Liberals: Many Types of Families

- **Liberals** define family diversity as positive and therefore support personal choice of family form.
- Liberals fear that locking people in "traditional families" will limit the ability of women to earn a living and trap some women in abusive relationships. **p. 374**

The Radical Left: Replace the Family

- **Radicals on the left** claim that conventional families support inequality based on class, gender, and sexual orientation.
- Radicals on the left support the abolition of the family as we know it. Child care should be a collective enterprise, and marriage should be a partnership with shared responsibility for housework and earning income. **p. 374**

Chapter 13
Education

Learning Objectives

13.1 Explain how schooling differs in low-income nations and high-income nations.

13.2 Discuss the causes and consequences of a number of problems with U.S. education.

13.3 Apply sociological theory to issues of education.

13.4 Analyze educational issues from various positions on the political spectrum.

Tracking the Trends

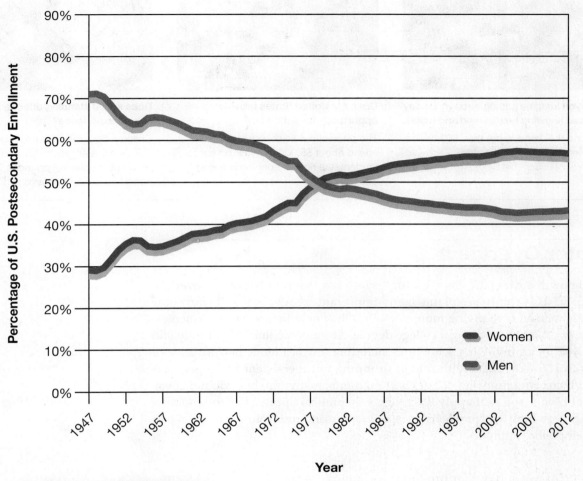

y

SOURCE: U.S. Department of Education (2014).

In 1950, college was largely for men, with males representing 70 percent of postsecondary enrollment in the United States. But women's share was on the rise and in 1979, for the first time in U.S. history, women made up half of all people attending college. That share continued to increase during the 1980s and 1990s, leveling off in recent years. In 2012, 57 percent of students enrolled in college were women and 43 percent were men. In your opinion, is this gender imbalance a problem? What do you think are some of the reasons more women than men continue their education after completing high school?

Constructing the Problem

Can you imagine getting through the day without knowing how to read and write?

Around the world, more than 800 million women and men are illiterate.

Does the United States provide equal opportunity for schooling?

The poorest public school districts spend about $5,000 per year on each student; the richest spend more than $20,000.

Does social standing affect a child's school experience?

Children from the poorest 25 percent of U.S. families are six times more likely to drop out of school than those from the richest 25 percent of families.

Chapter Overview

Do you know the dramatic changes our society has made in education over the last century? This chapter explains many important trends. You will learn how the average person is receiving more schooling than ever before, with an increasing share of adults now having a college degree. At the same time, our society still faces controversies involving schooling, including low academic performance of students in U.S. schools, a high rate of dropping out, persistent racial segregation, and increasing numbers of young immigrants, many of whom do not speak English at home. You will apply sociology's theoretical approaches to schooling issues and learn how the "problems" people identify and the "solutions" they favor reflect their political attitudes. ◼

May 17, 1954, was a day that promised to change the United States forever. It was on that day, now more than sixty years ago, that the U.S. Supreme Court handed down its landmark decision in the case known as *Brown v. Board of Education of Topeka*. With this decision, the Court declared that racially segregated schools, common in the United States at that time, violated the principles of the U.S. Constitution and were no longer lawful.

As the Court's decision was announced, a tall man stood on the steps of the Supreme Court building in Washington, D.C. Thurgood Marshall had been the lead lawyer for the National Association for the Advancement of Colored People (NAACP), the organization that had helped bring the lawsuit to the Supreme Court. Marshall, who went on to become a member of the Supreme Court (from 1967 until 1991), spoke to reporters and to the entire nation. He was quick to acknowledge that no statement from the Court would bring the needed change right away. On the contrary, he cautioned, there was still much work to be done in our nation's schools. But he

assured the country that thanks to the Supreme Court's decision, racial segregation in U.S. schools would be gone within five years (A. Cohen, 2004).

That event took place more than sixty years ago, and yet schools in the United States are almost as segregated today as they were back then. As this chapter explains, white children still attend schools with mostly white children, and black children still attend schools with mostly black children. The same holds for Latino children, who go to schools that enroll mostly children like themselves.

Racial segregation is only one problem in today's schools. Other issues include unequal funding that favors some students and disadvantages others, poor teaching in many school classrooms, high dropout rates, and violence in the school buildings.

All of these problems relate to **education**, *the social institution by which a society transmits knowledge—including basic facts and job skills, as well as cultural norms and values— to its members.* This chapter begins with a brief survey of education around the world and then assesses how well schools in the United States meet their goals of preparing young people for productive lives as adults.

Problems of Education: A Global Perspective

13.1 Explain how schooling differs in low-income nations and high-income nations.

Everywhere in the world, parents and neighbors in local communities join together to teach young people important knowledge and skills. One important type of education is **schooling**, *formal instruction carried out by specially trained teachers.* Although some form of education occurs everywhere, schooling is more widely available to young people living in high-income parts of the world than it is to those living in low-income regions.

Low-Income Countries: Too Little Schooling

Children in the United States take going to school for granted. But this opportunity is not available to some children living in the world's poorest countries. In the lowest-income nations in Central Africa and western Asia, about one-fourth of all youngsters never set foot in a classroom. A majority of the world's children do receive at least primary schooling—the first five or six grade levels. However, secondary education is less common. In much of sub-Saharan Africa and in a few Asian nations, half of all children receive no secondary education (World Bank, 2014).

Why is schooling in poor regions of the world so limited? Low-income countries have largely agrarian

(farming) economies, and one-third or more of the people live in rural communities. In traditional, rural settings, parents take most of the responsibility for teaching children the knowledge and skills needed for everyday life. Parents also gain an economic benefit by keeping children at home, where they can work to help support their families.

To encourage the economic growth that comes with replacing farming with industry and service work, governments in poor nations typically try to expand **literacy**, *the ability to read and write.* People need literacy skills to work in factories and offices. A literate workforce also helps countries attract foreign investment, which in turn expands the economy and creates more jobs.

But increasing literacy is not easy. Countries struggling to feed their people don't have a great deal of money to spend on schooling. This is the main reason that more than 800 million of the world's adults (about one in six) are still illiterate (World Bank, 2014). Global Map 13–1 on page 384 shows that illiteracy rates are high—often more than 50 percent—in poor regions of the world.

Gender also plays an important part in patterns of global literacy. In the poorest countries, females are far less likely than males to be literate. For example, in Nepal, a poor Asian nation, fewer than half of all women can read, compared with nearly three-fourths of the men (World Bank, 2014).

This gender disparity is declining. But change comes slowly in patriarchal societies where parents send far more boys than girls to school. The explanation of this typical pattern starts with the fact that poor countries are not only patriarchal (men have power over women) but also patrilocal (a newly married couple lives with the husband's parents). Because a new bride leaves her parents to live with her husband's family, the parents of girls view sending their daughters to school as a poor investment of their limited resources. Sons remain close to home after they grow up and marry, so parents are more willing to invest in their schooling. Parents get what they can from a daughter while she is young and living at home, typically by making her work for wages (International Labor Organization, 2013).

High illiteracy rates mean a low quality of life for hundreds of millions of the world's women. But a lack of schooling also contributes to other problems. Without the ability to read, mothers have difficulty providing nutrition and health care to their young children and have few opportunities to work in higher-income jobs. Women who lack economic opportunity also end up having more children, adding to the burden of a poor nation already struggling to feed its current population. Not only does this pattern hurt the women themselves, but it also slows economic development for the entire country.

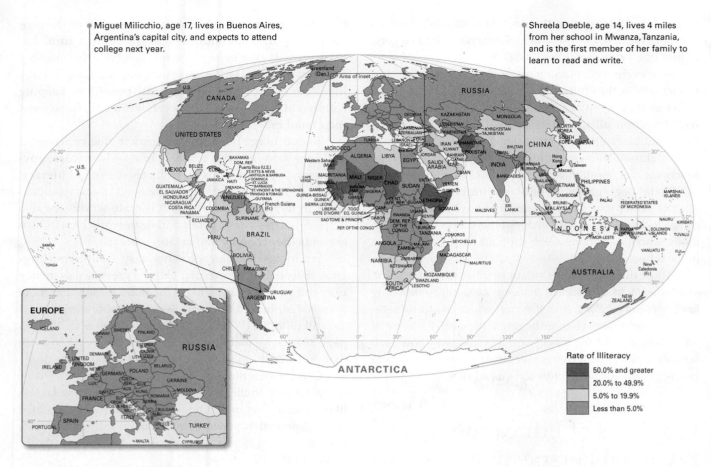

Miguel Milicchio, age 17, lives in Buenos Aires, Argentina's capital city, and expects to attend college next year.

Shreela Deeble, age 14, lives 4 miles from her school in Mwanza, Tanzania, and is the first member of her family to learn to read and write.

Rate of Illiteracy

- 50.0% and greater
- 20.0% to 49.9%
- 5.0% to 19.9%
- Less than 5.0%

Window on the World

Global Map 13–1 Illiteracy in Global Perspective

Illiteracy exists in the United States and other high-income nations, typically among the very poor. But in some of the world's lowest-income countries, half or more of the people cannot read and write.

SOURCES: United Nations Development Programme (2013); UNESCO (2013).

High-Income Countries: Unequal Schooling

In high-income countries, where most jobs require literacy and specialized skills, people think that children need schooling in order to be productive adults. In fact, most young people living in rich nations complete both primary and secondary school. In the United States, 88 percent of adults over the age of twenty-five have completed high school (U.S. Census Bureau, 2013).

In high-income nations, a significant share of people enroll in colleges and universities. The United States is second in the world (after Norway) in the share of its adult population that goes to college: Thirty-two percent of the U.S. population aged twenty-five and older has a four-year college or university degree (U.S. Census Bureau, 2013).

This national performance is a remarkable achievement, but the amount of schooling as well as the quality of schooling in this country is not equal for everyone.

Even with a large share of people going to college, the United States also has a surprisingly high level of illiteracy. Although the government officially claims that only a tiny percentage of the adult population is illiterate, estimates suggest that as many as 30 million people or 14 percent of the population have literacy skills that are weak to the point of considering them to be functionally illiterate (U.S. Department of Education, 2011).

In short, over the past century, our country has done a good job of increasing the extent of schooling for the population as a whole. At the same time, our nation's level of illiteracy is higher than that found in most other high-income nations (OECD, 2013).

Education in U.S. History

Early national leaders, including Thomas Jefferson, pointed to literacy as the key to making the United States a political democracy. At that time, the new nation was both rural and poor, and most people were unable to read newspapers or write letters.

Illiteracy was so common that it was not widely defined as a social problem. But other factors were also involved. For example, most people of the day saw no reason to school women, who, the thinking went, belonged in the home. White people saw little logic to schooling African Americans, most of whom lived as slaves; many whites actually feared that literacy would encourage people of color to organize a slave rebellion. Only after the Civil War, with the abolition of slavery, did school doors in the United States open to African Americans. In almost all cases, however, these schools were separate from and inferior to those enrolling white people.

By the late 1800s, as the Industrial Revolution increased demand for literate workers, our society started to define illiteracy as a social problem. The complex machinery used in factories demanded that workers have basic skills in reading, writing, and arithmetic. Another concern was the 1 million immigrants entering the country each year. Our society looked to public schools to give these newcomers not only the skills needed to work but also the cultural lessons—especially mastery of the English language—that would help them to become "Americanized."

Therefore, by about 1900, states were building more public schools and enacting laws that required children to attend for much of the year. Most people supported public education as a solution to the problems of illiteracy

This young girl working in the fields in the Nar Phu Valley in Nepal is evidence of a pattern common in low-income nations: Parents are more likely to send boys to school while girls go to work to earn income. Can you explain this double standard?

and cultural differences. Yet not all immigrants wanted to send their children to public schools. Catholic immigrants, in particular, wanted to preserve their traditions and their faith in what they saw as a mostly Protestant country. The Catholic Church responded by building and operating *parochial schools*, which still exist throughout the country.

By 1918, every state had enacted a mandatory education law requiring children to attend school until age sixteen or the completion of the eighth grade. Since then, as shown in Figure 13–1 the extent of schooling for the U.S. population has increased steadily. In 1920, just 16.4 percent of people age twenty-five or older had completed high school; a college degree was quite rare, earned by only 3.3 percent of adults. By 2013, as already noted, 88 percent of adults were high school graduates, and 32 percent had earned a college degree (U.S. Census Bureau, 2013).

Today, we *expect* young people to attend school. But although formal education is part of everyday life, today's schools face a number of serious problems. In fact, many people think that public education in the United States is in a state of crisis.

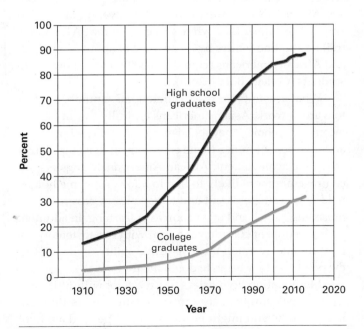

Figure 13–1 Schooling in the United States, 1910–2012

Today, the share of U.S. adults who complete college is more than twice as high as the share finishing high school back in 1910.

SOURCE: U.S. Census Bureau (2013).

Over the course of U.S. history, the doors of schools have opened wider for white people than for African Americans. The school pictured here might seem to be from the nineteenth century, but the photograph was taken in Georgia in 1941.

reading, twenty-seventh in science, and thirty-fifth in math. In short, many high-income nations seem to be schooling their children better than we do in the United States (OECD, 2013).

Another way to evaluate U.S. schooling is to look at trends in performance over time. Perhaps the best-known measure of academic performance is the college entrance examination taken by U.S. high school students. The Scholastic Assessment Test (SAT), which measures both verbal and mathematical achievement, shows little change over the past forty years. In 1967, average scores for U.S. students were 516 (out of a possible 800) on the mathematical test and 543 on the verbal test. By 2013, the average score in math had dropped two points to 514 and the average verbal score had fallen to 496 (College Board, 2013).

Problems with U.S. Education

13.2   Discuss the causes and consequences of a number of problems with U.S. education.

To understand what schools are up against, consider the scope of their task. Across the country, more than 55 million students, who speak more than 100 different languages, are enrolled in 132,000 public, parochial, and private schools (U.S. Department of Education, 2013).

The budget for the country's public schools, which enroll 90 percent of all students, is more than $650 billion. Yet many people across the country are dissatisfied with public schools. Surveys show that just 18 percent of U.S. adults give the nation's public schools a grade of A or B. A larger share of people evaluate their own local schools positively, with half giving a grade of A or B, but just as many give them a grade of C or below (Bushaw & Lopez, 2013). In the following pages, we survey the performance of U.S. schools and then consider a number of other problems and controversies surrounding schooling in the United States.

The Academic Performance of U.S. Schools

One way to assess U.S. education is to compare performance of our students to those in other countries. One recent study looked at sixty-five nations and compared how fifteen-year-olds perform in schools. The results show that the United States ranked twenty-third in

Academic Performance: Race, Class, and Gender

If the *average* performance of U.S. students has dropped a bit, the achievement of socially disadvantaged students remains a serious problem. There is evidence that our schools have failed whole segments of the U.S. population.

Although Asian American students average about seventy points higher than white students on the SAT, Latinos trail non-Latino whites by an average of about 220 points, and African Americans score about 300 points below white students (College Board, 2013).

What accounts for these differences? A number of factors are at work. Asian Americans typically live in higher-income households, they spend more time doing schoolwork, and they benefit from a home environment that emphasizes academic achievement. African American youngsters, by contrast, are more likely to live in a lower-income household with a single parent and to have less access to books, museums, travel, and other sources of learning. In addition, young people of color have to deal with racial stereotypes that call into question their academic ability, sometimes to the point that they begin to doubt themselves.

Many Latino youngsters begin school with little ability to speak English. If your only language is English, imagine how you might perform if you attended a school in which Spanish was spoken and almost every teacher and student was a native Spanish speaker. Although most Native Americans enter school speaking English, many view schools as representing an alien culture. Latino and Native Americans are the categories of the population least likely to complete a college education—only about 15 percent do (U.S. Census Bureau, 2013).

For all categories of people, the higher the share of children living in poverty, the lower the educational achievement. The poverty rates for African American children (38 percent), Native American children (37 percent), and Latino children (34 percent) are far greater than for Asian American children (14 percent) and non-Hispanic white children (12 percent) (U.S. Census Bureau, 2013). Obviously, families with higher incomes have more resources to support children's social and educational development.

The average income level also affects a local community's quality of schooling. Schools enrolling well-off students spend much more money per student than schools in low-income communities. This means that children from richer families have access to better teachers, are more likely to be taught in smaller classes, and have access to more educational technology. Not surprisingly, students from higher-income families end up performing better on achievement tests. On average, high school students from families earning more than $200,000 per year score 388 points higher on the combined SAT than those from families with incomes below $20,000 per year (College Board, 2013).

The Effects of Home and School

Children from low-income families face a double burden of fewer educational advantages at home and fewer opportunities at school. A recent study helps us understand how these two factors affect the learning performance of U.S. schoolchildren.

A research team led by Doug Downey calculated that students—who attend school six or seven hours a day, five days a week, with summers and vacation time off—spend only about 13 percent of their waking hours in school. For that reason, the researchers concluded, the factor that most affects a child's intellectual development is the *home* for the simple reason that children spend the vast majority of their time there (Downey, von Hippel, & Broh, 2004).

The research team then examined the pace at which high- and low-income children gained skills in reading and mathematics. Collecting data on school performance throughout the year, they confirmed that there are large differences in academic performance between children from high-income homes and those from low-income homes. Looking more closely, they noted that during the school year, children from high-income homes learn somewhat faster than children from low-income homes. But the gap grew the widest during the summer months, when children spend the most time in their home environment. This pattern points to the conclusion that schools matter, but the home environment matters *more*. Another way to say this is that schools reduce the learning gap that is created by differences in home communities, but schools do

not "level the playing field" between rich and poor children the way we sometimes think they do.

Dropping Out

The benefits of formal education end when some young people leave school. *Dropping out*—quitting school before earning a high school diploma—is a serious problem in this country.

How many have dropped out? Official government statistics show that 6.6 percent of the U.S. population aged sixteen to twenty-four (about 3 million people) have left school without graduating. The good news is that in the last fifty years, dropping out of school has become less common: In 1960, the rate was 14 percent. But dropping out is well above the average among certain segments of the U.S. population. Figure 13–2 shows that, while the

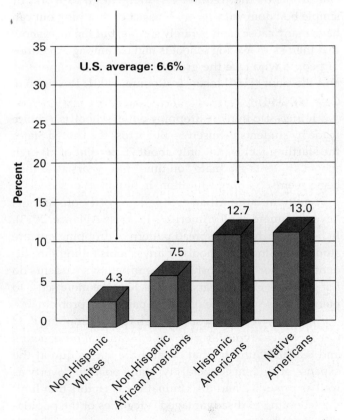

● Hispanic Americans are three times more likely than non-Hispanic whites to drop out of school.

Diversity Snapshot

Figure 13–2 Percentage of Dropouts among Categories of the U.S. Population, Ages 16 to 24

Dropping out of school is a problem for all categories of people. But the rates are especially high among Hispanics and Native Americans.

SOURCE: U.S. Department of Education (2014).

dropout rate is 4.3 percent for non-Hispanic whites, the rate is 7.5 percent among non-Hispanic African Americans, 12.7 percent among Latinos, and 13.0 percent among Native Americans (U.S. Department of Education, 2014).

Differences in income underlie much of this pattern. The dropout rate for young people from families with incomes of $100,000 and above is less than 2 percent; for those from families with incomes below $25,000, the dropout rate is about 12 percent (U.S. Department of Education, 2014).

Culture often plays a part when a student drops out of school. For people—including many recent immigrants—whose native language is not English, dropout rates are especially high. For example, 28 percent of Hispanic American students who were born outside the United States drop out of school. High dropout rates also are found among people—including many Native Americans—who have traditionally been uncomfortable sending their children to schools run by "outsiders."

In addition, the decision to leave school may be prompted by an unexpected pregnancy, a family's financial problems that require a student to go to work, or simple boredom with school. The act of dropping out can have many causes and is rarely simple, but the facts show that the risk of leaving school is highest among categories of people who face the greatest challenges—minorities and the poor (Hodkinson & Bloomer, 2001; Roscigno & Crowley, 2001).

It is easy to think of dropping out of school as a choice made by students themselves. But across the United States the startling fact is that only about 70 percent of all high school students graduate "on time" four years after they begin their secondary education. In hundreds of schools—especially in large urban areas—a majority of students never graduate at all (America's Promise Alliance, 2013). In light of such a widespread pattern of dropping out, are students failing the schools or are schools failing the students? In short, if almost half of our nation's students do not graduate in four years, it seems to make more sense to point to the school system itself as part of the problem.

How do we explain such a high rate of dropping out? Conservatives typically point to educational bureaucrats and teachers' unions that defend the status quo at the expense of students. Liberals typically point to poverty as well as prejudice and discrimination as factors that limit the schooling of disadvantaged categories of the population. But whatever its causes, dropping out has some serious consequences. Dropping out of high school raises the lifetime risks of unemployment, drug abuse, arrest, and poverty. For example, school dropouts account for more than half of all people receiving welfare assistance and 80 percent of this country's prison population (Christle, Jolivette, & Nelson, 2007). In short, dropping out of school can become one part of a multigenerational cycle in which children raised in a disadvantaged setting go on to become disadvantaged adults who pass on their situation to their own children.

Functional Illiteracy

The poor performance of many U.S. schools helps explain the fact that 14 percent of the U.S. adult population (about 30 million men and women) lack literacy skills to the point that they are considered to be functionally illiterate. The concept of **functional illiteracy** refers to *the inability to read and write or do basic arithmetic well enough to carry out daily responsibilities.*

Being functionally illiterate in the modern world turns many everyday activities into real challenges. Reading food labels, paying bills, understanding letters that children bring home from school, reading a newspaper, and making sense of the tables and graphs found in a textbook are all beyond the abilities of people who are functionally illiterate (U.S. Department of Education, 2009).

To the women and men who lack literacy skills, the problem goes beyond being able to cope. Functional illiteracy is also a source of personal embarrassment and shame. More important, in a world that demands more and more literacy skills with each passing year, functional illiteracy stands as a barrier to getting a good job, locking people into low-wage work or unemployment and often poverty. The fact that a sizable share of our national workforce cannot read or write well also wastes talent and reduces our country's competitive standing in a global economy (OECD, 2013).

School Segregation and Busing

Before the Civil War, few African Americans attended school. With the end of that war and the abolition of slavery in 1865, African Americans entered the classroom but typically in racially segregated schools. In 1896, in the case of *Plessy* v. *Ferguson*, the U.S. Supreme Court affirmed the principle of racial segregation, claiming that the facilities for blacks and whites could be separate if they were deemed to be "equal." In reality, of course, the principle of "separate but equal" was a sham and everyone knew it. Most white children attended schools with modern buildings, well-trained teachers, and up-to-date textbooks. By contrast, most African American children attended run-down schools with poorly trained teachers and outdated, hand-me-down books.

Racial segregation of this type was the norm throughout the post–Civil War South. The North, too, had racially segregated schools, due primarily to the fact that almost all African Americans were forced to live in mostly black neighborhoods, where local schools were underfunded.

Not until the 1950s, when the civil rights movement gained momentum, did activists challenge the system of racially segregated schools. They rallied around the case

CONSTRUCTING SOCIAL PROBLEMS
A DEFINING MOMENT

Linda Brown: Fighting to Desegregate the Schools

Sixty years ago, in Topeka, Kansas, a minister and his nine-year-old daughter walked hand in hand to the public elementary school four blocks from their home. The girl, Linda Brown, wanted to enroll in the fourth grade. But school officials refused, telling Reverend Brown to take his daughter to another school two miles away. Why? Topeka's public schools, like those in most of the United States, were segregated by race. Because she was African American, the rules stated, Linda Brown had to go to the school for "colored" children.

Linda Brown's parents thought that this policy was unjust. They were not alone. A civil rights movement was developing across the United States, and the Browns were soon at the center of what turned out to be a defining moment in U.S. schooling. They filed a lawsuit on behalf of Linda and other African Americans challenging laws that provided "separate but equal" schools for black and white children.

In 1954, the Supreme Court of the United States considered the case, and on May 17 of that year, the justices handed down an historic ruling. In *Brown* v. *Board of Education of Topeka*, the Court concluded that racially segregated schools provided African Americans with inferior schooling and declared the practice unlawful, overturning the doctrine of "separate but equal" schooling that an earlier Supreme Court had affirmed in 1896 in the case of *Plessy* v. *Ferguson*.

As noted in the opening to this chapter, the laws may have changed, but the reality of racially segregated schools continues in the United States sixty years after the *Brown* ruling. Why? The simple reason is that, as a result of differences in income and racial prejudice, black and white people typically live in different neighborhoods. The common practice in the United States is for children to attend schools near their homes. Thus residential segregation places children in schools that are filled almost

entirely with students of their own race. But Linda Brown and her father will long be celebrated as trailblazers in the drive for racial equality in U.S. schooling.

It has been more than half a century since Linda Brown lent her name to a landmark legal effort intended to desegregate U.S. public schools. How much has changed since then?

of Linda Brown, a nine-year-old girl in Topeka, Kansas. The Defining Moment box tells her story, which ultimately led the U.S. Supreme Court to define school segregation as unconstitutional.

After the Supreme Court ruled that separate schooling for blacks and whites was unconstitutional, some local governments did try to overcome racial segregation of schools. But how could a city or town achieve racial balance in schools if black people and white people lived in separate neighborhoods? One answer that emerged in the 1960s was to bus students from one neighborhood to another to achieve racial balance. White parents strongly opposed busing, objecting to the time their children had to spend on buses and the poor education the children received once they arrived. Black parents had a mixed reaction to busing: Some hoped the policy would improve their children's educational opportunities,

but others also objected to their children leaving local neighborhoods for another part of the city.

As the debate continued between more liberal supporters of "equal schooling" and more conservative supporters of "neighborhood schools," it became clear that the policy of busing would never succeed in integrating urban schools. In the 1960s, many white families moved from the central cities to suburbs—a pattern commonly called *white flight*—which placed their children beyond the reach of busing plans (S. J. L. Taylor, 1998). As described in Chapter 14 ("Urban Life"), the loss of urban population meant a decline in tax revenues, so schools in central cities actually became worse than before.

During the 1990s, the courts called an end to school busing. Because a majority of neighborhoods are still home to mostly people of the same race, schools today are just about

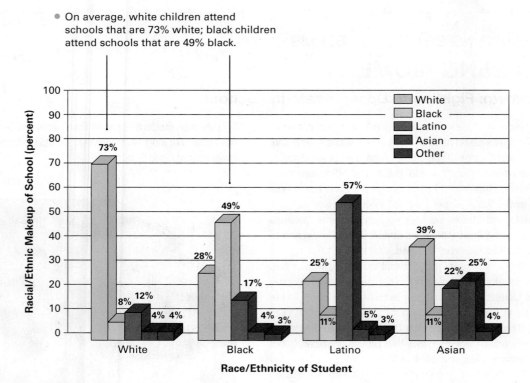

On average, white children attend schools that are 73% white; black children attend schools that are 49% black.

Diversity Snapshot

Figure 13–3 Racial Makeup of the Average Student's School, by Race and Ethnicity

Research shows that most students in the United States attend schools where most of the other students are of the same race and ethnic background as their own.

SOURCE: Orfield & Frankenberg (2014).

as racially segregated as they were in the 1960s. Figure 13–3 provides the results of one study showing that racial and ethnic segregation remains strong in today's schools.

Finally, as the suburban population continues to increase, suburbs have greater racial and ethnic diversity. Many of today's suburban schools have diverse student populations. Many, however, remain as racially segregated as inner-city schools have been for decades. As researchers recently reported, most white suburban students attend schools enrolling mostly white students. Three-fourths of African American students and 80 percent of Hispanic suburban students attend schools with nonwhite majorities. Furthermore, this study found, 43 percent of Latino students and 38 percent of African American students attend extremely segregated schools with a white population below 10 percent (Orfield, Kucsera, & Siegel-Hawley, 2012).

School Funding

Throughout the United States, schools differ not only in racial composition but also in the level of resources they offer to students. Why? Typically, the funding for a school system comes not just from the state but also from property taxes paid by people who live in the local community.

But some communities are far richer than others, and differences in tax revenues produce strikingly unequal school budgets. On a national scale today, per-student funding ranges from about $6,000 in a poor community such as Nampa, Idaho, to almost $20,000 in a high-income community such as Arlington, Virginia (U.S. Department of Education, 2014). Such differences in funding create vast differences in schooling. In a poor neighborhood, the school may be run-down, have few library and science facilities, place students in crowded classrooms, and offer only poorly trained teachers. The Diversity: Race, Class, & Gender box takes a closer look at Jonathan Kozol's account of what he calls the "savage inequalities" in U.S. education.

Is it possible to level the educational playing field? Doing so would require equalizing school funding in rich and poor communities. In 1997, Vermont enacted a policy called Act 60 to do exactly that. This law combines school taxes all across the state and redistributes funding on an equal per-student basis. This means that students in richer communities, with above-average property taxes, get the same amount in school funds as children in poorer communities. Such policies—described as "Robin Hood" laws because they take from the rich and give to the poor—do make funding more equal. But they are controversial,

DIVERSITY: RACE, CLASS, & GENDER
The "Savage Inequalities" of Schooling in the United States

"Excuse me," the man called out from his car window. "Do you know where P.S. 261 is?" "Sure," replies one of the two women on the sidewalk drawing shopping baskets behind them. "Go two more blocks and it's on the left. Look for the mortician's office."

The mortician's office? Jonathan Kozol (1991) shook his head as he looked for a parking spot across from the school. There was something deadly about the whole neighborhood: run-down buildings, trash strewn across empty lots, graffiti all over the walls, and the whole scene punctuated by the deafening sound of an elevated train thundering past along the overhead tracks.

In the center of this urban setting stands New York's Public School 261. You would not know it to see it, because the school has no sign.

Kozol walked to the building and introduced himself to a teacher as he stepped through the door. The teacher mentioned that the building used to be a roller-skating rink.

Kozol made his way to the principal's office. The principal explained that P.S. 261 serves a minority community of the North Bronx and that 90 percent of the students are African American or Latino. Officially, she continued, the school should have 900 students, but actual enrollment is about 1,300. City education guidelines state that a school's classrooms should hold no more than thirty-two students. Kozol will observe classes with as many as forty. The cafeteria seemed to be small, and it fed the children in three shifts. There was no playground, so after lunch, teachers tried to keep children in their cafeteria seats until it was time to return to the classrooms. As he walked throughout the school, Kozol saw only one classroom with a window.

A teacher complained about the temperature of her classroom, saying that in the winter it might be 55 degrees and in the summer it could be 90. Kozol then asked her what the children think of the school. She responded that they don't say much about it. But she added that they all have television and they know what schools are *supposed* to look like.

A few months later, Kozol visited a second school across town. Public School 24 is in New York's affluent Riverdale section of the Bronx. Like the other buildings in this upscale neighborhood, the school stands in good repair and is set back from the road by a green lawn with flowering trees. To the left, Kozol notes a playground for the youngest children; stretching out behind the school are playing fields where the older kids engage in team sports.

Kozol met with the principal, who proudly explained that many parents gladly pay the high cost of housing in Riverdale to be able to send their children to a school like this. Almost all the classes enroll less than thirty students. Looking up and down the halls, Kozol saw mostly white students, with a handful of Asian, Latino, and African American children. He found the building to be a wonderful learning facility, featuring bright and attractive classrooms, a large library, and even a planetarium.

By the end of the day, Kozol joined a group of children in one of the many classes for gifted students. He asked them what they were learning that day. A well-dressed young girl introduced herself as "Laurie" and explained that her class was doing problem solving. A tall, good-natured boy named David chimed in to say that he had learned that many problems have more than one good answer. Kozol asks the children if problem solving is a skill they were born with. The children respond that they knew some things when they started school. But, mostly, they have learned how to think and solve problems.

What Do You Think?

1. Some people claim that local communities have the right to spend whatever they can afford to educate their children, even though some school systems will have more funding than others. Do you agree or not? Why?

2. If you were in a position to decide how schools would be funded, what would you do?

3. If all children could attend schools that were exactly equal, do you think everyone's educational performance would be the same? Why or why not?

---

finding favor in poor school districts and criticism in wealthier communities (T. M. Edwards, 1998; Shlaes, 1998; Goodman, 1999; Komline, 2014).

Cultural Capital Funding is not the only way in which schools differ. Even if all schools were able to spend the same amount of money per child, the educational performance of richer and poorer children would still be unequal. This is because, as noted earlier, children have very different experiences in their homes. Parents with higher incomes are able to give their children greater *cultural capital*, the experiences and opportunities that shape a student's ability to learn and to succeed at school and elsewhere.

High-income parents are more likely to have a home that is spacious, quiet, and equipped with a personal computer and Internet access. Having more education themselves, well-off parents are more likely to teach young children language skills by, say, reading with them regularly. Low-income parents are more likely to have a smaller, more crowded home and are less likely to own a computer, books, and other learning materials. With less schooling (and a higher likelihood of speaking a language

One example of tracking is placing "gifted" students together in "enriched" classes. What effect might the label "gifted" have on the way teachers treat students?

other than English in the home), they can provide less help to children doing schoolwork (Coleman, 1966, 1988; McNeal, 1999).

The cultural capital a family gives its children has a lot to do with the family's income level, a point that is often made by political liberals. But cultural capital also includes the importance parents attach to schooling and academic achievement, a point often made by political conservatives. For example, Abigail and Stephan Thernstrom (2003) argue that parents (as well as schools) must foster a "culture of success" in order for children to do well. Their research suggests that, on average, black parents have lower expectations of their children than white parents do and that Asian parents are the most demanding of all. Such cultural differences explain why Asian Americans, a small minority of New York City's population, represent a majority of students at that city's most competitive high schools that admit students based solely on examination performance. In addition, according to the Thernstroms, a different cultural capital helps white children from low-income families to academically outperform African American children from families with much higher incomes.

Tracking

Schooling is unequal not only from one school or community to another. Inequality also exists within a single school as a result of **tracking**, *the policy of assigning students to different educational programs.*

The idea behind tracking is to place students in classes with others with a similar level of ability. In this way, less qualified students are not overwhelmed in classes above their abilities and more qualified students are not held back by work that they find too easy. In short, tracking

is based on a goal of schools meeting the abilities and interests of each child (Brantlinger, 1993; Loveless, 1999).

Critics of tracking claim that this policy amounts to a form of institutional discrimination because any student's ability has much to do with social standing. In practice, they say, tracking provides affluent children with the best a school has to offer, leaving children from lower-income families with a second-class education. In short, because family background affects how well a child performs in school, tracking transforms a *social* advantage into an *educational* advantage (Bowles & Gintis, 1976; Oakes, 1985; Cloud, 2003).

Typically, students in higher tracks attend classes that move them along quickly, with teaching that emphasizes critical thinking and creativity. Those in lower tracks are likely to progress more slowly, with a focus on basic skills and the importance of following directions.

To illustrate the difference in learning caused by tracking, imagine that children in two different tracks were studying the civil rights movement. Teachers in the advanced track might ask students to identify the strategies used by activists to bring about change and to identify strengths and weaknesses of each. Then they might ask the class to apply some of the same strategies to the struggle of today's immigrants to gain more economic security and a greater political voice. Teachers in a lower-track classroom, by contrast, might ask children only to identify the movement's leaders and highlight key events.

Researchers have shown that tracking can set in motion a **self-fulfilling prophecy**—*a situation in which people who are defined in a certain way eventually think and act as if the definition were true.* In this case, how the school defines children affects how the children see themselves. Children in higher tracks learn to see themselves as bright and able, which encourages them to work hard and to perform well. Children in lower tracks develop lower self-esteem, question their own abilities, and end up doing less well. In light of the controversy over tracking, schools across the country are now more careful about assigning children to different programs and allow more mobility from one track to another (Kozol, 1991; Loveless, 1999; Olin, 2003).

Gender Inequality

Gender also shapes the schooling of people in the United States. For generations, the two sexes followed different programs of study. Schools steered boys into courses such as woodworking and mechanical shop that would prepare them for industrial jobs in factories. Girls were tracked into courses such as home economics, typing, and shorthand that prepared them to be homemakers or to perform clerical work in offices. In college, men were encouraged to study the sciences, including physics, chemistry, biology, and mathematics. College women mainly majored in English, elementary education, foreign languages, and the social sciences.

School textbooks also reflected the two sexes in stereotypical roles. Books portrayed women working in the home and men in the paid workforce (Spender, 1989; Basow, 1992; Wood & Chesser, 1993). Even the organization of the school itself provided lessons concerning gender. Generations of students observed that most teachers (especially in the lower grades) were women, and most of the people in charge—principals and senior administrators—were men (Richardson, 1988; U.S. Department of Labor, 2013).

Over the course of the twentieth century, girls and women gradually gained more equal standing in schools. One important step occurred in 1972 when Congress passed Title IX of the Education Amendments to the Civil Rights Act. Title IX bans sex discrimination in education and requires schools receiving federal funding to provide male and female students with equal educational programs. Today, as a result of such efforts, girls are as likely as boys to be placed in classes for gifted students, and more young women than young men qualify for high school advanced placement courses, which provide better preparation for college. Since 1979, women have outnumbered men on this country's college and university campuses and, as shown in the figure at the beginning of this chapter, in 2012 women represented 57 percent of people enrolled in college. Not only did women represent 57 percent of all undergraduates, women also earned 60 percent of all master's degrees and 51 percent of all professional and doctoral degrees (U.S. Department of Education, 2014).

Despite this remarkable change, women are still concentrated in many traditionally feminine majors, such as library science (87 percent women), health professions (85 percent), education (80 percent), psychology (77 percent), and English (68 percent) (U.S. Department of Education, 2013).

Immigration: Increasing Diversity

Another challenge facing U.S. schools is meeting the needs of many of the more than 1 million immigrants who enter this country every year. As Chapter 3 ("Race and Ethnic Inequality") describes in detail, these immigrants represent more than 100 cultures and languages. Most of today's newcomers look to public schools to provide their children—and perhaps themselves—with the knowledge and skills needed to get good jobs.

English Immersion versus Bilingualism Many young immigrants and children of immigrants do well in school. But 22 percent of people under the age of eighteen speak a language other than English at home. How should schools meet the challenge of teaching students who know little English? Two opposing policies are being hotly debated. The first policy is **English immersion**, *the policy of teaching non–English speakers in English.* In many cases, a single class called English as a Second Language is taught in the student's native language with a native language teacher.

The second approach is **bilingual education**, *the policy of offering most classes in students' native language while also teaching them English.* In this case, schools must hire many teachers skilled not only in a particular subject matter but also in a non-English language. In school districts where students may speak dozens of different languages, as is common in California and other states, providing bilingual education is a tremendous challenge.

The debate over English immersion versus bilingual education is partly about how well students learn. Supporters of English immersion concede that students do learn more quickly in the short term when taught in their native language, but focusing on English helps students' long-term learning.

This nation's high rate of immigration creates challenges for schools. In this English as a Second Language (ESL) classroom, students who speak a wide range of languages at home come together to learn English.

Supporters of bilingualism point to evidence that becoming bilingual at a young age helps overall cognitive development. That is, young children who develop language skills in their native language and also in English go on to outperform one-language students on achievement tests. In addition, there can be little doubt of the value of gaining bilingual skills in today's global economy (Portes, 2002).

But there is even more at stake. The two policies have different political and cultural objectives. English immersion seeks to "Americanize" students by making English the central language and teaching them the dominant culture. By teaching in a student's native language, bilingual education places all cultural backgrounds on an equal footing and encourages acceptance of all ways of life. The Social Policy box takes a closer look at the politics underlying this debate.

Schooling People with Disabilities

The debate over whether schools meet the needs of students extends to people of all classes, colors, and cultures and people with mental or physical disabilities. In 2012, 6.4 million students with disabilities were enrolled in special-education programs in public schools, at a cost exceeding $12.5 billion (U.S. Department of Education, 2013).

SOCIAL POLICY

More Than Talk: The Politics of Bilingual Education

Schooling is not just about teaching children to read and write. Schooling is also a way to socialize children from diverse social backgrounds to find a place within U.S. society. A century ago, as immigration to the United States surged, our country expanded schooling to teach new arrivals the ways of their adopted land and to teach them the English language.

So important was the goal of teaching English that many states (Nebraska was the first in 1919) passed a law requiring all teachers in public schools to teach in English until at least the ninth grade. Public support for these laws was strong because, in the wake of World War I, people feared that immigrants who kept their native language might be disloyal to the United States should war break out again. But others opposed these laws claiming that they expressed little tolerance of cultural diversity. In 1923, this debate reached the U.S. Supreme Court, which settled the case of *Meyer* v. *State of Nebraska* by declaring English-only laws to be unconstitutional.

Jump ahead to 1971, when the San Francisco school system had 2,800 Chinese children but offered no classes in Chinese. A group of parents came together, defined this situation as a problem, and filed a lawsuit against the school district. The suit claimed that the lack of Chinese-language classes violated the Civil Rights Act of 1964, which bans any program receiving federal funds from discriminating on the basis of race, color, or national origin. This case also made its way to the U.S. Supreme Court, which ruled in *Lau* v. *Nichols* (1974) that all students have a right to be taught in a language they can understand. School administrators took this decision to mean that public schools had to create programs to give all children instruction in their native language, whether it is English or some other tongue. At that point, the policy of English immersion was replaced with the policy of bilingual education.

Supporters of bilingual education applaud treating all languages equally and respectfully. Critics of bilingualism claim that bilingual education encourages cultural division instead of emphasizing the cultural patterns most people share.

In 1998, the policy of English immersion gained ground in California when voters in that state passed Proposition 227, which bans bilingual programs in favor of the English immersion approach. In the years since then, the use of bilingual education has been sharply reduced, although schools throughout California report using a mix of approaches toward the goal of teaching English to some 1.5 million students who speak Spanish or some other language at home. Testing results show that students benefit the most from teaching them English while they also study in their native language. Such students also have the advantage of being bilingual, which in California and many other parts of the United States is very useful (Portes, 2002; Winerip, 2007; Garland, 2011; McGreevy, 2014; Myers, 2014). Even so, this debate symbolizes two visions of U.S. society: one pushing for a common culture and the other embracing cultural diversity. Therefore, the bilingual education debate is almost certain to continue.

What Do You Think?

1. Can you explain why the debate surrounding language instruction in schools goes beyond what is good for students to the issue of whether one favors cultural unity or cultural diversity?

2. What is your opinion about using English immersion or bilingual education to teach immigrant children? Explain.

3. What share of students in your high school spoke a language other than English as their first language? Do you recall how these students were taught?

Throughout most of U.S. history, few children with disabilities received any schooling at all. This pattern shifted in 1975, when Congress passed the Education for All Handicapped Children Act, which requires states to educate all children with disabilities. This law also directs schools to place students with disabilities in the "least restrictive environment," meaning that schools should try to treat them like anyone else while meeting their special needs.

This requirement to include students with disabilities in regular school programs led to the policy of **mainstreaming**, *integrating students with special needs into the overall educational program.* Supporters of mainstreaming argue that taking part in regular classes gives students with disabilities a better education. In addition, students without disabilities learn to interact with people who differ from themselves.

Critics of mainstreaming claim that there is little solid research showing that this policy improves anyone's academic performance. On the contrary, they argue, many students with disabilities find it difficult or even impossible to participate in regular classes. The alternative to mainstreaming is **special education**, *schooling children with physical or mental disabilities in separate classes with specially trained teachers.*

In general, which policy is better depends on the students. People with physical or mental disabilities that do not greatly restrict their activities can easily be mainstreamed. Those who are more severely challenged typically require special classes, which are more costly. In the United States, 60 percent of students with disabilities are mainstreamed, whereas the other 40 percent spend some or all of their time in special classes (U.S. Department of Education, 2014).

Finding Enough Teachers

Another problem for U.S. public schools is hiring enough teachers to fill the classrooms. Across the country, there are some 435,000 teaching vacancies each year, including about 360,000 in public schools and 75,000 in private schools. Looking ahead, there will be more than 4 million teachers working in the United States by 2021 (U.S. Department of Education, 2013). In practical terms, failing to fill teaching vacancies means greater demands placed on teachers and larger class sizes for students.

Why are there so many teaching vacancies? Most teachers like their work: Surveys show that close to 90 percent of current teachers are satisfied with their jobs (Primary Sources, 2014). But low salaries are one factor that discourages people from entering this career: Many districts simply pay too little to attract well-qualified teachers, especially in science and mathematics. National Map 13–1 on page 396 shows teacher salaries across the United States.

Low pay is not the only problem. Some people leave teaching due to frustration over extensive bureaucracy that makes the hiring process long and then imposes rigid rules on how classes are to be taught. Some holders of an education degree have had trouble passing state certification tests in specific fields, such as mathematics, biology, or English. An even greater number are turning away from teaching because of large class sizes and problems of discipline and violence in the schools.

Our society must ensure that classrooms are staffed with good teachers. One strategy to accomplish this goal is to force less qualified teachers to get the training they need in order to keep their jobs. A second part of the solution is to attract new and highly qualified people into this profession. In recent years, school systems have devised new recruitment strategies. Some are using incentives such as higher salaries and signing bonuses to attract people who have already established successful careers in other fields. Others are encouraging community colleges to provide more programs that will prepare people to become teachers. Finally, many school districts are going global, actively recruiting in countries such as Spain, India, and the Philippines, where talented educators are eager to be invited to work in U.S. classrooms (Lord, 2001; Evelyn, 2002; Ripley, 2008).

School Violence

In 2012, the killing of twenty children and six adults in the Sandy Hook Elementary School in Connecticut by a disturbed young man with firearms stunned the nation. This may be the worst case of school violence in our nation's history, but it is not the only one. Between 2000 and 2012, 214 young people were murdered while at school. Since 2000, the death toll from all incidents (including both killings and suicides) in school buildings totals 468 people of all ages.

Serious violence is not only limited to homicide but also includes offenses such as aggravated assault and forcible rape, both of which are more common than homicide. School violence also finds its way into most schools. According to the federal government, 74 percent of public schools reported at least one violent crime at school during the 2011–2012 school year (U.S. Department of Education, 2013).

In general, the larger the school is, the higher the risk of violence. The risk of serious violence is greater in large urban or suburban schools than it is in small, rural schools. More than 95 percent of schools enrolling more than 1,000 students reported at least one violent incident during the 2011–2012 school year. The risk of violence is also higher in low-income communities, especially in schools with mostly minority students. Research shows that males are twice as likely as females to be threatened in this way. In addition, compared to white students, African American and Latino students are at higher risk of being threatened

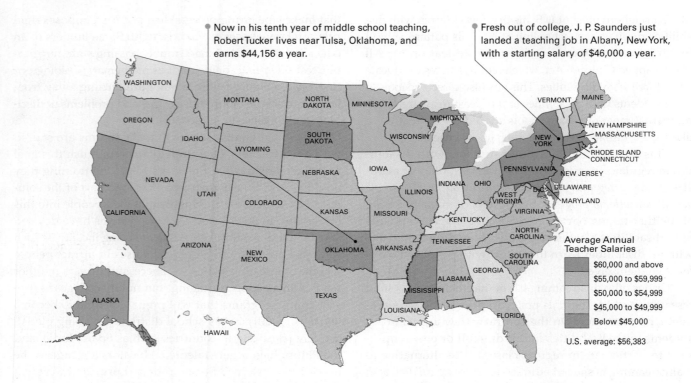

Now in his tenth year of middle school teaching, Robert Tucker lives near Tulsa, Oklahoma, and earns $44,156 a year.

Fresh out of college, J. P. Saunders just landed a teaching job in Albany, New York, with a starting salary of $46,000 a year.

Average Annual Teacher Salaries

$60,000 and above
$55,000 to $59,999
$50,000 to $54,999
$45,000 to $49,999
Below $45,000

U.S. average: $56,383

Seeing Ourselves

National Map 13–1 Public School Teachers' Pay across the United States

In the United States, teachers' pay has grown slowly in recent years, and many school districts have faced cutbacks and layoffs. Across the country, average pay in some states is far higher than it is in others and the dollar gap is increasing. Looking at the state-by-state averages, what pattern can you see?

SOURCE: U.S. Department of Education (2014).

or injured with a weapon on school property (U.S. Department of Education, 2013).

What can schools do to control violence? One recent approach is a *zero-tolerance policy* under which school officials severely punish or expel any student who brings a weapon, alcohol, or some other drug to school. Across the United States, 95 percent of schools now have adopted zero-tolerance policies for firearms, and 85 percent of high schools make use of security cameras, 60 percent make random checks of school property with drug-sniffing dogs, about half employ security guards, and 5 percent require students to pass through metal detectors as they enter the building (U.S. Department of Education, 2013).

Another policy is enacting a dress code to prevent students from wearing gang colors and insignia, which are symbols that can spark violence. About 20 percent of U.S. primary and middle schools require students to wear uniforms; about 10 percent of high schools have adopted this policy (U.S. Department of Education, 2013).

A final strategy used by many schools is a program in conflict resolution. In such programs, now widely used in public schools, teachers instruct children in ways to resolve conflict peacefully (U.S. Department of Education, 2013).

Are these policies working? Government data are encouraging. Between 1992 and 2011, annual victimization rates involving violence fell from 53 incidents to 24 incidents per 1,000 students. Similarly, the rate of victimization for property crimes fell dramatically from 101 incidents to 26 incidents per 1,000 students (U.S. Department of Education, 2013). But "get tough" zero-tolerance policies have been criticized for being racially biased, allegedly subjecting minority students to more frequent searches and more severe penalties than whites. In addition, critics claim, kicking students who misbehave out of school may reduce school violence, but it does little to help the troubled students who land back on the street and end up at even higher risk of involvement in violent crime (Skiba, 2000; Ballantine, 2001).

Theories of Education and Education-Related Problems

13.3 Apply sociological theory to issues of education.

Each of sociology's major theoretical approaches offers insights into the purposes and the problems of schooling. We begin with the structural-functional approach.

Structural-Functional Analysis: The Functions of Schooling

Structural-functional theory points out that the smooth operation of modern societies depends on schooling. Society must ensure young people learn a wide range of knowledge and skills so that they can take their place as productive adults. In a traditional society, instructing children is a responsibility of parents. As the U.S. economy changed from simple farming to more complex industry, however, responsibility for training the young moved from parents to specially trained teachers.

A second function of schooling is social placement. Our society looks to schools to help people assess their talents and develop their abilities so they can find their place in the labor force. For just about anyone, schooling increases employment opportunities. What people study in school—and how much schooling they have—are important factors in their pattern of lifetime earnings.

Throughout our nation's history, schooling has been a major avenue of upward social mobility for people in search of a better life. Researchers have learned that, among young people between the ages of twenty-five and thirty-two, those with only a high school diploma earn $28,000 a year on average. Those with a college degree average $45,000 (Caumont, 2014).

A third function of schooling is instilling common cultural beliefs and values. Shared culture is especially important in an "immigration society" that is so culturally diverse. For example, U.S. schools teach young people about the importance of achievement and the rules of fair play. In addition, U.S. society relies on schools to prepare people to participate in this country's political and economic systems. In short, schools help integrate individuals from many different cultural traditions into a united, national community (Fine, 1993; Ballantine, 2001).

Fourth, and finally, schooling also performs many latent, or less widely recognized, functions. For example, schools

provide child care for working parents. Schools also occupy young people who might otherwise have trouble finding jobs or might turn to crime. Given the great importance of schooling to the operation of modern societies, it is easy to understand why this approach leads to defining issues such as poor teaching, dropping out, and classroom violence as serious social problems (Fuller, Elmore, & Orfield, 1996; C. N. Stone, 1998).

EVALUATE

Structural-functional theory points out several critical functions that schooling performs for our modern society. But critics of this approach point out that the reality of schooling is different for different people, and some people find the experience much more positive than others. To understand how people experience school, we turn to symbolic-interaction theory, which highlights the interaction between students and school personnel.

CHECK YOUR LEARNING What functions of schooling are identified by structural-functional theory? What is one limitation of this theoretical approach?

Symbolic-Interaction Analysis: Labels in the Schools

Symbolic-interaction theory provides a micro-level look at how individuals experience the school system. One micro-level issue is how the labels used by school officials play a major part in defining the academic ability of each student.

Schools review student performance (typically, course grades and scores on standardized tests) and label students as, say, "gifted," "average," or "deficient." These

Violence is all too common in school buildings and campus communities across the United States. In 2014, a disturbed young man went on a killing spree in the area surrounding the University of California in Santa Barbara, leaving seven dead and seven wounded. Why do you think this country has such a high level of deadly violence?

labels do reflect the work students have done; at the same time, other factors including social class and race may play a part in the label attached to each child's performance.

These labels are more than just words in a document. They affect how teachers view students and how students think about themselves. The individuals that school officials label as exceptionally bright or as slow learners are likely, over time, to think of themselves in this way and perform accordingly. In short, tracking and other forms of labeling can set in motion a self-fulfilling prophecy.

The spoken and more subtle messages conveyed by teachers, coaches, and counselors to students can also shape their futures. For example, if school personnel consider some areas of study suitable for girls and others suitable for boys, or if they believe that certain majors or honors courses are expected of students in certain racial and ethnic categories but not students of other backgrounds, it is easy to see how students end up segregated into different areas of study (Sadker & Sadker, 1994; Sadker, 1999; Ballantine, 2001).

EVALUATE

The strength of symbolic-interaction theory lies in providing a "street-level" view of how, in social interaction, students and school personnel construct the reality they experience. Keep in mind, however, that the participants in any social situation are not all equal and the symbolic-interaction approach says little about social inequality. For example, teachers have more power to shape the reality of the classroom than students do. In the same way, larger social forces—such as social class—influence what different students may experience in the same school and generate different realities from school to school. These disparities bring us to social-conflict theory.

CHECK YOUR LEARNING What do we learn by applying symbolic-interaction theory to schooling? What is one limitation of this approach?

Social-Conflict Analysis: Schooling and Inequality

Social-conflict theory highlights the links between schooling and social inequality. As already explained, schooling in the United States is very unequal, to the benefit of some categories of students and to the disadvantage of others. Some students do very well in U.S. schools; others are left behind by our educational system through no fault of their own.

Earlier discussion highlighted one important dimension of differences—school funding—with some schools receiving far more money per student than others. Following this approach, the predictable result is that some schools are well equipped, beautifully maintained, and staffed by highly trained and motivated teachers. Other schools are run-down and lacking in basic facilities, with teachers who are poorly trained and ineffective in the classroom.

In addition, within any single school, the policy of tracking mandates that the best the school has to offer goes to the students who already have a lot going for them—those from higher-class backgrounds. On the other hand, children who are socially disadvantaged at the outset find that school only reaffirms their second-class standing (Oakes, 1985; Kozol, 1991, 2005, 2007).

Not only does schooling divide the population, but also schools train everyone to accept this outcome. The social-conflict approach views schooling as a system of social control that socializes all students to be obedient citizens who are respectful of authority. We might describe these messages as schooling's **hidden curriculum**, *explicit and subtle presentations of political or cultural ideas in the classroom that support the status quo.* Examples of these ideas include teaching students that social problems reflect the personal failings of individuals, that the existing economic and political systems are "right" or "natural," and that the United States is a better nation than any other. In short, rather than learning to think critically and creatively—especially about social justice—most students learn only to follow directions, to respect authority figures, and to fit into the system (Bowles & Gintis, 1976; Kozol, 1991; McLaren & Giarelli, 1995).

EVALUATE

A strength of social-conflict theory is that it highlights how schooling both reflects and perpetuates social inequality. But this approach, too, has its critics. One issue is that social-conflict theory overlooks how far our society has gone over the course of the last century in extending schooling to its people and, especially, in sending an increasing share of the population to college. In addition, schooling has opened the door to upward social mobility for generations of people of all social backgrounds, including immigrants. Finally, although schools teach beliefs and values that support the status quo, the fact that schools mix people of different cultures and class positions suggests that schooling is also a force for change.

CHECK YOUR LEARNING What do we learn by applying social-conflict theory to schooling? What is one limitation of this approach?

Feminist Analysis: Schooling and Gender

Feminist theory is one type of social-conflict theory that highlights patterns of inequality involving gender. In almost every aspect of our society, males have greater pay, power, and prestige than females. This is certainly true in the case of teaching. At the elementary school level, where teaching involves nurturing young children, 91 percent of all teachers are women. Among middle school teachers, 71 percent are women. Among high school teachers, 56 percent are women. Finally, among college teachers, where rewards are greatest of all, a majority of teachers—53 percent—are men. Among college faculty members who have earned the rank of full professor, 72 percent are men and 28 percent are women (Primary Sources, 2012).

Just as gender shapes the profession of teaching, so it shapes the learning of students. As this chapter has explained, for much of our nation's history, people considered schooling to be appropriate for men; there was little point to enhancing learning among women, whose lives centered in the home. Over time, the share of women in the classroom has steadily increased; however, the courses people take is largely guided by gender. In another form of tracking—this time involving sex rather than class—schools and colleges provide different instruction to the two sexes.

As we have already explained, schooling both reflects and perpetuates social inequality based on class. Feminist theory broadens our understanding by showing how schooling does exactly the same thing in terms of inequality based on gender.

Feminist theory shows us how gender shapes the social institution of education, just as it shapes other social institutions. The teaching positions that involve the youngest children are overwhelmingly held by women and the most highly rewarded positions in education are typically held by men. Society uses the concept of gender to define the types of people we are, providing a type of learning consistent with these definitions.

Critics of feminist theory point out that our society has made steady and quite remarkable progress in extending schooling to women. In fact, a larger share of women than men now graduates from high school, and women now outnumber men on college campuses across the country. In light of these facts, suggest some analysts, education may be one social institution where women are well on their way to securing a dominant position.

CHECK YOUR LEARNING   What do we learn by applying feminist theory to schooling? What is one limitation of this approach?

The Applying Theory table summarizes what we learn from each theoretical approach.

⭐ POLITICS AND EDUCATION

Constructing Problems and Defining Solutions

13.4 Analyze educational issues from various positions on the political spectrum.

The lesson from earlier chapters applies here as well: What people define as social problems and what policies they support as solutions reflect political attitudes. Now we

APPLYING THEORY
Education

	Structural-Functional Theory	Symbolic-Interaction Theory	Social-Conflict Theory	Feminist Theory
What is the level of analysis?	Macro-level	Micro-level	Macro-level	Macro-level
What is the importance of schooling to society?	Structural-functional theory explains that schooling performs numerous functions, including transmitting knowledge and skills young people need for work, social placement based on individual talents and interests, and uniting the population by teaching common values and beliefs. Schooling also performs many latent functions such as supervising young people during the day while parents work.	Symbolic-interaction theory focuses on the meanings and understandings that people construct in everyday social interactions. Using this approach, the experience of schooling is likely to be different in some ways for every individual. How a school labels a particular child—as, say, "gifted" or a "slow learner"—is likely to shape that child's experience of schooling and that child's personal identity.	Social-conflict theory links schooling to social inequality. Rather than showing how schooling helps the entire society operate, this approach highlights how schooling reflects existing divisions in society. Schooling both reflects patterns of social inequality and helps perpetuate this inequality by passing these differences from one generation to the next.	Schooling is a system of preparing young people to take on adult responsibilities. To the extent that society defines men and women as different types of people, the extent and content of schooling for the two sexes will differ. Schooling guides the learning and personal development of young people according to broad patterns of gender stratification.
What are important educational problems?	Because of the importance of schooling to the operation of society, anything that threatens the effectiveness of our schools—including poor teaching, classroom violence, and students dropping out of school—is likely to be defined as a social problem.	How we label children can create problems. Because labels can become real to us and have real consequences, a school's decision to label a child in a certain way can create a self-fulfilling prophecy. Children may come to think of themselves in terms of the labels used by school officials and perform accordingly.	Educational problems include the inequality in funding that sets some schools well above others and also the system of tracking that places young people from well-to-do families in the best classes and programs and those from disadvantaged families in the worst classes and programs.	Educational inequality also includes gender. Women were long excluded from higher education. Today, women have been empowered through education, but schooling continues to reflect gender inequality so that women remain relatively disadvantaged in terms of income and power.

examine conservative, liberal, and radical-left perspectives on the state of education in the United States.

Conservatives: Increase Competition

Schooling—specifically, public schooling under the control of government—is one area in which conservatives do not support the status quo. On the contrary, they are outspoken in their criticism of public education in the United States. As they see it, the poor performance of the nation's public school system has become a scandal, and they point to the failure of many big-city public school systems to graduate even half their students as tragic for the people involved and a huge problem for the nation as a whole.

The reason for the crisis, as conservatives see it, is that the government has monopoly control over the system of public education. This means that the nation's public schools do not have to compete for students. Schools receive tax money regardless of how schools perform, and parents living in districts with poor schools have few choices. A lack of competition has fostered rigid bureaucracy that defends the status quo and actively stands in the way of innovation and policies that would encourage excellence. For example, instead of linking teacher salaries to how much students learn, public education links teacher salaries to seniority (Thernstrom & Thernstrom, 2003).

No business operating as a monopoly feels competitive pressure to provide consumers with high value. Therefore, conservatives argue, we should expect this "one-provider system" to perform poorly. The solution to the problem of underperforming schools is to make schooling more competitive. If public schools had to compete for students, they would have to do a good job or go out of business.

Increased competition is the heart of the strategy of *school choice*. The most widespread policy to increase choice is the creation of **charter schools**, *public schools that are given the freedom to try out new policies and programs.* Charter schools are subject to less regulation than regular public schools as long as their students perform above the average. About 5,700 charter schools have been established in forty-one states, Washington, D.C., and Puerto Rico, and these schools enroll about 2 million students. These schools teach diverse students—64 percent are nonwhite—and many of these schools have established records of high academic achievement (U.S. Department of Education, 2014).

Adopting a similar strategy, some districts have developed **magnet schools**, *public schools that offer special facilities and programs in pursuit of educational excellence.* There are now some 3,000 magnet schools in the United States offering special instruction in areas including the sciences and foreign languages. Magnet schools enroll only 4.6 percent of public school students but have been able to improve learning for these students (U.S. Department of Education, 2014).

Conservatives also support increased competition by allowing private companies to engage in *schooling for profit.* Private schools are nothing new, of course: More than 25,000 private schools now operate in the United States. The point here is to let for-profit companies take over the operation of inefficient public schools, based on the claim that they can operate the school system more efficiently than government bureaucrats. A number of U.S. cities, including Baltimore, Miami, Hartford, and Boston, have experimented with for-profit schooling but have decided to go back to conventional public school systems. More recently, when Philadelphia's school system failed to graduate one-third of its students, the state took over the school system and brought in private companies to run most of the schools. Although there was some improvement in student performance, school officials were still dissatisfied and so, in 2010, they turned for assistance to independent companies that operate as nonprofit organizations. Emotions on both sides of the schooling-for-profit issue run high as everyone seeks to help those who are caught in a troubled system—the schoolchildren themselves (Garland, 2007; Richburg, 2008; Mezzacappa, 2010).

A final conservative policy is the **school voucher program**, *a program that provides parents with funds they can use at a public school or private school of their choice.* A voucher program says, in effect, "You are entitled to use your tax money to school your children wherever you want." Vouchers are especially popular among low-income families, who seek alternatives to the poor public schools in their neighborhoods. Many who have this option choose to send their children to parochial schools, which are run by a church (most are operated by the Roman Catholic Church), where there is greater discipline, less disruption, more learning, and fewer students dropping out. Many U.S. cities, including Cleveland, Indianapolis, Minneapolis, Milwaukee, Chicago, and Washington, D.C., have experimented with choice plans in recent years, and in 2002, the U.S. Supreme Court upheld Cleveland's voucher programs as lawful (Lord, 2002; Morse, 2002). The Personal Stories box takes a closer look at one family's experiences with vouchers.

Conservatives support school choice and the certification or testing of teachers as policies that would force all schools, both public and private, to show greater *accountability.* In 2002, President Bush signed an education bill, popularly called "No Child Left Behind," that required the testing of all public school students in grades three through eight in language arts, mathematics, and science; this law received wide support from conservatives. Schools in which students perform poorly are required to show improvement in coming years; if they do not, parents will get the option of moving their children to another school. By 2012, although some improvements in student performance are evident, almost half of the country's public schools have been labeled as failing. This stark reality has reduced support for "No Child Left

PERSONAL STORIES
School Choice: One Family's View

The poor performance of public school systems—especially in large urban areas—is a matter of controversy and debate. But for the people "on the ground" in places with poor local schools, the reality boils down to simply wanting something better.

Every morning, Delvoland Shakespeare walks out of his house in Cleveland, Ohio, buckles his two sons into the back seat of his gray Ford, and drives them about a mile to a Catholic school called Our Lady of Peace. Shakespeare thinks the school is the best opportunity his sons have ever had. Eight-year-old Landel has learned to use a computer; five-year-old Isaiah is learning to read. After dropping off the boys, Shakespeare parks the car and watches his sons line up to enter the building. "Seeing them going off to what I know is a good school," he says with a wide grin, "gives me the best feeling."

When Landel was ready to begin kindergarten, Shakespeare and his wife, Charlynn, decided to do some investigating. They knew that their city's public schools, like other inner-city schools across the United States, have serious problems, including the failure to graduate more than half of their students. So they planned a visit to the public school in their own neighborhood. On several corners around the school, they noticed drug dealers and prostitutes. Inside, they found the books to be in terrible shape—some without covers, many replaced by photocopies. Shakespeare's worst fears were confirmed when he entered the boys' restroom and a young man tried to sell him marijuana (Shlaes, 1998).

A few days conducting "fieldwork" was enough to convince the Shakespeares that they had to do whatever it took to find a better school for their children. They cut back on their spending, trying to save enough to afford a private school. But the cost of private schooling is high, and the tuition for two children was simply out of their reach. Then they heard about a new, experimental "choice" program: Low-income families could enter a lottery in the hope of winning a voucher worth $2,500 that could be used for tuition at a school of their choice. They signed up and were delighted when Landel won a school voucher. Three years later, when Isaiah was ready to start kindergarten, he also won a voucher.

The Shakespeares, like most low-income families who live in large cities, strongly support school choice. The simple reason is that they believe having a choice about schools has greatly benefited their children. But not everyone agrees that a voucher program is a good idea. Some people oppose any school choice program as weakening our nation's commitment to public education. Other people object to giving tax dollars to religious schools, seeing this policy as a violation of the constitutional separation of church and state. Others claim that voucher programs are drawing the best students from public schools, leaving the weakest students behind. Finally, some oppose vouchers simply because, as they see it, the real solution should be fixing our public schools, not abandoning them.

What Do You Think?

1. Older students have long used government grants and loans to attend colleges and universities affiliated with religious organizations. Should younger students be able to use vouchers to attend parochial schools? Why or why not?

2. What policy changes would you favor as a solution to the poor performance of public schools in the United States? Explain your position.

3. On balance, do you think a voucher program improves public schooling or not? Why?

Behind." Yet conservatives remain committed to the idea that student performance must be measured and public schools must be held accountable for how well or poorly students perform (Wallis & Steptoe, 2007; Dillon, 2011, 2011).

Liberals: Increase the Investment

Liberals consider public schools a vital part of U.S. society. Schooling is a necessary resource for everyone; for this reason, ensuring that good schools are available to all is one important responsibility of government.

Liberals concede that some schools are not doing their job very well, but they view struggling schools as a symptom of broader social problems, including economic inequality and racial discrimination. In light of the fact that some schools receive much more funding than others, year after year, should we be surprised that some students are left behind? Furthermore, given the striking class differences in U.S. society, some students benefit from greater cultural capital at home, just as others have the odds stacked against them long before they reach their first year in school. In addition, millions of young people face the challenge of speaking a first language other than English. Overcoming all of these challenges requires the full resources of the government. For this reason, liberals support government-funded programs such as Head Start, which provides early educational enrichment to children who need it most.

Some liberals support the idea of school choice (particularly charter schools and magnet schools, because they are still *public* schools), but the major liberal policy for improving schools is a greater investment of tax money in *all* schools so that they can better meet the needs of all students. Polls reveal solid majorities—not only among minorities but among whites as well—supporting the policy of poor minority children having the same educational resources as rich whites (Close, 2004).

it is far less costly to pay for good schools today than to pay the costs of dealing with the problems that result from poor schools—including crime, drug abuse, and functional illiteracy—later on.

The Radical Left: Attack Structural Inequality

Radicals on the left argue that most social problems, including problems of education, arise from basic flaws in the economic and political structure of the larger society. As long as the economic and political systems concentrate wealth and power in the hands of a few, this nation can never provide good schooling to all. From a radical-left point of view, schools are not the cause of the problem; the capitalist economy is. But schools do make the problem worse to the extent that they define the cause of poor academic performance, dropping out, and school violence as

Most people agree that inner-city schools have problems. Conservatives blame the government monopoly and teachers' unions that resist competition. Liberals call for greater spending on schools and more equal funding from district to district. Radicals claim that as long as striking inequality exists in society, schools will serve some students and fail to teach others.

the failure of *individuals* rather than the results of *structural inequality* in the United States.

A recent liberal initiative is called Common Core State Standards, a federally mandated set of standards that specifies skills that children should learn in each grade. First developed in 2010, these standards were quickly adopted by forty-five states and provide some welcome uniformity from state to state. They identify basic skills—such as understanding fractions and sentence structure—that the federal government claims should be "common" to everyone's schooling. Liberals support the Common Core as a way to raise student performance in the United States, which has lagged behind that of many other nations. Some conservatives, too, support this initiative as a way to make schools and teachers more accountable; many conservatives, however, fear an increasing federal government role in education, which they believe should be left up to the states and local communities. In the last year, however, a rising concern among parents that their children are facing an increasing workload to prepare for difficult tests has raised questions about the future of this program (Altman, 2014; Lahey, 2014; Lu, 2014).

At all levels of schooling, liberals voice strong support for bilingual programs, which conservatives oppose. Liberals claim that bilingual education not only allows students to progress in other subjects at the same time that they are learning English but also helps everyone recognize and value the full range of cultural diversity found in the United States (Ochoa, 1999; Portes, 2002).

Liberals support expanding the national investment in education to fund all these strategies. They claim that

Radicals on the left agree with liberals that public schools deserve more funding. At the very least, they argue, we need to eliminate the disparity of funding between wealthy schools and those in less affluent districts. A step in that direction is the action taken by the state of Vermont with equal funding to school districts statewide on a per-student basis. By ensuring that all schools receive the same amount of funding per student, states can follow Vermont's lead to increase educational equality.

Yet the Vermont program goes only so far. Even if schools were all exactly the same, some students would still have great advantages over others based on their social background. Radicals on the left conclude that the only way to make good education available to everyone is to eliminate the striking inequality found throughout society as a whole. This revolutionary idea would require basic changes to both the capitalist economy and the existing political system.

The Left to Right table summarizes the conservative, liberal, and radical-left perspectives on the state of U.S. schools.

Going On from Here

In one recent survey, seven out of ten U.S. adults said they would make improving the quality of education in the United States a top priority of our leaders in Washington,

LEFT TO RIGHT

The Politics of Education

	Radical-Left View	Liberal View	Conservative View
What is the problem?	Because schools operate within a social system marked by striking inequality of wealth and power, they fail much of the U.S. population and perpetuate class differences.	Although schools are educating more young people than ever before, they lack the funds and programs to meet the needs of some categories of the population.	Schools are a government monopoly that is neither efficient nor accountable. As a near government monopoly, schools fail to educate a significant share of young people.
What is the solution?	Equalize funding for all schools; ultimately, the solution lies in making radical changes in the economic and political systems to create a more egalitarian society.	Increase government funding for schools, especially in disadvantaged areas; expand Head Start and bilingual programs to improve schooling for minorities and low-income children.	Implement various strategies to make schools more competitive, including schooling for profit and using school vouchers. All schools must be made accountable for their performance.

JOIN THE DEBATE

1. All political perspectives agree on one thing: Schools in the United States are not getting the job done. In light of this fact, why do you think there has been little change in schools over recent decades?

2. Using each of the three political perspectives, respond to the following assertion: "Schooling in the United States advances the goal of equal opportunity by providing a learning program that matches a student's abilities and interests."

3. Which of the three political analyses of U.S. schooling included here do you find most convincing? Why?

D.C. People consider improving our schools to be so important because they think that education is the key that opens the door to economic opportunity: A high school diploma and a college degree (perhaps also a graduate degree) ensure both better jobs and higher income (Smith et al., 2013; Pew Research Center for the People & the Press, 2014). For this reason, we like to say that our schools provide every student not only with basic learning but also with the chance to discover individual interests and develop personal abilities.

In recent decades, the Information Revolution has further increased the importance of literacy skills, making schooling more important than ever. Yet as this chapter has shown, U.S. public schools are plagued by shortcomings: Measures of student performance have slipped over time and do not stand up well to those of other nations, and many young people (more than half in some large cities) drop out before finishing high school.

What are the prospects for change? People across the political spectrum agree that changes must be made. But there is far less agreement as to exactly what the problems and solutions are.

Conservatives focus on the school system itself. They argue that government does not manage schooling very well, especially when government has a near-monopoly over the process. Our society will have to provide more educational choice and competition before student performance will improve.

Liberals focus on government action to increase school funding. Liberals offer strong support for the idea that government should run high-quality schools and the public as a whole should bear the cost. They counter that school choice policies are likely to help some students—especially those with involved parents—but will leave other students behind and harm public schools overall. Liberals also note that in decades to come, this country's schoolchildren will become ever more culturally diverse, highlighting the importance of bilingual and multicultural programs.

Radicals on the left are also likely to shape the future of schooling. Vermont has already enacted a bold and controversial program to ensure that all school systems receive equal per-student funding. Yet sixteen years later, governments in other states have not enacted similar legislation. Will they in the years to come? Because the idea of equal funding challenges the long-established practice of local control of schools, change in this direction is likely to be slow and hotly contested. Yet given the extent of funding inequality noted in this chapter, public support for a more equal policy may well grow.

When it comes to schools in the United States, almost everyone is in favor of change. But precisely what changes are to come is a political decision that will be made as today's students take their places as adults.

Essay: Envisioning a Better Society The performance of schools in the United States—especially public schools—is controversial. What specific changes or policies would you suggest that would raise the academic performance of U.S. students? Explain why or how each policy would improve schooling in the future.

CHAPTER 13   Education

What can we do to improve the state of public schools in our large cities?

As this chapter has explained, the public is split on whether our urban schools are doing their job. The fact that official data show that 1,424 public schools across the United States failed to graduate at least 60 percent of their students is certainly cause for concern. Look at the two accompanying photos to see two approaches to solving this problem.

In general, liberals link poor performance to inadequate school funding. But an increasing number of liberals also see stifling bureaucracy as part of the problem and support the expansion of charter schools. Operating as public schools but not subject to the rigid rules and regulations of the larger public school system, charter schools are free to be creative in terms of organization, scheduling, and instruction. Because it is vital to liberals that excellence be created in public education, they see charter schools as one promising approach. How much do you support the concept of charter schools?

From a conservative point of view, the main reason that public schools do not function well is that they lack competition. In short, conservatives would like to see an educational marketplace, where parents and their children can choose the school that offers the greatest value. The policy that maximizes such choice is vouchers, which means that parents use public funds to pay for whatever school they wish, whether public or private. What do you see as strengths and weaknesses of a voucher system?

Hint: In the end, where you stand on the issue of our urban schools depends on how committed you are to the idea of public education. Vouchers, which would allow tax money to go to any school, public or private, would create the most choice but might well end up creating a bigger gap between the best- and worst-performing schools. For that reason, urban governments (almost all of which are overwhelmingly Democratic) have permitted only very limited voucher programs. Charter schools may represent a chance for political compromise because they offer some choice while also preserving the idea of keeping tax money in public education. Radicals on the left would be unlikely to sign on, however, because they look for greater change—toward a system of equally funded public education.

Getting Involved: Applications and Exercises

1. Most communities offer programs that train volunteers to teach adults to read. To find one in your area, ask about literacy programs at a local school or library or call a local social services agency. See how you can help others learn to read.

2. Head Start is a government program that helps disadvantaged children to succeed in school. Contact your county government and ask about volunteer opportunities with a Head Start program in your area.

3. Talk to your campus office that assists students with special needs. How does your campus deal with students with learning disabilities? What level of access to facilities on your campus do people with physical disabilities have?

4. Today, 57 percent of students on college and university campuses are women, and the gender gap in higher education has been increasing. Is there a gender gap on your campus? Check your school's website to see what you can learn. Try to account for any patterns you can identify.

A DEFINING MOMENT
Linda Brown: Fighting to Desegregate the Schools **p. 389**

Problems of Education: A Global Perspective

13.1   Explain how schooling differs in low-income nations and high-income nations.

- **Education** is the social institution by which a society transmits knowledge—including basic facts, job skills, and cultural norms and values—to its members.

- As societies industrialize, they require young people to attend schools where students receive instruction by specially trained teachers.

- In high-income countries, most people complete secondary school and a significant share completes college.

- In low-income countries, many young people, especially girls, receive little or no schooling; about one-sixth of adults in the world are illiterate. **pp. 383–84**

Education in U.S. History

- Only after the abolition of slavery did large numbers of African Americans attend school.

- With industrialization and the rise in immigration, all states had passed mandatory education laws by 1918.

- As women moved into the labor force over the course of the twentieth century, they also joined men at colleges and universities. **pp. 384–86**

education (p. 383) the social institution by which a society transmits knowledge—including basic facts and job skills, as well as cultural norms and values—to its members
schooling (p. 383) formal instruction carried out by specially trained teachers
literacy (p. 383) the ability to read and write

Problems with U.S. Education

13.2   Discuss the causes and consequences of a number of problems with U.S. education.

Academic Performance

- Of all industrialized nations, the United States has the second highest percentage of adults (about 32%) with college degrees. But on tests of literacy and science skills, U.S. students lag behind their counterparts in many other high-income nations.

- Socially disadvantaged categories of students score lower than students from affluent families on standardized tests. **pp. 386–87**

Dropping Out

- In 2012, 6.6% of young people (3 million) had dropped out before completing high school.

- African Americans (7.5%), Hispanics (12.7%), and Native Americans (13.0%) have higher dropout rates compared with whites (4.3%).

- Dropping out of school raises the risk of drug abuse, arrest, unemployment, and poverty as adults. **pp. 387–88**

Functional Illiteracy

- Functional illiteracy is a serious problem in the United States, where about 14% of adults cannot read or write well enough to carry out their daily tasks. **p. 388**

School Segregation and Busing

- The concept of "separate but equal" schools was established by the Supreme Court in 1896 (*Plessy* v. *Ferguson*).

- In 1954, the Court reversed itself and declared laws that racially segregate schools to be unconstitutional (*Brown* v. *Board of Education of Topeka*).

- When busing was used to integrate schools, "white flight" took many white families to the suburbs. As a result, public schools today remain about as racially segregated as they were in the 1960s. **pp. 388–90**

School Funding

- Because U.S. public schools are funded by state and local taxes, the richest school districts spend several times more per student than the poorest school districts.

- In addition to attending better schools, children from affluent families also benefit from greater *cultural capital*: experiences and opportunities at home that enhance learning. **pp. 390–92**

Tracking

- Tracking is a school policy that assigns children to various academic programs.
- Supporters claim that tracking provides students with schooling consistent with their interests and abilities.
- Critics claim that tracking assignments often are made according to social background, so that affluent students benefit and disadvantaged students are harmed. **p. 392**

Gender Inequality

- Today, a majority (57%) of college students are women.
- However, gender still operates as a form of tracking that guides women and men into different majors. **pp. 392–93**

Immigration: Increasing Diversity

- Cultural diversity is another challenge to U.S. schools. A debate centers on whether it is better to place non–English speakers in English immersion courses or to use a policy of bilingual education. **pp. 393–94**

Schooling People with Disabilities

- Some 6.4 million people with disabilities are enrolled in U.S. schools. Whether it is better to mainstream these students or to provide them with separate specialized programs is an ongoing issue. **pp. 394–95**

School Violence

- Violent crime is a serious problem in U.S. schools. In response, most schools have adopted a zero-tolerance policy toward both violence and bringing weapons and drugs to school. **pp. 395–96**

functional illiteracy (p. 388) the inability to read and write or do basic arithmetic well enough to carry out daily responsibilities

tracking (p. 392) the policy of assigning students to different educational programs

self-fulfilling prophecy (p. 392) a situation in which people who are defined in a certain way eventually think and act as if the definition were true

English immersion (p.393) the policy of teaching non–English speakers in English

bilingual education (p. 393) the policy of offering most classes in students' native language while also teaching them English

mainstreaming (p. 395) integrating students with special needs into the overall educational program

special education (p. 395) schooling children with physical or mental disabilities in separate classes with specially trained teachers

Theories of Education and Education-Related Problems

13.3   Apply sociological theory to issues of education.

Structural–Functional Analysis: The Functions of Schooling

Structural-functional theory highlights the importance of schools to the operation of society as a whole.

- Schooling prepares young people for the workforce and serves as a means of upward social mobility as students gain the knowledge and skills to perform jobs.
- Schooling teaches the dominant cultural values of a society.
- A latent function of schooling is providing child care for working parents. **p. 397**

Symbolic-Interaction Analysis: Labels in the Schools

Symbolic-interaction theory focuses on how the interaction of students and school personnel constructs reality, including how students come to see themselves.

- Schools' labeling of students as gifted or deficient can be a **self-fulfilling prophecy** with important consequences for what students expect of themselves. **pp. 397–98**

Social-Conflict Analysis: Schooling and Inequality

Social-conflict theory highlights the links between schooling and social inequality.

- Unequal funding from school to school and tracking within any single school perpetuate class differences from one generation to the next.
- Schooling's **hidden curriculum** socializes students to respect authority and not to challenge the status quo. **p. 398**

Feminist Analysis: Schooling and Gender

Feminist theory highlights the links between schooling and gender inequality.

- From elementary school to the college campus, the greater the rewards of teaching, the more likely men are to be found as classroom teachers.
- To the extent that our society defines females and males as different categories of people, gender guides how much schooling people receive as well as the content of the education. **pp. 398–99**

hidden curriculum (p. 398) explicit and subtle presentations of political or cultural ideas in the classroom that support the status quo

⭐ POLITICS AND EDUCATION

Constructing Problems and Defining Solutions

13.4   **Analyze educational issues from various positions on the political spectrum.**

Conservatives: Increase Competition

- **Conservatives** criticize U.S. public schools as inefficient and not accountable to the people they are supposed to serve.
- Conservatives propose making education competitive by giving parents choices about where to send their children through the use of charter schools, magnet schools, for-profit schools, and voucher programs. **pp. 400–1**

Liberals: Increase the Investment

- **Liberals** believe that the problems of schools are rooted in the larger society.
- Liberals support greater investment in schools, especially in programs such as Head Start and bilingual education, to enhance the cultural capital of disadvantaged students. **pp. 401–2**

The Radical Left: Attack Structural Inequality

- **Radicals on the left** argue that the shortcomings of U.S. schools are symptoms of the structural inequalities of U.S. society.
- Radicals on the left call for equalizing student funding in all schools. Ultimately, the radical goal is to bring about basic change in the direction of economic and political equality in the United States. **p. 402**

Chapter 14
Urban Life

Learning Objectives

14.1 Explain the historical development of cities in the United States.

14.2 Discuss the causes and consequences of a number of urban problems.

14.3 Apply sociological theory to urbanization and urban problems.

14.4 Analyze urban issues from various positions on the political spectrum.

Tracking the Trends

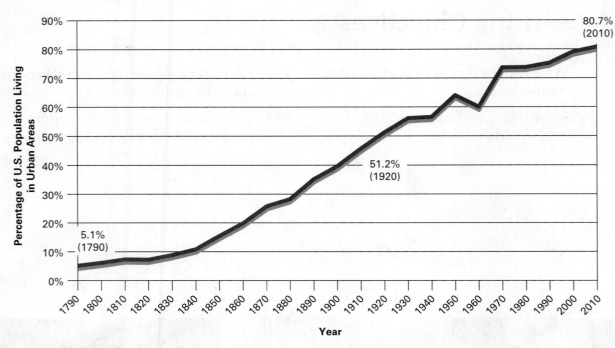

SOURCES: U.S. Census Bureau (1993, 2012).

The United States has not always been a nation of city dwellers. As the figure shows, when the government completed the first census in 1790, just 5 percent of people lived in cities. That share steadily increased after that and, in 1920, a majority of people were counted as city dwellers. Today, almost a century later, more than 80 percent of people in this country live in cities and their surrounding suburbs. Do you think that most of the social problems we face in the United States can also be thought of as *urban* problems?

Constructing the Problem

What is urban sprawl?

Urban sprawl is the rapid outward growth of cities. Atlanta, among our fastest-growing urban areas, has been gobbling up 500 acres of open ground each week.

Don't cities have plenty of jobs?

Yes, but in the inner-city neighborhoods of many large U.S. cities, a majority of adults cannot find work.

How big a problem is homelessness in the United States?

About 1.5 million people in the United States are homeless for at least some time during the course of a year.

Chapter Overview

Can you imagine the United States without its great cities, including New York, Chicago, and Los Angeles? This chapter explores urban life, explaining how cities developed over our nation's history. You will learn about many urban issues, including cities in financial crisis, the recent rise in home foreclosures, urban areas sprawling outward, substandard housing, racial segregation, and homelessness. You will carry out theoretical analysis of urban issues and learn how the urban issues people define as "problems" and the policies that they favor as "solutions" reflect their political attitudes. ■

The sun was almost down in Las Vegas, as Mary Saccacio walked slowly into the living room carrying the envelope in her right hand. Sensing Mary's presence, her husband, Vernon, looked up from the couch where he had been watching the news on television. "This just came from the bank." Mary spoke softly, a tremor in her voice.

When Mary and Vernon bought their modest house in Las Vegas, they knew it was a stretch. But at first, the monthly mortgage payments were low enough for the two retired teachers to afford. Because housing prices in Nevada had been going up so each year, they thought they would end up way ahead.

Then the housing bubble popped, and Nevada was among the states hardest hit. They were soon "underwater," meaning that the value of their home was now much less than what they owed on their mortgage. To make matters worse—much worse—the mortgage agreement they signed raised their interest rate after thirty-six months. This increased the monthly payment to more than they

could afford. Now that they were several months behind in their payments, the bank had written to announce the start of foreclosure proceedings.

As Mary read the letter, Vernon looked down at the floor. There was to be a court hearing. Unless they could come up with the money they owed the bank or negotiate

Seeing Ourselves

National Map 14–1 Foreclosures across the United States, 2008

The recession beginning in 2008 resulted in millions of people struggling to make payments on their home loans. For many unable to pay, foreclosure was the result. The map shows the rate of housing foreclosure for counties across the United States. What pattern do you see?

SOURCE: RealtyTrac (2009).

some settlement, they would be evicted. The house would then be sold to the highest bidder at a sheriff's sale (Saporito, 2008; El Boghdady & Cohen, 2009; Von Drehle, 2009; Robison, 2014).

As the economic recession intensified in 2008 and 2009, a housing crisis spread across the United States. The foreclosure rate peaked in 2010 and has fallen since then. But by 2013, more than 5 million homes across the country had been lost to foreclosure. National Map 14–1 shows the rate of foreclosure filings as the recession began.

The loss of homes and the disappearance of jobs are clear evidence that all is not well in the cities of the United States. In U.S. cities, we find beautiful architecture, brightly lit shopping districts, as well as famous universities, fascinating museums, and many other cultural centers. But cities also are concentrations of poverty, inadequate housing, homelessness, and crime.

The United States is a nation of cities; 81 percent of our population lives in an urban area (U.S. Census Bureau, 2013). This means that many of the problems we face as a society are problems of cities and urban life. This chapter examines cities in the United States and offers a brief look at the state of cities around the world. To understand the state of our

cities today, we begin with a brief look at how cities have grown and changed during our history.

Cities: Then and Now

14.1 Explain the historical development of cities in the United States.

It is not easy to imagine this country without great cities such as New York, Atlanta, Chicago, or Los Angeles. Four centuries ago—before this region of the world was called the United States—this continent was home to several million native people who made few permanent settlements. From coast to coast, there was not one tall structure or a single paved road.

Colonial Villages: 1565–1800

The first cities were created by Europeans who colonized what they called the "New World." The Spanish established the first settlement at Saint Augustine, Florida, in 1565. In 1607, the English founded Jamestown, Virginia. In 1624, the Dutch founded New Amsterdam—later renamed New York—at the southern tip of Manhattan Island. In 1630, the English settled Boston.

All of these settlements began as tiny villages, with narrow dirt streets, small houses, and just a few hundred residents. These communities provided a home for settlers in a new and unfamiliar world. People living there worked hard, and most managed to survive.

By the time the United States declared independence in 1776, barely 5 percent of the population lived in cities. The largest city in the new nation was Philadelphia, with 42,000 people—a far cry from the roughly 4.5 million in the Philadelphia metropolitan area today.

Westward Expansion: 1800–1860

After 1800, people began pushing westward, following new transportation routes, including the National Road (1818), the Baltimore & Ohio Railroad (1825), and the Erie Canal (1825). Along these routes, migrants formed settlements that grew into the great cities of the Midwest, including Buffalo, Cleveland, Detroit, and Chicago. During this time, the country experienced steady **urbanization** *the movement of people from the countryside to cities*. By the time of the Civil War in 1860, some 20 percent of the nation's people were urbanites.

The Industrial Metropolis: 1860–1950

The outbreak of the Civil War gave rise to many new factories to build weapons, which drew even more people from rural to urban places. In addition, about a million immigrants, mostly from Europe, were entering the United States each year, and almost all of them settled in cities. This mix of factories and surging population created the industrial *metropolis* (from Greek words meaning "mother city"). By 1900, Chicago boasted 2 million residents, and New York City had 4 million people, more than the entire nation's population in 1790.

Cities grew not just in number of people but also outward and upward. New train and trolley routes allowed city boundaries to move into the surrounding countryside. Steel beams replaced bricks and wood and ushered in the age of skyscrapers—tall buildings with elevators to move people up and down. By 1930, New York had expanded well beyond Manhattan Island and had a striking skyline, with the Empire State Building towering 102 stories above the streets.

Social Problems in Industrial Cities Industrialization changed cities, increasing their size and attracting a socially diverse population. By 1900, many people were coming to think of cities as a source of social problems. One reason for the bad image was a flood of immigrants. At that time, two-thirds of the people living in the nation's ten largest cities

City life was widely defined as a social problem by rural people in the nineteenth century. This drawing, depicting city streets as chaotic and dangerous, appeared in several rural newspapers in 1858.

had been born abroad or were the children of immigrants (Glaab, 1963). This high concentration of cultural diversity fueled both ethnic prejudice and antiurban bias. Especially among the majority of people who had lived for generations in rural communities, "city folk" were considered something less than "real Americans."

Most city residents were well aware of such feelings. But their immediate problems centered on basic needs such as housing. In 1900, more than one-third of New Yorkers lived in *tenements* buildings divided into many small apartments with few windows and shared bathrooms. Tenements filled up with recent immigrants, who were very poor.

To make matters worse, in industrial cities, the air was fouled by factory smoke, and sewage flowed freely into the streets, eventually reaching the same rivers and lakes used for drinking water. Children ran around dirty and unsupervised, epidemics raged in poor neighborhoods, and violent crime was rampant. The greatest suffering was experienced by the thousands of people—including children—who were so poor that they had no place to live at all except under a bridge or beneath a stairway.

In these industrial cities, there were plenty of jobs, but most demanded hard labor for ten or more hours a day and paid very low wages. Things got even worse with the onset of the Great Depression in 1929; at its worst point, one-fourth of all U.S. workers were thrown out of work and there were no unemployment benefits. Homelessness, breadlines, and begging on the streets were widespread in the United States. Not until the start of World War II (1939–1945) did the nation rise out of the depression. By the end of the war, a new era of prosperity was about to begin. But as we now explain, these "good times" were a mixed blessing for cities.

Postindustrial Cities and Suburbs: 1950–Present

By the end of the 1940s, the industrial metropolis reached its peak population. With the ending of World War II in 1945, soldiers returned home and many couples wasted little time before they started families. What became known as the baby boom was underway and it would soon change the face of our cities.

The postwar baby boom not only sent the U.S. birth rate soaring, but also it pushed many families to look for new housing. With the economy expanding, many families were earning more money than ever before and could afford to own at least one car. The federal government made automobiles more attractive by building the interstate highway system, including beltways around central cities. The search for new housing in the era of the "car culture" drew people away from the central cities into **suburbs**, *urban areas beyond the political boundaries of cities.*

In the 1950s, almost all new housing construction took place in the suburbs. Federal loan programs helped families buy new homes with just a small down payment, sometimes at irresistibly low prices. On New York's Long Island, a development called Levittown priced single-family houses at about $8,000 in 1948 (about $75,000 in today's dollars). Many people made fun of Levittown's small (720 square feet), identical "cookie-cutter" houses. But Abraham Levitt quickly sold all 17,447 of his houses in the first Levittown and then went on to build two more large developments in suburban Philadelphia (Wattel, 1958). Across the country, developers had little trouble selling new homes to families eager to own their own piece of leafy suburban real estate.

Economic changes helped suburbs grow even more in the 1960s and 1970s. The great metropolis had been created by industrial production, which centralized the population in cities centered on factories and transportation links. But the new postindustrial economy that emerged after the 1960s was characterized by service work and computer technology. This new economy relocated work from the old, downtown factories to office buildings, most of which were out in the suburbs. In short, the postindustrial economy *decentralized* the population. By 1970, most of the "urban" population of the United States lived not in central cities but in suburbs; by 2012, 52 percent of the *entire* country's population were suburbanites (U.S. Census Bureau, 2013).

Problems of Today's Cities

14.2 Discuss the causes and consequences of a number of urban problems.

The movement of people from central cities into suburbs created a number of urban problems, including bankruptcy, sprawl, and high rates of inner-city poverty.

Fiscal Problems of the 1970s

Is it possible for a city to go broke? During the 1970s, a number of U.S. cities flirted with bankruptcy. One was New York—the country's largest city, with a population exceeding 8 million. The trouble was that New York stood at the center of an even larger urban region that was expanding outward as people steadily crossed the city limits to live in outlying suburbs. Between 1970 and 1980, the population of New York actually declined by 860,000 people, a loss of more people than lived in the city of Boston. With the movement of industry from downtown factory districts to suburban industrial parks, the city lost not only residents but also half a million jobs. Corporate mergers and downsizing further reduced the demand for both industrial labor and office workers.

These trends combined to create a "perfect storm" that led to a fiscal crisis. The loss of people and fewer businesses meant that the city had a smaller tax base. To make matters worse, those who moved from the city were, on average, richer and better educated than those who stayed behind, including the poor and the unemployed, many of whom relied on social service programs. By the mid-1970s, the increasing costs of social service programs as well as the rising payroll for city employees was simply too much for New York to handle, and the city stood on the brink of bankruptcy. The picture was much the same in many other cities in the industrial regions of the Northeast and Midwest (Johnson & Lueck, 1996; U.S. Census Bureau, 2013).

The Postindustrial Revival

New York and other industrial metropolises such as Cleveland and Chicago managed to suffer through tough times. New sources of financing sent new money into the cities' coffers, some union contracts were revised, and welfare benefits were reduced to cut expenses.

Eventually, the old industrial cities were able to adapt to the new postindustrial economy. Many jobs were lost when older, industrial factories closed their doors. But millions of new jobs were created in the service sector of the economy, including entertainment, sales, financial services, law, consulting, publishing, and computer-based businesses. New York's midtown and downtown, which were once industrial regions, were transformed into postindustrial centers of finance and commerce.

A second factor that helped cities recover is rising immigration. After 1980, New York once again began gaining population as immigrants—many from Latin America and Asia—arrived in search of the same economic opportunities that drew people from Europe a century before. Most of these immigrants took service jobs in restaurants, hotels, and hospitals, working long hours for low wages and adding billions of dollars to the nation's economic output (Martin & Midgley, 2003).

The Recent Recession and New Fiscal Problems

The financial problems of cities have returned in recent years. In part, the cause is the Great Recession that began in 2008, causing cities to lose jobs, suffer devalued properties, and collect lower tax revenues. In addition, as noted earlier, the recession pushed millions of people out of their homes. To make matter worse, both factory and office jobs continue to move overseas, where labor costs are lower.

By 2012, the economy was showing signs of a slow recovery. Stock markets soared but, for the average person, there was little *feeling* of a recovery. The reason is that the economy has been adding jobs too slowly to provide work for everyone looking for a job. By late 2014, the official unemployment rate had dropped below 6 percent of the labor force. But counting people who have given up looking for work (and are therefore not counted in official unemployment numbers) puts the actual jobless rate as more likely at double the official number (Zakaria, 2011; U.S. Department of Labor, 2014).

These tough times have pushed some cities over the brink. In 2013, unable to deal with close to $20 billion in debt, Detroit declared bankruptcy. At the depth of the recent recession, Detroit's unemployment rate had soared to close to 20 percent—about the same as what the nation faced in the Great Depression of the 1930s. Some 80,000 properties in Detroit—roughly one in five—are vacant, and half of them are falling in a dangerous state of disrepair. Some buildings are falling down; many more will have to be demolished. Whole districts of the city look like a war zone.

A combination of declining population, falling tax revenues, nonpayment of water and sewer bills, and paying the increasing cost of social services and union contracts negotiated in better times presented the city with an impossible situation. Detroit has gained some economic strength from new immigration, including a vibrant Arab American community. Resolving this crisis will take many years, and some wonder whether the "motor city" will ever regain the economic strength it had half a century ago.

More than a dozen cities across the country have joined Detroit in bankruptcy court. Many more, including urban giant like Chicago and New Orleans, are struggling to pay their bills (Sullivan, 2009; Davey, 2014; Guyette, 2014; U.S. Department of Labor, 2014).

Urban Sprawl

One important reason that inner cities have had a tough time is that the larger urban areas have continued to expand. Beginning in the 1950s, cities began to spread outward resulting in sprawling urban regions. The French geographer Jean Gottman (1961) coined the term **megalopolis** to refer to *a vast urban region containing a number of cities and their surrounding suburbs.*

Flying south from Boston along the eastern seaboard on a clear night, you can look down on an unbroken carpet of lights all the way through New England down to northern Virginia, some 700 miles away. The same supercity pattern extends from Cleveland westward to Chicago, along the entire east coast of Florida, and up and down most of the nation's West Coast.

Megalopolis is the result of people moving from central cities to suburbs, with many of them following the increasing share of jobs now found in outlying office parks. Urban expansion has also resulted from several specific government policies. One is the interstate highway system, built by the federal government after World War II. These new highways, built during a prosperous era when more families were buying automobiles, fueled booming growth in distant suburbs served by urban "outerbelts." With the government offering low-cost housing loans as well, millions of people were quick to leave central cities for the expanding suburbs.

Urban sprawl is sure to remain a matter of controversy for decades to come. Should we define a suburban development like this one as a problem, or is it a solution for people who seek affordable housing in a residential area? Explain your position.

This decentralization of the urban population has led to **urban sprawl**, *unplanned, low-density development at the edge of expanding urban areas.* Urban sprawl is a mixed pattern of new construction, including roads, homes, schools, and shopping areas.

There is no doubt that many people are eager to buy into these developments. But most analysts consider urban sprawl a serious problem. Why? One reason is visual—the numbing sameness of much of this cityscape (Kunstler, 1996). Across North America, mass-produced housing developments and strip malls have no regional distinctiveness and often provide little that is pleasing to the eye. Driving through the urban sprawl around Atlanta, for example, you will see many of the same housing styles and stores that you would see outside of Columbus, Ohio; Portland, Oregon; Denver, Colorado; or any other large city.

A more serious problem is that sprawling urban developments have low densities (relatively few residents per acre) so that they consume land at a dizzying rate. Between 1980 and 2010, the population of the New York metropolitan area increased by 15 percent, but in the same twenty years, the area's population was occupying 60 percent more land. Atlanta, among the fasting-growing cities in the United States, is about 135 square miles, more than twice its size just twenty years ago. The entire Atlanta urban region, which gobbles up 500 acres of fields and farmland every week, now includes roughly 8,500 square miles. Similarly, the city of Phoenix now covers 517 square miles and the greater Phoenix urban region now sprawls across 14,600 square miles, an area larger than the state of Maryland (U.S. Census Bureau, 2013).

Although the rate of sprawl did slow during the recent recession, over the next fifty years development is projected to claim 3.5 million acres of California's Great Central Valley, its agricultural heartland. Nationwide, the building of housing developments, malls, parking lots, golf courses, and highways is likely to continue to consume as much as 1 million acres of open land each year (Cheslow, 2006; Davis, 2009; U.S. Census Bureau, 2011).

Another problem with urban sprawl is that the only way to get around these vast urban regions is by automobile, and commuting is both slow and expensive. Most suburban households need several automobiles and the cost of cars, insurance, and gasoline claims a large share of the typical family's income. In addition, today's suburbanites spend a great deal of their time on the road. The typical worker living in the Dallas, Atlanta, Philadelphia, or Los Angeles metropolitan area spends half an hour in the car getting to work (U.S. Census Bureau, 2013). Of course, when there are accidents—or simply when the traffic becomes especially heavy—the commute time can be considerably greater. The full consequences of sprawl, then, include the high costs of commuting, loss of personal time,

stress from dealing with traffic congestion, and increased air pollution.

Finally, from a rural family's point of view, sprawl threatens this country's farmland. According to the American Farmland Trust (2014), 78 percent of the vegetables and 91 percent of our fruit produced in the United States is grown near urban areas. This puts vital farm production directly in the path of urban sprawl.

At first glance, the answer to the many problems associated with sprawl may seem to be building more and bigger highways to help people move farther and faster. But is building more roads likely to solve the sprawl problem or to make it worse? The more roads we build, the more we encourage people to rely on their cars, and the more our urban areas are likely to expand outward.

Edge Cities

The movement of businesses away from the central city has created *edge cities*, business centers miles from the old downtowns. Unlike suburbs, which are made up mostly of homes, edge cities are mostly commercial developments, including corporate office buildings, shopping malls, hotels, and entertainment complexes. In suburbs, the population peaks at night; in edge cities, the population is greatest during the working day.

Most major urban areas in the United States now contain one or more edge cities. Examples include Tyson's Corner (in Virginia, near Washington, D.C.), King of Prussia (northwest of Philadelphia), and Las Colinas (near the Dallas–Fort Worth airport). Many edge cities do not have clear boundaries, and in some cases they even lack names and are known by the major highways that flow through them. Examples include Route 1 near Princeton, New Jersey, and Route 128 near Boston (Davis, 2009; Macionis & Parrillo, 2013).

Poverty

People who move away from central cities are typically more affluent than those left behind. The high costs of suburban, automobile-based living served as a barrier keeping most of the poor in central cities and out of suburbia. As more jobs relocated to outlying areas, economic opportunities for inner-city residents decreased. This is one reason that high concentrations of poverty are now found in central cities.

In Camden, New Jersey, for example, the decades after 1950 saw downtown businesses move to the suburbs. Many people—particularly those who were younger, more educated, and better off financially—followed the flow away from the central city. Camden saw its population fall from 125,000 in 1950 to about 77,000 today. Of the households that remain in the city, more than one-third (and half the households with children) are poor (U.S. Census

SOCIAL POLICY

When Work Disappears: Can We Rescue the Inner City?

William Julius Wilson, one of the nation's most influential social scientists, points out that most of the problems of the inner city can be traced to one major factor: a lack of jobs (Wilson, 1996a, 1996b). Over recent decades, as jobs have disappeared from the inner city, few of our national political leaders have paid much attention to this trend. In 1996, when Congress enacted welfare reform intended to move poor people from welfare to work, little was said about where people were to find jobs.

In 1950, when industrial cities were at their peak populations, Wilson explains, most adults in the African American community of Washington Park in Chicago were working at jobs that provided enough income to support their families. By the 1990s, after jobs had flowed out of the central cities, two-thirds were unemployed. Wilson found this pattern in other poor, inner-city communities from New York to Los Angeles.

One elderly woman, who moved to Washington Park in 1953, explained to Wilson that when she moved in to her neighborhood, it had beautiful homes—some were even mini-mansions—and there were many stores, a hotel, and even doctors' offices. It was, she explained, a middle-class neighborhood. But, as the years went by, Washington Park became a low-income neighborhood, a place many people simply call a "ghetto."

Why did this neighborhood and others like it decline? Based on eight years of research in Washington Park, Wilson points to a stark reality: There is almost no work to be found. The loss of jobs prompted some people to leave and pushed those who remained into desperate poverty. The economic decline weakened families and forced people to turn to welfare.

In Woodlawn, another Chicago community near Washington Park, more than 800 businesses operated in 1950; when Wilson surveyed the area forty years later, he found that only 100 remained. A number of big employers, including Western Electric and International Harvester, closed their plants in the late 1960s. As big employers closed their downtown factories and stopped paying wages, smaller businesses found fewer customers and the inner cities simply collapsed.

Wilson believes we can rescue the inner cities by creating jobs. But how? As a first step, the government can hire people to do all kinds of needed work, starting with clearing slums and building low-income housing. This strategy, modeled on the Works Progress Administration (WPA) enacted in 1935 during the Great Depression, can move people from welfare to work and, in the process, create much-needed hope.

A second step is to improve city schools. Doing this will require raising the necessary financing, attracting good teachers, and expecting students to meet challenging academic standards while learning the language and computer skills needed to succeed in today's postindustrial economy.

A third step involves improved regional public transportation. Workers without cars need train and subway links to get to job sites in suburban areas.

Finally, workers need affordable child care programs. Child care must be made available to help parents meet the responsibilities of parenting while also holding down a job.

Why have these steps not been taken already? Wilson explains that many people incorrectly believe that there is plenty of work in central cities, and they conclude that poor people simply don't want a job. Another concern is that Wilson's proposals, at least in the short term, require a huge increase in government spending beyond the current costs of providing welfare assistance to jobless communities.

In the long run, however, what are the costs of letting parts of our large cities decay? Can we afford to let our children grow up in hopeless and often violent surroundings where they join the ranks of the restless and often angry people who have no work?

What Do You Think?

1. Do you support Wilson's proposals for change? Why or why not? What changes do you expect to see in cities such as Chicago and Detroit over the next decade or so?

2. If the United States is willing to spend hundreds of billions of dollars bailing out big financial companies, should the government also spend the money it takes to bail out our cities?

3. Do you think continuing immigration will expand the economies of large cities in the decades to come? Why or why not?

Bureau, 2013). The future is bleak for Camden's children, as once busy streets stand empty and thousands of houses have been boarded up or torn down.

Camden is not the only city facing such problems. Across the United States, every large city contains low-income neighborhoods. Typically, the residents of low-income communities are African Americans, Latinos, or other disadvantaged minorities. Many of these neighborhoods were once thriving industrial areas, with retail stores, professional offices, and a population as likely to be middle class as working class. Today, many inner-city communities contain only the poor, who live cut off from economic opportunity, as the Social Policy box explains.

In 2012, the poverty rate for all urban regions in the United States was 14.5 percent. The poverty rate for central cities was higher at 19.7 percent; by contrast, the poverty rate in the suburbs was lower at 11.2 percent. In recent years, suburbs have become more diverse in terms of class, race, and ethnicity. But a stark economic difference between inner-city and suburb persists (U.S. Census Bureau, 2013).

Poverty across the urban landscape is uneven. Yet urban areas fare better than rural regions. The poverty rate was even higher—17.7 percent—in rural areas of the country, which are typically places with even fewer jobs. Although cities do contain high concentrations of poverty, urban areas generally provide more economic opportunity than rural areas do (U.S. Census Bureau, 2013).

Housing Problems

In the same way that people need work, they also need a place to live. Because our society defines housing as a commodity to be bought and sold on the open market, a family's income determines its quality of housing. The economic inequality of U.S. society creates enormous disparities in housing, a fact clearly evident in the history of our nation's cities.

Tenement Housing   Most people today would be shocked by the housing problems in the early industrial metropolis. In the final decades of the nineteenth century, developers built tenements to house the greatest number of families in the smallest amount of space. Not only were tenement apartments very small, but most had few windows and little ventilation as well. As many as six families shared a single bathroom. Insulation was poor, and rooms could be stifling in the summer and cold in the winter.

Because most of the 1 million immigrants entering the United States each year were poor, the public accepted the tenements as a necessary evil. But some people had the courage to speak out against the horror. The leading opponent of tenement housing a century ago was Jacob Riis, who managed single-handedly to sway public opinion and define poor housing as a serious social problem. The Defining Moment box tells his story.

While millions of people lived out their lives in tenements, the elite few who owned the industries and controlled the financial life of our nation lived in splendid luxury. These families, with names most people still recognize today—including Vanderbilt (railroads), Morgan (finance), and Rockefeller (oil) in New York, Ford (automobiles) in Detroit, and Armour and Swift (meatpacking) in Chicago—lived in spacious mansions staffed by dozens of servants.

This pattern of mansions for the few and miserable housing for the many continued for decades despite increasing public opposition to tenements. Not until

the 1930s did housing quality begin to improve. As part of President Franklin Roosevelt's New Deal, the federal government raised taxes to fund the construction of new housing and began to provide loans to help people buy homes. In addition, cities across the United States enacted housing codes with the goal of eliminating the worst conditions of the tenements. Despite these efforts, a 1940 government report found that 40 percent of houses in urban areas had some serious defect, such as inadequate heating or a lack of running water.

Urban Renewal   After World War II, as people migrated from central cities out to the new suburbs, many downtown neighborhoods fell into disrepair. The federal government responded by passing the Urban Housing Act of 1949, which began a policy called *urban renewal*. Urban renewal gave local city governments the right to seize a decaying neighborhood, forcing out the families who lived there paying only nominal compensation for their homes. The city then sold the properties to a developer, who tore down existing housing and rebuilt the area. Because developers were interested in profits, they built not low-income housing but commercial properties, including town houses and apartments for people with more money. Rarely was the housing produced by urban renewal within reach of the residents who had lived there before.

As this policy went into effect in cities across the United States, many so-called slum areas were rebuilt to "middle-class standards" to attract higher-income people back to the city. But urban renewal failed to provide housing for those who needed it the most. Critics saw urban renewal as little more than a form of "urban cleansing," pushing out poor people without providing housing alternatives. Many of the poor who were evicted by urban renewal crowded into whatever low-cost housing remained, creating worse slums in the process (Macionis & Parrillo, 2013).

Public Housing   With urban renewal clearing away block after block, city officials gradually owned up to the fact that many of the poor people displaced from their homes had nowhere to go. The need to house these people led to the creation of **public housing**, *high—density apartment buildings constructed to house poor people.*

From the outset, public housing was met with criticism from just about everybody. Liberals viewed it as a Band-Aid approach to the problem of cities with little affordable housing. In addition, they claimed, much public housing was actually worse than the neighborhoods that had been knocked down by the bulldozers during urban renewal.

For their part, conservatives objected to government getting into the housing business in the first place. They

CONSTRUCTING SOCIAL PROBLEMS
A DEFINING MOMENT

Jacob Riis: Revealing the Misery of the Tenements

In 1870, a young man of twenty-one climbed aboard a small ship, leaving his native Denmark for a journey to the United States, where he hoped to find a better life. Jacob Riis (1849–1914) shared the dreams of millions of other men and women. After weeks at sea, he arrived in New York harbor and soon settled in the Richmond Hill district, a neighborhood almost entirely populated by immigrants living in tenements.

Riis had a remarkable career as one of the earliest photojournalists. He spent a typical evening walking around the poorest neighborhoods of New York collecting stories, which became the basis for his writing, and taking photographs of urban life. He hoped that his essays—and especially his photos—would call public attention to the suffering of families in New York's tenements and other slum housing. They did just that. To more affluent people who never ventured into these areas, the photographs were eye-opening, sobering, even shocking.

Riis gave hundreds of public lectures and wrote many books featuring thousands of photographs, many of which are still widely viewed today. His lifetime of effort made a difference in defining tenement housing as a serious problem of urban life.

claimed that government-run housing would be no better than government-run schools.

But perhaps the most vocal critics of public housing were poor people themselves. Given how important owning a home is to our society's definition of success, few people—then or now—were likely to be proud of living in a government-owned apartment. On the contrary, many complained that living in "the projects" became a stigma. In addition, public housing was typically *bad* housing. Public housing projects in almost every major city were cheaply built, and they quickly became run-down. To make matters worse, many projects were plagued with illegal drug use, crime, and violence.

The Social Importance of Architecture A final concern, especially shared by architects and city planners, was the physical design of public housing. At the outset, because city officials wanted to house as many poor people in as little space as possible, they favored building high-rise towers. A pattern common to high-rise structures, however,

High-rise "superblocks" can be hazardous to your health. This claim became widespread by the 1970s, leading many cities to dynamite huge public housing projects. This demolition took place in 2001 in New Brunswick, New Jersey. What were some of the reasons cities took such drastic action?

was rampant crime. Was there something about this type of architectural design that encouraged lawbreaking?

In 1972, research by Oscar Newman provided an answer. In a study of New York public housing projects, Newman compared buildings that housed the same types of residents but used different architectural designs. Newman discovered that crime rates in high-rise buildings (those with more than six stories) were much greater than in low-rise buildings (with six or fewer stories). In general, he concluded, the taller the building, the higher the crime rate. Newman also discovered that most crimes took place not in people's apartments but in public spaces of the buildings, including parking lots, lobby entrances, hallways, stairways, and elevators.

What accounted for the difference in crime rates? High-rise buildings have higher crime rates, Newman explained, because they breed anonymity. Placed far above the ground, residents are likely to feel detached from their surroundings. Lower buildings, by contrast, encourage a greater sense of community and allow people to know their neighbors and, most important, to keep an eye on public spaces, informally "defending" their community.

In light of such findings, and the generally dismal quality of life in early public housing projects, public housing was soon transformed from a "solution" to a "social problem." The consequences of this new thinking were sometimes explosive. In 1972, the city of Saint Louis dynamited several high-rise towers of the Pruitt-Igoe

public housing complex, a stark indication that this type of public housing was simply not healthy for people. Decades later, the city of Chicago began tearing down Cabrini-Green, another tall project with lots of crime.

In many cities, "projects" still exist. But more recently social policy has shifted from building large-scale housing developments to providing financial assistance to families to rent apartments in the private housing market. Established in 1974, the Section 8 program directs federal government subsidies to developers who rehabilitate existing rental housing or build new apartments. In exchange for this subsidy, developers agree to allocate a share of the housing to low-income families. When low-income families move in, they pay 30 to 40 percent of their adjusted gross income for rent, with the government making up the difference. The advantages of this program include giving low-income families some choice about where to live and avoiding the past practice of creating housing in which all the residents are poor.

The Section 8 program did increase the availability of low-income housing. But funding has not been sufficient to meet the demand. A number of large cities in the United States have had tens of thousands of people on the waiting list for Section 8 vouchers, indicating that much more needs to be done (Thigpen, 2002; U.S. Department of Housing and Urban Development, 2012).

Racial Segregation

In cities across the United States, the poor—especially poor people of color—are isolated from the mainstream of society. In a classic study, Douglas Massey and Nancy Denton (1988, 1989) examined large cities across the United States and documented the existence of what they called *hypersegregation:* Entire districts of cities (commonly called "ghettos") contain only poor African Americans, and these people are cut off from the larger society in several ways. Data from the Census Bureau (2013) indicate that racial hypersegregation has declined only slightly in the decades since then.

Hypersegregation means that poor minority urbanites are isolated not only *spatially* (highly concentrated in certain neighborhoods typically in the inner-city) but also *socially* because they live almost entirely in these neighborhoods, rarely venturing out into the larger urban area. In the same way, richer people in other parts of the urban area rarely enter minority neighborhoods.

How common is hypersegregation? Massey and Denton estimated that about one in five African Americans lives cut off from the larger society. By contrast, holding income levels the same, hypersegregation characterizes a smaller share of Hispanic people and a very small share of Asian Americans (Jagarowsky & Bane, 1990; U.S. Census Bureau, 2013).

The fact that a large share of the African American population but few people of other categories experience hypersegregation shows that racial inequality is a key element in the problems of U.S. cities. Our cities remain racially divided; in fact, the urban decentralization of the past fifty or sixty years largely resulted from a desire by whites to distance themselves from people of color. The trend continues: The white share of the population of the 100 largest U.S. cities fell from 52 percent in 1990 to 40 percent in 2012 (U.S. Census Bureau, 2013). The pattern of largely white suburbs and largely African American inner cities persists throughout the United States.

Homelessness

A century ago, every large city in the United States had tens of thousands of homeless people. In fact, adults and children living under bridges, in alleyways, and on the streets were so much a part of the urban landscape that many people at that time considered homelessness a normal part of city life rather than a serious social problem.

Although the number of homeless people is now lower than it was a century ago, we expect everyone to have a safe and secure place to live. Therefore, homelessness is now widely viewed as a social problem in the United States. One might also say that homelessness is a greater tragedy today because our nation is now far richer than it was back then.

There is no precise count of the homeless population. In 2013, the Department of Housing and Urban Development (HUD) surveyed cities and towns across the country to estimate the number of people who were homeless for some period of time during that year. Surveys counted about 610,000 people, including people living on the streets, in shelters, and in transitional housing. Based on that finding, they estimate that as many as 1.5 million people may be homeless for some period of time over the course of a year; activist organizations suggest that the number may be higher (Ohlemacher, 2007; U.S. Department of Housing and Urban Development, 2013).

Homelessness is primarily an urban problem. At the same time, as the entire urban region becomes more socially diverse, officials have noted a steady increase in the number of people living in suburbs

requesting assistance in obtaining shelter. In a study by the U.S. Department of Housing and Urban Development (2013), researchers interviewed people in more than 400 communities across the United States—most of them homeless at the time—and reported that 70 percent reside in central cities, and 30 percent live in suburbs or in nearby rural areas.

This HUD study documented that homeless people are the poorest of the poor. In the survey, 30 percent of homeless people reported having no source of income and an additional 40 percent reported income of less than $1,000 per month. Another 25 percent reported monthly income between $1,000 and $2,000. Just 5 percent reported monthly income greater than $2,000. With so little income, it is easy to understand why people cannot afford housing.

Research also shows that most homeless people do not work, although about 20 percent report having at least a part-time job. Some people—typically conservatives—point to this lack of work and say that homeless people are themselves responsible for their situation. In addition, one-third of homeless people are substance abusers, and one-fourth are mentally ill (U.S. Department of Housing and Urban Development, 2011; U.S. Conference of Mayors, 2013).

Other people—typically liberals—see homelessness as caused mostly by our society. From this point of view, the main causes of homelessness are low wages, too few jobs, and a lack of affordable housing (Kozol, 1988; L. Kaufman, 2004).

However we define the problem, it is clear that the homeless need more income. But more than that, many homeless people also need social support and help with

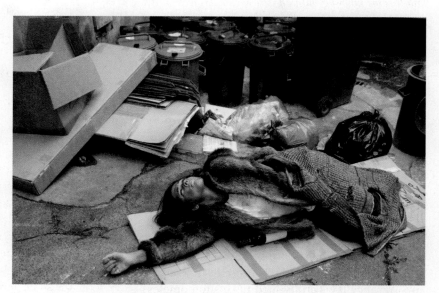

Everyone agrees that homeless people are poor. We also know that a substantial share of homeless people suffer from mental illness, just as many abuse alcohol or other drugs. But are these behaviors the cause of homelessness (as conservatives sometimes claim) or are they the consequences of homelessness (as liberals typically claim)?

Table 14–1 The Ten Largest Cities in the United States, 1950 and 2012

	1950			2012	
Rank	City	Population	Rank	City	Population
1	New York	7,892,000	1	New York	8,336,697
2	Chicago	3,621,000	2	Los Angeles	3,857,786
3	Philadelphia	2,072,000	3	Chicago	2,714,844
4	Los Angeles	1,970,000	4	Houston	2,161,686
5	Detroit	1,850,000	5	Philadelphia	1,547,607
6	Baltimore	950,000	6	Phoenix	1,488,759
7	Cleveland	915,000	7	San Antonio	1,383,194
8	Saint Louis	857,000	8	San Diego	1,338,354
9	Boston	801,000	9	Dallas	1,241,108
10	San Francisco	775,000	10	San Jose	982,783

NOTE: Cities shaded in blue are located in the Snowbelt; those shaded in yellow are in the Sunbelt.
SOURCE: U.S. Census Bureau (2014).

personal issues. Some of these problems—including depression and substance abuse—are themselves the result of living on the streets. But in other cases, the problems began in childhood as the result of a physical or mental disability or physical or sexual abuse.

The homeless, then, face many challenges. Yet research also provides grounds for hope. After receiving physical and mental health care services and substance abuse treatment, 75 percent of homeless people living in families and 60 percent of homeless individuals living alone are able to move to what government officials call "an improved living situation."

In some cases, the key to a more secure life is **supportive housing**, *a program that combines low-income housing with on–site social services.* With the help of such programs, most people with substance abuse problems, mental disabilities, or simply those bearing the scars of living poor and alone on the streets find they can hold a job and live independently.

Keep in mind that these programs, although costly, may actually end up saving money. Supporting one person with affordable housing and social services might cost $15,000 a year; yet, the bill for supporting a prison inmate is about three times greater.

Are we willing to help? Our society's policy for dealing with the homeless has not always been guided by a desire to assist. Especially in the 1990s, public opinion was critical of the homeless. Dozens of cities across the United States enacted antivagrancy laws and issued tickets to homeless people for sleeping in doorways, asking for money in public, or carrying open containers of alcohol. Many cities also conducted nightly "police sweeps" to get homeless people off the streets. In the tough economic times our society has faced during the past few years, it seems likely that attitudes toward the homeless—which include thousands of people who have lost their homes through foreclosure—have softened.

Snowbelt and Sunbelt Cities

Across the United States, the population has been moving from central cities to the larger urban regions. But the consequences of this migration for cities have been different in two regions of the country.

Take a look at the changing list of the ten largest cities in the United States, shown in Table 14–1. In 1950, eight of the top ten cities were in the Northeast and Midwest, a region often called the Snowbelt. By 2012, however, seven of ten were in the South and West, which is often called the Sunbelt (U.S. Census Bureau, 2013).

Snowbelt cities have lost population in the postindustrial era as people and businesses have decentralized across the city limits to suburbs. Not so in the Sunbelt, where cities are rapidly gaining population. In part, this is because our national population is shifting south and west. In 1940, the Snowbelt was home to 60 percent of the U.S. population; today, it is the Sunbelt that holds more than 60 percent of the people. National Map 14–2 shows recent population shifts that have occurred in the United States between 2000 and 2010.

Table 14–2 The Ten Largest Urban Areas in the World, 2011 and 2025

	2011			2025 (Projected)	
Rank	Urban Area	Population (in millions)	Rank	Urban Area	Population (in millions)
1	Tokyo-Yokohama, Japan	38.2	1	Tokyo-Yokohama, Japan	38.7
2	Delhi, India	25.6	2	Delhi, India	32.9
3	Shanghai, China	23.0	3	Shanghai, China	28.4
4	Mexico City, Mexico	21.7	4	Mumbai (Bombay), India	26.6
5	New York-Newark	21.3	5	Mexico City, Mexico	24.6
6	Mumbai (Bombay), India	21.2	6	New York-Newark	23.6
7	São Paulo, Brazil	21.0	7	São Paulo, Brazil	23.2
8	Beijing, China	18.1	8	Dhaka, Bangladesh	22.9
9	Dhaka, Bangladesh	17.4	9	Beijing, China	22.6
10	Karachi, Pakistan	15.5	10	Karachi, Pakistan	20.2

SOURCE: United Nations (2012).

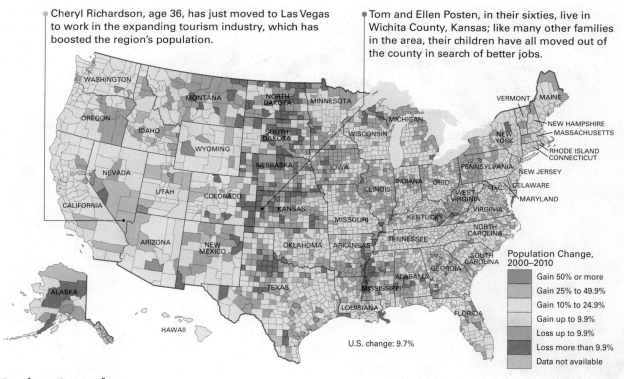

Cheryl Richardson, age 36, has just moved to Las Vegas to work in the expanding tourism industry, which has boosted the region's population.

Tom and Ellen Posten, in their sixties, live in Wichita County, Kansas; like many other families in the area, their children have all moved out of the county in search of better jobs.

Population Change, 2000–2010

- Gain 50% or more
- Gain 25% to 49.9%
- Gain 10% to 24.9%
- Gain up to 9.9%
- Loss up to 9.9%
- Loss more than 9.9%
- Data not available

U.S. change: 9.7%

Seeing Ourselves

National Map 14–2 Population Change across the United States, 2000–2010

The map shows areas of the country where population density went up or down between 2000 and 2010. What is the general pattern to this change? What problems does rapid population increase bring to a county? What about rapid population loss?

SOURCE: U.S. Census Bureau (2011).

Why hasn't decentralization hurt Sunbelt cities? The answer is a difference in their political geography. A century ago, Snowbelt cities were locked within a ring of politically independent suburbs. As the urban area decentralized, the cities lost population. But newer Sunbelt cities don't have this ring of independent suburbs; as population has grown, they have simply sprawled outward, annexing land as they expand. For this reason, Sunbelt cities are much larger physically than the older, industrial metropolises. Jacksonville, Florida, for example, now covers 758 square miles, more than three times the size of Columbus, Ohio, even though both cities have about 800,000 people. Sunbelt cities have expanded their city limits to maintain their tax base as people and jobs move outward.

Cities in Poor Countries

As we have seen in earlier chapters, many of the social problems found in the United States are far worse in the world's poor nations. The same is true of urban problems such as poverty, inadequate housing, and poor sanitation. The Social Problems in Global Perspective box on page 425 offers a look at the striking poverty in one of the world's major cities, Manila, capital of the Philippines.

Global Map 14–1 on page 424 shows the level of urbanization for all regions of the world. About 80 percent of the populations of rich nations live in and around cities. In the poorest countries, by contrast, fewer than 30 percent of people are urbanites. But everywhere in the world, the number of city dwellers is increasing. By 2011, for the first time in history, a majority of the world's people—3.6 billion out of a total of 7 billion—were living in urban places (United Nations, 2012; World Bank, 2014).

As explained in Chapter 15 ("Population and Global Inequality"), world population was 7.2 billion in 2013 and is increasing by about 87 million people each year. The urban population of the world is increasing about twice as fast. This is because, in Latin America, Africa, and Asia, people are migrating from rural areas to cities in search of economic opportunity, more schooling, and a better quality of life. As Table 14–2 on page 422 shows, eight of the ten largest cities in the world are now in economically developing nations. Only one of these large cities—New York—is in the United States. By 2025, according to current projections, most of the world's ten largest urban areas will reach unprecedented population size.

Mumbai (Bombay), Shanghai, Mexico City, and others on the list are becoming true megacities. Even a rich

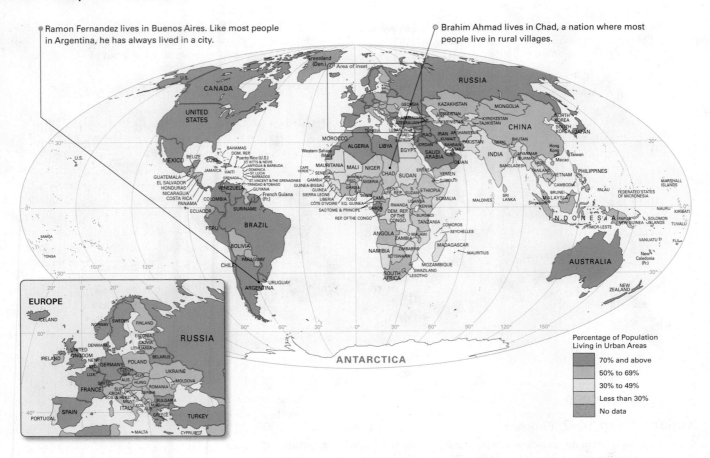

Ramon Fernandez lives in Buenos Aires. Like most people in Argentina, he has always lived in a city.

Brahim Ahmad lives in Chad, a nation where most people live in rural villages.

Percentage of Population Living in Urban Areas

- 70% and above
- 50% to 69%
- 30% to 49%
- Less than 30%
- No data

Window on the World

Global Map 14–1   Urbanization in Global Perspective

More than half of the world's people now live in cities. A nation's share of city dwellers depends on its level of economic development. In high-income nations such as the United States and Canada, more than three-fourths of the people live in urban places. By contrast, in low-income nations in Africa and Asia, only one-third of the population lives in cities. Even so, the largest cities in low-income countries are growing very rapidly.

SOURCE: Population Reference Bureau (2013).

nation such as the United States faces serious challenges in meeting the housing, transportation, and sanitation needs of the 21 million people in the sprawling New York urban region. How, then, will nations where incomes are much lower—such as Bangladesh and Mexico—be able to support their soaring urban populations?

Throughout history, cities have offered the promise of a better life. But cities provide no sure solution to social problems. The evidence to support this conclusion is found in the ever-present shantytowns, settlements where people have built makeshift homes from whatever materials they can find and where most people do not have clean water and sewerage. A pressing question is whether cities that so far have failed to meet the needs of so many millions of people will be able to meet the needs of many millions more.

Theories of Urbanization and Urban Problems

14.3 Apply sociological theory to urbanization and urban problems.

We now apply sociology's major theoretical approaches to the problems of cities. Each of these theoretical orientations provides insights into how urbanization shapes people's lives.

Structural-Functional Analysis: A Theory of Urbanism

The main contribution of structural-functional theory to our understanding of cities is the theory of urbanism. The theory emerged in the writings of two European

SOCIAL PROBLEMS IN GLOBAL PERSPECTIVE
World-Class Poverty: A Visit to Manila's Smokey Mountain

What caught my eye was how clean she was—a girl no more than seven or eight years old, hair carefully combed and wearing a freshly laundered dress. Her eyes followed us as we walked past; camera-toting Americans stand out here, in one of the poorest neighborhoods in the entire world.

Fed by methane from the decomposing garbage, the fires never go out on Smokey Mountain, Manila's vast garbage dump. The smoke envelops the hills of refuse like a thick fog. But Smokey Mountain is more than a dump. It is a neighborhood, a place that thousands of people call home.

The residents of Smokey Mountain are the poorest of the poor, and one is hard-pressed to imagine a setting more hostile to human life. Surrounded by smoke and squalor, men and women do what they can to survive, picking plastic bags from the city's garbage and washing them in the river, salvaging cardboard boxes that pile up alongside a family's plywood shack.

All over Smokey Mountain are children—kids who must already sense the enormous odds against them. The girls and boys we see are the lucky ones, of course. But what chance do they have, living in families that earn a dollar or two a day? With barely any opportunity for schooling? Year after year, breathing this air? Against this backdrop of human tragedy, one lovely little girl has put on a fresh dress and gone out to play. . . .

With Smokey Mountain behind us, our taxi driver threads his way through heavy traffic as we head for the other side of Manila. The contrast is amazing: The forbidding smoke and smells of the dump give way to polished neighborhoods one might find in Miami or Los Angeles. On the bay in the distance, a cluster of yachts floats silently at anchor. No more rutted streets; now we glide quietly along wide boulevards lined with trees and filled with expensive Japanese cars. On each side, we pass shopping plazas, upscale hotels, and high-rise office buildings. Every block or so stands the entrance to an exclusive residential enclave set off by gates and protected by armed guards. Here, in large, air-conditioned homes, the rich of Manila live—and many of the poor work.

What Do You Think?

1. To what extent does living in a place like Smokey Mountain differ from "living in poverty" in the United States? Explain.

2. How would you feel as a traveler from the United States witnessing such intense poverty? Why?

3. Using Google or another search engine, find images of Smokey Mountain, Manila. What do you think can be done to address such poverty?

SOURCE: The author's personal visit to Manila (October 1994).

---

sociologists, Ferdinand Tönnies and Emile Durkheim, and Louis Wirth of the United States.

Ferdinand Tönnies: *Gemeinschaft* and *Gesellschaft*

Tönnies (1855–1937) lived during the Industrial Revolution, and he tried to explain how social life changed as rural living gave way to life in the industrial metropolis. He built his answer around the contrasting concepts of *Gemeinschaft* and *Gesellschaft*.

Gemeinschaft is a German word (roughly translated as "community") meaning *a type of social organization in which people are closely bound by kinship and tradition*. Living in small rural villages, people have a strong sense of community based on kinship and shared traditions. At its best, explained Tönnies, rural living is guided by a concern for the needs of all rather than people pursuing their self-interest.

In the industrial city, however, traditional community is lost and life approximates *Gesellschaft* (roughly translated as "association"), *a type of social organization in which people interact on the basis of self-interest*. In the city, Tönnies explained, a person typically pays only passing attention to the welfare of the community. Typically, a person mostly "looks out for number one."

Emile Durkheim: Mechanical and Organic Solidarity

The French sociologist Emile Durkheim (1858–1917) agreed with Tönnies that the rise of cities brought changes to the organization of society. Durkheim characterized rural social ties as **mechanical solidarity**, *social bonds based on common sentiments and shared moral values*. Durkheim's concept of mechanical solidarity is similar to Tönnies's concept of *Gemeinschaft*.

Durkheim agreed that the rise of industrial cities weakened mechanical solidarity. But urban life also creates new connections between people. **Organic solidarity** consists of *social bonds based on specialization and mutual interdependence*. In the city, people work at different types of jobs and have less in common in terms of background and interests. At the same time, increasing economic specialization makes urban people need each other. As city dwellers, we look to others to meet just about all our everyday needs, from driving the bus to policing the

A common theme in the writings of Tönnies, Durkheim, and Simmel is the impersonality of cities. Urban living, it seems, makes people indifferent to those around them. Do you agree with this assessment? What evidence can you point to in support of your position?

streets to teaching our children in school. In short, rural society is held together by *likeness*, and urban society is held together by *difference*.

Durkheim's view of urban life is more positive than that of Tönnies. Although something may be lost in the process of urbanization, Durkheim concluded, urban people benefit from more individual choice, moral tolerance, and personal privacy than people who live in rural areas.

Louis Wirth: Urbanism as a Way of Life   From the ideas of Tönnies and Durkheim, the U.S. sociologist Louis Wirth (1897–1952) developed a formal theory of urban life. Wirth (1938) began by defining the city as a settlement with a large, dense, socially diverse population. These traits, he continued, make social ties within the city fleeting and impersonal. Because urbanites are surrounded by millions of other people, they never get to know most of the people they pass by every day.

When urbanites do think others, it is usually not in terms of *who they are* in any personal sense but simply in terms of *what they do*. In other words, urbanites recognize but know little about the bus driver, the school principal, the police officer on the beat, or the clerk in the grocery store on the corner. This limited knowledge of others, coupled to the social diversity of the city, makes urbanites more tolerant than rural villagers.

The major structural-functional argument about cities is that they generate urbanism, a distinctive form of social life. We can understand the popular conception of the city as a cold and heartless place and appreciate why at least many city dwellers seem to lack a sense of community. From this point of view, one reason that social problems are pronounced in urban areas is that cities encourage people to take an "I just don't care" attitude about their social surroundings.

But is Wirth's urbanism thesis correct? Herbert Gans (1968) argues that cities contain neighborhoods that differ much more than Wirth's theory suggests. Gans agrees that some people do have the detached, cosmopolitan attitude that Wirth describes. But what about "ethnic villagers" who live in traditional neighborhoods where almost everyone else is like them? The Italian and Polish communities that existed on New York's Lower East Side early in the twentieth century, as well as Korean and Vietnamese neighborhoods in Philadelphia and Los Angeles today, have many of the personal ties and long-standing traditions we link to rural living. Gans's research reminds us that class, race, ethnicity, and age create an urban mix far more complex than any single profile of "urbanites" will allow.

Claude Fischer (1975) points out that cities also encourage the formation of new social groups because large populations allow a critical mass of individuals of almost every type. Although every small town has some gay men and lesbians, for example, only large cities such as New York and San Francisco have gay *communities*, with thousands of residents and a distinctive subculture supported by gay newspapers, gay bars, and gay theater.

CHECK YOUR LEARNING   Explain Wirth's theory of urbanism. What is one criticism of this theory?

Symbolic-Interaction Analysis: Experiencing the City

On a micro-level, the reality of city living is a matter of personal experiences. How do people socially construct reality in the city?

Georg Simmel: Urban Stimulation and Selectivity   The German sociologist Georg Simmel (1858–1918) explained that people living in cities experience intense stimulation. The sights, sounds, and smells of city life—not to mention the vast number of people—all combine to overwhelm the senses. In other words, so much takes place around individuals in the city that they couldn't respond to most of it even if they wanted to. The result, claimed Simmel, is that urbanites develop a *blasé attitude* and they "tune out" much of what is around them.

Simmel explained that, experiencing urban overstimulation, people develop a blasé attitude as a strategy for survival. It does not mean that people lack concern for others. On the contrary, by responding selectively to only certain people and situations, urbanites focus their time and energy on what really matters.

Leo Srole: Mental Health in the Metropolis

If people have to tune out most of what goes on around them to survive in the city, are cities an unhealthy environment? Over the years, a number of researchers have tried to answer this question, and their general conclusion is that cities pose no harm to people's mental health.

In one of the largest studies, Leo Srole (1972) monitored the mental health of New Yorkers in the 1950s and again in the early 1970s. Srole found that overall, the mental health of people (especially women) living in New York was actually a little better than among people living in rural areas.

Later research has confirmed these results (Fischer, 1973; Hackler, 1979; Weisner, 1981; Kadushin, 1983). City living may involve more stimulation, but this does not contribute to problems of mental illness. On the contrary, many people thrive in an environment where they have access to many other people and activities and lots of choice about how to live.

The Industrial Revolution created great cities across the United States. In recent decades, however, the movement of industry abroad resulted in job losses and declining populations in Detroit and other older cities in the "Rustbelt." Yet today's high levels of immigration are bringing new life to many cities as a new generation of people join the urban mix. In the Detroit metropolitan area, much of a recent gain in population is due to surging Arab immigration.

EVALUATE

On a micro-level, we find that cities do differ from rural areas in the level of stimulation that people commonly experience. Yet contrary to the impression we get from Simmel's theory (and also that of Tönnies), cities turn out to be relatively healthful places.

But this upbeat conclusion has a major limitation: Some urbanites live far better than others. Any general conclusions about the quality of life in the city must take into account social inequality, which brings us to the social-conflict approach.

CHECK YOUR LEARNING How did Georg Simmel describe the experience of urban living? Is there evidence that city life is harmful to people's mental health?

Social-Conflict Analysis: Cities and Inequality

As in earlier chapters, social-conflict theory focuses on social inequality. In this case, the issue is how social stratification in the United States shapes the city and urban life.

Urban Political Economy The application of social-conflict theory to cities—urban political economy—differs from the approaches of Tönnies and Wirth, who treated the city as defined simply by its size, density, and social diversity. Rather than treating the city as self-defining, this approach asks how the economic and political structures of the larger society shape the city and give rise to its problems.

Following the lead of Karl Marx, this approach asserts that social class plays an important part in defining urbanism. Consider, in any city, how much the lives of the rich differ from those of working-class people and, even more, from those of the poor and the homeless. On another level, this approach seeks to explain how the physical development of the city reflects the private property and profit seeking central to a capitalist economy.

David Harvey: A Study of Baltimore David Harvey's study of Baltimore shows that the growth and decline of an urban area have much to do with the process of capital investment. Harvey (1973) found that banks had little interest in lending money to people living in inner-city Baltimore for housing or any other reason. As a result, poor people had to finance whatever housing they could afford through their own savings or through government programs. Under such conditions, this section of the city remained poor and run-down.

By contrast, banks were eager to lend money to people living in the affluent sections of Baltimore. Middle-class and upper-middle-class people had little trouble obtaining home mortgages, which banks viewed as good investments.

Harvey reports that even government programs end up serving the interests of investors. In Baltimore and elsewhere, urban renewal turned out to be a slum clearance program that forced out the poor, who often ended up in projects that were worse than the housing they had lived in before. The city turned over their old neighborhoods to profit-seeking developers who built housing and shopping centers that

APPLYING THEORY

Urban Life

	Structural-Functional Theory	Symbolic-Interaction Theory	Social-Conflict Theory
What is the level of analysis?	Macro-level	Micro-level	Macro-level
How do we understand urban life?	Using structural-functional analysis, Tönnies, Durkheim, and Wirth developed a theory of urbanism that contrasted social life in urban and rural places. Wirth explained that a large, dense, and socially diverse population generated a distinctive way of life marked by impersonal relationships and tolerance.	Symbolic-interaction theory focuses on the way we experience urban life. Simmel explained that urban life exposes us to intense stimulation, causing urbanites to develop a blasé attitude. Urbanites effectively tune out much of what goes on around them. Srole and others, however, found that urban living does not harm people's mental health.	Social-conflict theory claims that cities are not defined by their large, dense, and diverse populations but are actually shaped by the larger political economy. Marx pointed to capitalism and the economic inequality it creates as defining modern, urban life. Harvey explained how the search for profit guides government and banks to the benefit of the rich and the disadvantage of the poor.
Is urban life a problem?	As Tönnies saw it, urban life was something of a problem because *Gesellschaft* was based on self-interest and lacked the broader social bonds of *Gemeinschaft*. Durkheim was more optimistic, noting that cities give people more privacy and personal choice.	The common view of the city dweller as cold and heartless is based on a bit of truth, as urban people are selective about what they respond to. At the same time, however, nothing in the nature of modern cities inevitably causes problems for people in everyday life.	Social-conflict theory supports a radical view that urban problems are caused by the larger political economy. Solving problems like economic inequality requires changes to the capitalist economic system.

would attract people with more money. In short, patterns of investment—who makes money available to whom—go a long way toward explaining the differing fortunes of people across the urban area.

EVALUATE

The older structural-functional theories point to population size and density as defining urban life. The newer political-economy theory points to capitalism and its drive for profit as the defining factor. The power of money is at work not only in the rise and fall of neighborhoods in the central city but also in the decentralization of population as investment shifts from industrial production to newer information companies.

The economic system may well shape our cities. At the same time, as Wirth and others have argued, rural social life and urban social life do differ. Another criticism of this approach is that the effects of capital investment on urban life are not always clear. Too little investment may cause a community to decline, but too much investment can result in overbuilt areas and urban sprawl.

CHECK YOUR LEARNING   What do we learn by applying social-conflict theory to cities and urban life? What is one criticism of this approach?

The Applying Theory table summarizes what we learn from each theoretical approach to urban life. Then, in the final sections of this chapter, we examine how politics guides the ways in which people construct urban problems and define solutions.

⭐ POLITICS AND URBAN LIFE

Constructing Problems and Defining Solutions

14.4   Analyze urban issues from various positions on the political spectrum.

To hear some people tell it, our large cities are enjoying a rebirth; others see our cities in crisis. To better understand how people define urban problems—and what they see as solutions—we must look at today's urban issues from different political viewpoints.

Conservatives: The Market and Morality

In assessing the state of our cities, conservatives would have us consider where we have been and how far we have come. A century ago, when Jacob Riis walked the streets and alleyways of New York's Lower East Side, one-third of New Yorkers lived in desperate circumstances, with many families crowded together in dark tenement rooms. Sanitation was minimal. Two of every ten children born in the tenements did not survive for even a single year. Such a level of infant mortality is nearly three times higher than the rate today across sub-Saharan Africa, the poorest region of the world (Population Reference Bureau, 2013).

Today's urbanites live far longer, and most take for granted safe housing, dependable plumbing, electricity to operate lights and appliances, and good medical care. What has brought about this improvement? Conservatives would credit economic expansion. As the United States became an industrial society, the economy generated ever more products and services, so that cities grew and living standards rose for everyone.

More recently, the ups and downs in cities have also reflected economic trends. The rise of a service economy helped push population outward from the old central cities to the expanding suburbs. These same trends caused economic decline in the central cities, especially those located in the nation's Snowbelt. Today, in fact, this region of the country is sometimes called the Rustbelt because of all the obsolete factories that now stand empty and rusting.

Conservatives accept the operation of the market economy, and they view the decline of the inner cities as unfortunate but not permanent. As noted earlier, the expansion of the postindustrial economy has already transformed many old industrial areas into business centers or arts and entertainment districts. Examples of this inner-city comeback can be found in the lakefront of Cleveland, the Baltimore harbor area, and the riverfront of New Orleans. In time, even a city like Detroit, which is still reeling from the loss of industrial production, will be remade.

If economic forces shape cities, what can government do? Conservatives have supported the creation of **enterprise zones**, *areas in the inner city that attract new businesses with the promise of tax relief.* Under such programs, government reduces or eliminates taxes on businesses that relocate to an economically depressed area where jobs are needed. This incentive should attract business to areas of the cities where a large share of people do not have work (Kemp, 1994).

Beyond such limited policies, however, conservatives oppose the growth of government social welfare programs, which expanded in the 1960s. Consider, for example, this account by Senator Daniel P. Moynihan of New York City in 1943, the year he graduated from one of the city's high schools:

> By 1943, [the number of New Yorkers on welfare] was down to 73,000 persons.... In 1943, there were exactly forty-four homicides by gunshot in all of the City of New York.... In 1943, the illegitimacy rate was 3 percent. Last year, it was 45 percent. Ours was a much poorer city fifty years ago, but a much more stable one. (1993:119–20)

Fifty years later, when Moynihan wrote his account, New York's population had actually declined, but many urban problems had become much worse. Almost 1 million people (one in seven New Yorkers) were on welfare, and the number of murders had risen to almost 2,000 a year. By 2012, the number of households receiving food stamps was 647,000, the number of murders was 419, and 36 percent of babies were born to unwed mothers.

As conservatives see it, the expansion of the welfare state caused the long-term rise in public assistance and, indirectly, the gradual increase in crime and violence. Everyone agrees that the intention behind expanding government social programs was to help people. But as Charles Krauthammer (1995:15) puts it, "The growth in the size and power of the welfare state is the primary cause of the decline of society's...institutions—voluntary associations, local government, church, and, above all, the family." Conservatives link problems such as street violence and poverty to family breakdown; they blame the weakness of today's families on decades of welfare policies that gave money to people who could work but chose not to find a job and policies that provided child support for mothers as long as they did not have a husband.

Conservatives also direct criticism to the rest of the population as well. The recent economic downturn is in large measure "payback" for years of too much greed on Wall Street and in the nation's corporate boardrooms, as well as too much spending and too little saving among households at all income levels.

In short, a conservative approach claims that the strength of a city—and of an entire society—lies partly in

A generation ago, this downtown area of Cleveland was little more than abandoned factories—a place to avoid. Today, it is a thriving entertainment district, home to the Rock and Roll Hall of Fame. Conservatives claim that market forces are the key to reviving inner cities; liberals look to government intervention; radicals claim that capitalism can never save our cities. Which view do you find most convincing? Why?

its economic prosperity but mostly in the moral character of its people. From a conservative point of view, most economic indicators have gone up, but many moral indicators are way down (D. G. Myers, 2000; Andersen, 2009).

Liberals: Government Reform

From a liberal point of view, U.S. cities are beset with a number of serious social problems. As explained in Chapter 2 ("Poverty and Wealth"), economic inequality in the United States is increasing. People within the "1 percent" are becoming richer while the rest of us in the "99 percent" experience a lack of economic security. In big cities—from New York to Los Angeles and from Detroit to Houston—we find tens of millions of poor people, many neighborhoods of low-quality housing, and urban schools that do not teach students effectively. Economic differences have become so great that we can no longer consider this country to be a land of equal opportunity (Putnam, 2014, and personal communication).

Liberals believe that the root of these problems is social inequality, and they look to the government to take action. Enforcing antidiscrimination laws is one part of the liberal solution to urban problems. The law must ensure that racial prejudice does not prevent people of any color, ethnicity, gender, or sexual orientation from living where they choose, within the limits of their housing budget.

More broadly, liberals look to government to stabilize an economy that has become unbalanced by decades of anything-goes free-market policies. In part, then, the liberal solution to economic insecurity is greater government regulation of the economy. In addition, liberals look to government to reduce the income and wealth gaps that currently divide our society. Liberals support raising the taxes paid by the rich, who are the people benefitting the most from our way of life. At the bottom, reform involves a host of social supports and programs to increase economic opportunity, especially for people living in inner-city areas. The private sector has done little for our inner cities, liberals claim, so the government must step in to create needed jobs and provide transportation to suburbs and other outlying areas where jobs are more readily available.

In sum, liberals reject the conservative idea that our cities should rise and fall as the result of changing economic forces. As a counterpoint to the conservative view that government is part of the problem, liberals see government as the solution to the problems affecting our cities.

The Radical Left: The Need for Basic Change

Even more than liberals, radicals on the left believe that the cities of the United States are truly in crisis. So great is the economic inequality, so deep is the racism, and so limited are government efforts to improve matters, radicals argue, that nothing less than basic change in our economic and political systems will solve urban problems. Left radicals flatly reject the conservative reliance on the market system to guide the development of our cities. They claim that by giving free rein to market forces, the United States is simply making urban problems such as poverty, crime, and urban sprawl that much worse. At the same time, the reforms proposed by liberals do not go far enough because, as radicals see it, they rest on the same economic foundation of capitalism.

To apply the radical approach, recall the history of urban renewal in the United States. Government devised the policy of urban renewal with the goal of reversing the physical decline of the central cities. But rather than providing better housing for the poor, who by definition have the greatest need, the program turned poor neighborhoods over to private developers who used the land for their own profit by building shopping centers and housing for more affluent people. This process points to the conclusion that under a capitalist system, the government operates to serve the private sector and the capitalist class. Furthermore, because the private sector is concerned not with people but with profits, it will never be willing to meet the need for low-income housing.

As Marxists see it, the capitalist economy operates in the interest of the capitalist class and not the majority. Today, as a century ago, our economy operates to the benefit of those who own productive property. Most of our country's elite now live in suburbs and work there or in edge cities, leaving the poor to struggle for survival in the central cities. Districts of striking poverty remain in New York, Detroit, Saint Louis, Houston, Los Angeles, and just about every other major city in the country.

John Logan and Harvey Molotch (1987) argue that the new global economy benefits major corporations and their stockholders, but ordinary people in U.S. cities face declining prospects. As multinational corporations export industrial jobs to poor countries, for example, the urban poor are left with less and less. Social welfare programs may have grown over the course of the past century, but economic inequality continues to increase. On the contrary, as Manuel Castells (1977, 1983, 1989) argues, government programs only help to "extend" capitalism—that is, they keep a bad system from collapsing entirely.

Thus radicals conclude that under the present system, solutions will never be found. The radical perspective seeks more basic change in the economic foundation of U.S. society. Until the basic institutions of the United States operate to the benefit of the many rather than the few, urban problems will remain with us.

The Left to Right table sums up the state of U.S. cities from each of the three political perspectives.

LEFT TO RIGHT

The Politics of Urban Life

	Radical-Left View	Liberal View	Conservative View
What is the problem?	Cities are in crisis: Under capitalism, cities operate to support and benefit the few who own productive property, ignoring the needs of the majority; urban poverty, crime, and sprawl are all out of control.	Cities suffer from the effects of social inequality; poor people and minorities fare the worst with regard to housing, schools, and other resources.	Urban life is far better than it was a century ago because living standards have risen. Inner cities declined as economic forces relocated and replaced industry after 1950, but the postindustrial economy is reviving them.
What is the solution?	Neither the economy operating on its own nor government programs can bring about needed changes; capitalism itself must be transformed into a system that meets the needs of the many rather than the few.	Government must attack racial segregation by enforcing antidiscrimination laws, reduce income inequality, and bring more economic opportunity to the inner cities, where poverty is greatest.	The improvements in urban life result from this nation's productive market economy. Where needed, government can stimulate economic development with enterprise zones.

JOIN THE DEBATE

1. To what degree, from each of the political perspectives, are cities in the United States in serious trouble?

2. From the point of view of each political perspective, what is the proper role of the marketplace in meeting the needs of urbanites? What about the proper role of the government?

3. Which of the three political analyses of urban life included here do you find most convincing? Why?

Going On from Here

Cities have always generated controversy. One reason for this controversy is that cities are centers of change. More than a century ago, the Industrial Revolution occurred mostly in cities. Then, as now, most immigrants to the United States settled in cities.

Just as important, cities reflect and intensify the best and the worst of our way of life. On the one hand, the best hospitals and universities, the most celebrated museums, and the most popular mass media are all based in cities. Cities also offer the widest range of choices about how to live, the most jobs, and the greatest economic opportunity.

But cities also reveal the failings of U.S. society. Poverty can be found almost anywhere, but the greatest concentration of poor people is found in central cities. Much the same can be said for crime, low-quality housing, and bad schools.

For almost a century, the United States has been an urban nation, and no one doubts that cities will stand at the center of our way of life far into the future. From a conservative point of view, the major force shaping future cities should be a market economy. Today, the postindustrial economy is causing urban regions to spread across the United States. A liberal perspective suggests that the market-based economy alone will not solve many of the problems—such as increasing inequality and racial and ethnic conflict—that continue to plague us; government, too, must play an important part. As radicals on the left claim, the capitalist economy will never be a solution; it is actually the heart of the problem. From this point of view, as long as we let the economy shape cities, we rule out any meaningful solution.

The main question for the future, then, is this: How great a role should government take in shaping cities and urban life? With ever-increasing sprawl, mounting problems of pollution, and social inequality on the rise, perhaps the time is at hand to consider what kinds of cities we want our children and grandchildren to inherit. The debate will place those (typically conservatives) who want to limit government power in favor of letting market forces shape urban life against those (typically liberals) who favor giving government the power to reform or those (radicals on the left) who want to completely remake the urban landscape. How this debate is resolved holds the key to the cities of tomorrow.

Essay: Envisioning a Better Society Generally speaking, do you think life in our cities is getting better or worse? Why? What specific policies would you support in the effort to improve the cities of tomorrow? Explain how and why your suggestions would improve urban life.

CHAPTER 14 Urban Life

Have our nation's efforts to improve the quality of life in our large cities worked?

Who has benefited the most? Look at the accompanying photos to learn more about the policy of urban renewal, which led to redevelopment in many inner-city neighborhoods in the years after World War II.

In the 1950s, the policy of "urban renewal" was enacted in large, industrial cities, including Baltimore. The "problem" (for which urban renewal was to be a solution) was described by some as "slums" or "urban blight," which referred to low-income neighborhoods where dilapidated housing was thought to breed high levels of violent crime, drug trafficking, and other problems associated with poverty. To many liberals, however, the problem was not just substandard housing but the deeper issue of poverty as well. Can you see why?

Baltimore tore down blocks and blocks of "slums" and turned the land into the Inner Harbor development, a popular combination of trendy stores, upscale restaurants, and pricey residences. Redevelopment of this kind, also found in Philadelphia, Boston, and most other older, industrial cities, attracted wealthy people back to the city, raised tax revenues, and won a great deal of public support. Why would conservatives support this policy? Why would liberals be critical of it?

Hint: By constructing the problem of "urban blight" in terms of housing, politicians (with the enthusiastic help of developers) defined the solution as building new, more expensive commercial and residential developments. Projects like Baltimore's Inner Harbor have certainly been popular and they have made money for cities and developers alike. Therefore, conservatives praise this policy as showing the power of market forces to improve the city. At the same time, liberals counter that urban renewal simply pushed poor people away, often to high-rise "projects," and did little to address the more basic problem of poverty.

Getting Involved: Applications and Exercises

1. Do you know the extent of homelessness in your city? Answering this question is the first step in making a difference in terms of this problem. Contact a local social services agency or office of the city government, and ask for available information or an interview. What programs are in place to assist homeless people? What can others do to help?

2. Homelessness is often related to other social problems. As the chapter explains, homelessness results from both poverty and a lack of affordable housing. But homeless people often experience discrimination based on their housing status, by police, businesses, and medical services. Can you explain why? Homeless people also are at high risk of personal violence. Can you explain why?

3. A tour of your local community on foot, or on a bicycle, or in a car can be enlightening when you bring along a sociological perspective. Travel around your local area, making a sociological map as you go. Identify the commercial, industrial, and residential areas. From the apparent size and quality of housing, locate the rich and poor neighborhoods. Where do the rich and poor live in relation to commercial and industrial areas? Who lives on the area's highest ground and on the lowest ground? How far apart do rich people and poor people live?

4. About 81 percent of all people in the United States live in a place the government classifies as urban. In what ways, in your opinion, is urban living better than living in a rural area? What about the other way around: In what ways do you think rural living is better than city life?

Making the Grade

CHAPTER 14 Urban Life

A DEFINING MOMENT
Jacob Riis: Revealing the Misery of the Tenements **p. 419**

Cities: Then and Now

14.1 Explain the historical development of cities in the United States.

1700 ◄─────────── 1900 ──────────► 2014

U.S. cities evolved from small villages along the eastern seaboard. New cities sprang up as the nation pushed westward after 1800. The Civil War marked the rise of the industrial metropolis. **p. 412**

An antiurban bias grew stronger in the late nineteenth century as industrial cities swelled with immigrants. By 1920, a majority of the U.S. population lived in cities. **p. 412**

After 1950, urban decentralization rapidly expanded suburbs, which now contain a majority of the U.S. population. One consequence of the outward flow of people was fiscal crisis for central cities, especially in the Snowbelt. **pp. 412–14**

> **suburbs** (p. 414) urban areas beyond the political boundaries of cities

Problems of Today's Cities

14.2 Discuss the causes and consequences of a number of urban problems.

Fiscal Problems of the 1970s

- A declining tax base, coupled with a rising need for social services, led some cities to the brink of bankruptcy in the 1970s.

- Cities have rebounded since the 1970s, along with the growth of the postindustrial economy. But millions of urbanites—especially immigrants from Latin America and Asia—work in low-paying service jobs. **p. 414**

Urban Sprawl

The decentralization of cities has led to urban sprawl. This rapid, unplanned development has caused three problems:

- A boring sameness in the urban landscape
- A rapid loss of open spaces and loss of farmland

- Increasing reliance on automobiles, which consumes resources, pollutes the air, and causes personal stress **pp. 415–16**

Poverty

As more businesses move outward toward *edge cities*, the urban poor who remain in central cities find that their communities have fewer jobs.

- This loss of jobs is the key reason the poverty rate is twice as high in the central cities as in the suburbs. **pp. 416–18**

Housing Problems

Inadequate housing has always been a problem for some people in U.S. cities.

- At least one-third of people in the early industrial metropolis lived in overcrowded tenements.

- Not until the New Deal of the 1930s did the federal government act to improve urban housing.

- Urban renewal began in 1949 as an effort to improve declining central-city neighborhoods. In practice, cities claimed poor and working-class neighborhoods and sold the land to developers, who built profitable commercial districts and housing for more well-to-do people.

- Urban public housing—often called "projects"—was constructed to house poor people displaced by urban renewal. Problems with drugs and crime were widespread in projects, especially those containing high-rise buildings that discouraged neighborhood ties. **pp. 418–20**

Racial Segregation

- *Hypersegregation* affects one in five African Americans, who live in urban ghettos socially isolated from the larger society. **pp. 420–21**

Homelessness

- Estimates suggest that about 610,000 people are homeless on any given night; 1.5 million people in the United States are homeless for at least some time during any year.

- Research shows that homelessness is an urban problem, with 70% of homeless people living in central cities and 30% residing in suburbs or rural areas. **pp. 421–22**

Snowbelt and Sunbelt Cities

The U.S. population is now less concentrated in the *Snowbelt* (the North and Midwest) and more concentrated in the *Sunbelt* (the South and West).

- Snowbelt cities have fixed borders where they meet politically independent suburbs.
- Sunbelt cities have annexed surrounding territory to grow larger. **pp. 422–23**

Cities in Poor Countries

Half the planet's people live in urban areas. Most of the world's largest cities are in economically developing nations, and their populations are soaring. These cities cannot meet the needs of this surging population. **pp. 423–24**

> **urbanization** (p. 413) the movement of people from the countryside to cities
> **megalopolis** (p. 415) a vast urban region containing a number of cities and their surrounding suburbs
> **urban sprawl** (p. 416) unplanned, low-density development at the edge of expanding urban areas
> **public housing** (p. 418) high-density apartment buildings constructed to house poor people
> **supportive housing** (p. 418) a program that combines low-income housing with on-site social services

Theories of Urbanization and Urban Problems

14.3 Apply sociological theory to urbanization and urban problems.

Structural-Functional Analysis: A Theory of Urbanism

Structural-functional theory contrasts rural and urban living.

- In Europe, Tönnies used the concepts of *Gemeinschaft* and *Gesellschaft* to contrast these settings.
- Durkheim developed similar concepts of **mechanical solidarity** and **organic solidarity.**
- In the United States, Wirth set out a theory of urbanism stating that population size, density, and diversity generate impersonality and tolerance. **pp. 424–26**

Symbolic-Interaction Analysis: Experiencing the City

Symbolic-interaction theory takes a micro-level look at the reality of city living.

- Georg Simmel explained that cities expose people to intense stimulation. To cope, urbanites develop a blasé attitude, tuning out much of what goes on around them.
- Despite the widespread idea that cities threaten mental health, research reveals that urbanites have better mental health than people living in rural areas. **pp. 426–27**

Social-Conflict Analysis: Cities and Inequality

Social-conflict theory focuses on how social inequality shapes the city and urban life.

- Economic inequality generates very different neighborhoods in cities across the United States.
- Both government policies and economic investment favor affluent people while ignoring the needs of low-income people. **pp. 427–28**

> *Gemeinschaft* (p. 425) a type of social organization in which people are closely bound by kinship and tradition
> *Gesellschaft* (p. 425) a type of social organization in which people interact on the basis of self-interest
> **mechanical solidarity** (p. 425) social bonds based on common sentiments and shared moral values
> **organic solidarity** (p. 425) social bonds based on specialization and mutual interdependence

✪ POLITICS AND URBAN LIFE

Constructing Problems and Defining Solutions

14.4 Analyze urban issues from various positions on the political spectrum.

Conservatives: The Market and Morality

- **Conservatives** link the expansion of the welfare state to the rise of problems such as violence and the breakdown of the traditional family, which in turn have caused the deterioration of cities.
- Conservatives claim that most government programs to improve city life are ineffective or counterproductive. They look to the operation of the market economy to transform run-down cities into prosperous urban centers. **pp. 428–30**

Liberals: Government Reform

- **Liberals** point to increasing economic inequality in U.S. cities resulting in millions of people having to live in low-quality housing and attend inferior schools.
- Liberals praise government efforts to improve city life by reducing income inequality, making jobs available, and combating discrimination. **p. 430**

The Radical Left: The Need for Basic Change

- **Radicals on the left** blame the market economy for creating urban problems such as poverty, crime, and urban sprawl. They cite the history of urban renewal as an example of the harmful results of putting profits over people.
- Radicals on the left claim that only a basic change in the capitalist economy is likely to result in a better life for the majority. **p. 430**

Chapter 15
Population and Global Inequality

Tracking the Trends

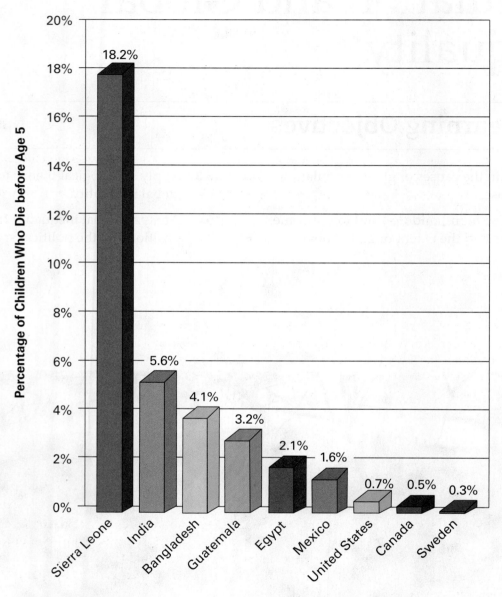

Percentage of Children Who Die before Age 5

- Sierra Leone — 18.2%
- India — 5.6%
- Bangladesh — 4.1%
- Guatemala — 3.2%
- Egypt — 2.1%
- Mexico — 1.6%
- United States — 0.7%
- Canada — 0.5%
- Sweden — 0.3%

SOURCE: UNICEF (2014).

Just as people are unequal within a society, so the nations of the world are unequal in their level of economic development. As a result, infants born in high-income nations such as Sweden, the United States, and Canada are almost certain to survive to the age of five. In fact, the odds are better than eight in ten of living past the age of sixty-five. By contrast, almost one of every five children born in the low-income nation of Sierra Leone dies before reaching the age of five. Can you see how global inequality is, in a basic sense, a matter of life or death?

Constructing the Problem

Is population increase a problem?

By 2014, Earth's population had exceeded 7 billion people, more than four times what the planet's population was a century ago.

In a rich world, do people really go hungry?

Around the world, almost 850 million people—about one in eight—experience daily hunger.

How does gender figure into the issue of global poverty?

Around the world, 70 percent of adults facing life-threatening poverty are women.

Chapter Overview

Why is the planet's population a matter of serious concern? To answer this question, this chapter introduces demography, the study of population, and makes use of important concepts such as fertility, mortality, and immigration. You will learn where on the planet population is increasing fastest and how population trends reflect global inequality. You will apply sociology's theoretical approaches to global inequality and learn how the "problems" people see in the world and the "solutions" they favor reflect their political attitudes. ■

Fatma Mint Mamadou looks out over the endless stretch of grass and sand that surrounds her. Night is coming to this desert community, and she is counting camels, as she does every evening.

Mamadou is a young woman living in North Africa's Islamic Republic of Mauritania. She has never been to school and cannot read or write. If you ask her age, she smiles and shakes her head. She doesn't know when she was born.

She has spent her life tending camels, herding sheep, hauling bags of water, sweeping the floor, and serving tea and food. For this work, she is paid nothing. She is a slave, one human being owned by another. This young woman is one of an estimated half a million slaves in Mauritania.

Mamadou accepts her situation, mostly because she has never known anything else. She explains without anger that she is a slave just like her mother before her and her grandmother before that. "Just as God created a camel to be a camel," she shrugs, "he created me to be a slave."

This young woman lives with her two children, her mother, and her brothers and sisters in a squatter settlement on the edge of Nouakchott, Mauritania's capital city. Their home is a 9-by-12-foot hut they built from wood scraps and other building materials they found at a construction site. The roof is a piece of cloth; there is no

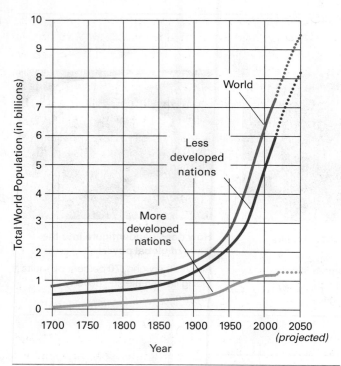

Figure 15–1 World Population, 1700–2050

Global population began to increase rapidly after about 1800. Although the *rate* of increase is now declining, the world is likely to have more than 9 billion people by 2040.

SOURCE: United Nations (2013).

plumbing and no furniture. The nearest water comes from a well a mile down the road.

A final question is more personal: "Are you and other girls ever raped?" Mamadou hesitates. With no hint of emotion, she responds, "Of course, in the night the men come to breed us. Is that what you mean by rape?" (Burkett, 1997).

The life of this young woman is powerful evidence of the extent of social inequality in the world. Living in a rich society, most of us take for granted going to school, having enough to eat, and making choices about how to live. But elsewhere, people struggle to survive, and the exploitation of some by others is both stunning and routine.

This chapter begins our survey of problems on a global scale, with an eye to the contrasts between rich and poor countries. We begin with the issue of population increase, which in low-income regions of the world is especially high. Then the focus turns to the causes of population increase and why too many people on the planet is widely considered to be a serious problem.

The chapter then turns to global inequality. After investigating the problems of global poverty and hunger, we examine various explanations for the striking inequalities found around the world and assess possible solutions to these problems.

Global Population Increase

15.1 Explain the causes of global population increase.

Global population has not always been a cause for concern. For most of human history, the world's population was both low and fairly steady. Only after the Industrial Revolution did the world's population begin to rise. And when it did, it skyrocketed.

Population by the Numbers

Some 12,000 years ago, when our distant ancestors were first creating permanent settlements, the population of the entire world was just 5 million, which is less than the population of New York City today. Global population increased very slowly, so that in about 1 c.e. the planet had about 300 million people, or roughly the population of the United States today.

Around 1750, just as the Industrial Revolution was beginning in Europe and the American colonies were moving toward a war of independence from Great Britain, the world's population began to increase sharply. Figure 15–1 shows that the world's population reached 1 billion by 1800. By 1930, not much more than a century later, it was 2 billion. At this point, not only was the population going up, but the rate of increase was itself increasing as well, like a car's gas pedal being pushed closer and closer to the floor. By 1962, just thirty-two years later, the world passed the 3 billion mark, and 4 billion people crowded the planet by 1974. No wonder that about this time, people began to talk about "overpopulation" as a serious problem.

By 1970, the *rate* of increase began to slow, but global population kept pushing upward. In terms of an automobile, the vehicle was accelerating more slowly but it was still going faster and faster. The world passed the 5 billion mark in 1987 and the 6 billion mark in 1999. This means that over the course of the twentieth century, global population quadrupled. In 2013, there were 7.2 billion people in the world (United Nations, 2013).

Most of the 87 million people being added to the world every year live in poor countries where the problem of poverty is already serious. Looking ahead, the United Nations (2013) projects that global population will surpass 8 billion in 2023 and climb to about 9.6 billion by 2050. Whether Earth can support 9 billion people or more—and at what standard of living—is one of the most serious questions we face today (Smail, 2007).

Causes of Population Increase

Tracking these trends is the focus of **demography**, *the study of human population*. Demography (from Greek words meaning "writing about people") is one branch of sociology that not only measures population levels but also tries to explain why they rise and fall. Demographers point to two basic reasons for the current population increase: high fertility and falling mortality.

High Fertility Fertility is *the incidence of childbearing in a country's population.* Demographers measure a society's fertility using the **crude birth rate**, *the number of live births in a given year for every 1,000 people in a population.* The crude birth rate is calculated by dividing the number of live births in a year by the society's total population and multiplying the result by 1,000. In the United States in 2012, there were 3.95 million live births in a population of 314 million, yielding a crude birth rate of 12.6 (Martin et al., 2013).

Demographers describe this measure as "crude" because it is based on the entire population, not just women in their childbearing years. But the crude birth rate is a good, easy-to-figure measure of a society's fertility. Figure 15–2 shows the crude birth rate for the major regions of the world.

All other factors being equal, the higher a nation's fertility, the faster its population increases. For the world as a whole, the crude birth rate is 20. Against this global average, the birth rate in the United States is low. Birth rates are higher in poor countries such as the Philippines (21) and still higher in many of the world's poorest nations, including Afghanistan (37) in Asia, Angola (47) in Central Africa, the Palestinian Territory in the Middle East (33), and Guatemala (32) in Latin America (Population Reference Bureau, 2013). The Diversity: Race, Class, & Gender box on page 442 explains how the lack of effective birth control contributes to high birth rates in poor countries.

Falling Mortality An even more important factor in the upward surge in global population is falling **mortality**, *the incidence of death in a country's population.* Demographers track mortality using the **crude death rate**, *the number of deaths in a given year for every 1,000 people in a population.* The number of deaths in a year is divided by the total population, and the result is multiplied by 1,000. In 2011 there were 2.5 million deaths in the U.S. population of 312 million, yielding a crude death rate of 8.1 (Hoyert & Xu, 2012).

Other factors being equal, the lower a nation's mortality, the faster its population increases. For the world as a whole, the crude death rate is 8, which makes the U.S. rate about average.

Why is the U.S. mortality rate not far below the world average? To answer this question, notice first that the global pattern of death rates is more complex than the pattern for birth rates. Common sense suggests that, the lower the crude death rate, the healthier the society. This is true to a point. Some very poor nations such as Moldova (11) and Mali (15) have high crude death rates. But poor nations also have populations that are, on average, very young because of the high birth rates we have already discussed. Rich nations such as the United States have populations that are, on average, much older. For this reason, the death rate for the United States is higher than you might at first expect. A society's average age also helps explain why the death rates in some poor countries, such as Malaysia (5) and Nicaragua (5), are lower than expected (Population Reference Bureau, 2013). The middle graph in Figure 15–2 shows the crude death rates for the major world regions.

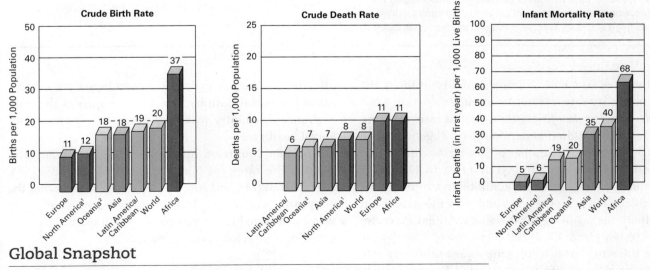

Global Snapshot

Figure 15–2 Three Population Statistics for World Regions

These figures provide a comparative look at the birth rates, death rates, and infant mortality rates for major regions of the world.

Notes: ¹United States and Canada
  ²Australia, New Zealand, and South Pacific islands

SOURCE: Population Reference Bureau (2013).

DIVERSITY: RACE, CLASS, & GENDER

Women, Power, and Contraception: The Key to Controlling Population

As recently as 1960, family planning was almost unknown in poor countries and not all that common even in the United States. Today, as women have gained greater control over their lives, birth rates are down, and about three-fourths of U.S. couples in their childbearing years use some form of contraception. Worldwide, however, patriarchy remains strong, and only about half of the world's women have access to effective birth control (Population Reference Bureau, 2013).

There are many reasons for not using contraception including religious beliefs and, especially in low-income nations, women's lack of social power. Another important factor is poverty: Women who live in poor societies cannot afford

contraception—and some women have not even heard about this technology.

The figure clearly shows the difference contraception makes in lowering fertility. The vertical axis shows the percentage of women using contraception; the horizontal axis shows the average number of children a woman bears during her lifetime. Each of the 175 dots represents a country in the world. The dots show a strong *correlation*, or association, between the two variables; the *regression line* is a statistical way of summarizing this linear relationship. In countries where contraception is widespread, women have about two children; in countries where it is not, women have five or more children. It is easy to imagine the consequences of each pattern for population increase (Population Reference Bureau, 2013).

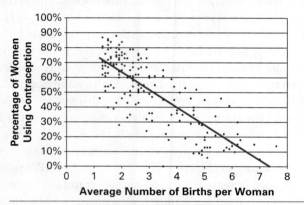

Contraceptive Use and Fertility in 159 Countries

This pattern shows a negative correlation represented by the regression line: As the share of women using contraception goes up, a woman's average number of children goes down.

What Do You Think?

1. In 1900, the average woman in the United States had about five children compared to about two today. What changes to our society over the last century do you think brought fertility down?

2. Looking around the world, women who live in societies that give them more choices about how to live are more likely to use contraception. What does this suggest about the need to raise the social standing of women?

3. If women everywhere in the world were to have five children, what consequences would there be for the planet as a whole?

A better measure of a nation's quality of life is the **infant mortality rate**, *the number of babies, of every 1,000 born, who die before their first birthday*. In this case, the number of deaths of children under one year of age in a given year is divided by the number of live births during that year, and the result is multiplied by 1,000. In 2011, there were 24,000 infant deaths and 4 million live births in the United States. Dividing the first number by the second and multiplying the result by 1,000 yields an infant mortality rate of 6.05 (Hoyert & Xu, 2012).

For the world as a whole, the infant mortality rate is 40, so quality of life in the United States is quite good. However, the U.S. infant mortality rate is still higher than that of most other rich countries, including Great Britain (4.2), Australia (3.4), Japan (2.2), and Sweden (2.6) (Population Reference Bureau, 2013). What explains the lower standing of the United States? For

one thing, social inequality is greater here than in most other industrial nations. For another, ours is the only high-income country without a program to provide universal health care.

In poor countries, infant mortality is dramatically higher. The rates for Nicaragua (18), Cambodia (45), Afghanistan (71), and Angola (98) reflect the fact that the people of these nations lack adequate nutrition and safe water and have little or no access to high-quality medical care (Population Reference Bureau, 2013).

Measuring Population Increase

Demographers can calculate a society's *natural growth rate* (or rate of natural increase) by combining fertility and mortality rates. To do this, simply subtract the crude death rate from the crude birth rate. In the case of the United States,

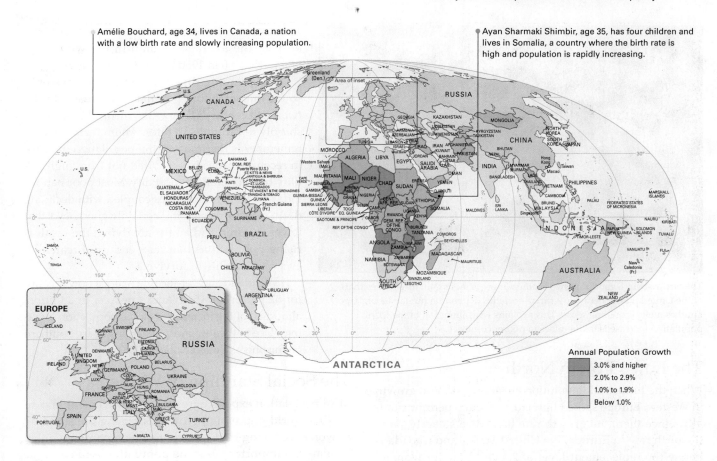

Amélie Bouchard, age 34, lives in Canada, a nation with a low birth rate and slowly increasing population.

Ayan Sharmaki Shimbir, age 35, has four children and lives in Somalia, a country where the birth rate is high and population is rapidly increasing.

Annual Population Growth
- 3.0% and higher
- 2.0% to 2.9%
- 1.0% to 1.9%
- Below 1.0%

Window on the World

Global Map 15–1 Population Growth in Global Perspective

The richest countries of the world—including the United States, Canada, and the nations of Europe—have growth rates below 1 percent. The nations of Latin America and Asia typically have growth rates around 1.3 percent, which double a population in fifty-four years. Africa has an overall growth rate of 2.6 percent (despite only small increases in countries with a high rate of AIDS), which cuts the doubling time to twenty-seven years. In global perspective, we see that a society's standard of living is closely related to its rate of population growth: Population is rising fastest in the world regions that can least afford to support more people.

SOURCE: Population Reference Bureau (2013).

a crude birth rate of 12.6 minus the crude death rate of 8.1 yields a natural growth rate of 4.5 per 1,000, or 0.45 percent annual growth.

For the world as a whole, population is increasing at the rate of 1.2 percent each year. Global Map 15–1 shows that population growth is slow in North America (0.4 percent annually), Europe (0.0 percent), and Oceania (1.1 percent), rich regions of the planet.

The annual growth rate can be used to calculate the *doubling time* for a nation's population: Simply divide the number 70 by the annual growth rate. The population of Central America, with an annual growth rate of 1.6 percent, will double in about forty-four years. The population of Central Africa, with a 3.0 percent growth rate, will double in twenty-three years. Clearly, a country that has trouble feeding the population it has now can hardly afford to let population double within one generation.

Based simply on natural increase, the population of the United States will double in 156 years (70 divided by 0.45). But another factor plays a major part in this country's rate of population increase—immigration. As explained in Chapter 3 ("Racial and Ethnic Inequality"), at least 1 million people enter the United States each year, both legally and illegally. The United States and other high-income nations grow as much or more from immigration as they do from natural increase. On the other hand, low-income nations such as Afghanistan grow almost entirely from natural increase, with births exceeding deaths.

We now turn to a survey of population patterns around the world. Generally speaking, population growth is slow or even absent in the Northern Hemisphere, where we find most of the high-income countries. But population is rapidly increasing in the Southern Hemisphere, which contains most of the world's low-income countries.

The birth rate in Uganda, a low-income nation, is more than three times that of the United States. Because agrarian societies depend on human labor, large families make economic sense. This explains why almost all of the world's population increase is taking place in poorer countries.

The Low-Growth North

When the Industrial Revolution began, population growth in Western Europe spiked upward to about 3 percent annually. Since then, the growth rate has fallen steadily. Now the birth rate in Europe, the United States, and Canada is below the replacement level of 2.1 children per woman. Demographers call this point **zero population growth**, *the level of reproduction that maintains population at a steady state.* Nearly eighty nations, almost all high-income nations, have dropped below the point of zero population growth (United Nations, 2012; Population Reference Bureau, 2013).

What explains the great decline in population increase? Important factors include the high cost of raising children, widespread use of contraceptives and abortion, the trend toward later marriage, the increasing popularity of staying single, and the fact that the typical family now has both partners in the labor force.

In sum, in high-income nations such as the United States, population increase is not a serious problem. In fact, twenty-five European nations are projected to *lose* population between now and 2050. Some analysts suggest that these nations may face a problem of *underpopulation* in the future because the increasing share of elderly people in these societies will have fewer and fewer young people to care for them and support them financially (United Nations, 2014). In this country, despite a low birth rate, our high rate of immigration almost guarantees that population will continue to increase in the decades to come.

The High-Growth South

Rising population is already a serious problem for many poor nations that lie in the Southern Hemisphere. The problem would certainly be worse if many low-income countries had not started programs to limit births. As a result of these efforts, the number of children born to the average woman in the world has fallen from 6.0 in 1950 to 2.5 children today.

But bringing down the birth rate goes only so far in controlling population increase. In the twentieth century, advances in medical technology sharply reduced death rates. An important fact to remember is that most of the population increase in recent decades has resulted not from high fertility but from falling mortality. Most poor nations today have high birth rates coupled with declining death rates. Although it is certainly good news that fewer children and adults are dying, the result is rising populations that may end up threatening everyone's ability to survive.

Worldwide, lower-income nations now account for 82 percent of the planet's people. In addition, almost all of the increase in global population is taking place in the low-income nations of the Southern Hemisphere (United Nations, 2012).

The Social Standing of Women

Most population experts agree that a key element in controlling world population growth is raising the standing of women. Making birth control technology more widely available is important, but the population will continue to increase as long as a culture defines women's primary responsibility as raising children.

Dr. Nafis Sadik, a Pakistani woman who headed the United Nations' efforts at population control, sums up the approach: Give a woman more choices about how to live, and she will have fewer children. A woman who has access to schooling and jobs can decide when and whether she wants to marry, and she will bear children as a matter of choice, not because it is the only option open to her. Under these conditions, evidence shows, women have fewer children (Axinn & Barber, 2001; Population Reference Bureau, 2011).

Explaining the Population Problem: Malthusian Theory

Thomas Robert Malthus (1766–1834) was an English economist, priest, and pioneering demographer who lived at just the time when global population began heading sharply upward. Malthus (1926, orig. 1798) offered a simple mathematical analysis of population increase that led to a troubling conclusion. Population, he predicted, would increase according to what mathematicians call a *geometric progression*, illustrated by the series of numbers 2, 4, 8, 16, 32, and so on. At such a rate, world population would soon soar out of control.

Food production would also increase, Malthus predicted, but only in *arithmetic progression* (as in the series 2, 3, 4, 5, 6). This limited increase reflects the fact that, no matter what new technology people invent, there is only so much farmland to grow food.

CONSTRUCTING SOCIAL PROBLEMS
A DEFINING MOMENT
Thomas Robert Malthus: Claiming Population Is a Problem

Probably no one in history has had more of an effect on how people look at the issue of population increase than Thomas Robert Malthus. Born in 1766 to a prosperous and highly educated family, Malthus was the second of eight children, a number not uncommon for his time.

Malthus became a priest and later a university professor. But he is remembered for the treatise on population that he published in 1798 under the full title "An Essay on the Principle of Population as It Affects the Future Improvement of Society, with Remarks on the Speculations of Mr. Godwin, M. Condorcet and Other Writers."

Perhaps sensing the controversy he would cause, Malthus originally published the work anonymously. Five years later, he republished his work under his name in a much expanded form. The key line of his treatise is this: "Population increases in a geometric ratio, while the means of subsistence increases in an arithmetic ratio." Malthus believed that human beings had two powerful needs—for sex and for food. Living at a time when families were very large and there was no reliable form of birth control, he reasoned that "the number of mouths to be fed will have no limit" so that "the food that is to supply them cannot keep pace."

Was there any hope? Malthus pointed out that crime, disease, and war might well slow population increase. But he rejected birth control on religious grounds and thought it highly unlikely that people would give up sex (Malthus himself had just three children). In the end, Malthus could imagine no escape from a future of "famine, distress, havoc, and dismay."

More than two centuries later, we can be thankful that Malthus was at least partly wrong. Especially in high-income nations, birth rates have fallen dramatically in recent decades, and thanks to advancements in technology, food production is far greater than Malthus imagined. But the fact remains that global population continues to increase and any rate of population increase is not sustainable in the long run. Is it possible that the Malthusian nightmare will never happen? Or has it just been delayed?

Thomas Robert Malthus lived in England at a time when population was beginning to soar. His prediction that population would increase far more quickly than food and other resources prompted one artist to imagine this future for his native country.

Putting the two patterns together, Malthus concluded that people would soon reproduce beyond what the planet could feed, leading to starvation and social chaos. The Defining Moment box takes a closer look at the warning sounded by Malthus.

EVALUATE

If Malthus had been right in his conclusion, we probably would not be here to think about his ideas. But Malthus failed to foresee that, as the Industrial Revolution took hold, it would unleash forces that would push birth rates downward. A decline in fertility occurred because once children were no longer needed to farm the land, they became very costly to raise. In addition, many people began using artificial birth control. Finally, Malthus underestimated how much food humanity would eventually produce. New technology in the form of irrigation, fertilizers, pesticides, and genetically modified foods has increased farm output far beyond what he imagined.

But was Malthus entirely wrong? Good land, clean water, and fresh air are all limited resources, so population cannot continue to increase indefinitely. In short, no level of population growth can go on forever. To avoid Malthus's dire prediction, humanity must work out ways to control its own numbers.

CHECK YOUR LEARNING Explain Malthus's prediction about the future of the world's population. What are several criticisms of his prediction?

A More Recent Approach: Demographic Transition Theory

A more recent analysis of population change is **demographic transition theory**, *a thesis linking demographic changes to a*

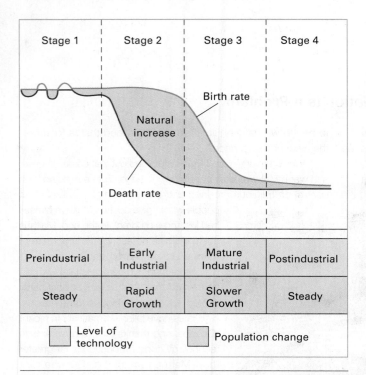

Stage 1	Stage 2	Stage 3	Stage 4
Preindustrial	Early Industrial	Mature Industrial	Postindustrial
Steady	Rapid Growth	Slower Growth	Steady

Level of technology   Population change

Figure 15–3   The Stages of Demographic Transition

Demographic transition theory shows the process by which societies move from high birth rates and high death rates (Stage 1) to low birth rates and low death rates (Stage 4).

society's level of technological development. Figure 15–3 shows a society's population dynamics at four levels of technological development. Preindustrial, agrarian societies—that is, almost the entire world before 1750—fall into Stage 1. These societies have high birth rates because families depend on the labor of children and because there is little effective birth control. Death rates are also high because poor people have little understanding of health and disease. Periodic outbreaks of plague and other infectious diseases cancel out any increase in births, so population bobs up and down remaining fairly steady over long periods of time.

Stage 2, the onset of industrialization, begins the demographic transition. Death rates fall because of higher living standards, including better nutrition and the benefits of scientific medicine. Because birth rates remain high, population begins increasing rapidly. Malthus lived during Europe's Stage 2, which helps explain his pessimistic view of the world's future. The poorest countries on the planet are in this high-growth stage today.

In Stage 3, a mature industrial economy, the birth rate falls into line with the death rate, and the rate of population increase slows. Fertility falls partly because families no longer have to bear many children just to ensure that a few of them will survive to adulthood. Also, mature industrial societies transform children from economic assets (people who work to contribute to their families' income) to economic liabilities (children's schooling and other needs strain

family finances). Effective birth control becomes widely available, and limiting family size is important to women who want to work outside the home.

Stage 4 corresponds to a postindustrial economy, which promotes stable population size once again. Both the birth rate and the death rate are low, so there is little or no natural increase in population size. As noted earlier, this is now the case in much of Western Europe and Japan (Population Reference Bureau, 2013).

EVALUATE

Compared with Malthus's alarming prediction, demographic transition theory offers a more hopeful view of our demographic future. In this analysis, advancing technology first sparks population increase but then brings it under control, all the while lifting living standards.

But will poor societies develop economically to the point that their birth rates drop? If they remain poor, there is little chance that the world will ever bring rising population under control. As shown in Figure 15–4, even if birth rates fall, the very young population of poor nations (such as Kenya) means that most people have yet to bear children. So, at least for some decades to come, population increase is inevitable.

CHECK YOUR LEARNING   In your own words, explain demographic transition theory. What is a criticism of this approach?

Global Inequality

15.2   Describe high-, middle-, and low-income nations and the extent of global poverty.

You have seen that population increase is a far greater problem in some parts of the world than it is in others. The same is true in terms of poverty and hunger. As you might guess, the most serious problems of population increase *and* hunger are found in the same parts of the world.

Chapter 2 ("Poverty and Wealth") explained that people in the United States are divided into classes, with some having far more wealth, income, prestige, and power than others. Social stratification is even greater if we broaden our view to include not just people in the United States but people all around the world as well.

Figure 15–5 on page 448 divides the world's total income by fifths of humanity. For comparison, recall (from Figure 2–1 on page 35) that the richest 20 percent of the U.S. population earns about 48.9 percent of the national income. The richest 20 percent of the world's people, however, receives about 77 percent of all income. In the United States, the poorest 20 percent of the population earns 3.8 percent of the national income; globally, the same proportion of the population struggles to survive on just 1.6 percent of all income (Milanovic, 2014).

The global distribution of wealth, as the second half of Figure 15–5 on page 448 shows, is even more unequal. The richest 20 percent of the world's adults own about 94 percent of the planet's wealth. The richest 1 percent of the

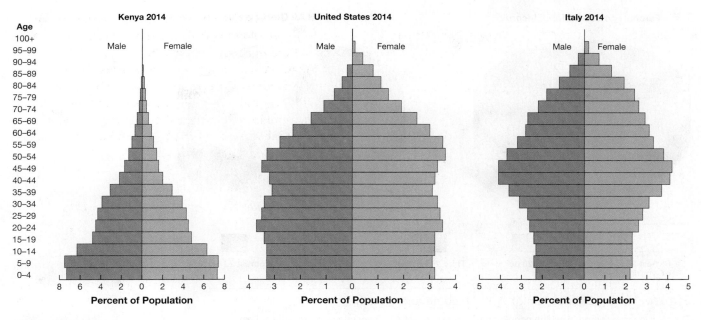

Global Snapshot

Figure 15–4 Population Pyramids: Kenya, United States, and Italy, 2014

Population pyramids are graphic representations of the population according to sex (male and female) and age (from birth to one hundred years and over). In a very poor nation such as Kenya, the youngest people make up the largest share of the society, guaranteeing that population increase will continue as children enter their childbearing years. The U.S. pyramid has a more boxlike shape because we are, on average, a much older population. (The average age in the United States is about thirty-eight, compared with about nineteen in Kenya.) Italy is one of the nations that is recording a slight population decrease. There are proportionately fewer young people in Italy with a larger share of elderly people. There the average age is forty-five and rising.

SOURCE: U.S. Census Bureau (2014).

world's people own about 46 percent of all wealth. At the same time, the poorest half of the world's adults own only 0.7 percent of all global wealth. In terms of dollars, about half the world's families have less than $4,000 in total wealth, far less than the $77,300 in wealth for the typical family in the United States (Davies, Lluberas, & Shorrocks, 2013).

With the world's income and wealth so unevenly distributed, even people who are counted among the poor in the United States live much better than most of the people of the world. At the same time, affluent men and women in rich countries live so well that many have trouble understanding just how serious the plight of others in the world really is. Each of the world's three richest people—Carlos Slim Helú in Mexico and Bill Gates and Warren Buffett in the United States—is worth more than $60 billion, which is more than the wealth of all the people in 110 of the world's 194 countries (*Forbes*, 2014; World Bank, 2014).

High-Income Nations

Just as people within a single society live at various class levels, the global system of inequality contains high-income, middle-income, and low-income nations. Global

Map 15–2 on page 449 shows which of the world's 194 nations fall in each category. There are now seventy-four high-income nations in the world, including the United States and Canada, Mexico, Argentina, and Chile, the countries of Western Europe, the Russian Federation, Israel, Saudi Arabia, Japan, South Korea, Australia, and New Zealand.

The world's rich nations benefit from high productivity resulting from advanced technology. It was in these nations that the Industrial Revolution steadily boosted productivity beginning more than two centuries ago. How much of a difference does advanced technology make? The high-income nation of Spain produces more than the mostly agrarian continent of Africa below the Sahara. Tiny Italy has just one-tenth the land of giant India, yet Italy out-produces India (World Bank, 2014).

In 2013, high-income nations were home to about 1.6 billion people, or 23 percent of Earth's population. Even at the bottom of this favored category (for instance, Lebanon), annual income is at least $13,000; the figure is more than four times that much in the world's richest countries, such as the United States and Singapore. Taken together, the people in the seventy-four high-income countries earn 64 percent of the income earned by all of humanity.

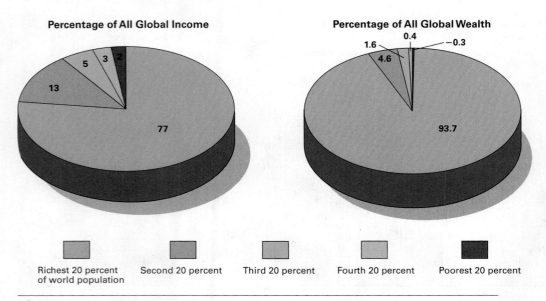

Figure 15–5 Distribution of World Income and Wealth

The total income earned by all the people of the world is distributed very unevenly, with the richest 20 percent of people receiving 77 percent of all income and owning 94 percent of all wealth.

SOURCES: Based on Milanovic (2009, 2011) and Davies, Lluberas, & Shorrocks (2013).

Middle-Income Nations

People living in middle-income countries have incomes ranging from $2,500 (in, say, Nicaragua in Latin America, Cape Verde in Africa, and Vietnam in Asia) to about $12,000 (in Costa Rica in Latin America, Serbia in Europe, and Iran in Asia). These nations—seventy-one in all—have significant industrialization, but about 48 percent of the people still live in rural areas and work in agriculture. In general, people in rural areas have less access to schooling, medical care, good housing, and safe water than those who live in cities.

In recent years, both India and China have entered the ranks of middle-income nations. In all, this middle category includes some 4.3 billion people, or about 60 percent of the global population. Overall, they earn about 33 percent of the entire world's income.

Low-Income Nations

The world's forty-nine low-income nations have populations that are, on average, agrarian and very poor. Most of these nations are found in Central Africa or Asia. In poor countries, about 65 percent of the people live in rural areas and farm as their ancestors have done for centuries. The remainder live in or near cities, where many work in factories. With limited industrial technology, low-income nations are not very productive, which is one reason that hunger, disease, poor schooling, and unsafe housing are so common.

In 2013, about 17 percent of the planet's population, or more than 1 billion people, lived in low-income nations earning only 3 percent of the world's income. For every dollar earned by people living in a rich nation, these

people earn just pennies. We now take a closer look at the problems of global poverty and hunger.

The World's Poverty Problem

Poverty is far more widespread in the world as a whole than it is in the United States. Around the world, about 850 million people do not have enough to eat. Over time, hunger leads to malnutrition and makes it hard to work; it also raises the risk of disease (United Nations, 2013).

In more scientific terms, the typical adult in a rich nation, such as the United States, consumes about 3,440 calories a day, which is too much for good health. The result of this high level of consumption is that about two-thirds of the people in this country are overweight. The typical adult in a low-income country, who performs a great deal of physical labor, consumes just 2,360 calories a day. This is too little for good health, especially among people who do lots of physical labor, and the result is hunger and undernourishment.

The long-term effects of poverty are deadly. In the ten minutes it takes to read through this section of the chapter, about 100 people in the world, sick and weakened from hunger, will die. This amounts to about 25,000 people each day, or 9 million people each year. Global hunger is among the most serious social problems facing the world today (United Nations Development Programme, 2013).

Relative versus Absolute Poverty Most of the poverty that we have in the United States is *relative poverty*, referring to a lack of the resources that most people take for granted. In global perspective, however, we face the problem of *absolute poverty*, a lack of resources that is life-threatening.

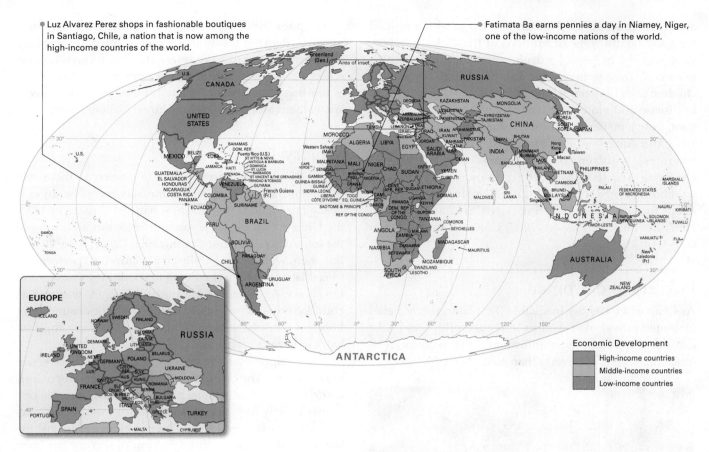

Luz Alvarez Perez shops in fashionable boutiques in Santiago, Chile, a nation that is now among the high-income countries of the world.

Fatimata Ba earns pennies a day in Niamey, Niger, one of the low-income nations of the world.

Economic Development

- High-income countries
- Middle-income countries
- Low-income countries

Window on the World

Global Map 15–2 Economic Development in Global Perspective

In high-income countries—including the United States, Canada, Chile, Argentina, the nations of Western Europe, Israel, Saudi Arabia, Australia, and Japan—a highly productive economy provides people, on average, with material plenty. Middle-income countries—including most of Latin America and Asia—are less economically productive, with a standard of living about average for the world as a whole but far below that of the United States. These nations also have a significant share of poor people who are barely able to feed and house themselves. In the low-income countries of the world, poverty is severe and widespread. Although small numbers of elites live very well in the poorest nations, most people struggle to survive on a small fraction of the income common in the United States.

Note: Data for this map are provided by the United Nations and the World Bank. Each country's economic productivity is measured in terms of its gross national income (GNI), which is the total value of all the goods and services produced by a country's economy within its borders in a given year, plus net compensation and property income from abroad. Dividing each country's GNI by the country's population gives us the per capita (per-person) GNI and allows us to compare the economic performance of countries of different population sizes. High-income countries have a per capita GNI of more than $12,500. Many are far richer than this, however; the figure for the United States exceeds $52,000. Middle-income countries have a per capita GNI ranging from $2,500 to $12,499. Low-income countries have a per capita GNI of less than $2,500. Figures used here reflect the United Nations' "purchasing power parities" system, which is an estimate of what people can buy using their income in the local economy.

SOURCES: Data from United Nations Development Programme (2013) and World Bank (2014).

Human beings in absolute poverty lack the nutrition necessary for health and long-term survival. There is no denying that some absolute poverty exists in the United States. But such immediately life-threatening poverty strikes only a tiny percentage of the U.S. population. By contrast, about 40 percent of the people in low-income countries are in what the United Nations (2013) calls "severe poverty." One way to see this difference is to contrast life expectancy in rich nations and low-income countries. In rich countries such as the United States, death typically occurs after age

seventy-eight. When absolute poverty is widespread, however, death comes early. For example, in very poor nations such as Sierra Leone and the Central African Republic, one-fourth of all children die before they complete their teens.

Poverty and Children

Poverty distorts the lives of young people, even those lucky enough to survive. In the low-income nations of the world, according to a United Nations (2012) estimate, about one-fourth of all children lack the nutrition needed for good health. Tens of millions of these children beg, steal, sell sex, or work for drug gangs to provide income needed by their families. But they pay a high price. Such children miss out on schooling and are likely to fall victim to disease and violence. Many young girls become pregnant, truly a matter of children having children.

Latin America faces the greatest problem of poor, homeless children: Brazil reports that millions of children are living on their own, underfed and unschooled, often sniffing glue or using other cheap drugs to numb their suffering (UNICEF, 2006; Leopold, 2007; Levinson & Bassett, 2007; Consortium for Street Children, 2011).

Poverty and Women

As Chapter 4 ("Gender Inequality") explains, rich societies give men power over women in a number of ways. One consequence of gender stratification is that women are at much higher risk of poverty than men.

For every dollar earned by the average person in the United States, people in India earn about 7 cents. Even though India is now a middle-income country, widespread poverty is evident on the streets of Chennai (formerly Madras) and other Indian cities as families beg for money. If you were a visitor from the United States, what degree of responsibility would you feel for the welfare of a family like this one?

In poor countries, men and women are even more unequal. Because traditional societies often are strongly patriarchal, women have fewer choices, receive limited schooling, and find little economic opportunity. As a result, as much as 70 percent of the adults facing absolute poverty are women (Moghadam, 2005; United Nations, 2010).

Slavery

Surely the greatest horror linked to poverty in the world is slavery. Many people assume slavery to be an evil of the past. The British Empire banned slavery in 1833; the United States did the same in 1865. But according to the International Labour Organization (2012), some 20 million men, women, and children are currently performing forced labor or otherwise living in conditions that amount to slavery. Another 168 million children are working as child laborers, whose childhoods are built around long hours of work for little or no pay. Half of these children work in hazardous conditions.

The chapter-opening story gives a picture of slavery in today's world. The case of Fatma Mint Mamadou represents *chattel slavery*, in which one person owns another. No one knows exactly how many chattel slaves exist because the practice of buying and selling human beings is against the law around the globe. But this form of slavery has been documented in many countries in Asia, the Middle East, and especially Africa and involves hundreds of thousands of people. Human trafficking is one of the most profitable forms of crime (next to selling guns and drugs) to organized crime syndicates around the world (Orhant, 2002).

A second type of bondage is slavery imposed by the state. In this type of slavery, the government forces people to perform labor, as punishment for criminal violations or simply because the state needs workers. China uses a policy of state slavery to deal with people addicted to drugs, and North Korea forces countless people to work in state-owned farms or factories.

A third type of servitude is *child slavery*, in which children living in desperately poor families hustle on the streets to bring in income. Millions of children, many in poor countries of Latin America, fall into this category.

A fourth type of bondage is *debt bondage*, in which employers enslave workers of all ages by paying them too little to cover the costs of their debts. This practice is common in sweatshops throughout the world, where workers receive a wage that is too little to pay for the food and housing their employers provide. As soon as they begin working, they fall into debt that they can never pay off. Because they are not free to leave their work, for practical purposes they have become slaves.

A fifth type of slavery is a *servile form of marriage*. In India, Thailand, and some African nations, families marry off women against their will. Many of these women end up as slaves performing work for their husband's family; in other cases, women are forced into prostitution.

In 1948, the United Nations issued the Universal Declaration of Human Rights, which states, "No one shall be held in slavery or servitude; slavery and the slave trade shall be prohibited in all their forms." Even though slavery is both morally wrong and against the law, it persists as part of the sad story of global poverty.

Theories of Global Inequality

15.3 Apply sociological theory to the issue of global inequality.

Both of sociology's macro-level theoretical approaches provide explanations for global poverty and insights into the problem of population increase.

Structural-Functional Analysis: The Process of Modernization

Modernization theory is *a model of economic and social development that explains global inequality in terms of technological and cultural differences between societies.* Modernization theory begins by pointing out that two centuries ago every nation in the world was very poor. As the Industrial Revolution gradually expanded the economies of the nations of Europe and soon after the United States, an increasing number of countries gradually became affluent. At first, new industrial wealth benefited just a few people. But industrial technology was so productive that gradually the living standards of even the poorest people began to rise.

Over the last century, living standards in high-income countries, including the United States, have jumped fivefold. This means dramatic improvements in housing quality, nutrition, and important measures of health. In addition, people do less physical work because of electrically operated household appliances, we travel in fast and comfortable automobiles and, most recently, we communicate with others virtually anywhere by using microelectronic computers and other high-tech devices. Industrialization has also transformed most of the countries in Latin America and Asia into middle-income societies, and there too, living standards have risen. But in low-income countries, where there is less industrial technology, a large share of people remains poor.

At this point, you might be wondering why every society does not simply adopt industrial technology. Modernization theory's answer is this: Every society *has* industrialized to some degree, but some societies are not eager to sacrifice tradition in favor of change toward higher living standards. Following this approach, then, tradition, which often takes the form of strong religious beliefs, is the greatest barrier to economic development.

A general pattern is that the poorer a nation is, the greater the domination of women by men. In a country like Afghanistan, how is this fact reflected in the number of children a woman has, as well as her opportunities for schooling and for paid work?

In traditional societies that have strong families that teach their new members to respect the past, culture acts as an anchor that discourages people from exploring new ways of life. Held in place by their traditions, these societies do not adopt new technologies or give their people the schooling that might improve their lives.

In today's world, there are many examples of societies that reject modernization, including the Amish of North America, the Semai of Malaysia, and fundamentalist Muslims in Iran, Afghanistan, and elsewhere. Typically, these societies reject industrial technology and other elements of modern culture as a threat to their family relationships, customs, and religious beliefs.

On the other hand, history shows that living standards went up the most in parts of the world eager to embrace change. Near the end of the Middle Ages, as the sociologist Max Weber (1958, orig. 1904–05) explained, the cultural environment of Western Europe was quite open to change. As Protestant religious beliefs (especially those of John Calvin) took hold in parts of Europe, a progress-oriented way of life emerged. People came to view getting rich—which the Catholic tradition regarded with suspicion—as a sign of personal virtue and as an indication of divine selection for eternal salvation. Under these circumstances, a new ethic of individual achievement and material comfort gradually replaced the traditional emphasis on kinship and community. Such cultural beliefs led people to seek out new technology and, together, these factors pushed societies forward into the Industrial Revolution. Before long, culture and technology had succeeded in lifting Western Europeans from poverty and creating widespread prosperity.

W. W. Rostow: The Stages of Modernization Modernization theory draws on the work of Max Weber, as well as the ideas of Ferdinand Tönnies and Emile Durkheim, which were discussed in Chapter 14 ("Urban Life"). But it was Walt Whitman Rostow (1960, 1978) who expressed modernization theory as an easy-to-understand series of stages.

1. **Traditional stage.** People living in traditional, agrarian societies raise their children to look to the past, respecting old ways. Such people do not easily imagine how life can be very different from what they have always known. Therefore, they build their lives around their families and local communities, following the ways of their ancestors with little personal choice or individual freedom. Such societies provide a life that is spiritually rich but poor in a material sense.

   Several centuries ago, most of the world was in this first stage of economic development. Today, nations such as Bangladesh, Niger, and Somalia are still stuck in the traditional stage and remain almost as poor as they were then.

2. **Take-off stage.** As societies begin to break free of cultural tradition, they allow people to develop their talents and imagination and to pursue new types of work. As a result, the economy begins to grow. People begin producing goods not just for their own consumption but also to trade with others for profit, which means a market takes form. Greater individualism, a willingness to take risks, and a desire for material goods are all new cultural patterns that encourage change toward material prosperity. In the process, of course, these forces also weaken family ties and time-honored norms and values.

   Great Britain and the United States reached take-off in the early 1800s. Thailand, a middle-income country in eastern Asia, is now in this stage. Reaching take-off sometimes depends on progressive influences that come from richer nations in the form of foreign aid, export-advanced technology and investment capital, and invitations to foreign students to take advantage of advanced schooling.

3. **Drive to technological maturity.** As this stage begins, people begin to define poverty as a problem, and they see technological progress and economic growth as

solutions. Industrialization is now under way; the economy grows and diversifies as new products are invented and markets expand. People begin to realize that their new way of life is weakening traditional family and local community life, but most abandon the ways of the past, which they come to see as "old-fashioned." Great Britain reached this point by about 1840; the United States, by 1860. Today, Mexico, the U.S. territory of Puerto Rico, and Poland are among the nations driving toward technological maturity.

   Once a society reaches Stage 3, there is much less absolute poverty. Cities swell with people who have left their rural villages in search of better jobs and schooling. Occupational specialization means people deal with countless others making relationships less personal. The rising importance of individual freedom and social equality sparks social movements demanding greater political rights for all, including women. Governments pass laws requiring everyone to attend school, and a small but increasing share of people go on to college or other advanced training.

4. **High mass consumption.** At this point, industrial technology is widespread, and the economy is growing rapidly with steadily rising living standards. Mass production of a vast assortment of new goods and services fuels mass consumption. Most people take affluence for granted and learn to "need" things their ancestors never imagined.

   The United States, Japan, and others of today's high-income nations moved into this stage of development by about 1900. Recently entering this level of economic development are two former British colonies that are now prosperous small societies of eastern Asia: Hong Kong (part of the People's Republic of China) and Singapore (independent since 1965).

Rostow explains that rich nations play an important part in helping poor countries move through the four stages. Rich nations can export high-tech farming methods to poor nations to help raise agricultural yields. Such techniques—part of what is commonly called the Green Revolution—include hybrid and genetically modified seeds, modern irrigation methods, chemical fertilizers, and pesticides for insect control. Poor countries also look to rich nations for industrial technology as well as computers and other new information technology.

Even an expanding economy will not lift living standards if poor societies do not control their population growth. Rich nations can help poor nations limit population increase by giving them birth control technology and educational programs to promote its use. Also, according to modernization theory, once economic development is under way, birth rates should decline as they have in industrialized nations because children are no longer an economic asset but become an economic liability (Lino, 2012).

Since it first emerged in the 1950s, modernization theory has shaped the foreign policy of the United States and other rich nations. Supporters point to rapid economic development in much of the world—especially the Asian nations of South Korea, Taiwan, Singapore, and Hong Kong—as evidence that the affluence created in Western Europe and North America is within reach of all countries (Parsons, 1966; Moore, 1977, 1979; Bauer, 1981; Berger, 1986; Firebaugh & Beck, 1994; Firebaugh, 1996; Firebaugh & Sandu, 1998).

But critics see modernization theory as simply a defense of capitalism. If modernization theory is correct, they ask, why is there still so much poverty in much of the world? They also ask why living standards in a number of nations, including Haiti and Nicaragua in Latin America and Sudan, Ghana, and Rwanda in Africa, are no better, and in some cases worse, than they were in 1960 (United Nations Development Programme, 2013).

Second, critics point out that modernization theory says little about how rich nations often try to prevent poor countries from developing. Centuries ago, European nations began a system of colonial control over much of the world that benefited the European conquerors at the expense of most of the world's people. Such exploitation continues to the present day, as later sections of the chapter explain.

Third, modernization theory sets up the world's most developed countries as the standard that guides the development of the rest of the world, as if we have nothing to learn from others. This ethnocentric (culturally self-serving) bias can have harmful consequences. The Western idea of "progress" encourages the exploitation of other nations and also fuels wasteful consumption, causing harm to the physical environment of the planet, the focus of Chapter 16 ("Technology and the Environment").

Fourth and finally, critics reject modernization theory's implication that poor societies are responsible for their own poverty. Instead of blaming the victims, critics want to shift the focus to the behavior of rich nations.

Such concerns point to a second major approach to understanding global inequality, called "world system theory." The Applying Theory table on page 455 summarizes what we learn from both of these approaches.

CHECK YOUR LEARNING In your own words, explain the basic ideas that make up modernization theory. What are Rostow's stages of modernization? What are several criticisms of this approach?

Social-Conflict Analysis: The Global Economic System

The social-conflict approach to global inequality centers on **world system theory**, *a model of economic development that explains global inequality in terms of the historical exploitation of poor societies by rich ones.* For centuries, rich nations have used the capitalist global economy to benefit themselves as they exploit poor nations.

This approach rejects the idea that poor nations are simply lagging behind other nations in the race for economic development. In this analysis, some nations have become rich only *because* others have become poor.

The origins of the capitalist world economy go back five centuries to the time when Europeans began establishing colonies, which eventually included the Americas to the west, Africa to the south, and Asia to the east. **Colonialism** is *the process by which some nations enrich themselves through political and economic control of other nations.* Great Britain established so many colonies around the world that by 1900 that nation controlled about one-fourth of the world's land and could boast, "The sun never sets on the British Empire." The United States, which was itself one of the early British colonies, eventually pushed westward across the continent, purchased Alaska, and gained control of Haiti, Puerto Rico, Guam, the Philippines, the Hawaiian Islands, and parts of Panama and Cuba.

Formal colonialism began to decline in the mid-nineteenth century. Today, colonialism has almost disappeared from the world. According to world system theory, however, exploitation continues in the form of **neocolonialism** (*neo* means "new"), *a new form of economic exploitation that involves the operation of multinational corporations rather than direct political control by foreign governments.* In the past, colonial powers directly ruled

Modernization theory claims that as rich nations colonized much of the world, they spread progressive culture and new technology. World system theory challenges this claim, charging that colonization did little more than make some nations rich while making others poor. Which approach do you find more convincing? Why?

SOCIAL PROBLEMS IN GLOBAL PERSPECTIVE
Sweatshop Safety: How Much Is a Life Worth?

The day was unfolding like any other: Thousands of people were sitting at sewing machines and other equipment making shirts and other clothing at one of the largest garment factories in Bangladesh. Suddenly a sickening rumble was accompanied by collapsing floors and ceilings. The four-story concrete structure simply fell in on itself, and most of the workers never had a chance.

It took days to dig through the rubble and locate all those who had been working there. When the job was done, 1,129 people were dead. More than 2,500 were injured, most of them seriously.

The government did an investigation of the collapse of the Rana Plaza building in Savar, a suburb of the nation's capital, Dhaka. The conclusion was chilling: The building had been constructed in an unsafe way with little regard for building codes. Upper floors of the building were not built to support the weight of people and equipment. Large power generators, needed to keep production going during frequent power blackouts, were heavy and shook the floor when they came on (Yardley, 2013; Greenhouse & Harris, 2014).

Millions of workers are employed in garment factories that have been widely described as "sweatshops." Found in Bangladesh and other lower-income nations, the worst of these sweatshops pay workers as little as 50 cents an hour. Yet they have no trouble finding people willing to work eight hours a day, six days a week, all year long, to earn perhaps $1,200 a year. Forget about any paid vacation or other benefits. As the collapse of the Rana Plaza factory suggests, many sweatshops were built at the lowest possible cost and lack even the most basic safety protections.

Sweatshop factories such as this one are big business in Bangladesh, where some 5,000 garment factories are operating. In that nation, garment making represents about 75 percent of the total economic exports. Approximately 60 percent of the garments shipped from Bangladesh end up in clothing stores in the United States. People who look for bargains on store clothing racks rarely stop to think that one reason for the low price may well be that the workers halfway around the world who made the garments are paid only pennies a day.

In the case of the Rana Plaza factory, there were widespread concerns that the building was unsafe. But, according to the government investigation, workers who expressed concerns were told by the factory owners that the building was safe and that they had to go to work. The government report painted a picture of placing profit above people that added up to a disaster waiting to happen. The company owners and the town mayor have been charged with numerous crimes and may face long prison sentences.

Perhaps most disturbing of all, this incident is just the latest of a long string of very deadly and very preventable accidents involving sweatshops in Bangladesh. Despite many previous disasters like this one, the pattern of sweatshop garment production goes on.

What Do You Think?

1. Some people view the wages paid by textile factories abroad as the "going rate" in low-income nations. Others see them as exploitation of poor people. Which is closer to your view? Why?

2. Most of the textile exports of Bangladesh come to the United States. Are consumers in this country partly responsible for situations such as that described in this box? Why or why not?

3. Apply modernization theory and dependency theory to industrial accidents such as the one described here. What conclusion is reached following each approach?

---

their colonies. Today, rich nations continue to exploit poor nations through the worldwide operation of multinational corporations (Bonanno, Constance, & Lorenz, 2000).

Immanuel Wallerstein: The Capitalist World Economy

Immanuel Wallerstein (1974, 1979, 1983, 1984) explains that the "capitalist world economy," which has been in operation for more than 500 years, is centered in today's rich nations. These high-income countries (see Global Map 15–2 on page 449) are the *core* of the world economy. These nations became rich as they established colonies and systematically collected gold, silver, and other raw materials from other countries. The resulting wealth helped them begin the Industrial Revolution. Today, multinational corporations dominate the global economy and continue to funnel wealth from around the world to North America, Western Europe, Australia, and Japan. In Wallerstein's analysis, low-income countries form the *periphery* of the world economy. Drawn into the world economy by colonial exploitation, poor nations continue to support rich ones in two ways. First, they provide inexpensive labor. The Social Problems in Global Perspective box provides a look at a familiar form of exploitation—the sweatshop. Recall from earlier chapters that multinational corporations have "exported" jobs from the United States to Bangladesh, the Philippines, Taiwan, China, and other countries where labor costs are low. Second, lower-income nations provide a vast market for industrial products sold by corporations that are based in rich countries.

APPLYING THEORY

Global Inequality

	Structural Functional Analysis: Modernization Theory	Social-Conflict Analysis: World System Theory
How has the world changed over the centuries?	People throughout the world were very poor until industrial technology started to raise living standards; although some nations are more productive than others, all nations today are better off compared to centuries ago.	People living around the world were roughly equal until the beginning of colonialism, a system of economic exploitation that made some nations rich and other nations poor.
Why is there global inequality?	Differences in culture and technology are the major reasons: While some countries have shown eagerness to change and adopt new technology, others remain more traditional.	Colonialism created inequality, and the world capitalist system, dominated by multinational corporations, continues to enrich some nations at the expense of others.
	The United States and other rich countries are part of the solution to global poverty because they help lower-income countries develop economically.	The United States and other rich countries are part of the problem because they benefit from the capitalist world economy while making other nations poor.
What is the political character of the theory?	Although liberals agree with the way modernization theory attacks traditions, this approach finds greatest support among conservatives who support the capitalist economy.	This theory is favored by Marxists and others on the political left: It calls for radical change to the world capitalist system in favor of a more egalitarian economic system.

The remaining countries that fall in between the "haves" and "have-nots" are called the *semiperiphery* of the world economy. They include middle-income countries such as Brazil, Honduras, and Indonesia that have close ties to the global economic core.

According to Wallerstein and others who use this approach (Delacroix & Ragin, 1981; Frank, 1981; Bergesen, 1983; Dixon & Boswell, 1996; Kentor, 1998, 2001), the world economy not only exploits people living in poor nations but also makes these low-income countries dependent on rich nations. For this reason, this approach is also called *dependency theory*. This dependency occurs in three ways:

1. **Poor countries have only narrow, export-oriented economies.** Poor nations produce only a few crops, which they sell to rich countries. For example, coffee and fruits from Latin American nations, petroleum from Nigeria, hardwoods from the Philippines, and palm oil from Malaysia are all consumed by affluent people in rich nations. With production under the control of multinational corporations, low-income countries develop little of their own industrial production.

2. **Poor countries lack industrial production.** Having little industrial base, poor nations depend on rich nations to buy their inexpensive raw materials. At the same time, they turn to rich countries for more expensive manufactured goods. For example, British colonialists encouraged the people of India to raise cotton but prevented them from weaving their own cloth. The British shipped Indian cotton to English textile mills in Birmingham and Manchester. The more expensive finished goods were then shipped back to India for sale.

   The same pattern applies today to agricultural products. What modernization theorists call the Green

Revolution involves poor countries selling cheap raw materials to rich nations and in turn buying expensive fertilizers, pesticides, and mechanical equipment from those same rich nations. Rich countries gain much more than poor nations from such trading.

3. **Poor countries are deeply in debt.** Given such unequal trade patterns, it is little wonder that poor countries have fallen into debt to rich nations. Altogether, the poor nations of the world owe rich countries $4.8 trillion. Such staggering debt leaves poor countries with little money to build economically; the result is high unemployment and high inflation (World Bank, 2014).

As Wallerstein and other social-conflict theorists see it, the causes of global poverty are the capitalist economy and the policies of rich nations. Modernization theorists claim that rich nations produce wealth through capital investment and technological innovation. As poor nations do business with rich nations and adopt pro-growth policies and more productive technology, they too will produce more wealth and prosper. World system theorists, by contrast, highlight how the global economy distributes wealth. They argue that the world's economic system only makes rich countries richer, leaving poor nations little or no opportunity to improve their living standards. In short, the global economy has *overdeveloped* rich nations and *underdeveloped* the rest of the world.

From this point of view, the problem of global population increase is likely to continue. As long as many of the world's nations remain poor, their fertility rates will remain high. Not until the world moves toward a more equal distribution of wealth and resources will there be a real chance for controlling population and ensuring the economic security of all.

The central point of world system theory or dependency theory is that no nation develops or fails to develop in isolation: The global economic system shapes the destiny of all nations. Citing Latin America, Africa, and other poor regions of the world, dependency theorists claim that there can be no development for the world's poor under the current market system dominated by rich countries and their capitalist, multinational corporations.

But critics disagree, claiming that the main assertion of this approach—that no nation gets richer without another nation getting poorer—is simply incorrect. They point out that—in countries rich or poor—enterprising individuals working on farms, in small businesses, and in large corporations can and do create new wealth through their hard work, imagination, and use of technology. This is precisely why the wealth of the world as a whole has increased tenfold since 1950.

Second, critics challenge the argument that rich nations are to blame for global poverty. As evidence for this assertion, they point to many of the world's poorest countries (such as Ethiopia) that have had little contact with rich countries. On the other hand, a long history of trade with rich nations has increasingly generated prosperity in Sri Lanka, Singapore, Hong Kong, and, more recently, India (E. F. Vogel, 1991; Firebaugh, 1992; Zakaria, 2004).

Third, critics say that by citing a single factor—world capitalism—as the cause of global inequality, world system theory treats poor societies as passive victims with no responsibility for their own situation (Worsley, 1990). They note that while the Taliban enforced fundamentalist Islam in Afghanistan, that nation had few economic ties with other countries and people there remained desperately poor. Similarly, many nations, including Panama, Haiti, the Democratic Republic of Congo, the Philippines,

Egypt, Iraq, Zaire, Zimbabwe, and Libya, have suffered from the actions of dictators who have looted national wealth. Capitalist societies, then, cannot be blamed for economic stagnation in these nations.

Fourth, critics say that world system theory is wrong to claim that global trade always makes rich nations richer and poor nations poorer. In 2013, the United States had a trade deficit of $704 billion, meaning that this nation imports nearly three-quarters of a trillion dollars more than it sells abroad. The single greatest debt (of $318 billion) was to China, whose profitable trade with rich nations such as the United States has now pushed that country into the ranks of middle-income nations (U.S. Census Bureau, 2014).

CHECK YOUR LEARNING In your own words, explain world system theory. What are several criticisms of this theory?

✪ POLITICS AND GLOBAL INEQUALITY

Constructing Problems and Defining Solutions

15.4 Analyze global inequality from various positions on the political spectrum.

What issues people see as "problems" and what policies they support as "solutions" reflect their political attitudes. This chapter concludes with three political perspectives on global poverty and the solutions each offers.

Conservatives praise the power of the marketplace and see world trade as benefiting all nations, rich and poor alike. Liberals argue that markets alone cannot ensure the well-being of a billion desperately poor people around the world—world governments, too, must take action. Radicals contend that global capitalism is incapable of lifting the living standards of the world as a whole; they call for a new, more equitable economic and political system. In your opinion, which viewpoint offers the greatest promise to people like these women, who work for a few dollars a day in sweatshops?

Conservatives: The Power of the Market

In his study of industrial capitalism, Peter Berger (1986:36) concludes, "Industrial capitalism has generated the greatest productive power in human history. To date, no other socioeconomic system has been able to generate comparable productive power." This statement provides a strong foundation for the conservative view of global inequality.

Conservatives believe that poverty is a serious problem throughout the world. But they remind us that the problem is much smaller today than in centuries past. For tens of thousands of generations, the vast majority of people in the world were poorly nourished, had primitive shelter, received little schooling, and had almost no medical care. Today, on average, people live longer and better than ever before. Some 3 billion—nearly half—of the world's people enjoy long, healthy, and comfortable lives well beyond the imagination of their ancestors. Another 3 billion people are not this well-off but still are more secure and comfortable than the average person who lived before the Industrial Revolution.

That leaves about 1.2 billion people whose lives are in serious danger as the result of poverty. Consistent with modernization theory, conservatives believe that the solution to global poverty lies in allowing the productive power of industrial capitalism—the force that lifted living standards of the majority—to continue to work its magic. They point to United Nations studies (United Nations Development Programme, 1994, 1996, 1998, 2003, 2005, 2008, 2011) that show that global progress is being made toward a better life: Daily calorie intake and average life expectancy are both up, and access to safe water and adult literacy are more widespread today than ever before. Worldwide, infant mortality has declined to half of what it was in 1960. In recent decades, astounding economic development has been recorded by many formerly poor nations of the world, including Mexico, Brazil, South Korea, Taiwan, Hong Kong, Singapore, India, and China.

Liberals: Governments Must Act

Liberals accept the fact that the capitalist market system is highly productive. Yet they differ from conservatives in claiming that the solution to global poverty involves more than the capitalist market operating *by itself*. According to the World Bank (2014), nations around the world should continue to pursue economic growth. But their governments should adopt policies that allocate a larger share of this increasing wealth to the poor.

One reason government help is needed is that modernizing influences, such as the use of high technology, have yet to reach many low-income nations, especially the desperately poor, rural regions. Liberals claim that governments of rich nations—the countries that benefit most from global economic production—have a moral obligation to provide economic assistance that will reach the world's poor to help improve nutrition, health care, and education.

A second issue is that global corporations as well as national businesses that operate in low-income nations typically increase their profits by using low-wage labor. For example, controversy arose with reports that companies contracting with Apple to assemble iPads and other products in China pay workers a fraction of what workers in the United States earn and may force extended overtime and provide unsafe working conditions (Bondreau & May, 2012). Liberals think that it is up to governments in both rich and poor countries to eliminate the exploitation that occurs in such businesses.

The worse cases of economic exploitation involve factories that operate as "sweatshops." The typical U.S. worker in manufacturing earns about $35 per hour. But across our southern border in Mexico, the comparable figure is about $6.50 and in the poorest countries of the world the hourly wage is less than $1 (U.S. Department of Labor, 2012). Sweatshops not only pay workers very little, but they are also extremely dangerous workplaces. The Social Problems in Global Perspective box on page 454 describes a recent and deadly example.

Finally, around the world, millions of peasants do not own the land they work. In Brazil, for example, three-fourths of all farmland is owned by wealthy landowners who make up less than 5 percent of the population (Galano, 1998). For this reason, as a step toward reducing global poverty, liberals support government action to give working families the opportunity to own land. In Brazil, for example, a social movement to put farmland into the hands of small farmers has succeeded in helping almost half a million families gain title to land they now both work and own (Field & Bell, 2013).

The Radical Left: End Global Capitalism

As radicals on the left see it, global poverty results from the operation of the worldwide capitalist economy. Hunger activists Frances Moore Lappé and Joseph Collins (Lappé, Collins, & Kinley, 1981; Lappé & Collins, 1986) claim that many people in the United States have been raised to think of global poverty as the inevitable result of "natural" disasters such as droughts and floods and also the lack of population control on the part of "backward" societies.

From the radical-left point of view, however, global poverty is tragic because it is *not* inevitable. Lappé and Collins point out that the world already produces plenty of food for everyone. In fact, if the world's total food supply were to be distributed and consumed equally, every person on the planet would soon be getting fat. Even poor regions of the world such as southern Africa actually *export* food, even though many people in these regions go hungry.

How, then, can we explain the existence of poverty amid plenty? Lappé and Collins see the problem as the capitalist economy through which rich nations direct the production of food for profits, not people. Corporations operating in poor nations typically produce export crops such as coffee, which bring high profits when sold in rich nations. But growing export crops produces fewer staples such as beans and corn that would feed local families. Government officials in poor countries also favor growing for export because they need the money to pay foreign debt. To break out of this vicious circle, the capitalist global economy must be changed.

LEFT TO RIGHT

The Politics of Global Inequality

	Radical-Left View	Liberal View	Conservative View
What is the problem?	Some of the world is overdeveloped, and much of the world is underdeveloped. The world's wealth is concentrated in a handful of very rich nations.	Most people in rich nations have more than they need, but 1.2 billion people around the world contend with a poor diet, inadequate housing, and little education.	Although more than 5 billion people in the world live far better than our ancestors several centuries ago, 1.2 billion of the world's people remain poor.
What is the solution?	Replace the capitalist world economy with a system that values people above profits, eliminate multinational corporations, use land to grow food for local consumption, and cancel foreign debt.	The rich of the world must share their wealth in the form of foreign aid that will improve health, schooling, and housing; oppose sweatshops; and support land reform.	Allow the productive power of the market to raise the living standards of poor nations today as it has done in the past; encourage capital investment and technology transfers to poor nations.

JOIN THE DEBATE

1. From each of the three political perspectives, what role do rich nations such as the United States have in addressing global poverty and hunger?

2. What importance does each political perspective assign to government? To a free market?

3. Which of the three political analyses of global inequality included here do you find most convincing? Why?

In the short term, from this point of view, the problem of global poverty is likely to get worse as the world's poorest nations sink deeper in debt to rich nations. The solution is the transformation of global capitalism toward a more socially conscious economic system. At the very least, poor nations should demand a cancellation of existing debt and end economic relations with multinational corporations. In addition, they should nationalize (that is, take control of) foreign-owned industries within their borders and place them under government ownership. In recent years, leftist leaders in a number of nations in South America have done just that. Of course, such action strikes at the very root of our global power structure. But from the radical-left point of view, nothing less is likely to work.

The Left to Right table summarizes the three political approaches to global poverty.

Going On from Here

The increase in world population remains one of the most serious problems facing humanity. During the twentieth century, global population soared. Looking ahead, although the *rate* of population increase will slow, projections state that billions more will be added to the planet during this century. The Social Problems in Focus box tracks predictions about the future.

The main reason that global population will continue to increase in coming decades is that half of the people in high-growth nations have yet to reach childbearing age. The projected increase will place greater demands on the limited resources in low-income nations, making the task of raising living standards more difficult. For this reason,

the United Nations and other organizations are working toward the goal of bringing a halt to global population increase. Some analysts argue that we need to go even further. They claim that we must *reduce* global population to perhaps half of what we have now if everyone in the world is to have a safe and secure life (Smail, 2007).

No less challenging is the problem of global inequality. Currently, the world's wealth is very unequally distributed, with a small share of humanity (including people living in the United States, Canada, Japan, and European nations) producing most of the goods and services and consuming most of the planet's resources.

As this chapter has explained, although almost everyone agrees that the situation is serious, there is disagreement about what to do about it. The official policy of the United States has been fairly close to modernization theory: Government leaders have long claimed that poor nations can and will develop economically as rich nations did in the past. To help poor nations make economic progress, the United States provides roughly $31 billion in foreign aid annually (plus an additional $17 billion in military assistance) to nations in every region of the world. In addition, the United States supports expanding trade with other nations—including policies such as the North American Free Trade Agreement (NAFTA)—in the belief that increasing market activity benefits all nations.

Critics of "free trade" agreements counter that manufacturing jobs are being lost in the United States (which hurts workers here) and most manufacturing now takes place in low-income nations (where workers are paid little). As they see it, free trade policies benefit corporations more than working people.

SOCIAL PROBLEMS IN FOCUS

Increasing Population: A Success Story or the Greatest Crisis?

What does the future hold for our planet? Can we continue to allow population to increase at the current rate? To continue to increase at *any* rate?

Think about this: By the time you finish reading this feature, more than 1,000 people will have been added to our planet. By this time tomorrow, global population will have risen by more than 237,000. Currently, as the table shows, there are more than four births for every two deaths on the planet, pushing the world's population upward by more than 86 million people annually. Put another way, global population increase amounts to adding the population of Germany to the world each year.

It is no wonder that many demographers and environmentalists are deeply concerned about the future. Earth has an unprecedented population: The 1.9 billion people we have added since 1990 alone exceed the planet's total population in 1900. Numbers like this make you think that Thomas Malthus—who predicted that overpopulation would push the world into war and suffering—might have been right after all.

Lester Brown and other *neo-Malthusians* predict a worldwide crisis if we do not change our ways. Brown (1995) concedes that Malthus failed to imagine how much technology (especially fertilizers and plant genetics) could boost the planet's agricultural output. But, all the same, he maintains that Earth's increasing population is rapidly outstripping its finite resources. In many low-income countries, families can find little firewood; in high-income countries, people are depleting the oil reserves. Everywhere, people are draining our supply of clean water and poisoning the planet with waste. These claims lead some analysts to argue that we have already passed Earth's "carrying capacity" for population. Therefore, we need to hold the line or even reduce global population to ensure our long-term survival (Brown, 1995; Scanlon, 2001; Smail, 2007).

But other analysts, the *anti-Malthusians*, have a more positive view. Julian Simon (1995) points out that, two centuries after Malthus predicted catastrophe, Earth supports almost six times as many people who, on average, live longer, healthier lives than ever before. With more advanced technology, not only have people devised ways to increase productivity, but they are also slowing population increase. As Simon sees it, these trends are cause for celebration. Human ingenuity has consistently proved the doomsayers wrong, and Simon is betting that it will continue to do so (Population Reference Bureau, 2013; U.S. Census Bureau, 2014).

What Do You Think?

1. Where do you place your bet? Do you think Earth can support 8 or 10 billion people? Explain.

2. What do you think should be done about global population increase? Point to specific policy directions.

3. Do you find the arguments made by the Malthusians or the anti-Malthusians more convincing? Why?

Global Population Increase, 2013

	Births	Deaths	Net Increase
Per year	142,634,000	55,973,000	86,661,000
Per month	11,886,167	4,664,417	7,221,750
Per day	390,778	153,351	237,427
Per hour	16,282	6,390	9,893
Per minute	271	106	165
Per second	4.5	1.8	2.8

What are the current global economic trends? The good news is that, over the past century, living standards rose in most of the world. Even the economic output of the poorest 25 percent of the world's people almost tripled during the last 100 years. This means that the number of people in the world living on less than $1.25 a day fell from about 1.9 billion in 1981 to about 1.2 billion in 2010 (Chen & Ravallion, 2012). Most people in the world are better off than ever before in *absolute* terms.

Then there is some troubling news. Although economic output has increased for both rich and poor nations, this growth has been uneven. As a result, in 2012, although living standards have risen everywhere, the *relative* gap between rich and poor in 2012 was more than five times bigger than it was back in 1900 (United Nations Development Programme, 2013). As Figure 15–6 on page 460 shows, the poorest of the world's people are being left behind.

Looking at specific regions of the world, the greatest reduction in poverty has taken place in Asia. Both China and India have joined the ranks of middle-income nations. Extreme poverty, which affected roughly three-fourths of China's people in 1980, had been reduced to about 10 percent of the people in 2010. In India, where half the people were extremely poor in 1980, just 30 percent were very poor in 2010. In recent decades, the economic growth of India and China has actually been

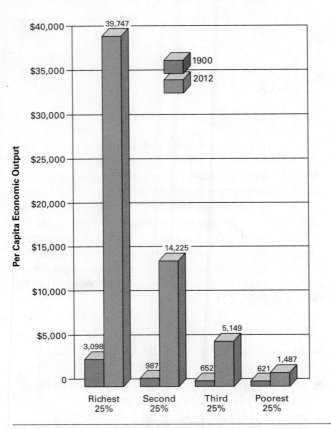

Figure 15–6 The World's Increasing Economic Inequality

The gap between the richest and poorest people in the world in 2012 was more than five times bigger than it was in 1900.

SOURCE: World Bank (2014).

great enough to reduce global economic inequality as the planet's concentration of wealth has shifted from North America and Europe to Asia (Sala-i-Martin, 2002; Chen & Ravallion, 2008; Davies et al., 2009; Milanovic, 2014).

In Latin America, the story is mixed. During the 1970s, this world region enjoyed significant economic growth; during the 1980s and 1990s, however, there was little overall improvement. But the rate of extreme poverty in Latin America, which was 12 percent in 2000, fell to about 6 percent by 2010 (Chen & Ravallion, 2008; World Bank, 2014).

Poverty rates in Africa—especially south of the Sahara—remain high. In this region, the rate of extreme poverty was almost 60 percent in 2000 but fell back to 48 percent by 2010. Most hopefully, analysts point out that six of the ten fastest-developing nations in the world now are in Africa (Chen & Ravallion, 2008; World Bank, 2014).

Daily hunger experienced by some 850 million people on the planet is reason enough for the world to take action. But something even bigger is at stake: Unless the world changes so that all people have a secure existence, can any of us expect the nations of the world to find peace?

Essay: Envisioning a Better Society What do you see as the future of global inequality? Fifty years from now, do you think that global inequality will be greater or lesser than it is now? Why? What specific policies would you support in pursuit of a better world?

CHAPTER 15   Population and Global Inequality

What should we do about the rapidly increasing population of our planet?

As this chapter has explained, Earth's population has increased sevenfold over the last 200 years, to the point that many analysts are pointing to a population crisis. Look at the two accompanying photos to see two different approaches to solving this problem.

From the left side of the political spectrum, the solution to social problems typically is action by the government. In China, a nation that was facing rapid population increase, the government enacted a one-child policy back in 1979. The government views this policy as a solution to the population problem, claiming that the nation's population is now about 250 million lower than it would have been without this policy. What do you see as advantages and disadvantages of such a policy?

From the right side of the political spectrum, conservatives claim that the market system will encourage economic development and, in time, put the brakes on population increase. As economies develop, children become more and more expensive to raise and more women join the labor force. As a result, birth rates fall—without heavy-handed government mandates.

Hint: China's government mandate has certainly reduced that nation's population increase. But critics point to increases in abortion and also female infanticide as unfortunate consequences. In addition, there is the question as to whether government or parents themselves should make decisions about having children. As for the conservative solution, economic development can take decades, allowing population to climb in the meantime. In addition, a free-market solution allows richer families to have more children than poorer families can afford, raising questions of equity. On the population question, which approach to a solution do you support?

Getting Involved: Applications and Exercises

1. Pay attention to mass media advertising that mentions low-income countries (ads selling, say, coffee from Colombia or exotic vacations to India). What images of life in low-income countries does the advertising present? In light of the facts presented in this chapter, do you think these images are accurate?

2. Explain the causes and solutions to the problem of global poverty using modernization theory. How does world system theory support a different analysis?

3. Looking over the various global maps in this text, identify social patterns (such as how many children women have, the level of life expectancy, the extent of illiteracy, and other factors) associated with the world's richest and poorest nations. Make use of both modernization theory and world system theory to explain the patterns you find.

4. Do some research on the Internet to explore the status of women in a number of low-income nations. One good source is the Human Development Report, published annually by the United Nations (http://www.undp.org). In poor countries, are women and men more unequal than they are in high-income nations such as the United States? In what ways are they unequal? Why are they unequal?

Making the Grade

CHAPTER 15 Population and Global Inequality

A DEFINING MOMENT
Thomas Robert Malthus: Claiming Population Is a Problem **p. 445**

Global Population Increase

15.1   **Explain the causes of global population increase.**

Factors Affecting Population Growth

High **fertility**, as measured by the **crude birth rate**

- Birth rates are highest in low-income nations, where access to birth control is limited and women have few choices about how many children to bear. **p. 441**

Low **mortality**, as measured by the **crude death rate**

- The lower a nation's mortality, the faster its population increases.

- Infant mortality is highest in poor nations, where people lack adequate nutrition and safe water and have little access to high-quality medical care. **pp. 441–42**

In global terms, U.S. population growth is low.

- Historically, world population grew slowly because high birth rates were mostly offset by high death rates.

- About 1750, a demographic transition began as world population rose sharply, mostly because of falling death rates.

- In 1798, Thomas Robert Malthus warned that population growth would outpace food production, resulting in starvation and social chaos.

- More recent **demographic transition theory** holds that technological advances gradually slow population increase. **pp. 442–46**

demography (p. 440) the study of human population

fertility (p. 441) the incidence of childbearing in a country's population

crude birth rate (p. 441) the number of live births in a given year for every 1,000 people in a population

mortality (p. 441) the incidence of death in a country's population

crude death rate (p. 441) the number of deaths in a given year for every 1,000 people in a population

infant mortality rate (p. 442) the number of babies, of every 1,000 born, who die before their first birthday

zero population growth (p. 444) the level of reproduction that maintains population at a steady state

demographic transition theory (p. 445) a thesis linking demographic changes to a society's level of technological development

Global Inequality

15.2   **Describe high-, middle-, and low-income nations and the extent of global poverty.**

Social inequality in the world as a whole is greater than in the United States.

- About 23% of the world's people live in high-income countries such as the United States and receive 64% of all income.

- Another 60% live in middle-income countries, receiving about 33% of all income.

- The remaining 17% of the world's population live in low-income countries that have yet to industrialize and earn only 3% of global income. **pp. 446–48**

Relative poverty is found everywhere, but poor nations contain widespread *absolute poverty* that is life-threatening.

- Worldwide, the lives of 842 million people are at risk because of poor nutrition.

- About 9 million people, most of them children, die annually from various causes brought on by hunger and lack of adequate nutrition. **pp. 448–49**

Nearly everywhere in the world, women are more likely than men to be poor. About 70% of adults facing absolute poverty are women.

- Gender stratification is most pronounced in poor societies, which tend to be strongly patriarchal.

- About 20 million men, women, and children live in conditions that can be described as slavery. **pp. 449–51**

Theories of Global Inequality

15.3   Apply sociological theory to the issue of global inequality.

Structural-Functional Analysis: The Process of Modernization

Structural-functional analysis is seen in **modernization theory**'s model of economic development, which explains global inequality in terms of differences among societies in level of technology and cultural patterns.

- Modernization theory maintains that economic development hinges on breaking free of traditional cultural patterns to seek material prosperity and adopt advanced technology.

- The modernization theorist W. W. Rostow identifies four stages of development: traditional, take-off, drive to technological maturity, and high mass consumption. **pp. 451–53**

- *Critics of modernization theory* say that rich nations do not encourage but actually prevent economic development around the world. Therefore, they claim, poor nations cannot follow the path to development taken by rich nations centuries ago. **p. 453**

Social-Conflict Analysis: The Global Economic System

Social-conflict analysis centers on **world system theory**, a model of economic development that explains global inequality in terms of the historical exploitation of poor societies by rich ones.

- World system theory (also called "dependency theory") claims that global wealth and poverty are the historical products of the capitalist world economy beginning with colonialism and continuing, more recently, with the operation of multinational corporations.

- Immanuel Wallerstein views the high-income countries as the advantaged core of the capitalist world economy, middle-income nations as the semiperiphery, and poor societies as the global periphery. Economic relations make poor nations dependent on rich ones. **pp. 453–56**

- *Critics of world system theory* argue that this approach overlooks the sixfold increase in the world's wealth since 1950. Furthermore, the world's poorest societies are not those with the strongest ties to rich countries. **p. 456**

modernization theory (p. 451) a model of economic and social development that explains global inequality in terms of technological and cultural differences between societies

world system theory (dependency theory) (p. 453) a model of economic development that explains global inequality in terms of the historical exploitation of poor societies by rich ones

colonialism (p. 453) the process by which some nations enrich themselves through political and economic control of other nations

neocolonialism (p. 453) a new form of economic exploitation that involves the operation of multinational corporations rather than direct political control by foreign governments

✪ POLITICS AND GLOBAL INEQUALITY

Constructing Problems and Defining Solutions

15.4   Analyze global inequality from various positions on the political spectrum.

Conservatives: The Power of the Market

- **Conservatives** believe that poverty is a problem around the world, but they focus on the improvements that have been made in recent centuries.

- Conservatives believe that the productive power of industrial capitalism will eventually solve the problem of global poverty. **pp. 456–57**

Liberals: Governments Must Act

- **Liberals** claim that the governments of rich nations have a moral responsibility to provide aid to poor nations, especially in the areas of health and education.

- Liberals want governments in both rich and poor countries to eliminate sweatshop exploitation. **p. 457**

The Radical Left: End Global Capitalism

- **Radicals on the left** blame the policies of rich nations for creating poverty in poor nations and keeping them in debt.

- Radicals on the left believe that poor nations should nationalize foreign-owned industries within their borders and demand a cancellation of their existing debt to rich nations. **pp. 457–58**

Technology and the Environment

Learning Objectives

16.1 Identify several key factors that affect the natural environment.

16.2 Discuss the causes and consequences of increasing pollution, global warming, and other environmental problems.

16.3 Apply sociological theory to issues involving the natural environment.

16.4 Analyze environmental problems and solutions from various positions on the political spectrum.

Tracking the Trends

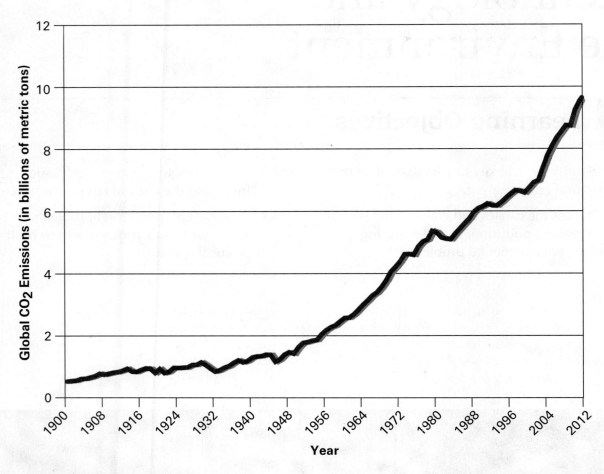

SOURCES: Adams (2013) and Boden, Marland, & Andres (2010).

Human societies rely on the burning of wood, coal, oil, natural gas, and other fossil fuels to generate energy. But humanity's increasing need for energy means expelling ever more carbon dioxide (CO_2) into the atmosphere. The figure shows the increasing annual output of CO_2 emission from 1900 to 2012. As you can see, the output level doubled by 1930 and doubled again by 1960. It doubled again by 1975 and more than doubled yet again by 2010. Scientists claim that the increasing levels of CO_2 emissions are raising the average temperature of the planet's atmosphere resulting in global warming, which has the potential to alter our planet dramatically. Are you concerned about how our way of life may be affecting the natural environment that supports life on this planet?

Constructing the Problem

Is trash a problem?

Every day, people in the United States generate 1.4 billion pounds of solid waste. What should we do with it?

Does living well hurt the environment?

The average person living in the United States uses about thirty-three times more energy each year than the typical person living in Bangladesh.

Why should we protect the planet's rain forests?

The world's rain forests, which support us in many ways, are shrinking by some 21,000 square miles each year.

Chapter Overview

Why is the state of the natural environment a social issue? The simple answer is that the biggest factor affecting the environment is how humanity organizes social life. This chapter looks at specific factors such as population increase, material affluence, technology, and cultural patterns, all of which shape the environment. You will learn about environmental issues involving solid waste, water supply, air and water pollution, and global warming. You will apply sociology's theoretical approaches to environmental issues and learn how the environmental "problems" that people see and the policies they favor as "solutions" reflect their political attitudes. ■

Grandma Macionis was a beautiful and loving woman who never threw anything away. Born in Lithuania—which she called the "old country"—Lillian Macionis grew up in a small village in which everyone was poor. Even after she came to the United States as a young woman, this social world shaped her entire life.

Each year, the family gathered together to celebrate her birthday. The occasion brought great amusement because, after opening each present, she would carefully put aside the box, refold the wrapping paper, and roll up the ribbon so that all these things could be used again. The packaging meant as much to her as the gift itself—possibly even more because, as far as we could tell, Grandma never wore any new clothes we gave her. Grandma Macionis lived a simple life guided by the belief that there was nothing wrong with what she already had. So, although she appreciated gifts as a symbol of her family's love, she viewed anything new in the material world as unnecessary and wasteful.

Grandma's kitchen knives were worn down from decades of sharpening, and every piece of furniture she ever owned stayed with her to the end of her life. (Carrying on

the family tradition, I still eat at the same round oak table she first placed in her kitchen almost a century ago.)

As curious as Grandma Macionis often seemed to her grandchildren, she was a product of her culture. The social world in which she grew up produced little "trash." If socks wore thin, people mended them, again and again. When clothes became worn beyond repair, people used them as cleaning rags or sewed them together to make a quilt. For people like Grandma, everything had value, if not in one way, then in another.

Grandma Macionis never thought of herself as an environmentalist. But she was: She used few resources and created almost no solid waste. Living this way may seem strange or old-fashioned to most people in the United States today. After all, most of us seem to measure social standing by how much we consume. And our modern way of life also favors "convenience," a value that leads us to buy our morning coffee in throw-away cups, to bundle our groceries in throw-away plastic bags, and to rely on private cars rather than public transit. As this chapter explains, most of us hold a materialistic, fast-paced view of the "good life." But living this way also places a great strain on our natural environment.

Ecology: Studying the Natural Environment

16.1 Identify several key factors that affect the natural environment.

Ecology is *the study of how living organisms interact with the natural environment.* Because ecology involves both human societies and the physical world, this field links the social sciences and natural sciences. This chapter focuses on how the operation of society shapes the natural environment.

The term **natural environment** refers to *Earth's surface and atmosphere, including air, water, soil, and other resources necessary to sustain living organisms.* Like every other living species, humans depend on the natural environment to survive.

Yet humans stand apart from other species in our capacity for culture. This means that we are the only species that takes deliberate action to remake the world according to our interests and desires. To do this, we rely on **technology**, *knowledge that people apply to the task of living in a physical environment.* As technology has become more complex and powerful, humans have gained the ability—for better or worse—to transform the world.

The Role of Sociology

Problems related to the environment include vast amounts of solid waste, various types of pollution, the effects of acid rain, the process of global warming, and the declining number of living species. None of these problems results from the natural world operating on its own. They are all products of the way humans organize their lives within societies. For this reason, environmental issues are *social problems.*

Sociologists examine how people consume natural resources and track the amount of waste and pollution that people produce. Sociologists track public opinion on issues ranging from natural gas "fracking" to global warming and identify what categories of people support one side or the other of various environmental issues. But the most important contribution sociologists make is in demonstrating how our society's technology, cultural patterns, and specific political and economic arrangements affect the natural environment.

The Global Dimension

Like the problems of rising population and world hunger, discussed in Chapter 15 ("Population and Global Inequality"), environmental problems are global in scope. Why? Because although humans have divided our planet into nations, it is a single **ecosystem**, *the interaction of all living organisms and their natural environment.*

The Greek meaning of *eco* is "house," which reminds us that our planet is our home, the setting in which living things and their natural environment are interconnected. Changes to any part of the natural environment ripple throughout the entire global ecosystem.

These connections can be illustrated by humans' use of chlorofluorocarbons (CFCs, marketed under the brand name Freon), once common as propellants in aerosol spray cans and as gas in refrigerators and air conditioners. CFCs were widely used because they are cheap, easy to use, nontoxic, and effective. But once released into the environment, they began to accumulate in the upper atmosphere, where they reacted with sunlight to form chlorine atoms. Chlorine destroys ozone, the layer of the atmosphere that filters out harmful ultraviolet radiation. This process caused a huge hole to open in the atmospheric ozone layer over Antarctica that led to an increase in the incidence of human skin cancers and caused harm to plants and animals. To protect the ozone layer, the United States and many other nations have banned the use of CFCs in favor of environmentally safer alternatives.

Population Increase

Sociologists point to a simple formula: $I = PAT$, where environmental impact (I) reflects a society's population (P), its level of affluence (A), and its level of technology (T). In short, the more people in a society, the richer their way of life, and the more complex their technology, the bigger the impact on the natural environment.

Let's look first at population. As Chapter 15 ("Population and Global Inequality") explained, 2,000 years ago, the world had about 300 million people—less than the population of the United States today (Population Reference Bureau, 2014).

In the nineteenth century, as a number of nations developed industrial technology and the medical science that goes along with it, living standards rose and death rates fell sharply. The predictable result was a sharp upward spike in world population. By 1800, global population had soared to 1 billion.

In the decades that followed, population increased ever more quickly, with the planet's population reaching 2 billion by 1930, 3 billion by 1962, 4 billion by 1974, 5 billion by 1987, and 6 billion by 1999. By the beginning of 2014, more than 7.1 billion people lived on the planet. Although the rate of increase has now slowed, we continue to add 87 million people to the world's total each year (more than 237,000 every day) (Population Reference Bureau, 2013).

A well-known riddle illustrates how runaway growth can suddenly overwhelm the natural environment (Milbrath, 1989:10):

> A pond has a single water lily growing on it. The lily doubles in size each day. In thirty days, it covers the entire pond. On which day did the lily cover half the pond?

The answer that comes readily to mind—the fifteenth day—is wrong. The lily was not increasing in size by the same amount every day; it was *doubling* in size each day. The correct answer, then, is that the lily covered half the pond on the twenty-ninth day, just one day earlier. The point is that for almost the entire month, the size of the growing lily seems manageable. Only on the twenty-ninth day, when the lily covers half the pond, are people likely to see the problem, but by then it is too late to do anything about it and the very next day, the lily chokes the life out of the entire pond.

Most experts predict that the world population will increase to about 9.6 billion people by 2050 (United Nations, 2013). The most rapid population growth is occurring in the poorest regions of the world. A glance back at Global Map 15–1 on page 470 shows the growth rates for nations around the world. Taken together, the nations of Africa are adding to their population at an annual rate of 2.6 percent, which will more than double Africa's population by 2050 (Population Reference Bureau, 2013).

Poverty and Affluence

Rapid population increase makes the problem of poverty worse. This is because a surging population can offset increases in productivity so that living standards stay the same. If a society's population doubles, doubling economic productivity amounts to no gain at all in standard of living.

But poverty also makes environmental problems worse. Preoccupied with survival, poor people have little choice but to consume the resources they have, without thinking about long-term environmental consequences.

But the long-term trend for the world is toward greater affluence. What are the environmental consequences of rising population and greater affluence taking place *together*? One way to answer this question is to consider the consequences of increasing affluence in India and China, which together contain 2.6 billion people. China is already the world's largest market for automobiles. Now that India is a middle-income nation, an ever-increasing share of its people own motor vehicles. In 2014, a year in which about 15 million automobiles were sold in the United States, sales reached 20 million vehicles in China (CBS News, 2014). What effect will this trend toward greater auto production and use have on the world's oil reserves? What about global air quality?

Simply put, if people all around the world were to live at the level of material abundance that most people in the United States take for granted, the natural environment would rapidly collapse. From an environmentalist point of view, our planet may suffer from economic underdevelopment in some places, but it also suffers from economic overdevelopment in others.

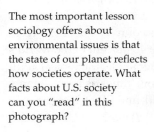

The most important lesson sociology offers about environmental issues is that the state of our planet reflects how societies operate. What facts about U.S. society can you "read" in this photograph?

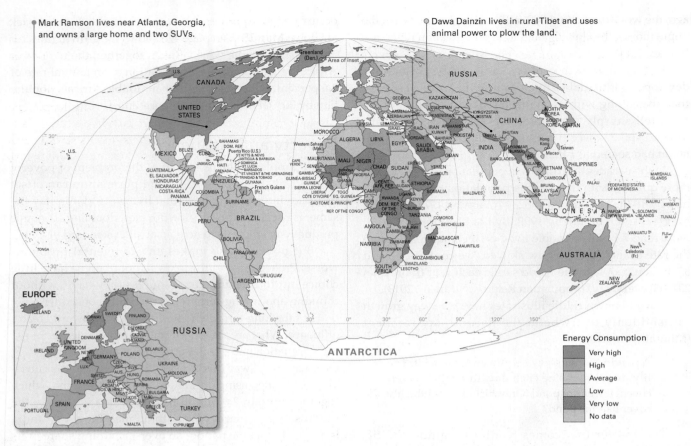

Mark Ramson lives near Atlanta, Georgia, and owns a large home and two SUVs.

Dawa Dainzin lives in rural Tibet and uses animal power to plow the land.

Energy Consumption

- Very high
- High
- Average
- Low
- Very low
- No data

Window on the World

Global Map 16–1 Energy Consumption in Global Perspective

People in high-income nations consume far more energy than those living in poor countries. The typical U.S. resident uses the same amount of energy in a year as 108 people in Ethiopia or 88 people in the Central African Republic. In general, the most economically productive nations are those that put the greatest burden on the natural environment. In fact, in recent years, the demand for energy in the United States has exceeded the available supply.

SOURCE: Central Intelligence Agency (2014).

Technology

We gain additional insight from considering the historical development of technology. Our earliest ancestors lived by hunting animals and gathering plants. With this simple technology, these people had little effect on the environment. They adapted their lives to the rhythms of nature, moving from place to place with the migration of animals and the changing seasons and in response to natural events such as fires, floods, and droughts.

People living in societies that gain the use of horticulture (small-scale farming), pastoralism (the herding of animals), or agriculture (with animal-drawn plows) have a greater capacity to affect the environment. But limited by the use of muscle power for energy, the environmental impact of these technologies is still quite small.

The Industrial Revolution changed everything by replacing muscles with vastly more powerful combustion engines that burn fossil fuels such as coal and oil. Using industrial technology, humans are capable of bending nature to their will, tunneling through mountains, damming rivers, irrigating deserts, and drilling for oil beneath the ocean floor. In the process, we consume more energy resources and also release more pollutants into the atmosphere. The overall result of new technology is that humans have brought more change to the planet's environment in the last two centuries than our ancestors did in all of human history before then.

Global Map 16–1 shows that high-income, high-technology countries consume a great deal of the world's energy. Although these nations account for just 23 percent of humanity, they represent about 40 percent of the world's energy consumption. From another angle, the typical adult in the United States uses about four times as much energy as the average person in the world, and fifty times as much as a person living in a low-income nation such as Eritrea (International Energy Agency, 2014).

Equally important, members of industrial and postindustrial societies produce 100 times more goods than people working in agrarian societies. Much of what we produce (such as packaging) is never consumed at all and is simply thrown away, creating vast amounts of solid waste.

The Environmental Deficit This short look at human history teaches an important lesson: The increase in human population, the rising level of affluence around the globe, and the development of more powerful technology have positive consequences, but they also put the lives of future generations at risk. The evidence is mounting that we are running up an **environmental deficit**, *serious, long-term harm to the environment caused by humanity's focus on short-term material affluence* (Bormann, 1990).

Facing up to the environmental deficit is important for three reasons. First, it reminds us that environmental quality is a *social issue,* reflecting choices people make about what technology to use, how many children to have, and how much to consume. Second, it suggests that much environmental damage may be *unintended.* By focusing on the short-term benefits of, say, cutting down forests or using throwaway packaging, we satisfy our desire for material goods and convenience. At the same time, however, we fail to see that such behavior has long-term, harmful environmental effects. Third, in some respects the environmental deficit is *reversible.* If members of modern societies make different choices, they can undo many (but not all) environmental problems.

Cultural Patterns: Growth and Limits

How we live is guided by culture. Our cultural outlook, especially how we think about "the good life," has important consequences for the natural environment.

The Logic of Growth Why does our society set off specific areas as parks or wildlife preserves? The unspoken message is that except for these special areas, people may freely use the planet and its resources for their own purposes (N. Myers, 1991). Most members of our society share this aggressive approach to the natural environment. Where does this thinking come from?

In the United States, our way of life is based on a quest for *material comfort.* Most people believe that money and the things it buys enrich our lives. Most of us also believe in *progress,* thinking that the future will be better than the present, and *science,* looking to experts and new technology to improve our lives. Taken together, these cultural values form an outlook that environmentalists call the *logic of growth.*

The logic of growth is rooted in an optimistic view of the world. In simple terms, this way of thinking amounts to certain key beliefs: Material things are "good," "people are clever," and "life will improve."

Of course, even optimists realize that progress can sometimes lead to unexpected problems. For example, the increasing number of motor vehicles in the world may make move people faster than ever, but this trend also threatens to drain the planet's oil reserves. The logic of growth argues that people—especially scientists and other experts—are inventive and will find a way around any problems. By the time oil supplies run short, which is likely by the end of this century, scientists will have invented vehicles powered by electricity, hydrogen, solar energy, or some as yet unknown type of power to free us from oil dependence.

The logic of growth is deeply linked to U.S. culture. However, environmentalists point to several flaws in this line of thinking (Milbrath, 1989). First, this approach fails to recognize that natural resources such as oil, clean air, fresh water, and topsoil are *finite* resources that can and will be used up. The greater the pursuit of economic growth, the sooner these resources will be gone.

Second, environmentalists say it is arrogant and dangerous to assume that human resourcefulness can solve all our problems. On the contrary, the more powerful and complex the technology—say, using nuclear reactors instead of gasoline engines or drilling for oil beneath the ocean floor rather than on land—the more serious the potential consequences of miscalculation or accident. Environmentalists therefore claim that we cannot support more and more people at higher living standards without exhausting finite resources, degrading the environment, and endangering ourselves in the process.

The Limits to Growth Environmentalists claim that, because we humans cannot invent our way out of the problems created by the logic of growth, we need another way of thinking about the world. Growth cannot continue indefinitely and must have limits. Simply stated, the *limits-to-growth thesis* is that humanity must limit population increase and the use of finite resources to avoid eventual environmental collapse.

A 1972 book called *The Limits to Growth* helped launch the environmental movement. In the book, Donella Meadows and her colleagues (1972; Meadows, Randers, & Meadows, 2004) devised a computer model that estimated the planet's available resources, rates of population increase, amount of land available for cultivation, levels of industrial and food production, and amount of pollutants released into the atmosphere. Based on historical trends, the model made projections to the end of the twenty-first century. The authors admit that such long-range predictions are, to some extent, guesswork, and some critics think they are plain wrong (J. Simon, 1981). But other researchers suggest that a global economic collapse due to using up limited resources could occur in as little as twenty years (Strauss, 2012). Right or wrong, Meadows's conclusions, shown in Figure 16–1, deserve serious consideration.

According to the limits-to-growth thesis, humans (especially those using industrial technology) are quickly consuming Earth's finite resources. Supplies of oil, natural gas, and other sources of energy are already falling sharply and will continue to drop, a little faster or more slowly depending on policies in rich nations and the speed at which other nations industrialize. Global population is likely to rise through the first half of this century, with a gradual decline after that. At this point, world hunger—caused by too many people and unequal distribution of food—will increase and may well reach a crisis level. And before long, the world will begin running out of water and other vital resources, reducing industrial output.

Environmentalists who support the limits-to-growth thesis are sometimes called neo-Malthusians because, like Thomas Robert Malthus, discussed in Chapter 15, ("Population and Global Inequality"), they are pessimistic about the future of humanity. Believing that current patterns of life are not sustainable through this century, they conclude that we face a basic choice: Either we make deliberate changes in how we live now, or a future crisis will force change upon us.

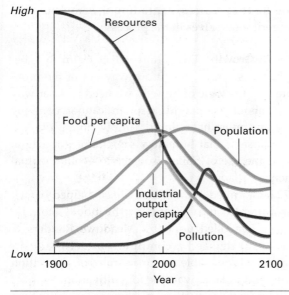

Figure 16–1   The Limits to Growth: Projections

This computer model predicts that humanity will deplete most of Earth's resources within a century. Although people disagree over the specifics of such predictions, most agree that significant change is needed to avoid environmental catastrophe.

SOURCE: Based on Meadows et al. (1972).

Environmental Problems

16.2 **Discuss the causes and consequences of increasing pollution, global warming, and other environmental problems.**

Environmentalists express serious worries about our future. About two-thirds of U.S. adults say they share a concern about the environment; most define pollution and other related issues as "dangerous" problems (Smith et al., 2013). This statistic is far higher than it was fifty years ago, when only a handful of people defined environmental issues as problems. The Defining Moment box takes a closer look at one of the first people who did.

What is the state of the natural environment today? The following sections briefly examine several environmental issues, with particular attention to problems in the United States.

Solid Waste: The Disposable Society

One environmental problem is waste—or more precisely, too much of it. The average person in the United States discards about 4.4 pounds of paper, metal, plastic, and other disposable materials daily; over a lifetime, that amounts to 64 tons. The country as a whole generates 1.4 billion pounds of solid waste *each and every day* (U.S. Environmental Protection Agency, 2014). Figure 16–2 on page 474 shows the composition of our national trash.

The problem of solid waste stems from a simple fact about our culture: We live in a *disposable society*. U.S. culture values material comfort and also efficiency. As a result, we consume more products than any nation on Earth, and many of these products come with lots of extra packaging that allows for ease of sale and "drive-through" convenience. The most familiar case is the cardboard, plastic, and Styrofoam containers that we buy with our fast food and throw away as soon as we finish the meal. Countless other products—from film to fishhooks, cosmetics to CD-ROMs—are elaborately packaged to appeal to the customer and to discourage tampering and theft. Manufacturers market soft drinks, beer, and fruit juices in easy-to-handle aluminum, glass, and plastic containers; yet all this packaging only uses up our finite resources and also generates mountains of solid waste. In addition, our way of life makes use of countless items that are disposable: pens, razors, flashlights, batteries, and even cameras. Other products, from computers to automobiles, are designed to have a short useful life. Much of what we create eventually becomes unwanted junk.

Living in a rich society, the average person in the United States consumes fifty to one hundred times more energy, plastics, lumber, and other resources than someone living in a low-income nation such as Bangladesh or Tanzania. At the same time, members of our society

CONSTRUCTING SOCIAL PROBLEMS

A DEFINING MOMENT

Rachel Carson: Sounding an Environmental Wake-Up Call

In the United States, the 1950s was a decade of rising prosperity. During these "good times," most people considered "growth" to be good for everyone. Few people expressed concerns about the future of the natural environment.

Rachel Carson saw things differently. Carson (1907–1964) grew up in a western Pennsylvania farm community, where she developed a lifelong passion for nature. After finishing college, she earned a master's degree in zoology. Then she went to work for the U.S. Bureau of Fisheries, preparing pamphlets on conservation. After her retirement, Carson wrote books about nature, gaining a national reputation as an environmentalist.

During the years that followed, Carson's attention turned to the rapidly increasing use of pesticides. After World War II, scientists created many new chemical pesticides that most people saw as a solution to the problem of insects damaging crops. As the use of pesticides in the United States skyrocketed, no one gave much thought to the harm these chemicals posed to the environment.

In 1962, Carson published her wake-up call in the book *Silent Spring*, which explained how the use of pesticides such as dichlorodiphenyltrichloroethane (DDT) was poisoning the streams, rivers, and lakes of the United States. Carson's book provoked a firestorm of controversy led by chemical companies, which tried to have the book banned from stores and libraries. But Carson's words went a long way to defining chemical pesticides not as a solution but as a problem that threatened the planet. She pulled no punches, asking, "Can anyone believe it is possible to lay down such a barrage of poisons on the surface of the earth without making it unfit for all life?" (1995:409).

Carson challenged the common view that science was always a force for good. In the process, she created a defining moment that helped launch the modern environmental movement.

Rachel Carson is credited with turning public attention to the environment. Her 1962 book *Silent Spring* documented the health and environmental hazards of pesticides (such as DDT) that were being widely used on farms and lawns. Rather than seeing chemicals as a solution, Carson defined them as a problem and helped spark the modern environmental movement.

also consume far more than people living in many other high-income countries such as Japan or Sweden. This high level of consumption means that we in the United States not only use a disproportionate share of the planet's natural resources but also generate most of the world's solid waste (United Nations, 2011).

We are quick to say that we "throw things away." But less than half of our solid waste is burned or recycled, leaving most (about 135 million tons in 2012) to end up in landfills (U.S. Environmental Protection Agency, 2014).

These dumping grounds pose several threats to the natural environment. First, landfills across the country are filling up. Already a number of municipalities in the United States are shipping trash to other countries to be discarded. Second, the material that ends up in landfills here or abroad contributes to water pollution. Although most localities have enacted laws that regulate what can

go in a landfill, the U.S. Environmental Protection Agency has identified 1,319 dump sites across the United States containing hazardous materials that are polluting water both above and below the ground. Third, what goes into landfills may end up remaining there for centuries. Tires, diapers, and plastic utensils do not readily decompose, and tens of millions of them will become an unwelcome environmental burden for generations to come.

Environmentalists argue that we should address the problem of solid waste by doing what Grandma Macionis and many of our ancestors did—turn "waste" into a resource. This is the basic idea behind *recycling*, reusing resources we would otherwise throw away. Recycling is a common practice in Japan and many other nations, and it is becoming more widespread in the United States, where we now recycle more than one-third of waste materials. The share is increasing as more and more states pass laws

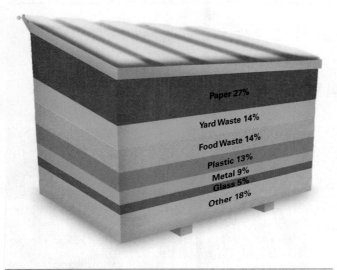

Figure 16–2 Composition of Household Trash

Here is a rough breakdown of the trash that U.S. society generates—a total of 1.4 billion pounds each day.

SOURCE: U.S. Environmental Protection Agency (2014).

requiring monetary deposits on glass bottles and aluminum cans or requiring that people recycle these materials. In addition, as more people recycle, the business of recycling is becoming more profitable. The Social Problems in Global Perspective box provides a look at one recycling success story in Egypt.

Preserving Clean Water

Oceans, lakes, and streams are the lifeblood of the global ecosystem. Humans depend on water for drinking, bathing, cooling, cooking, recreation, and a host of other activities.

According to what scientists call the *hydrologic cycle*, Earth naturally recycles water and refreshes the land. The process begins as heat from the sun causes water, 97 percent of which is in the planet's oceans, to evaporate and form clouds. Next, the clouds return water to Earth as rain, which drains into streams and rivers and rushes toward the seas. The hydrologic cycle not only renews the supply of water but also cleans it. Because water evaporates at lower temperatures than most pollutants, the water vapor that rises from the seas is pure, leaving contaminants behind. The hydrologic cycle generates clean water in the form of rain, leaving pollutants to steadily build up in the oceans.

There are two major problems associated with water: inadequate water supply and water pollution.

Inadequate Water Supply Even in the ancient civilizations of China, Egypt, and Rome, water rights were an important part of the law, reflecting the vital importance of water to any society. Some regions of the world, especially the tropics, enjoy a plentiful supply of water. However, in much of North America and Asia, people look to rivers rather than rainfall for their water, making supply a problem. In some regions of the United States, the main source is groundwater, which is water underground that is accessed using wells and springs. In many regions of the country, the supply is running low. For example, the Ogallala aquifer runs underground across seven states, from South Dakota to Texas. It is now being pumped so rapidly that it is already running dry in some places and may completely disappear within several decades (Egan, 2014).

In China, deep aquifers are dropping rapidly. In the Middle East, water supply is reaching a critical level. Iran is rationing water in its capital city. In Egypt, people can consume just one-sixth as much water from the Nile today as they could in 1900. Analysts project that by 2050, 3.9 billion people—or 40 percent of the world's population—will be living in water-stressed areas (OECD, 2012).

Soaring populations demand more and more water. Complex technology, especially in manufacturing and power-generating facilities, consumes more water, especially for cooling. The global use of water (estimated at 1 quadrillion gallons per year) is increasing even faster than the world's population. Underground water tables are rapidly dropping in countries all over the world (OECD, 2012; United Nations Food and Agricultural Organization, 2014).

In light of these trends, we must face the reality that water is a finite resource. Greater conservation of water by individuals can make a difference—currently the average person in the United States uses 2.8 million gallons of water over a lifetime. Around the world, however, individuals account for just 5 to 10 percent of all water use. More water is consumed by industry, which is responsible for 20 percent of global water use. The largest share of freshwater is directed at farm irrigation, amounting to more than 70 percent of the total. A water-supply crisis is coming quickly to the world's major agricultural regions including northeast China, northwest India, the Midwest of the United States, and California's central valley (U.S. Geological Survey, 2010; OECD, 2012).

More efficient irrigation technology may reduce water demand in the future. But here again, we see how population increase, advancing technology, and economic expansion combine to strain Earth's resources (United Nations Environment Programme, 2012).

Water Pollution In large cities from Mexico City to Cairo to Shanghai, people with no sure supply of fresh, safe water drink contaminated water every day. As a result, waterborne microorganisms cause infectious diseases, including diarrhea, intestinal worms, typhoid, cholera, and dysentery, which spread rapidly through these populations. The

SOCIAL PROBLEMS IN GLOBAL PERSPECTIVE

Turning the Tide: Reclaiming Solid Waste in Egypt

Half an hour from the center of Cairo, Egypt's capital city, the bus loaded with students from the United States bumped along a dirt road and then jerked to a stop. It was not quite dawn on that November morning, and the muezzins were soon to climb the minarets of Cairo's many mosques to call the Islamic faithful to morning prayers. The driver turned, genuinely bewildered, to face us. "Why," he asked, in labored English, "do you want to be *here*? And in the middle of the night?"

It was a good question. No sooner had one sociologist and several dozen students stepped off the bus than more smoke and stench than we had ever before encountered swirled around us. Eyes squinting, handkerchiefs pressed against noses and mouths, we slowly moved up the mountain of trash that extended for miles.

This is the Cairo dump, the final resting place for the trash generated by 20 million people in one of the world's largest cities. Gazing intently and walking with great care, we were guided by flickers of light from small fires that burned around us. Up ahead, through clouds of smoke, blazing piles of trash attracted local people warming themselves and talking.

As we approached, the fires cast a strange light on the people's faces. We stopped some distance from them, separated by a vast chasm of culture and circumstance. But smiles drew the two groups closer, and soon we all shared the comfort of the fire. At that moment, calls to prayer sounded across the city.

The Zebaleen ("rubbish people"), as they are called, number about 25,000 and are a religious minority—Coptic Christians—in a mostly Muslim society. Barred by religious discrimination from many jobs, the Zebaleen use donkey carts and small trucks to pick up Cairo's trash and haul it here. At dawn, hundreds of Zebaleen gather at the dump, swarming over the new piles in search of anything of value.

During this visit, we observed men, women, and children picking through Cairo's refuse and filling baskets with bits of metal, strips of ribbon, and even scraps of food. Every now and then, someone gleefully displayed a precious find that would bring the equivalent of a few dollars in the city. Watching in silence, we became keenly aware of our sturdy shoes and warm clothing and self-conscious that our watches and cameras represented more money than most of the Zebaleen earn in a whole year.

More than two decades later, the Cairo Zebaleen still work the city's streets collecting trash. But much has changed, and they are now one of the world's environmental success stories. The Zebaleen have a legal contract to perform their work and have built a large recycling center near the dump. Dozens of workers operate huge shredders that turn discarded cloth into stuffing to fill upholstered furniture, car seats, and pillows. Other workers separate plastic and metal into large bins for cleaning and resale. Using start-up loans from the World Bank and their own ingenuity, the Zebaleen have become successful business people.

The Zebaleen are still poor by U.S. standards. But they are prospering and now own the land on which they live and work. They have even built an apartment complex with electricity and running water. Many international environmental organizations hope their example will inspire others elsewhere (Garwood, 2003; Stack, 2009).

What Do You Think?

1. Why is the amount of recycling so limited in most societies?

2. Will recycling ever become big business in the United States? Why or why not?

3. How much recycling takes place on your campus? What can you do to get involved?

---

result is millions of deaths each year. This makes water *quality* just as serious a problem as *supply*.

By global standards, water quality in the United States is generally good. However, even here the problem of water pollution is growing steadily. According to the Sierra Club (2012), an environmental activist organization, this country produces hundreds of millions of pounds of toxic substances (including farm fertilizer, lawn treatments, and other chemicals) each year that end up in rivers and streams. Each year, the Mississippi River carries some 2 million tons of nitrogen—mostly from fertilizer washed from farmland—into the Gulf of Mexico. The buildup of nitrogen has created a "dead zone" the size of New Jersey in which almost nothing can live (Waterkeeper Alliance, 2013).

Air Pollution

The spread of industrial technology—including factories, power plants, and motor vehicles—has caused a decline in air quality. The problem was most serious a century ago, when thick, black smoke belched from factory smokestacks, often for twenty-four hours a day. In 1948, toxic smoke from the many factories killed seventy residents of Donora, Pennsylvania. On the other side of the country, exhaust fumes from automobiles hung over cities such as Los Angeles that had escaped the earlier rush of industrial development. Much the same was true of London, where smoke from factories and home coal fires combined with automobile emissions to create a deadly haze that the British

Seeing Ourselves

National Map 16–1 Risk of Cancer from Air Pollution across the United States

Air quality is better in rural areas than in urban places. Therefore, the risk of cancer from air pollution is greater in and around large cities. Across the country, the regions with both large urban areas and lots of industry (including the Los Angeles and New York metropolitan regions) have the highest risk of all.

SOURCE: U.S. Environmental Protection Agency (2011).

jokingly called "pea soup." During five days in 1952, an especially thick cloud of smoke covered the city of London and killed 4,000 people (Clarke, 1984).

In the last half century, great strides have been made in combating air pollution. Laws now forbid high-pollution factory emissions and there are far fewer of the coal fires that literally poisoned people in London. Technology, too, has advanced, with smokestack "scrubbers" greatly reducing noxious output of factories. Automobiles are far cleaner due to the adoption of unleaded gasoline in the early 1970s and changes in engine design and exhaust systems. Still, with more than 253 million vehicles in the United States alone, keeping the air clean remains a challenge. National Map 16–1 shows the risk of cancer from air pollution for counties throughout the continental United States.

The world's rich societies have entered a postindustrial era in which industrial technology is giving way to computer technology. Because this new type of production is far cleaner, air quality in these countries has been

improving. The benefit of cleaner air is very real: Experts estimate that improvement in U.S. air quality over the past several decades has added almost half a year to the average life span (Chang, 2009).

We may be breathing easier, but with more factory production overseas, the problem of air pollution in poor societies is getting worse. In addition, many people in low-income countries still rely on wood, coal, peat, or other "dirty" fuels for heat. Today, many low-income nations are so eager for short-term industrial development that they ignore the longer-term dangers of air pollution. As a result, many cities in Latin America, Eastern Europe, and Asia have air pollution as bad as London or Los Angeles seventy years ago.

Acid Rain

Across the 6 million acres of Adirondack Park in upstate New York, 400 lakes and ponds have been declared "dead" because they are too acidic to support fish or plant life.

This deadly trend could claim another 1,000 lakes and ponds by 2050.

The cause of this problem is **acid rain**, *precipitation, made acidic by air pollution, that destroys plant and animal life*. The complex reaction that creates acid rain and acid snow begins with power plants burning fossil fuels such as oil and coal to generate electricity. This combustion releases sulfur and nitrogen oxides into the air. Carried high into the atmosphere by winds, these gases react with the air to form sulfuric and nitric acid, which makes falling rain acidic. Figure 16–3 illustrates this process.

The process that causes acid rain is a case of one type of pollution causing another. In this case, air pollution from smokestacks ends up contaminating the rain that falls and collects in lakes and streams far away. Acid rain is a global phenomenon because many of the regions that suffer the harmful effects are thousands of miles from the original pollution. Here in the United States, power-generating facilities in the South and Midwest threaten all of New England. Abroad, tall chimneys of British power plants produce acid rain that has devastated forests and killed fish as far away as Norway and Sweden.

The Disappearing Rain Forests

Rain forests are *regions of dense forestation, most of which circle the globe close to the equator*. The largest rain forests are in South America, Central Africa, and Southeast Asia. In all, the world's rain forests cover some 3 billion acres, or 10 percent of the planet's total land surface.

Like other global resources, the rain forests are falling victim to the needs and appetites of the increasing human population. For example, to meet the demand for beef in North America, ranchers in Latin America burn down forests to gain more grazing land for cattle. Timber companies are cutting down forests to produce hardwood that ends up being used in high-income countries for furniture, wood floors and paneling, luxury yachts, and even high-grade coffins. Under this economic pressure, the world's rain forests are now just half their original size, and they continue to shrink by about 1 percent (21,000 square miles) annually. If this rate of destruction remains unchecked, these forests will vanish in about 250 years, taking with them much of the plant and animal biodiversity of this planet (United Nations, 2011).

Global Warming

Scientists have documented the fact that average temperatures throughout the world are rising, a trend called *global warming*. Over the last two centuries, as societies have developed industrial technology, the amount of

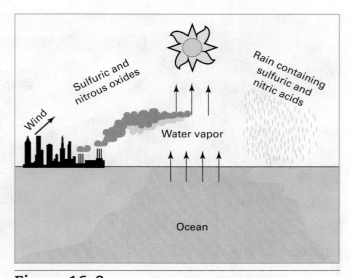

Figure 16–3   The Formation of Acid Rain

This figure illustrates the process of creating acid rain, which threatens plant and animal life in many parts of the world.

carbon dioxide (CO_2) released by factories and automobiles into the atmosphere has soared. Experts estimate that the current atmospheric concentration of carbon dioxide is 42 percent higher than it was 250 years ago (U.S. Department of Commerce, National Oceanic and Atmospheric Association, 2014).

The oceans absorb a certain amount of this CO_2. So do plants, which remove carbon dioxide from the air and expel oxygen. This process is one reason the rain forests are so important to our planet's future. But the production of carbon dioxide has gone up while the amount of plant life on Earth has gone down. The net result is that the concentration of CO_2 in the atmosphere is steadily rising.

As many see it, this change has pushed the planet to a dangerous point where the future of our species is threatened. How does carbon dioxide in the atmosphere threaten us? As carbon dioxide builds up in the atmosphere, it behaves much like the glass roof of a greenhouse, letting heat from the sun pass to Earth's surface while preventing much of it from radiating back away from the planet. This process is known as the *greenhouse effect*. Holding in some of the sun's heat is necessary to keep Earth warm, especially at night. But as the level of carbon dioxide in the atmosphere keeps going up, so does the amount of heat that the planet retains. This is the source of global warming.

Scientists report that over the past century, Earth's average temperature rose 1.67° to an average of 58.3° Fahrenheit. Before the end of this century, they expect the planet's average temperature to rise by 2° or more (Gore, 2006; Kluger, 2006; Adam, 2008; NASA, 2014).

More and more scientists are now convinced that global warming is a real threat to the environment. They note, for example, that polar ice is melting, which will raise the levels of the oceans. If the average temperature of the planet rises just a few degrees during this century, much of the coastal United States will be underwater. What are strategies to limit global warming?

Such a warming trend would melt vast portions of the polar ice caps. Ice is very reflective, sending much of the sun's heat back into space. As the ice caps melt, therefore, Earth will become warmer still. In addition, melting ice caps will raise the sea level, flooding low-lying land around the world. Low-lying nations such as Bangladesh will lose as much as one-fifth of its land by 2050. Projections are that the Carteret Islands of Papua New Guinea and the Maldives Islands in the Indian Ocean will become completely covered with water. Such a calamity would unleash a mass migration of perhaps 100 million "climate change refugees." In time, much of the coastal United States may also be flooded, with the Atlantic Ocean rising right up to the steps of the White House in Washington, D.C.

Weather patterns are likely to change. The Great Plains, in the midwestern United States, currently one of the most productive agricultural regions in the world, would probably lose so much rain that little would grow there (Gillis, 2011; McMahon, 2011; Reed, 2011).

Some analysts point out that that global temperature changes have been taking place throughout history, with no clear link to the status of the rain forests. Some maintain that the complexity of the natural environment renders any prediction about the future as speculative (Krauthammer, 2013). But the scientific community has reached a consensus that, first, the world is getting warmer; second, that temperature increase is due to human activity; and third, that global warming is a serious threat to the planet (Kluger, 2006; S. F. Singer, 2007; International Panel on Climate Change, 2012).

Declining Biodiversity

Another reason to worry about the planet's loss of rain forests is Earth's declining *biodiversity*. There are about 30 million different living species on the planet, counting all forms of life, from bacteria to plants and animals. Several dozen species of plants and animals cease to exist each day. But given such a vast number of living species, why is declining biodiversity a problem?

There are four reasons. First, Earth's biodiversity plays a major role in feeding the world's people. By cross-breeding familiar crops with more exotic plants, agricultural scientists make crops more plentiful and increase their resistance to insects and disease. Certain species of life are also vital for our food supply. Bees, for example, perform the task of pollinating plants. Today, however, the bee population of the United States has declined by one-third—probably due to new pesticides being used—and this loss of bees threatens future food supplies.

Second, Earth's biodiversity is a vital genetic resource. Medical and pharmaceutical researchers study the entire range of animal and plant life, which is where they find compounds that will cure disease and improve the quality of our lives. As examples, the oral birth control pill is a product of plant research involving the Mexican forest yam, and the Pacific yew tree is the basis for a drug that is widely used to treat breast cancer.

Third, with the loss of any species of life—from a tiny black ant to the magnificent California condor to the adorable Chinese panda—we lose part of the beauty and complexity of our natural environment. The warning signs are already posted: Three-fourths of the world's 10,000 bird species are declining in number, and more than 1,000 will disappear by the end of this century (Youth, 2003). Protecting the rain forests is vital to maintaining the planet's biodiversity because they are home to half of all living species.

Finally, the extinction of species is irreversible and final. Do we have the right to impoverish the world for those who will live tomorrow? (See E. O. Wilson, 1991; Brown et al., 1993; Stevens, 2003; Kluger, 2006.)

Theories of the Environment and Environmental Problems

16.3 Apply sociological theory to issues involving the natural environment.

Sociology's two macro-level approaches can help us gain a deeper understanding of environmental issues.

Structural-Functional Analysis: Highlighting Connections

Structural-functional theory links environmental issues to the overall operation of society. This approach offers three important lessons.

First, technology has a powerful effect on the environment. As noted earlier, the more powerful a society's technology, the greater the society's capacity to alter the natural world. This is the reason that environmental issues arise, not among technologically simple people, but among people who live in societies that use industrial technology.

Second, culture affects the state of the environment. A structural-functional analysis points out how values and beliefs guide human actions. Thus the state of the environment reflects our attitudes about the natural world. Members of industrial societies generally view nature as a resource to serve our needs (a point of view described earlier as the "logic of growth"). It was this vision that pushed our ancestors to clear forests for farmland, dam rivers for irrigation and water power, cover vast areas of Earth with asphalt and concrete, and erect tall buildings to make cities. In addition, our culture is materialistic, so that we look to *things* (as often as, say, family or spiritual beliefs) as a source of comfort and happiness. Our tendency toward what sociologists call "conspicuous consumption" leads us to purchase and display things not because we really need them but simply as a way to show off our social position (Veblen, 1953, orig. 1899). Guided by such values, our actions set the stage for environmental stress.

Third, structural-functional theory points up the interconnectedness of all social patterns. Our ideas that favor efficiency as well as independence, for example, go a long way toward explaining the U.S. fascination with personal automobiles. Building and operating hundreds of millions of vehicles has in turn put great stress on resources such as oil and polluted the atmosphere.

Given the connection between the natural environment and the operation of society, the solutions to environmental problems are complex. Is it possible to control the rate at which humanity consumes Earth's resources, for example, while we add more than 237,000 people to the global population each day? Limiting population increase, in turn, depends partly on expanding the range of occupational and educational opportunities available to women so they have alternatives to staying home and having more children.

No one doubts that solving environmental problems will be difficult. But structural-functional analysis provides grounds for optimism because of its view that systems adapt to changing conditions. Take the case of air pollution. Air quality declined sharply as nations developed industrial technology. But gradually, societies in Europe and North America recognized the problem, enacted new laws, and developed new technology to clean the air. In short, as long as we pay attention to the planet and remain creative, we can make the changes needed to ensure a livable environment.

EVALUATE

Structural-functional theory shows that problems of the natural environment are created by the operation of society itself. But as noted before, critics charge that structural-functional analysis pays little attention to social inequality. This means that, guided by this theory, we may recognize environmental problems but overlook the fact that burdens of pollution and scarcity fall disproportionately on people with less social power: the poor and minorities.

Critics also question structural-functionalism's optimistic view that society can resolve most environmental problems. For one thing, many people—particularly those operating large corporations—have vested interests in continuing past ways, even if they threaten the well-being of the general public. For another, many environmental problems, especially rapid population growth, are simply too far out of control to justify an optimistic outlook.

CHECK YOUR LEARNING What do we learn by applying structural-functional theory to environmental issues? What is a criticism of this approach?

Social-Conflict Analysis: Highlighting Inequality

Social-conflict theory highlights exactly the issues that structural-functionalism tends to overlook—power and inequality. Far from being inevitable, conflict theorists claim, problems of the natural environment result from social inequality. In other words, elites directly or indirectly make environmental problems worse as they advance their self-interest.

Marxist Class-Conflict Theory From a Marxist class-conflict point of view, the hierarchical organization of U.S. society gives a small number of people control over our society. As Chapter 10 ("Economy and Politics") describes, our capitalist economic system concentrates both wealth and power in a small elite who set the national agenda.

As the Industrial Revolution began, early capitalists eagerly funneled Earth's resources to feed their factories in search of immense profits. Just as they showed little regard for the social consequences of their actions, they paid little attention to the effects on the natural environment. In addition, capitalists and their managers are protected by laws that treat corporate pollution as a white-collar crime, as discussed in Chapter 6, ("Crime, Violence, and Criminal Justice"), so that any legal action usually results in fines paid by the company and not jail time served by individuals. For this reason, it is rare that corporate executives who order the release of pollutants into the air or the dumping of toxic

No one wants to live near factories where toxic chemicals are found. But because poor people have less power, they are the ones who usually end up living in hazardous areas. What effects has living near dangerous chemicals had on people in the past?

waste into bodies of water are held personally accountable for their actions.

Conflict theorists taking a Marxist view of society see capitalism itself as a threat to the environment. For one thing, capitalism demands the pursuit of profit, which in practice means continuous economic expansion—precisely the pattern that underlies the logic of growth. For another, strategies to maximize profits may include designing products with a limited useful life, a concept called *planned obsolescence*. Such policies may increase profits in the short term, but over the long haul they use up natural resources and produce mountains of solid waste.

A second issue raised by Marxist class-conflict theory involves global inequality. It is the people in rich countries who consume most of Earth's resources and who generate most air, water, and land pollution. In other words, not only do we maintain our affluent way of life by exploiting the poor in low-income countries, but we poison the world's air and water as well in the process. Researchers point to the conclusion that most of the harm done to the natural environment is directed at people living in low-income nations (Das Gupta, 2013).

In sum, a Marxist approach condemns rich nations as *overdeveloped* and consuming too much. As Chapter 15 ("Population and Global Inequality") explains, this social-conflict analysis suggests that the majority of the planet's people, who live in poor societies, will never raise their living standards under the current capitalist world economy. But from an environmental point of view, this would not even be desirable. What is needed is a more equitable distribution of the world's existing wealth among all its people, which would achieve greater social justice and better preserve the natural environment.

Environmental Racism Theory Another theory within the social-conflict approach links environmental issues with race. **Environmental racism** is *a pattern of discrimination in which environmental hazards are greatest for poor people, especially minorities*. This theory points out that, historically, factories that create pollution have been located in or near neighborhoods of the poor and people of color. Why? In part, this pattern exists because factories draw the poor, who are in search of work. Then, once hired, people with low incomes often find that the only housing they can afford stands in the very shadow of the plants and mills where they work.

Nobody wants to live next to a factory or a garbage dump, of course, but what choice do poor people have? Through the years, the most serious environmental hazards have been found around Newark, New Jersey, rather than in upscale Bergen County; on Chicago's South Side rather than in wealthy Lake Forest; and on or near Native American reservations in the West rather than in the affluent suburbs of Denver or Phoenix (Commission for Racial Justice, 1994; Bohon & Humphrey, 2000).

EVALUATE

Social-conflict theories raise important questions about who sets a society's agenda and who benefits—and who suffers—from the way society operates. From this point of view, environmental problems result from the institutions that enrich the few. These include economic inequality and also racial inequality within a society as well as a global hierarchy of nations.

Critics of this approach point out that, despite our capitalist economy, our nation's history shows a steady trend toward legal protection of the natural environment. Over the past half century, the United States has achieved significant improvements in air and water quality. Some analysts also argue that there is limited evidence to support the claim that environmental racism is widespread (Boerner & Lambert, 1995; Yandle & Burton, 1996).

Social-conflict theory charges that capitalism itself is particularly hostile to the natural world. There is no doubt that capitalism supports the logic of growth, which places stress on the

APPLYING THEORY

Technology and the Environment

	Structural Functional Theory	Social-Conflict Theory
What is the level of analysis?	Macro-level	Macro-level
How do we understand technology and the environment?	Structural-functional theory highlights links between the operation of society and the stress it puts on the natural environment. Complex technology raises the threat of damage to the environment, as do cultural values that encourage technological development, materialism, and economic growth.	Social-conflict theory links technology and the environment to social inequality. Marxist theory claims that capitalism places industrial technology under the control of a small elite who exploit natural resources as they exploit human labor. Environmental racism theory claims that minorities and the poor suffer the most from environmental hazards.
How do we understand environmental problems?	A society's technology and culture shape its environmental impact. These forces can harm the environment, but societies also adapt, thereby reducing environmental problems. In short, just as technology and cultural values can cause problems, they can also provide solutions.	Capitalism's demand for economic growth and profit is the key source of environmental problems, which are most serious for minorities and the poor. The solution to these problems lies in greater equality at home and redistribution of resources from the overdeveloped nations to underdeveloped nations.

environment. But capitalist societies in North America and Europe have made huge strides toward environmental protection. Consider, for example, that today's automobiles generate just a fraction of the pollution typical of a car in the 1960s. Therefore, critics say, capitalism can embrace environmental concerns. Just as important, the environmental record of socialist societies has been strikingly poor. Back when Europe was divided between capitalist countries to the west and socialist countries to the east, the strongest complaints about environmental quality came not from the capitalist nations in Western Europe but from the socialist nations of Eastern Europe, such as Poland and the Soviet Union (Dunlap, Gallup, & Gallup, 1992).

CHECK YOUR LEARNING What do we learn by applying social-conflict theory to environmental issues? What is a criticism of this approach?

The Applying Theory table summarizes what we can learn from each of these theoretical approaches to environmental issues.

⭐ POLITICS AND THE ENVIRONMENT

Constructing Problems and Defining Solutions

16.4 Analyze environmental problems and solutions from various positions on the political spectrum.

How do political attitudes shape the way people see environmental problems and define solutions? Conservatives typically support the free-market system and point to evidence that environmental problems are improving. Liberals tend to be more critical of our economic system and emphasize the need for greater government action to protect the environment. Radicals argue that the only way

to head off environmental collapse is to make fundamental changes to the capitalist system.

Conservatives: Grounds for Optimism

Like just about everyone else, conservatives are concerned about environmental issues. But they typically resist what they see as "alarmist" environmental claims, which (as they see it) only encourage a stronger role for government in directing social life (Krauthammer, 2013). In other words, fears about global warming can be used to expand government power to regulate everything from how we travel to the size of our shower heads (Will, 2014). More generally, conservatives take an optimistic view that businesses, various organizations, and the scientific community are able to recognize environmental problems and take action to solve them.

Conservatives point to the trend toward increasing environmental awareness found in all postindustrial societies (Pakulski, 1993; Jenkins & Wallace, 1996). Especially as production shifts from smoky factories to clean information technology, it is evident that societal concerns about environmental issues have caused people to take action to address them.

As to the warnings of environmental collapse in the near future, Julian Simon (1995) asks, "Why the doom and gloom?" He explains that ever since Malthus predicted social chaos, based on his belief that a rising population would consume the world's resources, people have warned society may collapse. But, today, the planet supports seven times as many people as when Malthus lived, and on average, they live better and longer than ever before. As Simon sees it, these facts are cause not for gloom but for celebration.

Why has the world done so well? Simon points to human ingenuity. More powerful technology certainly

What is our environmental future? Conservatives base their optimism on human ingenuity and the power of technology. Liberals, by contrast, look to government to mandate reforms. Radicals doubt that anything short of fundamental change will turn the tide. Which viewpoint do you support? Why?

increases a society's potential impact on the natural environment. But the development of new forms of energy and new productive technologies can also be good news for the environment. New energy sources and the modern factories are far cleaner than ever before. More broadly, today's economy is based on information technology, which is much more environmentally friendly than the industrial technology it is replacing. There is good reason to be optimistic that high technology will continue to reduce pollution from cars and from smokestacks (Dunlop, 2006).

Because this optimistic position opposes the pessimistic view of Malthus, it is often described as *anti-Malthusian*. This viewpoint, which is similar to the logic-of-growth viewpoint described earlier, is conservative because it expresses support for the status quo, in the belief that problems people create are problems people can solve.

Liberals: Grounds for Concern

Not everyone shares the optimism of people like Julian Simon. Most environmentalists are deeply concerned about problems such as population increase, resource consumption, and various types of pollution. Some openly predict catastrophe if humanity does not change its ways (Bright, 2003; Gore, 2006; Kluger, 2006). Given this prediction, it is easy to see why such activists are sometimes called *neo-Malthusians*. These people agree with the warnings sounded two centuries ago by Malthus and they support the limits-to-growth position described earlier in the chapter.

Neo-Malthusians concede that societies have been able to devise new, more productive technology, well beyond what Malthus could have imagined. Using these

technologies, the world now produces far more food and other goods than ever before. But the unequal distribution of these resources means that some people benefit far more than others, and as both production and population increase, we are steadily consuming the planet's finite resources. In many poor countries, there is little firewood for cooking or heating. Water supplies are already inadequate in much of the Middle East. The richer people on the planet are rapidly consuming Earth's supplies of oil and natural gas. Precisely when these supplies will give out is uncertain, but there is no doubt that some day they will be gone. Steadily increasing population also puts greater pressure on the planet's rain forests and undeveloped land continues to disappear.

In the same way, there is a limit to Earth's ability to absorb pollution. As both population and production rise, we can expect environmental quality to decline. Many analysts suggest that we have already passed the planet's *carrying capacity*, the number of people that it can support in the long term. In fact, some argue that our natural environment may only be able to support half of the world's present population (Smail, 2007).

In the face of such predictions, liberals call for reform on a number of fronts. Important steps include conservation efforts such as mandatory recycling programs, limiting carbon output into the atmosphere, and limiting the consumption of natural resources, such as clean water. These programs are especially important in rich countries because this is where most consumption takes place. These programs may involve costs but, liberals argue, these costs are far lower than the price of nonaction (OECD, 2012).

In practice, liberals are asking people in rich nations to make sacrifices in their living standards in the interest of the natural environment. The final piece of the solution lies in expanded efforts to reduce our reliance on "dirty" energy sources such as coal, coupled with "investment" in cleaner-burning fuels and engines for cars, power plants, and factories. Government should also mandate change toward lighter and more fuel-efficient motor vehicles. In short, heeding the warnings about global warming, liberals look to government to enact new policies and laws that will protect the environment.

The Radical Left: Grounds for Fundamental Change

Radicals on the left do not share conservatives' optimism about the future of the planet. Although radicals support the liberal agenda for an activist government, they believe that liberal reforms do not go far enough toward solving environmental problems.

LEFT TO RIGHT

The Politics of the Environment

	Radical-Left View	Liberal View	Conservative View
What is the problem?	The natural environment is in serious danger due to capitalism's ever-increasing appetite for growth and profits. Under the current economic and political system, the natural environment is likely to experience eventual collapse.	The natural environment is in danger. Both increasing pollution and the rapid use of natural resources including freshwater threaten people now and present societal patterns are not sustainable.	There are challenges but problems can be solved. Although humanity has created pollution and consumed natural resources, it has shown itself capable of devising new, "clean" technologies as well as alternative forms of energy.
What is the solution?	A healthy environment requires an economic system that delivers both equality and environmental awareness. Overconsumption in high-income nations must end, and global wealth must be distributed more equally.	Government must enact new policies and enforce laws to prevent further environmental damage in the United States. Individuals must conserve, recycle, and support global efforts to protect the remaining resources including rain forests.	Allow the market system to develop new technology. Human ingenuity and an economic system that encourages innovation will extend the human record of living longer, healthier, and richer lives. The market system can do this with limited government regulation.

JOIN THE DEBATE

1. Looking over the three political perspectives on the environment, do you see any areas of agreement? If so, what are they?
2. From the point of view of each of the three political perspectives, what changes should take place in the United States to protect the future of the planet?
3. Which of the three political analyses of the natural environment included here do you find most convincing? Why?

Those who follow a Marxist approach charge that significant environmental change is impossible under a capitalist system that places profits above all other concerns. This does not mean that we have to give up advanced technology. Most left radicals see technology as a useful tool if it is directed by economic and political systems that represent the interests of the people as a whole.

For radicals on the left, the key to solving environmental problems is replacing the capitalist economy. This process must occur worldwide because, as many radicals on the left see it, a key goal for our planet is reducing the extent of global stratification. Rich nations, they say, are already economically overdeveloped. In the interests of social justice and environmental safety, wealth must be redistributed more equitably around the world.

None of the political positions argues that things should stay exactly the way they are right now. Everyone recognizes environmental problems; the differences lie mainly in the degree of change people think is necessary to solve them. The Left to Right table summarizes the arguments that follow these three political positions.

Going On from Here

India's great leader Mahatma Gandhi believed that societies must provide for people's *need* but not for their *greed*. From an environmental point of view, this means that Earth will be able to sustain future generations only if people today slow their consumption of finite resources such as oil, hardwoods, and water. Nor can we go on polluting the air, water, and soil at anything close to current levels. We must stop cutting down our rain forests if we are to preserve the global climate. Finally, we cannot risk the future of the planet by adding people to the world at the rate of 87 million each year (Population Reference Bureau, 2013).

Recall the formula $I = PAT$, which tells us that a society's impact on the environment is a function of its level of population, its level of affluence, and its level of technology. Worldwide, population is increasing, living standards are rising, and technology is advancing. The predictable result is a larger environmental impact. Our planet's environmental deficit is increasing. In effect, our present way of life is borrowing against the future well-being of our children and their children. From a global perspective, members of rich societies who currently consume so much of Earth's resources are endangering the entire planet.

However the politics play out, the solution to the entire range of environmental problems described in this chapter must be for humanity to live in a way that does not make the environmental deficit any bigger. We need to develop an **ecologically sustainable culture**, *a way of life that meets the needs of the present generation without threatening the environment for future generations.*

To develop a sustainable way of life, we must adopt three basic strategies. First, the world must *conserve finite resources* by defining our present needs with a responsible eye to the future. Conservation involves using resources more efficiently, seeking alternative resources, and in some cases, learning to live with less.

SOCIAL PROBLEMS IN FOCUS
Getting Right with the Environment: How about You?

This chapter makes the case that the state of the natural environment depends on how we organize social life. In the end, each of us takes a stand on environmental issues by how we choose to live.

One key to creating an environmentally sustainable way of life is conserving finite resources. Are you willing to make personal choices that will advance this goal? What about driving a lighter and more efficient automobile? What about using public transportation, riding a bicycle, or walking more often?

Reducing waste is also important. One easy way to gain a better sense of how much waste you create is by carrying around a plastic bag for several days and filling it with everything you throw away. Willing to try? What about avoiding fast-food and other consumable products that use lots of packaging? How about recycling whatever you can?

Finally, keep in mind the wide gap between rich and poor nations in terms of consuming the planet's resources. Many environmentalists argue that it is people living in high-income nations who must change the most. Are you willing to accept a lower standard of living in pursuit of a more secure natural environment?

What Do You Think?

1. Why do you think most people in the United States have not yet defined environmental issues as serious social problems?

2. Has reading this chapter changed your opinions about environmental issues in any way? Explain.

3. What specific changes would you be willing to make in your own life in the interest of supporting a sustainable way of life?

The second strategy is to *reduce waste*. The best way to reduce waste is to use less in the first place. In addition, societies around the world need to expand recycling programs through education and legislation.

The third key element in any plan for a sustainable ecosystem is to *bring world population growth under control*. Our current population of more than 7.1 billion is already straining the natural environment. The higher world population climbs, the greater environmental problems will become. Controlling population increase requires immediate action in low-income regions of the world where growth rates are highest.

In the end, perhaps, solving environmental problems depends on all of us developing a new way of seeing the world. An *egocentric* outlook, common in rich nations today, is all about meeting an ever-expanding set of personal needs. But a sustainable environment demands an *ecocentric* outlook, one that highlights the environmental consequences of the choices we make. Such a point of view, which is especially important to those of us lucky enough to live in rich societies, reminds us that today's actions shape tomorrow's world.

In addition, instead of viewing humans as superior to other life forms and assuming that we have the right to dominate the planet, we must remember that all forms of life are interdependent. Ignoring this truth not only threatens the diversity of animal and plant life on the planet but also will eventually threaten our own well-being.

Finally, achieving a sustainable ecosystem will require global cooperation. The planet's rich and poor nations differ greatly in terms of economic interests, cultural beliefs, and living standards. Policies encouraging conservation and reducing waste have little impact among people who are desperately poor. The most difficult part of any effort to solve the world's environmental problems will be coming to terms with global inequality. Most environmentalists argue that the high-income countries of the world are already overdeveloped, using more resources than Earth can sustain over the long term. At the same time, low-income nations are underdeveloped, unable to meet the basic needs of many of their people. Establishing a sustainable ecosystem will depend on bold new programs of global cooperation. The Social Problems in Focus box helps you to decide where you stand on the question of whether our society should develop an environmentally sustainable way of life.

Although the challenge is enormous, it is nothing compared with the eventual consequences of allowing the environmental deficit to continue to build. We must make our choices in the knowledge that the state of tomorrow's world depends on the decisions we make today (Brown et al., 1993; Bright, 2003).

Essay: Envisioning a Better Society Looking ahead fifty years, do you think that problems involving the natural environment will become greater or smaller? Why? What specific policies would you support in pursuit of your vision of a better world?

CHAPTER 16 Technology and the Environment

What's the best way to address problems of the natural environment?

Look at the two accompanying photos to understand two different approaches to finding a solution to environmental problems.

From a liberal point of view, business as usual within the market system is unlikely to lead the country to an environmentally sustainable way of life. The solution, from this political perspective, is government legislation mandating changes in how we live. People sharing this viewpoint recently gathered near the U.S. Capitol to urge the federal government to take bold action limiting air pollution and consumption of energy. How much do you support this approach to a solution? Why?

The conservative approach is based on the belief that the market system is, indeed, capable of responding to the environmental challenge. Conservatives expect that by unleashing human ingenuity, and with the advantages of new technology, our current system will generate new solutions to many environmental problems. For example, recent years have seen the introduction of a host of new electric and hybrid (gasoline and electric) automobiles. How confident are you that our market system and innovative technology will bring about solutions to environmental problems?

prius goes plural

Hint: The conservative claim that our present system can "invent" us out of our current problems is at least partly true. As conservatives point out, over time, our society has made the air cleaner as cars use less fuel and generate fewer pollutants. At the same time, conservatives' confidence in the future may be overly optimistic. After all, liberals remind us, it is our current system that got us into this situation. The liberal claim is that government can "invest" us out of our current problems. What can government do better than private business? Perhaps it takes government to make decisions—like providing incentives for driving smaller cars and using less energy—that we as consumers are unlikely to make on our own. Where do you stand on this issue?

Getting Involved: Applications and Exercises

1. Carry a plastic trash bag around for an entire day, and fill it with everything you throw away. What is the weight of one day's trash? Are you surprised by how much material you discard?

2. In Genesis 1:28–29, God instructs humanity to "fill the earth and subdue it; rule over the fish of the sea and the birds of the air and over every living creature that moves on the ground....I give you every seed-bearing plant on the face of the whole earth and every tree that has fruit with seed in it. They will be yours for food." Do you think this statement gives humans the right to exploit the natural environment as they see fit? Does it give humanity the responsibility to care for it? Both? Explain your position.

3. In 2014, what motor vehicle do you think was the best seller in the United States? The answer is the Ford F-Series pickup, a brawny vehicle weighing some 5,000 pounds. Light-duty trucks make up 38 percent of motor vehicle sales, with cars accounting for 37 percent of sales, and SUVs and crossovers representing the remaining 25 percent. What do these data suggest about our society's view of transportation?

4. The United States exploded the first atomic bomb in 1945. Since then, there have been more than 2,000 nuclear explosions on the planet. Why, in your opinion, would humanity create nuclear weapons with the capacity to completely eliminate life on this planet?

CHAPTER 16 Technology and the Environment

A DEFINING MOMENT
Rachel Carson: Sounding an Environmental Wake-Up Call **p. 473**

Ecology: Studying the Natural Environment

16.1 Identify several key factors that affect the natural environment.

The state of the **natural environment** reflects how human beings organize social life.

- Ecologists therefore study how living organisms interact with their environment.

Analyzing environmental problems demands a global perspective.

- All parts of the **ecosystem**, including the air, soil, and water, are linked. Changes in one part of the world affect the natural environment elsewhere. **p. 468**

> **ecology** (p. 468) the study of how living organisms interact with the natural environment
>
> **natural environment** (p. 468) Earth's surface and atmosphere, including air, water, soil, and other resources necessary to sustain living organisms
>
> **technology** (p. 468) knowledge that people apply to the task of living in a physical environment
>
> **ecosystem** (p. 468) the interaction of all living organisms and their natural environment

Factors Affecting the Environment

Population increase affects the natural environment.

- Even though the rate of growth is slowing, world population threatens to overwhelm available resources. **pp. 468–69**

Global affluence and its emphasis on material abundance lead to pollution and rapid use of energy and other resources.

- **Technology** development gives societies greater control over the natural environment, for better or for worse.

- By focusing on short-term benefits and ignoring the long-term consequences brought on by their way of life, societies build up an **environmental deficit**. **pp. 469–71**

Global poverty also results in depletion of natural resources.

- Preoccupied with survival, poor people have little choice but to consume scarce resources. **p. 469**

Cultural patterns—how we as a society live and what we value—affect the environment.

- The *logic-of-growth* thesis supports economic development and asserts that people can solve whatever environmental problems may arise.

- The *limits-to-growth* thesis states that societies have little choice but to curb development in order to avoid environmental collapse. **pp. 471–72**

> **environmental deficit** (p. 471) serious, long-term harm to the environment caused by humanity's focus on short-term material affluence

Environmental Problems

16.2 Discuss the causes and consequences of increasing pollution, global warming, and other environmental problems.

Solid Waste

- As a "disposable society," the United States generates 1.4 billion pounds of solid waste each day, one-half of which ends up in landfills. **pp. 472–74**

Preserving Clean Water

- Water consumption is rapidly increasing everywhere. Much of the world, notably Africa and the Middle East, is reaching a water supply crisis. **pp. 474–75**

Air Pollution

- Since 1950, high-income countries have made significant progress in reducing air pollution. In poor nations, especially in cities, air pollution remains a serious problem because homes and factories burn "dirty" fuels. **pp. 475–76**

Acid Rain

- Acid rain, the product of pollutants entering the atmosphere mostly from industrial smokestacks, contaminates land and water thousands of miles away. **pp. 476–77**

Disappearing Rain Forests

- Rain forests serve the planet by removing carbon dioxide from the atmosphere and maintaining Earth's biodiversity. With millions of trees being cut down each year by logging companies and ranchers in search of grazing land for their livestock, global rain forests are now half their original size and are shrinking by about 1 percent annually. **p. 477**

Global Warming

Global warming is the rise in the average temperature of the planet, caused by increasing levels of carbon dioxide released into the atmosphere by factories and automobile engines. Destroying the rain forests makes the problem worse because plant life consumes carbon dioxide. **pp. 477–78**

acid rain (p. 477) precipitation, made acidic by air pollution, that destroys plant and animal life
rain forests (p. 477) regions of dense forestation, most of which circle the globe close to the equator

Theories of the Environment and Environmental Problems

16.3 **Apply sociological theory to issues involving the natural environment.**

Structural-Functional Analysis: Highlighting Connections

Structural-functional theory looks at the connection between environmental issues, technology, and culture.

- In the same way that the problems of the environment are created by the operation of society, society also has the ability to adapt to change or to correct environmental problems. **p. 479**

Social-Conflict Analysis: Highlighting Inequality

Social-conflict theory highlights the role of inequality in environmental problems.

- **Marxist class-conflict theory** claims that the capitalist economy harms the environment as elites increase economic productivity in search of greater personal profits.

- **Environmental racism theory** states that the poor—and especially minorities—suffer most from environmental hazards, a pattern known as **environmental racism. pp. 479–81**

environmental racism (p. 480) a pattern of discrimination in which environmental hazards are greatest for poor people, especially minorities
ecologically sustainable culture (p. 483) a way of life that meets the needs of the present generation without threatening the environment for future generations

✪ POLITICS AND THE ENVIRONMENT

Constructing Problems and Defining Solutions

16.4 **Analyze environmental problems and solutions from various positions on the political spectrum.**

Conservatives: Grounds for Optimism

- **Conservatives** acknowledge the reality of environmental problems, but they argue that human beings will use their ingenuity and technology to solve them, with little need for government regulation.

- Because conservatives take an optimistic view of the future, their position is described as *anti-Malthusian.* **pp. 481–82**

Liberals: Grounds for Concern

- **Liberals** believe that government reforms such as mandatory recycling and strategies to reduce solid waste and develop cleaner-burning fuels are necessary to avoid eventual environmental collapse.

- Because of their pessimistic view of the future, liberal environmentalists are sometimes called *neo-Malthusians.* **p. 482**

The Radical Left: Grounds for Fundamental Change

- **Radicals on the left** doubt that liberal reforms will be sufficient to solve the world's environmental problems.

- Radicals on the left believe that the capitalist economy, which places profits above all other concerns, must be replaced with a system that will safeguard the environment in the interest of all people. **pp. 482–83**

Chapter 17
War and Terrorism

Learning Objectives

17.1 Explain the causes and consequences of both war and peace.

17.2 Identify types of terrorism in the world as well as strategies to address terrorism.

17.3 Apply sociological theory to issues involving war and terrorism.

17.4 Analyze war, terrorism, and the pursuit of peace from various positions on the political spectrum.

Tracking the Trends

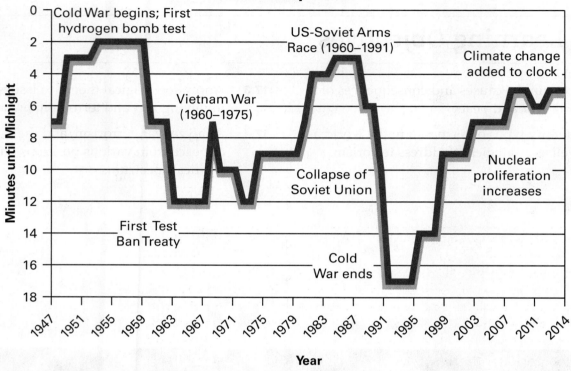

Doomsday Clock

SOURCE: Bulletin of Atomic Scientists (2014).

After World War II ended with the explosion of two nuclear bombs over cities in Japan, many of the scientists who had constructed these weapons were understandably fearful about the future. To assess the threat that humanity would unleash its own technology to destroy life on this planet, they constructed what they called the "doomsday clock." They characterized this danger by moving the hands of the clock closer to or farther away from "midnight." As you can see from the figure, they concluded that atomic weapons made the world far more dangerous. But the danger declined somewhat in the decades that followed, increasing again as the United States and the Soviet Union participated in an arms race. The fall of the Soviet Union brought the end of the Cold War and tensions again declined. But the recent trend is toward greater danger, especially because more nations now have nuclear weapons. Do you think nuclear weapons make us more safe or less safe?

Constructing the Problem

What are the financial costs of war?

In 2013, the world's nations spent $1.75 trillion for military purposes.

Is it only soldiers who die in war?

Most of war's casualties are civilians.

Do the world's armies include children?

Around the world, about 250,000 children—some as young as six years of age—are soldiers, and many take part in armed combat.

Chapter Overview

Why do countries go to war? This chapter explores social patterns related to war, peace, and terrorism. You will learn several reasons why wars happen and also discover the reasons that war has become more and more destructive. You will understand the economic and human costs of war. You will be able to explain how terrorism differs from conventional war and why war in an age of nuclear weapons poses unimaginable dangers. You will also be able to outline several strategies that promote peace. You will apply sociology's major theoretical approaches to war and terrorism and you will learn how the global issues people define as "problems" and the policies they favor as "solutions" reflect people's political attitudes. ■

It was one of those late-night "discussions" that sometimes happen in the dorms—the kind that use up a lot of energy but end up generating more heat than light. As Brandon (passionate Democrat) saw it, the two terms of the Obama administration have made the nation and its people much safer. "Thanks to Obama," he thundered, "the world is beginning to respect us again! We're cooperating with our allies, not going it alone the way we did with Bush and Cheney. We're using diplomacy rather than just sending in the Marines."

But Emma (passionate Republican) would hear none of it. "Obama has been a weak leader," she claimed. "He did not end the Iraq War in a way that made the sacrifice worth it. He's now planning to pull out of Afghanistan, whether or not we defeat the Taliban." "Sure, he got bin Laden," Emma added, "but that was the only real success he has had. He has failed to back up his warnings to Syria about killing its own people, he is letting Iran get nuclear weapons, and he has allowed Putin to seize Ukraine."

We've all been there, arguing back and forth about whether the country is safer or not, whether the United States is doing the right things around the world or making things worse. These are difficult questions that reflect people's political values and attitudes. At the same time, such discussions raise important questions about war—why nations get into

wars and whether armed conflict solves anything. In addition, everyone recognizes that terrorism has become common enough that it is often described as a new type of war.

In 2014, the United States had disengaged from military action in Iraq but still had soldiers in Afghanistan. In addition, our political leaders were trying to resolve a dozen other conflicts that threatened to break out into war in various regions of the world. In addition, the United States had military personnel stationed in about twenty nations in an effort to keep the peace.

Given how common and how controversial war is, we might well wonder why nations go to war in the first place. Some analysts suggest that the answer lies within ourselves—that is, humans, especially males, are naturally aggressive (Chagnon, 1997). If this were so, there would seem to be little that we can do to prevent war. But after decades of research on the causes of armed conflict, most social scientists reject the idea that war is caused by human nature and hold the view that the roots of war are to be found in society itself. To the extent that this is the case, understanding more about the social causes of war should help our leaders develop effective strategies to promote peace.

War and Peace: Basic Definitions

17.1 Explain the causes and consequences of both war and peace.

War is *violent conflict between nations or organized groups.* **Peace**, on the other hand, is *the absence of violent conflict.*

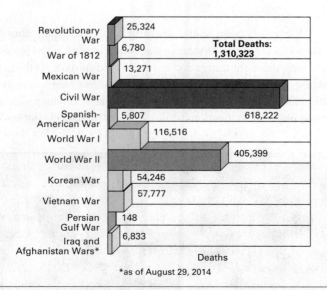

Figure 17–1   Deaths of Americans in Eleven U.S. Wars

Almost half of all U.S. deaths in war occurred during the Civil War (1861–65).

SOURCE: Compiled from various sources by Maris A. Vinovskis and the author.

Many people think of peace as the normal state of affairs. Yet wars have always been a part of human history. The United States has been involved in many large-scale wars, shown in Figure 17–1, as well as a number of minor conflicts played out in Grenada, Panama, Haiti, Somalia, and Bosnia. Throughout the twentieth century, there was no time at which there was not an armed conflict occurring somewhere around the world. In recent decades, civil wars have been the most common type of war. During the last decade, in only four of thirty-one major military conflicts has one nation sought to win territory from another nation; in twenty-seven of these conflicts, warring parties have sought control of the government within a single nation (Themnér & Wallensteen, 2014). Global Map 17–1 shows a recent assessment of the level of peacefulness around the world.

The Increasing Destruction of War

Over the centuries, the level of violence associated with war has sharply increased. Much of this increase is due to societies applying more powerful technology to warfare. A thousand years ago, the most a human could do in battle was to kill one person at a time by swinging a sword, throwing a spear, or launching an arrow. Around the beginning of the twelfth century, the development of guns using black powder made killing far more efficient but still ended one life at a time. By the early sixteenth century, black powder was fed into large cannons that had the power to launch heavy balls that would knock down stone walls, sometimes killing several people at once. Soon cannonballs were replaced by exploding shells that were able to kill even more people at one time. The U.S. Civil War, fought between 1861 and 1865, was this country's bloodiest conflict, in part because soldiers continued the time-honored strategy of standing near each other firing guns and cannons that were now far more powerful and accurate than ever before.

This trend toward more deadly weapons continued into the twentieth century. Single-shot rifles were replaced by automatic weapons that came to be known as "machine guns." In addition, armies were equipped with chemical weapons as well as more powerful explosive bombs. World War I introduced aircraft into military combat, and planes were joined by missiles in World War II, so that armies could rain death and destruction down on entire cities from miles above. In the case of the two atomic weapons, used by the United States against Japan to end World War II, more than 100,000 people died instantly by a blast that leveled an entire city.

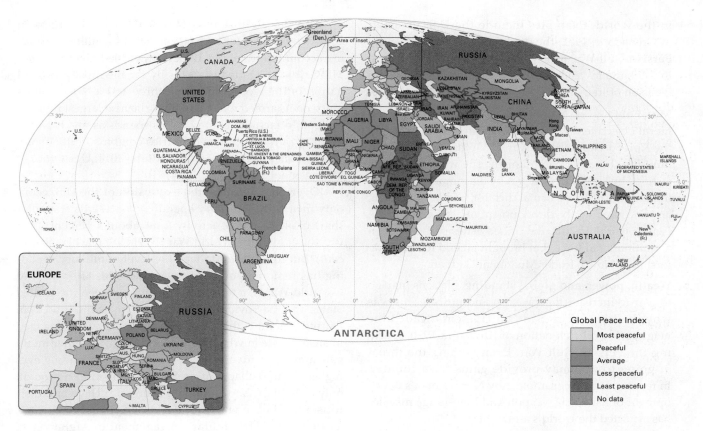

Window on the World

Global Map 17–1 Peace in Global Perspective, 2013

In 2014, the Institute for Economics and Peace assigned a "Peace Index" to nations of the world. The most peaceful nations not only had no active military conflict but also were marked by little or no terrorism, low military spending, and little violence based on drug trafficking or other causes. In general, higher-income countries are more peaceful than low-income nations. What other patterns do you see?

SOURCE: Institute for Economics and Peace (2014).

In short, the last century saw the invention of **weapons of mass destruction**, *weapons with the capacity to kill many thousands of people at one time*. Such weapons increase the destruction of war in two ways: First, they have far greater destructive power and, second, they target civilian populations. As the deadly potential of weapons increases and as weapons of mass destruction are available to more and more nations, the dangers of war become ever greater.

The Causes of War

Why do wars happen? Sociologists have identified seven factors that encourage the outbreak of war (Q. Wright, 1987; Kaldor, 1999; Van Evera, 1999):

1. **Perceived threats.** Societies mobilize their armed forces in response to perceived threats. In 1962, the United States prepared for war against the Soviet Union after learning that Soviet nuclear missiles had been set up on the island of Cuba, a nation just 90 miles south of Florida. Only after the Soviets agreed to remove the

missiles did the two nations step back from the brink of war. In recent years, Israel has invaded southern Lebanon after rocket attacks across their common border killed a number of Israeli civilians.

2. **Cultural and religious differences.** Another cause of war is cultural and religious differences. Often these differences become exaggerated as societies teach their members to "demonize" those in some other country or group—that is, to see some category of people not only as "the other" but as evil. At the extreme, one category of people may try to eliminate another from an entire geographic area. In the Balkan conflict of the 1990s, ethnic Serbs rounded up hundreds of thousands of Croats, Muslims, and ethnic Albanians, deported them, placed them in prison camps, or simply killed them in a process called "ethnic cleansing."

3. **Political objectives.** Political objectives can be an underlying factor in war. A periodic show of force can be one way for a nation to assert a leadership position

in the world. Examples include the U.S. invasion of Grenada in 1982, the deployment of troops in the Persian Gulf War in 1991–92, the bombing of Serbia in 1999, the invasion of Afghanistan in 2001, and the invasion of Iraq in 2003.

4. **Moral objectives.** Nations may go to war to achieve a moral objective. Leaders in the United States justified the Korean War and the war in Vietnam as efforts to limit the spread of communism. The war in Iraq was justified by U.S. leaders in part by the moral goal of ending the rule of Iraq's brutal dictator, Saddam Hussein, and encouraging the development of democracy in the Islamic world. In 2011, the United States participated in a multinational force that brought an end to the dictatorship of Libyan leader Muammar Gaddafi.

5. **Wealth, power, and global standing.** Nations may go to war to increase their wealth and power. This was why the Iraqi leader Saddam Hussein invaded the neighboring oil-rich nation of Kuwait in 1990, sparking the Persian Gulf War. Even making the threat of going to war may provide gains for a country. In recent years, for example, tiny North Korea's development of a nuclear weapon and long-range missiles has attracted the world's attention.

6. **Social problems.** Leaders sometimes use armed conflicts to divert attention from domestic social problems. For example, the People's Republic of China managed to turn attention away from great economic hardship by supporting military conflicts in Korea, Vietnam, and Tibet. Focusing national attention on an external threat can unify a population against a common enemy rather than directing blame for problems at their own government.

7. **Absence of alternatives.** Finally, nations go to war because of an absence of alternatives. A nation may simply have no diplomatic means to end a threat or to accomplish its political or moral objectives.

Typically, leaders draw on many of these factors in making claims about the need for military action. Of course, going to war is almost always controversial. Leaders may defend military action, say, as a response to a perceived threat or in pursuit of a moral objective. Critics, however, may define the military action quite differently, say, as a political strategy or an effort to gain wealth and power.

The Economic Costs of Militarism

In 2013, the nations of the world spent $1.75 trillion for military purposes, which amounts to $250 for every man, woman, and child on a planet where a billion people are desperately poor (Stockholm International Peace Research Institute, 2014).

The U.S. defense budget was almost $649 billion in 2014, about $2,066 for each citizen. Overall, military spending accounted for about 17 percent of the federal budget. Militarily, the United States is by far the most powerful nation in the world, spending three and a half times as much on its armed forces as China, the next largest military budget. In fact, the United States spends as much on the military as the next nine countries combined (Stockholm International Peace Research Institute, 2014; U.S. Office of Management and Budget, 2014).

Over past decades, the expansion of the U.S. economy means that military spending represents a smaller share of all economic activity (now about 4 percent) than was the case during World War II (when it reached 40 percent). But in terms of dollars, the level of military spending has remained quite high. For decades after the end of World War II, a tense relationship between the United States and the Soviet Union was known as the Cold War. During this time, these two world superpowers engaged in an *arms race* in which each side, fearing the other might gain a military advantage, pushed military spending ever higher. Yet the collapse of the Soviet Union in 1991 brought only a slight decline in military spending. The war on terrorism that began with the attacks on September 11, 2001, as well as the U.S. military engagement in Afghanistan, has kept military spending high. At the same time, the Obama administration pushed down military spending by 7.8 percent in 2013 (Stockholm International Peace Research Institute, 2014).

Some analysts claim that the United States—or more specifically, a powerful elite within this country—benefits from the traditionally high levels of military spending. They see the United States as dominated by a **military-industrial complex,** *the close association of the federal government, the military, and the defense industries* (Marullo, 1987). From this point of view, militarism in the United States is not only a matter of defense and national security but also a matter of profit and influence for the country's power elite (see Chapter 10, "Economy and Politics").

The Economic Costs of War

The economic costs of war involve more than military spending. War also destroys the *infrastructure* of a society: its homes and workplaces, water systems, electrical and communication networks, roads, bridges, railways, harbors, and airports. By the end of World War II, much of Europe lay in ruins and had to be rebuilt at the cost of hundreds of billions of dollars. In the wake of the war in Iraq, the United States has already spent more than $60 billion in efforts to rebuild that country.

Especially in tough economic times, many people wonder if this country can afford to spend so much on military objectives. After all, money spent on war takes economic resources away from programs that improve people's health care, nutrition, and education. Looking globally, if all nations were to use the funds currently spent on militarism and rebuilding after wars to assist the poor, this planet could go a long way toward ending the global problems of hunger and disease.

The Human Costs of War

The economic costs of war are huge. But the greatest loss is measured in human terms. Historically, armed conflicts have become ever more deadly. For example, the death toll in the U.S. Civil War was about 600,000. Fifty years later, World War I claimed almost 10 million lives. Thirty years after that, the death toll from World War II exceeded 50 million.

The most dramatic example of total war was the use of two atomic bombs by the United States against Japan at the end of World War II. The first bomb almost completely destroyed the industrial city of Hiroshima. The second wiped out Nagasaki (shown here). In each case, the death toll exceeded 100,000 people.

The main reason for this increase is the development of weapons of mass destruction. Such weapons kill not only more soldiers but civilians as well. Until the end of the nineteenth century, war was armed conflict between professional soldiers. From time to time, civilians were killed, but for the most part, these deaths were unintended. That has changed in the last century.

The Strategy of Total War The twentieth century witnessed the development of a new and more deadly strategy of **total war**, *deadly conflict that targets both population centers and military targets*. Military victory required reducing an enemy's ability to produce weapons. With airplanes, bombs, and missiles at their command, military leaders had the power to demolish the enemy's factories, which often meant leveling entire cities. In the process, of course, attacks killed not only the civilians who worked in the factories but also people who lived anywhere in the area. During World War II, for example, both the Germans and the Allied forces repeatedly bombed one another's cities with the objective of weakening the other's ability and will to fight. As a result, most of the people who died in World War II were not soldiers but civilians. Clearly, the strategy of total war blurs the lines between soldiers and civilians by putting all people at risk (Renner, 1993; Ehrenreich, 1997).

Concentration Camps During World War II, some nations set up **concentration camps**, *centers where prisoners are confined for purposes of state security, exploitation, punishment, or execution*. The United States imprisoned about 100,000 people of Japanese ancestry

between 1942 and 1944. These camps, set up within a year of the Japanese attack on Pearl Harbor, were an effort to control a segment of the U.S. population thought to represent a threat to national security.

In Europe, concentration camps took on a far more deadly mission. Both the Soviet leader Josef Stalin and the German leader Adolf Hitler operated labor camps that forced prisoners to work so hard, with so little food, that most inmates eventually died of disease brought on by starvation and sheer exhaustion. During World War II, Hitler's Nazis also operated numerous death camps, including those at Auschwitz and Buchenwald, in which they systematically exterminated some 6 million Jews, along with additional millions of political prisoners, Catholics, Gypsies, homosexuals, and anyone else defined as undesirable. The death toll under Stalin was greater still, reaching as high as 30 million.

War Crimes Strange as it may seem, there are rules of war. Each nation enacts standards for fighting and nations also came together to create formal agreements called the Geneva Conventions, which were negotiated in Geneva, Switzerland, between 1864 and 1949. Violation of these standards is a **war crime**, *an offense against the law of war as established by international agreements and international law*. In the wake of World War II, the Geneva Conventions recognized three categories of war crimes. *Crimes against peace* include preparing for or starting an unjust war against another nation. *Conventional war crimes* include the murder, rape, torture, deportation, or other ill treatment of a population in any occupied territory. And *crimes against humanity* include political, racial, or religious

A chilling fact is that around the world, hundreds of thousands of children work as soldiers. These young teenage boys train as regular soldiers in the Ugandan army. What factors, especially in poor societies, lead children to become involved in war?

persecution—including systematic killing—of any civilian population during war.

After World War II, an international war crimes tribunal tried twenty-four Nazi leaders at Nuremberg, Germany, convicting nineteen of war crimes. A separate tribunal tried and convicted twenty-five Japanese leaders. The sentences in each case ranged from lengthy prison terms to execution.

More recently, the United Nations International Criminal Tribunal has prosecuted a few officers for war crimes in Rwanda and the former Yugoslavia. However, because this tribunal's power depends on the political cooperation of individual nations and their willingness to aid in apprehending alleged criminals, many military leaders who may have engaged in war crimes manage to escape prosecution (R. J. Newman, 2002).

War-Related Disabilities Many war survivors suffer from mental and physical disabilities. Soldiers have long talked about "battle fatigue" or "shell shock." After the Vietnam War, about 15 percent of soldiers experienced *posttraumatic stress disorder* (PTSD), a war-related disability resulting from trauma or stress in battle. Symptoms of PTSD include nightmares, difficulty with concentration and sleeping, flashbacks to traumatic events, jumpiness and hyperalertness, guilt about surviving, and feelings of detachment from other people (American Psychiatric Association, 2002). An everyday event such as hearing an engine backfiring or seeing a helicopter flying overhead can trigger a PTSD episode, causing the person to relive the terror of combat.

Now that advanced medical technology is available to seriously wounded soldiers, more men and women

who would have died from battlefield injuries are now surviving. But, although they survive, many are left with serious disabilities. In all, some 3.5 million U.S. veterans have some disability resulting from an injury during active duty in the military. Of these, about 360,000 are totally disabled. To provide care for disabled veterans, the Department of Veterans Affairs (VA) operates the Veterans Health Administration, which is the nation's single largest health care system with more than 1,700 care sites. Care is provided free of charge to former prisoners of war, individuals with service-related injuries or disabilities, and veterans with income below the poverty line. Thousands of other veterans are treated on a space-available basis (Moakley, 1999; U.S. Department of Veterans Affairs, 2014).

The problems of illness and disability among veterans spill over into the world of work. Many veterans have difficulty finding and keeping jobs. This is one reason that 1.5 million veterans earn incomes below the poverty line. One veterans' organization claims that 58,000 vets are homeless at any given time and about twice that number are homeless for some time during any given year (National Coalition for Homeless Veterans, 2014).

War and Children Finally, the human toll of war falls heavily on children. During the last century, every major war left vast numbers of orphans. Hundreds of thousands of children also died in bombings and other attacks. More recently, children are actually taking part in combat. The Personal Stories box takes a closer look.

Social Class and the Military

During World War II, three-fourths of U.S. men in their late teens and twenties served in the military. These men became soldiers either voluntarily or by being *drafted*—called by the government to military service. Every male was expected to serve. Only those who had some physical or mental impairment were released from this obligation.

Today there is no draft. That policy ended in 1973 and was replaced by the concept of an all-volunteer military. But, given the differences in life chances linked to social class, not every member of our society is equally

PERSONAL STORIES

Children in Combat: Not Too Young to Kill

People call him "TS." To some, he may appear to be a boy of about twelve. But the look on his face shows that he is old beyond his years. TS is a soldier with six years of combat experience. He has fought on the front lines of Sierra Leone, a war-torn nation in western Africa. In raids of villages along the border of his country, TS has killed people, many people. He has seen so much violence that he finds it difficult to sleep and often wets his bed.

The story of this boy soldier began when rebels invaded TS's village. Soldiers killed his parents and kidnapped the boy, who was only six at the time. His captors taught him that he was now a freedom fighter. TS joined the ranks of thousands of child soldiers in Sierra Leone.

Military units that abduct children typically try to turn them against their own relatives and neighbors, a strategy that leaves the children with nowhere else to go. Socially isolated children are easily molded into fighters, and many develop a family-like loyalty to the military. Many children readily obey orders to shoot to kill and even serve as suicide bombers.

According to the Coalition to Stop the Use of Child Soldiers (2014), as many as 250,000 children work as soldiers in some twenty-two lower-income countries in South America, Africa, and Asia. Should people this young be in uniform? It is true that in many lower-income nations, adulthood begins much earlier than is typical in the United States. Many six- or seven-year-olds work for income; by thirteen or fourteen, many marry and take

on other adult roles. But most children who become soldiers have little choice in the matter. After as little as one year working as soldiers, they may become socialized to a life of violence and find it very hard to live any other way.

And what about rich countries? Some critics say they, too, exploit children. In Great Britain, for example, the navy recruits sixteen-year-olds, and people as young as seventeen join the army. The U.S. military also allows people as young as seventeen to sign up, with parental consent. According to the Department of Defense, in 2011, 3,651 seventeen-year-olds and 40,200 eighteen-year-olds joined the U.S. military (Hermes, 2005; United Nations, 2013; U.S. Department of Defense, 2014).

What Do You Think?

1. In poor countries, most young children work for income. In light of this fact, is joining the military so different? Explain your position.

2. Most high-income countries have laws that prohibit children from serving as soldiers, but many low-income countries either do not have such laws or do not enforce them. What should other nations do to assist children forced into military service?

3. U.S. soldiers currently serving in Iraq are as young as eighteen. Is that too young to be asked to perform such service? Why or why not?

---

likely to volunteer. One recent study concluded that the military has few young people who are rich and also few who are very poor. Rather, the military has become a job mostly for working-class men and women who hope to earn some money to go to college or who look for a way simply to get out of the small town where they grew up. Regionally, the largest share (42 percent) of young enlistees comes from the South, where local culture is more supportive of the military and where most military bases are located. The smallest share (13 percent) comes from the Northeast (U.S. Department of Defense, 2014). As two analysts put it, "America's military seems to resemble the makeup of a two-year commuter or trade school outside Birmingham or Biloxi far more than that of a ghetto or barrio or four-year university in Boston" (Halbfinger & Holmes, 2003:1).

In today's uncertain economy, the military has found that an increasing number of young men and women are interested in signing up. For some, the attraction lies in training and money to use later on for college. For others, there are few alternative jobs to be

found. In any case, our nation now has a "working-class army" (Glater, 2005). The Social Problems in Focus box on page 498 raises the question of whether or not our nation now has created a "warrior caste."

Mass Media and War

We view the world through stories and images provided by the mass media. Reporting war news is, of course, nothing new. But the Iraq War was the first war in which television crews actually traveled right along with U.S. troops, reporting what happened as the military operations unfolded. For several years, cable television channels broadcast live coverage of the war twenty-four hours a day, seven days a week.

The mass media not only *report* the events but also *frame* them, guiding how viewers understand and interpret what happens. Media outlets critical of the Iraqi war—especially the Arab news channel Al-Jazeera—tended to report the slow pace of the conflict, played up the casualties on the part of the U.S. and allied forces, and

SOCIAL PROBLEMS IN FOCUS

Has Our All-Volunteer Army Turned into a Warrior Caste?

Marine Sergeant Alex Lemons returned to his wife and home in Utah in 2008, after completing three tours of duty in Iraq. He was glad to put combat behind him. But his return to the United States did not feel like a homecoming. "I felt as alien here as I felt in Iraq," Lemons explained, sitting in his living room. After getting back, Lemons explained, he saw no evidence anywhere that this country was engaged in a war. Most people didn't think much about the fact that the United States had been at war in Iraq. Lemons felt that this amounted to a major problem: The vast majority of our people in society no longer are directly involved in the military.

It was not always that way. During World War II, about 9 percent of the U.S. population served in the military. Almost everyone who stayed at home was involved in the war effort by working in defense plants, participating in the rationing of vital materials, and buying bonds to finance the war effort. Today, by contrast, just one-half of 1 percent of our nation's population is in the military, and most families have no living member who has ever worn a military uniform. Since the September 2001 attacks, people over the age of eighteen who have served in the military represent just 1 percent of the population. That leaves 99 percent of us with no direct involvement in military service. This is the same level of inequality that mobilized the Occupy movement—in this case, however, it is the "1 percent" that is doing all the work.

There are many reasons that military service now involves a small share of the U.S. population. The most important factor is that, in 1973, as the Vietnam War was winding down, the draft was ended and replaced by the policy of the all-volunteer military. A second factor is gender because 85 percent of today's military personnel are males. Third, the military is overwhelmingly from certain parts of the country—with the South heavily represented. In fact, half of all active-duty military personnel are stationed in just five states: Virginia, North Carolina, Georgia, Texas, and California. Beyond this list, additional factors also come into play: Most young people would be ineligible to enlist even if they wanted to. Some have criminal records and many are overweight.

When we put all the factors together, today's military personnel are men from rural areas and small towns in more traditional regions of the country that hold to military values such as honor, discipline, and patriotism. Although almost none of these people grew up in poverty, the large majority are from working-class families. Typically, they see in military service a way to gain economic security and work experience.

The fact that military service falls on an ever-thinner slice of U.S. society is also evident in the country's leadership. At the end of the Vietnam War, almost 80 percent of members of Congress were veterans; today, that share has fallen to 19 percent. As for the people who work in the mass media, including newspapers, television, and films, virtually no one has served in the military.

With these facts in mind, it's easy to understand the frustration of one military wife, who lives in Washington State and whose husband served in Afghanistan. Several years ago, she recounted that the Taliban blew up "a bus last week and killed 17 people, and I didn't know anything about it because it wasn't on the news. It makes me think nobody cares. They're putting on things like Kardashians getting divorced—it's on the news constantly—but we have soldiers over there dying, and you just don't hear about it" (Thompson, 2011; Manning, 2014).

What Do You Think?

1. Do you think the responsibility of military service should be shouldered by just 1 percent of the adult population? Explain.
2. Would you support restoring the draft as a means of spreading this responsibility throughout the class structure? Why or why not?
3. How well do you think this nation treats our military veterans? Explain.

---

presented detailed accounts of the deaths and injuries suffered by Iraqi civilians. All this information and the accompanying "spin" was intended to increase pressure on the U.S. government to end the war. Media outlets supportive of the war—including most news organizations in the United States—tended to report the rapid pace of the war, to focus on the casualties to Saddam Hussein's forces, and to downplay harm to Iraqi civilians as minimal and unintended. Obviously, this "spin" was intended to encourage public support for the war.

For any point of view, the mass media now operate to provide selective information on armed conflicts to a worldwide audience. The power to shape the reality we perceive means that television and other media are almost as important to the outcome of a conflict as the military forces that are doing the actual fighting.

War in the Nuclear Age

In the mid-1940s, warfare became far more deadly with the development of **nuclear weapons**, *bombs that use atomic reactions to generate enormous destructive force*. Only twice have nuclear weapons been used in war. In 1945, at the conclusion of World War II, the United States dropped two atomic bombs on Japan. The first exploded over the city of Hiroshima; the second, dropped three days later,

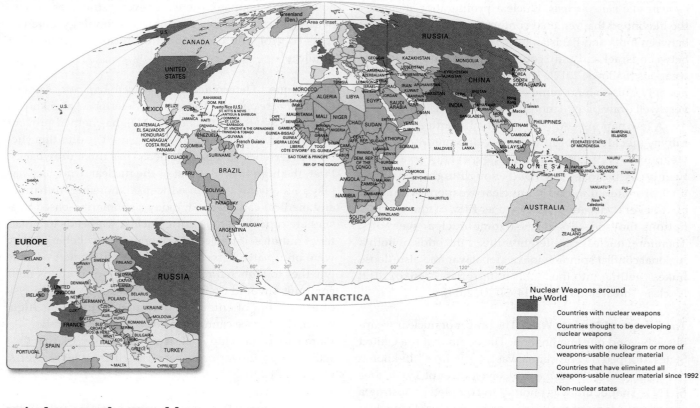

Window on the World

Global Map 17–2 Nuclear Weapons in Global Perspective

In 2014, nine countries possessed nuclear weapons. Many more, especially high-income nations, could build these weapons but have chosen not to. How many countries do you think will have nuclear weapons in the year 2050?

SOURCES: Stockholm International Peace Research Institute (2014) and Nuclear Threat Initiative (2014).

fell on Nagasaki. Each explosion instantly killed 100,000 people and leveled the city. Today, estimates suggest that there are some 17,270 nuclear weapons worldwide, and about 4,400 of them are operational. Most of these weapons are thousands of times more powerful than the bombs used against Japan (Stockholm International Peace Research Institute, 2013).

The Increase and Spread of Nuclear Weapons The arms race that followed World War II led the United States and the Soviet Union to build large arsenals of nuclear weapons. Since the end of World War II, the two superpowers have built about 125,000 nuclear bombs. These nuclear stockpiles reached their peak during the Cold War in the late 1960s and represented many times the number of weapons needed to wipe out all life on this planet.

After the collapse of the Soviet Union in 1991, the Russian Federation and the United States gradually reduced their nuclear arsenals. The latest Strategic Arms

Reduction Talks (2011) has led the two nations, in 2014, to hold about 3,100 nuclear warheads (1,585 in the United States and 1,512 in the Russian Federation), with an agreement to limit each nation to 1,550 operational warheads and allowing each country to verify the number of warheads through a system of inspections. These reductions have continued in 2014 despite rising tensions between Russia and the United States over Russian advances into Ukraine (Barnes & Entous, 2014; U.S. Department of State, 2014).

These superpowers are not the only nations that have nuclear weapons. Global Map 17–2 identifies the United States, Great Britain, France, Russia, Israel, India, Pakistan, the People's Republic of China, and North Korea as nations with a substantial nuclear capability. Available information suggests that China, India, and Pakistan are increasing the size of their nuclear arsenals (Stockholm International Peace Research Institute, 2013).

Recent decades have witnessed a pattern of **nuclear proliferation**, *the acquisition of nuclear weapon technology* *by more and more nations*. Nuclear proliferation increases the likelihood that regional conflicts, such as the tensions between India and Pakistan in 2002 or the current tensions between Israel and Iran, could trigger the use of nuclear weapons (Fallows, 2012). The use of such weapons would not only cause a huge number of casualties but also could very well draw other nations into the conflict.

A few nations—Argentina, Brazil, South Africa, and Libya—decided to stop their development of nuclear weapons. As of 2014, however, experts estimate that twenty-six nations now have enough highly enriched nuclear material to make a nuclear weapon. Within the next several decades, as many as fifty of the world's nations may possess at least some nuclear weapons. Therefore, nuclear proliferation raises the odds of both a regional conflict spinning into a global war and also "loose nukes" getting into the hands of terrorists (Zenko, 2012; Nuclear Threat Initiative, 2014; SIPRI, 2014).

The Effects of Nuclear War The power of nuclear weapons is beyond our imagination. The bomb that the United States dropped on Hiroshima was a "primitive" 15-kiloton device, meaning it had the explosive power of 15,000 tons of TNT. That bomb was enough to completely destroy a major city. Many of the warheads in the world's nuclear arsenals are rated at 50 megatons, equivalent to 50 million tons of TNT, which is 3,000 times more powerful than the Hiroshima bomb.

Even a relatively small nuclear weapon of a single megaton, if detonated, will produce temperatures that exceed the heat on the surface of the sun. Instantly, such heat will vaporize anything within about a mile's range nearby and the resulting firestorm will consume everything for 10 miles in every direction. The bomb also generates a shockwave that extends outward, destroying everything in its path and drawing debris upward into a giant mushroom cloud. In the days that follow, radioactive debris rains down over a vast area (Sagan & Turco, 1990).

Some scientists claim that exploding even a few nuclear bombs at one time would draw enough debris and dust into the atmosphere to block the sun's rays from reaching the planet's surface for months or even years. This event would trigger a *nuclear winter*, a cooling of Earth's atmosphere by as much as 50° Fahrenheit. The resulting semidarkness and subfreezing temperatures, together with radiation from nuclear fallout, might kill most of the planet's vegetation and animal life. Should multiple nuclear bombs ever be used in war, in short, all life on Earth might come to an end (Sagan & Turco, 1990).

Strategies for Peace

Given the unimaginable horrors of war in a nuclear age, the nations of the world must seek to live in peace. But how can this happen? There are several strategies to keep peace, including deterrence, high-technology defense, arms control, and diplomatic resolution of underlying conflicts.

Deterrence Deterrence is *a strategy to keep peace based on the threat of retaliation*. The logic of deterrence, also known as *mutual assured destruction* (MAD), has helped prevent all-out war for more than sixty years. Despite this success, deterrence as a path to peace has three drawbacks. First, the high financial cost of the nuclear arms race has taken money away from education, housing, nutrition, and medical care. Second, today's submarine-based missiles are capable of delivering nuclear warheads in a matter of minutes. If the leaders of one country believed they were under attack, they would have little time to decide whether to launch a retaliatory strike—or perhaps their computers would do it for them. In such a case, the risk of error—and of entering an unintended war—is high. Third, deterrence cannot control nuclear proliferation. As more nations develop nuclear weapons, the risk that they will be used in war or by terrorists increases (Kugler & Organski, 1989).

High-Technology Defense A second strategy to keep the peace is the use of new technology, including satellites, to defend against a nuclear attack. The Strategic Defense Initiative (SDI), first proposed by the Reagan administration in 1981, was just such a program. In principle, such a system would detect enemy missiles soon after launch and destroy them with lasers and particle beams before they reenter the atmosphere.

But the capacity to actually *do* this tests all current technologies. First, after spending more than $100 billion on this technology, preliminary tests of SDI did not show much success (Hsin, 2003). Second, even if one nation were to deploy such a system, other countries may see this effort as preparation for war. With this thinking in mind, the Obama administration turned away from SDI in favor of installing a missile defense system in Europe, based on sophisticated radar and rockets, to guard against any nuclear missiles fired toward Europe from Iran.

Arms Control A third strategy to keep the peace is **arms control**, *international agreements on the development, testing, production, and deployment of weapons*. Since World War II, the focus of arms control efforts has been on limiting the nuclear stockpiles held by the United States and the Soviet Union. In the 1970s, the two nations entered into the Strategic Arms Limitation Talks (SALT), which led to agreements freezing the number of nuclear weapons held by each side and limiting the development of antimissile defense systems. In the 1980s and 1990s, the

United States and the Soviet Union (after 1991, the Russian Federation) entered into the Strategic Arms Reduction Talks (START), which led both nations to reduce the number of their operational nuclear weapons (Norris & Kristensen, 2012).

Arms control has limitations. First, treaties focused on existing weapons may do little to slow the development of newer and even more powerful weapons. Second, even providing for inspections, it is difficult to verify whether nations are living up to arms control agreements. Third, despite recent progress toward arms control, enough nuclear weapons still remain to destroy the entire planet. The more important issue, therefore, is resolving the underlying conflicts that might end up causing their use.

Perhaps the greatest threat to the security of the world is the spread of nuclear weapons to more and more countries. Iran is enriching uranium, which could be used to create an atomic bomb. Do the United States and other "older" nuclear powers have a right to deny the same weapons to nations that wish to have them? Why or why not?

Diplomatic Resolution of Underlying Conflict The most effective path to peace is to resolve conflicts, the strategy of *diplomacy*. Peace depends on the efforts of national leaders and ambassadors posted in various countries as well as the work of international agencies such as the United Nations. In recent years, diplomats have used the term *peace process* to refer to the back-and-forth negotiations between parties in conflict, including the steps each side will take to end hostilities in exchange for a desired objective. Negotiating peace is always difficult, and not every participant in a conflict may want peace, at least not on terms that are agreeable to all. For example, the Middle East peace process has been going on for decades, but violent confrontations between Israelis and Palestinians continue.

Throughout the world today, there are hundreds of conflicts between nations and between groups within nations based on territorial disputes, ethnicity, religion, ideology, and inequality. To suppose that humankind can resolve all these conflicts may seem like wishful thinking. But the fact remains that the world spends far more money on weapons of war than on strategies for peace (Dedrick & Yinger, 1990; Kaplan & Schaffer, 2001).

There are individuals who have shown a lifetime commitment to the pursuit of peace. One of the most influential was the Indian leader Mohandas Gandhi (1869–1948), whose lessons are described in the Defining Moment box on page 502.

Terrorism

17.2 Identify types of terrorism in the world as well as strategies to address terrorism.

Terrorism involves *unlawful, typically random acts of violence or the threat of violence by an individual, group, or government to achieve a political goal*. Every day, a significant act of terrorism takes place somewhere in the world (U.S. Department of State, 2014).

War involves an ongoing conflict that usually follows international law and conventions. But terrorism involves sporadic and unpredictable acts of violence that cause widespread fear. Acts of terror, which include bombings, hijackings, and assassinations, are typically used by individuals or groups against a more powerful enemy.

Some terrorists are individual activists, but others are supported by a government. **State-sponsored terrorism** is *the practice by one government of providing money, weapons, and training to terrorists who engage in violence in another nation*. For example, when the Taliban regime had control of Afghanistan, that government provided military training and other support to members of al-Qaeda, who later engaged in terrorist attacks against the United States and other countries. For more than a decade after the attacks of September 11, 2001, the United States has been engaged in military action in Afghanistan in order to drive the Taliban from power and weaken the al-Qaeda network. The U.S. government identifies Iran, Cuba, Sudan, and Syria as nations that have sponsored terrorism (U.S. Department of State, 2013).

CONSTRUCTING SOCIAL PROBLEMS

A DEFINING MOMENT

Mohandas Gandhi: Sending a Message of Peace

Mohandas Karamchand Gandhi was a small man who carried a mighty message. He built his life around the idea that the most effective path to peace and justice is to practice not war but nonviolence.

Gandhi's primary goal was the liberation of his native country, India, from the colonial control of the British. Rather than attacking the British militarily or resorting to suicide bombers or other forms of terror common in today's world, he advocated a strategy of *nonviolent resistance*—encouraging everyone politely but firmly to refuse to cooperate with a system they believed to be wrong.

In one of his most effective tactics, Gandhi urged the people of India to make their own clothes rather than buy garments manufactured in England within what he saw as an exploitative colonial economic system. The spinning wheel became his symbol of resistance, and the Indian people admiringly nicknamed him "Mahatma" ("great soul").

Gandhi faced many challenges and was arrested many times during his life. But in 1947, the movement he founded succeeded in ending British colonial rule. Tragically, just one year later, this man of peace was shot and killed by a crazed opponent. But his message lives on, and it has been embraced by many others, including the U.S. civil rights leader, Martin Luther King Jr.

Mohandas Gandhi taught the world that it is possible to pursue justice using nonviolent means rather than war. In the years since Gandhi's death, how well has this lesson been learned?

Any discussion of terrorism is likely to involve claims and counterclaims. Organizations may use terrorism to focus world attention on their issues and demands, which they claim to be fair and good. They consider violence as a legitimate political response to injustice. For this reason, whether people condemn or celebrate an act of violence depends on which side of a dispute they are on. For example, the U.S. government condemns al-Qaeda for engaging in terrorism, and leaders of al-Qaeda say much the same thing about the United States. The United States also claims that Iran engages in state-sponsored terrorism for supporting Hezbollah fighters in Lebanon who are frequently at war with Israel; Iran counters that Israel, with the support of the United States, engages in terrorism against its neighbors. In short, whether we label actors as "terrorists" or "freedom fighters" is a matter of politics (Sheehan, 2000; J. C. Jenkins, 2003; U.S. Department of State, 2011).

Governments also use terrorism against their own people. **Repressive state terrorism** is *government use of violence within its own national borders to suppress political opposition.* Many governments have used kidnapping, torture, rape, and mass murder to stay in power. The Soviet dictator Josef Stalin used secret police and a system of concentration camps to control or kill anyone he considered a threat. Adolf Hitler used similar brutal methods to rule Germany during the Nazi era. In the 1970s, Pol Pot conducted a campaign of repressive state terrorism against the people of Cambodia. Until his overthrow by U.S. forces, Saddam Hussein used a brutal campaign of terror to maintain an iron grip on the people of Iraq. Since 2011, Bashar al-Assad has used violence in his efforts to remain in power in Syria (Blanford, 2014).

The Extent of Terrorism

In 2013, there were more than 9,700 terrorist attacks worldwide, which claimed 17,891 lives, including sixteen civilian U.S. citizens. Terrorism caused serious injury to more than 32,000 people. More than half of all attacks and a large majority of all deaths and injuries took place in just three countries—Iraq, Pakistan, and Afghanistan—but major terrorist attacks also occurred in other countries, including Nigeria, Syria, and India (U.S. Department of State, 2014).

Terrorism: A Global Perspective For at least a century, terrorism has played a part in efforts to end colonial rule in many nations of the world. In 1916, for example, Irish people opposed to British rule formed the Irish Republican Army (IRA) with the goal of forcing the British from Ireland. In 1922, the British gave up claim to most of Ireland but kept control of three counties that have been called Northern Ireland. For decades after that, the IRA used terrorism as part of its efforts to end British control there as well.

Many other terrorist campaigns took place around the world. After World War II, a militant faction of the Zionist movement that sought to establish a Jewish state in the Middle East used terrorism to drive the British from Palestine. In 1954, a group called the Mau Mau used terror in its efforts to force British colonialists from the African nation of Kenya. That same year, Algerian terrorists began a campaign of violence against French citizens in their country, which played a part in ending French colonial rule of Algeria in 1962. In recent decades, organizations committed to establishing a Palestinian state on land controlled by Israel have made Israelis the targets of terrorism (U.S. Department of State, 2003, 2014).

In 2012, the world witnessed a horrific example of state-sponsored terrorism as the Syrian government turned its military on its own people in an effort to crush a widely popular rebellion. Do you think that the United States has the obligation to come to the aid of people who are demanding greater freedom or should this country stay out of the internal affairs of other nations?

In recent years, a considerable amount of terrorism in the world has been carried out by radical Muslims who have directed their violence against the United States. In 1993, al-Qaeda members exploded a truck full of dynamite at the World Trade Center in New York's downtown business district, killing six people and injuring more than 1,000 (Hughes, 1998). In 1998, the same organization exploded bombs at the U.S. embassies in Tanzania and Kenya, killing 257 people and injuring more than 5,000. In 2001, the most deadly attack on the United States in history took almost 3,000 lives when al-Qaeda terrorists seized and crashed airliners loaded with passengers and fuel into the twin towers of the World Trade Center in New York and the Pentagon outside Washington, D.C. Another hijacked plane, in which passengers fought the terrorists, crashed in rural Pennsylvania.

The targeting of the United States reflects this nation's substantial military, economic, and political presence around the world. In addition, some radical organizations, including al-Qaeda, define the United States as an evil influence in the world (Thomas & Hirsh, 2000; U.S. Department of State, 2011).

Terrorism in U.S. History   Although many people here in the United States think of terrorists as people from other countries, the United States has a long history of homegrown terrorism. After the abolition of slavery, the Ku Klux Klan and other organizations used cross burnings, beatings, lynchings, and bombings to prevent African Americans from exercising their new political rights. In the century after the Civil War, historians estimate, more than 5,000 black men were lynched by white supremacist mobs (Williams, 2000).

Early in the twentieth century, many large businesses, sometimes with support by police, used violence to prevent union organizing. Some labor groups fought back. The Industrial Workers of the World (IWW), a radical-left labor union, began a war against capitalism that included violent strikes, bombings, and assassinations (Lukas, 1997). In the 1960s, some students who shared radical-left views formed the Weather Underground, a group committed to forming a classless society by destroying the nation's economic and military institutions. This group carried out a number of violent attacks, including a bombing of the Pentagon in 1975 (Finlayson, 1998).

On April 19, 1995, Timothy McVeigh, a military veteran, parked a truck full of homemade explosives in front of the Murrah Federal Building in Oklahoma City. McVeigh, on the radical right, was seeking revenge on the federal government for actions taken against Randy Weaver at Ruby Ridge, Idaho, and against the Branch Davidian compound in Waco, Texas, events discussed in Chapter 6 ("Crime, Violence, and Criminal Justice"). The explosion killed 168 people—many of them children—and injured hundreds more. McVeigh was executed for his crime in 2001.

The Costs of Terrorism

One great cost of terrorism is loss of life and physical injury: In recent years tens of thousands of people worldwide have been killed or injured by terrorism (U.S. Department of State, 2014). Hostages and other survivors of terror attacks, like soldiers who suffer from battlefield trauma, may well experience posttraumatic stress disorder. Just as important, such acts cause widespread fear. Everyone living in the United States at the time of the attacks on September 11, 2001, can recall the fear and anxiety caused by the events of that day. For people living in Iraq, where the pace of terrorism is far greater, fear and anxiety have been an almost daily occurrence.

The economic costs of terrorist attacks are impossible to measure, but they reach into the hundreds of billions of dollars. There is the immediate loss of property as well as the effects on the entire economy. In the area near where New York's World Trade Center stood before the September 11 attacks, the entire economy collapsed for several years. Similarly, in the aftermath of those plane hijackings, air travel fell dramatically, forcing several airlines into bankruptcy.

If we were to calculate the full costs of this country's "war on terrorism," including all the military spending that supports it, the total would surely be trillions of dollars. Such vast sums are hard to imagine, but they easily represent enough money to end poverty not only in this country but everywhere in the world as well.

Terrorism as a Type of War

Terrorism has emerged as a new type of war. Like war, terrorism is a form of armed conflict, but it differs from conventional war in four major ways (Ratnesar, 2003; Jenkins, 2012).

After winning the military campaign in Afghanistan, the United States faced a much tougher job—winning the hearts and minds of the Afghan people. How might you react to a foreign army occupying your country?

1. **The parties in conflict are not clearly known.** War is fought between nations known to one another. Terrorism is carried out by organized groups whose identity, leadership, membership, and location may or may not be known. Years after the United States launched its war on terrorism, there is still much to learn about the al-Qaeda organization.

2. **The objectives of the terrorist groups are not clearly stated.** Wars are usually fought with clear objectives, such as gaining territory. The goals of terrorist groups, by contrast, may not be clear. Although al-Qaeda clearly has the intention of harming the United States, the precise goals of the September 11 attacks and other terrorist acts have never been clearly stated.

3. **Terrorism is asymmetrical.** Conventional warfare is symmetrical, with two opposing powers sending their armies into battle. By contrast, terrorism is an asymmetrical or uneven conflict in which a small number of attackers use terror and their own willingness to die in order to take on a far more powerful enemy.

4. **Terrorism has no clear beginning or ending.** According to Brian Michael Jenkins, people in our country typically see military conflict as having a clear beginning and ending, even to the point of setting dates for these events. But, he explains, this precision is not always the case. Members of al-Qaeda typically see the current conflict with the United States as a continuation of a long, historical struggle between "believers and infidels." Therefore, although specific terrorist attacks may be located in time, the larger conflict is a process that may continue for generations.

Strategies for Dealing with Terrorism

Five strategies for dealing with terrorism are part of official U.S. policy and have widespread support elsewhere in the world: Make no concessions, prosecute terrorists, apply economic sanctions, use military force if necessary, and defend against terrorism. In addition to these responses, nations must address the root causes in order to counter terrorism (Tucker, 1998).

Make No Concessions Many national leaders say that they will never give in to demands by terrorist groups. This policy is based on the logic that giving terrorists what they want by, say, paying ransom, surrendering land, or freeing prisoners only encourages further violence. Some nations say they will not even negotiate with terrorists.

But critics claim that a no-concessions policy has little impact on terrorism. They point out that many terrorist organizations are not looking for concessions but simply want to inflict as much damage as possible. In addition, research suggests that whether a country makes concessions or not has little effect on the subsequent level of terrorism.

Prosecute or Kill Terrorists A second strategy to deal with terrorists is criminal prosecution. The federal government successfully prosecuted Timothy McVeigh for the Oklahoma City bombing; he was executed in 2001. In 2006, Zacarias Moussaoui, the alleged "twentieth hijacker" in the September 11, 2001, attacks, was sentenced to life in prison. In some cases, the U.S. military tries to kill terrorist leaders. In 2006, the U.S. military was successful in the effort to hunt down and kill Abu Musab al-Zarqawi, leader of al-Qaeda in Iraq. In 2011, U.S. military forces succeeded in tracking down and killing several senior al-Qaeda leaders, including Osama bin Laden in Pakistan. The recent use of drones to kill militants in Afghanistan, Pakistan, and elsewhere is another example of this policy (Nordland & Masood, 2013).

Apply Economic Sanctions The United States has applied *economic sanctions* or trade restrictions against a number of nations believed to be supporting terrorism, including Libya, Syria, Iraq, North Korea, and Iran. Economic sanctions may harm another country, but bringing about a desired change of behavior may take years, if it occurs at all. In addition, economic sanctions may harm the civilian population of a country while having little effect on leaders. Sanctions against Cuba, for example, have probably hurt the living standards of ordinary people and done little to threaten the power of that country's leaders, Fidel and Raul Castro.

Use Military Force A fourth strategy to punish terrorists and their supporters is direct use of military force. In 1986, the United States bombed Libya following terrorist attacks on U.S. citizens in Europe. After the Persian Gulf War, the United States bombed Iraq for attacking its own Kurdish population. After the September 11, 2001, attacks, the United States went to war in Afghanistan. In 2003, the United States invaded Iraq and ousted its leaders, claiming they were planning to engage in terrorism against this country. In 2011, a multinational force helped drive Libyan dictator and a reputed sponsor of terrorism, Muammar Gaddafi, from power.

Of course, any use of military force is risky because it may provoke further terrorist attacks. In addition, going to war is almost always controversial, as the largely negative response both among the U.S. public and among world leaders to the use of force by the United States in Iraq clearly showed.

Defend against Terrorism

A fifth strategy is to make terrorism harder to carry out. For more than twenty-five years, the U.S. government has used various security measures to protect airports, buildings, and personnel. In addition, the government gathers intelligence data in an effort to identify terrorist groups, monitor their activities, and prevent their attacks. Shortly after the attacks of September 11, 2001, the U.S. Congress passed the USA PATRIOT Act, which greatly expanded the power of government officials to monitor the behavior of people in the United States. Congress renewed this act in 2005 and provisions of the act were renewed again in 2011.

Government leaders claim the USA PATRIOT Act has worked, helping to prevent new attacks. Critics reply that giving such broad powers to government threatens people's civil liberties, which may be more harmful to the country than terrorism itself.

Address the Root Causes of Terrorism A final issue, which often gets little attention, may be the most important of all. It points to the need to examine the underlying conflicts and conditions that cause people to engage in terrorism in the first place.

This approach does not assume that the claims made by terrorists are valid, nor does it condone terrorists' use of violence against innocent people. But it does help us see that terrorism is a symptom of the passionate belief on the part of less powerful people that they are being treated unfairly. If there were greater opportunity for such people to express their grievances, and if the powerful nations of the world took greater interest in global inequality and showed greater respect for the cultures of less powerful people, perhaps fewer terrorist acts would occur.

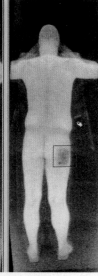

High security, including the use of full body scans, is now a fact of life in U.S. airports. How has today's heightened security affected you or members of your family? Are you willing to give up personal privacy in order to gain greater personal security?

Theories of War and Terrorism

17.3 Apply sociological theory to issues involving war and terrorism.

Theory involves organizing facts to gain understanding. The sections that follow first consider the value of biological theories and then apply sociology's various theoretical approaches to war and terrorism.

Biological Theories of Conflict

Is a tendency toward war and violence a natural part of being human? Some biological scientists claim that it is. Konrad Lorenz (1966, 1981) claims that just as some animals will defend a nest, den, or burrow, humans turn to war to defend their homeland.

Edward Wilson (1975) claims that certain types of human behavior, including war and aggression, result from competition among males in the process of reproduction. In the case of most animals, males fight with each other for sexual access to females. In the case of humans, however, the process is more complex. Wilson argues that more aggressive men typically achieve higher social standing, which in turn attracts females. On average, Wilson continues, more aggressive men are more likely than less aggressive men to reproduce. Over hundreds of generations, this process ensures that genetic traits favoring aggression will become more common in the human species.

EVALUATE

Most sociologists tend to dismiss claims that humans are naturally aggressive. They point out that people make choices about how to act and that we are not guided by biological instincts the way other animals are. Not surprisingly, sociologists point to culture and social structure as the greatest influences on human behavior. These factors, rather than biology, make some societies more warlike than others. If war is indeed natural to humans, why do nations have to go to such great lengths to convince their people to go to war? (Montagu, 1976)

CHECK YOUR LEARNING   How do biologists explain the aggressive tendency they see in human behavior? Why do sociologists reject this argument?

Structural-Functional Analysis: The Functions of Conflict

Structural-functional theory highlights the functions that war and other conflicts have for society. Although war has obvious costs in terms of the loss of lives and property, it may accomplish important goals.

Two centuries ago, the Prussian military theorist Carl von Clausewitz (1780–1831) studied the functions of warfare. War, he concluded, is simply politics carried on by other means. Nations go to war to achieve political goals, such as gaining land or increasing their international prestige. War may be a good strategy, Clausewitz (1968, orig. 1832) concluded, if nations expect that the gains of fighting will outweigh the likely costs—and only if, of course, the country's leaders are sure of winning.

History tells us that war is often not a winning strategy. For one thing, many countries that start wars end up in defeat. But today's sociologists point out that war continues to have important political consequences. Most of the world's territorial boundaries have been established by wars. Similarly, war and even terrorism have played a major part in creating new nations, including the United States. Throughout the twentieth century, war and terrorism have been strategies used by ethnic and religious minorities seeking their own nation-states. As already noted, terrorism can be used effectively by a group or nation in opposition to a much stronger enemy.

An important function of both war and terrorism is uniting the population of a nation to rally around a patriotic cause. Conflict with a nation or group with a differing way of life also helps clarify and strengthen a society's cultural values. Military efforts create tens of thousands of jobs, greatly expanding the economy. In addition, many of the technological developments we take for granted today, including interstate highways, high-speed jet travel, cellular telephones, and the Internet, were products of research first carried out for military purposes.

Finally, war has played a part in improving the social standing of women and other minorities. It was during World War II, for example, that African Americans and women of all racial categories first gained access to good jobs in factories turning out war equipment (Flexner, 1975; Chafe, 1977; Galbraith, 1985). The Diversity: Race, Class, & Gender box takes a look at the place of women in today's armed forces.

EVALUATE

Critics of structural-functional theory ask, first of all, how we can even think about war as having positive consequences when the weapons of war now threaten to devastate whole nations and possibly to destroy the entire planet. Second, by pointing out the positive functions of war and other violent conflict, this approach downplays the tremendous costs of war, including loss of life and property and damage to the environment. Third, the costs and benefits of war are not the same for everyone. Political and military leaders and the people who manufacture and sell weapons of war may benefit from conflict, but the ordinary people who actually do the fighting usually end up paying a high price. Finally, the reality of conflict is always a matter of how people define it, which brings us to symbolic-interaction theory.

DIVERSITY: RACE, CLASS, & GENDER
Women in the Military: An Equal Right to Kill?

Although most people think of the military as a man's world, women have served in the U.S. armed forces since colonial times. At the beginning of World War II, women represented 2 percent of the U.S. military forces. Today, women make up about 15 percent of the U.S. military, and they represent about 2 percent of nearly 6,800 soldiers killed in the wars in Iraq and Afghanistan (U.S. Department of Defense, 2014).

Nevertheless, some uneasiness remains regarding women serving in combat roles. Some people who oppose women in combat point to the fact that, on average, women have less physical strength than men. Others counter that in today's high-technology wars, physical strength plays a smaller and smaller role in armed conflict. Mental strength may matter more to today's soldiers, and data show that women in uniform are better educated and more intelligent than their male counterparts.

Just as important, in this age of high technology, it is hard to draw a line between combat and noncombat personnel. For example, a combat soldier who fires a missile at an enemy position may be miles away from the actual explosion. At the same time, a noncombatant team operating a helicopter may come under fire flying the wounded from a battlefield.

Perhaps the greatest resistance to having more women in combat is the traditional view of women as nurturers who give life and help to others. As long as U.S. culture defines women in this way (and as long as we engage in wars), it is likely that the military will resist putting women in harm's way.

What Do You Think?

1. Is the fact that women generally have less physical strength than men important in today's military? Why or why not?

2. What does the high level of sexual assault directed at women suggest about the culture of the military as far as gender goes?

3. What about the fact that women in combat may be taken as prisoners of war? Do you think enemy soldiers will treat women POWs differently from men who are POWs? Explain.

CHECK YOUR LEARNING What do we learn by applying structural-functional theory to war and terrorism? What are several criticisms of this approach?

Symbolic-Interaction Analysis: The Meanings of Conflict

Symbolic-interaction theory focuses attention on the meanings people attach to war and other types of violent conflict. The importance of meanings was illustrated earlier in the statement that one side's "terrorists" (people who are part of the problem) may well be the other side's "freedom fighters" (people who are part of the solution).

In general, national leaders use symbols and meanings as tools to "spin" the reality of war in a particular way. Leaders encourage the public to define their own country's cause as just, making claims that their soldiers march "with God on their side." In addition, leaders use symbols and meanings to demonize the enemy. A generation ago, President Ronald Reagan justified greater military spending by painting the Soviet Union as an "evil empire" that was a danger to the entire world. More recently, President George W. Bush characterized Iran, Iraq, and North Korea as an "axis of evil." The Iranian president returned the favor, characterizing the United States as "the great Satan."

The military trains recruits to define the enemy as less than human. In the Vietnam War, for example, many U.S. soldiers learned to dehumanize their Vietnamese counterparts as "gooks." The process of demonizing "the other," of course, makes killing them that much easier (Said, 1981; Aditjondro, 2000).

EVALUATE

Symbolic-interaction theory shows us that war is a battle waged not only using guns but also using words and other symbols as people define themselves as just and their opponents as unjust. But this theory says little about the role of power in international conflict. The side that turns out to be "right" typically is the side that is militarily stronger. In addition, within a society's population, some categories of people declare wars, and others fight them. Some categories make money from military campaigns, and some lose everything. To learn more about how inequality shapes war, we turn to the social-conflict theory.

CHECK YOUR LEARNING What do we learn by applying symbolic-interaction theory to war and terrorism? What are several limitations of this approach?

Social-Conflict Analysis: Inequality and Conflict

Social-conflict theory highlights the link between war and social inequality. Karl Marx, who helped develop the social-conflict approach, considered political leaders the servants of the capitalist class, the people who own the means of production. Capitalists want ever-increasing profits, which they get from finding new sources of raw materials, manufacturing new

About fifteen percent of the military personnel now deployed by the United States are women. Do you support women moving into combat roles in the military? Why or why not?

products, and selling them in new markets. In Marx's day, capitalists did all these things through colonizing the world, which led rich nations in Europe to conquer and control other countries.

Formal colonialism is now mostly a thing of the past, but the pattern of foreign control remains. Rich nations, including the United States, use their military power to protect and expand the global capitalist economy (Wallerstein, 1979; M. C. Hudson, 1992; Tabb, 1992). From this point of view, the war in Iraq was less about advancing the cause of freedom and justice in Iraq and securing freedom in the Middle East than it was about ensuring the flow of oil and opening more of the world to multinational corporations. Here at home, the rich are the primary beneficiaries of war, and working people represent most of the soldiers and sailors who do the fighting (Halbfinger & Holmes, 2003).

As noted earlier, the production of weapons and other military goods helps speed the growth of the capitalist economy, pushing up corporate profits. The arms race a generation ago or the war on terror today may or may not make the nation safer, but developing and producing new weapons and military technology is certainly highly profitable for those who control the U.S. economy (Mills, 1956).

And what of terrorism? Historically, poor nations have been no match for the military might of the countries that colonized them. For that reason, groups opposing colonial rule often act outside the established political

system. As noted earlier, terrorism can be an effective way for less powerful people to focus the world's attention on what they consider to be injustice. In short, war is the means by which powerful nations dominate the globe; terrorism is the means by which the powerless fight back (B. Hoffman, 1998; Kaldor, 1999; Stern, 1999; Zanini, 1999).

EVALUATE

By linking war and terrorism to social inequality, social-conflict theory helps explain ongoing support for militarism in the United States even during times of peace. One limitation of the claim that capitalism is the major cause of war is that socialist nations also engage in war. For example, the Soviet Union used military force to gain and maintain control of Eastern Europe following World War II, just as China has directed its military power against Vietnam, Cambodia, and Tibet. In addition, a broad view of history shows that wars break out not only because of economic concerns but also as the result of religious beliefs and ethnic pride.

CHECK YOUR LEARNING What do we learn by applying social-conflict theory to war and terrorism? What are several limitations of this approach?

The Applying Theory table summarizes what we can learn about war and terrorism from each of sociology's three major theoretical approaches.

⭐ POLITICS AND WAR

Constructing Problems and Defining Solutions

17.4 Analyze war, terrorism, and the pursuit of peace from various positions on the political spectrum.

Theory provides useful insights about war and terrorism, but the issues people identify as "problems" and the policies that they favor as "solutions" reflect their political attitudes. The following sections examine the conservative, liberal, and radical-left views of war and terrorism.

Conservatives: Peace through Strength

Conservatives believe that the United States represents good in the world; at the same time, they recognize that some other nations or their leaders threaten this good. Aware that the United States has enemies abroad, most conservatives favor military strength as the best way to keep the peace. Just as conservatives tend to have a

APPLYING THEORY

War and Terrorism

	Structural-Functional Theory	Symbolic-Interaction Theory	Social-Conflict Theory
What is the level of analysis?	Macro-level	Micro-level	Macro-level
How do we understand war and terrorism?	Structural-functional theory suggests that war is a strategy that a society may use to establish its independence, defend its way of life, or reach other objectives. Terrorism is a strategy used by groups or nations to oppose a much stronger enemy. Conflict helps unite a society and strengthen its core values. Militarism helps expand the economy. Many technological advances that improve our lives, including the Internet, were developed through military research.	Symbolic-interaction theory focuses on the meanings and understandings that people attach to conflict. National leaders use symbols to convince a population that their cause is just. Leaders also use symbols to demonize an enemy.	Social-conflict theory links war to social inequality. Marx explained militarism as efforts by the capitalist elite to gain ever-increasing profits through colonialism; today, the goal is to defend and expand the capitalist global economy. Strong nations use war to dominate the globe; the powerless use terrorism to fight back.
What does the theory say about war and terrorism as problems?	Like all social patterns, war has benefits and costs. Whether a particular conflict ends up being thought of as a problem or not has much to do with the outcomes, all of which may not be evident for some time.	Reality is socially constructed. Therefore, whether any military effort is celebrated as heroic or condemned as unjust depends on the definitions that are applied. Two parties in conflict may see the same situation in very different terms so that one party's "problem" is the other's "solution."	The question becomes: problems for whom? Elites often benefit from militarism and the wars that are fought by ordinary people who bear most of the suffering and loss.

law-and-order view that a strong police force is needed to fight crime at home, conservatives believe that a strong military protects the nation's interests against hostile forces beyond its borders. For this reason, most conservatives support U.S. military actions abroad—at least when our national interests are at stake—and this helps explain why this country currently stations troops in twenty nations.

During the Cold War, which lasted from the end of World War II until the collapse of the Soviet Union in 1991, conservatives supported increased military expenditures in the belief that in facing an enemy that opposed our core value of human liberty, nothing less than the freedom of the United States was at stake. As a result of the war against terror, President George W. Bush pushed military expenditures higher, claiming that a strong U.S. military presence in the world is vital both for ensuring the security of people here in the United States and for extending freedom to people living in countries that lack democracy. More recently, President Barack Obama has ended the country's military involvement in Iraq and is drawing down our military commitment in Afghanistan with a plan to remove most or all U.S. troops from that country by 2015.

Conservatives also take a hard line against terrorism. In general, they paint those who use violence against innocent people as criminals who oppose freedom and hold back their countries' economic development. People to the right of center think the United States should do whatever is necessary to identify those responsible for terrorism and bring them to justice, applauding the killing of Osama bin Laden in 2011.

In the 2012 presidential election, Republican Mitt Romney expressed the conservative position of "peace through strength." Accusing President Obama of "apologizing for America," Romney campaigned on the promise to acknowledge this country's greatness (Friedman, 2012).

Liberals: The Dangers of Militarism

Liberals agree with conservatives that the United States needs to be able to defend itself from attack. For this reason, liberals also support our nation's military. However, liberals typically favor a somewhat lower level of military spending than conservatives support. One reason is that, as liberals see it, the United States has not always used its military wisely. The Democratic victory in the 2006 congressional elections and the election of President Obama in 2008 were driven, in large part, by the voters' view that the Iraq War had turned world opinion against the United States and encouraged even greater terrorism.

A second disagreement centers on how a society should use its limited resources. Conservatives tend to make military spending a top priority, but liberals are keenly aware that military spending takes money away from education, health care, and other important programs. In short, liberals see militarism as draining

Conservatives regard the United States as a force for good in the world; from this perspective, the wars in Iraq and Afghanistan have been efforts to spread democracy. Liberals are more cautious in this regard; they voice greater support for multinational efforts led by the United Nations. Radicals see militarism as a strategy to extend capitalism; they typically oppose the use of U.S. military power.

resources that could be used to provide universal health insurance, reduce poverty, and improve run-down schools. Therefore, liberals typically offer strong support for arms reduction.

When it comes to international tensions as well as terrorism, liberals believe that our country's first response should be diplomacy and negotiation rather than the deployment of troops. For this reason, liberals emphasize the importance of international efforts at building peace, including the work of the United Nations. President Obama's decision to support rather than to lead an international effort to remove Libyan dictator Muammar Gadaffi signaled a shift to a more liberal strategy than that of his predecessor, President Bush, who was more willing to "go it alone" if necessary.

The Radical Left: Peace through Equality

Radicals on the political left believe that the root cause of war, terrorism, and militarism is inequality. Given the enormous gulf between the rich and the poor around the world, they ask, why should anyone expect people to live in peace? Radicals claim that the United States pours money into militarism not for national defense but to operate as a global police force, expanding U.S. influence and extending the global reach of capitalism throughout the world.

In practice, then, the United States engages in military action when any other nation or organization threatens

the operation of the world's capitalist economy. Radicals point to the economic boycott of Cuba after that country's socialist revolution in 1959; hostility toward the socialist Sandinistas in Nicaragua during the 1980s; the onset of the Gulf War in 1991, when the Iraqi army threatened our oil supply in Kuwait; and the 2003 Iraq War and the larger war on terrorism, both seen as efforts to stabilize the world and allow the expansion of corporate influence. Our leaders may justify wars on moral grounds, radicals claim, but the real motive amounts to little more than greed. Left radicals were as likely to see the United States as part of the problem (at least under the Bush administration) as they were to see our country as part of the solution to the world's problems. The radical left has been only mildly more supportive of President Obama, seeing his policies as more liberal but yet very similar to those of the previous administration.

Given their critical view of how U.S. society operates, it is not surprising that radicals on the left often express sympathy for the efforts of forces around the world that are seeking change. From this point of view, terrorism is a political response to powerlessness. As long as a handful of powerful nations rule the world, we should expect some oppressed groups to strike back.

In sum, radicals believe that war and terrorism will continue until the world moves toward greater social equality. Radicals therefore call for a national and international redistribution of wealth in favor of the poor majority. The Left to Right table summarizes the conservative, liberal, and radical-left views of war and terrorism.

Going On from Here

Albert Einstein, whose discoveries in physics led to the development of nuclear weapons, once observed, "The unleashed power of the atom has changed everything save our modes of thinking, and we thus drift toward unparalleled catastrophe." Given humanity's history of warfare and the stockpiles of nuclear weapons on the planet today, what are the odds that we'll get through the twenty-first century without a nuclear war? No one can say for sure, but it seems that the world has learned the skills of making war faster than the skills of creating a lasting peace. As we look to the future, the fact that more and more nations will have nuclear weapons and other weapons of mass destruction means that even local conflicts could threaten the entire planet.

As we move ahead, winning peace may well depend on implementing three strategies. First, the nations of the world must make significant efforts at arms control,

LEFT TO RIGHT

The Politics of War and Terrorism

	Radical-Left View	Liberal View	Conservative View
What is the problem?	The basic problem is capitalism, which encourages militarism in order to expand corporate profits at home and to defend the capitalist economy around the world.	There is a need for defense, but militarism itself can be a problem because an arms buildup provokes conflict; nuclear proliferation raises the risk of nuclear war; terrorism poses dangers to the United States.	The problem is that some nations and groups are hostile to the values and achievements of the United States; nuclear arms development by these nations threatens the security of the United States; terrorists engage in periodic attacks against the United States.
What is the solution?	The solution to militarism is ending the domination of the world by rich nations; eliminating capitalism will end the need for ongoing militarism as well as terrorism.	Reasonable military strength is necessary, but the United States should seek arms reductions and rely on diplomacy as much as possible. Addressing the grievances of less powerful people will reduce terrorism.	Maintaining military strength and strong counterterrorism measures will defeat enemies who are set on our destruction, encourage peace, and ensure the security of the United States.

JOIN THE DEBATE

1. Looking over the three political perspectives on war and terrorism, do you see any areas of agreement? If so, what are they?
2. From the point of view of each of the three political perspectives, what would be the proper role of the U.S. military around the world?
3. Which of the three political analyses of war and terrorism do you find most convincing? Why?

---

with the goal of greatly reducing the number of weapons of mass destruction. The United States and the Russian Federation have made good progress already. A challenge to this goal is that some nations such as North Korea, which almost certainly has one or more nuclear weapons, permit no inspections of their arms production facilities.

Second, controlling the spread of nuclear technology is equally important. No nation can be secure as long as nuclear weapons continue to spread around the world. It seems likely that Iran is in the process of developing nuclear technology that may lead to nuclear weapons. Although the U.S. and Iranian governments recently reached an agreement to limit the development of nuclear technology, Iran's nuclear ambitions are likely to continue. If so, the odds of military conflict aimed at preventing Iran from completing this work is high. Even then, what country will be next? How can we ensure that all nuclear weapons remain out of reach of terrorist organizations?

The third and final strategy—clearly the most difficult of all—is to address the underlying causes of war and terrorism. In part, this requires the leaders of all nations, rich and poor alike, to demonstrate genuine concern for the well-being of people everywhere, especially the poor. In addition, all world nations must be willing to participate in some forum, whether it be the United Nations or some other organization, in which national leaders can gather to present and discuss their goals and their grievances, with the overall purpose of replacing violence with negotiation and diplomacy. Idealistic? Of course. But in the end, necessary.

Finally, the planet's prospects for peace may hinge on real change that reduces the exploitation of poor people by the well-off. The greatest challenge on the road to peace may be confronting the tremendous problem of poverty and hunger, the focus of Chapter 15 ("Population and Global Inequality"). The goal must be to bring about economic development in regions of the world where at present widespread suffering prevents political stability. There is every reason to think that, given the will to succeed, world leaders can accomplish this goal. How the world responds to this challenge will shape the lives of us all.

Essay: Envisioning a Better Society Looking ahead fifty years, do you expect the world will have more or less military conflict? Why? What specific changes to our global way of life would you support in the pursuit of peace?

CHAPTER 17   War and Terrorism

What is your view of the U.S. military? What about the extent of militarism in the world?

Militarism has long been a controversial part of our society, sparking spirited critics as well as passionate defenders. Look at the two accompanying photos, which suggest two approaches to this country's military.

The further you move to the political left, the greater your criticism of the U.S. military. Liberals would support the idea of defending the nation against aggressors but are cautious and often critical about using the nation's military power. Radicals on the left oppose almost all use of U.S. military power, which they see as supporting capitalism. On the sixth anniversary of the U.S. invasion of Iraq, thousands of demonstrators gathered behind the Lincoln Memorial in the nation's capital to call for an end to the country's military presence in Iraq. Judging from the signs they are holding, what would these people rather do with some of the money that supports our military?

From the political right, the U.S. military is necessary to defend this nation against other nations or organized groups that threaten our way of life. In addition, some conservatives believe U.S. military power should be used to bring political freedom to countries around the globe. From this point of view, the military is worth supporting— even by joining up. These young people in Florida are completing their swearing-in ceremony making them part of the United States Marine Corps. Would you consider doing the same?

Hint: For some, the military is a problem; for others, it is a solution. On the left, there is support for our men and women in uniform, but support for militarism in general is usually limited to defending this country against attack. Beyond that, most liberals would prefer to see much of the billions spent on weapons channeled instead to schools, job creation programs, and other social services. On the right, patriotism is a more popular concept, and there is wide support for most U.S. military deployments. Then, too, for many young people—regardless of their political views—the armed forces is a solution, in that signing up is a way to get a steady paycheck and perhaps save some money to eventually go to college.

Getting Involved: Applications and Exercises

1. Do you know people who have served in the military? If so, speak to several of them about their military experiences. For those who were in combat, ask how the experience changed them and if it changed their attitudes toward war.

2. Contact a military recruiter in your area. See what you can learn about the categories of people (consider gender, age, race, ethnicity, and social class) who are most likely to join the military.

3. Watch two films of the Cold War era, *Fail-Safe* and *On the Beach*, to gain a better understanding of the height of the arms race between the United States and the Soviet Union. For a humorous yet insightful take on the arms race and the dangers of nuclear war, watch *Dr. Strangelove or: How I Learned to Stop Worrying and Love the Bomb*.

4. What student or community organizations on or near campus oppose war? Identify one or two, and try to learn what these organizations do. What are their positions regarding terrorism?

A DEFINING MOMENT

Mohandas Gandhi: Sending a Message of Peace **p. 502**

War and Peace: Basic Definitions

17.1 Explain the causes and consequences of both war and peace.

War has occurred throughout human history.

- During the twentieth century, the development of weapons of mass destruction made war far more deadly than ever before. **pp. 492–93**

Causes of war

- perceived threats
- cultural and religious differences
- political objectives
- moral objectives
- the desire to gain wealth and power
- the desire to turn a population's attention away from domestic social problems
- the absence of alternatives for resolving disputes **pp. 493–94**

The Economic Costs of War

- Each year the world spends $1.75 trillion on militarism; in 2014, the U.S. military budget was about $649 billion.
- The arms race and the war on terrorism pushed U.S. military spending upward; military spending has declined in recent years.
- War destroys a society's entire infrastructure—its roads, bridges, airports, water systems, and electrical and communications networks.
- Money spent on war is taken away from health care, education, and other programs that benefit a population. **pp. 494–95**

The Human Costs of War

- The development of more deadly weapons and the strategy of total war greatly increase the number of civilian casualties.
- Suffering from war continues after the end of hostilities in the form of posttraumatic stress disorder. In all, 3.5 million U.S. veterans suffer from war-related disabilities; of these, 360,000 are totally disabled.

- Wars leave vast numbers of children orphaned. Children today are often forced into combat in wars around the world. **pp. 495–96**

War in the Nuclear Age

The danger posed by war increased dramatically with the development of nuclear weapons at the end of World War II.

- A single nuclear bomb can destroy an entire city.
- Even with recent arms reductions, there are still about 4,400 operational nuclear weapons, more than enough destructive power to end life on the planet. **pp. 498–500**

Strategies for Peace

Given the horrors of all-out war, humanity must use strategies for peace. These include

- deterrence
- high-technology defense
- arms control
- resolving underlying conflicts **pp. 500–501**

---

war (p. 492) violent conflict between nations or organized groups

peace (p. 492) the absence of violent conflict

weapons of mass destruction (p. 493) weapons with the capacity to kill many thousands of people at one time

military-industrial complex (p. 494) the close association of the federal government, the military, and the defense industries

total war (p. 495) deadly conflict that targets both population centers and military targets

concentration camps (p. 495) centers where prisoners are confined for purposes of state security, exploitation, punishment, or execution

war crime (p. 495) an offense against the law of war as established by international agreements and international law

nuclear weapons (p. 498) bombs that use atomic reactions to generate enormous destructive force

nuclear proliferation (p. 499) the acquisition of nuclear weapon technology by more and more nations

deterrence (p. 500) a strategy to keep peace based on the threat of retaliation; also known as *mutual assured destruction* (MAD)

arms control (p. 500) international agreements on the development, testing, production, and deployment of weapons

Terrorism

17.2 Identify types of terrorism in the world as well as strategies to address terrorism.

Terrorism involves unlawful and typically random acts of violence in the pursuit of political goals.

- In 2013, there were 9,707 terrorist attacks worldwide, killing 17,891 people (including 16 private U.S. citizens) and injuring 32,577 more.
- In addition to the economic costs of defending against terrorism, such efforts may reduce our personal freedoms. **pp. 501–4**

Terrorism as a New Type of War

Terrorism involves armed conflict but differs from conventional war in that

- the parties in conflict are not clearly known
- the objectives of the terrorist groups are not clearly stated
- terrorism is asymmetrical **p. 504**

Strategies for Dealing with Terrorism

- prosecution
- a policy of making no concessions
- the application of economic sanctions to nations that support terrorism
- the use of military force
- defense against terrorism
- addressing the underlying causes of terrorism **pp. 504–5**

> **terrorism** (p. 501) unlawful, typically random acts of violence or the threat of violence by an individual, group, or government to achieve a political goal
> **state-sponsored terrorism** (p. 501) the practice by one government of providing money, weapons, and training to terrorists who engage in violence in another nation
> **repressive state terrorism** (p. 502) government use of violence within its own national borders to suppress political opposition

Theories of War and Terrorism

17.3 Apply sociological theory to issues involving war and terrorism.

Structural-Functional Analysis: The Functions of Conflict

Structural-functional theory looks at the functions that war and other types of conflict have for society.

- War is a strategy for pursuing political goals.
- War typically unifies a population and encourages economic growth and technological innovation. **p. 506**

Symbolic-Interaction Analysis: The Meanings of Conflict

Symbolic-interaction theory focuses on the meanings that people attach to war.

- Societies use symbols and meanings to define their cause as just and to demonize the enemy.
- At the individual level, learning to dehumanize the enemy makes killing easier. **p. 507**

Social-Conflict Analysis: Inequality and Conflict

Social-conflict theory highlights how both war and terrorism are linked to social inequality.

- Karl Marx saw militarism as fueling the capitalist economy at home and expanding the reach of capitalism abroad.
- It is the rich elites of a nation who benefit from wars; the troops who do the fighting typically come from the lower classes. **pp. 507–8**

⭐ POLITICS AND WAR
Constructing Problems and Defining Solutions

17.4 Analyze war, terrorism, and the pursuit of peace from various positions on the political spectrum.

Conservatives: Peace through Strength

- **Conservatives** favor a strong defense against forces in the world hostile to the United States.
- Conservatives supported the arms race and favor achieving peace through strength.
- Conservatives see terrorism as criminal acts opposing freedom. **pp. 508–9**

Liberals: The Dangers of Militarism

- **Liberals** support military defense of the United States but caution that a military buildup can provoke the very conflict it is intended to prevent.
- Liberals point out that spending on militarism takes money away from social programs that benefit the population.
- Liberals generally support diplomacy as a way to address the problems that lead to terrorism. **pp. 509–10**

The Radical Left: Peace through Equality

- **Radicals on the left** link war and militarism to social inequality.
- Radicals on the left believe that the United States and other rich nations use their military power to defend their economic interests and to support the global capitalist economy.
- Radicals on the left see terrorism as a form of rebellion, one way poor and powerless people can make their suffering known and force change. **p. 510**

Glossary

abortion   the intentional termination of a pregnancy

acid rain   precipitation, made acidic by air pollution, that destroys plant and animal life

activity theory   the idea that people enhance personal satisfaction in old age by keeping up a high level of social activity

acute disease   an illness that strikes suddenly

addiction   a physical or psychological craving for a drug

affirmative action   policies intended to improve the social standing of minorities subject to past prejudice and discrimination

age stratification   social inequality among various age categories within a society

ageism   prejudice and discrimination directed toward older people

alcoholism   addiction to alcohol

alienation (Marx)   powerlessness in the workplace resulting in the experience of isolation and misery

alienation (Weber)   depersonalization not just in the workplace but throughout society as well brought on by a rational focus on efficiency

anti-institutional violence   violence directed against the government in violation of the law

arms control   international agreements on the development, testing, production, and deployment of weapons

asexuality   the absence of sexual attraction to people of either sex

assimilation   the process by which minorities gradually adopt cultural patterns from the dominant majority population

authoritarianism   a political system that denies popular participation in government

bilingual education   the policy of offering most classes in students' native language while also teaching them English

bisexuality   sexual attraction to people of both sexes

blaming the victim   finding the cause of a social problem in the behavior of people who suffer from it

blended families   families in which children have some combination of biological parents and stepparents

capitalism   an economic system in which natural resources and the means of producing goods and services are privately owned

caregiving   informal and unpaid care provided to a dependent person by family members, other relatives, or friends

charter schools   public schools that are given the freedom to try out new policies and programs

chronic disease   an illness that has a long-term development

claims making   the process of convincing the public and important public officials that a particular issue or situation should be defined as a social problem

codependency   behavior on the part of others that helps a substance abuser continue the abuse

cohabitation   the sharing of a household by an unmarried couple

colonialism   the process by which some nations enrich themselves through political and economic control of other nations

community-based corrections   correctional programs that take place in society at large rather than behind prison walls

concentration camps   centers where prisoners are confined for purposes of state security, exploitation, punishment, or execution

conglomerate   a giant corporation composed of many smaller corporations

corporate crime   an illegal act committed by a corporation or by persons acting on its behalf

corporations   businesses with a legal existence, including rights and liabilities, separate from that of their members

crime against persons   crime that involves violence or the threat of violence against others

crime against property   crime that involves theft of property belonging to others

crime   the violation of a criminal law enacted by federal, state, or local government

criminal justice system   society's use of due process, police, courts, and punishment to enforce the law

criminal recidivism   later offenses by people previously convicted of crimes

crude birth rate   the number of live births in a given year for every 1,000 people in a population

crude death rate   the number of deaths in a given year for every 1,000 people in a population

cultural capital   skills, values, attitudes, and schooling that increase a person's chances of success

culture   a way of life including widespread values (about what is good and bad), beliefs (about what is true), and behavior (what people do every day)

culture of poverty   cultural patterns that encourage poverty as a way of life

decriminalization   removing the current criminal penalties that punish the manufacturing, sale, and personal use of drugs

deindustrialization   the decline of industrial production that occurred in the United States after about 1950

deinstitutionalization   the release of people from mental hospitals into local communities

democracy   a political system in which power is exercised by the people as a whole

demographic transition theory   a thesis linking demographic changes to a society's level of technological development

demography   the study of human population

dependency   a state in which a person's body has adjusted to regular use of a drug

depressants   drugs that slow the operation of the central nervous system

deterrence   a strategy to keep peace based on the threat of retaliation; also known as *mutual assured destruction* (MAD)

deterrence   using punishment to discourage further crime

direct-fee system   a medical care system in which patients or their insurers pay directly for the services of physicians and hospitals

disability   a physical or mental condition that limits everyday activities

discrimination   the unequal treatment of various categories of people

disengagement theory   the idea that modern societies operate in an orderly way by removing people from positions of responsibility as they reach old age

drug   any chemical substance other than food or water that affects the mind or body

ecologically sustainable culture   a way of life that meets the needs of the present generation without threatening the environment for future generations

ecology   the study of how living organisms interact with the natural environment

economic issues   political debates about how a society should produce and distribute material resources

economy   the social institution that organizes the production, distribution, and consumption of goods and services

ecosystem   the interaction of all living organisms and their natural environment

education   the social institution by which a society transmits knowledge—including basic facts and job skills, as well as cultural norms and values—to its members

English immersion   the policy of teaching non-English speakers in English

enterprise zones   areas in the inner city that attract new businesses with the promise of tax relief

environmental deficit   serious, long-term harm to the environment caused by humanity's focus on short-term material affluence

environmental racism   a pattern of discrimination in which environmental hazards are greatest for poor people, especially minorities

epidemic   the rapid spread of a disease through a population

ethnicity   a shared cultural heritage, which typically involves common ancestors, language, and religion

Eurocentrism   the practice of using European (particularly English) cultural standards to judge everyone

euthanasia   assisting in the death of a person suffering from an incurable disease

experiment   a research method for investigating cause-and-effect relationships under tightly controlled conditions

extended family   parents and children, and also grandparents, aunts, uncles, and cousins, who often live close to one another and operate as a family unit

families of affinity   people with or without legal or blood ties who feel they belong together and define themselves as a family

family   a social institution that unites individuals into cooperative groups that care for one another, including any children

felony   a more serious crime punishable by at least one year in prison

feminism   a political movement that seeks the social equality of women and men

feminization of poverty   the trend of women making up an increasing share of the poor

fertility   the incidence of childbearing in a country's population

field research (participant observation)   a research method for observing people while joining them in their everyday activities

functional illiteracy   the inability to read and write or do basic arithmetic well enough to carry out daily responsibilities

Gemeinschaft   a type of social organization in which people are closely bound by kinship and tradition

gender   the personal traits and life chances that a society links to being female or male

gender gap   the tendency for women and men to hold different opinions about certain issues and to support different candidates

gender stratification   the unequal distribution of wealth, power, and privilege between men and women

genocide   the systematic killing of one category of people by another

gerontocracy   a social system that gives a society's oldest members the most wealth, power, and prestige

gerontology   the study of aging and the elderly

Gesellschaft   a type of social organization in which people interact on the basis of self-interest

glass ceiling   subtle discrimination that effectively blocks the movement of women into the highest positions in organizations

globalization   the expansion of economic activity around the world with little regard for national borders

government   a formal organization that directs the political life of a society

hate crime   a criminal offense against a person, property, or society motivated by the offender's bias against a race, religion, disability, sexual orientation, or ethnicity or national origin

health   a state of complete physical, mental, and social well-being

health maintenance organizations (HMOs)   private insurance organizations that provide medical care to subscribers for a fixed fee

heterosexism   bias that treats heterosexuality as the norm while stigmatizing anyone who violates this norm as "queer"

heterosexuality   sexual attraction to someone of the other sex

hidden curriculum   explicit and subtle presentations of political or cultural ideas in the classroom that support the status quo

homelessness   the plight of poor people who lack shelter and live primarily on the streets

homophobia   an aversion to or hostility toward people thought to be gay, lesbian, or bisexual

homosexuality   sexual attraction to someone of the same sex

hospice   homelike care that provides physical and emotional comfort to dying people and their families

in vitro fertilization   uniting eggs and sperm in a laboratory

income   salary or wages from a job plus earnings from investments and other sources

infant mortality rate   the number of babies, of every 1,000 born, who die before their first birthday

institutional discrimination   discrimination that is built into the operation of social institutions, including the economy, schools, and the legal system

institutional racism   racism at work in the operation of social institutions, including the economy, schools, hospitals, the military, and the criminal justice system

institutional violence   violence carried out by government representatives under the law

interlocking directorates   social networks made up of people who serve as directors of several corporations at the same time

intersection theory   the investigation of the interplay of race, class, and gender, often resulting in multiple dimensions of disadvantage

juvenile delinquency   violation of the law by young people

kinship   a social bond, based on common ancestry, marriage, or adoption, that joins individuals into families

labeling theory   the idea that crime and all other forms of rule breaking result not so much from what people do as from how others respond to those actions

labor unions worker organizations that seek to improve wages and working conditions through various strategies, including negotiations and strikes

law a norm formally created through a society's political system

libertarians people who favor the greatest individual freedom possible

life course the socially constructed stages that people pass through as they live out their lives

life expectancy at birth the number of years, on average, people in a society can expect to live

life expectancy the average life span of a country's population

literacy the ability to read and write

lobbying the efforts of special-interest groups and their representatives to influence government officials

magnet schools public schools that offer special facilities and programs in pursuit of educational excellence

mainstreaming integrating students with special needs into the overall educational program

marriage a lawful relationship usually involving economic cooperation, sexual activity, and childbearing

Marxist political-economy model an analysis that sees the concentration of wealth and power in society as resulting from capitalism

mass murder the intentional, unlawful killing of four or more people at one time and place

matriarchy a social pattern in which females dominate males

McDonaldization defining work in terms of the principles of efficiency, predictability, uniformity, and automation

mechanical solidarity social bonds based on common sentiments and shared moral values

megalopolis a vast urban region containing a number of cities and their surrounding suburbs

mental disorder a condition involving thinking, mood, or behavior that causes distress and reduces a person's ability to function in everyday life

meritocracy a system of social inequality in which social standing corresponds to personal ability and effort

military-industrial complex the close association of the federal government, the military, and the defense industries

minority any category of people, identified by physical or cultural traits, that a society subjects to disadvantages

misdemeanor a less serious crime punishable by less than one year in prison

modernization theory a model of economic and social development that explains global inequality in terms of technological and cultural differences between societies

monarchy a political system in which a single family rules from generation to generation

monopoly the domination of an entire market by a single company

mortality the incidence of death in a country's population

multiculturalism educational programs designed to recognize cultural diversity in the United States and to promote respect for all cultural traditions

natural environment Earth's surface and atmosphere, including air, water, soil, and other resources necessary to sustain living organisms

neocolonialism a new form of economic exploitation that involves the operation of multinational corporations rather than direct political control by foreign governments

norms rules and expectations by which a society guides the behavior of its members

nuclear family one or two parents and their children

nuclear proliferation the acquisition of nuclear weapon technology by more and more nations

nuclear weapons bombs that use atomic reactions to generate enormous destructive force

oligopoly the domination of a market by a few companies

organic solidarity social bonds based on specialization and mutual interdependence

organized crime a business operation that supplies illegal goods and services

patriarchy a social pattern in which males dominate females

peace the absence of violent conflict

plea bargaining a negotiation in which the state reduces a defendant's charge in exchange for a guilty plea

pluralism a state in which people of all racial and ethnic categories have about the same overall social standing

pluralist model an analysis of the political system that sees power widely distributed among various groups and organizations in a society

political action committees (PACs) organizations formed by special-interest groups to raise and spend money in support of political goals

political economy the closely linked economic and political life of a nation or world region

political spectrum a continuum representing a range of political attitudes from "left" to "right"

politics the social institution that guides a society's decision making about how to live

pornography words or images intended to cause sexual arousal

poverty gap the difference between the actual income of the typical poor household and the official poverty line

poverty line an income level set by the U.S. government for the purpose of counting the poor

power-elite model an analysis of the political system that sees power as concentrated among members of a small elite

prejudice any rigid and unfounded generalization about an entire category of people

prenatal care health care for women during pregnancy

primary labor market jobs that provide good pay and extensive benefits to workers

progressive taxation a policy that raises tax rates as income increases

prostitution the selling of sexual services

psychotherapy an approach to mental health in which patients talk with trained professionals to gain insight into the cause of their problems

public housing high-density apartment buildings constructed to house poor people

queer theory a body of theory and research that challenges the heterosexual bias in U.S. society

race a socially constructed category of people who share biologically transmitted traits that members of a society define as important

racism the assertion that people of one race are less worthy than or even biologically inferior to others

rain forests   regions of dense forestation, most of which circle the globe close to the equator

rationalization of society (Weber)   the historical change from tradition to rationality and efficiency as the typical way people think about the world

rehabilitation   reforming an offender to prevent future offenses

repressive state terrorism   government use of violence within its own national borders to suppress political opposition

restorative justice   a response to crime seeking to restore the well-being of the victim, offender, and larger communities lost due to crime

retribution   moral vengeance by which society inflicts suffering on an offender comparable to that caused by the offense

school voucher program   a program that provides parents with funds they can use at a public school or private school of their choice

schooling   formal instruction carried out by specially trained teachers

secondary analysis   a research method that makes use of data originally collected by others

secondary labor market   jobs that provide low pay and few benefits to workers

segregation   the physical and social separation of categories of people

self-fulfilling prophecy   a situation in which people who are defined in a certain way eventually think and act as if the definition were true

serial murder   the killing of several people by one offender over a period of time

sex   the biological distinction between females and males; also, activity that leads to physical gratification and possibly reproduction

sexism   the belief that one sex is innately superior to the other

sexual harassment   unwanted comments, gestures, or physical contact of a sexual nature

sexual orientation   a person's romantic and emotional attraction to another person

sexually transmitted diseases (STDs)   diseases spread by sexual contact

sick role   a pattern of behavior expected of people defined as ill

social classes   categories of people who have similar access to resources and opportunities

social disorganization   a breakdown in social order caused by rapid social change

social epidemiology   the study of how health and disease are distributed throughout a society's population

social institution   a major sphere of social life, or a societal subsystem, organized to meet a basic human need

social issues   political debates involving moral judgments about how people should live

social movement   an organized effort at claims making that tries to shape the way people think about an issue in order to encourage or discourage social change

social policy   formal strategies that affect how society operates

social problem   a condition that undermines the well-being of some or all members of a society and is usually a matter of public controversy

social stratification   society's system of ranking categories of people in a hierarchy

social welfare programs   organized efforts by government, private organizations, or individuals to assist needy people considered worthy of assistance

social-conflict approach   a theoretical framework that sees society as divided by inequality and conflict

social-constructionist approach   the assertion that social problems arise as people define conditions as undesirable and in need of change

socialism   an economic system in which natural resources and the means of producing goods and services are collectively owned

socialized medicine   a medical care system in which the government owns and operates most medical facilities and employs most physicians

societal protection   protecting the public by rendering an offender incapable of further offenses through incarceration or execution

society   people who live within some territory and share many patterns of behavior

sociological imagination   a point of view that highlights how society affects the experiences we have and the choices we make

sociology   the systematic study of human societies

special education   schooling children with physical or mental disabilities in separate classes with specially trained teachers

special-interest groups   political alliances of people interested in some economic or social issue

stalking   repeated efforts by someone to establish or re-establish a relationship against the will of the victim

state-sponsored terrorism   the practice by one government of providing money, weapons, and training to terrorists who engage in violence in another nation

stereotype   an exaggerated description applied to every person in some category

stigma   a powerful, negative, social label that radically changes a person's self-concept and social identity

stimulants   drugs that increase alertness, changing a person's mood by increasing energy

structural-functional approach   a theoretical framework that sees society as a system of many interrelated parts

suburbs   urban areas beyond the political boundaries of cities

supportive housing   a program that combines low-income housing with on-site social services

surrogate motherhood   an arrangement by which one woman carries and bears a child for another woman

survey   a research method by which subjects respond to items on a questionnaire or in an interview

symbolic-interaction approach   a theoretical framework that sees society as the product of individuals interacting with one another

technology   knowledge that people apply to the task of living in a physical environment

terrorism   unlawful, typically random acts of violence or the threat of violence by an individual, group, or government to achieve a political goal

theoretical approach   a basic image of society that guides theory and research

theory   a statement of how and why specific facts are related

total war   deadly conflict that targets both population centers and military targets

tracking   the policy of assigning students to different educational programs

transgender   appearing or behaving in ways that challenge conventional cultural norms concerning how females and males should look and act

underclass   poor people who live in areas with high concentrations of poverty and limited opportunities for schooling or work

urban sprawl   unplanned, low-density development at the edge of expanding urban areas

urbanization   the movement of people from the countryside to cities

victimless crimes   offenses that directly harm only the person who commits them

violence   behavior that causes injury to people or damage to property

war crime   an offense against the law of war as established by international agreements and international law

war   violent conflict between nations or organized groups

wealth   the value of all the economic assets owned by a person or family, minus any debts

weapons of mass destruction   weapons with the capacity to kill many thousands of people at one time

welfare state   a range of policies and programs that transfer wealth from the rich to the poor and provide benefits to needy members of society

white-collar crime   illegal activities conducted by people of high social position during the course of their employment or regular business activities

world system theory (dependency theory)   a model of economic development that explains global inequality in terms of the historical exploitation of poor societies by rich ones

youth gangs   groups of young people who identify with one another and with a particular territory

zero population growth   the level of reproduction that maintains population at a steady state

References

*Blue type denotes reference citations new to this fifth edition.

Chapter 1

ANDERSON, ELIJAH. 1999. *Code of the Street: Decency, Violence, and the Moral Life of the Inner City*. New York: Norton.

BENJAMIN, LOIS. 1991. *The Black Elite: Facing the Color Line in the Twilight of the Twentieth Century*. Chicago: Nelson-Hall.

BLUMER, HERBERT G. 1969. "Collective Behavior." In Alfred McClung Lee, (ed.), *Principles of Sociology*, 3rd ed. (pp. 65–121). New York: Barnes & Noble.

DAVIS, NANETTE J. 1980. *Sociological Constructions of Deviance: Perspectives and Issues in the Field*, 2nd ed., Dubuque, IA: Brown.

DAVIS, NANETTE J. 2000. "From Victims to Survivors: Working with Recovering Street Prostitutes." In Ronald Weitzer, (ed.), *Sex for Sale: Prostitution, Pornography, and the Sex Industry* (pp. 139–55). New York: Routledge.

EHRENREICH, BARBARA. 2001. *Nickel and Dimed: On How (Not) to Get By in America*. New York: Holt.

FARIS, ROBERT E. L. 1967. *Chicago Sociology, 1920–1932*. Chicago: University of Chicago Press.

FITCH, G. A., S. A. SOCCOLICH, F. GUO, J. McCLAFFERTY, Y. FANG, R. L. OLSON, M. A. PEREZ, R. J. HANOWSKI, J. M. HANKEY, and T. A. DINGUS. "The Impact of Hand-Held and Hands-Free Cell Phone Use on Driving Performance and Safety-Critical Event Risk." National Highway Traffic Safety Administration. April 2013. [Online]. Available at http://www.nhtsa.gov/DOT/NHTSA/NVS/Crash%20Avoidance/Technical%20Publications/2013/811757.pdf

GALLUP. "Most Important Problem." 2013. [Online]. Available at http://www.gallup.com/poll/1675/Most-Important-Problem.aspx

GOLDMAN, HENRY. 1991. "The Plight of the Black Child." *Philadelphia Inquirer* (February 10): 5E.

GOVERNORS HIGHWAY SAFETY ASSOCIATION. "State Cell Phone Driving Laws." 2013. [Online]. Available at http://www.ghsa.org/html/stateinfo/laws/cellphone_laws.html

HANEY, CRAIG, W. CURTIS BANKS, and PHILIP G. ZIMBARDO. 1973. "Interpersonal Dynamics in a Simulated Prison." *International Journal of Criminology and Penology*. Vol. 1, No. 1: 69–95.

KOHUT, ANDREW. "Misreading Election 2012." *Wall Street Journal*, November 13, 2012. [Online]. Available at http://online.wsj.com/article/SB10001424127887323894704578113231375465160.html

MAUSS, ARMAND L. 1975. *Social Problems of Social Movements*. Philadelphia: Lippincott.

MILANOVIC, BRANKO. "Global Income Inequality: New Results and Implications for 21st Century Policy." World Bank. Spring 2011. [Online] Available at http://siteresources.worldbank.org/EXTABCDE/Resources/7455676-1292528456380/7626791-1303141641402/7878676-1306699356046/Parallel-Sesssion-6-Branko-Milanovic.pdf

MILANOVIC, BRANKO. "More or Less." *Finance & Development*, Vol. 48, No. 3, International Monetary Fund. September 2011. [Online] Available at http://www.imf.org/external/pubs/ft/fandd/2011/09/milanovic.htm

MILLS, C. WRIGHT. 1959. *The Sociological Imagination*. New York: Oxford University Press.

NATIONAL HIGHWAY TRAFFIC SAFETY ADMINISTRATION. "Fatality Analysis Reporting System (FARS)." 2013. [Online]. Available at http://www-fars.nhtsa.dot.gov/Main/index.aspx

NATIONAL HIGHWAY TRAFFIC SAFETY ADMINISTRATION."2011 Traffic Safety Annual Assessment—Alcohol-Impaired Driving Fatalities." 2013. [Online] Available at http://www.nrd.nhtsa.dot.gov/Pubs/811700.pdf

NORC. *General Social Surveys, 1972–2012: Cumulative Codebook*. Chicago: National Opinion Research Center, 2013. [Online] Available at http://www.norc.org/GSS+Website

ORTIZ, ISABEL, and MATTHEW CUMMINS. "Global Inequality: Beyond the Bottom Billion." UNICEF. 2011. [Online] Available at www.unicef.org/socialpolicy/files/Global_Inequality.pdf

PARK, ROBERT E., and ERNEST W. BURGESS. 1970 (orig. 1921). *Introduction to the Science of Sociology*. Chicago: University of Chicago Press.

PEW RESEARCH CENTER FOR THE PEOPLE & THE PRESS. "Changing Face of America Helps Assure Obama Victory." 2012. [Online] Available at http://www.people-press.org/2012/11/07/changing-face-of-america-helps-assure-obama-victory

POPULATION REFERENCE BUREAU. "Datafinder." 2013. [Online] Available at http://www.prb.org/DataFinder.aspx

SMITH, TOM W., PETER MARSDEN, MICHAEL HOUT, and JIBUM KIM. "General Social Surveys, 1972–2012." National Opinion Research Center; The Roper Center for Public Opinion Research, University of Connecticut; Computer-assisted Survey Methods Program, University of California. June 2013. [Online] Available at http://www.norc.org/GSS+Website

TILLY, CHARLES. 1978. *From Mobilization to Revolution*. Reading, Mass.: Addison-Wesley.

UNESCO (United Nations Educational, Scientific, and Cultural Organization). "Data Centre." 2013. [Online] Available at http://www.uis.unesco.org/Pages/default.aspx

U.S. CENSUS BUREAU. "Current Population Survey." 2013. [Online] Available at http://www.census.gov/cps

U.S. DEPARTMENT OF JUSTICE, FEDERAL BUREAU OF INVESTIGATION. "Crime in the United States, 2012." 2013. [Online] Available at http://www.fbi.gov/about-us/cjis/ucr/crime-in-the-u.s/2012/crime-in-the-u.s.-2012/tables

U.S. DEPARTMENT OF LABOR. "Labor Force Statistics from the Current Population Survey." 2013. [Online] Available at http://www.bls.gov/cps/cpsaat01.htm

WELCH, SANDY, MYRNA DAWSON, and ANNETTE NIEROBISZ. 2002. "Legal Factors, Extra-Legal Factors, or Changes in the Law? Using Criminal Justice Research to Understand the Resolution of Sexual Harassment Complaints." *Social Problems*. Vol. 49, No. 4 (November): 605–23.

WILSON, WILLIAM JULIUS. 1996a. *When Work Disappears: The World of the New Urban Poor*. New York: Knopf.

WORLD BANK. "PovcalNet." 2013. [Online] Available at http://iresearch.worldbank.org/PovcalNet/index.htm?1

WORLD BANK. "World DataBank: Education Statistics." 2012, 2013. [Online] Available at http://data.worldbank.org/data-catalog/ed-stats

ZIMBARDO, PHILIP G. 1972. "Pathology of Imprisonment." *Society*. Vol. 9 (April): 4–8.

Chapter 2

Adams, Patricia F., Whitney K. Kirzinger, and Michael E. Martinez. "Summary Health Statistics for the U.S. Population: National Health Interview Survey, 2011." *Vital Health Stat*. Vol. 10, No. 255 National Center for Health Statistics. November 2012. [Online] Available at http://www.cdc.gov/nchs/data/series /sr_10/sr10_255.pdf

America's Promise Alliance. "Cities in Crisis 2009: Closing the Graduation Gap." 2010. [Online] Available at http://www .americaspromise.org/Our-Work/Dropout-Prevention/Cities-in-Crisis.aspx

Anderson, Elijah. 1999. *Code of the Street: Decency, Violence, and the Moral Life of the Inner City*. New York: Norton.

Bennett, William J. 1995. "Redeeming Our Time." *Imprimis*. Vol. 24, No. 11 (November). Available January 14, 2007, at http://www .hillsdale.edu/imprimis/1995/11

Bork, Robert H. 2008. *A Time to Speak*. Wilmington, Del.: Intercollegiate Studies Institute, 2008.

Bourdieu, Pierre, and Jean-Claude Passeron. 1977. *Reproduction in Society, Education, and Culture*. Thousand Oaks, Calif.: Sage.

Burtless, Gary. "Life Expectancy and Rising Income Inequality: Why Connection Matters for Fixing Entitlements." Brookings Research. October 23, 2012. [Online] Available at http://www .brookings.edu/research/opinions/2012/10/23-inequality-life-expectancy-burtless

Center on Hunger and Poverty. 2000. *Paradox of Our Times: Hunger in a Strong Economy*. Medford, Mass: Tufts University Press.

Christie, Les. "Foreclosures Fall in Most U.S. Cities." CNN Money. July 28, 2011. [Online] Available at http://money.cnn .com/2011/07/28/real_estate/metro_area_foreclosures/index.htm

Congressional Budget Office. "Growing Disparities in Life Expectancy." April 17, 2008. [Online] Available at http://www.cbo .gov/ftpdocs/91xx/doc9104/04-17-LifeExpectancy_Brief.pdf

Connerly, Ward. 2000. "The Content of Our Children's Character." *Imprimis*. Vol. 29, No. 2 (February): 1–3, 5.

Corporate Library, The. "Executive Compensation." 2013. [Online] Available at http://www3.gmiratings.com/home/2013/10 /gmi-ratings-2013-ceo-pay-survey

Davis, Kingsley, and Wilbert Moore. "Some Principles of Stratification." *American Sociological Review*. Vol. 10, No. 2 (April 1945): 242–49.

DeCarlo, Scott. "Gravity-Defying CEO Pay." *Forbes*. April 4, 2012. [Online] Available at http://www.forbes.com/lists/2012/12 /ceo-compensation-12_land.html

Economic Policy Institute. "Family Budget Calculator." 2013. [Online] Available at http://www.epi.org/publication/ib368-basic -family-budgets

Ehrenreich, Barbara. 2001. *Nickel and Dimed: On How (Not) to Get By in America*. New York: Holt.

Forbes. "Lists and Profiles." 2013. [Online] Available at http://www .forbes.com/lists

Furstenberg, Frank F., Jr., and Andrew Cherlin. 1991. *Divided Families: What Happens to Children When Parents Part*. Cambridge, Mass.: Harvard University Press.

Gallup. "Economy." 2013. [Online] Available at http://www .gallup.com/poll/165584/fewer-believe-plenty-opportunity-ahead.aspx

Gans, Herbert J. 1971. "The Uses of Poverty: The Poor Pay All." *Social Policy*. Vol. 2, No. 4 (July–August): 20–24.

Hananel, Sam. "Plan to Hike Minimum Wage for Federal Contract Workers Wins Praise, But Impact May Be Limited." Associated

Press. January 29, 2014. [Online] Available at http://finance.yahoo .com/news/wage-hike-federal-contract-workers-082119522.html

Harrington, Michael. 1962. *The Other America: Poverty in the United States*. Baltimore: Penguin.

Helman, Christopher. "America's 25 Highest-Paid CEOs." *Forbes*. October 12, 2011. [Online] Available at http://www.forbes.com /sites/christopherhelman/2011/10/12/americas-25-highest-paid-ceos

Herrnstein, Richard J., and Charles Murray. 1994. *The Bell Curve: Intelligence and Class Structure in American Life*. New York: Free Press.

Holland, Joshua. "Hundreds of Wall Street Execs Went to Prison During the Last Fraud-Fueled Bank Crisis." Moyers & Company. September 13, 2013. [Online] Available at http://billmoyers .com/2013/09/17/hundreds-of-wall-street-execs-went-to-prison -during-the-last-fraud-fueled-bank-crisis

Internal Revenue Service. "Individual Statistical Tables by Tax Rate and Income Percentile." 2012. [Online] Available at http:// www.irs.gov/uac/SOI-Tax-Stats-Individual-Statistical-Tables-by-Tax-Rate-and-Income-Percentile#_grp2

Johnston, David Cay. 2005. "Richest Are Leaving Even the Rich Far Behind." *New York Times* (June 5): 1, 27.

Katz, Michael B. 1990. *The Undeserving Poor: From the War on Poverty to the War on Welfare*. New York: Pantheon.

———. 1996. *In the Shadow of the Poorhouse*. New York: Basic Books.

Kilgore, Sally B. 1991. "The Organizational Context of Tracking in Schools." *American Sociological Review*. Vol. 56, No. 2 (April): 189–203.

Kozol, Jonathan. 1991. *Savage Inequalities: Children in America's Schools*. New York: Crown.

Lewis, Oscar. *The Children of Sanchez*. New York: Random House, 1961.

Lewis, Oscar. 1966. *La Vida*. New York: Random House.

Liazos, Alexander. 1982. *People First: An Introduction to Social Problems*. Needham Heights, Mass.: Allyn & Bacon.

Lichter, Daniel T., and Martha L. Crowley. 2002. "Poverty in America: Beyond Welfare Reform." *Population Bulletin*. Vol. 57, No. 2 (June): 3–34.

Lichter, Daniel T., and Rukmalie Jayakody. 2002. "Welfare Reform: How Do We Measure Success?" *Annual Review of Sociology*. Vol. 28: 117–41.

Luhby, Tami. "Class Warfare: Who Pays Fair Share of Taxes?" *Yahoo News*. October 14, 2011. [Online] Available at http://finance .yahoo.com/news/Class-warfare-Who-pays-fair-cnnm-46718926. html?x=0&sec=topStories&pos=9&asset=&ccode=

Martin, Deanna. 2009. "Mayor to Indiana Governor: Send Stimulus Cash Fast." *MSNBC* (March 19). [Online] Available March 22, 2009, at http://www.msnbc.msn.com/id/29771876

Massey, Douglas S., and Nancy A. Denton. 1989. "Hypersegregation in U.S. Metropolitan Areas: Black and Hispanic Segregation along Five Dimensions." *Demography*. Vol. 26, No. 3 (August): 373–91.

Milanovic, Branko. "Global Inequality: From Class to Location, from Proletarians to Migrants." *World Bank Policy Research* working paper, No. WPS. 5820, September 2011. [Online] Available at http://go.worldbank.org/PWVINQBEH0

Moore, Stephen, and Lincoln Anderson. 2005. "Great American Dream Machine." *Wall Street Journal* (December 21): A18.

Morin, Rich. "Rising Share of Americans See Conflict Between Rich and Poor." Pew Research Center. January 11, 2012. [Online]

Available at http://www.pewsocialtrends.org/2012/01/11/rising-share-of-americans-see-conflict-between-rich-and-poor

Mouw, Ted. 2000. "Job Relocation and the Racial Gap in Unemployment in Detroit and Chicago, 1980 to 1990." *American Sociological Review*. Vol. 65, No. 5 (October): 730–53.

Murray, Charles. 1984. *Losing Ground: American Social Policy, 1950–1980*. New York: Basic Books.

Murray, Harry. 2000. "Deniable Degradation: The Finger-Imaging of Welfare Recipients." *Sociological Forum*. Vol. 15, No. 1 (March): 39–63.

Nord, Mark, Margaret Andrews, and Steven Carlson. 2002. *Household Food Security in the United States, 2001*. Washington, D.C.: Economic Research Service, U.S. Department of Agriculture.

Obama, Barack. "Remarks by the President on Economic Mobility." December 4, 2013. [Online] Available at http://www.whitehouse.gov/the-press-office/2013/12/04/remarks-president-economic-mobility

O'Hare, William P. 2002. "Tracking the Trends in Low-Income Working Families." *Population Today*. Vol. 30, No. 6 (August–September): 1–3.

Ohlemacher, Stephen. "Fact Check: Are Rich Taxed Less than Secretaries?" Associated Press. September 20, 2011. [Online] Available at http://news.yahoo.com/fact-check-rich-taxed-less-secretaries-070642868.html

Pew Research Center for the People & the Press. 2012, 2013. [Online] Available at http://www.people-press.org

Powell, Colin L., and Joseph E. Persico. 1995. *My American Journey*. New York: Random House.

Ritholtz, Barry. "The Minimum Wage and McDonald's Welfare." *Bloomberg*. December 17, 2013. [Online] Available at http://www.bloomberg.com/news/2013-12-17/the-minimum-wage-and-mcdonald-s-welfare.html

Roth, Zachary. "Labor: Lavish CEO Pay Still Rising." *The Lookout*. April 20, 2011. [Online] Available at http://news.yahoo.com/s/yblog_thelookout/20110420/ts_yblog_thelookout/labor-lavish-ceo-pay-still-rising

Ryan, William. 1976. *Blaming the Victim*, rev. ed. New York: Vintage Books.

Saint Jean, Yanick, and Joe R. Feagin. 1998. *Double Burden: Black Women and Everyday Racism*. Armonk, N.Y.: Sharpe.

Samuelson, Robert J. 2003. "The Rich and Everyone Else." *Newsweek* (January 27): 57.

Singh, Gopal K. "Child Mortality in the United States, 1935–2007: Large Racial and Socioeconomic Disparities Have Persisted Over Time." Rockville, Md.: U.S. Department of Health and Human Services. 2010. [Online] Available at http://www.hrsa.gov/healthit/images/mchb_child_mortality_pub.pdf

Smith, Tom W., Peter Marsden, Michael Hout, and Jibum Kim. "General Social Surveys, 1972–2012." National Opinion Research Center; The Roper Center for Public Opinion Research, University of Connecticut; Computer-assisted Survey Methods Program, University of California. June 2013. [Online] Available at http://www.norc.org/GSS+Website

Stanley, William D., and Thomas J. Danko. 1996. *The Millionaire Next Door: The Surprising Secrets of America's Wealthy*. New York: Pocket Books.

Taub, Stephen. "The Rich List." *Institutional Investor*. April 15, 2013. [Online] Available at http://www.institutionalinvestorsalpha.com/Article/3190499/The-Rich-List.html

Thornburgh, Nathan. 2006. "Dropout Nation." *Time*. Vol. 167, No. 16 (April 17): 30–40.

Trattner, Walter I. 1980. "Social Welfare." In Glenn Porter, ed., *Encyclopedia of American Economic History*, Vol. 3 (pp. 1155–67). New York: Scribner.

U.S. Bureau of Economic Analysis. "National Income and Product Account Tables." 2013. [Online] Available at http://www.bea.gov/iTable/iTable.cfm?ReqID=9&step=1#reqid=9&step=1&isuri=1

U.S. Census Bureau. "American Community Survey." 2013. [Online] Available at http://www.census.gov/acs

U.S. Census Bureau. "Current Population Survey." 2013. [Online] Available at http://www.census.gov/cps

U.S. Census Bureau. "Families and Living Arrangements." 2013. [Online] Available at http://www.census.gov/hhes/families

U.S. Census Bureau. "Small Area Income & Poverty Estimates: Maps." 2013. [Online] Available at http://www.census.gov/did/www/saipe/data/highlights/files/2012/F6_MP_2012.pdf

U.S. Census Bureau. "Voting and Registration." 2013. [Online] Available at http://www.census.gov/hhes/www/socdemo/voting/index.html

U.S. Conference of Mayors. "A Status Annual Report on Hunger and Homelessness in America's Cities." 2013. [Online] Available at http://www.usmayors.org/pressreleases/uploads/2013/1210-report-HH.pdf

U.S. Department of Agriculture. "Characteristics of Supplemental Nutrition Assistance Program Households [Annual]." 2012. [Online] Available at http://www.fns.usda.gov/ORA/menu/Published/SNAP/SNAP.htm

U.S. Department of Agriculture, Economic Research Service. "Food Security in the United States: Key Statistics and Graphics." 2013. [Online] Available at http://www.ers.usda.gov/topics/food-nutrition-assistance/food-security-in-the-us/key-statistics-graphics.aspx

U.S. Department of Housing and Urban Development, Office of Community Planning and Development. "The Annual Homeless Assessment Report to Congress." 2013. [Online] Available at http://www.onecpd.info/hdx/guides/ahar

U.S. Department of Labor, Wage and Hour Division. 2012. [Online] Available at http://www.dol.gov/whd/flsa/index.htm

Western, Bruce. 2002. "The Impact of Incarceration on Wage Mobility and Inequality." *American Sociological Review*. Vol. 67, No. 4 (August): 526–46.

Westervelt, Eric. "Silicon Valley Trailer Park Residents Fight to Stay." National Public Radio. (October 15, 2013). [Online] Available at http://www.npr.org/2013/10/15/227807022/silicon-valley-trailer-park-residents-fight-to-stay

Wilson, William Julius. 1996a. *When Work Disappears: The World of the New Urban Poor*. New York: Knopf.

Wolff, Edward N. "The Asset Price Meltdown and the Wealth of the Middle Class." 2012. [Online] Available at http://www.nber.org/papers/w18559

Zagorsky, Jay. 2006. "Divorce Drops a Person's Wealth by 77 Percent." Press release (January 18). [Online] Available January 19, 2006, at http://www.eurekalert.org/pub_releases/2006-01/osu-dda011806.php

Chapter 3

Adorno, T. W., et al. 1950. *The Authoritarian Personality*. New York: Harper.

Albon, Joan. 1971. "Retention of Cultural Values and Differential Urban Adaptation: Samoans and American Indians in a West Coast City." *Social Forces*. Vol. 49, No. 3 (March): 385–93.

Ali, Lorraine, and Vanessa Juarez. "We Love This Country." *Newsweek*. April 7, 2003.

ALI, LORRAINE, TAMARA LIPPER, and MOHAMMED MACK. "Voters: A Demographic Shift." *Newsweek*. October 25, 2004.

BARTLETT, DONALD L., and JAMES B. STEELE. "Wheel of Misfortune." *Time* (December 16, 2002): 44–58.

BENJAMIN, LOIS. 1991. *The Black Elite: Facing the Color Line in the Twilight of the Twentieth Century*. Chicago: Nelson-Hall.

BOGARDUS, EMORY S. 1925. "Social Distance and Its Origins." *Sociology and Social Research*. Vol. 9 (July–August): 216–25.

———. 1967. *A Forty-Year Racial Distance Study*. Los Angeles: University of Southern California Press.

BONILLA-SILVA, EDUARDO. 1999. "The Essential Social Fact of Race." *American Sociological Review*. Vol. 64, No. 6 (December): 899–906.

BOZA, TANYA GOLASH. 2002. "Proposed American Sociological Association Statement on Race." [Online] Available October 24, 2002, at http://www.unc.edu/~tatiana

BRODKIN, KAREN B. 2007. "How Did Jews Become White Folks?" In John J. Macionis and Nijole V. Benokraitis, eds., *Seeing Ourselves: Classic, Contemporary, and Cross-Cultural Readings in Sociology*, 7th ed. (pp. 274–83). Upper Saddle River, N.J.: Prentice Hall.

CAMARA, EVANDRO. Personal communication, 2000.

CARMICHAEL, STOKELY, and CHARLES V. HAMILTON. *Black Power: The Politics of Liberation in America*. New York: Vintage Books, 1967.

CARTER, STEPHEN. 1991. *Reflections of an Affirmative Action Baby*. New York: Basic Books.

CHUA-EOAN, HOWARD. 2000. "Profiles in Outrage." *Time*. Vol. 156, No. 13 (September 25): 38–39.

DOBYNS, HENRY F. 1966. "An Appraisal of Techniques with a New Hemispheric Estimate." *Current Anthropology*. Vol. 7, No. 4 (October): 395–446.

DOLLARD, JOHN et al. 1939. *Frustration and Aggression*. New Haven, Conn.: Yale University Press.

DU BOIS, W. E. B. 2001 (orig. 1903). "The Souls of Black Folk." In John J. Macionis and Nijole V. Benokraitis, eds., *Seeing Ourselves: Classic, Contemporary, and Cross-Cultural Readings in Sociology*, 5th ed. (pp. 226–30). Upper Saddle River, N.J.: Prentice Hall.

EMERSON, MICHAEL O., GEORGE YANCEY, and KAREN J. CHAI. 2001. "Does Race Matter in Residential Segregation? Exploring the Preferences of White Americans." *American Sociological Review*. Vol. 66, No. 6 (December): 922–35.

EWERS, JUSTIN. 2008. "Saving Symbols of Shame." *U.S. News & World Report*. Vol. 144, No. 7 (March 10): 31.

FINEMAN, HOWARD, and TAMARA LIPPER. 2003. "Spinning Race." *Newsweek* (January 27): 26–29.

FORDHAM, SIGNITHIA, and JOHN U. OGBU. 1992. "Black Students' School Success: Coping with the Burden of 'Acting White.'" In John J. Macionis and Nijole V. Benokraitis, eds., *Seeing Ourselves: Classic, Contemporary, and Cross-Cultural Readings in Sociology*, 2nd ed. (pp. 287–303). Englewood Cliffs, N.J.: Prentice Hall.

FRANKLIN, JOHN HOPE. 1967. *From Slavery to Freedom: A History of Negro Americans*, 3rd ed. New York: Vintage Books.

GAMBOA, SUZANNE. 2003. "INS: 7 Million Illegal Immigrants in U.S." *Yahoo News*. [Online] Available January 31, 2003, at http://www.yahoonews.com

GILBERTSON, GRETA A., and DOUGLAS T. GURAK. 1993. "Broadening the Enclave Debate: The Dual Labor Market Experiences of Dominican and Colombian Men in New York City." *Sociological Forum*. Vol. 8, No. 2 (June): 205–20.

GILDER, GEORGE. 1980. "The Myths of Racial and Sexual Discrimination." *National Review*. Vol. 32, No. 23 (November 14): 1381–90.

GLAAB, CHARLES N., and A. THEODORE BROWN. 1967. *A History of Urban America*. New York: Macmillan.

GLAESER, EDWARD, and JACOB VIGDOR. "The End of the Segregated Century: Racial Separation in America's Neighborhoods, 1890–2010." *Civic Report No. 66*. Manhattan Institute. 2012. [Online] Available at http://www.manhattan-institute.org/pdf/cr_66.pdf

HAGOPIAN, ELAINE C. 2004. *Civil Rights in Peril: The Targeting of Arabs and Muslims*. London: Photo Press.

HARRELL, EBEN. "How We See Immigration—And Why We're Wrong." *Time*. February 3, 2011. [Online] Available at http://www.time.com/time/world/article/0,8599,2045932,00.html

HARRIS, DAVID R., and JEREMIAH JOSEPH SIM. 2002. "Who Is Multiracial? Assessing the Complexity of Lived Race." *American Sociological Review*. Vol. 67, No. 4 (August): 614–27.

IGNATIEV, NOEL. 1995. *How the Irish Became White*. New York: Routledge.

JOHNSON, JACQUELINE, SHARON RUSH, and JOE R. FEAGIN. 2000. "Doing Anti-Racism: Toward an Egalitarian American Society." *Contemporary Sociology*. Vol. 29, No. 1 (January): 95–110.

JOHNSON, SCOTT. Personal communication. March 21, 2014.

KANTROWITZ, BARBARA, and PAT WINGERT. 2003. "What's at Stake." *Newsweek* (January 27): 30–37.

KEISTER, LISA A. 2003. "Religion and Wealth: The Role of Religious Affiliation and Participation in Early Adult Asset Accumulation." *Social Forces*. Vol. 82, No. 1 (September): 173–205.

KINKEAD, GWEN. 1992. *Chinatown: A Portrait of a Closed Society*. New York: HarperCollins.

KOZOL, JONATHAN. 2005. *The Shame of the Nation: The Restoration of Apartheid Schooling in America*. New York: Crown.

KRYSAN, MARIA. 2002. "Community Undesirability in Black and White: Examining Racial Residential Preferences through Community Perceptions." *Social Problems*. Vol. 49, No. 4 (November): 521–43.

LEE, JENNIFER, and FRANK D. BEAN. 2010. *The Diversity Paradox: Immigration and the Color Line in Twenty-First-Century America*. New York: Russell Sage Foundation.

LEWIS, OSCAR. 1966. *La Vida*. New York: Random House.

LIAZOS, ALEXANDER. 1982. *People First: An Introduction to Social Problems*. Needham Heights, Mass.: Allyn & Bacon.

MARABLE, MANNING. 1995. *Beyond Black and White: Transforming African-American Politics*. New York: Verso.

MARTIN, DOUGLAS. 1997. "The Medicine Woman of the Mohegans." *New York Times* (June 4): B1, B7.

MARX, KARL, and FRIEDRICH ENGELS. 1959 (orig. 1893). *Marx and Engels: Basic Writings on Politics and Philosophy*, ed. Lewis S. Feurer. Garden City, N.Y.: Anchor.

MARZÁN, GILBERT, ANDRÉS TORRES, and ANDREW LUECKE. "Puerto Rican Outmigration from New York City: 1995–2000." Centro de Estudios Puertorriqueños, Hunter College (CUNY), *Policy Report*, Vol. 2, No. 2 (2008). [Online] Available at http://www.centropr.org/documents/working_papers/Outmigration091108.pdf

MASSEY, DOUGLAS S., and NANCY A. DENTON. 1989. "Hypersegregation in U.S. Metropolitan Areas: Black and Hispanic Segregation along Five Dimensions." *Demography*. Vol. 26, No. 3 (August): 373–91.

MATTHIESSEN, PETER. 1984. *Indian Country*. New York: Viking.

MURRAY, CHARLES. 1984. *Losing Ground: American Social Policy, 1950–1980*. New York: Basic Books.

NAGEL, JOANE. 1996. *American Indian Ethnic Renewal: Red Power and the Resurgence of Identity and Culture*. New York: Oxford University Press.

NORC. *General Social Surveys, 1972–2006: Cumulative Codebook.* Chicago: National Opinion Research Center. 2007. [Online] Available March 19, 2008, at http://publicdata.norc.org/41000 /gss/Documents/Codebook/FINAL%202006%20CODEBOOK.pdf

OWEN, CAROLYN A., HOWARD C. ELSNER, and THOMAS R. McFAUL. 1977. "A Half-Century of Social Distance Research: National Replication of the Bogardus Studies." *Sociology and Social Research.* Vol. 66, No. 1: 80–98.

PARRILLO, VINCENT N. 2003. *Strangers to These Shores*, 7th ed. Boston: Allyn & Bacon.

PARRILLO, VINCENT N., and CHRISTOPHER DONOGHUE. 2005. "Updating the Bogardus Social Distance Studies: A New National Survey." *Social Science Journal.* Vol. 42, No. 2 (April): 257–71.

PARRILLO, VINCENT N., and CHRISTOPHER DONOGHUE. 2013. "The National Social Distance Study: Ten Years Later." *Sociological Forum.* Vol. 28, No. 3: 597–614.

PASSEL, JEFFREY, and D'VERA COHN. "Unauthorized Immigrant Population: National and State Trends, 2010." Pew Hispanic Center. February 2011. [Online] Available at http://www.pewhispanic .org/2011/02/01/unauthorized-immigrant-population-brnational -and-state-trends-2010/

PASSEL, JEFFREY, D'VERA COHN, and ANA GONZALEZ-BARRERA. "Population Decline of Unauthorized Immigrants Stalls, May Have Reversed." 2013. [Online] Available at http://www.pewhispanic .org/2013/09/23/2-number-and-trend

PEW RESEARCH CENTER. "'Borders First' Dividing Line in Immigration Debate." June 23, 2013. [Online] Available at http://www.people-press.org/2013/06/23/borders-first-a -dividing-line-in-immigration-debate

PEW RESEARCH CENTER. "King's Dream Remains Elusive Goal; Many Americans See Racial Disparities." August 22, 2013. [Online] Available at http://www.pewsocialtrends.org/2013/08/22 /kings-dream-remains-an-elusive-goal-many-americans-see -racial-disparities

PEW RESEARCH CENTER FOR THE PEOPLE & THE PRESS. "Question Search." 2013. [Online] Available at http://www.people-press .org/question-search

PEW RESEARCH CENTER, FACT TANK. "If They Could, How Many Unauthorized Immigrants Would Become U.S. citizens?" June 27, 2013. [Online] Available at http://www.pewresearch.org/fact -tank/2013/06/27/if-they-could-how-many-unauthorized -immigrants-would-become-u-s-citizens

PEW RESEARCH CENTER, FACT TANK. "Six Take-Aways from the Census Bureau's Voting Report." May 8, 2013. [Online] Available at http://www.pewresearch.org/fact-tank/2013/05/08/six -take-aways-from-the-census-bureaus-voting-report

PEW RESEARCH CENTER, HISPANIC TRENDS PROJECT. 2011, 2012, 2013. [Online] Available at http://www.pewhispanic.org

SALE, KIRKPATRICK. 1990. *The Conquest of Paradise: Christopher Columbus and the Columbian Legacy.* New York: Knopf.

SOWELL, THOMAS. 1981. *Ethnic America.* New York: Basic Books.

———. 1987. "Preferential Treatment," in Thomas Sowell, *Compassion versus Guilt and Other Essays* (pp. 197–99). New York: Morrow.

———. 1990. *Preferential Policies: An International Perspective.* New York: Morrow.

———. 1994. *Race and Culture.* New York: Basic Books.

———. 1995. "Ethnicity and IQ." In Steven Fraser, ed., *The Bell Curve Wars: Race, Intelligence and the Future of America* (pp. 70–79). New York: Basic Books.

STEELE, SHELBY. 1990. *The Content of Our Character: A New Vision of Race in America.* New York: St. Martin's Press.

STONE, BRAD LOWELL. 2000. "Robert Nisbet on Conservative Dogmatics." *Society.* Vol. 37, No. 3 (March-April): 68–74.

STOUT, DAVID. 2003. "Supreme Court Splits on Diversity Efforts at University of Michigan." *Yahoo News.* [Online] Available June 23, 2003, at http://www.yahoo.com/news

TANNENBAUM, FRANK. 1946. *Slave and Citizen: The Negro in the Americas.* New York: Vintage Books.

TOTENBERG, NINA. "Justices Seek 'Strict Scrutiny' in Affirmative Action Case." June 24, 2013. National Public Radio. [Online]. Available at http://www.npr.org/2013/06/24/195272169 /justices-send-affirmative-action-case-back-to-lower-court

TUMULTY, KAREN. 2006. "Should They Stay or Should They Go?" *Time.* Vol. 167, No. 15 (April 10): 30–40.

TYLER, S. LYMAN. 1973. *A History of Indian Policy.* Washington, D.C.: Bureau of Indian Affairs, U.S. Department of the Interior.

U.S. CENSUS BUREAU. "American Community Survey." 2011. [Online] Available at http://www.census.gov/acs

U.S. CENSUS BUREAU. "American Community Survey." 2013. [Online] Available at http://www.census.gov/acs

U.S. CENSUS BUREAU. "Census 2010." 2011. [Online] Available at http://factfinder2.census.gov

U.S. CENSUS BUREAU. "Current Population Survey." September 2011. [Online] Available at http://www.census.gov/cps/

U.S. CENSUS BUREAU. "Current Population Survey." 2013. [Online] Available at http://www.census.gov/cps

U.S. CENSUS BUREAU. "Families and Living Arrangements." 2013. [Online] Available at http://www.census.gov/hhes/families

U.S. CENSUS BUREAU. "Language Use." 2013. [Online] Available at http://www.census.gov/hhes/socdemo/language

U.S. CENSUS BUREAU. "Population Estimates." 2013. [Online] Available at http://www.census.gov/popest/data/index.html

U.S. DEPARTMENT OF LABOR, BUREAU OF LABOR STATISTICS. "International Labor Comparisons." 2013. [Online] Available at http://www.bls.gov/fls

U.S. DEPARTMENT OF LABOR. "Labor Force Statistics from the Current Population Survey." 2013. [Online] Available at http://www.bls .gov/cps/cpsatabs.htm

WEST, CORNEL. 2008. "The Obama Moment." *U.S. News & World Report* (November 17): 29.

WILKES, RIMA, and JOHN ICELAND. "Hypersegregation in the Twenty-First Century." *Demography.* Vol. 41, No. 1 (February 09, 2004): 23–26.

WILSON, WILLIAM JULIUS. 1996a. *When Work Disappears: The World of the New Urban Poor.* New York: Knopf.

WOODWARD, C. VANN. 1974. *The Strange Career of Jim Crow.* 3rd rev. ed. New York: Oxford University Press.

ZUBERI, TUKUFU. 2001. *Thicker than Blood: How Racial Statistics Lie.* Minneapolis: University of Minnesota Press.

Chapter 4

ABEND, LISA. 2013. "Boys Won't Be Boys." *Time.* Vol. 182, No. 25 (December 16): 40–42.

AMERICAN BAR ASSOCIATION. "Legal Education Statistics." 2010. [Online] Available at http://www.abanet.org/legaled/statistics /charts/stats%20-%206.pdf

ARMSTRONG, ELIZABETH. *The Retreat from Organization: U.S. Feminism Reconceptualized.* Albany: State University of New York Press, 2002.

ARRIGHI, BARBARA A., ed. 2001. *Understanding Inequality: The Intersection of Race/Ethnicity, Class, and Gender.* Lanham, Md.: Rowman & Littlefield.

Barry, Kathleen. 1983. "Feminist Theory: The Meaning of Women's Liberation." In Barbara Haber, ed., *The Women's Annual, 1982–1983* (pp. 35–78). Boston: Hall.

Bellas, Marcia L., and Barbara Thomas Coventry. 2001. "Salesmen, Saleswomen, or Sales Workers? Determinants of the Sex Composition of Sales Occupations." *Sociological Forum*. Vol. 16, No. 1 (March): 73–98.

Benokraitis, Nijole V., and Joe R. Feagin. 1995. *Modern Sexism: Blatant, Subtle, and Overt Discrimination*, 2nd ed. Upper Saddle River, N.J.: Prentice Hall.

Bernard, Jessie. 1982. *The Future of Marriage*, 2nd ed. New Haven, Conn.: Yale University Press.

Bernstein, David E. 2001. "Casey Martin Ruling Is Par for the Course." *Wall Street Journal* (May 30). [Online] Available May 18, 2006, at http://www.mason.gmu.edu/~dbernste/caseymartin.htm

Blankenhorn, David. 1995. *Fatherless America: Confronting Our Most Urgent Social Problem*. New York: HarperCollins.

Cantrell, Ashe. "10 Famous Films that Surprisingly Fail the Bechdel Test." Film School Rejects. November 11, 2013. [Online] Available at http://www.filmschoolrejects.com/features /10-famous-films-that-surprisingly-fail-the-bechdel-test.php

Catalyst. "Knowledge Center." 2014. [Online] Available at http://www.catalyst.org/knowledge

Ceci, Stephen J., and Wendy M. Williams. "Understanding Current Causes of Women's Underrepresentation in Science." *The Proceedings of the National Academy of Sciences*. 2011. [Online] Available at http://www.human.cornell.edu/hd/loader .cfm?csModule=security/getfile&PageID=60893

Center for American Women and Politics. "Women in Elective Office." 2013. [Online] Available at http://www.cawp.rutgers.edu /fast_facts/index.php

Chaker, Anne Marie, and Hilary Stout. 2004. "After Years Off, Women Struggle to Revive Careers." *Wall Street Journal* (May 5): A1, A8.

College Board, The. "2013 College-Bound Seniors: Total Group Profile Report." 2013. [Online] Available at http: //media.collegeboard.com/digitalServices/pdf/research/2013 /TotalGroup-2013.pdf

Collins, Patricia Hill. 2000. *Black Feminist Thought: Knowledge, Consciousness, and the Politics of Empowerment*, 2nd ed. New York: Routledge.

Cooper, Helene. "Pentagon Study Finds 50% Increase in Reports of Military Sexual Assaults." *New York Times*. May 1, 2014. [Online] Available at http://www.nytimes.com/2014/05/02/us /military-sex-assault-report.html?_r=0

Cortese, Anthony J. 1999. *Provocateur: Images of Women and Minorities in Advertising*. Lanham, Md.: Rowman & Littlefield.

Dworkin, Andrea. 1987. *Intercourse*. New York: Free Press.

Ehrenreich, Barbara. 1983. *The Hearts of Men: American Dreams and the Flight from Commitment*. Garden City, N.Y.: Anchor Doubleday.

———. 1999. "The Real Truth about the Female Body." *Time*. Vol. 153, No. 9 (March 15): 56–65.

Engels, Friedrich. 1902 (orig. 1884). *The Origin of the Family*. Chicago: Kerr.

England, Paula. 1992. *Comparable Worth: Theories and Evidence*. Hawthorne, N.Y.: Aldine de Grutyer.

England, Paula, Joan M. Hermsen, and David A. Cotter. 2000. "The Devaluation of Women's Work: A Comment on Tam." *American Journal of Sociology*. Vol. 105, No. 6 (May): 1741–60.

Freedman, Estelle B. 2002. *No Turning Back: The History of Feminism and the Future of Women*. New York: Ballantine.

Frias, Sonia M., and Ronald J. Angel. 2007. "Stability and Change in the Experience of Partner Violence among Low-Income Women." *Social Science Quarterly*. Vol. 88, No. 5 (May): 1281–1306.

Fryar, Cheryl D., Qiuping Gu, and Cynthia Ogden. 2012. "Anthropometric Reference Data for Children and Adults: United States, 2007–2010." National Center for Health Statistics. *Vital Health Stat*. Vol. 11, No. 252. [Online] Available at http://www.cdc .gov/nchs/data/series/sr_11/sr11_252.pdf

Gibson, Megan. "2013 Was a Good Year for Women in Movies. What Will 2014 Hold?" *Time*. January 9, 2014. [Online] Available at http://entertainment.time.com/2014/01/09/2013-was-a-good -year-for-women-in-movies-what-will-2014-hold

Goetting, Ann. 1999. *Getting Out: Life Stories of Women Who Left Abusive Men*. New York: Columbia University Press.

Goffman, Erving. 1979. *Gender Advertisements*. New York: Harper Colophon.

Goldberg, Steven. 1974. *The Inevitability of Patriarchy*. New York: Morrow.

Greenstone, Jody. "The Real Women's Issue: Time." *Wall Street Journal*. (March 9–10, 2013): C3.

Guardian. "Swedish Cinemas Take Aim at Gender Bias with Bechdel Test Rating." November 6, 2013. [Online] Available at http://www .theguardian.com/world/2013/nov/06/swedish-cinemas-bechdel -test-films-gender-bias

Hacker, Helen Mayer. 1951. "Women as a Minority Group." *Social Forces*. Vol. 30, No. 1 (October): 60–69.

Hadley, Janet. 1996. *Abortion: Between Freedom and Necessity*. Philadelphia: Temple University Press.

Henley, Nancy, Mykol Hamilton, and Barrie Thorne. 1992. "Womanspeak and Manspeak: Sex Differences in Communication, Verbal and Nonverbal." In John J. Macionis and Nijole V. Benokraitis, eds., *Seeing Ourselves: Classic, Contemporary, and Cross-Cultural Readings in Sociology*, 2nd ed. (pp. 10–15). Englewood Cliffs, N.J.: Prentice Hall.

Herman, Dianne F. 2001. "The Rape Culture." In John J. Macionis and Nijole V. Benokraitis, eds., *Seeing Ourselves: Classic, Contemporary, and Cross-Cultural Readings in Sociology*, 5th ed. (pp. 38–46). Upper Saddle River, N.J.: Prentice Hall.

Hewlett, Sylvia Ann. "As Careers Paths Change, Make On-Ramping Easy." 2009. [Online] Available at http://blogs.hbr.org /hbr/hewlett/2010/07/as_careers_paths_change_make_o.html

Hewlett, Sylvia Ann, and Carolyn Buck Luce. "Off-Ramps and On-Ramps: Keeping Talented Women on the Road to Success." *Harvard Business Review*. Vol. 83, Issue 3 (March 2005): 43–54.

Hooks, bell. 2000. *Feminist Theory: From Margin to Center*, 2nd ed. London: Pluto Press.

Huffman, Matt L., Steven C. Velasco, and William T. Bielby. 1996. "Where Sex Composition Matters Most: Comparing the Effects of Job versus Occupational Sex Composition of Earnings." *Sociological Focus*. Vol. 29, No. 3 (August): 189–207.

Inter-Parliamentary Union. "Women in National Parliaments." 2013. [Online] Available at http://www.ipu.org/wmn-e/classif .htm

Jackson, Sheri, and Sue Scott, eds. 1996. *Feminism and Sexuality: A Reader*. New York: Columbia University Press.

Jagger, Alison. 1983. "Political Philosophies of Women's Liberation." In Laurel Richardson and Verta Taylor, eds., *Feminist Frontiers: Rethinking Sex, Gender, and Society*. Reading, Mass.: Addison-Wesley.

JOHNSON, CATHRYN. 1994. "Gender, Legitimate Authority, and Leader-Subordinate Conversations." *American Sociological Review*. Vol. 59, No. 1 (February): 122–35.

KAUFMAN, WALTER. 1976. *Religions in Four Dimensions: Existential, Aesthetic, Historical, and Comparative*. Pleasantville, N.Y.: Reader's Digest Press.

LENGERMANN, PATRICIA MADOO, and RUTH A. WALLACE. 1985. *Gender in America: Social Control and Social Change*. Englewood Cliffs, N.J.: Prentice Hall.

LEWIN, TAMAR. "Girls' Gains Have Not Cost Boys, Report Says." *New York Times* (May 20, 2008). [Online] Available at http://www.nytimes.com/2008/05/20/education/20girls.html

LINDSAY, LINDA. 1994. *Gender Roles*, 2nd ed. Englewood Cliffs, N.J.: Prentice Hall.

MACCOBY, ELEANOR EMMONS, and CAROL NAGY JACKLIN. 1974. *The Psychology of Sex Differences*. Stanford, Calif.: Stanford University Press.

NIELSEN MEDIA RESEARCH. "The Cross-Platform Report." 2013. [Online] Available at http://www.nielsen.com/content/dam/corporate/us/en/reports-downloads/2013%20Reports/Nielsen-March-2013-Cross-Platform-Report.pdf

OHLEMACHER, STEPHEN. 2006. "Study Finds That Marriage Builds Wealth." *Yahoo News*. [Online] Available January 18, 2007, at http://news.yahoo.com

PARSONS, TALCOTT. 1942. "Age and Sex in the Social Structure of the United States." *American Sociological Review*. Vol. 7, No. 4 (August): 604–16.

———.1951. *The Social System*. New York: Free Press.

———. 1954. *Essays in Sociological Theory*. New York: Free Press.

PEW RESEARCH CENTER. "On Pay Gap, Millennial Women Near Parity—For Now." December 11, 2013. [Online] Available at http://www.pewsocialtrends.org/2013/12/11/on-pay-gap-millennial-women-near-parity-for-now

PHILLIPS, ANNE, ed. 1987. *Feminism and Equality*. New York: New York University Press.

PLANTY, MICHAEL, LYNN LANGTON, CHRISTOPHER KREBS, MARCUS BERZOFSKY, and HOPE SMILEY-MCDONALD. 2013. "Female Victims of Sexual Violence, 1994–2010." Bureau of Justice Statistics. (March). Washington, D.C.: U.S. Department of Justice.

POPENOE, DAVID. 1993a. "American Family Decline, 1960–1990: A Review and Appraisal." *Journal of Marriage and the Family*. Vol. 55, No. 3 (August): 527–55.

———. 1993b. "Parental Androgyny." *Society*. Vol. 30, No. 6 (September-October): 5–11.

PURCELL, PIPER, and LARA STEWART. 1990. "Dick and Jane in 1989." *Sex Roles*. Vol. 22, Nos. 3–4 (February): 177–85.

REILAND, RALPH. 1998. "Selecting Targets." *Free Market*. Vol. 16, No. 1 (January). [Online] Available May 15, 2006, at http://www.mises.org

SHEA, RACHEL HARTIGAN. 2002. "The New Insecurity." *U.S. News & World Report*. Vol. 132, No. 9 (March 25): 40.

SLAUGHTER, ANN-MARIE. "Why Women Sill Can't Have It All." *The Atlantic*. July/August 2012. [Online] Available at http://www.theatlantic.com/magazine/archive/2012/07/why-women-still-cant-have-it-all/309020

SMITH, TOM W., PETER MARSDEN, MICHAEL HOUT, and JIBUM KIM. "General Social Surveys, 1972–2012." National Opinion Research Center; The Roper Center for Public Opinion Research, University of Connecticut; Computer-assisted Survey Methods Program, University of California. June 2013. [Online] Available at http://www.norc.org/GSS+Website

SMITH-LOVIN, LYNN, and CHARLES BRODY. 1989. "Interruptions in Group Discussions: The Effects of Gender and Group Composition." *American Journal of Sociology*. Vol. 54, No. 3 (June): 424–35.

SMOLOWE, JILL. 1994. "When Violence Hits Home." *Time*. Vol. 144, No. 1 (July 4): 18–25.

SOMMERS, CHRISTINA HOFF. 2003. Lecture at Kenyon College (April 7).

STACEY, JUDITH. 1990. *Brave New Families: Stories of Domestic Upheaval in Late-Twentieth-Century America*. New York: Basic Books.

STEINHAUSER, JENNIFER. "Birth Control Is Covered and G.O.P. Vows a Fight." *New York Times*. February 8, 2012. Available at http://www.nytimes.com/2012/02/09/us/politics/boehner-vows-to-fight-contraception-rule.html?_r=1

TAVRIS, CAROL, and CAROL WADE. 2001. *Psychology in Perspective*, 3rd ed. Upper Saddle River, N.J.: Prentice Hall.

TAYLOR, FRANK. 2003. "Content Analysis and Gender Stereotypes in Children's Books." *Teaching Sociology*. Vol. 31, No. 3 (July): 300–11.

TONG, ROSEMARIE. 2009. *Feminist Thought: A More Comprehensive Introduction*, 3rd ed. Boulder, Colo.: Westview Press.

TVB. "TV Basics." August 2012. [Online] Available at http://www.tvb.org/trends/95487

UDRY, J. RICHARD. 2000. "Biological Limitations of Gender Construction." *American Sociological Review*. Vol. 65, No. 3 (June): 443–57.

———. 2001. "Feminist Critics Uncover Determinism, Positivism, and Antiquated Theory." *American Sociological Review*. Vol. 66, No. 4 (August): 611–18.

UNICEF. "Child Info Statistics by Area: Child Protection." 2013. [Online] Available at http://www.childinfo.org/fgmc_progress.html

UNITED NATIONS DEVELOPMENT PROGRAMME. "Gender Inequality Index." 2013. [Online] Available at http://hdrstats.undp.org/en/indicators/68606.html

U.S. CENSUS BUREAU. "Current Population Survey." 2013. [Online] Available at http://www.census.gov/cps

U.S. CENSUS BUREAU. "Families and Living Arrangements." 2013. [Online] Available at http://www.census.gov/hhes/families

U.S. DEPARTMENT OF DEFENSE. "Military Personnel Statistics." 2014. [Online] Available at https://www.dmdc.osd.mil/appj/dwp/reports.do?category=reports&subCat=milActDutReg

U.S. DEPARTMENT OF EDUCATION, NATIONAL CENTER FOR EDUCATION STATISTICS. "U.S. Digest of Education Statistics 2012." 2013. [Online] Available at http://nces.ed.gov/programs/digest/d12

U.S. DEPARTMENT OF EDUCATION, NATIONAL CENTER FOR EDUCATION STATISTICS. "U.S. Digest of Education Statistics 2013." 2013. [Online] Available at http://nces.ed.gov/programs/digest/2013menu_tables.asp

U.S. DEPARTMENT OF JUSTICE, BUREAU OF JUSTICE STATISTICS. "National Criminal Victimization Analysis Tool." 2014. [Online] Available at http://www.bjs.gov/index.cfm?ty=nvat

U.S. DEPARTMENT OF JUSTICE, NATIONAL INSTITUTE OF JUSTICE. "Sexual Assault on Campus." 2012. [Online] Available at http://www.ojp.usdoj.gov/nij/topics/crime/rape-sexual-violence/campus/measuring.htm

U.S. DEPARTMENT OF LABOR, BUREAU OF LABOR STATISTICS. "American Time Use Survey." 2012, 2013. [Online] Available at http://www.bls.gov/tus

U.S. DEPARTMENT OF LABOR, BUREAU OF LABOR STATISTICS. "Employment Characteristics of Families." 2013. [Online] Available at http://www.bls.gov/news.release/famee.toc.htm

U.S. Department of Labor, Bureau of Labor Statistics. "Highlights of Women's Earnings in 2012." 2013. [Online] Available at http://www.bls.gov/cps/cpswom2012.pdf

U.S. Department of Labor. "Labor Force Statistics from the Current Population Survey." 2013. [Online] Available at http://www.bls .gov/cps/cpsatabs.htm

van der Lippe, Tanja, and Liset van Dijk. 2002. "Comparative Research on Women's Employment." *Annual Review of Sociology.* Vol. 28: 221–41.

Vogel, Lise. 1983. *Marxism and the Oppression of Women: Toward a Unitary Theory.* New Brunswick, N.J.: Rutgers University Press.

Waite, Linda J., and Maggie Gallagher. 2000. *The Case for Marriage: Why Married People Are Happier, Healthier, and Better Off Financially.* New York: Doubleday.

Wolf, Naomi. 1990. *The Beauty Myth: How Images of Beauty Are Used against Women.* New York: Morrow.

Chapter 5

AARP Public Policy Institute. "Caregiving in the U.S.: A Focused Look at Caring for Someone Age 50 or Older." 2009. [Online] Available at http://assets.aarp.org/rgcenter/il/caregiving_09.pdf

American Health Care Association. "Nursing Facility Operational Characteristics Report." March 2013. [Online] Available at http://www.ahcancal.org/research_data/oscar_data/Pages /default.aspx

Arias, Elizabeth. "United States Life Tables, 2009." 2014. [Online] Available at http://www.cdc.gov/nchs/data/nvsr/nvsr62 /nvsr62_07.pdf

Arias, Elizabeth. "United States Life Tables, 2007." *National Vital Statistics Reports,* Vol. 59, No. 6. 2011. [Online] Available at http://www.cdc.gov/nchs/data/nvsr/nvsr59/nvsr59_09.pdf

Ariès, Philippe. 1974. *Western Attitudes toward Death: From the Middle Ages to the Present.* Baltimore, Md.: Johns Hopkins University Press.

Atchley, Robert C. 1982. "Retirement as a Social Institution." *Annual Review of Sociology.* Vol. 8: 263–87.

Barnett, Ola W., Cindy L. Miller-Perrin, and Robin D. Perrin. 1997. *Family Violence across the Lifespan: An Introduction.* Thousand Oaks, Calif.: Sage.

Barr, Bob. 2004. "Euthanasia . . . or a 'Dutch Treat'?" *Washington Times* (December 26). [Online] Available July 29, 2007, at http://www.bobbarr.org/default.asp?pt=newsdescr &RI=585

Bendick, M. F. 1992. "Reaching the Breaking Point: Dangers of Mistreatment in Elder Caregiving Situations." *Journal of Elder Abuse and Neglect.* Vol. 4, No. 3 (Fall): 39–59.

Benjamin, Bernard, and Chris Wallis. 1963. "The Mortality of Widowers." *Lancet.* Vol. 2 (August): 454–56.

Bosworth, Barry, and Gary Burtless. 1998. "Population Aging and American Economic Performance." In Barry Bosworth and Gary Burtless, eds., *Aging Societies: The Global Dimension* (pp. 267–310). Washington, D.C.: Brookings Institution.

Brown, Alyssa. "In U.S., Average Retirement Age Up to 61." Gallup Economy. January 15, 2014. [Online] Available at http://www .gallup.com/poll/162560/average-retirement-age.aspx

Butler, Robert N. 1975. *Why Survive? Being Old in America.* New York: Harper & Row, 1975.

———. 1994. "Dispelling Ageism: The Cross-Cutting Intervention." In Dena Shenk and W. Andrew Achenbaum, eds., *Changing Perceptions of Aging and the Aged.* New York: Springer.

Cohen, Elias. 2001. "The Complex Nature of Ageism: What Is It? Who Does It? Who Perceives It?" *Gerontologist.* Vol. 41, No. 5 (October): 576–78.

Cubanski, Juliette, Christina Swoope, Anthony Damico, and Tricia Neuman. "Health Care on a Budget: The Financial Burden of Health Spending by Medicare Households." Kaiser Family Foundation. 2014. [Online] Available at http://kff.org/medicare /issue-brief/health-care-on-a-budget-the-financial-burden-of -health-spending-by-medicare-households

Cumming, Elaine, and William E. Henry. 1961. *Growing Old: The Process of Disengagement.* New York: Basic Books.

Economist. "Hiring Grandpa." April 7, 2011. [Online] Available at http://www.economist.com/node/18474681?story_id=18474681

Federal Interagency Forum on Aging-Related Statistics. "Older Americans 2012: Key Indicators of Well-Being." 2012. [Online] Available at http://www.agingstats.gov/agingstatsdotnet /Main_Site/Data/2012_Documents/Docs/EntireChartbook.pdf

Fox, Susannah, Maeve Duggan, and Kristen Purcell. "Family Caregivers Wired for Health." June 20, 2013. Pew Research Center. [Online] Available at http://www.pewinternet.org/Reports/2013 /Family-Caregivers/Summary-of-Findings.aspx

Gall, Terry L., David R. Evans, and John Howard. 1997. "The Retirement Adjustment Process: Changes in the Well-Being of Male Retirees across Time." *Journal of Gerontology, Series B: Psychological Sciences.* Vol. 52B, No. 3 (May): 110–17.

Gendell, Murray. 2002. "Boomers' Retirement Wave Likely to Begin in Just Six Years." *Population Today.* Vol. 30, No. 3 (April): 1–2.

Gendell, Murray. 2008. "Older Workers: Increasing Their Labor Force Participation and Hours of Work." *Monthly Labor Review.* [Online] Available at http://bls.gov/opub/mlr/2008/01 /art3full.pdf

Gillon, Raanan. 1999. "Euthanasia in the Netherlands: Down the Slippery Slope?" *Journal of Medical Ethics.* Vol. 25, No. 1 (February): 3–4.

Goldman, Russell. "Deaf Twins Going Blind Euthanized." ABC News. January 14, 2013. [Online] Available at http://news.yahoo .com/deaf-twins-going-blind-euthanized-165500992--abc-news -topstories.html

Greenberg, Jan R., Martha McKibben, and Jane A. Raymond. 1990. "Dependent Adult Children and Elder Abuse." *Journal of Elder Abuse and Neglect.* Vol. 2, Nos. 1–2 (Spring–Summer): 73–86.

Havinghurst, Robert J., Bernice L. Neugarten, and Sheldon S. Tobin. 1968. "Disengagement and Patterns of Aging." In Bernice L. Neugarten, ed., *Middle Age and Aging: A Reader in Social Psychology* (pp. 161–72). Chicago: University of Chicago Press.

Himes, Christine L. 2001. "Elderly Americans." *Population Bulletin.* Vol. 56, No. 4 (December).

Hinrichsen, Gregory A., N. A. Hernandez, and S. Pollack. 1992. "Difficulties and Rewards in Family Care of Depressed Older Adults." *Gerontologist.* Vol. 32, No. 4 (August): 486–92.

Holmes, Ellen Rhoads, and Lowell D. Holmes. 1995. *Other Cultures, Elder Years,* 2nd ed. Thousand Oaks, Calif.: Sage.

Hoyert, Donna, and Jiaquan Xu. "Deaths: Preliminary Data for 2011." *National Vital Statistics Reports.* Vol. 61, No. 6. National Center for Health Statistics. 2012. [Online] Available at http://www.cdc .gov/nchs/data/nvsr/nvsr61/nvsr61_06.pdf

Kaiser Family Foundation. "Medicare Chartbook, 4th ed." 2010. [Online] Available at http://facts.kff.org/chartbook .aspx?cb=58

Kaiser Family Foundation. "Medicare Fact Sheet." 2012. [Online] Available at http://kff.org/medicare/fact-sheet/medicare-at-a -glance-fact-sheet

Kleinman, Arthur. 1997. "Intimations of Solidarity? The Popular Culture Responds to Assisted Suicide." *Hastings Center Report* (September–October): 34–36.

KOSTERLITZ, JULIE. 1997. "When We're 64." *National Journal*. Vol. 29, No. 39 (September 27): 1882–85.

LABATON, STEPHEN. 2000. "You Don't Have to Be Old to Sue for Age Discrimination." *New York Times* (February 16): A7.

LEE, FELICIA R. 2002. "Long Buried, Death Goes Public Again." *New York Times* Online. [Online] Available November 2, 2002, at http://www.researchnavigator.com

LEFF, LISA. 2008. "California Gay Marriage Vote Still Undecided." *Yahoo News* (November 5). [Online] Available November 5, 2008, at http://news.yahoo.com/s/ap/20081105/ap_on_el_ge/ballot_measures

LUND, DALE A. 1989. "Conclusions about Bereavement in Later Life and Implications for Interventions and Future Research." In Dale A. Lund, ed., *Older Bereaved Spouses: Research with Practical Applications* (pp. 217–31). London: Taylor & Francis/Hemisphere.

———. 1993. "Caregiving." *In Encyclopedia of Adult Development* (pp. 57–63). Phoenix, Ariz.: Oryx Press.

MANHEIMER, RONALD J., ed. 1994. *Older Americans Almanac: A Reference Work on Seniors in the United States*. Detroit: Gale Research.

MEDINA, JOHN J. 1996. *The Clock of Ages: Why We Age, How We Age, Winding Back the Clock*. Cambridge: Cambridge University Press.

MORRIS, DAVID C. 1997. "Older Adults' Perceptions of Dr. Kevorkian in Middletown, U.S.A." *Omega*. Vol. 35, No. 4: 405–12.

MYERHOFF, BARBARA. 1979. *Number Our Days*. New York: Dutton.

NATIONAL CENTER ON ELDER ABUSE. "Abuse of Adults Aged 60+: The 2004 Survey of Adult Protective Services." 2006. [Online] Available at http://www.ncea.aoa.gov/NCEAroot/Main_Site/pdf/2-14-06%2060FACT%20SHEET.pdf

NATIONAL CENTER FOR HEALTH STATISTICS, CDC. "Health Data Interactive." 2013. [Online] Available at http://www.cdc.gov/nchs/hdi.htm

NEUGARTEN, BERNICE L. 1996. "Retirement in the Life Course." In Dale A. Neugarten, ed., The Meanings of Age: Selected Papers of Bernice L. Neugarten (pp. 221–37). Chicago: University of Chicago Press.

NEW YORK TIMES. "Assisted Suicide." *New York Times*. 2013, 2014. [Online] Available at http://topics.nytimes.com/top/reference/timestopics/subjects/e/euthanasia/assisted_suicide/index.html

OECD (Organisation for Economic Co-operation and Development). "Employment Policies and Data." 2013. [Online] Available at http://www.oecd.org/els/emp

OGDEN, RUSSEL D. 2001. "Nonphysician-Assisted Suicide: The Technological Imperative of the Deathing Counterculture." *Death Studies*. Vol. 25, No. 5 (July): 387–402.

PALMORE, ERDMAN B. 1979. "Predictors of Successful Aging." *Gerontologist*. Vol. 19, No. 5 (October): 427–31.

———. 1998. "Ageism." In David E. Redburn and Robert P. McNamara, eds., *Social Gerontology* (pp. 29–41). Westport, Conn.: Auburn House.

PEAR, ROBERT. "Violations Reported at 94% of Nursing Homes." *New York Times*. September 29, 2008. [Online] Available at http://www.nytimes.com/2008/09/30/us/30nursing.html

PEW RESEARCH CENTER, INTERNET and AMERICAN LIFE PROJECT. "Pew Family Caregivers 2012." 2012. [Online] Available at http://www.pewinternet.org/Reports/2013/Family-Caregivers/Summary-of-Findings.aspx

PEW RESEARCH RELIGION and PUBLIC LIFE PROJECT. "To End Our Days: The Social, Legal and Political Dimensions of the End-of-Life Debate." 2013. [Online] Available at http://www.pewforum.org/2013/11/21/to-end-our-days

PEW RESEARCH CENTER. "Views on End-of-Life Medical Treatments." 2013. [Online] Available at http://www.pewforum.org/2013/11/21/views-on-end-of-life-medical-treatments

PHILLIPSON, CHRIS. 1982. *Capitalism and the Construction of Old Age*. London: Macmillan.

PITT, DAVID. 2009. "Economy Dampens Hope of a Comfortable Retirement." *Yahoo News* (April 14) [Online] Available April 14, 2009, at http://news.yahoo.com/s/ap/20090414/ap_on_bi_ge/retirement_confidence

POWELL, LAWRENCE ALFRED, KENNETH J. BRANCO, and JOHN B. WILLIAMSON. 1996. *The Senior Rights Movement: Framing the Policy Debate in America*. New York: Twayne.

REUTERS. "Factbox: Status of Euthanasia, Assisted Suicide in Europe." 2010. [Online] Available at http://www.reuters.com/article/2010/06/25/us-germany-court-suicide-factbox-idUSTRE65O2OI20100625?pageNumber=2

RICHE, MARTHA FARNSWORTH. 2000. "America's Diversity and Growth: Signposts for the 21st Century." *Population Bulletin*. Vol. 55, No. 2 (June).

ROBINSON, JOHN P., PERLA WERNER, and GEOFFREY GODBEY. 1997. "Freeing Up the Golden Years." *American Demographics*. Vol. 19, No. 10 (October): 20–24.

SMART, TIM. 2001. "Not Acting Their Age." *U.S. News & World Report*. Vol. 130, No. 22 (June 4): 54–60.

SMITH, TOM W., PETER MARSDEN, MICHAEL HOUT, and JIBUM KIM. "General Social Surveys, 1972–2012." National Opinion Research Center; The Roper Center for Public Opinion Research, University of Connecticut; Computer-assisted Survey Methods Program, University of California. June 2013. [Online] Available at http://www.norc.org/GSS+Website

SOMMERS, CHRISTINA HOFF. 2003. Lecture at Kenyon College (April 7).

SPILLMAN, BRENDA C. 2002. "New Estimates of Lifetime Nursing Home Use: Have Patterns of Use Changed?" *Medical Care*. Vol. 40, No. 10 (October): 965–1006.

SPITZER, STEVEN. 1980. "Toward a Marxian Theory of Deviance." In Delos H. Kelly, ed., *Criminal Behavior: Readings in Criminology* (pp. 175–91). New York: St. Martin's Press.

STATE OF OREGON, PUBLIC HEALTH DIVISION. "Death with Dignity Act Annual Report." 2013. [Online] Available at http://public.health.oregon.gov/ProviderPartnerResources/EvaluationResearch/DeathwithDignityAct/Pages/index.aspx

STROM, STEPHANIE. 2000. "In Japan, the Golden Years Have Lost Their Glow." *New York Times* (February 16): A7.

TAGLIABUE, JOHN. 2008. "Woman Who Sought Euthanasia Dies." *New York Times* (March 21). [Online] Available January 18, 2009, at http://query.nytimes.com/gst/fullpage.html?res=9A0DE1D61130F932A15750C0A96E9C8B63&sec=&spon=&partner=permalink&exprod=permalink

THOMPSON, MARK. 1998. "Shining a Light on Abuse." *Time*. Vol. 152, No. 5 (August 3): 42–43.

U.S. CENSUS BUREAU. "American Community Survey." 2013. [Online] Available at http://www.census.gov/acs

U.S. CENSUS BUREAU. "Current Population Survey." 2013. [Online] Available at http://www.census.gov/cps

U.S. CENSUS BUREAU. "International Data Base." 2014. [Online] Available at http://www.census.gov/population/international/data/idb/informationGateway.php

U.S. CENSUS BUREAU. "2012 National Population Projections: Tables and Charts." 2012. [Online] Available at http://www.census.gov/population/projections/data/national/2012/summarytables.html

U.S. CENSUS BUREAU. "Population Estimates." 2013. [Online] Available at http://www.census.gov/popest/data/index.html

U.S. CENSUS BUREAU. "Voting and Registration." 2013. [Online] Available at http://www.census.gov/hhes/www/socdemo/voting/index.html

U.S. Census Bureau. "International Data Base." 2012. [Online] Available at http://www.census.gov/ipc/www/idb

U.S. Department of Housing and Urban Development and U.S. Census Bureau. "American Housing Survey for the United States." 2011. [Online] Available at http://www.census.gov/hhes /www/housing/ahs/ahs09/ahs09.html

U.S. Department of Housing and Urban Development and U.S. Census Bureau. "2011 American Housing Survey for the United States." 2013. [Online] Available at http://factfinder2. census.gov/faces/nav/jsf/pages/programs.xhtml? program=ahs

U.S. Department of Housing and Urban Development. "A Picture of Subsidized Households for the Year 2009." 2013. [Online] Available at http://www.huduser.org/portal/datasets/assthsg .html

U.S. Equal Employment Opportunity Commission. "Enforcement & Litigation Statistics." 2013. [Online] Available at http://www1 .eeoc.gov/eeoc/statistics/enforcement/adea.cfm

U.S. House of Representatives. Minority Staff, Special Investigations Division, Committee on Government Reform. 2001. Abuse of Residents Is a Major Problem in U.S. Nursing Homes. Washington, D.C.: U.S. Government Printing Office.

Wise, David A. 1997. "Retirement against the Demographic Trend: More Older People Living Longer, Working Less, and Saving Less." Demography. Vol. 34, No. 1 (February): 83–95.

Wyatt, Edward. 2000. "Tenure Gridlock: When Professors Choose Not to Retire." New York Times (February 16): D11.

Chapter 6

Almasy, Steve, and Ashley Fantz. "One Piece Still Missing from Puzzle of Fatal Theater Shooting: Why?" CNN Justice. January 14, 2014. [Online] Available at http://www.cnn.com/2014/01/14 /justice/florida-movie-theater-shooting

American Gaming Association. "Fact Sheet: Types of Gaming by State." 2014. [Online] Available at http://www.americangaming. org/industry-resources/research/fact-sheets/states-gaming

American Medical Association. 1997. [Online] Available March 4, 1997, at http://www.ama-assn.org

Amnesty International. "List of Abolitionist and Retentionist Countries." 2013. [Online] Available at http://www.amnesty.org /en/death-penalty/abolitionist-and-retentionist-countries

Anderson, Elijah. 1994. "The Code of the Streets." Atlantic Monthly. Vol. 273 (May): 81–94.

———. 2002. "The Ideologically Driven Critique." American Journal of Sociology. Vol. 197, No. 6 (May): 1533–50.

Antlfinger, Carrie. "Homicides Down in Some Large U.S. Cities." Yahoo News. January 3, 2009. [Online] Available January 3, 2009, at http://news.yahoo.com/s/ap/20090103/ap_on_re_us /urban_homicides

Babwin, Dohn. 2003. "Illinois Governor to Commute Death-Row Sentences." Yahoo News. [Online] Available January 11, 2003, at http://dailynews.yahoo.com

Becker, Howard S. 1966. Outside: Studies in the Sociology of Deviance. New York: Free Press.

Berman, Douglas A., and Harlan Protass. "A Saner Approach to Sentencing." Wall Street Journal. (May 8, 2013): A17.

Brady Campaign to Prevent Gun Violence. 2012. [Online] Available at http://www.bradycampaign.org

Calabresi, Massimo, and Bill Saporito. "The Street Fighter." Time. Vol. 179, No. 6 (February 13, 2012): 22–27.

CAP Index. 2011. [Online] Available at http://www.capindex.com

Cloward, Richard A., and Lloyd E. Ohlin. 1966. Delinquency and Opportunity: A Theory of Delinquent Gangs. New York: Free Press.

Cohn, D'Vera, Paul Taylor, Mark Hugo Lopez, Catherine A. Gallagher, Kim Parker, and Kevin T. Maass. "Gun Homicide Rate Down 49% Since 1993 Peak; Public Unaware." Pew Research Center. May 7, 2013. [Online] Available at http:// www.pewsocialtrends.org/2013/05/07/gun-homicide-rate-down -49-since-1993-peak-public-unaware/#chapter-1-overview

Cole, George F., and Christopher E. Smith. 2002. Criminal Justice in America, 3rd ed. Belmont, Calif.: Wadsworth.

Cottom, Tressie McMillan. "What Legalizing Recreational Marijuana Could Mean for Minorities." Here & Now. National Public Radio. January 16, 2014. [Online] Available at http: //hereandnow.wbur.org/2014/01/16/legalizing-recreational -marijuana

Daly, Kathleen, and Meda Chesney-Lind. 1988. "Feminism and Criminology." Justice Quarterly. Vol. 5, No. 4 (December): 497–583.

Death Penalty Information Center. "The Death Penalty in 2013: Year End Report." 2014. [Online] Available at http: //deathpenaltyinfo.org/documents/YearEnd2013.pdf

Death Penalty Information Center. "Outlaw Death Penalty to Save Lives and Cash." November 8, 2010. [Online] Available at: http://www.deathpenaltyinfo.org/editorials-illinois-outlaw-death -penalty-save-lives-and-cash

DeFina, Robert H., and Thomas M. Arvanites. 2002. "The Weak Effect of Imprisonment on Crime, 1971–1998." Social Science Quarterly. Vol. 83, No. 3 (September): 635–53.

Deslatte, Melinda. 2003. "Serial Killing Suspect Returns to Louisiana." San Francisco Examiner (July 3). [Online] Available July 3, 2003, at http://www.examiner.com

Dinitz, Simon, F. R. Scarpitti, and Walter C. Reckless. 1962. "Delinquency and Vulnerability: A Cross-Group and Longitudinal Analysis." American Sociological Review. Vol. 25, No. 4 (August): 555–58.

Durkheim, Emile. 1964a (orig. 1895). The Division of Labor in Society. New York: Free Press.

———. 1964b (orig. 1893). The Rules of Sociological Method. New York: Free Press.

Eaglesham, Jean. "Missing: Stats on Crisis Convictions." Wall Street Journal. May 13, 2012. [Online] Available at http://online.wsj.com /news/articles/SB10001424052702303505504577401911741048088

Federal Communications Commission (FCC). "Violent Television Programming and Its Impact on Children." April 17, 2007. [Online] Available at http://hraunfoss.fcc.gov/edocs_public/attachmatch /FCC-07-50A1.pdf

Fishel, Justin, and Chad Pergram. "Fort Hood Shooting Repeat Renews Calls for Ending Gun Restrictions on Base." FoxNews.com. April 3, 2014. [Online] Available at http://www.foxnews.com /politics/2014/04/03/fort-hood-shooting-repeat-renews-calls-for -ending-gun-restrictions-on-base

Gelles, Richard J. 1997. Intimate Violence in Families, 3rd ed. Thousand Oaks, Calif.: Sage.

Glueck, Sheldon, and Eleanor Glueck. 1950. Unraveling Juvenile Delinquency. New York: Commonwealth Fund.

Goffman, Erving. 1963. Stigma: Notes on the Management of Spoiled Identity. Englewood Cliffs, N.J.: Prentice Hall.

Gray, Eliza. "Sexual Assault on Campus." Time. Vol. 183, No. 20 (May 26, 2014): 20–27.

Grillo, Ioan. "Drug War No More." New York Times, November 27, 2013. [Online] Available at http://www.nytimes.com/2013/11/28 /opinion/drug-war-no-more.html?ref=drugtrafficking

Groves, Betsy McAlister. 1997. "Growing Up in a Violent World: The Impact of Family and Community Violence on Young Children and Their Families." *Topics in Early Childhood Special Education.* Vol. 17, No. 1 (Spring): 74–101.

Herpertz, Sabine C., and Henning Sass. 2000. "Emotional Deficiency and Psychopathy." *Behavioral Sciences and the Law.* Vol. 18, No. 5 (September–October): 567–80.

Hill, John. "2009. Wong a Regular at Store's Gun Counter." *USA Today* (April 6): 4A.

Hirschi, Travis. 1969. *Causes of Delinquency.* Berkeley: University of California Press.

Hixon, Allen L. 1999. "Preventing Street Gang Violence." *American Family Physician.* Vol. 59, No. 8 (April 15): 2121–24.

Holmes, Ronald M., and Stephen T. Holmes. 1993. *Murder in America.* Thousand Oaks, Calif.: Sage.

———. 1998. *Serial Murder,* 2nd ed. Thousand Oaks, Calif.: Sage.

Inciardi, James A., ed. 2000. *Elements of Criminal Justice,* 2nd ed. New York: Oxford University Press.

International Centre for Prison Studies, University of Essex. "World Prison Brief." 2014. [Online] Available at http://www .prisonstudies.org/highest-to-lowest/prison-population-total

Irwin, Neil. "This Is a Complete List of Wall Street CEOs Prosecuted for Their Role in the Financial Crisis." *Washington Post.* September 12, 2013. [Online] Available at http://www.washingtonpost.com /blogs/wonkblog/wp/2013/09/12/this-is-a-complete-list-of-wall -street-ceos-prosecuted-for-their-role-in-the-financial-crisis

Jenkins, Philip. 1994. *Using Murder: The Social Construction of Serial Homicide.* Hawthorne, N.Y.: Aldine de Gruyter.

Jenness, Valerie. 1993. *Making It Work: The Prostitutes' Rights Movement in Perspective.* Hawthorne, N.Y.: Aldine de Gruyter.

Jenness, Valerie, and Ryken Grattet. 2001. *Making a Hate Crime: From Movement to Law Enforcement.* New York: Russell Sage Foundation.

Johnson, Kevin. 2000. "Serious Crime Down Again: 7% Dip in '99." *USA Today* (May 8): A1.

Justice Reinvestment. "Ending Mass Incarceration: Charting a New Justice Reinvestment." 2014. [Online] Available at http: //sentencingproject.org/doc/publications/sen_Charting%20a%20 New%20Justice%20Reinvestment.pdf

Kempe, C. Henry, et al. 1962. "The Battered Child Syndrome." *Journal of the American Medical Association.* Vol. 181 (July 7): 17–24.

Kitman, Jamie. 2003. "Tort Reform for Dummies." *Automobile* (April): 145.

Krebs, Christopher P., Christine H. Lindequist, Tara D. Warner, Bonnie S. Fisher, and Sandra L. Martin. 2007. The *Campus Sexual Assault Study: Final Report.* U.S. Justice Department, National Institute of Justice. [Online] Available at https://www.ncjrs.gov /pdffiles1/nij/grants/221153.pdf

Kromar, Marina, and Patti M. Valkenburg. 1999. "A Scale to Assess Children's Moral Interpretations of Justified and Unjustified Violence and Its Relationship to Television Viewing." *Communication Research.* Vol. 26, No. 5 (October): 608–35.

Krouse, William J. "Gun Control Legislation." Congressional Research Service, November 14, 2012. [Online] Available at https://www.fas.org/sgp/crs/misc/RL32842.pdf

LaFree, Gary. 1998. *Losing Legitimacy: Street Crime and the Decline of Social Institutions in America.* Boulder, Colo.: Westview Press.

Langbein, Laura, and Roseana Bess. 2002. "Sports in School: Source of Amity or Antipathy?" *Social Science Quarterly.* Vol. 83, No. 2 (June): 436–54.

Lavella, Marianna. 2002. "Payback Time." *U.S. News & World Report.* Vol. 132, No. 7 (March 11): 36–40.

Law Center to Prevent Gun Violence. "Concealed Weapons Permitting Policy." 2014. [Online] Available at http://smartgunlaws .org/concealed-weapons-permitting-policy-summary

Lemert, Edwin M. 1951. *Social Pathology.* New York: McGraw-Hill.

———. 1972. *Human Deviance, Social Problems, and Social Control,* 2nd ed. Englewood Cliffs, N.J.: Prentice Hall.

Lemonick, Michael D. 2003. "The Search for a Murder Gene." *Time.* Vol. 164, No. 3 (January 20): 100.

Liptak, Adam. "More Than 1 in 100 Adults Are Now in Prison in U.S." *New York Times* (February 28, 2008): A14.

Little, Craig, and Andrea Rankin. 2001. "Why Do They Start It? Explaining Reported Early-Teen Sexual Activity." *Sociological Forum.* Vol. 16, No. 4 (December): 703–29.

Lombroso, Cesare. 1911 (orig. 1876). *Crime: Its Causes and Remedies,* trans. H. P. Horton. Boston: Little, Brown.

Lott, John R., Jr. 2000. *More Guns, Less Crime: Understanding Crime and Gun Control Laws,* 2nd ed. Chicago: University of Chicago Press.

Lowney, Kathleen S., and Joel Best. 1995. "Stalking Strangers and Lovers: Changing Media Typifications of a New Crime Problem." In Joel Best, ed., *Images of Issues: Typifying Contemporary Social Problems,* 2nd ed. (pp. 33–57). Hawthore, N.Y.: Aldine de Gruyter.

Martin, Joyce A., Brady E. Hamilton, Michelle J. K. Osterman, Sally C. Curtin, and T. J. Mathews. "Births: Final Data for 2012." *National Vital Statistics Reports,* Vol. 62, No 9. 2013. [Online] Available at http://www.cdc.gov/nchs/data/nvsr/nvsr62 /nvsr62_09.pdf

Mauer, Marc. 1999. *The Crisis of the Young African American Male and the Criminal Justice System.* Report prepared for U.S. Commission on Civil Rights, Washington, D.C., April 15–16. [Online] Available January 8, 2007, at http://www.sentencingproject.org/Admin /Documents/publications/rd_crisisoftheyoung.pdf

Merton, Robert K. 1938. "Social Structure and Anomie." *American Sociological Review.* Vol. 3, No. 6 (October): 672–82.

———. 1968. *Social Theory and Social Structure.* New York: Free Press.

Miller, William J., and Rick A. Matthews. 2001. "Youth Employment, Differential Association, and Juvenile Delinquency." *Sociological Focus.* Vol. 34, No. 3 (August): 251–68.

National Conference of State Legislatures. "Stateline." January 2011. [Online] Available at http://www.ncsl.org/magazine /stateline-january-2011.aspx

National Conference of State Legislatures. "State Medical Marijuana Laws." 2014. [Online] Available at http://www.ncsl. org/research/health/state-medical-marijuana-laws.aspx

Padgett, Tim. "Day of the Dead." *Time.* Online edition. June 30, 2011. [Online] Available at http://www.time.com/time/world /article/0,8599,2080608,00.html

Palazzolo, Joe, and Ashby Jones. "Sentenced to Treatment, Instead of Prison." *Wall Street Journal.* (August 17–18, 2013): A3.

Parler, Karen F., and Matthew V. Pruitt. 2000. "Poverty, Poverty Concentration, and Homicide." *Social Science Quarterly.* Vol. 81, No. 2 (June): 555–70.

Petersilia, Joan. 1997. "Probation in the United States: Practices and Challenges." *National Institute of Justice Journal.* No. 233 (September): 4.

Pew Research Center for the People & the Press. "Public's Policy Priorities: 1994–2013." 2013. [Online] Available at http: //www.people-press.org/2013/01/24/deficit-reduction-rises-on -publics-agenda-for-obamas-second-term

PINKER, STEVEN. 2003. "Are Your Genes to Blame?" *Time.* Vol. 164, No. 3 (January 20): 98–100.

PIQUERO, ALEX R., JOHN M. MACDONALD, and KAREN F. PARKER. 2002. "Race, Local Life Circumstances, and Criminal Activity." *Social Science Quarterly.* Vol. 83, No. 3 (September): 654–70.

PITTMAN, DAVID. 2001. "Memories of Rape." [Online] Available April 13, 2001, at http://www.1gc.apc.org/spr

POZIOS, VASILIS K., PRAVEEN R. KAMBAM, and H. ERIC BENDER. "Does Media Violence Lead to the Real Thing?" *The New York Times.* August 23, 2013. [Online] Available at http://www.nytimes .com/2013/08/25/opinion/sunday/does-media-violence-lead-to -the-real-thing.html

RAINE, ADRIAN. "The Criminal Mind." *Wall Street Journal.* April 26, 2013. [Online] Available at http://online.wsj.com/news/articles /SB10001424127887323335404578444682892520530

RECKLESS, WALTER C. 1973. *The Crime Problem.* New York: Appleton-Century-Crofts.

RECKLESS, WALTER C., and SIMON DINITZ. 1972. *The Prevention of Juvenile Delinquency.* Columbus: Ohio State University Press.

RECKLESS, WALTER C., SIMON DINITZ, and E. MURRAY. 1956. "Self Concept as an Insulator against Delinquency." *American Sociological Review.* Vol. 21, No. 5 (October): 744–56.

———. 1957. "The 'Good Boy' in a High-Delinquency Area." *Journal of Criminal Law, Criminology, and Police Science.* Vol. 48, No. 1 (June-July): 18–25.

REIMAN, JEFFREY. 1998. *The Rich Get Richer and the Poor Get Prison: Ideology, Class, and Criminal Justice.* Boston: Allyn & Bacon.

RIDEOUT, VICTORIA. "Parents, Children & Media, a Kaiser Family Foundation Survey." June 2007. [Online] Available at http://www .kff.org/entmedia/upload/7638.pdf

RIDEOUT, VICTORIA J., ULLA G. FOEHR, and DONALD F. ROBERTS. "Generation M2: Media in the Lives of 8- to 18-Year-Olds." *Kaiser Family Foundation.* January 2010. [Online] Available at http://www .kff.org/entmedia/ 8010.cfm

RITTER, MALCOLM. 2003. "Children-TV Violence Link Has Effect." *Yahoo News.* [Online] Available March 9, 2003, at http://www .yahoonews.com

ROBERTSON, LINDSAY A., HELENA M. MCANALLY, and ROBERT K. HANCOX. "Childhood and Adolescent Television Viewing and Antisocial Behavior in Early Adulthood." *Pediatrics.* 2013. [Online] Available at http://pediatrics.aappublications.org/content /early/2013/02/13/peds.2012-1582

SARCHE, JON. 2006. "Colorado Man Says He Committed 48 Murders." *Yahoo News.* [Online] Available July 28, 2006, at http://news.yahoo .com

SAVAGE, CHARLIE. "Trend to Lighten Harsh Sentences Catches On in Conservative States." *New York Times.* August 12, 2011. [Online] Available at http://www.nytimes.com/2011/08/13/us/13penal .html?_r1

SHELDON, WILLIAM H., EMIL M. HARTL, and EUGENE MCDERMOTT. 1949. *Varieties of Delinquent Youth.* New York: Harper.

SIMPSON, SALLY S. 1989. "Feminist Theory, Crime, and Justice." *Criminology.* Vol. 27 (November): 605–31.

SMITH, DOUGLAS A. 1987. "Police Response to Interpersonal Violence: Defining the Parameters of Legal Control." *Social Forces.* Vol. 65, No. 3 (March): 767–82.

SMITH, DOUGLAS A., and CHRISTY A. VISHER. 1981. "Street-Level Justice: Situational Determinants of Police Arrest Decisions." *Social Problems.* Vol. 29, No. 2 (December): 167–77.

SMITH, TOM W., PETER MARSDEN, MICHAEL HOUT, and JIBUM KIM. "General Social Surveys, 1972–2012." National Opinion Research Center; The Roper Center for Public Opinion Research, University of Connecticut; Computer-assisted Survey Methods Program, University of California. June 2013. [Online] Available at http://www.norc.org/GSS+Website

STATISTICS CANADA. "Homicide in Canada, 2012." 2013. [Online] Available at http://www.statcan.gc.ca/pub/85-002-x/2013001 /article/11882-eng.htm?fpv=2693

SULLIVAN, ANDREW. 2002. Lecture given at Kenyon College.

SUTHERLAND, EDWIN H. 1940. "White Collar Criminality." *American Sociological Review.* Vol. 5, No. 1 (February): 1–12.

TAYLOR, LAWRENCE. 1984. *Born to Crime: The Genetic Causes of Criminal Behavior.* Westport, Conn.: Greenwood.

THORNBERRY, TERRANCE, and MARGARET FARNSWORTH. 1982. "Social Correlates of Criminal Involvement: Further Evidence on the Relationship between Social Status and Criminal Behavior." *American Sociological Review.* Vol. 47, No. 4 (August): 505–18.

TJADEN, PATRICIA. 1997. "The Crime of Stalking: How Big Is the Problem?" *National Institute of Justice Research Preview.* Washington, D.C.: U.S. Department of Justice.

TJADEN, PATRICIA, and NANCY THOENNES. 1998. *Stalking in America: Findings from the National Violence against Women Survey.* Washington, D.C.: U.S. Department of Justice.

U.S. DEPARTMENT OF HEALTH and HUMAN SERVICES, ADMINISTRATION ON CHILDREN, YOUTH and FAMILIES. "Child Maltreatment 2012." 2013. [Online] Available at http: //www.acf.hhs.gov/programs/cb/resource/child-maltreatment- 2012

U.S. DEPARTMENT OF JUSTICE, BUREAU OF JUSTICE STATISTICS. "Capital Punishment." 2013. [Online] Available at http://www.bjs.gov /index.cfm?ty=pbdetail&iid=2079

U.S. DEPARTMENT OF JUSTICE, BUREAU OF JUSTICE STATISTICS. "Criminal Victimization." 2014. [Online] Available at http://www .bjs.gov/index.cfm?ty=dcdetail&iid=245#

U.S. DEPARTMENT OF JUSTICE, BUREAU OF JUSTICE STATISTICS. "Federal Criminal Case Processing Statistics." 2014. [Online] Available at http://www.bjs.gov/fjsrc

U.S. DEPARTMENT OF JUSTICE, BUREAU OF JUSTICE STATISTICS. "Federal Justice Statistics Resource Center." 2014. [Online] Available at http://bjs.ojp.usdoj.gov/fjsrc/index.cfm

U.S. DEPARTMENT OF JUSTICE, BUREAU OF JUSTICE STATISTICS. "Stalking Victims in the United States—Revised." 2012. [Online] Available at http://www.bjs.gov/index.cfm?ty=pbdetail&iid =1211

U.S. DEPARTMENT OF JUSTICE, FEDERAL BUREAU OF INVESTIGATION. "Crime in the United States 2012." 2013. [Online] Available at http://www.fbi.gov/about-us/cjis/ucr/crime-in-the-u.s/2012 /crime-in-the-u.s.-2012/tables

U.S. DEPARTMENT OF JUSTICE, FEDERAL BUREAU OF INVESTIGATION. "Hate Crime Statistics 2012." 2013. [Online] Available at http://www.fbi.gov/about-us/cjis/ucr/hate-crime/2012

U.S. DEPARTMENT OF JUSTICE, OFFICE OF JUVENILE JUSTICE and DELINQUENCY PREVENTION. "Highlights of the 2011 National Youth Gang Survey." 2013. [Online] Available at http://www.ojjdp.gov /pubs/242884.pdf

U.S. OFFICE OF NATIONAL DRUG CONTROL POLICY. "Arrestee Drug Abuse Monitoring Program (ADAM II)." 2013. [Online] Available at http://www.whitehouse.gov/sites/default/files/ondcp /policy-and-research/adam_ii_2012_annual_rpt_web.pdf

VERA INSTITUTE OF JUSTICE. "The Price of Prisons: What Incarceration Costs Taxpayers." 2012. [Online] Available at http://www.vera .org/project/price-prisons

VITO, GENNARO F., and RONALD M. HOLMES. 1994. *Criminology: Theory, Research, and Policy.* Belmont, Calif.: Wadsworth.

WARF, BARNEY, and CYNTHIA WADDELL. 2002. "Heinous Spaces, Perfidious Places: The Sinister Landscapes of Serial Killers." *Social and Cultural Geography.* Vol. 3, No. 3 (September): 323–46.

WILLIAMS, JUAN. "Race and the Gun Debate." *Wall Street Journal.* (March 27, 2013): A17.

WOLFGANG, MARVIN E., TERRENCE P. THORNBERRY, and ROBERT M. FIGLIO. 1987. *From Boy to Man, from Delinquency to Crime.* Chicago: University of Chicago Press.

ZIMRING, FRANKLIN E. 1998. *American Youth Violence.* New York: Oxford University Press.

Chapter 7

ALAN GUTTMACHER INSTITUTE. "Induced Abortion in the United States." 2013. [Online] Available at http://www.guttmacher.org /pubs/fb_induced_abortion.html

ALAN GUTTMACHER INSTITUTE. "State Policies in Brief: An Overview of Abortion Laws." February 1, 2012. [Online] Available at http://www.guttmacher.org/statecenter/spibs/spib_OAL.pdf

ALAN GUTTMACHER INSTITUTE. "State Policies in Brief: An Overview of Abortion Laws." 2014. [Online] Available at http://www .guttmacher.org/statecenter/spibs/spib_OAL.pdf

ATTORNEY GENERAL'S COMMISSION ON PORNOGRAPHY (MEESE COMMISSION). 1986. *Final Report.* Washington, D.C.: U.S. Department of Justice.

BEARMAN, PETER S., and HANNAH BRÜCKNER. 2002. "Opposite-Sex Twins and Adolescent Same-Sex Attraction." *American Journal of Sociology.* Vol. 107, No. 5 (March): 1179–1205.

BEARMAN, PETER S., JAMES MOODY, and KATHERINE STOVEL. "Chains of Affection." *American Journal of Sociology.* Vol. 110, No. 1 (July 2004): 44–91.

BLACKWOOD, EVELYN, and SASKIA WIERINGA, eds. 1999. *Female Desires: Same-Sex Relations and Transgender Practices across Cultures.* New York: Columbia University Press.

BLUE, LAURA. New Insight into the (Epi)Genetic Roots of Homosexuality." *Time.* December 1, 2012. [Online] Available at http://healthland.time.com/2012/12/13/new-insight-into-the -epigenetic-roots-of-homosexuality

BOYER, DEBRA. 1989. "Male Prostitution and Homosexual Identity." *Journal of Homosexuality.* Vol. 17, Nos. 1–2 (January–February): 151–84.

CDC (Centers for Disease Control and Prevention). "HIV/AIDS Surveillance Report, 2011." Vol. 23. 2013. [Online] Available at http://www.cdc.gov/hiv/library/reports/surveillance/index.html

CDC (Centers for Disease Control and Prevention). "National Survey of Family Growth (NSFG)." Accessed January 2014. [Online] Available at http://www.cdc.gov/nchs/nsfg.htm

CDC (Centers for Disease Control and Prevention). "Sexually Transmitted Diseases." Accessed January 2014. [Online] Available at http://www.cdc.gov/std/stats/default.htm

CDC (Centers for Disease Control and Prevention). "Youth Risk Behavior Survey—Youth Online." Accessed January 2014. [Online] Available at http://nccd.cdc.gov/YouthOnline/App/Default.aspx

CDC (Centers for Disease Control and Prevention). "Youth Risk Behavior Survey 2009." *Morbidity and Mortality Weekly Report,* Vol. 59, No. SS-5 (June 2010). [Online] Available at http://www.cdc .gov/HealthyYouth/yrbs/index.htm

CHAPMAN, STEVE. "Is Pornography a Catalyst of Sexual Violence?" reason.com. November 5, 2007. [Online] Available at http://reason .com/archives/2007/11/05/is-pornography-a-catalyst-of-s

CHAUNCEY, GEORGE. 1994. *Gay New York: Gender, Urban Culture, and the Making of the Gay Male World, 1890–1940.* New York: Basic Books.

COYOTE (CALL OFF YOUR OLD TIRED ETHICS). 2012. [Online] Available February 23, 2012, at http://www.coyotela.org /what_is.html

DAVIS, KINGSLEY. 1971. "Sexual Behavior." In Robert K. Merton and Robert Nisbet, eds., *Contemporary Social Problems,* 3rd ed. (pp. 313–60). New York: Harcourt Brace Jovanovich.

DWORKIN, ANDREA. 1987. *Intercourse.* New York: Free Press.

———. 1991. "Against the Male Flood: Censorship, Pornography, and Equality." In Robert M. Baird and Stuart E. Rosenbaum, eds., *Pornography: Private Right or Public Menace?* (pp. 56–61). Buffalo, N.Y.: Prometheus.

ESTES, RICHARD J. 2001. "The Commercial Sexual Exploitation of Children in the U.S., Canada, and Mexico." Reported in "Study Explores Sexual Exploitation." *Yahoo News.* [Online] Available September 10, 2001, at http://dailynews.yahoo.com

FOUCAULT, MICHEL. 1990. *A History of Sexuality, Part 1.* New York: Vintage Books.

FREEDOM TO MARRY. "The Freedom to Marry Internationally." 2014. [Online] Available at http://www.freedomtomarry.org/landscape /entry/c/international

GALLUP. "2011 Values and Beliefs Poll." May 2011. [Online] Available at http://www.gallup.com/poll/147842/Doctor-Assisted-Suicide -Moral-Issue-Dividing-Americans.aspx

GATES, GARY. "How Many People Are Lesbian, Gay, Bisexual, and Transgender?" The Williams Institute. April 2011. [Online] Available at http://williamsinstitute.law.ucla.edu/wp-content /uploads/Gates-How-Many-People-LGBT-Apr-2011.pdf

GAVE, ELENI N. 2005. "In the Indigenous Muxe Culture of Mexico's Oaxaca State, Alternative Notions of Sexuality Are Not Only Accepted, They're Celebrated." *Travel and Leisure* (November). [Online] Available June 15, 2009, at http://travelandleisure.com /articles/stepping-out/page/2/print

GRADY, DENISE. 1992. "The Brains of Gay Men." *Discover.* Vol. 13, No. 1 (January): 29.

HAMER, DEAN, and PETER COPELAND. 1994. *The Search for the Gay Gene and the Biology of Behavior.* New York: Simon & Schuster.

HERDT, GILBERT H. 1993. "Semen Transactions in Sambian Culture." In David N. Suggs and Andrew W. Miracle, eds., *Culture and Human Sexuality* (pp. 298–327). Pacific Grove, Calif.: Brooks/Cole.

HEREK, GREGORY M. 1991. "Myths about Sexual Orientation: A Lawyer's Guide to Social Science Research." *Law and Sexuality.* Vol. 1: 133–72.

HERMAN, DIANNE F. 2001. "The Rape Culture." In John J. Macionis and Nijole V. Benokraitis, eds., *Seeing Ourselves: Classic, Contemporary, and Cross-Cultural Readings in Sociology,* 5th ed. (pp. 38–46). Upper Saddle River, N.J.: Prentice Hall.

ICE. "Fact Sheet: Operation Predator—Targeting Child Exploitation and Sexual Crimes." June 25, 2012. [Online] Available at http://www.ice.gov/news/library/factsheets/predator.htm

KINSEY, ALFRED, WARDELL BAXTER POMEROY, and CLYDE E. MARTIN. 1948. Sexual Behavior in the Human Male. Philadelphia: Saunders.

KINSEY, ALFRED, WARDELL BAXTER POMEROY, CLYDE E. MARTIN, and PAUL H. GEBHARD. 1953. *Sexual Behavior in the Human Female.* Philadelphia: Saunders.

KOTZ, DEBORAH. 2008. "Sex, Health, and Happiness." *U.S. News & World Report* (September 15): 50–53.

LACEY, MARC. 2008. "A Distinct Lifestyle: The Muxe of Mexico." *New York Times* (December 7): 4.

LAUMANN, EDWARD O., JOHN H. GAGNON, ROBERT T. MICHAELS, and STUART MICHAELS. 1994. *The Social Organization of Sexuality: Sexual Practices in the United States.* Chicago: University of Chicago Press.

Lee, Deborah. 2000. "Hegemonic Masculinity and Male Feminisation: The Sexual Harassment of Men at Work." *Journal of Gender Studies*. Vol. 9, No. 2 (July): 141–55.

LeVay, Simon. 1993. *The Sexual Brain*. Cambridge, Mass.: MIT Press.

Luker, Kristen. 1984. *Abortion and the Politics of Motherhood*. Berkeley: University of California Press.

MacKinnon, Catharine A. 2001. "Pornography: Not a Moral Issue." In John J. Macionis and Nijole V. Benokraitis, eds., *Seeing Ourselves: Classic, Contemporary, and Cross-Cultural Readings in Sociology*, 5th ed. (pp. 294–301). Upper Saddle River, N.J.: Prentice Hall.

Millet, Kate. 1970. *Sexual Politics*. Garden City, N.Y.: Doubleday.

Monto, Martin. 2001. "Prostitution and Fellatio." *Journal of Sex Research*. Vol. 38, No. 2 (May): 140–46.

National Bureau of Economic Research. Data presented in *The Economist*. "Tuned In, Turned Off." January 14, 2014. [Online] Available at http://www.economist.com/news/united -states/21594324-watching-reality-tv-may-deter-teens-becoming -moms-tuned-turned

National Campaign to Prevent Teen and Unplanned Pregnancy. "By the Numbers: The Public Costs of Teen Childbearing." June 2011. [Online] Available at http://www. thenationalcampaign.org/costs/default.aspx

National Coalition of Anti-Violence Programs. "Hate Violence Against Lesbian, Gay, Bisexual, Transgender, Queer and HIV-Affected Communities in the United States in 2012." 2013. [Online] Available at http://www.avp.org/resources/avp-resources/248

National Conference of State Legislatures. "Defining Marriage: State Defense of Marriage Laws and Same-Sex Marriage." 2014. [Online] Available at http://www.ncsl.org/research/human -services/same-sex-marriage-overview.aspx

Pew Research Center. "Support for Same-Sex Marriage Edges Upward." 2010. [Online] Available at http://www.people-press. org/2010/10/06/support-for-same-sex-marriage-edges-upward

Pew Research Center. "Widening Regional Divide Over Abortion Laws." July 29, 2013. [Online] Available at http://www.people -press.org/2013/07/29/widening-regional-divide-over-abortion -laws

Pew Research Center, Forum on Religion and Public Life. "Gay Marriage Around the World." 2014. [Online] Available at http://www.pewforum.org/2013/12/19/gay-marriage-around -the-world-2013

Pew Research Center, Religion & Public Life Project. "Public Opinion on Abortion, 1995–2013." 2013. [Online] Available at http://www.pewforum.org/2013/01/16/public-opinion-on -abortion-slideshow

Population Reference Bureau. "Datafinder." 2011. [Online] Available at http://www.prb.org/DataFinder.aspx

Rankin, Susan R. "Campus Climate for Gay, Lesbian, Bisexual, and Transgender People: A National Perspective." The National Gay and Lesbian Task Force Policy Institute, 2003. [Online] Available at http://thetaskforce.org/reports_and_research/campus_climate

Renton, Alex. "Learning the Thai Sex Trade." *Prospect*. Issue 110 (May 21, 2005). [Online] Available at http://www .prospectmagazine.co.uk/2005/05/learningthethaisextrade

Rice, W. R., U. Friberg, and S. Gavrilets. 2012. "Homosexuality as a Consequence of Epigenetically Canalized Sexual Development." *Quarterly Review of Biology*, Vol. 87: 343–68.

Ritter, Karl. 2008. "World Takes Notice of Swedish Prostitute Laws." Independent (March 17). [Online] Available April 24, 2009, at http://www.independent.co.uk/news/world/europe/world -takes-notice-of-swedish-prostitute-laws-796793.html

Rosenberg, Mica. 2008. "Mexican Transvestite Fiesta Rocks Indigenous Town." Reuters (November 23). [Online] Available June 15, 2009, at http://www.reuters.com/article/lifestyleMolt /idUSTRE4AM1PB20081123

Schmalz, J. 1993. "Poll Finds an Even Split on Homosexuality's Cause." *New York Times* (March 5): A14.

Smith, Tom W., Peter Marsden, Michael Hout, and Jibum Kim. "General Social Surveys, 1972–2012." National Opinion Research Center; The Roper Center for Public Opinion Research, University of Connecticut; Computer-assisted Survey Methods Program, University of California. June 2013. [Online] Available at http://www.norc.org/GSS+Website

Sommers, Christina Hoff. 2003. Lecture at Kenyon College (April 7).

Strong, Bryan, and Christine DeVault. 1994. *Human Sexuality*. Mountain View, Calif.: Mayfield.

Sullivan, Andrew. 2002. Lecture given at Kenyon College.

Tannahill, Reay. 1992. *Sex in History*. Chelsea, Mich.: Scarborough House.

Thomas, Evan. 2003. "The War over Gay Marriage." *Newsweek* (July 7): 38–44.

Thompson, William E., and Jackie L. Harrod. 1999. "Topless Dancers: Managing Stigma in a Deviant Occupation." In Henry N. Pontell, ed., *Social Deviance: Readings in Theory and Research*, 3rd ed. (pp. 277–87). Upper Saddle River, N.J.: Prentice Hall.

UNAIDS. "2010 Report on the Global AIDS Epidemic." 2011. [Online] Available at http://www.unaids.org/globalreport

UNAIDS Global Report, 2013. 2013. [Online] Available at http://www.unaids.org/en/media/unaids/contentassets /documents/epidemiology/2013/gr2013/UNAIDS_Global_ Report_2013_en.pdf

UNICEF. 2006. Violence against Children in the Community. New York: United Nations. [Online] Available April 28, 2009, at http://www.unicef.org/media/media_45451.html

U.S. Department of Justice, Child Exploitation and Obscenity Section. 2012. [Online] Available at http://www.justice.gov /criminal/ceos/sextour.html

U.S. Department of Justice, Federal Bureau of Investigation. "Crime in the United States 2012." 2013. [Online] Available at http://www.fbi.gov/about-us/cjis/ucr/crime-in-the-u.s/2012 /crime-in-the-u.s.-2012/tables

U.S. Department of Justice, Federal Bureau of Investigation. "Hate Crime Statistics 2012." 2013. [Online] Available at http://www.fbi.gov/about-us/cjis/ucr/hate-crime/2012

U.S. Equal Employment Opportunity Commission. 2006. "Sexual Harassment Charges." [Online] Available January 8, 2007, at http://www.eeoc.gov/stats/harass.html

U.S. Equal Employment Opportunity Commission. "Sexual Harassment." 2014. [Online] Available at http://www.eeoc.gov /eeoc/statistics/enforcement/sexual_harassment.cfm

Ventura, Stephanie J., Sally C. Curtin, Joyce C. Abma, and Stanley K. Henshaw. "Estimated Pregnancy Rates and Rate of Pregnancy Outcomes for the United States, 1990–2008." *National Vital Statistics Reports*, Vol. 60, No. 7. 2012. [Online] Available at http://www.cdc.gov/nchs/data/nvsr/nvsr60 /nvsr60_07.pdf

Waite, Linda, Edward O. Laumann, Aniruddha Das, and L. Philip Schumm. "Sexuality: Measures of Partnerships, Practices, Attitudes, and Problems in the National Social Life, Health, and Aging Study." *The Journals of Gerentology: Social Sciences*. Vol. 64, No. 1 (2009): 56–66.

WILLIAMSON, CELIA, and TERRY CLUSE-TOLAR. 2002. "Pimp-Controlled Prostitution: Still an Integral Part of Street Life." *Violence against Women*. Vol. 8, No. 9 (September): 1074–93.

WOMEN'S JUSTICE CENTER. 2009. "Sweden's Prostitution Solution: Why Hasn't Anyone Tried This Before?" [Online] Available April 23, 2009, at http://www.justicewomen

ZOGBY INTERNATIONAL. 2001. Poll reported in Sandra Yin, "Race and Politics." *American Demographics*. Vol. 23, No. 8 (August): 11–13.

Chapter 8

ABADINSKY, HOWARD. 1989. *Drug Abuse: An Introduction*. Chicago: Nelson Hall.

ALTER, JONATHAN. 2001. "The War on Addiction." *Newsweek* (February 12): 36–39.

BADENHAUSEN, KURT. "A-Rod Vs. Lance Armstrong In the Court of Public Opinion." *Forbes*. November 21, 2013. [Online] Available at http://www.forbes.com/sites/kurtbadenhausen/2013/11/21/a-rod-vs-lance-armstrong-in-the-court-of-public-opinion

BAUM, ALICE S., and DONALD W. BURNES. 1993. *A Nation in Denial: The Truth about Homelessness*. Boulder, Colo.: Westview Press.

BECKER, HOWARD S. 1966. *Outside: Studies in the Sociology of Deviance*. New York: Free Press.

BEGLEY, SHARON. 2001. "How It All Starts inside Your Brain." *Newsweek* (February 12): 40–42.

BERKOWITZ, JUSTIN. "Rolling Stoned." *Car and Driver*. Vol. 59, No. 9 (March 2014): 28.

BERTRAM, EVA, MORRIS BLACHMAN, KENNETH SHARPE, and PETER ANDREAS. 1996. *Drug War Politics: The Price of Denial*. Berkeley: University of California Press.

BLUMENSON, ERIC D. 1998. "The Drug War's Hidden Economic Agenda: Corrupting Effects of Financing Police Departments by Asset Forfeitures in Drug Cases." *Nation*. Vol. 266 (March 9): 1–12.

BOWERSOX, JOHN A. 1995. "Buprenorphine May Soon Be Heroin Treatment Option." NIDA Notes (January–February). [Online] Available May 3, 1999, at http://www.nih.gov/NIDANotes/NNVol10N1/Bupren.html

BROOKS, DAVID. "Weed: Been There. Done That." *New York Times*. January 2, 2014. [Online] Available at http://www.nytimes.com/2014/01/03/opinion/brooks-weed-been-there-done-that.html

BRUPPACHER, BALZ. 2008. "Swiss Approve Pioneering Legal Heroin Program." [Online] Available November 30, 2008, at http://news.yahoo.com/s/ap/20081130/ap_on_re_eu/eu_switzerland_heroin_vote

CAVE, DAMIEN. "Mexico Seizes Record Amount of Methamphetamine." *New York Times*. February 9, 2012. Available at: http://www.nytimes.com/2012/02/10/world/americas/mexico-15-tons-of-methamphetamine.html

CDC (Centers for Disease Control and Prevention). "Alcohol and Public Health." 2013. [Online] Available at http://www.cdc.gov/alcohol/fact-sheets/mens-health.htm

CDC (Centers for Disease Control and Prevention). "Behavior Risk Surveillance System Survey Data." 2014. [Online] Available at http://apps.nccd.cdc.gov/brfss

CDC (Centers for Disease Control and Prevention). "CDC WONDER Online Database." 2012, 2014. [Online] Available at http://wonder.cdc.gov/mcd-icd10.html

CDC (Centers for Disease Control and Prevention). "Fetal Alcohol Spectrum Disorders (FASDs): Data and Statistics." 2014. [Online] Available at http://www.cdc.gov/NCBDDD/fasd/data.html

CDC (Centers for Disease Control and Prevention). "State Tobacco Activities Tracking and Evaluation (STATE) System." 2012. [Online] Available at http://apps.nccd.cdc.gov/statesystem

CLOUD, JOHN. 1998. "Harassed or Hazed? Why the Supreme Court Ruled That Men Can Sue Men for Sex Harassment." *Time*. Vol. 151, No. 10 (March 16): 55.

COMMON SENSE FOR DRUG POLICY. 1999. "Drug War Facts: The Netherlands and the United States." [Online] Available May 10, 1999, at http://www.csdp.org/factbook/thenethe.htm

COTTOM, TRESSIE MCMILLAN. "What Legalizing Recreational Marijuana Could Mean For Minorities." *Here & Now*. National Public Radio. January 16, 2014. [Online] Available at http://hereandnow.wbur.org/2014/01/16/legalizing-recreational-marijuana

COWLEY, GEOFFREY. 2001. "New Ways to Stay Clean." Newsweek (February 12): 44–47.

CRATTY, CAROL. "New Rules Slashing Crack Cocaine Sentences Go into Effect." *CNN*. November 2, 2011. [Online] Available at http://www.cnn.com/2011/11/01/justice/crack-cocaine-sentencing

DEGENHARDT, LOUISA, and WAYNE HALL. 2012. "Extent of Illicit Drug Use and Dependence, and Their Contribution to the Global Burden of Disease." *The Lancet*. Vol. 379, No. 9810 (January): 55–70.

DILLON, LIAM, AND IAN LOVETT. "Tunnel for Smuggling Found Under the U.S.-Mexico Border; Tons of Drugs Seized." *The New York Times*. December 31, 2013. [Online] Available at http://www.nytimes.com/2013/11/01/us/tunnel-for-smuggling-found-under-border-tons-of-drugs-seized.html

ELDREDGE, DIRK CHASE. 1998. *Ending the War on Drugs: A Solution for America*. Lanham, Md.: National Book Network.

GALLUP. "Illegal Drugs." 2013. [Online] Available at http://www.gallup.com/poll/1657/Illegal-Drugs.aspx

GELLES, RICHARD J. 1997. *Intimate Violence in Families*, 3rd ed. Thousand Oaks, Calif.: Sage.

GELLES, RICHARD J., and MURRAY A. STRAUS. 1988. *Intimate Violence: The Causes and Consequences of Abuse in the American Family*. New York: Touchstone.

GOLDSTEIN, AVRAM. 1994. *Addiction: From Biology to Drug Policy*. New York: Freeman.

GOMBY, DEANNA S., and PATRICIA H. SHIONO. 1991. "Estimating the Number of Substance-Exposed Infants." *Future of Children*. Vol. 1, No. 1 (Spring): 17–25.

GÓMEZ, LAURA E. 1997. *Misconceiving Mothers: Legislators, Prosecutors, and the Politics of Prenatal Drug Exposure*. Philadelphia: Temple University Press.

GOODE, ERICH. 1993. *Drugs in American Society*, 4th ed. New York: McGraw-Hill.

GRAY, ELIZA. 2014. "Heroin's Resurgence." *Time*. Vol. 183, No. 6 (February 17): 14.

HANANEL, SAM. 2006. "Meth Still No. 1 Drug Problem, Study Finds." *Yahoo News*. [Online]. Available July 18, 2006, at http://news.yahoo.com

HARRIS, GARDINER. 2012. "F.D.A. Finds Short Supply of Attention Deficit Drugs." *The New York Times*. January 1. [Online] Available at http://www.nytimes.com/2012/01/01/health/policy/fda-is-finding-attention-drugs-in-short-supply.html

HENDERSON, DAMIEN. 2003. "Cannabis Cafés Face Ban on Smoking." *Glasgow Herald* (May 29). [Online]. Available September 4, 2003, at http://www.theherald.co.uk

HINGSON, RALPH, TIMOTHY HEEREN, MICHAEL WINTER, and HENRY WECHSLER. 2005. "Magnitude of Alcohol-Related Mortality and Morbidity among U.S. College Students Ages 18–24: Changes from 1998 to 2001." [Online] Available May 5, 2009, at http://www.collegedrinkingprevention.gov/NIAAACollegeMaterials/magandprev.aspx

HINGSON, RALPH W. "Magnitude and Prevention of College Drinking and Related Problems." *NIAA Alcohol Research & Health*. Vol. 33, Nos. 1 & 2. 2010. [Online] Available at http://pubs.niaaa.nih.gov/publications/arh40/toc33-1_2.htm

HOGE, WARREN. 2002. "Britain to Stop Arresting Most Private Users of Marijuana." *New York Times* (July 11). [Online]. Available September 4, 2003, at http://www.researchnavigator.com

HUBER, CHRISTIAN. 1994. "Needle Park: What Can We Learn from the Zurich Experience?" *Addiction*. Vol. 89, No. 5 (May): 413–517.

HUNT, GEOFFREY, and ANNA XIAO DONG SUN. 1998. "The Drug Treatment System in the United States: A Panacea for the Drug War?" In Harold Klingemann and Geoffrey Hunt, eds., *Drug Treatment Systems in an International Perspective: Drugs, Demons, and Delinquents* (pp. 3–19). Thousand Oaks, Calif.: Sage.

INCIARDI, JAMES A., ed. 1996. *Drug Control and the Courts*. Thousand Oaks, Calif.: Sage.

JOHNSTON, LLOYD D., PATRICK M. O'MALLEY, JERALD G. BACHMAN, and JOHN E. SCHULENBERG. "Monitoring the Future Study." Ann Arbor: Institute for Social Research, The University of Michigan. 2013. [Online] Available at http://www.monitoringthefuture.org/index.html

KIRN, WALTER. 1998. "Crank." *Time*. Vol. 153, No. 24 (June 22): 25–32.

LASSETER, TOM. 2009. "U.N.: Afghan Opium Is Top Killer, Finances Taliban Violence." *McClatchy*. October 21. Available at http://www.mcclatchydc.com/2009/10/21/77535/killer-crop-afghan-opium-fuels.html

LEGER, DONNA. 2011. "More Teens Using Synthetic Drugs." *USA Today*. (December 15): A1.

LEINWAND, DONNA. 2001. "A Strange New World of Teenage Drug Use." *USA Today* (August 28): 6D, 7D.

LÉONS, MADELINE BARBARA, AND HARRY SANABRIA. 1997. "Coca and Cocaine in Bolivia: Reality and Policy Illusion." In Madeline Barbara Léons and Harry Sanabria, eds., *Coca, Cocaine, and the Bolivian Reality* (pp. 1–46). Albany: State University of New York Press.

MACCOUN, ROBERT J. 2001. "American Distortion of Dutch Drug Statistics." *Society*. Vol. 38, No. 3 (March-April): 23–26.

MANCALL, PETER C. 1995. *Deadly Medicine: Indians and Alcohol in Early America*. Ithaca, N.Y.: Cornell University Press.

MEYER, JOSH. 2009. "Obama Administration Urges Equal Penalties for Crack, Powder Cocaine Dealers." *Los Angeles Times* (April 30). [Online] Available May 3, 2009, at http://www.latimes.com/news/nationworld/nation/la-na-crack30-2009 apr30,0,2194990.story

MILKMAN, HARVEY, and STANLEY SUNDERWIRTH. 1995. "Doorway to Excess." In James A. Inciardi and Karen McElrath, eds., *The American Drug Scene: An Anthology* (pp. 12–22). Los Angeles: Roxbury.

MINISTRY OF HEALTH, WELFARE and SPORT. 1998. "Policy on Soft Drugs and Coffee Shops." *Drug Policy in the Netherlands: Continuity and Change*. [Online] Available May 10, 1999, at http://www.thc.nl/Countries/nl/VWSdrugs.htm

MOHAMED, A. RAFIK, AND ERIK D. FRITSVOLD. 2011. *Dorm Room Dealers: Drugs and the Privileges of Race and Class*. Boulder, Colo.: Rienner.

MUMOLA, CHRISTOPHER, and JENNIFER C. KARBERG. "Drug Use and Dependence, State and Federal Prisoners, 2004." U.S. Department of Justice. October 2006. [Online] Available at http://bjs.ojp.usdoj.gov/content/pub/pdf/dudsfp04.pdf

NADELMANN, ETHAN. 1995. "Switzerland's Heroin Experiment." *National Review*. Vol. 47, No. 13 (July 19): 46–47.

NATIONAL CONFERENCE OF STATE LEGISLATURES. "State Medical Marijuana Laws." 2014. [Online] Available at http://www.ncsl.org/research/health/state-medical-marijuana-laws.aspx

NATIONAL HIGHWAY TRAFFIC SAFETY ADMINISTRATION. "Alcohol-Impaired Driving." 2013. [Online] Available at http://www-nrd.nhtsa.dot.gov/Pubs/811870.pdf

NIGHTENGALE, BOB. 2007. "Some of Sport's Top Stars Implicated." *USA Today* (December 14): 1A.

PADGETT, TIM. 2002. "Taking the Side of the Coca Farmer." *Time*. Vol. 160, No. 6 (August 5): 8.

PADGETT, TIM, and IOAN GRILLO. 2008. "Cocaine Capital." *Time* (August 25): 37–38.

PEW RESEARCH CENTER FOR THE PEOPLE & THE PRESS. "Majority Now Supports Legalizing Marijuana." 2013. [Online] Available at http://www.people-press.org/2013/04/04/majority-now-supports-legalizing-marijuana

PLECK, ELIZABETH. 1987. *Domestic Tyranny: The Making of Social Policy against Family Violence from Colonial Times to the Present*. New York: Oxford University Press.

RAND, MICHAEL, WILLIAM J. SABOL, MICHAEL SINCLAIR, and HOWARD N. SNYDER. "Alcohol and Crime: Data from 2002 to 2008." *U.S. Department of Justice, Bureau of Justice Statistics*. September 3, 2010. [Online] Available at http://bjs.ojp.usdoj.gov/index.cfm?ty_pbdetail&iid_2313

RECER, PAUL. 1999. "Teenage Smoking Harms Lungs Forever, Study Says." *Louisville Courier-Journal* (April 7): A8.

REMNICK, DAVID. "Going the Distance." *New Yorker*. January 27, 2014. [Online] Available at http://www.newyorker.com/reporting/2014/01/27/140127fa_fact_remnick

RICHMAN, JOSH, and THOMAS PEELE. "Attorney General Eric Holder Announces Drug-Sentencing Reform in San Francisco." *San Jose Mercury News*. August 12, 2013. [Online] Available at http://www.mercurynews.com/nation-world/ci_23844818/san-francisco-ag-eric-holder-announces-drug-sentencing

ROOSEVELT, MARGOT. 2001. "The War against the War on Drugs." *Time*. Vol. 157, No. 18 (May 7): 46–47.

ROSENBAUM, DENNIS. "Just Say No to D.A.R.E.," Available February 29, 2012 at http://dare.procon.org

SANDERS, KERRY. "Pot Buyers Add More than $1M to Colorado Tax Coffers." *Today Money*. February 3, 2014. [Online] Available at http://www.today.com/money/pot-buyers-add-more-1m-colorado-tax-coffers-2D12035047

SCHWARZ, ALAN. "Attention Disorder or Not, Pills to Help in School." *New York Times*. October 9, 2012. [Online] Available at http://www.nytimes.com/2012/10/09/health/attention-disorder-or-not-children-prescribed-pills-to-help-in-school.html

SCHWARZ, ALAN. 2013. "Drowned in a Stream of Prescriptions." *New York Times*. February 2. [Online] Available at http://www.nytimes.com/2013/02/03/us/concerns-about-adhd-practices-and-amphetamine-addiction.html

SEELYE, KATHERINE Q. 2014. "A Call to Arms on a Vermont Heroin Epidemic." *New York Times* (February 28): A1–A17.

STANNER, PETER. 2011. "Legal Marijuana Gets One Step Closer." *Copenhagen Post*. November 21. [Online] Available at http://www.cphpost.dk/news/local/legal-marijuana-gets-one-step-closer

TANDY, KAREN P. 2009. "Myth: Legalization of Marijuana in Other Countries Has Been a Success." About.com (March 23). [Online] Available May 3, 2009, at http://alcoholism.about.com/od/pot/a/bldea050426_3.htm

TIERNEY, JOHN. 2009. "Obama's Drug Policy." *New York Times* (May 3). [Online] Available May 3, 2009, at http://tierneylab.blogs.nytimes.com/2009/03/12/obamas-drug-policy

TREBACH, ARNOLD S., and JAMES A. INCIARDI. 1993. *Legalize It? Debating American Drug Policy.* Lanham, Md.: University of America Press.

UNRAU, WILLIAM E. 1996. White Man's Wicked Water: The Alcohol Trade and Prohibition in Indian Country, 1802–1892. Lawrence: University of Kansas Press.

U.S. DEPARTMENT OF HEALTH and HUMAN SERVICES. 2005. *NIDA InfoFacts: Steroids* (Anabolic—Androgenic). Washington, D.C.: National Institute on Alcohol Abuse and Alcoholism.

U.S. DEPARTMENT OF HEALTH and HUMAN SERVICES, NATIONAL INSTITUTES OF HEALTH, NATIONAL INSTITUTE ON DRUG ABUSE. "Drugs of Abuse Information." 2013. [Online] Available at http://www.drugabuse.gov/drugs-abuse

U.S. DEPARTMENT OF HEALTH and HUMAN SERVICES, NATIONAL INSTITUTES OF HEALTH, NATIONAL INSTITUTE ON ALCOHOL ABUSE and ALCOHOLISM. "A Snapshot of Annual High-Risk College Drinking Consequences." 2013. [Online] Available at http://www.collegedrinkingprevention.gov/StatsSummaries/snapshot.aspx

U.S. DEPARTMENT OF HEALTH and HUMAN SERVICES. 2008. "Mental Disorders Cost Society Billions in Unearned Income." Press release (May 7). [Online] Available May 18, 2009, at http://www.nimh.nih.gov/science-news/2008/mental-disorders-cost-societybillions-in-unearned-income.shtml

U.S. DEPARTMENT OF HEALTH and HUMAN SERVICES, NATIONAL INSTITUTES OF HEALTH, NATIONAL INSTITUTE ON DRUG ABUSE. "Drugs of Abuse." 2012. Available at http://www.drugabuse.gov/drugs-abuse

U.S. DEPARTMENT OF HEALTH and HUMAN SERVICES, SUBSTANCE ABUSE and MENTAL HEALTH SERVICES ADMINISTRATION (SAMHSA). "Results from the 2010 National Survey on Drug Use and Health: National Findings." 2011. [Online] Available at http://oas.samhsa.gov/NSDUHlatest.htm

U.S. DEPARTMENT OF HEALTH and HUMAN SERVICES, SUBSTANCE ABUSE and MENTAL HEALTH SERVICES ADMINISTRATION (SAMHSA). "Results from the 2012 National Survey on Drug Use and Health: National Findings." 2013, 2014. [Online] Available at http://www.samhsa.gov/data/NSDUH/2012SummNatFindDet Tables/NationalFindings/NSDUHresults2012.htm#TOC

U.S. DEPARTMENT OF JUSTICE, BUREAU OF JUSTICE STATISTICS. "Drugs and Crime Facts" 2012. [Online] Available at http://www.bjs.gov/content/dcf/duc.cfm

U.S. DEPARTMENT OF JUSTICE, BUREAU OF JUSTICE STATISTICS. "Prisoners in 2012: Trends in Admissions and Releases, 1991–2012." 2013. [Online] Available at http://www.bjs.gov/content/pub/pdf/p12tar9112.pdf

U.S. DEPARTMENT OF JUSTICE. 2000. *Compendium of Federal Justice Statistics, 1998.* Washington, D.C.: U.S. Government Printing Office.

U.S. DEPARTMENT OF JUSTICE, FEDERAL BUREAU OF INVESTIGATION. "Crime in the United States 2010." 2011. [Online] Available at http://www.fbi.gov/about-us/cjis/ucr/crime-in-the-u.s/2010/crime-in-the-u.s.-2010

U.S. DEPARTMENT OF JUSTICE, FEDERAL BUREAU OF INVESTIGATION. "Crime in the United States 2012." 2013. [Online] Available at http://www.fbi.gov/about-us/cjis/ucr/crime-in-the-u.s/2012/crime-in-the-u.s.-2012/tables

U.S. OFFICE OF NATIONAL DRUG CONTROL POLICY (ONDCP). "Research and Data." 2013, 2014. [Online] Available at http://www.whitehouse.gov/ondcp/research-and-data

U.S. OFFICE OF NATIONAL DRUG CONTROL POLICY. "ADAM II 2012 Annual Report." 2013. [Online] Available at http://www.whitehouse.gov/sites/default/files/ondcp/policy-and-research/adam_ii_2012_annual_rpt_web.pdf

VAN DEN HURK, ARIE A. 1999. "Europe: Drugs, Prisons, and Treatment." In THCi: The Netherlands Law.

WADLEY, JARED, and SUSAN BARNES. "American Teens More Cautious about Using Synthetic Drugs." *Michigan News.* December 18, 2013. [Online] Available at http://www.monitoringthefuture.org//pressreleases/13drugpr_complete.pdf

WEIL, ANDREW T., and WINIFRED ROSEN. 1983. *Chocolate to Morphine: Understanding Mind-Active Drugs.* Boston: Houghton Mifflin.

WEISS, ROGER D., MARGARET L. GRIFFIN, and STEVEN M. MIRIN. 1992. "Drug Abuse as Self-Medication for Depression: An Empirical Study." *American Journal of Alcohol Abuse.* Vol. 18, No. 1 (February): 121–29.

WHITE, JASON M. 1991. *Drug Dependence.* Englewood Cliffs, N.J.: Prentice Hall.

WISEMAN, JACQUELINE. 1991. *The Other Half: Wives of Alcoholics and Their Social-Psychological Situation.* New Brunswick: Transaction.

WORLD HEALTH ORGANIZATION. "Tobacco." 2013. [Online] Available at http://www.who.int/mediacentre/factsheets/fs339/en

WORLD HEALTH ORGANIZATION. "WHO Report on the Global Tobacco Epidemic 2013." 2013. [Online] Available at http://www.who.int/tobacco/global_report/2013/en

WREN, CHRISTOPHER S. 1996. "Study Poses a Medical Challenge to Disparity in Cocaine Sentences." *New York Times* (November 20): A1.

ZERNIKE, KATE. 2001. "Antidrug Program Says It Will Adopt a New Program." *New York Times* (February 15): A1, A23.

Chapter 9

AMERICAN ASSOCIATION OF COLLEGES OF NURSING (AACN). "Fact Sheet: Nursing Shortage." 2014. [Online] Available at http://www.aacn.nche.edu/media-relations/fact-sheets/nursing-shortage

AMERICAN COLLEGE HEALTH ASSOCIATION. "National College Health Assessment (ACHA-NCHA-II) Reference Group Data Report." 2013. [Online] Available at http://www.acha-ncha.org/pubs_rpts.html

AMERICAN PSYCHIATRIC ASSOCIATION. 2000. *Diagnostic and Statistical Manual of Mental Disorders,* 4th ed. (DSM-IV-TR). Arlington, Va.: American Psychiatric Association.

AMERICAN PSYCHIATRIC ASSOCIATION. 2013. *Diagnostic and Statistical Manual of Mental Disorders,* 5th ed. Arlington, Va.: American Psychiatric Association.

ANDERSON, ELIJAH. 1994. "The Code of the Streets." *Atlantic Monthly.* Vol. 273 (May): 81–94.

ANDREWS, MICHELLE. 2009. "The State of America's Health." *U.S. News & World Report* (February): 9–12.

BARTLETT, BRUCE. 2000. "Death, Wealth, and Taxes." *Public Interest.* Vol. 141 (Fall): 55–67.

BIRENBAUM, A. 1995. *Putting Health Care on the National Agenda.* Westport, Conn.: Praeger.

BLANK, ROBERT H. 1997. *The Price of Life: The Future of American Health Care.* New York: Columbia University Press.

CDC (CENTERS FOR DISEASE CONTROL AND PREVENTION). "Behavior Risk Surveillance System Survey Data." 2014. [Online] Available at http://apps.nccd.cdc.gov/brfs

CDC (CENTERS FOR DISEASE CONTROL AND PREVENTION). "Diabetes: Data and Trends." 2014. Available at http://www.cdc.gov/diabetes/surveillance/index.htm

CDC (CENTERS FOR DISEASE CONTROL AND PREVENTION). "HIV/AIDS Surveillance Report, 2011." Vol. 23. 2013. [Online] Available at http://www.cdc.gov/hiv/library/reports/surveillance/index.html

CDC (Centers for Disease Control and Prevention). "Mental Illness Surveillance." 2014. [Online] Available at http://www.cdc.gov/features/mentalhealthsurveillance

CDC (Centers for Disease Control and Prevention). "National Hospital Discharge Survey." 2013. [Online] Available at http://www.cdc.gov/nchs/nhds/nhds_tables.htm#number

CDC (Centers for Disease Control and Prevention). "Summary Health Statistics for U. S. Adults: National Health Interview Survey, 2012." 2014. [Online] Available at http://www.cdc.gov/nchs/data/series/sr_10/sr10_260.pdf

Centers for Medicare and Medicaid Services. "National Health Care Expenditure Data." 2014. [Online] Available at http://www.cms.gov/NationalHealthExpendData/01_Overview.asp

Chesler, Phyllis. 1989. *Women and Madness*. New York: Harcourt Brace Jovanovich.

Cockerham, William C. 2005. *Sociology of Mental Disorders*, 7th ed. Upper Saddle River, N.J.: Prentice Hall.

———. 2007. *Medical Sociology*, 10th ed. Upper Saddle River, N.J.: Prentice Hall.

Collins, Patricia Hill. 2009. *Another Kind of Public Education: Race, Schools, the Media, and Democratic Possibilities*. Boston, Mass.: Beacon Press.

Cowley, Geoffrey. 1995. "The Prescription That Kills." *Newsweek* (July 17): 54.

Drake, Bruce. "Views of Health Care Law Among Uninsured Americans Turn More Negative." Pew Research Center. January 30, 2014. [Online] Available at http://www.pewresearch.org/fact-tank/2014/01/30/views-of-health-care-law-among-uninsured-americans-turn-more-negative

Duffy, Tom. 1999. "Campus Crusader: Dartmouth College Nutritionist Gives Students Food for Thought." *People*. Vol. 51, No. 13 (April 12): 71–72.

Eaton, William W., Jr. 1980. "A Formal Theory of Selection for Schizophrenia." *American Journal of Sociology*. Vol. 86, No. 1 (July): 149–58.

Faris, Robert E. L., and H. Warren Dunham. 1939. *Mental Disorders in Urban Areas*. Chicago: University of Chicago Press.

Feagin, Joe R., and Vera Hernán. 1995. *White Racism: The Basics*. New York: Routledge.

Foucault, Michel. 1965. *Madness and Civilization: A History of Insanity in the Age of Reason*. New York: Pantheon.

Fujiura, Glenn T. 2001. "Emerging Trends in Disability." *Population Today*. Vol. 29, No. 6 (August–September): 10–11.

Fuller, Torrey, E. 2013. "Fifty Years of Failing America's Mentally Ill." *Wall Street Journal* (February 5): A15.

Gagné, Patricia. 1998. *Battered Women's Justice: The Movement for Clemency and the Politics of Self-Defense*. New York: Twayne.

Gingrich, Newt. 2009. "The Market Can Fix the Healthcare Problem." *U.S. News & World Report* (January 27): 7.

Gupta, Giri Raj. 1993. *Sociology of Mental Health*. Needham Heights, Mass.: Allyn & Bacon.

Hafner-Eaton, Chris. 1994. "When the Phoenix Rises, Where Will She Go? The Women's Health Agenda." In Pauline Vaillancourt Rosenau, ed., *Health Care Reform in the Nineties* (pp. 236–56). Thousand Oaks, Calif.: Sage.

Heron, Melonie. "Deaths: Leading Causes for 2010." *National Vital Statistics Reports*, Vol. 62, No. 6. 2013. [Online] Available at http://www.cdc.gov/nchs/data/nvsr/nvsr62/nvsr62_06.pdf

Hollingshead, August B., and Frederich C. Redlich. 1958. *Social Class and Mental Illness: A Community Study*. New York: Wiley.

Hoyert, Donna, and Jiaquan Xu. "Deaths: Preliminary Data for 2011." *National Vital Statistics Reports*. Vol. 61, No. 6, 2012. [Online] Available at http://www.cdc.gov/nchs/data/nvsr/nvsr61/nvsr61_06.pdf

Kaiser Family Foundation. "AIDS Drug Assistance Programs (ADAPs)." 2014. [Online] Available at http://kff.org/hivaids/fact-sheet/aids-drug-assistance-programs/

Kaiser Family Foundation. "State Health Facts." 2014. [Online] Available at http://kff.org/statedata

Kaiser Family Foundation. "U.S. Federal Funding for HIV/AIDS: Annual Budget Requests." 2014. [Online] Available at http://www.kff.org/hivaids/7029.cfm

Kaukas, Dick. 1999. "The Poor Struggle for Transplants." *Louisville Courier-Journal* (June 6): A1, A14.

Kelly, Kate. 2001. "Lost on the Campus." *Time*. Vol. 157, No. 2 (January 15): 51–53.

Kesler, Charles R. 2014. "The Tea Party, Conservatism, and the Constitution." *Imprimis*. Vol. 43, No. 1 (January): 1–7.

Kessler, Ronald C., et al. 1994. "Lifetime and 12-Month Prevalence of DSM-III-R Psychiatric Disorders in the United States: Results from the National Comorbidity Survey." *Archives of General Psychiatry*. Vol. 51, No. 1 (January): 8–19.

Lerner, Sharon. 1999. "Insurers Shortchange Bulimics and Anorexics." *Village Voice*. Vol. 44, No. 15 (April 20): 25.

Levy, Leo, and Louis Rowitz. 1973. *The Ecology of Mental Disorders*. New York: Behavioral Publications.

Macionis, John J., and Linda Gerber. 2014. *Sociology: Eighth Canadian Edition*. Scarborough, Ontario: Pearson Education.

Martin, Joyce A., Brady E. Hamilton, Michelle J. K. Osterman, Sally C. Curtin, and T. J. Mathews. "Births: Final Data for 2012." *National Vital Statistics Reports*. Vol. 62, No. 9. 2013. [Online] Available at http://www.cdc.gov/nchs/data/nvsr/nvsr62/nvsr62_09.pdf

Medscape. "Physician Compensation Report." 2013. [Online] Available at http://www.medscape.com/features/slideshow/compensation/2013/public

National Institute of Mental Health. "Statistics." 2012, 2014. [Online] Available at http://www.nimh.nih.gov/statistics/index.shtml

Parsons, Talcott. 1951. *The Social System*. New York: Free Press.

Pear, Robert, and Erik Eckholm. 1991. "When Healers Are Entrepreneurs: A Debate over Costs and Ethics." *New York Times* (June 2): 1, 17.

Politz, Karen, Cynthia Cox, Kevin Lucia, and Katie Keith. "Medical Debt Among People with Health Insurance." Kaiser Family Foundation. January 7, 2014. [Online] Available at http://kff.org/private-insurance/report/medical-debt-among-people-with-health-insurance

Population Reference Bureau. "Datafinder." 2013. [Online] Available at http://www.prb.org/DataFinder.aspx.

Roche, Timothy. 2000. "The Crisis of Foster Care." *Time*. Vol. 156, No. 20 (November 13): 74–82.

Ross, Catherine E., John Mirowsky, and William C. Cockerham. 1983. "Social Class, Mexican Culture, and Fatalism: Their Effects on Psychological Distress." *American Journal of Community Psychology*. Vol. 11: 383–99.

Rushing, W. 1969. "Two Patterns in the Relationship between Social Class and Mental Hospitalization." *American Sociological Review*. Vol. 34, No. 4 (August): 533–41.

Schur, Edwin M. 1984. *Labeling Women Deviant: Gender, Stigma, and Social Control*. Philadelphia: Temple University Press.

SHEA, RACHEL HARTIGAN. 2002. "The New Insecurity." *U.S. News & World Report*. Vol. 132, No. 9 (March 25): 40.

SROLE, LEO. 1975. "Measurements and Classification in Socio-Psychiatric Epidemiology: Midtown Manhattan Study I (1954) and Midtown Manhattan Study II (1974)." *Journal of Health and Social Behavior*. Vol. 16, No. 4 (December): 347–64.

SROLE, LEO, et al. 1962. *Mental Health in the Metropolis: The Midtown Manhattan Study*. New York: McGraw-Hill.

STARR, PAUL. 1982. The Social Transformation of American Medicine. New York: Basic Books.

SZASZ, THOMAS S. 1961. *The Manufacturer of Madness: A Comparative Study of the Inquisition and the Mental Health Movement*. New York: Dell.

———. 1970. *The Myth of Mental Illness: Foundations of a Theory of Personal Conduct*. New York: Harper & Row.

———. 1994. "Mental Illness Is Still a Myth." *Society*. Vol. 31, No. 4 (May-June): 34–39.

———. 1995. "Idleness and Lawlessness in the Therapeutic State." *Society*. Vol. 32, No. 4 (May-June): 30–35.

UNAIDS. "Global Report, 2013." 2013. [Online] Available at http://www.unaids.org/en/media/unaids/contentassets/documents/epidemiology/2013/gr2013/UNAIDS_Global_Report_2013_en.pdf

UNITED NATIONS DEVELOPMENT PROGRAMME. "International Human Development Indicators." 2013. [Online] Available at http://hdrstats.undp.org/en/indicators/default.html

UNITED NATIONS, DEPARTMENT OF ECONOMIC and SOCIAL AFFAIRS, POPULATION DIVISION. "World Population Prospects: The 2012 Revision." 2013. [Online] Available at http://esa.un.org/unpd/wpp/unpp/panel_indicators.htm

U.S. CENSUS BUREAU. "American Community Survey." 2013. [Online] Available at http://www.census.gov/acs

U.S. CENSUS BUREAU. "Current Population Survey." 2013. [Online] Available at http://www.census.gov/cps

U.S. CENSUS BUREAU. "International Data Base." 2014. [Online] Available at http://www.census.gov/population/international/data/idb/informationGateway.php

U.S. DEPARTMENT OF DEFENSE. "Military Casualty Information." 2014. [Online] Available at http://www.dmdc.osd.mil/dcas/pages/casualties.xhtml

U.S. DEPARTMENT OF HEALTH and HUMAN SERVICES, HEALTH RESOURCES and SERVICES ADMINISTRATION. "The U.S. Health Workforce Chartbook." 2013. [Online] Available at http://bhpr.hrsa.gov/healthworkforce/supplydemand/usworkforce/chartbook/index.html

U.S. DEPARTMENT OF HEALTH and HUMAN SERVICES, SUBSTANCE ABUSE and MENTAL HEALTH SERVICES ADMINISTRATION (SAMHSA). "Results from the 2010 National Survey on Drug Use and Health: Mental Health Findings." 2012. [Online] Available at http://www.samhsa.gov/data/NSDUH/2k10MH_Findings/2k10MHResults.pdf

U.S. DEPARTMENT OF HEALTH and HUMAN SERVICES, SUBSTANCE ABUSE and MENTAL HEALTH SERVICES ADMINISTRATION (SAMHSA). "Results from the 2012 National Survey on Drug Use and Health: Mental Health Findings." 2013. [Online] Available at http://www.samhsa.gov/data/NSDUH/2k12MH_FindingsandDetTables/2K12MHF/NSDUHmhfr2012.htm#ch2

U.S. DEPARTMENT OF JUSTICE, FEDERAL BUREAU OF INVESTIGATION. "Crime in the United States 2012." 2013. [Online] Available at http://www.fbi.gov/about-us/cjis/ucr/crime-in-the-u.s/2012/crime-in-the-u.s.-2012/tables

U.S. DEPARTMENT OF LABOR. "Labor Force Statistics from the Current Population Survey." 2013. [Online] Available at http://www.bls.gov/cps

WHITE, JACK E. 1999. "Prejudice? Perish the Thought." *Time*. Vol. 152, No. 8 (March 8): 36.

WIERSMA, D., R. GIEL, A. DEJONG, and C. SLOOFF. 1983. "Social Class and Schizophrenia in a Dutch Cohort." *Psychological Medicine*. Vol. 13, No. 1 (February): 141–50.

WILSON, WILLIAM JULIUS. 1987. *The Truly Disadvantaged: The Inner City, the Underclass, and Public Policy*. Chicago: University of Chicago Press.

WORLD HEALTH ORGANIZATION. 1946. *Constitution of the World Health Organization*. New York: World Health Organization Interim Commission.

WORLD HEALTH ORGANIZATION. 2008. "The Global Burden of Disease: 2004 Update, Summary Tables." October 2008. [Online] Available at http://www.who.int/healthinfo/global_burden_disease/estimates_regional/en/index.html

WORLD HEALTH ORGANIZATION. 2013. "WHO Report on the Global Tobacco Epidemic, 2013." [Online] Available at http://www.who.int/tobacco/global_report/en

ZUCKERMAN, MORTIMER B. 2006. "The Russian Conundrum." *U.S. News & World Report* (March 13): 64.

Chapter 10

AZOK, DAWN KENT. "Bill Targets Companies That Take State Incentives and Use Large Numbers of Temporary Workers." AL.com. February 7, 2014. [Online] Available at http://www.aol.com/business/index.ssf/2014/02/bill_targets_companies_that_ta.html

BARTLETT, DONALD L., and JAMES B. STEELE. 1998. "Corporate Welfare." *Time*. Vol. 152, No. 19 (November 9): 36–54.

BERFIELD, SUSAN. "More Than Half of Wal-Mart's Hourly Workers Make Less Than $25,000." *Bloomberg Business Week*, October 23, 2013. [Online] Available at http://www.businessweek.com/articles/2013-10-23/more-than-half-of-walmarts-hourly-workers-make-less-than-25-000

BERGER, PETER L. 1986. *The Capitalist Revolution: Fifty Propositions about Prosperity, Equality, and Liberty*. New York: Basic Books.

BERGSTEN, C. FRED, THOMAS HORST, and THEODORE MORAN. 1978. *American Multinationals and American Interests*. Washington, D.C.: Brookings Institution.

BIPARTISAN POLICY CENTER. 2012. "2012 Election Turnout Dips Below 2008 and 2004 Levels: Number of Eligible Voters Increases by Eight Million, Five Million Fewer Votes Cast." November 8. [Online] Available at http://bipartisanpolicy.org/sites/default/files/2012%20Voter%20Turnout%20Report.pdf

CENTER FOR RESPONSIVE POLITICS. "Lobbying Database." 2011. [Online] Available at http://www.opensecrets.org/lobby/index.php

CENTER FOR RESPONSIVE POLITICS. "Lobbying Database." 2014. [Online] Available at http://www.opensecrets.org/lobby

CENTER FOR RESPONSIVE POLITICS. 2014. "2012 Presidential Race." [Online] Available at http://www.opensecrets.org/pres12/index.php

CISNEROS, HENRY. 2009. "A Fence Can't Stop the Future." *Newsweek* (January 26). [Online] Available January 28, 2009, at http://www.newsweek.com/id/180037/output/print

CONWAY, M. MARGARET, and JOANNE CONNOR GREEN. 1998. "Political Action Committees and Campaign Finance." In Allan J. Cigler and Burdett A. Loomis, eds., *Interest Group Politics*, 5th ed. (pp. 193–214). Washington, D.C.: CQ Press.

CORTESE, AMY. 2011. "A Town Creates Its Own Department Store." *New York Times*. November 12. [Online] Available at http://www.nytimes.com/2011/11/13/business/a-town-in-new-york-creates-its-own-department-store.html

Dahl, Robert. 1961. *Who Governs?* New Haven, Conn.: Yale University Press.

———. 1982. *Dilemmas of Pluralist Democracy*. New Haven, Conn.: Yale University Press.

Domhoff, G. William. 1970. *Higher Circles: The Governing Class in America*. New York: Random House.

Drawbaugh, Kevin. 2009. "U.S. House Approves Crackdown on Financial Bailout." *Reuters* (January 21). [Online] Available May 6, 2009, at http://uk.reuters.com/article/americasRegulatoryNes /idUKN2150024420090121

Eby, John. 2009. "Ironies Abound as Obama Called Not Radical Enough." *Niles Daily Star* (March 10) [Online] Available May 6, 2009, at http://www.nilesstar.com/articles/2009/03/10 /columnists/ndcolumn03.txt

Federal Election Commission. 2009. "Congressional Candidates Raised $1.42 Billion in 2007–2008." December 29. [Online] Available at http://www.fec.gov/press/press2009/2009Dec29Cong /2allhistory2008.pdf

Federal Election Commission. "PAC Count—1974 to Present." January 2012. [Online] Available at http://www.fec.gov/press /cf_summaries.shtml

Federal Election Commission. "PAC Count—1974 to Present." 2014. [Online] Available at http://www.fec.gov/press /summaries/2011/2011paccount.shtml

Ferguson, Niall. "How America Lost Its Way." *Wall Street Journal* (June 8–9, 2013): C1–C2.

Freedom House. "Freedom in the World Comparative and Historical Data." 2009. [Online] Available at http://www.freedomhouse.org/ report-types/freedom-world

Gallup. 2013. "Americans' Confidence in Congress Falls to Lowest on Record." June 13. [Online] Available at http://www.gallup. com/poll/163052/americans-confidence-congress-falls-lowest -record.aspx

Gallup. 2014. "Congressional Job Approval at 12% in February." February 10. [Online] Available at http://www.gallup.com /poll/167375/congressional-job-approval-february.aspx

Herrnson, Paul S. 1998. "Parties and Interest Groups in Postreform Congressional Elections." In Allan J. Cigler and Burdett A. Loomis, eds., *Interest Group Politics*, 5th ed. (pp. 145–68). Washington, D.C.: CQ Press.

Internal Revenue Service. "SOI Tax Stats—Business Tax Statistics." 2014. [Online] Available at http://www.irs.gov/uac/SOI-Tax -Stats-Business-Tax-Statistics

Jones, Jeffrey. 2014. "Record-High 42% of Americans Identify as Independents." Gallup, January 8. [Online] Available at http: //www.gallup.com/poll/166763/record-high-americans-identify -independents.aspx

Lipset, Seymour M. 1994. "The Social Requisites of Democracy Revisited: Presidential Address." *American Sociological Review*. Vol. 59, No. 1 (February): 1–22.

Liptak, Adam. 2012. "Campaign Finance (Super PACs)" *New York Times: Times Topics*. Updated February 27. [Online] Available at http://topics.nytimes.com/top/reference/timestopics/subjects/c /campaign_finance/index.html

Liptak, Adam. 2014. "Justices, 5–4, Kill Key Spending Cap in Politgical Races." *New York Times* (April 3): A1, A16.

Marx, Karl. 1964 (orig. 1844). *Economic and Philosophic Manuscripts of 1844*. New York: International Publishers.

McDonald, Michael P. "2012 General Election Turnout Rates." United States Elections Project. Accessed February 28, 2014. [Online] Available at http://elections.gmu.edu/Turnout_2012G .html

Mills, C. Wright. 1956. *The Power Elite*. New York: Oxford University Press.

Parenti, Michael. 1995. *Democracy by the Few*, 6th ed. New York: St. Martin's Press.

Perry, Mitch. "Mitt Romney Has Spent $41.9 Million Less of His Own Money in This Campaign." *Daily Loaf*. February 22, 2012. Available at http://cltampa.com/dailyloaf/archives/2012/02/22/mitt-romney -has-spent-419-million-less-of-his-own-money-in-this-campaign

Pew Research Center for the People & the Press. "Changing Face of America Helps Assure Obama Victory." November 7, 2012. [Online] Available at http://www.people-press.org/2012/11/07 /changing-face-of-america-helps-assure-obama-victory

Pew Research Center for the People & the Press. "Public Trust in Government, 1958–2013." October 18, 2013. [Online] Available at http://www.people-press.org/2013/10/18/trust-in-government -interactive

Polsby, Nelson W. 1959. "Three Problems in the Analysis of Community Power." *American Sociological Review*. Vol. 24, No. 6 (December): 796–803.

Riley, Charles. 2012. "Election 2012: How Rich Are These Guys?" *Money*. January 14. [Online] Available at http://finance.yahoo .com/news/election-2012--how-rich-are-these-guys.html

Rosenbloom, Stephanie, and Michael Barbaro. 2009. "Green-Light Specials, Now at Wal-Mart." *New York Times*. January 24. [Online] Available at http://www.nytimes.com/2009/01/25 /business/25walmart.html

Rothman, Stanley, and Amy E. Black. 1998. "Who Rules Now? American Elites in the 1990s." *Society*. Vol. 35, No. 6 (September–October): 17–20.

Rueschemeyer, Dietrich, Evelyn H. Stephens, and John D. Stephens. 1992. *Capitalist Development and Democracy*. Chicago: University of Chicago Press.

Sachs, Jeffrey D. 2009. "The Case for Bigger Government." *Time* (January 19): 34–36.

Sentencing Project. "Felony Disenfranchisement: A Primer." 2013. [Online] Available at http://www.sentencingproject.org/doc /publications/fd_Felony%20Disenfranchisement%20Primer.pdf

Smith, Adam. 1937 (orig. 1776). *An Inquiry into the Nature and Causes of the Wealth of Nations*. New York: Modern Library.

U.S. Census Bureau. "Voting and Registration." 2013. [Online] Available at http://www.census.gov/hhes/www/socdemo/ voting/index.html

Viser, Matt. "This Congress Going Down as Least Productive." *Boston Globe*. December 4, 2013. [Online] Available at http://www .bostonglobe.com/news/politics/2013/12/04/congress-course-make -history-least-productive/kGAVEBskUeqCB0htOUG9GI/story.html

Wall Street Journal/Heritage Foundation. "Index of Economic Freedom, 2014." 2014. [Online] Available at http://www.heritage .org/index

Walmart Stores Inc. "Corporate and Financial Facts." August 2011. [Online] Available at http://walmartstores.com/media/factsheets /fs_2230.pdf

Walmart Stores Inc. "Data Sheet: Worldwide Unit Details." January 2011. [Online] Available at http://walmartstores.com /pressroom/news/10532.aspx

Wilson, Reid. 2014. "Southwestern States Bidding for $5 billion Tesla Factory." *Washington Post*. February 27. [Online] Available at http://www.washingtonpost.com/blogs/govbeat/wp/2014/02/27 /southwestern-states-bidding-for-5-billion-tesla-factory

World Bank. "World DataBank: World Development Indicators." 2013. [Online] Available at http://data.worldbank.org/data -catalog/world-development-indicators.

Chapter 11

ALLEN, MIKE. 2009. "Card Check Battle Starts Tomorrow." *Politico.* [Online] Available May 8, 2009, at http://www.politico.com/news/stories/0309/19786.html

ANDERSEN, KURT. 2009a. "Don't Pretend We Didn't See This Coming for a Long, Long, Time." *Time* (April 6): 34–38.

———. 2009b. "That Was Then . . . and This Is Now." *Time* (April 6): 32–33.

ARMITAGE, JIM. 2014. "'Even Worse than Foxconn': Apple Rocked by Child Labor Claims." *The Independent.* March 18. [Online] Available at http://www.independent.co.uk/life-style/gadgets-and-tech/even-worse-than-foxconn-apple-rocked-by-child-labour-claims-8736504.html

BUI, QUOCTRUNG. 2013. "The Job Market Is Still Awful, In 3 Graphs." National Public Radio. December 5. [Online] Available at http://www.npr.org/blogs/money/2013/12/05/249022241/the-job-market-is-still-awful-in-3-graphs

CARROLL, JAMES R. 1999a. "Three Congressional Panels Probe Uranium Plant." *Louisville Courier-Journal* (September 14): 4B.

———. 1999b. "U.S. Warns of Uranium, Officials Cite Problems Linked to Waste Storage." *Louisville Courier-Journal* (September 15): 1A.

CASSELMAN, BEN. 2013. "Job Gap Widens in Uneven Recovery." *Wall Street Journal* (November 12): A1–2.

CHRONICLE OF HIGHER EDUCATION. 2012. "Survey Finds a Drop in Minority Presidents Leading Colleges." March 12. [Online] Available at http://chronicle.com/article/Who-Are-College-Presidents-/131138

DALMIA, SHIKHA. 2008. "Obama and Big Labor." Forbes (October 29). [Online] Available May 8, 2009, at http://www.forbes.com/2008/10/28/obama-card-check-oped-cx_sd_1029dalmia.html

DOLAN, MATTHEW. 2011. "UAW Set a Strategy on Foreign Car Plants." *Wall Street Journal* (January 3): B1, B5.

EHRENREICH, BARBARA. 2001. *Nickel and Dimed: On How (Not) to Get By in America.* New York: Holt.

FOROOHAR, RANA. 2014. "The Flat-Paycheck Recovery." *Time.* Vol. 183, No. 1 (January 13): 34.

GRAY, STEPHEN. 2011. "In Ohio, an Era Nears Its End." *Time.* Vol. 177, No. 11 (March 21): 15.

GREENHOUSE, STEVEN. 2000. "Despite Defeat on China Bill, Labor Is on the Rise." *New York Times* (May 20): A1, A18.

GUMBEL, PETER. 2009. "A World of Troubles." *Time* (April 6): 24–25.

GUP, TED. 1991. "The Curse of Coal." *Time.* Vol. 138, No. 18 (November 4): 54–64.

HORWITZ, STEVEN. 2008. "Government Regulation, Not Free-Market Greed, Caused This Crisis." *Christian Science Monitor* (October 22). [Online] Available May 8, 2009, at http://www.csmonitor.com/2008/1022/p09s01-coop.html

ITU (INTERNATIONAL TELECOMMUNICATIONS UNION). 2013. "ICT Database." [Online] Available at http://www.itu.int/net4/itu-d/icteye/AdvancedDataSearch.aspx

KESLER, CHARLES R. 2014. "The Tea Party, Conservatism, and the Constitution." *Imprimis.* Vol. 43, No. 1 (January): 1–7.

KIVANT, BARBARA. 2008. "Reassessing Risk." *Time* (November 17): Global 1–4.

KURTZ, ANNALYN. 2014. "Job Growth Remains Weak." *CNN Money.* February 7. [Online] Available at http://money.cnn.com/2014/02/07/news/economy/january-jobs-report/?iid=EL

LEVIN, ALAN, THOMAS FRANK, and PAUL OVERBERG. 2006. "Mine Had Hundreds of Violations." *USA Today* (January 4). [Online] Available July 27, 2009, at http://www.usatoday.com/news/nation/2006-01-04-mine-violations_x.htm

MCGEEHAN, PATRICK. 2009. "Adding to Recession's Pain, Thousands to Lose Job Benefits." *The New York Times* (January 11). [Online] Available January 12, 2009, at http://www.nytimes.com/2009/01/12/nyregion/12benefits.html

MINE SAFETY and HEALTH ADMINISTRATION. 2006. "Fatality Information." [Online] Available July 21, 2009, at http://www.msha.gov

MORATH, ERIC. 2014. "Sperling: Obama Won't Backtrack on $10.10 Minimum Wage." *Wall Street Journal.* March 4. [Online] Available at http://blogs.wsj.com/washwire/2014/03/04/sperling-obama-wont-backtrack-on-10-10-minimum-wage

MURPHY, MIKE. 2011. "The Real Stakes in Wisconsin." *Time.* Vol. 177, No. 10 (March 14): 24.

NATIONAL CONFERENCE OF STATE LEGISLATURES. "State Right-to-Work Laws." 2014. [Online] Available at http://www.ncsl.org/research/labor-and-employment/right-to-work-laws-and-bills.aspx

PIERSON, DAVID. 2008. "Americans Want More Regulation of Economy, Poll Finds." *Los Angeles Times* (October 15). [Online] Available May 8, 2009, at http://articles.latimes.com/2008/oct/15/business/fi-econpoll15

PIVEN, FRANCES FOX, and RICHARD A. CLOWARD. 1971. *Regulating the Poor: The Functions of Public Welfare.* New York: Vintage Books.

READ, RICHARD. "GM Announces Big Profits; First Time Detroit's Been in the Black Since 2004." *Washington Post.* February 16, 2012. [Online] Available at http://www.washingtonpost.com/cars/gm-announces-big-profits-first-time-detroits-been-in-the-black-since-2004/2012/02/16/gIQAC5dpHR_story.html

RIPLEY, AMANDA. "Meet Your Government Workers." *Time.* Vol. 177, No. 9 (March 7, 2011): 40–44.

RITZER, GEORGE. 1993. *The McDonaldization of Society: An Investigation into the Changing Character of Contemporary Social Life.* Thousand Oaks, Calif.: Pine Forge Press.

———. 1998. *The McDonaldization Thesis: Explorations and Extensions.* Thousand Oaks, Calif.: Sage.

SULZBERGER, A. G. "Union Bill Is Law, but Debate Is Far From Over." *New York Times.* [Online] Available March 11, 2011, at http://www.nytimes.com/2011/03/12/us/12wisconsin.html

U.S. CENSUS BUREAU. "Current Population Survey." 2013. [Online] Available at http://www.census.gov/cps

U.S. DEPARTMENT OF LABOR, BUREAU OF LABOR STATISTICS. "American Time Use Survey, 2012." 2013. [Online] Available at http://www.bls.gov/news.release/archives/atus_06202013.htm

U.S. DEPARTMENT OF LABOR, BUREAU OF LABOR STATISTICS. "American Time Use Survey." 2013. [Online] Available at http://www.bls.gov/tus

U.S. DEPARTMENT OF LABOR, BUREAU OF LABOR STATISTICS. "Current Employment Statistics - CES (National)." 2014. [Online] Available at http://www.bls.gov/ces/home.htm

U.S. DEPARTMENT OF LABOR, BUREAU OF LABOR STATISTICS. "Employment Situation." 2014. [Online] Available at http://www.bls.gov/news.release/pdf/empsit.pdf

U.S. DEPARTMENT OF LABOR, BUREAU OF LABOR STATISTICS. "Injuries, Illnesses, and Fatalities." 2013. [Online] Available at http://www.bls.gov/iif

U.S. DEPARTMENT OF LABOR, BUREAU OF LABOR STATISTICS. "International Labor Comparisons." 2012, 2013. [Online] Available at http://www.bls.gov/fls

U.S. DEPARTMENT OF LABOR, BUREAU OF LABOR STATISTICS. "Labor Force Statistics from the Current Population Survey. 2013, 2014. [Online] Available at http://www.bls.gov/cps/cpsaat01.htm

U.S. Department of Labor, Bureau of Labor Statistics. "Major Work Stoppages in 2013." 2014. [Online] Available at http://www.bls.gov/news.release/pdf/wkstp.pdf

U.S. Department of Labor, Mine Safety and Health Administration. "Mine Safety and Health at a Glance." 2013. [Online] Available at http://www.msha.gov/MSHAINFO/FactSheets/MSHAFCT10.HTM

U.S. Department of Labor. "Occupational Outlook Handbook." 2011. [Online] Available at http://www.bls.gov/oco

Vanden Brook, Tom, and Bill Nichols. 2006. "Tragic Turn Stuns Families." *USA Today* (January 4). [Online] Available July 27, 2009, at http://www.usatoday.com/news/nation/2006-01-04-mine-cover_x.htm

von Drehle, David. "The Fire Next Time." *Time*. Vol. 177, No. 13 (April 4, 2011): 78.

Wessel, David. "What's Wrong with America's Job Engine?" *Wall Street Journal*. July 27, 2011. [Online] Available at http://finance.yahoo.com/banking-budgeting/article/113206/americas-job-engine-wsj?mod+bb-budgeting%20&sec+topStories&pos=4&asset=&code=

White, Joseph B. 2009. "How Detroit's Automakers Went from King of the Hill to Roadkill." *Imprimis*. Vol. 38, No. 2 (February): 1–7.

Wingfield, Nick. "Apple's Job Creation Data Spurs an Economic Debate." *New York Times*. March 5, 2012. [Online] Available at: http://finance.yahoo.com/news/apple-job-creation-data-spurs-145604450.html

Zakaria, Fareed. "Why It's Different This Time." *Time*. Vol. 177, No. 8 (February 28, 2011): 30–31.

Chapter 12

Amato, Paul R., and Juliana M. Sobolewski. 2001. "The Effects of Divorce and Marital Discord on Adult Children's Psychological Well-Being." *American Sociological Review*. Vol. 66, No. 6 (December): 900–21.

Bernard, Jessie. 1982. *The Future of Marriage*, 2nd ed. New Haven, Conn.: Yale University Press.

Brines, Julie, and Kara Joyner. 1999. "The Ties That Bind: Principles of Cohesion in Cohabitation and Marriage." *American Sociological Review*. Vol. 64, No. 3 (June): 333–55.

Broude, Gwen J. 1996. "The Realities of Day Care." *Public Interest*. No. 125 (Fall): 95–105.

Bruni, Frank. "One Country's Big Gay Leap." *New York Times*, October 8, 2011. [Online] Available at http://www.nytimes.com/2011/10/09/opinion/sunday/bruni-same-sex-marriage-in-portugal.html

CDC (Centers for Disease Control and Prevention). "Assisted Reproductive Technology (ART) National Summary Reports." 2014. [Online] Available at http://www.cdc.gov/art

CDC (Centers for Disease Control and Prevention). "Marriage and Divorce Data." 2014. [Online] Available at http://www.cdc.gov/nchs/nvss/marriage_divorce_tables.htm

CDC (Centers for Disease Control and Prevention). "Marriages and Divorces: Detailed State Tables." 2012. [Online] Available at http://www.cdc.gov/nchs/mardiv.htm#state_tables

CDC (Centers for Disease Control and Prevention). "National Survey of Family Growth (NSFG)." 2012, 2013. [Online] Available at http://www.cdc.gov/nchs/nsfg.htm

Clemetson, Lynette. 2000. "Grandma Knows Best." *Newsweek* (June 12): 60–61.

Copen, Casey E., Kimberly Daniels, and William D. Mosher. "First Premarital Cohabitation in the United States: 2006–2010 National Survey of Family Growth." 2013. [Online] Available at http://www.cdc.gov/nchs/data/nhsr/nhsr064.pdf

England, Paula. 2001. "Three Reviews on Marriage." *Contemporary Sociology*. Vol. 30, No. 6 (November): 564–65.

European Union, European Communities Statistical Office. "Eurostat Database." 2013, 2014. [Online] Available at http://epp.eurostat.ec.europa.eu/portal/page/portal/population/data/database

Faludi, Susan. 1991. *Backlash: The Undeclared War against American Women*. New York: Crown.

Fleming, Jillian, Paul Mullen, and Gabriele Bammer. 1997. "A Study of Potential Risk Factors for Sexual Abuse in Childhood." *Child Abuse and Neglect*. Vol. 21, No. 1 (January): 49–58.

Fustos, Kata. "Marriage Benefits Men's Health." Population Reference Bureau. September 2010. [Online] Available at http://www.prb.org/Articles/2010/usmarriage-menshealth.aspx

Gates, Gary J. "GBT Parenting in the United States." The Williams Institute. February 2013. [Online] Available at http://williams institute.law.ucla.edu/wp-content/uploads/LGBT-Parenting.pdf

Glenn, Norval, and Thomas Sylvester. 2005. *The Denial: Downplaying the Consequences of Family Structure for Children*. New York: Institute for American Values.

Hewlett, Sylvia Ann, and Cornel West. 1998. *The War against Parents*. Boston: Houghton Mifflin.

Holden, Karen C., and Pamela J. Smock. 1991. "The Economic Costs of Marital Dissolution: Why Do Women Bear a Disproportionate Cost?" *Annual Review of Sociology*. Vol. 17: 51–78.

Kain, Edward L. 1990. *The Myth of Family Decline: Understanding Families in a World of Rapid Social Change*. Lexington, Mass.: Lexington Books.

Kana, Johnathan. "Aubrey Ireland, Helicopter Parents and Christian Surrender." *Think Christian*. January 7, 2013. [Online] Available at http://thinkchristian.reframemedia.com/aubrey-ireland-helicopter-parents-and-christian-surrender

Kantrowitz, Barbara, and Pat Wingert. 2001. "Unmarried with Children." *Newsweek* (May 28): 46–52.

Knight, Robert H. 1998. "How Domestic Partnerships and 'Gay Marriage' Threaten the Family." In Robert T. Francoeur and William J. Taverner, eds., *Taking Sides: Clashing Views on Controversial Issues in Human Sexuality*, 6th ed. (pp. 196–206). New York: Dushkin/McGraw-Hill.

Koontz, Stephanie. 1992. *The Way We Never Were: American Families and the Nostalgia Trap*. New York: Basic Books.

Kuruvilla, Carol. "21-Year-Old Ohio Honor Student Wins Stalking Order Against Helicopter Parents Who Monitored Her Internet Use and Phone Calls." *New York Daily News*. December 27, 2012. [Online] Available at http://www.nydailynews.com/news/national/21-year-old-stalker-parents-tracked-calls-web-article-1.1228274

Lewin, Tamar. 2000. "Now a Majority: Families with Two Parents Who Work." *New York Times* (October 24): A20.

Lofquist. Daphne A. "Multigenerational Household: 2009–2011. American Community Service Briefs." U.S. Census Bureau. October 2012. [Online] Available at http://www.census.gov/prod/2012pubs/acsbr11-03.pdf

Macionis, John J. 1978. "Intimacy: Structure and Process in Interpersonal Relationships." *Alternative Lifestyles*. Vol. 1, No. 1 (February): 113–30.

———. 2001. "Welcome to Cyber-Society." In John J. Macionis and Nijole V. Benokraitis, eds., *Seeing Ourselves: Classic, Contemporary, and Cross-Cultural Readings in Sociology*, 5th ed. (pp. 62–67). Upper Saddle River, N.J.: Prentice Hall.

Manlove, Jennifer. Cited in Rana Foroohar, "For Richer or Poorer." *Time*. Vol. 179, No. 10 (March 12, 2012): 23.

Martin, Joyce A., Brady E. Hamilton, Michelle J. K. Osterman, Sally C. Curtin, and T. J. Mathews. "Births: Final Data for 2012." *National Vital Statistics Reports*, Vol. 62, No 9. 2013. [Online] Available at http://www.cdc.gov/nchs/data/nvsr/nvsr62/nvsr62_09.pdf

McLanahan, Sara. 2002. "Life without Father: What Happens to the Children?" *Contexts*. Vol. 1, No. 1 (Spring): 35–44.

Murdock, George Peter. 1949. *Social Structure*. New York: Free Press.

National Conference of State Legislatures. "Defining Marriage: State Defense of Marriage Laws and Same-Sex Marriage." 2014. [Online] Available at http://www.ncsl.org/research/human-services/same-sex-marriage-overview.aspx

National Conference of State Legislatures. "Marriages." 2014. [Online] Available at http://www.ncsl.org/research/human-services/marriage-issues-family-law.aspx#covmar

Nock, Steven L., James D. Wright, and Laura Sanchez. 1999. "America's Divorce Problem." *Society*. Vol. 36, No. 4 (May-June): 43–52.

Norton, Eleanor Holmes. 1985. "Restoring the Traditional Black Family." *New York Times Magazine* (June 2): 43–98.

OECD (Organisation for Economic Co-operation and Development). "Society at a Glance 2014." 2014. [Online] Available at http://www.oecd-ilibrary.org/social-issues-migration-health/society-at-a-glance-2014/family_soc_glance-2014-10-en

Parkman, Allen M. 1992. *No-Fault Divorce: What Went Wrong?* Boulder, Colo.: Westview Press.

Pew Research Center. "The Decline of Marriage and Rise of / New Families." November 18, 2010. Available at http://www.pewsocialtrends.org/files/2010/11/pew-social-trends-2010-families.pdf

Pew Research Center. "Millenials in Adulthood: Detached from Institutions, Networked with Friends." March 2014. [Online] Available at http://www.pewsocialtrends.org/files/2014/03/2014-03-07_generations-report-version-for-web.pdf

Pew Research Center for the People & the Press. "The Generation Gap and the 2012 Election (Section 8: Domestic and Foreign Policy Views)." 2011. [Online] Available at http://www.people-press.org/2011/11/03/section-8-domestic-and-foreign-policy-views

Pew Research Center, Social and Demographic Trends. "As Marriage and Parenthood Drift Apart, Public Is Concerned about Social Impact." July 1, 2007. [Online] Available at http://pewsocialtrends.org/pubs/526/marriage-parenthood

Pew Research Center, Social and Demographic Trends. "The Public Renders a Split Verdict on Changes in Family Structure." 2011. [Online] Available at http://www.pewsocialtrends.org/files/2011/02/Pew-Social-Trends-Changes-In-Family-Structure.pdf

Pew Research Center for the People & the Press. "In Gay Marriage Debate, Both Supporters and Opponents See Legal Recognition as 'Inevitable'." 2013. [Online] Available at http://www.people-press.org/2013/06/06/in-gay-marriage-debate-both-supporters-and-opponents-see-legal-recognition-as-inevitable

Pew Research Center Global Attitudes Project. "The Global Divide on Homosexuality." June 4, 2013. [Online] Available at http://www.pewglobal.org/2013/06/04/the-global-divide-on-homosexuality

Pew Research Center Religion and Public Life Project. "Gay Marriage Around the World." 2014. [Online] Available at http://www.pewforum.org/2013/12/19/gay-marriage-around-the-world-2013

Phillips, Melanie. 2001. "What about the Overclass?" *Public Interest*. No. 145 (Fall): 38–43.

Polgreen, Lydia, and Robert F. Worth. 2003. "Children with Foster Parents Found Starving in New Jersey." *International Herald Tribune Online* (October 28). [Online] Available October 28, 2003, at http://www.ith.com/articles/115312.html

Popenoe, David. 1988. *Disturbing the Nest: Family Change and Decline in Modern Societies*. Hawthorne, N.Y.: Aldine de Gruyter.

———. 1993a. "American Family Decline, 1960–1990: A Review and Appraisal." *Journal of Marriage and the Family*. Vol. 55, No. 3 (August): 527–55.

———. 1999. *Life without Father: Compelling New Evidence That Fatherhood and Marriage Are Indispensable for the Good of Children and Society*. Cambridge, Mass.: Harvard University Press.

Popenoe, David, and Barbara Dafoe Whitehead. 1999. *Should We Live Together? What Young Adults Need to Know about Cohabitation before Marriage*. New Brunswick, N.J.: National Marriage Project.

Roche, Timothy. 2000. "The Crisis of Foster Care." *Time*. Vol. 156, No. 20 (November 13): 74–82.

Scommegna, Paola. 2002. "Increased Cohabitation Changing Children's Family Settings." *Population Today*. Vol. 30, No. 7 (July): 3, 6.

Simon, Roger W. 2002. "Revisiting the Relationship among Gender, Marital Status, and Mental Health." *American Journal of Sociology*. Vol. 107, No. 4 (January): 1065–96.

Smith, Tom W., Peter Marsden, Michael Hout, and Jibum Kim. "General Social Surveys, 1972–2012." National Opinion Research Center; The Roper Center for Public Opinion Research, University of Connecticut; Computer-assisted Survey Methods Program, University of California. June 2013. [Online] Available at http://www.norc.org/GSS+Website

Solomon-Fears, Carmen. "Fatherhood Initiatives: Connecting Fathers to Their Children." Congressional Research Service. January 28, 2014. [Online] Available at https://www.fas.org/sgp/crs/misc/RL31025.pdf

Stacey, Judith. 1990. *Brave New Families: Stories of Domestic Upheaval in Late-Twentieth-Century America*. New York: Basic Books.

———. 1993. "Good Riddance to 'The Family': A Response to David Popenoe." *Journal of Marriage and the Family*. Vol. 55, No. 3 (August): 545–47.

Stack, Carol B. 1975. *All Our Kin: Strategies for Survival in a Black Community*. New York: Harper & Row.

U.S. Census Bureau. "American Community Survey." 2010, 2011. [Online] Available at http://www.census.gov/acs/www

U.S. Census Bureau. "American Community Survey." 2013. [Online] Available at http://www.census.gov/acs

U.S. Census Bureau. "Current Population Survey." September 2011. [Online] Available at http://www.census.gov/cps

U.S. Census Bureau. "Current Population Survey." 2013. [Online] Available at http://www.census.gov/cps

U.S. Census Bureau. "Current Population Survey, Table MS 1." 2014. [Online] Available at http://www.census.gov/hhes/families/data/marital.html

U.S. Census Bureau. "Families and Living Arrangements." 2011. [Online] Available at http://www.census.gov/population/www/socdemo/hh-fam.html

U.S. Census Bureau. "Families and Living Arrangements." 2013, 2014. [Online] Available at http://www.census.gov/hhes/families

U.S. Census Bureau. "Survey of Income and Program Participation (SIPP)." 2011. [Online] Available at http://www.census.gov/hhes /childcare/index.html

U.S. Census Bureau. "Survey of Income and Program Participation (SIPP)." 2013. [Online] Available at http://www.census.gov/hhes /childcare/data/sipp/2011/tables.html

U.S. Department of Labor, Bureau of Labor Statistics. "American Time Use Survey." 2013. [Online] Available at http://www.bls.gov/tus

U.S. Department of Labor, Bureau of Labor Statistics. "Employment Characteristics of Families—2013." 2014. [Online] Available at http://www.bls.gov/news.release/pdf/famee.pdf

Von Drehle, David. "How Gay Marriage Won." *Time*. Vol. 181, No. 13 (April 8, 2013): 16–24.

Waite, Linda J., and Maggie Gallagher. 2000. *The Case for Marriage: Why Married People Are Happier, Healthier, and Better Off Financially*. New York: Doubleday.

Weitzman, Lenore J. 1985. *The Divorce Revolution: The Unexpected Social and Economic Consequences for Women and Children in America*. New York: Free Press.

———. 1996. "The Economic Consequences of Divorce Are Still Unequal: Comment on Peterson." *American Sociological Review*. Vol. 61, No. 3 (June): 537–38.

Whitehead, Barbara Defoe. 1997. *The Divorce Culture*. New York: Knopf.

Wilson, William Julius. 1987. *The Truly Disadvantaged: The Inner City, the Underclass, and Public Policy*. Chicago: University of Chicago Press.

———. 1996a. *When Work Disappears: The World of the New Urban Poor*. New York: Knopf.

———. 1996b. "Work." *New York Times Magazine* (August 18): 26–31, 40, 48, 52, 54.

Chapter 13

Altman, Alex. "Skipping Out." *Time*. Vol. 183, No. 15. (April 21, 2014): 12.

America's Promise Alliance. "Building a Grad Nation." 2013. [Online] Available at http://www.americaspromise.org/dropout -crisis-facts

Ballantine, Jeanne H. 2001. *The Sociology of Education: A Systematic Analysis*, 5th ed. Upper Saddle River, N.J.: Prentice Hall.

Basow, Susan A. 1992. *Gender Stereotypes and Roles*, 3rd ed. Pacific Grove, Calif.: Brooks/Cole.

Belluck, Pam. 2000. "Indian Schools, Long Failing, Press for Money and Quality." *New York Times*. (May 18): A1.

Bowles, Samuel, and Herbert Gintis. 1976. Schooling in Capitalist America: Educational Reform and the Contradictions of Economic Life. New York: Basic Books.

Brantlinger, Ellen A. 1993. *The Politics of Social Class in Secondary School: Views of Affluent and Impoverished Youth*. New York: Teachers College Press.

Bushaw, William, and Shane Lopez. "Public Education in the United States: Which Way Do We Go?" *Kappan Magazine*, Vol. 95, No. 1, 2013(9–25). [Online] Available at http://pdkintl.org /noindex/2013_PDKGallup.pdf

Caumont, Andrea. "Six Key Findings About Going to College." Pew Research Center. February 11, 2014. [Online] Available at http://www.pewresearch.org/fact-tank/2014/02/11/6-key -findings-about-going-to-college

Christle, Christine, Kristine Jolivette, and C. Michael Nelson. 2007. "School Characteristics Related to High School Dropout Rates." *Remedial and Special Education*. Vol. 28, No. 6: 325–39.

Close, Ellis. 2004. "A Dream Deferred." *Newsweek* (May 17): 52–59.

Cloud, John. 2003. "Inside the New SAT." *Time*. Vol. 162, No. 17 (October 27): 48–56.

Cohen, Adam. 2004. "The Supreme Struggle." *New York Times* (January 18): sec. 4A, 22–24, 38.

Coleman, James S. 1966. *Equality of Educational Opportunity*. Washington, D.C.: U.S. Government Printing Office.

———. 1988. "Social Capital in the Creation of Human Capital." *American Journal of Sociology*. Vol. 94, No. 1 (July): 95–120.

College Board. "2013 College-Bound Seniors: Total Group Profile Report." 2013. [Online] Available at http://media.collegeboard .com/digitalServices/pdf/research/2013/TotalGroup-2013.pdf

College Board. "2011 College-Bound Seniors: Total Group Profile Report." 2011. [Online] Available at http://professionals .collegeboard.com/profdownload/cbs2011_total_group_report.pdf

Dillon, Sam. 2011a. "Failure Rate of Schools Overstated, Study Says." *New York Times*. December 15, 2011. [Online] Available at http://www.nytimes.com/2011/12/15/education/education -secretary-overstated-failing-schools-under-no-child-left-behind -study-says.html

Dillon, Sam. 2011b. "Most Public Schools May Miss Targets, Education Secretary Says." *New York Times*. March 9, 2011. [Online] Available at http://www.nytimes.com/2011/03/10 /education/10education.html

Downey, Douglas B., Paul T. von Hippel, and Beckett A. Broh. 2004. "Are Schools the Great Equalizer? Cognitive Inequality during the Summer Months and School Year." *American Sociological Review*. Vol. 69, No. 5 (October): 613–35.

Edwards, Tamala M. 1998. "Revolt of the Gentry." *Time*. Vol. 151, No. 23 (June 15): 34–35.

Evelyn, Jamilah. 2002. "Community Colleges Play Too Small a Role in Teacher Education, Report Concludes." *Chronicle of Higher Education Online*. [Online] Available October 24, 2002, at http://chronicle.com/daily/2002/10/2002102403n.htm

Fine, Melinda. 1993. "'You Can't Just Say That the Only Ones Who Can Speak Are Those Who Agree with Your Position': Political Discourse in the Classroom." *Harvard Educational Review*. Vol. 63, No. 4 (Winter): 421–33.

Fuller, Bruce, Richard F. Elmore, and Gary Orfield. 1996. "Policy-Making in the Dark: Illuminating the School Choice Debate." In Bruce Fuller, Richard F. Elmore, and Gary Orfield, eds., *Who Chooses? Who Loses? Culture, Institutions, and the Unequal Effects of School Choice* (pp. 1–24). New York: Teachers College Press.

Garland, Sarah. 2007. "Study Backs Results of For-Profit Schools." New York Sun Online (April 11). [Online] Available March 31, 2008, at http://www2.nysun.com/article/52198

Garland, Sarah. "English Learners Still Far Behind under English-Only Law." *The Hechinger Report*. October 24, 2011. Available at http://hechingerreport.org/content/english-learners-still-far -behind-under-english-only-methods_6590/

Goodman, David. 1999. "America's Newest Class War." *Mother Jones*. Vol. 24, No. 5 (September–October): 68–75.

Hodkinson, Paul, and Martin Bloomer. 2001. "Dropping Out of Further Education: Complex Causes and Simplistic Policy Assumptions." *Research Papers in Education*. Vol. 16, No. 2 (July): 117–41.

International Labour Organization. "Global Child Labour Trends 2008 to 2012." 2013. [Online] Available at http://www.ilo .org/ipecinfo/product/viewProduct.do?productId=23015

Komline, Patti. "My Turn: The Time to Fix Vermont's School Funding System Is Now." *Burlington Free Press*. April 9, 2014. [Online] Available at http://www.burlingtonfreepress.com

/article/20140410/OPINION02/304100025/My-Turn-time
-Vermont-s-fix-school-funding-system-now

Kozol, Jonathan. 1991. *Savage Inequalities: Children in America's School*. New York: Crown.

———. 2005. *The Shame of the Nation: The Restoration of Apartheid Schooling in America*. New York: Crown.

———. 2007. *Letters to a Young Teacher*. New York: Crown.

Lahey, Jessica. "A Lesson in the Common Core." *New York Times*. February 27, 2014. [Online] Available at: http://parenting.blogs.nytimes.com/2014/02/27/a-lesson-on-the-common-core/?_php=true&_type=blogs&smid=pl-share&_r=0

Lord, Mary. 2001. "Good Teachers the Newest Imports." *U.S. News & World Report*. Vol. 130, No. 13 (April 9): 54.

———. 2002. "A Battle for Children's Futures." *U.S. News & World Report*. Vol. 132, No. 6 (March 4): 35–36.

Loveless, Tom. 1999. "Will Tracking Reform Promote Social Equity?" *Educational Leadership*. Vol. 56, No. 7 (April): 28–32.

Lu, Adrienne. "State Reconsider Common Core Tests." Stateline: The Daily News Service of the Pew Charitable Trusts. January 24, 2014. [Online] Available at http://www.pewstates.org/projects/stateline/headlines/states-reconsider-common-core-tests-85899535255

McGreevy, Patrick. "California Senator Proposed Restoring Bilingual Education." *Los Angeles Times*. February 20, 2014. [Online] Available at http://www.latimes.com/local/political/la-me-pc-california-senator-proposes-restoring-bilingual-education-20140220,0,6194709.story#axzz2uZbSdGc

McLaren, Peter L., and James M. Giarelli, eds. 1995. *Critical Theory and Educational Research*. Albany: State University of New York Press.

McNeal, Ralph B., Jr. 1999. "Parental Involvement as Social Capital: Differential Effectiveness on Science Achievement, Truancy, and Dropping Out." *Social Forces*. Vol. 78, No. 1 (October): 117–44.

Mezzacappa, Dale. "Only Six Providers Approved for 'Turnaround.'" *Philadelphia Public Schools: The Notebook*. (March 5, 2010) [Online] Available at http://thenotebook.org/blog/102296/six-providers-approved-turnaround

Morse, Jodie. 2002. "Learning while Black." *Time*. Vol. 159, No. 21 (May 27): 50–52.

Myers, Andrew. "Students Learning English Benefit More in Two-Language Instructional Programs than English Immersion, Stanford Research Finds." *Stanford News*. March 25, 2014. [Online] Available at http://news.stanford.edu/news/2014/march/teaching-english-language-032514.html

National Education Association. "Rankings & Estimates: Rankings of the States 2011 and Estimates of School Statistics 2012." Washington, DC: National Education Association. December 2011. [Online] Available at http://www.nea.org/assets/docs/NEA_Rankings_And_Estimates_FINAL_20120209.pdf

Oakes, Jeannie. 1985. *Keeping Track: How Schools Structure Inequality*. New Haven, Conn.: Yale University Press.

Ochoa, Rachel. 1999. "Bilingual Education Challenged Again." *Hispanic*. Vol. 12, No. 10 (October): 12–13.

OECD (Organisation for Economic Co-operation and Development). "Education at a Glance 2013: OECD Indicators." 2013. [Online] Available at http://www.oecd.org/edu/educationataglance2013-indicatorsandannexes.htm

OECD (Organisation for Economic Co-operation and Development). "PISA 2012 Results." 2013. [Online] Available at http://www.oecd.org/pisa/keyfindings/pisa-2012-results.htm

Olin, Dirk. 2003. "The Tracking System." *New York Times* (September 28). [Online] Available October 12, 2003, at http://www.researchnavigator.com

Orfield, Gary and Erica Frankenberg, with Jongyeon Ee and John Kuscera. "Brown at 60: Great Progress, a Long Retreat and an Uncertain Future." Civil Rights Project/Proyecto Derechos Civiles, UCLA, May 2014 (revised version 5-15-14). Available at http://civilrightsproject.ucla.edu/research/k-12-education/integration-and-diversity/brown-at-60-great-progress-a-long-retreat-and-an-uncertain-future/Brown-at-60-051814.pdf (Table 4, p. 12)

Orfield, Gary, and Chungmei Lee. 2007. *Racial Transformation and the Changing Nature of Segregation*. Cambridge, Mass.: Civil Rights Project at Harvard University.

Pew Research Center for the People & the Press. "January 2014 Political Survey." January 23, 2014. [Online] Available at http://www.people-press.org/files/legacy-questionnaires/1-23-14%20Poverty_Inequality%20topline%20for%20release.pdf

Portes, Alejandro. 2002. "English Only Triumphs, but the Costs Are High." *Contexts*. Vol. 1 No. 1 (Spring): 10–15.

Primary Sources. "Primary Sources: America's Teachers on the Teaching Profession." 2012, 2014. [Online] Available at http://mediaroom.scholastic.com/files/ps_fullreport.pdf

Richardson, Laurel. 1988. *The Dynamics of Sex and Gender: A Sociological Perspective*, 3rd ed. New York: HarperCollins.

Richburg, Keith B. 2008. "School Privatization Plan Sputters." *Washington Post* (June 29). [Online] Available February 3, 2009, at http://www.boston.com/news/education/k_12/articles/2008/06/29/school_privatization_plan_sputters

Ripley, Amanda. 2008. "Can She Save Our Schools?" *Time* (December 8): 36–44.

Roscigno, Vincent J., and Martha L. Crowley. 2001. "Rurality, Institutional Disadvantage, and Achievement/Attainment." *Rural Sociology*. Vol. 66, No. 2 (June): 268–92.

Sadker, David. 1999. "Gender Equity: Still Knocking at the Classroom Door." *Educational Leadership*. Vol. 56, No. 7 (April): 22–26.

Sadker, David, and Myra Sadker. 1994. *Failing at Fairness: How America's Schools Cheat Girls*. New York: Scribner.

Shlaes, Amity. 1998. "A Chance to Equip My Child." *Wall Street Journal* (February 23): A22.

Skiba, Russell. 2000. "No to Zero Tolerance." *Louisville Courier-Journal* (January 16): D3.

Smith, Tom W., Peter Marsden, Michael Hout, and Jibum Kim. "General Social Surveys, 1972–2012." National Opinion Research Center; The Roper Center for Public Opinion Research, University of Connecticut; Computer-assisted Survey Methods Program, University of California. June 2013. [Online] Available at http://www.norc.org/GSS+Website

Spender, Dale. 1989. *Invisible Women: The Schooling Scandal*. London: Women's Press.

Stone, Clarence N. 1998. "Linking Civic Capacity and Human Capital Formation." In Marilyn J. Gittell, ed., *Strategies for School Equity: Creating Productive Schools in a Just Society* (pp. 163–76). New Haven, Conn.: Yale University Press.

Taylor, Steven J. L. 1998. *Desegregation in Boston and Buffalo: The Influence of Local Leaders*. Albany: State University of New York Press.

Thernstrom, Abigail, and Stephan Thernstrom. 2003. *No Excuses: Closing the Racial Gap in Learning*. New York: Simon & Schuster.

United Nations Development Programme. *Human Development Report 2011*. Statistical Tables. [Online] Available at http://hdr.undp.org/en/statistics/data/

U.S. Census Bureau. "American Community Survey." 2013. [Online] Available at http://www.census.gov/acs

U.S. Census Bureau. "Current Population Survey." 2013. [Online] Available at http://www.census.gov/cps

U.S. Census Bureau. "Families and Living Arrangements." 2013. [Online] Available at http://www.census.gov/hhes/families

U.S. Department of Education, National Center for Education Statistics. "2003 National Assessment of Adult Literacy." 2008, 2009. [Online] Available at http://nces.ed.gov/naal/index.asp

U.S. Department of Education, National Center for Education Statistics. "The Condition of Education." May 2011. [Online] Available at http://nces.ed.gov/programs/coe

U.S. Department of Education, National Center for Education Statistics. "The Condition of Education." 2014. [Online] Available at http://nces.ed.gov/programs/coe

U.S. Department of Education, National Center for Education Statistics. "Indicators of School Crime and Safety: 2011." February 2012. [Online] Available at http://nces.ed.gov/programs/crimeindicators/crime indicators2011/tables.asp

U.S. Department of Education, National Center for Education Statistics. "Indicators of School Crime and Safety: 2012." 2013. [Online] Available at http://nces.ed.gov/programs/crimeindicators/crimeindicators2012/tables.asp

U.S. Department of Education, National Center for Education Statistics. "Projections of Education Statistics to 2020." 2011. [Online] Available at http://nces.ed.gov/programs/projections/projections2020/tables.asp

U.S. Department of Education, National Center for Education Statistics. "Projections of Education Statistics to 2021." 2013. [Online] Available at http://nces.ed.gov/programs/projections/projections2021/index.asp

U.S. Department of Education, National Center for Education Statistics. "Trends in High School Dropout and Completion Rates in the United States: 1972–2009, Compendium Report." October 2011. [Online] Available at http://nces.ed.gov/pubs2012/2012006.pdf

U.S. Department of Education, National Center for Education Statistics. "U.S. Digest of Education Statistics 2010." April 2011. [Online] Available at http://nces.ed.gov/programs/digest/2010menu_tables.asp

U.S. Department of Education, National Center for Education Statistics. "U.S. Digest of Education Statistics 2012." 2013. [Online] Available at http://nces.ed.gov/programs/digest/d12

U.S. Department of Education, National Center for Education Statistics. "U.S. Digest of Education Statistics 2013." 2014. [Online] Available at http://nces.ed.gov/programs/digest/2013menu _tables.asp

U.S. Department of Education. "EdData Express: Data about elementary and secondary schools in the U.S." 2014. [Online] Available at http://eddataexpress.ed.gov/index.cfm

Wallis, Claudia, and Sonja Steptoe. 2007. "How to Fix No Child Left Behind." *Time* (June 4): 34–41.

Winerip, Michael. 2007. "Diversity as Normal as Speaking Chinese." *New York Times* (October 7). [Online] Available May 21, 2009, at http://www.nytimes.com/2007/10/07/nyregion/nyregionspecial2/07Rparenting.html?_r=1

Wood, Peter B., and Michelle Chesser. 1993. "Black Stereotyping in a University Population." *Sociological Focus*. Vol. 27, No. 1 (January): 17–34.

World Bank. "World DataBank: Education Statistics." 2014. [Online] Available at http://data.worldbank.org/data-catalog/ed-stats

World Bank. "World DataBank: World Development Indicators." 2014. [Online] Available at http://data.worldbank.org/data-catalog/world-development-indicators

Chapter 14

American Farmland Trust. "Threatened Farmland." 2014. [Online] Available at http://www.farmland.org

Andersen, Kurt. 2009a. "Don't Pretend We Didn't See This Coming for a Long, Long, Time." *Time* (April 6): 34–38.

———. 2009b. "That Was Then . . . and This Is Now." *Time* (April 6): 32–33.

Castells, Manuel. 1977. *The Urban Question*. Cambridge, Mass.: MIT Press.

———. 1983. *The City and the Grass Roots*. Berkeley: University of California Press.

———. 1989. *The Informational City*. Oxford: Blackwell.

Cheslow, Jerry. 2006. "Loving the Landscape but Not the Sprawl." *New York Times Online*. [Online] Available July 17, 2006, at http://www.researchnavigator.com

Davey, Monica. "A Picture of Detroit Ruin, Street by Forlorn Street." *New York Times*. February 17, 2014. [Online] Available at http://www.nytimes.com/2014/02/18/us/detroit-tries-to-get-a-clear-picture-of-its-blight.htm

Davis, Lisa Selin. 2009. "A (Radical) Way to Fix Urban Sprawl." *Time* (June 22): 54–57.

El Boghdady, Dina, and Sarah Cohen. 2009. "The Growing Foreclosure Crisis." Washington Post (January 17). [Online] Available May 13, 2009, at http://www.washingtonpost.com/wp-dyn/content/article/2009/01/16/AR2009011604724.html

Fischer, Claude. 1973. "Urban Malaise." *Social Problems*. Vol. 52, No. 2 (May): 221–35.

———. 1975. "Toward a Subcultural Theory of Urbanism." *American Journal of Sociology*. Vol. 80, No. 6 (May): 1319–41.

Gans, Herbert J. 1968. *People and Plans: Essays on Urban Problems and Solutions*. New York: Basic Books.

Glaab, Charles N. 1963. *The American City: A Documentary History*. Homewood, Ill.: Dorsey.

Gottmann, Jean. 1961. *Megalopolis*. New York: Twentieth Century Fund.

Guyette, Curt. "Examining the Body of Evidence in Detroit's Bankruptcy Trial." *Metrotimes*. April 1, 2014. [Online] Available at http://metrotimes.com/covers/examining-the-body-of-evidence-in-detroit-s-bankruptcy-trial-1.1660471

Hackler, Tim. 1979. "The Big City Has No Corners on Mental Illness." *New York Times Magazine* (December 19): A1.

Harvey, David. 1973. *Social Justice and the City*. Baltimore: Johns Hopkins University Press.

Jagarowsky, Paul A., and Mary Jo Bane. 1990. *Neighborhood Poverty: Basic Questions*. Discussion Paper Series H-90-3. John F. Kennedy School of Government. Cambridge, Mass.: Harvard University Press.

Johnson, Kirk, and Thomas L. Lueck. 1996. "Region's Economy in Fundamental Shift." *New York Times* (February 19): A1.

Kadushin, Charles. 1983. "Mental Health and the Interpersonal Environment." *American Sociological Review*. Vol. 48, No. 2 (April): 188–98.

Kaufman, Leslie. 2004. "Surge in Homeless Families Sets Off Debate on Cause." *New York Times* (June 29).

Kemp, Jack. 1994. "A Cultural Renaissance." *Imprimis*. Vol. 23, No. 8 (August): 1–5.

Kozol, Jonathan. 1988. *Rachel and Her Children: Homeless Families in America*. New York: Fawcett Columbine.

Krauthammer, Charles. 1995. "A Social Conservative Credo." *Public Interest*. Vol. 121 (Fall): 15–22.

KUNSTLER, JAMES HOWARD. 1996. "Home from Nowhere." *Atlantic Monthly*. Vol. 278 (September): 43–66.

LOGAN, JOHN, and HARVEY MOLOTCH. 1987. *Urban Fortunes: The Political Economy of Place*. Berkeley: University of California Press.

MACIONIS, JOHN J., and VINCENT R. PARRILLO. 2013. *Cities and Urban Life* (6th ed.). Upper Saddle River: Pearson.

MARTIN, PHILIP, and ELIZABETH MIDGLEY. 2003. "Immigration: Shaping and Reshaping America." *Population Bulletin*. Vol. 58, No. 2 (June). Washington, D.C.: Population Reference Bureau.

MASSEY, DOUGLAS S., and NANCY A. DENTON. 1988. "Suburbanization and Segregation in U.S. Metropolitan Areas." *American Journal of Sociology*. Vol. 94, No. 3 (November): 592–626.

———. 1989. "Hypersegregation in U.S. Metropolitan Areas: Black and Hispanic Segregation along Five Dimensions." *Demography*. Vol. 26, No. 3 (August): 373–91.

MOYNIHAN, DANIEL PATRICK. 1993. "Toward a New Intolerance." *Public Interest*. No. 112 (Summer): 119–22.

MYERS, DAVID G. 2000. *The American Paradox: Spiritual Hunger in an Age of Plenty*. New Haven, Conn.: Yale University Press.

OHLEMACHER, STEPHEN. 2007. "Official Count: 754,000 People Believed Homeless in U.S." *Seattle Times* (February 28). [Online] Available March 9, 2007, at http://seattletimes.nwsource.com /html/nationworld/2003592874_homeless28.html

POPULATION REFERENCE BUREAU. "Datafinder." 2013, 2014. [Online] Available at http://www.prb.org/DataFinder.aspx

PUTNAM, ROBERT D. "Inequality of Opportunity." Presentation at Kenyon College. April 10, 2014.

REALTYTRAC, INC. "Foreclosure Market Reports." 2009. [Online] Available at http://www.realtytrac.com/content/foreclosure-market-report

ROBISON, JENNIFER. "Firm Ranks Nevada No. 2 Nationwide for Foreclosures in '13." *Las Vegas Review-Journal*. April 13, 2014. [Online] Available at http://www.reviewjournal.com/business /firm-ranks-nevada-no-2-nationwide-foreclosures-13

SAPORITO, BILL. 2008. "Is Housing Nearing the Floor?" *Time* (November 10): 56–57.

SROLE, LEO. 1972. "Urbanization and Mental Health: Some Reformulations." *American Scientist*. Vol. 60: 576–83.

SULLIVAN, AMY. 2009. "Postcard from Detroit." *Time* (April 30). [Online] Available May 14, 2009, at http://www.time.com/time /magazine/article/0,9171,1894943,00.html

THIGPEN, DAVID E. 2002. "The Long Way Home." *Time*. Vol. 160, No. 6 (August 5): 42–44.

UNITED NATIONS, DEPARTMENT OF ECONOMIC AND SOCIAL AFFAIRS. "World Population Prospects: The 2012 Revision." 2013. [Online] Available at http://esa.un.org/unpd/wpp/unpp/panel _indicators.htm

UNITED NATIONS, DEPARTMENT OF ECONOMIC AND SOCIAL AFFAIRS. "World Urbanization Prospects: The 2011 Revision." March 2012. [Online] Available at http://esa.un.org/unpd/wup/pdf /WUP2011_Highlights.pdf

U.S. CENSUS BUREAU. "American Community Survey." 2011. [Online] Available at http://www.census.gov/acs

U.S. CENSUS BUREAU. "American Community Survey." 2013. [Online] Available at http://www.census.gov/acs

U.S. CENSUS BUREAU. "Census 2010." 2011. [Online] Available at http://factfinder2.census.gov/faces/nav/jsf/pages/index.xhtml

U.S. CENSUS BUREAU. "Current Population Survey." September 2011. [Online] Available at http://www.census.gov/cps

U.S. CENSUS BUREAU. "Current Population Survey." 2013. [Online] Available at http://www.census.gov/cps

U.S. CENSUS BUREAU. "Population Division." *Population Estimates*. 2011. [Online] Available at http://www.census.gov/popest /estimates.html

U.S. CENSUS BUREAU. "Population Estimates." 2013, 2014. [Online] Available at http://www.census.gov/popest/data/index.html

U.S. CENSUS BUREAU. "State and County QuickFacts." 2011. [Online] Available at http://quickfacts.census.gov/qfd/states/00000.html

U.S. CENSUS BUREAU. "State and County QuickFacts." 2014. [Online] Available at http://quickfacts.census.gov/qfd

U.S. CONFERENCE OF MAYORS. "A Status Annual Report on Hunger and Homelessness in America's Cities." 2013. [Online] Available at http://www.usmayors.org/pressreleases/uploads/2013/1210 -report-HH.pdf

U.S. DEPARTMENT OF HOUSING and URBAN DEVELOPMENT, OFFICE OF COMMUNITY PLANNING AND DEVELOPMENT. "The Annual Homeless Assessment Report to Congress." June 2011. [Online] Available at http://www.hudhre.info/index. cfm?do=viewResource&ResourceId_4450

U.S. DEPARTMENT OF HOUSING AND URBAN DEVELOPMENT, OFFICE OF COMMUNITY PLANNING AND DEVELOPMENT. "The Annual Homeless Assessment Report to Congress." 2013. [Online] Available at http://www.onecpd.info/hdx/guides/ahar

U.S. DEPARTMENT OF HOUSING AND URBAN DEVELOPMENT. "Housing Choice Vouchers Fact Sheet." 2012. [Online] Available at http://portal.hud.gov/hudportal/HUD?src_/topics/housing _choice_voucher_program_8

U.S. DEPARTMENT OF LABOR, BUREAU OF LABOR STATISTICS. "Local Area Unemployment Statistics." 2014. [Online] Available at http://www.bls.gov/lau

VON DREHLE, DAVID. 2009a. "House of Cards." *Time* (March 9): 22–29.

———. 2009b. "The Moment: 4/5/09, New York." *Time* (April 20): 11.

WATTEL, H. 1958. "Levittown: A Suburban Community." In William Dobriner, ed., *The Suburban Community* (pp. 287–313). New York: Putnam.

WEISNER, THOMAS S. 1981. "Cities, Stress, and Children." In Ruth H. Moore, Robert I. Monroe, and Beatrice B. Whiting, eds., *Handbook of Cross-Cultural Human Development* (pp. 783–803). New York: Garland.

WILSON, WILLIAM JULIUS. 1996a. *When Work Disappears: The World of the New Urban Poor*. New York: Knopf.

———. 1996b. "Work." *New York Times Magazine* (August 18): 26–31, 40, 48, 52, 54.

WIRTH, LOUIS. 1938. "Urbanism as a Way of Life." *American Journal of Sociology*. Vol. 44, No. 1 (July): 1–24.

WORLD BANK. "World DataBank: World Development Indicators." 2014. [Online] Available at http://data.worldbank.org/data -catalog/world-development-indicators

ZAKARIA, FAREED. "Why It's Different This Time." *Time*. Vol. 177, No. 8 (February 28, 2011): 30–31.

Chapter 15

AXINN, WILLIAM G., and JENNIFER S. BARBER. 2001. "Mass Education and Fertility Transition." *American Sociological Review*. Vol. 66, No. 4 (August): 481–505.

BAUER, P. T. 1981. *Equality, the Third World, and Economic Delusion*. Cambridge, Mass.: Harvard University Press.

BERGER, PETER L. 1986. *The Capitalist Revolution: Fifty Propositions about Prosperity, Equality, and Liberty*. New York: Basic Books.

BERGESEN, ALBERT, ed. 1983. *Crises in the World-System*. Thousand Oaks, Calif.: Sage.

BONDREAU, JOHN, and PATRICK MAY. "New Report Finds Worker Abuses at Apple's Supplier in China." MercuryNews.com March 30, 2012. [Online] Available at http://www.mercurynews.com /business/ci_20286152/apple-china-worker-abuses-audit-factories -ipad-iphone

BONNANO, ALESSANDRO, DOUGLAS H. CONSTANCE, and HEATHER LORENZ. 2000. "Powers and Limits of Transnational Corporations: The Case of ADM." *Rural Sociology*. Vol. 65, No. 3 (September): 171–90.

BROWN, LESTER R. "Reassessing the Earth's Population." *Society*. Vol. 32, No. 4 (May/June 1995): 7–10.

BURKETT, ELINOR. 1997. "'God Created Me to Be a Slave.'" *New York Times Magazine* (October 12): 56–60.

CHEN, SHAOHUA, and MARTIN RAVALLION. "The Developing World Is Poorer Than We Thought, But No Less Successful in the Fight against Poverty." August 2008. [Online] Available at http://go.worldbank.org/C9GR27WRJ0

CONSORTIUM FOR STREET CHILDREN. "Street Children Statistics." 2011. [Online] Available at http://www.streetchildren.org.uk /_uploads/resources/Street_Children_Stats_FINAL.pdf

DAVIES, JAMES, RODRIGO LLUBERAS, and ANTHONY SHORROCKS. "Credit Suisse Global Wealth Databook 2013." 2013. [Online] Available at https://infocus.credit-suisse.com/data/_product _documents/_shop/369553/2012_global_wealth_databook.pdf

DAVIES, JAMES B., SUSANNA SANDSTROM, ANTHONY SHORROCKS, and EDWARD N. WOLFF. "The Level and Distribution of Global Household Wealth." September 2009. [Online] Available at http://economics.uwo.ca/centres/epri/wp2009/Davies_ Sandstrom_Shorrocks_Wolff_01.pdf

DELACROIX, JACQUES, and CHARLES C. RAGIN. 1981. "Structural Blockage: A Cross-National Study of Economic Dependency, State Efficacy, and Underdevelopment." *American Journal of Sociology*. Vol. 86, No. 6 (May): 1311–47.

DIXON, WILLIAM J., and TERRY BOSWELL. 1996. "Dependency, Disarticulation, and Denominator Effects: Another Look at Foreign Capital Penetration." *American Journal of Sociology*. Vol. 102, No. 2 (September): 543–62.

FIELD, TORY, and BEVERLY BELL. "Inherit the Earth: Land Reform in Brazil." *Huffington Post*, August 7, 2013. [Online] Available at http://www.huffingtonpost.com/beverly-bell/inherit-the-earth -land-re_b_3720875.html

FIREBAUGH, GLENN. 1992. "Growth Effects of Foreign and Domestic Investment." *American Journal of Sociology*. Vol. 98, No. 1 (July): 105–30.

———. 1996. "Does Foreign Capital Harm Poor Nations? New Estimates Based on Dixon and Boswell's Measures of Capital Penetration." *American Journal of Sociology*. Vol. 102, No. 2 (September): 563–75.

FIREBAUGH, GLENN, and FRANK D. BECK. 1994. "Does Economic Growth Benefit the Masses? Growth, Dependence, and Welfare in the Third World." *American Sociological Review*. Vol. 59, No. 5 (October): 631–53.

FIREBAUGH, GLENN, and DUMITRU SANDU. 1998. "Who Supports Marketization and Democratization in Post-Communist Romania?" *Sociological Forum*. Vol. 13, No. 3 (September): 521–41.

FORBES. "The World's Billionaires." 2014. [Online] Available at http://www.forbes.com/billionaires

FRANK, ANDRÉ GUNDER. 1981. *Reflections on the World Economic Crisis*. New York: Monthly Review Press.

GALANO, ANA MARIA. "Land Hungry in Brazil." UNESCO Courier. July–August, 1998. [Online] Available at http://www.unesco.org /courier/1998_08/uk/somm/intro.htm

GREENHOUSE, STEVEN, and ELIZABETH A. HARRIS. "Battling for a Safer Bangladesh." *New York Times*. April 21, 2014. [Online] Available at http://www.nytimes.com/2014/04/22/business/international /battling-for-a-safer-bangladesh.html

HOYERT, DONNA, and JIAQUAN XU. "Deaths: Preliminary Data for 2011." *National Vital Statistics Reports*. Vol. 61, No. 6. 2012. [Online] Available at http://www.cdc.gov/nchs/data/nvsr/nvsr61 /nvsr61_06.pdf

INTERNATIONAL LABOUR ORGANIZATION. "Forced Labour, Human Trafficking, and Slavery." 2012. [Online] Available at http://www .ilo.org/global/topics/forced-labour/lang--en/index.htm

KENTOR, JEFFREY. 1998. "The Long-Term Effects of Foreign Investment Dependence on Economic Growth, 1940–1990." *American Journal of Sociology*. Vol. 103, No. 4 (January): 1024–46.

———. 2001. "The Long-Term Effects of Globalization on Income Inequality, Population Growth, and Economic Development." *Social Problems*. Vol. 48, No. 4 (November): 435–55.

LAPPÉ, FRANCES MOORE, and JOSEPH COLLINS. 1986. *World Hunger: Twelve Myths*. New York: Grove Press/Food First Books.

LAPPÉ, FRANCES MOORE, JOSEPH COLLINS, and DAVID KINLEY. 1981. *Aid as Obstacle: Twenty Questions about Our Foreign Policy and the Hungry*. San Francisco: Institute for Food and Development Policy.

LEOPOLD, EVELYN. 2007. "Sudan's Young Endure 'Unspeakable' Abuse: Report." [Online] Available April 19, 2007, at http://www .news.yahoo.com

LEVINSON, F. JAMES, and LUCY BASSETT. 2007. "Malnutrition Is Still a Major Contributor to Child Deaths." [Online] Available December 4, 2008, at http://www.prb.org/pdf07/Nutrition2007.pdf

LINO, MARK. "Expenditures on Children by Families, 2011." U.S. Department of Agriculture Center for Nutrition Policy and Promotion. 2012. [Online] Available at http://www.cnpp.usda .gov/Publications/CRC/crc2011.pdf

MALTHUS, THOMAS ROBERT. 1926 (orig. 1798). *First Essay on Population 1798*. London: Macmillan.

MARTIN, JOYCE A., BRADY E. HAMILTON, MICHELLE J. K. OSTERMAN, SALLY C. CURTIN, and T. J. MATHEWS. "Births: Final Data for 2012." *National Vital Statistics Reports*, Vol. 62, No 9. 2013. [Online] Available at http://www.cdc.gov/nchs/data/nvsr/nvsr62 /nvsr62_09.pdf

MILANOVIC, BRANKO. "Global Inequality Recalculated: The Effect of New 2005 PPP Estimates on Global Inequality." World Bank. 2009. [Online] Available at http://siteresources.worldbank.org /INTDECINEQ/Resources/Global_Inequality_Recalculated.pdf

MILANOVIC, BRANKO. "Global Income Inequality: New Results and Implications for 21st Century Policy." World Bank. 2011. [Online] Available at http://siteresources.worldbank.org/EXTABCDE /Resources/ 7455676-1292528456380/7626791-1303141641402/7878676 -1306699356046/Parallel-Sesssion-6-Branko-Milanovic.pdf

MILANOVIC, BRANKO. "Global Perspectives on Inequality." Presentation at Kenyon College, April 10, 2014.

MOGHADAM, VALENTINE M. "The 'Feminization of Poverty' and Women's Human Rights." UNESCO, Gender Equality and Development Section. July 2005. [Online] Available at http://portal.unesco.org/shs/en/files/8282/11313736811 Feminization_of_Poverty.pdf

MOORE, WILBERT E. 1977. "Modernization as Rationalization: Processes and Restraints." In Manning Nash, ed., *Essays on Economic Development and Cultural Change in Honor of Bert F. Hoselitz* (pp. 29–42). Chicago: University of Chicago Press.

———. 1979. *World Modernization: The Limits of Convergence*. New York: Elsevier.

ORHANT, MELANIE. 2002. "Human Trafficking Exposed." *Population Today*. Vol. 30, No. 1 (January): 1, 4.

PARSONS, TALCOTT. 1966. *Societies: Evolutionary and Comparative Perspectives*. Englewood Cliffs, N.J.: Prentice Hall.

POPULATION REFERENCE BUREAU. "Datafinder." 2011. [Online] Available at http://www.prb.org/DataFinder.aspx

POPULATION REFERENCE BUREAU. "World Population Data Sheet (annual)." 2011. [Online] Available at http://www.prb.org/Publications/Datasheets/2011/world-population-data-sheet.aspx

POPULATION REFERENCE BUREAU. "Datafinder." 2013, 2014. [Online] Available at http://www.prb.org/DataFinder.aspx

POPULATION REFERENCE BUREAU. "World Population Data Sheet 2013." 2013. [Online] Available at http://www.prb.org/pdf13/2013-population-data-sheet_eng.pdf

ROSTOW, WALT W. 1960. *The Stages of Economic Growth: A Non-Communist Manifesto*. Cambridge: Cambridge University Press.

———. 1978. *The World Economy: History and Prospect*. Austin: University of Texas Press.

SALA-I-MARTIN, XAVIER. 2002. *The World Distribution of Income*. Working Paper No. 8933. Cambridge, Mass.: National Bureau of Economic Research.

SCANLON, STEPHAN J. "Food Availability and Access in Less Industrialized Societies: A Test and Interpretation of Neo-Malthusian and Technoecological Theories." *Sociological Forum*. Vol. 16, No. 2 (June 2001): 231–62.

SIMON, JULIAN. 1995. "More People, Greater Wealth, More Resources, Healthier Environment." In Theodore D. Goldfarb, ed., *Taking Sides: Clashing Views on Controversial Environmental Issues*, 6th ed. Guilford, Conn.: Dushkin.

SMAIL, J. Kenneth. 2007. "Let's Reduce Global Population!" In John J. Macionis and Nijole V. Benokraitis, eds., *Seeing Ourselves: Classic, Contemporary, and Cross-Cultural Readings in Sociology*, 7th ed. Upper Saddle River, N.J.: Prentice Hall.

UNICEF. 2006. *Violence against Children in the Community*. New York: United Nations. [Online] Available April 28, 2009, at http://www.unicef.org/media/media_45451.html

UNITED NATIONS DEVELOPMENT PROGRAMME. 1994. *Human Development Report 1994*. New York: Oxford University Press.

———. 1996. *Human Development Report 1996*. New York: Oxford University Press.

———. 1998. *Human Development Report 1998*. New York: Oxford University Press.

———. 2003. *Human Development Report 2003*. New York: Oxford University Press.

———. 2005. *Human Development Report, 2005*. New York: Oxford University Press.

———. 2008. *Human Development Report, 2008*. New York: Oxford University Press.

UNITED NATIONS DEVELOPMENT PROGRAMME. *Human Development Report 2011*. Statistical Tables. [Online] Available at http://hdr.undp.org/en/statistics/data/

UNITED NATIONS DEVELOPMENT PROGRAMME. "International Human Development Indicators." 2013. [Online] Available at http://hdr.undp.org/en/data

UNITED NATIONS, DEPARTMENT OF ECONOMIC and SOCIAL AFFAIRS. "World Population Prospects: The 2012 Revision." 2013. [Online] Available at http://esa.un.org/unpd/wpp/unpp/panel_indicators.htm

UNITED NATIONS, DEPARTMENT OF ECONOMIC and SOCIAL AFFAIRS. "World Urbanization Prospects: The 2011 Revision." March 2012. [Online] Available at http://esa.un.org/unpd/wup/pdf/WUP2011_Highlights.pdf

UNITED NATIONS, FOOD AND AGRICULTURE ORGANIZATION (FAO). "The State of Food Insecurity in the World 2013." 2013. [Online] Available at http://www.fao.org/publications/sofi/en

UNITED NATIONS, STATISTICS DIVISION. "The World's Women 2010: Trends and Statistics." October 20, 2010. [Online] Available at http://unstats.un.org/unsd/demographic/products/Worldswomen/WW2010pub.htm

UNITED NATIONS, WORLD FOOD PROGRAMME. "Hunger Statistics." 2014. [Online] Available at http://www.wfp.org/hunger/stats

U.S. CENSUS BUREAU. "International Data Base." 2014. [Online] Available at http://www.census.gov/population/international/data/idb/informationGateway.php

U.S. CENSUS BUREAU. "Population Estimates." 2013, 2014. [Online] Available at http://www.census.gov/popest/data/index.html

U.S. DEPARTMENT OF LABOR, BUREAU OF LABOR STATISTICS. "International Labor Comparisons." 2012. [Online] Available at http://www.bls.gov/fls

VOGEL, EZRA F. 1991. *The Four Little Dragons: The Spread of Industrialization in East Asia*. Cambridge, Mass.: Harvard University Press.

WALLERSTEIN, IMMANUEL. 1974. *The Modern World-System: Capitalist Agriculture and the Origins of the European World-Economy in the Sixteenth Century*. New York: Academic Press.

———. 1979. *The Capitalist World-Economy*. New York: Cambridge University Press.

———. 1983. "Crises: The World Economy, the Movements, and the Ideologies." In Albert Bergesen, ed., *Crises in the World-System* (pp. 21–36). Beverly Hills, Calif.: Sage.

———. 1984. *The Politics of the World Economy: The States, the Movements, and the Civilizations*. Cambridge: Cambridge University Press.

WEBER, MAX. 1958 (orig. 1904–05). *The Protestant Ethic and the Spirit of Capitalism*. New York: Scribner.

WORLD BANK. "The State of the Poor: Where Are the Poor and Where Are They Poorest?" April 17, 2014. [Online] Available at http://www.worldbank.org/content/dam/Worldbank/document/State_of_the_poor_paper_April17.pdf

WORLD BANK. "World DataBank: World Development Indicators." 2014. [Online] Available at http://data.worldbank.org/data-catalog/world-development-indicators

WORSLEY, PETER. 1990. "Models of the World System." In Mike Featherstone, ed., *Global Culture: Nationalism, Globalization, and Modernity* (pp. 83–95). Newbury Park, Calif.: Sage.

YARDLEY, JIM. "Report on Deadly Factory Collapse in Bangladesh Finds Widespread Blame." *New York Times*, May 22, 2013. [Online] Available at http://www.nytimes.com/2013/05/23/world/asia/report-on-bangladesh-building-collapse-finds-widespread-blame.html

ZAKARIA, FAREED. 2004. "Bigger than Both of Them." *Newsweek* (January 19): 39.

Chapter 16

ADAM, DAVID. 2008. "World CO2 Levels at Record High, Scientists Warn." *Guardian* (May 12). [Online] Available July 16, 2008, at http://www.guardian.co.uk/environment/2008/may/12/climatechange.carbonemissions

BOERNER, CHRISTOPHER, and THOMAS LAMBERT. 1995. "Environmental Injustice." *Public Interest*. Vol. 118 (Winter): 61–82.

BOHON, STEPHANIE A., and CRAIG R. HUMPHREY. 2000. "Courting LULUs: Characteristics of Suitor and Objector Communities." *Rural Sociology*. Vol. 65, No. 3 (September): 376–95.

BORMANN, F. HERBERT. "The Global Environmental Deficit." *BioScience*. Vol. 40, No. 2 (1990): 74.

BRIGHT, CHRIS. 2003. "A History of Our Future." In *Worldwatch Institute, State of the World, 2003* (pp. 3–13). New York: Norton.

BROWN, LESTER R., et al., eds. 1993. *State of the World, 1993: A Worldwatch Institute Report on Progress toward a Sustainable Society*. New York: Norton.

CARSON, RACHEL. 1995 (orig. 1962). "Silent Spring." In John J. Macionis and Nijole V. Benokraitis, eds., *Seeing Ourselves: Classic, Contemporary, and Cross-Cultural Readings in Sociology*, 3rd ed. (pp. 407–10). Upper Saddle River, N.J.: Prentice Hall.

CBS NEWS. "China Breaks World Record for Car Sales in 2013." January 31, 2014. [Online] Available at http://www.cbsnews.com/news/china-breaks-world-record-for-car-sales-in-2013

CENTRAL INTELLIGENCE AGENCY. *CIA World Factbook*. 2014. [Online] Available at https://www.cia.gov/library/publications/the-world-factbook/index.html

CHANG, ALICIA. 2009. "Study: Cleaner Air Adds 5 Months to U.S. Life Span." *Yahoo News* (January 21). [Online] Available April 10, 2009, at http://www.newsvine.com/_news/2009/01/21/2339450-study-cleaner-air-adds-5-months-to-us-life-span

CLARKE, ROBIN. 1984. "Atmospheric Pollution." In Sir Edmund Hillary, ed., *Ecology 2000: The Changing Face of the Earth* (pp. 130–48). New York: Beaufort.

COMMISSION FOR RACIAL JUSTICE, UNITED CHURCH OF CHRIST. 1994. *CRJ Reporter*. New York: Commission for Racial Justice, United Church of Christ.

DAS GUPTA, MONICA. "Population, Poverty, and Climate Change." The World Bank. October 1, 2013. [Online] Available at http://documents.worldbank.org/curated/en/2013/10/18338481/population-poverty-climate-change

DUNLAP, RILEY E., GEORGE H. GALLUP Jr., and ALEC M. GALLUP. 1992. *The Health of the Planet Survey*. Princeton, N.J.: George H. Gallup International Institute.

DUNLOP, BECKY NORTON. 2006. "Conservation Ethics." *Society*. Vol. 43, No. 3 (March–April): 13–18.

EGAN, TIMOTHY. "How to Heal the Heartland." *New York Times*. April 10, 2014. [Online] Available at http://www.nytimes.com/2014/04/11/opinion/egan-how-to-heal-the-heartland.html

GARWOOD, PAUL. 2003. "Garbage Collectors Trash Governor's Plan." *Middle Eastern Times*. [Online] Available November 29, 2003, at http://www.metimes.com/2K1/issue2001-20/eq/garbage_collectors_trash.htm

GILLIS, JUSTIN. "Sea-Level Science." *Conservation*. Vol. 12, No. 1 (Spring 2011): 44–45.

GORE, AL. 2006. *An Inconvenient Truth*. Emmaus, Pa.: Rodale Books.

INTERGOVERNMENTAL PANEL ON CLIMATE CHANGE. "Special Report on Managing the Risks of Extreme Events and Disasters to Advance Climate Change Adaptation." 2012. [Online] Available at http://www.ipcc-wg2.gov/SREX

INTERNATIONAL ENERGY AGENCY. "Key World Energy Statistics 2013." 2014. [Online] Available at http://www.iea.org/publications/freepublications/publication/KeyWorld2013.pdf

JENKINS, J. CRAIG, and MICHAEL WALLACE. 1996. "The Generalized Action Potential of Protest Movements: The New Class, Social Trends, and Political Exclusion Explanations." *Sociological Forum*. Vol. 11, No. 2 (June): 183–207.

KLUGER, JEFFREY. 2006. "The Tipping Point." *Time*. Vol. 167, No. 14 (April 3): 34–42.

KRAUTHAMMER, CHARLES. 2013. *Things That Matter: Three Decades of Passions, Pastimes, and Politics*. New York: Crown Forum.

McMAHON, BUCKY. "Vanishing Point." *Conservation*. Vol. 12, No. 1 (Spring 2011): 40–48.

MEADOWS, DONELLA H., DENNIS L. MEADOWS, JORGEN RANDERS, and WILLIAM W. BEHRENS III. 1972. *The Limits to Growth: A Report on the Club of Rome's Project on the Predicament of Mankind*. New York: Universe.

MEADOWS, DONELLA H., JORGEN RANDERS, and DENNIS L. MEADOWS. 2004. *Limits to Growth: The 30-Year Update*. White River Junction, Vt.: Chelsea Green.

MILBRATH, LESTER W. 1989. *Envisioning a Sustainable Society: Learning Our Way Out*. Albany: State University of New York Press.

MYERS, NORMAN. 1991. "Biological Diversity and Global Security." In F. Herbert Bormann and Stephen R. Kellert, eds., *Ecology, Economics, and Ethics: The Broken Circle* (pp. 11–25). New Haven, Conn.: Yale University Press.

NASA GODDARD INSTITUTE FOR SPACE STUDIES. "GISS Surface Temperature Analysis (GISTEMP)." 2014. [Online] Available at http://data.giss.nasa.gov/gistemp

OECD (ORGANISATION FOR ECONOMIC CO-OPERATION AND DEVELOPMENT). "Environmental Outlook to 2050: The Consequences of Inaction." 2012. [Online] Available at www.oecd.org/environment/outlookto2050

OECD (ORGANISATION FOR ECONOMIC CO-OPERATION AND DEVELOPMENT). "Stat.Extracts." 2012. [Online] Available at http://stats.oecd.org/index.aspx

PAKULSKI, JAN. 1993. "Mass Social Movements and Social Class." *International Sociology*. Vol. 8, No. 2 (June): 131–58.

POPULATION REFERENCE BUREAU. "Datafinder." 2013, 2014. [Online] Available at http://www.prb.org/DataFinder.aspx

POPULATION REFERENCE BUREAU. "World Population Data Sheet 2013." 2013. [Online] Available at http://www.prb.org/pdf13/2013-population-data-sheet_eng.pdf

REED, BRIAN. "Could People from Kiribati Be 'Climate Change Refugees'?" *The Two-Way*. National Public Radio news blog. [Online] Available February 17, 2011, at http://www.npr.org/templates/archives/archive.php?thingId_131216964

SIERRA CLUB. "Clean Water." 2012. [Online] Available at http://www.sierraclub.org/watersentinels

SIMON, JULIAN. 1981. *The Ultimate Resource*. Princeton, N.J.: Princeton University Press.

———. 1995. "More People, Greater Wealth, More Resources, Healthier Environment." In Theodore D. Goldfarb, ed., *Taking Sides: Clashing Views on Controversial Environmental Issues*, 6th ed. Guilford, Conn.: Dushkin.

SINGER, S. FRED. 2007. "Global Warming: Man-Made or Natural?" *Imprimis*. Vol. 36, No. 8 (August): 1–5.

SMAIL, J. KENNETH. 2007. "Let's Reduce Global Population!" In John J. Macionis and Nijole V. Benokraitis, eds., *Seeing Ourselves: Classic, Contemporary, and Cross-Cultural Readings in Sociology*, 7th ed. Upper Saddle River, N.J.: Prentice Hall.

SMITH, TOM W., PETER MARSDEN, MICHAEL HOUT, and JIBUM KIM. "General Social Surveys, 1972–2012." National Opinion Research Center; The Roper Center for Public Opinion Research, University of Connecticut; Computer-assisted Survey Methods Program, University of California. June 2013. [Online] Available at http://www.norc.org/GSS+Website

STACK, LIAM. "For Egypt's Christians, Pig Cull Has Lasting effects." *Christian Science Monitor*. September 3, 2009. Available at: http://www.csmonitor.com/World/Middle-East/2009/0903/p17s01-wome.html

STEVENS, HELEN. 2003. Declining Biodiversity and Unsustainable Agricultural Production: Common Cause, Common Solution?

Research Paper No. 2, 2001–2002. Department of the Parliamentary Library, Australia. [Online] Available October 31, 2003, at http://www.aph.gov.au/library/pubs/rp/2001-02/02RP02.pdf

STRAUSS, MARK. "Looking Back on the Limits of Growth." *Smithsonian*. April, 2012. Available at http://www.smithsonianmag.com/science-nature/Looking-Back-on-the-Limits-of-Growth.html

UNITED NATIONS ENVIRONMENT PROGRAMME (UNEP). "Climate Neutral Network." [Online] Available April 2012 at http://www.unep.org/climateneutral

UNITED NATIONS STATISTICS DIVISION. "Environmental Indicators." 2011. [Online] Available at http://unstats.un.org/unsd/ENVIRONMENT/qindicators.htm

UNITED NATIONS, DEPARTMENT OF ECONOMIC AND SOCIAL AFFAIRS. "World Population Prospects: The 2012 Revision." 2013. [Online] Available at http://esa.un.org/unpd/wpp/unpp/panel_indicators.htm

UNITED NATIONS, FOOD AND AGRICULTURE ORGANIZATION (FAO). "The State of Forests in the Amazon Basin, Congo Basin and Southeast Asia." 2011. [Online] Available at http://www.fao.org/forestry/fra/70893/en/

UNITED NATIONS, FOOD AND AGRICULTURE ORGANIZATION (FAO). "AQUASTAT Database." 2014. [Online] Available at http://www.fao.org/nr/water/aquastat/main/index.stm

U.S. DEPARTMENT OF COMMERCE, NATIONAL OCEANIC and ATMOSPHERIC ADMINISTRATION. "Trends in Atmospheric Carbon Dioxide, Mauna Loa." 2014. [Online] Available at http://www.esrl.noaa.gov/gmd/ccgg/trends

U.S. ENVIRONMENTAL PROTECTION AGENCY. "Municipal Solid Waste (MSW) in the United States: Facts and Figures." 2011. [Online] Available at http://www.epa.gov/epawaste/nonhaz/municipal/msw99.htm

U.S. ENVIRONMENTAL PROTECTION AGENCY. "Municipal Solid Waste (MSW) in the United States: Facts and Figures." 2014. [Online] Available at http://www.epa.gov/epawaste/nonhaz/municipal/msw99.htm

U.S. ENVIRONMENTAL PROTECTION AGENCY. "National Priorities List (NPL)." Superfund Sites. 2014. [Online] Available at http://www.epa.gov/superfund/sites/npl/index.htm

U.S. ENVIRONMENTAL PROTECTION AGENCY. "2005 National-Scale Air Toxics Assessment (NATA)." 2011. [Online] Available at http://www.epa.gov/ttn/atw/natamain

U.S. GEOLOGICAL SURVEY. "Estimated Use of Water in the United States." 2010. [Online] Available at http://water.usgs.gov/watuse

VEBLEN, THORSTEIN. 1953 (orig. 1899). *The Theory of the Leisure Class*. New York: New American Library.

WATERKEEPER ALLIANCE. "Annual Report 2013." 2013. [Online] Available at http://waterkeeper.org

WILL, GEORGE. "Will: 'Global Warming' Is Socialism by the Back Door." *The Foundry*. April 30, 2014. [Online] Available at http://blog.heritage.org/2014/04/30/will-global-warming-socialism-back-door

WILSON, EDWARD O. 1991. "Biodiversity, Prosperity, and Value." In F. Herbert Bormann and Stephen R. Kellert, eds., *Ecology, Economics, and Ethics: The Broken Circle* (pp. 3–10). New Haven, Conn.: Yale University Press.

YANDLE, TRACY, and DUDLEY BURTON. 1996. "Reexamining Environmental Justice: A Statistical Analysis of Historical Hazardous Waste Landfill Siting in Metropolitan Texas." *Social Science Quarterly*. Vol. 77, No. 3 (September): 477–92.

YOUTH, HOWARD. 2003. "Watching Birds Disappear." In Worldwatch Institute, *State of the World, 2003* (pp. 14–37). New York: Norton.

Chapter 17

ADITJONDRO, GEORGE J. 2000. "Ninjas, Nanggalas, Monuments, and Mossad Manuals: An Anthropology of Indonesian State Terror in East Timor." In Jeffrey A. Sluka, ed., *Death Squad: The Anthropology of State Terror* (pp. 158–88). Philadelphia: University of Pennsylvania Press.

AMERICAN PSYCHIATRIC ASSOCIATION. 2002. "Practice Guideline for the Treatment of Patients with Eating Disorders." In *Facts about Eating Disorders and the Search for Solutions*. Arlington, Va.: American Psychiatric Association.

BARNES, JULIAN E., and ADAM ENTOUS. "U.S. Planning Cuts to Nuclear Forces Under Pact with Russia." *Wall Street Journal*. April 8, 2014. [Online] Available at http://online.wsj.com/news/articles/SB10001424052702304819004579489502893002072

BLANFORD, NICHOLAS. "Town by Town, Assad Regime Retakes Southwestern Syria." *Christian Science Monitor*. April 8, 2014. [Online] Available at http://www.csmonitor.com/World/Middle-East/2014/0408/Town-by-town-Assad-regime-retakes-southwestern-Syria-video

CENTER FOR CONSTITUTIONAL RIGHTS. 2003. [Online] Available November 19, 2003, at http://www.ccr-ny.org

CHAFE, WILLIAM. 1977. *Women and Equality: Changing Patterns in American Culture*. New York: Oxford University Press.

CHAGNON, NAPOLEON A. 1997. *Yanomamö*. Fort Worth, Tex.: Harcourt Brace.

CLAUSEWITZ, CARL VON. 1968 (orig. 1832). *On War*. ed. Anatol Rapaport. Baltimore: Penguin.

COALITION TO STOP THE USE OF CHILD SOLDIERS. 2014. [Online] Available at http://www.child-soldiers.org/faq.php

DEDRICK, DENNIS K., and RICHARD E. YINGER. 1990. "MAD, SDI, and the Nuclear Arms Race." Unpublished manuscript. Georgetown, Ky.: Georgetown College.

EHRENREICH, BARBARA. 1997. *Blood Rites: Origins and History of the Passions of War*. New York: Holt.

FALLOWS, JAMES. "An Exchange with Jeffrey Goldberg on 'Bluffing,' Israel, and Iran." March 21, 2012. [Online] Available at http://www.theatlantic.com/international/archive/2012/03/an-exchange-with-jeffrey-goldberg-on-bluffing-israel-and-iran/254895

FINLAYSON, JOHN. 1998. "Student Terror: The Weathermen." In *Encyclopedia of World Terrorism*. Vol. 3 (pp. 534–35). Armonk, N.Y.: Sharpe.

FLEXNER, ELEANOR. 1975. *Century of Struggle: The Women's Rights Movement in the United States*, rev. ed. Cambridge, Mass.: Belknap Press.

FRIEDMAN, EMILY. "Romney on President Obama: Instead of Apologizing FOR America, Apologize TO America." Fox Nation. March 24, 2012. [Online] Available at http://nation.foxnews.com/mitt-romney/2012/03/24/romney-president-obama-instead-apologizing-america-apologize-america

GALBRAITH, JOHN KENNETH. 1985. *The New Industrial State*, 4th ed. Boston: Houghton Mifflin.

GLATER, JONATHAN D. 2005. "Blue Collars in Olive Drab." *New York Times* (May 22). [Online] Available June 12, 2009, at http://www.nytimes.com/2005/05/22/national/class/MILITARY-FINAL.html

HALBFINGER, DAVID M., and STEVEN A. HOLMES. 2003. "Military Mirrors Working-Class America." *New York Times on the Web* (March 30). [Online] Available September 8, 2003, at http://www.resrearchnavigator.com/content/nyt/2003/03/30/82.htm

HERMES, WILL. 2005. "Straight Out of Sudan: A Child Soldier Raps." *New York Times Online*. [Online] Available July 27, 2006, at http://www.researchnavigator.com

HOFFMAN, BRUCE. 1998. *Inside Terrorism.* New York: Columbia University Press.

HSIN, HONOR. 2003. "Episode II." *Harvard International Review.* Vol. 25, No. 3 (Fall): 15–16.

HUDSON, MICHAEL C. 1992. "The Middle East under Pax Americana: How New, How Orderly?" *Third World Quarterly.* Vol. 13, No. 2 (February–March): 301–16.

HUGHES, MATTHEW. 1998. "The World Trade Center Bombing." In *Encyclopedia of World Terrorism.* Vol. 3 (pp. 540–41). Armonk, N.Y.: Sharpe.

INSTITUTE FOR ECONOMICS AND PEACE. "Global Peace Index." 2012. [Online] Available at http://economicsandpeace.org/research /iep-indices-data/global-peace-index

JENKINS, J. CRAIG. 2003. *Images of Terror: What We Can and Can't Know about Terrorism.* Hawthorne, N.Y.: Aldine de Gruyter.

JENKINS, BRIAN MICHAEL. "Al Qaeda in Its Third Decade: Irreversible Decline or Imminent Victory?" Santa Monica, CA: Rand Corporation. 2012.

KALDOR, MARY. 1999. *New and Old Wars: Organized Violence in a Global Era.* Stanford, Calif.: Stanford University Press.

KAPLAN, DAVID E., and MICHAEL SCHAFFER. 2001. "Losing the Psywar." *U.S. News & World Report* (October 8): 46.

KUGLER, JACEK, and A. F. K. ORGANSKI. 1989. "The Power Transition: A Retrospective and Prospective Evaluation." In Manus I. Midlarskky, ed., *Handbook of War Studies* (pp. 171–94). Boston: Unwin Hyman.

LORENZ, KONRAD. 1966. *On Aggression.* New York: Harcourt Brace.

———. 1981. *The Foundations of Ethology.* New York: Springer-Verlag.

LUKAS, J. ANTHONY. 1997. *Big Trouble.* New York: Simon & Schuster.

MANNING, JENNIFER E. "Membership of the 113th Congress: A Profile." Congressional Research Service. March 14, 2014. [Online] Available at http://www.fas.org/sgp/crs/misc/R42964.pdf

MILLS, C. WRIGHT. 1956. *The Power Elite.* New York: Oxford University Press.

MOAKLEY, TERRY. 1999. "The Thanks of a Grateful Nation? The Numbers Don't Lie When It Comes to VA Shortfalls." *WE Magazine.* Vol. 3, No. 5 (September–October): 106.

MONTAGU, ASHLEY. 1976. *The Nature of Human Aggression.* New York: Oxford University Press.

NATIONAL COALITION FOR HOMELESS VETERANS. "Background & Statistics." 2014. [Online] Available at http://nchv.org/index.php /news/media/background_and_statistics

NEWMAN, RICHARD J. 2002. "Hunters and Hunted." *U.S. News & World Report.* Vol. 132, No. 2 (January 21): 30.

NORDLAND, ROD, and SALMAN MASOOD. "Recent Drone Strikes Strain U.S. Ties with Afghanistan and Pakistan." *New York Times.* November 29, 2013. [Online] Available at http://www.nytimes. com/2013/11/30/world/asia/drone-strike-pakistan.html

NORRIS, ROBERT S., and HANS M. KRISTENSEN. "Nuclear Pursuits, 2012." *Bulletin of the Atomic Scientists.* Vol. 68, No. 1, (January/ February 2012): 94–98.

RATNESAR, ROMESH. 2003. "Al-Qaeda's New Home." *Time* (September 15). [Online] Available May 23, 2009, at http://www .time.com/time/magazine/article/0,9171,1005665,00.html

RENNER, MICHAEL. 1993. *Critical Juncture: The Future of Peacekeeping.* Washington, D.C.: Worldwatch Institute.

SAGAN, CARL, and RICHARD TURCO. 1990. *A Path Where No Man Thought: Nuclear Winter and the End of the Arms Race.* New York: Random House.

SAID, EDWARD. 1981. *Covering Islam: How the Media and the Experts Determine How We See the Rest of the World.* New York: Pantheon.

SAVAGE, CHARLIE. "Democratic Senators Issue Strong Warning about Use of the Patriot Act." *New York Times.* March 16, 2012. [Online] Available at http://www.nytimes.com/2012/03/16/us/politics /democratic-senators-warn-about-use-of-patriot-act.html

SHEEHAN, MICHAEL A. 2000. "Post-Millennium Terrorism Review." Speech at the Brookings Institution, Washington, D.C. (February 10). [Online] Available March 13, 2000, at http://www.state.gov /www/policy_remarks/2000/000210_sheehan_brookings.html

STERN, JESSICA. 1999. *The Ultimate Terrorists.* Cambridge, Mass.: Harvard University Press.

STOCKHOLM INTERNATIONAL PEACE RESEARCH INSTITUTE (SIPRI). "Military Expenditures Database." 2014. [Online] Available at http://www.sipri.org/research/armaments/milex/milex_database

STOCKHOLM INTERNATIONAL PEACE RESEARCH INSTITUTE (SIPRI). "Nuclear Forces Database." 2014. [Online] Available at http://www.sipri.org/research/armaments/nuclear-forces

STOCKHOLM INTERNATIONAL PEACE RESEARCH INSTITUTE. "SIPRI Yearbook 2010." 2011. [Online] Available at http://www.sipri.org /yearbook

STOCKHOLM INTERNATIONAL PEACE RESEARCH INSTITUTE (SIPRI). "SIPRI Yearbook 2013." 2013. [Online] Available at http://www .sipri.org/yearbook

STOLBERG, SHERYL GAY. 2006. "Patriot Act Revisions Pass House, Sending Measure to President." *New York Times Online* (March 8). [Online] Available July 28, 2006, at http://www.researchnavigator. com

TABB, WILLIAM K. 1992. "Vampire Capitalism." *Socialist Review.* Vol. 22, No. 1 (January): 81–93.

THEMNÉR, LOTTA, and PETER WALLENSTEEN. "Armed Conflict, 1946–2013." *Journal of Peace Research* 2014. Vol. 51, No. 4.

THOMAS, EVAN, and MICHAEL HIRSH. 2000. "The Future of Terror." *Newsweek* (January 10): 34–37.

THOMPSON, MARK. "The Other 1%." *Time.* Vol. 178, No. 20 (November 1, 2011): 33–39.

TUCKER, DAVID. 1998. "Responding to Terrorism." *Washington Quarterly.* Vol. 21, No. 1 (Winter): 103–17.

UNITED NATIONS. "Children and Armed Conflict." 2013. [Online] Available at http://childrenandarmedconflict.un.org/effects-of -conflict/six-grave-violations/child-soldiers

U.S. DEPARTMENT OF DEFENSE. "Military Casualty Information." 2014. [Online] Available at http://www.dmdc.osd.mil/dcas /pages/casualties.xhtml

U.S. DEPARTMENT OF DEFENSE. "Military Personnel Statistics." 2014. [Online] Available at https://www.dmdc.osd.mil/appj/dwp /reports.do?category=reports&subCat=milActDutReg

U.S. DEPARTMENT OF DEFENSE. "Population Representation in the Military Services." 2014. [Online] Available at http://prhome .defense.gov/RFM/MPP/AP/POPREP.aspx

U.S. DEPARTMENT OF STATE. 2003. *Patterns of Global Terrorism, 2002.* [Online] Available December 26, 2006, at http://www.usis.usemb. se/terror/rpt2002/index.html

U.S. DEPARTMENT OF STATE, NATIONAL COUNTERTERRORISM CENTER. "2011 Report on Terrorism." 2011. [Online] Available at http://www.nctc.gov/docs/2011_NCTC_Annual_Report_Final.pdf

U.S. DEPARTMENT OF STATE. "Country Reports on Terrorism." 2011. [Online] Available at http://www.state.gov/j/ct/rls/crt/2010 /index.htm

U.S. DEPARTMENT OF STATE. "Country Reports on Terrorism." 2013. [Online] Available at http://www.state.gov/j/ct/rls/crt/2013 /index.htm

U.S. DEPARTMENT OF STATE. "New START Treaty." 2014. [Online] Available at http://www.state.gov/t/avc/newstart/index.htm

U.S. Department of State, National Counterterrorism Center. "Counterterrorism 2014 Calendar." 2014. [Online] Available at http://www.nctc.gov/site/calendar/index.html

U.S. Department of Veterans Affairs, Veterans Health Administration. "Veterans Health Administration Facilities by State." 2014. [Online] Available at http://www1.va.gov/health /MedicalCenters.asp

U.S. Office of Management and Budget. "The Budget for Fiscal Year 2014." 2014. [Online] Available at http://www.gpo.gov /fdsys/granule/BUDGET-2014-PER/BUDGET-2014-PER-1-6-1

Van Evera, Stephen. 1999. *Causes of War: Power and the Roots of Conflict*. Ithaca, N.Y.: Cornell University Press.

Wallerstein, Immanuel. 1979. *The Capitalist World-Economy*. New York: Cambridge University Press.

Williams, Patricia J. 2000. "Without Sanctuary." *Nation*. Vol. 270, No. 6 (February 14): 9.

Wilson, Edward O. 1975. *Sociobiology: The New Synthesis*. Cambridge, Mass.: Belknap Press.

Wright, Quincy. 1987. "Causes of War in the Atomic Age." In William M. Evan and Stephen Hilgartner, eds., *The Arms Race and Nuclear War* (pp. 7–10). Englewood Cliffs, N.J.: Prentice Hall.

Zanini, Michele. 1999. "Middle Eastern Terrorism and Netwar." *Studies in Conflict and Terrorism*. Vol. 22, No. 3 (July–September): 247–56.

Zenko, Micah. "The 2012 Nuclear Security Summit: Obama's Work in Progress." Blog. March 27, 2012. [Online] Available at http://blogs.cfr.org/zenko/2012/03/27/the-2012-nuclear-security -summit-obamas-work-in-progress

Credits

Photo Credits

Chapter 1 1: LHB Photo/Alamy; 3: William Thomas Cain/Stringer/Getty Images; 3: DC Stock/Alamy; 3: Conor Caffrey/Science Source; 3: Blend Images/SuperStock; 8: Bao Dandan Xinhua News Agency/Newscom; 10: The Granger Collection, NYC; 10: Andy Cross/The Denver Post/Getty Images; 13: Dean Conger/Corbis; 16: Joe Koshellek/MCT/Newscom; 23: Bill Pugliano/Stringer/Getty Images; 23: Mario Anzuoni/Reuters/Landov; 25: Bettmann/Corbis; 26: Jim West/Alamy; 27: Jeff Greenberg/Alamy.

Chapter 2 31: Davis Turner MCT/Newscom; 33: Slim Aarons/Getty Images; 33: Con Tanasiuk/Design Pics/Alamy; 33: Mario Tama/Getty Images; 33: Jerzy Dabrowski/picture-alliance/dpa/AP Images; 44: John Sturrock/Alamy; 46: Gale Zucker/Aurora Photos/Alamy; 47: Eduardo Munoz/Reuters/Landov; 48: The Gazette, Bill Olmsted/AP Images; 50: Jim West Image Broker/Newscom; 52: H William Tetlow/Getty Images; 52: Cecil Stoughton/Corbis; 53: Esbin-Anderson/The Image Works; 55: Zurijeta/Shutterstock; 56: Jeff Greenberg/Alamy; 59: Alison Wright/Corbis; 61: Everett Collection/Newscom; 61: Tomas Abad/Alamy; 62: Jeff Greenberg/The Image Works.

Chapter 3 65: Bettmann/CORBIS; 67: Mark Duncan/AP Images; 67: Jack Hollingsworth/Corbis; 67: Stuart Franklin/Magnum Photos; 67: Norma Jean Gargasz/Alamy; 68: PhotoDisc/Getty Images, Inc.; 73: JEFF TOPPING/Reuters/Landov; 74: Gene Herrick/AP Images; 76: Kevin Fleming/Corbis; 78: AP Images/Bill Hudson; 79: Bettmann/Corbis; 82: Jerry Holt/Zumapress/Newscom; 85: Rich Legg/E+/Getty images; 86: Mark Peterson/Redux Pictures; 87: AP Images; 87: AP Photo/PRNewsFoto/McDonald's; 91: Steve Debenport/E+/Getty Images; 94: Davis Barber/PhotoEdit; 95: Kevin G. Hall/KRT/Newscom.

Chapter 4 99: Thinkstock/Stockbyte/Getty Images; 101: Laurence Mouton/PhotoAlto Agency/Getty Images; 101: Krista Greco/Pearson Education; 101: moodboard/Corbis; 101: Warner Bros.Pictures/Close, Murray/Album/Al/SuperStock; 102: JODI BIEBER/AFP/Getty Images/Newscom; 104: Everett Collection Inc/Alamy; 109: Francois Pesant/Polaris/Newscom; 118: Janet Wishnetsky/Corbis; 121: AMER HILABI/AFP/Getty Images/Newscom; 122: The Granger Collection, NYC; 123: MNStudio/Fotolia; 125: iofoto/Fotolia; 127: Danny Hooks/Alamy; 128: Sports Illustrated/Getty Images.

Chapter 5 132: New York City/Alamy; 134: Sally Greenhill/Alamy; 134: Jean Michel Foujols/Corbis; 134: Zoran Milich/Masterfile; 134: Markus Schreiber/AP Images; 135: B.S.P.I./Terra/Corbis; 139: Chris O'Meara/AP Images; 141: John Birdsall/The Image Works; 143: Robin Nelson/PhotoEdit; 145: Golden Pixels LLC/Alamy; 147: Baxter/BSIP; 148: Frank Barratt/Hulton Archive/Getty Images; 150: Monalyn Gracia/Corbis; 154: Dennis MacDonald/PhotoEdit, Inc.; 155: Bettmann/Corbis; 156: Tibanna79/Shutterstock.

Chapter 6 159: AP Photo/Jessica Hill, File; 161: Richard Lord/The Image Works; 161: PFC Donald Watkins/Landov; 161: RubberBall/Alamy; 161: Andy Jones/AP Images; 167: Robert Padgett/Reuters; 169: Bill Aron/PhotoEdit; 173: Mike Powell/Allsport Concepts/Getty Images; 174: Bettmann/Corbis; 175: Pictorial Press Ltd/Alamy; 177: Splash News/Newscom; 179: Angel Zayas/Demotix/Corbis; 181: A. Ramey/PhotoEdit; 182: moodboard/Alamy; 186: Mark Duncan/AP Images; 188: Bill Losh/Getty Images; 189: Enigma/Alamy; 191: Michael Matthews/Police Images/Alamy; 194: AP Photo/Damian Dovarganes; 195: Jim Wright/Star Ledger/Corbis.

Chapter 7 199: Kristoffer Tripplaar/Alamy; 201: H. Armstrong Roberts/ClassicStock/Corbis; 201: Jack Star/PhotoLink/Photodisc/Getty Images; 201: Will Hart/PhotoEdit, Inc; 202: Bettmann/Corbis; 204: Hulton Archive/Getty Images; 210: Piero Cruciatti/Alamy; 212: Sergei Supinsky/AFP/Getty Images; 219: Picture Contact BV/Alamy; 222: Aman Rahman/AFP/Getty Images; 223: Chad Ehlers/Alamy; 225: J Andrews/Alamy Limited; 227: Alison Yin/AP Images; 228: Marvi Lacar/Getty Images.

Chapter 8 232: James Chance/Polaris/Newscom; 234: Underwood & Underwood/Corbis; 234: Image Source/Getty Images; 234: George Doyle/Stockbyte/Getty Images; 234: Falko Updarp/AGE Fotostock; 235: National Library of Medicine; 236: Terry Vine/AGE Fotostock; 241: Toby Talbot/AP Images; 243: Bob Berg/Getty Images Entertainment/Getty Images; 245: Stephane Bidouze/Shutterstock; 246: Ernesto Benavides/AFP/Getty Images; 249: LARRY MULVEHILL/Getty Images; 253: Marta NASCIMENTO/REA/Redux; 253: Michel Porro/AP Images; 256: ZUMA Wire Service/Alamy; 259: Scott Houston/Alamy; 260: Carl J. Single/Syracuse Newspapers/The Image Works.

Chapter 9 264: Tao Associates/Getty Images; 266: Juan Silva/The Image Bank/Getty Images; 266: Kevin Fleming/Corbis; 266: David kelly Crow/PhotoEdit; 266: Innovated Captures/Fotolia; 269: Heiner Heine/imagebroker/Alamy; 276: SAUL LOEB/AFP/Getty Images/Newscom; 278: Andreea Angelescu/Corbis; 279: Davis Barber/PhotoEdit; 281: blickwinkel/Alamy; 283: Jerry Cooke/Science Source; 288: Ferdinando Scianna/Magnum Photos; 290: Kim Ritzenthaler/KRT/Newscom; 291: Digital Vision/Getty Images.

Chapter 10 295: Dennis MacDonald/Alamy; 297: John Crowe/Alamy; 297: LJ Wilson-Knight/Alamy; 297: Robert Sullivan/AFP/Getty Images; 297: Patrick Eckersley/arabianEye/Corbis; 299: Ronald Zak/AP Images; 299: Jay Directo/AFP/Getty Images; 303: Mike Groll/AP Images; 305: Library of Congress Prints and Photographs Division[LC-DIG-ppmsca-25813]; 307: James Steidl/Shutterstock; 311: Bob Daemmrich/Alamy; 312: Bettmann/Corbis; 313: Tom Williams/CQ Roll Call/Newscom; 315: Tom Olmscheid/AP Images; 318: Billy E. Barnes/PhotoEdit; 319: Jeff Greenberg 5 of 6/Alamy.

Chapter 11 322: Jim West/Alamy; 324: George Frey/epa/Corbis; 324: Octavio Jones/Tampa Bay Tim/ZUMA Press, Inc./Alamy; 324: CandyBox Images/Fotolia; 324: Jim Young/Reuters/Landov; 326: Randy Duchaine/Alamy; 328: Craig Aurness/Corbis/Glow Images; 332: Cala Molodovan/Krt/Newscom; 334: David Bacon/The Image Works; 337: Fotosearch/Getty Images; 341: Jim Craigmyle/Corbis; 342: Sonda Dawes/The Image Works; 343: Jeff Greenberg/PhotoEdit; 346: Zuma Wire Service/Alamy; 349: Joe Raedle/Getty Images News/Getty Images; 350: Gilles Mingasson/Getty Images News/Getty Images.

Chapter 12 354: Visual Ideas/Camilo Morales/Getty Images; 356: Bruce Ayres/The Image Bank/Getty Images; 356: Courtney Keating/E+/Getty Images; 356: David Turnley/Corbis; 356: Peter Bernik/Shutterstock; 358: Peter Hopper Stone/ABC/Getty Images; 360: Spencer Grant/PhotoEdit; 367: Elise Amendola/AP Images; 369: Eric Audras/Getty Images; 370: Dmac/Alamy; 372: Vibe Images/Fotolia; 373: Larry Williams/Bridge/Corbis; 376: Mitch Haddad/Disney ABC Television Group/Getty Images; 377: Moviestore collection/Alamy.

Chapter 13 380: Minerva Studio/Fotolia; 382: Jake Lyell/Alamy; 382: Jeff Greenberg 1of6/Alamy; 382: Iris Coppola/Creative/Corbis; 382: AP Images; 382: nik wheeler/Alamy; 386: Library of Congress Prints & Photographs Division Washington, DC 20540 http://hdl.loc.gov/loc.pnp/pp.print; 389: Carl Iwasaki//Time Life Pictures/Getty Images; 392: Gabbro/Alamy; 393: Gideon Mendel/Corbis; 397: Splash News/Newscom; 402: David Martin/AP Images; 404: Chris Hondros/Newsmakers/Getty Images; 405: Peter Cavanagh/Alamy.

Chapter 14 409: David Grossman/Alamy; 411: Benjamin Rondel/Flirt/Corbis; 411: Bill Aron/PhotoEdit; 411: Journal Courier/The Image Works; 411: Mark Avery/Reuters; 413: The Granger Collection, NYC; 415: Condor 36/Shutterstock; 419: Library of Congress Prints and Photographs Division Washington, D.C. 20540 USA; 419: Jacob Riis/Jacob Riis Picture History/Newscom; 419: Jacob Riis/Newscom; 420: Joe McLaughlin/AP Images; 421: Stéphane Bidouze/Fotolia; 426: Lee Snider/The Image Works; 427: Clark Brennan/Alamy; 429: Phil Long/Ap images; 432: Mark Kauffman/The LIFE Picture Collection/Getty Images; 433: Steve Ruark/AP Images.

Chapter 15 437: Gavriel Jecan/DanitaDelimont.com "Danita Delimont Photography"/Newscom; 439: K.M. Choudary/AP Images; 439: David Turnley/Turnley/Corbis; 439: Jeremy Horner/Documentary/Corbis; 439: Malcolm Linton/Hulton Archive/Getty Images; 444: Sean Sprague/The Image Works; 445: The Granger Collection, NYC; 450: Paul W. Liebhardt; 451: Ton Koene/Horizons WWP/Alamy; 453: Mary Evans Picture Library/The Image Works; 456: Michael S. Yamashita/Corbis; 461: Tim Graham/Alamy.

Chapter 16 465: Wilfried Krecichwost/Bridge/Corbis; 467: Kuni Takahashi/MCT/Newscom; 467: Wayne Lawler/Encyclopedia/Corbis; 467: Jonh Macionis; 469: Huguette Roe/Shutterstock; 473: RHS/AP Images; 478: Daniel Beltra/Greenpeace International Support Services; 478: Kevin Elsby/Alamy; 480: Bloomberg/Getty Images; 482: Peter Macdiarmid/Getty Images News/Getty Images; 484: Lain Masterton/Alamy; 486: Alex Wong/Getty Images News/Getty Images; 486: Paul Sancya/AP Images.

Chapter 17 489: Bettmann/Corbis; 491: Leif Skoogfors/Documentary Value/Corbis; 491: AP Images; 491: Jason Reed/Reuters/Corbis; 491: Gary Conner/PhotoEdit; 495: United States Marine Corps; 496: Mike Goldwater/Alamy; 501: Farzaneh Khademian/Abacausa.com/Newscom; 503: Kaveh Kazemi/Getty Images; 502: AP Images; 504: U.S. Air Force; 505: PAUL ELLIS/AFP/Getty Images/Newscom; 508: United States Marine Corps; 510: Sarah Conard/Reuters; 512: Saul Loeb/AFP/Getty Images.

Text Credits

Chapter 1 4: Mills, C. Wright. 1959. *The Social Imagination*. New York: Oxford University Press. p. 3; 5: Gallup (1935, 2013); 8: Rogers, TIME magazine, 2013; 8: Blumer, Herbert G. 1969. "Collective Behavior." In Alfred McClung Lee, (ed.), *Principles of Sociology*, 3rd ed. (pp. 65–121). New York: Barnes & Noble.; Mauss, Armand L. 1975. *Social Problems of Social Movements*. Philadelphia: Lippincott.; Tilly, Charles. 1978. *From Mobilization to Revolution*. Reading, MA: Addison-Wesley; 12: Data from Hamilton, Martin, & Ventura (2013), Population Reference Bureau (2013); 19: Karl Marx, Theses On Feuerbach, (1845) in, "The German Ideology" (1938), Lawrence and Wishart edition. Translated by Cyril Smith 2002, based on work done jointly with Don Cuckson; 19: Data from U.S. Department of Labor (2013); 20: Benjamin Franklin quoted in February 4, 1735 edition of the Pennsylvania Gazette; 20: Goldman, Henry. 1991:5. "The Plight of the Black Child." *Philadelphia Inquirer* (February 10): 5E; 21: The data in this figure are from General Social Surveys, 1972–2012. (Chicago: National Opinion Research Center, 2013).

Chapter 2 32: Gallup, October 25, 2013, In U.S., Fewer Believe "Plenty of Opportunity" to Get Ahead; 35: Internal Revenue Service (2013); U.S. Census Bureau (2013); 35: U.S. Census Bureau (2013); 37: Estimates based on Wolff (2012); 36: Morin, Rich. "Rising Share of Americans See Conflict Between Rich and Poor." Pew Research Center. January 11, 2012. Available at: http://www.pewsocialtrends.org/2012/01/11/rising-share-of-americans-see-conflict-between-rich-and-poor/; 38: Data from Saez, Emmanuel and Thomas Piketty. "Income Inequality in the United States, 1913–2012." updated 2013. Available at http://eml.berkeley.edu/~saez/TabFig2012prel.xls; 39: Remarks by the President Obama on Economic Mobility, 2013; 39: Internal Revenue Service, "Statistics of income", 2012; 40: U.S. Census Bureau (2013); 42: U.S. Census Bureau (2013); 43: U.S. Census Bureau (2013); 44: Ehrenreich, Barbara. 2001:220. Nickel and Dimed: On How (Not) to Get By in America. New York: Holt; 50: William J. Clinton: "Address Accepting the Presidential Nomination at the Democratic National Convention in New York," July 16, 1992. Online by Gerhard Peters and John T. Woolley, The American Presidency Project. http://www.presidency.ucsb.edu/ws/?pid=25958; 51: President Franklin D. Roosevelt, in second inaugural address, on January 20, 1937; 52: Kingsley Davis and Wilbert E. Moore, Some Principles of Stratification, *American Sociological Review*, Vol. 10, No. 2, 1944 Annual Meeting Papers (Apr., 1945), 242–249; 53: Based on Ryan, William. 1976. *Blaming the victim*, rev.ed. New York: Vintage Books.

Chapter 3 70: U.S. Census Bureau (2013); 75: U.S. Census Bureau (2013); 77: U.S. Census Bureau (2013); 78: U.S.

Census Bureau (2013); 79: U.S. Census Bureau (2013); 80: U.S. Census Bureau (2013); 81: U.S. Census Bureau (2013); 82: U.S. Census Bureau (2013); 83: Parrillo, Vincent N., and Christopher Donoghue. 2005. "Updating the Bogardus Social Distance Studies: A New National Survey." *Social Science Journal*. Vol. 42, No. 2 (April): 257–71.; Parrillo & Donoghue (2013); 84: Parrillo, Vincent N., and Christopher Donoghue. 2005. "Updating the Bogardus Social Distance Studies: A New National Survey." *Social Science Journal*. Vol. 42, No. 2 (April): 257–71.; Parrillo & Donoghue (2013); 88: Albon, Joan. 1971:387. "Retention of Cultural Values and Differential Urban Adaptation: Samoans and American Indians in a West Coast City." *Social Forces*, Vol. 49, No. 3 (March): 385–93; 88–89: Du Bois, W. E. B. 2001:227 (orig. 1903). "The Souls of Black Folk." In John J. Macionis and Nijole V. Benokraitis, eds., *Seeing Ourselves: Classic, Contemporary, and Cross-Cultural Readings in Sociology*, 5th ed. (pp. 226–30). Upper Saddle River, N.J.: Prentice Hall; 89: Manning Marable (1995:1). *Beyond Black and White: Transforming African-American Politics*. (Verso, 1995); 89: Marx, Karl., and Friedrich Engels. (1959:458, orig. 1893). *Marx and Engels: Basic Writings on Politics and Philosophy*, ed. Lewis S. Feurer. Garden City, N.Y.: Anchor; 91: Johnson, Jacqueline, Sharon Rush, and Joe R. Feagin, 2000:101. "Doing AntiRacism: Toward an Egalitarian American Society." *Contemporary Sociology*. Vol. 29, No. 1 (January): 95–110.

Chapter 4   103: Data from United Nations Development Programme (2013); 107: 1 Corinthians 11:7–9; 107: 1 Corinthians 11:7–9; 107: Ephesians 5:22–24; 107: Daily prayer among Orthodox Jewish men; 108: Center for American Women and Politics (2013); 109: Helene Cooper, 2014, Pentagon Study Finds 50% Increase in Reports of Military Sexual Assaults, *The New York Times*; 110: U.S. Department of Labor (2013); 110: U.S. Department of Labor (2013); 112: Pew Research Center, 2013. On Pay Gap, Millennial Women Near Parity - For Now; 112: U.S. Department of Labor (2013); 113: Based on Chaker, Anne Marie, and Hilary Stout, 2004. "After Years Off, Women Struggle to Revive Careers." *Wall Street Journal* (May 5): A1, A8; 114: U.S. Department of Labor (2013); 117: Wallis Simpson, Duchess of Windsor; 120: Equal Rights Amendment; 123: United States Declaration of Independence, In Congress, July 4, 1776; 125: Stacey, Judith (1990:269–70). *Brave New Families: Stories of Domestic Upheaval in Late-Twentieth-Century America*. New York: Basic Books.

Chapter 5   136: Strom, Stephanie. (2000). "In Japan, the Golden Years Have Lost Their Glow." *New York Times* (February 16): A7.; U.S. Census Bureau (2014); 137: U.S. Census Bureau (2012, 2013); 138: U.S. Census Bureau (2013); 141: Palmore, Erdman B. 1998:30–31. "Ageism." In David E. Redburn and Robert P. McNamara, eds., *Social Gerontology* (pp. 29–41). Westport, Conn.: Auburn House; 144: U.S. Census Bureau (2013); 151: U.S. Census Bureau (2013).

Chapter 6   163: U.S. Department of Justice (2013); 164: U.S. Department of Justice, Federal Bureau of Investigation (2013); 166: CAP Index, Inc. (2011). www.capindex.com; 170: U.S. Department of Justice, Federal Bureau of Investigation (2013); 176: U.S. Department of Justice, Federal Bureau of Investigation (2013); 178: Brady Campaign to Prevent Gun Violence. 2012 [Online] Available at http://www.bradycampaign.org/ and Law Center to Prevent Gun Violence (2014); 178: Fifth Amendment to the United States Constitution; 178: Smith, Douglas A., and Christy A. Visher.

1981. "Street-Level Justice: Situational Determinants of Police Arrest Decisions." *Social Problems*. Vol. 29, No. 2 (December): 167–77.; Smith, Douglas A. 1987. "Police Response to Interpersonal Violence: Defining the Parameters of Legal Control." *Social Forces*. Vol. 65, No. 3 (March): 767–82; 180: U.S. Department of Justice (2013) and International Centre for Prison Studies (2014); 183: Based on data from Abolitionist & Retentionist Countries, Amnesty International (2013), http://www.amnesty.org/en/death-penalty/abolitionist-and-retentionist-countries; 185: U.S. Department of Justice (2013); 186: Durkheim, Emile. 1964a (orig. 1895). *The Division of Labor in Society*. New York: Free Press; Durkheim, Emile. 1964b (orig. 1893). *The Rules of Sociological Method*. New York: Free Press; 187: Created by the author, based on Merton, Robert K. (1968). *Social Theory and Social Structure*. New York: Free Press; 187: Hirschi, Travis. 1969. *Causes of Delinquency*. Berkeley: University of California Press.

Chapter 7   201: Bearman et al. (2004); 203: Laumann, Edward O., John H. Gagnon, Robert T. Michaels, and Stuart Michaels. 1994. The Social Organization of Sexuality: Sexual Practices in the United States. Chicago: University of Chicago Press; 204: Sharon Moalem, *How sex works : why we look, smell, taste, feel, and act the way we do* (New York : Harper Perennial, 2010); 205: Adapted from Storms, Michael D. "Theories of Sexual Orientation." *Journal of Personality and Social Psychology*. Vol. 38, No. 5 (May 1980): 783–92; 206: Centers for Disease Control and Prevention, (2014); 208: Data from Smith et al. (2013); 215: Data from Population Reference Bureau. "Datafinder." 2011. [Online] Available at http://www.prb.org/DataFinder.aspx; 216: Based on data from Guttmacher Institute variable "Pregnancy Rate" in Table 1.3 "State-specific rates of pregnancy, birth and abortion among women aged 15–19, by year" in document "U.S. Teenage Pregnancies, Births and Abortions, 2008: State Trends by Age, Race, and Ethnicity" by Kathryn Kost and Stanley Henshaw, March 2013. http://www.guttmacher.org/pubs/USTPtrendsState08.pdf; 218: U.S. Attitudes toward Abortion; 220: UNAIDS (2013); 220: Based on CDC (Centers for Disease Control and Prevention), "Youth Risk Behavior Survey 2009." Morbidity and Mortality Weekly Report, Vol 59, No. SS-5 (June 2010). [Online] Available at http://www.cdc.gov/HealthyYouth/yrbs/index.htm; 221: Centers for Disease Control and Prevention (2013).

Chapter 8   234: Remnick, David. "Going the Distance." The New Yorker. January 27, 2014. Available at: http://www.newyorker.com/reporting/2014/01/27/140127fa_fact_remnick?currentPage=all; 235: Goldstein, Avram. 1994. *Addiction: From Biology to Drug Policy*. New York: Freeman; 237: U.S. Department of Health and Human Services (2013); 239: CDC (Centers for Disease Control and Prevention), "State Tobacco Activities Tracking and Evaluation (STATE) System." 2012. [Online] Available at http://apps.nccd.cdc.gov/statesystem and World Health Organization (2013); 248: United States Code, Title 21, Sec. 841 (2010); 250: U.S. Bureau of Justice Statistics (2008, 2013); 252: Data from National Conference of State Legislatures, 2014.

Chapter 9   267: World Health Organization (1946:3), Constitution of the World Health Organization. New York: World Health Organization Interim Commission; 268: Based on data from Population Reference Bureau variable "Infant Mortality Rate" http://www.prb.org/DataFinder/Topic/Rankings.aspx?ind=5; 270: Centers for Disease Control and Prevention (2013); 272: United Nations Development Programme (2013); 273: Based on data from the variable "Health expenditure, public (% of total health expenditure)" in the Health, Nutrition and Population Statistics section of the World Bank's World DataBank, http://databank.worldbank.org/data/views/variableSelection/selectvariables.aspx?source=health-nutrition-and-population-statistics#s_h; 278: Data from Hoyert, Donna, and Jiaquan Xu. "Deaths: Preliminary Data for 2011." National Vital Statistics Reports. Vol. 61, No. 6. 2012. Available at http://www.cdc.gov/nchs/data/nvsr/nvsr61/nvsr61_06.pdf; 281: American Psychiatric Association. 2000. *Diagnostic and Statistical Manual of Mental Disorders*, 4th ed. (DSM-IV-TR). Arlington, Va: American Psychiatric Association; American Psychiatric Association, 2013; 282: Based on U.S. Department of Health and Human Services (2013).

Chapter 10   300: Based on data from *The Wall Street Journal*/Heritage Foundation (2014); 301: Data from World Development Indicators (2013); 308: McDonald, Michael P. (2013) "2012 General Election Turnout Rates." United States Elections Project. Accessed 2/28/2014. Available at http://elections.gmu.edu/Turnout_2012G.html; 309: Data from Gallup. "Americans' Confidence in Congress Falls to Lowest on Record." June 13, 2013. Available at http://www.gallup.com/poll/163052/americans-confidence-congress-falls-lowest-record.aspx; 310: U.S. Census Bureau (2013).

Chapter 11   326: Based on U.S. Department of Labor (2013); 327: U.S. Department of Labor (2013); 330: U.S. Department of Labor (2013); 330: Gup, Ted. 1991:55. "The Curse of Coal." *Time*. Vol. 138, No. 18 (November 4): 54–64; 333: U.S. Department of Labor (2014); 336: U.S. Department of Labor (2014); 338: U.S. Department of Labor (2014); 338: John Kasich, Ohio governor, On March 8, 2011 in his first "state of the state" speech; 339: National Conference of State Legislatures (2014); 340: Based on data from International Telecommunication Union's ICT Database 2013, variable "VAR 3. Percentage of individuals using the Internet, fixed (wired) Internet subscriptions, fixed (wired)-broadband subscriptions" http://www.itu.int/net4/itu-d/icteye/AdvancedDataSearch.aspx

Chapter 12   359: U.S. Census Bureau (2013); 360: Pew Research Center. "The Decline of Marriage and Rise of New Families." November 18, 2010. Available at http://www.pewsocialtrends.org/files/2010/11/pew-social-trends-2010-families.pdf; 362: Centers for Disease Control and Prevention (2013); 363: CDC (Centers for Disease Control and Prevention), National Center for Health Statistics. "Marriage and Divorce Data." 2012. [Online] Available at http://www.cdc.gov/nchs/nvss/marriage_divorce_tables.htm; 364: OECD (2013), European Union (2013), Centers for Disease Control and Prevention (2013), United Nations (2014); 367: Goodridge et al. v. Department of Public Health 798 N.E.2d 941 (Mass. 2003); 367: President George W Bush, Second Presidential Debate, October 11, 2000; 367: President George W Bush, State of the Union Address, January 20, 2004; 368: Bruni, Frank. "One Country's Big Gay Leap." *New York Times*. October 8, 2011; European Union (2014), Pew Research Center Project on Religion and Public Life (2014).

Chapter 13   384: United Nations Development Programme. Human Development Report 2011. Statistical Tables [Online] Available at http://hdr.undp.org/en/statistics/

data/; UNESCO (2013); 385: U.S. Census Bureau (2013); 387: U.S. Department of Education (2014); 390: Based on data from Orfield, Gary and and Erica Frankenberg, with Jongyeon Ee and John Kuscera. Brown at 60: Great Progress, a Long Retreat and an Uncertain Future. The Civil Rights Project/Proyecto Derechos Civiles, UCLA, May 2014 (revised version 5–15-14). http://civilrightsproject.ucla.edu/research/k-12-education/integration-and-diversity/brown-at-60-great-progress-a-long-retreat-and-an-uncertain-future/Brown-at-60–051814.pdf (Table 4, p. 12); 396: U.S. Department of Education (2014).

Chapter 14   412: Renwood RealtyTrac, LLC. (www.realtytrac.com); 423: U.S. Census Bureau, "Population Division." Population Estimates (2011). [Online] Available at http://www.census.gov/popest/estimates.html; 422: U.S. Census Bureau (2014); 424: Based on data from Population Reference Bureau variable "Urban Population" http://www.prb.org/DataFinder/Topic/Rankings.aspx?ind=12; 422: Data from United Nations, Department of Economic and Social Affairs. "World Urbanization Prospects: The 2011 Revision." March 2012. Available at http://esa.un.org/unpd/wup/pdf/WUP2011_Highlights.pdf; 429: Moynihan, Daniel Patrick, 1993. "Toward a New Intolerance." *Public Interest*. No. 112 (Summer): 119–22; 429: Krauthammer, Charles, 1995:15. "A Social Conservative Credo." *Public Interest*. Vol. 121 (Fall): 15–22.

Chapter 15   440: Based on Burkett, Elinor. 1997. "God Created Me to Be a Slave." *New York Times Magazine* (October 12): 56–60; 440: Data from United Nations, Department of Economic and Social Affairs. "World Population Prospects: The 2012 Revision." 2013. Available at http://esa.un.org/unpd/wpp/unpp/panel_indicators.htm; 441: Data from Population Reference Bureau (2013); 443: Data from Population Reference Bureau (2013); 445: Thomas Robert Malthus (1798), An Essay on the Principle of Population as It Affects the Future Improvement of Society, with Remarks on the Speculations of Mr. Godwin, M. Condorcet and Other Writers; 447: U.S. Census Bureau (2014); 448: Based on Milanovic, Branko, "Global Inequality Recalculated: The Effect of New 2005 PPP Estimates on Global inequality." World Bank 2009. Available at http://siteresources.worldbank.org/INTDECINEQ/Resources/Global_Inequality_Recalculated.pdf; Milanovic (2011) and Davies, Lluberas, & Shorrocks (2013); 449: Data from United Nations Development Programme (2013) and World Bank (2014); 451: Universal Declaration of Human Rights, 1948, Article 4; 455: The Haves and the Have-Nots : A Brief and Idiosyncratic History of Global Inequality by Milanovic, Branko. Reproduced with permission of Basic Books in the format Republish in a book via Copyright Clearance Center; 456: Berger, Peter L. (1986:36), *The Capitalist Revolution: Fifty Prepositions about Prosperity, Equality, and Liberty*. New York: Basic Books; 460: Data from World Bank. "World DataBank: World Development Indicators." 2014. Available at http://data.worldbank.org/data-catalog/world-development-indicators.

Chapter 16   469: Milbrath, Lester W. 1989:10, *Envisioning a Sustainable Society: Learning Our Way out*. Albany: State University of New York Press; 470: Central Intelligence Agency (2014); 471: Ernest G. Bormann, *Small group communication: theory and practice* (Harper & Row, 1990); 472: Based on Meadows, Donella H., Dennis L. Meadows,

Jorgen Randers, and William W. Behrens III. 1972. *The Limits to Growth: A Report on the Club of Rome's project on the Predicament of Mankind.* New York: Universe; 473: Carson, Rachel. (1995:409) (orig. 1962). "Silent Spring" In John J. Macionis and Nijole V. Benokraitis, eds., *Seeing Ourselves: Classic, Contemporary, and Cross-Cultural Readings in Sociology,* 3rd ed. (pp. 407–10). Upper Saddle River, N.J.: Prentice Hall; 474: U.S. Environmental Protection Agency (2014); 476: U.S. Environmental Protection Agency. "2005 National-Scale Air Toxics Assessment (NATA)." 2011. [Online] Available at http://www.epa.gov/ttn/atw/nata2005/tables.html; 481: Julian Simon (1995). "More People, Greater Wealth, More Resources, Healthier Environment." In Theodore D. Goldfarb, ed., *Taking Sides: Clashing Views on Controversial Environmental Issues,* 6th ed. Guilford, Conn.: Dushkin; 486: Genesis 1: 28–29.

Chapter 17 492: Compiled from various sources by Maris A. Vinovskis and the author; 493: Institute for Economics and Peace. "Global Peace Index." 2012. [Online] Available at http://economicsandpeace.org/research/iep-indices-data/global-peace-index; 493: Wright, Quincy. 1987. "Causes of War in the Atomic Age." In William M. Evan and Stephen Hilgartner, eds., *The Arms Race and Nuclear War* (pp. 7–10). Englewood Cliffs, NJ: Prentice Hall; Kaldor, Mary. 1999. *New and Old Wars: Organized Violence in a Global Era.* Stanford, Calif.: Stanford University Press; Van Evera, Stephen. 1999. *Causes of War: Power and the Roots of Conflict.* Ithaca, N.Y.: Cornell University Press; 494: Marullo, Sam. 1987. "The Functions and Dysfunctions of Preparations for Fighting Nuclear War." *Sociological Focus.* Vol. 20, No. 2 (April): 135–53; 497: Halbfinger, David M., and Steven A. Holmes, (2003:1). "Military Mirrors Working-Class America." New York Times on the Web (March 30). [Online] Available September 8, 2003, at http://www.resresearchnavigator.com/contentnyt/2003/03/30/82.htm; 497: Glater, Jonathan D. 2005. "Blue Collars in Olive Drab." *New York Times* (May 22). [Online] Available June 12, 2009, at http://www.nytimes.com/2005/05/22/national/class/MILITARY-FINAL.html; 499: Based on data from SIPRI, http://www.sipri.org/research/armaments/nuclear-forces and http://www.sipri.org/media/pressreleases/2014/nuclear_May_2014, and NTI Nuclear Materials Security Index, http://ntiindex.org/data-results/interactive-map/> TABLE VIEW; 504: Ratnesar, Romesh. 2003. "Al-Qaeda's New Home." Time (September 15). [Online] Available May 23, 2009, at http://www.time.com/time/magazine/article/0,9171,1005665,00.html; Jenkins, Brian Michael. "Al Qaeda in Its Third Decade: Irreversible Decline or Imminent Victory?" Santa Monica, CA: Rand Corporation. 2012; 510: Albert Einstein, Einstein on Peace, p. 576.

Name Index

Subject Index